# *the dramatic moment*

EUGENE M. WAITH

*Yale University*

Prentice-Hall, Inc., *Englewood Cliffs, N.J.*

PRENTICE-HALL INTERNATIONAL, INC., *London*
PRENTICE-HALL OF AUSTRALIA, PTY. LTD., *Sydney*
PRENTICE-HALL OF CANADA, LTD., *Toronto*
PRENTICE-HALL OF INDIA (PRIVATE), LTD., *New Delhi*
PRENTICE-HALL OF JAPAN, INC., *Tokyo*

Prentice-Hall English Literature Series
Maynard Mack, *Editor*

LIBRARY OF CONGRESS CATALOG CARD NO.: 67–10313

PRINTED IN THE UNITED STATES OF AMERICA: 21925-C

Current printing (last digit):
10  9  8  7  6  5  4  3  2  1

# Preface

Much of the great drama of the past was written for theaters very different from those of the twentieth century. Its form was affected not only by these theaters but by the literary conventions of the various periods. Some knowledge of this background material is an invaluable aid in approaching the drama written before our own time. There are certain problems to be faced in studying any drama, however, especially when plays are read rather than seen in the theater. Since it is easier to deal with some of these problems without the distraction of an unfamiliar idiom, the first section of this volume contains two twentieth-century plays. The accessibility of the first play, *Major Barbara*, is increased by Shaw's novelistic stage directions—a special concession to the reader of drama. The second play, *The Zoo Story*, though briefer than the first and more strictly contemporary, is not provided with the same sort of aids. Both plays present problems of interpretation, but those in the second play are in several respects more difficult.

The second section is arranged chronologically, so that each play may contribute something to the understanding of the next. This section includes plays written for the theaters of classical Greece, the Middle Ages, the Renaissance, and the late nineteenth century. In the third section there are three theatrical experiments which have exercised a significant influence on the drama of today. Pirandello's *Six Characters in Search of an Author*, which concludes the volume, is in one sense an inquiry into the nature of drama—a play concerned with the issues that underlie the interpretation of all the other plays. Thus, the end is also another beginning; for it is to be hoped that the historical section as well as the more recent experiments will illuminate the two plays with which the volume opens.

The general introduction discusses the distinctive nature of drama and the special problems faced by the spectator or reader in understanding it. Each play is preceded by a brief introduction containing the chief biographical facts about the playwright. The introductions in the first section also translate the problems discussed in the general introduction into more specific suggestions of what to look for in the plays. The introductions in the second and third sections provide background material relating to the physical characteristics of the various theaters and to the dramatic principles underlying the plays. In the first and second sections the plays are followed by discussions of genre and technique, with specific reference to the plays themselves. Though there are no complete interpretations, these discussions point to some of the questions that should be answered. Both introductions and discussions are interrelated so as to give coherence to the sequence of plays and some basis of comparison between them. The appendix consists of writings on the theater which, like the plays in the third section, have an important bearing on recent developments.

I am particularly indebted to conversations with Maynard Mack and to the able assistance of Robert L. Reid. The sections on modern drama owe much to the work of Eric Bentley, Robert Brustein, John Gassner, and Maurice Valency.

E.M.W.

# Contents

# Introduction

The distinctive feature of the drama is that it is designed to be presented by actors, whose voices, gestures, and movements are the chief means of conveying to an audience some idea, some feeling. There may or may not be a written text. At the simple level of the parlor game, the members of one team may decide on only the general outlines of a brief scene whose meaning is to be guessed by the others. The details are improvised at the moment of acting. A somewhat similar procedure was followed in the sixteenth, seventeenth, and eighteenth centuries by professional actors of the *commedia dell' arte*, who performed their plays from scenarios which gave only the plots and occasional scraps of dialogue. Even when every word is written down, every entrance and exit carefully marked, and many indications of stage business given, the actors are still responsible for conveying the meaning of the play to the audience in the theater.

This essential fact about the drama has many consequences. One is the extraordinary impact that a play may have. Every work of art, whether it is in the medium of words or paint or stone or musical sound, gives life to the artist's conception through the form he has created, but the vitality of a play is of a special sort. Enactment by human beings gives the play unique immediacy, not only because we are in the actual presence of those who seem to be living through the experience presented, but also because every performance is a new creation of the experience. What we see is not a mechanical reproduction of an event that has already taken place; the event is being shaped during the time that we are there, and we to some extent participate in its formation.

The written form of a play is therefore less final than the words of a poem or a novel. What any author writes is susceptible of some variety of interpretation, but whereas the poet and the novelist can expect their words to confront the reader directly, the playwright designs his speeches to be delivered by actors who will interpret them according to their understanding of what he has written. In this respect the playwright is like the composer, whose music will be heard as interpreted by various performers. In modern productions the director plays a large part in the interpretation, for he normally is responsible for the basic conception, determines the pace, blocks out every movement on the stage, and discusses with each actor the rendition of his role. It would be wrong to exaggerate the fluidity of dramatic texts, for the playwright has many ways of making clear the essential pattern of meaning and thus of setting limits to the variety of legitimate interpretation. Nevertheless, the effect of a particular inflection or gesture should not be underestimated. Strindberg said: "I have seen parts created that were better than my original conception of them."[1]

The author of a play, therefore, speaks less directly to us than do other authors, though the play itself speaks with singular directness. Because of the playwright's special relationship to his creation, his own voice is never heard in the speeches he has written. We may sometimes suspect that a certain character is his mouthpiece for a moment or during an entire play, but such suspicions are difficult to prove. In the preface to *Major Barbara* Shaw expresses a number of opinions which are almost identical with those of his heroine, but he refers to her as a being quite independent of him: ". . . when Major Barbara says that

---

[1] "Notes to Members of the Intimate Theatre," *The Chamber Plays* (New York: E. P. Dutton & Co., Inc., 1962), p. 209.

1

there are no scoundrels, she is right..." and so forth. If we compared what she says throughout the play with Shaw's known beliefs, the separateness of her identity would be even more apparent. In speaking of Bill Walker, another character, Shaw comments that in real life he would not be aware of certain aspects of his situation as he is in the play. But as a dramatist, Shaw says it is his business "to shew the connexion between things that seem apart and unrelated in the haphazard order of events in real life." Hence he has contrived to give his character the awareness he would not have had as an actual person. These are excellent illustrations of the way the playwright manipulates his characters, allowing them to share more or less fully his own vision of the truth. But unless he writes about them as Shaw does in his prefaces, his opinions must be deduced from the play as a whole. He does not have the novelist's privilege of telling the reader what he thinks about a character or exactly what is going on in a character's mind. If Shakespeare had written a novel about Hamlet, several acres of printed commentary on the character would have been made unnecessary; and quite conceivably, Hamlet would not have had such a compelling reality. What is lost in precision of analysis may be gained in the imaginative appeal of a character whom we encounter directly.

Distinctions of the kind that are made in the last two paragraphs are far from being absolute. It is easy to think of short stories and parts of novels told almost entirely in dialogue, or of lyrics in which the poet has assumed a personality distinct from his own. There are also plays in which a crucial episode is narrated, as in the messengers' speeches in *Oedipus Rex*. Nevertheless, it is useful to keep in mind how each genre characteristically operates and to look for explanations when the author makes use of techniques from another genre.

If the characters in the play stand on their own, seemingly independent of their creator, it is legitimate to ask how we are to know when to take them at their own word and when to suspect an ironical contrast between their views and the playwright's. The question cannot be easily answered, and it is closely related to the matter of varying interpretations by actors. There is still a considerable difference of opinion on the part of actors and critics about Shylock's self-defense: should the audience respond to it with complete sympathy, with the hostile view that it is hypocritical, or with some combination of the two? Since the actor has already made his decision, the audience must in effect decide whether this interpretation is justified.

In making a decision we may, of course, use some of the same criteria as for actual people: are their words matched by their deeds? is there anything suspect about the way they express themselves? But it will be even more important to see how one speech or one action is related to many other speeches and actions of the same character and of others; to see it in relation to the outcome of the play; to fit it in with any ideas which the play seems to emphasize. In other words, the final decision about the proper interpretation of a character will depend on seeing the relationship of this part to the whole design. General knowledge of the period in which the play was written will contribute to our understanding. Familiarity with the thought of the time, with the special meaning of a word, with literary or dramatic conventions, or with the kind of theater for which the play was written—any of these kinds of knowledge will increase our awareness of the alternatives between which we must choose in interpreting the part of the design on which we are concentrating. However, the interpretation of this detail will still have to be checked against our understanding of the rest. Interpretations of the component parts must add up to a coherent interpretation of the whole play, and only in the play grasped as a totality will we hear what might be called the "voice" of the playwright.

The process of coming to understand a play is similar to the interpretation of any kind of literature except in one major respect: in the theater there is no turning back to see what was said a moment ago, and no glancing ahead to see how this episode evolves. The task of relating parts to each other and to the whole is therefore complicated by the necessity of responding to each moment as it comes and thus of experiencing the play as a continuous flow of present time. A greater demand is made on the memory, and in this respect the spectator in less literate times had an advantage over us. More accustomed to memorizing whatever he found notable, he probably retained without effort more of what he heard. If so, it was easier for him than for us to see the connections which make up the design of the play as a whole.

Not only are we unable to stop the flow of the action on the stage but, because of the greater immediacy of its emotional impact, we are even more absorbed by what is happening at the moment than when we are reading a story or a poem. In discussing the play with others who have seen it, we are apt to recall scenes or moments which struck us with particular force.

The playwright, fully aware that his play must succeed or fail with the audience on the basis of a succession of transient impressions, seeks to produce moments of special intensity. Though such moments serve the purpose of holding attention, they should not be thought of primarily as attention-getters. No playwright wishes to bore the spectators, and he tries, like any author, to maintain continuous interest by moving, shocking, entertaining, or challenging them. The moments on which he truly depends, however, are like what are often called "dramatic moments" in actual life. These are the moments in which more is at stake than is immediately apparent—the exchange of remarks which echoes for anyone who knows the speakers some crucial incident in their past, a quarrel or a love affair; the comment which unexpectedly explains a person's past behavior; the announcement which commits him to a future course of action.

What may be called the dramatic moments in a play may be either comic or serious, but not every pratfall or pistol shot will be charged with enough significance to constitute such a moment. One cannot be dogmatic about which passages in a play can properly be called dramatic moments, and again much will depend on the actors and the director. But it is generally agreed that a building up of intensity, followed by a subsiding, is characteristic of all drama. It is sometimes discussed in terms of plot—a "rising action," a "climax," and a "falling action." Or it may be put in terms of the relative intensity of emotional response to what is happening on the stage. A director has written of the structure of a play as "a series of peaks and valleys which builds to a climax and recedes to the resolution."[2] These peaks may be equated with what are called here dramatic moments. Thus considered, a moment of maximum intensity is led up to by moments of somewhat lesser intensity, which themselves rise above the level of what surrounds them. In a play which makes any claim upon the intellect, the dramatic moment derives much of its intensity from the insight it provides into the meaning of the situation. The scene in which Macbeth reaches for the "air-drawn dagger" is engrossing not merely because it dramatizes the supernatural, but also because it prefigures the murder of Duncan, suggests the

[2] Frank McMullan, *The Directorial Image* (Hamden, Conn.: The Shoestring Press, 1962), p. 45.

emotional tension of the hero, and presents a brilliant emblem of his grasping for power. It is an omen and a revelation.

As this example shows, the dramatic moment is a means by which the dramatist may introduce intimations of both past and future into the continual present of his play and in this way offer the spectator a glimpse of the total design. Sometimes the effect may be achieved largely through the management of the plot, as in *Oedipus Rex*, where each added piece of information given to the King makes the truth about his past more clear. In these dramatic moments one is increasingly aware, as the play progresses, of the fitting together of the pieces in a tragic design. Some playwrights draw upon the resources of poetry to bring out the full significance of the moment, as Shakespeare does in *Macbeth* (for example in the "Tomorrow and tomorrow and tomorrow" speech) or *King Lear* (perhaps most notably in the storm scenes on the heath). The repeated use of images, such as those of suffering and torture in *King Lear*, or symbols, such as Chekhov's seagull, gives them a cumulative force which makes them particularly effective in enhancing the significance of the moments in which they appear.

Our examination of the relations between the playwright, the audience, and the play as acted in the theater has brought out some of the reasons why a succession of these moments of intensity is characteristic of dramatic form. It may also have suggested why they are especially useful to the interpreter of drama in his effort to grasp the play as a whole. It remains to look at certain aspects of drama which are evident both in the whole play and in the moments of which it is composed.

First is the necessity for action. Something must be done. The Greek word "drama" originally meant "deed" and derives from a verb meaning "to do." The action may be of many sorts. It need not be a story of many happenings, stretched out over a considerable period of time, though it sometimes is. More often, when the dramatist is drawing upon such a story, he chooses to present only its culmination, contriving to inform the spectators of what has gone before. The effect thus obtained is, of course, more concentrated, and therefore in the strictest sense more in accord with dramatic form. For this reason certain puristic critics, associating themselves with the dramatic traditions of Greece and Rome, insisted on what were called the three unities—the requirements that there be only one plot (unity of action), that it take place in one day (unity of time), and in one location (unity of place). Nevertheless, many plays with more loosely articulated structures have succeeded not only with the public at large but also with discriminating critics.

At the opposite extreme from the play which presents a long and complicated story is that in which the characters seem to do very little but talk to each other. Such a play may seem at first to be a mere gallery of speaking portraits, but a second look will usually reveal that at least one character in the play has been brought to see the truth about another or about himself or his situation; again something has happened.

The basic importance of action is closely related to structure and to the moments of intensity already discussed; for the action is what gives the play its shape and makes possible the dramatic moments. Books on playwriting frequently discuss the action in terms of a conflict between certain characters or between the principal character and his environment. By increasing the tensions in such a struggle the dramatist builds up intensity; by decreasing them he leads toward a resolution. The term *dénouement*, often used of the final resolution, literally means "the unknotting." Although such discussions of the craft of the playwright sound rather mechanical and formulaic, they describe some of the basic movements of the action of a play. An awareness of them contributes to the understanding of dramatic structure.

It is sometimes debated whether action or character is the more important in drama, but the dilemma is unreal. Though, as has been shown, it is the nature of drama to present an action, there can be no action without characters. The question of whether the action determines the characters or vice versa is more debatable and requires various answers in reference to various plays. In a thriller, for example, the simplified types exist largely for the benefit of the plot, which is the source of the thrills. In other plays the characters may be so fully developed that they seem to generate the plot. But finally we must conclude that in all drama action and character function together to fulfill the particular purpose of each individual play.

The purpose of a play has often been thought of in terms of entertainment or instruction, following a famous distinction made by Horace in his *Ars Poetica*. Years of inconclusive discussion suggest, however, that these are not the most useful terms. In extreme cases one or the other of these purposes may clearly seem dominant, but more often neither "instruction" nor "entertainment" seems quite applicable, or both purposes are served in proportions which are difficult to determine. It is preferable to think of the purpose of a play as the expression of a meaning inherent in the dramatic action. Comprehension of this meaning is, of course, the object of all interpretation.

In connection with meaning, the theme of the play becomes a major consideration. *Theme* may legitimately be equated with *topic*, as when we say that the *theme* of *Romeo and Juliet* is love, but this does not advance our understanding of the meaning by much. It will be more useful to think of themes as *ideas*. If we say that the tragic brevity of young love is one theme in *Romeo and Juliet*, we state at least part of the meaning. To discuss the interaction of several such themes would lead to a fuller statement of the meaning. In the case of a primarily didactic play the theme might best be expressed as a *thesis*—that man must repent in order to be saved, that slaves must be set free, that justice must be done to all. It is a mistake to suppose that any such statement of theme, even the most comprehensive, is the equivalent of the total meaning, for that is to be found only in the entire experience of the play. No topic or idea or thesis abstracted from the experience is a substitute, but any interpretation of the meaning will certainly necessitate thematic analysis.

The interpretation of action, character, and theme will be affected by certain other aspects of the play, less easily defined and less clearly separable than those already discussed. To begin with one of the least definable but most important, the mood or atmosphere of a play is often a substantial factor in the impression it creates. The pervasive atmosphere of evil in *Macbeth* or that of fiery haste in *Romeo and Juliet* amounts to considerably more than background. It becomes part of the meaning of each tragedy. Similarly, the gaiety or bitterness of a comedy may be one of its distinguishing features. The mood may be established in many different ways. It may be in part the result of the playwright's choice of characters (as the witches in *Macbeth*) or his management of the action (as the sudden quarrels and love-affairs in *Romeo and Juliet*). If the play is in poetry, imagery can contribute to the effect. And, since the earliest drama, music has been used to create or reinforce the desired mood. In the English theater since the end of the seventeenth century, and somewhat earlier on the Continent, scenery has also been used for this purpose, for the appearance of the stage can be made to suggest much more than the locale. In the contemporary theater a most important refinement of visual appeal is lighting, which perhaps vies with music in the immediacy of its effect.

Not wholly distinct from mood or atmosphere is what is often called the "world" of the play. By this is meant not only the setting (such as ancient Greece or contemporary America), but whether this is a world of heroes or of ordinary citizens, a world dominated by religious values or social conventions or materialism. An action which would seem noble in one of these worlds might seem ridiculous in another and thus demand a different interpretation of the character.

The world the playwright has chosen to depict will ordinarily influence his style, though this will also be affected by the conventions of the theater for which he is writing. "Style" is another inclusive term. It is sometimes used to refer to the conventions themselves, as when one speaks of a play in the "French classical style" or in the "style of a Japanese Noh play." But more often it refers to the manner of verbal expression to be found in the play. Many sorts of distinctions may be made, such as "florid," "simple," "realistic," or "extravagant," but one of the most useful is the distinction between a formal style—that is, highly patterned (as in symmetrical repartee or rhyming lines)—and a familiar style (as when the language seems to fall naturally into the cadences of conversation). A formal style may or may not involve what is called "elevated language"—a literary diction and the frequent use of figures of speech. A familiar style normally uses everyday language. Whether elevated or not, a formal verbal style is normally accompanied in drama by gestures and movements which are also removed from those of every day. Sometimes the terms "formalized" or "stylized" are used for a production of this sort. It used to be thought that a formal, elevated style was the only proper one for tragedy, and a familiar style for comedy, but in the contemporary theater, where the familiar style is most often used for both tragedy and comedy, the occasional use of formal techniques is apt to be dictated by other considerations, some of which will be mentioned in the introductions to Shaw and Strindberg.

Up to this point the play has been discussed as something experienced in the theater, since theatrical performance is the natural medium of drama and determines its characteristic form. When we read a play, we must keep the conditions of theatrical performance in mind and, whenever possible, imagine what differences they might make in the total effect. In the effort of visualizing a play we shall be helped by the kind of stage directions which most modern playwrights put in their printed texts. They are there only in part for the actor or director and in part for the reader, of whom the modern playwright is much more aware than were his predecessors. Some Elizabethan playwrights thought little or not at all of possible readers, and intended their directions, if any, entirely for the stage. Though modern editors of such plays frequently supply additional directions, more effort is required of us in envisaging the stage performance. For example, when a character in one of these older plays says "yes" or "oh," and does not elaborate further, we must decide whether these words are to be said "almost inaudibly," "complacently," or as if "amazed," "troubled," or "much perplexed," to quote a few of Shaw's directions from Act I of *Major Barbara*. We may have to decide whether the tone of an entire scene is bitterly satirical or farcical (a problem raised by one scene in *Volpone* to which attention is called in the discussion, "Satirical Comedy"). Even in a much more recent play, such as Chekhov's *The Seagull*, the tone and pace of a speech or a scene may be open to question.

Such problems can be resolved only by referring to our gradually increasing perception of the general design of the play—to our understanding of the potentialities and limits of each character and of the themes which the interaction of the characters suggest. As we attempt to grasp the significance of each scene and even of each speech within the scene, we supply for ourselves many of the aids to interpretation which the director and the actors give us on the stage.

As readers of a play, however, we enjoy two advantages which are some compensation for what we miss by not being spectators. One is the opportunity to pause at any time to consider the significance of a particular speech or scene, comparing it if we choose with something which precedes or follows it. The other, partly dependent on our freedom to regulate the pace, is the close attention we can give to the verbal texture. If the play is in verse, and especially if the language is highly figurative, we shall undoubtedly be aware of certain fine points which would escape us in the theater. Though, as was said before, a better-trained memory would retain more in the theater and hence would greatly increase such awareness, there is no reason to deny that there are some subtleties which might never be apparent except to a reader. If the meaning were dependent on such effects, the play would have to be considered unperformable—an example of "closet drama." But if, as is often the case with Shakespeare, the play is eminently actable and yet contains passages whose total meaning cannot be adequately projected on the stage, one must conclude that it has a literary value in addition to its dramatic value.

While taking advantage of his special privileges, the reader of drama will nevertheless profit greatly by making an effort to imagine the stage presentation. If the scene can be visualized and if, above all, the inflections of a voice can be guessed, some of the immediacy of the theatrical experience will be felt. In this way the reader can aim toward a comprehensive view of the play which does full justice to its dramatic moments.

*two
twentieth-century
plays*

SECTION I

# George Bernard Shaw

George Bernard Shaw, like Swift, Sheridan, and Yeats, was a Dubliner who had a major effect upon English letters. Born in 1856, he left school in 1871, and took a job with a Dublin real-estate agent. Five years later he went to London, where his mother had already established herself as a music teacher. With her support, a small allowance from his father, and occasional earnings from literary hack-work, he continued to live there and soon began writing novels. By 1883 he had written five of them, none successful. Though he also dabbled in psychical research at this period, his greatest interest was in social and economic problems. In 1884 he joined the Fabian Society and helped to channel its aims in the direction of practical socialism. Some of the ideas expressed in his early plays were obviously formed at this time, and his style was indebted to the lecturing and debating he did. Two other activities occupied much of his time in the eighties and nineties—the reviewing of music and drama. In each field he championed a highly controversial artist, in whom he saw an apostle of socialistic ideas like his own. Though Shaw often forced his interpretations, *The Quintessence of Ibsenism* (1891) and *The Perfect Wagnerite* (1898) remain stimulating and instructive criticism. Particularly important for his development as a playwright was his interest in Ibsen, whose technique of dealing dramatically with social problems influenced Shaw profoundly. Shaw's first play, *Widowers' Houses* (1892), which had to do with slum landlords, was started in collaboration with William Archer, a drama critic and translator of Ibsen. However, in spite of Shaw's continuing interest in social problems, his plays cannot be neatly encompassed in the pigeon-hole of what were called "problem plays." Their great variety in tone and theme can be suggested by a few examples. *Candida* (1894), thanks to the sympathetic portrayal of the heroine, is warm-hearted comedy, whereas *Saint Joan* (1923), for all its witty presentation of the historical issues, approaches tragedy. *Back to Methuselah* (1920) is fantasy; *Major Barbara* (1905) is firmly rooted in the London of its day. By the time of his death in 1950 Shaw had written fifty-seven plays and playlets, and established his position as the foremost contemporary dramatist writing in English.

The opening stage direction of *Major Barbara* is a good example of the help given to the reader as well as to the director and actor by many modern playwrights. Not only does Shaw go into considerable detail in his description of Lady Britomart's house; he as good as invites the reader to imagine himself on the stage, sitting on the "large and comfortable settee." Indications of right and left on the stage are normally given from the point of view of the actor and hence are backwards for a person facing the stage. The reader has to adjust to "stage right" and "stage left," as they are called. But Shaw, by saying "a person sitting on it . . . would have, on his right . . ." spares his reader this momentary confusion.

The details of the furniture Shaw mentions all tell something about the moneyed upper-class milieu with which the poverty of the working-class section of London is later to be contrasted. The dialogue of the play is equally indicative. The vocabulary, grammar, and sentence structure of each character reveal not only his social station, education, and often age, but sometimes an individual peculiarity. Lomax is distinguished by his almost meaningless strings of well-bred exclamations: "But really, don't you know! Oh I say!"

Bill Walker's lower-class background is immediately clear from his way of speaking. His dialect is reproduced with as much phonetic care as the better-known speech habits of Eliza Doolittle in *Pygmalion*. However, once again, Shaw gives special aid to the reader. In the manner of a novelist he supplies at the outset a brief psychological analysis of Lady Britomart, explaining her behavior by relating it to her social background. As other characters enter, he gives his reader similar insights which would otherwise have to be inferred.

In paying close attention to details of setting and speech, Shaw proclaims his connection with the tradition of realism, the implications of which are discussed at greater length in the introduction to Ibsen's *Hedda Gabler*. It is the tradition with which we are most familiar in the twentieth century, closely related to the dominant mode of fiction. Realism always reproduces the surface of life with maximum fidelity in order to facilitate belief in the truth of situation and character. When Shaw speaks as he does about a room in Lady Britomart's house or about the lady herself, he encourages us to suppose that his characters live in a world as real as our own.

It soon becomes apparent, however, that Shaw is not exclusively concerned with mirror-images of people. His names are one indication. "Lady Britomart" and "Andrew Undershaft" hardly sound like the names of real people. They are ways of expressing an attitude toward these characters—of putting them in a certain light. The associations of Britomart with classical legend and with Spenser's *Faerie Queene* seem to constitute a satirical thrust at the lady's aristocratic bearing. Undershaft, with its suggestions of pushing up from below, is almost a ticket name of the sort Ben Jonson or Charles Dickens might use for comic purposes.

Thus, from the outset we know that we are being invited to look at the characters from the special angle of the satirist and to examine with care the society in which they move. Soon we become aware that Shaw is maneuvering them into opposition with each other, and we are listening to exchanges of wit and eloquence unlike any that life ordinarily affords. As the style moves from realistic familiarity to a more formal pattern, more attention is called to what is being said and less to who is saying it. It will be our business as interpreters to understand how the setting and situation, the characters and their ideas, fit into the total design of the play.

# Major Barbara

*A DISCUSSION IN THREE ACTS*

## GEORGE BERNARD SHAW

### ACT I

*It is after dinner in January 1906, in the library in* LADY BRITOMART UNDERSHAFT's *house in Wilton Crescent. A large and comfortable settee is in the middle of the room, upholstered in dark leather. A person sitting on it (it is vacant at present) would have, on his right,* LADY BRITOMART's *writing table, with the lady herself busy at it; a smaller writing table behind him on his left; the door behind him on* LADY BRITOMART's *side; and a window with a window seat directly on his left. Near the window is an armchair.*

LADY BRITOMART *is a woman of fifty or there-abouts, well dressed and yet careless of her dress, well bred and quite reckless of her breeding, well mannered and yet appallingly outspoken and indifferent to the opinion of her interlocutors, amiable and yet peremptory, arbitrary, and high-tempered to the last bearable degree, and withal a very typical managing matron of the upper class, treated as a naughty child until she grew into a scolding mother, and finally settling down with plenty of practical ability and worldly experience, limited in the oddest way with domestic and class limitations, conceiving the universe exactly as if it were a large house in Wilton Crescent, though handling her corner of it very effectively on that assumption, and being quite enlightened and liberal as to the books in the library, the pictures on the walls, the music in the portfolios, and the articles in the papers.*

*Her son,* STEPHEN, *comes in. He is a gravely correct young man under 25, taking himself very seriously, but still in some awe of his mother, from childish habit and bachelor shyness rather than from any weakness of character.*

---

Reprinted by permission of The Society of Authors, London

STEPHEN. Whats the matter?

LADY BRITOMART. Presently, Stephen.

(STEPHEN *submissively walks to the settee and sits down. He takes up a Liberal weekly called* The Speaker.)

LADY BRITOMART. Dont begin to read, Stephen. I shall require all your attention.

STEPHEN. It was only while I was waiting—

LADY BRITOMART. Dont make excuses, Stephen. (*He puts down* The Speaker.) Now! (*She finishes her writing; rises; and comes to the settee.*) I have not kept you waiting very long, I think.

STEPHEN. Not at all, mother.

LADY BRITOMART. Bring me my cushion. (*He takes the cushion from the chair at the desk and arranges it for her as she sits down on the settee.*) Sit down. (*He sits down and fingers his tie nervously.*) Dont fiddle with your tie, Stephen: there is nothing the matter with it.

STEPHEN. I beg your pardon. (*He fiddles with his watch chain instead.*)

LADY BRITOMART. Now are you attending to me, Stephen?

STEPHEN. Of course, mother.

LADY BRITOMART. No: it's not of course. I want something much more than your everyday matter-of-course attention. I am going to speak to you very seriously, Stephen. I wish you would let that chain alone.

STEPHEN (*hastily relinquishing the chain*). Have I done anything to annoy you, mother? If so, it was quite unintentional.

LADY BRITOMART (*astonished*). Nonsense! (*With some remorse.*) My poor boy, did you think I was angry with you?

STEPHEN. What is it, then, mother? You are making me very uneasy.

LADY BRITOMART (*squaring herself at him rather aggressively*). Stephen: may I ask how soon you intend to realize that you are a grown-up man, and that I am only a woman?

STEPHEN (*amazed*). Only a—

LADY BRITOMART. Dont repeat my words, please: it is a most aggravating habit. You must learn to face life seriously, Stephen. I really cannot bear the whole burden of our family affairs any longer. You must advise me: you must assume the reponsibility.

STEPHEN. I!

LADY BRITOMART. Yes, you, of course. You were 24 last June. Youve been at Harrow and Cambridge. Youve been to India and Japan. You must know a lot of things, now; unless you have wasted your time most scandalously. Well, advise me.

STEPHEN (*much perplexed*). You know I have never interfered in the household—

LADY BRITOMART. No: I should think not. I dont want you to order the dinner.

STEPHEN. I mean in our family affairs.

LADY BRITOMART. Well, you must interfere now; for they are getting quite beyond me.

STEPHEN (*troubled*). I have thought sometimes that perhaps I ought; but really, mother, I know so little about them; and what I do know is so painful! it is so impossible to mention some things to you—(*he stops, ashamed*).

LADY BRITOMART. I suppose you mean your father.

STEPHEN (*almost inaudibly*). Yes.

LADY BRITOMART. My dear: we cant go on all our lives not mentioning him. Of course you were quite right not to open the subject until I asked you to; but you are old enough now to be taken into my confidence, and to help me to deal with him about the girls.

STEPHEN. But the girls are all right. They are engaged.

LADY BRITOMART (*complacently*). Yes: I have made a very good match for Sarah. Charles Lomax will be a millionaire at 35. But that is ten years ahead; and in the meantime his trustees cannot under the terms of his father's will allow him more than £800 a year.

STEPHEN. But the will says also that if he increases his income by his own exertions, they may double the increase.

LADY BRITOMART. Charles Lomax's exertions are much more likely to decrease his income than to increase it. Sarah will have to find at least another £800 a year for the next ten years; and even then they will be as poor as church mice. And what about Barbara? I thought Barbara was going to make the most brilliant career of all of you. And what does she do? Joins the Salvation Army; discharges her maid; lives on a pound a week; and walks in one evening with a professor of Greek whom she has picked up in the street, and who pretends to be a Salvationist, and actually plays the big drum for her in public because he has fallen head over ears in love with her.

STEPHEN. I was certainly rather taken aback when I heard they were engaged. Cusins is a very nice fellow, certainly: nobody would ever guess that he was born in Australia; but—

LADY BRITOMART. Oh, Adolphus Cusins will make a very good husband. After all, nobody can say a word against Greek: it stamps a man at once as an educated gentleman. And my family, thank Heaven, is not a pig-headed Tory one. We are Whigs, and believe in liberty. Let snobbish people say what they please: Barbara shall marry, not the man they like, but the man *I* like.

STEPHEN. Of course I was thinking only of his income. However, he is not likely to be extravagant.

LADY BRITOMART. Dont be too sure of that, Stephen. I know your quiet, simple, refined, poetic people like Adolphus: quite content with the best of everything! They cost more than your extravagant people, who are always as mean as they are second rate. No: Barbara will need at least £2000 a year. You see it means two additional households. Besides my dear, you must marry soon. I dont approve of the present fashion of philandering bachelors and late marriages; and I am trying to arrange something for you.

STEPHEN. It's very good of you, mother; but perhaps I had better arrange that for myself.

LADY BRITOMART. Nonsense! you are much too young to begin matchmaking: you would be taken in by some pretty little nobody. Of course I dont mean that you are not to be consulted: you know that as well as I do.

(STEPHEN *closes his lips and is silent.*) Now dont sulk, Stephen.

STEPHEN. I am not sulking, mother. What has all this got to do with—with—with my father?

LADY BRITOMART. My dear Stephen: where is the money to come from? It is easy enough for you and the other children to live on my income as long as we are in the same house; but I cant keep four families in four separate houses. You know how poor my father is: he has barely seven thousand a year now; and really, if he were not the Earl of Stevenage, he would have to give up society. He can do nothing for us. He says, naturally enough, that it is absurd that he should be asked to provide for the children of a man who is rolling in money. You see, Stephen, your father must be fabulously wealthy, because there is always a war going on somewhere.

STEPHEN. You need not remind me of that, mother. I have hardly ever opened a newspaper in my life without seeing our name in it. The Undershaft torpedo! The Undershaft quick firers! The Undershaft ten inch! the Undershaft disappearing rampart gun! the Undershaft submarine! and now the Undershaft aerial battleship! At Harrow they called me the Woolwich Infant.[1] At Cambridge it was the same. A little brute at King's who was always trying to get up revivals, spoilt my Bible—your first birthday present to me—by writing under my name, "Son and heir to Undershaft and Lazarus, Death and Destruction Dealers: address Christendom and Judea." But that was not so bad as the way I was kowtowed to everywhere because my father was making millions by selling cannons.

LADY BRITOMART. It is not only the cannons, but the war loans that Lazarus arranges under cover of giving credit for the cannons. You know, Stephen, it's perfectly scandalous. Those two men, Andrew Undershaft and Lazarus, positively have Europe under their thumbs. That is why your father is able to behave as he does. He is above the law. Do you think Bismarck or Gladstone or Disraeli

could have openly defied every social and moral obligation all their lives as your father has? They simply wouldnt have dared. I asked Gladstone to take it up. I asked The Times to take it up. I asked the Lord Chamberlain to take it up. But it was just like asking them to declare war on the Sultan. They wouldnt. They said they couldnt touch him. I believe they were afraid.

STEPHEN. What could they do? He does not actually break the law.

LADY BRITOMART. Not break the law! He is always breaking the law. He broke the law when he was born: his parents were not married.

STEPHEN. Mother! Is that true?

LADY BRITOMART. Of course it's true: that was why we separated.

STEPHEN. He married without letting you know this!

LADY BRITOMART (*rather taken aback by this inference*). Oh no. To do Andrew justice, that was not the sort of thing he did. Besides, you know the Undershaft motto: Unashamed. Everybody knew.

STEPHEN. But you said that was why you separated.

LADY BRITOMART. Yes, because he was not content with being a foundling himself: he wanted to disinherit you for another foundling. That was what I couldnt stand.

STEPHEN (*ashamed*). Do you mean for—for —for—

LADY BRITOMART. Dont stammer, Stephen. Speak distinctly.

STEPHEN. But this is so frightful to me, mother. To have to speak to you about such things!

LADY BRITOMART. It's not pleasant for me, either, especially if you are still so childish that you must make it worse by a display of embarrassment. It is only in the middle classes, Stephen, that people get into a state of dumb helpless horror when they find that there are wicked people in the world. In our class, we have to decide what is to be done with wicked people; and nothing should disturb our self-possession. Now ask your question properly.

STEPHEN. Mother: have you no consideration for me? For Heaven's sake either treat

---

[1] *Woolwich Infant* a cannon named for the Woolwich arsenal

me as a child, as you always do, and tell me nothing at all; or tell me everything and let me take it as best I can.

LADY BRITOMART. Treat you as a child! What do you mean? It is most unkind and ungrateful of you to say such a thing. You know I have never treated any of you as children. I have always made you my companions and friends, and allowed you perfect freedom to do and say whatever you liked, so long as you liked what I could approve of.

STEPHEN (*desperately*). I daresay we have been the very imperfect children of a very perfect mother; but I do beg you to let me alone for once, and tell me about this horrible business of my father wanting to set me aside for another son.

LADY BRITOMART (*amazed*). Another son! I never said anything of the kind. I never dreamt of such a thing. This is what comes of interrupting me.

STEPHEN. But you said—

LADY BRITOMART (*cutting him short*). Now be a good boy, Stephen, and listen to me patiently. The Undershafts are descended from a foundling in the parish of St Andrew Undershaft in the city. That was long ago, in the reign of James the First. Well, this foundling was adopted by an armorer and gun-maker. In the course of time the foundling succeeded to the business; and from some notion of gratitude, or some vow or something, he adopted another foundling, and left the business to him. And that foundling did the same. Ever since that, the cannon business has always been left to an adopted foundling named Andrew Undershaft.

STEPHEN. But did they never marry? Were there no legitimate sons?

LADY BRITOMART. Oh yes: they married just as your father did; and they were rich enough to buy land for their own children and leave them well provided for. But they always adopted and trained some foundling to succeed them in the business; and of course they always quarrelled with their wives furiously over it. Your father was adopted in that way; and he pretends to consider himself bound to keep up the tradition and adopt somebody to leave the business to. Of course I was not going to stand that. There

may have been some reason for it when the Undershafts could only marry women in their own class, whose sons were not fit to govern great estates. But there could be no excuse for passing over my son.

STEPHEN (*dubiously*). I am afraid I should make a poor hand of managing a cannon foundry.

LADY BRITOMART. Nonsense! you could easily get a manager and pay him a salary.

STEPHEN. My father evidently had no great opinion of my capacity.

LADY BRITOMART. Stuff, child! you were only a baby: it had nothing to do with your capacity. Andrew did it on principle, just as he did every perverse and wicked thing on principle. When my father remonstrated, Andrew actually told him to his face that history tells us of only two successful institutions: one the Undershaft firm, and the other the Roman Empire under the Antonines. That was because the Antonine emperors all adopted their successors. Such rubbish! The Stevenages are as good as the Antonines, I hope; and you are a Stevenage. But that was Andrew all over. There you have the man! Always clever and unanswerable when he was defending nonsense and wickedness: always awkward and sullen when he had to behave sensibly and decently!

STEPHEN. Then it was on my account that your home life was broken up, mother. I am sorry.

LADY BRITOMART. Well, dear, there were other differences. I really cannot bear an immoral man. I am not a Pharisee, I hope; and I should not have minded his merely doing wrong things: we are none of us perfect. But your father didnt exactly do wrong things: he said them and thought them: that was what was so dreadful. He really had a sort of religion of wrongness. Just as one doesnt mind men practising immorality so long as they own that they are in the wrong by preaching morality; so I couldnt forgive Andrew for preaching immorality while he practised morality. You would all have grown up without principles, without any knowledge of right and wrong, if he had been in the house. You know, my dear, your father was a very attractive man in some ways. Children did not dislike him; and he took advantage of it to put the wickedest ideas into their heads, and make them quite unmanageable. I did not dislike him myself: very far from it; but nothing can bridge over moral disagreement.

STEPHEN. All this simply bewilders me, mother. People may differ about matters of opinion, or even about religion; but how can they differ about right and wrong? Right is right; and wrong is wrong; and if a man cannot distinguish them properly, he is either a fool or a rascal: thats all.

LADY BRITOMART (*touched*). Thats my own boy (*she pats his cheek*)! Your father never could answer that: he used to !augh and get out of it under cover of some affectionate nonsense. And now that you understand the situation, what do you advise me to do?

STEPHEN. Well, what can you do?

LADY BRITOMART. I must get the money somehow.

STEPHEN. We cannot take money from him. I had rather go and live in some cheap place like Bedford Square or even Hampstead than take a farthing of his money.

LADY BRITOMART. But after all, Stephen, our present income comes from Andrew.

STEPHEN (*shocked*). I never knew that.

LADY BRITOMART. Well, you surely didnt suppose your grandfather had anything to give me. The Stevenages could not do everything for you. We gave you social position. Andrew had to contribute something. He had a very good bargain, I think.

STEPHEN (*bitterly*). We are utterly dependent on him and his cannons, then?

LADY BRITOMART. Certainly not: the money is settled. But he provided it. So you see it is not a question of taking money from him or not: it is simply a question of how much. I dont want any more for myself.

STEPHEN. Nor do I.

LADY BRITOMART. But Sarah does; and Barbara does. That is, Charles Lomax and Adolphus Cusins will cost them more. So I must put my pride in my pocket and ask for it, I suppose. That is your advice, Stephen, is it not?

STEPHEN. No.

LADY BRITOMART (*sharply*). Stephen!

STEPHEN. Of course if you are determined—

LADY BRITOMART. I am not determined: I ask your advice; and I am waiting for it. I will not have all the responsibility thrown on my shoulders.

STEPHEN (*obstinately*). I would die sooner than ask him for another penny.

LADY BRITOMART (*resignedly*). You mean that *I* must ask him. Very well, Stephen: it shall be as you wish. You will be glad to know that your grandfather concurs. But he thinks I ought to ask Andrew to come here and see the girls. After all, he must have some natural affection for them.

STEPHEN. Ask him here!!!

LADY BRITOMART. Do not repeat my words, Stephen. Where else can I ask him?

STEPHEN. I never expected you to ask him at all.

LADY BRITOMART. Now dont tease, Stephen. Come! you see that it is necessary that he should pay us a visit, dont you?

STEPHEN (*reluctantly*). I suppose so, if the girls cannot do without his money.

LADY BRITOMART. Thank you, Stephen: I knew you would give me the right advice when it was properly explained to you. I have asked your father to come this evening. (STEPHEN *bounds from his seat.*) Dont jump, Stephen: it fidgets me.

STEPHEN (*in utter consternation*). Do you mean to say that my father is coming here tonight—that he may be here at any moment?

LADY BRITOMART (*looking at her watch*). I said nine. (*He gasps. She rises.*) Ring the bell, please. (STEPHEN *goes to the smaller writing table; presses a button on it; and sits at it with his elbows on the table and his head in his hands, outwitted and overwhelmed.*) It is ten minutes to nine yet; and I have to prepare the girls. I asked Charles Lomax and Adolphus to dinner on purpose that they might be here. Andrew had better see them in case he should cherish any delusions as to their being capable of supporting their wives. (*The butler enters:* LADY BRITOMART *goes behind the settee to speak to him.*) Morrison: go up to the drawing room and tell everybody to come down here at once. (MORRISON *withdraws.* LADY BRITOMART *turns to* STEPHEN). Now remember, Stephen: I shall need all your countenance and authority. (*He rises and tries to recover some vestige of these attributes.*) Give me a chair, dear. (*He pushes a chair forward from the wall to where she stands, near the smaller writing table. She sits down; and he goes to the armchair, into which he throws himself.*) I dont know how Barbara will take it. Ever since they made her a major in the Salvation Army she has developed a propensity to have her own way and order people about which quite cows me sometimes. It's not ladylike: I'm sure I dont know where she picked it up. Anyhow, Barbara shant bully me; but still it's just as well that your father should be here before she has time to refuse to meet him or make a fuss. Dont look nervous, Stephen: it will only encourage Barbara to make difficulties. *I* am nervous enough, goodness knows; but I dont shew it.

(SARAH *and* BARBARA *come in with their respective young men,* CHARLES LOMAX *and* ADOLPHUS CUSINS. SARAH *is slender, bored, and mundane.* BARBARA *is robuster, jollier, much more energetic.* SARAH *is fashionably dressed:* BARBARA *is in Salvation Army uniform.* LOMAX, *a young man about town, is like many other young men about town. He is afflicted with a frivolous sense of humor which plunges him at the most inopportune moments into paroxysms of imperfectly suppressed laughter.* CUSINS *is a spectacled student, slight, thin haired, and sweet voiced, with a more complex form of* LOMAX's *complaint. His sense of humor is intellectual and subtle, and is complicated by an appalling temper. The lifelong struggle of a benevolent temperament and a high conscience against impulses of inhuman ridicule and fierce impatience has set up a chronic strain which has visibly wrecked his constitution. He is a most implacable, determined, tenacious, intolerant person who by mere force of character presents himself as—and indeed actually is—considerate, gentle, explanatory, even mild and apologetic, capable possibly of murder, but not of cruelty or coarseness. By the operation of some instinct which is not merciful enough to blind him with the illusions of love, he is obstinately bent on marrying* BARBARA. LOMAX *likes* SARAH *and thinks it will be rather a lark to marry her. Consequently he has not attempted to resist* LADY BRITOMART's *arrangements to that end.*

*All four look as if they had been having a good deal of fun in the drawing room. The girls enter first, leaving the swains outside.* SARAH *comes to the settee.* BARBARA *comes in after her and stops at the door.*)

BARBARA. Are Cholly and Dolly to come in?

LADY BRITOMART (*forcibly*). Barbara: I will not have Charles called Cholly: the vulgarity of it positively makes me ill.

BARBARA. It's all right, mother: Cholly is quite correct nowadays. Are they to come in?

LADY BRITOMART. Yes, if they will behave themselves.

BARBARA (*through the door*). Come in, Dolly; and behave yourself.

(BARBARA *comes to her mother's writing table.* CUSINS *enters smiling, and wanders towards* LADY BRITOMART.)

SARAH (*calling*). Come in, Cholly. (LOMAX *enters, controlling his features very imperfectly, and places himself vaguely between* SARAH *and* BARBARA.)

LADY BRITOMART (*peremptorily*). Sit down, all of you. (*They sit.* CUSINS *crosses to the window and seats himself there.* LOMAX *takes a chair.* BARBARA *sits at the writing table and* SARAH *on the settee.*) I dont in the least know what you are laughing at, Adolphus. I am surprised at you, though I expected nothing better from Charles Lomax.

CUSINS (*in a remarkably gentle voice*). Barbara has been trying to teach me the West Ham Salvation March.

LADY BRITOMART. I see nothing to laugh at in that; nor should you if you are really converted.

CUSINS (*sweetly*). You were not present. It was really funny, I believe.

LOMAX. Ripping.

LADY BRITOMART. Be quiet, Charles. Now listen to me, children. Your father is coming here this evening.

(*General stupefaction.* LOMAX, SARAH, *and* BARBARA *rise:* SARAH *scared, and* BARBARA *amused and expectant.*)

LOMAX (*remonstrating*). Oh I say!

LADY BRITOMART. You are not called on to say anything, Charles.

SARAH. Are you serious, mother?

LADY BRITOMART. Of course I am serious. It is on your account, Sarah, and also on Charles's. (*Silence.* SARAH *sits, with a shrug.*

CHARLES *looks painfully unworthy.*) I hope you are not going to object, Barbara.

BARBARA. I! why should I? My father has a soul to be saved like anybody else. He's quite welcome as far as I am concerned. (*She sits on the table, and softly whistles "Onward, Christian Soldiers."*)

LOMAX (*still remonstrant*). But really, dont you know! Oh I say!

LADY BRITOMART (*frigidly*). What do you wish to convey, Charles?

LOMAX. Well, you must admit that this is a bit thick.

LADY BRITOMART (*turning with ominous suavity to* CUSINS). Adolphus: you are a professor of Greek. Can you translate Charles Lomax's remarks into reputable English for us?

CUSINS (*cautiously*). If I may say so, Lady Brit, I think Charles has rather happily expressed what we all feel. Homer, speaking of Autolycus,[2] uses the same phrase. πυκινόν δόμον ἐλθεῖν means a bit thick.

LOMAX (*handsomely*). Not that I mind, you know, if Sarah dont.[3] (*He sits.*)

LADY BRITOMART (*crushingly*). Thank you. Have I your permission, Adolphus, to invite my own husband to my own house?

CUSINS (*gallantly*). You have my unhesitating support in everything you do.

LADY BRITOMART. Tush! Sarah: have you nothing to say?

SARAH. Do you mean that he is coming regularly to live here?

LADY BRITOMART. Certainly not. The spare room is ready for him if he likes to stay for a day or two and see a little more of you; but there are limits.

SARAH. Well, he cant eat us, I suppose. *I* dont mind.

LOMAX (*chuckling*). I wonder how the old man will take it.

LADY BRITOMART. Much as the old woman will, no doubt, Charles.

LOMAX (*abashed*). I didnt mean—at least—

LADY BRITOMART. You didnt think, Charles. You never do; and the result is, you never mean anything. And now please attend to me,

Your father will be quite a stranger to us.

LOMAX. I suppose he hasnt seen Sarah since she was a little kid.

LADY BRITOMART. Not since she was little kid, Charles, as you express it with that elegance of diction and refinement of thought that seem never to desert you. Accordingly— er—(*impatiently*) Now I have forgotten what I was going to say. That comes of your provoking me to be sarcastic, Charles. Adolphus: will you kindly tell me where I was.

CUSINS (*sweetly*). You were saying that as Mr Undershaft has not seen his children since they were babies, he will form his opinion of the way you have brought them up from their behavior tonight, and that therefore you wish us all to be particularly careful to conduct ourselves well, especially Charles.

LADY BRITOMART (*with emphatic approval*). Precisely.

LOMAX. Look here, Dolly: Lady Brit didnt say that.

LADY BRITOMART (*vehemently*). I did, Charles. Adolphus's recollection is perfectly correct. It is most important that you should be good; and I do beg you for once not to pair off into opposite corners and giggle and whisper while I am speaking to your father.

BARBARA. All right, mother. We'll do you credit. (*She comes off the table, and sits in her chair with ladylike elegance.*)

LADY BRITOMART. Remember, Charles, that Sarah will want to feel proud of you instead of ashamed of you.

LOMAX. Oh I say! theres nothing to be exactly proud of, dont you know.

LADY BRITOMART. Well, try and look as if there was.

(MORRISON, *pale and dismayed, breaks into the room in unconcealed disorder.*)

MORRISON. Might I speak a word to you, my lady?

LADY BRITOMART. Nonsense! Shew him up.

MORRISON. Yes, my lady. (*He goes.*)

LOMAX. Does Morrison know who it is?

LADY BRITOMART. Of course. Morrison has always been with us.

LOMAX. It must be a regular corker for him, dont you know.

LADY BRITOMART. Is this a moment to get

2 *Autolycus* a son of Hermes noted for trickery
3*if Sarah dont* "don't" was an acceptable substitute for "doesn't" in familiar speech

on my nerves, Charles, with your outrageous expressions?

LOMAX. But this is something out of the ordinary, really—

MORRISON (*at the door*). The—er—Mr Undershaft. (*He retreats in confusion.*)

(ANDREW UNDERSHAFT *comes in. All rise.* LADY BRITOMART *meets him in the middle of the room behind the settee.*

ANDREW *is, on the surface, a stoutish, easygoing elderly man, with kindly patient manners, and an engaging simplicity of character. But he has a watchful, deliberate, waiting, listening face, and formidable reserves of power, both bodily and mental, in his capacious chest and long head. His gentleness is partly that of a strong man who has learnt by experience that his natural grip hurts ordinary people unless he handles them very carefully, and partly the mellowness of age and success. He is also a little shy in his present very delicate situation.*)

LADY BRITOMART. Good evening, Andrew.

UNDERSHAFT. How d'ye do, my dear.

LADY BRITOMART. You look a good deal older.

UNDERSHAFT (*apologetically*). I am somewhat older. (*Taking her hand with a touch of courtship.*) Time has stood still with you.

LADY BRITOMART (*throwing away his hand*). Rubbish! This is your family.

UNDERSHAFT (*surprised*). Is it so large? I am sorry to say my memory is failing very badly in some things. (*He offers his hand with paternal kindness to* LOMAX.)

LOMAX (*jerkily shaking his hand*). Ahdedoo.

UNDERSHAFT. I can see you are my eldest. I am very glad to meet you again, my boy.

LOMAX (*remonstrating*). No, but look here dont you know—(*Overcome.*) Oh I say!

LADY BRITOMART (*recovering from momentary speechlessness*). Andrew: do you mean to say that you dont remember how many children you have?

UNDERSHAFT. Well, I am afraid I—. They have grown so much—er. Am I making any ridiculous mistake? I may as well confess: I recollect only one son. But so many things have happened since, of course—er—

LADY BRITOMART (*decisively*). Andrew: you are talking nonsense. Of course you have only one son.

UNDERSHAFT. Perhaps you will be good enough to introduce me, my dear.

LADY BRITOMART. That is Charles Lomax, who is engaged to Sarah.

UNDERSHAFT. My dear sir, I beg your pardon.

LOMAX. Notatall. Delighted, I assure you.

LADY BRITOMART. This is Stephen.

UNDERSHAFT (*bowing*). Happy to make your acquaintance, Mr Stephen. Then (*going to* CUSINS) you must be my son. (*Taking* CUSINS' *hands in his.*) How are you, my young friend? (*To* LADY BRITOMART.) He is very like you, my love.

CUSINS. You flatter me, Mr Undershaft. My name is Cusins: engaged to Barbara. (*Very explicitly.*) That is Major Barbara Undershaft, of the Salvation Army. That is Sarah, your second daughter. This is Stephen Undershaft, your son.

UNDERSHAFT. My dear Stephen, I beg your pardon.

STEPHEN. Not at all.

UNDERSHAFT. Mr Cusins: I am much indebted to you for explaining so precisely. (*Turning to* SARAH.) Barbara, my dear—

SARAH (*prompting him*). Sarah.

UNDERSHAFT. Sarah, of course. (*They shake hands. He goes over to* BARBARA.) Barbara—I am right this time, I hope?

BARBARA. Quite right. (*They shake hands.*)

LADY BRITOMART (*resuming command*). Sit down, all of you. Sit down, Andrew. (*She comes forward and sits on the settee.* CUSINS *also brings his chair forward on her left.* BARBARA *and* STEPHEN *resume their seats.* LOMAX *gives his chair to* SARAH *and goes for another.*)

UNDERSHAFT. Thank you, my love.

LOMAX (*conversationally, as he brings a chair forward between the writing table and the settee, and offers it to* UNDERSHAFT). Takes you some time to find out exactly where you are, dont it?

UNDERSHAFT (*accepting the chair, but remaining standing*). That is not what embarrasses me, Mr Lomax. My difficulty is that if I play the part of a father, I shall produce the effect of an intrusive stranger; and if I play the part of a discreet stranger, I may appear a callous father.

LADY BRITOMART. There is no need for you

to play any part at all, Andrew. You had much better be sincere and natural.

UNDERSHAFT (*submissively*). Yes, my dear: I daresay that will be best. (*He sits down comfortably.*) Well, here I am. Now what can I do for you all?

LADY BRITOMART. You need not do anything, Andrew. You are one of the family. You can sit with us and enjoy yourself.

(*A painfully conscious pause.* BARBARA *makes a face at* LOMAX, *whose too long suppressed mirth immediately explodes in agonized neighings.*)

LADY BRITOMART (*outraged*). Charles Lomax: if you can behave yourself, behave yourself. If not, leave the room.

LOMAX. I'm awfully sorry, Lady Brit; but really you know, upon my soul! (*He sits on the settee between* LADY BRITOMART *and* UNDERSHAFT, *quite overcome.*)

BARBARA. Why dont you laugh if you want to, Cholly? It's good for your inside.

LADY BRITOMART. Barbara: you have had the education of a lady. Please let your father see that; and dont talk like a street girl.

UNDERSHAFT. Never mind me, my dear. As you know, I am not a gentleman; and I was never educated.

LOMAX (*encouragingly*). Nobody'd know it, I assure you. You look all right, you know.

CUSINS. Let me advise you to study Greek, Mr Undershaft. Greek scholars are privileged men. Few of them know Greek; and none of them know anything else; but their position is unchallengeable. Other languages are the qualifications of waiters and commercial travellers: Greek is to a man of position what the hallmark is to silver.

BARBARA. Dolly: dont be insincere. Cholly: fetch your concertina[4] and play something for us.

LOMAX (*jumps up eagerly, but checks himself to remark doubtfully to* UNDERSHAFT). Perhaps that sort of thing isnt in your line, eh?

UNDERSHAFT. I am particularly fond of music.

LOMAX (*delighted*). Are you? Then I'll get it. (*He goes upstairs for the instrument.*)

UNDERSHAFT. Do you play, Barbara?

BARBARA. Only the tambourine. But Cholly's teaching me the concertina.

UNDERSHAFT. Is Cholly also a member of the Salvation Army?

BARBARA. No: he says it's bad form to be a dissenter.[5] But I dont despair of Cholly. I made him come yesterday to a meeting at the dock gates, and take the collection in his hat.

UNDERSHAFT (*looks whimsically at his wife*)!!

LADY BRITOMART. It is not my doing, Andrew. Barbara is old enough to take her own way. She has no father to advise her.

BARBARA. Oh yes she has. There are no orphans in the Salvation Army.

UNDERSHAFT. Your father there has a great many children and plenty of experience, eh?

BARBARA (*looking at him with quick interest and nodding*). Just so. How did you come to understand that? (LOMAX *is heard at the door trying the concertina.*)

LADY BRITOMART. Come in, Charles. Play us something at once.

LOMAX. Righto! (*He sits down in his former place, and preludes.*)

UNDERSHAFT. One moment, Mr Lomax. I am rather interested in the Salvation Army. Its motto might be my own: Blood and Fire.

LOMAX (*shocked*). But not your sort of blood and fire, you know.

UNDERSHAFT. My sort of blood cleanses: my sort of fire purifies.

BARBARA. So do ours. Come down tomorrow to my shelter—the West Ham shelter—and see what we're doing. We're going to march to a great meeting in the Assembly Hall at Mile End. Come and see the shelter and then march with us: it will do you a lot of good. Can you play anything?

UNDERSHAFT. In my youth I earned pennies, and even shillings occasionally, in the streets and in public house parlors by my natural talent for stepdancing.[6] Later on, I became a member of the Undershaft orchestral society, and performed passably on the tenor trombone.

LOMAX (*scandalized—putting down the concertina*). Oh I say!

---

[4] *concertina* hand accordian

[5] *dissenter* i.e., member of any of the "dissenting" sects which broke away from the established church [6] *stepdancing* a kind of dancing performed by one person, displaying special steps

BARBARA. Many a sinner has played himself into heaven on the trombone, thanks to the Army.

LOMAX (to BARBARA, *still rather shocked*). Yes; but what about the cannon business, dont you know? (*To* UNDERSHAFT.) Getting into heaven is not exactly in your line, is it?

LADY BRITOMART. Charles!!!

LOMAX. Well; but it stands to reason, dont it? The cannon business may be necessary and all that: we cant get on without cannons; but it isnt right, you know. On the other hand, there may be a certain amount of tosh about the Salvation Army—I belong to the Established Church myself—but still you cant deny that it's religion; and you cant go against religion, can you? At least unless youre downright immoral, dont you know.

UNDERSHAFT. You hardly appreciate my position, Mr Lomax—

LOMAX (*hastily*). I'm not saying anything against you personally—

UNDERSHAFT. Quite so, quite so. But consider for a moment. Here I am, a profiteer in mutilation and murder. I find myself in a specially amiable humor just now because, this morning, down at the foundry, we blew twenty-seven dummy soldiers into fragments with a gun which formerly destroyed only thirteen.

LOMAX (*leniently*). Well, the more destructive war becomes, the sooner it will be abolished, eh?

UNDERSHAFT. Not at all. The more destructive war becomes the more fascinating we find it. No, Mr Lomax: I am obliged to you for making the usual excuse for my trade; but I am not ashamed of it. I am not one of those men who keep their morals and their business in watertight compartments. All the spare money my trade rivals spend on hospitals, cathedrals, and other receptacles for conscience money, I devote to experiments and researches in improved methods of destroying life and property. I have always done so; and I always shall. Therefore your Christmas card moralities of peace on earth and goodwill among men are of no use to me. Your Christianity, which enjoins you to resist not evil, and to turn the other cheek, would make me a bankrupt. My morality—my religion—must have a place for cannons and torpedoes in it.

STEPHEN (*coldly—almost sullenly*). You speak as if there were half a dozen moralities and religions to choose from, instead of one true morality and one true religion.

UNDERSHAFT. For me there is only one true morality; but it might not fit you, as you do not manufacture aerial battleships. There is only one true morality for every man; but every man has not the same true morality.

LOMAX (*overtaxed*). Would you mind saying that again? I didnt quite follow it.

CUSINS. It's quite simple. As Euripides says, one man's meat is another man's poison morally as well as physically.

UNDERSHAFT. Precisely.

LOMAX. Oh, that! Yes, yes, yes. True. True.

STEPHEN. In other words, some men are honest and some are scoundrels.

BARBARA. Bosh! There are no scoundrels.

UNDERSHAFT. Indeed? Are there any good men?

BARBARA. No. Not one. There are neither good men nor scoundrels: there are just children of one Father; and the sooner they stop calling one another names the better. You neednt talk to me: I know them. Ive had scores of them through my hands: scoundrels, criminals, infidels, philanthropists, missionaries, county councillors, all sorts. Theyre all just the same sort of sinner; and theres the same salvation ready for them all.

UNDERSHAFT. May I ask have you ever saved a maker of cannons?

BARBARA. No. Will you let me try?

UNDERSHAFT. Well, I will make a bargain with you. If I go to see you tomorrow in your Salvation Shelter, will you come the day after to see me in my cannon works?

BARBARA. Take care. It may end in your giving up the cannons for the sake of the Salvation Army.

UNDERSHAFT. Are you sure it will not end in your giving up the Salvation Army for the sake of the cannons?

BARBARA. I will take my chance of that.

UNDERSHAFT. And I will take my chance of the other. (*They shake hands on it.*) Where is your shelter?

BARBARA. In West Ham. At the sign of the cross. Ask anybody in Canning Town. Where are your works?

UNDERSHAFT. In Perivale St Andrews. At the sign of the sword. Ask anybody in Europe.

LOMAX. Hadnt I better play something?

BARBARA. Yes. Give us Onward, Christian Soldiers.

LOMAX. Well, thats rather a strong order to begin with, dont you know. Suppose I sing Thourt passing hence, my brother. It's much the same tune.

BARBARA. It's too melancholy. You get saved, Cholly; and youll pass hence, my brother, without making such a fuss about it.

LADY BRITOMART. Really, Barbara, you go on as if religion were a pleasant subject. Do have some sense of propriety.

UNDERSHAFT. I do not find it an unpleasant subject, my dear. It is the only one that capable people really care for.

LADY BRITOMART (looking at her watch). Well, if you are determined to have it, I insist on having it in a proper and respectable way. Charles: ring for prayers.

(General amazement. STEPHEN rises in dismay.)

LOMAX (rising). Oh I say!

UNDERSHAFT (rising). I am afraid I must be going.

LADY BRITOMART. You cannot go now, Andrew: it would be most improper. Sit down. What will the servants think?

UNDERSHAFT. My dear: I have conscientious scruples. May I suggest a compromise? If Barbara will conduct a little service in the drawing room, with Mr Lomax as organist, I will attend it willingly. I will even take part, if a trombone can be procured.

LADY BRITOMART. Dont mock, Andrew.

UNDERSHAFT (shocked—to BARBARA). You dont think I am mocking, my love, I hope.

BARBARA. No, of course not; and it wouldnt matter if you were: half the Army came to their first meeting for a lark. (Rising.) Come along. (She throws her arm round her father and sweeps him out, calling to the others from the threshold.) Come, Dolly. Come, Cholly.

(CUSINS rises.)

LADY BRITOMART. I will not be disobeyed by everybody. Adolphus: sit down. (He does

not.) Charles: you may go. You are not fit for prayers: you cannot keep your countenance.

LOMAX. Oh I say! (He goes out.)

LADY BRITOMART (continuing). But you, Adolphus, can behave yourself if you choose to. I insist on your staying.

CUSINS. My dear Lady Brit: there are things in the family prayer book that I couldnt bear to hear you say.

LADY BRITOMART. What things, pray?

CUSINS. Well, you would have to say before all the servants that we have done things we ought not to have done, and left undone things we ought to have done, and that there is no health in us. I cannot bear to hear you doing yourself such an injustice, and Barbara such an injustice. As for myself, I flatly deny it: I have done my best. I shouldnt dare to marry Barbara—I couldnt look you in the face—if it were true. So I must go to the drawing room.

LADY BRITOMART (offended). Well, go. (He starts for the door.) And remember this, Adolphus (he turns to listen): I have a very strong suspicion that you went to the Salvation Army to worship Barbara and nothing else. And I quite appreciate the very clever way in which you systematically humbug me. I have found you out. Take care Barbara doesnt. Thats all.

CUSINS (with unruffled sweetness). Dont tell on me. (He steals out.)

LADY BRITOMART. Sarah: if you want to go, go. Anything's better than to sit there as if you wished you were a thousand miles away.

SARAH (languidly). Very well, mamma. (She goes.)

(LADY BRITOMART, with a sudden flounce, gives way to a little gust of tears.)

STEPHEN (going to her). Mother: whats the matter?

LADY BRITOMART (swishing away her tears with her handkerchief). Nothing. Foolishness. You can go with him, too, if you like, and leave me with the servants.

STEPHEN. Oh, you mustnt think that, mother. I—I dont like him.

LADY BRITOMART. The others do. That is the injustice of a woman's lot. A woman has to bring up her children; and that means to restrain them, to deny them things they want, to set them tasks, to punish them when they do wrong, to do all the unpleasant things. And then the father, who has nothing to do but pet them and spoil them, comes in when all her work is done and steals their affection from her.

STEPHEN. He has not stolen our affection from you. It is only curiosity.

LADY BRITOMART (*violently*). I wont be consoled, Stephen. There is nothing the matter with me. (*She rises and goes towards the door.*)

STEPHEN. Where are you going, mother?

LADY BRITOMART. To the drawing room, of course. (*She goes out. Onward, Christian Soldiers, on the concertina, with tambourine accompaniment, is heard when the door opens.*) Are you coming, Stephen?

STEPHEN. No. Certainly not. (*She goes. He sits down on the settee, with compressed lips and an expression of strong dislike.*)

## ACT II

*The yard of the West Ham shelter of the Salvation Army is a cold place on a January morning. The building itself, an old warehouse, is newly whitewashed. Its gabled end projects into the yard in the middle, with a door on the ground floor, and another in the loft above it without any balcony or ladder, but with a pulley rigged over it for hoisting sacks. Those who come from this central gable end into the yard have the gateway leading to the street on their left, with a stone horse-trough just beyond it, and on the right, a penthouse shielding a table from the weather. There are forms[7] at the table; and on them are seated a man and a woman, both much down on their luck, finishing a meal of bread (one thick slice each, with margarine and golden syrup) and diluted milk.*

*The man, a workman out of employment, is young, agile, a talker, a poser, sharp enough to be capable of anything in reason except honesty or altruistic considerations of any kind. The woman is a commonplace old bundle of poverty and hard-worn humanity. She looks sixty and probably is forty-five.*

*If they were rich people, gloved and muffed and well wrapped up in furs and overcoats, they would be numbed and miserable; for it is a grindingly cold raw January day; and a glance at the background of grimy warehouses and leaden sky visible over the whitewashed walls of the yard would drive any idle rich person straight to the Mediterranean. But these two, being no more troubled with visions of the Mediterranean than of the moon, and being compelled to keep more of their clothes in the pawnshop, and less on their persons, in winter than in summer, are not depressed by the cold: rather are they stung into vivacity, to which their meal has just now given an almost jolly turn. The man takes a pull at his mug, and then gets up and moves about the yard with his hands deep in his pockets, occasionally breaking into a stepdance.*

THE WOMAN. Feel better arter your meal, sir?

THE MAN. No. Call that a meal! Good enough for you, praps; but wot is it to me, an intelligent workin man.

THE WOMAN. Workin man! Wot are you?

THE MAN. Painter.

THE WOMAN (*sceptically*). Yus, I dessay.

THE MAN. Yus, you dessay! I know. Every loafer that cant do nothink calls isself a painter. Well, I'm a real painter: grainer, finisher, thirty-eight bob a week when I can get it.

THE WOMAN. Then why dont you go and get it?

THE MAN. I'll tell you why. Fust: I'm intelligent—ff ff f! it's rotten cold here (*he dances a step or two*)—yes: intelligent beyond the station o life into which it has pleased the capitalists to call me; and they dont like a man that sees through em. Second, an intelligent bein needs a doo share of appiness; so I drink somethink cruel when I get the chawnce. Third, I stand by my class and do as little as I can so's to leave arf the job for me fellow workers. Fourth, I'm fly[8] enough to know wots inside the law and wots outside it; and inside it I do as the capitalists do: pinch wot I can lay me ands on. In a proper state of society I am sober, industrious and honest: in Rome, so to speak, I do as the Romans do. Wots the consequence? When trade is bad—

---

[7] *forms* benches

[8] *fly* knowing, "hip"

and it's rotten bad just now—and the employers az to sack arf their men, they generally start on me.

THE WOMAN. Whats your name?

THE MAN. Price. Bronterre O'Brien Price. Usually called Snobby Price, for short.

THE WOMAN. Snobby's a carpenter,[9] aint it? You said you was a painter.

PRICE. Not that kind of snob,[10] but the genteel sort. I'm too uppish, owing to my intelligence, and my father being a Chartist[11] and a reading, thinking man: a stationer, too. I'm none of your common hewers of wood and drawers of water; and dont you forget it. (*He returns to his seat at the table, and takes up his mug.*) Wots your name?

THE WOMAN. Rummy[12] Mitchens,[13] sir.

PRICE (*quaffing the remains of his milk to her*). Your elth, Miss Mitchens.

RUMMY (*correcting him*). Missis Mitchens.

PRICE. Wot! Oh Rummy, Rummy! Respectable married woman, Rummy, gittin rescued by the Salvation Army by pretendin to be a bad un. Same old game!

RUMMY. What am I to do? I cant starve. Them Salvation lesses is dear good girls; but the better you are, the worse they likes to think you were before they rescued you. Why shouldnt they av a bit o credit, poor loves? theyre worn to rags by their work. And where would they get the money to rescue us if we was to let on we'er no worse than other people? You know what ladies and gentlemen are.

PRICE. Thievin swine! Wish I ad their job, Rummy, all the same. Wot does Rummy stand for? Pet name praps?

RUMMY. Short for Romola.

PRICE. For wot!?

RUMMY. Romola. It was out of a new book. Somebody me mother wanted me to grow up like.

PRICE. We're companions in misfortune, Rummy. Both on us got names that nobody cawnt pronounce. Consequently I'm Snobby and youre Rummy because Bill and Sally wasnt good enough for our parents. Such is life!

RUMMY. Who saved you, Mr Price? Was it Major Barbara?

PRICE. No: I come here on my own. I'm going to be Bronterre O'Brien Price, the converted painter. I know wot they like. I'll tell em how I blasphemed and gambled and wopped my poor old mother—

RUMMY (*shocked*). Used you to beat your mother?

PRICE. Not likely. She used to beat me. No matter: you come and listen to the converted painter, and youll hear how she was a pious woman that taught me me prayers at er knee, an how I used to come home drunk and drag her out o bed be er snow white airs, an lam into er with the poker.

RUMMY. Thats whats so unfair to us women. Your confessions is just as big lies as ours: you dont tell what you really done no more than us; but you men can tell your lies right out at the meetins and be made much of for it; while the sort o confessions we az to make az to be wispered to one lady at a time. It aint right, spite of all their piety.

PRICE. Right! Do you spose the Army'd be allowed if it went and did right? Not much. It combs our air and makes us good little blokes to be robbed and put upon. But I'll play the game as good as any of em. I'll see somebody struck by lightnin, or hear a voice sayin "Snobby Price: where will you spend eternity?" I'll av a time of it, I tell you.

RUMMY. You wont be let drink, though.

PRICE. I'll take it out in gorspellin, then. I dont want to drink if I can get fun enough any other way.

(JENNY HILL, *a pale, overwrought, pretty Salvation lass of 18, comes in through the yard gate, leading* PETER SHIRLEY, *a half hardened, half wornout elderly man, weak with hunger.*)

JENNY (*supporting him*). Come! pluck up. I'll get you something to eat. Youll be all right then.

PRICE (*rising and hurrying officiously to take the old man off* JENNY's *hands*). Poor old man! Cheer up, brother: youll find rest and peace and appiness ere. Hurry up with the food, miss: e's fair done. (JENNY *hurries into the shelter.*) Ere,

---

[9] *Snobby's a carpenter* in the sense the woman is thinking of (see note 10) [10] *snob* ordinarily meant "cobbler" rather than "carpenter" [11] *Chartist* Chartism was a nineteenth-century democratic movement for social and political reform [12] *Rummy* (Br. slang) odd, strange, queer [13] *Mitchens* (from "miche" — Middle English "mychen"— obsolete British dialect) to pilfer; to skulk; to play truant

buck up, daddy! she's fetchin y'a thick slice
o breadn treacle, an a mug o skyblue. (*He
seats him at the corner of the table.*)

RUMMY (*gaily*). Keep up your old art! Never
say die!

SHIRLEY. I'm not an old man. I'm ony 46.
I'm as good as ever I was. The grey patch
come in my hair before I was thirty. All it
wants is three pennorth o hair dye: am I to
be turned on the streets to starve for it? Holy
God! Ive worked ten to twelve hours a day
since I was thirteen, and paid my way all
through; and now am I to be thrown into the
gutter and my job given to a young man
that can do it no better than me because Ive
black hair that goes white at the first change?

PRICE (*cheerfully*). No good jawrin about it.
Youre ony a jumped-up,[14] jerked-off, orspittle-
turned-out incurable of an ole workin man:
who cares about you? Eh? Make the thievin
swine give you a meal: theyve stole many a
one from you. Get a bit o your own back. (JEN-
NY *returns with the usual meal.*) There you are,
brother. Awsk a blessin an tuck that into you.

SHIRLEY (*looking at it ravenously but not
touching it, and crying like a child*). I never took
anything before.

JENNY (*petting him*). Come, come! the Lord
sends it to you: he wasnt above taking bread
from his friends; and why should you be?
Besides, when we find you a job you can pay
us for it if you like.

SHIRLEY (*eagerly*). Yes, yes: thats true. I can
pay you back: it's only a loan. (*Shivering.*) Oh
Lord! oh Lord! (*He turns to the table and attacks
the meal ravenously.*)

JENNY. Well, Rummy, are you more comfortable now?

RUMMY. God bless you, lovey! youve fed my
body and saved my soul, havnt you? (JENNY,
*touched, kisses her.*) Sit down and rest a bit: you
must be ready to drop.

JENNY. Ive been going hard since morning.
But theres more work than we can do. I
mustnt stop.

RUMMY. Try a prayer for just two minutes.
Youll work all the better after.

JENNY (*her eyes lighting up*). Oh isnt it wonderful how a few minutes prayer revives you!

---

[14] *jumped-up* conceited

I was quite lightheaded at twelve o'clock, I
was so tired; but Major Barbara just sent me
to pray for five minutes; and I was able to go
on as if I had only just begun. (*To* PRICE.) Did
you have a piece of bread?

PRICE (*with unction*). Yes, miss; but Ive got
the piece that I value more; and thats the
peace that passeth hall hannerstennin.

RUMMY (*fervently*). Glory Hallelujah!

(BILL WALKER, *a rough customer of about 25,
appears at the yard gate and looks malevolently at*
JENNY.)

JENNY. That makes me so happy. When
you say that, I feel wicked for loitering here.
I must get to work again.

(*She is hurrying to the shelter, when the new-
comer moves quickly up to the door and intercepts
her. His manner is so threatening that she retreats as
he comes as her truculently, driving her down the
yard.*)

BILL. Aw knaow you. Youre the one that
took awy maw girl. Youre the one that set
er agen me. Well, I'm gowin to ev er aht. Not
that Aw care a carse for er or you: see? Bat
Aw'll let er knaow; and Aw'll let you knaow.
Aw'm gowing to give her a doin thatll teach
er to cat awy from me. Nah in wiv you and tell
er to cam aht afore Aw cam in and kick er aht.
Tell er Bill Walker wants er. She'll knaow
wot thet means; and if she keeps me witin
itll be worse. You stop to jawr beck at me;
and Aw'll stawt on you: d'ye eah? Theres your
wy. In you gow. (*He takes her by the arm and
slings her towards the door of the shelter. She falls
on her hand and knee.* RUMMY *helps her up again.*)

PRICE (*rising, and venturing irresolutely towards* BILL). Easy there, mate. She aint doin
you no arm.

BILL. Oo are you callin mite? (*Standing
over him threateningly.*) Youre gowin to stend
ap for er, aw yer? Put ap your ends.

RUMMY (*running indignantly to him to scold
him*). Oh, you great brute—(*He instantly
swings his left hand back against her face. She
screams and reels back to the trough, where she sits
down, covering her bruised face with her hands and
rocking herself and moaning with pain.*)

JENNY (*going to her*). Oh, God forgive you!
How could you strike an old woman like
that?

BILL (*seizing her by the hair so violently that*

*she also screams, and tearing her away from the old woman*). You Gawd forgimme again an Aw'll Gawd forgive you one on the jawr thetll stop you pryin for a week. (*Holding her and turning fiercely on* PRICE.) Ev you ennything to sy agen it?

PRICE (*intimidated*). No, matey: she aint anything to do with me.

BILL. Good job for you! Aw'd pat two meals into you and fawt you with one finger arter, you stawved cur. (*To* JENNY.) Nah are you gowin to fetch aht Mog Ebbijem; or em Aw to knock your fice off you and fetch her meself?

JENNY (*writhing in his grasp*). Oh please someone go in and tell Major Barbara—(*She screams again as he wrenches her head down; and* PRICE *and* RUMMY *flee into the shelter.*)

BILL. You want to gow in and tell your Mijor of me, do you?

JENNY. Oh please dont drag my hair. Let me go.

BILL. Do you or downt you? (*She stifles a scream.*) Yus or nao?

JENNY. God give me strength—

BILL (*striking her with his fist in the face*). Gow an shaow her thet, and tell her if she wants one lawk it to cam and interfere with me. (JENNY, *crying with pain, goes into the shed. He goes to the form and addresses the old man.*) Eah: finish your mess; an git aht o maw wy.

SHIRLEY (*springing up and facing him fiercely, with the mug in his hand*). You take a liberty with me, and I'll smash you over the face with the mug and cut your eye out. Aint you satisfied—young whelps like you—with takin the bread out o the mouths of your elders that have brought you up and slaved for you, but you must come shovin and cheekin and bullyin in here, where the bread o charity is sickenin in our stummicks?

BILL (*contemptuously, but backing a little*). Wot good are you, you aold palsy mag?[15] Wot good are you?

SHIRLEY. As good as you and better. I'll do a day's work agen you or any fat young soaker[16] of your age. Go and take my job at Horrockses, where I worked for ten year.

They want young men there: they cant afford to keep men over forty-five. Theyre very sorry—give you a character and happy to help you to get anything suited to your years—sure a steady man wont be long out of a job. Well, let em try you. Theyll find the differ. What do you know? Not as much as how to beeyave yourself—layin your dirty fist across the mouth of a respectable woman!

BILL. Downt provowk me to ly it acrost yours: d'ye eah?

SHIRLEY (*with blighting contempt*). Yes: you like an old man to hit, dont you, when youve finished with the women. I aint seen you hit a young one yet.

BILL (*stung*). You loy, you aold soupkitchener, you. There was a yang menn eah. Did Aw offer to itt him or did Aw not?

SHIRLEY. Was he starvin or was he not? Was he a man or only a crosseyed thief an a loafer? Would you hit my son-in-law's brother?

BILL. Oo's ee?

SHIRLEY. Todger Fairmile o Balls Pond. Him that won £20 off the Japanese wrastler at the music hall by standin out 17 minutes 4 seconds agen him.

BILL (*sullenly*). Aw'm nao music awl wrastler. Ken he box?

SHIRLEY. Yes: an you cant.

BILL. Wot! Aw cawnt, cawnt Aw? Wots thet you sy? (*Threatening him.*)

SHIRLEY (*not budging an inch*). Will you box Todger Fairmile if I put him on to you? Say the word.

BILL (*subsiding with a slouch*). Aw'll stend ap to enny menn alawv, if he was ten Todger Fairmawls. But Aw dont set ap to be a perfeshnal.

SHIRLEY (*looking down on him with unfathomable disdain*). You box! Slap an old woman with the back o your hand! You hadnt even the sense to hit her where a magistrate couldnt see the mark of it, you silly young lump of conceit and ignorance. Hit a girl in the jaw and ony make her cry! If Todger Fairmile'd done it, she wouldnt a got up inside o ten minutes, no more than you would if he got on to you. Yah! I'd set about you myself if I had a week's feedin in me instead o two months'

---

[15] *mag* chatterbox    [16] *soaker* drunkard

starvation. (*He turns his back on him and sits down moodily at the table.*)

BILL (*following him and stooping over him to drive the taunt in*). You loy! youve the bread and treacle in you that you cam eah to beg.

SHIRLEY (*bursting into tears*). Oh God! it's true: I'm only an old pauper on the scrap heap. (*Furiously.*) But youll come to it yourself; and then youll know. Youll come to it sooner than a teetotaller like me, fillin yourself with gin at this hour o the mornin!

BILL. Aw'm nao gin drinker, you oald lawr; bat wen Aw want to give my girl a bloomin good awdin Aw lawk to ev a bit o devil in me: see? An eah Aw emm, talkin to a rotten aold blawter like you sted o givin her wot for. (*Working himself into a rage.*) Aw'm gowin in there to fetch her aht. (*He makes vengefully for the shelter door.*)

SHIRLEY. Youre going to the station on a stretcher, more likely; and theyll take the gin and the devil out of you there when they get you inside. You mind what youre about: the major here is the Earl o Stevenage's granddaughter.

BILL (*checked*). Garn!

SHIRLEY. Youll see.

BILL (*his resolution oozing*). Well, Aw aint dan nathin to er.

SHIRLEY. Spose she said you did! who'd believe you?

BILL (*very uneasy, skulking back to the corner of the penthouse*). Gawd! theres no jastice in this cantry. To think wot them people can do! Aw'm as good as er.

SHIRLEY. Tell her so. It's just what a fool like you would do.

(BARBARA, *brisk and businesslike, comes from the shelter with a note book, and addresses herself to* SHIRLEY. BILL, *cowed, sits down in the corner on a form, and turns his back on them.*)

BARBARA. Good morning.

SHIRLEY (*standing up and taking off his hat*). Good morning, miss.

BARBARA. Sit down: make yourself at home. (*He hesitates; but she puts a friendly hand on his shoulder and makes him obey.*) Now then! since youve made friends with us, we want to know all about you. Names and addresses and trades.

SHIRLEY. Peter Shirley. Fitter. Chucked out two months ago because I was too old.

BARBARA (*not at all surprised*). Youd pass still. Why didnt you dye your hair?

SHIRLEY. I did. Me age come out at a coroner's inquest on me daughter.

BARBARA. Steady?

SHIRLEY. Teetotaller. Never out of a job before. Good worker. And sent to the knackers[17] like an old horse!

BARBARA. No matter: if you did your part God will do his.

SHIRLEY (*suddenly stubborn*). My religion's no concern of anybody but myself.

BARBARA (*guessing*). *I* know. Secularist?[18]

SHIRLEY (*hotly*). Did I offer to deny it?

BARBARA. Why should you? My own father's a Secularist, I think. Our Father— yours and mine—fulfils himself in many ways; and I daresay he knew what he was about when he made a Secularist of you. So buck up, Peter! we can always find a job for a steady man like you. (SHIRLEY, *disarmed and a little bewildered, touches his hat. She turns from him to* BILL.) Whats your name?

BILL (*insolently*). Wots thet to you?

BARBARA (*calmly making a note*). Afraid to give his name. Any trade?

BILL. Oo's afride to give is nime? (*Doggedly, with a sense of heroically defying the House of Lords in the person of Lord Stevenage.*) If you want to bring a chawge agen me, bring it. (*She waits, unruffled.*) Moy nime's Bill Walker.

BARBARA (*as if the name were familiar: trying to remember how*). Bill Walker? (*Recollecting.*) Oh, I know: youre the man that Jenny Hill was praying for inside just now. (*She enters his name in her note book.*)

BILL. Oo's Jenny 'Ill. And wot call as she to pry for me?

BARBARA. I dont know. Perhaps it was you that cut her lip.

BILL (*defiantly*). Yus, it was me that cat her lip. Aw aint afride o you.

BARBARA. How could you be, since youre not afraid of God? Youre a brave man, Mr

---

[17] *knacker* a person who buys and slaughters worn-out horses and sells their flesh as dog's meat
[18] *Secularist* one who believes that morality should have nothing to do with religious belief

Walker. It takes some pluck to do our work here; but none of us dare lift our hand against a girl like that, for fear of her father in heaven.

BILL (*sullenly*). I want nan o your kentin jawr. I spowse you think Aw cam eah to beg from you, like this demmiged lot eah. Not me. Aw downt want your bread and scripe and ketlep. Aw dont blieve in your Gawd, no more than you do yourself.

BARBARA (*sunnily apologetic and ladylike, as on a new footing with him*). Oh, I beg your pardon for putting your name down, Mr Walker. I didnt understand. I'll strike it out.

BILL (*taking this as a slight, and deeply wounded by it*). Eah! you let maw nime alown. Aint it good enaff to be in your book?

BARBARA (*considering*). Well, you see, theres no use putting down your name unless I can do something for you, is there? Whats your trade?

BILL (*still smarting*). Thets nao concern o yours.

BARBARA. Just so. (*Very businesslike.*) I'll put you down as (*writing*) the man who—struck—poor little Jenny Hill—in the mouth.

BILL (*rising threateningly*). See eah. Awve ed enaff o this.

BARBARA (*quite sunny and fearless*). What did you come to us for?

BILL. Aw cam for maw gel, see? Aw cam to tike her aht o this and to brike er jawr for er.

BARBARA (*complacently*). You see I was right about your trade. (BILL, *on the point of retorting furiously, finds himself, to his great shame and terror, in danger of crying instead. He sits down again suddenly.*) Whats her name?

BILL (*dogged*). Er nime's Mog Ebbijem: thets wot her nime is.

BARBARA. Mog Habbijam! Oh, she's gone to Canning Town, to our barracks there.

BILL (*fortified by his resentment of* MOG's *perfidy*). Is she? (*Vindictively.*) Then Aw'm gowin to Kennintahn arter her. (*He crosses to the gate; hesitates; finally comes back at* BARBARA.) Are you loyin to me to git shat o me?

BARBARA. I dont want to get shut of you. I want to keep you here and save your soul. Youd better stay: youre going to have a bad time today, Bill.

BILL. Oo's gowin to give it to me? You, preps?

BARBARA. Someone you dont believe in. But youll be glad afterwards.

BILL (*slinking off*). Aw'll gow to Kennintahn to be aht o reach o your tangue. (*Suddenly turning on her with intense malice.*) And if Aw downt fawnd Mog there, Aw'll cam beck and do two years for you, selp me Gawd if Aw downt!

BARBARA (*a shade kindlier, if possible*). It's no use, Bill. She's got another bloke.

BILL. Wot!

BARBARA. One of her own converts. He fell in love with her when he saw her with her soul saved, and her face clean, and her hair washed.

BILL (*surprised*). Wottud she wash it for, the carroty slat? It's red.

BARBARA. It's quite lovely now, because she wears a new look in her eyes with it. It's a pity youre too late. The new bloke has put your nose out of joint, Bill.

BILL. Aw'll put his nowse aht o joint for him. Not that Aw care a carse for er, mawnd thet. But Aw'll teach her to drop me as if Aw was dirt. And Aw'll teach him to meddle with maw judy.[19] Wots iz bleedin nime?

BARBARA. Sergeant Todger Fairmile.

SHIRLEY (*rising with grim joy*). I'll go with him, miss. I want to see them two meet. I'll take him to the infirmary when it's over.

BILL (*to* SHIRLEY, *with undissembled misgiving*). Is thet im you was speakin on?

SHIRLEY. Thats him.

BILL. Im that wrastled in the music awl?

SHIRLEY. The competitions at the National Sportin Club was worth nigh a hundred a year to him. He's gev em up now for religion; so he's a bit fresh for want of the exercise he was accustomed to. He'll be glad to see you. Come along.

BILL. Wots is wight?

SHIRLEY. Thirteen four.[20] (BILL's *last hope expires.*)

BARBARA. Go and talk to him, Bill. He'll convert you.

---

[19] *judy* (slang) girl   [20] *thirteen four* i.e., thirteen stone four pounds (one stone is fourteen pounds)

SHIRLEY. He'll convert your head into a mashed potato.

BILL (*sullenly*). Aw aint afride of im. Aw aint afride of ennybody. Bat e can lick me. She's dan me. (*He sits down moodily on the edge of the horse trough.*)

SHIRLEY. You aint going. I thought not. (*He resumes his seat.*)

BARBARA (*calling*). Jenny!

JENNY (*appearing at the shelter door with a plaster on the corner of her mouth*). Yes, Major.

BARBARA. Send Rummy Mitchens out to clear away here.

JENNY. I think she's afraid.

BARBARA (*her resemblance to her mother flashing out for a moment*). Nonsense! she must do as she's told.

JENNY (*calling into the shelter*). Rummy: the Major says you must come.

(JENNY *comes to* BARBARA, *purposely keeping on the side next* BILL, *lest he should suppose that she shrank from him or bore malice.*)

BARBARA. Poor little Jenny! Are you tired? (*Looking at the wounded cheek.*) Does it hurt?

JENNY. No: it's all right now. It was nothing.

BARBARA (*critically*). It was as hard as he could hit, I expect. Poor Bill! You dont feel angry with him, do you?

JENNY. Oh no, no, no: indeed I dont, Major, bless his poor heart! (BARBARA *kisses her; and she runs away merrily into the shelter.* BILL *writhes with an agonizing return of his new and alarming symptoms, but says nothing.* RUMMY MITCHENS *comes from the shelter.*)

BARBARA (*going to meet* RUMMY). Now Rummy, bustle. Take in those mugs and plates to be washed; and throw the crumbs about for the birds.

(RUMMY *takes the three plates and mugs; but* SHIRLEY *takes back his mug from her, as there is still some milk left in it.*)

RUMMY. There aint any crumbs. This aint a time to waste good bread on birds.

PRICE (*appearing at the shelter door*). Gentleman come to see the shelter, Major. Says he's your father.

BARBARA. All right. Coming. (SNOBBY *goes back into the shelter, followed by* BARBARA.)

RUMMY (*stealing across to* BILL *and addressing him in a subdued voice, but with intense conviction*). I'd av the lor of you, you flat eared pignosed potwalloper, if she'd let me. Youre no gentleman, to hit a lady in the face. (BILL, *with greater things moving in him, takes no notice.*)

SHIRLEY (*following her*). Here! in with you and dont get yourself into more trouble by talking.

RUMMY (*with hauteur*). I aint ad the pleasure o being hintroduced to you, as I can remember. (*She goes into the shelter with the plates.*)

SHIRLEY. Thats the—

BILL (*savagely*). Downt you talk to me, d'ye eah? You lea me alown, or Aw'll do you a mischief. Aw'm not dirt under your feet, ennywy.

SHIRLEY (*calmly*). Dont you be afeered. You aint such prime company that you need expect to be sought after. (*He is about to go into the shelter when* BARBARA *comes out, with* UNDERSHAFT *on her right.*)

BARBARA. Oh, there you are, Mr Shirley! (*Between them.*) This is my father: I told you he was a Secularist, didnt I? Perhaps youll be able to comfort one another.

UNDERSHAFT (*startled*). A Secularist! Not the least in the world: on the contrary, a confirmed mystic.

BARBARA. Sorry, I'm sure. By the way, papa, what is your religion? in case I have to introduce you again.

UNDERSHAFT. My religion? Well, my dear, I am a Millionaire. That is my religion.

BARBARA. Then I'm afraid you and Mr Shirley wont be able to comfort one another after all. Youre not a Millionaire, are you, Peter?

SHIRLEY. No; and proud of it.

UNDERSHAFT (*gravely*). Poverty, my friend, is not a thing to be proud of.

SHIRLEY (*angrily*). Who made your millions for you? Me and my like. Whats kep us poor? Keepin you rich. I wouldnt have your conscience, not for all your income.

UNDERSHAFT. I wouldnt have your income, not for all your conscience, Mr Shirley. (*He goes to the penthouse and sits down on a form.*)

BARBARA (*stopping* SHIRLEY *adroitly as he is about to retort*). You wouldnt think he was my father, would you, Peter? Will you go into the shelter and lend the lasses a hand for a while: we're worked off our feet.

SHIRLEY (*bitterly*). Yes: I'm in their debt for a meal, aint I?

BARBARA. Oh, not because youre in their debt, but for love of them, Peter, for love of them. (*He cannot understand, and is rather scandalized.*) There! dont stare at me. In with you; and give that conscience of yours a holiday. (*Bustling him into the shelter.*)

SHIRLEY (*as he goes in*). Ah! it's a pity you never was trained to use your reason, miss. Youd have been a very taking lecturer on Secularism.

(BARBARA *turns to her father.*)

UNDERSHAFT. Never mind me, my dear. Go about your work; and let me watch it for a while.

BARBARA. All right.

UNDERSHAFT. For instance, whats the matter with that outpatient over there?

BARBARA (*looking at* BILL, *whose attitude has never changed, and whose expression of brooding wrath has deepened*). Oh, we shall cure him in no time. Just watch. (*She goes over to* BILL *and waits. He glances up at her and casts his eyes down again, uneasy, but grimmer than ever.*) It would be nice to just stamp on Mog Habbijam's face, wouldnt it, Bill?

BILL (*starting up from the trough in consternation*). It's a loy: Aw never said so. (*She shakes her head.*) Oo taold you wot was in moy mawnd?

BARBARA. Only your new friend.

BILL. Wot new friend?

BARBARA. The devil, Bill. When he gets round people they get miserable, just like you.

BILL (*with a heartbreaking attempt at devil-may-care cheerfulness*). Aw aint miserable. (*He sits down again, and stretches his legs in an attempt to seem indifferent.*)

BARBARA. Well, if youre happy, why dont you look happy, as we do?

BILL (*his legs curling back in spite of him*). Aw'm eppy enaff, Aw tell you. Woy cawnt you lea me alown? Wot ev I dan to you? Aw aint smashed your fice, ev Aw?

BARBARA (*softly: wooing his soul*). It's not me thats getting at you, Bill.

BILL. Oo else is it?

BARBARA. Somebody that doesnt intend you to smash women's faces, I suppose. Somebody or something that wants to make a man of you.

BILL (*blustering*). Mike a menn o me! Aint Aw a menn? eh? Oo sez Aw'm not a menn?

BARBARA. Theres a man in you somewhere, I suppose. But why did he let you hit poor little Jenny Hill? That wasnt very manly of him, was it?

BILL (*tormented*). Ev dan wiv it, Aw tell you. Chack it. Aw'm sick o your Jenny Ill and er silly little fice.

BARBARA. Then why do you keep thinking about it? Why does it keep coming up against you in your mind? Youre not getting converted, are you?

BILL (*with conviction*). Not ME. Not lawkly.

BARBARA. Thats right, Bill. Hold out against it. Put out your strength. Dont lets get you cheap. Todger Fairmile said he wrestled for three nights against his salvation harder than he ever wrestled with the Jap at the music hall. He gave in to the Jap when his arm was going to break. But he didnt give in to his salvation until his heart was going to break. Perhaps youll escape that. You havnt any heart, have you?

BILL. Wot d'ye mean? Woy aint Aw got a awt the sime as ennybody else?

BARBARA. A man with a heart wouldnt have bashed poor little Jenny's face, would he?

BILL (*almost crying*). Ow, will you lea me alown? Ev Aw ever offered to meddle with you, that you cam neggin and provowkin me lawk this? (*He writhes convulsively from his eyes to his toes.*)

BARBARA (*with a steady soothing hand on his arm and a gentle voice that never lets him go*). It's your soul thats hurting you, Bill, and not me. Weve been through it all ourselves. Come with us, Bill. (*He looks wildly round.*) To brave manhood on earth and eternal glory in heaven. (*He is on the point of breaking down.*) Come. (*A drum is heard in the shelter; and* BILL, *with a gasp, escapes from the spell as* BARBARA *turns quickly.* ADOLPHUS *enters from the shelter with a big drum.*) Oh! there you are, Dolly. Let me introduce a new friend of mine, Mr Bill Walker. This is my bloke,

Bill: Mr Cusins. (CUSINS *salutes with his drumstick.*)

BILL. Gowin to merry im?

BARBARA. Yes.

BILL (*fervently*). Gawd elp im! Gaw-aw-aw-awd elp im!

BARBARA. Why? Do you think he wont be happy with me?

BILL. Awve aony ed to stend it for a mawnin: e'll ev to stend it for a lawftawm.

CUSINS. That is a frightful reflection, Mr Walker. But I cant tear myself away from her.

BILL. Well, Aw ken. (*To* BARBARA.) Eah! do you knaow where Aw'm gowin to, and wot Aw'm gowin to do?

BARBARA. Yes: youre going to heaven; and youre coming back here before the week's out to tell me so.

BILL. You loy. Aw'm gowin to Kennintahn, to spit in Todger Fairmawl's eye. Aw beshed Jenny Ill's fice; an nar Aw'll git me aown fice beshed and cam beck and shaow it to er. Ee'll itt me ardern Aw itt her. Thatll mike us square. (*To* ADOLPHUS.) Is thet fair or is it not? Youre a genlmn: you oughter knaow.

BARBARA. Two black eyes wont make one white one, Bill.

BILL. Aw didnt awst you. Cawnt you never keep your mahth shat? Oy awst the genlmn.

CUSINS (*reflectively*). Yes: I think youre right, Mr Walker. Yes: I should do it. It's curious: it's exactly what an ancient Greek would have done.

BARBARA. But what good will it do?

CUSINS. Well, it will give Mr Fairmile some exercise; and it will satisfy Mr Walker's soul.

BILL. Rot! there aint nao sach a thing as a saoul. Ah kin you tell wevver Awve a saoul or not? You never seen it.

BARBARA. Ive seen it hurting you when you went against it.

BILL (*with compressed aggravation*). If you was maw gel and took the word aht o me mahth lawk thet, Aw'd give you sathink youd feel urtin, Aw would. (*To* ADOLPHUS.) You tike maw tip mite. Stop er jawr; or youll doy afoah your tawm. (*With intense expression.*) Wore aht: thets wot youll be: wore aht. (*He goes away through the gate.*)

CUSINS (*looking after him*). I wonder!

BARBARA. Dolly! (*Indignant, in her mother's manner.*)

CUSINS. Yes, my dear, it's very wearing to be in love with you. If it lasts, I quite think I shall die young.

BARBARA. Should you mind?

CUSINS. Not at all. (*He is suddenly softened, and kisses her over the drum, evidently not for the first time, as people cannot kiss over a big drum without practice.* UNDERSHAFT *coughs.*)

BARBARA. It's all right, papa, weve not forgotten you. Dolly: explain the place to papa: I havnt time. (*She goes busily into the shelter.*)

(UNDERSHAFT *and* ADOLPHUS *now have the yard to themselves.* UNDERSHAFT, *seated on a form, and still keenly attentive, looks hard at* ADOLPHUS. ADOLPHUS *looks hard at him.*)

UNDERSHAFT. I fancy you guess something of what is in my mind, Mr Cusins. (CUSINS *flourishes his drumsticks as if in the act of beating a lively rataplan, but makes no sound.*) Exactly so. But suppose Barbara finds you out!

CUSINS. You know, I do not admit that I am imposing on Barbara. I am quite genuinely interested in the views of the Salvation Army. The fact is, I am a sort of collector of religions; and the curious thing is that I find I can believe them all. By the way, have you any religion?

UNDERSHAFT. Yes.

CUSINS. Anything out of the common?

UNDERSHAFT. Only that there are two things necessary to Salvation.

CUSINS (*disappointed, but polite*). Ah, the Church Catechism. Charles Lomax also belongs to the Established Church.

UNDERSHAFT. The two things are—

CUSINS. Baptism and—

UNDERSHAFT. No. Money and gunpowder.

CUSINS (*surprised, but interested*). That is the general opinion of our governing classes. The novelty is in hearing any man confess it.

UNDERSHAFT. Just so.

CUSINS. Excuse me: is there any place in your religion for honor, justice, truth, love, mercy and so forth?

UNDERSHAFT. Yes: they are the graces and luxuries of a rich, strong, and safe life.

CUSINS. Suppose one is forced to choose between them and money or gunpowder?

UNDERSHAFT. Choose money and gunpowder: for without enough of both you cannot afford the others.

CUSINS. That is your religion?

UNDERSHAFT. Yes.

(*The cadence of this reply makes a full close in the conversation.* CUSINS *twists his face dubiously and contemplates* UNDERSHAFT. UNDERSHAFT *contemplates him.*)

CUSINS. Barbara wont stand that. You will have to choose betweeen your religion and Barbara.

UNDERSHAFT. So will you, my friend. She will find out that that drum of yours is hollow.

CUSINS. Father Undershaft: you are mistaken: I am a sincere Salvationist. You do not understand the Salvation Army. It is the army of joy, of love, of courage: it has banished the fear and remorse and despair of the old hellridden evangelical sects: it marches to fight the devil with trumpet and drum, with music and dancing, with banner and palm, as becomes a sally from heaven by its happy garrison. It picks the waster out of the public house and makes a man of him: it finds a worm wriggling in a back kitchen, and lo! a woman! Men and women of rank too, sons and daughters of the Highest. It takes the poor professor of Greek, the most artificial and self-suppressed of human creatures, from his meal of roots, and lets loose the rhapsodist in him; reveals the true worship of Dionysos to him; sends him down the public street drumming dithyrambs. (*He plays a thundering flourish on the drum.*)

UNDERSHAFT. You will alarm the shelter.

CUSINS. Oh, they are accustomed to these sudden ecstasies. However, if the drum worries you—(*He pockets the drumsticks; unhooks the drum; and stands it on the ground opposite the gateway.*)

UNDERSHAFT. Thank you.

CUSINS. You remember what Euripides says about your money and gunpowder?

UNDERSHAFT. No.

CUSINS (*declaiming*).

> One and another
> In money and guns may outpass his
>     brother;

> And men in their millions float
>     and flow
> And seethe with a million hopes as
>     leaven;
> And they win their will; or they
>     miss their will;
> And their hopes are dead or are
>     pined for still;
>     But whoe'er can know
>     As the long days go
> That to live is happy, has found
>     his heaven.[21]

My translation: what do you think of it?

UNDERSHAFT. I think, my friend, that if you wish to know, as the long days go, that to live is happy, you must first acquire money enough for a decent life, and power enough to be your own master.

CUSINS. You are damnably discouraging. (*He resumes his declamation.*)

> Is it so hard a thing to see
> That the spirit of God—
>     whate'er it be—
> The law that abides and changes
>     not, ages long,
> The Eternal and Nature-born:
>     these things be strong?
> What else is Wisdom? What of
>     Man's endeavor,
> Or God's high grace so lovely and
>     so great?
> To stand from fear set free? to
>     breathe and wait?

---

21 *One and another . . . heaven* With regard to this quotation and the following one, Shaw placed this note at the beginning of the play: "The Euripidean verses in the second act of *Major Barbara* are not by me, nor even directly by Euripides. They are by Professor Gilbert Murray, whose English version of *The Bacchae* came into our dramatic literature with all the impulsive power of an original work shortly before *Major Barbara* was begun. The play, indeed, stands indebted to him in more ways than one." The first passage corresponds to ll. 904–11, the second to ll. 893–901. In *The Bacchae* Pentheus refuses to believe in the cult of Dionysus which his mother has joined. He is tricked by the god into attending one of their revels and is torn to pieces.

To hold a hand uplifted over Fate?
And shall not Barbara be loved
   for ever?

UNDERSHAFT. Euripides mentions Barbara, does he?

CUSINS. It is a fair translation. The word means Loveliness.

UNDERSHAFT. May I ask—as Barbara's father—how much a year she is to be loved for ever on?

CUSINS. As Barbara's father, that is more your affair than mine. I can feed her by teaching Greek: that is about all.

UNDERSHAFT. Do you consider it a good match for her?

CUSINS (*with polite obstinacy*). Mr Undershaft: I am in many ways a weak, timid, ineffectual person; and my health is far from satisfactory. But whenever I feel that I must have anything, I get it, sooner or later. I feel that way about Barbara. I dont like marriage: I feel intensely afraid of it; and I dont know what I shall do with Barbara or what she will do with me. But I feel that I and nobody else must marry her. Please regard that as settled. —Not that I wish to be arbitrary; but why should I waste your time in discussing what is inevitable?

UNDERSHAFT. You mean that you will stick at nothing: not even the conversion of the Salvation Army to the worship of Dionysos.

CUSINS. The business of the Salvation Army is to save, not to wrangle about the name of the pathfinder. Dionysos or another: what does it matter?

UNDERSHAFT (*rising and approaching him*). Professor Cusins: you are a young man after my own heart.

CUSINS. Mr Undershaft: you are, as far as I am able to gather, a most infernal old rascal; but you appeal very strongly to my sense of ironic humor.

(UNDERSHAFT *mutely offers his hand. They shake.*)

UNDERSHAFT (*suddenly concentrating himself*). And now to business.

CUSINS. Pardon me. We are discussing religion. Why go back to such an uninterest-ing and unimportant subject as business?

UNDERSHAFT. Religion is our business at present, because it is through religion alone that we can win Barbara.

CUSINS. Have you, too, fallen in love with Barbara?

UNDERSHAFT. Yes, with a father's love.

CUSINS. A father's love for a grown-up daughter is the most dangerous of all infatuations. I apologize for mentioning my own pale, coy, mistrustful fancy in the same breath with it.

UNDERSHAFT. Keep to the point. We have to win her; and we are neither of us Methodists.

CUSINS. That doesnt matter. The power Barbara wields here—the power that wields Barbara herself—is not Calvinism, not Presbyterianism, not Methodism—

UNDERSHAFT. Not Greek Paganism either, eh?

CUSINS. I admit that. Barbara is quite original in her religion.

UNDERSHAFT (*triumphantly*). Aha! Barbara Undershaft would be. Her inspiration comes from within herself.

CUSINS. How do you suppose it got there?

UNDERSHAFT (*in towering excitement*). It is the Undershaft inheritance. I shall hand on my torch to my daughter. She shall make my converts and preach my gospel—

CUSINS. What! Money and gunpowder!

UNDERSHAFT. Yes, money and gunpowder. Freedom and power. Command of life and command of death.

CUSINS (*urbanely: trying to bring him down to earth*). This is extremely interesting, Mr Undershaft. Of course you know that you are mad.

UNDERSHAFT (*with redoubled force*). And you?

CUSINS. Oh, mad as a hatter. You are welcome to my secret since I have discovered yours. But I am astonished. Can a madman make cannons?

UNDERSHAFT. Would anyone else than a madman make them? And now (*with surging energy*) question for question. Can a sane man translate Euripides?

CUSINS. No.

UNDERSHAFT (*seizing him by the shoulder*).

Can a sane woman make a man of a waster or a woman of a worm?

CUSINS (*reeling before the storm*). Father Colossus—Mammoth Millionaire—

UNDERSHAFT (*pressing him*). Are there two mad people or three in this Salvation shelter today?

CUSINS. You mean Barbara is as mad as we are?

UNDERSHAFT (*pushing him lightly off and resuming his equanimity suddenly and completely*). Pooh, Professor! let us call things by their proper names. I am a millionaire; you are a poet: Barbara is a savior of souls. What have we three to do with the common mob of slaves and idolators? (*He sits down again with a shrug of contempt for the mob.*)

CUSINS. Take care! Barbara is in love with the common people. So am I. Have you never felt the romance of that love?

UNDERSHAFT (*cold and sardonic*). Have you ever been in love with Poverty, like St Francis? Have you ever been in love with Dirt, like St Simeon! Have you ever been in love with disease and suffering, like our nurses and philanthropists? Such passions are not virtues, but the most unnatural of all the vices. This love of the common people may please an earl's granddaughter and a university professor; but I have been a common man and a poor man; and it has no romance for me. Leave it to the poor to pretend that poverty is a blessing: leave it to the coward to make a religion of his cowardice by preaching humility: we know better than that. We three must stand together above the common people: how else can we help their children to climb up beside us? Barbara must belong to us, not to the Salvation Army.

CUSINS. Well, I can only say that if you think you will get her away from the Salvation Army by talking to her as you have been talking to me, you dont know Barbara.

UNDERSHAFT. My friend: I never ask for what I can buy.

CUSINS (*in a white fury*). Do I understand you to imply that you can buy Barbara?

UNDERSHAFT. No; but I can buy the Salvation Army.

CUSINS. Quite impossible.

UNDERSHAFT. You shall see. All religious organizations exist by selling themselves to the rich.

CUSINS. Not the Army. That is the Church of the poor.

UNDERSHAFT. All the more reason for buying it.

CUSINS. I dont think you quite know what the Army does for the poor.

UNDERSHAFT. Oh yes I do. It draws their teeth: that is enough for me as a man of business.

CUSINS. Nonsense! It makes them sober—

UNDERSHAFT. I prefer sober workmen. The profits are larger.

CUSINS.—honest—

UNDERSHAFT. Honest workmen are the most economical.

CUSINS.—attached to their homes—

UNDERSHAFT. So much the better: they will put up with anything sooner than change their shop.

CUSINS.—happy—

UNDERSHAFT. An invaluable safeguard against revolution.

CUSINS.—unselfish—

UNDERSHAFT. Indifferent to their own interests, which suits me exactly.

CUSINS.—with their thoughts on heavenly things—

UNDERSHAFT (*rising*). And not on Trade Unionism nor Socialism. Excellent.

CUSINS (*revolted*). You really are an infernal old rascal.

UNDERSHAFT (*indicating* PETER SHIRLEY, *who has just come from the shelter and strolled dejectedly down the yard between them*). And this is an honest man!

SHIRLEY. Yes; and what av I got by it? (*He passes on bitterly and sits on the form, in the corner of the penthouse.*)

(SNOBBY PRICE, *beaming sanctimoniously, and* JENNY HILL, *with a tambourine of coppers, come from the shelter and go to the drum, on which* JENNY *begins to count the money.*)

UNDERSHAFT (*replying to* SHIRLEY). Oh, your employers must have got a good deal by it from first to last. (*He sits on the table, with one foot on the side form.* CUSINS, *overwhelmed, sits down on the same form nearer the shelter.* BARBARA *comes from the shelter to the middle of the yard. She is excited and a little overwrought.*)

BARBARA. Weve just had a splendid experience meeting at the other gate in Cripps's Lane. Ive hardly ever seen them so much moved as they were by your confession, Mr Price.

PRICE. I could almost be glad of my past wickedness if I could believe that it would elp to keep hathers straight.

BARBARA. So it will, Snobby. How much, Jenny?

JENNY. Four and tenpence, Major.

BARBARA. Oh Snobby, if you had given your poor mother just one more kick, we should have got the whole five shillings!

PRICE. If she heard you say that, miss, she'd be sorry I didnt. But I'm glad. Oh what a joy it will be to her when she hears I'm saved!

UNDERSHAFT. Shall I contribute the odd twopence, Barbara? The millionaire's mite,[22] eh? (He takes a couple of pennies from his pocket.)

BARBARA. How did you make that twopence?

UNDERSHAFT. As usual. By selling cannons, torpedoes, submarines, and my new patent Grand Duke hand grenade.

BARBARA. Put it back in your pocket. You cant buy your salvation here for twopence: you must work it out.

UNDERSHAFT. Is twopence not enough? I can afford a little more, if you press me.

BARBARA. Two million millions would not be enough. There is bad blood on your hands; and nothing but good blood can cleanse them. Money is no use. Take it away. (She turns to CUSINS.) Dolly: you must write another letter for me to the papers. (He makes a wry face.) Yes: I know you dont like it; but it must be done. The starvation this winter is beating us: everybody is unemployed. The General says we must close this shelter if we cant get more money. I force the collections at the meetings until I am ashamed: dont I, Snobby?

PRICE. It's a fair treat to see you work it, miss. The way you got them up from three-and-six to four-and-ten with that hymn, penny by penny and verse by verse, was a caution.

Not a Cheap Jack on Mile End Waste could touch you at it.

BARBARA. Yes; but I wish we could do without it. I am getting at last to think more of the collection than of the people's souls. And what are those hatfuls of pence and halfpence? We want thousands! tens of thousands! hundreds of thousands! I want to convert people, not to be always begging for the Army in a way I'd die sooner than beg for myself.

UNDERSHAFT (in profound irony). Genuine unselfishness is capable of anything, my dear.

BARBARA (unsuspectingly, as she turns away to take the money from the drum and put it in a cash bag she carries). Yes, isnt it? (UNDERSHAFT looks sardonically at CUSINS.)

CUSINS (aside to UNDERSHAFT). Mephistopheles! Machiavelli!

BARBARA (tears coming into her eyes as she ties the bag and pockets it). How are we to feed them? I cant talk religion to a man with bodily hunger in his eyes. (Almost breaking down.) It's frightful.

JENNY (running to her). Major, dear—

BARBARA (rebounding). No: dont comfort me. It will be all right. We shall get the money.

UNDERSHAFT. How?

JENNY. By praying for it, of course. Mrs Baines says she prayed for it last night; and she has never prayed for it in vain: never once. (She goes to the gate and looks out into the street.)

BARBARA (who has dried her eyes and regained her composure). By the way, dad, Mrs Baines has come to march with us to our big meeting this afternoon; and she is very anxious to meet you, for some reason or other. Perhaps she'll convert you.

UNDERSHAFT. I shall be delighted, my dear.

JENNY (at the gate: excitedly). Major! Major! heres that man back again.

BARBARA. What man?

JENNY. The man that hit me. Oh, I hope he's coming back to join us.

(BILL WALKER, with frost on his jacket, comes through the gate, his hands deep in his pockets and his chin sunk between his shoulders, like a cleaned-out gambler. He halts between BARBARA and the drum.)

BARBARA. Hullo, Bill! Back already!

BILL (nagging at her). Bin talkin ever sence, ev you?

22 millionaire's mite ironic reference to Biblical tale of the widow's mite (Mark 12: 41–44; Luke 21: 1–4)

BARBARA. Pretty nearly. Well, has Todger paid you out for poor Jenny's jaw?

BILL. Nao e aint.

BARBARA. I thought your jacket looked a bit snowy.

BILL. Sao it is snaowy. You want to knaow where the snaow cam from, downt you?

BARBARA. Yes.

BILL. Well, it cam from orf the grahnd in Pawkinses Corner in Kennintahn. It got rabbed orf be maw shaoulders: see?

BARBARA. Pity you didnt rub some off with your knees, Bill! That would have done you a lot of good.

BILL (*with sour mirthless humor*). Aw was sivin anather menn's knees at the tawm. E was kneelin on moy ed, e was.

JENNY. Who was kneeling on your head?

BILL. Todger was. E was pryin for me: pryin camfortable wiv me as a cawpet. Sow was Mog. Sao was the aol bloomin meetin. Mog she sez "Ow Lawd brike is stabborn sperrit; bat downt urt is dear art." Thet was wot she said. "Downt urt is dear art"! An er blowk—thirteen stun four—kneelin wiv all is wight on me. Fanny, aint it?

JENNY. Oh no. We're so sorry, Mr Walker.

BARBARA (*enjoying it frankly*). Nonsense! of course it's funny. Served you right, Bill! You must have done something to him first.

BILL (*doggedly*). Aw did wot Aw said Aw'd do. Aw spit in is eye. E looks ap at the skoy and sez, "Ow that Aw should be fahnd worthy to be spit upon for the gospel's sike!" e sez; an Mog sez "Glaory Allelloolier!"; an then e called me Braddher, an dahned me as if Aw was a kid and e was me mather worshin me a Setterda nawt. Aw ednt jast nao shaow wiv im at all. Arf the street pryed; an the tather arf larfed fit to split theirselves. (*To* BARBARA.) There! are you settisfawd nah?

BARBARA (*her eyes dancing*). Wish I'd been there, Bill.

BILL. Yus: youd a got in a hextra bit o talk on me, wouldnt you?

JENNY. I'm so sorry, Mr Walker.

BILL. (*fiercely*). Downt you gow being sorry for me: youve no call. Listen eah. Aw browk your jawr.

JENNY. No, it didnt hurt me: indeed it didnt, except for a moment. It was only that I was frightened.

BILL. Aw downt want to be forgive be you, or be ennybody. Wot Aw did Aw'll py for. Aw trawd to gat me aown jawr browk to settisfaw you—

JENNY (*distressed*). Oh no—

BILL (*impatiently*). Tell y' Aw did: cawnt you listen to wots bein taold you? All Aw got be it bein mide a sawt of in the pablic street for me pines. Well, if Aw cawnt settisfaw you one wy, Aw ken anather. Listen eah! Aw ed two quid sived agen the frost; an Awve a pahnd of it left. A mite o mawn last week ed word with the judy e's gowin to merry. E give er wot-for; an e's bin fawnd fifteen bob. E ed a rawt to itt er cause they was gowin to be merrid; but Aw ednt nao rawt to itt you; sao put anather fawv bob on an call it a pahnd's worth. (*He produces a sovereign.*[23]) Eahs the manney. Tike it; and lets ev no more o your forgivin an pryin and your Mijor jawrin me. Let wot Aw dan be dan an pide for; and let there be a end of it.

JENNY. Oh, I couldnt take it, Mr Walker. But if you would give a shilling or two to poor Rummy Mitchens! you really did hurt her; and she's old.

BILL (*contemptuously*). Not lawkly. Aw'd give her anather as soon as look at er. Let her ev the lawr o me as she threatened! She aint forgiven me: not mach. Wot Aw dan to er is not on me mawnd—wot she (*indicating* BARBARA) mawt call on me conscience—no more than stickin a pig. It's this Christian gime o yours that Aw wownt ev plyed agen me: this bloomin forgivin an neggin an jawrin that mikes a menn thet sore that iz lawf's a burdn to im. Aw wownt ev it, Aw tell you; sao tike your manney and stop thraowin your silly beshed fice hap agen me.

JENNY. Major: may I take a little of it for the Army?

BARBARA. No: the Army is not to be bought We want your soul, Bill; and we'll take nothing less.

BILL (*bitterly*). Aw knaow. Me an maw few shillins is not good enaff for you. Youre a earl's

---

[23] *sovereign* gold coin worth one pound

grendorter, you are. Nathink less than a andered pahnd for you.

UNDERSHAFT. Come, Barbara! you could do a great deal of good with a hundred pounds. If you will set this gentleman's mind at ease by taking his pound, I will give the other ninety-nine.

(BILL, *dazed by such opulence, instinctively touches his cap.*)

BARBARA. Oh, youre too extravagant, papa. Bill offers twenty pieces of silver. All you need offer is the other ten. That will make the standard price to buy anybody who's for sale. I'm not; and the Army's not. (*To* BILL.) Youll never have another quiet moment, Bill, until you come round to us. You cant stand out against your salvation.

BILL (*sullenly*). Aw cawnt stend aht agen music awl wrastlers and awtful tangued women. Awve offered to py. Aw can do no more. Tike it or leave it. There it is. (*He throws the sovereign on the drum, and sits down on the horse-trough. The coin fascinates* SNOBBY PRICE, *who takes an early opportunity of dropping his cap on it.*)

(MRS BAINES *comes from the shelter. She is dressed as a Salvation Army Commissioner. She is an earnest looking woman of about 40, with a caressing, urgent voice, and an appealing manner.*)

BARBARA. This is my father, Mrs Baines. (UNDERSHAFT *comes from the table, taking his hat off with marked civility.*) Try what you can do with him. He wont listen to me, because he remembers what a fool I was when I was a baby. (*She leaves them together and chats with* JENNY.)

MRS BAINES. Have you been shewn over the shelter, Mr Undershaft? You know the work we're doing, of course.

UNDERSHAFT (*very civilly*). The whole nation knows it, Mrs Baines.

MRS BAINES. No, sir: the whole nation does not know it, or we should not be crippled as we are for want of money to carry our work through the length and breadth of the land. Let me tell you that there would have been rioting this winter in London but for us.

UNDERSHAFT. You really think so?

MRS BAINES. I know it. I remember 1886, when you rich gentlemen hardened your hearts against the cry of the poor. They broke the windows of your clubs in Pall Mall.

UNDERSHAFT (*gleaming with approval of their method*). And the Mansion House Fund went up next day from thirty thousand pounds to seventy-nine thousand! I remember quite well.

MRS BAINES. Well, wont you help me to get at the people? They wont break windows then. Come here, Price. Let me shew you to this gentleman (PRICE *comes to be inspected.*) Do you remember the window breaking?

PRICE. My ole father thought it was the revolution, maam.

MRS BAINES. Would you break windows now?

PRICE. Oh no, maam. The windows of eaven av bin opened to me. I know now that the rich man is a sinner like myself.

RUMMY (*appearing above at the loft door*). Snobby Price!

SNOBBY. Wot is it?

RUMMY. Your mother's askin for you at the other gate in Cripps's Lane. She's heard about your confession. (PRICE *turns pale.*)

MRS BAINES. Go, Mr Price; and pray with her.

JENNY. You can go through the shelter, Snobby.

PRICE (*to* MRS BAINES). I couldnt face her now, maam, with all the weight of my sins fresh on me. Tell her she'll find her son at ome, waitin for her in prayer. (*He skulks off through the gate, incidentally stealing the sovereign on his way out picking up his cap from the drum.*)

MRS BAINES (*with swimming eyes*). You see how we take the anger and the bitterness against you out of their hearts, Mr Undershaft.

UNDERSHAFT. It is certainly most convenient and gratifying to all large employers of labor, Mrs Baines.

MRS BAINES. Barbara: Jenny: I have good news: most wonderful news. (JENNY *runs to her.*) My prayers have been answered. I told you they would Jenny, didnt I?

JENNY. Yes, yes.

BARBARA (*moving nearer to the drum*). Have we got money enough to keep the shelter open?

MRS BAINES. I hope we shall have enough to

keep all the shelters open. Lord Saxmundham has promised us five thousand pounds—

BARBARA. Hooray!

JENNY. Glory!

MRS BAINES. —if—

BARBARA. "If!" If what?

MRS BAINES. —if five other gentlemen will give a thousand each to make it up to ten thousand.

BARBARA. Who is Lord Saxmundham? I never heard of him.

UNDERSHAFT (who has pricked up his ears at the peer's name, and is now watching BARBARA curiously). A new creation, my dear. You have heard of Sir Horace Bodger?

BARBARA. Bodger! Do you mean the distiller? Bodger's whisky!

UNDERSHAFT. That is the man. He is one of the greatest of our public benefactors. He restored the cathedral at Hakington. They made him a baronet for that. He gave half a million to the funds of his party: they made him a baron for that.

SHIRLEY. What will they give him for the five thousand?

UNDERSHAFT. There is nothing left to give him. So the five thousand, I should think, is to save his soul.

MRS BAINES. Heaven grant it may! Oh Mr Undershaft, you have some very rich friends. Cant you help us towards the other five thousand? We are going to hold a great meeting this afternoon at the Assembly Hall in the Mile End Road. If I could only announce that one gentleman had come forward to support Lord Saxmundham, others would follow. Dont you know somebody? couldnt you? wouldnt you? (Her eyes fill with tears.) oh, think of those poor people, Mr Undershaft: think of how much it means to them, and how little to a great man like you.

UNDERSHAFT (sardonically gallant). Mrs Baines: you are irresistible. I cant disappoint you; and I cant deny myself the satisfaction of making Bodger pay up. You shall have your five thousand pounds.

MRS BAINES. Thank God!

UNDERSHAFT. You dont thank me?

MRS BAINES. Oh sir, dont try to be cynical: dont be ashamed of being a good man. The Lord will bless you abundantly; and our prayers will be like a strong fortification round you all the days of your life. (With a touch of caution.) You will let me have the cheque to shew at the meeting, wont you? Jenny: go in and fetch a pen and ink. (JENNY runs to the shelter door.)

UNDERSHAFT. Do not disturb Miss Hill: I have a fountain pen. (JENNY halts. He sits at the table and writes the cheque. CUSINS rises to make room for him. They all watch him silently.)

BILL (cynically, aside to BARBARA, his voice and accent horribly debased). Wot prawce selvytion nah?

BARBARA. Stop. (UNDERSHAFT stops writing: they all turn to her in surprise.) Mrs Baines: are you really going to take this money?

MRS BAINES (astonished). Why not, dear?

BARBARA. Why not! Do you know what my father is? Have you forgotten that Lord Saxmundham is Bodger the whisky man? Do you remember how we implored the County Council to stop him from writing Bodger's Whisky in letters of fire against the sky; so that the poor drink-ruined creatures on the Embankment could not wake up from their snatches of sleep without being reminded of their deadly thirst by that wicked sky sign? Do you know that the worst thing I have had to fight here is not the devil, but Bodger, Bodger, Bodger, with his whisky, his distilleries, and his tied houses?[24] Are you going to make our shelter another tied house for him, and ask me to keep it?

BILL. Rotten dranken whisky it is too.

MRS BAINES. Dear Barbara: Lord Saxmundham has a soul to be saved like any of us. If heaven has found the way to make a good use of his money, are we to set ourselves up against the answer to our prayers?

BARBARA. I know he has a soul to be saved. Let him come down here; and I'll do my best to help him to his salvation. But he wants to send his cheque down to buy us, and go on being as wicked as ever.

UNDERSHAFT (with a reasonableness which CUSINS alone perceives to be ironical). My dear Barbara: alcohol is a very necessary article. It heals the sick—

[24] tied houses i.e., taverns which sell only his liquor

BARBARA. It does nothing of the sort.

UNDERSHAFT. Well, it assists the doctor: that is perhaps a less questionable way of putting it. It makes life bearable to millions of people who could not endure their existence if they were quite sober. It enables Parliament to do things at eleven at night that no sane person would do at eleven in the morning. Is it Bodger's fault that this inestimable gift is deplorably abused by less than one per cent of the poor? (*He turns again to the table; signs the cheque; and crosses it.*)

MRS BAINES. Barbara: will there be less drinking or more if all those poor souls we are saving come tomorrow and find the doors of our shelters shut in their faces? Lord Saxmundham gives us the money to stop drinking —to take his own business from him.

CUSINS (*impishly*). Pure self-sacrifice on Bodger's part, clearly! Bless dear Bodger! (BARBARA *almost breaks down as* ADOLPHUS, *too, fails her.*)

UNDERSHAFT (*tearing out the cheque and pocketing the book as he rises and goes past* CUSINS *to* MRS BAINES). I also, Mrs Baines, may claim a little distinterestedness. Think of my business! think of the widows and orphans! the men and lads torn to pieces with shrapnel and poisoned with lyddite! (MRS BAINES *shrinks; but he goes on remorselessly.*) the oceans of blood, not one drop of which is shed in a really just cause! the ravaged crops! the peaceful peasants forced, women and men, to till their fields under the fire of opposing armies on pain of starvation! the bad blood of the fierce little cowards at home who egg on others to fight for the gratification of their national vanity! All this makes money for me: I am never richer, never busier than when the papers are full of it. Well, it is your work to preach peace on earth and good will to men. (MRS BAINES's *face lights up again.*) Every convert you make is a vote against war. (*Her lips move in prayer.*) Yet I give you this money to help you to hasten my own commercial ruin. (*He gives her the cheque.*)

CUSINS (*mounting the form in an ecstasy of mischief*). The millennium will be inaugurated by the unselfishness of Undershaft and Bodger. Oh be joyful! (*He takes the drum-sticks from his pocket and flourishes them.*)

MRS BAINES (*taking the cheque*). The longer I live the more proof I see that there is an Infinite Goodness that turns everything to the work of salvation sooner or later. Who would have thought that any good could have come out of war and drink? And yet their profits are brought today to the feet of salvation to do its blessed work. (*She is affected to tears.*)

JENNY (*running to* MRS BAINES *and throwing her arms round her*). Oh dear! how blessed, how glorious it all is!

CUSINS (*in a convulsion of irony*). Let us seize this unspeakable moment. Let us march to the great meeting at once. Excuse me just an instant. (*He rushes into the shelter.* JENNY *takes her tambourine from the drum head.*)

MRS BAINES. Mr Undershaft: have you ever seen a thousand people fall on their knees with one impulse and pray? Come with us to the meeting. Barbara shall tell them that the Army is saved, and saved through you.

CUSINS (*returning impetuously from the shelter with a flag and a trombone, and coming between* MRS BAINES *and* UNDERSHAFT). You shall carry the flag down the first street, Mrs Baines. (*He gives her the flag.*) Mr Undershaft is a gifted trombonist: he shall intone an Olympian diapason to the West Ham Salvation March. (*Aside to* UNDERSHAFT, *as he forces the trombone on him.*) Blow, Machiavelli, blow.

UNDERSHAFT (*aside to him, as he takes the trombone*). The trumpet in Zion![25] (CUSINS *rushes to the drum, which he takes up and puts on.* UNDERSHAFT *continues, aloud.*) I will do my best. I could vamp[26] a bass if I knew the tune.

CUSINS. It is a wedding chorus from one of Donizetti's operas; but we have converted it. We convert everything to good here, including Bodger. You remember the chorus. "For thee immense rejoicing—immenso giubilo— immenso giubilo." (*With drum obbligato.*) Rum tum ti tum tum, tum tum ti ta—

BARBARA. Dolly: you are breaking my heart.

---

[25] *trumpet in Zion* "Blow ye the trumpet in Zion, and sound an alarm in my holy mountain: let all the inhabitants of the land tremble: for the day of the Lord cometh, for it is nigh at hand" (*Joel* 2: 1). [26] *vamp* to improvise (an accompaniment)

CUSINS. What is a broken heart more or less here? Dionysos Undershaft has descended. I am possessed.

MRS BAINES. Come, Barbara: I must have my dear Major to carry the flag with me.

JENNY. Yes, yes, Major darling.

CUSINS (*snatches the tambourine out of* JENNY's *hand and mutely offers it to* BARBARA).

BARBARA (*coming forward a little as she puts the offer behind her with a shudder, whilst* CUSINS *recklessly tosses the tambourine back to* JENNY *and goes to the gate*). I cant come.

JENNY. Not come!

MRS BAINES (*with tears in her eyes*). Barbara: do you think I am wrong to take the money?

BARBARA (*impulsively going to her and kissing her*). No, no: God help you, dear, you must: you are saving the Army. Go; and may you have a great meeting!

JENNY. But arnt you coming?

BARBARA. No. (*She begins taking off the silver S brooch from her collar.*)

MRS BAINES. Barbara: what are you doing?

JENNY. Why are you taking your badge off? You cant be going to leave us, Major.

BARBARA (*quietly*). Father: come here.

UNDERSHAFT (*coming to her*). My dear! (*Seeing that she is going to pin the badge on his collar, he retreats to the penthouse in some alarm.*)

BARBARA (*following him*). Dont be frightened. (*She pins the badge on and steps back towards the table, shewing him to the others.*) There! It's not much for £5000, is it?

MRS BAINES. Barbara: if you wont come and pray with us, promise me you will pray for us.

BARBARA. I cant pray now. Perhaps I shall never pray again.

MRS BAINES. Barbara!

JENNY. Major!

BARBARA (*almost delirious*). I cant bear any more. Quick march!

CUSINS (*calling to the procession in the street outside*). Off we go. Play up, there! Immenso giubilo. (*He gives the time with his drum; and the band strikes up the march, which rapidly becomes more distant as the procession moves briskly away.*)

MRS BAINES. I must go, dear. Youre overworked: you will be all right tomorrow. We'll never lose you. Now Jenny: step out with the

old flag. Blood and Fire! (*She marches out through the gate with her flag.*)

JENNY. Glory Hallelujah! (*Flourishing her tambourine and marching.*)

UNDERSHAFT (*to* CUSINS, *as he marches out past him easing the slide of his trombone*). "My ducats and my daughter!"

CUSINS (*following him out*). Money and gunpowder!

BARBARA. Drunkenness and Murder! My God: why hast thou forsaken me?

(*She sinks on the form with her face buried in her hands. The march passes away into silence.* BILL WALKER *steals across to her.*)

BILL (*taunting*). Wot prawce selvytion nah?

SHIRLEY. Dont you hit her when she's down.

BILL. She itt me wen Aw wiz dahn. Waw shouldnt Aw git a bit o me aown beck?

BARBARA (*raising her head*). I didnt take your money, Bill. (*She crosses the yard to the gate and turns her back on the two men to hide her face from them.*)

BILL (*sneering after her*). Naow, it warnt enaff for you. (*Turning to the drum, he misses the money.*) Ellow! If you aint took it sammun else ez. Weres it gorn? Bly me if Jenny Ill didnt tike it arter all!

RUMMY (*screaming at him from the loft*). You lie, you dirty blackguard! Snobby Price pinched it off the drum when he took up his cap. I was up here all the time an see im do it.

BILL. Wot! Stowl maw manney! Waw didnt you call thief on him, you silly aold macker you?

RUMMY. To serve you aht for ittin me acrost the fice. It's cost y'pahnd, that az. (*Raising a pæan[27] of squalid triumph.*) I done you. I'm even with you. Uve ad it aht o y—(BILL *snatches up* SHIRLEY's *mug and hurls it at her. She slams the loft door and vanishes. The mug smashes against the door and falls in fragments.*)

BILL (*beginning to chuckle*). Tell us, aol menn, wot o'clock this mawnin was it wen im as they call Snobby Prawce was sived?

BARBARA (*turning to him more composedly, and with unspoiled sweetness*). About half past twelve, Bill. And he pinched your pound at

---

[27] *paean* song of joy, triumph

a quarter to two. *I* know. Well, you cant afford to lose it. I'll send it to you.

BILL (*his voice and accent suddenly improving*). Not if Aw wiz to stawve for it. Aw aint to be bought.

SHIRLEY. Aint you? Youd sell yourself to the devil for a pint o beer; only there aint no devil to make the offer.

BILL (*unashamed*). Sao Aw would, mite, and often ev, cheerful. But she cawnt baw me. (*Approaching* BARBARA.) You wanted maw soul, did you? Well, you aint got it.

BARBARA. I nearly got it, Bill. But weve sold it back to you for ten thousand pounds.

SHIRLEY. And dear at the money!

BARBARA. No, Peter: it was worth more than money.

BILL (*salvationproof*). It's nao good: you cawnt get rahnd me nah. Aw downt blieve in it; and Awve seen tody that Aw was rawt. (*Going.*) Sao long, aol soupkitchener! Ta, ta, Mijor Earl's Grendorter! (*Turning at the gate.*) Wot prawce selvytion nah? Snobby Prawce! Ha! ha!

BARBARA (*offering her hand*). Goodbye, Bill.

BILL (*taken aback, half plucks his cap off; then shoves it on again defiantly*). Git aht. (BARBARA *drops her hand, discouraged. He has a twinge of remorse.*) But thets aw rawt, you knaow. Nathink pasnl. Naow mellice. Sao long, Judy. (*He goes.*)

BARBARA. No malice. So long, Bill.

SHIRLEY (*shaking his head*). You make too much of him, miss, in your innocence.

BARBARA (*going to him*). Peter: I'm like you now. Cleaned out, and lost my job.

SHIRLEY. Youve youth an hope. Thats two better than me.

BARBARA. I'll get you a job, Peter. Thats hope for you: the youth will have to be enough for me. (*She counts her money.*) I have just enough left for two teas at Lockharts, a Rowton doss[28] for you, and my tram and bus home. (*He frowns and rises with offended pride. She takes his arm.*) Dont be proud, Peter: it's sharing between friends. And promise me

youll talk to me and not let me cry. (*She draws him towards the gate.*)

SHIRLEY. Well, I'm not accustomed to talk to the like of you—

BARBARA (*urgently*). Yes, yes: you must talk to me. Tell me about Tom Paine's books and Bradlaugh's[29] lectures. Come along.

SHIRLEY. Ah, if you would only read Tom Paine in the proper spirit, miss! (*They go out through the gate together.*)

## ACT III

*Next day after lunch* LADY BRITOMART *is writing in the library in Wilton Crescent.* SARAH *is reading in the armchair near the window.* BARBARA, *in ordinary fashionable dress, pale and brooding, is on the settee.* CHARLES LOMAX *enters. He starts on seeing* BARBARA *fashionably attired and in low spirits.*

LOMAX. Youve left off your uniform!

(BARBARA *says nothing; but an expression of pain passes over her face.*)

LADY BRITOMART (*warning him in low tones to be careful*). Charles!

LOMAX (*much concerned, coming behind the settee and bending sympathetically over* BARBARA). I'm awfully sorry, Barbara. You know I helped you all I could with the concertina and so forth. (*Momentously.*) Still, I have never shut my eyes to the fact that there is a certain amount of tosh about the Salvation Army. Now the claims of the Church of England—

LADY BRITOMART. Thats enough, Charles. Speak of something suited to your mental capacity.

LOMAX. But surely the Church of England is suited to all our capacities.

BARBARA (*pressing his hand*). Thank you for your sympathy, Cholly. Now go and spoon with Sarah.

LOMAX (*dragging a chair from the writing table and seating himself affectionately by* SARAH's *side*). How is my ownest today?

SARAH. I wish you wouldnt tell Cholly to do things, Barbara. He always comes straight

---

[28] *Rowton doss* Rowton houses, named after their designer, Baron Rowton (1838–1903), were hotels for the poor; *doss* cheap lodging

[29] *Bradlaugh* late nineteenth-century social reformer

and does them. Cholly: we're going to the works this afternoon.

LOMAX. What works?

SARAH. The cannon works.

LOMAX. What? your governor's shop!

SARAH. Yes.

LOMAX. Oh I say!

(CUSINS *enters in poor condition. He also starts visibly when he see* BARBARA *without her uniform.*)

BARBARA. I expected you this morning, Dolly. Didnt you guess that?

CUSINS (*sitting down beside her*). I'm sorry. I have only just breakfasted.

SARAH. But weve just finished lunch.

BARBARA. Have you had one of your bad nights?

CUSINS. No: I had rather a good night: in fact, one of the most remarkable nights I have ever passed.

BARBARA. The meeting?

CUSINS. No: after the meeting.

LADY BRITOMART. You should have gone to bed after the meeting. What were you doing?

CUSINS. Drinking.

LADY BRITOMART. } { Adolphus!
SARAH. } { Dolly!
BARBARA. } { Dolly!
LOMAX. } { Oh I say!

LADY BRITOMART. What were you drinking, may I ask?

CUSINS. A most devilish kind of Spanish burgundy, warranted free from added alcohol: a Temperance burgundy in fact. Its richness in natural alcohol made any addition superfluous.

BARBARA. Are you joking, Dolly?

CUSINS (*patiently*). No I have been making a night of it with the nominal head of this household: that is all.

LADY BRITOMART. Andrew made you drunk!

CUSINS. No: he only provided the wine. I think it was Dionysos who made me drunk. (*To* BARBARA.) I told you I was possessed.

LADY BRITOMART. Youre not sober yet. Go home to bed at once.

CUSINS. I have never before ventured to reproach you, Lady Brit; but how could you marry the Prince of Darkness?

LADY BRITOMART. It was much more excusable to marry him than to get drunk with him. That is a new accomplishment of Andrew's, by the way. He usent to drink.

CUSINS. He doesnt now. He only sat there and completed the wreck of my moral basis, the rout of my convictions, the purchase of my soul. He cares for you, Barbara. That is what makes him so dangerous to me.

BARBARA. That has nothing to do with it, Dolly. There are larger loves and diviner dreams than the fireside ones. You know that, dont you?

CUSINS. Yes: that is our understanding. I know it. I hold to it. Unless he can win me on that holier ground he may amuse me for a while; but he can get no deeper hold, strong as he is.

BARBARA. Keep to that; and the end will be right. Now tell me what happened at the meeting?

CUSINS. It was an amazing meeting. Mrs Baines almost died of emotion. Jenny Hill simply gibbered with hysteria. The Prince of Darkness played his trombone like a madman: its brazen roarings were like the laughter of the damned. 117 conversions took place then and there. They prayed with the most touching sincerity and gratitude for Bodger, and for the anonymous donor of the £5000. Your father would not let his name be given.

LOMAX. That was rather fine of the old man, you know. Most chaps would have wanted the advertisement.

CUSINS. He said all the charitable institutions would be down on him like kites on a battle-field if he gave his name.

LADY BRITOMART. Thats Andrew all over. He never does a proper thing without giving an improper reason for it.

CUSINS. He convinced me that I have all my life been doing improper things for proper reasons.

LADY BRITOMART. Adolphus: now that Barbara has left the Salvation Army, you had better leave it too. I will not have you playing that drum in the streets.

CUSINS. Your orders are already obeyed, Lady Brit.

BARBARA. Dolly: were you ever really in earnest about it? Would you have joined if you had never seen me?

CUSINS (*disingenuously*). Well—er—well, possibly, as a collector of religions—

LOMAX (*cunningly*). Not as a drummer,

though, you know. You are a very clear-headed brainy chap, Dolly; and it must have been apparent to you that there is a certain amount of tosh about—

LADY BRITOMART. Charles: if you must drivel, drivel like a grown-up man and not like a schoolboy.

LOMAX (*out of countenance*). Well, drivel is drivel, dont you know, whatever a man's age.

LADY BRITOMART. In good society in England, Charles, men drivel at all ages by repeating silly formulas with an air of wisdom. Schoolboys make their own formulas out of slang, like you. When they reach your age, and get political private secretaryships and things of that sort, they drop slang and get their formulas out of the Spectator or The Times. You had better confine yourself to The Times. You will find that there is a certain amount of tosh about The Times; but at least its language is reputable.

LOMAX (*overwhelmed*). You are so awfully strong-minded, Lady Brit—

LADY BRITOMART. Rubbish! (MORRISON *comes in.*) What is it?

MORRISON. If you please, my lady, Mr Undershaft has just drove up to the door.

LADY BRITOMART. Well, let him in. (MORRISON *hesitates.*) Whats the matter with you?

MORRISON. Shall I announce him, my lady; or is he at home here, so to speak, my lady?

LADY BRITOMART. Announce him.

MORRISON. Thank you, my lady. You wont mind my asking, I hope. The occasion is in a manner of speaking new to me.

LADY BRITOMART. Quite right. Go and let him in.

MORRISON. Thank you, my lady. (*He withdraws.*)

LADY BRITOMART. Children: go and get ready. (SARAH *and* BARBARA *go upstairs for their out-of-door wraps.*) Charles: go and tell Stephen to come down here in five minutes: you will find him in the drawing room. (CHARLES *goes.*) Adolphus: tell them to send round the carriage in about fifteen minutes. (ADOLPHUS *goes.*)

MORRISON (*at the door*). Mr Undershaft.

(UNDERSHAFT *comes in.* MORRISON *goes out.*)

UNDERSHAFT. Alone! How fortunate!

LADY BRITOMART (*rising*). Dont be senti-mental, Andrew. Sit down. (*She sits on the settee: he sits beside her, on her left. She comes to the point before he has time to breathe.*) Sarah must have £800 a year until Charles Lomax comes into his property. Barbara will need more, and need it permanently, because Adolphus hasnt any property.

UNDERSHAFT (*resignedly*). Yes, my dear: I will see to it. Anything else? for yourself, for instance?

LADY BRITOMART. I want to talk to you about Stephen.

UNDERSHAFT (*rather wearily*). Dont, my dear. Stephen doesnt interest me.

LADY BRITOMART. He does interest me. He is our son.

UNDERSHAFT. Do you really think so? He has induced us to bring him into the world; but he chose his parents very incongruously, I think. I see nothing of myself in him, and less of you.

LADY BRITOMART. Andrew: Stephen is an excellent son, and a most steady, capable, highminded young man. You are simply trying to find an excuse for disinheriting him.

UNDERSHAFT. My dear Biddy: the Undershaft tradition disinherits him. It would be dishonest of me to leave the cannon foundry to my son.

LADY BRITOMART. It would be most un-natural and improper of you to leave it to anyone else, Andrew. Do you suppose this wicked and immoral tradition can be kept up for ever? Do you pretend that Stephen could not carry on the foundry just as well as all the other sons of the big business houses?

UNDERSHAFT. Yes: he could learn the office routine without understanding the business, like all the other sons; and the firm would go on by its own momentum until the real Undershaft—probably an Italian or a German—would invent a new method and cut him out.

LADY BRITOMART. There is nothing that any Italian or German could do that Stephen could not do. And Stephen at least has breeding.

UNDERSHAFT. The son of a foundling! Nonsense!

LADY BRITOMART. My son, Andrew! And even you may have good blood in your veins for all you know.

UNDERSHAFT. True. Probably I have. That is another argument in favor of a foundling.

LADY BRITOMART. Andrew: dont be aggravating. And dont be wicked. At present you are both.

UNDERSHAFT. This conversation is part of the Undershaft tradition, Biddy. Every Undershaft's wife has treated him to it ever since the house was founded. It is mere waste of breath. If the tradition be ever broken it will be for an abler man than Stephen.

LADY BRITOMART (*pouting*). Then go away.

UNDERSHAFT (*deprecatory*). Go away!

LADY BRITOMART. Yes: go away. If you will do nothing for Stephen, you are not wanted here. Go to your foundling, whoever he is; and look after him.

UNDERSHAFT. The fact is, Biddy—

LADY BRITOMART. Dont call me Biddy. I dont call you Andy.

UNDERSHAFT. I will not call my wife Britomart: it is not good sense. Seriously, my love, the Undershaft tradition has landed me in a difficulty. I am getting on in years; and my partner Lazarus has at last made a stand and insisted that the succession must be settled one way or the other; and of course he is quite right. You see, I havent found a fit successor yet.

LADY BRITOMART (*obstinately*). There is Stephen.

UNDERSHAFT. Thats just it: all the foundlings I can find are exactly like Stephen.

LADY BRITOMART. Andrew!!

UNDERSHAFT. I want a man with no relations and no schooling: that is, a man who would be out of the running altogether if he were not a strong man. And I cant find him. Every blessed foundling nowadays is snapped up in his infancy by Barnardo homes, or School Board officers, or Boards of Guardians; and if he shews the least ability he is fastened on by schoolmasters; trained to win scholarships like a racehorse; crammed with second-hand ideas; drilled and disciplined in docility and what they call good taste; and lamed for life so that he is fit for nothing but teaching. If you want to keep the foundry in the family, you had better find an eligible foundling and marry him to Barbara.

LADY BRITOMART. Ah! Barbara! Your pet! You would sacrifice Stephen to Barbara.

UNDERSHAFT. Cheerfully. And you, my dear, would boil Barbara to make soup for Stephen.

LADY BRITOMART. Andrew: this is not a question of our likings and dislikings: it is a question of duty. It is your duty to make Stephen your successor.

UNDERSHAFT. Just as much as it is your duty to submit to your husband. Come, Biddy! these tricks of the governing class are of no use with me. I am one of the governing class myself; and it is waste of time giving tracts to a missionary. I have the power in this matter; and I am not to be humbugged into using it for your purposes.

LADY BRITOMART. Andrew: you can talk my head off; but you cant change wrong into right. And your tie is all on one side. Put it straight.

UNDERSHAFT (*disconcerted*). It wont stay unless it's pinned (*He fumbles at it with childish grimaces.*)

(STEPHEN *comes in.*)

STEPHEN (*at the door*). I beg your pardon. (*About to retire.*)

LADY BRITOMART. No: come in, Stephen. (STEPHEN *comes forward to his mother's writing table.*)

UNDERSHAFT (*not very cordially*). Good afternoon.

STEPHEN (*coldly*). Good afternoon.

UNDERSHAFT (*to* LADY BRITOMART). He knows all about the tradition, I suppose?

LADY BRITOMART. Yes. (*To* STEPHEN.) It is what I told you last night, Stephen.

UNDERSHAFT (*sulkily*). I understand you want to come into the cannon business.

STEPHEN. *I* go into trade! Certainly not.

UNDERSHAFT (*opening his eyes, greatly eased in mind and manner*). Oh! in that case—

LADY BRITOMART. Cannons are not trade, Stephen. They are enterprise.

STEPHEN. I have no intention of becoming a man of business in any sense. I have no capacity for business and no taste for it. I intend to devote myself to politics.

UNDERSHAFT (*rising*). My dear boy: this is an immense relief to me. And I trust it may prove an equally good thing for the country. I was afraid you would consider yourself disparaged and slighted. (*He moves towards* STEPHEN *as if to shake hands with him.*)

LADY BRITOMART (*rising and interposing*). Stephen: I cannot allow you to throw away an enormous property like this.

STEPHEN (*stiffly*). Mother: there must be an end of treating me as a child, if you please. (LADY BRITOMART *recoils, deeply wounded by his tone.*) Until last night I did not take your attitude seriously, because I did not think you meant it seriously. But I find now that you left me in the dark as to matters which you should have explained to me years ago. I am extremely hurt and offended. Any further discussion of my intentions had better take place with my father, as between one man and another.

LADY BRITOMART. Stephen! (*She sits down again, her eyes filling with tears.*)

UNDERSHAFT (*with grave compassion*). You see, my dear, it is only the big men who can be treated as children.

STEPHEN. I am sorry, mother, that you have forced me—

UNDERSHAFT (*stopping him*). Yes, yes, yes, yes: thats all right, Stephen. She wont interfere with you any more: your independence is achieved: you have won your latchkey. Dont rub it in; and above all, dont apologize. (*He resumes his seat.*) Now what about your future, as between one man and another— I beg your pardon, Biddy: as between two men and a woman.

LADY BRITOMART (*who has pulled herself together strongly*). I quite understand, Stephen. By all means go your own way if you feel strong enough. (STEPHEN *sits down magisterially in the chair at the writing table with an air of affirming his majority.*)

UNDERSHAFT. It is settled that you do not ask for the succession to the cannon business.

STEPHEN. I hope it is settled that I repudiate the cannon business.

UNDERSHAFT. Come, come! dont be so devilishly sulky: it's boyish. Freedom should be generous. Besides, I owe you a fair start in life in exchange for disinheriting you. You cant become prime minister all at once. Havnt you a turn for something? What about literature, art, and so forth?

STEPHEN. I have nothing of the artist about me, either in faculty or character, thank Heaven!

UNDERSHAFT. A philosopher, perhaps? Eh?

STEPHEN. I make no such ridiculous pretension.

UNDERSHAFT. Just so. Well, there is the army, the navy, the Church, the Bar. The Bar requires some ability. What about the Bar?

STEPHEN. I have not studied law. And I am afraid I have not the necessary push—I believe that is the name barristers give to their vulgarity—for success in pleading.

UNDERSHAFT. Rather a difficult case, Stephen. Hardly anything left but the stage, is there? (STEPHEN *makes an impatient movement.*) Well, come! is there anything you know or care for?

STEPHEN (*rising and looking at him steadily*). I know the difference between right and wrong.

UNDERSHAFT (*hugely tickled*). You dont say so! What! no capacity for business, no knowledge of law, no sympathy with art, no pretension to philosophy; only a simple knowledge of the secret that has puzzled all the philosophers, baffled all the lawyers, muddled all the men of business, and ruined most of the artists: the secret of right and wrong. Why, man, youre a genius, a master of masters, a god! At twentyfour, too!

STEPHEN (*keeping his temper with difficulty*). You are pleased to be facetious. I pretend to nothing more than any honorable English gentleman claims as his birthright. (*He sits down angrily.*)

UNDERSHAFT. Oh, thats everybody's birthright. Look at poor little Jenny Hill, the Salvation lassie! she would think you were laughing at her if you asked her to stand up in the street and teach grammar or geography or mathematics or even drawing room dancing; but it never occurs to her to doubt that she can teach morals and religion. You are all alike, you respectable people. You cant tell me the bursting strain of a ten-inch gun, which is a very simple matter; but you all think you can tell me the bursting strain of a man under temptation. You darent handle high explosives; but youre all ready to handle honesty and truth and justice and the whole duty of man, and kill one another at that game. What a country! What a world!

LADY BRITOMART (*uneasily*). What do you think he had better do, Andrew?

UNDERSHAFT. Oh, just what he wants to do. He knows nothing and he thinks he knows everything. That points clearly to a political career. Get him a private secretaryship to someone who can get him an Under Secretaryship; and then leave him alone. He will find his natural and proper place in the end on the Treasury Bench.

STEPHEN (*springing up again*). I am sorry, sir, that you force me to forget the respect due to you as my father. I am an Englishman and I will not hear the Government of my country insulted. (*He thrusts his hands in his pockets, and walks angrily across to the window.*)

UNDERSHAFT (*with a touch of brutality*). The government of your country! *I* am the government of your country: I, and Lazarus. Do you suppose that you and half a dozen amateurs like you, sitting in a row in that foolish gabble shop, can govern Undershaft and Lazarus? No, my friend: you will do what pays us. You will make war when it suits us, and keep peace when it doesnt. You will find out that trade requires certain measures when we have decided on those measures. When I want anything to keep my dividends up, you will discover that my want is a national need. When other people want something to keep my dividends down, you will call out the police and military. And in return you shall have the support and applause of my newspapers, and the delight of imagining that you are a great statesman. Government of your country! Be off with you, my boy, and play with your caucuses and leading articles and historic parties and great leaders and burning questions and the rest of your toys. *I* am going back to my counting-house to pay the piper and call the tune.

STEPHEN (*actually smiling, and putting his hand on his father's shoulder with indulgent patronage*). Really, my dear father, it is impossible to be angry with you. You dont know how absurd all this sounds to me. You are very properly proud of having been industrious enough to make money; and it is greatly to your credit that you have made so much of it. But it has kept you in circles where you are valued for your money and deferred to for it, instead of in the doubtless very old-fashioned and behind-the-times public school and university where I formed my habits of mind. It is natural for you to think that money governs England; but you must allow me to think I know better.

UNDERSHAFT. And what does govern England, pray?

STEPHEN. Character, father, character.

UNDERSHAFT. Whose character? Yours or mine?

STEPHEN. Neither yours nor mine, father, but the best elements in the English national character.

UNDERSHAFT. Stephen: Ive found your profession for you. Youre a born journalist. I'll start you with a high-toned weekly review. There!

(*Before* STEPHEN *can reply* SARAH, BARBARA, LOMAX, *and* CUSINS *come in ready for walking. Barbara crosses the room to the window and looks out.* CUSINS *drifts amiably to the armchair.* LOMAX *remains near the door, whilst* SARAH *comes to her mother.*

STEPHEN *goes to the smaller writing table and busies himself with his letters.*)

SARAH. Go and get ready, mamma: the carriage is waiting. (LADY BRITOMART *leaves the room.*)

UNDERSHAFT (*to* SARAH). Good day, my dear. Good afternoon, Mr Lomax.

LOMAX (*vaguely*). Ahdedoo.

UNDERSHAFT (*to* CUSINS). Quite well after last night, Euripides, eh?

CUSINS. As well as can be expected.

UNDERSHAFT. Thats right. (*To* BARBARA.) So you are coming to see my death and devastation factory, Barbara?

BARBARA (*at the window*). You came yesterday to see my salvation factory. I promised you a return visit.

LOMAX (*coming forward between* SARAH *and* UNDERSHAFT). Youll find it awfully interesting. Ive been through the Woolwich Arsenal; and it gives you a ripping feeling of security, you know, to think of the lot of beggars we could kill if it came to fighting. (*To* UNDERSHAFT, *with sudden solemnity.*) Still, it must be rather an awful reflection for you, from the religious point of view as it were. Youre getting on, you know, and all that.

SARAH. You dont mind Cholly's imbecility, papa, do you?

LOMAX (*much taken aback*). Oh I say!

UNDERSHAFT. Mr Lomax looks at the matter in a very proper spirit, my dear.

LOMAX. Just so. Thats all I meant, I assure you.

SARAH. Are you coming, Stephen?

STEPHEN. Well, I am rather busy—er—(*Magnanimously.*) Oh well, yes: I'll come. That is, if there is room for me.

UNDERSHAFT. I can take two with me in a little motor I am experimenting with for field use. You wont mind its being rather unfashionable. It's not painted yet; but it's bullet proof.

LOMAX (*appalled at the prospect of confronting* WILTON CRESCENT *in an unpainted motor*). Oh I say!

SARAH. The carriage for me, thank you. Barbara doesnt mind what she's seen in.

LOMAX. I say, Dolly, old chap: do you really mind the car being a guy?[30] Because of course if you do I'll go in it. Still—

CUSINS. I prefer it.

LOMAX. Thanks awfully, old man. Come, my ownest. (*He hurries out to secure his seat in the carriage.* SARAH *follows him.*)

CUSINS (*moodily walking across to* LADY BRITOMART'*s writing table*). Why are we two coming to this Works Department of Hell? that is what I ask myself.

BARBARA. I have always thought of it as a sort of pit where lost creatures with blackened faces stirred up smoky fires and were driven and tormented by my father? Is it like that, dad?

UNDERSHAFT (*scandalized*). My dear! It is a spotlessly clean and beautiful hillside town.

CUSINS. With a Methodist chapel? Oh do say theres a Methodist chapel.

UNDERSHAFT. There are two: a Primitive one and a sophisticated one. There is even an Ethical Society; but it is not much patronized, as my men are all strongly religious. In the High Explosives Sheds they

object to the presence of Agnostics as unsafe.

CUSINS. And yet they dont object to you!

BARBARA. Do they obey all your orders?

UNDERSHAFT. I never give them any orders. When I speak to one of them it is "Well, Jones, is the baby doing well? and has Mrs Jones made a good recovery?" "Nicely, thank you, sir." And thats all.

CUSINS. But Jones has to be kept in order. How do you maintain discipline among your men?

UNDERSHAFT. I dont. They do. You see, the one thing Jones wont stand is any rebellion from the man under him, or any assertion of social equality between the wife of the man with 4 shillings a week less than himself, and Mrs Jones! Of course they all rebel against me, theoretically. Practically, every man of them keeps the man just below him in his place. I never meddle with them. I never bully them. I dont even bully Lazarus. I say that certain things are to be done; but I dont order anybody to do them. I dont say, mind you, that there is no ordering about and snubbing and even bullying. The men snub the boys and order them about; the carmen snub the sweepers; the artisans snub the unskilled laborers; the foremen drive and bully both the laborers and artisans; the assistant engineers find fault with the foremen; the chief engineers drop on the assistants; the departmental managers worry the chiefs; and the clerks have tall hats and hymnbooks and keep up the social tone by refusing to associate on equal terms with anybody. The result is a colossal profit, which comes to me.

CUSINS (*revolted*). You really are a—well, what I was saying yesterday.

BARBARA. What was he saying yesterday?

UNDERSHAFT. Never mind, my dear. He thinks I have made you unhappy. Have I?

BARBARA. Do you think I can be happy in this vulgar silly dress? I! who have worn the uniform. Do you understand what you have done to me? Yesterday I had a man's soul in my hand. I set him in the way of life with his face to salvation. But when we took your money he turned back to drunkenness and derision. (*With intense conviction.*) I will never forgive you that. If I had a child,

---

[30] *guy* person of grotesque looks

and you destroyed its body with your explosives—if you murdered Dolly with your horrible guns—I could forgive you if my forgiveness would open the gates of heaven to you. But to take a human soul from me, and turn it into the soul of a wolf! that is worse than any murder.

UNDERSHAFT. Does my daughter despair so easily? Can you strike a man to the heart and leave no mark on him?

BARBARA (*her face lighting up*). Oh, you are right: he can never be lost now: where was my faith?

CUSINS. Oh, clever clever devil!

BARBARA. You may be a devil; but God speaks through you sometimes. (*She takes her father's hands and kisses them.*) You have given me back my happiness: I feel it deep down now, though my spirit is troubled.

UNDERSHAFT. You have learnt something. That always feels at first as if you had lost something.

BARBARA. Well, take me to the factory of death; and let me learn something more. There must be some truth or other behind all this frightful irony. Come, Dolly. (*She goes out.*)

CUSINS. My guardian angel! (*To* UNDERSHAFT.) Avaunt![31] (*He follows* BARBARA.)

STEPHEN (*quietly, at the writing table*). You must not mind Cusins, father. He is a very amiable good fellow; but he is a Greek scholar and naturally a little eccentric.

UNDERSHAFT. Ah, quite so, Thank you, Stephen. Thank you. (*He goes out.*)

(STEPHEN *smiles patronizingly; buttons his coat responsibly; and crosses the room to the door.* LADY BRITOMART, *dressed for out-of-doors, opens it before he reaches it. She looks round for others; looks at* STEPHEN; *and turns to go without a word.*)

STEPHEN (*embarrassed*). Mother—

LADY BRITOMART. Dont be apologetic, Stephen. And dont forget that you have outgrown your mother. (*She goes out.*)

(*Perivale St Andrews lies between two Middlesex hills, half climbing the northern one. It is an almost smokeless town of white walls, roofs of narrow green slates or red tiles, tall trees, domes, campaniles, and slender chimney shafts, beautifully situated and* beautiful in itself. The best view of it is obtained from the crest of a slope about half a mile to the east, where the high explosives are dealt with. The foundry lies hidden in the depths between, the tops of its chimneys sprouting like huge skittles into the middle distance. Across the crest runs an emplacement of concrete, with a firestep, and a parapet which suggests a fortification, because there is a huge cannon of the obsolete Woolwich Infant pattern peering across it at the town. The cannon is mounted on an experimental gun carriage: possibly the original model of the Undershaft disappearing rampart gun alluded to by STEPHEN. The firestep, being a convenient place to sit, is furnished here and there with straw disc cushions; and at one place there is the additional luxury of a fur rug.*

BARBARA *is standing on the firestep, looking over the parapet towards the town. On her right is the cannon; on her left the end of a shed raised on piles, with a ladder of three or four steps up to the door, which opens outwards and has a little wooden landing at the threshold, with a fire bucket in the corner of the landing. Several dummy soldiers more or less mutilated, with straw protruding from their gashes, have been shoved out of the way under the landing. A few others are nearly upright against the shed; and one has fallen forward and lies, like a grotesque corpse, on the emplacement. The parapet stops short of the shed, leaving a gap which is the beginning of the path down the hill through the foundry to the town. The rug is on the firestep near this gap. Down on the emplacement behind the cannon is a trolley carrying a huge conical bombshell with a red band painted on it. Further to the right is the door of an office, which, like the sheds, is of the lightest possible construction.*

CUSINS *arrives by the path from the town.*)

BARBARA. Well!

CUSINS. Not a ray of hope. Everything perfect! wonderful! real! It only needs a cathedral to be a heavenly city instead of a hellish one.

BARBARA. Have you found out whether they have done anything for old Peter Shirley?

CUSINS. They have found him a job as gatekeeper and timekeeper. He's frightfully miserable. He calls the timekeeping brain-work, and says he isnt used to it; and his gate lodge is so splendid that he's ashamed to use the rooms, and skulks in the scullery.

BARBARA. Poor Peter!

---

[31] *avaunt* begone, go away

(STEPHEN *arrives from the town. He carries a fieldglass.*)

STEPHEN (*enthusiastically*). Have you two seen the place? Why did you leave us?

CUSINS. I wanted to see everything I was not intended to see; and Barbara wanted to make the men talk.

STEPHEN. Have you found anything discreditable?

CUSINS. No. They call him Dandy Andy and are proud of his being a cunning old rascal; but it's all horribly, frightfully, immorally, unanswerably perfect.

(SARAH *arrives.*)

SARAH. Heavens! what a place! (*She crosses to the trolley.*) Did you see the nursing home!? (*She sits down on the shell.*)

STEPHEN. Did you see the libraries and schools!?

SARAH. Did you see the ball room and the banqueting chamber in the Town Hall!?

STEPHEN. Have you gone into the insurance fund, the pension fund, the building society, the various applications of cooperation!?

(UNDERSHAFT *comes from the office, with a sheaf of telegrams in his hand.*)

UNDERSHAFT. Well, have you seen everything? I'm sorry I was called away. (*Indicating the telegrams.*) Good news from Manchuria.

STEPHEN. Another Japanese victory?

UNDERSHAFT. Oh, I dont know. Which side wins does not concern us here. No: the good news is that the aerial battleship is a tremendous success. At the first trial it has wiped out a fort with three hundred soldiers in it.

CUSINS (*from the platform*). Dummy soldiers?

UNDERSHAFT (*striding across to* STEPHEN *and kicking the prostrate dummy brutally out of his way*). No: the real thing.

(CUSINS *and* BARBARA *exchange glances. Then* CUSINS *sits on the step and buries his face in his hands.* BARBARA *gravely lays her hand on his shoulder. He looks up at her in whimsical desperation.*)

UNDERSHAFT. Well, Stephen, what do you think of the place?

STEPHEN. Oh, magnificent. A perfect triumph of modern industry. Frankly, my dear father, I have been a fool: I had no idea of what it all meant: of the wonderful forethought, the power of organization, the administrative capacity, the financial genius, the colossal capital it represents. I have been repeating to myself as I came through your streets "Peace hath her victories no less renowned than War." I have only one misgiving about it all.

UNDERSHAFT. Out with it.

STEPHEN. Well, I cannot help thinking that all this provision for every want of your workmen may sap their independence and weaken their sense of responsibility. And greatly as we enjoyed our tea at that splendid restaurant —how they gave us all that luxury and cake and jam and cream for threepence I really cannot imagine!—still you must remember that restaurants break up home life. Look at the continent, for instance! Are you sure so much pampering is really good for the men's characters?

UNDERSHAFT. Well you see, my dear boy, when you are organizing civilization you have to make up your mind whether trouble and anxiety are good things or not. If you decide that they are, then, I take it, you simply dont organize civilization; and there you are, with trouble and anxiety enough to make us all angels! But if you decide the other way, you may as well go through with it. However, Stephen, our characters are safe here. A sufficient dose of anxiety is always provided by the fact that we may be blown to smithereens at any moment.

SARAH. By the way, papa, where do you make the explosives?

UNDERSHAFT. In separate little sheds, like that one. When one of them blows up, it costs very little; and only the people quite close to it are killed.

(STEPHEN, *who is quite close to it, looks at it rather scaredly, and moves away quickly to the cannon. At the same moment the door of the shed is thrown abruptly open; and a foreman in overalls and list slippers comes out on the little landing and holds the door for* LOMAX, *who appears in the doorway.*)

LOMAX (*with studied coolness*). My good fellow: you neednt get into a state of nerves. Nothing's going to happen to you; and I suppose it wouldnt be the end of the world if anything did. A little bit of British pluck is what you want, old chap. (*He descends and strolls across to* SARAH.)

UNDERSHAFT (*to the foreman*). Anything wrong, Bilton?

BILTON (*with ironic calm*). Gentleman walked into the high explosives shed and lit a cigaret, sir: thats all.

UNDERSHAFT. Ah, quite so. (*Going over to* LOMAX.) Do you happen to remember what you did with the match?

LOMAX. Oh come! I'm not a fool. I took jolly good care to blow it out before I chucked it away.

BILTON. The top of it was red hot inside, sir.

LOMAX. Well, suppose it was! I didn't chuck it into any of your messes.

UNDERSHAFT. Think no more of it, Mr Lomax. By the way, would you mind lending me your matches.

LOMAX (*offering his box*). Certainly.

UNDERSHAFT. Thanks. (*He pockets the matches.*)

LOMAX (*lecturing to the company generally*). You know, these high explosives dont go off like gunpowder, except when theyre in a gun. When theyre spread loose, you can put a match to them without the least risk: they just burn quietly like a bit of paper. (*Warming to the scientific interest of the subject.*) Did you know that, Undershaft? Have you ever tried?

UNDERSHAFT. Not on a large scale, Mr Lomax. Bilton will give you a sample of gun cotton when you are leaving if you ask him. You can experiment with it at home. (BILTON *looks puzzled.*)

SARAH. Bilton will do nothing of the sort, papa. I suppose it's your business to blow up the Russians and Japs; but you might really stop short of blowing up poor Cholly. (*Bilton gives it up and retires into the shed.*)

LOMAX. My ownest, there is no danger. (*He sits beside her on the shell.*

LADY BRITOMART *arrives from the town with a bouquet.*)

LADY BRITOMART (*impetuously*). Andrew: you shouldnt have let me see this place.

UNDERSHAFT. Why, my dear?

LADY BRITOMART. Never mind why: you shouldnt have: thats all. To think of all that (*indicating the town*) being yours! and that you have kept it to yourself all these years!

UNDERSHAFT. It does not belong to me. I belong to it. It is the Undershaft inheritance.

LADY BRITOMART. It is not. Your ridiculous cannons and that noisy banging foundry may be the Undershaft inheritance; but all that plate and linen, all that furniture and those houses and orchards and gardens belong to us. They belong to me: they are not a man's business. I wont give them up. You must be out of your senses to throw them all away; and if you persist in such folly, I will call in a doctor.

UNDERSHAFT (*stooping to smell the bouquet*). Where did you get the flowers, my dear?

LADY BRITOMART. Your men presented them to me in your William Morris Labor Church.

CUSINS. Oh! It needed only that. A Labor Church! (*He mounts the firestep distractedly, and leans with his elbows on the parapet, turning his back to them.*)

LADY BRITOMART. Yes, with Morris's words in mosaic letters ten feet high round the dome. NO MAN IS GOOD ENOUGH TO BE ANOTHER MAN'S MASTER. The cynicism of it!

UNDERSHAFT. It shocked the men at first, I am afraid. But now they take no more notice of it than of the ten commandments in church.

LADY BRITOMART. Andrew: you are trying to put me off the subject of the inheritance by profane jokes. Well, you shant. I dont ask it any longer for Stephen: he has inherited far too much of your perversity to be fit for it. But Barbara has rights as well as Stephen. Why should not Adolphus succeed to the inheritance? I could manage the town for him; and he can look after the cannons, if they are really necessary.

UNDERSHAFT. I should ask nothing better if Adolphus were a foundling. He is exactly the sort of new blood that is wanted in English business. But he's not a foundling; and theres an end of it. (*He makes for the office door.*)

CUSINS (*turning to them*). Not quite. (*They all turn and stare at him.*) I think—Mind! I am not committing myself in any way as to my future course—but I think the foundling difficulty can be got over. (*He jumps down to the emplacement.*)

UNDERSHAFT (*coming back to him*). What do you mean?

CUSINS. Well, I have something to say. which is in the nature of a confession.

SARAH.
LADY BRITOMART. }Confession!
BARBARA.
STEPHEN.

LOMAX. Oh I say!

CUSINS. Yes, a confession. Listen, all. Until I met Barbara I thought myself in the main an honorable, truthful man, because I wanted the approval of my conscience more than I wanted anything else. But the moment I saw Barbara, I wanted her far more than the approval of my conscience.

LADY BRITOMART. Adolphus!

CUSINS. It is true. You accused me yourself, Lady Brit, of joining the Army to worship Barbara; and so I did. She bought my soul like a flower at a street corner; but she bought it for herself.

UNDERSHAFT. What! Not for Dionysos or another?

CUSINS. Dionysos and all the others are in herself. I adored what was divine in her, and was therefore a true worshipper. But I was romantic about her too. I thought she was a woman of the people, and that a marriage with a professor of Greek would be far beyond the wildest social ambitions of her rank.

LADY BRITOMART. Adolphus!!

LOMAX. Oh I say!!!

CUSINS. When I learnt the horrible truth—

LADY BRITOMART. What do you mean by the horrible truth, pray?

CUSINS. That she was enormously rich; that her grandfather was an earl; that her father was the Prince of Darkness—

UNDERSHAFT. Chut!

CUSINS. —and that I was only an adventurer trying to catch a rich wife, then I stooped to deceive her about my birth.

BARBARA (*rising*). Dolly!

LADY BRITOMART. Your birth! Now Adolphus, dont dare to make up a wicked story

for the sake of these wretched cannons. Remember: I have seen photographs of your parents; and the Agent General for South Western Australia knows them personally and has assured me that they are most respectable married people.

CUSINS. So they are in Australia; but here they are outcasts. Their marriage is legal in Australia, but not in England. My mother is my father's deceased wife's sister; and in this island I am consequently a foundling.

(*Sensation.*)

BARBARA. Silly! (*She climbs to the cannon, and leans, listening, in the angle it makes with the parapet.*)

CUSINS. Is the subterfuge good enough, Machiavelli?

UNDERSHAFT (*thoughtfully*). Biddy: this may be a way out of the difficulty.

LADY BRITOMART. Stuff! A man cant make cannons any the better for being his own cousin instead of his proper self. (*She sits down on the rug with a bounce that expresses her downright contempt for their casuistry.*)

UNDERSHAFT (*to* CUSINS). You are an educated man. That is against the tradition.

CUSINS. Once in ten thousand times it happens that the schoolboy is a born master of what they try to teach him. Greek has not destroyed my mind: it has nourished it. Besides, I did not learn it at an English public school.

UNDERSHAFT. Hm! Well, I cannot afford to be too particular: you have cornered the foundling market. Let it pass. You are eligible, Euripides: you are eligible.

BARBARA. Dolly: yesterday morning, when Stephen told us all about the tradition, you became very silent; and you have been strange and excited ever since. Were you thinking of your birth then?

CUSINS. When the finger of Destiny suddenly points at a man in the middle of his breakfast, it makes him thoughtful.

UNDERSHAFT. Aha! You have had your eye on the business, my young friend, have you?

CUSINS. Take care! There is an abyss of moral horror between me and your accursed aerial battleships.

UNDERSHAFT. Never mind the abyss for the present. Let us settle the practical details and leave your final decision open. You know that you will have to change your name. Do you object to that?

CUSINS. Would any man named Adolphus— any man called Dolly!—object to be called something else?

UNDERSHAFT. Good. Now, as to money! I propose to treat you handsomely from the beginning. You shall start at a thousand a year.

CUSINS (*with sudden heat, his spectacles twinkling with mischief*). A thousand! You dare offer a miserable thousand to the son-in-law of a millionaire! No, by Heavens, Machiavelli! you shall not cheat me. You cannot do without me; and I can do without you. I must have two thousand five hundred a year for two years. At the end of that time, if I am a failure, I go. But if I am a success, and stay on, you must give me the other five thousand.

UNDERSHAFT. What other five thousand?

CUSINS. To make the two years up to five thousand a year. The two thousand five hundred is only half pay in case I should turn out a failure. The third year I must have ten per cent on the profits.

UNDERSHAFT (*taken aback*). Ten per cent! Why, man, do you know what my profits are?

CUSINS. Enormous, I hope: otherwise I shall require twenty-five per cent.

UNDERSHAFT. But, Mr Cusins, this is a serious matter of business. You are not bringing any capital into the concern.

CUSINS. What! no capital! Is my mastery of Greek no capital? Is my access to the subtlest thought, the loftiest poetry yet attained by humanity, no capital? My character! my intellect! my life! my career! what Barbara calls my soul! are these no capital? Say another word: and I double my salary.

UNDERSHAFT. Be reasonable—

CUSINS (*peremptorily*). Mr Undershaft: you have my terms. Take them or leave them.

UNDERSHAFT (*recovering himself*). Very well. I note your terms; and I offer you half.

CUSINS (*disgusted*). Half!

UNDERSHAFT (*firmly*). Half.

CUSINS. You call yourself a gentleman; and you offer me half!!

UNDERSHAFT. I do not call myself a gentleman; but I offer you half.

CUSINS. This to your future partner! your successor! your son-in-law!

BARBARA. You are selling your own soul, Dolly, not mine. Leave me out of the bargain, please.

UNDERSHAFT. Come! I will go a step further for Barbara's sake. I will give you three fifths; but that is my last word.

CUSINS. Done!

LOMAX. Done in the eye! Why, *I* get only eight hundred, you know.

CUSINS. By the way, Mac, I am a classical scholar, not an arithmetical one. Is three fifths more than half or less?

UNDERSHAFT. More, of course.

CUSINS. I would have taken two hundred and fifty. How you can succeed in business when you are willing to pay all that money to a University don who is obviously not worth a junior clerk's wages!—well! What will Lazarus say?

UNDERSHAFT. Lazarus is a gentle romantic Jew who cares for nothing but string quartets and stalls at fashionable theatres. He will be blamed for your rapacity in money matters, poor fellow! as he has hitherto been blamed for mine. You are a shark of the first order, Euripides. So much the better for the firm!

BARBARA. Is the bargain closed, Dolly? Does your soul belong to him now?

CUSINS. No: the price is settled: that is all. The real tug of war is still to come. What about the moral question?

LADY BRITOMART. There is no moral question in the matter at all, Adolphus. You must simply sell cannons and weapons to people whose cause is right and just, and refuse them to foreigners and criminals.

UNDERSHAFT (*determinedly*). No: none of that. You must keep the true faith of an Armorer, or you dont come in here.

CUSINS. What on earth is the true faith of an Armorer?

UNDERSHAFT. To give arms to all men who offer an honest price for them, without respect of persons or principles: to aristocrat and republican, to Nihilist and Tsar, to Capitalist and Socialist, to Protestant and Catholic, to burglar and policeman, to black man, white man and yellow man, to all sorts and conditions, all nationalities, all faiths, all follies, all causes and all crimes. The first Undershaft wrote up in his shop IF GOD GAVE THE HAND, LET NOT MAN WITHHOLD THE SWORD. The second wrote up ALL HAVE THE RIGHT TO FIGHT: NONE HAVE THE RIGHT TO JUDGE. The third wrote up TO MAN THE WEAPON: TO HEAVEN THE VICTORY. The fourth had no literary turn; so he did not write up anything; but he sold cannons to Napoleon under the nose of George the Third. The fifth wrote up PEACE SHALL NOT PREVAIL SAVE WITH A SWORD IN HER HAND. The sixth, my master, was the best of all. He wrote up NOTHING IS EVER DONE IN THIS WORLD UNTIL MEN ARE PREPARED TO KILL ONE ANOTHER IF IT IS NOT DONE. After that, there was nothing left for the seventh to say. So he wrote up, simply, UNASHAMED.

CUSINS. My good Machiavelli, I shall certainly write something up on the wall; only, as I shall write it in Greek, you wont be able to read it. But as to your Armorer's faith, if I take my neck out of the noose of my own morality I am not going to put it into the noose of yours. I shall sell cannons to whom I please and refuse them to whom I please. So there!

UNDERSHAFT. From the moment when you become Andrew Undershaft, you will never do as you please again. Dont come here lusting for power, young man.

CUSINS. If power were my aim I should not come here for it. You have no power.

UNDERSHAFT. None of my own, certainly.

CUSINS. I have more power than you, more will. You do not drive this place: it drives you. And what drives the place?

UNDERSHAFT (enigmatically). A will of which I am a part.

BARBARA (startled). Father! Do you know what you are saying; or are you laying a snare for my soul?

CUSINS. Dont listen to his metaphysics, Barbara. The place is driven by the most rascally part of society, the money hunters, the pleasure hunters, the military promotion hunters; and he is their slave.

UNDERSHAFT. Not necessarily. Remember the Armorer's Faith. I will take an order from a good man as cheerfully as from a bad one. If you good people prefer preaching and shirking to buying my weapons and fighting the rascals, dont blame me. I can make cannons: I cannot make courage and conviction. Bah! you tire me, Euripides, with your morality mongering. Ask Barbara: she understands. (He suddenly reaches up and takes BARBARA's hands, looking powerfully into her eyes.) Tell him, my love, what power really means.

BARBARA (hypnotized). Before I joined the Salvation Army, I was in my own power; and the consequence was that I never knew what to do with myself. When I joined it, I had not time enough for all the things I had to do.

UNDERSHAFT (approvingly). Just so. And why was that, do you suppose?

BARBARA. Yesterday I should have said, because I was in the power of God. (She resumes her self-possession, withdrawing her hands from his with a power equal to his own.) But you came and shewed me that I was in the power of Bodger and Undershaft. Today I feel—oh! how can I put it into words? Sarah: do you remember the earthquake at Cannes, when we were little children?—how little the surprise of the first shock mattered compared to the dread and horror of waiting for the second? That is how I feel in this place today. I stood on the rock I thought eternal; and without a word of warning it reeled and crumbled under me. I was safe with an infinite wisdom watching me, an army marching to Salvation with me; and in a moment, at a stroke of your pen in a cheque book, I stood alone; and the heavens were empty. That was the first shock of the earthquake: I am waiting for the second.

UNDERSHAFT. Come, come, my daughter! dont make too much of your little tinpot tragedy. What do we do here when we spend years of work and thought and thousands of pounds of solid cash on a new gun or an aerial battleship that turns out just a hairsbreadth wrong after all? Scrap it. Scrap it without wasting another hour or another pound on it. Well, you have made for yourself something that you call a morality or a religion or what not. It doesnt fit the facts. Well, scrap it. Scrap it and get one that does fit. That is what is wrong with the world at present. It scraps its obsolete steam engines and dynamos; but it wont scrap its old prejudices and its old moralities and its old religions and its old political constitutions. Whats the result? In machinery it does very well; but in morals and religion and politics it is working at a loss that brings it nearer bankruptcy every year. Dont persist in that folly. If your old religion broke down yesterday, get a newer and a better one for tomorrow.

BARBARA. Oh how gladly I would take a better one to my soul! But you offer me a worse one. (*Turning on him with sudden vehemence.*) Justify yourself: shew me some light through the darkness of this dreadful place, with its beautifully clean workshops, and respectable workmen, and model homes.

UNDERSHAFT. Cleanliness and respectability do not need justification, Barbara: they justify themselves. I see no darkness here, no dreadfulness. In your Salvation shelter I saw poverty, misery, cold and hunger. You gave them bread and treacle and dreams of heaven. I give from thirty shillings a week to twelve thousand a year. They find their own dreams; but I look after the drainage.

BARBARA. And their souls?

UNDERSHAFT. I save their souls just as I saved yours.

BARBARA (*revolted*). You saved my soul! What do you mean?

UNDERSHAFT. I fed you and clothed you and housed you. I took care that you should have money enough to live handsomely—more than enough; so that you could be wasteful, careless, generous. That saved your soul from the seven deadly sins.

BARBARA (*bewildered*). The seven deadly sins!

UNDERSHAFT. Yes, the deadly seven. (*Counting on his fingers.*) Food, clothing, firing, rent, taxes, respectability and children. Nothing can lift those seven millstones from Man's neck but money; and the spirit cannot soar until the millstones are lifted. I lifted them from your spirit. I enabled Barbara to become Major Barbara; and I saved her from the crime of poverty.

CUSINS. Do you call poverty a crime?

UNDERSHAFT. The worst of crimes. All the other crimes are virtues beside it: all the other dishonors are chivalry itself by comparison. Poverty blights whole cities; spreads horrible pestilences; strikes dead the very souls of all who come within sight, sound, or smell of it. What you call crime is nothing: a murder here and a theft there, a blow now and a curse then: what do they matter? they are only the accidents and illnesses of life: there are not fifty genuine professional criminals in London. But there are millions of poor people, abject people, dirty people, ill fed, ill clothed people. They poison us morally and physically: they kill the happiness of society: they force us to do away with our own liberties and to organize unnatural cruelties for fear they should rise against us and drag us down into their abyss. Only fools fear crime: we all fear poverty. Pah! (*turning on* BARBARA) you talk of your half-saved ruffian in West Ham: you accuse me of dragging his soul back to perdition. Well, bring him to me here; and I will drag his soul back again to salvation for you. Not by words and dreams; but by thirty eight shillings a week, a sound house in a handsome street, and a permanent job. In three weeks he will have a fancy waistcoat; in three months a tall hat and a chapel sitting; before the end of the year he will shake hands with a duchess at a Primrose League meeting, and join the Conservative Party.

BARBARA. And will he be the better for that?

UNDERSHAFT. You know he will. Dont be a hypocrite, Barbara. He will be better fed, better housed, better clothed, better behaved; and his children will be pounds heavier and bigger. That will be better than an American cloth mattress in a shelter, chopping firewood, eating bread and treacle, and being forced to kneel down from time to time to thank heaven for it: knee drill, I think you call it. It is cheap work converting starving men with a Bible in one hand and a slice of bread in the other. I will undertake to convert West Ham to Mahometanism on the same terms. Try your hand on my men: their souls are hungry because their bodies are full.

BARBARA. And leave the east end to starve?

UNDERSHAFT (*his energetic tone dropping into one of bitter and brooding remembrance*). I was an east ender. I moralized and starved until one day I swore that I would be a full-fed free man at all costs; that nothing should stop me except a bullet, neither reason nor morals nor the lives of other men. I said "Thou shalt starve ere I starve"; and with that word I became free and great. I was a dangerous man until I had my will: now I am a useful, beneficent, kindly person. That is the history of most self-made millionaires, I fancy. When it is the history of every Englishman we shall have an England worth living in.

LADY BRITOMART. Stop making speeches, Andrew. This is not the place for them.

UNDERSHAFT (*punctured*). My dear: I have no other means of conveying my ideas.

LADY BRITOMART. Your ideas are nonsense. You got on because you were selfish and unscrupulous.

UNDERSHAFT. Not at all. I had the strongest scruples about poverty and starvation. Your moralists are quite unscrupulous about both: they make virtues of them. I had rather be a thief than a pauper. I had rather be a murderer than a slave. I dont want to be either; but if you force the alternative on me, then, by Heaven, I'll choose the braver and more moral one. I hate poverty and slavery worse than any other crimes whatsoever. And let me tell you this. Poverty and slavery have stood up for centuries to your sermons and leading articles: they will not stand up to my machine guns. Dont preach at them: dont reason with them. Kill them.

BARBARA. Killing. Is that your remedy for everything?

UNDERSHAFT. It is the final test of conviction, the only lever strong enough to overturn a social system, the only way of saying Must. Let six hundred and seventy fools loose in the streets; and three policemen can scatter them. But huddle them together in a certain house in Westminster; and let them go through certain ceremonies and call themselves certain names until at last they get the courage to kill; and your six hundred and seventy fools become a government. Your pious mob fills up ballot papers and imagines it is governing its masters; but the ballot paper that really governs is the paper that has a bullet wrapped up in it.

CUSINS. That is perhaps why, like most intelligent people, I never vote.

UNDERSHAFT. Vote! Bah! When you vote, you only change the names of the cabinet. When you shoot, you pull down governments, inaugurate new epochs, abolish old orders and set up new. Is that historically true, Mr Learned Man, or is it not?

CUSINS. It is historically true. I loathe having to admit it. I repudiate your sentiments. I abhor your nature. I defy you in every possible way. Still, it is true. But it ought not to be true.

UNDERSHAFT. Ought! ought! ought! ought! ought! Are you going to spend your life saying ought, like the rest of our moralists? Turn your oughts into shalls, man. Come and make explosives with me. Whatever can blow men up can blow society up. The history of the world is the history of those who had courage enough to embrace this truth. Have you the courage to embrace it, Barbara?

LADY BRITOMART. Barbara: I positively forbid you to listen to your father's abominable wickedness. And you, Adolphus, ought to know better than to go about saying that wrong things are true. What does it matter whether they are true if they are wrong?

UNDERSHAFT. What does it matter whether they are wrong if they are true?

LADY BRITOMART (*rising*). Children: come home instantly. Andrew: I am exceedingly sorry I allowed you to call on us. You are wickeder than ever. Come at once.

BARBARA (*shaking her head*). It's no use running away from wicked people, mamma.

LADY BRITOMART. It is every use. It shews your disapprobation of them.

BARBARA. It does not save them.

LADY BRITOMART. I can see that you are going to disobey me. Sarah: are you coming home or are you not?

SARAH. I daresay it's very wicked of papa to make cannons; but I dont think I shall cut him on that account.

LOMAX (*pouring oil on the troubled waters*). The

fact is, you know, there is a certain amount of tosh about this notion of wickedness. It doesnt work. You must look at facts. Not that I would say a word in favor of anything wrong; but then, you see, all sorts of chaps are always doing all sorts of things; and we have to fit them in somehow, dont you know. What I mean is that you cant go cutting everybody; and thats about what it comes to. (*Their rapt attention to his eloquence makes him nervous.*) Perhaps I dont make myself clear.

LADY BRITOMART. You are lucidity itself, Charles. Because Andrew is successful and has plenty of money to give to Sarah, you will flatter him and encourage him in his wickedness.

LOMAX (*unruffled*). Well, where the carcase is, there will the eagles be gathered, dont you know. (*To* UNDERSHAFT.) Eh? What?

UNDERSHAFT. Precisely. By the way, may I call you Charles?

LOMAX. Delighted. Cholly is the usual ticket.

UNDERSHAFT (*to* LADY BRITOMART). Biddy—

LADY BRITOMART (*violently*). Dont dare call me Biddy. Charles Lomax: you are a fool. Adolphus Cusins: you are a Jesuit. Stephen: you are a prig. Barbara: you are a lunatic. Andrew: you are a vulgar tradesman. Now you all know my opinion; and my conscience is clear, at all events. (*She sits down with a vehemence that the rug fortunately softens.*)

UNDERSHAFT. My dear: you are the incarnation of morality. (*She snorts.*) Your conscience is clear and your duty done when you have called everybody names. Come, Euripides! it is getting late; and we all want to go home. Make up your mind.

CUSINS. Understand this, you old demon—

LADY BRITOMART. Adolphus!

UNDERSHAFT. Let him alone, Biddy. Proceed, Euripides.

CUSINS. You have me in a horrible dilemma. I want Barbara.

UNDERSHAFT. Like all young men, you greatly exaggerate the difference between one young woman and another.

BARBARA. Quite true, Dolly.

CUSINS. I also want to avoid being a rascal.

UNDERSHAFT (*with biting contempt*). You lust for personal righteousness, for self-approval, for what you call a good conscience, for what Barbara calls salvation, for what I call patronizing people who are not so lucky as yourself.

CUSINS. I do not: all the poet in me recoils from being a good man. But there are things in me that I must reckon with. Pity—

UNDERSHAFT. Pity! The scavenger of misery.

CUSINS. Well, love.

UNDERSHAFT. I know. You love the needy and the outcast: you love the oppressed races, the negro, the Indian ryot, the underdog everywhere. Do you love the Japanese? Do you love the French? Do you love the English?

CUSINS. No. Every true Englishman detests the English. We are the wickedest nation on earth; and our success is a moral horror.

UNDERSHAFT. That is what comes of your gospel of love, is it?

CUSINS. May I not love even my father-in-law?

UNDERSHAFT. Who wants your love, man? By what right do you take the liberty of offering it to me? I will have your due heed and respect, or I will kill you. But your love! Damn your impertinence!

CUSINS (*grinning*). I may not be able to control my affections, Mac.

UNDERSHAFT. You are fencing, Euripides. You are weakening: your grip is slipping. Come! try your last weapon. Pity and love have broken in your hand: forgiveness is still left.

CUSINS. No: forgiveness is a beggar's refuge. I am with you there: we must pay our debts.

UNDERSHAFT. Well said. Come! you will suit me. Remember the words of Plato.

CUSINS (*starting*). Plato! You dare quote Plato to me!

UNDERSHAFT. Plato says, my friend, that society cannot be saved until either the Professors of Greek take to making gunpowder, or else the makers of gunpowder become Professors of Greek.

CUSINS. Oh, tempter, cunning tempter!

UNDERSHAFT. Come! choose, man, choose.

CUSINS. But perhaps Barbara will not marry me if I make the wrong choice.

BARBARA. Perhaps not.

CUSINS (*desperately perplexed*). You hear!

BARBARA. Father: do you love nobody?

UNDERSHAFT. I love my best friend.

LADY BRITOMART. And who is that, pray?

UNDERSHAFT. My bravest enemy. That is the man who keeps me up to the mark.

CUSINS. You know, the creature is really a sort of poet in his way. Suppose he is a great man, after all!

UNDERSHAFT. Suppose you stop talking and make up your mind, my young friend.

CUSINS. But you are driving me against my nature. I hate war.

UNDERSHAFT. Hatred is the coward's revenge for being intimidated. Dare you make war on war? Here are the means: my friend Mr Lomax is sitting on them.

LOMAX (*springing up*). Oh I say! You dont mean that this thing is loaded, do you? My ownest: come off it.

SARAH (*sitting placidly on the shell*). If I am to be blown up, the more thoroughly it is done the better. Dont fuss, Cholly.

LOMAX (*to* UNDERSHAFT, *strongly remonstrant*). Your own daughter, you know!

UNDERSHAFT. So I see. (*To* CUSINS.) Well, my friend, may we expect you here at six tomorrow morning?

CUSINS (*firmly*). Not on any account. I will see the whole establishment blown up with its own dynamite before I will get up at five. My hours are healthy, rational hours: eleven to five.

UNDERSHAFT. Come when you please: before a week you will come at six and stay until I turn you out for the sake of your health. (*Calling.*) Bilton! (*He turns to* LADY BRITOMART, *who rises.*) My dear: let us leave these two young people to themselves for a moment. (BILTON *comes from the shed.*) I am going to take you through the gun cotton shed.

BILTON (*barring the way*). You cant take anything explosive in here, sir.

LADY BRITOMART. What do you mean? Are you alluding to me.

BILTON (*unmoved*). No, maam. Mr Undershaft has the other gentleman's matches in his pocket.

LADY BRITOMART (*abruptly*). Oh! I beg your pardon. (*She goes into the shed.*)

UNDERSHAFT. Quite right, Bilton, quite right: here you are. (*He gives* BILTON *the box of matches.*) Come, Stephen. Come, Charles. Bring Sarah. (*He passes into the shed.*)

(BILTON *opens the box and deliberately drops the matches into the fire-bucket.*)

LOMAX. Oh! I say. (BILTON *stolidly hands him the empty box.*) Infernal nonsense! Pure scientific ignorance! (*He goes in.*)

SARAH. Am I all right, Bilton?

BILTON. Youll have to put on list slippers, miss: thats all. Weve got em inside. (*She goes in.*)

STEPHEN (*very seriously to* CUSINS). Dolly, old fellow, think. Think before you decide. Do you feel that you are a sufficiently practical man? It is a huge undertaking, an enormous responsibility. All this mass of business will be Greek to you.

CUSINS. Oh, I think it will be much less difficult than Greek.

STEPHEN. Well, I just want to say this before I leave you to yourselves. Dont let anything I have said about right and wrong prejudice you against this great chance in life. I have satisfied myself that the business is one of the highest character and a credit to our country. (*Emotionally.*) I am very proud of my father. I—(*Unable to proceed, he presses* CUSINS' *hand and goes hastily into the shed, followed by* BILTON.)

(BARBARA *and* CUSINS, *left alone together, look at one another silently.*)

CUSINS. Barbara: I am going to accept this offer.

BARBARA. I thought you would.

CUSINS. You understand, dont you, that I had to decide without consulting you. If I had thrown the burden of the choice on you, you would sooner or later have despised me for it.

BARBARA. Yes: I did not want you to sell your soul for me any more than for this inheritance.

CUSINS. It is not the sale of my soul that troubles me: I have sold it too often to care about that. I have sold it for a professorship. I have sold it for an income. I have sold it to escape being imprisoned for refusing to pay taxes for hangmen's ropes and unjust wars and things that I abhor. What is all human conduct but the daily and hourly sale of our souls for trifles? What I am now selling it for is neither money nor position nor comfort, but for reality and for power.

BARBARA. You know that you will have no power, and that he has none.

CUSINS. I know. It is not for myself alone. I want to make power for the world.

BARBARA. I want to make power for the world too; but it must be spiritual power.

CUSINS. I think all power is spiritual: these cannons will not go off by themselves. I have tried to make spiritual power by teaching Greek. But the world can never be really touched by a dead language and a dead civilization. The people must have power; and the people cannot have Greek. Now the power that is made here can be wielded by all men.

BARBARA. Power to burn women's houses down and kill their sons and tear their husbands to pieces.

CUSINS. You cannot have power for good without having power for evil too. Even mother's milk nourishes murderers as well as heroes. This power which only tears men's bodies to pieces has never been so horribly abused as the intellectual power, the imaginative power, the poetic, religious power that can enslave men's souls. As a teacher of Greek I gave the intellectual man weapons against the common man. I now want to give the common man weapons against the intellectual man. I love the common people. I want to arm them against the lawyers, the doctors, the priests, the literary men, the professors, the artists, and the politicians, who, once in authority, are more disastrous and tyrannical than all the fools, rascals, and impostors. I want a power simple enough for common men to use, yet strong enough to force the intellectual oligarchy to use its genius for the general good.

BARBARA. Is there no higher power than that? (*Pointing to the shell.*)

CUSINS. Yes; but that power can destroy the higher powers just as a tiger can destroy a man: therefore Man must master that power first. I admitted this when the Turks and Greeks were last at war. My best pupil went out to fight for Hellas. My parting gift to him was not a copy of Plato's Republic, but a revolver and a hundred Undershaft cartridges. The blood of every Turk he shot —if he shot any—is on my head as well as on Undershaft's. That act committed me to this place for ever. Your father's challenge has beaten me. Dare I make war on war? I must. I will. And now, is it all over between us?

BARBARA (*touched by his evident dread of her answer*). Silly baby Dolly! How could it be!

CUSINS (*overjoyed*). Then you—you—you— Oh for my drum! (*He flourishes imaginary drumsticks.*)

BARBARA (*angered by his levity*). Take care, Dolly, take care. Oh, if only I could get away from you and from father and from it all! if I could have the wings of a dove and fly away to heaven!

CUSINS. And leave me!

BARBARA. Yes, you, and all the other naughty mischievous children of men. But I cant. I was happy in the Salvation Army for a moment. I escaped from the world into a paradise of enthusiasm and prayer and soul saving; but the moment our money ran short, it all came back to Bodger: it was he who saved our people: he, and the Prince of Darkness, my papa. Undershaft and Bodger: their hands stretch everywhere: when we feed a starving fellow creature, it is with their bread, because there is no other bread; when we tend the sick, it is in the hospitals they endow; if we turn from the churches they build, we must kneel on the stones of the streets they pave. As long as that lasts, there is no getting away from them. Turning our backs on Bodger and Undershaft is turning our backs on life.

CUSINS. I thought you were determined to turn your back on the wicked side of life.

BARBARA. There is no wicked side: life is all one and I never wanted to shirk my share in whatever evil must be endured, whether it be sin or suffering. I wish I could cure you of middle-class ideas, Dolly.

CUSINS (*gasping*). Middle cl—! A snub! A social snub to me! from the daughter of a foundling!

BARBARA. That is why I have no class, Dolly: I come straight out of the heart of the whole people. If I were middle-class I should turn my back on my father's business; and we should both live in an artistic drawing room, with you reading the reviews in one corner, and I in the other at the piano, playing Schumann: both very superior persons, and neither of us a bit of use. Sooner than that, I would sweep out the guncotton shed, or be one of Bodger's barmaids. Do you know what would have happened if you had refused papa's offer?

CUSINS. I wonder!

BARBARA. I should have given you up and married the man who accepted it. After all, my dear old mother has more sense than any of you. I felt like her when I saw this place—felt that I must have it—that never, never, never could I let it go; only she thought it was the houses and the kitchen ranges and the linen and china, when it was really all the human souls to be saved: not weak souls in starved bodies, sobbing with gratitude for a scrap of bread and treacle, but fullfed, quarrelsome, snobbish, uppish creatures, all standing on their little rights and dignities, and thinking that my father ought to be greatly obliged to them for making so much money for him—and so he ought. That is where salvation is really wanted. My father shall never throw it in my teeth again that my converts were bribed with bread. (*She is transfigured.*) I have got rid of the bribe of bread. I have got rid of the bribe of heaven. Let God's work be done for its own sake: the work he had to create us to do because it cannot be done except by living men and women. When I die, let him be in my debt, not I in his; and let me forgive him as becomes a woman of my rank.

CUSINS. Then the way of life lies through the factory of death?

BARBARA. Yes, through the raising of hell to heaven and of man to God, through the unveiling of an eternal light in the Valley of The Shadow. (*Seizing him with both hands.*) Oh, did you think my courage would never come back? did you believe that I was a deserter? that I, who have stood in the streets, and taken my people to my heart, and talked of the holiest and greatest things with them, could ever turn back and chatter foolishly to fashionable people about nothing in a drawing room? Never, never, never, never: Major Barbara will die with the colors. Oh! and I have my dear little Dolly boy still; and he has found me my place and my work. Glory Hallelujah! (*She kisses him.*)

CUSINS. My dearest: consider my delicate health. I cannot stand as much happiness as you can.

BARBARA. Yes: it is not easy work being in love with me, is it? But it's good for you. (*She runs to the shed, and calls, childlike.*) Mamma! Mamma! (BILTON *comes out of the shed, followed by* UNDERSHAFT.) I want Mamma.

UNDERSHAFT. She is taking off her list slippers, dear. (*He passes on to* CUSINS.) Well? What does she say?

CUSINS. She has gone right up into the skies.

LADY BRITOMART (*coming from the shed and stopping on the steps, obstructing* SARAH, *who follows with* LOMAX. BARBARA *clutches like a baby at her mother's skirt*). Barbara: when will you learn to be independent and to act and think for yourself? I know as well as possible what that cry of "Mamma, Mamma," means. Always running to me!

SARAH (*touching* LADY BRITOMART's *ribs with her finger tips and imitating a bicycle horn*). Pip! pip!

LADY BRITOMART (*highly indignant*). How dare you say Pip! pip! to me, Sarah? You are both very naughty children. What do you want, Barbara?

BARBARA. I want a house in the village to live in with Dolly. (*Dragging at the skirt.*) Come and tell me which one to take.

UNDERSHAFT (*to* CUSINS). Six o'clock tomorrow morning, Euripides.

THE END

## The Play of Ideas

There might seem to be no action at all in *Major Barbara*. It is clearly an example of the sort of play mentioned in the Introduction, in which the characters do little but talk. Yet there is an intense intellectual and emotional conflict, as a result of which something very important happens to Barbara. Shaw called the play "A Discussion in Three Acts." What he meant by this unusual terminology can be seen in the expanded form of *The Quintessence of Ibsenism* published in 1913. In a chapter called "The Technical Novelty in Ibsen's Plays" he wrote: "Formerly you had in what was called a well made play an exposition in the first act, a situation in the second, an unravelling in the third. Now you have exposition, situation, and discussion; and the discussion is the test of the playwright."[1] If we attempted to apply this scheme to *Major Barbara* we might say that in the exposition (Act I) we are introduced to the problems of Lady Britomart, a representative of the upper-class outlook, with a husband who is socially inferior and mentally her opposite, and with Barbara, who has committed the grave impropriety of joining the Salvation Army. Lady Britomart is the first onstage, is next to the last to leave it, and dominates the proceedings up to the entrance of Undershaft. He and Barbara then take the spotlight, and we see contrasted two views of life which are both departures from the norm of Lady Britomart: the evangelism of the Salvation Army and the materialism of the munitions maker.

The situation (Act II) would then be the conflict between Barbara and her father, ending in his destruction of her faith in the Salvation Army. We might call Act III, especially its second scene, the discussion of the issues raised by the situation—the capacity of Undershaft's philosophy, as compared with any other, to deal with the evils of the social and economic situation.

Such an analysis of the play has the advantage of explaining why the peak of emotional excitement is reached at the end of the second act, while the third act is the most conversational of all—a kind of Platonic dialogue on an abstract topic. However, to see the play only in this way is not to do it justice. Important as the characters are in Acts I and II, it is their ideas which are in conflict, and hence even the exposition and the situation are permeated by discussion. The play is a play of ideas. Not only do the characters fight, flatter, and seduce for the sake of ideas, but the audience is led to approve first of one idea, then of another. It seems obvious enough at first that Undershaft is thoroughly immoral (Martin Meisel has shown how much this character owes to the "heavy" villain of melodrama[2]). At the end his morality seems at least as valid as any other. Often such reversals occur as one speech follows and refutes another, the simplest and most pat examples being such repartee as:

SHIRLEY. . . . I wouldnt have your conscience, not for all your income.

UNDERSHAFT. I wouldnt have your income, not for all your conscience, Mr. Shirley.

An equally unexpected reply of Undershaft's points to a more complicated reappraisal of the topic under discussion, though it appears at first to be mere flippancy. This is his answer to Barbara's question about his religion: "My religion? Well, my dear, I am a Millionaire. That is my religion."

---

[1] (New York: Hill and Wang, 1957), p. 171.
[2] *Shaw and the Nineteenth-Century Theater* (Princeton, N. J.: Princeton University Press, 1963), pp. 32–3, 296–303.

Witty repartee is one of the standard comic devices. In a comedy such as *Major Barbara*, which is also a play of ideas, these sudden turns bring the underlying conflicts to the surface, call our attention to them, compress them into a few words. The wit thus becomes much more than a diversion or an ornament. It provides a special form of dramatic moment appropriate to this kind of play.

Calling *Major Barbara* a "discussion" and leaving it at that has the further disadvantage of overlooking the emotional appeal of certain scenes. The end of the second act is an example. Throughout the act the triumphs of the Salvation Army, though partly comic, have a latent emotional persuasiveness, both because of the effective rhetoric of evangelism, perfectly reproduced by Shaw, and because of his depiction of Barbara's idealism and courage. Her crucial encounter with Bill Walker is shrewdly calculated to enlist sympathy for her and hence for her cause. At the end the cause is saved by the contributions of Bodger and Undershaft and the triumphal procession marchs off to the accompaniment of the band, but the nature of this triumph costs Barbara her faith and elicits her agonized quotation of Christ's words on the cross: "My God: why hast thou forsaken me?" The chief turning point in the conflict of ideas is made an intensely moving moment—doubtless the most effective dramatic moment of the play. Because of its strong emotional appeal we are able to feel the force of the conflicting ideas.

In the dialectic of a Shaw play one view rarely has an unqualified victory over its opponents. Sometimes it appears in variant forms which command different degrees of assent or condemnation. In *Major Barbara* standard upperclass morality is represented not only by Lady Britomart, whom Undershaft calls "the incarnation of morality," but also by Stephen, who reduces it to absurd simplicity, and Lomax, who makes it meaningless with his muddleheaded clichés. Sometimes the pros and cons for one course of action are presented almost simultaneously with almost equal force, as in the question of accepting money made by whisky and munitions to further the cause of the Salvation Army. The triumphal march is balanced by Barbara's resignation, the practicality of both millionaires and the Army leaders by her idealism.

Though Undershaft succeeds in his scheme of winning Barbara to his side, it is by no means certain that the play constitutes an endorsement of all he stands for. At times Undershaft's speeches seem to be based on patent sophistry, at other times on the hardest of hard sense. At the end, Barbara's exaltation over what is to her a new and better religion seems to go considerably beyond the pragmatic doctrine of wealth which he has successfully preached. Thus the term "play of ideas" may also be used to suggest the way ideas are played off against one another. What validity is left to each one at the final curtain is one of the problems to be faced by any interpretation.

Another sort of complexity in this play of ideas is suggested by the constant use of a religious frame of reference in connection not only with the evangelism of the Salvation Army but also with the secular views of Undershaft. He denies that he is a Secularist, insisting that he is a "confirmed mystic." His mystic side is called to our attention by the increasingly frequent allusions to Dionysus, which at first seem comically inappropriate, but later provide an alternative to the Christian view of Undershaft as the "Prince of Darkness." Cusin's disquisition on the Salvation Army as a Dionysiac "army of joy" suggests a surprising connection between one aspect of the Army and Undershaft's belief that material happiness is a basic requirement for spiritual health. It also helps to explain how Barbara can make the switch from evangelical Christianity to her father's "religion." Her ecstatic speech about "raising hell to heaven" is surely visionary and possibly Dionysiac in character. In some sense, then, this is a religious play. Just how the religious implications are to be fitted in with other kinds of ideas in the total meaning is another problem of interpretation.

## Selected Reading List for Shaw

Eric Bentley, *Bernard Shaw*. New York: New Directions, 1947.

Robert Brustein, "Bernard Shaw," *The Theatre of Revolt*. Boston: Little, Brown & Co., 1964, pp. 183–227.

John Gassner, "Shaw on Ibsen and the Drama of Ideas," *Ideas in the Drama*. New York: Columbia University Press, 1964, pp. 71–100.

Martin Meisel, *Shaw and the Nineteenth-Century Theater*. Princeton, N. J.: Princeton University Press, 1963.

# Edward Albee

Edward Albee was born in 1928 and was adopted by a family well known in the theatrical world. He was named for his adopted grandfather, who founded with B. F. Keith a chain of vaudeville theaters in the 1880's. Albee grew up in New York City and Connecticut, and after finishing his secondary schooling, attended college for a year and a half. By this time he had decided to be a writer. For the next several years he wrote poetry while working at a succession of jobs in New York. During a year in Florence he wrote a novel which he did not consider successful enough to publish. Then in 1958, when he was just under thirty, he turned to writing for the theater. He left the job he then had with Western Union, and in three weeks wrote *The Zoo Story*. It was first performed with Samuel Beckett's *Krapp's Last Tape* in Berlin in 1959; in 1960 the two plays were given their American premières in New York at an off-Broadway theater. Albee achieved almost instant recognition. Since that time *The American Dream* and *The Death of Bessie Smith* have been performed off Broadway and *Who's Afraid of Virginia Woolf*, *The Ballad of the Sad Café*, and *Tiny Alice* on Broadway.

In *The Zoo Story* Albee does not give the reader the same kind of assistance that Shaw gives. His stage directions are strictly stage directions, intended primarily for the director and the actors. The setting is very simple compared to Lady Britomart's library, and is hardly intended to tell us much about the characters. In fact Central Park is important to the play largely because it is a neutral ground on which two such different people as Peter and Jerry might meet. In passing, it is important to notice that Albee makes minimal demands on the stage-designer. The play could be produced on the simplest stage imaginable. The few details about the appearance of the two characters help to visualize them, but there are no such character sketches as Shaw's. Albee sometimes gives the impression that he could not give such a sketch if he wanted to. Jerry's "fall from physical grace should not suggest debauchery," he writes; "he has, to come closest to it, a great weariness." A slight element of mystery is present in the stage direction, as if the playwright himself did not know everything about his character.

We are teased with another minor mystery during most of the play—the question of what happened at the zoo. But the chief mystery is the meaning of Jerry's behavior. Although there is no difficulty in understanding what he says, we are increasingly aware that this has only an indirect relation to what he means. Instead of following a debate carried on in the open, as in *Major Barbara*, we are obliged to look beneath the surface of the dialogue for the substance of a conflict which is never made quite explicit. The tone, the emotional coloring of many of the speeches, communicates more than the sense of the words. Because so much is said by means of understatement and suggestion, the design of the play, though much simpler than that of *Major Barbara*, is less easy to discern and less definite in outline. It is possible to be precise about the issues raised in Shaw's play. The underlying meaning of *The Zoo Story* is open to a greater variety of interpretation.

# The Zoo Story

## EDWARD ALBEE

### THE PLAYERS

PETER. A man in his early forties, neither fat nor gaunt, neither handsome nor homely. He wears tweeds, smokes a pipe, carries horn-rimmed glasses. Although he is moving into middle age, his dress and his manner would suggest a man younger.

JERRY. A man in his late thirties, not poorly dressed, but carelessly. What was once a trim and lightly muscled body has begun to go to fat; and while he is no longer handsome, it is evident that he once was. His fall from physical grace should not suggest debauchery; he has, to come closest to it, a great weariness.

### THE SCENE

It is Central Park; a Sunday afternoon in summer; the present. There are two park benches, one toward either side of the stage; they both face the audience. Behind them: foliage, trees, sky. At the beginning, Peter is seated on one of the benches.

### STAGE DIRECTIONS

As the curtain rises, PETER is seated on the bench stage-right. He is reading a book. He stops reading, cleans his glasses, goes back to reading. JERRY enters.

JERRY. I've been to the zoo. (PETER doesn't notice.) I said, I've been to the zoo. MISTER, I'VE BEEN TO THE ZOO!

PETER. Hm?...What?...I'm sorry, were you talking to me?

JERRY. I went to the zoo, and then I walked until I came here. Have I been walking north?

PETER (puzzled). North? Why...I...I think so. Let me see.

JERRY (pointing past the audience). Is that Fifth Avenue?

PETER. Why yes; yes, it is.

JERRY. And what is that cross street there; that one, to the right?

PETER. That? Oh, that's Seventy-fourth Street.

JERRY. And the zoo is around Sixty-fifth Street; so, I've been walking north.

PETER (anxious to get back to his reading). Yes; it would seem so.

JERRY. Good old north.

PETER (lightly, by reflex). Ha, ha.

JERRY (after a slight pause). But not due north.

PETER. I...well, no, not due north; but, we...call it north. It's northerly.

JERRY (watches as PETER, anxious to dismiss him, prepares his pipe). Well, boy; you're not going to get lung cancer, are you?

PETER (looks up, a little annoyed, then smiles). No, sir. Not from this.

JERRY. No, sir. What you'll probably get is cancer of the mouth, and then you'll have to wear one of those things Freud wore after they took one whole side of his jaw away. What do they call those things?

PETER (*uncomfortable*). A prosthesis?

JERRY. The very thing! A prosthesis. You're an educated man, aren't you? Are you a doctor?

PETER. Oh, no; no. I read about it somewhere; *Time* magazine, I think. (*He turns to his book.*)

JERRY. Well, *Time* magazine isn't for blockheads.

PETER. No, I suppose not.

JERRY (*after a pause*). Boy, I'm glad that's Fifth Avenue there.

PETER (*vaguely*). Yes.

JERRY. I don't like the west side of the park much.

PETER. Oh? (*Then, slightly wary, but interested.*) Why?

JERRY (*offhand*). I don't know.

PETER. Oh. (*He returns to his book*).

JERRY (*he stands for a few seconds, looking at* PETER, *who finally looks up again, puzzled*). Do you mind if we talk?

PETER (*obviously minding*). Why . . . no, no.

JERRY. Yes you do; you do.

PETER (*puts his book down, his pipe out and away, smiling*). No, really; I don't mind.

JERRY. Yes you do.

PETER (*finally decided*). No; I don't mind at all, really.

JERRY. It's . . . it's a nice day.

PETER (*stares unnecessarily at the sky*). Yes. Yes, it is; lovely.

JERRY. I've been to the zoo.

PETER. Yes, I think you said so . . . didn't you?

JERRY. You'll read about it in the papers tomorrow, if you don't see it on your TV tonight. You have TV, haven't you?

PETER. Why yes, we have two; one for the children.

JERRY. You're married!

PETER (*with pleased emphasis*). Why, certainly.

JERRY. It isn't a law, for God's sake.

PETER. No . . . no, of course not.

JERRY. And you have a wife.

PETER (*bewildered by the seeming lack of communication*). Yes!

JERRY. And you have children.

PETER. Yes; two.

JERRY. Boys?

PETER. No, girls . . . both girls.

JERRY. But you wanted boys.

PETER. Well . . . naturally, every man wants a son, but . . .

JERRY (*lightly mocking*). But that's the way the cookie crumbles?

PETER (*annoyed*). I wasn't going to say that.

JERRY. And you're not going to have any more kids, are you?

PETER (*a bit distantly*). No. No more. (*Then back, and irksome.*) Why did you say that? How would you know about that?

JERRY. The way you cross your legs, perhaps; something in the voice. Or maybe I'm just guessing. Is it your wife?

PETER (*furious*). That's none of your business! (*A silence.*) Do you understand? (JERRY *nods.* PETER *is quiet now.*) Well, you're right. We'll have no more children.

JERRY (*softly*). That *is* the way the cookie crumbles.

PETER (*forgiving*). Yes . . . I guess so.

JERRY. Well, now; what else?

PETER. What were you saying about the zoo . . . that I'd read about it, or see . . . ?

JERRY. I'll tell you about it, soon. Do you mind if I ask you questions?

PETER. Oh, not really.

JERRY. I'll tell you why I do it; I don't talk to many people—except to say like: give me a beer, or where's the john, or what time does the feature go on, or keep your hands to yourself, buddy. You know—things like that.

PETER. I must say I don't . . .

JERRY. But every once in a while I like to talk to somebody, really *talk*; like to get to know somebody, know all about him.

PETER (*lightly laughing, still a little uncomfortable*). And am I the guinea pig for today?

JERRY. On a sun-drenched Sunday afternoon like this? Who better than a nice married man with two daughters and . . . uh . . . a dog? (PETER *shakes his head.*) No? Two dogs. (PETER *shakes his head again.*) Hm. No dogs? (PETER *shakes his head, sadly.*) Oh, that's a shame. But you look like an animal man. CATS? (PETER *nods his head, ruefully.*) Cats! But, that can't be your idea. No, sir. Your wife and daughters? (PETER *nods his head.*) Is there anything else I should know?

PETER (*he has to clear his throat*). There are . . . there are two parakeets. One . . . uh . . . one for each of my daughters.

JERRY. Birds.

PETER. My daughters keep them in a cage in their bedroom.

JERRY. Do they carry disease? The birds.

PETER. I don't believe so.

JERRY. That's too bad. If they did you could set them loose in the house and the cats could eat them and die, maybe. (PETER *looks blank for a moment, then laughs.*) And what else? What do you do to support your enormous household?

PETER. I . . . uh . . . I have an executive position with a . . . a small publishing house. We . . . uh . . . we publish textbooks.

JERRY. That sounds nice; very nice. What do you make?

PETER (*still cheerful*). Now look here!

JERRY. Oh, come on.

PETER. Well, I make around eighteen thousand a year, but I don't carry more than forty dollars at any one time . . . in case you're a . . . a holdup man . . . ha, ha, ha.

JERRY (*ignoring the above*). Where do you live? (PETER *is reluctant.*) Oh, look; I'm not going to rob you, and I'm not going to kidnap your parakeets, your cats, or your daughters.

PETER (*too loud*). I live between Lexington and Third Avenue, on Seventy-fourth Street.

JERRY. That wasn't so hard, was it?

PETER. I didn't mean to seem . . . ah . . . it's that you don't really carry on a conversation; you just ask questions, and I'm . . . I'm normally . . . . uh . . . reticent. Why do you just stand there?

JERRY. I'll start walking around in a little while, and eventually I'll sit down. (*Recalling.*) Wait until you see the expression on his face.

PETER. What? Whose face? Look here; is this something about the zoo?

JERRY (*distantly*). The what?

PETER. The zoo; the zoo. Something about the zoo.

JERRY. The zoo?

PETER. You've mentioned it several times.

JERRY (*still distant, but returning abruptly*).

The zoo? Oh, yes; the zoo. I was there before I came here. I told you that. Say, what's the dividing line between upper-middle-middle-class and lower-upper-middle-class?

PETER. My dear fellow, I . . .

JERRY. Don't my dear fellow me.

PETER (*unhappily*). Was I patronizing? I believe I was; I'm sorry. But, you see, your question about the classes bewildered me.

JERRY. And when you're bewildered you become patronizing?

PETER. I . . . I don't express myself too well, sometimes. (*He attempts a joke on himself.*) I'm in publishing, not writing.

JERRY (*amused, but not at the humor*). So be it. The truth *is: I* was being patronizing.

PETER. Oh, now; you needn't say that.

(*It is at this point that* JERRY *may begin to move about the stage with slowly increasing determination and authority, but pacing himself, so that the long speech about the dog comes at the high point of the arc.*)

JERRY. All right. Who are your favorite writers? Baudelaire and J. P. Marquand?

PETER (*wary*). Well, I like a great many writers; I have a considerable . . . catholicity of taste, if I may say so. Those two men are fine, each in his way. (*Warming up.*) Baudelaire, of course . . . uh . . . is by far the finer of the two, but Marquand has a place . . . in our . . . uh . . . national . . .

JERRY. Skip it.

PETER. I . . . sorry.

JERRY. Do you know what I did before I went to the zoo today? I walked all the way up Fifth Avenue from Washington Square; all the way.

PETER. Oh, you live in the Village! (*This seems to enlighten* PETER.)

JERRY. No, I don't. I took the subway down to the Village so I could walk all the way up Fifth Avenue to the zoo. It's one of those things a person has to do; sometimes a person has to go a very long distance out of his way to come back a short distance correctly.

PETER (*almost pouting*). Oh, I thought you lived in the Village.

JERRY. What were you trying to do? Make sense out of things? Bring order? The old pigeonhole bit? Well, that's easy; I'll tell you. I live in a four-story brownstone room-inghouse on the upper West Side between Columbus Avenue and Central Park West. I live on the top floor; rear; west. It's a laughably small room, and one of my walls is made of beaverboard; this beaverboard separates my room from another laughably small room, so I assume that the two rooms were once one room, a small room, but not necessarily laughable. The room beyond my beaverboard wall is occupied by a colored queen who always keeps his door open; well, not always, but *always* when he's plucking his eyebrows, which he does with Buddhist concentration. This colored queen has rotten teeth, which is rare, and he has a Japanese kimono, which is also pretty rare; and he wears this kimono to and from the john in the hall, which is pretty frequent. I mean, he goes to the john a lot. He never bothers me, and he never brings anyone up to his room. All he does is pluck his eyebrows, wear his kimono and go to the john. Now, the two front rooms on my floor are a little larger, I guess; but they're pretty small, too. There's a Puerto Rican family in one of them, a husband, a wife, and some kids; I don't know how many. These people entertain a lot. And in the other front room, there's somebody living there, but I don't know who it is. I've never seen who it is. Never. Never ever.

PETER (*embarrassed*). Why . . . why do you live there?

JERRY (*from a distance again*). I don't know.

PETER. It doesn't sound like a very nice place . . . where you live.

JERRY. Well, no; it isn't an apartment in the East Seventies. But, then again I, don't have one wife, two daughters, two cats and two parakeets. What I do have, I have toilet articles, a few clothes, a hot plate that I'm not supposed to have, a can opener, one that works with a key, you know; a knife, two forks, and two spoons, one small, one large; three plates, a cup, a saucer, a drinking glass, two picture frames, both empty, eight or nine books, a pack of pornographic playing cards, regular deck, an old Western Union typewriter that prints nothing but capital letters, and a small strongbox without a lock which has in it . . . what? Rocks! Some rocks . . . sea-rounded rocks I picked up on the beach when I was a kid. Under which . . . weighed down . . . are some letters . . . please letters . . . please why don't you do this, and please when will you do that letters. And when letters, too. When will you write? When will you come? When? These letters are from more recent years.

PETER (*stares glumly at his shoes, then*). About those two empty picture frames . . . ?

JERRY. I don't see why they need any explanation at all. Isn't it clear? I don't have pictures of anyone to put in them.

PETER. Your parents . . . perhaps . . . a girl friend . . .

JERRY. You're a very sweet man, and you're possessed of a truly enviable innocence. But good old Mom and good old Pop are dead . . . you know? . . . I'm broken up about it, too . . . I mean really. BUT. That particular vaudeville act is playing the cloud circuit now, so I don't see how I can look at them, all neat and framed. Besides, or, rather, to be pointed about it, good old Mom walked out on good old Pop when I was ten and a half years old; she embarked on an adulterous turn of our southern states . . . a journey of a year's duration . . . and her most constant companion . . . among others, among many others . . . was a Mr. Barley-corn. At least, that's what good old Pop told me after he went down . . . came back . . . brought her body north. We'd received the news between Christmas and New Year's, you see, that good old Mom had parted with the ghost in some dump in Alabama. And, without the ghost . . . she was less welcome. I mean, what was she? A stiff . . . a northern stiff. At any rate, good old Pop cele-brated the New Year for an even two weeks and then slapped into the front of a somewhat moving city omnibus, which sort of cleaned things out family-wise. Well no; then there was Mom's sister, who was given neither to sin nor the consolations of the bottle. I moved in on her, and my memory of her is slight excepting I remember still that she did all things dourly: sleeping, eating, working, praying. She dropped dead on the stairs to her apartment, my apartment then, too, on the afternoon of my high school graduation. A terribly middle-European joke, if you ask me.

PETER. Oh, my; oh, my.

JERRY. Oh, your what? But that was a long time ago, and I have no feeling about any of it that I care to admit to myself. Perhaps you can see, though, why good old Mom and good old Pop are frameless. What's your name? Your first name?

PETER. I'm Peter.

JERRY. I'd forgotten to ask you. I'm Jerry.

PETER (with a slight, nervous laugh). Hello, Jerry.

JERRY (nods his hello). And let's see now; what's the point of having a girl's picture, especially in two frames? I have two picture frames, you remember. I never see the pretty little ladies more than once, and most of them wouldn't be caught in the same room with a camera. It's odd, and I wonder if it's sad.

PETER. The girls?

JERRY. No. I wonder if it's sad that I never see the little ladies more than once. I've never been able to have sex with, or, how is it put? . . . make love to anybody more than once. Once; that's it. . . . Oh, wait; for a week and a half, when I was fifteen . . . and I hang my head in shame that puberty was late . . . I was a h-o-m-o-s-e-x-u-a-l. I mean, I was queer . . . (very fast) . . . queer, queer, queer . . . with bells ringing, banners snapping in the wind. And for those eleven days, I met at least twice a day with the park superintendent's son . . . a Greek boy, whose birthday was the same as mine, except he was a year older. I think I was very much in love. . . maybe just with sex. But that was the jazz of a very special hotel, wasn't it? And now; oh, do I love the little ladies; really, I love them. For about an hour.

PETER. Well, it seems perfectly simple to me. . . .

JERRY (angry). Look! Are you going to tell me to get married and have parakeets?

PETER (angry himself). Forget the parakeets! And stay single if you want to. It's no business of mine. I didn't start this conversation in the . . .

JERRY. All right, all right. I'm sorry. All right? You're not angry?

PETER (laughing). No, I'm not angry.

JERRY (relieved). Good. (Now back to his previous tone.) Interesting that you asked me about the picture frames. I would have thought that you would have asked me about the pornographic playing cards.

PETER (with a knowing smile). Oh, I've seen those cards.

JERRY. That's not the point. (Laughs.) I suppose when you were a kid you and your pals passed them around, or you had a pack of your own.

PETER. Well, I guess a lot of us did.

JERRY. And you threw them away just before you got married.

PETER. Oh, now; look here. I didn't need anything like that when I got older.

JERRY. No?

PETER (embarrassed). I'd rather not talk about these things.

JERRY. So? Don't. Besides, I wasn't trying to plumb your post-adolescent sexual life and hard times; what I wanted to get at is the value difference between pornographic playing cards when you're a kid, and pornographic playing cards when you're older. It's that when you're a kid you use the cards as a substitute for a real experience, and when you're older you use real experience as a substitute for the fantasy. But I imagine you'd rather hear about what happened at the zoo.

PETER (enthusiastic). Oh, yes; the zoo. (Then, awkward.) That is . . . if you. . . .

JERRY. Let me tell you about why I went . . . well, let me tell you some things. I've told you about the fourth floor of the rooming-house where I live. I think the rooms are better as you go down, floor by floor. I guess they are; I don't know. I don't know any of the people on the third and second floors. Oh, wait! I do know that there's a lady living on the third floor, in the front. I know because she cries all the time. Whenever I go out or come back in, whenever I pass her door, I always hear her crying, muffled, but . . . very determined. Very determined indeed. But the one I'm getting to, and all about the dog, is the landlady. I don't like to use words that are too harsh in describing people. I don't like to. But the landlady is a fat, ugly, mean, stupid, unwashed, misanthropic, cheap, drunken bag of garbage. And you may have noticed that I very seldom use profanity, so I can't describe her as well as I might.

PETER. You describe her . . . vividly.

JERRY. Well, thanks. Anyway, she has a dog, and I will tell you about the dog, and she and her dog are the gatekeepers of my dwelling. The woman is bad enough; she leans around in the entrance hall, spying to see that I don't bring in things or people, and when she's had her midafternoon pint of lemon-flavored gin she always stops me in the hall, and grabs ahold of my coat or my arm, and she presses her disgusting body up against me to keep me in a corner so she can talk to me. The smell of her body and her breath . . . you can't imagine it . . . and somewhere, somewhere in the back of that pea-sized brain of hers, an organ developed just enough to let her eat, drink, and emit, she has some foul parody of sexual desire. And I, Peter, I am the object of her sweaty lust.

PETER. That's disgusting. That's . . . horrible.

JERRY. But I have found a way to keep her off. When she talks to me, when she presses herself to my body and mumbles about her room and how I should come there, I merely say: but, Love; wasn't yesterday enough for you, and the day before? Then she puzzles, she makes slits of her tiny eyes, she sways a little, and then, Peter . . . and it is at this moment that I think I might be doing some good in that tormented house . . . a simple-minded smile begins to form on her unthinkable face, and she giggles and groans as she thinks about yesterday and the day before; as she believes and relives what never happened. Then, she motions to that black monster of a dog she has, and she goes back to her room. And I am safe until our next meeting.

PETER. It's so . . . unthinkable. I find it hard to believe that people such as that really *are*.

JERRY (*lightly mocking*). It's for reading about, isn't it?

PETER (*seriously*). Yes.

JERRY. And fact is better left to fiction. You're right, Peter. Well, what I have been meaning to tell you about is the dog; I shall, now.

PETER (*nervously*). Oh, yes; the dog.

JERRY. Don't go. You're not thinking of going, are you?

PETER. Well . . . no, I don't think so.

JERRY (*as if to a child*). Because after I tell you about the dog, do you know what then? Then . . . then I'll tell you about what happened at the zoo.

PETER (*laughing faintly*). You're . . . you're full of stories, aren't you?

JERRY. You don't *have* to listen. Nobody is holding you here; remember that. Keep that in your mind.

PETER (*irritably*). I know that.

JERRY. You do? Good.

(*The following long speech, it seems to me, should be done with a great deal of action, to achieve a hypnotic effect on Peter, and on the audience, too. Some specific actions have been suggested, but the director and the actor playing Jerry might best work it out for themselves.*)

ALL RIGHT. (*As if reading from a huge billboard.*) THE STORY OF JERRY AND THE DOG! (*Natural again.*) What I am going to tell you has something to do with how sometimes it's necessary to go a long distance out of the way in order to come back a short distance correctly; or, maybe I only think that it has something to do with that. But, it's why I went to the zoo today, and why I walked north . . . northerly, rather . . . until I came here. All right. The dog, I think I told you, is a black monster of a beast: an oversized head, tiny, tiny ears, and eyes . . . bloodshot, infected, maybe; and a body you can see the ribs through the skin. The dog is black, all black; all black except for the bloodshot eyes, and . . . yes . . . and an open sore on its . . . *right* forepaw; that is red, too. And, oh yes; the poor monster, and I do believe it's an old dog . . . it's certainly a misused one . . . almost always has an

erection ... of sorts. That's red, too. And
... what else? ... oh, yes; there's a gray-
yellow-white color, too, when he bares his
fangs. Like this: Grrrrrrr! Which is what he
did when he saw me for the first time ... the
day I moved in. I worried about that animal
the very first minute I met him. Now, animals
don't take to me like Saint Francis had birds
hanging off him all the time. What I mean
is: animals are indifferent to me ... like
people (*he smiles slightly.*) ... most of the time.
But this dog wasn't indifferent. From the
very beginning he'd snarl and then go for me,
to get one of my legs. Not like he was rabid,
you know; he was sort of a stumbly dog, but
he wasn't half-assed, either. It was a good,
stumbly run; but I always got away. He got
a piece of my trouser leg, look, you can see
right here, where it's mended; he got that
the second day I lived there; but, I kicked
free and got upstairs fast, so that was that.
(*Puzzles.*) I still don't know to this day how
the other roomers manage it, but you know
what I *think*: I think it had to do only with
me. Cozy. So. Anyway, this went on for over
a week, whenever I came in; but never when
I went out. That's funny. Or, it *was* funny.
I could pack up and live in the street for all
the dog cared. Well, I thought about it up in
my room one day, one of the times after I'd
bolted upstairs, and I made up my mind. I
decided: First, I'll kill the dog with kindness,
and if that doesn't work ... I'll just kill him.
(PETER *winces.*) Don't react, Peter; just listen.
So, the next day I went out and bought a bag
of hamburgers, medium rare, no catsup, no
onion; and on the way home I threw away
all the rolls and kept just the meat.

(*Action for the following, perhaps.*)

When I got back to the roominghouse the
dog was waiting for me. I half opened the
door that led into the entrance hall, and
there he was; waiting for me. It figured.
I went in, very cautiously, and I had the
hamburgers, you remember; I opened the
bag, and I set the meat down about twelve
feet from where the dog was snarling at me.
Like so! He snarled; stopped snarling;
sniffed; moved slowly; then faster; then
faster toward the meat. Well, when he got to
it he stopped, and he looked at me. I smiled;

but tentatively, you understand. He turned
his face back to the hamburgers, smelled,
sniffed some more, and then ... RRRAA
AAGGGGGHHHH, like that ... he tore
into them. It was as if he had never eaten
anything in his life before, except like garbage. Which might very well have been
the truth. I don't think the landlady ever
eats anything but garbage. But. He ate all the
hamburgers, almost all at once, making
sounds in his throat like a woman. *Then,*
when he'd finished the meat, the hamburger,
and tried to eat the paper, too, he sat down
and smiled. I think he smiled; I know cats do.
It was a very gratifying few moments. Then,
BAM, he snarled and made for me again.
He didn't get me this time, either. So, I got
upstairs, and I lay down on my bed and
started to think about the dog again. To be
truthful, I was offended, and I was damn
mad, too. It was six perfectly good hamburgers with not enough pork in them to
make it disgusting. I was offended. But,
after a while, I decided to try it for a few
more days. If you think about it, this dog had
what amounted to an antipathy toward me;
really. And, I wondered if I mightn't overcome this antipathy. So, I tried it for five
more days, but it was always the same: snarl,
sniff; move; faster; stare; gobble; RAAGGG
HHH; smile; snarl; BAM. Well, now; by
this time Columbus Avenue was strewn with
hamburger rolls and I was less offended
than disgusted. So, I decided to kill the dog.

(PETER *raises a hand in protest.*)

Oh, don't be so alarmed, Peter; I didn't
succeed. The day I tried to kill the dog I
bought only one hamburger and what I
thought was a murderous portion of rat
poison. When I bought the hamburger I
asked the man not to bother with the roll, all
I wanted was the meat. I expected some
reaction from him, like: we don't sell no
hamburgers without rolls; or, wha' d'ya
wanna do, eat it out'a ya han's? But no; he
smiled benignly, wrapped up the hamburger
in waxed paper, and said: A bite for ya
pussy-cat? I wanted to say: No, not really;
it's part of a plan to poison a dog I know.
But, you can't say "a dog I know" without
sounding funny; so I said, a little too loud,

I'm afraid, and too formally: YES, A BITE FOR MY PUSSY-CAT. People looked up. It always happens when I try to simplify things; people look up. But that's neither hither nor thither. So. On my way back to the roominghouse, I kneaded the hamburger and the rat poison together between my hands, at that point feeling as much sadness as disgust. I opened the door to the entrance hall, and there the monster was, waiting to take the offering and then jump me. Poor bastard; he never learned that the moment he took to smile before he went for me gave me time enough to get out of range. BUT, there he was; malevolence with an erection, waiting. I put the poison patty down, moved toward the stairs and watched. The poor animal gobbled the food down as usual, which made me almost sick, and then, BAM. But, I sprinted up the stairs, as usual, and the dog didn't get me, as usual. AND IT CAME TO PASS THAT THE BEAST WAS DEATHLY ILL. I knew this because he no longer attended me, and because the landlady sobered up. She stopped me in the hall the same evening of the attempted murder and confided the information that God had struck her puppy-dog a surely fatal blow. She had forgotten her bewildered lust, and her eyes were wide open for the first time. They looked like the dog's eyes. She sniveled and implored me to pray for the animal. I wanted to say to her: Madam, I have myself to pray for, the colored queen, the Puerto Rican family, the person in the front room whom I've never seen, the woman who cries deliberately behind her closed door, and the rest of the people in all roominghouses, everywhere; besides, Madam, I don't understand how to pray. But . . . to simplify things . . . I told her I would pray. She looked up. She said that I was a liar, and that I probably wanted the dog to die. I told her, and there was so much truth here, that I didn't want the dog to die. I didn't, and not just because I'd poisoned him. I'm afraid that I must tell you I wanted the dog to live so that I could see what our new relationship might come to.

(PETER *indicates his increasing displeasure and slowly growing antagonism.*)

Please understand, Peter; that sort of thing is important. You must believe me; it *is* important. We have to know the effect of our actions. (*Another deep sigh.*) Well, anyway; the dog recovered. I have no idea why, unless he was a descendant of the puppy that guarded the gates of hell or some such resort. I'm not up on my mythology. (*He pronounces the word myth-o-log-y.*) Are you?

(PETER *sets to thinking, but* JERRY *goes on.*)

At any rate, and you've missed the eight-thousand-dollar question, Peter; at any rate, the dog recovered his health and the landlady recovered her thirst, in no way altered by the bow-wow's deliverance. When I came home from a movie that was playing on Forty-second Street, a movie I'd seen, or one that was very much like one or several I'd seen, after the landlady told me puppykins was better, I was so hoping for the dog to be waiting for me. I was . . . well, how would you put it . . . enticed? . . . fascinated? . . . no, I don't think so . . . heart-shatteringly anxious, that's it; I was heart-shatteringly anxious to confront my friend again.

(PETER *reacts scoffingly.*)

Yes, Peter; friend. That's the only word for it. I was heart-shatteringly et cetera to confront my doggy friend again. I came in the door and advanced, unafraid, to the center of the entrance hall. The beast was there . . . looking at me. And, you know, he looked better for his scrape with the never-mind. I stopped; I looked at him; he looked at me. I think . . . I think we stayed a long time that way . . . still, stone-statue . . . just looking at one another. I looked more into his face than he looked into mine. I mean, I can concentrate longer at looking into a dog's face than a dog can concentrate at looking into mine, or into anybody else's face, for that matter. But during that twenty seconds or two hours that we looked into each other's face, we made contact. Now, here is what I had wanted to happen: I loved the dog now, and I wanted him to love me. I had tried to love, and I had tried to kill, and both had been unsuccessful by themselves. I hoped . . . and I don't really know why I expected the dog to understand anything, much less my motivations . . . I hoped that the dog would understand.

(PETER *seems to be hypnotized.*)

It's just . . . it's just that . . . (JERRY *is abnormally tense, now*) . . . it's just that if you can't deal with people, you have to make a start somewhere. WITH ANIMALS! (*Much faster now, and like a conspirator.*) Don't you see? A person has to have some way of dealing with SOMETHING. If not with people . . . if not with people . . . SOMETHING. With a bed, with a cockroach, with a mirror . . . no, that's too hard, that's one of the last steps. With a cockroach, with a . . . with a . . . with a carpet, a roll of toilet paper . . . no, not that, either . . . that's a mirror, too; always check bleeding. You see how hard it is to find things? With a street corner, and too many lights, all colors reflecting on the oily-wet streets . . . with a wisp of smoke, a wisp . . . of smoke . . . with . . . with pornographic playing cards, with a strongbox . . . WITH-OUT A LOCK . . . with love, with vomiting, with crying, with fury because the pretty little ladies aren't pretty little ladies, with making money with your body which is an act of love and I could prove it, with howling because you're alive; with God. How about that? WITH GOD WHO IS A COLORED QUEEN WHO WEARS A KIMONO AND PLUCKS HIS EYEBROWS, WHO IS A WOMAN WHO CRIES WITH DETERMINATION BEHIND HER CLOSED DOOR . . . with God who, I'm told, turned his back on the whole thing some time ago . . . with . . . some day, with people. (JERRY *sighs the next word heavily.*) People. With an idea; a concept. And where better, where ever better in this humiliating excuse for a jail, where better to communicate one single, simple-minded idea than in an entrance hall? Where? It would be A START! Where better to make a beginning . . . to understand and just possibly be understood . . . a beginning of an understanding, than with . . .

(*Here* JERRY *seems to fall into almost grotesque fatigue.*)

. . . than with A DOG. Just that; a dog.

(*Here there is a silence that might be prolonged for a moment or so; then* JERRY *wearily finishes his story.*)

A dog. It seemed like a perfectly sensible idea. Man is a dog's best friend, remember. So: the dog and I looked at each other. I longer than the dog. And what I saw then has been the same ever since. Whenever the dog and I see each other we both stop where we are. We regard each other with a mixture of sadness and suspicion, and then we feign indifference. We walk past each other safely; we have an understanding. It's very sad, but you'll have to admit that it is an understanding. We had made many attempts at contact, and we had failed. The dog has returned to garbage, and I to solitary but free passage. I have not returned. I mean to say, I have *gained* solitary free passage, if that much further loss can be said to be gain. I have learned that neither kindness nor cruelty by themselves, independent of each other, creates any effect beyond themselves; and I have learned that the two combined, together, at the same time, are the teaching emotion. And what is gained is loss. And what has been the result: the dog and I have attained a compromise; more of a bargain, really. We neither love nor hurt because we do not try to reach each other. And, *was* I trying to feed the dog an act of love? And, perhaps, was the dog's attempt to bite me *not* an act of love? If we can so misunderstand, well then, why have we invented the word love in the first place?

(*There is silence.* JERRY *moves to* PETER'S *bench and sits down beside him. This is the first time* JERRY *has sat down during the play.*)

The Story of Jerry and the Dog: the end.

(PETER *is silent.*)

Well, Peter? (JERRY *is suddenly cheerful.*) Well, Peter? Do you think I could sell that story to the *Reader's Digest* and make a couple of hundred bucks for *The Most Unforgettable Character I've Ever Met?* Huh?

(JERRY *is animated, but* PETER *is disturbed.*)

Oh, come on now, Peter; tell me what you think.

PETER (*numb*). I . . . I don't understand what . . . I don't think I . . . (*Now, almost tearfully.*) Why did you tell me all of this?

JERRY. Why not?

PETER. I DON'T UNDERSTAND!

JERRY (*furious, but whispering*). That's a lie.

PETER. No. No, it's not.

JERRY (*quietly*). I tried to explain it to you as I went along. I went slowly; it all has to do with . . .

PETER. I DON'T WANT TO HEAR ANY MORE. I don't understand you, or your landlady, or her dog. . . .

JERRY. *Her* dog! I thought it was my . . . No. No, you're right. It *is* her dog. (*Looks at* PETER *intently, shaking his head.*) I don't know what I was thinking about; of course you don't understand. (*In a monotone, wearily.*) I don't live in your block; I'm not married to two parakeets, or whatever your setup is. I am a *permanent transient*, and my home is the sickening roominghouses on the West Side of New York City, which is the greatest city in the world. Amen.

PETER. I'm . . . I'm sorry; I didn't mean to . . .

JERRY. Forget it. I suppose you don't quite know what to make of me, eh?

PETER (*a joke*). We get all kinds in publishing. (*Chuckles.*)

JERRY. You're a funny man. (*He forces a laugh.*) You know that? You're a very . . . a richly comic person.

PETER (*modestly, but amused*). Oh, now, not really. (*Still chuckling.*)

JERRY. Peter, do I annoy you, or confuse you?

PETER (*lightly*). Well, I must confess that this wasn't the kind of afternoon I'd anticipated.

JERRY. You mean, I'm not the gentleman you were expecting.

PETER. I wasn't expecting anybody.

JERRY. No, I don't imagine you were. But I'm here, and I'm not leaving.

PETER (*consulting his watch*). Well, you may not be, but I must be getting home soon.

JERRY. Oh, come on; stay a while longer.

PETER. I really should get home; you see . . .

JERRY (*tickles* PETER's *ribs with his fingers*). Oh, come on.

PETER. (*he is very ticklish; as* JERRY *continues to tickle him his voice becomes falsetto*). No, I . . . OHHHHH! Don't do that. Stop, Stop. Ohhh, no, no.

JERRY. Oh, come on.

PETER (*as* JERRY *tickles*). Oh, hee, hee, hee. I must go. I . . . hee, hee, hee. After all, stop, hee, hee, hee, after all, the parakeets will be getting dinner ready soon. Hee, hee. And the cats are setting the table. Stop, stop, and, and . . . (PETER *is beside himself now*) . . . and we're having . . . hee, hee . . . uh . . . ho, ho, ho.

(JERRY *stops tickling* PETER, *but the combination of the tickling and his own mad whimsy has* PETER *laughing almost hysterically. As his laughter continues, then subsides,* JERRY *watches him, with a curious fixed smile.*)

JERRY. Peter?

PETER. Oh, ha, ha, ha, ha, ha. What? What?

JERRY. Listen, now.

PETER. Oh, oh, oh. What . . . what is it, Jerry? Oh, my.

JERRY (*mysteriously*). Peter, do you want to know what happened at the zoo?

PETER. Ah, ha, ha. The what? Oh, yes; the zoo. Oh, ho, ho. Well, I had my own zoo there for a moment with . . . hee, hee, the parakeets getting dinner ready, and the . . . ha, ha, whatever it was, the . . .

JERRY (*calmly*). Yes, that was very funny, Peter. I wouldn't have expected it. But do you want to hear about what happened at the zoo, or not?

PETER. Yes. Yes. by all means; tell me what happened at the zoo. Oh, my. I don't know what happened to me.

JERRY. Now I'll let you in on what happened at the zoo; but first, I should tell you why I went to the zoo. I went to the zoo to find out more about the way people exist with animals, and the way animals exist with each other, and with people too. It probably wasn't a fair test, what with everyone separated by bars from everyone else, the animals for the most part from each other, and always the people from the animals. But, if it's a zoo, that's the way it is. (*He pokes* PETER *on the arm.*) Move over.

PETER (*friendly*). I'm sorry, haven't you enough room? (*He shifts a little.*)

JERRY (*smiling slightly*). Well, all the animals are there, and all the people are there, and it's Sunday and all the children are there. (*He pokes* PETER *again.*) Move over.

PETER (*patiently, still friendly*). All right.

(*He moves some more, and* JERRY *has all the room he might need.*)

JERRY. And it's a hot day, so all the stench is there, too, and all the balloon sellers, and all the ice cream sellers, and all the seals are barking, and all the birds are screaming. (*Pokes* PETER *harder.*) Move over!

PETER (*beginning to be annoyed.*) Look here, you have more than enough room! (*But he moves more, and is now fairly cramped at one end of the bench.*)

JERRY. And I am there, and it's feeding time at the lions' house, and the lion keeper comes into the lion cage, one of the lion cages, to feed one of the lions. (*Punches* PETER *on the arm, hard.*) MOVE OVER!

PETER (*very annoyed*). I can't move over any more, and stop hitting me. What's the matter with you?

JERRY. Do you want to hear the story? (*Punches* PETER's *arm again.*)

PETER (*flabbergasted*). I'm not so sure! I certainly don't want to be punched in the arm.

JERRY (*punches* PETER's *arm again*). Like that?

PETER. Stop it! What's the matter with you?

JERRY. I'm crazy, you bastard.

PETER. That isn't funny.

JERRY. Listen to me, Peter. I want this bench. You go sit on the bench over there, and if you're good I'll tell you the rest of the story.

PETER (*flustered*). But ... whatever for? What *is* the matter with you? Besides, I see no reason why I should give up this bench. I sit on this bench almost every Sunday afternoon, in good weather. It's secluded here; there's never anyone sitting here, so I have it all to myself.

JERRY (*softly*). Get off this bench, Peter; I want it.

PETER (*almost whining*). No.

JERRY. I said I want this bench, and I'm going to have it. Now get over there.

PETER. People can't have everything they want. You should know that; it's a rule; people can have some of the things they want, but they can't have everything.

JERRY (*laughs*). Imbecile! You're slow-witted!

PETER. Stop that!

JERRY. You're a vegetable! Go lie down on the ground.

PETER (*intense*). Now *you* listen to me. I've put up with you all afternoon.

JERRY. Not really.

PETER. LONG ENOUGH. I've put up with you long enough. I've listened to you because you seemed ... well, because I thought you wanted to talk to somebody.

JERRY. You put things well; economically, and yet, ... oh, what is the word I want to put justice to your ... JESUS, you make me sick ... get off here and give me my bench.

PETER. MY BENCH!

JERRY (*pushes* PETER *almost, but not quite, off the bench*). Get out of my sight.

PETER (*regaining his position*). God da ... mn you. That's enough! I've had enough of you. I will not give up this bench; you can't have it, and that's that. Now, go away.

(JERRY *snorts but does not move.*)

Go away, I said.

(JERRY *does not move.*)

Get away from here. If you don't move on ... you're a bum ... that's what you are. ... If you don't move on, I'll get a policeman here and make you go.

(JERRY *laughs, stays.*)

I warn you, I'll call a policeman.

JERRY (*softly*). You won't find a policeman around here; they're all over on the west side of the park chasing fairies down from trees or out of the bushes. That's all they do. That's their function. So scream your head off; it won't do you any good.

PETER. POLICE! I warn you, I'll have you arrested. POLICE! (*Pause.*) I said POLICE! (*Pause.*) I feel ridiculous.

JERRY. You look ridiculous: a grown man screaming for the police on a bright Sunday afternoon in the park with nobody harming you. If a policeman *did* fill his quota and come sludging over this way he'd probably take you in as a nut.

PETER (*with disgust and impotence*). Great God, I just came here to read, and now you want me to give up the bench. You're mad.

JERRY. Hey, I got news for you, as they say. I'm on your precious bench, and you're never going to have it for yourself again.

PETER (*furious*). Look, you; get off my bench. I don't care if it makes any sense or not. I want this bench to myself; I want you OFF IT!

JERRY (*mocking*). Aw ... look who's mad.

PETER. GET OUT!

JERRY. No.

PETER. I WARN YOU!

JERRY. Do you know how ridiculous you look *now?*

PETER (*his fury and self-consciousness have possessed him*). It doesn't matter. (*He is almost crying.*) GET AWAY FROM MY BENCH!

JERRY. Why? You have everything in the world you want; you've told me about your home, and your family, and *your own* little zoo. You have everything, and now you want this bench. Are these the things men fight for? Tell me, Peter, is this bench, this iron and this wood, is this your honor? Is this the thing in the world you'd fight for? Can you think of anything more absurd?

PETER. Absurd? Look, I'm not going to talk to you about honor, or even try to explain it to you. Besides, it isn't a question of honor; but even if it were, you wouldn't understand.

JERRY (*contemptuously*). You don't even know what you're saying, do you? This is probably the first time in your life you've had anything more trying to face than changing your cat's toilet box. Stupid! Don't you have any idea, not even the slightest, what other people *need?*

PETER. Oh, boy, listen to you; well, you don't need this bench. That's for sure.

JERRY. Yes; yes, I do.

PETER (*quivering*). I've come here for years; I have hours of great pleasure, great satisfaction, right here. And that's important to a man. I'm a responsible person, and I'm a GROWNUP. This is my bench, and you have no right to take it away from me.

JERRY. Fight for it, then. Defend yourself; defend your bench.

PETER. You've *pushed* me to it. Get up and fight.

JERRY. Like a man?

PETER (*still angry*). Yes, like a man, if you insist on mocking me even further.

JERRY. I'll have to give you credit for one thing: you *are* a vegetable, and a slightly nearsighted one, I think . . .

PETER. THAT'S ENOUGH. . . .

JERRY. . . . but, you know, as they say on TV all the time—you know—and I mean this, Peter, you have a certain dignity; it surprises me. . . .

PETER. STOP!

JERRY (*rises lazily*). Very well, Peter, we'll battle for the bench, but we're not evenly matched.

(*He takes out and clicks open an ugly-looking knife.*)

PETER (*suddenly awakening to the reality of the situation*). You *are* mad! You're stark raving mad! YOU'RE GOING TO KILL ME!

(*But before* PETER *has time to think what to do,* JERRY *tosses the knife at* PETER'*s feet.*)

JERRY. There you go. Pick it up. You have the knife and we'll be more evenly matched.

PETER (*horrified*). No!

JERRY (*rushes over to* PETER, *grabs him by the collar;* PETER *rises; their faces almost touch*). Now you pick up that knife and you fight with me. You fight for your self-respect; you fight for that goddamned bench.

PETER (*struggling*). No! Let . . . let go of me! He . . . Help!

JERRY (*slaps* PETER *on each "fight"*). You fight, you miserable bastard; fight for that bench; fight for your parakeets; fight for your cats, fight for your two daughters; fight for your wife; fight for your manhood, you pathetic little vegetable. (*Spits in* PETER'*s face.*) You couldn't even get your wife with a male child.

PETER. (*breaks away, enraged*). It's a matter of genetics, not manhood, you . . . you monster.

(*He darts down, picks up the knife and backs off a little; he is breathing heavily.*)

I'll give you one last chance; get out of here and leave me alone!

(*He holds the knife with a firm arm, but far in front of him, not to attack, but to defend.*)

JERRY (*sighs heavily*). So be it!

(*With a rush he charges* PETER *and impales himself on the knife. Tableau: For just a moment, complete silence,* JERRY *impaled on the knife at the end of* PETER'*s still firm arm. Then* PETER *screams, pulls away, leaving the knife in* JERRY. JERRY *is motionless, on point. Then he, too, screams, and it must be the sound of an infuriated and fatally wounded animal. With the knife in him, he stumbles back to the bench that* PETER *had vacated. He crumbles there, sitting, facing* PETER *his eyes wide in agony, his mouth open.*)

PETER (*whispering*). Oh my God, oh my God, oh my God. . . .

(*He repeats these words many times, very rapidly.*)

JERRY (JERRY *is dying; but now his expression seems to change. His features relax, and while his voice varies, sometimes wrenched with pain, for the most part he seems removed from his dying. He smiles*). Thank you, Peter. I mean that, now; thank you very much.

(PETER's *mouth drops open. He cannot move; he is transfixed.*)

Oh, Peter, I was so afraid I'd drive you away. (*He laughs as best he can.*) You don't know how afraid I was you'd go away and leave me. And now I'll tell you what happened at the zoo. I think . . . I think this is what happened at the zoo . . . I think. I think that while I was at the zoo I decided that I would walk north . . . northerly, rather . . . until I found you . . . or somebody . . . and I decided that I would talk to you . . . I would tell you things . . . and things that I would tell you would . . . Well, here we are. You see? Here we *are*. But . . . I don't know . . . could I have planned all this? No . . . no, I couldn't have. But I think I did. And now I've told you what you wanted to know, haven't I? And now you know all about what happened at the zoo. And now you know what you'll see in your TV, and the face I told you about . . . you remember . . . the face I told you about . . . my face, the face you see right now. Peter . . . Peter? . . . Peter . . . thank you. I came unto you (*he laughs, so faintly*) and you have comforted me. Dear Peter.

PETER (*almost fainting*). Oh my God!

JERRY. You'd better go now. Somebody might come by, and you don't want to be here when anyone comes.

PETER (*does not move, but begins to weep*). Oh my God, oh my God.

JERRY (*most faintly, now; he is very near death*). You won't be coming back here any more, Peter; you've been dispossessed. You've lost your bench, but you've defended your honor. And Peter, I'll tell you something now; you're not really a vegetable; it's all right, you're an animal. You're an animal, too. But you'd better hurry now, Peter. Hurry, you'd better go . . . see?

(JERRY *takes a handkerchief and with great effort and pain wipes the knife handle clean of fingerprints.*)

Hurry away, Peter.

(PETER *begins to stagger away.*)

Wait . . . wait, Peter. Take your book . . . book. Right here . . . beside me . . . on your bench . . . my bench, rather. Come . . . take your book.

(PETER *starts for the book, but retreats.*)

Hurry . . . Peter.

(PETER *rushes to the bench, grabs the book, retreats.*)

Very good, Peter . . . very good. Now . . . hurry away.

(PETER *hesitates for a moment, then flees, stage-left.*)

Hurry away. . . . (*His eyes are closed now.*) Hurry away, your parakeets are making the dinner . . . the cats . . . are setting the table . . .

PETER (*off stage*). (*A pitiful howl.*) OH MY GOD!

JERRY (*his eyes still closed, he shakes his head and speaks; a combination of scornful mimicry and supplication*). Oh . . . my . . . God.

(*He is dead.*)

CURTAIN

## Understatement and Suggestion

Shaw engages the minds of his audience by means of brilliant dialectic, leading them first in one direction then in another. Although he does not overlook emotional response, the game he is playing is essentially intellectual. Albee makes a totally different approach to his audience. His situation is apparently a casual encounter of strangers. The dialogue, at least at first, seems casual too, and in no way out of the ordinary. No ideas are presented. We are occupied solely with finding out who the two speakers are. Jerry, the talker, is much more informative about himself, but the few details he manages to pry out of Peter give us a reasonably clear picture of the kind of life he leads. His personality is revealed by some of his answers and especially by the tone in which he gives them. Albee is careful to point out in a stage direction for instance, that when Peter says he doesn't mind talking to Jerry, he really does. By the time that Jerry launches into his long story about the dog we know enough about the two men to be fully aware of the contrast between them.

In this part of the play we may have the impression that Albee's technique is an entirely realistic one. He is obliging us to observe his characters as we would any strangers, inferring whatever we can from their words and behavior. However, the latter part of the play derives some of its effectiveness from the fact that it is unexpected. By means of the final violent action Albee shocks us into a concern with the motives for Jerry's behavior and with more basic problems of human existence exemplified by his life and death. In fact, from the very beginning there are suggestions of the meaning underlying this seemingly casual conversation, though they may not be apparent the first time the play is seen or read.

It may be toward the end of the dog story that a part of the pattern of meaning first becomes clear. Albee's stage directions suggest how the climactic importance of this story is to be heightened by Jerry's movements on the stage. The story is striking first of all because of its strangeness and humor. It confirms previous impressions of what an odd type Jerry is. But when Jerry describes how he looked at the dog after the failure of his attempt to kill it, he makes a revealing comment: ". . . during that twenty seconds or two hours that we looked into each other's face, we made contact. Now, here is what I had wanted to happen: I loved the dog now, and I wanted him to love me." Later he says, "And *was* trying to feed the dog an act of love? And perhaps, was the dog's attempt to bite me *not* an act of love?" These comments bring Jerry's conversation with Peter into a new perspective. Peter's initial effort to put Jerry off, Jerry's occasionally hostile probing of Peter's private life take on a significance they did not have at the time. Because of these connections, "The Story of Jerry and the Dog" is an impressive dramatic moment. The interpretation of the entire play hinges on it.

The other important moment in *The Zoo Story* is of course the one in which Jerry tricks Peter into killing him. The meaning of the play is to be found by lining up the suggestions of these moments with other details. It has been pointed out that the play contains a number of Christian references and some to pagan mythology. For example, the dying Jerry says, "I came unto you . . . and you have comforted me." The dog in his apartment house resembles the guardian of the underworld, Cerberus.[1] One of the chief tasks of interpretation is to decide whether such references constitute a coherent framework which give the play a consistent religious or mythic meaning or whether they merely add a dimension to an episode here and there. In either case it will be clear, especially upon a second reading or viewing, that most of the speeches and actions are charged with more meaning than is immediately apparent. The unpretentious façade of the play is an understatement.

## Selected Reading List for Albee

Lee Baxandall, "The Theatre of Edward Albee," *Tulane Drama Review*, IX (1965), 19–40.

Rose A. Zimbardo, "Symbolism and Naturalism in Edward Albee's *The Zoo Story*," *Twentieth Century Literature*, VIII (1962), 10–17.

---

[1] See Rose A. Zimbardo, "Symbolism and Naturalism in Edward Albee's *The Zoo Story*," *Twentieth Century Literature*, VIII (1962), 10–17.

*plays for the
great theaters
of the past*

SECTION II

# Sophocles and the Greek Theater

Sophocles was born in the first years of the fifth century B.C., in about 496, and died in 406, having lived through the period of the greatest power and the greatest cultural achievement of Athens. Two years later came the surrender to Sparta at the end of the Peloponnesian War. Though he held various public offices, his great contribution to the life of Athens was the writing of plays from 468 B.C. until his death. He wrote one hundred and twenty-three of them, only seven of which have survived complete. *Oedipus Rex* was probably written in about 425.

The theater for which he wrote differed in almost every respect from the one with which we are familiar today. Even plays as unlike as *Major Barbara* and *The Zoo Story* are equally designed for the standard indoor theater with a raised stage separated from the auditorium by a curtain or, when the curtain is raised, by a marked contrast between the lighting of the two areas. In the Greek theater the spectators sat in the open air in broad daylight on tiers of seats surrounding a little more than half of a flat circular area called the *orchestra* or "dancing place." The curve of the hill into which the seats were built provided excellent acoustics for a very large audience. The Theater of Dionysus at Athens, where the plays of Aeschylus, Sophocles, and Euripides were performed, seated 14,000 and had an orchestra sixty feet in diameter. On the other side of this circle from the spectators was the wooden stage building, probably one story high in the time of Sophocles, with a door in the center and possibly columns—a simple architectural façade which would readily suggest the palace in *Oedipus Rex*. In plays that required scenery there were apparently painted screens or cloths which could be fastened to the building, but for many plays the architectural façade sufficed. In front of the building and adjoining the circular orchestra was an area where much of the action took place. It may have been raised on a low platform or may have been level with the orchestra. Between the ends of the stage building and the seats of the spectators were entrances into the orchestra.

The crowds which frequented the theater of Dionysus represented a cross section of the citizens of Athens. Their coming was a religious observance, for the plays were performed at the annual festival in honor of the god for whom the theater was named. Every day for three days the spectators saw five plays between sunrise and sunset—three tragedies and a satyr play (in which heroic myths were treated farcically) by one author and a comedy by another. At the end, prizes were awarded to the dramatists. The occasion was at once solemn and festive.

It has usually been assumed that the dancing which was performed by the masked chorus in the orchestra was a direct descendant of ritual dances which were a part of the worship of Dionysus and hence that tragedy itself derived, as Aristotle said it did, from Dionysiac rites. Some scholars doubt that there was a direct connection, since so few extant tragedies have any observable connection with the myth of Dionysus, but the religious context of Greek tragedy is nonetheless apparent. Not only were the plays performed exclusively at religious festivals but there was an altar in the middle of the orchestra, and the choral odes were often, as in *Oedipus Rex*, prayers or religious reflections.

Whatever the origins of the chorus may have been, the choral odes, sung by the dancers to the accompaniment of the flute, were the basis upon which tragedy was built. Tragedy began when Thespis added an actor, called *hypokrites*, the

*The photograph of the Theater at Epidaurus by Max Hirmer appears in Berve and Gruben,*
Greek Temples, Theaters and Shrines *(New York: Harry N. Abrams, Inc., n.d) and is*
*reproduced by permission of the Hirmer Verlag in Munich. In the center of the circular orchestra*
*can be seen a small circular stone where the altar was probably set. At the right are the ruins of*
*the stage buidings, and beyond them is the west párados.*

"response-giver," because he entered into a dialogue with the leader of the chorus. The word later came to mean "actor" and gave us our word "hypocrite."
Aeschylus added a second actor, Sophocles a third, and it is important to note
that no more are required for *Oedipus Rex,* since several of the speaking parts can
be doubled. The actors also wore masks. Facial expression on which we count
so much in the modern theater could hardly have been seen by the nearest
spectators, and those in the back rows were three hundred feet from the acting
area. Masks had the advantage of indicating by their bold design whether the
actor was impersonating a slave, a citizen (young or old), a hero, or some other

standard type. Oedipus probably had a second mask to wear in his last scene when he had blinded himself. The actors, all of whom were men, wore costumes appropriate to their roles, with the royal characters dressed in gorgeous robes. At a somewhat later date the principal characters wore high-soled boots which added to their stature, but this development had not occurred at the time of Sophocles. It is obvious that characters thus typed by mask and costume would be portrayed by the dramatist with more attention to broad generic distinctions than we are accustomed to in the modern theater. The emphasis fell on what was suitable for a subject or a king, an old man or a boy. In this regard the requirements of the theater accorded with poetic theory, which also insisted on such distinctions. Not only was one kind of character set off from another kind in the same play, but the characters in tragedy, which dealt with illustrious people, were presented in a more dignified and elevated style than those of comedy, which dealt with ordinary people.

Although the actors took the roles of the principal personages in the story, the chorus long remained a central feature of tragedy and determined its structure. Often, as in *Oedipus Rex*, it represented a group of elder citizens, and as such, provided a kind of link between the world of the play and the world of the audience, who could be expected to agree with the sentiments expressed by the chorus. Its first appearance, called the *párados*, or "entrance," marks the end of the prologue and the beginning of the play proper. Before this, in *Oedipus Rex*, the King has come out of the central door to talk with the priest and the suppliants who have gathered near the altar in the orchestra. They have been joined by Creon, and the dialogue has explained the present situation. Then the chorus marches into the orchestra through the space between the stage building and the seats. They remain until the end of the play, sometimes singing and dancing by themselves, sometimes engaging in conversation with the actors. Each of their odes marks the end of one episode or scene, and is set off from the dialogue by being written in the meter and diction of lyric poetry. The last section of the play, the *éxodos*, receives its name from their final departure. The pattern of the action, like the delineation of character, is clear and bold.

To visualize the continual presence of the chorus is to be aware of the weight of the opinions of these old men who represent the community, and hence in one sense represent the audience. When they seem to turn against the hero as they do in their second ode, they oblige us to decide where our sympathies lie— with this god-fearing chorus or with the lonely figure of Oedipus. Thus they not only reveal the structure of the play but help to formulate its central problems.

The chorus performs one further task which the reader must try to imagine: by means of its chanting and dancing it brings out the extraordinary intensity of feeling in the lyric odes, so that these moments of philosophical reflection become almost as eloquent as the speeches of the principal characters.

# Oedipus Rex

## SOPHOCLES

### CHARACTERS

| | |
|---|---|
| OEDIPUS | MESSENGER |
| A PRIEST | SHEPHERD OF LAÏOS |
| CREON | SECOND MESSENGER |
| TEIRESIAS | CHORUS OF THEBAN ELDERS |
| IOCASTÊ | |

SCENE: *Before the palace of* OEDIPUS, *King of Thebes. A central door and two lateral doors open onto a platform which runs the length of the façade. On the platform, right and left, are altars; and three steps lead down into the "orchestra," or chorus-ground. At the beginning of the action these steps are crowded by suppliants who have brought branches and chaplets of olive leaves and who lie in various attitudes of despair.* OEDIPUS *enters.*

### PROLOGUE

OEDIPUS. My children, generations of the living
In the line of Kadmos, nursed at his ancient hearth:
Why have you strewn yourselves before these altars
In supplication, with your boughs and garlands?
The breath of incense rises from the city   5
With a sound of prayer and lamentation.
                        Children,
I would not have you speak through messengers,
And therefore I have come myself to hear you—

The Oedipus Rex of Sophocles: An English Version by Dudley Fitts and Robert Fitzgerald, copyright, 1949, by Harcourt, Brace & World, Inc. and reprinted with their permission.

2 *line of Kadmos* (or Cadmus) Phoenician prince who founded Thebes; Oedipus is a descendant of Cadmus, which he does not suspect

I, Oedipus, who bear the famous name.
                (*To a* PRIEST.)
You, there, since you are eldest in the company,   10
Speak for them all, tell me what preys upon you,
Whether you come in dread, or crave some blessing:
Tell me, and never doubt that I will help you
In every way I can; I should be heartless
Were I not moved to find you suppliant here.   15
    PRIEST. Great Oedipus, O powerful King of Thebes!
You see how all the ages of our people
Cling to your altar steps: here are boys
Who can barely stand alone, and here are priests
By weight of age, as I am a priest of God,  20
And young men chosen from those yet unmarried;
As for the others, all that multitude,
They wait with olive chaplets in the squares,
At the two shrines of Pallas, and where Apollo
Speaks in the glowing embers.
                    Your own eyes   25
Must tell you: Thebes is in her extremity
And can not lift her head from the surge of death.
A rust consumes the buds and fruits of the earth;
The herds are sick; children die unborn,
And labor is vain. The god of plague and pyre   30
Raids like detestable lightning through the city,
And all the house of Kadmos is laid waste,
All emptied, and all darkened: Death alone
Battens upon the misery of Thebes.

24 *Pallas* Athena

You are not one of the immortal gods, we
    know;           35
Yet we have come to you to make our prayer
As to the man of all men best in adversity
And wisest in the ways of God. You saved
    us
From the Sphinx, that flinty singer, and the
    tribute
We paid to her so long; yet you were
    never         40
Better informed than we, nor could we teach
    you:
It was some god breathed in you to set us
    free.

Therefore, O mighty King, we turn to you:
Find us our safety, find us a remedy,
Whether by counsel of the gods or men.   45
A king of wisdom tested in the past
Can act in a time of troubles, and act well.
Noblest of men, restore
Life to your city! Think how all men call you
Liberator for your triumph long ago;   50
Ah, when your years of kingship are remem-
    bered,
Let them not say We rose, but later fell—
Keep the State from going down in the storm!
Once, years ago, with happy augury,
You brought us fortune; be the same
    again!       55
No man questions your power to rule the
    land:
But rule over men, not over a dead city!
Ships are only hulls, citadels are nothing,
When no life moves in the empty passage-
    ways.
    OEDIPUS. Poor children! You may be sure
    I know      60
All that you longed for in your coming here.
I know that you are deathly sick; and yet,
Sick as you are, not one is as sick as I.
Each of you suffers in himself alone
His anguish, not another's; but my spirit   65
Groans for the city, for myself, for you.

I was not sleeping, you are not waking me.
No, I have been in tears for a long while
And in my restless thought walked many
    ways.
In all my search, I found one helpful
    course,     70

And that I have taken: I have sent Creon,
Son of Menoikeus, brother of the Queen,
To Delphi, Apollo's place of revelation,
To learn there, if he can,
What act or pledge of mine may save the
    city.     75
I have counted the days, and now, this very
    day,
I am troubled, for he has overstayed his time.
What is he doing? He has been gone too long.
Yet whenever he comes back, I should do ill
To scant whatever hint the god may give.   80
    PRIEST. It is a timely promise. At this
    instant
They tell me Creon is here.
    OEDIPUS.         O Lord Apollo!
May his news be fair as his face is radiant!
    PRIEST. It could not be otherwise: he is
    crowned with bay,
The chaplet is thick with berries.
    OEDIPUS.       We shall soon know;   85
He is near enough to hear us now.
            (Enter CREON.)
                       O Prince:
Brother: son of Menoikeus:
What answer do you bring us from the god?
    CREON. It is favorable. I can tell you, great
    afflictions
Will turn out well, if they are taken well.   90
    OEDIPUS. What was the oracle? These vague
    words
Leave me still hanging between hope and
    fear.
    CREON. Is it your pleasure to hear me with
    all these
Gathered around us? I am prepared to speak,
But should we not go in?
    OEDIPUS.       Let them all hear it.   95
It is for them I suffer, more than for myself.
    CREON. Then I will tell you what I heard
    at Delphi.

In plain words
The god commands us to expel from the land
    of Thebes
An old defilement that it seems we shel-
    ter.     100
It is a deathly thing, beyond expiation.
We must not let it feed upon us longer.
    OEDIPUS. What defilement? How shall we
    rid ourselves of it?

CREON. By exile or death, blood for blood.
It was
Murder that brought the plague-wind on the
city.                                              105
OEDIPUS. Murder of whom? Surely the god
has named him?
CREON. My lord: long ago Laïos was our
king,
Before you came to govern us.
OEDIPUS.                    I know;
I learned of him from others; I never saw
him.
CREON. He was murdered; and Apollo
commands us now                          110
To take revenge upon whoever killed him.
OEDIPUS. Upon whom? Where are they?
Where shall we find a clue
To solve that crime, after so many years?
CREON. Here in this land, he said.
                                If we make enquiry,
We may touch things that otherwise escape
us.                                               115
OEDIPUS. Tell me: Was Laïos murdered in
his house,
Or in the fields, or in some foreign country?
CREON. He said he planned to make a pil-
grimage.
He did not come home again.
OEDIPUS.                  And was there no one,
No witness, no companion, to tell what hap-
pened?                                           120
CREON. They were all killed but one, and
he got away
So frightened that he could remember one
thing only.
OED. What was that one thing? One may
be the key
To everything, if we resolve to use it.
CREON. He said that a band of highway-
men attacked them,                         125
Outnumbered them, and overwhelmed the
King.
OEDIPUS. Strange, that a highwayman
should be so daring—
Unless some faction here bribed him to do it.
CREON. We thought of that. But after
Laïos' death
New troubles arose and we had no
avenger.                                         130
OEDIPUS. What troubles could prevent your
hunting down the killers?

CREON. The riddling Sphinx's song
Made us deaf to all mysteries but her own.
OEDIPUS. Then once more I must bring
what is dark to light.
It is most fitting that Apollo shows,      135
As you do, this compunction for the dead.
You shall see how I stand by you, as I should,
To avenge the city and the city's god,
And not as though it were for some distant
friend,
But for my own sake, to be rid of evil.    140
Whoever killed King Laïos might—who
knows?—
Decide at any moment to kill me as well.
By avenging the murdered king I protect
myself.
Come, then, my children: leave the altar
steps,
Lift up your olive boughs!
                              One of you go  145
And summon the people of Kadmos to
gather here.
I will do all that I can; you may tell them
that.
                              (*Exit a* PAGE.)
So, with the help of God,
We shall be saved—or else indeed we are lost.
PRIEST. Let us rise, children. It was for this
we came,                                        150
And now the King has promised it himself.
Phoibos has sent us an oracle; may he
descend
Himself to save us and drive out the plague.
(*Exeunt* OEDIPUS *and* CREON *into the palace by
the central door. The* PRIEST *and the* SUPPLIANTS
*disperse R and L. After a short pause the* CHORUS
*enters the orchestra.*)

## PÁRODOS

(STROPHE 1.)
CHORUS. What is the god singing in his
profound
Delphi of gold and shadow?                 155

---

152 *Phoibos* Apollo  154 *strophe* in ancient
Greek theater: 1. (a) the movement of the
chorus in turning from right to left; (b) that
part of the choric song performed during this;
2. in a Pindaric ode, the stanza which is answered by the antistrophe

What oracle for Thebes, the sunwhipped
city?

Fear unjoints me, the roots of my heart tremble.
Now I remember, O Healer, your power,
and wonder:
Will you send doom like a sudden cloud, or
weave it
Like nightfall of the past?                          160

Ah no: be merciful, issue of holy sound:
Dearest to our expectancy: be tender!

(ANTISTROPHE 1.)
Let me pray to Athenê, the immortal daugh-
ter of Zeus,
And to Artemis her sister
Who keeps her famous throne in the market
ring,                                                165
And to Apollo, bowman at the far butts of
heaven—

O gods, descend! Like three streams leap
against
The fires of our grief, the fires of darkness;
Be swift to bring us rest!

As in the old time from the brilliant
house                                                170
Of air you stepped to save us, come again!

(STROPHE 2.)
Now our afflictions have no end,
Now all our stricken host lies down
And no man fights off death with his mind;

The noble plowland bears no grain,          175
And groaning mothers can not bear—

See, how our lives like birds take wing,
Like sparks that fly when a fire soars,
To the shore of the god of evening.

(ANTISTROPHE 2.)
The plague burns on, it is pitiless,          180
Though pallid children laden with death
Lie unwept in the stony ways,

And old gray women by every path
Flock to the strand about the altars

---

164 *Artemis* Apollo's twin sister; goddess of
the moon, wild animals, and hunting

There to strike their breasts and cry          185
Worship of Zeus in wailing prayers:
Be kind, God's golden child!

(STROPHE 3.)
There are no swords in this attack by fire,
No shields, but we are ringed with cries.

Send the besieger plunging from our
homes                                                190
Into the vast sea-room of the Atlantic
Or into the waves that foam eastward of
Thrace—

For the day ravages what the night spares—

Destroy our enemy, lord of the thunder!
Let him be riven by lightning from heav-
en!                                                    195

(ANTISTROPHE 3.)
Phoibos Apollo, stretch the sun's bowstring,
That golden cord, until it sing for us,
Flashing arrows in heaven!
                              Artemis, Huntress,
Race with flaring lights upon our mountains!

O scarlet god, O golden-banded brow,      200
O Theban Bacchos in a storm of Maenads,
          (*Enter* OEDIPUS, *center.*)
Whirl upon Death, that all the Undying
hate!
Come with blinding cressets, come in joy!

## SCENE I

OEDIPUS. Is this your prayer? It may be
answered. Come,
Listen to me, act as the crisis demands,      205
And you shall have relief from all these evils.

Until now I was a stranger to this tale,
As I had been a stranger to the crime.
Could I track down the murderer without
a clue?

---

201 *Bacchos* Dionysus, god of the vine and of
fertility, honored by festivals at which plays
were performed  201 *Maenads* frenzied female
participants in the cult of Dionysus  203 *cressets*
torches

But now, friends,                                        210
As one who became a citizen after the murder,
I make this proclamation to all Thebans:
If any man knows by whose hand Laïos, son
   of Labdakos,
Met his death, I direct that man to tell me
   everything,
No matter what he fears for having so long
   withheld it.                                          215
Let it stand as promised that no further trou-
   ble
Will come to him, but he may leave the land
   in safety.

Moreover: If anyone knows the murderer to
   be foreign,
Let him not keep silent: he shall have his
   reward from me.
However, if he does conceal it; if any
   man                                                   220
Fearing for his friend or for himself disobeys
   this edict,
Hear what I propose to do:

I solemnly forbid the people of this country,
Where power and throne are mine, ever to
   receive that man
Or speak to him, no matter who he is, or let
   him                                                   225
Join in sacrifice, lustration, or in prayer.
I decree that he be driven from every house,
Being, as he is, corruption itself to us: the
   Delphic
Voice of Zeus has pronounced this revelation.
Thus I associate myself with the oracle         230
And take the side of the murdered king.

As for the criminal, I pray to God—
Whether it be a lurking thief, or one of a
   number—
I pray that that man's life be consumed in
   evil and wretchedness.
And as for me, this curse applies no less     235
If it should turn out that the culprit is my
   guest here,
Sharing my hearth.
                    You have heard the penalty.
I lay it on you now to attend to this
For my sake, for Apollo's, for the sick
Sterile city that heaven has abandoned.       240

---

226 *lustration* ceremonial purification

Suppose the oracle had given you no com-
   mand:
Should this defilement go uncleansed for
   ever?
You should have found the murderer: your
   king,
A noble king, had been destroyed!
                                     Now I,
Having the power that he held before me,   245
Having his bed, begetting children there
Upon his wife, as he would have, had he
   lived—
Their son would have been my children's
   brother,
If Laïos had had luck in fatherhood!
(But surely ill luck rushed upon his
   reign)—                                              250
I say I take the son's part, just as though
I were his son, to press the fight for him
And see it won! I'll find the hand that
   brought
Death to Labdakos' and Polydoros' child,
Heir of Kadmos' and Agenor's line.             255
And as for those who fail me,
May the gods deny them the fruit of the
   earth,
Fruit of the womb, and may they rot utterly!
Let them be wretched as we are wretched,
   and worse!

For you, for loyal Thebans, and for all       260
Who find my actions right, I pray the favor
Of justice, and of all the immortal gods.
   CHORAGOS. Since I am under oath, my
      lord, I swear
I did not do the murder, I can not name
The murderer. Might not the oracle            265
That has ordained the search tell where to
   find him?
   OEDIPUS. An honest question. But no man
      in the world
Can make the gods do more than the gods
   will.
   CHORAGOS. There is one last expedient—
   OEDIPUS.                     Tell me what it is.
Though it seem slight, you must not hold it
   back.                                                270
   CHORAGOS. A lord clairvoyant to the lord
      Apollo,

---

263 Stage direction: *Choragos* the leader of the
chorus

As we all know, is the skilled Teiresias.
One might learn much about this from him,
Oedipus.
  OEDIPUS. I am not wasting time:
Creon spoke of this, and I have sent for
him—                                                      275
Twice, in fact; it is strange that he is not
here.
  CHORAGOS. The other matter—that old
report—seems useless.
  OEDIPUS. Tell me. I am interested in all
reports.
  CHORAGOS. The King was said to have
been killed by highwaymen.
  OEDIPUS. I know. But we have no witnesses
to that.                                                     280
  CHORAGOS. If the killer can feel a particle
of dread,
Your curse will bring him out of hiding!
  OEDIPUS.                                      No.
The man who dared that act will fear no
curse.
  (Enter the blind seer TEIRESIAS, led by a PAGE.)
  CHORAGOS. But there is one man who may
detect the criminal.
This is Teiresias, this is the holy prophet   285
In whom, alone of all men, truth was born.
  OEDIPUS. Teiresias: seer: student of mys-
teries,
Of all that's taught and all that no man
tells,
Secrets of Heaven and secrets of the earth:
Blind though you are, you know the city
lies                                                          290
Sick with plague; and from this plague, my
lord,
We find that you alone can guard or save us.

Possibly you did not hear the messengers?
Apollo, when we sent to him,
Sent us back word that this great pes-
tilence                                                       295
Would lift, but only if we established clearly
The identity of those who murdered Laïos.
They must be killed or exiled.
                              Can you use
Birdflight or any art of divination
To purify yourself, and Thebes, and me   300
From this contagion? We are in your hands.
There is no fairer duty

Than that of helping others in distress.
  TEIRESIAS. How dreadful knowledge of the
truth can be
When there's no help in truth! I knew this
well,                                                         305
But did not act on it: else I should not have
come.
  OEDIPUS. What is troubling you? Why are
your eyes so cold?
  TEIRESIAS. Let me go home. Bear your own
fate, and I'll
Bear mine. It is better so: trust what I say.
  OEDIPUS. What you say is ungracious and
unhelpful                                          ·        310
To your native country. Do not refuse to
speak.
  TEIRESIAS. When it comes to speech, your
own is neither temperate
Nor opportune. I wish to be more prudent.
  OEDIPUS. In God's name, we all beg you—
  TEIRESIAS.              You are all ignorant.
No; I will never tell you what I know.       315
Now it is my misery; then, it would be yours.
  OEDIPUS. What! You do know something,
and will not tell us?
You would betray us all and wreck the State?
  TEIRESIAS. I do not intend to torture myself,
or you.
Why persist in asking? You will not persuade
me.                                                           320
  OEDIPUS. What a wicked old man you are!
You'd try a stone's
Patience! Out with it! Have you no feeling
at all?
  TEIRESIAS. You call me unfeeling. If you
could only see
The nature of your own feelings . . .
  OEDIPUS.                                      Why,
Who would not feel as I do? Who could
endure                                                       325
Your arrogance toward the city?
  TEIRESIAS.                    What does it matter!
Whether I speak or not, it is bound to
come.
  OEDIPUS. Then, if "it" is bound to come,
you are bound to tell me.
  TEIRESIAS. No, I will not go on. Rage as
you please.
  OEDIPUS. Rage? Why not!
          And I'll tell you what I think:   330

You planned it, you had it done, you all but
Killed him with your own hands: if you had
eyes,
I'd say the crime was yours, and yours alone.
TEIRESIAS. So? I charge you, then,
Abide by the proclamation you have
made:    335
From this day forth
Never speak again to these men or to me;
You yourself are the pollution of this coun-
try.
OEDIPUS. You dare say that! Can you pos-
sibly think you have
Some way of going free, after such insol-
ence?    340
TEIRESIAS. I have gone free. It is the truth
sustains me.
OEDIPUS. Who taught you shamelessness?
It was not your craft.
TEIRESIAS. You did. You made me speak.
I did not want to.
OEDIPUS. Speak what? Let me hear it again
more clearly.
TEIRESIAS. Was it not clear before? Are you
tempting me?    345
OEDIPUS. I did not understand it. Say it
again.
TEIRESIAS. I say that you are the murderer
whom you seek.
OEDIPUS. Now twice you have spat out
infamy. You'll pay for it!
TEIRESIAS. Would you care for more? Do
you wish to be really angry?
OEDIPUS. Say what you will. Whatever you
say is worthless.    350
TEIRESIAS. I say that you live in hideous
love with her
Who is nearest you in blood. You are blind
to the evil.
OEDIPUS. It seems you can go on mouthing
like this for ever.
TEIRESIAS. I can, if there is power in truth.
OEDIPUS.             There is:
But not for you, not for you,    355
You sightless, witless, senseless, mad old
man!
TEIRESIAS. You are the madman. There is
no one here
Who will not curse you soon, as you curse
me.

OEDIPUS. You child of endless night!
You can not hurt me
Or any other man who sees the sun.    360
TEIRESIAS. True: it is not from me your
fate will come.
That lies within Apollo's competence,
As it is his concern.
OEDIPUS.           Tell me:
Are you speaking for Creon, or for yourself?
TEIRESIAS. Creon is no threat. You weave
your own doom.    365
OEDIPUS. Wealth, power, craft of states-
manship!
Kingly position, everywhere admired!
What savage envy is stored up against these,
If Creon, whom I trusted, Creon my friend,
For this great office which the city once    370
Put in my hands unsought—if for this power
Creon desires in secret to destroy me!

He has bought this decrepit fortune-teller,
this
Collector of dirty pennies, this prophet
fraud—
Why, he is no more clairvoyant than I am!
                  Tell us:    375
Has your mystic mummery ever approached
the truth?
When that hellcat the Sphinx was performing
here,
What help were you to these people?
Her magic was not for the first man who
came along:
It demanded a real exorcist. Your birds—    380
What good were they? or the gods, for the
matter of that?
But I came by,
Oedipus, the simple man, who knows noth-
ing—
I thought it out for myself, no birds helped
me!
And this is the man you think you can des-
troy,    385
That you may be close to Creon when he's
king!
Well, you and your friend Creon, it seems
to me,
Will suffer most. If you were not an old man,
You would have paid already for your
plot.

CHORAGOS. We can not see that his words or yours          390
Have been spoken except in anger, Oedipus,
And of anger we have no need. How can God's will
Be accomplished best? That is what most concerns us.

TEIRESIAS. You are a king. But where argument's concerned
I am your man, as much a king as you.          395
I am not your servant, but Apollo's.
I have no need of Creon to speak for me.

Listen to me. You mock my blindness, do you?
But I say that you, with both your eyes, are blind:
You can not see the wretchedness of your life,          400
Nor in whose house you live, no, nor with whom.
Who are your father and mother? Can you tell me?
You do not even know the blind wrongs
That you have done them, on earth and in the world below.
But the double lash of your parents' curse will whip you          405
Out of this land some day, with only night
Upon your precious eyes.
Your cries then—where will they not be heard?
What fastness of Kithairon will not echo them?
And that bridal-descant of yours—you'll know it then,          410
The song they sang when you came here to Thebes
And found your misguided berthing.
All this, and more, that you can not guess at now,
Will bring you to yourself among your children.
Be angry, then. Curse Creon. Curse my words.          415
I tell you, no man that walks upon the earth
Shall be rooted out more horribly than you.

---

409 *Kithairon* a mountain in Boeotia

OEDIPUS. Am I to bear this from him?—
Damnation
Take you! Out of this place! Out of my sight!

TEIRESIAS. I would not have come at all if you had not asked me.          420

OEDIPUS. Could I have told that you'd talk nonsense, that
You'd come here to make a fool of yourself, and of me?

TEIRESIAS. A fool? Your parents thought me sane enough.

OEDIPUS. My parents again!—Wait: who were my parents?

TEIRESIAS. This day will give you a father, and break your heart.          425

OEDIPUS. Your infantile riddles! Your damned abracadabra!

TEIRESIAS. You were a great man once at solving riddles.

OEDIPUS. Mock me with that if you like; you will find it true.

TEIRESIAS. It was true enough. It brought about your ruin.

OEDIPUS. But if it saved this town?
                              (*To the* PAGE.)
TEIRESIAS. Boy, give me your hand.          430
OEDIPUS. Yes, boy; lead him away
                    —While you are here
We can do nothing. Go; leave us in peace.

TEIRESIAS. I will go when I have said what I have to say.
How can you hurt me? And I tell you again:
The man you have been looking for all this time,          435
The damned man, the murderer of Laïos,
That man is in Thebes. To your mind he is foreign-born,
But it will soon be shown that he is a Theban,
A revelation that will fail to please.
                    A blind man,
Who has his eyes now; a penniless man, who is rich now;          440
And he will go tapping the strange earth with his staff.
To the children with whom he lives now he will be
Brother and father—the very same; to her
Who bore him, son and husband—the very same

Who came to his father's bed, wet with his
father's blood.                                    445
Enough. Go think that over.
If later you find error in what I have said,
You may say that I have no skill in prophecy.
(*Exit* TEIRESIAS, *led by his* PAGE. OEDIPUS *goes
into the palace.*)

## ODE I

(STROPHE 1.)
CHORUS. The Delphic stone of prophe-
cies
Remembers ancient regicide                         450
And a still bloody hand.
That killer's hour of flight has come.
He must be stronger than riderless
Coursers of untiring wind,
For the son of Zeus armed with his father's
thunder                                            455
Leaps in lightning after him;
And the Furies follow him, the sad Furies.

(ANTISTROPHE 1.)
Holy Parnassos' peak of snow
Flashes and blinds that secret man,
That all shall hunt him down:                      460
Though he may roam the forest shade
Like a bull gone wild from pasture
To rage through glooms of stone.
Doom comes down on him; flight will not
avail him;
For the world's heart calls him desolate,          465
And the immortal Furies follow, for ever fol-
low.

(STROPHE 2.)
But now a wilder thing is heard
From the old man skilled at hearing Fate in
the wingbeat of a bird.
Bewildered as a blown bird, my soul hovers
and can not find
Foothold in this debate, or any reason or rest
of mind.                                           470
But no man ever brought—none can bring
Proof of strife between Thebes' royal house,

---

457 *Furies* three female divinities (Alecto, Tisi-
phone, and Megaera) who punished doers of
unavenged crimes   458 *Parnassos* sacred mountain
at Delphi

Labdakos' line, and the son of Polybos;
And never until now has any man brought
word
Of Laïos' dark death staining Oedipus the
King.                                              475

(ANTISTROPHE 2.)
Divine Zeus and Apollo hold
Perfect intelligence alone of all tales ever
told;
And well though this diviner works, he works
in his own night;
No man can judge that rough unknown or
trust in second sight,
For wisdom changes hands among the
wise.                                              480
Shall I believe my great lord criminal
At a raging word that a blind old man let
fall?
I saw him, when the carrion woman faced
him of old,
Prove his heroic mind! These evil words are
lies.

## SCENE II

(*Enter* CREON)
CREON. Men of Thebes:                              485
I am told that heavy accusations
Have been brought against me by King
Oedipus.

I am not the kind of man to bear this tamely.

If in these present difficulties
He holds me accountable for any harm to
him                                                490
Through anything I have said or done—
why, then,
I do not value life in this dishonor.
It is not as though this rumor touched upon
Some private indiscretion. The matter is
grave.
The fact is that I am being called disloyal     495
To the State, to my fellow citizens, to my
friends.
    CHORAGOS. He may have spoken in anger,
    not from his mind.
    CREON. But did you not hear him say I was
    the one

---

474 Cf. ll. 255–6, 733   483 *carrion woman* sphinx

Who seduced the old prophet into lying?

CHORAGOS. The thing was said; I do not
know how seriously.                          500

CREON. But you were watching him!
Were his eyes steady?
Did he look like a man in his right mind?

CHORAGOS.                    I do not know.
I can not judge the behavior of great men.
But here is the King himself.

(*Enter* OEDIPUS.)

OEDIPUS.            So you dared come back.
Why? How brazen of you to come to my
house,                                        505
You murderer!

Do you think I do not know
That you plotted to kill me, plotted to steal
my throne?
Tell me, in God's name: am I coward, a fool,
That you should dream you could accom-
plish this?
A fool who could not see your slippery
game?                                         510
A coward, not to fight back when I saw it?
You are the fool, Creon, are you not? hoping
Without support or friends to get a throne?
Thrones may be won or bought: you could
do neither.

CREON. Now listen to me. You have talked;
let me talk, too.                             515
You can not judge unless you know the facts.

OEDIPUS. You speak well: there is one fact;
but I find it hard
To learn from the deadliest enemy I have.

CREON. That above all I must dispute with
you.

OEDIPUS. That above all I will not hear
you deny.                                     520

CREON. If you think there is anything good
in being stubborn
Against all reason, then I say you are wrong.

OEDIPUS. If you think a man can sin
against his own kind
And not be punished for it, I say you are
mad.

CREON. I agree. But tell me: what have I
done to you?                                  525

OEDIPUS. You advised me to send for that
wizard, did you not?

CREON. I did. I should do it again.

OEDIPUS.            Very well. Now tell me:
How long has it been since Laïos—

CREON.                    What of Laïos?

OEDIPUS. Since he vanished in that onset
by the road?

CREON. It was long ago, a long time.

OEDIPUS.            And this prophet,     530
Was he practicing here then?

CREON.    He was; and with honor, as now.

OEDIPUS. Did he speak of me at that time?

CREON.                    He never did;
At least, not when I was present.

OEDIPUS.            But . . . the enquiry?
I suppose you held one?

CREON. We did, but we learned nothing.

OEDIPUS. Why did the prophet not speak
against me then?                              535

CREON. I do not know; and I am the kind
of man
Who holds his tongue when he has no facts
to go on.

OEDIPUS. There's one fact that you know,
and you could tell it.

CREON. What fact is that? If I know it, you
shall have it.

OEDIPUS. If he were not involved with you,
he could not say                              540
That it was I who murdered Laïos.

CREON. If he says that, you are the one
that knows it!—
But now it is my turn to question you.

OEDIPUS. Put your questions. I am no murderer.

CREON. First, then: You married my sister?

OEDIPUS.        I married your sister.     545

CREON. And you rule the kingdom equally
with her?

OEDIPUS. Everything that she wants she has
from me.

CREON. And I am the third, equal to both
of you?

OEDIPUS. That is why I call you a bad
friend.

CREON. No. Reason it out, as I have
done.                                         550
Think of this first: Would any sane man
prefer
Power, with all a king's anxieties,
To that same power and the grace of sleep?
Certainly not I.
I have never longed for the king's power—
only his rights.                              555
Would any wise man differ from me in this?
As matters stand, I have my way in everything

With your consent, and no responsibilities.
If I were king, I should be a slave to policy.
How could I desire a scepter more   560
Than what is now mine—untroubled influence?
No, I have not gone mad; I need no honors,
Except those with the perquisites I have now.
I am welcome everywhere; every man salutes me,
And those who want your favor seek my ear,   565
Since I know how to manage what they ask.
Should I exchange this ease for that anxiety?
Besides, no sober mind is treasonable.
I hate anarchy
And never would deal with any man who likes it.   570

Test what I have said. Go to the priestess
At Delphi, ask if I quoted her correctly.
And as for this other thing: if I am found
Guilty of treason with Teiresias,
Then sentence me to death! You have my word   575
It is a sentence I should cast my vote for—
But not without evidence!
              You do wrong
When you take good men for bad, bad men for good.
A true friend thrown aside—why, life itself
Is not more precious!
        In time you will know this well:  580
For time, and time alone, will show the just man,
Though scoundrels are discovered in a day.
    CHORAGOS. This is well said, and a prudent man would ponder it.
Judgments too quickly formed are dangerous.
    OEDIPUS. But is he not quick in his duplicity?  585
And shall I not be quick to parry him?
Would you have me stand still, hold my peace, and let
This man win everything, through my inaction?
    CREON. And you want—what is it, then?
To banish me?
    OEDIPUS. No, not exile. It is your death I want,  590

So that all the world may see what treason means.
    CREON. You will persist, then? You will not believe me?
    OEDIPUS. How can I believe you?
    CREON.           Then you are a fool.
    OEDIPUS. To save myself?
    CREON.         In justice, think of me.
    OEDIPUS. You are evil incarnate.
    CREON.      But suppose that you are wrong?  595
    OEDIPUS. Still I must rule.
    CREON.      But not if you rule badly.
    OEDIPUS. O city, city!
    CREON.         It is my city, too!
    CHORAGOS. Now, my lords, be still. I see the Queen,
Iocastê, coming from her palace chambers;
And it is time she came, for the sake of you both.  600
This dreadful quarrel can be resolved through her.
         (*Enter* IOCASTÊ.)
    IOCASTÊ. Poor foolish men, what wicked din is this?
With Thebes sick to death, is it not shameful
That you should rake some private quarrel up?
             (*To* OEDIPUS.)
Come into the house.
      —And you, Creon, go now: 605
Let us have no more of this tumult over nothing.
    CREON. Nothing? No, sister: what your husband plans for me
Is one of two great evils: exile or death.
    OEDIPUS. He is right.
    Why, woman I have caught him squarely
Plotting against my life.
    CREON.      No! Let me die 610
Accurst if ever I have wished you harm!
    IOCASTÊ. Ah, believe it, Oedipus!
In the name of the gods, respect this oath of his
For my sake, for the sake of these people here!

              (STROPHE 1.)
    CHORAGOS. Open your mind to her, my lord. Be ruled by her, I beg you!  615

OEDIPUS. What would you have me do?

CHORAGOS. Respect Creon's word. He has never spoken like a fool,

And now he has sworn an oath.

OEDIPUS. You know what you ask?

CHORAGOS. I do.

OEDIPUS. Speak on, then.

CHORAGOS. A friend so sworn should not be baited so, 620

In blind malice, and without final proof.

OEDIPUS. You are aware, I hope, that what you say

Means death for me, or exile at the least.

(STROPHE 2.)

CHORAGOS. No, I swear by Helios, first in Heaven!

May I die friendless and accurst, 625

The worst of deaths, if ever I meant that!

It is the withering fields

That hurt my sick heart:

Must we bear all these ills,

And now your bad blood as well? 630

OEDIPUS. Then let him go. And let me die, if I must,

Or be driven by him in shame from the land of Thebes.

It is your unhappiness, and not his talk,

That touches me.

As for him—

Wherever he is, I will hate him as long as I live. 635

CREON. Ugly in yielding, as you were ugly in rage!

Natures like yours chiefly torment themselves.

OEDIPUS. Can you not go? Can you not leave me?

CREON. I can.

You do not know me; but the city knows me,

And in its eyes I am just, if not in yours. 640

(Exit CREON.)

(ANTISTROPHE 1.)

CHORAGOS. Lady Iocastê, did you not ask the King to go to his chambers?

IOCASTÊ. First tell me what has happened.

CHORAGOS. There was suspicion without evidence; yet it rankled

As even false charges will.

IOCASTÊ. On both sides?

CHORAGOS. On both.

IOCASTÊ. But what was said?

CHORAGOS. Oh let it rest, let it be done with! 645

Have we not suffered enough?

OEDIPUS. You see to what your decency has brought you:

You have made difficulties where my heart saw none.

(ANTISTROPHE 2.)

CHORAGOS. Oedipus, it is not once only I have told you— 650

You must know I should count myself unwise

To the point of madness, should I now forsake you—

You, under whose hand,

In the storm of another time,

Our dear land sailed out free. 655

But now stand fast at the helm!

IOCASTÊ. In God's name, Oedipus, inform your wife as well:

Why are you so set in this hard anger?

OEDIPUS. I will tell you, for none of these men deserves

My confidence as you do. It is Creon's work, 660

His treachery, his plotting against me.

IOCASTÊ. Go on, if you can make this clear to me.

OEDIPUS. He charges me with the murder of Laïos.

IOCASTÊ. Has he some knowledge? Or does he speak from hearsay?

OEDIPUS. He would not commit himself to such a charge, 665

But he has brought in that damnable soothsayer

To tell his story.

IOCASTÊ. Set your mind at rest.

If it is a question of soothsayers, I tell you

That you will find no man whose craft gives knowledge

Of the unknowable.

Here is my proof: 670

An oracle was reported to Laïos once

(I will not say from Phoibos himself, but from

His appointed ministers, at any rate)

That his doom would be death at the hands of his own son—

His son, born of his flesh and of mine! 675

Now, you remember the story: Laïos was
  killed
By marauding strangers where three highways meet;
But his child had not been three days in this
  world
Before the King had pierced the baby's
  ankles
And had him left to die on a lonely mountain.            680

Thus, Apollo never caused that child
To kill his father, and it was not Laïos' fate
To die at the hands of his son, as he had
  feared.
This is what prophets and prophecies are
  worth!
Have no dread of them.
                It is God himself  685
Who can show us what he wills, in his own
  way.
  OEDIPUS. How strange a shadowy memory
  crossed my mind,
Just now while you were speaking; it chilled
  my heart.
  IOCASTÊ. What do you mean? What
  memory do you speak of?
  OEDIPUS. If I understand you, Laïos was
  killed                  690
At a place where three roads meet.
  IOCASTÊ.            So it was said;
We have no later story.
  OEDIPUS.         Where did it happen?
  IOCASTÊ. Phokis, it is called: at a place
  where the Theban Way
Divides into the roads toward Delphi and
  Daulia.
  OEDIPUS. When?
  IOCASTÊ.      We had the news not long
  before you came           695
And proved the right to your succession here.
  OEDIPUS. Ah, what net has God been weav-
  ing for me?
  IOCASTÊ. Oedipus! Why does this trouble
  you?
  OEDIPUS.          Do not ask me yet.
First, tell me how Laïos looked, and tell me
How old he was.
  IOCASTÊ.     He was tall, his hair just
  touched               700
With white; his form was not unlike your own.

  OEDIPUS. I think that I myself may be
  accurst
By my own ignorant edict.
  IOCASTÊ.          You speak strangely.
It makes me tremble to look at you, my
  King.
  OEDIPUS. I am not sure that the blind man
  can not see.           705
But I should know better if you were to tell
  me—
  IOCASTÊ. Anything—though I dread to
  hear you ask it.
  OEDIPUS. Was the King lightly escorted, or
  did he ride
With a large company, as a ruler should?
  IOCASTÊ. There were five men with him in
  all: one was a herald;      710
And a single chariot, which he was driving.
  OEDIPUS. Alas, that makes it plain enough!
                       But who—
Who told you how it happened?
  IOCASTÊ.         A household servant,
The only one to escape.
  OEDIPUS.         And is he still
A servant of ours?
  IOCASTÊ.       No; for when he came
  back at last           715
And found you enthroned in the place of the
  dead king,
He came to me, touched my hand with his,
  and begged
That I would send him away to the frontier
  district
Where only the shepherds go—
As far away from the city as I could send
  him.            720
I granted his prayer; for although the man
  was a slave,
He had earned more than this favor at my
  hands.
  OEDIPUS. Can he be called back quickly?
  IOCASTÊ.                   Easily.
But why?
  OEDIPUS.     I have taken too much upon
  myself
Without enquiry; therefore I wish to con-
  sult him.           725
  IOCASTÊ. Then he shall come.
                    But am I not one also
To whom you might confide these fears of
  yours?

OEDIPUS. That is your right; it will not be denied you,
Now least of all; for I have reached a pitch
Of wild foreboding. Is there anyone          730
To whom I should sooner speak?

Polybos of Corinth is my father.
My mother is a Dorian: Meropê.
I grew up chief among the men of Corinth
Until a strange thing happened—          735
Not worth my passion, it may be, but strange.

At a feast, a drunken man maundering in his cups
Cries out that I am not my father's son!

I contained myself that night, though I felt anger
And a sinking heart. The next day I visited          740
My father and mother, and questioned them. They stormed,
Calling it all the slanderous rant of a fool;
And this relieved me. Yet the suspicion
Remained always aching in my mind;
I knew there was talk; I could not rest;   745
And finally, saying nothing to my parents,
I went to the shrine at Delphi.

The god dismissed my question without reply;
He spoke of other things.
                              Some were clear,
Full of wretchedness, dreadful, unbear-
able:          750
As, that I should lie with my own mother, breed
Children from whom all men would turn their eyes;
And that I should be my father's murderer.

I heard all this, and fled. And from that day
Corinth to me was only in the stars          755
Descending in that quarter of the sky,
As I wandered farther and farther on my way
To a land where I should never see the evil
Sung by the oracle. And I came to this country
Where, so you say, King Laïos was killed.   760

I will tell you all that happened there, my lady.

There were three highways
Coming together at a place I passed;
And there a herald came towards me, and a chariot
Drawn by horses, with a man such as you describe          765
Seated in it. The groom leading the horses
Forced me off the road at his lord's com-
mand;
But as this charioteer lurched over towards me
I struck him in my rage. The old man saw me
And brought his double goad down upon my head          770
As I came abreast.
                    He was paid back, and more!
Swinging my club in this right hand I knocked him
Out of his car, and he rolled on the ground.
                              I killed him.

I killed them all.
Now if that stranger and Laïos were—
kin,          775
Where is a man more miserable than I?
More hated by the gods? Citizen and alien alike
Must never shelter me or speak to me—
I must be shunned by all.
                              And I myself
Pronounced this malediction upon my-
self!          780

Think of it: I have touched you with these hands,
These hands that killed your husband. What defilement!

Am I all evil, then? It must be so,
Since I must flee from Thebes, yet never again
See my own countrymen, my own coun-
try,          785
For fear of joining my mother in marriage
And killing Polybos, my father.
                              Ah,

If I was created so, born to this fate,
Who could deny the savagery of God?

O holy majesty of heavenly powers!                790
May I never see that day! Never!
Rather let me vanish from the race of men
Than know the abomination destined me!
  CHORAGOS. We too, my lord, have felt
    dismay at this.
But there is hope: you have yet to hear the
  shepherd.                                       795
  OEDIPUS. Indeed, I fear no other hope is left
    me.
  IOCASTÊ. What do you hope from him
    when he comes?
  OEDIPUS.            This much:
If his account of the murder tallies with
    yours,
Then I am cleared.
  IOCASTÊ.            What was it that I said
Of such importance?
  OEDIPUS. Why, "marauders," you said,  800
Killed the King, according to this man's
    story.
If he maintains that still, if there were several,
Clearly the guilt is not mine: I was alone.
But if he says one man, singlehanded,
    did it,
Then the evidence all points to me.          805
  IOCASTÊ. You may be sure that he said
    there were several;
And can he call back that story now? He
    cán not.
The whole city heard it as plainly as I.
But suppose he alters some detail of it:
He can not ever show that Laïos' death       810
Fulfilled the oracle: for Apollo said
My child was doomed to kill him; and my
    child—
Poor baby!—it was my child that died first.

No. From now on, where oracles are con-
    cerned,
I would not waste a second thought on
    any.                                          815
  OEDIPUS. You may be right.
            But come: let someone go
For the shepherd at once. This matter must
  be settled.
  IOCASTÊ. I will send for him.

I would not wish to cross you in anything,
And surely not in this.—Let us go in.        820
                (*Exeunt into the palace.*)

## ODE II

                            (STROPHE 1.)
  CHORUS. Let me be reverent in the ways
    of right,
Lowly the paths I journey on;
Let all my words and actions keep
The laws of the pure universe
From highest Heaven handed down.              825
For Heaven is their bright nurse,
Those generations of the realms of light;
Ah, never of mortal kind were they begot,
Nor are they slaves of memory, lost in sleep:
Their Father is greater than Time, and ages
    not.                                         830

                            (ANTISTROPHE 1.)
The tyrant is a child of Pride
Who drinks from his great sickening cup
Recklessness and vanity,
Until from his high crest headlong
He plummets to the dust of hope.              835
That strong man is not strong.
But let no fair ambition be denied;
May God protect the wrestler for the State
In government, in comely policy,
Who will fear God, and on His ordinance
    wait.                                        840

                            (STROPHE 2.)
Haughtiness and the high hand of disdain
Tempt and outrage God's holy law;
And any mortal who dares hold
No immortal Power in awe
Will be caught up in a net of pain:           845
The price for which his levity is sold.
Let each man take due earnings, then,
And keep his hands from holy things,
And from blasphemy stand apart—
Else the crackling blast of heaven            850
Blows on his head, and on his desperate
    heart;
Though fools will honor impious men,
In their cities no tragic poet sings.

                            (ANTISTROPHE 2.)
Shall we lose faith in Delphi's obscurities,
We who have heard the world's core          855

Discredited, and the sacred wood
Of Zeus at Elis praised no more?
The deeds and the strange prophecies
Must make a pattern yet to be understood.
Zeus, if indeed you are lord of all,          860
Throned in light over night and day,
Mirror this in your endless mind:
Our masters call the oracle
Words on the wind, and the Delphic vision
     blind!
Their hearts no longer know Apollo,        865
And reverence for the gods has died away.


## SCENE III

*(Enter* IOCASTÊ.*)*

IOCASTÊ. Princes of Thebes, it has occurred
     to me
To visit the altars of the gods, bearing
These branches as a suppliant, and this in-
     cense.
Our King is not himself: his noble soul     870
Is overwrought with fantasies of dread,
Else he would consider
The new prophecies in the light of the old.
He will listen to any voice that speaks disas-
     ter,
And my advice goes for nothing.            875
          *(She approaches the altar, R.)*
          To you, then, Apollo,
Lycean lord, since you are nearest, I turn in
     prayer.

Receive these offerings, and grant us deliver-
     ance
From defilement. Our hearts are heavy with
     fear
When we see our leader distracted, as help-
     less sailors
Are terrified by the confusion of their helms-
     man.                                     880
          *(Enter* MESSENGER.*)*
MESSENGER. Friends, no doubt you can
     direct me:
Where shall I find the house of Oedipus,
Or, better still, where is the King himself?
     CHORAGOS. It is this very place, stranger;
     he is inside.
This is his wife and mother of his child-
     ren.                                      885

MESSENGER. I wish her happiness in a happy
     house,
Blest in all the fulfillment of her marriage.
     IOCASTÊ. I wish as much for you: your
     courtesy
Deserves a like good fortune. But now, tell
     me:
Why have you come? What have you to say
     to us?                                    890
     MESSENGER. Good news, my lady, for your
     house and your husband.
     IOCASTÊ. What news? Who sent you here?
     MESSENGER.                I am from Corinth.
The news I bring ought to mean joy for
     you,
Though it may be you will find some grief
     in it.
     IOCASTÊ. What is it? How can it touch us
     in both ways?                             895
     MESSENGER. The people of Corinth, they
     say,
Intend to call Oedipus to be their king.
     IOCASTÊ. But old Polybos—is he not reign-
     ing still?
     MESSENGER. No. Death holds him in his
     sepulchre.
     IOCASTÊ. What are you saying? Polybos is
     dead?                                     900
     MESSENGER. If I am not telling the truth,
     may I die myself.
     IOCASTÊ. Go in, go quickly; tell this to your
     master.          *(To a* MAIDSERVANT.*)*

O riddlers of God's will, where are you
     now!
This was the man whom Oedipus, long ago,
Feared so, fled so, in dread of destroying
     him—                                      905
But it was another fate by which he died.
          *(Enter* OEDIPUS, *center.)*
     OEDIPUS. Dearest Iocastê, why have you
     sent for me?
     IOCASTÊ. Listen to what this man says, and
     then tell me
What has become of the solemn prophecies.
     OEDIPUS. Who is this man? What is his
     news for me?                              910
     IOCASTÊ. He has come from Corinth to an-
     nounce your father's death!
     OEDIPUS. Is it true, stranger? Tell me in
     your own words.

MESSENGER. I can not say it more clearly:
the King is dead.

OEDIPUS. Was it by treason? Or by an attack of illness?

MESSENGER. A little thing brings old men to
their rest.                                    915

OEDIPUS. It was sickness, then?

MESSENGER.        Yes, and his many years.

OEDIPUS. Ah!

Why should a man respect the Pythian
hearth, or

Give heed to the birds that jangle above his
head?

They prophesied that I should kill Polybos,                                          920

Kill my own father; but he is dead and buried,

And I am here—I never touched him, never,

Unless he died of grief for my departure,

And thus, in a sense, through me. No. Polybos

Has packed the oracles off with him under-
gound.                                        925

They are empty words.

IOCASTÊ.            Had I not told you so?

OEDIPUS. You had; it was my faint heart
that betrayed me.

IOCASTÊ. From now on never think of those
things again.

OEDIPUS. And yet—must I not fear my
mother's bed?

IOCASTÊ. Why should anyone in this world
be afraid,                                     930

Since Fate rules us and nothing can be foreseen?

A man should live only for the present day.

Have no more fear of sleeping with your
mother:

How many men, in dreams, have lain with
their mothers!

No reasonable man is troubled by such
things.                                        935

OEDIPUS. That is true; only—

If only my mother were not still alive!

But she is alive. I can not help my dread.

IOCASTÊ. Yet this news of your father's
death is wonderful.

OEDIPUS. Wonderful. But I fear the living
woman.                                         940

MESSENGER. Tell me, who is this woman
that you fear?

OEDIPUS. It is Meropê, man; the wife of
King Polybos.

MESSENGER. Meropê? Why should you be
afraid of her?

OEDIPUS. An oracle of the gods, a dreadful
saying.

MESSENGER. Can you tell me about it or are
you sworn to silence?                          945

OEDIPUS. I can tell you, and I will.

Apollo said through his prophet that I was
the man

Who should marry his own mother, shed his
father's blood

With his own hands. And so, for all these
years

I have kept clear of Corinth, and no harm
has come—                                      950

Though it would have been sweet to see my
parents again.

MESSENGER. And is this the fear that drove
you out of Corinth?

OEDIPUS. Would you have me kill my
father?

MESSENGER.                    As for that

You must be reassured by the news I gave you.

OEDIPUS. If you could reassure me, I would
reward you.                                    955

MESSENGER. I had that in mind, I will confess: I thought

I could count on you when you returned to
Corinth.

OEDIPUS. No: I will never go near my parents again.

MESSENGER. Ah, son, you still do not know
what you are doing—

OEDIPUS. What do you mean? In the name
of God tell me!                                960

MESSENGER. —If these are your reasons for
not going home.

OEDIPUS. I tell you, I fear the oracle may
come true.

MESSENGER. And guilt may come upon you
through your parents?

OEDIPUS. That is the dread that is always
in my heart.

MESSENGER. Can you not see that all your
fears are groundless?                          965

OEDIPUS. How can you say that? They are
my parents, surely?

MESSENGER. Polybos was not your father.

OEDIPUS.                    Not my father?

MESSENGER. No more your father than the man speaking to you.

OEDIPUS. But you are nothing to me!

MESSENGER.              Neither was he.

OEDIPUS. Then why did he call me son?

MESSENGER.              I will tell you: 970 Long ago he had you from my hands, as a gift.

OEDIPUS. Then how could he love me so, if I was not his?

MESSENGER. He had no children, and his heart turned to you.

OEDIPUS. What of you? Did you buy me? Did you find me by chance?

MESSENGER. I came upon you in the crooked pass of Kithairon.          975

OEDIPUS. And what were you doing there?

MESSENGER.              Tending my flocks.

OEDIPUS. A wandering shepherd?

MESSENGER. But your savior, son, that day.

OEDIPUS. From what did you save me?

MESSENGER.   Your ankles should tell you that.

OEDIPUS. Ah, stranger, why do you speak of that childhood pain?

MESSENGER. I cut the bonds that tied your ankles together.          980

OEDIPUS. I have had the mark as long as I can remember.

MESSENGER. That was why you were given the name you bear.

OEDIPUS. God! Was it my father or my mother who did it?
Tell me!

MESSENGER.          I do not know. The man who gave you to me
Can tell you better than I.          985

OEDIPUS. It was not you that found me, but another?

MESSENGER. It was another shepherd gave you to me.

OEDIPUS. Who was he? Can you tell me who he was?

MESSENGER. I think he was said to be one of Laïos' people.

OEDIPUS. You mean the Laïos who was king here years ago?          990

MESSENGER. Yes. King Laïos; and the man was one of his herdsmen.

OEDIPUS. Is he still alive? Can I see him?

MESSENGER.              These men here
Know best about such things.

OEDIPUS.              Does anyone here
Know this shepherd that he is talking about?
Have you seen him in the fields, or in the town?          995
If you have, tell me. It is time things were made plain.

CHORAGOS. I think the man he means is that same shepherd
You have already asked to see. Iocastê perhaps
Could tell you something.

OEDIPUS.              Do you know anything
About him, Lady? Is he the man we have summoned?          1000
Is that the man this shepherd means?

IOCASTÊ.              Why think of him?
Forget this herdsman. Forget it all.
This talk is a waste of time.

OEDIPUS.              How can you say that,
When the clues to my true birth are in my hands?

IOCASTÊ. For God's love, let us have no more questioning!          1005
Is your life nothing to you?
My own is pain enough for me to bear.

OEDIPUS. You need not worry. Suppose my mother a slave,
And born of slaves: no baseness can touch you.

IOCASTÊ. Listen to me, I beg you: do not do this thing!          1010

OEDIPUS. I will not listen; the truth must be made known.

IOCASTÊ. Everything that I say is for your own good!

OEDIPUS.              My own good
Snaps my patience, then; I want none of it.

IOCASTÊ. You are fatally wrong! May you never learn who you are!

OEDIPUS. Go, one of you, and bring the shepherd here.          1015
Let us leave this woman to brag of her royal name.

IOCASTÊ. Ah, miserable!
That is the only word I have for you now.
That is the only word I can ever have.

(*Exit into the palace.*)

---

982 *name you bear* his name means, literally, "swollen foot"

CHORAGOS. Why has she left us, Oedipus?
Why has she gone                                   1020
In such a passion of sorrow? I fear this sil-
ence:
Something dreadful may come of it.
OEDIPUS.                                    Let it come!
However base my birth, I must know about
it.
The Queen, like a woman, is perhaps
ashamed
To think of my low origin. But I              1025
Am a child of Luck; I cannot be dishonored.
Luck is my mother; the passing months, my
brothers,
Have seen me rich and poor.
                               If this is so,
How could I wish that I were someone else?
How could I not be glad to know my
birth?                                            1030

## ODE III

(STROPHE.)

CHORUS. If ever the coming time were
known
To my heart's pondering,
Kithairon, now by Heaven I see the torches
At the festival of the next full moon,
And see the dance, and hear the choir
sing                                              1035
A grace to your gentle shade:
Mountain where Oedipus was found,
O mountain guard of a noble race!
May the god who heals us lend his aid,
And let that glory come to pass               1040
For our king's cradling-ground.

(ANTISTROPHE.)

Of the nymphs that flower beyond the
years,
Who bore you, royal child,
To Pan of the hills or the timberline Apollo,
Cold in delight where the upland clears, 1045
Or Hermês for whom Kyllenê's heights are
piled?
Or flushed as evening cloud,
Great Dionysos, roamer of mountains,
He—was it he who found you there,
And caught you up in his own proud       1050
Arms from the sweet god-ravisher
Who laughed by the Muse's fountains?

## SCENE IV

OEDIPUS. Sirs: though I do not know the
man,
I think I see him coming, this shepherd we
want:
He is old, like our friend here, and the
men                                               1055
Bringing him seem to be servants of my
house.
But you can tell, if you have ever seen him.
(Enter SHEPHERD escorted by servants.)
CHORAGOS. I know him, he was Laïos' man.
You can trust him.
OEDIPUS. Tell me first, you from Corinth:
is this the shepherd
We were discussing?
MESSENGER.     This is the very man.    1060
OEDIPUS. (To SHEPHERD.) Come here. No,
look at me. You must answer
Everything I ask.—You belonged to Laïos?
SHEPHERD. Yes: born his slave, brought up
in his house.
OEDIPUS. Tell me: what kind of work did
you do for him?
SHEPHERD. I was a shepherd of his, most
of my life.                                       1065
OEDIPUS. Where mainly did you go for
pasturage?
SHEPHERD. Sometimes Kithairon, some-
times the hills near-by.
OEDIPUS. Do you remember ever seeing this
man out there?
SHEPHERD. What would he be doing there?
This man?
OEDIPUS. This man standing here. Have
you ever seen him before?                      1070
SHEPHERD. No. At least, not to my recol-
lection.
MESSENGER. And that is not strange, my
lord. But I'll refresh
His memory: he must remember when we
two
Spent three whole seasons together, March
to September,
On Kithairon or thereabouts. He had two
flocks;                                           1075
I had one. Each autumn I'd drive mine
home
And he would go back with his to Laïos'
sheepfold.—

Is this not true, just as I have described it?

SHEPHERD. True, yes; but it was all so long ago.

MESSENGER. Well, then: do you remember, back in those days,                1080

That you gave me a baby boy to bring up as my own?

SHEPHERD. What if I did? What are you trying to say?

MESSENGER. King Oedipus was once that little child.

SHEPHERD. Damn you, hold your tongue!

OEDIPUS.                No more of that!

It is your tongue needs watching, not this man's.                1085

SHEPHERD. My King, my Master, what is it I have done wrong?

OEDIPUS. You have not answered his question about the boy.

SHEPHERD. He does not know. . . . He is only making trouble. . . .

OEDIPUS. Come, speak plainly, or it will go hard with you.

SHEPHERD. In God's name, do not torture an old man!                1090

OEDIPUS. Come here, one of you; bind his arms behind him.

SHEPHERD. Unhappy king! What more do you wish to learn?

OEDIPUS. Did you give this man the child he speaks of?

SHEPHERD.                I did.

And I would to God I had died that very day.

OEDIPUS. You will die now unless you speak the truth.                1095

SHEPHERD. Yet if I speak the truth, I am worse than dead.

OEDIPUS. Very well; since you insist upon delaying—

SHEPHERD. No! I have told you already that I gave him the boy.

OEDIPUS. Where did you get him? From your house? From somewhere else?

SHEPHERD. Not from mine, no. A man gave him to me.                1100

OEDIPUS. Is that man here? Do you know whose slave he was?

SHEPHERD. For God's love, my King, do not ask me any more!

OEDIPUS. You are a dead man if I have to ask you again.

SHEPHERD. Then . . . Then the child was from the palace of Laïos.

OEDIPUS. A slave child? or a child of his own line?                1105

SHEPHERD. Ah, I am on the brink of dreadful speech!

OEDIPUS. And I of dreadful hearing. Yet I must hear.

SHEPHERD. If you must be told, then . . .

                They said it was Laïos' child;

But it is your wife who can tell you about that.

OEDIPUS. My wife!—Did she give it to you?

SHEPHERD.                My lord, she did.                1110

OEDIPUS. Do you know why?

SHEPHERD.                I was told to get rid of it.

OEDIPUS. An unspeakable mother!

SHEPHERD. There had been prophecies . . .

OEDIPUS. Tell me.

SHEPHERD.                It was said that the boy would kill his own father.

OEDIPUS. Then why did you give him over to this old man?

SHEPHERD. I pitied the baby, my King, 1115

And I thought that this man would take him far away

To his own country.

                He saved him—but for what a fate!

For if you are what this man says you are,

No man living is more wretched than Oedipus.

OEDIPUS. Ah God!                1120

It was true!

                All the prophecies!

                —Now,

O Light, may I look on you for the last time!

I, Oedipus,

Oedipus, damned in his birth, in his marriage damned,

Damned in the blood he shed with his own hand!                1125

(*He rushes into the palace.*)


## ODE IV

(STROPHE 1.)

CHORUS. Alas for the seed of men.

What measure shall I give these generations
That breathe on the void and are void
And exist and do not exist?

Who bears more weight of joy          1130
Than mass of sunlight shifting in images,
Or who shall make his thoughts stay on
That down time drifts away?

Your splendor is all fallen.

O naked brow of wrath and tears,          1135
O change of Oedipus!
I who saw your days call no man blest—
Your great days like ghósts góne.

(ANTISTROPHE 1.)
That mind was a strong bow.

Deep, how deep you drew it then, hard
    archer,          1140
At a dim fearful range,
And brought dear glory down!

You overcame the stranger—
The virgin with her hooking lion claws—
And though death sang, stood like a
    tower          1145
To make pale Thebes take heart.

Fortress against our sorrow!

Divine king, giver of laws,
Majestic Oedipus!
No prince in Thebes had ever such
    renown,          1150
No prince won such grace of power.

(STROPHE 2.)
And now of all men ever known
Most pitiful is this man's story:
His fortunes are most changed, his state
Fallen to a low slave's          1155
Ground under bitter fate.

O Oedipus, most royal one!
The great door that expelled you to the
    light
Gave at night—ah, gave night to your
    glory:
As to the father, to the fathering son.          1160

All understood too late.

How could that queen whom Laïos won,
The garden that he harrowed at his height,
Be silent when that act was done?

(ANTISTROPHE 2.)
But all eyes fail before time's eye,          1165
All actions come to justice there.
Though never willed, though far down the
    deep past,
Your bed, your dread sirings,
Are brought to book at last.

Child by Laïos doomed to die,          1170
Then doomed to lose that fortunate little
    death,
Would God you never took breath in this air
That with my wailing lips I take to cry:

For I weep the world's outcast.
Blind I was, and can not tell why;          1175
Asleep, for you had given ease of breath;
A fool, while the false years went by.

## ÉXODOS

(*Enter, from the palace,* SECOND MESSENGER.)
2ND MESSENGER. Elders of Thebes, most
    honored in this land,
What horrors are yours to see and hear,
    what weight
Of sorrow to be endured, if, true to your
    birth,          1180
You venerate the line of Labdakos!
I think neither Istros nor Phasis, those great
    rivers,
Could purify this place of the corruption
It shelters now, or soon must bring to
    light—
Evil not done unconsciously, but willed.    1185

The greatest griefs are those we cause our-
    selves.
    CHORAGOS. Surely, friend, we have grief
    enough already;
What new sorrow do you mean?
    2ND MESSENGER.          The Queen is dead.
    CHORUS. Iocastê? Dead? But at whose
    hand?
    2ND MESSENGER.          Her own.
The full horror of what happened you can
    not know,          1190
For you did not see it; but I, who did, will
    tell you
As clearly as I can how she met her death.

When she had left us,
In passionate silence, passing through the court,
She ran to her apartment in the house,   1195
Her hair clutched by the fingers of both hands.
She closed the doors behind her; then, by that bed
Where long ago the fatal son was conceived—
That son who should bring about his father's death—
We heard her call upon Laïos, dead so many years,   1200
And heard her wail for the double fruit of her marriage,
A husband by her husband, children by her child.

Exactly how she died I do not know:
For Oedipus burst in moaning and would not let us
Keep vigil to the end: it was by him   1205
As he stormed about the room that our eyes were caught.
From one to another of us he went, begging a sword,
Cursing the wife who was not his wife, the mother
Whose womb had carried his own children and himself.
I do not know: it was none of us aided him,   1210
But surely one of the gods was in control!
For with a dreadful cry
He hurled his weight, as though wrenched out of himself,
At the twin doors: the bolts gave, and he rushed in.
And there we saw her hanging, her body swaying   1215
From the cruel cord she had noosed about her neck.
A great sob broke from him, heartbreaking to hear,
As he loosed the rope and lowered her to the ground.

I would blot out from my mind what happened next!

For the King ripped from her gown the golden brooches   1220
That were her ornament, and raised them, and plunged them down
Straight into his own eyeballs, crying, "No more,
No more shall you look on the misery about me,
The horrors of my own doing! Too long you have known
The faces of those whom I should never have seen,   1225
Too long been blind to those for whom I was searching!
From this hour, go in darkness!" And as he spoke,
He struck at his eyes—not once, but many times;
And the blood spattered his beard,
Bursting from his ruined sockets like red hail.   1230

So from the unhappiness of two this evil has sprung,
A curse on the man and woman alike. The old
Happiness of the house of Labdakos
Was happiness enough: where is it today?
It is all wailing and ruin, disgrace, death —all   1235
The misery of mankind that has a name—
And it is wholly and for ever theirs.
   CHORAGOS. Is he in agony still? Is there no rest for him?
   2ND MESSENGER. He is calling for someone to lead him to the gates
So that all the children of Kadmos may look upon   1240
His father's murderer, his mother's—no,
I can not say it!
            And then he will leave Thebes,
Self-exiled, in order that the curse
Which he himself pronounced may depart from the house.
He is weak, and there is none to lead him,   1245
So terrible is his suffering.
            But you will see:
Look, the doors are opening; in a moment
You will see a thing that would crush a heart of stone.

(*The central door is opened;*
OEDIPUS, *blinded, is led in.*)
CHORAGOS. Dreadful indeed for men to see.
Never have my own eyes                    1250
Looked on a sight so full of fear.

Oedipus!
What madness came upon you, what daemon
Leaped on your life with heavier
Punishment than a mortal man can
    bear?                    1255
No; I can not even
Look at you, poor ruined one.
And I would speak, question, ponder,
If I were able. No.
You make me shudder.                    1260
    OEDIPUS. God.        God.
Is there a sorrow greater?
Where shall I find harbor in this world?
My voice is hurled far on a dark wind.
What has God done to me?                    1265
    CHORAGOS. Too terrible to think of, or to see.

(STROPHE 1.)
OEDIPUS. O cloud of night,
Never to be turned away: night coming on,
I can not tell how: night like a shroud!

My fair winds brought me here.
                 O God. Again    1270
The pain of the spikes where I had sight,
The flooding pain
Of memory, never to be gouged out.
    CHORAGOS. This is not strange.
You suffer it all twice over, remorse in
    pain,                    1275
Pain in remorse.

(ANTISTROPHE 1.)
OEDIPUS. Ah dear friend
Are you faithful even yet, you alone?
Are you still standing near me, will you stay
    here,
Patient, to care for the blind?
             The blind man!    1280
Yet even blind I know who it is attends me,
By the voice's tone—
Though my new darkness hide the comforter.
    CHORAGOS. Oh fearful act!
What god was it drove you to rake black    1285
Night across your eyes?

(STROPHE 2.)
OEDIPUS. Apollo. Apollo. Dear
Children, the god was Apollo.
He brought my sick, sick fate upon me.
But the blinding hand was my own!    1290
How could I bear to see
When all my sight was horror everywhere?
    CHORUS. Everywhere; that is true.
    OEDIPUS. And now what is left?
Images? Love? A greeting even,    1295
Sweet to the senses? Is there anything?
Ah, no, friends: lead me away.
Lead me away from Thebes.
             Lead the great wreck
And hell of Oedipus, whom the gods hate.
    CHORUS. Your fate is clear, you are not
    blind to that.                    1300
Would God you had never found it out!

(ANTISTROPHE 2.)
OEDIPUS. Death take the man who un-
    bound
My feet on that hillside
And delivered me from death to life!
    What life?
If only I had died,                    1305
This weight of monstrous doom
Could not have dragged me and my darlings
    down.
    CHORUS. I would have wished the same.
    OEDIPUS. Oh never to have come here
With my father's blood upon me! Never    1310
To have been the man they call his mother's
    husband!
Oh accurst! Oh child of evil,
To have entered that wretched bed—
             the selfsame one!
More primal than sin itself, this fell to me.
    CHORAGOS. I do not know how I can
    answer you.                    1315
You were better dead than alive and blind.
    OEDIPUS. Do not counsel me any more.
    This punishment
That I have laid upon myself is just.
If I had eyes,
I do not know how I could bear the sight    1320
Of my father, when I came to the house of
    Death,
Or my mother: for I have sinned against
    them both

So vilely that I could not make my peace
By strangling my own life.

                 Or do you think my children,
Born as they were born, would be sweet to
   my eyes?                        1325
Ah never, never! Nor this town with its high
   walls,
Nor the holy images of the gods.

                          For I,
Thrice miserable!—Oedipus, noblest of all
   the line
Of Kadmos, have condemned myself to enjoy
These things no more, by my own maledic-
   tion                              1330
Expelling that man whom the gods declared
To be a defilement in the house of Laïos.
After exposing the rankness of my own guilt,
How could I look men frankly in the eyes?
No, I swear it,                     1335
If I could have stifled my hearing at its
   source,
I would have done it and made all this body
A tight cell of misery, blank to light and
   sound:
So I should have been safe in a dark agony
Beyond all recollection.

                   Ah Kithairon!    1340
Why did you shelter me? When I was cast
   upon you,
Why did I not die? Then I should never
Have shown the world my execrable birth.

Ah Polybos! Corinth, city that I believed
The ancient seat of my ancestors: how
   fair                          1345
I seemed, your child! And all the while this
   evil
Was cancerous within me!

                   For I am sick
In my daily life, sick in my origin.

O three roads, dark ravine, woodland and
   way
Where three roads met: you, drinking my
   father's blood,             1350
My own blood, spilled by my own hand:
   can you remember
The unspeakable things I did there, and the
   things
I went on from there to do?

                 O marriage, marriage!

The act that engendered me, and again the
   act
Performed by the son in the same bed—
                  Ah, the net   1355
Of incest, mingling fathers, brothers, sons,
With brides, wives, mothers: the last evil
That can be known by men: no tongue can
   say
How evil!

           No. For the love of God, conceal me
Somewhere far from Thebes; or kill me; or
   hurl me                  1360
Into the sea, away from men's eyes for ever.

Come, lead me. You need not fear to touch
   me.
Of all men, I alone can bear this guilt.
             (*Enter* CREON.)
   CHORAGOS. We are not the ones to decide;
     but Creon here
May fitly judge of what you ask. He only  1365
Is left to protect the city in your place.
   OEDIPUS. Alas, how can I speak to him?
     What right have I
To beg his courtesy whom I have deeply
   wronged?
   CREON. I have not come to mock you,
     Oedipus,
Or to reproach you, either.
                  (*To* ATTENDANTS.)
            —You, standing there:  1370
If you have lost all respect for man's dignity,
At least respect the flame of Lord Helios:
Do not allow this pollution to show itself
Openly here, an affront to the earth
And Heaven's rain and the light of day. No,
   take him              1375
Into the house as quickly as you can.
For it is proper
That only the close kindred see his grief.
   OEDIPUS. I pray you in God's name, since
     your courtesy
Ignores my dark expectation, visiting    1380
With mercy this man of all men most execra-
   ble:
Give me what I ask—for your good, not for
   mine.
   CREON. And what is it that you would
     have me do?
   OEDIPUS. Drive me out of this country as
     quickly as may be

To a place where no human voice can ever
  greet me.                                                   1385
  CREON. I should have done that before
  now—only,
God's will had not been wholly revealed to me.
  OEDIPUS. But his command is plain: the
  parricide
Must be destroyed. I am that evil man.
  CREON.—That is the sense of it, yes; but as
  things are,                                                 1390
We had best discover clearly what is to be
  done.
  OEDIPUS. You would learn more about a
  man like me?
  CREON. You are ready now to listen to the
  god.
  OEDIPUS. I will listen. But it is to you
That I must turn for help. I beg you, hear
  me.                                                         1395

The woman in there—
Give her whatever funeral you think proper:
She is your sister.
                    —But let me go, Creon!
Let me purge my father's Thebes of the pol-
  lution
Of my living here, and go out to the wild
  hills,                                                      1400
To Kithairon, that has won such fame with
  me,
The tomb my mother and father appointed
  for me,
And let me die there, as they willed I should.
And yet I know
Death will not ever come to me through
  sickness                                                    1405
Or in any natural way: I have been preserved
For some unthinkable fate. But let that be.

As for my sons, you need not care for them.
They are men, they will find some way to live.
But my poor daughters, who have shared
  my table,                                                  1410
Who never before have been parted from
  their father—
Take care of them, Creon; do this for me.
And will you let me touch them with my
  hands
A last time, and let us weep together?
Be kind, my lord,                                            1415
Great prince, be kind!

          Could I but touch them,
They would be mine again, as when I had
  my eyes.
  (*Enter* ANTIGONE *and* ISMENE, *attended.*)
Ah, God!
Is it my dearest children I hear weeping?
Has Creon pitied me and sent my daughters?
  CREON. Yes, Oedipus: I knew that they
  were dear to you                                            1421
In the old days, and know you must love
  them still.
  OEDIPUS. May God bless you for this—and
  be a friendlier
Guardian to you than he has been to me!

Children, where are you?                                     1425
Come quickly to my hands: they are your
  brother's—
Hands that have brought your father's once
  clear eyes
To this way of seeing—
                         Ah dearest ones,
I had neither sight nor knowledge then, your
  father
By the woman who was the source of his own
  life!                                                       1430
And I weep for you—having no strength to
  see you—,
I weep for you when I think of the bitterness
That men will visit upon you all your lives.
What homes, what festivals can you attend
Without being forced to depart again in
  tears?                                                      1435
And when you come to marriageable age,
Where is the man, my daughters, who would
  dare
Risk the bane that lies on all my children?
Is there any evil wanting? Your father killed
His father; sowed the womb of her who bore
  him;                                                        1440
Engendered you at the fount of his own exist-
  ence!

That is what they will say of you.

                               Then, whom
Can you ever marry? There are no bride-
  grooms for you,
And your lives must wither away in sterile
  dreaming.

O Creon, son of Menoikeus!                     1445

You are the only father my daughters have,

Since we, their parents, are both of us gone
    for ever.

They are your own blood: you will not let
    them

Fall into beggary and loneliness;

You will keep them from the miseries that
    are mine!                                        1450

Take pity on them; see, they are only child-
    ren,

Friendless except for you. Promise me this,

Great Prince, and give me your hand in token
    of it.

               (CREON *clasps his right hand.*)

Children:

I could say much, if you could understand
    me,                                              1455

But as it is, I have only this prayer for you:

Live where you can, be as happy as you can—

Happier, please God, than God has made
    your father!

    CREON. Enough. You have wept enough.
      Now go within.

    OEDIPUS. I must; but it is hard.

    CREON.         Time eases all things.  1460

    OEDIPUS. But you must promise—

    CREON.         Say what you desire.

    OEDIPUS. Send me from Thebes!

    CREON.         God grant that I may!

    OEDIPUS. But since God hates me . . .

    CREON.      No, he will grant your wish.

    OEDIPUS. You promise?

    CREON.         I can not speak beyond
      my knowledge.

    OEDIPUS. Then lead me in.

    CREON.        Come now, and leave
      your children.                                 1465

    OEDIPUS. No! Do not take them from me!

    CREON.        Think no longer

That you are in command here, but rather
    think

How, when you were, you served your own
    destruction.

    (*Exeunt into the house all but the* CHORUS;
    *the* CHORAGOS *chants directly to the audience.*)

    CHORUS. Men of Thebes: look upon
      Oedipus.

This is the king who solved the famous
    riddle                                            1470

And towered up, most powerful of men.

No mortal eyes but looked on him with envy,

Yet in the end ruin swept over him.

Let every man in mankind's frailty

Consider his last day; and let none          1475

Presume on his good fortune until he find

Life, at his death, a memory without pain.

## Oedipus Rex and Aristotle's Concept of Tragedy

    One passage in Aristotle's *Poetics* has affected critical discussion of tragedy ever since, and, however imperfectly understood, forms the basis of what many people think tragedy should be. In his discussion of the ideal tragedy Aristotle describes the tragic hero as (in Butcher's translation) "a man who is not emi-nently good and just, yet whose misfortune is brought about not by vice or depravity, but by some error or frailty." The last three words are an attempt to encompass the chief possible meanings of *hamartía*, about which scholars are still battling. It is generally interpreted as a moral failing rather than a simple mis-take, and is frequently referred to as the "tragic flaw." If this interpretation is accepted, Aristotle is saying that the ideal kind of hero for tragedy is one who is neither perfect nor vicious, but yet is morally responsible for his downfall. He adds that the hero should be a famous and well-born man like Oedipus or Thyestes. In recent times this last qualification is often brushed aside as an aristocratic prejudice, but the remainder is widely accepted as a tragic norm.

    Did Aristotle, who greatly admired *Oedipus Rex*, think that its hero exemplified his ideal? And if so, was he correct? The answer to the first of these questions

can never be known. The answer to the second is an important part of any interpretation of the play, for if the hero is to some extent a sinner who is punished,
the meaning of the play is not at all the same as if the hero, though entirely virtuous, is destroyed by forces beyond his control. In order to reach a decision
several related problems must be faced. Since the terrible crimes of regicide,
parricide, and incest were committed in ignorance, they can hardly be considered as the consequences of a tragic flaw, unless anger, which occasioned the
murder "where three highways meet," were that flaw; and Oedipus' anger at
the old man who struck him is at least understandable if not justifiable. A better
case could be made for overweening self-confidence as the tragic flaw—what
the Greeks called *hubris*, a word which had some of the same connotations as
"pride," and was applied to one who, for example, defied the gods. When
Oedipus is angered by Teiresias and Creon he treats them arrogantly, boasting
of his success against the Sphinx. The chorus in its second ode seems to be
accusing him of *hubris* (translated here as "pride") and irreverence for the gods.
However, Iocastê is more scornful of oracles than Oedipus, and he has tried not
so much to oppose the gods as to avoid committing the crimes which were
prophesied for him. If he is guilty of hubris, it is ironically manifested in his
attempt to follow the path of virtue.

It soon becomes clear that it is not easy to say whether Oedipus is guilty of a
tragic flaw in any usual sense of that term. If he is innocent, other problems open
up. The play has sometimes been called a tragedy of fate, implying that the hero
is a helpless victim of the gods, but against this view it has been pointed out that
Oedipus is directly responsible for what happens, pursuing the inquiry into the
murder of Laïos relentlessly even after he has begun to suspect part of the truth
and in spite of the reluctance of those whom he questions. His courage, his energy, his initiative do not give the impression of a person merely buffeted by
fate. But if he is both innocent of any tragic flaw and yet responsible for what
happens to him, the nature of the tragedy becomes more mysterious. We seem
to be confronted with paradoxes — a man both self-sufficient and helpless,
famous for his wisdom and yet ignorant of the crucial facts about himself. A
satisfactory interpretation must make sense of these apparent contradictions.

Another part of Aristotle's description of the ideal tragedy can be applied to
*Oedipus Rex* more easily than the concept of hamartia. He speaks of the ideal
plot as one in which the events seem to follow each other inevitably as cause and
effect and yet bring about an unexpected reversal of the situation and a "recognition," or "change from ignorance to knowledge." No one who has ever seen
or read the play has failed to experience its terrible logic. Whether or not one
knows at the beginning what the outcome will be (as the first audience presumably did), the irony of Oedipus' pursuit of the truth is inescapable at the end
when he is blind and begging for exile. Not only has he found out who he is, but
he has had to accept the awful responsibility for what he has done. No more
complete reversal or devastating recognition can be imagined, and yet it increases, rather than diminishes, the stature of the hero. The moments in which
part and then all the truth strikes him have an intensity achieved by few other
plays.

To incorporate into the interpretation the effect of Oedipus' acquisition of
self-knowledge is to deal with the relation of hubris to limitation. One must
decide whether the emphasis of the play falls upon the extraordinary worth of
the hero or upon the insufficiency of even that worth.

## Selected Reading List for Sophocles

Bernard Knox, *Oedipus at Thebes*. New Haven: Yale University Press, 1957.

H.D.F. Kitto, *Greek Tragedy*. Garden City, New York: Doubleday & Company, Inc., n.d., pp. 121–92.

Richard B. Sewall, "*Oedipus the King*," *The Vision of Tragedy*. New Haven, Conn.: Yale University Press, 1959, pp. 25–43.

Cedric Whitman, *Sophocles*. Cambridge, Mass.: Harvard University Press, 1951.

## Selected Reading List for the Greek Theater

Peter Arnott, *An Introduction to the Greek Theatre*. Bloomington, Ind.: Indiana University Press, 1959.

Margarete Bieber, *The History of the Greek and Roman Theater*. Princeton, N. J.: Princeton University Press, 1961.

T. B. L. Webster, *Greek Theatre Production*. London: Methuen and Co., Ltd., 1956.

# Everyman and The Medieval Theater

The development of medieval drama from religious observance can be traced much more circumstantially than that of Greek drama. The Mass of the Christian church is dramatic in itself, not only in its use of dialogue between the priest and the faithful, but also in the re-enactment of the Last Supper at Communion and in many other parts of the liturgy which recall events of Old Testament history and the life of Christ. It is not surprising that certain passages in the liturgy were elaborated dramatically and then separated from the Mass to be acted as little plays. The earliest one we know, the tenth-century *Quem Quaeritis* trope, was introduced into the opening of the Easter Mass. At that time the musical development of the Mass had reached the point where one syllable of the text was often prolonged over many notes of music, and the "tropes" were new words to be sung on these notes. The *Quem Quaeritis* trope was a dialogue between the three Marys and the angel at the tomb, who asks them "Whom seek ye?" (*quem quaeritis?*) and tells them that Jesus has risen from the tomb. This simple dramatization of the core of the Easter story was then moved from the Mass to matins or vespers, members of the clergy taking the parts of the Marys and the angel and going through the appropriate actions. Soon other episodes, such as the nativity, were given a similar treatment, and there came to be a repertory of liturgical drama performed in the church in Latin by the clergy.

The next important step was taken in the twelfth and thirteenth centuries when such plays, translated into the vernacular, began to be acted outside the church by laymen. By this time the high points of Old Testament history had also been dramatized, so that the Bible story from the creation through the life of Christ to the prophecy of the Last Judgment could be performed. Such plays were known as mystery or miracle plays. Considering their source, the term "scriptural drama" is perhaps more useful today.

There were two chief ways of performing scriptural drama. One was in a city square, where the various locations required were represented by separate structures, called "mansions," all visible at once. On this "simultaneous set" the actors in one episode revealed themselves at the door of their mansion (often by drawing back a curtain), acted out their part of the story, and withdrew again as others appeared at the door of another mansion, indicating a shift of locality.

However, some scriptural drama was performed in a very different manner. In fourteenth-century England it became customary in certain towns to celebrate the feast of Corpus Christi with a cycle of plays, each one put on by one of the trade guilds. For this purpose the guild fitted up a stage and dressing rooms on a wagon (known as a "pageant wagon"), which was hauled first to one and then another of the open places in the city as that particular play was performed over and over. As the pageant wagons of the various guilds moved through the city, the people gathered at each of the stopping-places were able to see the entire cycle of plays. Performances of this kind went on in England until late in the sixteenth century, in the lifetime of Shakespeare.

In the fifteenth century another kind of religious drama became popular, developing not from the liturgy but from the sermon. This was the morality play. From the beginning it was in the vernacular. Its object was to teach religious doctrine rather than to tell a story. Influenced by the literary vogue of that

111

era, it took the form of allegory, depicting man's encounters with the vices and virtues which struggle for possession of his soul. Thus, morality plays differed from the scriptural drama not only in having as characters personifications instead of historical personages, but also in being dominated by a theme rather than by a narrative. The emphasis of these plays fell normally upon the salvation possible through God's grace if man repented properly for his misdeeds.

Another distinctive characteristic of the morality play was its performance by professional actors instead of amateurs. Groups of strolling players went about the country giving performances for money in the towns or in the homes of the nobility. Although they normally wore the livery of some lord whose servants they were considered to be, they did so largely in order to avoid being arrested as vagrants according to the laws of the time. Their livelihood came mainly from the money they could make as actors. They were thus the prototypes of the acting companies of Shakespeare's day who were also under the patronage of some lord, and were known as "the Lord Chamberlain's Men" or "the Lord Admiral's Men." At first these companies of strolling players were very small—often four men and a boy (to play the women's parts); later they were somewhat larger. Many of the morality plays which survive were written especially to be acted by such groups, and show how, by the doubling of parts, they may be played by a certain number of actors—four or five or eight, as the case may be.

When a company of players arrived in a town they might set up in the main square the simplest of platforms with a curtained booth in back as a dressing room, from which entrances would be made. Or in some cases they might arrange mansions similar to those used in some of the scriptural dramas. *The Castle of Perseverance* has separate platforms, or "scaffolds," for God, the World, the Flesh, Belial, and Covetise, and a castle where Mankind defends himself against besieging sins. The players might also be hired by some neighboring lord to perform in his banquet hall. Since plays were sometimes given between the courses of a feast, they came to be called "interludes," and "moral interlude" is an alternative term for the morality play. The staging in a hall need not have been very different from that on a platform in the town square. In the hall a platform would not have been strictly necessary, though doubtless one was sometimes used. If the play was put on at one end of the hall, the doors in that wall might serve for entrances and obviate the necessity for any curtained booth. There were many possible arrangements, but the text of a play such as *Everyman* shows that the requirements were the simplest. An acting space was all these players needed.

*Everyman*, like most of the morality plays, was published anonymously. It was probably performed in about 1495, and may be a translation of a Dutch play, *Elckerlyk*, to which it is very similar. The full title of the English play is *The Summoning of Everyman*, and its subject is the last hours of Everyman's life, when he is faced with the problem of making his "reckoning" before God. Although there is no pitched battle, as in *The Castle of Perseverance*, between the virtues and vices, Everyman's summoning by death poses the basic problems of the moral life as dramatically as any morality play. Much shorter than many of them, and lacking the humorous, often low-comical episodes found in most, *Everyman* is usually considered the best representive of the genre because of its compactness and consistent tone.

The bare platform where Everyman confronts Death is the visual expression of a world of essences where only the most important questions are asked.

If we can imagine this simplest of stages, devoid of any scenic illusion, we are already part way into the play, and prepared to deal with its staggering simplicities. By contrast, it will help to ask ourselves what the play loses if it is played behind footlights.

## The Text Of Everyman

The text of *Everyman* is based on the Britwell copy of the Skot edition, reprinted by Sir Walter Greg (Louvain: 1904), with occasional readings taken from the other Skot and Pynson editions according to the procedure suggested by Greg in his reprint of the Pynson editions (Louvain: 1910), pp. 60-68. Spellings have been modernized, though most distinct archaic forms of words have been preserved. A few verb forms have been slightly modernized; for example, "lend" (as a past participle) to "lent." Although modern spelling obscures some of the rhymes, even the old spelling does not make all of them clear without an additional indication of early sixteenth-century pronunciation, when, for example, "tempestes" and "beestes" made an acceptable rhyme. Since many rhymes are lost with modern vowel sounds, it has not seemed worthwhile to indicate only a few of them by occasionally retaining the old spellings. Editorial additions appear in brackets.

# The Summoning of Everyman

### CHARACTERS

| | |
|---|---|
| MESSENGER | GOOD DEEDS |
| GOD: *Adonai* | KNOWLEDGE |
| DEATH | CONFESSION |
| EVERYMAN | BEAUTY |
| FELLOWSHIP | STRENGTH |
| COUSIN | DISCRETION |
| KINDRED | FIVE WITS |
| GOODS | ANGEL |
| DOCTOR | |

*Here beginneth a treatise how the High Father of Heaven sendeth Death to summon every creature to come and give account of their lives in this world, and is in manner of a moral play.*

MESSENGER. I pray you all give your audience,
And hear this matter with reverence,
By figure a moral play—
*The Summoning of Everyman* called it is,
That of our lives and ending shows 5
How transitory we be all day.
This matter is wondrous precious,
But the intent of it is more gracious,
And sweet to bear away.
The story saith: Man, in the beginning, 10
Look well, and take good heed to the ending,
Be you never so gay!
Ye think sin in the beginning full sweet,
Which in the end causeth the soul to weep,

---

3 *By figure* in form   6 *all day* always

When the body lieth in clay.                                    15
Here shall you see how Fellowship and Jollity,
Both Strength, Pleasure, and Beauty,
Will fade from thee as flower in May.
For ye shall hear how our Heaven King
Calleth Everyman to a general reckoning.  20
Give audience, and hear what he doth say.
                                                    [*Exit.*]
(GOD *speaketh.*)
GOD. I perceive, here in my majesty,
How that all creatures be to me unkind,
Living without dread in worldly prosperity.
Of ghostly sight the people be so blind,          25
Drowned in sin, they know me not for their
    God.
In worldly riches is all their mind,
They fear not my rightwiseness, the sharp rod;
My law that I showed when I for them died
They forget clean, and shedding of my blood
    red;                                                    30
I hanged between two thieves, it cannot be
    denied;
To get them life I suffered to be dead;
I healed their feet, with thorns hurt was my
    head.
I could do no more than I did, truly;
And now I see the people do clean forsake
    me.                                                      35
They use the seven deadly sins damnable,
As pride, covetise, wrath, and lechery,
Now in the world be made commendable;
And thus they leave of angels the heavenly
    company.
Every man liveth so after his own plea-
    sure,                                                    40
And yet of their life they be nothing sure.
I see the more that I them forbear
The worse they be from year to year;
All that liveth appaireth fast.
Therefore I will, in all the haste,              45
Have a reckoning of every man's person;
For, and I leave the people thus alone
In their life and wicked tempests,
Verily they will become much worse than
    beasts;
For now one would by envy another up
    eat;                                                      50
Charity they all do clean forget.

I hoped well that every man
In my glory should make his mansion,
And thereto I had them all elect;
But now I see, like traitors deject,              55
They thank me not for the pleasure that I to
    them meant,
Nor yet for their being that I them have lent.
I proffered the people great multitude of
    mercy,
And few there be that asketh it heartily;
They be so cumbered with worldly riches,  60
That needs on them I must do justice,
On every man living without fear.
Where art thou, Death, thou mighty mes-
    senger?
                        [*Enter* DEATH.]
DEATH. Almighty God, I am here at your
    will,
Your commandment to fulfil.                      65
GOD. Go thou to Everyman,
And show him, in my name,
A pilgrimage he must on him take,
Which he in no wise may escape;
And that he bring with him a sure reckon-
    ing                                                      70
Without delay or any tarrying. [*Exit* GOD.]
DEATH. Lord, I will in the world go run over
    all,
And cruelly out search both great and small.
Every man will I beset that liveth beastly
Out of God's laws, and dreadeth not folly. 75
He that loveth riches I will strike with my
    dart,
His sight to blind, and from heaven to depart,
Except that alms deeds be his good friend,
In hell for to dwell, world without end.
                    [*Enter* EVERYMAN.]
Lo, yonder I see Everyman walking;            80
Full little he thinketh on my coming.
His mind is on fleshly lusts and his treasure,
And great pain it shall cause him to endure
Before the Lord, Heaven King.
Everyman, stand still! Whither art thou go-
    ing                                                      85
Thus gaily? Hast thou thy Maker forget?
EVERYMAN. Why askest thou?
Wouldest thou wete?
DEATH. Yea, sir, I will show you:

---

23 *unkind* unnatural   25 *ghostly* spiritual   37
*covetise* avarice   44 *appaireth* degenerates   47 *and*
if

54 *elect* chosen   55 *deject* abject   69 *wise* manner, way   72 *over all* everywhere   77 *depart* separate  86 *forget* forgotten   88 *wete* know

In great haste I am sent to thee                    90
From God out of his Majesty.
EVERYMAN. What, sent to me?
DEATH. Yea, certainly.
Though thou have forget him here,
He thinketh on thee in the heavenly
    sphere,                                         95
As, ere we depart, thou shalt know.
EVERYMAN. What desireth God of me?
DEATH. That shall I show thee:
A reckoning he will needs have
Without any longer respite.                         100
EVERYMAN. To give a reckoning, longer
    leisure I crave.
This blind matter troubleth my wit.
DEATH. On thee thou must take a long
    journey;
Therefore thy book of count with thee thou
    bring;
For turn again thou can not by no way.   105
And look thou be sure of thy reckoning,
For before God thou shalt answer and show
Thy many bad deeds, and good but a few,
How thou hast spent thy life, and in what wise,
Before the Chief Lord of paradise.       110
Have ado that we were in that way,
For, wete thou well, thou shalt make none
    attorney.
EVERYMAN. Full unready I am such reckon-
    ing to give.
I know thee not. What messenger art thou?
DEATH. I am Death, that no man dread-
    eth.                                            115
For every man I 'rest, and no man spareth;
For it is God's commandment
That all to me should be obedient.
EVERYMAN. O Death! thou comest when
    I had thee least in mind!
In thy power it lieth me to save.                   120
Yet of my good will I give thee, if thou will be
    kind;
Yea, a thousand pound shalt thou have,
And defer this matter till another day.
DEATH. Everyman, it may not be, by no
    way!

I set not by gold, silver, nor riches,              125
Ne by pope, emperor, king, duke, ne princes.
For, and I would receive gifts great,
All the world I might get;
But my custom is clean contrary.
I give thee no respite. Come hence, and not
    tarry.                                          130
EVERYMAN. Alas! shall I have no longer
    respite?
I may say Death giveth no warning.
To think on thee, it maketh my heart sick,
For all unready is my book of reckoning.
But twelve year and I might have a bid-
    ing,                                            135
My counting-book I would make so clear,
That my reckoning I should not need to
    fear.
Wherefore, Death, I pray thee, for God's
    mercy,
Spare me till I be provided of remedy.
DEATH. Thee availeth not to cry, weep, and
    pray;                                           140
But haste thee lightly that thou were gone
    that journey,
And prove thy friends if thou can.
For wete thou well the tide abideth no man;
And in the world each living creature
For Adam's sin must die of nature.                  145
EVERYMAN. Death, if I should this pilgri-
    mage take,
And my reckoning surely make,
Show me, for saint charity,
Should I not come again shortly?
DEATH. No, Everyman; and thou be once
    there,                                          150
Thou mayst never more come here,
Trust me verily.
EVERYMAN. O gracious God, in the high
    seat celestial,
Have mercy on me in this most need!
Shall I have no company from this vale
    terrestrial                                     155
Of mine acquaintance that way me to lead?
DEATH. Yea, if any be so hardy,
That would go with thee and bear thee com-
    pany.

---

102 *blind . . . wit* dark problem puzzles my
mind   104 *count* accounts   105 *turn again* return
111 *Have . . . way* get ready to go   112 *none attorney*
no one to appear in your place   115 *that . . .
dreadeth* who fears no man   116 *'rest* arrest   121
*good* goods

---

125 *set not by* care not for   126 *Ne* nor   127 *and* if
135 *But . . . biding* if I could remain only twelve
years   139 *of remedy* with help   141 *lightly* quickly
142 *prove* test   145 *of nature* naturally

Hie thee that thou were gone to God's mag-
nificence,
Thy reckoning to give before his presence. 160
What! weenest thou thy life is given thee,
And thy worldly goods also?

EVERYMAN. I had weened so, verily.

DEATH. Nay, nay; it was but lent thee;
For, as soon as thou art go,           165
Another a while shall have it, and then go
therefro
Even as thou hast done.
Everyman, thou art mad! Thou hast thy wits
five,
And here on earth will not amend thy life;
For suddenly I do come.           170

EVERYMAN. O wretched caitiff! whither
shall I flee,
That I might 'scape this endless sorrow?
Now, gentle Death, spare me till tomorrow,
That I may amend me
With good advisement.           175

DEATH. Nay, thereto I will not consent,
Nor no man will I respite,
But to the heart suddenly I shall smite
Without any advisement.
And now out of thy sight I will me hie;    180
See thou make thee ready shortly,
For thou mayst say this is the day
That no man living may 'scape away.
                    [Exit DEATH.]

EVERYMAN. Alas! I may well weep with
sighs deep.
Now have I no manner of company      185
To help me in my journey and me to keep;
And also my writing is full unready.
How shall I do now for to excuse me?
I would to God I had never be get!
To my soul a full great profit it had be,  190
For now I fear pains huge and great.
The time passeth; Lord, help, that all
wrought.
For though I mourn it availeth naught.
The day passeth, and is almost ago;
I wot not well what for to do.       195
To whom were I best my complaint to make?
What and I to Fellowship thereof spake,

And showed him of this sudden chance?
For in him is all mine affiance,
We have in the world so many a day     200
Be good friends in sport and play.
I see him yonder, certainly;
I trust that he will bear me company;
Therefore to him will I speak to ease my
sorrow.          [Enter FELLOWSHIP.]
Well met, good Fellowship, and good mor-
row!           205

(FELLOWSHIP speaketh.)

FELLOWSHIP. Everyman, good morrow, by
this day!
Sir, why lookest thou so piteously?
If any thing be amiss, I pray thee me say,
That I may help to remedy.

EVERYMAN. Yea, good Fellowship, yea,   210
I am in great jeopardy.

FELLOWSHIP. My true friend, show to me
your mind.
I will not forsake thee to my life's end
In the way of good company.

EVERYMAN. That was well spoken, and
lovingly.           215

FELLOWSHIP. Sir, I must needs know your
heaviness;
I have pity to see you in any distress;
If any have you wronged, ye shall revenged be,
Though I on the ground be slain for thee,
Though that I know before that I should
die.           220

EVERYMAN. Verily, Fellowship, gramercy.

FELLOWSHIP. Tush! by thy thanks I set
not a straw!
Show me your grief, and say no more.

EVERYMAN. If I my heart should to you
break,
And then to turn you your mind from
me,           225
And would not me comfort when ye hear me
speak,
Then should I ten times sorrier be.

FELLOWSHIP. Sir, I say as I will do indeed.

EVERYMAN. Then be you a good friend at
need;
I have found you true here before.     230

FELLOWSHIP. And so ye shall evermore;
For, in faith, and thou go to hell,

---

159 *Hie . . . gone* hurry and go   161 *weenest*
supposest   165 *go* gone   166 *therefro* from it   168
*wits* senses   175 *advisement* warning   187 *writing*
account   189 *be get* been begotten   194 *ago* gone
by   195 *wot* know   196 *complaint* lament

---

199 *affiance* trust   216 *heaviness* sorrow   224
*break* reveal   225 *to* were to   232 *and* if

I will not forsake thee by the way!

EVERYMAN. Ye speak like a good friend.
I believe you well;
I shall deserve it, and I may.                          235

FELLOWSHIP. I speak of no deserving, by
this day!
For he that will say and nothing do
Is not worthy with good company to go;
Therefore show me the grief of your mind,
As to your friend most loving and kind.     240

EVERYMAN. I shall show you how it is:
Commanded I am to go a journey,
A long way, hard and dangerous,
And give a strait count without delay
Before the high judge, Adonai.                   245
Wherefore, I pray you, bear me company,
As ye have promised, in this journey.

FELLOWSHIP. That is matter indeed! Prom-
ise is duty;
But, and I should take such a voyage on me,
I know it well, it should be to my pain.     250
Also it maketh me afeared, certain.
But let us take counsel here as well as we can,
For your words would fear a strong man.

EVERYMAN. Why, ye said if I had need,
Ye would me never forsake, quick ne dead,   255
Though it were to hell, truly.

FELLOWSHIP. So I said, certainly,
But such pleasures be set aside, the sooth to
say.
And also, if we took such a journey,
When should we come again?                     260

EVERYMAN. Nay, never again till the day of
doom.

FELLOWSHIP. In faith, then will not I come
there!
Who hath you these tidings brought?

EVERYMAN. Indeed, Death was with me
here.

FELLOWSHIP. Now, by God that all hath
bought,                                                        265
If Death were the messenger,
For no man that is living today
I will not go that loath journey—
Not for the father that begat me!

EVERYMAN. Ye promised otherwise, par-
die.                                                                 270

FELLOWSHIP. I wot well I said so, truly;
And yet if thou wilt eat, and drink, and make
good cheer,
Or haunt to women the lusty company,
I would not forsake you while the day is clear,
Trust me verily!                                            275

EVERYMAN. Yea, thereto ye would be ready.
To go to mirth, solace, and play,
Your mind will sooner apply
Than to bear me company in my long jour-
ney.

FELLOWSHIP. Now, in good faith, I will not
that way.                                                        280
But and thou wilt murder, or any man kill,
In that I will help thee with a good will!

EVERYMAN. O, that is a simple advice in-
deed!
Gentle fellow, help me in my necessity;
We have loved long, and now I need,        285
And now, gentle Fellowship, remember me!

FELLOWSHIP. Whether ye have loved me
or no,
By Saint John, I will not with thee go.

EVERYMAN. Yet, I pray thee, take the labor,
and do so much for me
To bring me forward, for saint charity,       290
And comfort me till I come without the town.

FELLOWSHIP. Nay, and thou would give me
a new gown,
I will not a foot with thee go;
But, and thou had tarried, I would not have
left thee so.
And as now God speed thee in thy jour-
ney,                                                                 295
For from thee I will depart as fast as I may.

EVERYMAN. Whither away, Fellowship?
Will thou forsake me?

FELLOWSHIP. Yea, by my fay, to God I
betake thee.

EVERYMAN. Farewell, good Fellowship! For
thee my heart is sore;
Adieu for ever! I shall see thee no more.    300

FELLOWSHIP. In faith, Everyman, farewell
now at the end!
For you I will remember that parting is
mourning.

[*Exit* FELLOWSHIP.]

---

235 *deserve* repay; *and if*    244 *strait count* strict
accounting 245 *Adonai* i.e., God  253 *fear* frighten
258 *pleasures* pleasantries 265 *bought* redeemed
268 *loath* loathsome 270 *pardie* by God (par dieu)

273 *haunt . . . company* frequent the pleasant
company of women 289 *take* undertake 290 *bring
me forward* escort me    298 *fay* faith; *betake*
commend   302 *For* because of

EVERYMAN. Alack! shall we thus depart indeed
(Ah, Lady, help!) without any more comfort?
Lo, Fellowship forsaketh me in my most need.                                         305
For help in this world whither shall I resort?
Fellowship here before with me would merry make,
And now little sorrow for me doth he take.
It is said, "In prosperity men friends may find,
Which in adversity be full unkind."                                              310
Now whither for succor shall I flee,
Sith that Fellowship hath forsaken me?
To my kinsmen I will, truly,
Praying them to help me in my necessity;
I believe that they will do so,                                                   315
For "kind will creep where it may not go."
I will go say, for yonder I see them go.
Where be ye now, my friends and kinsmen?

[*Enter* KINDRED *and* COUSIN.]

KINDRED. Here be we now, at your commandment.
Cousin, I pray you show us your intent     320
In any wise, and not spare.
COUSIN. Yea, Everyman, and to us declare
If ye be disposed to go any whither,
For, wete you well, we will live and die together.
KINDRED. In wealth and woe we will with you hold,                                   325
For over his kin a man may be bold.
EVERYMAN. Gramercy, my friends and kinsmen kind.
Now shall I show you the grief of my mind.
I was commanded by a messenger
That is a high king's chief officer;       330
He bade me go a pilgrimage, to my pain,
And I know well I shall never come again;
Also I must give reckoning strait,
For I have a great enemy that hath me in wait,
Which intendeth me for to hinder.           335

KINDRED. What account is that which ye must render?
That would I know.
EVERYMAN. Of all my works I must show
How I have lived, and my days spent;
Also of ill deeds that I have used          340
In my time, sith life was me lent;
And of all virtues that I have refused.
Therefore I pray you go thither with me,
To help to make mine account, for saint charity.
COUSIN. What, to go thither? Is that the matter?                                    345
Nay, Everyman, I had liefer fast bread and water
All this five year and more.
EVERYMAN. Alas, that ever I was bore!
For now shall I never be merry
If that you forsake me.                     350
KINDRED. Ah, sir, what! Ye be a merry man!
Take good heart to you, and make no moan.
But one thing I warn you, by Saint Anne,
As for me, ye shall go alone.
EVERYMAN. My Cousin, will you not with me go?                                        355
COUSIN. No, by our Lady! I have the cramp in my toe.
Trust not to me, for, so God me speed,
I will deceive you in your most need.
KINDRED. It availeth not us to tice.
Ye shall have my maid with all my heart;    360
She loveth to go to feasts, there to be nice,
And to dance, and abroad to start;
I will give her leave to help you in that journey,
If that you and she may agree.
EVERYMAN. Now show me the very effect of your mind.                                 365
Will you go with me, or abide behind?
KINDRED. Abide behind? Yea, that will I, and I may!
Therefore, farewell till another day.

[*Exit* KINDRED.]

EVERYMAN. How should I be merry or glad?
For fair promises men to me make,          370
But when I have most need, they me forsake.
I am deceived; that maketh me sad.
COUSIN. Cousin Everyman, farewell now,

---

312 *Sith* since   313 *will* will go   316 *"kind . . .
go"* "kinship will creep where it may not walk";
i.e., "blood is thicker than water"   317 *say* assay,
make trial   320 *Cousin* any relative, except brother
or sister   333 *strait* strict   334 *I have . . . wait* i.e.,
Satan lies in wait for me   335 *hinder* harm

---

340 *used* practiced   341 *sith* since   357 *speed*
prosper   359 *tice* entice   361 *nice* wanton   362
*start* gad about

For verily I will not go with you;
Also of mine own an unready reckoning    375
I have to account; therefore I make tarrying.
Now, God keep thee, for now I go.

       *[Exit* COUSIN.]
 EVERYMAN. Ah, Jesus! is all come hereto?
Lo, fair words maketh fools fain;
They promise and nothing will do, cer-
 tain.    380
My kinsmen promised me faithfully
For to abide with me steadfastly,
And now fast away do they flee.
Even so Fellowship promised me.
What friend were best me of to provide?    385
I lose my time here longer to abide.
Yet in my mind a thing there is:
All my life I have loved riches;
If that my Good now help me might,
It would make my heart full light.    390
I will speak to him in this distress.
Where art thou, my Goods and riches?
 GOODS *[within].* Who calleth me? Every-
 man? What, hast thou haste?
I lie here in corners, trussed and piled so high,
And in chests I am locked full fast,    395
Also sacked in bags—thou mayest see with
 thine eye—
I cannot stir; in packs low I lie.
What would ye have? Lightly me say.
 EVERYMAN. Come hither, Good, in all the
 haste thou may.
For of counsel I must desire thee.    400
      *[Enter* GOODS.]
 GOODS. Sir, and ye in the world have sorrow
 or adversity,
That can I help you to remedy shortly.
 EVERYMAN. It is another disease that
 grieveth me;
In this world it is not, I tell thee so.
I am sent for another way to go,    405
To give a strait count general
Before the highest Jupiter of all;
And all my life I have had joy and pleasure
 in thee,
Therefore I pray thee go with me,
For, peradventure, thou mayst before God
 Almighty    410
My reckoning help to clean and purify;
For it is said ever among,

That money maketh all right that is wrong.
 GOODS. Nay, Everyman; I sing another
 song,
I follow no man in such voyages;    415
For, and I went with thee,
Thou shouldst fare much the worse for me;
For because on me thou did set thy mind,
Thy reckoning I have made blotted and blind,
That thine account thou cannot make
 truly;    420
And that hast thou for the love of me.
 EVERYMAN. That would grieve me full sore,
When I should come to that fearful answer.
Up, let us go thither together.
 GOODS. Nay, not so! I am too brittle, I may
 not endure;    425
I will follow no man one foot, be ye sure.
 EVERYMAN. Alas! I have thee loved, and
 had great pleasure
All my life-days on good and treasure.
 GOODS. That is to thy damnation, without
 lesing!
For my love is contrary to the love everlast-
 ing.    430
But if thou had me loved moderately during,
As to the poor to give part of me,
Then shouldst thou not in this dolor be,
Nor in this great sorrow and care.
 EVERYMAN. Lo, now was I deceived ere I
 was ware,    435
And all I may wyte my spending of time.
 GOODS. What, weenest thou that I am
 thine?
 EVERYMAN. I had weened so.
 GOODS. Nay, Everyman, I say no;
As for a while I was lent thee,    440
A season thou hast had me in prosperity.
My condition is man's soul to kill;
If I save one, a thousand I do spill;
Weenest thou that I will follow thee?
Nay, from this world, not verily.    445
 EVERYMAN. I had weened otherwise.
 GOODS. Therefore to thy soul Good is a
 thief;
For when thou art dead, this is my guise,
Another to deceive in the same wise

---

376 *make tarrying* tarry 379 *fain* joyful 389 *Good*
goods 398 *Lightly* quickly 406 *strait* strict

419 *blind* obscure 429 *lesing* lie 431 *during*
while living 435 *ware* aware 436 *wyte . . . time*
blame on the way I spent my time 443 *spill* ruin
448 *guise* custom

As I have done thee, and all to his soul's
    reprief.                                    450
EVERYMAN. O false Good, cursed thou be!
Thou traitor to God, that hast deceived me
And caught me in thy snare.
    GOODS. Marry! thou brought thyself in care,
Whereof I am glad.                              455
I must needs laugh, I cannot be sad.
    EVERYMAN. Ah, Good, thou hast had long
    my heartly love;
I gave thee that which should be the Lord's
    above.
But wilt thou not go with me indeed?
I pray thee truth to say.                       460
    GOODS. No, so God me speed!
Therefore farewell, and have good day.
                        [Exit GOODS.]
    EVERYMAN. O, to whom shall I make my
    moan
For to go with me in that heavy journey?
First Fellowship said he would with me
    gone;                                       465
His words were very pleasant and gay,
But afterward he left me alone.
Then spake I to my kinsmen, all in despair,
And also they gave me words fair,
They lacked no fair speaking,                   470
But all forsake me in the ending.
Then went I to my Goods, that I loved best,
In hope to have comfort, but there had I least;
For my Goods sharply did me tell
That he bringeth many into hell.                475
Then of myself I was ashamed,
And so I am worthy to be blamed;
Thus may I well myself hate.
Of whom shall I now counsel take?
I think that I shall never speed                480
Till that I go to my Good Deed.
But alas! she is so weak
That she can neither go nor speak.
Yet will I venture on her now.
My Good Deeds, where be you?                    485
        [GOOD DEEDS speaks from below.]
    GOOD DEEDS. Here I lie, cold in the ground.
Thy sins hath me sore bound,
That I cannot stir.
    EVERYMAN. O Good Deeds, I stand in fear!
I must you pray of counsel,                     490

For help now should come right well.
    GOOD DEEDS. Everyman, I have understand-
    ing
That ye be summoned account to make
Before Messias, of Jerusalem King;
And you do by me, that journey with you
    will I take.                                495
    EVERYMAN. Therefore I come to you my
    moan to make;
I pray you that ye will go with me.
    GOOD DEEDS. I would full fain, but I cannot
    stand, verily.
    EVERYMAN. Why, is there anything on you
    fall?
    GOOD DEEDS. Yea, sir, I may thank you of
    all;                                        500
If ye had perfectly cheered me,
Your book of count full ready had be.
Look, the books of your works and deeds eke.
Behold how they lie under the feet,
To your soul's heaviness.                       505
    EVERYMAN. Our Lord Jesus help me!
For one letter here I can not see.
    GOOD DEEDS. There is a blind reckoning in
    time of distress!
    EVERYMAN. Good Deeds, I pray you, help
    me in this need,
Or else I am for ever damned indeed.            510
Therefore help me to make my reckoning
Before the Redeemer of all thing,
That King is, and was, and ever shall.
    GOOD DEEDS. Everyman, I am sorry of your
    fall,
And fain would I help you, and I were
    able.                                       515
    EVERYMAN. Good Deeds, your counsel I
    pray you give me.
    GOOD DEEDS. That shall I do verily;
Though that on my feet I may not go,
I have a sister that shall with you also,
Called Knowledge, which shall with you
    abide,                                      520
To help you to make that dreadful reckoning.
                        [Enter KNOWLEDGE.]
    KNOWLEDGE. Everyman, I will go with thee,
    and be thy guide,
In thy most need to go by thy side.

-----

450 *reprief* shame  464 *heavy* sad  465 *gone* go
480 *speed* prosper  483 *go* walk  484 *venture* gamble
491 *come right well* be welcome  495 *And you do
by me* if you do as I say  500 *of all* for every
thing  501 *perfectly cheered* properly cared for
503 *eke* also  505 *heaviness* distress  518 *go* walk

EVERYMAN. In good condition I am now in every thing,
And am wholly content with this good thing;  525
Thanked be God my Creator.
GOOD DEEDS. And when she hath brought you there,
Where thou shalt heal thee of thy smart,
Then go you with your reckoning and your Good Deeds together
For to make you joyful at heart  530
Before the blessed Trinity.
EVERYMAN. My Good Deeds, gramercy!
I am well content, certainly,
With your words sweet.
KNOWLEDGE. Now go we together lovingly  535
To Confession, that cleansing river.
EVERYMAN. For joy I weep; I would we were there!
But, I pray you, give me cognition
Where dwelleth that holy man, Confession.
KNOWLEDGE. In the house of salvation,  540
We shall find him in that place,
That shall us comfort, by God's grace.
[KNOWLEDGE leads EVERYMAN to CONFESSION.]
Lo, this is Confession. Kneel down and ask mercy,
For he is in good conceit with God almighty.
EVERYMAN. O glorious fountain, that all uncleanness doth clarify,  545
Wash from me the spots of vices unclean,
That on me no sin may be seen.
I come, with Knowledge, for my redemption,
Redempt with hearty and full contrition;
For I am commanded a pilgrimage to take,  550
And great accounts before God to make.
Now, I pray you, Shrift, mother of salvation,
Help my Good Deeds for my piteous exclamation.
CONFESSION. I know your sorrow well, Everyman.
Because with Knowledge ye come to me,  555
I will you comfort as well as I can,
And a precious jewel I will give thee,
Called penance, voider of adversity.

Therewith shall your body chastised be
With abstinence and perseverance in God's service.  560
Here shall you receive that scourge of me
[Gives EVERYMAN a scourge.]
Which is penance strong that ye must endure
To remember thy Savior was scourged for thee
With sharp scourges and suffered it patiently.
So must thou ere thou 'scape that painful pilgrimage.  565
Knowledge, keep him in this voyage,
And by that time Good Deeds will be with thee.
But in any wise be seker of mercy,
For your time draweth fast, and ye will saved be;
Ask God mercy, and He will grant truly;  570
When with the scourge of penance man doth him bind,
The oil of forgiveness then shall he find.
[Exit CONFESSION.]
EVERYMAN. Thanked be God for his gracious work!
For now I will my penance begin;
This hath rejoiced and lighted my heart,  575
Though the knots be painful and hard within.
KNOWLEDGE. Everyman, look your penance that ye fulfil,
What pain that ever it to you be,
And Knowledge shall give you counsel at will
How your account ye shall make clearly.  580
EVERYMAN. O eternal God! O heavenly figure!
O way of rightwiseness! O goodly vision!
Which descended down in a virgin pure
Because he would every man redeem,
Which Adam forfeited by his disobedience.  585
O blessed Godhead! elect and high divine,
Forgive me my grievous offence;
Here I cry thee mercy in this presence.
O ghostly treasure! O ransomer and redeemer!
Of all the world hope and conductor,  590
Mirror of joy, founder of mercy,
Which illumineth heaven and earth thereby,

---

527 *she* (*he* in early editions)  528 *smart* pain
538 *cognition* knowledge  544 *conceit* esteem  549
*Redempt with* redeemed by (?)  552 *Shrift* confession

565 *'scape* finish  566 *in this voyage* i.e., moving
in this direction  568 *seker* confident  569 *fast* to
an end  579 *at will* whenever you desire it  589
*ghostly* spiritual  591 *foundator* founder

Hear my clamorous complaint, though it
late be.

Receive my prayers; unworthy in this heavy
life.

Though I be a sinner most abominable,  595
Yet let my name be written in Moses' table.

O Mary! pray to the Maker of all thing,

Me for to help at my ending,

And save me from the power of my enemy,

For Death assaileth me strongly.  600

And, Lady, that I may by mean of thy prayer

Of your Son's glory to be partner,

By the mean of his passion I it crave.

I beseech you, help my soul to save.

Knowledge, give me the scourge of penance.  605

My flesh therewith shall give a quittance.

I will now begin, if God give me grace.

   KNOWLEDGE. Everyman, God give you time
and space.

Thus I bequeath you in the hands of our
Savior,

Now may you make your reckoning sure.  610

   EVERYMAN. In the name of the Holy
Trinity,

My body sore punished shall be.

              [*Scourges himself.*]

Take this, body, for the sin of the flesh.

Also thou delightest to go gay and fresh,

And in the way of damnation thou did me
bring;  615

Therefore suffer now strokes of punishing.

Now of penance I will wade the water clear,

To save me from purgatory, that sharp fire.

       [GOOD DEEDS *rises from below.*]

   GOOD DEEDS. I thank God, now I can walk
and go,

And am delivered of my sickness and woe.  620

Therefore with Everyman I will go, and not
spare;

His good works I will help him to declare.

   KNOWLEDGE. Now, Everyman, be merry
and glad!

Your Good Deeds cometh now, ye may not
be sad.

Now is your Good Deeds whole and
sound,  625

Going upright upon the ground.

   EVERYMAN. My heart is light, and shall be
evermore.

Now will I smite faster than I did before.

   GOOD DEEDS. Every man, pilgrim, my special friend,

Blessed be thou without end.  630

For thee is preparate the eternal glory.

Ye have me made whole and sound,

Therefore I will bide by thee in every stound.

   EVERYMAN. Welcome, my Good Deeds;
now I hear thy voice,

I weep for very sweetness of love.  635

   KNOWLEDGE. Be no more sad, but ever
rejoice;

God seeth thy living in his throne above.

Put on this garment to thy behove,

          [*Handing* EVERYMAN *a cloak.*]

Which is wet with your tears,

Or else before God you may it miss,  640

When you to your journey's end come shall.

   EVERYMAN. Gentle Knowledge, what do ye
it call?

   KNOWLEDGE. It is the garment of sorrow;

From pain it will you borrow;

Contrition it is  645

That getteth forgiveness;

It pleaseth God passing well.

   GOOD DEEDS. Everyman, will you wear it
for your heal?

        [EVERYMAN *puts on the cloak.*]

   EVERYMAN. Now blessed be Jesu, Mary's
Son,

For now have I on true contrition.  650

And let us go now without tarrying;

Good Deeds, have we clear our reckoning?

   GOOD DEEDS. Yea, indeed I have it here.

   EVERYMAN. Then I trust we need not fear.

Now, friends, let us not part in twain.  655

   KNOWLEDGE. Nay, Everyman, that will we
not, certain.

   GOOD DEEDS. Yet must thou lead with thee

Three persons of great might.

   EVERYMAN. Who should they be?

   GOOD DEEDS. Discretion and Strength they
hight,  660

And thy Beauty may not abide behind.

   KNOWLEDGE. Also ye must call to mind

---

596 *table* tablets, i.e., among the saved  606
*quittance* satisfaction (for sins)  614 *gay and fresh*
handsomely dressed

631 *preparate* prepared  633 *stound* trial  637 *living*
way of living  638 *behove* advantage  640 *miss*
lack (when you need it)  644 *borrow* redeem
649 *heal* welfare  660 *hight* are called

Your Five Wits as for your counselors.

GOOD DEEDS. You must have them ready at all hours.

EVERYMAN. How shall I get them hither? 665

KNOWLEDGE. You must call them all together,

And they will hear you incontinent.

EVERYMAN. My friends, come hither and be present,

Discretion, Strength, my Five Wits, and Beauty.

[*Enter* DISCRETION, STRENGTH, FIVE WITS, *and* BEAUTY.]

BEAUTY. Here at your will we be ready. 670

What would ye that we should do?

GOOD DEEDS. That ye would with Everyman go,

And help him in his pilgrimage.

Advise you, will ye with him or not in that voyage?

STRENGTH. We will bring him all thither, 675

To his help and comfort, ye may believe me.

DISCRETION. So will we go with him all together.

EVERYMAN. Almighty God, loved may thou be!

I give thee laud that I have hither brought

Strength, Discretion, Beauty, and Five Wits.

Lack I naught. 680

And my Good Deeds, with Knowledge clear,

All be in company at my will here.

I desire no more to my business.

STRENGTH. And I, Strength, will by you stand in distress,

Though thou would in battle fight on the ground. 685

FIVE WITS. And though it were through the world round,

We will not depart for sweet nor sour.

BEAUTY. No more will I, unto death's hour,

Whatsoever thereof befall.

DISCRETION. Everyman, advise you first of all, 690

Go with a good advisement and deliberation.

We all give you virtuous monition

That all shall be well.

EVERYMAN. My friends, hearken what I will tell:

I pray God reward you in his heavenly sphere. 695

Now hearken, all that be here,

For I will make my testament

Here before you all present:

In alms half my good I will give with my hands twain

In the way of charity, with good intent, 700

And the other half still shall remain,

In queth to be returned there it ought to be.

This I do in despite of the fiend of hell,

To go quit out of his peril

Ever after and this day. 705

KNOWLEDGE. Everyman, hearken what I say;

Go to Priesthood, I you advise,

And receive of him in any wise

The holy sacrament and ointment together;

Then shortly see ye turn again hither; 710

We will all abide you here.

FIVE WITS. Yea, Everyman, hie you that ye ready were.

There is no emperor, king, duke, ne baron,

That of God hath commission

As hath the least priest in the world being; 715

For of the blessed sacraments pure and benign

He beareth the keys, and thereof hath the cure

For man's redemption—it is ever sure—

Which God for our soul's medicine

Gave us out of his heart with great pain, 720

Here in this transitory life, for thee and me.

The blessed sacraments seven there be:

Baptism, confirmation, with priesthood good,

And the sacrament of God's precious flesh and blood,

Marriage, the holy extreme unction, and penance. 725

These seven be good to have in remembrance,

Gracious sacraments of high divinity.

EVERYMAN. Fain would I receive that holy body

And meekly to my ghostly father I will go.

FIVE WITS. Everyman, that is the best that ye can do. 730

---

663 *Wits* senses   667 *incontinent* at once   674 *Advise you* take thought   679 *laud* praise   687 *for sweet nor sour* i.e., no matter what   690 *advise you* take thought   692 *monition* prediction

702 *In queth* as a legacy; *there* where   704 *quit . . . peril* free of danger from him   709 *holy sacrament and ointment* communion and extreme unction   717 *cure* care

God will you to salvation bring,
For priesthood exceedeth all other thing;
To us Holy Scripture they do teach,
And converteth man from sin, heaven to reach;
God hath to them more power given,      735
Than to any angel that is in heaven.
With five words he may consecrate
God's body in flesh and blood to make,
And handleth his Maker between his hands.
The priest bindeth and unbindeth all bands,      740
Both in earth and in heaven.
Thou ministers all the sacraments seven,
Though we kiss thy feet, thou were worthy;
Thou art surgeon that cureth sin deadly:
No remedy we find under God      745
But all only priesthood.
Everyman, God gave priests that dignity,
And setteth them in his stead among us to be;
Thus be they above angels in degree.

[*Exit* EVERYMAN.]

KNOWLEDGE. If priests be good, it is so, surely.      750
But when Jesus hanged on the cross with great smart,
There he gave out of his blessed heart
The same sacrament in great torment.
He sold them not to us, that Lord omnipotent.
Therefore Saint Peter the Apostle doth say 755
That Jesus' curse hath all they
Which God their Savior do buy or sell,
Or they for any money do take or tell.
Sinful priests giveth the sinners example bad;
Their children sitteth by other men's fires, I have heard;      760
And some haunteth women's company
With unclean life, as lusts of lechery.
These be with sin made blind.

FIVE WITS. I trust to God no such may we find.

Therefore let us priesthood honor,      765
And follow their doctrine for our souls' succour.
We be their sheep, and they shepherds be
By whom we all be kept in surety.
Peace! for yonder I see Everyman come,
Which hath made true satisfaction.      770

GOOD DEEDS. Methinketh it is he indeed.

[*Re-enter* EVERYMAN.]

EVERYMAN. Now Jesu be your alder speed.
I have received the sacrament for my redemption,
And then mine extreme unction.
Blessed be all they that counseled me to take it!      775
And now, friends, let us go without longer respite.
I thank God that ye have tarried so long.
Now set each of you on this rood your hand,
And shortly follow me.
I go before, there I would be. God be our guide.      780

STRENGTH. Everyman, we will not from you go,
Till ye have gone this voyage long.

DISCRETION. I, Discretion, will bide by you also.

KNOWLEDGE. And though this pilgrimage be never so strong,
I will never part you fro.      785
Everyman, I will be as sure by thee
As ever I did by Judas Maccabee.

[*They go to a grave.*]

EVERYMAN. Alas! I am so faint I may not stand,
My limbs under me do fold.
Friends, let us not turn again to this land, 790
Not for all the world's gold;
For into this cave must I creep
And turn to the earth, and there to sleep.

BEAUTY. What, into this grave? Alas!

EVERYMAN. Yea, there shall ye consume, more and less.      795

BEAUTY. And what, should I smother here?

EVERYMAN. Yea, by my faith, and never more appear.

---

737 *five words* "For this is my body" (Christ's words, repeated by the priest at the consecration of the wafer in the Mass)   740 *bindeth ... bands* Christ promised St. Peter that whatever he bound or unbound on earth would be bound or unbound in heaven.   742 *Thou ministers* you administer   751 *smart* pain   757 *Which ... sell* (alluding to simony, the sale or purchase of the sacraments)   758 *Or they ... tell* or those who, for any sacrament, take or count out money

772 *your ... speed* the helper of you all   778 *rood* cross   780 *there* where   787 *Judas Maccabee* great warrior who defended Israel against the Syrians   790, 793 *turn* return   795 *consume ... less* decay, all of you

In this world live no more we shall,
But in heaven before the highest Lord of all.
    BEAUTY. I cross out all this; adieu, by Saint
      John!                      800
I take my tape in my lap and am gone.
    EVERYMAN. What, Beauty, whither will ye?
    BEAUTY. Peace! I am deaf. I look not be-
      hind me,
Not and thou would give me all the gold in
    thy chest.          [*Exit* BEAUTY.]
    EVERYMAN. Alas, whereto may I trust?  805
Beauty goeth fast away from me;
She promised with me to live and die.
    STRENGTH. Everyman, I will thee also for-
    sake and deny.
Thy game liketh me not at all.
    EVERYMAN. Why, then ye will forsake me
    all?                      810
Sweet Strength, tarry a little space.
    STRENGTH. Nay, sir, by the rood of grace,
I will hie me from thee fast,
Though thou weep till thy heart to-brast.
    EVERYMAN. Ye would ever bide by me, ye
    said.                    815
    STRENGTH. Yea, I have you far enough con-
    veyed.
Ye be old enough, I understand,
Your pilgrimage to take on hand.
I repent me that I hither came.
    EVERYMAN. Strength, you to displease I am
    to blame;                 820
Yet promise is debt, this ye well wot.
    STRENGTH. In faith, I care not!
Thou art but a fool to complain.
You spend your speech and waste your brain.
Go, thrust thee into the ground.      825
                  [*Exit* STRENGTH.]
    EVERYMAN. I had weened surer I should
    you have found.
He that trusteth in his Strength
She him deceiveth at the length.
Both Strength and Beauty forsaketh me,
Yet they promised me fair and lovingly.  830
    DISCRETION. Everyman, I will after Strength
    be gone;
As for me I will leave you alone.

---

800 *all this* i.e., his former promises  801 *I take
. . . gone* "I tuck my skirts in my belt and am off"
(Donaldson)  814 *to-brast* break in pieces  821 *wot*
know

    EVERYMAN. Why, Discretion, will ye forsake
    me?
    DISCRETION. Yea, in faith, I will go from
    thee;
For when Strength goeth before      835
I follow after evermore.
    EVERYMAN. Yet, I pray thee, for the love
    of the Trinity,
Look in my grave once piteously.
    DISCRETION. Nay, so nigh I will not come.
Farewell, every one!  [*Exit* DISCRETION.]  840
    EVERYMAN. O all thing faileth, save God
    alone,
Beauty, Strength, and Discretion;
For when Death bloweth his blast,
They all run from me full fast.
    FIVE WITS. Everyman, of thee now my leave
    I take;                  845
I will follow the other, for here I thee forsake.
    EVERYTHING. Alas! then may I wail and
    weep,
For I took you for my best friend.
    FIVE WITS. I will no longer thee keep;
Now farewell, and there an end.      850
                [*Exit* FIVE WITS.]
    EVERYMAN. O Jesu, help! All hath forsaken
    me!
    GOOD DEEDS. Nay, Everyman; I will bide
    with thee,
I will not forsake thee indeed;
Thou shalt find me a good friend at need.
    EVERYMAN. Gramercy, Good Deeds! Now
    may I true friends see.      855
They have forsaken me, every one;
I loved them better than my Good Deeds
    alone.
Knowledge, will ye forsake me also?
    KNOWLEDGE. Yea, Everyman, when ye to
    death shall go;
But not yet, for no manner of danger.  860
    EVERYMAN. Gramercy, Knowledge, with
    all my heart.
    KNOWLEDGE. Nay, yet I will not from hence
    depart
Till I see where ye shall be come.
    EVERYMAN. Methinketh, alas, that I must
    be gone
To make my reckoning and my debts pay,  865
For I see my time is nigh spent away.

---

838 *piteously* with pity

Take example, all ye that this do hear or see,
How they that I loved best do forsake me,
Except my Good Deeds that bideth truly.
  GOOD DEEDS. All earthly things is but vanity. 870
Beauty, Strength, and Discretion do man forsake,
Foolish friends and kinsmen, that fair spake,
All fleeth save Good Deeds, and that am I.
  EVERYMAN. Have mercy on me, God most mighty;
And stand by me, thou Mother and Maid, holy Mary! 875
  GOOD DEEDS. Fear not, I will speak for thee.
  EVERYMAN. Here I cry God mercy!
  GOOD DEEDS. Short our end, and 'minish our pain.
Let us go and never come again.
  EVERYMAN. Into thy hands, Lord, my soul I commend. 880
Receive it, Lord, that it be not lost.
As thou me boughtest, so me defend,
And save me form the fiend's boast,
That I may appear with that blessed host
That shall be saved at the day of doom. 885
In manus tuas—of might's most
For ever—commendo spiritum meum.
  [EVERYMAN and GOOD DEEDS go into the grave.]
  KNOWLEDGE. Now hath he suffered that we all shall endure;
The Good Deeds shall make all sure.
Now hath he made ending. 890
Methinketh that I hear angels sing
And make great joy and melody
Where Everyman's soul shall received be.
  ANGEL. Come, excellent elect spouse to Jesu!

Here above thou shalt go 895
Because of thy singular virtue.
Now thy soul is taken thy body fro,
Thy reckoning is crystal clear.
Now shalt thou into the heavenly sphere,
Unto the which all ye shall come 900
That liveth well before the day of doom.
  [Exit KNOWLEDGE. Enter DOCTOR.]
  DOCTOR. This memorial men may have in mind;
Ye hearer's, take it of worth, old and young,
And forsake Pride, for he deceiveth you in the end,
And remember Beauty, Five Wits, Strength, and Discretion, 905
They all at the last do Everyman forsake,
Save his Good Deeds there doth he take.
But beware, for and they be small,
Before God he hath no help at all.
None excuse may be there for Everyman. 910
Alas, how shall he do then?
For, after death, amends may no man make,
For then mercy and pity doth him forsake.
If his reckoning be not clear when he doth come,
God will say, "Ite, maledicti, in ignem aeternum." 915
And he that hath his account whole and sound,
High in heaven he shall be crowned.
Unto which place God bring us all thither,
That we may live body and soul together.
Thereto help the Trinity! 920
Amen, say ye, for saint charity.

FINIS

THUS ENDETH THIS MORAL PLAY OF EVERYMAN.

878 Short our end shorten our dying; 'minish diminish 882 boughtest redeemed 886–87 In manus ... meum "Into thy hands, o greatest of powers, I commend my spirit forever" 894 elect chosen

901 Stage direction: Enter Doctor a theologian comes to explain the meaning of the play 902 memorial reminder 903 take it of worth value it 915 "Ite ... aeternum" "Depart, ye cursed, into everlasting fire"

## Allegory and Didacticism

It is often thought today that good drama requires characters who are recognizable human beings, and there is a marked preference for individuals distinguished from their fellow human beings by traits which are not even typical of any large group but are more nearly peculiar to one person. The dramatic vitality of *Everyman* is sufficient proof that the theater makes no such demands. Its central character is deliberately generalized to make him as typical as possible of the "average man," and most of the rest of the characters are personifications, such as Death or Knowledge, or representatives of categories of people, such as Everyman's relatives and friends. No one of them gives us more than a hint of an individual person, and yet several of them are memorable characters. Moreover some of the scenes not only give immediacy to the problems they present but make a strong emotional appeal.

The effectiveness of the scene in which Knowledge makes her famous promise, "Everyman, I will go with thee, and be thy guide, / In thy most need to go by thy side" (ll. 522–23), does not seem to be in the slightest impaired by the fact that she represents an abstraction. What makes this statement of allegiance moving is not the personality of the speaker but the situation. We have seen Everyman deserted by his friends, his kinsmen, and his material possessions—gradually stripped of everything outside his individual being—and we have seen that Good Deeds, though well disposed, is as yet too feeble to walk. By these simple means the radical loneliness of every human being at the approach of death is powerfully presented, and the gesture of Knowledge comes with the force of an unexpected offer of friendship.

When Everyman approaches the grave, the pattern of stripping away is repeated. He is accompanied by his Good Deeds, whose strength he has revived through confession and penance, and by his various bodily faculties and characteristics. But now he finds that even these parts of himself can go no further: "All earthly things is but vanity. / Beauty, Strength, and Discretion do man forsake . . ." (ll. 870–71). Even Knowledge, though she will continue to the edge of the grave, must finally leave. Only Everyman's positive accomplishments can remain with him: "All fleeth save Good Deeds, and that am I" (l. 873). There is an almost heroic ring about this second statement of allegiance.

These moments are moving not because we are attracted to the characters as individuals, but because the situation of the generalized Everyman is one in which anyone can imagine himself. Something comparable might be said about the amusing scene in which the falseness of Fellowship is satirically revealed. Fellowship is a tempter, but he is made neither subtle nor complex. Though he is more of a person than Knowledge or Good Deeds and is more particularized than Everyman, he is a *kind* of person rather than an individual. The emphasis falls on his cheerful camaraderie, the quality for which he stands. The satirical humor of the scene derives from his patent hypocrisy and from his casual offer to distract Everyman with wine and women or help him kill someone. The shocking inadequacy of such good fellowship is the focus of attention.

These scenes recreate certain basic situations in human life, and where such universality is the aim, the drastically simplified and schematized characterization of allegory is clearly appropriate. It makes possible the special effect of the scenes, while at the same time the general scheme of the play makes the characters acceptable.

Another way of explaining the appropriateness of the allegorical characters is in terms of the didactic purpose of the play. They make the moral lesson clear in every episode, even before the "Doctor" sums it up at the end. They are also the means by which our responses to certain basic situations are related to the lesson, so that it has a force quite different from that of a moral treatise. In *Everyman* the relation of character to theme is particularly close.

The inescapable didacticism of the play raises other problems in interpretation. Keats said, "We hate poetry which has a palpable design upon us," and there are those who would apply his comment to all literature including the drama, finding something repellent in the crudity of a clear-cut lesson. Such critics might be much more favorable to *Major Barbara* because Shaw, for all his concern with ideas, does not force any one idea upon us, but by his dialectical method obliges us to reconsider several. Yet it must be pointed out that many great literary works, such as *The Divine Comedy* and *Paradise Lost*, are clearly didactic. The mere fact of a didactic intention cannot be used as evidence of artistic inferiority.

One objection to the didactic author is that, like the sentimentalist or the propagandist, he is apt to distort his material in order to elicit the single response he desires. The questions raised by such objections are too numerous and complicated to be dealt with briefly. We can only suggest here that although some distortion of life is inevitable in every artistic treatment (through selectivity, simplification, and arrangement, for example), the important question is whether or not the work as a whole corresponds in some way with our knowledge or experience of life. Where we are aware of falsity we may legitimately complain of distortion. Where we assent to the portrayal of a situation, we must agree that whatever distortion there may be is justified.

It is a curious fact that one may respond sympathetically to a didactic work without accepting the truth of the specific lesson it teaches. The high regard of critics of all shades of belief and unbelief for Dante and Milton proves the point. Readers and spectators are apparently capable of suspending both belief and disbelief, and of accepting hypothetically an author's belief and even his lesson so long as they are reading his words or watching his play.[1] For some the didactic purpose may serve chiefly as one of the forces which give coherence to the work. Thus the members of an audience who are not persuaded by *Everyman* to "forsake Pride" may have no difficulty in accepting this lesson as part of the experience of the play, and they may even be aware of how materially it contributes to the effectiveness of each situation. The world of the play, to which the characters are carefully shaped, is a world of Christian doctrine. If it is the characters and their interaction which give this dramatized sermon its force, the sermon in return augments the urgency of the situations and heightens the significance of the characters. The mutual dependence of the parts of the play and the lesson they teach is a fact with which interpretation must deal as it must deal with the closely related fact of allegorical characterization. The recognition of both facts is a prerequisite to understanding what kind of play *Everyman* is.

### Selected Reading List for the Morality Play

W. Bridges-Adams, "Moralities and Interludes," *The Irresistible Theatre*. London: Secker & Warburg, 1957, pp. 61–81.

J. A. Cormican, "Morality Tradition and the Interludes," *The Age of Chaucer*, Pelican *Guide to English Literature*, I. Baltimore, Md.: Penguin Books, Inc., 1963, 188–96.

---

[1] See M. H. Abrams, "Belief and the Suspension of Disbelief," *Literature and Belief*, ed. M. H. Abrams (New York: Columbia University Press, 1958), pp. 1–30.

Willard Farnham, "Tragedy and the English Moral Play," *The Medieval Heritage of Elizabethan Tragedy*. Oxford: Basil Blackwell, 1963, pp. 173–270.

Bernard Spivack, *Shakespeare and the Allegory of Evil*. New York: Columbia University Press, 1958, pp. 60–205.

# Shakespeare and The Elizabethan Theater

By the last decade of the sixteenth century, when Shakespeare began to write, a number of the companies of strolling players, which had been performing moralities and other plays in the provinces, had settled down in London, where they had become larger and more stable organizations. The nucleus of a company might still be no more than eight men. They held a royal patent to act and were shareholders in the company. William Shakespeare was such a shareholder in the Lord Chamberlain's company, later the King's company, when James I came to the throne. In addition to the shareholders, who took all the principal male parts, there were a few apprentices, boys of six or eight to eighteen, who played the parts of women, and hired men who performed such functions as prompting, collecting admissions, playing music, and acting in minor roles. Even with this larger company, there was often some doubling of parts as in the Greek and medieval theaters. The companies performed in inns, halls, or public squares as they always had until 1576 when the first permanent playhouse, called the Theater, was built by the father of Richard Burbage, the principal actor in Shakespeare's company. Other playhouses followed, including the most famous of all, the Globe, built by Shakespeare's company in 1599. Though the companies continued to make occasional tours in the provinces, especially in years when the plague closed the London theaters, these new playhouses became their permanent homes.

We have disappointingly meager evidence about what an Elizabethan public playhouse was like. From contemporary depictions such as Hollar's "Long View of London" (1647), we know that it was roughly circular in shape, with a central yard open to the sky and surrounded by covered galleries. The most important single piece of evidence about the appearance of the stage is a copy of a letter from Johannes de Witt, a Dutch visitor to London in about 1596, containing a sketch and a description of the Swan, a theater near the Globe. The rest of what we know or can guess depends on woodcuts ornamenting the title pages of a few plays, on brief descriptions, building contracts, and the printed texts of the plays with their stage directions. The De Witt sketch shows a large platform stage projecting into the middle of the yard where, as we know from other sources, those who paid only a penny for admission stood, while those who paid a little more sat on benches in the covered galleries. Both the seated audience and the standees were on three sides of the stage. On the fourth side was a wall separating it from the "tiring house," where the actors dressed and from which they made their entrances. De Witt's sketch shows two doors for this purpose; in some theaters there must have been three, as we can tell from certain stage directions. We also know that part or all of the tiring-house wall must often have been hung with an arras or curtains, and that there must have been some enclosed space where, by drawing a curtain or opening a door, a character might be revealed, or a spectacle like Volpone's gold (in the first scene of Ben Jonson's play). This space is sometimes called the "inner stage" today, though such a term was not used in Elizabethan times. It may have been recessed in the wall or built out like a booth. Above the entrances to the stage in the De Witt sketch are openings from which people are looking down. When the play required a character to speak or appear "above," this gallery is where the action would occur. If the space was not needed in a particular play, it is probable that spectators were allowed there. The De Witt sketch shows part of the stage covered by a roof, known as the "heavens" or the "shadow," a feature of most public playhouses, though it was not always supported by two large posts as at the Swan. On the roof De Witt drew the flag which advertised a performance that day, and on a high platform the trumpeter who would announce the beginning of the performance and provide the offstage flourishes so often called for in Elizabethan plays. Other musicians were probably stationed near the trumpeter in the third floor over the stage to play incidental music when it was needed. In the latter part of Shakespeare's life music was often played between the acts, though earlier this custom was rarely observed in the public theaters. After the play there was usually a jig, accompanied, of course, by music.

Even though many details remain a matter of guesswork, the main features of the Elizabethan public playhouse are clear. The large acting area of the platform stage could be supplemented when necessary by the enclosed space at the back, the gallery above, or even the musicians' gallery in the third floor. The stage was lit by daylight only (performances were in the afternoon), and there was no scenery, though there were sometimes rather elaborate props such as an arbor or a canopied throne. Spectacle was provided by colorful costumes and sometimes by machinery which could lower an actor from the "heavens" or raise him through a trap door in the floor. As in the Greek theater, little effort was made to create the illusion of a particular place, and there was no barrier between the audience and the players such as the artificial lighting of the modern stage imposes. The audience was large (the theater probably held between two and three thousand people) and constituted a cross section of the population. Toward the end of Shakespeare's career, his company acquired what was called a "private house"—an indoor theater charging higher prices, and hence catering to a more select audience. Here the lighting was artificial, and illusionistic scenery may even have been used on occasion. But it was for the public playhouse that Shakespeare wrote the great majority of his plays, and we should have in mind the conditions of that theater in reading *King Lear*. Shakespeare takes full advantage of its opportunities, allowing his characters to speak directly to the audience at times, and moving the action rapidly from indoors to outdoors and from one place to another. Nothing more than a throne or a table and bench is needed to indicate that we are in Lear's palace or in Albany's castle, and when the scene is the heath, the poetry conjures up not only a grim landscape but a furious storm as well. Drums and other sound effects undoubtedly helped to suggest the thunder and wind, but in such a theater as this, words have undisputed primacy.

Although the stage of the Elizabethan public theater was somewhat less bare than the platform where *Everyman* was performed, its simplicity carried with it some of the same universal suggestiveness. The playwright was free to go straight to the heart of a human problem without pausing to explain in detail how the problem arose. The reader of the strange opening scene of *King Lear*, so like an old folk tale of good and wicked daughters, will do well to take a hint from the simplicity of the original staging, and concentrate his attention on the basic issues of Lear's choice, rather than worry about the unlikelihood that such a family scene ever took place. He will also do well to ask himself what is likely to become of these basic issues in a mode of presentation that insists on the everyday credibility of the scene.

Shakespeare probably wrote *King Lear* in 1605 or 1606, after he had been

*Johannes de Witt's letter containing a sketch of the Swan Theater, written in about 1596, was copied by its recipient, Arend van Buchel. In 1888 the copy was discovered in the Utrecht University library. The letter was in Latin, and De Witt labeled various parts of his sketch with Latin terms which also served to support the resemblance he found between the Elizabethan and Roman theaters. Part of his letter appears at the foot of the sketch. Translations of the terms follow:* planities sive arena *flat place or arena;* proscaenium *stage;* mimorum aedes *tiring house (literally, "the actors' house");* ingressus *entrance (note that there is another one opposite);* orchestra *a term used in the Roman theater for the best seats, occupied by the senators;* sedilia *seats;* porticus *gallery;* tectum *roof.*

132

writing for the stage for about fifteen years. Born in Stratford-upon-Avon in 1564, he was married in 1582 and apparently went to London without his wife sometime between 1585 and 1592. Soon he was connected with an acting company as both actor and playwright, but it was as a shareholder that he made money, for authors received a modest flat fee and no royalties for their plays. Shakespeare's share of the company's profits was great enough to allow him to buy a better house for his family in Stratford before the end of the century. His improved social status was marked by the grant of a coat of arms. In 1598 Francis Meres considered him one of the outstanding English writers, worthy of comparison with the best Roman poets and playwrights. He seems to have done his last writing for the theater in the season of 1612–13. He died at Stratford April 23, 1616.

### The Text of King Lear

There are two authoritative texts of *King Lear*, the First Quarto (1608—the earliest edition) and the First Folio (1623—the first collected edition of Shakespeare's plays). The Folio is generally regarded as the more reliable, and contains some 100 lines not in the First Quarto, but it omits some 300 lines which are in the First Quarto and appear quite authentic. The omission may reflect a text cut for performance. The text printed in this volume is based on the Folio; all additions appear in brackets. Many of these are stage directions supplied by modern editors (that is, in the eighteenth to twentieth centuries). A few added stage directions come from the First Quarto; these are listed in the Textual Notes at the end of the play. All the additions to the dialogue derive from the First Quarto. Occasionally a First Folio reading has been replaced by what seems a better one from the First Quarto or later editions. All such substitutions are indicated in the Textual Notes. Exact information about the emendations of modern editors can be found in "The Arden Shakespeare" or "The Signet Classic Shakespeare."

A few typographical errors in the Folio text have been silently corrected, and both spelling and punctuation have been modernized. Occasionally the lineation has been altered, and the location of a few stage directions has been moved, usually by no more than two lines. Speech headings have been normalized and spelled out. The act and scene division is that of the Folio except in Act IV, where the Folio omits the third scene. In Act II the modern division of the Folio's Scene 2 into three scenes is indicated in the margin for convenience of reference, though there is no need for such a subdivision, since the action is continuous. In the Folio the numbering of the acts and scenes is in Latin. To make the metrical pattern clear, an indication is given when the "ed" of a past participle must be pronounced as a separate syllable (*endurèd*), or when an abnormal accentuation is required (*revénues*).

# The Tragedy of King Lear

## WILLIAM SHAKESPEARE

### CHARACTERS

LEAR, *King of Britain*
KING OF FRANCE
DUKE OF BURGUNDY
DUKE OF CORNWALL
DUKE OF ALBANY
EARL OF KENT
EARL OF GLOUCESTER
EDGAR, *son to* GLOUCESTER
EDMUND, *bastard son to* GLOUCESTER
CURAN, *a courtier*
OLD MAN, *tenant to* GLOUCESTER
DOCTOR
LEAR'S FOOL
OSWALD, *steward to* GONERIL
A CAPTAIN *under* EDMUND'S *command*
GENTLEMEN
A HERALD
SERVANTS *to* CORNWALL
GONERIL ⎫
REGAN  ⎬ *daughters to* LEAR
CORDELIA ⎭
KNIGHTS *attending on* LEAR, OFFICERS,
    MESSENGERS, SOLDIERS, ATTENDANTS
SCENE: *Britain*

### ACT I. *Scene 1*

(*Enter* KENT, GLOUCESTER, *and* EDMUND.)

KENT. I thought the King had more affected the Duke of Albany than Cornwall.

GLOUCESTER. It did always seem so to us; but now, in the division of the kingdom, it appears not which of the dukes he values 5 most, for equalities are so weighed that curiosity in neither can make choice of either's moiety.

KENT. Is not this your son, my lord?

GLOUCESTER. His breeding, sir, hath 10 been at my charge. I have so often blushed to acknowledge him that now I am brazed to't.

KENT. I cannot conceive you.

GLOUCESTER. Sir, this young fellow's 15 mother could; whereupon she grew round-wombed, and had indeed, sir, a son for her cradle ere she had a husband for her bed. Do you smell a fault?

KENT. I cannot wish the fault undone, 20 the issue of it being so proper.

GLOUCESTER. But I have a son, sir, by order of law, some year elder than this who yet is no dearer in my account: though this knave came something saucily to the 25 world before he was sent for, yet was his mother fair, there was good sport at his making, and the whoreson must be acknowledged. Do you know this noble gentleman, Edmund? 30

EDMUND. No, my lord.

GLOUCESTER. My Lord of Kent. Remember him hereafter as my honorable friend.

EDMUND. My services to your lordship.

---

*Act I. Scene 1* It will be noticed that no locality is given for the action here or at the opening of other scenes. Occasionally a property (such as a throne) suggests the locality; more often it is to be inferred from the dialogue. With no alteration the stage may represent a palace in one scene and a heath in the next. I.1.1 *affected* liked 2 *Albany* i.e., Scotland (once the domain of Albanacte)

6–8 *equalities . . . moiety* i.e., the shares are so equal that careful examination cannot make either one prefer the other's share 10 *breeding* upbringing 12 *brazed* brazened 14 *conceive* understand (Gloucester then puns on the sexual meaning) 21 *proper* handsome 24 *account* estimation 25 *knave* fellow (affectionate abuse); *saucily* presumptuously 28 *whoreson* more affectionate abuse, but literally accurate—bastard

KENT. I must love you, and sue to 35
know you better.

EDMUND. Sir, I shall study deserving.

GLOUCESTER. He hath been out nine
years, and away he shall again. (*[Sound a]
sennet.*) The King is coming. 40

(*Enter [one bearing a coronet, then]* KING
LEAR, *[then the* DUKES OF*]* CORNWALL *[and]*
ALBANY, *[next]* GONERIL, REGAN, COR-
DELIA, *and* ATTENDANTS.)

LEAR. Attend the lords of France and
Burgundy, Gloucester.

GLOUCESTER. I shall, my lord.

(*Exit [with* EDMUND*].*)

LEAR. Meantime we shall express our
darker purpose.

Give me the map there. Know that we have
divided

In three our kingdom; and 'tis our fast
intent 45

To shake all cares and business from our
age,

Conferring them on younger strengths while
we

Unburdened crawl toward death. Our son
of Cornwall,

And you our no less loving son of Albany,

We have this hour a constant will to publish 50

Our daughters' several dowers, that future
strife

May be prevented now. The princes, France
and Burgundy,

Great rivals in our youngest daughter's
love,

Long in our court have made their amorous
sojourn,

And here are to be answered. Tell me, my
daughters 55

(Since now we will divest us both of rule,

Interest of territory, cares of state),

Which of you shall we say doth love us
most,

That we our largest bounty may extend

Where nature doth with merit challenge.
Goneril, 60

Our eldest-born, speak first.

GONERIL. Sir, I love you more than word
can wield the matter;

Dearer than eyesight, space, and liberty;

Beyond what can be valuèd, rich or rare;

No less than life, with grace, health, beauty,
honor; 65

As much as child e'er loved, or father found;

A love that makes breath poor, and speech
unable.

Beyond all manner of so much I love you.

CORDELIA *[aside]*. What shall Cordelia
speak? Love, and be silent.

LEAR. Of all these bounds, even from this
line to this, 70

With shadowy forests and with champains
riched,

With plenteous rivers and wide-skirted
meads,

We make thee lady. To thine and Albany's
issues

Be this perpetual.—What says our second
daughter,

Our dearest Regan, wife of Cornwall?
[Speak] 75

REGAN. I am made of that self mettle as
my sister,

And prize me at her worth. In my true
heart

I find she names my very deed of love;

Only she comes too short, that I profess

Myself an enemy to all other joys 80

Which the most precious square of sense
possesses,

And find I am alone felicitate

In your dear Highness' love.

CORDELIA *[aside]*. Then poor Cordelia;

And yet not so, since I am sure my love's

More ponderous than my tongue. 85

LEAR. To thee and thine hereditary ever

---

38 *out* away 39–40 Stage direction: *sennet* trumpet
flourish (signalizing a procession); the pageantry
of this entrance emphasizes the ceremony of Lear's
court 43 *darker purpose* hidden intention 45 *fast*
firm 50 *constant will to publish* fixed determination
to proclaim 51 *several* individual 57 *interest*
legal right

60 *nature . . . challenge* the claims of natural
affection are matched by desert 62 *wield* handle
63 *space* i.e., in which to be free 67 *breath* language; *unable* impotent 71 *champains riched* plains
enriched 72 *wide-skirted meads* extensive meadows
73 *issues* descendants 76 *self* same 77 *prize* value
78 *my . . . love* the love by which I am bound (as
by a contract) 81 *which . . . possesses* which the
choicest estimate of sense values 82 *felicitate* made
happy 85 *ponderous* weighty

Remain this ample third of our fair kingdom,
No less in space, validity, and pleasure
Than that conferred on Goneril.—Now, our joy,
Although our last and least; to whose young love          90
The vines of France and milk of Burgundy
Strive to be interested; what can you say to draw
A third more opulent than your sisters? Speak.

    CORDELIA. Nothing, my lord.
    LEAR. Nothing?          95
    CORDELIA. Nothing.
    LEAR. Nothing will come of nothing. Speak again.
    CORDELIA. Unhappy that I am, I cannot heave
My heart into my mouth. I love your Majesty
According to my bond, no more nor less.          100
    LEAR. How, how, Cordelia? Mend your speech a little,
Lest you may mar your fortunes.
    CORDELIA.              Good my lord,
You have begot me, bred me, loved me. I
Return those duties back as are right fit,
Obey you, love you, and most honor you.          105
Why have my sisters husbands if they say
They love you all? Haply, when I shall wed,
That lord whose hand must take my plight shall carry
Half my love with him, half my care and duty.
Sure I shall never marry like my sisters,          110
[To love my father all.]
    LEAR. But goes thy heart with this?
    CORDELIA.          Ay, my good lord.
    LEAR. So young, and so untender?
    CORDELIA. So young, my lord, and true.
    LEAR. Let it be so, thy truth then be thy dower!          115
For, by the sacred radiance of the sun,
The mysteries of Hecate and the night,
By all the operation of the orbs

From whom we do exist and cease to be,
Here I disclaim all my paternal care,          120
Propinquity and property of blood,
And as a stranger to my heart and me
Hold thee from this for ever. The barbarous Scythian,
Or he that makes his generation messes
To gorge his appetite, shall to my bosom          125
Be as well neighbored, pitied, and relieved,
As thou my sometime daughter.
    KENT.              Good my liege—
    LEAR. Peace, Kent!
Come not between the dragon and his wrath.
I loved her most, and thought to set my rest          130
On her kind nursery.—Hence and avoid my sight!—
So be my grave my peace as here I give
Her father's heart from her! Call France. Who stirs?
Call Burgundy. Cornwall and Albany,
With my two daughters' dowers digest the third;          135
Let pride, which she calls plainness, marry her.
I do invest you jointly with my power,
Preeminence, and all the large effects
That troop with majesty. Ourself, by monthly course,
With reservation of an hundred knights,          140
By you to be sustained, shall our abode
Make with you by due turn. Only we shall retain
The name, and all th' addition to a king. The sway,
Revénue, execution of the rest,
Belovèd sons, be yours; which to confirm,          145
This coronet part between you.
    KENT.              Royal Lear,
Whom I have ever honored as my king,
Loved as my father, as my master followed,
As my great patron thought on in my prayers—

---

88 *validity* value  90 *least* smallest, youngest  92 *interested* closely connected  100 *bond* filial obligation  104 *Return . . . back* am dutiful in return  108 *plight* i.e., troth-plight  117 *Hecate* (pronounced Héccat) goddess of the underworld and patroness of witchcraft  118 *operation . . . orbs* astrological influences

---

121 *Propinquity . . . blood* relationship and commonblood  124 *generation* offspring; *messes* portions of food  127 *sometime* former  130 *set my rest* (1) rely with confidence (term derived from the card game of primero); (2) find my repose  131 *nursery* nursing, care  133 *Who stirs?* Who is in attendance?  138 *effects* perquisites  139 *Ourself* the royal "we"  143 *addition* titles, prerogatives

LEAR. The bow is bent and drawn; make from the shaft. 150

KENT. Let it fall rather, though the fork invade
The region of my heart. Be Kent unmannerly
When Lear is mad. What wouldst thou do, old man?
Think'st thou that duty shall have dread to speak
When power to flattery bows? To plainness honor's bound 155
When majesty falls to folly. Reserve thy state,
And in thy best consideration check
This hideous rashness. Answer my life my judgment,
Thy youngest daughter does not love thee least,
Nor are those empty-hearted whose low sounds 160
Reverb no hollowness.

LEAR.             Kent, on thy life, no more!

KENT. My life I never held but as [a] pawn
To wage against thine enemies; ne'er fear to lose it,
Thy safety being motive.

LEAR.             Out of my sight!

KENT. See better, Lear, and let me still remain 165
The true blank of thine eye.

LEAR. Now by Apollo—

KENT.             Now by Apollo, King,
Thou swear'st thy gods in vain.

LEAR.             O vassal! Miscreant!
        [Grasping his sword.]

ALBANY, CORNWALL. Dear sir, forbear!

KENT. Kill thy physician, and thy fee bestow 170
Upon the foul disease. Revoke thy gift,
Or, whilst I can vent clamor from my throat,
I'll tell thee thou dost evil.

LEAR.             Hear me, recreant,
On thine allegiance, hear me!

That thou hast sought to make us break our vows, 175
Which we durst never yet, and with strained pride
To come betwixt our sentence and our power,
Which nor our nature nor our place can bear,
Our potency made good, take thy reward.
Five days we do allot thee for provision 180
To shield thee from disasters of the world,
And on the sixth to turn thy hated back
Upon our kingdom. If, on the tenth day following,
Thy banished trunk be found in our dominions,
The moment is thy death. Away. By Jupiter, 185
This shall not be revoked.

KENT. Fare thee well, King. Sith thus thou wilt appear,
Freedom lives hence, and banishment is here.
[To CORDELIA.] The gods to their dear shelter take thee, maid,
That justly think'st and hast most rightly said. 190
[To REGAN and GONERIL.] And your large speeches may your deeds approve,
That good effects may spring from words of love.
Thus Kent, O princes, bids you all adieu;
He'll shape his old course in a country new.
        (Exit.)

(Flourish. Enter GLOUCESTER, with FRANCE and BURGUNDY; ATTENDANTS.)

GLOUCESTER. Here's France and Burgundy, noble lord. 195

LEAR. My Lord of Burgundy,
We first address toward you, who with this king
Hath rivalled for our daughter. What in the least
Will you require in present dower with her,
Or cease your quest of love?

BURGUNDY.             Most royal Majesty, 200
I crave no more than hath your Highness offered,

---

150 *make* get away; *shaft* arrow  151 *fall* strike; *fork* forked head  156 *Reserve thy state* keep your kingly authority  158 *Answer my life* Let my life be answerable for  161 *Reverb no hollowness* do not resound (like a drum) from emptiness  162 *pawn* stake  163 *wage* wager  164 *motive* moving cause  165 *still* always  166 *blank* white spot in the center of the target (for Lear to aim at)  168 *Miscreant* literally, infidel  173 *recreant* traitor

175 *That* in that, since  176 *strained* excessive  177 *sentence* decree  179 *Our . . . good* if my authority is to be maintained  184 *trunk* body  187 *Sith* since  191 *approve* prove true  194 *shape . . . course* pursue his customary ways (of plainspeaking)

Nor will you tender less.

LEAR.                    Right noble Burgundy,
When she was dear to us, we did hold her so;
But now her price is fallen. Sir, there she
    stands.
If aught within that little seeming sub-
    stance,                                      205
Or all of it, with our displeasure pieced
And nothing more, may fitly like your Grace,
She's there, and she is yours.

BURGUNDY.                 I know no answer.

LEAR. Will you, with those infirmities she
    owes,
Unfriended, new adopted to our hate,    210
Dow'red with our curse, and strangered with
    our oath,
Take her, or leave her?

BURGUNDY.           Pardon me, royal sir.
Election makes not up on such conditions.

LEAR. Then leave her, sir, for by the pow'r
    that made me
I tell you all her wealth. [To FRANCE.] For
    you, great King,                            215
I would not from your love make such a stray
To match you where I hate; therefore beseech
    you
T' avert your liking a more worthier way
Than on a wretch whom nature is ashamed
Almost t' acknowledge hers.

FRANCE.              This is most strange,    220
That she whom even but now was your [best]
    object,
The argument of your praise, balm of your
    age,
The best, the dearest, should in this trice of
    time
Commit a thing so monstrous to dismantle
So many folds of favor. Sure her offense    225
Must be of such unnatural degree
That monsters it, or your fore-vouched affec-
    tion
Fall'n into taint; which to believe of her
Must be a faith that reason without miracle

Should never plant in me.

CORDELIA.   I yet beseech your Majesty, 230
If for I want that glib and oily art
To speak and purpose not, since what I well
    intend
I'll do't before I speak, that you make known
It is no vicious blot, murder, or foulness,
No únchaste action or dishonored step,   235
That hath deprived me of your grace and
    favor;
But even for want of that for which I am
    richer—
A still-soliciting eye, and such a tongue
That I am glad I have not, though not to
    have it
Hath lost me in your liking.

LEAR.                    Better thou 240
Hadst not been born than not t' have pleased
    me better.

FRANCE. Is it but this! A tardiness in nature
Which often leaves the history unspoke
That it intends to do. My Lord of Burgundy,
What say you to the lady? Love's not
    love                                         245
When it is mingled with regards that
    stands
Aloof from th' éntire point. Will you have her?
She is herself a dowry.

BURGUNDY.           Royal King,
Give but that portion which yourself proposed,
And here I take Cordelia by the hand,    250
Duchess of Burgundy.

LEAR. Nothing. I have sworn. I am firm.

BURGUNDY. I am sorry then you have so
    lost a father
That you must lose a husband.

CORDELIA.           Peace be with Burgundy.
Since that respects of fortune are his love, 255
I shall not be his wife.

FRANCE. Fairest Cordelia, that art most rich
    being poor,
Most choice forsaken, and most loved
    despised,
Thee and thy virtues here I seize upon.
Be it lawful I take up what's cast away.    260

---

205 *little seeming* (1) appearing small; (2) making no pretense  206 *pieced* joined  209 *owes* owns
211 *strangered with* made a stranger by  213 *Election
...up* a choice cannot be made  216 *make...
stray* turn so far away as  221 *best object* main
object of love  222 *argument* theme  224 *dismantle*
strip off  227 *monsters it* makes it monstrous  228
*taint* decay

231 *for I want* because I lack  238 *still-soliciting*
always begging  242 *tardiness* reticence  246–47
*mingled...point* mixed with considerations
irrelevant to what is essential  255 *respects of
fortune* mercenary considerations

Gods, gods! 'Tis strange that from their
  cold'st neglect
My love should kindle to inflamed respect.
Thy dow'rless daughter, King, thrown to my
  chance,
Is queen of us, of ours, and our fair France.
Not all the dukes of wat'rish Burgundy      265
Can buy this únprized precious maid of me.
Bid them farewell, Cordelia, though unkind.
Thou losest here, a better where to find.

  LEAR. Thou hast her, France; let her be
    thine, for we
Have no such daughter, nor shall ever
  see                                        270
That face of hers again. Therefore be gone
Without our grace, our love, our benison.
Come, noble Burgundy.

    (*Flourish. Exeunt* [LEAR, BURGUNDY, CORN-
    WALL, ALBANY, GLOUCESTER, *and* ATTEN-
                                    DANTS].)

  FRANCE. Bid farewell to your sisters.
  CORDELIA. The jewels of our father, with
    washed eyes                             275
Cordelia leaves you. I know you what you
  are;
And, like a sister, am most loath to call
Your faults as they are named. Love well our
  father.
To your professèd bosoms I commit him;
But yet, alas, stood I within his grace,    280
I would prefer him to a better place.
So farewell to you both.
  REGAN. Prescribe not us our duty.
  GONERIL.                    Let your study
Be to content your lord, who hath received
  you
At fortune's alms. You have obedience
  scanted,                                  285
And well are worth the want that you have
  wanted.
  CORDELIA. Time shall unfold what plighted
    cunning hides;

Who covers faults, at last with shame derides.
Well may you prosper.
  FRANCE.              Come, my fair Cordelia.
    (*Exit* FRANCE *and* CORDELIA.)
  GONERIL. Sister, it is not little I have to  290
say of what most nearly appertains to us both.
I think our father will hence to-night.
  REGAN. That's most certain, and with you;
next month with us.
  GONERIL. You see how full of changes      295
his age is. The observation we have made of
it hath [not] been little. He always loved our
sister most, and with what poor judgment he
hath now cast her off appears too grossly.
  REGAN. 'Tis the infirmity of his age; yet  300
he hath ever but slenderly known himself.
  GONERIL. The best and soundest of his time
hath been but rash; then must we look from
his age to receive not alone the imperfections
of long-ingraffed condition, but there-     305
withal the unruly waywardness that infirm
and choleric years bring with them.
  REGAN. Such unconstant starts are we like
to have from him as this of Kent's banishment.
  GONERIL. There is further compliment      310
of leave-taking between France and him.
Pray you let us hit together; if our father carry
authority with such disposition as he bears,
this last surrender of his will but offend us.
  REGAN. We shall further think of it.      315
  GONERIL. We must do something, and i' th'
heat.                                    (*Exeunt.*)


                    *Scene 2*


  (*Enter* BASTARD, [*solus, with a letter*].)
  EDMUND. Thou, Nature, art my goddess; to
    thy law

---

262 *inflamed respect* ardent regard   265 *wat'rish*
(1) full of rivers; (2) diluted   266 *únprized* un-
valued   268 *here* this place; *where* other place
272 *benison* blessing   275 *The jewels* i.e., your prized
possessions; *washed* i.e., with tears   277 *like* as
278 *as . . . named* by their true names   279 *professèd* i.e., professing love   281 *prefer* advance   285
*alms* small charitable gift   286 *worth . . . wanted*
deserving of the same lack of affection that you
have shown   287 *plighted* folded

288 *Who covers* i.e., time, who . . . etc.   299
*grossly* obviously   305 *long-ingraffed condition* firmly
imbedded temperament   308 *unconstant starts* impulsive moves   310 *compliment* ceremony   312 *hit*
agree   312–13 *carry . . . bears* continues to exercise
authority in this way   314 *last* recent   316–17 *i' th'
heat* i.e., while the iron is hot
I.2.1 *Nature* Edmund's Nature is almost the
equivalent of animal nature or instinct, as opposed
to the broader concept which equates nature
with the orderly scheme of the entire created
universe. By his definition he is indeed a "natural
son"; by the other he is most unnatural in breaking the bonds of family and society

My services are bound. Wherefore should I
Stand in the plague of custom, and permit
The curiosity of nations to deprive me,
For that I am some twelve or fourteen moon-
    shines                             5
Lag of a brother? Why bastard? Wherefore
    base,
When my dimensions are as well compact,
My mind as generous, and my shape as true,
As honest madam's issue? Why brand they us
With base? with baseness? bastardy? Base,
    base?                              10
Who, in the lusty stealth of nature, take
More composition and fierce quality
Than doth, within a dull, stale, tired bed,
Go to th' creating a whole tribe of fops
Got 'tween asleep and wake? Well then,     15
Legitimate Edgar, I must have your land.
Our father's love is to the bastard Edmund
As to th' legitimate. Fine word, "legitimate."
Well, my legitimate, if this letter speed,
And my invention thrive, Edmund the
    base                              20
Shall top th' legitimate. I grow, I prosper.
Now, gods, stand up for bastards.

             (*Enter* GLOUCESTER.)

    GLOUCESTER. Kent banished thus? and
    France in choler parted?
And the King gone to-night? prescribed his
    pow'r?
Confined to exhibition? All this done     25
Upon the gad? Edmund, how now? What
    news?
    EDMUND. So please your lordship, none.
    GLOUCESTER. Why so earnestly seek you to
put up that letter?
    EDMUND. I know no news, my lord.     30
    GLOUCESTER. What paper were you reading?
    EDMUND. Nothing, my lord.
    GLOUCESTER. No? What needed then that

terrible dispatch of it into your pocket?
The quality of nothing hath not such     35
need to hide itself. Let's see. Come, if it
be nothing, I shall not need spectacles.
    EDMUND. I beseech you, sir, pardon me. It
is a letter from my brother that I have not
all o'er-read; and for so much as I have    40
perused, I find it not fit for your o'erlooking.
    GLOUCESTER. Give me the letter, sir.
    EDMUND. I shall offend, either to detain or
give it. The contents, as in part I understand
them, are to blame.     45
    GLOUCESTER. Let's see, let's see.
    EDMUND. I hope, for my brother's justifi-
cation, he wrote this but as an essay or taste
of my virtue.
    GLOUCESTER (*reads*). "This policy and    50
reverence of age makes the world bitter to the
best of our times; keeps our fortunes from us
till our oldness cannot relish them. I begin to
find an idle and fond bondage in the op-
pression of aged tyranny, who sways, not    55
as it hath power, but as it is suffered. Come
to me, that of this I may speak more. If our
father would sleep till I waked him, you
should enjoy half his revenue for ever, and
live the beloved of your brother,    60
                              EDGAR."
Hum! Conspiracy? "Sleep till I waked him,
you should enjoy half his revenue." My son
Edgar! Had he a hand to write this? A heart
and brain to breed it in? When came    65
this to you? Who brought it?
    EDMUND. It was not brought me, my lord;
there's the cunning of it. I found it thrown
in at the casement of my closet.
    GLOUCESTER. You know the character    70
to be your brother's?
    EDMUND. If the matter were good, my lord,
I durst swear it were his; but in respect of
that, I would fain think it were not.
    GLOUCESTER. It is his.    75
    EDMUND. It is his hand, my lord; but I hope
his heart is not in the contents.

---

3 *Stand . . . custom* be afflicted by convention   4
*curiosity of nations* nice distinctions of society  5 *For
that* because   5–6 *moonshines Lag of* months behind
(Edmund is not only illegitimate but a younger
brother)   6 *base* it was supposed (wrongly) that
"bastard" was derived from "base"   7 *dimensions
. . . compact* body is as proportionally framed  8
*generous* befitting a gentleman   12 *composition* com-
pleteness; *fierce* mettlesome   15 *got* begotten   19
*speed* succeed  20 *invention* plot  24 *prescribed* limited
25 *exhibition* an allowance  26 *gad* spur (of the
moment)   34 *terrible dispatch* hasty putting away

---

41 *o'erlooking* examination  48 *essay or taste* trial
or test  50–51 *policy and reverence* policy of rever-
encing  54 *idle and fond* vain and foolish  55 *sways*
rules  56 *suffered* allowed  69 *closet* room  70
*character* handwriting  73–74 *in respect of that* considering what it is  74 *fain* prefer to

GLOUCESTER. Has he never before sounded you in this business?

EDMUND. Never, my lord. But I have ⁸⁰ heard him oft maintain it to be fit that, sons at perfect age, and fathers declined, the father should be as ward to the son, and the son manage his revenue.

GLOUCESTER. O villain, villain! His very ⁸⁵ opinion in the letter. Abhorred villain, unnatural, detested, brutish villain; worse than brutish! Go, sirrah, seek him. I'll apprehend him. Abominable villain! Where is he?

EDMUND. I do not well know, my lord. ⁹⁰ If it shall please you to suspend your indignation against my brother till you can derive from him better testimony of his intent, you should run a certain course; where, if you violently proceed against him, mistaking ⁹⁵ his purpose, it would make a great gap in your own honor and shake in pieces the heart of his obedience. I dare pawn down my life for him that he hath writ this to feel my affection to your honor, and to no other ¹⁰⁰ pretense of danger.

GLOUCESTER. Think you so?

EDMUND. If your honor judge it meet, I will place you where you shall hear us confer of this and by an auricular assurance ¹⁰⁵ have your satisfaction, and that without any further delay than this very evening.

GLOUCESTER. He cannot be such a monster.

[EDMUND. Nor is not, sure.

GLOUCESTER. To his father, that so ¹¹⁰ tenderly and entirely loves him. Heaven and earth!] Edmund, seek him out; wind me into him, I pray you; frame the business after your own wisdom. I would unstate myself to be in a due resolution. ¹¹⁵

EDMUND. I will seek him, sir, presently; convey the business as I shall find means, and acquaint you withal.

GLOUCESTER. These late eclipses in the sun and moon portend no good to us. ¹²⁰ Though the wisdom of nature can reason it thus and thus, yet nature finds itself scourged by the sequent effects. Love cools, friendship falls off, brothers divide. In cities, mutinies; in countries, discord; in palaces, treason; ¹²⁵ and the bond cracked 'twixt son and father. This villain of mine comes under the prediction, there's son against father; the King falls from bias of nature, there's father against child. We have seen the best ¹³⁰ of our time. Machinations, hollowness, treachery, and all ruinous disorders follow us disquietly to our graves. Find out this villain, Edmund, it shall lose thee nothing; do it carefully. And the noble and true-hearted ¹³⁵ Kent banished; his offense, honesty. 'Tis strange. (Exit.)

EDMUND. This is the excellent foppery of the world, that when we are sick in fortune, often the surfeits of our own behavior, we ¹⁴⁰ make guilty of our disasters the sun, the moon, and stars; as if we were villains on necessity; fools by heavenly compulsion; knaves, thieves, and treachers by spherical predominance; drunkards, liars, and ¹⁴⁵ adulterers by an enforced obedience of planetary influence; and all that we are evil in, by a divine thrusting on. An admirable evasion of whoremaster man, to lay his goatish disposition on the charge of a ¹⁵⁰ star. My father compounded with my mother under the Dragon's Tail, and my nativity was

---

78–79 *sounded you* sounded you out  82 *at perfect age* (being) in the prime of life  88 *sirrah* (pronounced seár-a) familiar form of address used by masters to servants, parents to children, etc.  94 *run . . . course* proceed without danger of making a mistake  99 *feel* test  101 *pretense of danger* dangerous purpose  103 *meet* fitting  112–13 *wind . . . him* worm your way into his confidence  for me  113 *frame* plan  114–15 *unstate . . . resolution* give up my rank to know the truth  116 *presently* at once  117 *convey* manage  118 *withal* therewith

121 *wisdom of nature* scientific knowledge  121–23 *can . . . effects* can provide explanations, yet the consequences (of eclipses, etc.) are disruptions of the natural order. Belief in astrology was not confined to the superstitious. Though Shakespeare makes fun of superstitious extravagance, it is noteworthy that those who scoff at astrology, such as Edmund and Cassius (in *Julius Caesar*), are not Shakespeare's most dependable characters  122 *scourged* whipped, punished  127–28 *comes . . . prediction* i.e., his villainy was foretold by the omens  129 *bias of nature* natural inclination  134 *lose thee nothing* cause you no loss  138 *foppery* foolishness  139–40 *we are . . . surfeits* things go badly, often because of our excesses  144 *treachers* traitors  144–45 *spherical predominance* ascendancy of some planet or star  150 *goatish* lecherous  152–53 *Dragon's Tail, Ursa Major* constellations chosen for their sexual suggestiveness

under Ursa Major, so that it follows I am rough and lecherous. [Fut!] I should have been that I am, had the maidenliest star 155 in the firmament twinkled on my bastardizing. [Edgar—]

(*Enter* edgar.)

[and] pat he comes, like the catastrophe of the old comedy. My cue is villainous melancholy, with a sigh like Tom o' Bedlam. 160 —O, these eclipses do portend these divisions. Fa, sol, la, mi.

edgar. How now, brother Edmund; what serious contemplation are you in?

edmund. I am thinking, brother, of a 165 prediction I read this other day, what should follow these eclipses.

edgar. Do you busy yourself with that?

edmund. I promise you, the effects he writes of succeed unhappily: [as of un- 170 naturalness between the child and the parent; death, dearth, dissolutions of ancient amities; divisions in state, menaces and maledictions against king and nobles; needless diffidences, banishment of friends, dissipation of 175 cohorts, nuptial breaches, and I know not what.

edgar. How long have you been a sectary astronomical?

edmund. Come, come,] when saw you 180 my father last?

edgar. The night gone by.

edmund. Spake you with him?

edgar. Ay, two hours together.

edmund. Parted you in good terms? 185 Found you no displeasure in him by word nor countenance?

edgar. None at all.

edmund. Bethink yourself wherein you may have offended him; and at my entreaty 190 forbear his presence until some little time hath qualified the heat of his displeasure, which at this instant so rageth in him that with the

mischief of your person it would scarcely allay. 195

edgar. Some villain hath done me wrong.

edmund. That's my fear. I pray you have a continent forbearance till the speed of his rage goes slower; and, as I say, retire with me to my lodging, from whence I will 200 fitly bring you to hear my lord speak. Pray ye, go; there's my key. If you do stir abroad, go armed.

edgar. Armed, brother?

edmund. Brother, I advise you to the 205 best: [go armed.] I am no honest man if there be any good meaning toward you. I have told you what I have seen and heard; but faintly, nothing like the image and horror of it. Pray you, away. 210

edgar. Shall I hear from you anon?

edmund. I do serve you in this business.

(*Exit* [edgar].)

A credulous father, and a brother noble,
Whose nature is so far from doing harms
That he suspects none; on whose foolish honesty 215
My practices ride easy. I see the business.
Let me, if not by birth, have lands by wit;
All with me's meet that I can fashion fit.

(*Exit.*)

*Scene 3*

(*Enter* goneril *and* steward [oswald].)

goneril. Did my father strike my gentleman for chiding of his fool?

oswald. Ay, madam.

goneril. By day and night, he wrongs me!
Every hour
He flashes into one gross crime or other
That sets us all at odds. I'll not endure it. 5
His knights grow riotous, and himself upbraids us
On every trifle. When he returns from hunting,

---

154 *Fut!* (God)'s foot! 158 *catastrophe* conclusion 160 *Tom o' Bedlam* common name for wandering beggars who came, or pretended to come, from the London madhouse, Bethlehem (Bedlam) Hospital 170 *succeed* follow 174 *diffidences* suspicions 175–76 *dissipation of cohorts* melting away of supporters 178–79 *sectary astronomical* believer in astrology 192 *qualified* moderated

195 *allay* be appeased 197–98 *have . . . forbearance* restrain yourself and keep out of sight 201 *fitly* at a suitable time 209–10 *image and horror* horrible true picture 211 *anon* soon 216 *practices* plots 218 *meet* proper; *fashion fit* frame to suit my purposes
I.3.1. Stage direction: *Steward* the head of an Elizabethan household, often a gentleman by birth 3 *By day and night* an oath 6 *riotous* unruly

I will not speak with him. Say I am sick.
If you come slack of former services,
You shall do well; the fault of it I'll
   answer.                  10
                  [*Horns within.*]
OSWALD. He's coming, madam; I hear him.
GONERIL. Put on what weary negligence
   you please,
You and your fellows. I'd have it come to
   question.
If he distaste it, let him to my sister,
Whose mind and mine I know in that are
   one,                15
[Not to be overruled. Idle old man,
That still would manage those authorities
That he hath given away. Now, by my life,
Old fools are babes again, and must be used
With checks as flatteries, when they are
   seen abused.]          20
Remember what I have said.
   OSWALD.          Well, madam.
GONERIL. And let his knights have colder
   looks among you.
What grows of it, no matter; advise your
   fellows so.
[I would breed from hence occasions, and
   I shall,
That I may speak.] I'll write straight to my
   sister             25
To hold my [very] course. Prepare for dinner.
                (*Exeunt.*)

### Scene 4

(*Enter* KENT [*disguised*].)

KENT. If but as well I other accents borrow
That can my speech defuse, my good intent
May carry through itself to that full issue
For which I razed my likeness. Now, ban-
   ished Kent,
If thou canst serve where thou dost stand
   condemned,         5

So may it come, thy master whom thou lov'st
Shall find thee full of labors.
(*Horns within. Enter* LEAR *and* ATTENDANTS.)
LEAR. Let me not stay a jot for dinner;
go get it ready. [*Exit an* ATTENDANT. ] How
now, what art thou?         10
KENT. A man, sir.
LEAR. What dost thou profess? What
wouldst thou with us?
KENT. I do profess to be no less than I seem,
to serve him truly that will put me in  15
trust, to love him that is honest, to converse
with him that is wise and says little, to fear
judgment, to fight when I cannot choose,
and to eat no fish.
LEAR. What art thou?      20
KENT. A very honest-hearted fellow, and as
poor as the King.
LEAR. If thou be'st as poor for a subject as
he's for a king, thou art poor enough. What
wouldst thou?      25
KENT. Service.
LEAR. Who wouldst thou serve?
KENT. You.
LEAR. Dost thou know me, fellow?
KENT. No, sir, but you have that in  30
your countenance which I would fain call
master.
LEAR. What's that?
KENT. Authority.
LEAR. What services canst thou do?  35
KENT. I can keep honest counsel, ride, run,
mar a curious tale in telling it and deliver a
plain message bluntly. That which ordinary
men are fit for I am qualified in, and the
best of me is diligence.    40
LEAR. How old art thou?
KENT. Not so young, sir, to love a woman
for singing, nor so old to dote on her for
anything. I have years on my back forty-
eight.     45
LEAR. Follow me; thou shalt serve me. If I
like thee no worse after dinner, I will not
part from thee yet. Dinner, ho, dinner!

---

9 *come . . . services* serve him less well than formerly  10 *answer* answer for  13 *come to question*
become an issue  14 *distaste* dislike  16 *Idle* foolish
20 *checks . . . abused* restraints as well as cajolery
when they are seen to be misguided  24 *breed*
create; *occasions* opportunities
I.4.2 *defuse* confuse, disguise  3 *full issue* fulfillment  4 *razed my likeness* obliterated my normal
appearance

---

7 Stage direction: *within* offstage  8 *stay a jot*
wait a moment  12 *dost . . . profess* is your profession  14 *profess* claim  16 *converse* consort  18
*judgment* i.e., divine judgment  19 *eat no fish* i.e.,
be a good Protestant (anachronism)  31 *fain* like
to  36 *keep . . . counsel* respect honorable con-
fidences  37 *curious* elaborate

Where's my knave? my fool? Go you and
call my fool hither. (*Exit an* ATTENDANT.) 50
    (*Enter* STEWARD [OSWALD].)
You, you, sirrah, where's my daughter?
  OSWALD. So please you— (*Exit.*)
  LEAR. What says the fellow there? Call the
clotpoll back. [*Exit* KNIGHT.] Where's my fool?
Ho. I think the world's asleep. 55
    [*Re-enter* KNIGHT.]
How now? Where's that mongrel?
  KNIGHT. He says, my lord, your daughter
is not well.
  LEAR. Why came not the slave back to me
when I called him? 60
  KNIGHT. Sir, he answered me in the
roundest manner, he would not.
  LEAR. He would not?
  KNIGHT. My lord, I know not what the
matter is; but to my judgment your 65
Highness is not entertained with that cere-
monious affection as you were wont. There's
a great abatement of kindness appears as
well in the general dependants as in the Duke
himself also and your daughter. 70
  LEAR. Ha? Say'st thou so?
  KNIGHT. I beseech you pardon me, my
lord, if I be mistaken; for my duty cannot be
silent when I think your Highness wronged.
  LEAR. Thou but rememb'rest me of 75
mine own conception. I have perceived a
most faint neglect of late, which I have rather
blamed as mine own jealous curiosity than
as a very pretense and purpose of unkindness.
I will look further into't. But where's my 80
fool? I have not seen him this two days.
  KNIGHT. Since my young lady's going into
France, sir, the fool hath much pined away.
  LEAR. No more of that; I have noted it
well. Go you and tell my daughter I 85
would speak with her. [*Exit* KNIGHT.] Go you,
call hither my fool. (*Exit an* ATTENDANT.]
    (*Enter* STEWARD [OSWALD].)
O, you, sir, you! Come you hither, sir. Who
am I, sir?
  OSWALD. My lady's father. 90
  LEAR. "My lady's father"? My lord's
knave, you whoreson dog, you slave, you cur!

  OSWALD. I am none of these, my lord;
I beseech your pardon.
  LEAR. Do you bandy looks with me, 95
you rascal? [*Strikes him.*]
  OSWALD. I'll not be strucken, my lord.
  KENT. Nor tripped neither, you base
football player. [*Trips up his heels.*]
  LEAR. I thank thee, fellow. Thou serv'st 100
me, and I'll love thee.
  KENT. Come, sir, arise, away. I'll teach
you differences. Away, away. If you will
measure your lubber's length again, tarry;
but away. Go to! Have you wisdom? So. 105
    [*Pushes him out.*]
  LEAR. Now, my friendly knave, I thank
thee. There's earnest of thy service.
    [*Gives money.*]
    (*Enter* FOOL.)
  FOOL. Let me hire him too. Here's my
coxcomb. [*Offers* KENT *his cap.*]
  LEAR. How now, my pretty knave? 110
How dost thou?
  FOOL. Sirrah, you were best take my
coxcomb.
  KENT. Why, fool?
  FOOL. Why? For taking one's part 115
that's out of favor. Nay, an' thou canst not
smile as the wind sits, thou'lt catch cold
shortly. There, take my coxcomb. Why, this
fellow has banished two on's daughters, and
did the third a blessing against his will. 120
If thou follow him, thou must needs wear my
coxcomb.—How now, nuncle? Would I had
two coxcombs and two daughters.
  LEAR. Why, my boy?
  FOOL. If I gave them all my living, 125
I'ld keep my coxcombs myself. There's mine;
beg another of thy daughters.
  LEAR. Take heed, sirrah—the whip.
  FOOL. Truth's a dog must to kennel; he
must be whipped out, when the Lady 130
Brach may stand by th' fire and stink.
  LEAR. A pestilent gall to me.

---

49 *knave* boy  54 *clotpoll* clodpoll, blockhead
62 *roundest* plainest  66 *entertained* treated  75 *re-memb'rest* remind  77 *faint neglect* cf. "weary neg-ligence" (I.3.12)  78 *jealous curiosity* suspicious watchfulness  79 *very pretense* deliberate intention

95 *bandy* exchange  97 *strucken* struck  99 *football* considered a low game for street urchins, etc. 103 *differences* distinctions of rank  107 *earnest* a part payment to bind a bargain  109 *coxcomb* jester's cap, crested with imitation comb  116 *an'* if  117 *smile...sits* make friends with those in power  119 *banished* i.e., alienated by making them independent; *on's* of his  122 *nuncle* uncle (from "mine uncle")  131 *Brach* hound bitch 132 *gall* irritation

FOOL. Sirrah, I'll teach thee a speech.

LEAR. Do.

FOOL. Mark it, nuncle.    135

Have more than thou showest,
Speak less than thou knowest,
Lend less than thou owest,
Ride more than thou goest,
Learn more than thou trowest,    140
Set less than thou throwest;
Leave thy drink and thy whore,
And keep in-a-door,
And thou shalt have more
Than two tens to a score.    145

KENT. This is nothing, fool.

FOOL. Then 'tis like the breath of an unfee'd lawyer—you gave me nothing for't. Can you make no use of nothing, nuncle?

LEAR. Why, no, boy. Nothing can be    150 made out of nothing.

FOOL (to KENT). Prithee tell him, so much the rent of his land comes to; he will not believe a fool.

LEAR. A bitter fool.    155

FOOL. Dost thou know the difference, my boy, between a bitter fool and a sweet one?

LEAR. No, lad; teach me.

FOOL. [That lord that counselled thee
To give away thy land,    160
Come place him here by me—
Do thou for him stand.
The sweet and bitter fool
Will presently appear;
The one in motley here,    165
The other found out there.

LEAR. Dost thou call me fool, boy?

FOOL. All thy other titles thou hast given away; that thou wast born with.

KENT. This is not altogether fool, my    170 lord.

FOOL. No, faith; lords and great men will not let me. If I had a monopoly out, they would have part on't. And ladies too, they will not let me have all the fool to    175 myself; they'll be snatching.] Nuncle, give me an egg, and I'll give thee two crowns.

LEAR. What two crowns shall they be?

FOOL. Why, after I have cut the egg i' th'    180 middle and eat up the meat, the two crowns of the egg. When thou clovest thy crown i' th' middle and gav'st away both parts, thou bor'st thine ass on thy back o'er the dirt. Thou hadst little wit in thy bald crown when thou gav'st thy golden one    185 away. If I speak like myself in this, let him be whipped that first finds it so.

[Sings.] Fools had ne'er less grace in a year,
For wise men are grown foppish,
And know not how their wits to wear,    190
Their manners are so apish.

LEAR. When were you wont to be so full of songs, sirrah?

FOOL. I have used it, nuncle, e'er since thou mad'st thy daughters thy mothers; for    195 when thou gav'st them the rod, and put'st down thine own breeches,

[Sings.] Then they for sudden joy did weep,
And I for sorrow sung,
That such a king should play bo-
peep    200
And go the fools among.

Prithee, nuncle, keep a schoolmaster that can teach thy fool to lie. I would fain learn to lie.

LEAR. An' you lie, sirrah, we'll have you whipped.    205

FOOL. I marvel what kin thou and thy daughters are. They'll have me whipped for speaking true; thou'lt have me whipped for lying; and sometimes I am whipped for holding my peace. I had rather be any    210 kind o' thing than a fool, and yet I would not be thee, nuncle: thou hast pared thy wit o' both sides and left nothing i' th' middle. Here comes one o' the parings.

(Enter GONERIL.)

LEAR. How now, daughter? What    215 makes that frontlet on? You are too much of late i' th' frown.

FOOL. Thou wast a pretty fellow when thou hadst no need to care for her frowning. Now

---

139 goest walk    140 trowest believe    141 Set . . . throwest bet less than you throw for (i.e., get odds)    150–51 Nothing . . . nothing cf I.1.97    165 motley cloth of mixed colors worn by jesters    166 found out revealed    173 let me (be all the fool there is)    176 snatching (probably referring to the belief that fools had large sexual organs)

180 eat eaten    183–84 bor'st . . . dirt (a reversal of sensible procedure)    186 like myself i.e., like a fool    186–87 let . . . so i.e., let anyone who thinks this is foolishness be whipped as a fool    188 grace favor    189 foppish foolish    194 used it made this practice    200 bo-peep a children's hiding game    204 an' if    216 frontlet frown (literally a band worn across the brow)

thou art an O without a figure. I am 220
better than thou art now: I am a fool, thou
art nothing. [*To* GONERIL.] Yes, forsooth, I
will hold my tongue. So your face bids me,
though you say nothing. Mum, mum,
    He that keeps nor crust nor crum, 225
    Weary of all, shall want some.—
(*Points at* LEAR.) That's a shealed peascod.
    GONERIL. Not only, sir, this your all-li-
    censed fool,
But other of your insolent retinue
Do hourly carp and quarrel, breaking
    forth 230
In rank and not-to-be-endurèd riots. Sir,
I had thought by making this well known
    unto you
To have found a safe redress, but now grow
    fearful,
By what yourself too late have spoke and
    done,
That you protect this course, and put it
    on 235
By your allowance; which if you should,
    the fault
Would not 'scape censure, nor the redresses
    sleep,
Which, in the tender of a wholesome weal,
Might in their working do you that
    offense,
Which else were shame, that then neces-
    sity 240
Will call discreet proceeding.
    FOOL. For you know, nuncle,
    The hedge-sparrow fed the cuckoo so
      long
    That it had it head bit off by it
      young.
So out went the candle, and we were left
    darkling. 245
    LEAR. Are you our daughter?

---

220 *0 . . . figure* cipher with no figure in front
of it to give it value  226 *want* need  227 *shealed
peascod* shelled peapod  228 *all-licensed* all-privi-
leged  230 *carp* find fault  231 *rank* gross  233 *safe*
sure  235 *put it on* encourage it  236 *allowance*
approval  237 *redresses sleep* corrective actions lie
dormant  238 *tender of* care for; *weal* state  239–41
*Might . . . proceeding* might otherwise seem humiliating but in these circumstances will be called
prudent  243–44 *hedge-sparrow . . . young* an example of ingratitude: the cuckoo lays eggs in the
nests of other birds; the young cuckoos are said
to kill their foster parents  244 *it* its  245 *darkling*
in the dark

    GONERIL. I would you would make use of
    your good wisdom
(Whereof I know you are fraught) and put
    away
These dispositions which of late transport you
From what you rightly are. 250
    FOOL. May not an ass know when the cart
    draws the horse?
Whoop, Jug, I love thee!
    LEAR. Does any here know me? This is not
    Lear.
Does Lear walk thus? speak thus? Where
    are his eyes?
Either his notion weakens, [or] his discern-
    ings 255
Are lethargied—Ha! Waking? 'Tis not so.
Who is it that can tell me who I am?
    FOOL. Lear's shadow.
    [LEAR. I would learn that; for, by the marks
of sovereignty, knowledge, and reason, 260
I should be false persuaded I had daughters.
    FOOL. Which they will make an obedient
    father.]
    LEAR. Your name, fair gentlewoman?
    GONERIL. This admiration, sir, is much o'
    th' savor
Of other your new pranks. I do beseech
    you 265
To understand my purposes aright.
As you are old and reverend, should be wise.
Here do you keep a hundred knights and
    squires,
Men so disordered, so deboshed, and
    bold
That this our court, infected with their man-
    ners, 270
Shows like a riotous inn. Epicurism and lust
Makes it more like a tavern or a brothel
Than a graced palace. The shame itself doth
    speak
For instant remedy. Be then desired
By her that else will take the thing she
    begs 275
A little to disquantity your train,

---

248 *fraught* laden  249 *dispositions* moods  252
*Jug* nickname for Joan (part of a popular refrain?)
255 *notion* understanding  256 *Waking?* i.e., Am
I awake?  259 *marks* outward signs  264–65 *admiration* air of wonderment; *o' th' savor . . . your* like
some of your other  269 *deboshed* debauched  271
*Epicurism* gluttony  273 *graced* honored  276
*disquantity* reduce in size

And the remainders that shall still depend
To be such men as may besort your age,
Which know themselves, and you.
    LEAR.          Darkness and devils!
Saddle my horses; call my train together. 280
Degenerate bastard, I'll not trouble thee:_
Yet have I left a daughter.
    GONERIL. You strike my people, and your
      disordered rabble
Make servants of their betters.
          (Enter ALBANY.)
    LEAR. Woe that too late repents.—[O, sir,
      are you come?] 285
Is it your will? Speak, sir.—Prepare my
    horses.
Ingratitude! thou marble-hearted fiend,
More hideous when thou show'st thee in a
    child
Than the sea-monster.
    ALBANY.        Pray, sir, be patient.
    LEAR. Detested kite, thou liest. 290
My train are men of choice and rarest parts,
That all particulars of duty know
And in the most exact regard support
The worships of their name. O most small
    fault,
How ugly didst thou in Cordelia show! 295
Which, like an engine, wrenched my frame
    of nature
From the fixed place; drew from my heart
    all love
And added to the gall. O Lear, Lear, Lear!
Beat at this gate that let thy folly in
          [Strikes his head.]
And thy dear judgment out. Go, go, my
    people. 300
    ALBANY. My lord, I am guiltless, as I am
    ignorant
Of what hath moved you.
    LEAR.        It may be so, my lord.
Hear, Nature, hear; dear goddess, hear:
Suspend thy purpose if thou didst intend
To make this creature fruitful. 305
Into her womb convey sterility,
Dry up in her the organs of increase,

And from her derogate body never spring
A babe to honor her. If she must teem,
Create her child of spleen, that it may
    live 310
And be a thwart disnatured torment to her.
Let it stamp wrinkles in her brow of youth,
With cadent tears fret channels in her cheeks,
Turn all her mother's pains and benefits
To laughter and contempt, that she may
    feel 315
How sharper than a serpent's tooth it is
To have a thankless child. Away, away!
          (Exit.)
    ALBANY. Now, gods that we adore, whereof
    comes this?
    GONERIL. Never afflict yourself to know
    more of it,
But let his disposition have that scope 320
As dotage gives it.
          (Enter LEAR.)
    LEAR. What, fifty of my followers at a
    clap?
Within a fortnight?
    ALBANY.        What's the matter, sir?
    LEAR. I'll tell thee. [To GONERIL.] Life and
    death, I am ashamed
That thou hast power to shake my manhood
    thus! 325
That these hot tears, which break from me
    perforce,
Should make thee worth them. Blasts and
    fogs upon thee!
Th' untented woundings of a father's curse
Pierce every sense about thee! Old fond
    eyes,
Beweep this cause again I'll pluck ye out 330
And cast you, with the waters that you loose,
To temper clay. [Yea, is't come to this?]
Ha! Let it be so. I have another daughter,
Who I am sure is kind and comfortable.
When she shall hear this of thee, with her
    nails 335
She'll flay thy wolvish visage. Thou shalt find
That I'll resume the shape which thou dost
    think

---

277 *depend* be attached  278 *besort* suit  290 *kite* bird of prey  291 *parts* accomplishments  293 *in the most exact regard* with the most careful attention  294 *worships* honor  296 *engine* instrument of torture or war machine; *frame of nature* Lear's body or his whole being, either of which may be compared to a building  298 *gall* bitterness

308 *derogate* degraded  309 *teem* be pregnant 310 *spleen* spitefulness  311 *thwart disnatured* perverse unnatural  313 *cadent* falling; *fret* wear  314 *benefits* loving care  326 *perforce* by force, against my will  328 *untented* untentable: too deep to be cleaned with a *tent*, a roll of lint  329 *fond* foolish 330 *Beweep* i.e., if you beweep  332 *temper* soften 334 *comfortable* disposed to give comfort  337 *shape* i.e., role of king

I have cast off for ever.

(*Exit* [LEAR *with* KENT *and* ATTENDANTS].)

GONERIL.                Do you mark that?

ALBANY. I cannot be so partial, Goneril,

To the great love I bear you—                340

GONERIL. Pray you, content.—What, Oswald, ho!

[*To* FOOL.] You, sir, more knave than fool, after your master!

FOOL. Nuncle Lear, nuncle Lear, tarry. Take the fool with thee.

A fox, when one has caught her,                345
And such a daughter,
Should sure to the slaughter,
If my cap would buy a halter.
So the fool follows after.        (*Exit.*)

GONERIL. This man hath had good counsel —a hundred knights!                350

'Tis politic and safe to let him keep
At point a hundred knights—yes, that on every dream,
Each buzz, each fancy, each complaint, dislike,
He may enguard his dotage with their pow'rs
And hold our lives in mercy.—Oswald, I say!                355

ALBANY. Well, you may fear too far.

GONERIL.                Safer than trust too far.

Let me still take away the harms I fear,
Not fear still to be taken. I know his heart.
What he hath uttered I have writ my sister.
If she sustain him and his hundred knights,                360
When I have showed th' unfitness—

(*Enter* STEWARD [OSWALD].)

How now, Oswald?
What, have you writ that letter to my sister?

OSWALD. Ay, madam.

GONERIL. Take you some company, and away to horse.

Inform her full of my particular fear,                365
And thereto add such reasons of your own
As may compact it more. Get you gone,
And hasten your return. [*Exit* OSWALD.] No, no, my lord,

This milky gentleness and course of yours,
Though I condemn not, yet under pardon,    370
You are much more atasked for want of wisdom
Than praised for harmful mildness.

ALBANY. How far your eyes may pierce I cannot tell;
Striving to better, oft we mar what's well.

GONERIL. Nay then—                375

ALBANY. Well, well; th' event.        (*Exeunt.*)

## Scene 5

(*Enter* LEAR, KENT, *and* FOOL.)

LEAR. Go you before to Gloucester with these letters. Acquaint my daughter no further with anything you know than comes from her demand out of the letter. If your diligence be not speedy, I shall be there    5 afore you.

KENT. I will not sleep, my lord, till I have delivered your letter.        (*Exit.*)

FOOL. If a man's brains were in's heels, were't not in danger of kibes?                10

LEAR. Ay, boy.

FOOL. Then I prithee be merry. Thy wit shall not go slipshod.

LEAR. Ha, ha, ha.

FOOL. Shalt see thy other daughter will    15 use thee kindly; for though she's as like this as a crab's like an apple, yet I can tell what I can tell.

LEAR. What canst tell, boy?

FOOL. She will taste as like this as a    20 crab does to a crab. Thou canst tell why one's nose stands i' th' middle on's face?

LEAR. No.

FOOL. Why, to keep one's eyes of either side's nose, that what a man cannot smell out    25 he may spy into.

LEAR. I did her wrong.

---

339–40 *partial ... To* made so partial ... by  348–49 *halter ... after* rhymed with slaughter, etc.  351 *politic* good policy, wise (ironic)  352 *At point* armed  353 *buzz* rumor  355 *in mercy* at his mercy  357 *still* always  358 *taken* overtaken (by them)  364 *some company* an escort  365 *particular* own  367 *compact* confirm

369 *gentleness and course* gentle course  371 *atasked* censured  372 *harmful* dangerous, potentially harmful  376 *th'event* the outcome (will show who's right)
I.5.4 *demand out of* questioning suggested by  10 *kibes* chilblains  13 *slipshod* in slippers; i.e., your brains, being nonexistent, will not require such protection  15 *Shalt* thou shalt  16 *kindly* with a play on the meaning "according to her nature"  17 *crab* crabapple  22 *on's* of his  27 *her* i.e., Cordelia; from this time on, Lear's inner preoccupations come out with increasing frequency

FOOL. Canst tell how an oyster makes his shell?

LEAR. No.                                                30

FOOL. Nor I neither; but I can tell why a snail has a house.

LEAR. Why?

FOOL. Why, to put 's head in; not to give it away to his daughters, and leave his   35 horns without a case.

LEAR. I will forget my nature. So kind a father!—Be my horses ready?

FOOL. Thy asses are gone about 'em. The reason why the seven stars are no moe   40 than seven is a pretty reason.

LEAR. Because they are not eight.

FOOL. Yes indeed. Thou wouldst make a good fool.

LEAR. To take 't again perforce—   45 Monster ingratitude!

FOOL. If thou wert my fool, nuncle, I'd have thee beaten for being old before thy time.

LEAR. How's that?                                        50

FOOL. Thou shouldst not have been old till thou hadst been wise.

LEAR. O, let me not be mad, not mad, sweet heaven!
Keep me in temper; I would not be mad!
[*Enter a* GENTLEMAN.]
How now, are the horses ready?            55

GENTLEMAN. Ready, my lord.

LEAR. Come, boy.

FOOL. She that's a maid now, and laughs at my departure,
Shall not be a maid long, unless things be cut shorter.

(*Exeunt.*)

## ACT II.   *Scene 1*

(*Enter* BASTARD *and* CURAN *severally.*)

EDMUND. Save thee, Curan.

CURAN. And you, sir. I have been with your father, and given him notice that the Duke of Cornwall and Regan his Duchess will be here with him this night.      5

EDMUND. How comes that?

CURAN. Nay, I know not. You have heard of the news abroad—I mean the whispered ones, for they are yet but ear-kissing arguments?      10

EDMUND. Not I. Pray you, what are they?

CURAN. Have you heard of no likely wars toward, 'twixt the Dukes of Cornwall and Albany?

EDMUND. Not a word.      15

CURAN. You may do, then, in time. Fare you well, sir.      (*Exit.*)

EDMUND. The Duke be here to-night? The better best!
This weaves itself perforce into my business.
My father hath set guard to take my brother,      20
And I have one thing of a queasy question
Which I must act. Briefness and fortune, work!
Brother, a word: descend. Brother, I say!
(*Enter* EDGAR.)
My father watches. O sir, fly this place.
Intelligence is given where you are hid.      25
You have now the good advantage of the night.
Have you not spoken 'gainst the Duke of Cornwall?
He's coming hither; now i' th' night, i' th' haste,
And Regan with him. Have you nothing said
Upon his party 'gainst the Duke of Albany?      30
Advise yourself.

EDGAR.      I am sure on't, not a word.

EDMUND. I hear my father coming. Pardon me:
In cunning I must draw my sword upon you.
Draw, seem to defend yourself; now quit you well.—

37 *nature* paternal instinct   40 *seven stars* Pleiades; *moe* more   45 *take 't again* take back what he has given   54 *in temper* balanced   58 *departure* rhymed with "shorter"   59 *things ... shorter* another sexual joke
II.1 Stage direction: *severally* separately; i.e., from two entrances to the stage. Elizabethan theaters normally had two or three doors in the back wall of the stage   1 *Save* God save

9–10 *ear-kissing arguments* whispered topics   13 *toward* impending   18 *better* i.e., even better than   21 *of ... question* whose outcome is uncertain (*queasy* literally, on the point of vomiting)   22 *Briefness* immediate action   30 *Upon his party 'gainst* about his enmity to   31 *Advise yourself* consider   33 *in cunning* as a ruse   34 *quit you* acquit yourself

Yield! Come before my father! Light ho,
here!—                                    35
Fly, brother.—Torches, torches!—So fare-
well.                              (*Exit* EDGAR.)
Some blood drawn on me would beget opin-
ion
Of my more fierce endeavor. [*Wounds his arm.*]
I have seen drunkards
Do more than this in sport.—Father, father!
Stop, stop! No help?              40
   (*Enter* GLOUCESTER, *and* SERVANTS *with
               torches.*)
   GLOUCESTER. Now, Edmund, where's the
   villain?
   EDMUND. Here stood he in the dark, his
   sharp sword out,
Mumbling of wicked charms, conjuring the
moon
To stand auspicious mistress.
   GLOUCESTER.          But where is he?
   EDMUND. Look, sir, I bleed.
   GLOUCESTER.          Where is the villain,
   Edmund?                        45
   EDMUND. Fled this way, sir, when by no
   means he could—
   GLOUCESTER. Pursue him, ho! Go after.
[*Exeunt some* SERVANTS.] By no means what?
   EDMUND. Persuade me to the murder of
   your lordship;
But that I told him the revenging gods
'Gainst parricides did all the thunder
bend;                              50
Spoke with how manifold and strong a bond
The child was bound to th' father—sir, in
fine,
Seeing how loathly opposite I stood
To his unnatural purpose, in fell motion
With his preparèd sword he charges home 55
My unprovided body, lanched mine arm;
But when he saw my best alarumed spirits
Bold in the quarrel's right, roused to th'
encounter,
Or whether gasted by the noise I made,
Full suddenly he fled.
   GLOUCESTER.          Let him fly far.   60
Not in this land shall he remain uncaught;

And found—dispatch. The noble Duke my
master,
My worthy arch and patron, comes to-night:
By his authority I will proclaim it
That he which finds him shall deserve our
thanks,                            65
Bringing the murderous coward to the stake;
He that conceals him, death.
   EDMUND. When I dissuaded him from his
   intent
And found him pight to do it, with curst
speech
I threatened to discover him. He replied, 70
"Thou unpossessing bastard; dost thou think,
If I would stand against thee, would the
reposal
Of any trust, virtue, or worth in thee
Make thy words faithed? No. What I should
deny
(As this I would, ay, though thou didst
produce                            75
My very character) I'd turn it all
To thy suggestion, plot, and damnèd practice;
And thou must make a dullard of the world,
If they not thought the profits of my
death
Were very pregnant and potential spirits 80
To make thee seek it."
   GLOUCESTER.          O strange and fastened
   villain!
Would he deny his letter, said he? [I never
got him.]                    (*Tucket within.*)
Hark, the Duke's trumpets. I know not why
he comes.
All ports I'll bar; the villain shall not
'scape;
The Duke must grant me that. Besides, his
picture                            85
I will send far and near, that all the kingdom
May have due note of him; and of my land,
Loyal and natural boy, I'll work the means
To make thee capable.

───────

50 *bend* aim   52 *in fine* finally   53 *loathly opposite*
loathingly opposed   54 *fell* deadly   56 *unprovided*
unprotected; *lanched* lanced   57 *best alarumed* fully
aroused   58 *Bold . . . right* emboldened by the
rightness of my cause   59 *gasted* struck aghast

62 *dispatch* death (to him)   63 *arch and patron*
chief patron   69 *pight* determined   70 *discover*
reveal   71 *unpossessing* landless   72 *reposal* placing
74 *faithed* believed   76 *character* handwriting   77
*practice* devising   78 *make . . . world* think the world
stupid   80 *pregnant* urgent (from Fr. *preindre*, to
press); *potential* powerful   81 *fastened* hardened
82 *got* begot   82 Stage direction: *Tucket* (Cornwall's) special trumpet-call; Stage direction: *within*
offstage   89 *capable* i.e., of inheriting

(*Enter* CORNWALL, REGAN, *and* ATTENDANTS.)

CORNWALL. How now, my noble friend?
Since I came hither                                    90
(Which I can call but now) I have heard
strange news.

REGAN. If it be true, all vengeance comes
too short
Which can pursue th' offender. How dost,
my lord?

GLOUCESTER. O madam, my old heart is
cracked, it's cracked.

REGAN. What, did my father's godson seek
your life?                                             95
He whom my father named, your Edgar?

GLOUCESTER. O lady, lady, shame would
have it hid.

REGAN. Was he not companion with the
riotous knights
That tended upon my father?

GLOUCESTER. I know not, madam. 'Tis too
bad, too bad.                                          100

EDMUND. Yes, madam, he was of that
consort.

REGAN. No marvel then though he were
ill affected.
'Tis they have put him on the old man's death,
To have th' expense and waste of his
revénues.
I have this present evening from my sister   105
Been well informed of them, and with such
cautions
That, if they come to sojourn at my house,
I'll not be there.

CORNWALL.    Nor I, assure thee, Regan.
Edmund, I hear that you have shown your
father
A childlike office.

EDMUND.         It was my duty, sir.       110

GLOUCESTER. He did bewray his practice,
and received
This hurt you see, striving to apprehend him.

CORNWALL. Is he pursued?

GLOUCESTER.            Ay, my good lord.

CORNWALL. If he be taken, he shall never
more
Be feared of doing harm. Make your own
purpose,                                               115

How in my strength you please. For you,
Edmund,
Whose virtue and obedience doth this instant
So much commend itself, you shall be ours.
Natures of such deep trust we shall much
need;
You we first seize on.

EDMUND.              I shall serve you, sir,   120
Truly, however else.

GLOUCESTER.    For him I thank your Grace.

CORNWALL. You know not why we came to
visit you?

REGAN. Thus out of season, threading dark-
eyed night.
Occasions, noble Gloucester, of some prize,
Wherein we must have use of your
advice.                                                125
Our father he hath writ, so hath our sister,
Of differences, which I best thought it fit
To answer from our home. The several mes-
sengers
From hence attend dispatch. Our good old
friend,
Lay comforts to your bosom, and bestow   130
Your needful counsel to our businesses,
Which craves the instant use.

GLOUCESTER.           I serve you, madam.
Your Graces are right welcome.

                          (*Exeunt. Flourish.*)


*Scene 2*

(*Enter* KENT *and* STEWARD [OSWALD],
*severally.*)

OSWALD. Good dawning to thee, friend. Art
of this house?

KENT. Ay.

OSWALD. Where may we set our horses?

KENT. I' th' mire.                                     5

---

101 *consort* company   102 *affected* disposed   103
*put him on* put him up to   104 *expense and waste*
wasteful expenditure   110 *childlike* filial   111 *bewray his practice* reveal his plot   115 *of doing* be-

cause he might do   115–16 *Make . . . please* make
any use you please of my powers for your purposes   117 *virtue and obedience* virtuous obedience
124 *prize* moment   127 *differences* disputes; *which*
(referring to the letters)   128 *from* away from   129
*attend dispatch* are waiting to be sent back   130
*Lay . . . bosom* be comforted   131 *needful* needed
132 *craves . . . use* need to be dealt with immediately (a third person singular verb was often
used for the plural)
II.2.1 *dawning* (though still dark, it is just before dawn)   1–2 *Art . . . house* are you a servant
here

OSWALD. Prithee, if thou lov'st me, tell me.

KENT. I love thee not.

OSWALD. Why then, I care not for thee.

KENT. If I had thee in Lipsbury Pinfold, I would make thee care for me. 10

OSWALD. Why dost thou use me thus? I know thee not.

KENT. Fellow, I know thee.

OSWALD. What dost thou know me for?

KENT. A knave, a rascal, an eater of 15 broken meats; a base, proud, shallow, beggarly, three-suited, hundred-pound, filthy worsted-stocking knave; a lily-livered, action-taking, whoreson, glass-gazing, superserviceable, finical rogue; one-trunk-inheriting 20 slave; one that wouldst be a bawd in way of good service, and art nothing but the composition of a knave, beggar, coward, pander, and the son and heir of a mongrel bitch; one whom I will beat into clamorous whining 25 if thou deny'st the least syllable of thy addition.

OSWALD. Why, what a monstrous fellow art thou, thus to rail on one that is neither known of thee nor knows thee! 30

KENT. What a brazen-faced varlet art thou to deny thou knowest me! Is it two days ago since I tripped up thy heels and beat thee before the King? [Draws his sword.] Draw, you rogue, for though it be night, yet the 35 moon shines. I'll make a sop o' th' moonshine of you. You whoreson cullionly barbermonger, draw!

OSWALD. Away, I have nothing to do with thee. 40

KENT. Draw, you rascal. You come with letters against the King, and take Vanity the

puppet's part against the royalty of her father. Draw, you rogue, or I'll so carbonado your shanks. Draw, you rascal. Come your 45 ways!

OSWALD. Help, ho! Murder! Help!

KENT. Strike, you slave! Stand, rogue! Stand, you neat slave! Strike! [Beats him.]

OSWALD. Help, ho! Murder, murder! 50

(Enter BASTARD [with his rapier drawn], CORNWALL, REGAN, GLOUCESTER, SERVANTS.)

EDMUND. How now? What's the matter? Part!

KENT. With you, goodman boy, if you please! Come, I'll flesh ye; come on, young master. 55

GLOUCESTER. Weapons? Arms? What's the matter here?

CORNWALL. Keep peace, upon your lives. He dies that strikes again. What is the matter? 60

REGAN. The messengers from our sister and the King.

CORNWALL. What is your difference? Speak.

OSWALD. I am scarce in breath, my lord.

KENT. No marvel, you have so bestirred 65 your valor. You cowardly rascal, nature disclaims in thee. A tailor made thee.

CORNWALL. Thou art a strange fellow. A tailor make a man?

KENT. A tailor, sir. A stonecutter or a 70 painter could not have made him so ill, though they had been but two years o' th' trade.

CORNWALL. Speak yet, how grew your quarrel? 75

OSWALD. This ancient ruffian, sir, whose life I have spared at suit of his gray beard—

KENT. Thou whoreson zed, thou unnecessary letter! My lord, if you will give me leave, I will tread this unbolted villain into 80 mortar and daub the wall of a jakes with him.

9 in Lipsbury Pinfold slang for "between my teeth" or "in my clutches" (pinfold pound for stray animals) 16 broken meats scraps 17 three-suited i.e., with the number of suits allotted to servants; hundred-pound (the least that a gentleman would have, and hence a sneer at Oswald's pretensions) 18 worsted-stocking (worn by servants) 18–19 action-taking i.e., one who would sue rather than fight 19 glass-gazing i.e., vain 19–20 super-serviceable overobliging 20 finical fussy, foppish; one-trunk-inheriting i.e., having only one trunkful of goods 22–23 composition composite 27 addition titles 36 sop o' th' moonshine something which will sop up moonshine through the holes Kent will make 37–38 cullionly barbermonger rascally patron of hairdressers 42–43 Vanity the puppet in the

popular puppet shows of Shakespeare's time there were sometimes personified abstractions like those of the morality plays 44 carbonado cut crosswise like a piece of meat for broiling 45–46 Come your ways come along 49 neat foppish 53 With you a challenge (to Oswald): "My quarrel is with you!"; goodman form of address used to an inferior 54 flesh ye give you your first taste of blood 67 disclaims claims no part 78 zed "z" (little used and often omitted from dictionaries of the time) 80 unbolted unsifted, crude 81 jakes privy

Spare my gray beard? you wagtail.
CORNWALL. Peace, sirrah!
You beastly knave, know you no reverence?
KENT. Yes, sir, but anger hath a privi-
    lege.        85
CORNWALL. Why art thou angry?
KENT. That such a slave as this should wear
    a sword,
Who wears no honesty. Such smiling
    rogues as these
Like rats oft bite the holy cords atwain
Which are too intrinse t' unloose; smooth
    every passion    90
That in the natures of their lords rebel,
Being oil to fire, snow to the colder moods;
Renege, affirm, and turn their halcyon
    beaks
With every gale and vary of their masters,
Knowing naught, like dogs, but following. 95
A plague upon your epileptic visage!
Smile you my speeches, as I were a fool?
Goose, if I had you upon Sarum Plain,
I'ld drive ye cackling home to Camelot.
CORNWALL. What, art thou mad, old
    fellow?    100
GLOUCESTER. How fell you out? Say that.
KENT. No contraries hold more antipathy
Than I and such a knave.
CORNWALL. Why dost thou call him knave?
    What is his fault?
KENT. His countenance likes me not.    105
CORNWALL. No more perchance does mine,
    nor his, nor hers.
KENT. Sir, 'tis my occupation to be plain:
I have seen better faces in my time
Than stands on any shoulder that I see
Before me at this instant.
CORNWALL.        This is some fellow 110
Who, having been praised for bluntness,
    doth affect

A saucy roughness, and constrains the garb
Quite from his nature. He cannot flatter, he;
An honest mind and plain—he must speak
    truth.
An' they will take it, so; if not, he's plain. 115
These kind of knaves I know which in this
    plainness
Harbor more craft and more corrupter ends
Than twenty silly-ducking óbservants
That stretch their duties nicely.
CORNWALL. Sir, in good faith, in síncere
    verity,    120
Under th' allowance of your great aspéct,
Whose influence, like the wreath of radiant
    fire
On flick'ring Phoebus' front—
CORNWALL.        What mean'st by this?
KENT. To go out of my dialect, which you
discommend so much. I know, sir, I am 125
no flatterer. He that beguiled you in a plain
accent was a plain knave, which, for my part,
I will not be, though I should win your
displeasure to entreat me to't.
CORNWALL. What was th' offense you    130
gave him?
OSWALD. I never gave him any.
It pleased the King his master very late
To strike at me, upon his misconstruction;
When he, compact, and flattering his dis-
    pleasure,    135
Tripped me behind; being down, insulted,
    railed,
And put upon him such a deal of man
That worthied him, got praises of the
    King

---

82 *wagtail* kind of bird that jerks its tail up and down, perhaps suggesting obsequiousness; cf. *silly-ducking óbservants*, 1.118  85 *anger hath a privilege* cf. *noble anger*, II.4.280  89 *holy cords* sacred bonds (as between husband and wife, parent and child, etc.)  90 *intrinse* entangled, intricate; *smooth* flatter, cater to  93 *Renege* deny; *halcyon* kingfisher (if hung up by the beak, it was believed that it would turn with every wind like a weathervane)  94 *gale and vary* varying gale  96 *epileptic* twitching with an attempt to smile (?)  97 *Smile you* do you smile at  98 *Sarum* Salisbury  99 *Camelot* legendary seat of King Arthur

112–13 *constrains . . . nature* forces the style (of sincerity) beyond its true nature; carries it to an extreme  115 *An'* if  118 *silly-ducking óbservants* foolishly bowing obsequious attendants  119 *nicely* fussily  120–23 *Sir . . . front* (Kent parodies a more courtly style)  121 *allowance* approval; *aspéct* (1) appearance; (2) position in the heavens  122 *influence* astrological power  123 *Phoebus'* the sun's  126 *He* the sort of person Cornwall has described, who conceals craft beneath his plainness  128–29 *though . . . to't* though I pushed your displeasure to the point where it prompted me to retaliate by being a plain knave (?)  133 *very late* quite recently  134 *misconstruction* misunderstanding  135 *compact* in league with the King  137 *put . . . man* affected such virility  138 *worthied* reflected credit on

For him attempting who was self-subdued;
And, in the fleshment of this dread ex-
    ploit,                                    140
Drew on me here again.

    KENT.    None of these rogues and cowards
But Ajax is their fool.

    CORNWALL.    Fetch forth the stocks!
You stubborn ancient knave, you reverent
    braggart,
We'll teach you.

    KENT.    Sir, I am too old to learn.
Call not your stocks for me, I serve the
    King—                                     145
On whose employment I was sent to you;
You shall do small respect, show too bold
    malice
Against the grace and person of my
    master,
Stocking his messenger.

    CORNWALL. Fetch forth the stocks. As I
    have life and honor,                      150
There shall he sit till noon.

    REGAN. Till noon? Till night, my lord,
    and all night too.

    KENT. Why, madam, if I were your
    father's dog,
You should not use me so.

    REGAN.    Sir, being his knave, I will.
                 (*Stocks brought out.*)

    CORNWALL. This is a fellow of the selfsame
    color                                     155
Our sister speaks of. Come, bring away the
    stocks.

    GLOUCESTER. Let me beseech your Grace
    not to do so.
[His fault is much, and the good King his
    master
Will check him for't. Your purposed low
    correction
Is such as basest and contemnèd'st
    wretches                                  160
For pilf'rings and most common trespasses
Are punished with.]
The King his master needs must take it ill

That he, so slightly valued in his messenger,
Should have him thus restrained.

    CORNWALL.        I'll answer that.  165

    REGAN. My sister may receive it much more
    worse,
To have her gentleman abused, assaulted,
[For following her affairs. Put in his legs.]
             [KENT *is put in the stocks.*]

    CORNWALL. Come, my lord, away!
    (*Exit* [*with all but* GLOUCESTER *and* KENT].)

    GLOUCESTER. I am sorry for thee, friend.
'Tis the Duke's pleasure,                     170
Whose disposition all the world well knows
Will not be rubbed nor stopped. I'll entreat
    for thee.

    KENT. Pray do not, sir. I have watched
    and travelled hard.
Some time I shall sleep out, the rest I'll
    whistle.
A good man's fortune may grow out at
    heels.                                    175
Give you good morrow.

    GLOUCESTER. The Duke's to blame in this.
'Twill be ill taken.           (*Exit.*)

    KENT. Good King, that must approve the
    common saw,
Thou out of heaven's benediction com'st
To the warm sun.                              180
Approach, thou beacon to this under globe,
That by thy comfortable beams I may
Peruse this letter. Nothing almost sees miracles
But misery. I know 'tis from Cordelia,
Who hath most fortunately been informed 185
Of my obscurèd course. And shall find time
From this enormous state, seeking to give
Losses their remedies.—All weary and o'er-
    watched,

---

139 *him . . . self-subdued* attacking him (Oswald) who refused to fight 140 *fleshment of* bloodthirstiness excited by 141–42 *None . . . fool* rogues and cowards like Oswald always speak of a warrior like Ajax as a fool 143 *stubborn* rough; *reverent* aged 148 *grace* royalty; i.e., position as king 155 *color* kind 156 *away* along 159 *check* reprove 160 *contemnèd'st* most despised

164 *slightly valued in* little respected in the person of 165 *answer* answer for 171 *disposition* inclination 172 *rubbed* deflected (bowling term) 173 *watched* gone without sleep 175 *A good man's* even a good man's; *grow . . . heels* wear out, i.e., decline 176 *Give* God give 178 *approve* prove true; *saw* saying 179–80 *Thou . . . sun* to leave the shade, often referred to as "God's blessing," to expose oneself to the hot sun was a proverbial example of bad judgment 181 *beacon . . . globe* i.e., the sun, which is about to rise 182 *comfortable* helpful 183–84 *Nothing . . . misery* i.e., wretchedness prepares us to see miracles(?) 186 *obscurèd* disguised 186–88 *And . . . remedies* i.e., Cordelia will intervene to try to restore order. The text may be corrupt or Kent may be reading phrases from the letter 187 *enormous* abnormal, monstrous

Take vantage, heavy eyes, not to behold
This shameful lodging. Fortune, good
   night;                  190
Smile once more, turn thy wheel.   [*Sleeps.*]
       (*Enter* EDGAR.)         II. 3
EDGAR. I heard myself proclaimed,
And by the happy hollow of a tree
Escaped the hunt. No port is free, no place
That guard and most unusual vigilance
Does not attend my taking. Whiles I may
   'scape,                  5
I will preserve myself; and am bethought
To take the basest and most poorest shape
That ever penury, in contempt of man,
Brought near to beast: my face I'll grime
   with filth,
Blanket my loins, elf all my hairs in knots,  10
And with presented nakedness outface
The winds and persecutions of the sky.
The country gives me proof and precedent
Of Bedlam beggars, who, with roaring voices,
Strike in their numbed and mortified [bare]
   arms                 15
Pins, wooden pricks, nails, sprigs of rose-
   mary;
And with this horrible object, from low
   farms,
Poor pelting villages, sheepcotes, and mills,
Sometimes with lunatic bans, sometime with
   prayers,

---

189 *vantage* advantage (of sleep)
II.3 Stage direction: *Enter Edgar* the scene divisions here and after Edgar's exit are preserved in the margin for convenience of reference because they appear in most modern editions. They are not in the Folio, and on the Elizabethan stage the action was presumably continuous. Though Kent remains asleep onstage, Edgar, who ignores his presence, may be imagined as in a different place just as heaven and hell were simultaneously represented on the stage in some of the old scriptural dramas, the action shifting from one to the other  2 *happy* lucky  5 *attend my taking* await to capture me  6 *am bethought* have in mind  9 *Brought . . . beast* i.e., reduced (man) to the level of a beast by imposing such a shape upon him. The form of Edgar's disguise is integrally related to the imagery and thought of the play as the heath scenes of Act III make clear  10 *elf* tangle (in "elf-locks")  11 *presented* exposed; *outface* brave  13 *proof* example  14 *Bedlam* see I.2.160  15 *Strike* stick; *mortified* insensible to pain  16 *pricks* skewers  17 *object* spectacle; *low* humble  18 *pelting* paltry  19 *bans* curses

Enforce their charity. Poor Turlygod, poor
   Tom,                 20
That's something yet: Edgar I nothing am.
               (*Exit.*)
(*Enter* LEAR, FOOL, *and* GENTLEMAN.)   II. 4
LEAR. 'Tis strange that they should so
   depart from home,
And not send back my messenger.
GENTLEMAN.            As I learned,
The night before there was no purpose in
   them
Of this remove.
KENT.       Hail to thee, noble master.
LEAR. Ha!                 5
Mak'st thou this shame thy pastime?
KENT.             No, my lord.
FOOL. Ha, ha, he wears cruel garters.
Horses are tied by the heads, dogs and bears
by th' neck, monkeys by th' loins, and men
by th' legs. When a man's over-lusty at   10
legs, then he wears wooden nether-stocks.
LEAR. What's he that hath so much thy
   place mistook
To set thee here?
KENT.         It is both he and she,
Your son and daughter.
LEAR. No.                 15
KENT. Yes.
LEAR. No, I say.
KENT. I say yea.
[LEAR. No, no, they would not.
KENT. Yes, they have.]          20
LEAR. By Jupiter, I swear no!
KENT. By Juno, I swear ay!
LEAR.           They durst not do't;
They could not, would not do't. 'Tis worse
   than murder
To do upon respect such violent outrage.
Resolve me with all modest haste which
   way                25
Thou mightst deserve or they impose this
   usage,

---

20 *Poor Turlygod* presumably a name, like *poor Tom*, which beggars often gave themselves
II.4 Stage direction: *Enter Lear* see note at II.3 *Enter Edgar*; with the arrival of Lear the action involving Kent resumes  4 *remove* removal  7 *cruel* pun on "crewel," a yarn used in garters  10 *over-lusty at* overactive with  11 *nether-stocks* stockings (as opposed to "upper-stocks" or breeches)  24 *respect* i.e., due to the King  25 *Resolve* explain to; *modest* seemly

Coming from us.

KENT.                    My lord, when at their home
I did commend your Highness' letters to
    them,
Ere I was risen from the place that showed
My duty kneeling,  came there a reeking
    post,                                                    30
Stewed in his haste,  half breathless, panting
    forth
From Goneril his mistress salutations;
Delivered letters, spite of intermission,
Which presently they read; on whose contents
They summoned up their meiny,  straight
    took horse,                                          35
Commanded me to follow and attend
The leisure of their answer, gave me cold
    looks;
And meeting here the other messenger,
Whose welcome I perceived had poisoned
    mine,
Being the very fellow which of late          40
Displayed so saucily against your Highness,
Having more man than wit about me, drew;
He raised the house with loud and coward
    cries.
Your son and daughter found this trespass
    worth
The shame which here it suffers.            45

    FOOL. Winter's not gone yet, if the wild
geese fly that way.
        Fathers that wear rags
            Do make their children blind,
        But fathers that bear bags           50
            Shall see their children kind.
        Fortune, that arrant whore,
        Ne'er turns the key to th' poor.
    But for all this, thou shalt have as many
dolors for thy daughters as thou canst tell   55
in a year.

LEAR. O, how this mother swells up toward
    my heart!
Hysterica passio, down, thou climbing sor-
    row;
Thy element's below. Where is this daughter?
    KENT. With the Earl, sir, here within.
    LEAR.                    Follow me not;     60
Stay here.                              (Exit.)
    GENTLEMAN. Made you no more offense but
what you speak of?
    KENT. None.
    How chance the King comes with so       65
small a number?
    FOOL. An' thou hadst been set i' th' stocks
for that question, thou'dst well deserved it.
    KENT. Why, fool?
    FOOL. We'll set thee to school to an       70
ant, to teach thee there's no laboring i' th'
winter. All that follow their noses are led by
their eyes but blind men, and there's not a
nose among twenty but can smell him that's
stinking. Let go thy hold when a great       75
wheel runs down a hill, lest it break thy neck
with following. But the great one that goes
upward, let him draw thee after. When a
wise man gives thee better counsel, give me
mine again. I would have none but          80
knaves follow it since a fool gives it.
    That sir which serves and seeks for gain,
        And follows but for form,
    Will pack when it begins to rain
        And leave thee in the storm.          85
    But I will tarry; the fool will stay,
        And let the wise man fly.
    The knave turns fool that runs away;
        The fool no knave, perdy.
    KENT. Where learned you this, fool?       90
    FOOL. Not i' th' stocks, fool.
        (Enter LEAR and GLOUCESTER.)
    LEAR. Deny to speak with me? They are
    sick, they are weary,

---

28 *commend* present  30 *reeking post* sweating
messenger  31 *Stewed* steaming  33 *spite of intermission* regardless of interrupting me  34 *presently*
immediately; *on* as the result of  35 *meiny* retinue
41 *Displayed* showed off  42 *man than wit* valor
than discretion  46–47 *Winter's . . . way* i.e., our
season of bad luck is not over yet if that's the
way Cornwall and Regan are acting  49 *make . . .
blind* encourage their children to neglect them
50 *bags* (of gold)  53 *turns the key* i.e., opens the
door  55 *dolors* sorrows (with pun on "dollars");
*tell* count

---

57–58 *mother, Hysterica passio* two terms for hysteria
believed to originate in the womb or belly  59
*element* proper place  71–72 *no laboring . . . winter*
Lear's small retinue is equated with the grasshopper's lack of provisions for the winter, whereas
the ant wisely provides for herself during the summer  74–75 *him that's stinking* i.e., a person whose
fortune has decayed  83 *form* show  84 *pack* be off
88 *The knave . . . away* i.e., the faithless man is the
true fool  89 *perdy* literally "by God" (*par
dieu*)

They have travelled all the night? Mere
fetches,
The images of revolt and flying off!
Fetch me a better answer.

GLOUCESTER.                    My dear lord,    95
You know the fiery quality of the Duke,
How unremovable and fixed he is
In his own course.

LEAR. Vengeance, plague, death, confusion!
Fiery? What quality? Why, Gloucester,
Gloucester,
I'ld speak with the Duke of Cornwall and
his wife.                                        100

GLOUCESTER. Well, my good lord, I have
informed them so.

LEAR. Informed them? Dost thou understand me, man?

GLOUCESTER. Ay, my good lord.

LEAR. The King would speak with
Cornwall. The dear father
Would with his daughter speak, commands
her service.                                     105
Are they informed of this? My breath and
blood!
Fiery? The fiery Duke, tell the hot Duke
that—
No, but not yet. May be he is not well.
Infirmity doth still neglect all office
Whereto our health is bound. We are not
ourselves                                        110
When nature, being oppressed, commands
the mind
To suffer with the body. I'll forbear;
And am fallen out with my more headier will
To take the indisposed and sickly fit
For the sound man.—Death on my state!
Wherefore                                        115
Should he sit here? [Pointing to KENT.]
                    This act persuades me
That this remotion of the Duke and her
Is practice only. Give me my servant forth.
Go tell the Duke and 's wife I'd speak with
them!

Now, presently! Bid them come forth and
hear me,                                         120
Or at their chamber door I'll beat the drum
Till it cry sleep to death.

GLOUCESTER. I would have all well betwixt
you.                                      (Exit.)

LEAR. O me, my heart, my rising heart!
But down!

FOOL. Cry to it, nuncle, as the cockney  125
did to the eels when she put 'em i' th' paste
alive. She knapped 'em o' th' coxcombs with
a stick and cried, "Down, wantons, down!"
'Twas her brother that, in pure kindness to
his horse, buttered his hay.                     130

(Enter CORNWALL, REGAN, GLOUCESTER,
SERVANTS.)

LEAR. Good morrow to you both.

CORNWALL.                    Hail to your Grace.
(KENT here set at liberty.)

REGAN. I am glad to see your Highness.

LEAR. Regan, I think you are. I know what
reason
I have to think so. If thou shouldst not be
glad,
I would divorce me from thy mother's
tomb,                                            135
Sepulchring an adultress. [To KENT] O, are
you free?
Some other time for that.—Beloved Regan,
Thy sister 's naught. O Regan, she hath tied
Sharp-toothed unkindness, like a vulture,
here.
I can scarce speak to thee. Thou'lt not
believe                                          140
With how depraved a quality—O Regan!

REGAN. I pray you, sir, take patience.
I have hope
You less know how to value her desert
Than she to scant her duty.

LEAR.                    Say? how is that?

REGAN. I cannot think my sister in the
least                                            145

---

93 fetches tricks    94 images exact likenesses;
flying off desertion  96 quality disposition  109
office duties  110 Whereto . . . bound which we are
bound to perform when well  113 fallen out angry;
headier i.e., headstrong  115 state royal position
116 he i.e., Kent  117 remotion removal  118 practice deceptive policy

120 presently immediately   122 cry follow (like
a pack or "cry" of hunting dogs)  125 cockney
city-dweller  126 paste pastry pie  127 knapped
rapped; coxcombs heads  128 wantons i.e., impudent
or "fresh" things  135–36 divorce . . . adultress not
believe you were my own child, and hence refuse
to be buried with your mother  138 naught wicked
141 quality disposition  142–44 I have . . . her duty
a double negative, but meaning "I hope it's a

Would fail her obligation. If, sir, perchance
She have restrained the riots of your followers,
'Tis on such ground, and to such wholesome
    end,
As clears her from all blame.
    LEAR. My curses on her!
    REGAN.         O, sir, you are old;   150
Nature in you stands on the very verge
Of his confine. You should be ruled, and led
By some discretion that discerns your state
Better than you yourself. Therefore I pray
    you
That to our sister you do make return;   155
Say you have wronged her.
    LEAR.         Ask her forgiveness?
Do you but mark how this becomes the house:
"Dear daughter, I confess that I am old.
                     [Kneels.]
Age is unnecessary. On my knees I beg
That you'll vouchsafe me raiment, bed,
    and food."   160
    REGAN. Good sir, no more. These are un-
    sightly tricks.
Return you to my sister.
    LEAR [rises].         Never, Regan.
She hath abated me of half my train,
Looked black upon me, struck me with her
    tongue
Most serpent-like upon the very heart.   165
All the stored vengeances of heaven fall
On her ingrateful top! Strike her young
    bones,
You taking airs, with lameness.
    CORNWALL.         Fie, sir, fie!
    LEAR. You nimble lightnings, dart your
    blinding flames
Into her scornful eyes! Infect her beauty,  170
You fen-sucked fogs drawn by the pow'rful
    sun
To fall and blister.
    REGAN.         O the blest gods!
So will you wish on me when the rash mood
    is on.
    LEAR. No, Regan, thou shalt never have
    my curse.

Thy tender-hefted nature shall not give   175
Thee o'er to harshness. Her eyes are fierce,
    but thine
Do comfort, and not burn. 'Tis not in thee
To grudge my pleasures, to cut off my train,
To bandy hasty words, to scant my sizes,
And, in conclusion, to oppose the bolt   180
Against my coming in. Thou better know'st
The offices of nature, bond of childhood,
Effects of courtesy, dues of gratitude.
Thy half o' th' kingdom hast thou not
    forgot,
Wherein I thee endowed.
    REGAN.       Good sir, to th' purpose.  185
                  (Tucket within.)
    LEAR. Who put my man i' th' stocks?
    CORNWALL.         What trumpet's that?
    REGAN. I know't—my sister's. This ap-
    proves her letter,
That she would soon be here.
        (Enter STEWARD [OSWALD].)
                  Is your lady come?
    LEAR. This is a slave, whose easy-borrowed
    pride
Dwells in the fickle grace of her he fol-
    lows.   190
Out, varlet, from my sight.
    CORNWALL.         What means your Grace?
    LEAR. Who stocked my servant? Regan,
    I have good hope
Thou didst not know on't.
            (Enter GONERIL.)
            Who comes here? O heavens!
If you do love old men, if your sweet sway
Allow obedience, if you yourselves are
    old,   195
Make it your cause. Send down, and take
    my part.
[To GONERIL.] Art not ashamed to look upon
    this beard?
O Regan, will you take her by the hand?
    GONERIL. Why not by th' hand, sir?
    How have I offended?
All's not offense that indiscretion finds   200

matter of your undervaluing her rather than of
her falling short in her duty."   152 *confine* limit
(i.e., allotted life-span)  153 *discretion* i.e., discreet
person; *state* condition   157 *house* family decorum
163 *abated* curtailed   167 *ingrateful top* ungrateful
head   168 *taking* infectious  172 *fall and blister*
i.e., fall on people and cause blisters

175 *tender-hefted* moved by tenderness  179 *sizes*
allowances  180 *oppose the bolt* i.e., fasten the door
182 *offices* duties  183 *Effects* actions  185 Stage
direction: *Tucket* see note at II.1. 82  187 *approves*
confirms  189 *easy-borrowed* borrowed on small
security  191 *varlet* base fellow  195 *Allow* approve
of  196 *it* i.e., my cause

And dotage terms so.

LEAR.                 O sides, you are too tough!
Will you yet hold? How came my man i' th'
    stocks?

CORNWALL. I set him there, sir; but his
    own disorders
Deserved much less advancement.

LEAR.                 You? Did you?

REGAN. I pray you, father, being weak,
    seem so.                                          205
If till the expiration of your month
You will return and sojourn with my sister,
Dismissing half your train, come then to me.
I am now from home, and out of that provi-
    sion
Which shall be needful for your entertain-
    ment.                                              210

LEAR. Return to her, and fifty men dis-
    missed?
No, rather I abjure all roofs, and choose
To wage against the enmity o' th' air,
To be a comrade with the wolf and owl,
Necessity's sharp pinch. Return with her? 215
Why, the hot-blooded France, that dowerless
    took
Our youngest born, I could as well be brought
To knee his throne, and, squire-like, pension
    beg
To keep base life afoot. Return with her?
Persuade me rather to be slave and sump-
    ter                                                220
To this detested groom.

GONERIL.              At your choice, sir.

LEAR. I prithee, daughter, do not make
    me mad.
I will not trouble thee, my child; farewell.
We'll no more meet, no more see one another.
But yet thou art my flesh, my blood, my
    daughter;                                          225
Or rather a disease that's in my flesh,
Which I must needs call mine. Thou art a
    boil,
A plague-sore, or embossèd carbuncle
In my corrupted blood. But I'll not chide
    thee.
Let shame come when it will, I do not call
    it.                                                230

I do not bid the thunder-bearer shoot,
Nor tell tales of thee to high-judging Jove.
Mend when thou canst, be better at thy
    leisure;
I can be patient, I can stay with Regan,
I and my hundred knights.

REGAN.               Not altogether so. 235
I looked not for you yet, nor am provided
For your fit welcome. Give ear, sir, to my
    sister;
For those that mingle reason with your pas-
    sion
Must be content to think you old, and so—
But she knows what she does.

LEAR.                 Is this well spoken? 240

REGAN. I dare avouch it, sir. What, fifty
    followers?
Is it not well? What should you need of more?
Yea, or so many, sith that both charge and
    danger
Speak 'gainst so great a number? How in
    one house
Should many people, under two com-
    mands,                                             245
Hold amity? 'Tis hard, almost impossible.

GONERIL. Why might not you, my lord, re-
    ceive attendance
From those that she calls servants, or from
    mine?

REGAN. Why not, my lord? If then they
    chanced to slack ye,
We could control them. If you will come to
    me                                                 250
(For now I spy a danger), I entreat you
To bring but five-and-twenty. To no more
Will I give place or notice.

LEAR. I gave you all.

REGAN.        And in good time you gave it.

LEAR. Made you my guardians, my deposi-
    taries,                                            255
But kept a reservation to be followed
With such a number. What, must I come to
    you
With five-and-twenty? Regan, said you so?

REGAN. And speak't again, my lord. No
    more with me.

213 wage fight   215 Necessity's . . . pinch i.e., and
thus endure necessity's, etc.   216 hot-blooded
choleric (cf. I.2.23)   218 knee kneel at   220 sumpter
packhorse   228 embossèd come to a head

231 thunder-bearer i.e., Jupiter   238 mingle . . .
passion interpret your passionate words in the
light of reason   243 sith that since; charge expense
253 notice recognition   255 depositaries trustees 256
kept . . . to be made a condition that I be

LEAR. Those wicked creatures yet do look
well-favored                                                    260
When others are more wicked; not being the
worst
Stands in some rank of praise. [*To* GONERIL.]
I'll go with thee.
Thy fifty yet doth double five-and-twenty,
And thou art twice her love.
    GONERIL.                    Hear me, my lord.
What need you five-and-twenty? ten? or
five?                                                          265
To follow in a house where twice so many
Have a command to tend you?
    REGAN.                    What need one?
    LEAR. O reason not the need! Our basest
beggars
Are in the poorest thing superfluous.
Allow not nature more than nature needs, 270
Man's life is cheap as beast's. Thou art a lady:
If only to go warm were gorgeous,
Why, nature needs not what thou gorgeous
wear'st,
Which scarcely keeps thee warm. But, for
true need—
You heavens, give me that patience, patience
I need.                                                        275
You see me here, you gods, a poor old man,
As full of grief as age, wretched in both.
If it be you that stirs these daughters' hearts
Against their father, fool me not so much
To bear it tamely; touch me with noble
anger,                                                         280
And let not women's weapons, water drops,
Stain my man's cheeks. No, you unnatural
hags!
I will have such revenges on you both
That all the world shall—I will do such
things—
What they are, yet I know not; but they
. shall be                                                       285

The terrors of the earth. You think I'll weep.
No, I'll not weep.              (*Storm and tempest.*)
I have full cause of weeping, but this heart
Shall break into a hundred thousand flaws
Or ere I'll weep. O fool, I shall go mad!  290
(*Exeunt* [LEAR, FOOL, KENT, *and* GLOUCESTER].)
    CORNWALL. Let us withdraw; 'twill be a
storm.
    REGAN. This house is little; the old man
and's people
Cannot be well bestowed.
    GONERIL. 'Tis his own blame hath put
himself from rest,
And must needs taste his folly.              295
    REGAN. For his particular, I'll receive him
gladly,
But not one follower.
    GONERIL.          So am I purposed.
Where is my Lord of Gloucester?
    CORNWALL. Followed the old man forth.
            (*Enter* GLOUCESTER.)
                        He is returned.
    GLOUCESTER. The King is in high rage.
    CORNWALL.          Whither is he going? 300
    GLOUCESTER. He calls to horse, but will I
know not whither.
    CORNWALL. 'Tis best to give him way;
he leads himself.
    GONERIL. My lord, entreat him by no
means to stay.
    GLOUCESTER. Alack, the night comes on,
and the high winds
Do sorely ruffle. For many miles about     305
There's scarce a bush.
    REGAN.              O, sir, to willful men
The injuries that they themselves procure
Must be their schoolmasters. Shut up your
doors.
He is attended with a desperate train,
And what they may incense him to, being
apt                                                            310
To have his ear abused, wisdom bids fear.
    CORNWALL. Shut up your doors, my lord;
'tis a wild night.
My Regan counsels well. Come out o' th'
storm.                                         (*Exeunt.*)

---

260 *well-favored* attractive, good  268 *reason not*
don't argue on the basis of  269 *Are . . . superfluous*
i.e., the most trifling thing they have is, strictly
speaking, unnecessary  270 *Allow not* i.e., if you
do not allow; *needs* i.e., for mere survival  272–74
*If . . . warm* i.e., if wearing just enough to keep
warm were considered gorgeous, there would be
no need for wearing such gorgeous clothes as
yours, which hardly keep you warm  279 *fool*
humiliate

---

289 *flaws* fragments  290 *Or ere* before  294 *rest*
i.e., a place to rest  295 *must* i.e., he must; *taste*
test or experience the results of  296 *particular* own
person  305 *ruffle* rage  310 *apt* inclined

ACT III. *Scene 1*

(*Storm still. Enter* KENT *and a* GENTLEMAN
*severally.*)

KENT. Who's there besides foul weather?
GENTLEMAN. One minded like the weather,
  most unquietly.
KENT. I know you. Where's the King?
GENTLEMAN. Contending with the fretful
  elements;
Bids the wind blow the earth into the sea,     5
Or swell the curlèd waters 'bove the main,
That things might change or cease; [tears
  his white hair,
Which the impetuous blasts, with eyeless rage,
Catch in their fury and make nothing of;
Strives in his little world of man to out-
  scorn                                        10
The to-and-fro-conflicting wind and rain.
This night, wherein the cub-drawn bear
  would couch,
The lion and the belly-pinchèd wolf
Keep their fur dry, unbonneted he runs,
And bids what will take all.]
  KENT.           But who is with him?     15
GENTLEMAN. None but the fool, who labors
  to outjest
His heart-struck injuries.
  KENT.           Sir, I do know you,
And dare upon the warrant of my note
Commend a dear thing to you. There is divi-
  sion,
Although as yet the face of it is covered     20
With mutual cunning, 'twixt Albany and
  Cornwall;
Who have—as who have not, that their great
  stars
Throned and set high?—servants, who seem
  no less,

Which are to France the spies and specula-
  tions
Intelligent of our state. What hath been
  seen,                                        25
Either in snuffs and packings of the Dukes,
Or the hard rein which both of them hath
  borne
Against the old kind King, or something
  deeper,
Whereof, perchance, these are but furnish-
  ings—
[But, true it is, from France there comes a
  power                                        30
Into this scattered kingdom, who already,
Wise in our negligence, have secret feet
In some of our best ports and are at point
To show their open banner. Now to you:
If on my credit you dare build so far         35
To make your speed to Dover, you shall find
Some that will thank you, making just report
Of how unnatural and bemadding sorrow
The King hath cause to plain.
I am a gentleman of blood and breeding,     40
And from some knowledge and assurance offer
This office to you.]
  GENTLEMAN. I will talk further with you.
  KENT.                     No, do not.
For confirmation that I am much more
Than my out-wall, open this purse and
  take                                         45
What it contains. If you shall see Cordelia,
As fear not but you shall, show her this
  ring,
And she will tell you who your fellow is
That yet you do not know. Fie on this storm!
I will go seek the King.                       50
  GENTLEMAN. Give me your hand. Have you
  no more to say?
  KENT. Few words, but, to effect, more than
  all yet:

---

III.1.2 *minded . . . unquietly* i.e., with an unquiet
mind  6 *main* mainland  10 *little world* "microcosm" as opposed to the "macrocosm," or universe, to which it was supposed to correspond
12 *cub-drawn* sucked dry by her cubs (and so
ravenous); *couch* lie in its lair  13 *belly-pinchèd*
starved  15 *take all* (as the gambler cries, staking
all he has left)  18 *warrant . . . note* assurance of
my knowledge  19 *Commend . . . thing* entrust an
important matter  22 *that* whom; *stars* destinies
23 *seem no less* appear truly so

---

24–25 *speculations Intelligent of* intelligence agents
in  26 *snuffs and packings* quarrels and intrigues
27 *hard rein* harsh curbs; *hath borne* have exercised
(see note at II.1.132)  29 *furnishings* pretexts  30
*power* army  31 *scattered* divided  35 *credit* relia-
bility  38 *bemadding* maddening  39 *plain* complain of  40 *blood and breeding* good family  42
*office* official employment (i.e., the trip to Dover)
45 *out-wall* Kent is still in disguise  52 *to effect* in
importance

That when we have found the King—in which your pain
That way, I'll this—he that first lights on him
Holla the other.    (*Exeunt* [*severally*].)    55

### Scene 2

(*Storm still. Enter* LEAR *and* FOOL.)

LEAR. Blow, winds, and crack your cheeks. Rage, blow.
You cataracts and hurricanoes, spout
Till you have drenched our steeples, drowned the cocks.
You sulph'rous and thought-executing fires,
Vaunt-couriers to oak-cleaving thunder-bolts,    5
Singe my white head. And thou, all-shaking thunder,
Strike flat the thick rotundity o' th' world,
Crack Nature's moulds, all germens spill at once,
That makes ingrateful man.

FOOL. O nuncle, court holy-water in a    10
dry house is better than this rain water out o' door. Good nuncle, in; ask thy daughters blessing. Here's a night pities neither wise men nor fools.

LEAR. Rumble thy bellyful. Spit, fire. Spout, rain.    15
Nor rain, wind, thunder, fire are my daughters.
I tax not you, you elements, with unkindness.
I never gave you kingdom, called you children;
You owe me no subscription. Then let fall
Your horrible pleasure. Here I stand your slave,    20
A poor, infirm, weak, and despised old man.
But yet I call you servile ministers,
That will with two pernicious daughters join
Your high-engendered battles 'gainst a head
So old and white as this. O, ho! 'tis foul.    25

FOOL. He that has a house to put's head in has a good headpiece.
  The codpiece that will house
    Before the head has any,
  The head and he shall louse:    30
    So beggars marry many.
  The man that makes his toe
    What he his heart should make
  Shall of a corn cry woe,
    And turn his sleep to wake.    35
For there was never yet fair woman but she made mouths in a glass.

(*Enter* KENT.)

LEAR. No, I will be the pattern of all patience;
I will say nothing.

KENT. Who's there?    40

FOOL. Marry, here's grace and a codpiece; that's a wise man and a fool.

KENT. Alas, sir, are you here? Things that love night
Love not such nights as these. The wrathful skies
Gallow the very wanderers of the dark    45
And make them keep their caves. Since I was man,
Such sheets of fire, such bursts of horrid thunder,
Such groans of roaring wind and rain, I never
Remember to have heard. Man's nature cannot carry
Th' affliction nor the fear.

LEAR.                Let the great gods    50
That keep this dreadful pudder o'er our heads
Find out their enemies now. Tremble, thou wretch,
That hast within thee undivulgèd crimes

---

53–54 *your pain . . . this* you expend your efforts in that direction while I go this way
III.2.2 *hurricanoes* waterspouts  3 *cocks* weather-cocks  4 *thought-executing* executing the thoughts of the "thunder-bearer"(?)  5 *Vaunt-couriers* heralds  8 *Nature's moulds* i.e., in which men are formed; *germens* seeds  10 *court holy-water* flattery  17 *tax* charge  19 *subscription* allegiance  20 *pleasure* will  22 *ministers* agents  24 *high-engendered battles* battalions formed in the heavens

28–30 *The codpiece . . . louse* i.e., the man who takes care of his sexual needs before he has a roof over his head (which should be his primary concern) will be reduced to poverty—and lice; *codpiece* flap covering front opening in a man's breeches; hence euphemism for "penis"  32–35 *The man . . . wake* a parallel case of inverted values  37 *made . . . glass* i.e., practiced facial expressions in a mirror. The Fool's speeches are unpredictable combinations of pertinence and irrelevance as are the later mad speeches of Lear  41 *grace and a codpiece* i.e., a king and a fool (a fool often wore a conspicuous codpiece; also he carried a somewhat phallic baton called a "bauble")  45 *Gallow* frighten  46 *keep* stay in  47 *horrid* horrifying  49 *carry* bear  51 *pudder* turmoil

Unwhipped of justice. Hide thee, thou bloody
  hand,
Thou perjured, and thou simular of virtue 55
That art incestuous. Caitiff, to pieces shake,
That under covert and convenient seeming
Has practiced on man's life. Close pent-up
  guilts,
Rive your concealing continents and cry
These dreadful summoners grace. I am a
  man     60
More sinned against than sinning.
  KENT.             Alack, bareheaded?
Gracious my lord, hard by here is a hovel;
Some friendship will it lend you 'gainst the
  tempest.
Repose you there, while I to this hard
  house
(More harder than the stones whereof 'tis
  raised,     65
Which even but now, demanding after you,
Denied me to come in) return, and force
Their scanted courtesy.
  LEAR.           My wits begin to turn.
Come on, my boy. How dost, my boy?
  Art cold?
I am cold myself. Where is this straw, my
  fellow?     70
The art of our necessities is strange,
And can make vile things precious. Come,
  your hovel.
Poor fool and knave, I have one part in my
  heart
That's sorry yet for thee.
  FOOL [sings].
He that has and a little tiny wit,     75
  With, heigh-ho, the wind and the rain,
  Must make content with his fortunes fit
    Though the rain it raineth every day.
  LEAR. True, boy. Come, bring us to this
  hovel.
                    (Exit [with KENT].)
  FOOL. This is a brave night to cool a   80

courtesan. I'll speak a prophecy ere I go:
  When priests are more in word than
    matter;
  When brewers mar their malt with
    water;
  When nobles are their tailors'
    tutors,
  No heretics burned, but wenches'
    suitors;     85
  When every case in law is right,
  No squire in debt nor no poor knight;
  When slanders do not live in tongues,
  Nor cutpurses come not to throngs;
  When usurers tell their gold i' th' field, 90
  And bawds and whores do churches
    build—
  Then shall the realm of Albion
  Come to great confusion.
  Then comes the time, who lives to
    see't,
  That going shall be used with feet.   95
This prophecy Merlin shall make, for I live
before his time.            (Exit.)

### Scene 3

(Enter GLOUCESTER and EDMUND [with lights].)
  GLOUCESTER. Alack, alack, Edmund, I like
not this unnatural dealing. When I desired
their leave that I might pity him, they took
from me the use of mine own house, charged
me on pain of perpetual displeasure   5
neither to speak of him, entreat for him, or
any way sustain him.
  EDMUND. Most savage and unnatural.
  GLOUCESTER. Go to; say you nothing. There
is division between the Dukes, and a   10
worse matter than that. I have received a
letter this night—'tis dangerous to be spoken
—I have locked the letter in my closet. These

---

55 simular simulator   57 covert . . . seeming cover
of a proper appearance   58 practiced on plotted
against   59 Rive split open; continents containers
60 summoners officers who summoned offenders to
an ecclesiastical court; grace mercy   62 Gracious
my lord my gracious lord   64 hard both literally
and figuratively; house i.e., Gloucester's castle and
its inhabitants   66 demanding (as I was) inquiring
71 art magic powers (as in alchemy)   77 make . . .
fit i.e., be content with his fortune   80 brave fine

81 prophecy the fool's "prophecy" of confusion is
itself a nonsensical mixture of things as they are
and as they ideally might be   85 suitors (who are
"burned" with venereal disease)   90 i' th'field i.e.,
in the open   92 Albion England   95 going . . . used
walking shall be done   96 Merlin King Arthur's
magician
III.3 Stage direction: with lights since performances in the public playhouses were given by
daylight, one of the chief ways of indicating darkness on the stage was by carrying torches   3 pity
show pity to   10 division contention   13 closet
room

injuries the King now bears will be revenged
home; there is part of a power already    15
footed; we must incline to the King. I will
look him and privily relieve him. Go you and
maintain talk with the Duke, that my charity
be not of him perceived. If he ask for me,
I am ill and gone to bed. If I die for it,    20
as no less is threatened me, the King my old
master must be relieved. There is strange
things toward, Edmund; pray you be careful.
                                      (*Exit.*)
  EDMUND. This courtesy forbid thee shall
    the Duke
Instantly know, and of that letter too.    25
This seems a fair deserving, and must draw
    me
That which my father loses—no less than all.
The younger rises when the old doth fall.
                                      (*Exit.*)


                    *Scene 4*

        (*Enter* LEAR, KENT, *and* FOOL.)
  KENT. Here is the place, my lord. Good
    my lord, enter.
The tyranny of the open night's too rough
For nature to endure.        (*Storm still.*)
  LEAR.              Let me alone.
  KENT. Good my lord, enter here.
  LEAR.            Wilt break my heart?
  KENT. I had rather break mine own.
    Good my lord, enter.                5
  LEAR. Thou think'st 'tis much that this
    contentious storm
Invades us to the skin. So 'tis to thee,
But where the greater malady is fixed
The lesser is scarce felt. Thou'dst shun a bear;
But if thy flight lay toward the roaring
    sea,                              10
Thou'dst meet the bear i' th' mouth.
    When the mind's free,
The body's delicate. The tempest in my mind
Doth from my senses take all feeling else
Save what beats there. Filial ingratitude,

Is it not as this mouth should tear this
    hand                              15
For lifting food to't? But I will punish home.
No, I will weep no more. In such a night
To shut me out! Pour on; I will endure.
In such a night as this! O Regan, Goneril,
Your old kind father, whose frank heart
    gave all—                         20
O, that way madness lies; let me shun that.
No more of that.
  KENT.          Good my lord, enter here.
  LEAR. Prithee go in thyself; seek thine
    own ease.
This tempest will not give me leave to ponder
On things would hurt me more, but I'll go
    in.                               25
[*To the* FOOL] In, boy; go first. You houseless
    poverty—
Nay, get thee in. I'll pray, and then I'll
    sleep.                   (*Exit* [FOOL].)
Poor naked wretches, wheresoe'er you are,
That bide the pelting of this pitiless storm,
How shall your houseless heads and unfed
    sides,                            30
Your looped and windowed raggedness,
    defend you
From seasons such as these? O, I have ta'en
Too little care of this! Take physic, pomp;
Expose thyself to feel what wretches feel,
That thou mayst shake the superflux to
    them                              35
And show the heavens more just.
  EDGAR [*within*]. Fathom and half, fathom
and half! Poor Tom!
  FOOL [*within*]. Come not in here, nuncle;
here's a spirit. Help me, help me!     40
  KENT. Give me thy hand. Who's there?
              [*Enter* FOOL.]
  FOOL. A spirit, a spirit. He says his name's
poor Tom.
  KENT. What art thou that dost grumble
there i' th' straw? Come forth.        45
      (*Enter* EDGAR [*as* TOM O' BEDLAM].)
  EDGAR. Away! the foul fiend follows me.

---

15 *home* to the hilt; *power* army (i.e., of France)
16 *footed* landed; *incline to* side with    17 *look* look
for; *privily* secretly    23 *toward* impending    24
*courtesy . . . thee* kindness you have been forbidden
to show    26 *fair deserving* action deserving reward
III.4.8 *fixed* lodged    11 *i' th' mouth* i.e., in the
teeth; *free* i.e., from care

---

16 *home* to the hilt    20 *frank* liberal    26 *poverty*
i.e., poor people    31 *looped* loopholed    33 *Take . . .*
*pomp* purge (hence cure) yourselves, vainglorious
people    35 *superflux* superfluities    37 *Fathom and*
*half* because of the deluge Edgar pretends to take
soundings    40 *spirit* devil

Through the sharp hawthorn blow the winds.
Humh! go to thy bed, and warm thee.

LEAR. Didst thou give all to thy daughters?
And art thou come to this? 50

EDGAR. Who gives anything to poor Tom?
whom the foul fiend hath led through fire
and through flame, through ford and whirlpool, o'er bog and quagmire; that hath laid
knives under his pillow and halters in his 55
pew, set ratsbane by his porridge, made him
proud of heart, to ride on a bay trotting horse
over four-inched bridges, to course his own
shadow for a traitor. Bless thy five wits, Tom's
acold. O, do, de, do, de, do, de. Bless 60
thee from whirlwinds, star-blasting, and
taking. Do poor Tom some charity, whom
the foul fiend vexes. There could I have him
now—and there—and there again—and
there— (Storm still.) 65

LEAR. Has his daughters brought him to
this pass?
Couldst thou save nothing? Wouldst thou
give 'em all?

FOOL. Nay, he reserved a blanket, else we
had been all shamed.

LEAR. Now all the plagues that in the pendulous air 70
Hang fated o'er men's faults light on thy
daughters!

KENT. He hath no daughters, sir.

LEAR. Death, traitor; nothing could have
subdued nature
To such a lowness but his unkind daughters.
Is it the fashion that discarded fathers 75
Should have thus little mercy on their flesh?
Judicious punishment—'twas this flesh begot
Those pelican daughters.

EDGAR. Pillicock sat on Pillicock Hill. Alow,
alow, loo, loo! 80

FOOL. This cold night will turn us all to
fools and madmen.

EDGAR. Take heed o' th' foul fiend; obey
thy parents; keep thy words' justice; swear
not; commit not with man's sworn 85
spouse; set not thy sweet heart on proud
array. Tom's acold.

LEAR. What hast thou been?

EDGAR. A servingman, proud in heart and
mind; that curled my hair, wore gloves in 90
my cap; served the lust of my mistress' heart,
and did the act of darkness with her; swore
as many oaths as I spake words, and broke
them in the sweet face of heaven. One that
slept in the contriving of lust, and waked 95
to do it. Wine loved I deeply, dice dearly;
and in woman out-paramoured the Turk.
False of heart, light of ear, bloody of hand;
hog in sloth, fox in stealth, wolf in greediness,
dog in madness, lion in prey. Let not the 100
creaking of shoes nor the rustling of silks
betray thy poor heart to woman. Keep thy
foot out of brothels, thy hand out of plackets,
thy pen from lenders' books, and defy the
foul fiend. Still through the hawthorn 105
blows the cold wind; says suum, mun, nonny.
Dolphin my boy, boy, sesey! let him trot by.
(Storm still.)

LEAR. Thou wert better in a grave than to
answer with thy uncovered body this extremity
of the skies. Is man no more than this? 110
Consider him well. Thou ow'st the worm no
silk, the beast no hide, the sheep no wool, the
cat no perfume. Ha! here's three on's are
sophisticated. Thou art the thing itself; unaccommodated man is no more but such 115
a poor, bare, forked animal as thou art. Off,
off, you lendings! Come, unbutton here.

[Tearing off his clothes.]

---

47 Through . . . winds (a line from a ballad) 55–
56 knives, halters, ratsbane i.e., as means of committing suicide 56 pew balcony outside a window
57–58 ride . . . bridges i.e., take crazy risks 58
course chase 59 for as 61 star-blasting being
harmed by an evil star 62 taking infection 68
blanket (which covers his loins) 70 pendulous overhanging 71 fated o'er destined to punish 78
pelican the young of the pelican were supposed to
feed on the blood of the parent 79 Pillicock . . .
Hill a nursery rhyme (?) 79–80 Alow . . . loo a refrain or hunting cry (?)

85 commit not (i.e., adultery) 90–91 gloves in my
cap (favors from his mistress) 97 out-paramoured
the Turk had more women than the Sultan 98
light of ear ready to listen to evil 101 creaking of
shoes (fashionable, hence seductive) 103 plackets
slits in skirts 104 lenders' i.e., moneylenders' 107
Dolphin Dauphin (?) (allusion to a ballad); sesey
(from Fr. cessez, "stop, be quiet" [?]) 109 answer
bear the brunt of; extremity violence 111 Thou
ow'st you have taken from 113 cat civet cat (from
which perfume is derived) 114 sophisticated made
artificial (literally "adulterated") 114–15 unaccommodated unprovided, uncivilized 116 forked
i.e., two-legged 117 lendings borrowed clothes

FOOL. Prithee, nuncle, be contented; 'tis a naughty night to swim in. Now a little fire in a wild field were like an old lecher's 120 heart—a small spark, all the rest on's body cold. Look, here comes a walking fire.

(*Enter* GLOUCESTER *with a torch.*)

EDGAR. This is the foul Flibbertigibbet. He begins at curfew, and walks till the first cock. He gives the web and the pin, squints the 125 eye, and makes the harelip; mildews the white wheat, and hurts the poor creature of earth.

> Swithold footed thrice the 'old;
> He met the nightmare, and her
>     nine fold; 130
> Bid her alight
> And her troth plight,
> And aroint thee, witch, aroint thee!

KENT. How fares your Grace?
LEAR. What's he? 135
KENT. Who's there? What is't you seek?
GLOUCESTER. What are you there? Your names?

EDGAR. Poor Tom, that eats the swimming frog, the toad, the todpole, the wall-newt 140 and the water; that in the fury of his heart, when the foul fiend rages, eats cow-dung for sallets, swallows the old rat and the ditch-dog, drinks the green mantle of the standing pool; who is whipped from tithing to tithing, 145 and stocked, punished and imprisoned; who hath had three suits to his back, six shirts to his body,

> Horse to ride, and weapon to wear,
> But mice and rats, and such small deer, 150
> Have been Tom's food for seven long year.

Beware my follower! Peace, Smulkin, peace, thou fiend!

GLOUCESTER. What, hath your Grace no better company? 155

---

119 *naughty* wicked   120 *wild* barren   123 *Flibbertigibbet* (a devil)   124 *curfew* 9 P.M.; *first cock* midnight   125 *web . . . pin* cataract; *squints* crosses   129 *Swithold* St. Withold (who exorcized demons); *footed* walked over; *'old* wold (upland plain)   130 *nightmare* demon; *fold* offspring   131 *alight* i.e., from her horse   132 *her troth plight* pledge her word   133 *aroint thee* get away   140 *todpole* tadpole   141 *water* i.e., water-newt   143 *sallets* salads; *ditch-dog* dead dog in a ditch   144 *mantle* scum; *standing* stagnant   145 *tithing* tenfamily district   150 *deer* game   152–57 *Smulkin, Modo, Mahu* (devils)

EDGAR. The prince of darkness is a gentleman.
Modo he's called, and Mahu.
GLOUCESTER. Our flesh and blood, my lord, is grown so vile
That it doth hate what gets it.
EDGAR. Poor Tom's acold. 160
GLOUCESTER. Go in with me. My duty cannot suffer
T' obey in all your daughters' hard commands.
Though their injunction be to bar my doors
And let this tyrannous night take hold upon you,
Yet have I ventured to come seek you out 165
And bring you where both fire and food is ready.
LEAR. First let me talk with this philosopher.
What is the cause of thunder?
KENT. Good my lord, take his offer; go into th' house.
LEAR. I'll talk a word with this same learnèd Theban. 170
What is your study?
EDGAR. How to prevent the fiend, and to kill vermin.
LEAR. Let me ask you one word in private.
KENT. Impórtune him once more to go, my lord.
His wits begin t' unsettle.
GLOUCESTER.    Canst thou blame him? 175
(*Storm still.*)
His daughters seek his death. Ah, that good Kent,
He said it would be thus, poor banished man!
Thou say'st the King grows mad—I'll tell thee, friend,
I am almost mad myself. I had a son,
Now outlawed from my blood; he sought my life 180
But lately, very late. I loved him, friend,
No father his son dearer. True to tell thee,
The grief hath crazed my wits. What a night's this!
I do beseech your Grace—
LEAR.              O, cry you mercy, sir.

---

159 *gets* begets   161 *suffer* allow itself   170 *Theban* i.e., philosopher   172 *prevent* thwart   180 *outlawed . . . blood* disinherited   184 *cry you mercy* I beg your pardon

Noble philosopher, your company.                185

EDGAR. Tom's acold.

GLOUCESTER. In, fellow, there, into th'
hovel; keep thee warm.

LEAR. Come, let's in all.

KENT.                This way, my lord.

LEAR.                With him!
I will keep still with my philosopher.

KENT. Good my lord, soothe him; let him
take the fellow.                190

GLOUCESTER. Take him you on.

KENT. Sirrah, come on; go along with us.

LEAR. Come, good Athenian.

GLOUCESTER. No words, no words! Hush.

EDGAR. Child Rowland to the dark tower
came;                195

His word was still, "Fie, foh, and fum,
I smell the blood of a British man."
                (Exeunt.)

### Scene 5

(Enter CORNWALL and EDMUND.)

CORNWALL. I will have my revenge ere
I depart his house.

EDMUND. How, my lord, I may be censured,
that nature thus gives way to loyalty, something fears me to think of.                5

CORNWALL. I now perceive it was not
altogether your brother's evil disposition made
him seek his death; but a provoking merit,
set awork by a reproveable badness in himself.

EDMUND. How malicious is my fortune                10
that I must repent to be just! This is the
letter which he spoke of, which approves him
an intelligent party to the advantages of
France. O heavens, that this treason were not!
or not I the detector!                15

CORNWALL. Go with me to the Duchess.

EDMUND. If the matter of this paper be

certain, you have mighty business in hand.

CORNWALL. True or false, it hath made thee
Earl of Gloucester. Seek out where thy                20
father is, that he may be ready for our apprehension.

EDMUND [aside]. If I find him comforting
the King, it will stuff his suspicion more fully.
—I will persevere in my course of                25
loyalty, though the conflict be sore between
that and my blood.

CORNWALL. I will lay trust upon thee, and
thou shalt find a dearer father in my love.
                (Exeunt.)

### Scene 6

(Enter KENT and GLOUCESTER.)

GLOUCESTER. Here is better than the open
air; take it thankfully. I will piece out the
comfort with what addition I can. I will
not be long from you.

KENT. All the power of his wits have                5
given way to his impatience. The gods reward
your kindness.                (Exit [GLOUCESTER].)

(Enter LEAR, EDGAR, and FOOL.)

EDGAR. Frateretto calls me, and tells me
Nero is an angler in the lake of darkness.
Pray, innocent, and beware the foul fiend.                10

FOOL. Prithee, nuncle, tell me whether
a madman be a gentleman or a yeoman.

LEAR. A king, a king.

FOOL. No, he's a yeoman that has a
gentleman to his son; for he's a mad yeo-                15
man that sees his son a gentleman before him.

LEAR. To have a thousand with red burning
spits
Come hizzing in upon em'—

[EDGAR. The foul fiend bites my back.

FOOL. He's mad that trusts in the                20
tameness of a wolf, a horse's health, a boy's
love, or a whore's oath.

LEAR. It shall be done; I will arraign them
straight.

[To EDGAR.] Come, sit thou here, most
learned justice.

---

191 *Take him you* i.e., you take him    193 *Athenian*
i.e., philosopher    195 *Child . . . came* (a line from
a lost ballad [?]); *Child* candidate for knighthood;
*Rowland* the Roland of Charlemagne legends
196–97 *word* motto; *still* always; *"Fie . . . man"*
(from "Jack the Giant-Killer")
III.5.3 *censured* judged    4–5 *something fears* somewhat alarms    8 *provoking merit* virtue which
incited him to action    9 *himself* i.e., Edgar. The
idea seems to be that though it may have been
virtuous to be angry with Gloucester it was
wickedness which enlisted such feelings in the attempted parricide    12 *approves* proves    13 *intelligent . . . advantages* spy for the cause

21–22 *ready . . . apprehension* at hand for us to
arrest him    27 *blood* instinctive feelings    28 *lay . . .
thee* put you in a position of trust
III.6.8 *Frateretto* (a devil)    9 *Nero* in Chaucer's
"Monk's Tale" Nero's fishing is referred to    18
*hizzing* hissing    23 *arraign* bring to trial; *straight*
straightaway

[*To the* FOOL.] Thou, sapient 'r, sit here.
Now, you she-foxes—                                    25
EDGAR. Look, where he stands and glares.
Want'st thou eyes at trial, madam?
Come o'er the bourn, Bessy, to me.
FOOL.    Her boat hath a leak,
And she must not speak                         30
Why she dares not come over to thee.
EDGAR. The foul fiend haunts poor Tom in
the voice of a nightingale. Hoppedance cries
in Tom's belly for two white herring. Croak
not, black angel; I have no food for thee.    35
KENT. How do you, sir? Stand you not so
amazed.
Will you lie down and rest upon the cushions?
LEAR. I'll see their trial first. Bring in their
evidence.
[*To* EDGAR.] Thou, robèd man of justice,
take thy place.
[*To the* FOOL.] And thou, his yokefellow of
equity,                                          40
Bench by his side. [*To* KENT.] You are o' th'
commission;
Sit you too.
EDGAR.                    Let us deal justly.
Sleepest or wakest thou, jolly shepherd?
Thy sheep be in the corn;
And for one blast of thy minikin mouth    45
Thy sheep shall take no harm.
Purr, the cat is gray.
LEAR. Arraign her first. 'Tis Goneril, I here
take my oath before this honorable assembly,
kicked the poor King her father.              50
FOOL. Come hither, mistress. Is your name
Goneril?
LEAR. She cannot deny it.
FOOL. Cry you mercy, I took you for a
joint-stool.                                      55

LEAR. And here's another, whose warped
looks proclaim
What store her heart is made on. Stop her
there!
Arms, arms, sword, fire! Corruption in the
place!
False justicer, why hast thou let her 'scape?]
EDGAR. Bless thy five wits!                    60
KENT. O pity! Sir, where is the patience
now
That you so oft have boasted to retain?
EDGAR [*aside*]. My tears begin to take his
part so much
They mar my counterfeiting.
LEAR. The little dogs and all,                 65
Tray, Blanch, and Sweetheart—see, they
bark at me.
EDGAR. Tom will throw his head at them.
Avaunt, you curs.
Be thy mouth or black or white,
Tooth that poisons if it bite;                 70
Mastiff, greyhound, mongrel grim,
Hound or spaniel, brach or lym,
Or bobtail tike, or trundle-tail—
Tom will make him weep and wail;
For, with throwing thus my head,           75
Dogs leaped the hatch, and all are fled.
Do, de, de, de. Sese! Come, march to wakes
and fairs and market towns. Poor Tom, thy
horn is dry.
LEAR. Then let them anatomize Regan.   80
See what breeds about her heart. Is there any
cause in nature that makes these hard hearts?
[*To* EDGAR.] You, sir, I entertain for one of
my hundred; only I do not like the fashion
of your garments. You will say they are    85
Persian; but let them be changed.
KENT. Now, good my lord, lie here and rest
awhile.
LEAR. Make no noise, make no noise; draw
the curtains.                                      90

---

26 *he* i.e., one of the devils (?)  28 *bourn* brook
(the line is from a popular ballad, which the Fool
proceeds to parody)  33 *Hoppedance* (a devil)  36
*amazed* bewildered  41 *commission* those commis-
sioned as justices by the King  43–46 *Sleepest . . .
harm* (fragment of an old song[?])  44 *corn* wheat-
field  45 *minikin* shrill; *mouth* i.e., the shepherd's
pipe (?)  47 *cat is gray* it was thought that devils
often took the forms of gray cats  55 *joint-stool*
low stool made by a joiner (woodworker). Presumably, two such stools are on the stage to represent Goneril and Regan in this scene (see l. 55).
The Fool takes advantage of the situation to give
a special point to a standard humorous apology
for overlooking someone

---

57 *store* stuff  58 *Corruption . . . place* bribery in
the court  72 *brach* hound bitch; *lym* bloodhound
73 *bobtail . . . trundle-tail* cur with short or long tail
76 *hatch* lower half of a "Dutch door"  77 *Sese* like
*sesey* (III.4.107), be quiet, sh! (?); *wakes* parish
feasts  79 *horn* horn bottle (used in begging drink)
86 *Persian* it is ironical for Lear to speak thus
of Edgar's rags, since "Persian" suggested "gorgeous"  90 *curtains* Lear imagines he is in a bed
with curtains

So, so. We'll go to supper i' th' morning.

FOOL. And I'll go to bed at noon.

(*Enter* GLOUCESTER.)

GLOUCESTER. Come hither, friend. Where
is the King my master?

KENT. Here, sir, but trouble him not;
his wits are gone.

GLOUCESTER. Good friend, I prithee take
him in thy arms.                                      95

I have o'erheard a plot of death upon him.

There is a litter ready; lay him in't

And drive toward Dover, friend, where thou
shalt meet

Both welcome and protection. Take up thy
master.

If thou shouldst dally half an hour, his life, 100

With thine and all that offer to defend him,

Stand in assurèd loss. Take up, take up,

And    follow    me,    that    will    to    some
provision

Give thee quick conduct.

[KENT.                    Oppressèd nature sleeps.

This rest might yet have balmed thy broken
sinews,                                                   105

Which, if convenience will not allow,

Stand in hard cure. [*To the* FOOL.] Come,
help to bear thy master.

Thou must not stay behind.]

GLOUCESTER.              Come, come, away!

(*Exeunt [all but* EDGAR].)

[EDGAR. When we our betters see bearing
our woes,

We scarcely think our miseries our foes.   110

Who alone suffers suffers most i' th' mind,

Leaving free things and happy shows behind;

But then the mind much sufferance doth
o'erskip

When grief hath mates, and bearing fellowship.

How    light   and   portable   my   pain   seems
now,                                                        115

When that which makes me bend makes the
King bow.

He childed as I fathered. Tom, away.

Mark the high noises, and thyself bewray

When false opinion, whose wrong thoughts
defile thee,

In thy just proof repeals and reconciles
thee.                                                        120

What will hap more to-night, safe 'scape the
King!

Lurk, lurk.]                                      [*Exit.*]


*Scene 7*

(*Enter* CORNWALL, REGAN, GONERIL,
BASTARD, *and* SERVANTS.)

CORNWALL [*to* GONERIL]. Post speedily to my
lord your husband; show him this letter. The
army of France is landed. [*To* SERVANTS.]
Seek out the traitor Gloucester.

[*Exeunt some* SERVANTS.]

REGAN. Hang him instantly.                          5

GONERIL. Pluck out his e es.

CORNWALL. Leave him to my displeasure.
Edmund, keep you our sister company. The
revenges we are bound to take upon your
traitorous father are not fit for your be-   10
holding. Advise the Duke where you are
going, to a most festinate preparation. We are
bound to the like. Our posts shall be swift and
intelligent betwixt us. Farewell, dear sister;
farewell, my Lord of Gloucester.                   15

(*Enter* STEWARD [OSWALD].)

How now? Where's the King?

OSWALD. My Lord of Gloucester hath conveyed him hence.

Some five or six and thirty of his knights,

Hot questrists after him, met him at gate;

Who, with some other of the lord's depend-
ants,                                                         20

Are gone with him toward Dover, where
they boast

To have well-armèd friends.

CORNWALL.       Get horses for your mistress.

(*Exit* [OSWALD].)

---

92 *And . . . noon* (the Fool's last words in the
play) 103 *provision* supplies 105 *broken sinews*
racked nerves 106 *convenience* a suitable arrangement 107 *Stand . . . cure* will be hard to cure 109
*our woes* i.e., woes like ours 112 *free* carefree; *shows*
appearances, looks 113 *sufferance* suffering 114
*bearing* endurance 115 *portable* bearable

---

118 *Mark . . . noises* take note of the rumors of
great doings (?); *bewray* reveal 120 *In . . . thee*
proving your innocence, repeals your banishment
and reconciles you to your father 121 *What . . .
more* whatever else happens 122 *Lurk* i.e., keep
in hiding

III.7.2 *letter* see III.5.12 12 *festinate* speedy
14 *intelligent* informative 15 *Lord of Gloucester* see
III.5.20 19 *questrists* seekers

GONERIL. Farewell, sweet lord, and sister.
CORNWALL. Edmund, farewell.
[*Exeunt* GONERIL *and* EDMUND.]
Go seek the traitor Gloucester,
Pinion him like a thief, bring him before
us.                                          25
[*Exeunt other* SERVANTS.]
Though well we may not pass upon his life
Without the form of justice, yet our power
Shall do a court'sy to our wrath, which men
May blame, but not control.
(*Enter* GLOUCESTER *and* SERVANTS.)
Who's there, the traitor?
REGAN. Ingrateful fox, 'tis he.            30
CORNWALL. Bind fast his corky arms.
GLOUCESTER. What means your Graces?
Good my friends, consider
You are my guests. Do me no foul play,
friends.
CORNWALL. Bind him, I say.
[SERVANTS *bind him.*]
REGAN.       Hard, hard! O filthy traitor.
GLOUCESTER. Unmerciful lady as you are,
I'm none.                                    35
CORNWALL. To this chair bind him.
Villain, thou shalt find—
[REGAN *plucks his beard.*]
GLOUCESTER. By the kind gods, 'tis most
ignobly done
To pluck me by the beard.
REGAN. So white, and such a traitor?
GLOUCESTER.             Naughty lady,
These hairs which thou dost ravish from my
chin                                         40
Will quicken and accuse thee. I am your host.
With robber's hands my hospitable favors
You should not ruffle thus. What will you do?
CORNWALL. Come, sir, what letters had you
late from France?
REGAN. Be simple-answered, for we know
the truth.                                   45
CORNWALL. And what confederacy have
you with the traitors
Late footed in the kingdom?
REGAN. To whose hands you have sent the
lunatic King.

Speak.
GLOUCESTER. I have a letter guessingly set
down,                                        50
Which came from one that's of a neutral
heart,
And not from one opposed.
CORNWALL.             Cunning.
REGAN.                        And false.
CORNWALL. Where hast thou sent the king?
GLOUCESTER. To Dover.
REGAN. Wherefore to Dover? Wast thou
not charged at peril—                        55
CORNWALL. Wherefore to Dover? Let him
answer that.
GLOUCESTER. I am tied to th' stake, and I
must stand the course.
REGAN. Wherefore to Dover?
GLOUCESTER. Because I would not see thy
cruel nails
Pluck out his poor old eyes; nor thy fierce
sister                                       60
In his anointed flesh stick boarish fangs.
The sea, with such a storm as his bare head
In hell-black night endured, would have
buoyed up
And quenched the stellèd fires.
Yet, poor old heart, he holp the heavens to
rain.                                        65
If wolves had at thy gate howled that stern
time,
Thou shouldst have said, "Good porter, turn
the key."
All cruels else subscribe. But I shall see
The wingèd vengeance overtake such children.
CORNWALL. See't shalt thou never. Fellows,
hold the chair.                              70
Upon these eyes of thine I'll set my foot.
GLOUCESTER. He that will think to live till
he be old,
Give me some help.—O cruel! O ye gods!
REGAN. One side will mock another.
Th' other too.

55 *charged at peril* ordered on peril of your life
57 *I am tied . . . course* Gloucester compares him
self to a bear baited by dogs; a *course* was the
"running" of the dogs at the tied bear 61 *anointed* touched with oil at the coronation 63 *buoyed*
risen 64 *stellèd fires* stars 65 *holp* helped 67 *turn
the key* i.e., open the gate 68 *All . . . subscribe* all
other cruelties yield to this one—are as nothing
to it (?) 69 *wingèd* heavenly or swift 74 *mock*
make ridiculous

26 *pass upon* i.e., pass judgment on 28 *do a
court'sy to* defer to, be guided by 31 *corky* i.e.,
shrunken with age 39 *Naughty* wicked 41 *quicken*
come to life 42 *favors* features 43 *ruffle* tear at
44 *late* lately 47 *footed* landed

CORNWALL. If you see vengeance—
1. SERVANT.   Hold your hand, my lord! 75
I have served you ever since I was a child;
But better service have I never done you
Than now to bid you hold.
 REGAN.    How now, you dog?
 1. SERVANT. If you did wear a beard upon
  your chin,
I'd shake it on this quarrel. What do you
  mean!         80
 CORNWALL. My villain!  [Draw and fight.]
 1. SERVANT. Nay, then, come on, and take
  the chance of anger.
 REGAN. Give me thy sword. A peasant
  stand up thus?
  [She takes a sword and runs at him behind,
            kills him.]
 1. SERVANT. O, I am slain! My lord, you
  have one eye left
To see some mischief on him. O!  85
 CORNWALL. Lest it see more, prevent it.
  Out, vile jelly.
Where is thy lustre now?
 GLOUCESTER. All dark and comfortless.
  Where's my son Edmund?
Edmund, enkindle all the sparks of nature
To quit this horrid act.
 REGAN.   Out, treacherous villain;  90
Thou call'st on him that hates thee. It was he
That made the overture of thy treasons to us;
Who is too good to pity thee.
 GLOUCESTER. O my follies! Then Edgar was
  abused.
Kind gods, forgive me that, and prosper
  him.          95
 REGAN. Go thrust him out at gates, and
  let him smell
His way to Dover.
     (Exit [one] with GLOUCESTER.)
    How is't, my lord? How look you?
 CORNWALL. I have received a hurt.
  Follow me, lady.
Turn out that eyeless villain. Throw this
  slave
Upon the dunghill. Regan, I bleed apace.  100

Untimely comes this hurt. Give me your arm.
          (Exeunt.)
 [2. SERVANT. I'll never care what wickedness I do,
If this man come to good.
 3. SERVANT.    If she live long,
And in the end meet the old course of death,
Women will all turn monsters.  105
 2. SERVANT. Let's follow the old Earl,
  and get the bedlam
To lead him where he would. His roguish
  madness
Allows itself to anything.
 3. SERVANT. Go thou. I'll fetch some flax
  and whites of eggs
To apply to his bleeding face. Now heaven
  help him.]       110
       [Exeunt severally.]

ACT IV. Scene 1

(Enter EDGAR.)
 EDGAR. Yet better thus, and known to be
  contemned,
Than still contemned and flattered. To be
  worst,
The lowest and most dejected thing of for-
  tune,
Stands still in esperance, lives not in fear.
The lamentable change is from the best; 5
The worst returns to laughter. Welcome then,
Thou unsubstantial air that I embrace:
The wretch that thou hast blown unto the
  worst
Owes nothing to thy blasts.
  (Enter GLOUCESTER and an OLD MAN.)
       But who comes here?
My father, poorly led? World, world, O
  world!        10
But that thy strange mutations make us hate
  thee,

---

80 on this quarrel in this cause; What . . . mean
i.e., how can you do such a thing? 81 villain
(punning on the old meaning of "serf") 85
mischief injury 89 nature natural feeling 90 quit
avenge; horrid horrible 92 overture revelation 97
How look you how are you

---

104 meet . . . death i.e., die a ntaural death 108
Allows . . . anything lends itself to any suggestion or
use
IV.1.1 contemned scorned 3 dejected . . . fortune
cast down by fortune 4 esperance hope 6 The
worst . . . laughter i.e., the worst situation can only
change for the better 9 Owes nothing i.e., is indebted for no favors 10 poorly (1) by only one
attendant; (2) by a poorly dressed man 11–12
But . . . age only hate, prompted by incomprehensible reverses of fortune, reconciles us to growing old (and dying)

Life would not yield to age.

OLD MAN.                    O my good lord,
I have been your tenant, and your father's
     tenant,
These fourscore years.

GLOUCESTER. Away, get thee away. Good
     friend, be gone.                              15
Thy comforts can do me no good at all;
Thee they may hurt.

OLD MAN.          You cannot see your way.

GLOUCESTER. I have no way, and therefore
     want no eyes;
I stumbled when I saw. Full oft 'tis seen
Our means secure us, and our mere
     defects                                       20
Prove our commodities. O dear son Edgar,
The food of thy abusèd father's wrath,
Might I but live to see thee in my touch
I'd say I had eyes again!

OLD MAN.          How now? Who's there?

EDGAR [aside]. O gods! Who is't can say
     "I am at the worst"?                          25
I am worse than e'er I was.

OLD MAN.                    'Tis poor mad Tom.

EDGAR [aside]. And worse I may be yet.
     The worst is not
So long as we can say "This is the worst."

OLD MAN. Fellow, where goest?

GLOUCESTER.               Is it a beggarman?

OLD MAN. Madman and beggar too.           30

GLOUCESTER. He has some reason, else he
     could not beg.
I' th' last night's storm I such a fellow saw,
Which made me think a man a worm.
     My son
Came then into my mind, and yet my mind
Was then scarce friends with him. I have
     heard more since.                             35
As flies to wanton boys are we to th' gods;
They kill us for their sport.

---

EDGAR [aside].          How should this be?
Bad is the trade that must play fool to sorrow,
Ang'ring itself and others.—Bless thee, master.

GLOUCESTER. Is that the naked fellow?

OLD MAN.               Ay, my lord.        40

GLOUCESTER. Get thee away. If for my sake
Thou wilt o'ertake us hence a mile or twain
I' th' way toward Dover, do it for ancient love;
And bring some covering for this naked soul,
Which I'll entreat to lead me.

OLD MAN.          Alack, sir, he is mad.    45

GLOUCESTER. 'Tis the time's plague when
     madmen lead the blind.
Do as I bid thee, or rather do thy pleasure.
Above the rest, be gone.

OLD MAN. I'll bring him the best 'parel
     that I have,
Come on't what will.          (Exit.)        50

GLOUCESTER. Sirrah naked fellow—

EDGAR. Poor Tom's acold. [Aside.] I
     cannot daub it further.

GLOUCESTER. Come hither, fellow.

EDGAR [aside]. And yet I must.—Bless thy
     sweet eyes, they bleed.

GLOUCESTER. Know'st thou the way to
     Dover?                                        55

EDGAR. Both stile and gate, horseway and
footpath. Poor Tom hath been scared out of
his good wits. Bless thee, good man's son,
from the foul fiend. [Five fiends have been in
poor Tom at once: of lust, as Obidicut;      60
Hobbididence, prince of dumbness; Mahu,
of stealing; Modo, of murder; Flibbertigibbet, of mopping and mowing, who since
possesses chambermaids and waiting women.
So, bless thee, master.]                       65

GLOUCESTER. Here, take this purse, thou
     whom the heavens' plagues
Have humbled to all strokes. That I am
     wretched
Makes thee the happier. Heavens, deal so still!
Let the superfluous and lust-dieted man,

---

16 *comforts* attempts to help me   18 *want* need
20–21 *Our means ... commodities* i.e., our advantages give us false confidence, and our very
disadvantages turn out to be blessings   22 *food*
i.e., object; *abusèd* deceived   23 *in* i.e., by
means of   27–28 *The worst ... worst* (because
we can never know what is coming)   31 *reason*
rationality   33–34 *My son ... mind* though by
stage convention disguise is normally assumed to
be impenetrable in *King Lear*, Gloucester is here
allowed, realistically, to suspect the truth   36
*wanton* playful, irresponsible

37 *How ... be* how could this have happened (?)
39 *Ang'ring* offending   43 *ancient love* i.e., old
times' sake   46 *time's plague* disorder typical of
the times   52 *daub it* lay it on, pretend   60 *Obidicut*
(a devil, as are the four following)   61 *dumbness*
muteness   63 *mopping and mowing* making faces
67 *humbled* reduced to bearing humbly   69–73
*Let ... enough* cf. III. 4.33–36   69 *superfluous* possessed of more than he needs; *lust-dieted* whose
desires are fully fed

That slaves your ordinance, that will not
    see                                      70
Because he does not feel, feel your pow'r
    quickly;
So distribution should undo excess,
And each man have enough. Dost thou know
    Dover?
    EDGAR. Ay, master.
    GLOUCESTER. There is a cliff, whose high
    and bending head                 75
Looks fearfully in the confinèd deep.
Bring me but to the very brim of it,
And I'll repair the misery thou dost bear
With something rich about me. From that
    place
I shall no leading need.
    EDGAR.             Give me thy arm.    80
Poor Tom shall lead thee.       (Exeunt.)

### Scene 2

(Enter GONERIL and BASTARD.)
    GONERIL. Welcome, my lord. I marvel our
    mild husband
Not met us on the way.
        [Enter STEWARD.]
           Now, where's your master?
    OSWALD. Madam, within, but never man
    so changed.
I told him of the army that was landed:
He smiled at it. I told him you were com-
    ing:                                  5
His   answer   was,   "The   worse."   Of
    Gloucester's treachery
And of the loyal service of his son
When I informed him, then he called me sot
And told me I had turned the wrong side out.
What most he should dislike seems pleasant
    to him;                    10
What like, offensive.
    GONERIL [to EDMUND].    Then shall you go
    no further.
It is the cowish terror of his spirit,
That dares not undertake. He'll not feel
    wrongs

Which tie him to an answer. Our wishes on
    the way
May prove effects. Back, Edmund, to my
    brother.                    15
Hasten his musters and conduct his pow'rs.
I must change names at home, and give the
    distaff
Into my husband's hands. This trusty servant
Shall pass between us. Ere long you are like
    to hear
(If you dare venture in your own behalf)   20
A mistress's command. Wear this. Spare
    speech.                 [Gives a favor.]
Decline your head. This kiss, if it durst speak,
Would stretch thy spirits up into the air.
Conceive, and fare thee well.
    EDMUND. Yours in the ranks of death.
                                (Exit.)
    GONERIL.     My most dear Gloucester.  25
O, the difference of man and man:
To thee a woman's services are due;
My fool usurps my body.
    OSWALD.      Madam, here comes my lord.
                      [Exit STEWARD.]
    (Enter ALBANY.)
    GONERIL. I have been worth the whistle.
    ALBANY.              O Goneril,
You are not worth the dust which the rude
    wind                      30
Blows in your face. [I fear your disposition:
That nature which contemns its origin
Cannot be bordered certain in itself.
She that herself will sliver and disbranch
From her material sap, perforce must
    wither                   35
And come to deadly use.
    GONERIL. No more; the text is foolish.
    ALBANY. Wisdom and goodness to the vile
    seem vile:

---

70 *slaves* enslaves, i.e., spurns; *ordinance* (to give
to the needy)  75 *bending* overhanging  76 *in . . .
deep* at the sea, which it holds back
IV.2.2 *Not met* did not meet  8 *sot* fool  11 *What
like* what he should like  12 *cowish* cowardly  13
*undertake* venture

14 *an answer* retaliatory action  14–15 *Our
wishes . . . effects* i.e., the wishes (that you might
be my husband) discussed on the way here may
materialize  16 *musters* enlistments; *conduct his
pow'rs* lead his army  17 *change names* i.e., play
the man's role; *distaff* spinning-staff (hence symbol
of the wife)  21 *mistress* i.e., the adored woman
for whom, in chivalric romances, the knight does
battle  24 *conceive* understand fully  28 *fool* i.e.,
the despised Albany  29 *I . . . whistle* i.e., I used
to be at least worth whistling for (like a good
dog)  32 *contemns* despises  33 *bordered certain* safely
contained  34 *sliver* cut off  35 *material sap* source
of life

Filths savor but themselves. What have you
    done?
Tigers not daughters, what have you per-
    formèd?                 40
A father, and a gracious agèd man,
Whose reverence even the head-lugged bear
    would lick,
Most barbarous, most degenerate, have you
    madded.
Could my good brother suffer you to do it?
A man, a prince, by him so benefited!    45
If that the heavens do not their visible spirits
Send quickly down to tame these vile offenses,
It will come,
Humanity must perforce prey on itself,
Like monsters of the deep.]
    GONERIL.           Milk-livered man,   50
That bear'st a cheek for blows, a head for
    wrongs;
Who hast not in thy brows an eye discerning
Thine honor from thy suffering; [that not
    know'st
Fools do those villains pity who are punished
Ere they have done their mischief. Where's
    thy drum?                55
France spreads his banners in our noiseless
    land,
With plumèd helm thy state begins to threat,
Whilst thou, a moral fool, sits still and cries
"Alack, why does he so?"]
    ALBANY.          See thyself, devil:
Proper deformity seems not in the fiend   60
So horrid as in woman.
    GONERIL.          O vain fool!
    [ALBANY. Thou changèd and self-covered
    thing, for shame
Bemonster not thy feature. Were't my fitness
To let these hands obey my blood,
They are apt enough to dislocate and tear   65

Thy flesh and bones. Howe'er thou art a fiend,
A woman's shape doth shield thee.
    GONERIL. Marry, your manhood—mew!]
        (Enter a MESSENGER.)
    [ALBANY. What news?]
    MESSENGER. O, my good lord, the Duke of
    Cornwall's dead,             70
Slain by his servant, going to put out
The other eye of Gloucester.
    ALBANY.             Gloucester's eyes?
    MESSENGER. A servant that he bred, thrilled
    with remorse,
Opposed against the act, bending his sword
To his great master; who, thereat enraged,  75
Flew on him, and amongst them felled him
    dead;
But not without that harmful stroke which
    since
Hath plucked him after.
    ALBANY.        This shows you are above,
You justicers, that these our nether crimes
So speedily can venge. But, O poor
    Gloucester,            80
Lost he his other eye?
    MESSENGER.         Both, both, my lord.
This letter, madam, craves a speedy answer.
'Tis from your sister.
    GONERIL [aside].    One way I like this well;
But being widow, and my Gloucester with
    her,
May all the building in my fancy pluck    85
Upon my hateful life. Another way
The news is not so tart.—I'll read, and an-
    swer.                  [Exit.]
    ALBANY. Where was his son when they did
    take his eyes?
    MESSENGER. Come with my lady hither.
    ALBANY.            He is not here.
    MESSENGER. No, my good lord; I met him
    back again.            90

---

39 *savor* relish  42 *head-lugg'd* tugged by the
head (hence mean)  43 *degenerate* unnatural;
*madded* made mad  46 *visible spirits* spiritual agents
in visible form  48 *It will come* i.e., the following
will come to pass, happen  50 *milk-livered* cowardly
52–53 *discerning ... suffering* able to distinguish
between honor and ignominious acceptance of
injury  54 *Fools* i.e., only fools  56 *noiseless* i.e.,
not noisy with drums and trumpets  57 *helm* war-
helmet; *threat* threaten  60 *proper* fair-seeming
62 *changèd* i.e., into a very devil; *self-covered* i.e.,
covered by an appearance of humanity  63 *Bemonster ... feature* don't contort your face like a
fiend; *my fitness* fit for me  64 *blood* passion, instinct

---

68 *Marry* (oath, from "By Mary"); *mew* (contemptuous interjection, imitating a cat)  71 *going
to* i.e., as Cornwall was about to  73 *bred* reared;
*thrilled with remorse* pierced with compassion  76
*amongst them* i.e., aided by the others  78 *plucked
him after* drawn Cornwall along (to death)  79
*nether crimes* i.e., those committed here below  82
*craves* demands  85–86 *May ... life* may bring my
dream-castles crashing down on me, making life
hateful  86 *Another way* (actually the way mentioned in l. 83: presumably Cornwall's death gives
freer reign to Goneril's ambitions)  87 *tart* distasteful  90 *back* i.e., on his way back

ALBANY. Knows he the wickedness?

MESSENGER. Ay, my good lord. 'Twas he informed against him,
And quit the house on purpose, that their punishment
Might have the freer course.

ALBANY.                    Gloucester, I live
To thank thee for the love thou showed'st the King,                                      95
And to revenge thine eyes. Come hither, friend.
Tell me what more thou know'st.     (*Exeunt.*)


*Scene 3*


[(*Enter* KENT *and a* GENTLEMAN.)

KENT. Why the King of France is so suddenly gone back know you no reason?

GENTLEMAN. Something he left imperfect in the state, which since his coming forth is thought of, which imports to the kingdom        5
so much fear and danger that his personal return was most required and necessary.

KENT. Who hath he left behind him general?

GENTLEMAN. The Marshal of France,     10
Monsieur La Far.

KENT. Did your letters pierce the Queen to any demonstration of grief?

GENTLEMAN. Ay, sir. She took them, read them in my presence,
And now and then an ample tear trilled down                                            15
Her delicate cheek. It seemed she was a queen
Over her passion, who, most rebel-like,
Sought to be king o'er her.

KENT.                    O, then it moved her?

GENTLEMAN. Not to a rage. Patience and sorrow strove
Who should express her goodliest. You have seen                                          20
Sunshine and rain at once—her smiles and tears
Were like a better way: those happy smilets
That played on her ripe lip seemed not to know

What guests were in her eyes, which parted thence
As pearls from diamonds dropped. In brief,                                         25
Sorrow would be a rarity most beloved,
If all could so become it.

KENT.          Made she no verbal question?

GENTLEMAN. Faith, once or twice she heaved the name of father
Pantingly forth, as if it pressed her heart;
Cried "Sisters, sisters, shame of ladies, sisters!                                        30
Kent, father, sisters? What, i' th' storm i' th' night?
Let pity not be believed!" There she shook
The holy water from her heavenly eyes,
And clamor moistened; then away she started
To deal with grief alone.

KENT.                    It is the stars,     35
The stars above us govern our conditions;
Else one self mate and make could not beget
Such different issues. You spoke not with her since?

GENTLEMAN. No.

KENT. Was this before the King returned?

GENTLEMAN.                    No, since.     40

KENT. Well, sir, the poor distressèd Lear's i' th' town;
Who sometime, in his better tune, remembers
What we are come about, and by no means
Will yield to see his daughter.

GENTLEMAN.                    Why, good sir?

KENT. A sovereign shame so elbows him; his own unkindness,                                 45
That stripped her from his benediction, turned her
To foreign casualties, gave her dear rights
To his dog-hearted daughters—these things sting
His mind so venomously that burning shame
Detains him from Cordelia.

_____

IV.3.3 *Something . . . imperfect* he left some unfinished business  5 *imports* portends  12 *pierce* move  15 *trilled* trickled  20 *goodliest* most suitably  22 *Were . . . way* i.e., improved upon that spectacle

27 *If . . . it* if it were so becoming to all; *verbal question* oral conversation  32 *believed* i.e., believed to exist (in a world where such things happen)  34 *clamor moistened* moistened (and thus muted) lamentation  36 *govern our conditions* determine our characters  37 *one . . . make* the same husband and wife  42 *sometime* sometimes; *in . . . tune* i.e., in his more composed moments  45 *sovereign* overruling; *elbows* nudges, reminds  47 *casualties* chances

GENTLEMAN. Alack, poor gentleman.  50

KENT. Of Albany's and Cornwall's powers
you heard not?

GENTLEMAN. 'Tis so; they are afoot.

KENT. Well, sir, I'll bring you to our master Lear

And leave you to attend him. Some dear
cause

Will in concealment wrap me up awhile.  55

When I am known aright, you shall not grieve

Lending me this acquaintance. I pray you go

Along with me.]                    [*Exeunt.*]


*Scene 4*

(*Enter, with Drum and Colors,* CORDELIA,
GENTLEMEN, [DOCTOR], *and* SOLDIERS.)

CORDELIA. Alack, 'tis he! Why, he was
met even now

As mad as the vexed sea, singing aloud,

Crowned with rank femiter and furrow weeds,

With hardocks, hemlock, nettles, cuckoo
flow'rs,

Darnel, and all the idle weeds that grow  5

In our sustaining corn. A century send forth!

Search every acre in the high-grown field

And bring him to our eye. [*Exit an* OFFICER.]
What can man's wisdom

In the restoring his bereavèd sense?

He that helps him take all my outward
worth.  10

DOCTOR. There is means, madam.

Our foster nurse of nature is repose,

The which he lacks. That to provoke in him

Are many simples operative, whose power

Will close the eye of anguish.

CORDELIA.        All blest secrets,  15

All you unpublished virtues of the earth,

Spring with my tears; be aidant and remediate

54 *dear cause* important purpose or reason (never
revealed)
IV.4.3 *femiter* fumitory; *furrow weeds* weeds that
grow in the furrow  4 *hardocks* burdocks(?); *cuckoo
flowers* a variety of water cress  5 *Darnel* tares;
*idle* useless  6 *sustaining corn* life-giving wheat;
*century* troop of a hundred men  8 *What . . . wisdom*
what can man's science accomplish  9 *bereavèd*
impaired  10 *outward worth* material possessions
12 *foster* fostering  13 *provoke* induce  14 *Are . . .
operative* many herbs are effective  16 *unpublished
virtues* i.e., little-known remedial herbs  17 *spring*
grow; *remediate* remedial

In the good man's distress. Seek, seek for him,

Lest his ungoverned rage dissolve the life

That wants the means to lead it.

[*Enter* MESSENGER.]

MESSENGER.        News, madam.  20

The British pow'rs are marching hitherward.

CORDELIA. 'Tis known before. Our preparation stands

In expectation of them. O dear father,

It is thy business that I go about.

Therefore great France  25

My mourning, and importuned tears hath
pitied.

No blown ambition doth our arms incite,

But love, dear love, and our aged father's
right.

Soon may I hear and see him!  (*Exeunt.*)


*Scene 5*

(*Enter* REGAN *and* STEWARD [OSWALD].)

REGAN. But are my brother's pow'rs set
forth?

OSWALD.        Ay, madam.

REGAN. Himself in person there?

OSWALD.        Madam, with much ado.

Your sister is the better soldier.

REGAN. Lord Edmund spake not with your
lord at home?

OSWALD. No, madam.  5

REGAN. What might import my sister's
letter to him?

OSWALD. I know not, lady.

REGAN. Faith, he is posted hence on serious
matter.

It was great ignorance, Gloucester's eyes being out,

To let him live. Where he arrives he
moves  10

All hearts against us. Edmund, I think, is
gone,

In pity of his misery, to dispatch

His nighted life; moreover, to descry

The strength o' th' enemy.

OSWALD. I must needs after him, madam,
with my letter.  15

20 *wants* lacks; *means* i.e., reason  26 *importuned*
importunate  27 *blown* swollen
IV.5.2 *with much ado* as a result of much bother
and persuasion  6 *import* signify, say  8 *is posted* has
sped  9 *ignorance* folly  13 *nighted* (1) benighted;
(2) blinded

REGAN. Our troops set forth to-morrow.
Stay with us.
The ways are dangerous.
    OSWALD.         I may not, madam.
My lady charged my duty in this business.
    REGAN. Why should she write to Edmund?
Might not you
Transport her purposes by word? Belike,   20
Some things—I know not what. I'll love thee
much,
Let me unseal the letter.
    OSWALD.       Madam, I had rather—
    REGAN. I know your lady does not love her
husband,
I am sure of that; and at her late being here
She gave strange eliads and most speaking
looks         25
To noble Edmund. I know you are of her
bosom.
    OSWALD. I, madam?
    REGAN. I speak in understanding—y'are,
I know't—
Therefore I do advise you take this note:
My lord is dead; Edmund and I have
talked,         30
And more convenient is he for my hand
Than for your lady's. You may gather more.
If you do find him, pray you give him this;
And when your mistress hears thus much
from you,
I pray desire her call her wisdom to her.   35
So fare you well.
If you do chance to hear of that blind traitor,
Preferment falls on him that cuts him off.
    OSWALD. Would I could meet [him], mad-
am! I should show
What party I do follow.
    REGAN.      Fare thee well. (*Exeunt.*)   40

*Scene 6*

[*Enter* GLOUCESTER *and* EDGAR.]
    GLOUCESTER. When shall I come to th' top
of that same hill?
    EDGAR. You do climb up it now. Look how
we labor.

GLOUCESTER. Methinks the ground is even.
    EDGAR.         Horrible steep.
Hark, do you hear the sea?
    GLOUCESTER.         No, truly.
    EDGAR. Why, then, your other senses grow
imperfect        5
By your eyes' anguish.
    GLOUCESTER.      So may it be indeed.
Methinks thy voice is altered, and thou
speak'st
In better phrase and matter than thou didst.
    EDGAR. Y'are much deceived. In nothing
am I changed
But in my garments.
    GLOUCESTER.      Methinks y'are better
spoken.        10
    EDGAR. Come on, sir; here's the place.
Stand still. How fearful
And dizzy 'tis to cast one's eyes so low!
The crows and choughs that wing the mid-
way air
Show scarce so gross as beetles. Halfway down
Hangs one that gathers sampire—dreadful
trade;        15
Methinks he seems no bigger than his head.
The fishermen that walk upon the beach
Appear like mice; and yond tall anchoring
bark,
Diminished to her cock; her cock, a buoy
Almost too small for sight. The murmuring
surge        20
That on th' unnumb'red idle pebble chafes
Cannot be heard so high. I'll look no more,
Lest my brain turn, and the deficient sight
Topple down headlong.
    GLOUCESTER.     Set me where you stand.
    EDGAR. Give me your hand. You are now
within a foot        25
Of th' extreme verge. For all beneath the
moon

---

18 *charged my duty* commanded my obedience
20 *Belike* probably   25 *eliads* (*oeillades*) amorous
glances   26 *of her bosom* in her confidence   29
*take this note* note this   31 *convenient* suitable   32
*gather* guess   33 *this* presumably some token
38 *Preferment* advancement

IV.6.3 *Methinks . . . even* the absence of scenery
on the stage makes Edgar's deception of his father
somewhat easier to accept. In other situations we,
too, must imagine that what is described is there
6 *anguish* suffering   13 *choughs* jackdaws; *midway*
i.e., halfway down   14 *gross* large   15 *sampire*
samphire (an herb)   19 *cock* cockboat   21 *unnumb-
bered* innumerable; *idle* barren (?), uselessly
moving (?); *pebble* (used as a plural)   23–24
*the deficient . . . headlong* i.e., I fall because of
dizziness

Would I not leap upright.

GLOUCESTER.            Let go my hand.

Here, friend, 's another purse; in it a jewel
Well worth a poor man's taking. Fairies and
   gods
Prosper it with thee. Go thou further off;   30
Bid me farewell, and let me hear thee going.

EDGAR.  Now fare ye well, good sir.

GLOUCESTER.          With all my heart.

EDGAR [aside].  Why I do trifle thus with
   his despair
Is done to cure it.

GLOUCESTER.    O you mighty gods!

                      [He kneels.]

This world I do renounce, and in your
   sights                            35
Shake patiently my great affliction off.
If I could bear it longer and not fall
To quarrel with your great opposeless wills,
My snuff and loathèd part of nature should
Burn itself out. If Edgar live, O bless him!  40
Now, fellow, fare thee well.     [He falls.]

EDGAR.            Gone, sir—farewell.

And yet I know not how conceit may rob
The treasury of life when life itself
Yields to the theft. Had he been where he
   thought,
By this had thought been past. Alive or
   dead?                      45
Ho you, sir! Friend! Hear you, sir? Speak!
Thus might he pass indeed. Yet he revives.
What are you, sir?

GLOUCESTER.       Away, and let me die.

EDGAR.  Hadst thou been aught but gos-
   samer, feathers, air,
So many fathom down precipitating,    50
Thou'dst shivered like an egg; but thou dost
   breathe,
Hast heavy substance, bleed'st not, speak'st,
   art sound.
Ten masts at each make not the altitude
Which thou hast perpendicularly fell.

Thy life's a miracle. Speak yet again.    55

GLOUCESTER.  But have I fall'n, or no?

EDGAR.  From the dread summit of this
   chalky bourn.
Look up a-height. The shrill-gorged lark so far
Cannot be seen or heard. Do but look up.

GLOUCESTER.  Alack, I have no eyes.   60

Is wretchedness deprived that benefit
To end itself by death? 'Twas yet some com-
   fort
When misery could beguile the tyrant's rage
And frustrate his proud will.

EDGAR.             Give me your arm.

Up—so. How is't? Feel you your legs?
   You stand.                        65

GLOUCESTER.  Too well, too well.

EDGAR.        This is above all strangeness.

Upon the crown o' th' cliff what thing was
   that
Which parted from you?

GLOUCESTER.    A poor unfortunate beggar.

EDGAR.  As I stood here below, methought
   his eyes
Were two full moons; he had a thousand
   noses,                   70
Horns welked and waved like the enridgèd
   sea.
It was some fiend. Therefore, thou happy
   father,
Think that the clearest gods, who make them
   honors
Of men's impossibilities, have preserved thee.

GLOUCESTER.  I do remember now.
   Henceforth I'll bear             75
Affliction till it do cry out itself
"Enough, enough," and die. That thing you
   speak of,
I took it for a man. Often 'twould say
"The fiend, the fiend"—he led me to that
   place.

EDGAR.  Bear free and patient thoughts.

   (Enter LEAR [fantastically crowned with
               wild flowers.])

                But who comes here?   80

---

27 upright i. e., even up in the air, not to mention forward   29 Fairies (thought to guard treasure)   33–34 Why . . . cure it the reason I play this
trick on him is to cure his despair   37–38 fall To
quarrel i.e., fall into the sin of quarreling   39 snuff
a guttering candle-wick (to which the end of his
life is compared)   42 conceit imagination (whose
operation is puzzling—"I know not how"—but
powerful)   44 Yields to allows   53 at each end to
end

---

55 life survival   57 bourn boundary (of the sea)
58 a-height on high; gorged throated   63 beguile
cheat (as by suicide)   71 welked corrugated;
enridgèd furrowed into waves   72 happy father lucky
old man   73 clearest purest   73–74 who . . . impossibilities i.e., who make themselves honored by
doing what is impossible for men.   80 free (of
despair)

The safer sense will ne'er accommodate
His master thus.

LEAR. No, they cannot touch me for coining;
I am the King himself.

EDGAR. O thou side-piercing sight! 85

LEAR. Nature's above art in that respect.
There's your press money. That fellow
handles his bow like a crow-keeper. Draw me
a clothier's yard. Look, look, a mouse! Peace,
peace; this piece of toasted cheese will 90
do't. There's my gauntlet; I'll prove it on a
giant. Bring up the brown bills. O, well flown,
bird. I' th' clout, i' th' clout—hewgh! Give
the word.

EDGAR. Sweet marjoram. 95

LEAR. Pass.

GLOUCESTER. I know that voice.

LEAR. Ha! Goneril with a white beard?
They flattered me like a dog, and told me
I had the white hairs in my beard ere the 100
black ones were there. To say "ay" and "no"
to everything that I said! "Ay" and "no"
too was no good divinity. When the rain came
to wet me once, and the wind to make me
chatter; when the thunder would not 105
peace at my bidding; there I found 'em,
there I smelt 'em out. Go to, they are not men
o' their words. They told me I was everything. 'Tis a lie—I am not ague-proof.

GLOUCESTER. The trick of that voice I do
well remember. 110
Is't not the King?

LEAR. Ay, every inch a king.
When I do stare, see how the subject quakes.
I pardon that man's life. What was thy
cause?
Adultery? Thou shalt not die. Die for adul-
tery?
No; the wren goes to't, and the small gilded
fly 115
Does lecher in my sight.
Let copulation thrive; for Gloucester's bas-
tard son
Was kinder to his father than my daughters
Got 'tween the lawful sheets.
To't, luxury, pell-mell, for I lack soldiers. 120
Behold yond simp'ring dame,
Whose face between her forks presages snow,
That minces virtue, and does shake the head
To hear of pleasure's name.
The fitchew nor the soilèd horse goes to't 125
With a more riotous appetite.
Down from the waist they are centaurs,
Though women all above.
But to the girdle do the gods inherit,
Beneath is all the fiend's. 130
There's hell, there's darkness, there is the
sulphurous pit; burning, scalding, stench,
consumption. Fie, fie, fie! pah, pah! Give me
an ounce of civet, good apothecary, [to]
sweeten my imagination! There's money 135
for thee.

GLOUCESTER. O, let me kiss that hand.

LEAR. Let me wipe it first; it smells of
mortality.

GLOUCESTER. O ruined piece of nature;
this great world 140
Shall so wear out to naught. Dost thou know
me?

LEAR. I remember thine eyes well enough.
Dost thou squiny at me? No, do thy worst,

---

81 *safer* sounder; *accommodate* dress 82 *His* its
83 *touch* i.e., arrest; *coining* minting coins (the king's
prerogative) 86 *Nature's . . . respect* i.e., a born
king is superior to his image on a coin, which
may be counterfeit (?). As Kittredge says, this is
a "madly philosophical reflection." It bears on
the familiar topic of the relative merits of art and
nature 87 *press money* token payment to conscripted soldiers 88 *like a crow-keeper* i.e., as clumsily
as a boy stationed to scare off crows 89 *clothier's
yard* arrow (a yard long) 91 *gauntlet* (thrown
down as a challenge); *prove it on* maintain it in a
fight with 92 *brown bills* varnished halberds; *well
flown* (falconer's cry) 93 *clout* mark shot at 94
*word* password 99 *like a dog* i.e., fawningly 100–
101 *I had . . . there* i.e., I was wise before I had a
beard 101 *To say . . . "no"* i.e., to agree 103
*no good divinity* cf. II Corinthians 1:18: ". . . our
word to you was not yea and nay" 110 *trick*
special intonation 113 *cause* offense

116 *lecher* copulate 119 *Got* begotten 120
*luxury* lechery 122 *between . . . snow* seems to indicate sexual coldness; *forks* legs 123 *minces* coyly
pretends to 124 *pleasure* i.e., sexual pleasure 125
*fitchew* polecat (also slang for "prostitute"); *soilèd*
pastured (and hence wanton with feeding) 127
*centaurs* lustful mythological creatures, half man,
half horse 129 *girdle* waist; *inherit* hold sway 134
*civet* perfume 139 *mortality* mortal existence or
death 140–41 *this . . . naught* i.e., the universe
(macrocosm) will fall into ruin as the little world
(microcosm) of Lear has already done 143 *squiny*
squint, wink

blind Cupid; I'll not love. Read thou this
challenge; mark but the penning of it.     145

GLOUCESTER. Were all thy letters suns,
I could not see.

EDGAR [*aside*]. I would not take this from
report—it is,
And my heart breaks at it.

LEAR. Read.

GLOUCESTER. What, with the case of
eyes?                                      150

LEAR. O, ho, are you there with me? No
eyes in your head, nor no money in your
purse? Your eyes are in a heavy case, your
purse in a light; yet you see how this world
goes.                                      155

GLOUCESTER. I see it feelingly.

LEAR. What, art mad? A man may see how
this world goes with no eyes. Look with thine
ears. See how yond justice rails upon yond
simple thief. Hark in thine ear. Change   160
places and, handy-dandy, which is the
justice, which is the thief? Thou hast seen
a farmer's dog bark at a beggar?

GLOUCESTER. Ay, sir.

LEAR. And the creature run from the   165
cur. There thou mightst behold the great
image of authority—a dog's obeyed in office.
Thou rascal beadle, hold thy bloody hand!
Why dost thou lash that whore? Strip thy
own back.
Thou hotly lusts to use her in that kind   170
For which thou whip'st her. The usurer
hangs the cozener.
Through tattered clothes small vices do appear;
Robes and furred gowns hide all. Plate sin
with gold,
And the strong lance of justice hurtless
breaks;

Arm it in rags, a pygmy's straw does pierce
it.                                        175
None does offend, none—I say none! I'll
able 'em.
Take that of me, my friend, who have the
power
To seal th' accuser's lips. Get thee glass eyes
And, like a scurvy politician, seem
To see the things thou dost not. Now, now,
now, now!                                  180
Pull off my boots. Harder, harder! So.

EDGAR. O, matter and impertinency mixed;
Reason in madness.

LEAR. If thou wilt weep my fortunes, take
my eyes.
I know thee well enough; thy name is
Gloucester.                                185
Thou must be patient. We came crying
hither;
Thou know'st, the first time that we smell
the air
We wawl and cry. I will preach to thee. Mark.

GLOUCESTER. Alack, alack the day.

LEAR. When we are born, we cry that we
are come                                   190
To this great stage of fools.—This' a good
block.
It were a delicate stratagem to shoe
A troop of horse with felt. I'll put't in proof,
And when I have stol'n upon these son-in-
laws,
Then kill, kill, kill, kill, kill, kill!   195
(*Enter a* GENTLEMAN [*with* ATTENDANTS].)

GENTLEMAN. O, here he is! Lay hand upon
him.—Sir,
Your most dear daughter—

LEAR. No rescue? What, a prisoner?
I am even
The natural fool of fortune. Use me well;
You shall have ransom. Let me have sur-
geons;                                     200
I am cut to th' brains.

---

144 *blind Cupid* the sign hung outside a brothel
147 *take* believe   150 *case* sockets   151 *are . . . me*
is that your situation   153 *heavy case* sad plight
160 *simple* common   161 *handy-dandy* (phrase from a
well-known child's game of guessing which hand
is holding something)   167 *image* emblem, symbol;
*a dog . . . office* i.e., whoever is in power is obeyed
168 *beadle* parish constable   170 *that kind* i.e., the
sexual act   171 *The usurer . . . cozener* i.e., a magistrate guilty of usury puts a petty cheat to death
172 *appear* show   173 *furred gowns* (e.g., those
worn by judges)   174 *hurtless* without hurting

176 *able* authorize   177 *that* i.e., assurance of
immunity   179 *scurvy politician* vile schemer (who
follows Machiavellian policy)   182 *matter and impertinency* sense and nonsense   191 *This'* this is;
*block* i.e., a rock or stump on which Lear has
mounted to preach, and which reminds him of a
mounting-block (?)   192 *delicate* subtle   193 *in
proof* to the test;   199 *natural fool* born victim   201
*cut* wounded

GENTLEMAN.    You shall have anything.

LEAR. No seconds? All myself?

Why, this would make a man a man of salt,

To use his eyes for garden waterpots,

[Ay, and laying autumn's dust.] I will die bravely,                                              205

Like a smug bridegroom. What, I will be jovial!

Come, come, I am a king; masters, know you that?

GENTLEMAN. You are a royal one, and we obey you.

LEAR. Then there's life in't. Come, an you get it, you shall get it by running. Sa, sa,   210 sa, sa!

(*Exit* [*running, followed by* ATTENDANTS].)

GENTLEMAN. A sight most pitiful in the meanest wretch,

Past speaking of in a king. Thou hast one daughter

Who redeems nature from the general curse

Which twain have brought her to.            215

EDGAR. Hail, gentle sir.

GENTLEMAN.            Sir, speed you. What's your will?

EDGAR. Do you hear aught, sir, of a battle toward?

GENTLEMAN. Most sure and vulgar. Every one hears that

Which can distinguish sound.

EDGAR.            But, by your favor,

How near's the other army?                    220

GENTLEMAN. Near and on speedy foot. The main descry

Stands on the hourly thought.

EDGAR.            I thank you, sir. That's all.

GENTLEMAN. Though that the Queen on special cause is here,

Her army is moved on.

EDGAR.            I thank you, sir.

(*Exit* [GENTLEMAN].)

GLOUCESTER. You ever-gentle gods, take my breath from me;                               225

Let not my worser spirit tempt me again

To die before you please.

EDGAR.            Well pray you, father.

GLOUCESTER. Now, good sir, what are you?

EDGAR. A most poor man, made tame to fortune's blows,

Who, by the art of known and feeling sorrows,                                                     230

Am pregnant to good pity. Give me your hand;

I'll lead you to some biding.

GLOUCESTER.            Hearty thanks.

The bounty and the benison of heaven

To boot, and boot.

(*Enter* STEWARD [OSWALD].)

OSWALD.            A próclaimed prize! Most happy;

That eyeless head of thine was first framed flesh                                                  235

To raise my fortunes. Thou old unhappy traitor,

Briefly thyself remember. The sword is out

That must destroy thee.

GLOUCESTER.            Now let thy friendly hand

Put strength enough to't. [EDGAR *interposes*.]

OSWALD.            Wherefore, bold peasant,

Dar'st thou support a published traitor? Hence,                                                   240

Lest that th' infection of his fortune take

Like hold on thee. Let go his arm.

EDGAR. Chill not let go, zir, without vurther 'casion.

OSWALD. Let go, slave, or thou diest.        245

EDGAR. Good gentleman, go your gait, and let poor voke pass. An chud ha' bin zwaggered out of my life, 'twould not ha' bin zo long as 'tis by a vortnight. Nay, come not near th'

---

203 *salt* i.e., tears    205 *bravely* (1) courageously; (2) handsomely    206 *smug* spruce, trim; *bridegroom* (who "dies" at the climax of the sexual act)    209 *life* i.e., hope    210–11 *Sa . . . sa* (a hunting cry, to incite dogs, etc.)    214 *curse* condemnation    215 *twain* i.e., Goneril and Regan (whose behavior has made nature itself seem evil)    216 *gentle* noble; *speed* God speed    217 *toward* impending    218 *vulgar* i.e., known to everyone    221 *on speedy foot* rapidly advancing    221–22 *main . . . thought* the main body is hourly expected to come in view

226 *worser spirit* i.e., bad angel (who made him despair)    227 *father* old man    229 *tame* submissive    230 *art . . . sorrows* i.e., instruction of sorrows known and felt    231 *pregnant to* capable of    232 *biding* place to stay    233 *benison* blessing    234 *To boot, and boot* in addition, and for your advantage; *próclaimed prize* man with a price on his head; *happy* lucky    235 *framed flesh* created    237 *thyself remember* pray for yourself    238 *friendly* (since Gloucester longs for death)    240 *published* proclaimed    243 *Chill* I'll (in speaking to Oswald, Edgar adds a rustic dialect to his role of a "most poor man")    244 *vurther 'casion* further occasion    246 *gait* way    247 *voke* folk; *An chud* if I could; *zwaggered* swaggered

old man. Keep out, che vore ye, or Ise 250
try whether your costard or my ballow be
the harder. Chill be plain with you.
    OSWALD. Out, dunghill!     [*They fight.*]
    EDGAR. Chill pick your teeth, zir. Come.
No matter vor your foins. [OSWALD *falls.*] 255
    OSWALD. Slave, thou hast slain me.
      Villain, take my purse.
If ever thou wilt thrive, bury my body,
And give the letters which thou find'st about
    me
To Edmund Earl of Gloucester. Seek him out
Upon the English party. O, untimely
    death!       260
Death!       [*He dies.*]
    EDGAR. I know thee well. A serviceable vil-
    lain,
As duteous to the vices of thy mistress
As badness would desire.
    GLOUCESTER.     What, is he dead?
    EDGAR. Sit you down, father; rest you. 265
Let's see these pockets; the letters that he
    speaks of
May be my friends. He's dead; I am only
    sorry
He had no other deathsman. Let us see.
Leave, gentle wax; and, manners, blame us
    not;
To know our enemies' minds, we rip their
    hearts;     270
Their papers is more lawful.
      (*Reads the letter.*)
    "Let our reciprocal vows be remembered.
You have many opportunities to cut him off.
If your will want not, time and place will be
fruitfully offered. There is nothing done, 275
if he return the conqueror. Then am I the
prisoner, and his bed my jail; from the
loathed warmth whereof deliver me, and
supply the place for your labor.

---

250 *che vore ye* I warrant you; *Ise* I shall 251
*costard* head; *ballow* cudgel 254 *pick* i.e., knock
out 255 *foins* thrusts 256 *Villain* serf 258 *letters*
only one letter (Goneril's) is used in the ensuing
action; if Oswald also has a letter from Regan
(see IV.5.33), it is never mentioned. *about* upon
260 *party* side 264 *duteous . . . mistress* cf. Edgar's
false description of himself (III.4.89–97) as a
servingman 268 *deathsman* executioner 269 *Leave*
by your leave; *wax* (sealing the letter) 271 *Their
papers* i.e., to rip their papers 274 *want not* is not
deficient

"Your (wife, so I would say) affec- 280
    tionate servant,
        "GONERIL."
O indistinguished space of woman's will—
A plot upon her virtuous husband's life,
And the exchange my brother! Here in the
    sands     285
Thee I'll rake up, the post unsanctified
Of murderous lechers; and in the mature time
With this ungracious paper strike the sight
Of the death-practiced Duke. For him 'tis
    well
That of thy death and business I can tell. 290
    GLOUCESTER. The King is mad. How stiff
    is my vile sense,
That I stand up, and have ingenious feeling
Of my huge sorrows! Better I were distract;
So should my thoughts be severed from my
    griefs,
And woes by wrong imaginations lose 295
The knowledge of themselves.
      (*Drum afar off.*)
    EDGAR.     Give me your hand.
Far off methinks I hear the beaten drum.
Come, father, I'll bestow you with a friend.
      (*Exeunt.*)

*Scene 7*

(*Enter* CORDELIA, KENT, [DOCTOR,] *and*
    GENTLEMAN.)
    CORDELIA. O thou good Kent, how shall
    I live and work
To match thy goodness? My life will be too
    short
And every measure fail me.
    KENT. To be acknowledged, madam, is
    o'erpaid.
All my reports go with the modest truth; 5
Nor more nor clipped, but so.
    CORDELIA.     Be better suited.

---

280 *would* i.e., would like to 283 *indistinguished*
unlimited; *will* specifically "lust" (also implied in
l. 274 above) 285 *exchange* substitute 286 *rake
up* cover, bury; *post unsanctified* unholy messenger
287 *mature* ripe 288 *strike* blast 289 *death-practiced* whose death is plotted 291 *stiff* obstinate;
*vile sense* loathed consciousness 292 *ingenious feeling* acute awareness 293 *distract* mad 298 *bestow*
lodge
IV.7.5 *go* conform 6 *clipped* curtailed; *suited*
dressed

These weeds are memories of those worser
  hours.
I prithee put them off.
  KENT.                Pardon, dear madam.
Yet to be known shortens my made intent.
My boon I make it that you know me
  not                                   10
Till time and I think meet.
  CORDELIA. Then be't so, my good lord.
  [To the DOCTOR.] How does the King?
  DOCTOR. Madam, sleeps still.
  CORDELIA. O you kind gods,
Cure this great breach in his abusèd na-
  ture!                              15
Th' untuned and jarring senses, O, wind up
Of this child-changèd father!
  DOCTOR.           So please your Majesty
That we may wake the King? He hath slept
  long.
  CORDELIA. Be governed by your knowledge,
  and proceed
I' th' sway of your own will. Is he ar-
  rayed?                            20
  (Enter LEAR in a chair carried by SERVANTS.)
  DOCTOR. Ay, madam. In the heaviness of
  sleep
We put fresh garments on him.
  GENTLEMAN. Be by, good madam, when
  we do awake him.
I doubt [not] of his temperance.
  [CORDELIA.             Very well.
                           [Music.]
  DOCTOR. Please you draw near. Louder
  the music there.]               25
  CORDELIA. O my dear father, restoration
  hang
Thy medicine on my lips, and let this kiss
Repair those violent harms that my two sis-
  ters
Have in thy reverence made.
  KENT.           Kind and dear princess.

CORDELIA. Had you not been their father,
  these white flakes          30
Did challenge pity of them. Was this a face
To be opposed against the jarring winds?
[To stand against the deep dread-bolted
  thunder?
In the most terrible and nimble stroke
Of quick cross lightning to watch, poor
  perdu,                      35
With this thin helm?] Mine enemy's dog,
Though he had bit me, should have stood
  that night
Against my fire; and wast thou fain, poor
  father,
To hovel thee with swine and rogues forlorn
In short and musty straw? Alack, alack,   40
'Tis wonder that thy life and wits at once
Had not concluded all.—He wakes. Speak
  to him.
  DOCTOR. Madam, do you; 'tis fittest.
  CORDELIA. How does my royal lord? How
  fares your Majesty?
  LEAR. You do me wrong to take me out o'
  th' grave.                 45
Thou art a soul in bliss; but I am bound
Upon a wheel of fire, that mine own tears
Do scald like molten lead.
  CORDELIA.         Sir, do you know me?
  LEAR. You are a spirit, I know. Where did
  you die?
  CORDELIA. Still, still, far wide!      50
  DOCTOR. He's scarce awake. Let him alone
  awhile.
  LEAR. Where have I been? Where am I?
  Fair daylight?
I am mightily abused. I should e'en die with
  pity
To see another thus. I know not what to say.
I will not swear these are my hands.
  Let's see—               55
I feel this pin prick. Would I were assured
Of my condition.

---

7 *weeds* clothes; *memories* reminders   9 *Yet ...
intent* to be recognized as yet cuts my plan short;
the plan is never made clear, but it is dramatically
effective to leave Lear's recognition of Kent for
the very end   10 *My boon ... it* the favor I ask is
11 *meet* proper   15 *abused* (1) confused; (2) ill-
treated   16 *jarring* discordant; *wind up* put in tune
17 *child-changed* changed (1) to a child; (2) by the
cruelty of his children   20 *I' th' sway of* according
to   24 *temperance* sanity   29 *reverence* revered person

30 *flakes* strands of hair   31 *challenge* demand   33
*deep dread-bolted* deep-voiced and furnished with
terrifying bolts   35 *perdu* sentry in a perilous
position (also "lost one" [?])   36 *helm* helmet,
i.e., hair   38 *fain* obliged   40 *short* i.e., broken
with use (?)   47 *wheel of fire* (suggesting the
tortures of hell)   50 *wide* away from the mark
53 *abused* deluded

CORDELIA.      O look upon me, sir,
And hold your hand in benediction o'er me.
You must not kneel.
    LEAR.            Pray, do not mock me.
I am a very foolish fond old man,     60
Fourscore and upward, not an hour more
    nor less;
And, to deal plainly,
I fear I am not in my perfect mind.
Methinks I should know you, and know this
    man;
Yet I am doubtful, for I am mainly igno-
    rant     65
What place this is; and all the skill I have
Remembers not these garments; nor I know
    not
Where I did lodge last night. Do not laugh
    at me;
For, as I am a man, I think this lady
To be my child Cordelia.
    CORDELIA.         And so I am! I am!    70
    LEAR. Be your tears wet? Yes, faith.
      I pray weep not.
If you have poison for me, I will drink it.
I know you do not love me; for your sisters
Have, as I do remember, done me wrong.
You have some cause, they have not.
    CORDELIA.         No cause, no cause.    75
    LEAR. Am I in France?
    KENT.            In your own kingdom, sir.
    LEAR. Do not abuse me.
    DOCTOR. Be comforted, good madam.
      The great rage
You see is killed in him; [and yet it is danger
To make him even o'er the time he has
    lost.]     80
Desire him to go in. Trouble him no more
Till further settling.
    CORDELIA. Will't please your Highness
      walk?
    LEAR.            You must bear with me.
Pray you now, forget and forgive. I am old
    and foolish.

(*Exeunt.*) [*Mane*[*n*]*t* KENT *and* GENTLEMAN.]

    [GENTLEMAN. Holds it true, sir, that the    85
Duke of Cornwall was so slain?
    KENT. Most certain, sir.
    GENTLEMAN. Who is conductor of his people?
    KENT. As 'tis said, the bastard son of
Gloucester.     90
    GENTLEMAN. They say Edgar, his banished
son, is with the Earl of Kent in Germany.
    KENT. Report is changeable. 'Tis time to
look about; the powers of the kingdom approach apace.     95
    GENTLEMAN. The arbitrement is like to be
bloody. Fare you well, sir.    [*Exit.*]
    KENT. My point and period will be
    throughly wrought,
Or well or ill, as this day's battle's fought.
                       *Exit.*]

## ACT V. *Scene 1*

(*Enter, with Drum and Colors,* EDMUND,
REGAN, GENTLEMEN, *and* SOLDIERS.)

    EDMUND. Know of the Duke if his last
      purpose hold,
Or whether since he is advised by aught
To change the course. He's full of alteration
And self-reproving. Bring his constant pleas-
    ure.
          [*To a* GENTLEMAN *who goes out.*]
    REGAN. Our sister's man is certainly mis-
      carried.     5
    EDMUND. 'Tis to be doubted, madam.
    REGAN.            Now, sweet lord,
You know the goodness I intend upon you.
Tell me, but truly—but then speak the
    truth—
Do you not love my sister?
    EDMUND.            In honored love.
    REGAN. But have you never found my
      brother's way     10
To the forfended place?
    [EDMUND.            That thought abuses you.

---

60 *fond* silly    65 *mainly* entirely    67 *Remembers
. . . garments* the "fresh garments" in which Lear
is dressed provide a striking visual equivalent to
the spiritual transformation dramatized in this
scene    77 *abuse* deceive    78 *rage* frenzy    80 *even
o'er* fill in    82 *settling* calming    84 Stage direction:
*Mane*[*n*]*t* remain

94 *powers* armies    96 *arbitrement* decisive encounter    98 *My point . . . wrought* the aim and end
of my life will be thoroughly worked out    99 *or*
either
V.1.1 *Know* learn; *last purpose* most recent intention (i.e., to fight)    2 *advised* induced    4 *constant pleasure* fixed decision    5 *is . . . miscarried* has
certainly come to grief—run into difficulties    6
*doubted* feared    7 *goodness . . . you* honor or favor I
mean to do you    9 *honored* honorable    11 *forfended*
forbidden; *abuses* deceives

REGAN. I am doubtful that you have been
conjunct
And bosomed with her, as far as we call
hers.]

EDMUND. No, by mine honor, madam.

REGAN. I never shall endure her. Dear my
lord,                                                    15
Be not familiar with her.

EDMUND.                     Fear [me] not.
She and the Duke her husband!
*(Enter, with Drum and Colors, ALBANY,
GONERIL, SOLDIERS.)*

[GONERIL [aside]. I had rather lose the battle than that sister
Should loosen him and me.]

ALBANY. Our very loving sister, well
bemet.                                                    20
Sir, this I heard: the King is come to his
daughter,
With others whom the rigor of our state
Forced to cry out. [Where I could not be
honest,
I never yet was valiant. For this business,
It touches us as France invades our land,    25
Not bolds the King with others, whom I fear
Most just and heavy causes make oppose.

EDMUND. Sir, you speak nobly.]

REGAN.                     Why is this reasoned?

GONERIL. Combine together 'gainst the
enemy;
For these domestic and particular broils    30
Are not the question here.

ALBANY.                     Let's then determine
With th' ancient of war on our proceeding.

[EDMUND. I shall attend you presently at
your tent.]

REGAN. Sister, you'll go with us?

GONERIL. No.                                          35

REGAN. 'Tis most convenient. Pray go with
us.

---

12 *doubtful* fearful    12–13 *conjunct . . . hers* intimately associated with her in every way    16 *fear*
distrust    20 *bemet* met    22 *rigor . . . state* tyranny
of our rule    23 *honest* honorable    25 *touches us as*
concerns me in that    26–27 *Not . . . oppose* not because France encourages the King and others,
whom true and serious grievances, I fear, have
forced into opposition    28 *reasoned* argued    30
*particular broils* individual quarrels    32 *th' ancient
of war* the experienced officers    33 *presently* immediately    34 *us* me (not Edmund)    36 *convenient*
proper, fitting

GONERIL. O ho, I know the riddle.—
I will go.              *(Exeunt both the Armies.)*
*(Enter EDGAR.)*

EDGAR [to Albany]. If e'er your Grace had
speech with man so poor,
Hear me one word.

ALBANY [to those departing]. I'll overtake you.
[To EDGAR.] Speak.

EDGAR. Before you fight the battle, ope this
letter.                                                    40
If you have victory, let the trumpet sound
For him that brought it. Wretched though
I seem,
I can produce a champion that will prove
What is avouchèd there. If you miscarry,
Your business of the world hath so an end,    45
And machination ceases. Fortune love you.

ALBANY. Stay till I have read the letter.

EDGAR.                     I was forbid it.
When time shall serve, let but the herald cry,
And I'll appear again.

ALBANY. Why, fare thee well. I will o'erlook thy paper.        *(Exit [EDGAR].)*    50
*(Enter EDMUND.)*

EDMUND. The enemy's in view; draw up
your powers.
Here is the guess of their true strength and
forces
By diligent discovery; but your haste
Is now urged on you.

ALBANY.                     We will greet the time.
*(Exit.)*

EDMUND. To both these sisters have I sworn
my love;                                                  55
Each jealous of the other, as the stung
Are of the adder. Which of them shall I take?
Both? One? Or neither? Neither can be en-
joyed,
If both remain alive. To take the widow
Exasperates, makes mad her sister Goneril;    60
And hardly shall I carry out my side,
Her husband being alive. Now then, we'll use
His countenance for the battle, which being
done,
Let her who would be rid of him devise

---

37 *riddle* i.e., explanation of Regan's request
43 *prove* (in trial by combat)    45 *of* in    46 *machination* plotting    50 *o'erlook* look over    53 *discovery*
reconnoitering    54 *greet* i.e., meet the demands of
56 *jealous* suspicious    61 *hardly . . . side* it will be
difficult to win my game    63 *countenance* authority

His speedy taking off. As for the mercy    65
Which he intends to Lear and to Cordelia—
The battle done, and they within our power,
Shall never see his pardon; for my state
Stands on me to defend, not to debate.

                              *(Exit.)*

#### Scene 2

*(Alarum within. Enter, with Drum and
Colors, LEAR [held by the hand by] CORDELIA;
and SOLDIERS [of France], over the stage and
exeunt.)*
    *(Enter EDGAR and GLOUCESTER.)*
EDGAR. Here, father, take the shadow of
    this tree
For your good host. Pray that the right
    may thrive.
If ever I return to you again,
I'll bring you comfort.
    GLOUCESTER.         Grace go with you, sir.
                    *(Exit [EDGAR].)*
*(Alarum and retreat within. Enter EDGAR.)*
EDGAR. Away, old man! Give me thy
    hand. Away!                     5
King Lear hath lost, he and his daughter
    ta'en.
Give me thy hand. Come on.
    GLOUCESTER. No further, sir. A man may
    rot even here.
    EDGAR. What, in ill thoughts again? Men
    must endure
Their going hence, even as their coming
    hither;                         10
Ripeness is all. Come on.
    GLOUCESTER.         And that's true too.
                    *(Exeunt.)*

#### Scene 3

*(Enter, in conquest, with Drum and Colors,
EDMUND; LEAR and CORDELIA as prisoners;
SOLDIERS, CAPTAIN.)*

---

68–69 *my state . . . debate* to maintain my position I must fight for it, not quibble about right
and wrong
V.2.4 Stage direction: *Alarum and retreat* (trumpet calls signaling the beginning of the battle and
then a retreat)  9 *ill* i.e., despairing  11 *Ripeness*
(1) maturity; (2) readiness for death (as the ripe
fruit is ready to fall)

EDMUND. Some officers take them away.
    Good guard
Until their greater pleasures first be known
That are to censure them.
    CORDELIA.             We are not the first
Who with best meaning have incurred the
    worst.
For thee, oppressèd king, I am cast down;    5
Myself could else outfrown false Fortune's
    frown.
Shall we not see these daughters and these
    sisters?
    LEAR. No, no, no, no! Come, let's away to
    prison.
We two alone will sing like birds i' th' cage.
When thou dost ask me blessing, I'll kneel
    down                        10
And ask of thee forgiveness. So we'll live,
And pray, and sing, and tell old tales, and
    laugh
At gilded butterflies, and hear poor rogues
Talk of court news; and we'll talk with
    them too—
Who loses and who wins; who's in, who's
    out—                       15
And take upon's the mystery of things
As if we were God's spies; and we'll wear out,
In a walled prison, packs and sects of great
    ones
That ebb and flow by th' moon.
    EDMUND.            Take them away.
    LEAR. Upon such sacrifices, my Cor-
    delia,                       20
The gods themselves throw incense. Have
    I caught thee?
He that parts us shall bring a brand from
    heaven
And fire us hence like foxes. Wipe thine eyes.

---

V.3.1 *good guard* i.e., keep a good guard  2 *their
greater pleasures* will of those in command  3
*censure* judge  13 *gilded butterflies* gorgeously
dressed courtiers; *poor rogues* wretched creatures
16–17 *take . . . spies* profess to understand the mystery of existence and of fortune's changes as if
gifted with divine insight  17 *wear out* outlast
18–19 *packs . . . moon* plotters and factions among
the "great," whose fortunes rise and fall like the
tides  20 *such sacrifices* (as Lear's and Cordelia's
renunciation of the world)  21 *throw incense* i.e., act
as priests  22–23 *He . . . foxes* since no human
agency can separate us, it will have to be done
with a heavenly torch, as foxes are driven from
their holes by fire and smoke

The goodyears shall devour them, flesh and
fell,
Ere they shall make us weep! We'll see 'em
starved first.                                      25
Come.
    (*Exeunt* [LEAR *and* CORDELIA, *guarded*].)
EDMUND.      Come hither, captain; hark.
Take thou this note. [*Gives a paper.*] Go
follow them to prison.
One step I have advanced thee. If thou dost
As this instructs thee, thou dost make thy way
To noble fortunes. Know thou this, that
men                                                 30
Are as the time is. To be tender-minded
Does not become a sword. Thy great employ-
ment
Will not bear question. Either say thou'lt
do't,
Or thrive by other means.
    CAPTAIN.        I'll do't, my lord.
    EDMUND. About it; and write happy when
th' hast done.                                      35
Mark, I say instantly, and carry it so
As I have set it down.
    [CAPTAIN. I cannot draw a cart, nor eat
dried oats—
If it be man's work, I'll do't.]    (*Exit.*)
    (*Flourish. Enter* ALBANY, GONERIL, REGAN,
[*another* CAPTAIN, *and*] SOLDIERS.)
    ALBANY. Sir, you have showed to-day
your valiant strain,                                40
And fortune led you well. You have the
captives
Who were the opposites of this day's strife.
I do require them of you, so to use them
As we shall find their merits and our safety
May equally determine.
    EDMUND.      Sir, I thought it fit    45
To send the old and miserable King
To some retention [and appointed guard];
Whose age had charms in it, whose title
more,
To pluck the common bosom on his side
And turn our impressed lances in our eyes    50

Which do command them. With him I sent
the Queen,
My reason all the same; and they are ready
To-morrow, or at further space, t' appear
Where you shall hold your session. [At this
time
We sweat and bleed, the friend hath lost his
friend,                                             55
And the best quarrels, in the heat, are cursed
By those that feel their sharpness.
The question of Cordelia and her father
Requires a fitter place.]
    ALBANY.      Sir, by your patience,
I hold you but a subject of this war,              60
Not as a brother.
    REGAN.      That's as we list to grace him.
Methinks our pleasure might have been de-
manded
Ere you had spoke so far. He led our powers,
Bore the commission of my place and person,
The which immediacy may well stand up    65
And call itself your brother.
    GONERIL.      Not so hot!
In his own grace he doth exalt himself
More than in your addition.
    REGAN.      In my rights
By me invested, he compeers the best.
    ALBANY. That were the most if he should
husband you.                                        70
    REGAN. Jesters do oft prove prophets.
    GONERIL.      Holla, holla!
That eye that told you so looked but asquint.
    REGAN. Lady, I am not well; else I should
answer
From a full-flowing stomach. General,
Take thou my soldiers, prisoners, patri-
mony;                                               75
Dispose of them, of me; the walls is thine.
Witness the world that I create thee here
My lord and master.

---

53 *further space* a later time  54 *session* trials  56
*quarrels* causes; *cursed* (hence unfairly judged)  57
*sharpness* i.e., painful effects  59 *Requires . . . place*
i.e., only somewhere else can it be tried fairly
60 *subject of* subordinate in  61 *list to grace* please
to honor  65 *immediacy* i.e., status as my immediate representative  68 *your addition* honors you
have given him  69 *compeers* equals  70 *most* i.e.,
fullest sharing of your rights  72 *asquint* crookedly
74 *From . . . stomach* with a stream of angry words
76 *walls is thine* i.e., you have captured the fortress
(of myself)

---

24 *goodyears* forces of evil (common phrase of
uncertain origin); *fell* hide  31 *as the time is*
i.e., heartless in wartime  32 *become a sword* befit
a soldier  33 *bear question* admit discussion  35
*write happy* consider yourself fortunate  42 *opposites
of* enemies in  47 *retention and* confinement under
49 *pluck . . . bosom* win popular sympathy  50 *impressed . . . eyes* conscripted lancers against us

GONERIL.                    Mean you to enjoy him?

ALBANY. The let-alone lies not in your good will.

EDMUND. Nor in thine, lord.

ALBANY.         Half-blooded fellow, yes.     80

REGAN [*to* EDMUND]. Let the drum strike, and prove my title thine.

ALBANY. Stay yet; hear reason. Edmund, I arrest thee

On capital treason; and, in thy attaint,

This gilded serpent. [*Points to* GONERIL.] For your claim, fair sister,

I bar it in the interest of my wife.     85

'Tis she is subcontracted to this lord,

And I, her husband, contradict your banes.

If you will marry, make your loves to me;

My lady is bespoke.

GONERIL.            An interlude!

ALBANY. Thou art armed, Gloucester. Let the trumpet sound.     90

If none appear to prove upon thy person

Thy heinous, manifest, and many treasons,

There is my pledge. [*Throws down a glove.*] I'll make it on thy heart,

Ere I taste bread, thou art in nothing less

Than I have here proclaimed thee.

REGAN.                  Sick, O, sick!     95

GONERIL [*aside*]. If not, I'll ne'er trust medicine.

EDMUND. There's my exchange. [*Throws down a glove.*] What in the world he is

That names me traitor, villain-like he lies.

Call by the trumpet. He that dares approach,

On him, on you, who not? I will maintain     100

My truth and honor firmly.

ALBANY. A herald, ho!

[EDMUND.           A herald, ho, a herald!]

ALBANY. Trust to thy single virtue; for thy soldiers,

All levied in my name, have in my name

Took their discharge.

REGAN.        My sickness grows upon me.  105

ALBANY. She is not well. Convey her to my tent.            [*Exit* REGAN, *attended.*]
            (*Enter a* HERALD.)

Come hither, herald. Let the trumpet sound,

And read out this.

[CAPTAIN. Sound, trumpet!]
                    (*A trumpet sounds.*)

HERALD (*reads*). "If any man of quality     110

or degree within the lists of the army will maintain upon Edmund, supposed Earl of Gloucester, that he is a manifold traitor, let him appear by the third sound of the trumpet. He is bold in his defense."     115

[EDMUND. Sound!]            (*First trumpet.*)

HERALD. Again!            (*Second trumpet.*)

Again!                (*Third trumpet.*)
            (*Trumpet answers within.*)
(*Enter* EDGAR, *armed,* [*at the third sound, a trumpet before him*].)

ALBANY. Ask him his purposes, why he appears

Upon this call o' th' trumpet.

HERALD.            What are you?     120

Your name, your quality, and why you answer

This present summons?

EDMUND.            Know my name is lost,

By treason's tooth bare-gnawn and canker-bit;

Yet am I noble as the adversary

I come to cope.

ALBANY.        Which is that adversary?  125

EDGAR. What's he that speaks for Edmund Earl of Gloucester?

EDMUND. Himself. What say'st thou to him?

EDGAR.                Draw thy sword.

That, if my speech offend a noble heart,

Thy arm may do thee justice. Here is mine.

Behold it is my privilege,            130

The privilege of mine honors,

My oath, and my profession. I protest—

Maugre thy strength, place, youth, and eminence,

Despite thy victor sword and fire-new fortune,

---

79 *let-alone* permission  80 *Half-blooded* i.e., half noble-blooded (because a bastard)  81 *my title thine* your right to my title  83 *in thy attaint* as part to your treachery  86 *subcontracted* i.e., engaged though already married  87 *contradict your banes* forbid the banns  88 *loves* love-suits  89 *interlude* play (a sarcastic comment on Albany's ironic speech)  93 *make* prove  94 *nothing less* i.e., no respect less guilty  96 *medicine* i.e., poison  103 *single virtue* unaided valor (Lat. *virtus*)

111 *lists* muster  123 *canker-bit* eaten, as by the rose-caterpillar  125 *cope* encounter  130–32 *it . . . profession* I am entitled to challenge you by my position, my knightly oath and my profession of knighthood  133 *maugre* despite  134 *fire-new* brand-new

Thy valor and thy heart—thou art a traitor, 135
False to thy gods, thy brother, and thy father,
Conspirant 'gainst this high illustrious prince,
And from th' extremest upward of thy head
To the descent and dust below thy foot
A most toad-spotted traitor. Say thou "no," 140
This sword, this arm, and my best spirits are bent
To prove upon thy heart, whereto I speak,
Thou liest.

EDMUND.          In wisdom I should ask thy name,
But since thy outside looks so fair and warlike,
And that thy tongue some say of breeding breathes, 145
What safe and nicely I might well delay
By rule of knighthood I disdain and spurn.
Back do I toss these treasons to thy head,
With the hell-hated lie o'erwhelm thy heart,
Which—for they yet glance by and scarcely bruise— 150
This sword of mine shall give them instant way
Where they shall rest for ever. Trumpets, speak!     (*Alarums. Fights.*) [EDMUND *falls.*]

ALBANY. Save him, save him.

GONERIL.          This is practice, Gloucester.
By th' law of war thou wast not bound to answer
An unknown opposite. Thou art not vanquished, 155
But cozened and beguiled.

ALBANY.          Shut your mouth, dame,
Or with this paper shall I stop it.—Hold, sir.—

[*To* GONERIL.] Thou worse than any name, read thine own evil.
No tearing, lady! I perceive you know it.

GONERIL. Say if I do—the laws are mine, not thine. 160
Who can arraign me for't?

ALBANY.          Most monstrous! O,
Know'st thou this paper?

GONERIL.          Ask me not what I know.
(*Exit.*)

ALBANY. Go after her. She's desperate; govern her.          [*Exit an* OFFICER.]

EDMUND. What you have charged me with, that have I done,
And more, much more. The time will bring it out. 165
'Tis past, and so am I.—But what art thou
That hast this fortune on me? If thou'rt noble,
I do forgive thee.

EDGAR.          Let's exchange charity.
I am no less in blood than thou art, Edmund;
If more, the more th' hast wronged me. 170
My name is Edgar and thy father's son.
The gods are just, and of our pleasant vices
Make instruments to plague us.
The dark and vicious place where thee he got
Cost him his eyes.

EDMUND.          Th' hast spoken right; 'tis true. 175
The wheel is come full circle; I am here.

ALBANY [*to* EDGAR.] Methought thy very gait did prophesy
A royal nobleness. I must embrace thee.
Let sorrow split my heart if ever I
Did hate thee, or thy father.

EDGAR.          Worthy prince, I know't. 180

ALBANY. Where have you hid yourself?
How have you known the miseries of your father?

EDGAR. By nursing them, my lord. List a brief tale;
And when 'tis told, O that my heart would burst!
The bloody proclamation to escape 185

---

135 *heart* courage   137 *conspirant* conspirator
138 *extremest upward* very top   139 *To . . . dust* i.e., all the way down to the dust   140 *toad-spotted* The spots of the toad were thought to exude venom.
141 *bent* directed   143 *wisdom* prudence (see ll. 154–55 below)   145 *say* proof   146 *nicely* punctiliously   148 *treasons* accusations of treason   149 *hell-hated* hateful as hell; *o'erwhelm* i.e., to overwhelm   150–52 *Which . . . ever* i.e., my sword will guide these accusations of treason, which do not harm you as yet, to your heart, where they will stick   153 *practice* trickery   156 *cozened* cheated   157 *Hold* wait (presumably addressed to Edmund as Albany turns to his wife)

---

160 *mine* (as Lear's daughter)   163 *govern* control   167 *fortune on* lucky victory over   168 *charity* love, forgiveness   174 *got* begot   176 *wheel* (of fortune); *here* i.e., (1) at the bottom of the wheel, and (2) facing those against whom he plotted   177 *prophesy* promise

That followed me so near (O, our lives'
    sweetness!
That we the pain of death would hourly die
Rather than die at once) taught me to shift
Into a madman's rags, t' assume a semblance
That very dogs disdained; and in this
    habit                   190
Met I my father with his bleeding rings,
Their precious stones new lost; became his
    guide,
Led him, begged for him, saved him from
    despair;
Never—O fault!—revealed myself unto him
Until some half hour past, when I was
    armed,                 195
Not sure, though hoping of this good success,
I asked his blessing, and from first to last
Told him our pilgrimage. But his flawed
    heart—
Alack, too weak the conflict to support—
'Twixt two extremes of passion, joy and
    grief,                 200
Burst smilingly.
    EDMUND.        This speech of yours hath
    moved me,
And shall perchance do good; but speak
    you on—
You look as you had something more to say.
    ALBANY. If there be more, more woeful,
    hold it in,
For I am almost ready to dissolve,     205
Hearing of this.
    [EDGAR.   This would have seemed a period
To such as love not sorrow; but another,
To amplify too much, would make much
    more,
And top extremity.
Whilst I was big in clamor, came there in a
    man,                 210
Who, having seen me in my worst estate,
Shunned my abhorred society; but then,
    finding
Who 'twas that so endured, with his strong
    arms

He fastened on my neck, and bellowed out
As he'd burst heaven, threw him on my
    father,                215
Told the most piteous tale of Lear and him
That ever ear received; which in recounting
His grief grew puissant, and the strings of life
Began to crack. Twice then the trumpets
    sounded,
And there I left him tranced.
    ALBANY.           But who was this?  220
    EDGAR. Kent, sir, the banished Kent; who
    in disguise
Followed his enemy king and did him service
Improper for a slave.]
    (*Enter a* GENTLEMAN [*with a bloody knife*].)
    GENTLEMAN. Help, help! O, help!
    EDGAR.      What kind of help?
    ALBANY.                Speak, man.
    EDGAR. What means this bloody knife?
    GENTLEMAN.        'Tis hot, it smokes.  225
It came even from the heart of—O, she's dead.
    ALBANY. Who dead? Speak, man.
    GENTLEMAN. Your lady, sir, your lady; and
    her sister
By her is poisoned; she confesses it.
    EDMUND. I was contracted to them both.
    All three                  230
Now marry in an instant.
    EDGAR.           Here comes Kent.
        (*Enter* KENT.)
    ALBANY. Produce the bodies, be they alive
    or dead.          [*Exit* GENTLEMAN.]
This judgment of the heavens, that makes
    us tremble,
Touches us not with pity.—O, is this he?
The time will not allow the compliment  235
Which very manners urges.
    KENT.               I am come
To bid my king and master aye good night.
Is he not here?
    ALBANY.       Great thing of us forgot!
Speak, Edmund, where's the King? and
    where's Cordelia?
    (GONERIL *and* REGAN's *bodies brought out.*)
Seest thou this object, Kent?          240

---

187 *That . . . die* that we prefer to live even in
hourly fear of death  190 *habit* attire  191 *rings*
sockets  195 *armed* in armor  198 *pilgrimage*
journey; *flawed* cracked 205 *dissolve* melt in tears
206 *period* limit  207 *another* i.e., sorrow  208
*To . . . much* if I described it too fully  209 *top
extremity* exceed the limit  210 *big in clamor* loud
in lamentation  211 *estate* state

---

218 *puissant* powerful  220 *tranced* in a faint  222
*enemy* hostile  225 *smokes* steams  231 *marry* (i.e.,
in death)  235 *compliment* ceremony  236 *very
manners* ordinary civility  237 *aye* forever  238
*thing of* matter by  240 *object* sight

KENT. Alack, why thus?

EDMUND.          Yet Edmund was beloved.
The one the other poisoned for my sake,
And after slew herself.

ALBANY. Even so. Cover their faces.

EDMUND. I pant for life. Some good I
mean to do,                                    245
Despite of mine own nature. Quickly send—
Be brief in it—to the castle, for my writ
Is on the life of Lear and on Cordelia.
Nay, send in time.

ALBANY.          Run, run, O, run!

EDGAR. To who, my lord? Who has the
office? Send                                   250
Thy token of reprieve.

EDMUND. Well thought on. Take my sword;
Give it the captain.

EDGAR.          Haste thee for thy life.
                    [Exit OFFICER.]

EDMUND. He hath commission from thy
wife and me
To hang Cordelia in the prison and       255
To lay the blame upon her own despair
That she fordid herself.

ALBANY. The gods defend her! Bear him
hence awhile.          [EDMUND is borne off.]
(Enter LEAR, with CORDELIA in his arms,
    [GENTLEMAN, and others following].)

LEAR. Howl, howl, howl! O, you are men
of stones.
Had I your tongues and eyes, I'd use them
so                                             260
That heaven's vault should crack. She's gone
for ever.
I know when one is dead, and when one lives.
She's dead as earth. Lend me a looking glass.
If that her breath will mist or stain the stone,
Why then she lives.

KENT.          Is this the promised end?   265

EDGAR. Or image of that horror?

ALBANY.                    Fall and cease.

LEAR. This feather stirs; she lives! If it be so,
It is a chance which does redeem all sorrows
That ever I have felt.

KENT.                    O my good master.

LEAR. Prithee away.

EDGAR.     'Tis noble Kent, your friend.  270

LEAR. A plague upon you murderers, trai-
tors all;
I might have saved her; now she's gone for
ever.
Cordelia, Cordelia, stay a little. Ha.
What is't thou say'st? Her voice was ever soft,
Gentle, and low—an excellent thing in
woman.                                         275
I killed the slave that was a-hanging thee.

GENTLEMAN. 'Tis true, my lords, he did.

LEAR.                    Did I not, fellow?
I have seen the day, with my good biting fal-
chion
I would have made them skip. I am old now,
And these same crosses spoil me. Who are
you?                                           280
Mine eyes are not o' th' best. I'll tell you
straight.

KENT. If fortune brag of two she loved and
hated,
One of them we behold.

LEAR. This is a dull sight. Are you not
Kent?

KENT.     The same:
Your servant Kent; where is your servant
Caius?                                         285

LEAR. He's a good fellow, I can tell you
that.
He'll strike, and quickly too. He's dead and
rotten.

KENT. No, my good lord; I am the very man.

LEAR. I'll see that straight.

KENT. That from your first of difference
and decay                                      290
Have followed your sad steps.

LEAR.                    You are welcome hither.

---

278 *falchion* small curved sword  280 *crosses* ad-
versities; *spoil me* i.e., impair my swordsmanship
281 *straight* in a moment  282 *two* variously interpreted; probably refers to Lear and some hypo-
thetical other example of fortune's inconstancy.
284 *This . . . sight* i.e., I see dimly (because of failing eyesight and tears); or possibly, "This is a
melancholy spectacle"  285 *Caius* Kent's name in
disguise; pronounced "Keys")  289 *see . . . straight*
have that shown to me straightaway (?) (Lear is
at first incredulous)  290 *your . . . decay* beginning
of your change and decline in fortune

---

241 *Yet* after all, in spite of everything  247
*writ* i.e., order of execution  250 *office* commission
257 *fordid* destroyed  264 *stone* glass  265 *promised
end* i.e., Doomsday  266 *Fall and cease* i.e., let the
heavens fall and everything come to an end  268
*redeem* atone for

KENT. Nor no man else. All's cheerless, dark, and deadly.

Your eldest daughters have fordone themselves,
And desperately are dead.

LEAR.                    Ay, so I think.

ALBANY. He knows not what he says; and vain is it                                    295
That we present us to him.

EDGAR.                    Very bootless.

(*Enter a* MESSENGER.)

MESSENGER. Edmund is dead, my lord.

ALBANY.                    That's but a trifle here.
You lords and noble friends, know our intent.
What comfort to this great decay may come
Shall be applied. For us, we will resign,     300
During the life of this old Majesty,
To him our absolute power; [*To* EDGAR *and*
    KENT.] you to your rights,
With boot and such addition as your honors
Have more than merited. All friends shall taste
The wages of their virtue, and all foes     305
The cup of their deservings.—O, see, see!

LEAR. And my poor fool is hanged: no, no, no life?

Why should a dog, a horse, a rat, have life,
And thou no breath at all? Thou'lt come no more,
Never, never, never, never, never.     310
Pray you undo this button. Thank you, sir.

───────

292 *Nor no man else* it is really I (cf. l. 288)   293 *fordone* destroyed   294 *desperately* despairingly   296 *bootless* useless   299 *this . . . decay* this great ruined man, Lear   303 *boot* good measure; *addition* titles and rights   307 *fool* i.e., Cordelia; it is a term of endearment   311 *Pray . . . button* (presumably to ease Lear's feeling of suffocation)

Do you see this? Look on her! Look her lips,
Look there, look there—          (*He dies.*)

EDGAR.          He faints. My lord, my lord—

KENT. Break, heart, I prithee break!

EDGAR.                    Look up, my lord.

KENT. Vex not his ghost. O, let him pass!
He hates him                                    315
That would upon the rack of this tough world
Stretch him out longer.

EDGAR.                    He is gone indeed.

KENT. The wonder is, he hath endured so long.

He but usurped his life.

ALBANY. Bear them from hence. Our present business                         320
Is general woe. [*To* KENT *and* EDGAR.] Friends of my soul, you twain
Rule in this realm, and the gored state sustain.

KENT. I have a journey, sir, shortly to go.
My master calls me; I must not say no.

EDGAR. The weight of this sad time we must obey,                              325
Speak what we feel, not what we ought to say.
The oldest hath borne most; we that are young
Shall never see so much, nor live so long.

(*Exeunt with a dead march.*)

───────

312–13 *Look . . . there* it is usually assumed that Lear thinks he sees her lips move, and that, like Gloucester, he dies " 'twixt two extremes of passion, joy and grief"   315 *Vex . . . ghost* do not trouble his departing spirit   316 *rack . . . world* i.e., comparing the world to the instrument of torture   319 *usurped* possessed contrary to natural law   325 *obey* submit to

## Textual Notes

*The following list comprises substitutions in the dialogue of the First Folio (F1) of words or phrases from the quarto editions (Q1, 1608, or Q2, 1619), the Second Folio (F2, 1632) or from modern editions (M, i.e., editions of the eighteenth to twentieth centuries). The reading of the present text is given first in italics, followed by the designation of its source. The second reading is that of F1 unless it is followed by "Q1," as in passages omitted from the Folio.*

I. 1.6    *equalities* Q1; qualities
I. 1.81    *possesses* Q1; professes
I. 1.117    *mysteries* F2; miseries
I. 1.177    *sentence* Q1; sentences
I. 1.195    *Gloucester* Q1; Cor.

I. 1.213    *on* Q1; in
I. 1.228    *Fall'n* Q1; Fall
I. 1.232    *well* Q1; will
I. 1.255    *respects of fortune* Q1; respect and Fortunes

I. 1.312  *hit* Q1; sit
I. 2.21  *top th'*M; to'th'
I. 2.58  *waked* Q1; wake
I. 2.66  *this to you* Q1; you to this
I. 4.1  *well* Q1; will
I. 4.57  *daughter* Q1; Daughters
I. 4.114  *Kent. Why, fool?* Q1; Lear.
        Why my Boy?
I. 4.182  *crown* Q1; Crownes
I. 4.201  *fools* Q1; Foole
I. 4.244  *it had* Q1; it's had
I. 4.371  *You* F2; Your
I. 4.371  *ataskt* Q1; at task
II. 1.56  *lanched* Q1; latch'd
II. 1.57  *But* Q1; And
II. 1.74  *I should* Q1; should I
II. 1.83  *why* Q1; wher
II. 1.91  *strange news* Q1; strangenesse
II. 1.119  *Natures* Q1; Nature's
II. 2.25  *clamorous* Q1; clamours
II. 2.93  *Renege* Q1; Revenge
II. 2.94  *gale* Q1; gall
II. 2.123  *flick'ring* Q1; flicking
II. 2.140  *dread* Q1; dead
II. 2.147  *respect* Q1; respects
II. 2.160  *contemnèdst* M; temnest Q1
II. 2.170  *Duke's* Q1; Duke
II. 3.18  *sheepcotes* Q1; Sheeps-Coates
II. 4.2  *messenger* Q1; Messengers
II. 4.10  *man's* Q1; man
II. 4.31  *panting* Q1; painting
II. 4.34  *whose* Q1; those
II. 4.105  *her* Q1; tends
II. 4.135  *mother's* Q1; Mother
III. 1.48  *your* Q1; that
III. 2.3  *drowned* Q1; drown
III. 4.10  *thy* Q1; they
III. 4.53  *ford* Q1; Sword

III. 4.96  *deeply* Q1; deerely
III. 4.124  *till the* Q1; at
III. 6.25  *Now* Q2; no Q1
III. 6.28  *bourn* M; broome Q1
III. 6.72  *lym* M; Hym
III. 6.73  *tike* Q1; tight
III. 6.82  *makes* Q1; make
IV. 1.62  *Flibbertigibbet* M; Stiberdigebit
        Q1
IV. 1.63  *mopping and mowing* M;
        Mobing, & Mohing
IV. 2.47  *these* M; this Q1
IV. 2.57  *to threat* M; threat Q1
IV. 2.75  *thereat* Q1; threat
IV. 2.79  *justicers* Q1; Justices
IV. 3.14  *sir* M; say Q1
IV. 3.19  *strove* M; streme Q1
IV. 3.23  *seemed* M; seeme Q1
IV. 3.34  *moistened* M; moystened her Q1
IV. 4.3  *femiter* Q1 Fenitar
IV. 4.18  *distress* Q1; desires
IV. 6.17  *walk* Q1; walk'd
IV. 6.71  *enridgèd* Q1; enraged
IV. 6.83  *coining* Q1; crying
IV. 6.172  *small* Q1; great
IV. 6.173  *Plate* M; Place
IV. 6.213  *one* Q1; a
IV. 7.13  *Doctor* Q1; Gent.
IV. 7.17  *Doctor* Q1; Gent.
IV. 7.21  *Doctor* Q1; Gent.
IV. 7.43  *Doctor* Q1; Gent.
IV. 7.51  *Doctor* Q1; Gent.
V. 1.46  *love* Q1; loves
V. 3.83  *attaint* Q1; arrest
V. 3.84  *sister* Q1; Sisters
V. 3.97  *he is* Q1; he's
V. 3.162  *Goneril* Q1; Bast.
V. 3.259  *you* Q1; your

## Stage Directions

Stage directions printed in brackets are the additions of modern editors except in the following instances:

Stage directions taken from Q1 occur at: I. 1. 40, I. 2.212, II. 2.50, III. 3.1, IV. 2.28, IV. 2.87, IV. 4.1, IV. 6.34, IV. 6.41, IV. 6.253 and 261, IV. 7.1, IV. 7.84, V. 3.118, V. 3.223.

Stage directions suggested by Q1:

I. 2.1 *Enter Bastard [solus, with a letter]*; Enter Bastard solus Q1

III. 7.110 *[Exeunt severally]*; Exit Q1.

IV. 6.211 Exit *[running, followed by Attendants]*; Exit King running Q1

V. 2.1 *Lear [held by the hand by] Cordelia;* Cordelia with her father in her hand Q1

The following stage directions have been substituted for directions given in the Folio:

I. 5.1 *Enter Lear, Kent, and Fool* Q2; Enter Lear, Kent, Gentleman, and Foole F1

IV. 2.1 *Enter Goneril and Bastard* Q1; Enter Goneril, Bastard, and Steward F1

IV. 2.2 *Enter Steward* Q1.

## Poetry and Action

There are no better examples of the range of effects possible on the Elizabethan stage than the third and fourth acts of *King Lear*. In successive scenes the stage represents the heath, a room in Gloucester's castle, and the heath again, with a hovel in which Edgar is at first concealed (presumably the enclosed space upstage). Later the action is to be imagined as in Gloucester's castle again, or Albany's castle, or the French camp, or the country near Dover; yet each one of the "scene changes" is accomplished by nothing more than the clearing of the stage followed by the entrance of other characters and occasionally by the placing of a few pieces of furniture. The dialogue does all the rest, and the absence of pauses between scenes makes possible the rapid pace characteristic of Elizabethan drama.

The poetry of these scenes does a great deal more than provide them with a setting. It extends the significance of the action into the microcosm and the macrocosm—into the "little world" of man and into the "great world," or cosmos, in which man lives. In the "Gentleman's" description of the old king, "contending with the fretful elements," we see Lear matching his fury to that of the storm, as he

> Strives in his little world of man to outscorn
> The to-and-fro-conflicting wind and rain. (III.1.10–11)

The language makes us aware of the storm in Lear's mind, which has brought him to the verge of madness, and of the seemingly human malice of the storm. In this one image are caught the implications of Lear's situation as he sees it—a confrontation with the power of not only wicked daughters but an entire universe. At the same time the description of the winds tearing the king's white hair "with eyeless rage" may remind us that he initiated this terrible series of events with an act of "eyeless rage" in his blind fury against Cordelia.

Throughout this section of the play poetic images alternate with actual stage images. In the following scene King Lear comes onstage exactly as described, shouting at the winds, accusing the elements of conspiracy with his daughters, and protesting that he is "more sinned against than sinning" (III.2.61). In the fourth scene occurs a most remarkable correspondence between poetic image and stage image. Lear's suffering has led him to pity the "naked wretches" who have no protection from the storm and to see for the first time that he has been partly to blame, living in the luxury of his courtly world of appearances:

> O, I have ta'en
> Too little care of this! Take physic, pomp;
> Expose thyself to feel what wretches feel,
> That thou mayst shake the superflux to them
> And show the heavens more just. (III.4.32–36)

A moment later the almost naked Edgar enters, playing his role of a mad beggar. At first Lear can see him only as a father like himself, who has given away everything to his daughters, but a more shocking vision follows. This "naked wretch" becomes the image of man reduced to his essential characteristics: "Thou art the thing itself; unaccommodated man is no more but such a poor, bare, forked animal as thou art" (III. 4.114–16). In his disillusionment Lear begins to tear off his own clothes, not in order to "shake the superflux" to the needy, but because he sees no use in trying to be more than a "forked animal."

The image of naked man which serves in this brief sequence to express both Lear's movement toward compassion and his profound disillusionment carries a heavy load of meaning because of the emphasis in earlier scenes on the contrast between appearance and reality. Kent has urged Lear to "see better," when he was deceived by the appearance of love in his elder daughters. Flattering words have been made to hide the truth just as, in Lear's words on a later occasion, "robes and furred gowns" conceal vice. However, Lear has defended what might be called the symbolic value of clothes in his speech to Regan (II.4.268–75), explaining that they serve not only to keep man warm but even more importantly to distinguish his life from that of the beasts. Nakedness thus has a double meaning by the time King Lear meets Edgar on the heath. It represents truth stripped of false appearances but also life reduced to the level of brute existence. Our awareness of all these issues gives a tremendous emotional impact to the dramatic moment in which Lear begins to strip himself.

Another remarkable sequence of scenes enforces the parallels between the stories of Gloucester and Lear while developing some of the main themes of the play. Again the poetry extends the meaning of the action, and the action gives physical reality to certain images in the poetry. Lear's desire to see his enemies punished is dramatized in the mad trial scene (III.6) in which Kent, "Tom o' Bedlam," and the Fool are made judges. The vindictive cruelty mixed with the king's longing for justice is brought out in his fantasy just before he summons the judges:

> To have a thousand with red burning spits
> Come hizzing in upon 'em— (III.6.17–18)

Throughout the play ferocity is expressed in images of animal assault and torture. In the scene following the mad trial we see a far worse travesty of justice in the putting out of Gloucester's eyes where cruelty is no longer mere fantasy. As this scene comments in some ways on the preceding one, it prepares for another of the great dramatic moments in the tragedy when the blind Gloucester says: "I have no way, and therefore want no eyes; / I stumbled when I saw" (IV.1.18–19). This short speech goes to the heart of Gloucester's—and Lear's—tragedy, reminding us of their earlier blindness to the truth beneath the deceptive appearance, and pointing to the wisdom gained through suffering.

The poetry of *King Lear* is not merely that part of the language which is written in verse form. Many of the prose speeches are so full of figurative language and so rich in imaginative appeal that their failure to scan as regular pentameters is irrelevant. In fact some of them are printed as verse in one of the two early editions and as prose in the other. The entire verbal texture of the play is poetic. Furthermore, the very structure of the play is poetic, relying as it does upon certain images to make essential connections and thus build the thematic pattern. Hence, though we may speak of the poetry as complementary to the action, we must do so with the awareness that it is not added to or superimposed upon something which exists quite independently of it. The action often seems designed to actualize what has been implicit in a figure of speech. No dramatist has ever exploited more fully than Shakespeare the connections between verbal texture, action, character, and theme, and no stage was ever better suited to such a kind of drama than the Elizabethan.

## *Heroism and Repentance*

King Lear is in some ways an Everyman figure. Confronted with characters who represent, almost allegorically, truth and falsehood, he foolishly makes the wrong choice, because he is blinded by pride and anger. He is then brought to see the nature of his error. First he learns the truth about his daughters, then more gradually the truth about himself. Suffering the fury of the storm, he knows he has taken too little care of the "naked wretches" in his kingdom. Later his humility deepens. He calls himself "a very foolish fond old man," and begs forgiveness of Cordelia (IV.7). This process of redemption through suffering is analogous to the action of a morality play even though *King Lear* ends with the tragic irony that the acquisition of wisdom and humility does not insure perfect justice in the world. The innocent may still suffer with the guilty. But terrible as this recognition may be, it does not wipe out the spiritual gain made by Lear and by the parallel figure of Gloucester.

Recognition of error and loss of pride are also part of the pattern of *Oedipus Rex*, but Oedipus, unlike Everyman, is a great individual rather than a generalized representation of mankind. In this respect Lear is more like the hero of the Greek tragedy. Both are men whose great will power contributes to our impression of their extraordinary stature, and in interpreting their tragedies, much depends on how much blame is attached to their exercise of will. Though Lear does not murder, the banishment of Cordelia is a less excusable mistake than the killing of Laius. However, Lear's anger has certain positive connotations not found in the tragedy of Oedipus. Lear believes, however mistakenly, that he is protesting against the disruption of natural bonds both when he banishes Cordelia and when he curses his elder daughters. What we see to be caused in large part by his desire for flattery he considers as righteous wrath, and by the time that Goneril and Regan have turned him out in the storm, it begins to seem at least partly righteous. As Oedipus seems to be both responsible for what happens to him and a victim of circumstance, so Lear seems both culpable and the victim of malice. The pattern of error, repentance, and redemption is overlaid with a pattern of a different sort.

King Lear appeals to our pity when those whom he has trusted turn against him, and to our admiration when he refuses to accept this conduct tamely. In an older Elizabethan play on the same story Lear is wholly pathetic—a tearful victim of cruel daughters. Shakespeare's Lear determines not to weep after his first outburst at Goneril, and later begs the gods to touch him "with noble anger" rather than let tears stain his cheeks (II.4.280). This "noble anger," associated in his mind with the defense of the natural order, of the prerogatives of kingship, and of the dignity of man, makes Shakespeare's Lear even more hero than victim. While pity for him as a repentant evil-doer would be completely consonant with the doctrinal implications of the morality-play pattern, and with the Aristotelian conception of *hamartía*, or tragic flaw, admiration for his stubborn self-assertion goes with a somewhat different sort of tragic experience.

An interpretation of the play must come to grips with the paradoxical significance of Lear's anger. As a consequence of his blindness and a sympton of his pride it is the chief manifestation of his error and the direct cause of the tragic series of events. As evidence of his ideals and his fortitude it is one of the chief means by which he commands our respect and even our awe. In some way room must be found in an interpretation of this tragedy for both the nobility of angry self-assertion and protest and the nobility of acceptance and humble recognition of error. In the last act Lear gives the most touching evidence of his repentance in his speech to Cordelia as they are led away to prison (V.3.8–19), but he is still capable of impassioned protest at the absolute injustice of Cordelia's death when he enters again with her body in his arms.

The tragic dénouement obliges us not only to strike some sort of balance in our estimate of the character of the hero but also to make a closely related adjustment of almost contrary clues to the meaning of the play as a whole. After his victory over Edmund, Edgar asserts divine providence in support of the good:

> The gods are just, and of our pleasant vices
> Make instruments to plague us. (V.3.172–73)

But this is hardly the impression left after the death of Cordelia. One might feel that Gloucester was right in his earlier statement:

> As flies to wanton boys are we to th' gods;
> They kill us for their sport. (IV.1.36–37)

Yet not all the deaths in the play are random, and Gloucester himself recovers from the profound cynicism of this view. Neither pure chance nor malice nor absolute justice prevails. A recognition of this puzzling fact must be included in whatever meaning the tragedy is found to have.

## Selected Reading List for King Lear

A. C. Bradley, *"King Lear," Shakespearean Tragedy.* Greenwich, Conn.: Fawcett Publications Inc., 1965, pp. 200–74.

John F. Danby, *Shakespeare's Doctrine of Nature.* London: Faber & Faber, Ltd., 1961.

Robert B. Heilman, *This Great Stage.* Seattle, Wash.: University of Washington Press, 1963.

G. Wilson Knight, *"King Lear* and the Comedy of the Grotesque," "The Lear Universe," *The Wheel of Fire.* Cleveland: The World Publishing Company, 1963, pp. 160–206.

L. C. Knights, *"King Lear* and the Great Tragedies," *The Age of Shakespeare, The Pelican Guide to English Literature,* II. Baltimore, Md.: Penguin Books, Inc., 1963, 228–56.

Maynard Mack, *King Lear in our Time.* Berkeley and Los Angeles: University of California Press, 1965.

Richard B. Sewall, *"King Lear," The Vision of Tragedy.* New Haven: Yale University Press, 1959, pp.68–79.

## Selected Reading List for The Elizabethan Theater

Bernard Beckerman, *Shakespeare at the Globe.* New York: The Macmillan Company, 1962.

A. M. Nagler, *Shakespeare's Stage.* New Haven: Yale University Press, 1958.

# Jonson and Renaissance Classicism

Ben Jonson was born in 1572, eight years after Shakespeare. By the time he was twenty-five he, too, was in the theater world of London, acting in a rival company of players and occasionally writing or doctoring plays for them. His first dramatic success, however, was a play performed in 1598 by the Lord Chamberlain's company, *Every Man in His Humor*, in which Shakespeare took a part. In the years immediately following, Jonson was busily employed writing plays for this company, for another adult company, and for a company of boy actors who catered to a more élite audience at a "private house" (see p. 131). During this period he also began another dramatic activity which was to occupy a large proportion of his time and win him great fame. This was the composition of masques, those combinations of ballet, pantomime, and poetry, which were increasingly in demand at the court of James I. In this work he collaborated with one of the great architects of the day, Inigo Jones, whose magnificent settings introduced into England the painted scenery which had become the fashion in Italy. King James recognized Jonson's contributions to royal entertainment by awarding him an annual pension, thus making him in effect the first Poet Laureate, though the title was first given to Dryden.

Jonson's greatest comedies were written during an eight-year period. *Volpone*, written in 1606 for the King's company, was followed by *Epicene* for a boys' company, and two more for the King's company, *The Alchemist* and *Bartholomew Fair*. After 1614 he enjoyed no major successes with his plays, and in the latter part of his life he was no longer favored at court as he had been. Though he continued to be a literary dictator, surrounded by admiring disciples, he already seemed to belong to the past by the time of his death in 1637.

To the poets and playwrights who followed them, Shakespeare and Jonson appeared as neatly opposed types: Shakespeare the untutored genius, the inspired imitator of nature; Jonson the scholar whose hard work made him a master of his art. The pigeon-holes of art and nature are too confining, but the comparison still has its value. There is no doubt that Jonson prided himself on his classical learning and no doubt that it was great. His famous statement that Shakespeare had "small Latine and lesse Greeke," though qualified by Jonson's great admiration for Shakespeare's art, no doubt reflected an important difference in the extent of Shakespeare's familiarity with the classics. Jonson was the more conscious artist of the two and by far the more concerned with the rules of playwriting.

In both the dedicatory epistle and the prologue to *Volpone* we see that it was Jonson's ambition to write a comedy which would be no mere collection of amusing incidents and lines, but a well-constructed work which would both entertain and instruct. His ideal of what a comedy should be is largely derived from the great classical critics, Aristotle and Horace, and from the commentators on them who were responsible for the distinctive characteristics of Renaissance classicism. He offers

> . . . quick comedy refined,
> As best critics have designed;
> The laws of time, place, persons he observeth,
> From no needful rule he swerveth. (Prologue, ll.29–32)

198

The "laws of time" and "place" refer to two of the "three unities," the most famous of all neoclassical rules (see the Introduction, p. 4). To the unity of action stipulated by Aristotle and the unity of time, about which he was less definite, Renaissance critics added the unity of place. By the law of "persons" Jonson refers to the conviction of Renaissance critics that certain kinds of characters were proper for each genre—the most illustrious for tragedy, the more ordinary for comedy. A concomitant of this distinction was the concern with decorum: the speech and actions of each character should accord exactly with his position in society, his age, sex, and occupation. In the prologue to *Every Man in His Humor* Jonson speaks of

> ... deeds, and language, such as men do use,
> And persons, such as Comedy would choose,
> When she would show an image of the times,
> And sport with human follies, not with crimes . . . . (ll.21–24)

The idea that comedy should reflect life as we know it was also characteristic of Renaissance poetic theory, and was derived from classical writers.

Another article of Jonson's artistic credo, deeply rooted in classical tradition but also reminiscent of the morality play, is the didactic function of poetry. Horace wrote that the poet who combined the useful with the enjoyable deserved universal acclaim, and Renaissance critics echoed him endlessly. Jonson boasts in the prologue to *Volpone* that it has always been his aim "To mix profit with your pleasure" (l.8). In the dedicatory epistle he goes a step further by insisting that the good poet must be a good man in order to be able to show others the path to virtue. So seriously does Jonson take his responsibility to emphasize moral instruction that he punishes the scoundrels in his play with a severity which he fears may make the ending too somber for a comedy. This fear of impropriety is as classical as the desire to combine instruction with pleasure.

No one who reads *Volpone* or sees it on the stage is likely to come away with the idea that it is an academic exercise. The vitality of the characters, the bite of the satire, the cleverness of the situations project a comic vision which could not be the result of merely following a set of rules. Jonson's familiarity with classical comedy and with the dramatic criticism which derived from Aristotle and Horace shaped his idea of what comedy should be, but the comedies he wrote are original creations, quite different in their totality from any of the plays which he admired. He was able to revivify classical ideals by combining an active imagination with rigorous self-discipline.

*Volpone* was played on the same stage as *King Lear*, and quite possibly during the same theatrical season. Although a twentieth-century critic will not make the same sort of distinctions which seventeenth-century critics made between Jonson and Shakespeare, yet he will be struck by the different uses each playwright made of the conventions of this theater. For reasons which should now be clear, Jonson did not use the freedom to move the action constantly from place to place, nor did he write poetry with the cosmic overtones of the heath scenes in *King Lear*. However, even more than Shakespeare, he exploited the effectiveness of the simplified character. King Lear's good and evil daughters may suggest Truth and Falsehood in the first scene of the play, but in *Volpone* many characters are limited throughout the play to a quality proclaimed by their names—fox, vulture, raven. On a stage where no effort is made to reproduce the setting with scrupulous exactitude such characters are not out of place nor do they appear totally fantastic. A striking feature of the Elizabethan stage is the way in which it promotes an easy commerce between fantasy and reality.

## The Text of Volpone[1]

The text of *Volpone* is based on the folio volume of Jonson's *Works* published in 1616, which was seen through the press by Jonson himself, and therefore represents to a degree unusual for dramatic texts of the period what the dramatist intended us to have. To provide a readable text it has been necessary to revise some of the printing conventions of the seventeenth-century editions. In order to identify himself with the classical tradition of comedy, Jonson used as a model for his *Works* the first printed editions of Plautus, Terence, and Aristophanes, heading each scene with a list of all characters appearing in it, without marking individual entrances and exits. The present edition follows the more familiar practice of listing only those characters on stage at the beginning of a scene and indicates all entrances and exits. Stage directions, kept to an absolute minimum, have also been added where understanding of the dialogue depends on an implied but not explicit action, or on an unspecified location. With the exception of the first speech ascription in each scene, which is usually omitted by Jonson, all such additions and all other material not in the original text have been enclosed in square brackets.

Where Jonson printed all verse in the metrical unit of the line, whether or not it represents the speech of one or more than one character, this edition divides the parts of such lines according to the speaker, and indicates the metrical unit by echeloning the parts of the line.

The original punctuation has been followed where its rhetorical effect has a dramatic value, but modern pointing has been used wherever necessary to clarify syntactical obscurities and to eliminate obvious errors or mere eccentricity. Spelling has been modernized except where orthographical change affects either meaning or meter. For example, where Jonson prints 'd to indicate an unstressed ending of a past participle, this edition prints -ed, and where Jonson printed -ed to indicate stress this edition prints -èd. Jonson's frequent elisions, e.g., th' or i', are retained, and all unusual accents are marked.

In the original text the entrance of a new character usually, though not invariably, initiates a new scene, so that there are many more scenes than a fully modernized text would allow. This edition retains Jonson's act and scene divisions in the belief that in most cases they represent the linking effect, the *liaison des scènes*, characteristic of the developing neoclassic drama; in all cases they represent Jonson's own conception of dramatic form; and the fact of form is part of the meaning of his plays.

---

[1]This note on the text is derived, with Mr. Kernan's permission, from the "Preface of the General Editors" in *the Yale Ben Jonson*.

# Volpone,
# or The Fox

*A COMEDY*

## BEN JONSON

To the
Most Noble And Most Equal Sisters,
The Two Famous Universities,
For Their
Love and Acceptance Shown to His Poem
In The Presentation;
Ben. Jonson,
The Grateful Acknowledger,
Dedicates Both It And Himself.
There follows an Epistle, if
you dare venture on the length.

Never, most equal Sisters, had any man a wit so presently excellent as that it could raise itself; but there must come both matter, occasion, commenders, and favorers to it. If this be true, and that the fortune of all 5 writers doth daily prove it, it behooves the careful to provide well toward these accidents, and, having acquired them, to preserve that part of reputation most tenderly wherein the benefit of a friend is also defended. Hence 10 is it that I now render myself grateful and am studious to justify the bounty of your act, to which, though your mere authority were satisfying, yet, it being an age wherein poetry and the professors of it hear so ill on all 15 sides, there will a reason be looked for in the subject. It is certain, nor can it with any forehead be opposed, that the too much license of poetasters in this time hath much deformed their mistress, that, every day, their 20 manifold and manifest ignorance doth stick unnatural reproaches upon her; but for their petulancy it were an act of the greatest injustice either to let the learned suffer, or so divine a skill (which indeed should not be 25

From *Ben Jonson: Volpone*, edited by Alvin B. Kernan (New Haven: Yale University Press, 1962). Copyright ©1962 by Yale University Press. Reprinted by permission of the editor and Yale University Press. The footnotes include both the glosses which appear at the foot of the page in Mr. Kernan's edition and excerpts from his notes.

*Equal* of equal merit, and in the Latin sense: *aequus*, just. *Two Famous Universities* Oxford and Cambridge *Presentation* At some time after *Volpone* had been played in London by the King's Men (Shakespeare's company) in the winter of 1605–6, the play was presented at Oxford and Cambridge. The probable date of these performances is the summer of 1606 *There . . . length* in Quarto only  1 *wit* intelligence  2 *presently* immediately  3 *matter* subject matter

5 *that* i.e., "that it be the truth"  7 *toward* for; *accidents* chance occurrences, incidental additions to wit rather than innate characteristics  10 *benefit* kindness, i.e., the "love and acceptance shown to his poem"  13 *mere* absolute  14 *satisfying* sufficient  15 *professors* practitioners; *hear so ill* are spoken of in such an ill manner  18 *forehead* assurance, command of countenance  19 *poetasters* petty poets  20 *mistress* the poetic muse, i.e., poetry  22 *for* because of  23 *petulancy* insolence

attempted with unclean hands) to fall under the least contempt. For, if men will impartially, and not asquint, look toward the offices and function of a poet, they will easily conclude to themselves the impossibility 30 of any man's being the good poet without first being a good man. He that is said to be able to inform young men to all good disciplines, inflame grown men to all great virtues, keep old men in their best and supreme 35 state, or, as they decline to childhood, recover them to their first strength; that comes forth the interpreter and arbiter of nature, a teacher of things divine no less than human, a master in manners; and can alone, or 40 with a few, effect the business of mankind: this, I take him, is no subject for pride and ignorance to exercise their railing rhetoric upon. But it will here be hastily answered that the writers of these days are other things: 45 that not only their manners, but their natures, are inverted, and nothing remaining with them of the dignity of poet but the abused name, which every scribe usurps; that now, especially in dramatic, or, as they term 50 it, stage poetry, nothing but ribaldry, profanation, blasphemy, all license of offense to God and man is practiced. I dare not deny a great part of this, and am sorry I dare not, because in some men's abortive features 55 (and would they had never boasted the light) it is overtrue; but that all are embarked in this bold adventure for hell is a most uncharitable thought, and, uttered, a more malicious slander. For my particular, I 60 can, and from a most clear conscience, affirm, that I have ever trembled to think toward the least profaneness, have loathed the use of such foul and unwashed bawdry as is now made the food of the scene. And, howso- 65

ever I cannot escape, from some, the imputation of sharpness, but that they will say I have taken a pride, or lust, to be bitter, and not my youngest infant but hath come into the world with all his teeth; I would 70 ask of these supercilious politics, what nation, society, or general order, or state I have provoked? what public person? whether I have not in all these preserved their dignity, as mine own person, safe? My works are 75 read, allowed (I speak of those that are entirely mine); look into them. What broad reproofs have I used? where have I been particular? where personal? except to a mimic, cheater, bawd, or buffoon, 80 creatures for their insolencies worthy to be taxed? Yet to which of these so pointingly as he might not either ingenuously have confessed or wisely dissembled his disease? But it is not rumour can make men guilty, 85 much less entitle me to other men's crimes. I know that nothing can be so innocently writ or carried, but may be made obnoxious to construction; marry, whilst I bear mine innocence about me, I fear it not. Appli- 90 cation is now grown a trade with many, and there are that profess to have a key for the

68 *lust* liking  69 *youngest infant* Jonson's recent play, *Sejanus*, which had caused him some difficulty with the authorities  70 *with all his teeth* capable of biting, satiric. Richard III was popularly believed to have been born with a full set of teeth, and Shakespeare, following tradition, makes of this a fearful omen of Richard's later unnatural behavior. See *Rich. III*, II.4.  71 *politics* shrewd persons, with the additional sense of cunning contrivers  76 *allowed* licensed for public production by the Master of the Revels, a court official who acted as censor in Elizabethan times. This power later passed to the Lord Chamberlain, who, through a deputy called the censor, still exercises it  76–77 *those . . . mine* Jonson was the part author of a number of plays, among them *Eastward Ho* (1604), which he wrote with Chapman and Marston. This play, though it was produced, was definitely not allowed, and Jonson went to jail, along with Chapman and Marston, for certain passages in it which offended King James  77 *broad* indecent  80 *mimic* actor or perhaps plagiarist  82 *taxed* censured; *pointingly* specifically  88 *carried* managed  89 *to construction* by interpretation  90–91 *application* specific identification (of persons and events in plays)  92 *there are* there are those

33 *inform* form, mold  41 *effect . . . mankind* "perform the proper functions of man"  42 *I take him* "as I understand it"  43 *railing* abusive  49–53 *that . . . practiced* Blasphemy, obscenity, and lack of moral purpose were the standard charges leveled by the Puritans in their continuing war against the theaters. By 1606 there was some substance to their accusations, as Jonson admits. . .  55 *abortive features* premature and malformed plays—plays are here considered the offspring of the poet  65 *food* substance

deciphering of everything; but let wise and noble persons take heed how they be too credulous, or give leave to these invading 95 interpreters to be overfamiliar with their fames, who cunningly, and often, utter their own virulent malice under other men's simplest meanings. As for those that will (by faults which charity hath raked up, or 100 common honesty concealed) make themselves a name with the multitude, or (to draw their rude and beastly claps) care not whose living faces they entrench with their petulant styles, may they do it without a rival, 105 for me. I choose rather to lie graved in obscurity than share with them in so preposterous a fame. Nor can I blame the wishes of those severe and wiser patriots, who, providing the hurts these licentious 110 spirits may do in a state, desire rather to see fools, and devils, and those antique relics of barbarism retrieved, with all other ridiculous and exploded follies, than behold the wounds of private men, of princes, and nations. 115 For, as Horace makes Trebatius speak, among these,

—Sibi quisque timet, quamquam est intactus, et odit.

And men may justly impute such rages, if continued, to the writer, as his sports. 120 The increase of which lust in liberty, together with the present trade of the stage, in all their misc'line interludes, what learned or liberal soul doth not already abhor? where nothing but the filth of the time is uttered, 125 and that with such impropriety of phrase,

such plenty of solecisms, such dearth of sense, so bold prolepses, so racked metaphors, with brothelry able to violate the ear of a pagan, and blasphemy to turn the blood of a 130 Christian to water. I cannot but be serious in a cause of this nature, wherein my fame and the reputations of divers honest and learned are the question; when a name so full of authority, antiquity, and all great 135 mark, is, through their insolence, become the lowest scorn of the age; and those men subject to the petulancy of every vernaculous orator that were wont to be the care of kings and happiest monarchs. This it is that hath 140 not only rapt me to present indignation, but made me studious heretofore, and by all my actions to stand off from them; which may most appear in this my latest work—which you, most learned Arbitresses, have seen, 145 judged, and, to my crown, approved— wherein I have labored, for their instruction and amendment, to reduce not only the ancient forms, but manners of the scene: the easiness, the propriety, the innocence, 150 and last, the doctrine, which is the principal end of poesie, to inform men in the best reason of living. And though my catastrophe may in the strict rigor of comic law meet with censure, as turning back to my promise; 155 I desire the learned and charitable critic to have so much faith in me to think it was done of industry: for with what ease I could have varied it nearer his scale (but that I fear to boast my own faculty) I could here 160 insert. But my special aim being to put the

97 *utter* used in the special sense of circulating false money 100 *raked up* covered over 101–102 *make . . . name* by insisting that they are caricatured in some play 103 *claps* applause 104 *entrench* mark 109 *patriots* those concerned for the nation's welfare 110 *providing* foreseeing 112 *fools and devils* the reference here is to the old-fashioned morality plays and early Elizabethan drama modeled on these, in which fools of the slapstick variety, clowning devils, and melodramatic Vices were stocks in trade. . .; *antique* grotesque 114 *exploded* literally "to clap and hoot off the stage" (*OED*) 118 *Sibi . . . odit* "Although he is uninjured, everyone fears for himself and is angry" (Horace, *Sermones* 2.1.23) 121 *lust* pleasure; *liberty* unrestrained freedom 123 *misc'line* mixed, jumbled

134 *question* topic; *a name* Horace. Thomas Dekker in his play *Satiromastix* (1601) presented Jonson, in a ridiculous manner, under the name of Horace. Jonson had previously used Horace as the satirist in his *Poetaster* 136 *mark* note 138 *vernaculous* ill bred, scurrilous 141 *rapt* carried by force 148 *reduce* bring back 150 *innocence* harmlessness 153 *catastrophe* climax of the play 155 *as . . . promise* "because it fails to fulfill my promise (to reduce . . . the ancient forms)"; According to the critics, comedy was supposed to end joyfully. This "comic law" was purportedly derived from the practice of classical comedy, but as Jonson points out a few lines later, not all the plays of Aristophanes, Plautus, and Terence end on a happy note 158 *of industry* purposely

snaffle in their mouths that cry out: We never punish vice in our interludes, &c. I took the more liberty, though not without some lines of example, drawn even in the ancients 165 themselves, the goings out of whose comedies are not always joyful, but oft times the bawds, the servants, the rivals, yea, and the masters are mulcted, and fitly, it being the office of a comic poet to imitate justice, and 170 instruct to life, as well as purity of language, or stir up gentle affections. To which I shall take the occasion elsewhere to speak. For the present, most reverenced Sisters, as I have cared to be thankful for your affections 175 past, and here made the understanding acquainted with some ground of your favors, let me not despair their continuance, to the maturing of some worthier fruits; wherein, if my muses be true to me, I shall raise the 180 despised head of poetry again, and stripping her out of those rotten and base rags wherewith the times have adulterated her form, restore her to her primitive habit, feature, and majesty, and render her worthy to 185 be embraced and kissed of all the great and master-spirits of our world. As for the vile and slothful, who never affected an act worthy of celebration, or are so inward with their own vicious natures, as they worthily 190 fear her and think it a high point of policy to keep her in contempt with their declamatory and windy invectives; she shall out of just rage incite her servants (who are *genus irritabile*) to spout ink in their faces that 195 shall eat, farther than their marrow, into their fames, and not Cinnamus the barber

with his art shall be able to take out the brands, but they shall live, and be read, till the wretches die, as things worst deserving 200 of themselves in chief, and then of all mankind.

From my house in the Blackfriars, this 11th day of February, 1607

## THE PERSONS OF THE PLAY

VOLPONE, *a magnifico*
MOSCA, *his parasite*
VOLTORE, *an advocate*
CORBACCIO, *an old gentleman*
CORVINO, *a merchant*
AVOCATORI, *four magistrates*
NOTARIO, *the register*
NANO, *a dwarf*
CASTRONE, *a eunuch*
[SIR] POLITIC WOULDBE, *a knight*
PEREGRINE, *a gent[leman]-traveler*
BONARIO, *a young gentleman [son of* CORBACCIO]
FINE MADAME WOULDBE, *the knight's wife*
CELIA, *the merchant's wife*
COMMENDATORI, *officers*
MERCATORI, *three merchants*
ANDROGYNO, *a hermaphrodite*
SERVITORE, *a servant*
GREGE
WOMEN

---

162–163 *We . . . interludes* another common Puritan complaint against the theater 163 *interludes* plays 166 *goings out* conclusions 171–72 *as . . . affections* Jonson's parallelism breaks down in the last two grammatical elements 172 *To* about 172–73 *To . . . speak* Jonson probably refers to his commentary on Horace's *Ars Poetica*, on which he had announced a year or two before that he was working. The commentary does not survive, and it seems likely that it was lost when Jonson's library burned several years later 176 *the understanding* the intelligent 184 *primitive* original, first; *habit* clothing 197 *Cinnamus the barber* In Elizabethan days the barber often was a surgeon as well and would be called on to remove such marks as Jonson,

figuratively, plans to make on the poetasters who have whored the Muse. Martial in one of his epigrams (6.64.26) mentions the skill of Cinnamus in removing "stigmata" 199 *brands* scars, marks 201 *in chief* first of all 202–203 *from . . . 1607* in quarto only 202 *Blackfriars* a fashionable residential area in the heart of the City of London. Several indoor theaters were in this area. *Volpone* At the basis of this play is a beast fable. *. . .* The names of the chief characters are forms of animal names: Volpone, the fox; Mosca, the fly; Voltore, the vulture; Corbaccio and Corvino, ravens; Sir Pol, the parrot; and *Peregrine*, a hunting hawk *magnifico* rich and distinguished man *parasite* a flatterer, hanger-on *advocate* lawyer *register* clerk of the court [*Sir*] *Politic* "Politic" here has the meaning of crafty and skilled in diplomacy *Grege* crowd

## THE SCENE

*Venice*

## THE ARGUMENT

V olpone, childless, rich, feigns sick, despairs,

O ffers his state to hopes of several heirs,

L ies languishing; his Parasite receives

P resents of all, assures, deludes; then weaves

O ther cross plots, which ope themselves, are told.                    5

N ew tricks for safety are sought; they thrive; when, bold,

E ach tempts th' other again, and all are sold.

## PROLOGUE

Now, luck yet send us, and a little wit

  Will serve to make our play hit;

According to the palates of the season,

  Here is rhyme not empty of reason.

This we were bid to credit from our poet,                    5

  Whose true scope, if you would know it,

In all his poems still hath been this measure:

  To mix profit with your pleasure;

And not as some, whose throats their envy failing,

  Cry hoarsely, "All he writes is railing,"          10

And when his plays come forth, think they can flout them,

  With saying, "He was a year about them."

To these there needs no lie but this his creature,

  Which was two months since no feature;

And though he dares give them five lives to mend it,          15

'Tis known, five weeks fully penned it,

From his own hand, without a coadjutor,

  Novice, journeyman, or tutor.

Yet thus much I can give you as a token

  Of his play's worth: no eggs are broken,          20

Nor quaking custards with fierce teeth affrighted,

  Wherewith your rout are so delighted;

Nor hales he in a gull old ends reciting,

  To stop gaps in his loose writing,

With such a deal of monstrous and forced action,          25

  As might make Bedlam a faction;

Nor made he 'his play for jests stol'n from each table,

  But makes jests to fit his fable.

And so presents quick comedy refined,

  As best critics have designed;          30

The laws of time, place, persons he observeth,

  From no needful rule he swerveth.

All gall and copperas from his ink he draineth,

---

17 *coadjutor* a co-writer who wrote part of a play ... 18 *Novice* an apprentice doing parts under a master's direction...; *journeyman* a specialist called in to repair plays and rewrite parts...; *tutor* a guide and corrector of what others wrote... 21 *quaking custards* ...John Marston writes, "Let custards quake, my rage must freely run," in his satirical poem *The Scourge of Villainy* (1598–99), and the word "custards" refers to the bumbling fools whom he is prepared to attack in his fierce satiric style (Satire II, line 4).... In 1599, when the further printing of verse satire was forbidden, Marston carried his satiric style to the theater, where for a number of years his dramatic satirists proceeded with "fierce teeth" to frighten "quaking custards." It is, I believe, such satiric plays as Marston's *Histriomastix* and *The Malcontent* that Jonson is referring to here  22 *rout* mob  23 *hales* hauls; *gull* simple dupe; *old ends* bits and pieces of poetry—Shakespeare's Pistol is the most remarkable reciter of old ends in Elizabethan drama  26 *make ... faction* "add a new party to the madhouse"; *bedlam* St. Mary of Bethlehem, a religious institution which became the London insane asylum  27–28 "He does not construct his plays to accommodate stolen jokes, but makes his own jokes to fit his plays"  27 *stol'n from each table* The comparison is to scraps stolen from a feast. The Elizabethan playwright was notorious for lifting material from the classics and from his contemporaries... 28 *fable* plot  29 *quick* lively  31 *laws ..persons* See p. 199  33 *copperas* an acid

---

*Venice* In Jonson's time Venice was known not only for its connection with trade but also for its wealth, luxury, sophistication, and political cunning...
2 *state* property  5 *ope* open; *told* exposed  7 *sold* enslaved
5 *credit* believe, understand  6 *scope* aim  8 *To ... pleasure* the Horatian formula, *utile dulci*, which Jonson refers to frequently  10 *railing* carping, abusive language  12 *"He ... them"* It was one of Jonson's boasts that he was a craftsman who worked and reworked his plays rather than turning them out hurriedly, as most Elizabethan playwrights apparently did... 13 *To ... creature* "this play answers the charge"  14 *was ... feature* "was not begun two months ago"

Only a little salt remaineth,
Wherewith he'll rub your cheeks, till red
   with laughter,      35
They shall look fresh a week after.

ACT I. *Scene 1*

[VOLPONE's *house*.]
[VOLPONE.] Good morning to the day; and
   next, my gold!
Open the shrine that I may see my saint.

[MOSCA *opens a curtain disclosing piles of gold*.]
Hail the world's soul, and mine! More glad
   than is
The teeming earth to see the longed-for sun
Peep through the horns of the celestial Ram, 5
Am I, to view thy splendor darkening his;
That lying here, amongst my other hoards,
Show'st like a flame by night, or like the day
Struck out of chaos, when all darkness fled
Unto the center. O thou son of Sol,   10
But brighter than thy father, let me kiss,
With adoration, thee, and every relic
Of sacred treasure in this blessed room.
Well did wise poets by thy glorious name
Title that age which they would have the
   best,      15
Thou being the best of things, and far tran-
   scending
All style of joy in children, parents, friends,

Or any other waking dream on earth.
Thy looks when they to Venus did ascribe,
They should have giv'n her twenty thousand
   cupids,      20
Such are thy beauties and our loves! Dear
   saint,
Riches, the dumb god that giv'st all men
   tongues,
That canst do nought, and yet mak'st men
   do all things;
The price of souls; even hell, with thee to boot,
Is made worth heaven! Thou art virtue,
   fame,      25
Honor, and all things else. Who can get thee,
He shall be noble, valiant, honest, wise—
  MOSCA. And what he will, sir. Riches are
   in fortune
A greater good than wisdom is in nature.
  VOLPONE. True, my belovèd Mosca. Yet,
   I glory      30
More in the cunning purchase of my wealth
Than in the glad possession, since I gain
No common way: I use no trade, no venture;
I wound no earth with ploughshares; fat no
   beasts
To feed the shambles; have no mills for
   iron,      35
Oil, corn, or men, to grind 'em into powder;
I blow no subtle glass; expose no ships
To threat'nings of the furrow-facèd sea;
I turn no monies in the public bank,
Nor usure private—
  MOSCA.        No, sir, nor devour   40
Soft prodigals. You shall ha' some will
   swallow
A melting heir as glibly as your Dutch

---

I.1. [*Volpone*] Jonson does not provide a speech ascription for the first speech in a scene but simply lists the characters present at the beginning of the scene. In this edition the lists of characters are deleted and the necessary speech ascriptions added, without further comment  4 *teeming* filled with life and ready to bear  5 *Peep . . . Ram* The Ram is the sign of Aries in the zodiac. The sun enters Aries on the 21st of March, the spring equinox, and from this time the "teeming" earth can look forward to increasing light, warmth, and growth  7 *That* Gold is the understood subject of this clause  8–9 *day . . . chaos* the day of creation  10 *center* center of the earth; *son of Sol* In alchemy gold was considered the offspring of the sun  15 *that age* A number of classical poets, Ovid particularly (see *Metamorphoses* 1.89–112), looked back to a mythical golden age when men lived simpler and more honest lives, and which, according to the myth, was distinguished by its lack of precious metals. . . . Volpone completely misunderstands the metaphorical meaning of "gold" in the traditional term; *have* argue to be  17 *style* form

19 *they . . . ascribe* Venus was frequently styled "golden" (aurea Venus) by the Latin poets  22 *the dumb god* "silence is golden"  28 *what* whatever  31 *purchase* getting  32 *gain* make money in  33 *common* ordinary; *use* employ; *venture* risky business enterprise  35 *shambles* slaughterhouse  36 *corn* grain  37 *subtle* intricately wrought  39 *turn* "to keep passing in a course of exchange or traffic"  40 *usure* Volpone refers here to the practice of men loaning money at exorbitant rates to individuals in need, particularly to young men of fashion living beyond their means, the "soft prodigals" of line 41. . .; *private* privately  41 *soft prodigals* easy spendthrifts  42–43 *Dutch . . . butter* The Dutch were famous for their delight in eating butter

Will pills of butter, and ne'er purge for 't;
Tear forth the fathers of poor families
Out of their beds, and coffin them, alive,      45
In some kind, clasping prison, where their
     bones
May be forthcoming, when the flesh is rotten.
But, your sweet nature doth abhor these
     courses;
You loathe the widow's or the orphan's tears
Should wash your pavements, or their
     piteous cries                                      50
Ring in your roofs, and beat the air for
     vengeance—
   VOLPONE. Right, Mosca, I do loathe it.
   MOSCA                    And, besides, sir,
You are not like the thresher that doth stand
With a huge flail, watching a heap of corn,
And, hungry, dares not taste the smallest
     grain,                                            55
But feeds on mallows and such bitter herbs;
Nor like the merchant, who hath filled his
     vaults
With Romagnìa and rich Candian wines,
Yet drinks the lees of Lombard's vinegar.
You will not lie in straw, whilst moths and
     worms                                             60
Feed on your sumptuous hangings and soft
     beds.
You know the use of riches, and dare give,
     now,
From that bright heap, to me, your poor
     observer,
Or to your dwarf, or your hermaphrodite,
Your eunuch, or what other household
   : trifle                                            65
Your pleasure allows maintenance—
   VOLPONE.                    Hold thee, Mosca,
                    [ gives him money ]
Take, of my hand; thou strik'st on truth in all,
And they are envious term thee parasite.
Call forth my dwarf, my eunuch, and my fool,
And let 'em make me sport. What should
     I do                    [ exit MOSCA ]   70
But cocker up my genius and live free

To all delights my fortune calls me to?
I have no wife, no parent, child, ally,
To give my substance to; but whom I make
Must be my heir, and this makes men
     observe me.                                       75
This draws new clients, daily, to my house,
Women and men of every sex and age,
That bring me presents, send me plate, coin,
     jewels,
With hope that when I die (which they
     expect
Each greedy minute) it shall then return     80
Tenfold upon them; whilst some, covetous
Above the rest, seek to engross me, whole,
And counterwork the one unto the other,
Contend in gifts, as they would seem in love.
All which I suffer, playing with their
     hopes,                                            85
And am content to coin 'em into profit,
And look upon their kindness, and take more,
And look on that; still bearing them in hand,
Letting the cherry knock against their lips,
And draw it by their mouths, and back
     again,                                            90
How now!

*Scene 2*

[MOSCA *enters with* NANO, ANDROGYNO, *and*
CASTRONE *prepared to put on an entertainment.*]
   NANO. Now, room for fresh gamesters, who
     do will you to know,
They do bring you neither play nor university
     show;

---

74 *whom I make* whomever I designate   75 *observe*
be obsequious to   76 *clients* followers. Although
Volpone uses the word in the general
sense of "dependents," the word also looks back
to the original Latin meaning: free men who
lacking Roman citizenship, placed themselves
under the protection of a wealthy Roman who
then became their "patron" ...   78 *plate* dishes
and utensils made of silver or gold   82 *engross* to
absorb entirely   83 *unto* against   84 *as* ... *love*
"in order to try to show that they love me"   85
*suffer* allow   88 *bearing* ... *hand* leading them on
I.2.2 *play* ... *show* Nano is pointing out—in
mockingly humble tones—that his entertainment
is a small affair and not to be judged by the
standards applicable to a play put on in the
public playhouses or to one of the learned productions of the students at the universities. ...

---

43 *purge* take a laxative   56 *mallows* a variety of
coarse, harsh plants   58 *Romagnìa* wine from Greece
(Romanie) often referred to as "Rumney"; note
accent on next to last syllable; *Candian wines* from
Candy, i.e., Crete   59 *Lombard's vinegar* cheap,
acid wine from Lombardy   68 *term* that term   71
*cocker up* encourage; *genius* innate talents

And therefore do entreat you that whatsoever
    they rehearse,
May not fare a whit the worse, for the false
    pace of the verse.
If you wonder at this, you will wonder more
    ere we pass,                5
For know, here is enclosed the soul of
    Pythagoras,    [pointing to ANDROGYNO]
That juggler divine, as hereafter shall follow;
Which soul, fast and loose, sir, came first
    from Apollo,
And was breathed into Aethalides, Mercurius
    his son,
Where it had the gift to remember all that
    ever was done.            10
From thence it fled forth, and made quick
    transmigration
To goldy-locked Euphorbus, who was killed
    in good fashion,
At the siege of old Troy, by the cuckold of
    Sparta.
Hermotimus was next (I find it in my charta)
To whom it did pass, where no sooner it was
    missing,               15
But with one Pyrrhus of Delos it learned to
    go afishing;
And thence did it enter the sophist of Greece.
From Pythagore, she went into a beautiful
    piece,

Hight Aspasia, the meretrix; and the next toss
    of her
Was again of a whore, she became a philoso-
    pher,               20
Crates the Cynic, as itself doth relate it.
Since, kings, knights, and beggars, knaves,
    lords, and fools gat it,
Besides ox and ass, camel, mule, goat, and
    brock,
In all which it hath spoke, as in the Cobbler's
    cock.
But I come not here to discourse of that
    matter,             25
Or his one, two, or three, or his great oath,
    "By Quater!"
His musics, his trigon, his golden thigh,
Or his telling how elements shift; but I
Would ask, how of late thou hast suffered
    translation,
And shifted thy coat in these days of refor-
    mation?            30
  ANDROGYNO. Like one of the reformèd, a
    fool, as you see,
Counting all old doctrine heresy.
  NANO. But not on thine own forbid meats
    hast thou ventured?
  ANDROGYNO. On fish, when first a Carth-
    usian I entered.
  NANO. Why, then thy dogmatical silence
    hath left thee?           35

---

4 *false pace* referring to the doggerel rhythms
and forced rhymes of this speech  6 *Pythagoras*
Greek philosopher of sixth century B.C., and
founder of a school which had for one of its tenets
a belief in transmigration, the passage of the soul
from one body to another after death  8 *fast and
loose* a gambling trick, somewhat like our "shell
game," in which a leather belt was folded clev-
erly a number of times, and a dagger driven in
between the folds. Bets were then made on
whether the belt was fast or loose, i.e., around the
dagger or free of it  9 *Aethalides* herald for Jason's
Argonauts; *Mercurius his* a common Elizabethan
form of third person singular possessive  12
*Euphorbus* the Trojan who first wounded Patroclus,
*Iliad* 17  13 *cuckold of Sparta* Menelaus, whose
wife, Helen, was stolen by Paris  14 *Hermotimus*
a Greek philosopher of Claizomene who lived
about 500 B.C.; *charta* paper; either the part he
is reading or the source of this information,
Lucian's "Dialogue of the Cobbler and the Cock"
16 *Pyrrhus of Delos* This could be one of several
classical philosophers  17 *sophist* philosopher—
Pythagoras is meant

---

19 *Aspasia* the mistress of Pericles, leader of
Athens in the fifth century; *meretrix* courtesan
21 *Crates* Crates of Thebes, a pupil of the Cynic
philosopher Diogenes; *itself* The neuter pronoun
suggests that Nano may here point to Androgyno
who is playing the part of the soul  23 *brock*
badger  24 *Cobbler's cock* the cock who speaks in
Lucian's dialogue  26 *"By Quater"* Pythagoras
believed that number was the principle of harmony in the universe, and he therefore attached
supernatural significance to the geometrical relationships. The "quater" referred to here is the
triangle made with four dots as its base  27 *trigon*
triangle; *golden thigh* Pythagoras was believed by
his followers to have had a golden thigh  29
*translation* change, transmigration  30 *reformation*
i.e., The Protestant Reformation  31 *reformèd*
Puritans  33 *forbid meats* forbidden foods—the
Pythagoreans did not eat fish  34 *Carthusian* a
religious order famed for the severity of its diet
35 *silence* The Pythagoreans were bound to a
five-year silence

ANDROGYNO. Of that an obstreperous lawyer bereft me.

NANO. O wonderful change! When Sir
Lawyer forsook thee,

For Pythagore's sake, what body then took
thee?

ANDROGYNO. A good, dull moyle.

NANO.                     And how! by that means
Thou wert brought to allow of the eating
of beans?                                    40

ANDROGYNO. Yes.

NANO.              But from the moyle into
whom didst thou pass?

ANDROGYNO. Into a very strange beast,
by some writers called an ass;

By others, a precise, pure, illuminate brother,
Of those devour flesh, and sometimes one
another,

And will drop you forth a libel, or a sancti-
fied lie,                                    45

Betwixt every spoonful of a nativity pie.

NANO. Now quit thee, for heaven, of that
profane nation,

And gently report thy next transmigration.

ANDROGYNO. To the same that I am.

NANO.                  A creature of delight,
And what is more than a fool, an hermaphrodite?                                    50

Now, 'pray thee, sweet soul, in all thy varia-
tion,

Which body wouldst thou choose to take up
thy station?

ANDROGYNO. Troth, this I am in, even here
would I tarry.

NANO. 'Cause here the delight of each sex
thou canst vary?

ANDROGYNO. Alas, those pleasures be stale
and forsaken;                                55

No, 'tis your fool wherewith I am so taken,
The only one creature that I can call blessèd,
For all other forms I have proved most
distressèd.

NANO. Spoke true, as thou wert in Pythagoras still.

This learned opinion we celebrate will,   60

Fellow eunuch, as behooves us, with all our
wit and art,

To dignify that whereof ourselves are so great
and special a part.

VOLPONE. Now, very, very pretty! Mosca,
this

Was thy invention?

MOSCA.              If it please my patron,
Not else.

VOLPONE. It doth, good Mosca.

MOSCA.                  Then it was, sir.   65

SONG

Fools, they are the only nation
Worth men's envy or admiration;
Free from care or sorrow-taking,
Selves and others merry making,
All they speak or do is sterling.          70
Your fool, he is your great man's dearling,
And your ladies' sport and pleasure;
Tongue and bable are his treasure.
E'en his face begetteth laughter,
And he speaks truth free from slaughter.   75
He's the grace of every feast,
And, sometimes, the chiefest guest:
Hath his trencher and his stool,
When wit waits upon the fool.
  O, who would not be                       80
  Hee, hee, hee?      (One knocks without.)

VOLPONE. Who's that? Away! Look, Mosca.

MOSCA.                  Fool, begone!

[Exeunt NANO, CASTRONE, ANDROGYNO.]
'Tis Signior Voltore, the advocate;
I know him by his knock.

VOLPONE.              Fetch me my gown,
My furs, and night-caps; say my couch is
changing,                                    85

And let him entertain himself awhile
Without i' th' gallery. [Exit MOSCA.] Now,
now, my clients

Begin their visitation! Vulture, kite,
Raven, and gorcrow, all my birds of prey,

---

36 *obstreperous* in the Latin sense, "to make a noise" 39 *moyle* mule 43 *precise* Puritanical; *illuminate* illuminated, i.e., one who has had a vision of religious truth 46 *nativity pie* Christmas pie 47 *quit thee* get out 52 *to . . . station* to stay in 53 *Troth* in truth

62 *that* i.e., folly 65 *Song* Volpone and Mosca may join the three grotesques in this song, or the latter may sing it alone as a conclusion to their entertainment 70 *sterling* excellent 71 *dearling* darling 73 *bable* bauble, the mock scepter carried by a jester or professional fool—also slang for the male organ; the word also suggests "babble" 75 *free from slaughter* without fear of consequences 85 *furs* warm robes worn by the sick man; *my couch is changing* my bed is being changed 89 *gorcrow* carrion crow

That think me turning carcass, now they
    come. 90
I am not for 'em yet.[*Enter* MOSCA.]
                 How now? the news?
MOSCA. A piece of plate, sir.
VOLPONE.       Of what bigness?
MOSCA.                    Huge,
Massy, and antique, with your name inscribed,
And arms engraven.
    VOLPONE.       Good! and not a fox
Stretched on the earth, with fine delusive
    sleights 95
Mocking a gaping crow? ha, Mosca!
    MOSCA.             Sharp, sir.
    VOLPONE. Give me my furs. Why dost thou
    laugh so, man?
    MOSCA. I cannot choose, sir, when I ap-
    prehend
What thoughts he has, without, now, as he
    walks:
That this might be the last gift he should
    give; 100
That this would fetch you; if you died today,
And gave him all, what he should be tomor-
    row;
What large return would come of all his
    ventures;
How he should worshipped be, and rever-
    enced;
Ride with his furs, and foot-cloths; waited
    on 105
By herds of fools and clients; have clear way
Made for his moyle, as lettered as himself;
Be called the great and learnèd advocate:
And then concludes, there's nought impossi-
    ble.
    VOLPONE. Yes, to be learnèd, Mosca.
    MOSCA.            O, no; rich 110
Implies it. Hood an ass with reverend pur-
    ple,
So you can hide his two ambitious ears,
And he shall pass for a cathedral doctor.
    VOLPONE. My caps, my caps, good Mosca.
    Fetch him in.

---

91 *for'em* ready for them, i.e., not yet "made
up" as a dying man   103 *ventures* business enter-
prises; specifically here, the gifts he has given
Volpone  107 *lettered* learned  111 *Hood . . . purple*
the purple hood worn on the academic gown by
Doctors of Philosophy

MOSCA. Stay, sir; your ointment for your
    eyes.
VOLPONE.              That's true; 115
Dispatch, dispatch. I long to have possession
Of my new present.
    MOSCA.         That, and thousands more,
I hope to see you lord of.
    VOLPONE.         Thanks, kind Mosca.
    MOSCA. And that, when I am lost in blend-
    ed dust,
And hundreds such as I am, in succes-
    sion— 120
    VOLPONE. Nay, that were too much, Mosca.
    MOSCA.            You shall live
Still to delude these harpies.
    VOLPONE.          Loving Mosca!
                   [*Looking into a mirror.*]
'Tis well. My pillow now, and let him enter.
                      [*Exit* MOSCA.]
Now, my feigned cough, my phthisic, and
    my gout,
My apoplexy, palsy, and catarrhs, 125
Help, with your forcèd functions, this my
    posture,
Wherein, this three year, I have milked their
    hopes.
He comes, I hear him—uh! uh! uh! uh! O—

---

115 *ointment . . . eyes* to make them look rheumy
116 *Dispatch* hurry  120 *in succession* following me,
i.e., other servants to Volpone  122 *Still* always
123 *'Tis . . . now* Volpone is satisfied with the
make-up and costume he has, like an actor, been
donning. He now settles into his sick bed.
Throughout the remainder of this scene Volpone
remains in bed. The bed might have been placed
in a small curtained space at the rear of the
platform stage, but since most of the action takes
place around the bed it would seem more likely
that it was placed somewhere toward the front,
where the facial expression of the "sick man"
could have been seen and his low, faltering words
heard. To meet this dramatic problem a bed
could have been set up on the stage proper
or within a small tent, or "mansion," placed
forward of the tiring-house wall...  124–27
*Now . . . hopes* These four lines constitute a
mock invocation. Where the poet or petitioner
usually calls on the gods for inspiration, Volpone,
abusing poetry as he abuses other institutions of
mankind, calls on sickness. For another example
of Volpone's sacrilegious poetry see the mock
aubade—song to the dawn—with which the play
begins  124 *phthisic* consumption  126 *posture* imposture  127 *this three year* for three years

*Scene 3*

[*Enter* MOSCA *with* VOLTORE. VOLPONE *in bed.*]
MOSCA. You still are what you were, sir.
Only you,
Of all the rest, are he commands his love,
And you do wisely to preserve it thus,
With early visitation, and kind notes
Of your good meaning to him, which, I
know,                                              5
Cannot but come most grateful. Patron, sir.
Here's Signior Voltore is come—
  VOLPONE [*faintly*].          What say you?
MOSCA. Sir, Signior Voltore is come this
  morning
To visit you.
  VOLPONE. I thank him.
  MOSCA.             And hath brought
A piece of antique plate, bought of St.
  Mark,                                            10
With which he here presents you.
  VOLPONE.            He is welcome.
Pray him to come more often.
  MOSCA.          Yes.
  VOLTORE.          What says he?
MOSCA. He thanks you and desires you see
  him often.
  VOLPONE. Mosca.
  MOSCA.        My patron?
  VOLPONE.           Bring him near,
  where is he?
I long to feel his hand.
  MOSCA [*directing* VOLPONE'S *groping hands*].
                 The plate is here, sir. 15
  VOLTORE. How fare you, sir?
  VOLPONE.   I thank you, Signior Voltore.
Where is the plate? mine eyes are bad.
  VOLTORE [*putting it into his hands*]. I'm sorry
To see you still thus weak.
  MOSCA [*aside*].      That he is not weaker.
  VOLPONE. You are too munificent.
  VOLTORE.       No, sir; would to heaven
I could as well give health to you as that
  plate!                                           20

I.3.2 *are he* are that man  5 *good meaning* well
wishing  10 *of St. Mark* at a goldsmith's shop
in the Square of St. Mark  12 *What says he*
Throughout this scene Volpone speaks in a very
low voice, and pretends that he can neither see
nor hear very well

VOLPONE. You give, sir, what you can.
  I thank you. Your love
Hath taste in this, and shall not be unan-
  swered.
I pray you see me often.
  VOLTORE.          Yes, I shall, sir.
  VOLPONE. Be not far from me.
  MOSCA [*to Voltore*]. Do you observe that, sir?
  VOLPONE. Harken unto me still; it will
  concern you.                                     25
  MOSCA. You are a happy man, sir; know
  your good.
  VOLPONE. I cannot now last long—
  MOSCA.          You are his heir, sir.
  VOLTORE. Am I?
  VOLPONE.     I feel me going, uh! uh!
  uh! uh!
I am sailing to my port, uh! uh! uh! uh!
And I am glad I am so near my haven.      30
  MOSCA. Alas, kind gentleman. Well, we
  must all go—
  VOLTORE. But, Mosca—
  MOSCA.      Age will conquer.
  VOLTORE.             Pray thee,
  hear me.
Am I inscribed his heir for certain?
  MOSCA.             Are you?
I do beseech you, sir, you will vouchsafe
To write me i' your family. All my hopes  35
Depend upon your worship. I am lost
Except the rising sun do shine on me.
  VOLTORE. It shall both shine and warm
  thee, Mosca.
  MOSCA.                   Sir,
I am a man that have not done your love
All the worst offices. Here I wear your
  keys,                                            40
See all your coffers and your caskets locked,
Keep the poor inventory of your jewels,
Your plate, and monies; am your steward, sir,
Husband your goods here.
  VOLTORE.       But am I sole heir?
  MOSCA. Without a partner, sir, confirmed
  this morning;                                    45
The wax is warm yet, and the ink scarce dry
Upon the parchment.
  VOLTORE.        Happy, happy me!

21–22 *Your ... this* "this (the plate) gives an
idea of how much you love me"  22 *unanswered*
unrewarded  35 *To ... family* "make me a
member of your household"

By what good chance, sweet Mosca?
MOSCA.                    Your desert, sir;
I know no second cause.
    VOLTORE.                    Thy modesty
Is loth to know it; well, we shall requite
    it.                                                     50
    MOSCA. He ever liked your course, sir; that
        first took him.
I oft have heard him say how he admired
Men of your large profession, that could speak
To every cause, and things mere contraries,
Till they were hoarse again, yet all be
    law;                                                   55
That, with most quick agility, could turn,
And re-turn; make knots, and undo them;
Give forkèd counsel; take provoking gold
On either hand, and put it up. These men,
He   knew,   would   thrive   with   their
    humility.                                              60
And, for his part, he thought he should be
    bless'd
To have his heir of such a suffering spirit,
So wise, so grave, of so perplexed a tongue,
And loud withal, that would not wag, nor
    scarce
Lie still, without a fee; when every word        65
Your worship but lets fall, is a chequin!
                        (*Another knocks.*)
Who's that? One knocks. I would not have
    you seen, sir.
And yet—pretend you came and went in
    haste;
I'll fashion an excuse. And, gentle sir,
When you do come to swim in golden
    lard,                                                  70
Up to the arms in honey, that your chin
Is borne up stiff with fatness of the flood,
Think on your vassal; but remember me:
I ha' not been your worst of clients.
    VOLTORE.                         Mosca—
    MOSCA. When will you have your inventory
        brought, sir?                                      75

Or see a copy of the will? [*Calling out to the
    one knocking.*] Anon.
I'll bring 'em to you, sir. Away, be gone,
Put business i' your face.      [*Exit* VOLTORE.]
    VOLPONE.                    Excellent, Mosca!
Come hither, let me kiss thee.
    MOSCA.                         Keep you still, sir.
Here is Corbaccio.
    VOLPONE.         Set the plate away.          80
The vulture's gone, and the old raven's come.

### Scene 4

    MOSCA. Betake you to your silence, and
        your sleep.
[*Sets the plate aside.*] Stand there and mul-
    tiply. Now shall we see
A wretch who is indeed more impotent
Than this can feign to be, yet hopes to hop
Over his grave. [*Enter* CORBACCIO.] Signior
    Corbaccio!                                             5
You're very welcome, sir.
    CORBACCIO.         How does your patron?
    MOSCA. Troth, as he did, sir; no amends.
    CORBACCIO [*cupping his ear*].            What?
        mends he?
    MOSCA [*shouting*]. No, sir. He is rather
        worse.
    CORBACCIO.             That's well. Where
        is he?
    MOSCA. Upon his couch, sir, newly fall'n
        asleep.
    CORBACCIO. Does he sleep well?
    MOSCA.         No wink, sir, all this night, 10
Nor yesterday, but slumbers.
    CORBACCIO.             Good! he should take
Some counsel of physicians. I have brought
    him
An opiate here, from mine own doctor—
    MOSCA. He will not hear of drugs.
    CORBACCIO.                    Why? I myself
Stood by while 't was made, saw all th'
    ingredients,                                          15
And know it cannot but most gently work.
My life for his, 'tis but to make him sleep.
    VOLPONE [*aside*]. Ay, his last sleep, if he
        would take it.
    MOSCA.                              Sir,
He has no faith in physic.

---

51 *course* manner of acting; *took him* took his
fancy  53 *large* liberal  53–54 *speak . . . contraries*
defend any case and argue for exactly opposite
causes  54 *mere* absolute  58 *forkèd* fork-tongued;
*provoking* "provoke . . . To call to a judge or court
to take up one's cause" (*OED*)  59 *put it up*
pocket it  63 *perplexed* intricate (in the sense of
being double, speaking on either side)  66 *chequin*
a gold coin  73 *but* simply

78 *Put . . . face* "look as if you were here on a
matter of business"
I.4.4 *this* Volpone  11 *but slumbers* only dozes
19 *physic* medicine

CORBACCIO.　　　　　Say you, say you?

MOSCA. He has no faith in physic: he does think　　20

Most of your doctors are the greater danger,
And worse disease t' escape. I often have
Heard him protest that your physician
Should never be his heir.

CORBACCIO.　　　　　Not I his heir?

MOSCA. Not your physician, sir.

CORBACCIO.　　　　　O, no, no, no, 25
I do not mean it.

MOSCA.　　　　　No, sir, nor their fees
He cannot brook; he says they flay a man
Before they kill him.

CORBACCIO.　　　　　Right, I do conceive you.

MOSCA. And then, they do it by experiment,
For which the law not only doth absolve
　'em,　　30
But gives them great reward; and he is loth
To hire his death so.

CORBACCIO.　　　　　It is true, they kill
With as much license as a judge.

MOSCA.　　　　　Nay, more;
For he but kills, sir, where the law condemns,
And these can kill him too.

CORBACCIO.　　　　　Ay, or me,　　35
Or any man. How does his apoplex?
Is that strong on him still?

MOSCA.　　　　　Most violent.
His speech is broken, and his eyes are set,
His face drawn longer than 't was wont—

CORBACCIO.　　　　　How! how!
Stronger than he was wont?

MOSCA.　　　　　No, sir; his face　　40
Drawn longer than 't was wont.

CORBACCIO.　　　　　O, good.

MOSCA.　　　　　His mouth
Is ever gaping, and his eyelids hang.

CORBACCIO.　　　　　Good.

MOSCA. A freezing numbness stiffens all his joints,
And makes the color of his flesh like lead.

CORBACCIO.　　　　　'Tis good.

MOSCA. His pulse beats slow and dull.

CORBACCIO.　　Good symptoms still.　　45

---

MOSCA. And from his brain—

CORBACCIO.　　　　　Ha! How? not from his brain?

MOSCA. Yes, sir, and from his brain—

CORBACCIO.　　　　　I conceive you; good.

MOSCA. Flows a cold sweat, with a continual rheum,
Forth the resolvèd corners of his eyes.

CORBACCIO. Is't possible? Yet I am better, ha!　　50
How does he with the swimming of his head?

MOSCA. O, sir, 'tis past the scotomy; he now
Hath lost his feeling, and hath left to snort;
You hardly can perceive him that he breathes.

CORBACCIO. Excellent, excellent; sure I shall outlast him!　　55
This makes me young again, a score of years.

MOSCA. I was a-coming for you, sir.

CORBACCIO.　　　　　Has he made his will?
What has he given me?

MOSCA.　　　　　No, sir.

CORBACCIO.　　　　　Nothing? ha!

MOSCA. He has not made his will, sir.

CORBACCIO.　　　　　Oh, oh, oh.
What then did Voltore, the lawyer, here?　　60

MOSCA. He smelled a carcass, sir, when he but heard
My master was about his testament;
As I did urge him to it for your good—

CORBACCIO. He came unto him, did he? I thought so.

MOSCA. Yes, and presented him this piece of plate.　　65

CORBACCIO. To be his heir?

MOSCA.　　　　　I do not know, sir.

CORBACCIO.　　　　　True,
I know it too.

---

21 *your* used not to refer to Corbaccio's doctor, but in vague and contemptuous reference to doctors in general　26 *mean* intend　27 *flay* skin alive　28 *conceive* understand　29 *by experiment* by trying out various remedies on the patient

46 *from his brain* Drainage of fluid from the brain was believed to be one of the final stages of the disease, strong apoplexy, which Mosca is describing so carefully, symptom by symptom. . . 49 *resolvèd* relaxed　52 *scotomy* dimness of sight accompanied by dizziness　53 *left* ceased　54 *perceive him that* perceive that　56 *This . . . years* "This news makes me feel twenty years younger"　66–67 *True . . . too* Corbaccio pays no attention to what Mosca says, or does not hear him, and assumes that he has agreed that Voltore came to be made heir

MOSCA [*aside*]. By your own scale, sir.

CORBACCIO.                                          Well,
I shall prevent him yet. See, Mosca, look,
Here I have brought a bag of bright
   chequins,
Will quite weigh down his plate.

MOSCA [*taking the bag*].   Yea, marry, sir. 70
This is true physic, this your sacred medicine;
No talk of opiates to this great elixir.

   CORBACCIO. 'Tis aurum palpabile, if not
     potabile.

   MOSCA. It shall be ministered to him, in
     his bowl?

   CORBACCIO. Ay, do, do, do.

   MOSCA.                     Most blessed cordial! 75
This will recover him.

   CORBACCIO.            Yes, do, do, do.

   MOSCA. I think it were not best, sir.

   CORBACCIO.            What?

   MOSCA.                     To recover him.

   CORBACCIO. O, no, no, no; by no means.

   MOSCA.                     Why, sir, this
Will work some strange effect if he but feel it.

   CORBACCIO. 'Tis true, therefore forbear;
     I'll take my venture;                    80
Give me 't again.

   MOSCA.            At no hand. Pardon me.
You shall not do yourself that wrong, sir. I
Will so advise you, you shall have it all.

   CORBACCIO. How?

   MOSCA.            All, sir; 'tis your right,
     your own; no man
Can claim a part; 'tis yours without a
   rival,                                    85
Decreed by destiny.

   CORBACCIO.       How, how, good Mosca?

   MOSCA. I'll tell you, sir. This fit he shall
     recover—

   CORBACCIO. I do conceive you.

---

67 *By . . . scale* "measuring by your own standard"
68 *prevent* get ahead of—literally "come before"
70 *weigh down* outweigh in scales; *marry* indeed
72 *No . . . to* "There is no comparing other
medicines to . . ."; *elixir* a drug supposed to be
capable of prolonging life indefinitely  73 *aurum
palpabile* gold which can be felt; *potabile* drinkable.
Medicine having gold as its principle ingredient
was believed to be a sovereign remedy for all
diseases, and it is this compound which Mosca
and Corbaccio discuss in the following lines
75 *cordial* a medicine which stimulates the heart
80 *venture* i.e., the bag of gold  87 *recover* recover
from

---

   MOSCA.            And on first advantage
Of his gained sense, will I re-importune
   him
Unto the making of his testament,            90
And show him this. [*Points to the bag of gold.*]

   CORBACCIO.       Good, good.

   MOSCA.                     'Tis better yet,
If you will hear, sir.

   CORBACCIO.       Yes, with all my heart.

   MOSCA. Now would I counsel you, make
     home with speed;
There, frame a will whereto you shall inscribe
My master your sole heir.

   CORBACCIO.            And disinherit 95
My son?

   MOSCA. O, sir, the better; for that color
Shall make it much more taking.

   CORBACCIO.            O, but color?

   MOSCA. This will, sir, you shall send it unto
     me.
Now, when I come to enforce, as I will do,
Your cares, your watchings, and your many
   prayers,                                 100
Your more than many gifts, your this day's
   present,
And, last, produce your will; where, with-
   out thought
Or least regard unto your proper issue,
A son so brave and highly meriting,
The stream of your diverted love hath
   thrown you                               105
Upon my master, and made him your heir:
He cannot be so stupid, or stone dead,
But out of conscience and mere gratitude—

   CORBACCIO. He must pronounce me his?

   MOSCA.                     'Tis true.

   CORBACCIO.            This plot
Did I think on before.

   MOSCA.            I do believe it.    110

   CORBACCIO. Do you not believe it?

   MOSCA.                     Yes, sir—

   CORBACCIO.            Mine own project.

   MOSCA. Which, when he hath done, sir—

   CORBACCIO.       Published me his heir?

---

88 *first advantage* first opportunity  89 *gained*
regained  94 *frame* devise, write; *whereto* wherein
96 *color* pretense, outward appearance concealing
truth  97 *taking* attractive; *O, but color?* "O, is
it only pretense?"  99 *enforce* urge  103 *proper
issue* true child  108 *mere* complete  110 *think on
before* think of earlier

MOSCA. And you so certain to survive him—

CORBACCIO. Ay.

MOSCA. Being so lusty a man—

CORBACCIO. 'Tis true.

MOSCA. Yes, sir—

CORBACCIO. I thought on that too. See, how he should be   115
The very organ to express my thoughts!

MOSCA. You have not only done yourself a good—

CORBACCIO. But multiplied it on my son?

MOSCA. 'Tis right, sir.

CORBACCIO. Still my invention.

MOSCA. 'Las, sir, heaven knows
It hath been all my study, all my care,   120
(I e'en grow grey withal) how to work things—

CORBACCIO. I do conceive, sweet Mosca.

MOSCA. You are he
For whom I labor here.

CORBACCIO. Ay, do, do, do.
I'll straight about it.   [Going.]

[MOSCA now begins to bow and smile while speaking too softly for CORBACCIO to hear.]

MOSCA. Rook go with you, raven!

CORBACCIO. I know thee honest.

MOSCA. You do lie, sir.

CORBACCIO. And—   125

MOSCA. Your knowledge is no better than your ears, sir.

CORBACCIO. I do not doubt to be a father to thee.

MOSCA. Nor I to gull my brother of his blessing.

CORBACCIO. I may ha' my youth restored to me, why not?

MOSCA. Your worship is a precious ass—

CORBACCIO. What sayst thou?   130

MOSCA. I do desire your worship to make haste, sir.

CORBACCIO. 'Tis done, 'tis done, I go.
[Exit.]

VOLPONE [leaping up]. O, I shall burst!
Let out my sides, let out my sides.

MOSCA. Contain
Your flux of laughter, sir. You know this hope
Is such a bait it covers any hook.   135

VOLPONE. O, but thy working, and thy placing it!
I cannot hold; good rascal, let me kiss thee.
I never knew thee in so rare a humor.

MOSCA. Alas, sir, I but do as I am taught;
Follow your grave instructions; give 'em words;   140
Pour oil into their ears, and send them hence.

VOLPONE. 'Tis true, 'tis true. What a rare punishment
Is avarice to itself!

MOSCA. Ay, with our help, sir.

VOLPONE. So many cares, so many maladies,
So many fears attending on old age.   145
Yea, death so often called on as no wish
Can be more frequent with 'em. Their limbs faint,
Their senses dull, their seeing, hearing, going,
All dead before them; yea, their very teeth,
Their instruments of eating, failing them.   150
Yet this is reckoned life! Nay, here was one,
Is now gone home, that wishes to live longer!
Feels not his gout, nor palsy; feigns himself
Younger by scores of years, flatters his age
With confident belying it; hopes he may   155
With charms, like Aeson have his youth restored;
And with these thoughts so battens, as if fate
Would be as easily cheated on as he,

(another knocks)

115 See...be "Look, and if he isn't..." 116 very organ exact instrument 119 Still my invention "Again my idea!" (?); 'Las Alas 120 study concern 124 straight at once; Rook go with you "May you be cheated (rooked)" 126 Your... ears "Your understanding is no better than your hearing"—referring to Corbaccio's deafness and perhaps suggesting that being an ass, he has the ears of that animal 128 gull cheat; my brother Corbaccio's son. There is a glancing but significant reference here to the biblical story (Genesis 27) in which Jacob defrauds his brother Esau of Isaac's blessing by disguising himself in the skin of a goat

134 flux flood—the word also means "dysentery"; this hope i.e., to inherit Volpone's wealth 138 rare excellent; humor fanciful mood 140 grave wise 141 pour...ears flatter them with soft, easy words 148 going ability to walk 149 before them before they are 152 is (who) is 156 Aeson the father of Jason, captain of the Argonauts, who was restored to youth by the black magic of Medea 157 battens grows fat

And all turns air! Who's that, there, now?
  a third?
MOSCA. Close to your couch again; I hear
  his voice. 160
It is Corvino, our spruce merchant.
VOLPONE [lies down]. Dead.
MOSCA. Another bout, sir, with your eyes.
Who's there?

### Scene 5

[Enter CORVINO.]
MOSCA. Signior Corvino! come most wished
  for! O,
How happy were you, if you knew it, now!
CORVINO. Why? what? wherein?
MOSCA. The tardy hour is come, sir.
CORVINO. He is not dead?
MOSCA. Not dead, sir, but as good;
He knows no man.
CORVINO. How shall I do then?
MOSCA. Why, sir? 5
CORVINO. I have brought him here a pearl.
MOSCA. Perhaps he has
So much remembrance left as to know you,
  sir.
He still calls on you, nothing but your name
Is in his mouth. Is your pearl orient, sir?
CORVINO. Venice was never owner of the
  like. 10
VOLPONE [faintly]. Signior Corvino.
MOSCA. Hark.
VOLPONE. Signior Corvino.
MOSCA. He calls you; step and give it him.
  He is here, sir.
And he has brought you a rich pearl.
CORVINO. How do you, sir?
Tell him it doubles the twelfth caract.
MOSCA. Sir,
He cannot understand, his hearing's gone, 15
And yet it comforts him to see you—
CORVINO. Say
I have a diamond for him, too.
MOSCA. Best show 't, sir,
Put it into his hand; 'tis only there

He apprehends, he has his feeling yet.
[VOLPONE seizes the pearl.]
See how he grasps it!
CORVINO. 'Las, good gentleman. 20
How pitiful the sight is!
MOSCA. Tut, forget, sir.
The weeping of an heir should still be
  laughter
Under a visor.
CORVINO. Why, am I his heir?
MOSCA. Sir, I am sworn, I may not show
  the will
Till he be dead. But here has been Cor-
  baccio, 25
Here has been Voltore, here were others
  too,
I cannot number 'em, they were so many;
All gaping here for legacies; but I,
Taking the vantage of his naming you,
"Signior Corvino, Signior Corvino," took 30
Paper, and pen, and ink, and there I asked
  him
Whom he would have his heir? "Corvino."
  Who
Should be executor? "Corvino." And
To any question he was silent to,
I still interpreted the nods he made, 35
Through weakness, for consent; and sent
  home th' others,
Nothing bequeathed them but to cry and
  curse. (They embrace.)
CORVINO. O, my dear Mosca. Does he not
  perceive us?
MOSCA. No more than a blind harper.
  He knows no man,
No face of friend, nor name of any servant, 40
Who 't was that fed him last, or gave him
  drink;
Not those he hath begotten, or brought up,
Can he remember.
CORVINO. Has he children?
MOSCA. Bastards,
Some dozen, or more, that he begot on
  beggars,
Gypsies, and Jews, and black-moors when
  he was drunk. 45

159 all turns air everything becomes nothing
162 bout turn—Mosca again puts ointment in
Volpone's eyes
I.5.1 come most "arrived, just when you are
most..." 9 orient precious and lustrous 14 caract
carat 17 diamond trisyllabic: di-a-mond

23 visor mask 30 Signior Corvino Mosca imitates
Volpone's feeble voice 35 still continually 39
blind harper proverbial term for member of a
crowd

Knew you not that, sir? 'Tis the common fable,
The dwarf, the fool, the eunuch are all his;
He's the true father of his family,
In all save me, but he has given 'em nothing.

CORVINO. That's well, that's well. Art sure he does not hear us?          50

MOSCA. Sure, sir? why, look you, credit your own sense.          [*Shouts in* VOLPONE'*s ear.*]
The pox approach and add to your diseases,
If it would send you hence the sooner, sir,
For, your incontinence, it hath deserved it
Throughly and throughly, and the plague to boot.          55
You may come near, sir—Would you would once close
Those filthy eyes of yours that flow with slime
Like two frog-pits, and those same hanging cheeks,
Covered with hide instead of skin—Nay, help, sir—
That look like frozen dish-clouts set on end.          60

CORVINO. Or, like an old smoked wall, on which the rain
Ran down in streaks.

MOSCA.          Excellent, sir, speak out.
You may be louder yet; a culverin
Dischargéd in his ear would hardly bore it.

CORVINO. His nose is like a common sewer, still running.          65

MOSCA. 'Tis good! And what his mouth?

CORVINO.          A very draught.

MOSCA. O, stop it up—[*Starting to smother him.*]

CORVINO.          By no means.

MOSCA.          Pray you, let me.
Faith I could stifle him rarely with a pillow,
As well as any woman that should keep him.

CORVINO. Do as you will, but I'll be gone.

MOSCA.          Be so.          70

It is your presence makes him last so long.

CORVINO. I pray you, use no violence.

MOSCA.          No, sir? why?
Why should you be thus scrupulous, pray you, sir?

CORVINO. Nay, at your discretion.

MOSCA.          Well, good sir, be gone.

CORVINO. I will not trouble him now to take my pearl?          75

MOSCA. Puh! nor your diamond. What a needless care          [*taking the jewels*]
Is this afflicts you! Is not all here yours?
Am not I here, whom you have made? Your creature?
That owe my being to you?

CORVINO.          Grateful Mosca!
Thou art my friend, my fellow, my companion,          80
My partner, and shalt share in all my fortunes.

MOSCA. Excepting one.

CORVINO.          What's that?

MOSCA.          Your gallant wife, sir.
          [*Exit* CORVINO *hurriedly.*]
Now is he gone; we had no other means
To shoot him hence but this.

VOLPONE.          My divine Mosca!
Thou hast today outgone thyself. (*Another knocks.*)
          Who's there?          85
I will be troubled with no more. Prepare
Me music, dances, banquets, all delights;
The Turk is not more sensual in his pleasures
Than will Volpone.          [*Exit* MOSCA.]
          Let me see: a pearl!
A diamond! plate! chequins! good morning's purchase.          90
Why, this is better than rob churches, yet,
Or fat, by eating once a month a man.
          [*Enter* MOSCA.]
Who is 't?

MOSCA. The beauteous Lady Wouldbe, sir,
Wife to the English knight, Sir Politic Wouldbe—

---

46 *fable* story—not used here in the modern sense of "something invented or made up"  52 *pox* the great pox, i.e., syphilis  54 *it ... it* incontinence ... the pox  55 *Throughly ... throughly* through and through  56 *You ... sir* Mosca speaks here to Corvino  58 *frog-pits* stagnant puddles in which frogs live  60 *clouts* rags  63 *culverin* musket or a cannon  68 *rarely* excellently

---

73 *scrupulous* overly nice  75 *pearl* Volpone has the pearl and diamond clutched in his hand  88 *Turk* The Turks were noted for their extreme sensuality as well as their cruelty  90 *purchase* catch  92 *fat* grow fat

This is the style, sir, is directed me—        95
Hath sent to know how you have slept
      tonight,
And if you would be visited?
      VOLPONE.                    Not now.
Some three hours hence.—
      MOSCA.          I told the squire so much.
      VOLPONE. When I am high with mirth and
      wine, then, then.
'Fore heaven, I wonder at the desperate
      valor                                100
Of the bold English, that they dare let loose
Their wives to all encounters!
      MOSCA.                    Sir, this knight
Had not his name for nothing; he is *politic*,
And knows, howe'er his wife affect strange
      airs,
She hath not yet the face to be dishonest.  105
But had she Signior Corvino's wife's
      face—
      VOLPONE. Has she so rare a face?
      MOSCA.                    O, sir, the wonder,
The blazing star of Italy, a wench
O' the first year! a beauty ripe as harvest!
Whose skin is whiter than a swan, all
      over!                                110
Than silver, snow, or lilies! a soft lip,
Would tempt you to eternity of kissing!
And flesh that melteth in the touch to blood!
Bright as your gold! and lovely as your gold!
      VOLPONE. Why had not I known this
      before?
      MOSCA.                    Alas, sir,  115
Myself but yesterday discovered it.
      VOLPONE. How might I see her?
      MOSCA.                    O, not possible;
She's kept as warily as is your gold,
Never does come abroad, never takes air
But at a window. All her looks are sweet  120
As the first grapes or cherries, and are
      watched
As near as they are.
      VOLPONE.          I must see her—

---

95 *style* manner of speaking; *is directed me* "that
I am ordered to use"  100–102 The English were
much laughed at abroad for the freedom with
which they allowed their ladies to come and go
as they pleased and without supervision  105
*dishonest* unchaste  109 *O' the first year* of the finest
order  113 *to blood* to blushes  119 *abroad* out of
the house  122 *near* closely

      MOSCA.                              Sir,
There is a guard, of ten spies thick, upon her;
All his whole household; each of which is set
Upon his fellow, and have all their
      charge,                            125
When he goes out, when he comes in,
      examined.
      VOLPONE. I will go see her, though but at
      her window.
      MOSCA. In some disguise then.
      VOLPONE.                    That is true. I must
Maintain mine own shape still the same:
      we'll think.                    [*Exeunt.*]

### ACT II. *Scene 1*

[*The public square, before* CORVINO'S *house.*]
[*Enter* POLITIC WOULDBE, PEREGRINE.]
      SIR POLITIC. Sir, to a wise man, all the
      world's his soil.
It is not Italy, nor France, nor Europe,
That must bound me, if my fates call me
      forth.
Yet, I protest, it is no salt desire
Of seeing countries, shifting a religion,        5
Nor any disaffection to the state
Where I was bred, and unto which I owe
My dearest plots, hath brought me out;
      much less
That idle, antique, stale, grey-headed project
Of knowing men's minds, and manners,
      with Ulysses;                          10

---

124–25 *set Upon* set to watch  125 *charge* responsibility  126 *he* Corvino. On entering and
leaving his house Corvino questions his guards on
each particular of their instructions. He has, the
passage suggests, turned his house into a fortress
to guard his wife  129 *Maintain . . . shape* In a
play in which changing shape—i.e., appearance
—is a leading theme, this line is thoroughly
ambiguous; but Volpone's surface meaning is
that he agrees with Mosca that he must wear a
disguise when he goes out, for if the bilking of
the fools is to succeed he must always be thought
of as a dying man
II.1.1 *soil* country  4 *salt* keen  6 *disaffection to*
dissatisfaction with  8 *plots* schemes, projects  10
*Ulysses* Ulysses is described in the opening lines
of *The Odyssey* as a man who "roamed the wide
world and saw the cities of many peoples and
learned their ways." He became for the Renaissance the prototype of the curious traveler . . .

But a peculiar humor of my wife's,
Laid for this height of Venice, to observe,
To quote, to learn the language, and so forth.
I hope you travel, sir, with license?

PEREGRINE.                              Yes.

SIR POLITIC. I dare the safelier converse.
How long, sir,                                    15
Since you left England?

PEREGRINE.              Seven weeks.

SIR POLITIC.                    So lately!
You ha' not been with my lord ambassador?

PEREGRINE. Not yet, sir.

SIR POLITIC.              'Pray you, what
news, sir, vents our climate?
I heard, last night, a most strange thing
reported
By some of my lord's followers, and I long  20
To hear how 'twill be seconded.

PEREGRINE.              What was't, sir?

SIR POLITIC. Marry, sir, of a raven, that
should build
In a ship royal of the King's.

PEREGRINE [aside].          —This fellow,
Does he gull me, trow? or is gulled?—Your
name, sir?

SIR POLITIC. My name is Politic Wouldbe.

PEREGRINE[aside]. —O, that speaks him—  25
A knight, sir?

SIR POLITIC. A poor knight, sir.

PEREGRINE.              Your lady
Lies here, in Venice, for intelligence
Of tires, and fashions, and behavior
Among the courtesans? The fine Lady
Wouldbe?

SIR POLITIC. Yes, sir, the spider and the
bee ofttimes                                      30

Suck from one flower.

PEREGRINE.          Good Sir Politic!
I cry you mercy; I have heard much of you.
'Tis true, sir, of your raven.

SIR POLITIC.              On your knowledge?

PEREGRINE. Yes, and your lion's whelping
in the Tower.

SIR POLITIC. Another whelp!

PEREGRINE.          Another, sir.

SIR POLITIC.              Now heaven!   35
What prodigies be these? The fires at
Berwick!
And the new star! These things concurring,
strange!
And full of omen! Saw you those meteors?

PEREGRINE. I did, sir.

SIR POLITIC.              Fearful! Pray you,
sir, confirm me,
Were there three porpoises seen above the
bridge,                                            40
As they give out?

PEREGRINE.      Six, and a sturgeon, sir.

SIR POLITIC. I am astonished!

PEREGRINE.              Nay, sir, be not so;
I'll tell you a greater prodigy than these—

SIR POLITIC. What should these things
portend?

PEREGRINE.              The very day
(Let me be sure) that I put forth from
London,                                            45
There was a whale discovered in the river,
As high as Woolwich, that had waited there,
Few know how many months, for the subver-
sion

---

11 *humor* passion  12 *Laid ... height* aimed for
the latitude. Sir Politic uses an elaborate manner
of speech, and avoids the plain word whenever
he can  13 *quote* note down (the peculiarities of
the country)  14 *license* passport  17 *my lord ambassador* Sir Henry Wotton, King James' ambassador at Venice, was himself a noted intriguer
18 *vents our climate* comes from our country.
Another of Sir Pol's circumlocutions  21 *seconded*
confirmed  22 *raven* bird of ill omen; *should* used
here to mark reported speech  24 *gull* fool; *trow*
a mild expletive  25 *speaks* defines  27 *Lies* stays;
*intelligence* knowledge  28 *tires* attires, clothes
29 *courtesans* fashionable prostitutes. Venice was
famous for its courtesans

32 *cry you mercy* "ask your pardon" (for not
recognizing you)  33 *your* used indeterminately,
or to mean roughly, "that you know of"  34
*lion's whelping in the Tower* A lioness, Elizabeth,
was at this time kept in the Tower of London,
and she produced cubs in 1604 and again in 1605
36 *prodigies* strange omens  36–37 *fires ... star* In
1604 there were reports of ghostly armies fighting
at Berwick, on the Scottish border, and Kepler
discovered a new star in the constellation Ser-
pentarius ...  37 *concurring* coinciding  38 *meteors*
Meteors, because they are a disruption of the
ordinary pattern of the heavens, were taken as
ominous portents of impending social disorder
40 *the bridge* London Bridge  41 *give out* report
46 *whale* A whale did come up the Thames at
this time, within eight miles of London, and the
fearful believed that it intended to pump all the
water from the river onto the land

Of the Stode fleet.

SIR POLITIC.     Is't possible? Believe it,
'Twas either sent from Spain, or the
Archduke's!                                          50
Spinola's whale, upon my life, my credit!
Will they not leave these projects? Worthy
sir,
Some other news.

PEREGRINE.     Faith, Stone the fool is dead,
And they do lack a tavern fool extremely.

SIR POLITIC. Is Mas' Stone dead?

PEREGRINE.     He's dead, sir; why, I hope 55
You thought him not immortal? [Aside.]—
O, this knight,
Were he well known, would be a precious
thing
To fit our English stage. He that should write
But such a fellow, should be thought to feign
Extremely, if not maliciously.—

SIR POLITIC.                         Stone dead! 60

PEREGRINE. Dead. Lord, how deeply, sir,
you apprehend it!
He was no kinsman to you?

SIR POLITIC.                         That I know of.
Well, that same fellow was an unknown fool.

PEREGRINE. And yet you know him, it
seems?

SIR POLITIC.                         I did so. Sir,
I knew him one of the most dangerous
heads                                          65
Living within the state, and so I held him.

PEREGRINE. Indeed, sir?

SIR POLITIC.     While he lived, in action.
He has received weekly intelligence,
Upon my knowledge, out of the Low Coun-
tries,
For all parts of the world, in cabbages; 70

And those dispensed, again, t' ambassadors,
In oranges, musk-melons, apricots,
Lemons, pome-citrons, and suchlike; some-
times
In Colchester oysters, and your Selsey
cockles.

PEREGRINE. You make me wonder.

SIR POLITIC.     Sir, upon my knowledge. 75
Nay, I have observed him at your public
ordinary
Take his advertisement from a traveler,
A concealed statesman, in a trencher of meat;
And, instantly, before the meal was done,
Convey an answer in a toothpick.

PEREGRINE.                         Strange!     80
How could this be, sir?

SIR POLITIC.          Why, the meat was cut
So like his chàracter, and so laid as he
Must easily read the cipher.

PEREGRINE.                         I have heard
He could not read, sir.

SIR POLITIC.          So 'twas given out,
In policy, by those that did employ him; 85
But he could read, and had your languages,
And to 't, as sound a noddle—

PEREGRINE.                         I have heard, sir,
That your baboons were spies, and that
they were
A kind of subtle nation near to China.

SIR POLITIC. Ay, ay, your Mamuluchi.
Faith, they had                              90
Their hand in a French plot, or two; but
they
Were so extremely given to women as

_____

49 _Stode_ city at the mouth of the Elbe 50 _Archduke_ ruler of the Spanish Netherlands 51 _Spinola_ the Spanish general in the Netherlands at this time. He was extremely successful and was believed by the gullible in England to be fantastically clever in devising cunning schemes and "secret weapons" 53 _Stone_ a well-known London clown who had been flogged not long before _Volpone_ was written for making mocking speeches about the Lord Admiral 55 _Mas'_ master 61 _apprehend_ both "feel" and "understand" 62 _That_ not that 63 _unknown_ misinterpreted 65 _dangerous heads_ sub- versive persons 67 _action_ doing—i.e., he was an active spy, not merely passively unfriendly to the state

73 _pome-citrons_ lemon-like fruit 76 _ordinary_ tavern 77 _advertisement_ information 78 _concealed statesman_ disguised agent; _trencher_ platter 80 _toothpick_ All of Sir Politic's descriptions of plots, spies, and methods of espionage are burlesques not of genuine activities but of those imagined by the foolish and timorous in the days immediately after the discovery of the Gunpowder Plot, a Catholic attempt to blow up King James and the assembled Parliament on November 5, 1605 82 _chàracter_ handwriting, code—accented on second syllable, cha-ràc-ter 85 _policy_ craft 86 _had . . . languages_ was a skilled linguist 87 _to't_ in addtion; _noddle_ head, intelligence 89 _subtle_ cunning and devious 90 _Mamuluchi_ plural form of "Mameluke," former Christian slaves of the Turks who became rulers of Egypt during the thirteenth century . . . 92 _given to_ fond of

They made discovery of all; yet I
Had my advices here, on Wednesday last,
From one of their own coat, they were
    returned,           95
Made their relations, as the fashion is,
And now stand fair for fresh employment.
    PEREGRINE [aside].—       'Heart!
This Sir Pol will be ignorant of nothing—
It seems, sir, you know all.
    SIR POLITIC.      Not all, sir. But
I have some general notions; I do love    100
To note and to observe: though I live out,
Free from the active torrent, yet I'd mark
The currents and the passages of things
For mine own private use; and know the ebbs
And flows of state.
    PEREGRINE.    Believe it, sir, I hold   105
Myself in no small tie unto my fortunes
For casting me thus luckily upon you,
Whose knowledge, if your bounty equal it,
May do me great assistance in instruction
For my behavior, and my bearing, which   110
Is yet so rude and raw.
    SIR POLITIC.    Why? came you forth
Empty of rules for travel?
    PEREGRINE.      Faith, I had
Some common ones, from out that vulgar
    grammar,
Which he that cried Italian to me, taught
    me.
    SIR POLITIC. Why, this it is that spoils all
    our brave bloods,       115
Trusting our hopeful gentry unto pedants,
Fellows of outside, and mere bark. You seem
To be a gentleman, of ingenuous race—
I not profess it, but my fate hath been

To be where I have been consulted with  120
In this high kind, touching some great
    men's sons,
Persons of blood and honor—
    PEREGRINE.        Who be these, sir?

*Scene 2*

[*Enter* MOSCA *and* NANO, *disguised as mounte-
bank's attendants, with materials to erect
a scaffold stage. A crowd follows them.*]
    MOSCA. Under that window, there 't must
    be. The same.
    SIR POLITIC. Fellows to mount a bank!
    Did your instructor
In the dear tongues, never discourse to
    you
Of the Italian mountebanks?
    PEREGRINE.       Yes, sir.
    SIR POLITIC.         Why,
Here shall you see one.
    PEREGRINE.    They are quacksalvers,  5
Fellows that live by venting oils and drugs.
    SIR POLITIC. Was that the character he
    gave you of them?
    PEREGRINE. As I remember.
    SIR POLITIC.       Pity his ignorance.
They are the only knowing men of Europe!
Great general scholars, excellent phy-
    sicians,       10
Most admired statesmen, professed favorites
And cabinet counselors to the greatest
    princes!
The only languaged men of all the world!
    PEREGRINE. And I have heard they are
    most lewd impostors,

---

93 *discovery* disclosure  94 *advices* dispatches  95 *coat* party, faction  96 *relations* reports  97 *stand fair* are ready; *'Heart* God's Heart; curses were frequently formed in this manner, e.g., 'swounds, God's wounds  101–102 *though . . . torrent* "though I am not actively engaged in political affairs"  106 *in . . . tie* much obliged  108 *if . . . it* "if you are as generous as you are wise"  113 *vulgar grammar* ordinary grammar book  114 *cried* pronounced, i.e., taught  115 *brave bloods* gallants, well-born young men  117 *outside . . . bark* mere show and pretense—"bark" seems also to be a poor pun going back to "cried"  118 *ingenuous race* noble lineage  119 *I . . . it* "It [the education of high-born young men] is not my profession"

121 *high kind* important matter; *touching* bearing on.  122 *blood* nobility
II.2. Stage direction: there is no longer any exact equivalent of the mountebank and his show, but the old-fashioned Indian Medicine Man with his traveling wagon, his show, his "snake oil," and his "spiel" was in the direct line of descent from the mountebank . . . 2 *bank* Sir Pol is apparently correct, for the accepted etymology of "mountebank" is the Italian *monta in banco*. Bench (Italian, *banco*) here means the basic platform stage—simply boards laid on trestles with perhaps a cloth backdrop . . . 3 *dear* esteemed  6 *venting* vending  12 *cabinet counselors* close advisers  14 *lewd* ignorant

Made all of terms and shreds; no less
beliers                                                  15
Of great men's favors than their own vile
medicines;
Which they will utter upon monstrous oaths,
Selling that drug for twopence, ere they
part,
Which they have valued at twelve crowns
before.
SIR POLITIC. Sir, calumnies are answered
best with silence.                              20
Yourself shall judge. Who is it mounts, my
friends?
MOSCA. Scoto of Mantua, sir.
SIR POLITIC.                         Is't he? Nay, then
I'll proudly promise, sir, you shall behold
Another man than has been phantasied to
you.
I wonder, yet, that he should mount his
bank                                                      25
Here, in this nook, that has been wont
t'appear
In face of the Piazza! Here he comes
[*Enter* VOLPONE, *disguised as a mountebank.*]
VOLPONE [*to* NANO]. Mount, zany.
GREGE.                                        Follow,
follow, follow, follow, follow.
                    [VOLPONE *mounts the stage.*]
SIR POLITIC. See how the people follow
him! He's a man
May write ten thousand crowns in bank
here. Note,                                         30
Mark but his gesture. I do use to observe
The state he keeps in getting up!
PEREGRINE.                         'Tis worth it, sir.
VOLPONE. Most noble gentlemen, and my
worthy patrons, it may seem strange that
I, your Scoto Mantuano, who was ever      35
wont to fix my bank in face of the public

Piazza, near the shelter of the Portico to
the Procuratia, should now, after eight
months' absence from this illustrious city
of Venice, humbly retire myself into an      40
obscure nook of the Piazza.
SIR POLITIC. Did not I now object the
same?
PEREGRINE.                                    Peace, sir.
VOLPONE. Let me tell you: I am not, as
your Lombard proverb saith, cold on my
feet, or content to part with my com-      45
modities at a cheaper rate than I accustomed.
Look not for it. Nor that the calumnious
reports of that impudent detractor, and
shame to our profession, Allessandro Buttone
I mean, who gave out, in public, I was      50
condemned a *sforzato* to the galleys, for
poisoning the Cardinal Bembo's—cook, hath
at all attached, much less dejected me.
No, no, worthy gentlemen; to tell you true,
I cannot endure to see the rabble of these      55
ground *ciarlitani* that spread their cloaks
on the pavement as if they meant to do
feats of activity, and then come in lamely
with their moldy tales out of Boccaccio,
like stale Tabarin, the fabulist: some of      60
them discoursing their travels, and of their
tedious captivity in the Turk's galleys, when,
indeed, were the truth known, they were

38 *Procuratia* residence, along the north side of the
Piazza del San Marco, for the Procurators, important civic officials   42 *object* bring before the
eyes, visualize—another of Sir Pol's extravagant
words   44–45 *cold on my feet* (*Aver freddo a 'piedi*)
"to have cold at the feet," be forced to sell cheap
49 *Buttone* a rival mountebank   51 *sforzato* galley
slave   52 *Bembo's*—the dash suggests that Volpone
is about to say "mistress." Cardinal Bembo (1470–
1547) was a famous Italian humanist noted for
his pure Latin style and for the beautiful culmi-
nating speech he delivers in Castiglione's *Il
Cortegiano* (1528) on the progress from love of
earthly beauty to love of the spiritual . . .   53
*attached* caused me to be arrested (?)   56 *ground
ciarlitani* literally "ground charlatans," i.e., the
poorer quacks who performed on the pavement
rather than on a platform   58 *feats of activity*
tumbling   59–60 *Boccaccio . . . fabulist* Giovanni
Boccaccio (1313?–1375) whose collection of tales
(fables) *The Decameron* was a storehouse for later
storytellers   60 *Tabarin* a famous zany in an
Italian traveling company of comedians—the
name means "short cloak"   61 *discoursing* talking of

15 *terms* technical expressions; *shreds* bits and
pieces of language such as proverbs, quotations
from the classics   15–16 *beliers . . . favors* men who
lie about the esteem in which they are held by
the great   17 *utter* sell   22 *Scoto of Mantua* a
sixteenth-century Italian actor and leader of a
troupe of players licensed by the Duke of Mantua.
Scoto was a renowned juggler and sleight-of-
hand artist . . .   24 *phantasied* fancied, presented
to the imagination   27 *In face of* in the front,
or main, part   28 *zany* clown—see note to line
60 below   32 *state* formality of bearing

the Christian's galleys, where very temperately they eat bread, and drunk 65 water, as a wholesome penance enjoined them by their confessors, for base pilferies.

SIR POLITIC. Note but his bearing and contempt of these.

VOLPONE. These turdy-facy-nasty-paty-lousy-fartical rogues, with one poor 70 groats-worth of unprepared antimony, finely wrapped up in several *scartoccios*, are able, very well, to kill their twenty a week, and play; yet these meager, starved spirits, who have half stopped the organs of their 75 minds with earthy oppilations, want not their favorers among your shriveled salad-eating artisans, who are overjoyed that they may have their half-pe'rth of physic; though it purge 'em into another world, 't makes 80 no matter.

SIR POLITIC. Excellent! ha' you heard better language, sir?

VOLPONE. Well, let 'em go. And, gentlemen, honorable gentlemen, know that for this time our bank, being thus removed 85 from the clamors of the *canaglia*, shall be the scene of pleasure and delight; for I have nothing to sell, little or nothing to sell.

SIR POLITIC. I told you, sir, his end.

PEREGRINE.                     You did so, sir.

VOLPONE. I protest, I and my six ser- 90 vants are not able to make of this precious liquor so fast as it is fetched away from my lodging by gentlemen of your city, strangers of the Terra Firma, worshipful merchants, ay, and senators too, who, ever since 95 my arrival, have detained me to their uses by their splendidous liberalities. And worthily. For what avails your rich man to have

his magazines stuft with *moscadelli*, or of the purest grape, when his physicians pre- 100 scribe him, on pain of death, to drink nothing but water cocted with aniseeds? O health! health! the blessing of the rich! the riches of the poor! who can buy thee at too dear a rate, since there is no enjoying this 105 world without thee? Be not then so sparing of your purses, honorable gentlemen, as to abridge the natural course of life—

PEREGRINE. You see his end?

SIR POLITIC.                 Ay, is't not good?

VOLPONE. For, when a humid flux, or 110 catarrh, by the mutability of air falls from your head into an arm or shoulder, or any other part, take you a ducat, or your chequin of gold, and apply to the place affected: see, what good effect it can work. No, 115 no, 'tis this blessed *unguento*, this rare extraction, that hath only power to disperse all malignant humors that proceed either of hot, cold, moist, or windy causes—

PEREGRINE. I would he had put in dry too.

SIR POLITIC.         'Pray you, observe. 120

VOLPONE. To fortify the most indigest and crude stomach, ay, were it of one that through extreme weakness vomited blood, applying only a warm napkin to the place, after the unction and fricace; for the 125 vertigine in the head, putting but a drop into your nostrils, likewise behind the ears; a most sovereign and approved remedy: the *mal caduco*, cramps, convulsions, paralyses, epilepsies, *tremor cordia*, retired 130 nerves, ill vapours of the spleen, stoppings

65 *eat* ate  66–67 *enjoined them* prescribed for them 71 *unprepared* not made fit for human use  72 *several* separate; *scartoccios* papers—used to contain medicines, but may here refer also to plays 75–76 *stopped . . . oppilations* "have become so concerned with gross, mundane activities that their minds have ceased to work"; *oppilations* obstructions  77 *salad* probably has meaning here of "raw, unprepared vegetables"  78 *artisans* workers 79 *half-pe'rth* half-pennyworth; *physic* medicine 86 *canaglia* canaille, rabble  94 *Terra Firma* Venetian possessions on the mainland  97–98 *worthily* properly

99 *magazines* storehouses; *moscadelli* muscatel wines 102 *cocted* boiled  109 *end* goal  110–12 *flux, or catarrh* Volpone's medicine throughout this speech is based on the medieval and Renaissance theory of the four humors: . . . blood, phlegm, choler, and melancholy. . . . When the humors became seriously unbalanced, sickness resulted, and the "humid flux" Volpone refers to is an excess of heavy wetness flowing out of the head into the body—we should probably call it arthritis . . .  116 *unguento* salve  118 *humors* see note to lines 110–12  122 *crude* sour  125 *fricace* massage  126 *vertigine* dizziness; Volpone is now simply reeling off medical jargon in the manner of a pitchman  129 *mal caduco* epilepsy  130 *tremor cordia* palpitation of the heart  130–31 *retired nerves* shrunken sinews

of the liver, the stone, the strangury, *hernia
ventosa, iliaca passio;* stops a *dysenteria* immediately; easeth the torsion of the small
guts; and cures *melancholia hypocondriaca,* 135
being taken and applied according to my
printed receipt. (*Pointing to his bill and his
glass.*) For, this is the physician, this the
medicine; this counsels, this cures; this
gives the direction, this works the effect; 140
and, in sum, both together may be termed
an abstract of the theoric and practic in the
Aesculapian art. 'Twill cost you eight crowns.
And, Zan Fritada, pray thee sing a verse,
extempore, in honor of it.                              145

    SIR POLITIC. How do you like him, sir?
    PEREGRINE.                       Most strangely, I!
    SIR POLITIC. Is not his language rare?
    PEREGRINE.                           But alchemy
I never heard the like, or Broughton's books.

SONG

Had old Hippocrates or Galen,
That to their books put med'cines all in, 150
But known this secret, they had never,
Of which they will be guilty ever,
Been murderers of so much paper,
Or wasted many a hurtless taper.
No Indian drug had e'er been famèd, 155
Tobacco, sassafras not namèd;
Ne yet of guacum one small stick, sir,
Nor Raymond Lully's great elixir.

———

132 *the stone* kidney stone; *strangury* difficult
urination 132–33 *hernia ventosa* tumor containing
gas 133 *iliaca passio* cramps of the small intestine
137 *receipt* recipe 137–38 Stage direction: *bill*
prescription; *glass* bottle containing medicine 138
*this . . . this* he points first to the bill and then to
the glass 142 *abstract* compendium; *theoric* theory;
*practic* practice 143 *Aesculapian art* medicine;
Aesculapius was the Roman god of medicine 144
*Zan Fritada* a famous Italian comedian. The order
is probably addressed to Nano, who is playing
zany to Volpone's mountebank 147 *But* except
for 148 *Broughton's books* Hugh Broughton (1549–
1617) was a Puritan minister and scholar who
wrote a number of strange books on religious
subjects. Jonson's intense dislike of the Puritans
regularly finds expression in his plays 149 *Hippocrates or Galen* two famous Greek physicians
154 *hurtless* harmless 156 *Tobacco, sassafras* both
used as medicines 157 *Ne* nor; *guacum* drug extracted from resin of guacium tree 158 *Raymond
Lully* renowned medieval alchemist supposed to

Ne had been known the Danish Gonswart,
Or Paracelsus, with his long sword.      160
    PEREGRINE. All this, yet, will not do; eight
crowns is high.
    VOLPONE. No more. Gentlemen, if I had
but time to discourse to you the miraculous
effects of this my oil, surnamed *Oglio del
Scoto,* with the countless catalogue of 165
those I have cured of th'aforesaid, and
many more diseases; the patents and privileges of all the princes and commonwealths
of Christendom; or but the depositions of
those that appeared on my part, before 170
the signiory of the *Sanita* and most learned
college of physicians; where I was authorized,
upon notice taken of the admirable virtues
of my medicaments, and mine own excellency in matter of rare and unknown 175
secrets, not only to disperse them publicly
in this famous city, but in all the territories
that happily joy under the government of
the most pious and magnificent states of Italy.
But may some other gallant fellow say, 180
"O, there be divers that make profession to
have as good and as experimented receipts
as yours." Indeed, very many have assayed,
like apes, in imitation of that, which is really
and essentially in me, to make of this 185
oil; bestowed great cost in furnaces, stills,
alembics, continual fires, and preparation
of the ingredients (as indeed there goes
to it six hundred several simples, besides some
quantity of human fat, for the con- 190

———

have discovered the elixir; *elixir* a drug believed
by alchemists to be capable of prolonging life
and health indefinitely 159 *Gonswart* identity
not known certainly, but perhaps the theologian Johannes Wessel of Gansfort (1420–1489)
160 *Paracelsus . . . long sword* Paracelsus was one
of the strangest and most noted of the early
Renaissance physician-magicians. Alchemy and
physic were for him but part of one subject. He
was supposed to have kept his secret "essences"
in the handle of his sword 164–65 *Oglio del Scoto*
"Dr. Scoto's Oil" 167 *patents* official certificates
conferring certain rights 167–68 *privileges* special
ordinances giving honors to an individual 171
*signiory . . . Sanita* Venetian board for granting
medical licenses 181 *divers* many 182 *experimented*
tested 186–87 *furnaces, stills, alembics* pieces of
alchemical equipment 189 *several simples* separate
herbs

glutination, which we buy of the anatomists),
but, when these practitioners come to the
last decoction, blow, blow, puff, puff, and
all flies in fumo. Ha, ha ha! Poor wretches!
I rather pity their folly and indiscretion  195
than their loss of time and money; for those
may be recovered by industry; but to be a
fool born is a disease incurable. For myself,
I always from my youth have endeavoured
to get the rarest secrets, and book  200
them, either in exchange or for money; I
spared nor cost nor labor where anything
was worthy to be learned. And gentlemen,
honorable gentlemen, I will undertake, by
virtue of chemical art, out of the  205
honorable hat that covers your head to
extract the four elements, that is to say, the
fire, air, water, and earth, and return you
your felt without burn or stain. For, whilst
others have been at the balloo, I have  210
been at my book, and am now past the
craggy paths of study, and come to the
flowery plains of honor and reputation.

SIR POLITIC. I do assure you, sir, that is
his aim.

VOLPONE. But to our price—

PEREGRINE. And that withal, Sir Pol. 215

VOLPONE. You all know, honorable gentlemen, I never valued this *ampulla*, or vial,
at less than eight crowns, but for this time
I am content to be deprived of it for six; six
crowns is the price, and less in courtesy  220
I know you cannot offer me; take it or
leave it, howsoever, both it and I am at your
service. I ask you not as the value of the
thing, for then I should demand of you a
thousand crowns; so the Cardinals  225
Montalto, Farnese, the great Duke of Tus-
cany, my gossip, with divers other princes
have given me; but I despise money. Only

to show my affection to you, honorable gentlemen, and your illustrious state here,  230
I have neglected the messages of these princes,
mine own offices, framed my journey hither,
only to present you with the fruits of my
travels. [*To* NANO *and* MOSCA.] Tune your
voices once more to the touch of your  235
instruments, and give the honorable assembly some delightful recreation.

PEREGRINE. What monstrous and most
painful circumstance
Is here, to get some three or four *gazets*!
Some threepence i' th' whole, for that 'twill
come to.  240

SONG

You that would last long, list to my
song,
Make no more coil, but buy of this oil.
Would you be ever fair? and young?
Stout of teeth? and strong of tongue?
Tart of palate? quick of ear?  245
Sharp of sight? of nostril clear?
Moist of hand? and light of foot?
Or I will come nearer to't,
Would you live free from all diseases?
Do the act your mistress pleases,  250
Yet fright all aches from your bones?
Here's a med'cine for the nones.

VOLPONE. Well, I am in a humor, at this
time, to make a present of the small quantity
my coffer contains to the rich, in  255
courtesy, and to the poor, for God's sake.
Wherefore, now mark: I asked you six crowns,
and six crowns at other times you have paid
me; you shall not give me six crowns, nor
five, nor four, nor three, nor two, nor  260
one; nor half a ducat; no, nor a *moccenigo*.
Six-pence it will cost you, or six hundred
pound—expect no lower price, for by the
banner of my front, I will not bate a baga-

193 *decoction* boiling to extract the essences;
*blow ... puff* Volpone is imitating the alchemist
blowing on his fire to get it to the proper heat
194 *fumo* smoke  199 *from* since  200 *book* note
201 *in exchange* by trading (secret for secret)  202
*nor ... nor* neither ... nor  205 *chemical* alchemical
210 *balloo* a Venetian game in which a large ball
was tossed high in the air  211 *at my book* in
careful study  215 *withal* as well  217 *ampulla*
container  223 *as the value* as (the oil) is valued;
what it is worth  227 *gossip* godfather

232 *offices* duties; *framed* directed  238 *painful circumstance* careful arrangement of details, i.e.,
setting the scene in preparation for the sale  239
*gazets* Venetian coin worth a penny  240 *i' th'
whole* altogether  242 *coil* row, fuss  245 *Tart*
keen  248 *come nearer to't* "get down to what is
most important"  251 *aches* disyllabic, "aitches"
252 *nones* nonce, occasion  253 *humor* mood
261 *moccenigo* small coin  264 *banner ... front* the
mountebank's banner displayed before his stand
which lists diseases and cures; *bate* abate, subtract

tine; that I will have, only, a pledge of 265
your loves, to carry something from amongst
you to show I am not contemned by you.
Therefore, now, toss your handkerchiefs,
cheerfully, cheerfully; and be advertised that
the first heroic spirit that deigns to grace 270
me with a handkerchief, I will give it a little
remembrance of something beside, shall please
it better than if I had presented it with a
double pistolet.

PEREGRINE. Will you be that heroic spark,
Sir Pol? 275

(CELIA *at the window throws down her
handkerchief*.)

O see! the window has prevented you.

VOLPONE. Lady, I kiss your bounty, and
for this timely grace you have done your poor
Scoto of Mantua, I will return you, over and
above my oil, a secret of that high and 280
inestimable nature shall make you forever
enamored on that minute wherein your eye
first descended on so mean, yet not altogether to be despised, an object. Here is a poulder concealed in this paper of which, 285
if I should speak to the worth, nine thousand
volumes were but as one page, that page as a
line, that line as a word: so short is this pilgrimage of man, which some call life, to the
expressing of it. Would I reflect on the 290
price? Why, the whole world were but as an
empire, that empire as a province, that province as a bank, that bank as a private purse
to the purchase of it. I will, only, tell you:
it is the poulder that made Venus a 295
goddess (given her by Apollo), that kept her
perpetually young, cleared her wrinkles,
firmed her gums, filled her skin, colored her
hair. From her derived to Helen, and at the
sack of Troy unfortunately lost; till now, 300
in this our age, it was as happily recovered

by a studious antiquary out of some ruins of
Asia, who sent a moiety of it to the court of
France (but much sophisticated), wherewith
the ladies there now color their hair. 305
The rest, at this present, remains with me;
extracted to a quintessence, so that wherever
it but touches in youth it perpetually pre-
serves, in age restores the complexion; seats
your teeth, did they dance like virginal 310
jacks, firm as a wall; makes them white as
ivory, that were black as—

### Scene 3

[*Enter* CORVINO.]

CORVINO [*shouting up to* CELIA]. Spite o' the
devil, and my shame! [*To* VOLPONE.]
Come down here;
Come down! No house but mine to make
your scene?

(*He beats away the mountebank, etc.*)

Signior Flaminio, will you down, sir?
down?
What, is my wife your Franciscina, sir?
No windows on the whole Piazza, here, 5
To make your properties, but mine? but
mine?
Heart! ere tomorrow I shall be new chris-
tened,
And called the Pantalone di Besogniosi
About the town. [*Exit.*]

PEREGRINE. What should this mean, Sir
Pol?

---

265 *only* alone 267 *contemned* despised 269 *be
advertised* understand 271 *it* him 274 *double
pistolet* valuable Spanish gold coin 275 *spark* man
of fashion 275 Stage direction: *Celia at window*
Celia is on the upper stage above and at the rear
of the Elizabethan stage, or at a windowed pro-
jection to the side of this balcony 276 *prevented*
literally "come before," anticipated 281 *shall*
which shall—Jonson, like other Elizabethan
writers, frequently omits the relative pronoun
284–85 *poulder* powder 286 *to* of 299 *Helen*
Helen of Troy

302 *antiquary* scholar 303 *moiety* part 304 *sophisticated* adulterated 307 *extracted . . . quintessence*
"refined to its pure essence" 310–11 *virginal jacks*
The virginal was a small spinet without legs,
and its "jack" was a board with quills which
plucked the strings as the keys were played. But
the reference here is probably to the keys, which
resemble teeth
II.3.1 *Spite . . . devil* "manifestation of the devil's
hatred of man," i.e., woman 2 *scene* Although
the literal meaning applies well enough here, the
larger meaning of "scene" as "setting for a play"
should not be overlooked, for Volpone has just
acted out a play of his own devising 3–8
*Flaminio . . . Franciscina . . . Pantalone* These are all
names connected with the *commedia dell' arte*, the
popular Italian street comedy of the sixteenth
and seventeenth centuries . . . 6 *properties* stage
properties, set

SIR POLITIC. Some trick of state, believe it.
I will home.                                      10
PEREGRINE. It may be some design on you.
SIR POLITIC                           I know not.
I'll stand upon my guard.
PEREGRINE.              It is your best, sir.
SIR POLITIC. This three weeks all my advices,
all my letters,
They have been intercepted.
PEREGRINE.                  Indeed, sir?
Best have a care.
SIR POLITIC.    Nay, so I will.      [*Exit.*]
PEREGRINE.                    This knight, 15
I may not lose him for my mirth, till
night.                                 [*Exit.*]


                  *Scene 4*

[VOLPONE's *house.* VOLPONE *and* MOSCA.]
VOLPONE. O, I am wounded!
MOSCA.              Where, sir?
VOLPONE.                  Not without;
Those blows were nothing, I could bear
them ever.
But angry Cupid, bolting from her eyes,
Hath shot himself into me like a flame;
Where, now, he flings about his burning
heat,                                      5
As in a furnace an ambitious fire
Whose vent is stopped. The fight is all within
me.
I cannot live except thou help me, Mosca;
My liver melts, and I, without the hope
Of some soft air from her refreshing
breath,                                    10
Am but a heap of cinders.
MOSCA.              'Las, good sir!
Would you had never seen her!
VOLPONE.            Nay, would thou
Hadst never told me of her.
MOSCA.              Sir, 'tis true;
I do confess I was unfortunate,

And you unhappy; but I'm bound in
conscience,                                15
No less than duty, to effect my best
To your release of torment, and I will, sir.
VOLPONE. Dear Mosca, shall I hope?
MOSCA.                Sir, more than dear,
I will not bid you to despair of aught
Within a human compass.
VOLPONE.            O, there spoke 20
My better angel. Mosca, take my keys,
Gold, plate, and jewels, all's at thy devotion;
Employ them how thou wilt; nay, coin
me too,
So thou in this but crown my longings—
Mosca?
MOSCA. Use but your patience.
VOLPONE.            So I have.
MOSCA.              I doubt not   25
To bring success to your desires.
VOLPONE.                Nay, then,
I not repent me of my late disguise.
MOSCA. If you can horn him, sir, you
need not.
VOLPONE.                    True.
Besides, I never meant him for my heir.
Is not the color o' my beard and eyebrows 30
To make me known?
MOSCA.          No jot.
VOLPONE.            I did it well.
MOSCA. So well, would I could follow you
in mine,
With half the happiness; and, yet, I would
Escape your epilogue.
VOLPONE.        But were they gulled
With a belief that I was Scoto?
MOSCA.              Sir,      35

---

20 *compass* reach, possibility of achievement  22
*devotion* use   23 *coin* mint, turn to gold—but the
word often had the meaning of counterfeiting
24 *crown* satisfy, bring to fulfillment. A crown was
also a coin;—*Mosca?* A delay is indicated here;
Mosca says nothing for a time until Volpone
impatiently queries him  27 *not* do not  28 *horn*
"give him a pair of horns," i.e., cuckold him
30–31 *Is . . . known* "Will not the distinctive color
[red] . . . identify me?"  31 *No jot* not a bit  32
*mine* i.e., "my disguise and playing"  34 *your
epilogue* your end, i.e., the beating. But Mosca's
comment refers on another level to the "epilogue" he plans to all Volpone's deception:
bilking him of his fortune  34 *gulled* fooled,
taken in

---

10 *home* go home  11 *design* plot  12 *It . . . best*
"You were best to do so"
II.4.1 *without* outside, on the body  2 *Those blows*
(given him by Corvino)  3 *bolting* springing, but
also "shooting." A bolt is an arrow, and "Cupid's
bolt" was a standard figure of speech; *her* Celia's
6 *ambitious* swelling  9 *liver* the supposed seat of
violent passions such as love or hate

Scoto himself could hardly have distinguished!
I have not time to flatter you now; we'll
part,
And as I prosper, so applaud my art.

[*Exeunt.*]

### Scene 5

[corvino's *house.*]

[*Enter* corvino, celia.]

corvino. Death of mine honor, with the
city's fool?
A juggling, tooth-drawing, prating mounte-
bank?
And at a public window? where, whilst he,
With his strained action, and his dole of faces,
To his drug-lecture draws your itching
ears,                                                5
A crew of old, unmarried, noted lechers
Stood leering up like satyrs: and you smile
Most graciously, and fan your favors forth,
To give your hot spectators satisfaction!
What, was your mountebank their call?
their whistle?                                    10
Or were y' enamored on his copper rings?
His saffron jewel, with the toad stone in 't?
Or his embroider̀ed suit, with the cope-stitch,
Made of a hearse cloth? or his old tilt-
feather?
Or his starched beard! Well, you shall have
him, yes.                                         15

He shall come home and minister unto you
The fricace for the mother. Or, let me see,
I think you'd rather mount? would you
mount?
Why, if you'll mount, you may; yes truly,
you may,
And so you may be seen, down to th' foot.  20
Get you a cittern, Lady Vanity,
And be a dealer with the virtuous man;
Make one. I'll but protest myself a cuckold,
And save your dowry. I am a Dutchman, I!
For if you thought me an Italian,            25
You would be damned ere you did this,
you whore!
Thou'dst tremble to imagine that the murder
Of father, mother, brother, all thy race,
Should follow as the subject of my justice.
celia. Good sir, have patience!
corvino.   What couldst thou propose   30
Less to thyself than in this heat of wrath,
And stung with my dishonor, I should strike
[ *waves his sword* ]
This steel into thee, with as many stabs
As thou wert gazed upon with goatish eyes?
celia. Alas, sir, be appeased! I could
not think                                         35
My being at the window should more now
Move your impatience than at other times.
corvino. No? not to seek and entertain
a parley
With a known knave? before a multitude?
You were an actor with your handker-
chief,                                            40

---

II.5.2 *tooth-drawing* one of the major activities of
itinerant quacks   3 *public* i.e., opening on the
square   4 *strained action* overdone theatrical
gestures; *dole of faces* repertory of masks or facial
expressions   7 *satyrs* mythological demi-gods
noted for their cruelty and lechery   10 *call* "a
cry used to attract birds" (*OED*)   11–15 *copper
rings . . . starched beard* The mountebank then, like
all pitchmen still, wore elaborate costume and
make-up to attract his audience   12 *toad stone*
Many believed that the toad had a jewel between
his eyes which had magical properties   13 *cope-
stitch* The exact meaning is uncertain but doubtless it was a fancy, large stitch of some type
which stood out on the ornate embroidered suit
14 *hearse-cloths* rich hangings supported by the
hearse, the framework over a tomb. The implication here is that the mountebank has stolen,
or at least bought second-hand, these funeral
draperies for his clothes; *tilt-feather* a large, ornate
feather or plume worn in helmets   15 *starched
beard* one of the extreme fashions of the time

17 *fricace . . . mother* massage for an attack of
hysteria—perhaps a standard medical treatment,
but Corvino is also suggesting that Volpone
will seduce Celia   18 *mount* Corvino is again
punning in an unpleasant manner. Celia, he
suggests, may join the mountebank's troupe,
mount the bank; and may also mount the
mountebank   21 *cittern* zither; *Lady Vanity* stock
character in English morality plays   22 *dealer*
prostitute; *virtuous man* pun on "virtuoso"
23 *Make one* "make a bargain"; *protest* declare
24 *save . . . dowry* By law if a husband could show
that his wife had been unfaithful, he gained
possession of her dowry, which otherwise
remained in the wife's control during her lifetime
24–25 *Dutchman . . . Italian* By popular belief the
Dutch were phlegmatic while the Italians were
quick to anger and terrible in revenge   30–31
*What . . . thyself* "What less could you expect?"
38 *parley* conversation

Which he, most sweetly, kissed in the receipt.
And might, no doubt, return it with a letter,
And point the place where you might meet:
your sister's,
Your mother's, or your aunt's might serve
the turn.
    CELIA. Why, dear sir, when do I make these
    excuses?                                         45
Or ever stir abroad but to the church?
And that so seldom—
    CORVINO.              Well, it shall be less;
And thy restraint before was liberty
To what I now decree, and therefore mark
me.
First, I will have this bawdy light dammed
up;                                                  50
And till't be done, some two, or three yards
off
I'll chalk a line, o'er which if thou but chance
To set thy desp'rate foot, more hell, more
horror,
More wild, remorseless rage shall seize on thee
Than on a conjurer that had heedless left  55
His circle's safety ere his devil was laid.
Then, here's a lock which I will hang upon
thee,
And, now I think on 't, I will keep thee back-
wards;
Thy lodging shall be backwards, thy walks
backwards,
Thy prospect—all be backwards, and no
pleasure,                                            60
That thou shalt know but backwards. Nay,
since you force
My honest nature, know it is your own
Being too open makes me use you thus.
Since you will not contain your subtle nostrils
In a sweet room, but they must snuff the
air                                                  65
Of rank and sweaty passengers—( *knock
within* )
                              One knocks.

Away, and be not seen, pain of thy life;
Not look toward the window; if thou dost—
                    [CELIA *starts to leave.*]
Nay, stay, hear this, let me not prosper,
whore,
But I will make thee an anatomy,            70
Dissect thee mine own self, and read a lecture
Upon thee to the city, and in public.
Away! [*Exit* CELIA.] Who's there? [*Enter*
    SERVANT.]
    SERVANT.              'Tis Signior Mosca, sir.


                    *Scene 6*

    CORVINO. Let him come in, his master's
    dead. There's yet
Some good to help the bad.   [*Enter* MOSCA.]
                    My Mosca, welcome!
I guess your news.
    MOSCA.         I fear you cannot, sir.
    CORVINO. Is't not his death?
    MOSCA.              Rather the contrary.
    CORVINO. Not his recovery?
    MOSCA.                   Yes, sir.
    CORVINO.                I am cursed, 5
I am bewitched, my crosses meet to vex me.
How? how? how? how?
    MOSCA.        Why, sir, with Scoto's oil!
Corbaccio and Voltore brought of it,
Whilst I was busy in an inner room—
    CORVINO. Death! that damned mounte-
    bank! but for the law,                  10
Now, I could kill the rascal; 't cannot be
His oil should have that virtue. Ha' not I
Known him a common rogue, come fiddling
in
To th' *osteria*, with a tumbling whore,
And, when he has done all his forced tricks,
been glad                                      15
Of a poor spoonful of dead wine, with flies
in 't?

---

41 *in the receipt* "when he received it"   43 *point*
appoint   44 *serve the turn* "do the trick"   46 *abroad*
out of doors   49 *To* compared to; *mark* pay close
attention to   53 *desp'rate* reckless, violent   55–56
*conjurer . . . laid* The conjurer (magician) who
desired to raise a devil drew a magic circle within
which he was safe until the devil was returned
to hell, i.e., "laid"   57 *lock* chastity belt   60
*prospect* view   64 *subtle* cunning (to smell out lust)
65 *air* odor   66 *passengers* passersby

67 *pain* on pain   68 *Not* do not   70 *make . . .
anatomy* "anatomize you," i.e., describe your
moral character detail by detail. So great is
Corvino's fury, however, that he is also threatening literal dissection
II.6.6 *crosses* troubles   8 *of* "some of"   14 *osteria*
inn. Scoto is now being described as an itinerant
entertainer singing and performing for his
supper; *tumbling whore* female acrobat and dancer
15 *forced* strained, awkwardly apparent

It cannot be. All his ingredients
Are a sheep's gall, a roasted bitch's marrow,
Some few sod earwigs, pounded caterpillars,
A little capon's grease, and fasting spittle;　20
I know 'em to a dram.

MOSCA.　　　　I know not, sir;
But some on 't, there, they poured into his ears,
Some in his nostrils, and recovered him,
Applying but the fricace.

CORVINO.　　　　Pox o' that fricace.

MOSCA. And since, to seem the more officious　25
And flatt'ring of his health, there they have had,
At extreme fees, the college of physicians
Consulting on him how they might restore him;
Where one would have a cataplasm of spices,
Another a flayed ape clapped to his breast,　30
A third would ha' it a dog, a fourth an oil
With wild cats' skins. At last, they all resolved
That to preserve him was no other means
But some young woman must be straight sought out,
Lusty, and full of juice, to sleep by him;　35
And to this service, most unhappily
And most unwillingly, am I now employed,
Which here I thought to pre-acquaint you with,
For your advice, since it concerns you most,
Because I would not do that thing might cross　40
Your ends, on whom I have my whole dependence, sir.
Yet, if I do it not they may delate
My slackness to my patron, work me out
Of his opinion; and there all your hopes,

Ventures, or whatsoever, are all frustrate.　45
I do but tell you, sir. Besides, they are all
Now striving who shall first present him.
　Therefore,
I could entreat you, briefly, conclude some-
　what.
Prevent 'em if you can.

CORVINO.　　　　Death to my hopes!
This is my villainous fortune! Best to hire　50
Some common courtesan?

MOSCA.　　　　Ay, I thought on that, sir.
But they are all so subtle, full of art,
And age again doting and flexible,
So as—I cannot tell—we may perchance
Light on a quean may cheat us all.

CORVINO.　　　　'Tis true.　55

MOSCA. No, no; it must be one that has no tricks, sir,
Some simple thing, a creature made unto it;
Some wench you may command. Ha' you no kinswoman?
God's so—Think, think, think, think, think, think, think, sir.
One o' the doctors offered there his daughter.　60

CORVINO. How!

MOSCA.　　　　Yes, Signior Lupo, the physician.

CORVINO. His daughter!

MOSCA.　　　　And a virgin, sir. Why, alas,
He knows the state of's body, what it is;
That nought can warm his blood, sir, but a fever;
Nor any incantation raise his spirit;　65
A long forgetfulness hath seized that part.
Besides, sir, who shall know it? Some one or two—

CORVINO. I pray thee give me leave.

　　[*Walks up and down and talks to himself.*]
　　　　　　　　If any man

---

17 *It* i.e., Volpone's recovery by means of the oil
19 *sod earwigs* boiled insects. The earwig was supposed to creep into the ear and the word came to have the figurative meaning of "flatterer."
20 *fasting spittle* fasting man's saliva; the implication being that Scoto is starving and poverty stricken　22 *on 't* of it; *there* i.e., in Volpone's house　24 *Pox* the great pox, i.e., syphilis　25 *officious* dutiful　27 *extreme fees* enormous expense　29 *cataplasm* large plaster　33 *was* "there was"　34 *straight* instantly　36 *to* on　41 *ends* aims, intentions　42 *delate* report　43–44 *work ... opinion* "persuade him out of his high regard for me"

---

45 *frustrate* frustrated　46 *I ... sir* "I only tell what may happen"　47 *present him* i.e., with the young woman prescribed　48 *briefly* quickly; *conclude somewhat* decide something, form some plan　49 *Prevent* in both the sense of "stop" and the literal meaning of "come before" or "anticipate"　52 *subtle* cunning, tricky; *art* wiles　53 *age again* "old age on the other hand"; *flexible* pliable, gullible　55 *quean* whore　57 *made unto* forced to, directed　59 *God's so* God's soul(?); also a corruption of Italian, *cazzo*, the male organ　61 *Lupo* wolf　68 *give me leave* "excuse me"

But I had had this luck—The thing in 't self,
I know, is nothing—Wherefore should
not I                                              70
As well command my blood and my affec-
tions
As this dull doctor? In the point of honor
The cases are all one of wife and daughter.
MOSCA [aside]. I hear him coming.
CORVINO.          She shall do 't. 'Tis done.
'Slight, if this doctor, who is not engaged,   75
Unless 't be for his counsel, which is nothing,
Offer his daughter, what should I that am
So deeply in? I will prevent him; Wretch!
Covetous wretch! Mosca, I have determined.
MOSCA. How, sir?
CORVINO.          We'll make all sure. The
party you wot of                                  80
Shall be mine own wife, Mosca.
MOSCA.                        Sir, the thing
But that I would not seem to counsel you,
I should have motioned to you at the first.
And make your count, you have cut all their
throats.
Why, 'tis directly taking a possession!     85
And in his next fit, we may let him go.
'Tis but to pull the pillow from his head,
And he is throttled; 't had been done before
But for your scrupulous doubts.
CORVINO.                    Ay, a plague on 't,
My conscience fools my wit! Well, I'll be
brief,                                             90
And so be thou, lest they should be before
us.
Go home, prepare him, tell him with what
zeal
And willingness I do it; swear it was
On the first hearing, as thou mayst do, truly,
Mine own free motion.
MOSCA.                Sir, I warrant you, 95

---

71 *blood* spirit; *affections* feelings  72 *point* matter
73 *cases . . . of* "it is the same with"  74 *coming*
"coming round," taking the bait  75 *'Slight* God's
light; *engaged* deeply involved  79 *determined* decided  80 *wot* know  81 *the thing* 'the very thing"
83 *motioned* suggested  84 *make your count* "inventory Volpone's goods which you are sure to
get"(?)  85 *possession* in law "the detention or
enjoyment of a thing by a person himself or another in his name" (*OED*)  87 *'Tis but* "we
need only"; *from* from under  89 *scrupulous* overly
nice  90 *wit* reason; *brief* quick  91 *before* ahead
of  95 *free motion* unprompted proposal

I'll so possess him with it that the rest
Of his starved clients shall be banished all;
And only you received. But come not, sir,
Until I send, for I have something else
To ripen for your good, you must not
know 't.                                          100
CORVINO. But do not you forget to send
now.
MOSCA.                              Fear not.
[*Exit* MOSCA.]

*Scene 7*

CORVINO. Where are you, wife? My
Celia? wife?
[*Enter* CELIA *crying.*]
                    What, blubbering?
Come, dry those tears. I think thou thought'st
me in earnest?
Ha? by this light I talked so but to try thee.
Methinks the lightness of the occasion
Should ha' confirmed thee. Come, I am not
jealous.                                           5
CELIA. No?
CORVINO. Faith I am not, I, nor never
was;
It is a poor unprofitable humor.
Do not I know if women have a will
They'll do 'gainst all the watches o' the
world?
And that the fiercest spies are tamed with
gold?                                              10
Tut, I am confident in thee, thou shalt see 't;
And see I'll give thee cause too, to believe
it.
Come, kiss me. Go, and make thee ready
straight
In all thy best attire, thy choicest jewels,
Put 'em all on, and, with 'em, thy best
looks.                                             15
We are invited to a solemn feast
At old Volpone's, where it shall appear
How far I am free from jealousy or
fear.                                  [*Exeunt.*]

---

II.7.3 *try* test  4 *lightness* triviality; *occasion* i.e.,
leaning out the window, dropping handkerchief
5 *confirmed* reassured  6 *Faith* "in faith"  8 *will*
sexual appetite  9 *'gainst* despite; *watches* precautions  10 *tamed* bribed  16 *solemn feast* formal
banquet

## ACT III. *Scene 1*

[*A street.* mosca *alone.*]

mosca. I fear I shall begin to grow in love
With my dear self and my most prosp'rous
    parts,
They do so spring and burgeon; I can feel
A whimsy i' my blood. I know not how,
Success hath made me wanton. I could skip   5
Out of my skin, now, like a subtle snake,
I am so limber. O! your parasite
Is a most precious thing, dropped from above,
Not bred 'mongst clods and clodpolls, here
    on earth.
I muse the mystery was not made a
    science,          10
It is so liberally professed! Almost
All the wise world is little else in nature
But parasites or sub-parasites. And yet,
I mean not those that have your bare
    town-art,
To know who's fit to feed 'em; have no
    house,        15
No family, no cáre, and therefore mold
Tales for men's ears, to bait that sense; or get
Kitchen-invention, and some stale receipts
To please the belly, and the groin; nor those,
With their court-dog-tricks, that can fawn
    and fleer,    20
Make their revènue out of legs and faces,
Echo my lord, and lick away a moth.

---

III.1.2 *prosp'rous parts* flourishing talents  4 *whimsy*
dizziness, whirling  5 *wanton* playful  6 *subtle*
cunning; also dexterous, elusive  9 *clodpolls* dolts
10 *mystery* craft; *science* a term formerly applied
to certain philosophical studies required for a
degree in the School of *Literae Humaniores*, the
Liberal Arts—see "liberally professed" in line 11.
Mosca is lamenting that the art of the flatterer
should be considered only a "mystery" . . .  11
*liberally professed* freely practiced. See note to
line 10  14 *bare town-art* i.e., crude skill  16–17
*mold Tales* invent gossip and slander  18 *Kitchen-
invention* recipes for elaborate dishes; *receipts*
recipes  19 *groin* Mosca implies that pandering,
or perhaps, considering the word "receipts,"
retailing new varieties of sensual pleasure, is
among the activities of the "unattached" parasite . . .  20 *fleer* smile obsequiously  21 *revènue*
accented on second syllable; *legs and faces* bows
and smirks  22 *lick . . . moth* Mosca is carrying to
the extreme that form of servility, common in

---

But your fine, elegant rascal, that can rise
And stoop, almost together, like an arrow;
Shoot through the air as nimbly as a star;   25
Turn short as doth a swallow; and be here,
And there, and here, and yonder, all at once;
Present to any humor, all occasion;
And change a visor swifter than a thought,
This is the creature had the art born with
    him;        30
Toils not to learn it, but doth practice it
Out of most excellent nature: and such
    sparks
Are the true parasites, others but their zanies.

## *Scene 2*

[*Enter* bonario.]

mosca. Who's this? Bonario? Old
    Corbaccio's son?
The person I was bound to seek. Fair sir,
You are happ'ly met.
bonario.          That cannot be by thee.
mosca. Why, sir?
bonario.         Nay, 'pray thee know
    thy way and leave me:
I would be loth to interchange discourse   5
With such a mate as thou art.
mosca.          Courteous sir,
Scorn not my poverty.
bonario.        Not I, by heaven;
But thou shalt give me leave to hate thy
    baseness.
mosca. Baseness?
bonario.         Ay, answer me, is not
    thy sloth
Sufficient argument? thy flattery?     10
Thy means of feeding?
mosca.         Heaven be good to me!
These imputations are too common, sir,
And eas'ly stuck on virtue when she's poor.
You are unequal to me, and howe'er

---

all ages, in which the flatterer picks threads or
other objects from the coats of those he is trying
to please . . .  28 *Present . . . occasion* "ready to
satisfy any whim and meet any situation"  29
*visor* mask, i.e., personality  33 *zanies* clowns,
assistants—see II.2, where Nano plays Scoto's
zany
III.2.2 *bound* on my way  6 *mate* low person
10 *argument* reason  14 *unequal* unjust; *howe'er* no
matter how much

Your sentence may be righteous, yet you
  are not,         15
That ere you know me, thus proceed in
  censure.
St. Mark bear witness 'gainst you, 'tis inhu-
  man.         [*He cries.*]
  BONARIO [*aside*]. What? does he weep?
    the sign is soft and good.
I do repent me that I was so harsh.
  MOSCA. 'Tis true that swayed by strong
    necessity,         20
I am enforced to eat my carefull bread
With too much obsequy; 'tis true, beside,
That I am fain to spin mine own poor raiment
Out of my mere observance, being not born
To a free fortune; but that I have done   25
Base offices, in rending friends asunder,
Dividing families, betraying counsels,
Whispering false lies, or mining men with
  praises,
Trained their credulity with perjuries,
Corrupted chastity, or am in love     30
With mine own tender ease, but would not
  rather
Prove the most rugged and laborious course,
That might redeem my present estimation,
Let me here perish, in all hope of goodness.
  BONARIO [*aside*].—This cannot be a per-
    sonated passion—      35
I was to blame, so to mistake thy nature;
Pray thee forgive me and speak out thy
  business.
  MOSCA. Sir, it concerns you, and though
    I may seem
At first to make a main offence in manners,
And in my gratitude unto my master,   40
Yet, for the pure love which I bear all right,
And hatred of the wrong, I must reveal it.
This very hour your father is in purpose
To disinherit you—
  BONARIO.      How!
  MOSCA.        And thrust you forth
As a mere stranger to his blood; 'tis true,
  sir.         45

The work no way engageth me, but as
I claim an interest in the general state
Of goodness and true virtue, which I hear
T' abound in you, and for which mere
  respect,
Without a second aim, sir, I have done it.   50
  BONARIO. This tale hath lost thee much of
    the late trust
Thou hadst with me; it is impossible.
I know not how to lend it any thought
My father should be so unnatural.
  MOSCA. It is a confidence that well be-
    comes      55
Your piety, and formed, no doubt, it is
From your own simple innocence, which
  makes
Your wrong more monstrous and abhorred.
  But, sir,
I now will tell you more. This very minute
It is, or will be doing; and if you     60
Shall be but pleased to go with me, I'll bring
  you,
I dare not say where you shall see, but where
Your ear shall be a witness of the deed;
Hear yourself written bastard and professed
The common issue of the earth.
  BONARIO.         I'm mazed! 65
  MOSCA. Sir, if I do it not, draw your just
    sword
And score your vengeance on my front and
  face;
Mark me your villain. You have too much
  wrong,
And I do suffer for you, sir. My heart
Weeps blood in anguish—
  BONARIO.      Lead, I follow thee. 70
             [*Exeunt.*]

*Scene 3*

[VOLPONE's *house.*]
  VOLPONE. Mosca stays long, methinks.
    Bring forth your sports
And help to make the wretched time more
  sweet.

---

20 *swayed* controlled  21 *carefull* full of care, i.e.,
gotten with pain  22 *obsequy* humility  23 *fain*
obliged; *spin . . . raiment* get clothing  24 *mere
observance* service alone  28 *mining* undermining
32 *Prove* endure  33 *estimation* reputation  35
*personated* pretended; *passion* strong feeling  39
*main* great  45 *mere* complete

49 *for . . . respect* only for this reason  50 *second
aim* concealed purpose  53 *lend . . . thought* believe
it at all  56 *piety* filial love (Latin, *pietas*)  64
*professed* proclaimed  65 *common . . . earth* a man
without family or position; *mazed* bewildered,
confused  67 *score* mark; *front* forehead

[*Enter* NANO, CASTRONE, ANDROGYNO.]

NANO. Dwarf, fool, and eunuch, well met
here we be.

A question it were now, whether of us three,
Being, all, the known delicates of a rich man, 5
In pleasing him, claim the precedency can?

CASTRONE. I claim for myself.

ANDROGYNO.                    And so doth the fool.

NANO. 'Tis foolish indeed, let me set you
both to school.

First for your dwarf, he's little and witty,
And everything, as it is little, is pretty; 10
Else, why do men say to a creature of my
shape,
So soon as they see him, "It's a pretty little
ape"?
And, why a pretty ape? but for pleasing
imitation
Of greater men's action, in a ridiculous
fashion.
Beside, this feat body of mine doth not crave 15
Half the meat, drink, and cloth one of your
bulks will have.
Admit your fool's face be the mother of
laughter,
Yet, for his brain, it must always come after;
And though that do feed him, it's a pitiful case
His body is beholding to such a bad face. 20

(*One knocks.*)

VOLPONE. Who's there? My couch, away,
look, Nano, see;
Give me my caps first—go, inquire.

[*Exeunt* CASTRONE, ANDROGYNO.]
[VOLPONE *lies down in his bed.*]
Now Cupid
Send it be Mosca, and with fair return.

NANO. It is the beauteous madam—

VOLPONE.                    Wouldbe—is it?

NANO. The same.

VOLPONE.          Now, torment on me;
squire her in, 25
For she will enter, or dwell here forever.
Nay, quickly, that my fit were past. I fear

[*Exit* NANO.]

A second hell too: that my loathing this
Will quite expel my appetite to the other.
Would she were taking, now, her tedious
leave. 30
Lord, how it threats me, what I am to suffer!

*Scene 4*

[*Enter* NANO *with* LADY WOULDBE.]

LADY WOULDBE [*to* NANO]. I thank you,
good sir. Pray you signify
Unto your patron I am here—This band
Shows not my neck enough.—I trouble you,
sir;
Let me request you bid one of my women
Come hither to me. In good faith, I am
dressed 5
Most favourably today! It is no matter;
'Tis well enough. (*Enter* 1ST WOMAN.) Look,
see these petulant things!
How they have done this!

VOLPONE [*aside*].          —I do feel the fever
Ent'ring in at mine ears. O for a charm
To fright it hence—

LADY WOULDBE.          Come nearer. Is this
curl 10
In his right place? or this? Why is this
higher
Than all the rest? You ha' not washed your
eyes yet?
Or do they not stand even i' your head?
Where's your fellow? Call her.

[*Exit* 1ST WOMAN.]

NANO [*aside*].          Now, St. Mark
Deliver us! Anon she'll beat her women 15
Because her nose is red. [*Re-enter* 1ST WOMAN
*with* 2ND WOMAN.]

LADY WOULDBE.          I pray you, view
This tire, forsooth; are all things apt, or no?

1ST WOMAN. One hair a little, here, sticks
out, forsooth.

LADY WOULDBE. Dost so, forsooth? And
where was your dear sight
When it did so, forsooth? What now!
Bird-eyed? 20
And you too? Pray you both approach and
mend it.

---

III.3.4 *whether* which  5 *known delicates* acknowledged favourites  8 *set . . . to school* instruct  10 *as*
to the degree that  15 *feat* elegant  18 *come after*
follow, i.e., be second, less important  19 *that* i.e.,
the face, the mouth  23 *fair return* good luck—
the phrase has commercial suggestions: a "fair
return" on a venture

28 *this* i.e., Lady Wouldbe  29 *other* i.e., Celia
III.4.2 *band* ruff  5–6 *I . . . favourably* ironic  12–13
*You . . . head* "Can't you see straight?"  17 *tire*
hair arrangement  20 *Bird-eyed* frightened(?)

Now, by that light, I muse you're not
  ashamed!
I, that have preached these things, so oft,
  unto you,
Read you the principles, argued all the
  grounds,
Disputed every fitness, every grace,    25
Called you to counsel of so frequent dress-
  ings—
  NANO [aside]. More carefully than of your
    fame or honor.
  LADY WOULDBE. Made you acquainted what
    an ample dowry
The knowledge of these things would be unto
  you,
Able, alone, to get you noble husbands   30
At your return; and you, thus, to neglect it!
Besides, you seeing what a curious nation
Th' Italians are, what will they say of me?
"The English lady cannot dress herself."
Here's a fine imputation to our country!   35
Well, go your ways, and stay i' the next
  room.
This fucus was too coarse, too; it's no matter.
Good sir, you'll give 'em entertainment?
      [Exit NANO with WOMEN.]
  VOLPONE. The storm comes toward me.
  LADY WOULDBE.     How does my Volp?
  VOLPONE. Troubled with noise, I cannot
    sleep; I dreamt   40
That a strange fury entered, now, my house,
And, with the dreadful tempest of her breath,
Did cleave my roof asunder.
  LADY WOULDBE.     Believe me, and I
Had the most fearful dream, could I remem-
  ber 't—
  VOLPONE [aside]. Out on my fate! I ha'
    giv'n her the occasion   45
How to torment me. She will tell me hers.
  LADY WOULDBE. Methought the golden
    mediocrity,

Polite, and delicate—
  VOLPONE.     Oh, if you do love me,
No more; I sweat, and suffer, at the mention
Of any dream; feel how I tremble yet.   50
    [Placing her hand on his heart.]
  LADY WOULDBE. Alas, good soul! the passion
  of the heart,
Seed-pearl were good now, boiled with syrup
  of apples,
Tincture of gold, and coral, citron-pills,
Your elecampane root, myrobalanes—
  VOLPONE [aside]. Ay me, I have ta'en
    a grasshopper by the wing!   55
  LADY WOULDBE. Burnt silk and amber.
  You have muscadel
Good in the house—
  VOLPONE.     You will not drink and part?
  LADY WOULDBE. No, fear not that. I doubt
  we shall not get
Some English saffron, half a dram would
  serve,
Your sixteen cloves, a little musk, dried
  mints,   60
Burgloss, and barley-meal—
  VOLPONE [aside].     She's in again.
Before I feigned diseases, now I have one.
  LADY WOULDBE. And these applied with
  a right scarlet cloth.
  VOLPONE [aside]. Another flood of words!
  a very torrent!
  LADY WOULDBE. Shall I, sir, make you a
  poultice?
  VOLPONE.     No, no, no. 65
I'm very well, you need prescribe no more.
  LADY WOULDBE. I have, a little, studied
  physic; but now
I'm all for music, save, i' the forenoons
An hour or two for painting. I would have
A lady, indeed, to have all letters and arts,  70
Be able to discourse, to write, to paint,
But principal, as Plato holds, your music,
And so does wise Pythagoras, I take it,
Is your true rapture, when there is concent

---

24 grounds fundamentals—dressing is treated here
like a science or the art of government   27 fame
reputation   31 return i.e., to England   32 curious
particular in small details   37 fucus cosmetic for
covering up complexion, "pancake makeup"
38 give 'em entertainment look out for them   45
occasion means and opportunity   47 golden mediocrity . . . the "golden mean," that classic guide
to conduct which dictates "nothing in excess,"
and which has been lost completely in Volpone's
world where men pursue gold and power and

lust to the exclusion of all else, becoming in
the process "golden mediocrities"   51 passion of
the heart stomach gas pressing on the heart
52–56 Seed-pearl . . . muscadel a catalogue of popular
remedies   55 grasshopper referring to constant
whirring noise made by captive grasshoppers
58 doubt fear   63 right true   67 physic medicine
74 concent agreement, harmony

In face, in voice, and clothes, and is, indeed,                                         75
Our sex's chiefest ornament.
    VOLPONE.        The poet
As old in time as Plato, and as knowing,
Says that your highest female grace is silence.
    LADY WOULDBE. Which o' your poets?
      Petrarch? or Tasso? or Dante?
Guarini? Ariosto? Aretine?                                         80
Cieco di Hadria? I have read them all.
    VOLPONE [aside]. Is everything a cause to
      my destruction?
    LADY WOULDBE. I think I ha' two or three
      of 'em about me.
    VOLPONE [aside]. The sun, the sea, will
      sooner both stand still
Than her eternal tongue! Nothing can scape
    it.                                         85
    LADY WOULDBE. Here's *Pastor Fido*—
             [*Producing a book.*]
    VOLPONE [aside]. Profess obstinate silence;
That's now my safest.
    LADY WOULDBE.   All our English writers,
I mean such as are happy in th' Italian,
Will deign to steal out of this author, mainly;
Almost as much as from Montagniè.                                         90
He has so modern and facile a vein,
Fitting the time, and catching the court-ear.
Your Petrarch is more passionate, yet he,
In days of sonneting, trusted 'em with much.
Dante is hard, and few can understand
    him.                                         95
But for a desperate wit, there's Aretine!
Only, his pictures are a little obscene—
You mark me not.

VOLPONE.    Alas, my mind's perturbed.
LADY WOULDBE. Why, in such cases, we
    must cure ourselves,
Make use of our philosophy—
    VOLPONE.       O'y me!   100
    LADY WOULDBE. And as we find our
      passions do rebel,
Encounter 'em with reason, or divert 'em
By giving scope unto some other humor
Of lesser danger: as, in politic bodies
There's nothing more doth overwhelm the
    judgment,                                         105
And clouds the understanding, than too much
Settling and fixing, and, as 'twere, subsiding
Upon one object. For the incorporating
Of these same outward things into that part
Which we call mental, leaves some certain
    feces                                         110
That stop the organs, and, as Plato says,
Assassinates our knowledge.
    VOLPONE [aside].    Now, the spirit
Of patience help me!
    LADY WOULDBE.   Come, in faith, I must
Visit you more adays and make you well;
Laugh and be lusty.
    VOLPONE [aside].   My good angel save
    me!                                         115
    LADY WOULDBE. There was but one sole
    man in all the world
With whom I e'er could sympathize; and he
Would lie you often, three, four hours
    together
To hear me speak, and be sometime so rapt,
As he would answer me quite from the
    purpose,                                         120
Like you, and you are like him, just. I'll
    discourse,
An 't be but only, sir, to bring you asleep,
How we did spend our time and loves
    together,
For some six years.
    VOLPONE.    Oh, oh, oh, oh, oh, oh.
    LADY WOULDBE. For we were *coaetanei*,
    and brought up—                                         125
    VOLPONE. Some power, some fate, some
    fortune rescue me!

76 *poet* Sophocles, *Ajax* 293  80–81 *Aretine? Cieco di Hadria?* The other names Lady Wouldbe reels off are major Italian poets, but Luigi Groto, known as Cieco di Hadria, is a distinctly minor writer, while Pietro Aretino was a writer of powerful but extremely scurrilous and obscene verses ... 86 *Pastor Fido* "The Faithful Shepherd" (1590), Guarini's pastoral play  88 *happy* fluent  90 *Montagniè* Montaigne, the French essayist. Pronounced with four syllables here  92 *court-ear* ear of courtiers  93–94 *Petrarch ... much* Petrarch was most famous for his love sonnets, which were imitated by generations of poets, ... and this extensive imitation and borrowing are perhaps the basis for the statement "trusted 'em with much"  96 *desperate* outrageous  97 *pictures* Aretino wrote poems to accompany a series of obscene drawings

102 *Encounter* battle  103 *scope* free play; *humor* desire  104 *politic bodies* kingdoms  109 *outward things* the object on which the mind has fixed  118 *lie you* lie  120 *from the purpose* nothing to the point  125 *coaetanei* of the same age

## Scene 5

[*Enter* MOSCA.]

MOSCA. God save you, madam!

LADY WOULDBE.     Good sir.

VOLPONE.          Mosca, welcome!

Welcome to my redemption.

MOSCA.               Why, sir?

VOLPONE.                     Oh,

Rid me of this my torture quickly, there,

My madam with the everlasting voice;

The bells in time of pestilence ne'er made     5

Like noise, or were in that perpetual motion!

The cock-pit comes not near it. All my house,

But now, steamed like a bath with her thick
  breath.

A lawyer could not have been heard; nor
  scarce

Another woman, such a hail of words     10

She has let fall. For hell's sake, rid her hence.

MOSCA. Has she presented?

VOLPONE.                Oh, I do not care;

I'll take her absence upon any price,

With any loss.

MOSCA.     Madam—

LADY WOULDBE.     I ha' brought your
  patron

A toy, a cap here, of mine own work.

MOSCA.                'Tis well.  15

I had forgot to tell you I saw your knight

Where you'd little think it.

LADY WOULDBE.       Where?

MOSCA.                    Marry,

Where yet, if you make haste, you may
  apprehend him,

Rowing upon the water in a gondole,

With the most cunning courtesan of
  Venice.                                 20

LADY WOULDBE. Is't true?

MOSCA.                Pursue 'em, and
  believe your eyes.

Leave me to make your gift. [*Exit* LADY
  WOULDBE.] I knew 'twould take.

For lightly, they that use themselves most
  license,

Are still most jealous.

VOLPONE.          Mosca, hearty thanks

For thy quick fiction and delivery of me.   25

Now to my hopes, what sayst thou?

[*Re-enter* LADY WOULDBE.]

LADY WOULDBE.     But do you hear, sir?

VOLPONE. Again! I fear a paroxysm.

LADY WOULDBE.              Which way

Rowed they together?

MOSCA.          Toward the Rialto.

LADY WOULDBE. I pray you lend me your
  dwarf.

MOSCA.            I pray you, take him.

[*Exit* LADY WOULDBE.]

Your hopes, sir, are like happy blossoms:
  fair,                                    30

And promise timely fruit, if you will stay

But the maturing; keep you at your couch.

Corbaccio will arrive straight with the will;

When he is gone, I'll tell you more.

[*Exit* MOSCA.]

VOLPONE.              My blood,

My spirits are returned; I am alive;      35

And, like your wanton gamester at primero,

Whose thought had whispered to him, not
  go less,

Methinks I lie, and draw—for an encounter.

[*He draws the curtains across his bed.*]

## Scene 6

[MOSCA *leads* BONARIO *on stage and hides him.*]

MOSCA. Sir, here concealed you may hear
  all. But pray you

( *one knocks* )

Have patience, sir; the same's your father
  knocks.

I am compelled to leave you.

BONARIO.             Do so. Yet

Cannot my thought imagine this a truth.

## Scene 7

[MOSCA *opens door and admits* CORVINO
*and* CELIA.]

MOSCA. Death on me! you are come too
  soon, what meant you?

---

III.5.5 *bells . . . pestilence* The bells in London rang almost without ceasing during times of the plague    7 *cock-pit* where cock fights were put on    12 *presented* given a present    23 *lightly* commonly; *use . . . license* are most free (morally)

24 *still* always    36 *wanton gamester* reckless gambler; *primero* a popular card game of the day. Volpone makes use of the technical terms of the game—"go less" (i.e., wager less), "draw," and "encounter"—as metaphors for his coming meeting with Celia

Did not I say I would send?

CORVINO.                          Yes, but I feared
You might forget it, and then they prevent
     us.

MOSCA. Prevent! [*Aside.*]—Did e'er man
     haste so for his horns?

A courtier would not ply it so for a
     place.—                                        5

Well, now there's no helping it, stay here;
I'll presently return. [*He moves to one side.*]

CORVINO.                   Where are you, Celia?
You know not wherefore I have brought you
     hither?

CELIA. Not well, except you told me.

CORVINO.                          Now I will:
Hark hither. [*He leads her aside and whispers
                                              to her.*]

MOSCA (*to* BONARIO). Sir, your father hath
     sent word,                                      10
It will be half an hour ere he come;
And therefore, if you please to walk the
     while
Into that gallery—at the upper end
There are some books to entertain the time.
And I'll take care no man shall come unto
     you, sir.                                       15

BONARIO. Yes, I will stay there. [*Aside.*]
     I do doubt this fellow.          [*Exit.*]

MOSCA. There, he is far enough; he can hear
     nothing.
And for his father, I can keep him off.
     [*Returns to VOLPONE's couch, opens the
          curtains, and whispers to him.*]

CORVINO. Nay, now, there is no starting
     back, and therefore
Resolve upon it: I have so decreed.           20
It must be done. Nor would I move 't afore,
Because I would avoid all shifts and tricks,
That might deny me.

CELIA.                          Sir, let me beseech you,
Affect not these strange trials; if you doubt
My chastity, why, lock me up forever;        25
Make me the heir of darkness. Let me live

Where I may please your fears, if not your
     trust.

CORVINO. Believe it, I have no such
     humor, I.
All that I speak I mean; yet I am not mad;
Not horn-mad, see you? Go to, show
     yourself                                        30
Obedient, and a wife.

CELIA.                          O heaven!

CORVINO.                               I say it,
Do so.

CELIA. Was this the train?

CORVINO.                     I've told you reasons:
What the physicians have set down: how
     much
It may concern me; what my engagements
     are;
My means, and the necessity of those
     means                                           35
For my recovery; wherefore, if you be
Loyal and mine, be won, respect my venture.

CELIA. Before your honor?

CORVINO.                     Honor! tut, a breath.
There's no such thing in nature; a mere term
Invented to awe fools. What, is my gold     40
The worse for touching? clothes for being
     looked on?
Why, this 's no more. An old, decrepit
     wretch,
That has no sense, no sinew; takes his meat
With others' fingers; only knows to gape
When you do scald his gums; a voice, a
     shadow;                                         45
And what can this man hurt you?

CELIA.                          Lord, what spirit
Is this hath entered him?

CORVINO.                     And for your fame,
That's such a jig; as if I would go tell it,
Cry it, on the Piazza! Who shall know it
But he that cannot speak it, and this fellow, 50
Whose lips are i' my pocket, save yourself.
—If you'll proclaim 't, you may—I know no
     other

---

III.7.2 *send* send word when to come    3 *they* i.e.,
the other legacy hunters    4 *horns* the symbol of
the cuckold    5 *ply . . . place* work so hard for an
office at court    7 *presently* immediately    9 *except*
except what    14 *entertain* pass    21 *move* suggest
22 *shifts* evasions    24 *Affect . . . trials* "do not pretend to make such unusual tests" (of her virtue)

30 *horn-mad* with fear of being a cuckold    32 *train*
trap    34 *engagements* financial commitments    35
*means* i.e., becoming Volpone's heir    36 *recovery*
regaining financial stability    37 *venture* commercial enterprise    43 *sense* sensory perception    47
*fame* reputation    48 *jig* farce    51 *lips . . . pocket*
Mosca will not speak because Corvino owns him

Should come to know it.

CELIA.                    Are heaven and saints
then nothing?
Will they be blind, or stupid?

CORVINO.                    How?

CELIA.                    Good sir,
Be jealous still, emulate them, and think 55
What hate they burn with toward every sin.

CORVINO. I grant you. If I thought it were
a sin
I would not urge you. Should I offer this
To some young Frenchman, or hot Tuscan
blood
That had read Aretine, conned all his
prints,                    60
Knew every quirk within lust's labyrinth,
And were professed critic in lechery;
And I would look upon him, and applaud
him,
This were a sin; but here, 'tis contrary,
A pious work, mere charity, for physic 65
And honest policy to assure mine own.

CELIA. O heaven! canst thou suffer such a
change?

VOLPONE. Thou art mine honor, Mosca,
and my pride,
My joy, my tickling, my delight! Go, bring
'em.

MOSCA. Please you draw near, sir.

CORVINO.                    Come on, what— 70
                    [She hangs back.]
You will not be rebellious? By that light—
                    [He drags her to the bed.]

MOSCA [to VOLPONE]. Sir, Signior Corvino,
here, is come to see you.

VOLPONE. Oh!

MOSCA.          And hearing of the con-
sultation had,
So lately, for your health, is come to offer,
Or rather, sir, to prostitute—

CORVINO.          Thanks, sweet Mosca. 75

MOSCA. Freely, unasked, or unentreated—

CORVINO.                    Well.

MOSCA. As the true, fervent instance of his
love,
His own most fair and proper wife, the
beauty

Only of price in Venice—

CORVINO.                    'Tis well urged.

MOSCA. To be your comfortress, and to
preserve you.                    80

VOLPONE. Alas, I'm past already! Pray you,
thank him
For his good care and promptness; but for
that,
'Tis a vain labor e'en to fight 'gainst heaven;
Applying fire to a stone, uh, uh, uh, uh!
Making a dead leaf grow again. I take 85
His wishes gently, though; and you may
tell him
What I've done for him. Marry, my state
is hopeless!
Will him to pray for me, and t' use his
fortune
With reverence when he comes to 't.

MOSCA.                    Do you hear, sir?
Go to him with your wife.

CORVINO [to CELIA]. Heart of my father! 90
Wilt thou persist thus? Come, I pray thee,
come.
Thou seest 'tis nothing, Celia. By this hand
                    [raising his hand]
I shall grow violent. Come, do 't, I say.

CELIA. Sir, kill me rather. I will take down
poison,
Eat burning coals, do anything—

CORVINO.                    Be damned! 95
Heart! I will drag thee hence home by
the hair,
Cry thee a strumpet through the streets, rip
up
Thy mouth unto thine ears, and slit thy nose,
Like a raw rotchet!—Do not tempt me,
come.
Yield, I am loth—Death! I will buy some
slave                    100
Whom I will kill, and bind thee to him, alive;
And at my window hang you forth, devising
Some monstrous crime, which I, in capital
letters,
Will eat into thy flesh with aquafortis,
And burning cor'sives, on this stubborn
breast.                    105

---

57 *I grant you* "Agreed"    60 *prints* the obscene
pictures referred to above    62 *professed critic* con-
noisseur    63 *And if*    66 *own* i.e., inheritance

79 *Only of price* uniquely beautiful    84 *Applying . . .
stone* proverbial statement of absolute futility
95 *Eat burning coals* method of suicide used by
Portia, Brutus' wife    99 *rotchet* a variety of fish
104 *aquafortis* acid    105 *cor'sives* corrosives

Now, by the blood thou hast incensed, I'll
  do 't!
    CELIA. Sir, what you please, you may;
    I am your martyr.
    CORVINO. Be not thus obstinate, I ha' not
    deserved it.
Think who it is entreats you. Pray thee,
  sweet;
Good faith, thou shalt have jewels, gowns,
  attires,                    110
What thou wilt, think and ask. Do, but go
  kiss him.
Or touch him, but. For my sake. At my suit.
This once. [*She refuses.*] No? Not? I shall
  remember this.
Will you disgrace me thus? D' you thirst my
  undoing?
    MOSCA. Nay, gentle lady, be advised.
    CORVINO.            No, no.  115
She has watched her time. God's precious,
  this is scurvy,
'Tis very scurvy; and you are—
    MOSCA.            Nay, good sir.
    CORVINO. An errant locust, by heaven, a
    locust! Whore,-
Crocodile, that hast thy tears prepared,
Expecting how thou'lt bid 'em flow.
    MOSCA.         Nay, pray you, sir!  120
She will consider.
    CELIA.        Would my life would serve
To satisfy.
    CORVINO. 'Sdeath! if she would but speak
    to him,
And save my reputation, 'twere somewhat;
But spitefully to effect my utter ruin!
    MOSCA. Ay, now you've put your fortune
    in her hands.                  125
Why i' faith, it is her modesty, I must quit her.
If you were absent, she would be more
  coming;
I know it, and dare undertake for her.
What woman can before her husband?
  Pray you,
Let us depart and leave her here.

---

115 *advised* persuaded by the argument   116
*watched her time* waited for her moment   118 *errant*
either "far roving" or a form of "arrant"   119
*Crocodile . . . tears* The crocodile was proverbially
believed to shed tears in order to lure his victims
126 *quit* excuse   127 *coming* agreeable   128 *undertake for* warrant

    CORVINO.           Sweet Celia,  130
Thou may'st redeem all yet; I'll say no more.
If not, esteem yourself as lost.
              [*She begins to leave with him.*]
                    Nay, stay there.
           [*Exeunt* MOSCA *and* CORVINO.]
    CELIA. O God, and his good angels!
    whither, whither,
Is shame fled human breasts? that with such
  ease
Men dare put off your honors, and their
  own?                          135
Is that, which ever was a cause of life,
Now placed beneath the basest circumstance,
And modesty an exile made, for money?
    VOLPONE. Ay, in Corvino, and such
    earth-fed minds, (*he leaps off from the couch*)
That never tasted the true heaven of love.  140
Assure thee, Celia, he that would sell thee,
Only for hope of gain, and that uncertain,
He would have sold his part of Paradise
For ready money, had he met a cope-man.
Why art thou mazed to see me thus
  revived?                          145
Rather applaud thy beauty's miracle;
'Tis thy great work, that hath, not now
  alone,
But sundry times raised me in several shapes,
And, but this mornng, like a mountebank,
To see thee at thy window. Ay, before  150
I would have left my practice for thy love,
In varying figures I would have contended
With the blue Proteus, or the hornèd flood.
Now, art thou welcome.
    CELIA.         Sir!
    VOLPONE.        Nay, fly me not.
Nor let thy false imagination    155
That I was bed-rid, make thee think I am so:
Thou shalt not find it. I am, now, as fresh,
As hot, as high, and in as jovial plight

---

135 *your* i.e., God's and his angels'   137 *circumstance* matter of little importance   144 *cope-man*
merchant   145 *mazed* amazed   151 *practice* schem-
ing   152 *figures* shapes, disguises   153 *blue Proteus*
the "old man of the sea" who could change
himself at will into any shape . . .; *hornèd flood*
refers to the river Achelous—"horned" because
it branches and roars—which struggled with
Hercules in three forms: bull, serpent, and
man-ox . . . . 158 *jovial plight* happy condition,
but Jove and his love for earthly maidens is
referred to

As when in that so celebrated scene
At recitation of our comedy,                                    160
For entertainment of the great Valois,
I acted young Antinous, and attracted
The eyes and ears of all the ladies present,
T' admire each graceful gesture, note, and
   footing.

           SONG                                                165
   Come, my Celia, let us prove,
   While we can, the sports of love;
   Time will not be ours forever,
   He, at length, our good will sever;
   Spend not then his gifts in vain.                           170
   Suns that set may rise again;
   But if once we lose this light,
   'Tis with us perpetual night.
   Why should we defer our joys?
   Fame and rumor are but toys.                                175
   Cannot we delude the eyes
   Of a few poor household spies?
   Or his easier ears beguile,
   Thus removèd by our wile?
   'Tis no sin love's fruits to steal,                         180
   But the sweet thefts to reveal:
   To be taken, to be seen,
   These have crimes accounted been.
CELIA. Some serene blast me, or dire
   lightning strike
This my offending face.
   VOLPONE.          Why droops my Celia?    185
Thou hast in place of a base husband found
A worthy lover; use thy fortune well,
With secrecy and pleasure. See, behold,
   [pointing to his treasure]
What thou art queen of; not in expectation,
As I feed others, but possessed and
   crowned.                                                    190
See, here, a rope of pearl, and each more
   orient

Than that the brave Egyptian queen
   caroused;
Dissolve and drink 'em. See, a carbuncle
May put out both the eyes of our St. Mark;
A diamond would have bought Lollia
   Paulina                                                     195
When she came in like star-light, hid with
   jewels
That were the spoils of provinces; take these,
And wear, and lose 'em; yet remains an
   earring
To purchase them again, and this whole
   state.
A gem but worth a private patrimony       200
Is nothing; we will eat such at a meal.
The heads of parrots, tongues of nightingales,
The brains of peacocks, and of estriches
Shall be our food, and, could we get the
   phoenix,
Though nature lost her kind, she were our
   dish.                                                       205
   CELIA. Good sir, these things might move
   a mind affected
With such delights; but I, whose innocence
Is all I can think wealthy, or worth th'
   enjoying,
And which, once lost, I have nought to lose
   beyond it,
Cannot be taken with these sensual baits.    210
If you have conscience—
   VOLPONE.          'Tis the beggar's virtue;
If thou hast wisdom, hear me, Celia.
Thy baths shall be the juice of July-flowers,
Spirit of roses, and of violets,

---

192 *Egyptian queen* Cleopatra, who at an extravagant banquet drank pearls dissolved in vinegar; *caroused* drank   193 *carbuncle* rounded red gem, e.g., a ruby   194 *May . . . St. Mark* It may be that some image of St. Mark, the patron saint of Venice, had jewels for eyes, and that the jewel Volphone holds up makes them seem trivial, "puts out," by comparison. But at the same time, the jewel "puts out" or obliterates the eyes of the Saint in the same way that Volpone's gold in the opening scene "darkens" the light of the sun (line 6)   195 *Lollia Paulina* wife of a Roman governor of a province who covered herself with jewels taken from the province   200 *private patrimony* single inheritance   204 *phoenix* mythical bird. Only one was believed to exist at a time, and from his ashes another was born   205 *nature . . . kind* (the phoenix) became extinct   213 *July-flowers* gillyflowers

---

161 *great Valois* Henry of Valois, later Henry III of France, was magnificently entertained in Venice in 1524. Plays were one of the standard features of such entertainments   162 *Antinous* usually identified as the Roman Emperor Hadrian's favorite courtier, noted for his physical beauty   164 *footing* movement   165 *Song* this is an imitation of and partly translated from the famous fifth ode of Catullus beginning, *Vivamus, mea Lesbia, atque amemus . . .*   166 *prove* try, test   175 *toys* trifles   184 *serene* poisonous mist   185 *offending* i.e., because its beauty attracts Volpone   191 *orient* precious

The milk of unicorns, and panthers'
    breath              215
Gathered in bags and mixed with Cretan
    wines.
Our drink shall be preparèd gold and amber,
Which we will take until my roof whirl
    round
With the vertigo; and my dwarf shall dance,
My eunuch sing, my fool make up the
    antic.             220
Whilst we, in changèd shapes, act Ovid's
    tales,
Thou like Europa now, and I like Jove,
Then I like Mars, and thou like Erycine;
So of the rest, till we have quite run through,
And wearied all the fables of the gods.   225
Then will I have thee in more modern forms,
Attirèd like some sprightly dame of France,
Brave Tuscan lady, or proud Spanish beauty;
Sometimes unto the Persian Sophy's wife,
Or the Grand Signior's mistress; and, for
    change,            230
To one of our most artful courtesans,
Or some quick Negro, or cold Russian;
And I will meet thee in as many shapes;
Where we may, so, transfuse our wand'ring
    souls          [*kissing her*]
Out at our lips and score up sums of
    pleasures,           235
      That the curious shall not know
      How to tell them as they flow;
      And the envious, when they find
      What their number is, be pined.
    CELIA. If you have ears that will be pierced,
    or eyes           240
That can be opened, a heart may be touched,
Or any part that yet sounds man about you;
If you have touch of holy saints, or heaven,
Do me the grace to let me 'scape. If not,
Be bountiful and kill me. You do know   245

I am a creature hither ill betrayed
By one whose shame I would forget it were.
If you will deign me neither of these graces,
Yet feed your wrath, sir, rather than your
    lust,
It is a vice comes nearer manliness,   250
And punish that unhappy crime of nature,
Which you miscall my beauty: flay my face,
Or poison it with ointments for seducing
Your blood to this rebellion. Rub these hands
With what may cause an eating leprosy,  255
E'en to my bones and marrow; anything
That may disfavor me, save in my honor,
And I will kneel to you, pray for you, pay
    down
A thousand hourly vows, sir, for your health;
Report, and think you virtuous—
    VOLPONE.          Think me old,   260
Frozen, and impotent, and so report me?
That I had Nestor's hernia thou wouldst
    think.
I do degenerate and abuse my nation
To play with opportunity thus long;
I should have done the act, and then have
    parleyed.          265
Yield, or I'll force thee.     [*He seizes her.*]
    CELIA.        O! just God!
    VOLPONE.           In vain—
    BONARIO. Forbear, foul ravisher! libid-
inous swine! (*He leaps out from where*
MOSCA *had placed him.*)
Free the forced lady, or thou diest, impostor.
But that I am loth to snatch thy punishment
Out of the hand of justice, thou shouldst
    yet          270
Be made the timely sacrifice of vengeance,
Before this altar, and this dross, thy idol.
          [*Points to the gold.*]
Lady, let's quit the place, it is the den
Of villainy; fear nought, you have a guard;
And he ere long shall meet his just re-
    ward.    [*Exeunt* BONARIO *and* CELIA.]  275
    VOLPONE. Fall on me, roof, and bury me
    in ruin!

---

215 *panthers' breath* . . . Panthers were popularly
believed to have an extraordinarily sweet smell
which attracted their prey, like the tears of the
crocodile referred to in the note to line 119
above . . . 220 *antic* grotesque dance   221 *Ovid's
tales* "The Metamorphoses," a series of stories
dealing with human transformations  223 *Erycine*
Venus  229 *Sophy* ruler  230 *Grand Signior* Sultan
of Turkey, noted for cruelty  232 *quick* lively
237 *tell* count   239 *pined* eaten up with envy
242 *sounds man* announces you to be a man
(rather than beast)

---

254 *rebellion* i.e., because reason and virtue should
control passion, "blood"  255 *leprosy* any serious
disease of the skin  257 *disfavor* make the face
ugly  262 *Nestor's hernia* Nestor is the very old
and wise Greek of the *Iliad*—the hernia suggests
impotence  268 *impostor* pretender  275 *he* i.e.,
Volpone

Become my grave, that wert my shelter! O!
I am unmasked, unspirited, undone,
Betrayed to beggary, to infamy—

Suspect what they deserve still. [MOSCA *opens
door.*]

Signior Corbaccio!

### Scene 8

[*Enter* MOSCA, *bleeding.*]

MOSCA. Where shall I run, most wretched
shame of men,
To beat out my unlucky brains?
VOLPONE.                    Here, here.
What! dost thou bleed?
MOSCA.              O, that his well-driven
sword
Had been so courteous to have cleft me down
Unto the navel, ere I lived to see          5
My life, my hopes, my spirits, my patron, all
Thus desperately engagèd by my error.
VOLPONE. Woe on thy fortune!
MOSCA.                    And my follies, sir.
VOLPONE. Th' hast made me miserable.
MOSCA.                    And myself, sir.
Who would have thought he would have
hearkened so?                          10
VOLPONE. What shall we do?
MOSCA.              I know not; if my heart
Could expiate the mischance, I'd pluck it
out.
Will you be pleased to hang me, or cut my
throat?
And I'll requite you, sir. Let's die like
Romans,
Since we have lived like Grecians. (*They
knock without.*)
VOLPONE.              Hark! who's there?  15
I hear some footing; officers, the *Saffi*,
Come to apprehend us! I do feel the brand
Hissing already at my forehead; now,
Mine ears are boring.
MOSCA.              To your couch, sir; you
Make that place good, however. Guilty
men              [VOLPONE *lies down.*]  20

---

III.8.7 *engagèd* trapped    10 *he* i.e., Bonario;
*hearkened* listened    14 *requite* do the same for;
*Romans* referring to Roman custom of committing
suicide in adversity    15 *Grecians* noted for dis-
solute living    16 *footing* footsteps; *Saffi* police
17–19 *brand . . . boring* Branding on the forehead
and cutting the ears was common punishment
for criminals    20 *Make . . . however* Maintain your
disguise as a sick man whatever happens

### Scene 9

[*Enter* CORBACCIO.]
CORBACCIO. Why, how now, Mosca?
MOSCA.              O, undone, amazed, sir.
Your son, I know not by what accident,
Acquainted with your purpose to my patron,
Touching your will, and making him your
heir,
Entered our house with violence, his sword
drawn,                                  5
Sought for you, called you wretch, unnatural,
Vowed he would kill you.
CORBACCIO.        Me?
MOSCA.              Yes, and my patron.
CORBACCIO. This act shall disinherit him
indeed.
Here is the will.
MOSCA.        'Tis well, sir.
CORBACCIO.              Right and well.
Be you as careful now for me.
              [*Enter* VOLTORE *behind.*]
MOSCA.                    My life, sir,  10
Is not more tendered; I am only yours.
CORBACCIO. How does he? Will he die
shortly, think'st thou?
MOSCA.                    I fear
He'll outlast May.
CORBACCIO.        Today?
MOSCA [*shouting*].        No, last out May, sir.
CORBACCIO. Couldst thou not gi' him a
dram?
MOSCA.              O, by no means, sir.
CORBACCIO. Nay, I'll not bid you.
VOLTORE [*stepping forward*].        This is a
knave, I see.                          15
MOSCA [*aside*]. How! Signior Voltore! Did
he hear me?
VOLTORE.              Parasite!
MOSCA. Who's that? O, sir, most timely
welcome.
VOLTORE.                    Scarce
To the discovery of your tricks, I fear.

---

III.9.1 *amazed* confused    3 *purpose* intention    10
*careful* concerned for benefit    11 *tendered* watched
over    14 *dram* drink (of poison)

You are his, only? And mine, also, are you
not?

[CORBACCIO *wanders to the side of the stage
and stands there.*]

MOSCA. Who? I, sir?

VOLTORE. You, sir. What device is this 20
About a will?

MOSCA. A plot for you, sir.

VOLTORE. Come,
Put not your foists upon me; I shall scent 'em.

MOSCA. Did you not hear it?

VOLTORE. Yes, I hear Corbaccio
Hath made your patron, there, his heir.

MOSCA. 'Tis true,
By my device, drawn to it by my plot, 25
With hope—

VOLTORE. Your patron should
reciprocate?
And you have promised?

MOSCA. For your good I did, sir.
Nay, more, I told his son, brought, hid him
here,
Where he might hear his father pass the
deed;
Being persuaded to it by this thought, sir: 30
That the unnaturalness, first, of the act,
And then his father's oft disclaiming in him,
Which I did mean t' help on, would sure
enrage him
To do some violence upon his parent.
On which the law should take sufficient
hold, 35
And you be stated in a double hope.
Truth be my comfort, and my conscience,
My only aim was to dig you a fortune
Out of these two old, rotten sepulchres—

VOLTORE. I cry thee mercy, Mosca.

MOSCA. Worth your patience, 40
And your great merit, sir. And see the
change!

VOLTORE. Why, what success?

MOSCA. Most hapless! you
must help, sir.
Whilst we expected th' old raven, in comes

Corvino's wife, sent hither by her husband—

VOLTORE. What, with a present?

MOSCA. No, sir, on visitation; 45
I'll tell you how anon—and staying long,
The youth he grows impatient, rushes forth,
Seizeth the lady, wounds me, makes her
swear—
Or he would murder her, that was his vow—
T' affirm my patron to have done her rape, 50
Which how unlike it is, you see! and hence,
With that pretext he's gone t' accuse his
father,
Defame my patron, defeat you—

VOLTORE. Where's her husband?
Let him be sent for straight.

MOSCA. Sir, I'll go fetch him.

VOLTORE. Bring him to the *Scrutineo.*

MOSCA. Sir, I will. 55

VOLTORE. This must be stopped.

MOSCA. O, you do nobly, sir.
Alas, 'twas labored all, sir, for your good;
Nor was there want of counsel in the plot.
But Fortune can, at any time, o'erthrow
The projects of a hundred learned clerks,
sir. 60

CORBACCIO. What's that?

[*Suddenly becoming aware that others are
present.*]

VOLTORE [*to* CORBACCIO]. Will 't please
you, sir, to go along?

[*Exeunt* CORBACCIO *and* VOLTORE.]

MOSCA [*to* VOLPONE]. Patron, go in and pray
for our success.

VOLPONE. Need makes devotion; heaven
your labor bless!

ACT IV. *Scene 1*

[*A street in Venice.*]

[*Enter* SIR POLITIC *and* PEREGRINE.]

SIR POLITIC. I told you, sir, it was a plot;
you see
What observation is! You mentioned me

---

20 *device* scheme 22 *foists* tricks, but word also
means "odor" 32 *oft . . . him* frequent denial of
kinship 35 *sufficient hold* i.e., punish him in such
a way that he could not inherit 36 *stated*
settled; *double hope* i.e., inheriting Volphone's and
Corbaccio's fortunes 40 *cry . . . mercy* beg your
pardon 42 *success* result

55 *Scrutineo* law court in Senate House 60 *clerks*
learned men
IV.1.1 *it* Sir Pol apparently takes the entire
mountebank scene as a plot 2 *observation* careful
scrutiny of events; *mentioned* asked(?). In the
advice to Peregrine which Sir Politic delivers in
the remainder of the scene he details the perfect
formula for becoming an arrant fop and fool . . .

For some instructions: I will tell you, sir,
Since we are met here in this height of Venice,
Some few particulars I have set down    5
Only for this meridian, fit to be known
Of your crude traveler; and they are these.
I will not touch, sir, at your phrase, or clothes,
For they are old.

PEREGRINE.    Sir, I have better.

SIR POLITIC.    Pardon,
I meant as they are themes.

PEREGRINE.    O, sir, proceed.    10
I'll slander you no more of wit, good
    sir.

SIR POLITIC. First, for your garb, it must be
    grave and serious,
Very reserved and locked; not tell a secret
On any terms, not to your father; scarce
A fable but with caution; make sure choice    15
Both of your company and discourse; beware
You never speak a truth—

PEREGRINE.    How!

SIR POLITIC.    Not to strangers,
For those be they you must converse with
    most;
Others I would not know, sir, but at distance,
So as I still might be a saver in 'em.    20
You shall have tricks, else, passed upon you
    hourly.
And then, for your religion, profess none,
But wonder at the diversity of all;
And, for your part, protest were there no
    other
But simply the laws o' th' land, you could
    content you.    25
Nick Machiavel and Monsieur Bodin both
Were of this mind. Then must you learn the
    use

_____

4 *height* latitude    8 *touch ... at* deal with; *phrase*
manner of speaking    10 *themes* topics for discussion    12 *garb* bearing    13 *not* do not    15 *fable*
story    19 *know* acknowledge    20 *So ... 'em* "so
I might retain their friendship"(?)    24–25
*were ... you* "you could be quite content if
there were no religion, only the law" ...    26
*Machiavel ... Bodin* two advanced thinkers of
the age whose books were as popular among the
intellectuals and their imitators as Nietzsche and
Freud are today. Niccolò Machiavelli was the
author of *The Prince,* a handbook of *Realpolitik;*
and Jean Bodin had argued in his writings for
religious toleration on the grounds that it was
obviously impossible to achieve religious agreement

And handling of your silver fork at meals,
The metal of your glass (these are main
    matters
With your Italian), and to know the hour    30
When you must eat your melons and your
    figs.

PEREGRINE. Is that a point of state too?

SIR POLITIC.    Here it is.
For your Venetian, if he see a man
Preposterous in the least, he has him straight;
He has, he strips him. I'll acquaint you,
    sir.    35
I now have lived here 'tis some fourteen
    months;
Within the first week of my landing here,
All took me for a citizen of Venice,
I knew the forms so well—

PEREGRINE [*aside*].    And nothing else.

SIR POLITIC. I had read Contarini, took me
    a house,    40
Dealt with my Jews to furnish it with
    movables—
Well, if I could but find one man, one
    man
To mine own heart, whom I durst trust,
    I would—

PEREGRINE. What, what, sir?

SIR POLITIC    Make him rich, make
    him a fortune:
He should not think again. I would command
    it.    45

PEREGRINE. As how?

SIR POLITIC.    With certain projects
    that I have,
Which I may not discover.

PEREGRINE [*aside*].    If I had
But one to wager with, I would lay odds,
    now,
He tells me instantly.

SIR POLITIC.    One is, and that
I care not greatly who knows, to serve the
    state    50

_____

28 *fork* forks were fairly common in Italy, but
not in England, at this time    29 *metal* material;
*main* primary    34 *preposterous* incorrect; *straight* at
once    40 *Contarini* Cardinal Contarini (1483–
1542) wrote a book on Venice which was translated into English in 1599    41 *movables* furnishings    46 *projects* Sir Politic is an example of the
type of man known as a projector, the idea man
of his time who proposed schemes—projects—
for making money    47 *discover* disclose

Of Venice with red herrings for three
years,
And at a certain rate, from Rotterdam,
Where I have correspondence. There's a letter
        *[showing a greasy sheet of paper]*
Sent me from one o' th' States, and to that
purpose;
He cannot write his name, but that's his
mark.    55
   PEREGRINE. He is a chandler?
   SIR POLITIC.      No, a cheesemonger.
There are some other too with whom I treat
About the same negotiation;
And I will undertake it: for 'tis thus
I'll do 't with ease, I've cast it all. Your
hoy    60
Carries but three men in her, and a boy;
And she shall make me three returns a year.
So, if there come but one of three, I save;
If two, I can defalk. But this is now
If my main project fail.
   PEREGRINE.   Then you have others? 65
   SIR POLITIC. I should be loath to draw the
subtle air
Of such a place without my thousand aims.
I'll not dissemble, sir; where'er I come
I love to be considerative, and 'tis true
I have at my free hours thought upon   70
Some certain goods unto the state of Venice,
Which I do call my cautions; and, sir, which
I mean, in hope of pension, to propound
To the Great Council, then unto the Forty,
So to the Ten. My means are made
already—    75
   PEREGRINE. By whom?
   SIR POLITIC.     Sir, one that though
his place be obscure,
Yet he can sway, and they will hear him.
He's
A *commendatore.*
   PEREGRINE.   What, a common sergeant?

   SIR POLITIC. Sir, such as they are put it in
their mouths
What they should say, sometimes, as well as
greater.    80
I think I have my notes to show you—
        *[Searching his pockets.]*
   PEREGRINE.        Good sir.
   SIR POLITIC. But you shall swear unto me,
on your gentry,
Not to anticipate—
   PEREGRINE.   I, sir?
   SIR POLITIC.     Nor reveal
A circumstance—My paper is not with me.
   PEREGRINE. O, but you can remember, sir.
   SIR POLITIC.     My first is  85
Concerning tinderboxes. You must know
No family is here without its box.
Now, sir, it being so portable a thing,
Put case that you or I were ill affected
Unto the state; sir, with it in our pockets  90
Might not I go into the Arsenal?
Or you? Come out again? And none the
wiser?
   PEREGRINE. Except yourself, sir.
   SIR POLITIC.    Go to, then. I therefore
Advertise to the state how fit it were
That none but such as were known
patriots,    95
Sound lovers of their country, should be
suffered
T' enjoy them in their houses; and even
those
Sealed at some office, and at such a bigness
As might not lurk in pockets.
   PEREGRINE.       Admirable!
   SIR POLITIC. My next is, how t' inquire, and
be resolved    100
By present demonstration, whether a ship
Newly arrivèd from Syria, or from
Any suspected part of all the Levant,
Be guilty of the plague. And where they use
To lie out forty, fifty days, sometimes,  105
About the *Lazaretto* for their trial,

---

53 *correspondence* commercial connections  54 *States* Holland; *that purpose* i.e., selling herring to Venice  56 *chandler* seller of candles. Peregrine is commenting on the greasiness of the paper  60 *cast* figured; *hoy* small Dutch coastal boat  64 *defalk* retrench financially  69 *considerative* inquiring and thoughtful  72 *cautions* precautions  73 *pension* he hopes for a pension from the state as reward for his projects  74–75 *Great . . . Ten* the ruling bodies of Venice in order of importance

---

79–80 "Common sergeants as well as more important people sometimes tell the powerful what to think and say"  89 *Put case* "say for example"  91 *Arsenal* famous Venetian building which housed all their ships and weapons  94 *Advertise* make known  97 *them* i.e., tinderboxes  101 *present demonstration* immediate experiment  104 *guilty of* infected with; *use* are accustomed  106 *Lazaretto* a quarantine hospital

I'll save that charge and loss unto the
merchant,
And in an hour clear the doubt.
PEREGRINE.                         Indeed, sir!
SIR POLITIC. Or—I will lose my labor.
PEREGRINE.           My faith, that's much.
SIR POLITIC. Nay, sir, conceive me.
'Twill cost me, in onions,            110
Some thirty livres—
PEREGRINE.   Which is one pound sterling.
SIR POLITIC.   Beside   my   waterworks.
For this I do, sir:
First, I bring in your ship 'twixt two brick
walls—
But those the state shall venture. On the one
I strain me a fair tarpaulin, and in that   115
I stick my onions, cut in halves; the other
Is full of loopholes, out at which I thrust
The noses of my bellows; and those bellows
I keep, with waterworks, in perpetual motion,
Which is the easiest matter of a hundred.   120
Now, sir, your onion, which doth naturally
Attract th' infection, and your bellows
blowing
The air upon him, will show instantly
By his changed color if there be contagion,
Or else remain as fair as at the first.   125
Now 'tis known, 'tis nothing.
PEREGRINE.                 You are right, sir.
SIR POLITIC. I would I had my note.
                    [Searching his pockets.]
PEREGRINE                  Faith, so would I.
But you ha' done well for once, sir.
SIR POLITIC.                    Were I false,
Or would be made so, I could show you
reasons
How I could sell this state, now, to the
Turk—                               130
Spite of their galleys, or their—
         [Still frantically searching his pocket.]
PEREGRINE.              Pray you, Sir Pol.
SIR POLITIC. I have 'em not about me.
PEREGRINE.                  That I feared.
They're there, sir? [Pulling a book from SIR
POL's pocket.]

SIR POLITIC.            No, this is my diary,
Wherein I note my actions of the day.
  PEREGRINE. Pray you let's see, sir. What is
here?—"Notandum,               135
A rat had gnawn my spur leathers; notwith-
standing,
I put on new and did go forth; but first
I threw three beans over the threshold. Item,
I went and bought two toothpicks, whereof
one
I burst, immediately, in a discourse   140
With a Dutch merchant 'bout ragion del stato.
From him I went and paid a moccenigo
For piecing my silk stockings; by the way
I cheapened sprats, and at St. Mark's
I urined."
Faith, these are politic notes!
SIR POLITIC.              Sir, I do slip 145
No action of my life, thus but I quote it.
PEREGRINE. Believe me it is wise!
SIR POLITIC.              Nay, sir, read forth.

*Scene 2*

[*Enter* LADY WOULDBE, NANO, *and two*
WOMEN.]
LADY WOULDBE. Where should this loose
knight be, trow? Sure, he's housed.
NANO. Why, then he's fast.
LADY WOULDBE.      Ay, he plays both
with me.
I pray you stay. This heat will do more harm
To my complexion than his heart is worth.
I do not care to hinder, but to take him.   5
How it comes off!      [Rubbing her makeup.]
1ST WOMAN.      My master's yonder.
                                [Pointing.]
LADY WOULDBE.                  Where?

133 *diary* Jonson is burlesquing the many trave-
lers of his time who kept and published journals
in which they noted every trivial detail of their
journeys, like that meticulous observer of petty
facts, Captain Lemuel Gulliver   138 *three beans*
...Beans were traditionally believed to have
an expiatcry value, something like "knocking
on wood"   141 *ragion del stato* political affairs
142 *moccenigo* coin of small value   143 *piecing*
mending   144 *cheapened* bargained for   145 *slip*
allow to pass   146 *thus* but but in this manner;
*quote* note   147 *forth* on
IV.2.1 *loose* lascivious; *housed* i.e., in a bawdy
house   2 *fast* caught; *both* fast and loose, see
note to I.2.8

108 *clear the doubt* make sure (whether they are
infected)   111 *livre* French coin   114 *venture* pay
for   121–22 *naturally Attract* Onions were believed
to collect plague infection   128 *false* traitorous
129 *reasons* feasible methods(?)   131 *their* i.e., the
Venetians'

2ND WOMAN. With a young gentleman.

LADY WOULDBE.                 That same's the party!
In man's apparel! Pray you, sir, jog my
    knight.
I will be tender to his reputation,
However he demerit.

SIR POLITIC.                 My lady!

PEREGRINE.                     Where?     10

SIR POLITIC. 'Tis she indeed; sir, you shall
    know her. She is,
Were she not mine, a lady of that merit
For fashion, and behavior, and for beauty
I durst compare—

PEREGRINE.    It seems you are not jealous,
That dare commend her.

SIR POLITIC.                 Nay, and for
    discourse—                         15

PEREGRINE. Being your wife, she cannot
    miss that.

SIR POLITIC [the parties join].       Madam,
Here is a gentleman; pray you, use him fairly;
He seems a youth, but he is—

LADY WOULDBE.            None?

SIR POLITIC.                   Yes, one
Has put his face as soon into the world—

LADY WOULDBE. You mean, as early? But
    today?

SIR POLITIC.                 How's this?   20

LADY WOULDBE. Why, in this habit, sir;
    you apprehend me!
Well, Master Wouldbe, this doth not become
    you.
I had thought the odor, sir, of your good
    name
Had been more precious to you; that you
    would not
Have done this dire massàcre on your
    honor,                              25
One of your gravity, and rank besides!
But knights, I see, care little for the oath
They make to ladies, chiefly their own ladies.

SIR POLITIC. Now, by my spurs, the symbol
    of my knighthood—

PEREGRINE [aside]. Lord, how his brain is
    humbled for an oath!                30

SIR POLITIC. I reach you not.

LADY WOULDBE.           Right sir, your policy
May bear it through thus. [To PEREGRINE.]
    Sir, a word with you,
I would be loath to contest publicly
With any gentlewoman, or to seem
Froward, or violent, as The Courtier says.   35
It comes too near rusticity in a lady,
Which I would shun by all means. And,
    however
I may deserve from Master Wouldbe, yet
T' have one fair gentlewoman, thus, be
    made
Th' unkind instrument to wrong another,   40
And one she knows not, ay, and to persèver,
In my poor judgment, is not warranted
From being a solecism in our sex,
If not in manners.

PEREGRINE.       How is this!

SIR POLITIC.                   Sweet madam,
Come nearer to your aim.

LADY WOULDBE.     Marry, and will, sir.   45
Since you provoke me with your impudence
And laughter of your light land-siren here,
Your Sporus, your hermaphrodite—

PEREGRINE.                   What's here?
Poetic fury and historic storms!

SIR POLITIC. The gentleman, believe it, is
    of worth,                          50
And of our nation.

LADY WOULDBE.        Ay, your Whitefriars
    nation!

—————

31 reach understand; policy craft  32 bear it through
carry it off  35 Froward perverse; The Courtier Il
Cortegiano (1528), by Baldassare Castiglione, the
most famous of the Renaissance handbooks on
the conduct becoming to a gentleman or gentlewoman . . .  36 rusticity country manners, vulgarity  41 persèver accented on second syllable
42 warranted guaranteed (against)  43 solecism . . .
sex sexual impropriety—the lady's language is
overcharged  45 Come . . . aim make your point
more clearly  47 light immoral  48 Sporus a
young man whom Nero fancied. He had him
castrated and then married him with full ceremony. Volpone has Castrone in his private zoo
51 Whitefriars nation Whitefriars was a "liberty"
within the City of London, one of those areas
exempted by Royal Charter in times past from
the control of the town. In Jonson's day the
outcasts and those fleeing from the law who had
taken refuge here had set up a state of their
own. . . .

—————

8 jog poke(?), remind  10 demerit does not deserve (care for his reputation)  15 discourse conversation  16 miss lack  21 habit dress  25 massàcre
accented on second syllable  30 humbled literally,
brought low, i.e., all the way down to his spurs . . .

Come, I blush for you, Master Wouldbe, ay;
And am ashamed you should ha' no more
　　forehead
Than thus to be the patron, or St. George,
To a lewd harlot, a base fricatrice,　　　55
A female devil in a male outside.
　　SIR POLITIC.　　　　　　　　Nay,
And you be such a one, I must bid adieu
To your delights. The case appears too liquid.
　　　　　　　　　　　　　　　[*Exit.*]
　　LADY WOULDBE. Ay, you may carry't clear,
　　with your state-face!
But for your carnival concupiscence,　　60
Who here is fled for liberty of conscience,
From furious persecution of the marshal,
Her will I disc'ple.
　　PEREGRINE.　　　This is fine, i' faith!
And do you use this often? Is this part
Of your wit's exercise, 'gainst you have
　　occasion?　　　　　　　　　　　65
Madam—
　　LADY WOULDBE. Go to sir.
　　PEREGRINE.　　　Do you hear me, lady?
Why, if your knight have set you to beg
　　shirts,
Or to invite me home, you might have done
　　it
A nearer way by far.
　　LADY WOULDBE.　This cannot work you
Out of my snare.
　　PEREGRINE.　　Why, am I in it, then?　70
Indeed, your husband told me you were fair,
And so you are; only your nose inclines—
That side that's next the sun—to the queen-
　　apple.
　　LADY WOULDBE. This cannot be endured by
　　any patience.

---

53 *forehead* shame　55 *fricatrice* literally a massage, but also slang for whore　59 *carry't clear* carry on your pretense (of innocence); *state-face* grave, official manner—Lady Wouldbe seems to take her husband's pretenses to statesmanship seriously　60 *carnival concupiscence* licentious wench—Lady Wouldbe is close to using malapropisms　61 *liberty of conscience* i.e., freedom to practice her bawdy trade　62 *marshal* court officer and keeper of prisons　63 *disc'ple* discipline　64 *use this* act in this way　65 *'gainst* in preparation for a time when; *occasion* real need　69 *nearer* more direct　71 *fair* light complexioned—considered an attribute of beauty　72 *inclines* tends　73 *queen-apple* i.e., bright red

*Scene 3*

[*Enter* MOSCA.]
　　MOSCA. What's the matter, madam?
　　LADY WOULDBE.　　　　　If the Senate
Right not my quest in this, I will protest 'em
To all the world no aristocracy.
　　MOSCA. What is the injury, lady?
　　LADY WOULDBE.　　　　Why, the callet
You told me of, here I have ta'en
　　disguised.　　　　　　　　　　5
　　MOSCA. Who? This! What means your
　　ladyship? The creature
I mentioned to you is apprehended, now
Before the Senate. You shall see her—
　　LADY WOULDBE.　　　　　　Where?
　　MOSCA. I'll bring you to her. This young
　　gentleman,
I saw him land this morning at the port.　10
　　LADY WOULDBE. Is't possible? How has
　　my judgment wandered!
Sir, I must, blushing, say to you, I have
　　erred;
And plead your pardon.
　　PEREGRINE.　What, more changes yet?
　　LADY WOULDBE. I hope y' ha' not the
　　malice to remember
A gentlewoman's passion. If you stay　　15
In Venice, here, please you to use me, sir—
　　MOSCA. Will you go, madam?
　　LADY WOULDBE.　　　　Pray you, sir,
　　use me. In faith,
The more you see me, the more I shall
　　conceive
You have forgot our quarrel.
　　　[*Exeunt* LADY WOULDBE, MOSCA, NANO,
　　　　　　　　　　　　*and* WOMEN.]
　　PEREGRINE.　　　　　This is rare!
Sir Politic Wouldbe? No, Sir Politic Bawd,　20
To bring me, thus, acquainted with his
　　wife!
Well, wise Sir Pol, since you have practiced
　　thus

---

IV.3.2 *quest* petition; *protest* publish　4 *callet* prostitute　16 *use* employ, make use of in social matters; but the word has also a sexual meaning, as does "conceive" in line 18, which Peregrine picks up quickly. Lady Wouldbe is as clumsy as her husband in her choice of language　20 *Bawd* pander　21 *bring* make　22 *practiced* intrigued

Upon my freshmanship, I'll try your salt-
head,
What proof it is against a counterplot.

[Exit.]

Scene 4

[The Scrutineo, the Venetian court of law.]
[Enter VOLTORE, CORBACCIO, CORVINO,
and MOSCA.]

VOLTORE. Well, now you know the carriage
of the business,
Your constancy is all that is required,
Unto the safety of it.
  MOSCA.             Is the lie
Safely conveyed amongst us? Is that sure?
Knows every man his burden?
  CORVINO.          Yes.
  MOSCA.            Then shrink not. 5
  CORVINO [aside to MOSCA]. But knows the
advocate the truth?
  MOSCA.          O sir,
By no means. I devised a formal tale
That salved your reputation. But be valiant,
sir.
  CORVINO. I fear no one but him, that this
his pleading
Should make him stand for a co-heir—
  MOSCA.          Co-halter! 10
Hang him, we will but use his tongue, his
noise,
As we do Croaker's here. [Pointing to COR-
BACCIO.]
  CORVINO.       Ay, what shall he do?
  MOSCA. When we ha' done, you mean?
  CORVINO.          Yes.
  MOSCA.         Why, we'll think:
Sell him for mummia, he's half dust already.

[Turns away from CORVINO and speaks to
VOLTORE.]

Do not you smile to see this buffalo,    15
How he doth sport it with his head?—I
should,
If all were well and past. (To CORBACCIO.)
Sir, only you
Are he that shall enjoy the crop of all,
And these not know for whom they toil.
  CORBACCIO.         Ay, peace.
  MOSCA (to CORVINO). But you shall eat it.
—Much!—
         (To VOLTORE.) Worshipful sir,   20
Mercury sit upon your thund'ring tongue,
Or the French Hercules, and make your
language
As conquering as his club, to beat along,
As with a tempest, flat, our adversaries;
But much more yours, sir.
  VOLTORE.        Here they come,
  ha' done.                  25
  MOSCA. I have another witness if you
need, sir,
I can produce.
  VOLTORE.   Who is it?
  MOSCA.          Sir, I have her.

Scene 5

[Enter four AVOCATORI, BONARIO, CELIA,
NOTARIO, COMMENDATORI, and OTHERS.]

1ST AVOCATORE. The like of this the Senate
never heard of.
2ND AVOCATORE. 'Twill come most strange
to them when we report it.
4TH AVOCATORE. The gentlewoman has
been ever held
Of unreprovèd name.
3RD AVOCATORE.   So the young man.
4TH AVOCATORE. The more unnatural part,
that of his father.         5
2ND AVOCATORE. More of the husband.
1ST AVOCATORE.     I not know to give
His act a name, it is so monstrous!
4TH AVOCATORE. But the impostor, he is a
thing created

---

23 freshmanship newness, greenness—Peregrine
seems to believe that Sir Pol has been having
a joke at his expense; salt-head experienced in the
world—spoken ironically
IV.4.1 carriage management, way of handling
4 conveyed spread to all  5 burden refrain in a song,
i.e., what he is to say at the right moment  7
formal "elaborately constructed, circumstantial"
(OED)  8 salved saved  14 mummia the juice
that oozes from embalmed human bodies. It was
much prized until fairly recent times as an ingredient for certain medicines . . .

15 buffalo referring to Corvino's horns  16 sport
. . . head play about unconscious of his horns
20 eat it i.e., enjoy all the gold; Much! not at all
21 Mercury god of eloquence, but also of thieves
22 French Hercules another symbol of eloquence
27 her i.e., Lady Wouldbe
IV.5.5 part i.e., to disinherit his son  7 monstrous
trisyllabic: mon-ster-ous

T' exceed example.

1ST AVOCATORE.        And all after-times!

2ND AVOCATORE. I never heard a true voluptuary        10
Described but him.

3RD AVOCATORE.   Appear yet those were cited?

NOTARIO. All but the old magnifico, Volpone.

1ST AVOCATORE. Why is not he here?

MOSCA.        Please your fatherhoods,
Here is his advocate. Himself's so weak,
So feeble—

4TH AVOCATORE. What are you?

BONARIO.        His parasite, 15
His knave, his pander! I beseech the court
He may be forced to come, that your grave eyes
May bear strong witness of his strange impostures.

VOLTORE. Upon my faith and credit with your virtues,
He is not able to endure the air.        20

2ND AVOCATORE. Bring him, however.

3RD AVOCATORE.        We will see him.

4TH AVOCATORE.        Fetch him.

VOLTORE. Your fatherhoods' fit pleasures be obeyed,
But sure the sight will rather move your pities
Than indignation. May it please the court,
In the meantime he may be heard in me!        25
I know this place most void of prejudice,
And therefore crave it, since we have no reason
To fear our truth should hurt our cause.

3RD AVOCATORE.        Speak free.

VOLTORE. Then know, most honored fathers, I must now
Discover to your strangely abusèd ears        30
The most prodigious and most frontless piece
Of solid impudence, and treachery,
That ever vicious nature yet brought forth
To shame the state of Venice. This lewd woman,        [pointing to CELIA]
That wants no artificial looks or tears        35

To help the visor she has now put on,
Hath long been known a close adulteress
To that lascivious youth, there; [pointing to BONARIO]
                                not suspected,
I say, but known, and taken, in the act,
With him; and by this man, the easy husband,        [pointing to CORVINO] 40
Pardoned; whose timeless bounty makes him now
Stand here, the most unhappy, innocent person
That ever man's own goodness made accused.
For these, not knowing how to owe a gift
Of that dear grace but with their shame, being placed        45
So above all powers of their gratitude,
Began to hate the benefit, and in place
Of thanks, devise t' extirp the memory
Of such an act. Wherein, I pray your fatherhoods
To observe the malice, yea, the rage of creatures        50
Discovered in their evils; and what heart
Such take, even from their crimes. But that anon
Will more appear. This gentleman, the father,        [pointing to CORBACCIO]
Hearing of this foul fact, with many others,
Which daily struck at his too tender ears,        55
And grieved in nothing more than that he could not
Preserve himself a parent (his son's ills
Growing to that strange flood) at last decreed
To disinherit him.

1ST AVOCATORE.   These be strange turns!

2ND AVOCATORE. The young man's fame was ever fair and honest.        60

---

36 *visor* mask. Celia is crying and distraught, and Voltore is accusing her of pretending        37 *close secret*        45 *dear grace* rich value        45–46 *being . . . gratitude* "forgiveness is so rare a virtue that these base creatures cannot comprehend it and be grateful"        47 *benefit* i.e., Corvino's forgiveness        48 *extirp* eradicate        54 *fact* crime—Latin *facinus*        56 *grieved . . . more* "nothing grieved him more"        57 *ills* wrongdoings        58 *Growing . . . flood* increasing to such great unnaturalness        59 *turns* events        60 *fame* reputation

---

9 *example* the outstanding instances provided by art and history; *after-times* the future        11 *cited* summoned        12 *magnifico* nobleman        27 *it* i.e., to be heard        31 *frontless* shameless        35 *wants* lacks

VOLTORE. So much more full of danger is
his vice,
That can beguile so under shade of virtue.
But as I said, my honored sires, his father
Having this settled purpose—by what means
To him betrayed, we know not—and this
day                                                    65
Appointed for the deed, that parricide,
I cannot style him better, by confederacy
Preparing this his paramour to be there,
Entered Volpone's house—who was the man,
Your fatherhoods must understand, de-
signed                                              70
For the inheritance—there sought his father.
But with what purpose sought he him, my
lords?
I tremble to pronounce it, that a son
Unto a father, and to such a father,
Should have so foul, felonious intent:    75
It was, to murder him! When, being pre-
vented
By his more happy absence, what then did
he?
Not check his wicked thoughts? No, now new
deeds—
Mischief doth ever end where it begins—
An act of horror, fathers! He dragged
forth                                                 80
The agèd gentleman, that had there lain
bed-rid
Three years, and more, out off his innocent
couch,
Naked, upon the floor, there left him;
wounded
His servant in the face; and, with this
strumpet,
The stale to his forged practice, who was
glad                                                    85
To be so active—I shall here desire
Your fatherhoods to note but my collections
As most remarkable—thought at once to
stop
His father's ends, discredit his free choice
In the old gentleman, redeem themselves    90
By laying infamy upon this man,

To whom, with blushing, they should owe
their lives.
1ST AVOCATORE. What proofs have you of
this?
BONARIO.                 Most honored fathers,
I humbly crave there be no credit given
To this man's mercenary tongue.
2ND AVOCATORE.                    Forbear.  95
BONARIO. His soul moves in his fee.
3RD AVOCATORE.                        O, sir!
BONARIO.                           This fellow,
For six sols more would plead against his
Maker.
1ST AVOCATORE.You do forget yourself.
VOLTORE.            Nay, nay, grave fathers,
Let him have scope. Can any man imagine
That he will spare's accuser, that would
not                                                     100
Have spared his parent?
1ST AVOCATORE.        Well, produce your
proofs.
CELIA. I would I could forget I were a
creature!
VOLTORE. Signior Corbaccio!
4TH AVOCATORE.              What is he?
VOLTORE.                     The father.
2ND AVOCATORE. Has he had an oath?
NOTARIO.        Yes.
CORBACCIO.          What must I do now?
NOTARIO. Your testimony's craved.
CORBACCIO [cupping his ear].   Speak to the
knave?                                             105
I'll ha' my mouth first stopped with earth.
My heart
Abhors his knowledge. I disclaim in him.
1ST AVOCATORE. But for what cause?
CORBACCIO.    The mere portent of nature.
He is an utter stranger to my loins.
BONARIO. Have they made you to this?
CORBACCIO.          I will not hear thee,  110
Monster of men, swine, goat, wolf, parricide!
Speak not, thou viper.
BONARIO.              Sir, I will sit down,
And rather wish my innocence should
suffer,

---

62 *shade* cover, pretense   65 *him* i.e., Bonario
67 *confederacy* secret agreement   70 *designed* desig-
nated   85 *stale* lure; *forged practice* contrived
scheme   87 *collections* conclusions   89 *ends* intentions   90 *In* of; *old gentleman* i.e., Volpone   91
*this man* i.e., Corvino

92 *owe* acknowledge due   97 *sols* coins of small
value   99 *scope* freedom (to insult)   107 *his
knowledge* knowing him; *disclaim in him* deny
kinship to him   108 *mere portent* complete monster
110 *made . . . this* wrought you to this shape (i.e.,
a parent denying his son)

Than I resist the authority of a father.

VOLTORE. Signior Corvino!

2ND AVOCATORE.     This is strange.

1ST AVOCATORE.          Who's this?  115

NOTARIO. The husband.

4TH AVOCATORE.   Is he sworn?

NOTARIO.                He is.

3RD AVOCATORE.          Speak, then.

CORVINO. This woman, please your fatherhoods, is a whore

Of most hot exercise, more than a partridge,

Upon recòrd—

1ST AVOCATORE. No more.

CORVINO.               Neighs like a jennet.

NOTARIO. Preserve the honor of the court.

CORVINO.                    I shall,  120

And modesty of your most reverend ears.

And, yet, I hope that I may say these eyes

Have seen her glued unto that piece of cedar,

That fine, well-timbered gallant; and that
here               [tapping his forehead]

The letters may be read, thorough the
horn,                              125

That make the story perfect.

MOSCA.               Excellent, sir.

          [MOSCA and CORVINO whisper.]

CORVINO. There is no shame in this now, is
there?

MOSCA.                    None.

CORVINO. Or if I said I hoped that she
were onward

To her damnation, if there be a hell

Greater than whore and woman; a good
Catholic                             130

May make the doubt.

_____

118 *hot exercise* frequent and passionate activity;
*partridge* believed to be an extremely lecherous
bird   119 *Upon recòrd* generally known and acknowledged   124 *well-timbered gallant* handsome
young man (i.e., Bonario)   125 *letters . . . horn*
an elaborate but common play on the cuckold
and his horns. The letter is the "V" which
Corvino makes with his fingers on his forehead
to manifest his horns. But the joke also involves
the "hornbook," the Elizabethan primer from
which the schoolboy learned his letters. These
books were single printed sheets covered with
thin transparent horn to preserve them . . . ;
*thorough* through   126 *perfect* complete   128
*onward* well along   131 *make the doubt* question
(whether whore, woman, and hell be not equivalent)

3RD AVOCATORE.    His grief hath made
him frantic.

1ST AVOCATORE. Remove him hence.

                    (*She* [CELIA] *swoons.*)

2ND AVOCATORE.   Look to the woman.

CORVINO.                    Rare!

Prettily feigned! Again!

4TH AVOCATORE.    Stand from about her.

1ST AVOCATORE. Give her the air.

3RD AVOCATORE [*to* MOSCA]. What can
you say?

MOSCA.                 My wound,

May 't please your wisdoms, speaks for me,
received                           135

In aid of my good patron, when he missed

His sought-for father, when that well-taught
dame

Had her cue given her to cry out a rape.

BONARIO.  O most laid impudence!
Fathers—

3RD AVOCATORE.          Sir, be silent,

You had your hearing free, so must they
theirs.                             140

2ND AVOCATORE. I do begin to doubt th'
imposture here.

4TH AVOCATORE. This woman has too
many moods.

VOLTORE.               Grave fathers,

She is a creature of a most professed

And prostituted lewdness.

CORVINO.             Most impetuous,

Unsatisfied, grave fathers!

VOLTORE.            May her feignings  145

Not take your wisdoms; but this day she
baited

A stranger, a grave knight, with her loose
eyes

And more lascivious kisses. This man saw
'em

Together on the water in a gondola.

MOSCA. Here is the lady herself that saw
'em too,                            150

Without; who, then, had in the open streets

Pursued them, but for saving her knight's
honor.

1ST AVOCATORE. Produce that lady.

          [MOSCA *beckons to the wings.*]

_____

136 *he* i.e., Bonario   139 *laid* carefully planned
140 *free* without interference   143 *professed* open
146 *but* only; *baited* enticed   147 *loose* lewd   151
*Without* outside

2ND AVOCATORE. Let her come.
4TH AVOCATORE.    These things.
They strike with wonder!
3RD AVOCATORE.  I am turned a stone!

### Scene 6

[*Enter* LADY WOULDBE.]
MOSCA. Be resolute, madam.
LADY WOULDBE [*pointing to* CELIA]. Ay, this
 same is she.
Out, thou chameleon harlot! Now thine eyes
Vie tears with the hyena. Dar'st thou look
Upon my wrongèd face? I cry your pardons.
         [*To the Court.*]
I fear I have forgettingly transgressed  5
Against the dignity of the court—
2ND AVOCATORE.    No, madam.
LADY WOULDBE. And been exorbitant—
4TH AVOCATORE.  You have not, lady.
These proofs are strong.
LADY WOULDBE.  Surely, I had no
 purpose
To scandalize your honors, or my sex's.
3RD AVOCATORE. We do believe it.
LADY WOULDBE.   Surely, you may
 believe it.          10
2ND AVOCATORE. Madam, we do.
LADY WOULDBE.    Indeed, you may;
 my breeding
Is not so coarse—
4TH AVOCATORE.  We know it.
LADY WOULDBE.     To offend
With pertinacy—
3RD AVOCATORE. Lady—
LADY WOULDBE.   Such a presence.
No, surely,
1ST AVOCATORE. We well think it.
LADY WOULDBE.   You may think it.
1ST AVOCATORE. Let her o'ercome.
[*To* BONARIO.] What witnesses have you 15

To make good your report?
BONARIO.    Our consciences.
CELIA. And heaven, that never fails the
 innocent.
4TH AVOCATORE. These are no testimonies.
BONARIO.    Not in your courts,
Where multitude and clamor overcomes.
1ST AVOCATORE. Nay, then you do wax
 insolent.
 (VOLPONE *is brought in, as impotent.*)
VOLTORE.    Here, here, 20
The testimony comes that will convince,
And put to utter dumbness their bold tongues.
See here, grave fathers, here's the ravisher,
The rider on men's wives, the great impostor,
The grand voluptuary! Do you not think 25
These limbs should affect venery? Or these
 eyes
Covet a concubine? Pray you, mark these
 hands.
Are they not fit to stroke a lady's breasts?
Perhaps he doth dissemble!
BONARIO.    So he does.
VOLTORE. Would you ha' him tortured?
BONARIO. I would have him proved. 30
VOLTORE. Best try him, then, with
 goads, or burning irons;
Put him to the strappado. I have heard
The rack hath cured the gout. Faith, give it
 him
And help him of a malady; be courteous.
I'll undertake, before these honored fa-
 thers,           35
He shall have yet as many left diseases
As she has known adulterers, or thou strum-
 pets.
O my most equal hearers, if these deeds,
Acts of this bold and most exorbitant strain,
May pass with sufferance, what one
 citizen         40
But owes the forfeit of his life, yea, fame,

---

IV.6.2 *chameleon* . . . The chameleon was considered a "fraudulent, ravening, and gluttonous
beast," and was famed then as now for its ability
to change color to suit its circumstances 3
*hyena* The hyena was predominantly a symbol
of treachery, but it was believed able to imitate
the voices of human beings . . . 7 *exorbitant* dis-
orderly 8 *These proofs* i.e., those offered for
Celia and Bonario's guilt 13 *pertinacy* pertinacity
15 *o'ercome* conquer (in exchange of formalities)

16 *make good* verify 19 *multitude* the larger number (swearing the same story); *clamor* loudness
*Stage direction: impotent* completely disabled—
he is presumably lying in a litter 26 *affect venery*
care for lust 30 *proved* tested 32 *strappado* a
form of torture in which the victim is hoisted up
by his arms, which are first tied behind him,
and then dropped 34 *of* be rid of 39 *exorbitant
strain* disordered type 40 *pass . . . sufferance* be
permitted and condoned

To him that dares traduce him? Which of
you
Are safe, my honored fathers? I would ask,
With leave of your grave fatherhoods, if
their plot
Have any face or color like to truth?  45
Or if, unto the dullest nostril here,
It smell not rank and most abhorrèd slander?
I crave your care of this good gentleman,
Whose life is much endangered by their
fable;
And as for them, I will conclude with this:  50
That vicious persons when they are hot and
fleshed
In impious acts, their constancy abounds:
Damned deeds are done with greatest
confidence.
1ST AVOCATORE. Take 'em to custody, and
sever them.
        [CELIA and BONARIO are taken out.]
2ND AVOCATORE. 'Tis pity two such prodigies should live.  55
1ST AVOCATORE. Let the old gentleman be
returned with care.
I'm sorry our credulity wronged him.
        [Exeunt OFFICERS with VOLPONE.]
4TH AVOCATORE. These are two creatures!
3RD AVOCATORE.    I have an earthquake
in me!
2ND AVOCATORE. Their shame, even in
their cradles, fled their faces.
4TH AVOCATORE [to VOLTORE]. You've
done a worthy service to the state, sir,  60
In their discovery.
1ST AVOCATORE.   You shall hear ere night
What punishment the court decrees upon
'em.
VOLTORE. We thank your fatherhoods.—
        [Exeunt COURT OFFICIALS.]
        How like you it?
MOSCA.                Rare.
I'd ha' your tongue, sir, tipped with gold for
this;
I'd ha' you be the heir to the whole city;  65
The earth I'd have want men, ere you want
living.

They're bound to erect your statue in
St. Mark's.  [VOLTORE moves to one side.]
Signior Corvino, I would have you go
And show yourself, that you have conquered.
CORVINO.                    Yes.
MOSCA. It was much better that you should
profess  70
Yourself a cuckold, thus, than that the other
Should have been proved.
CORVINO.              Nay, I considered that.
Now, it is her fault.
MOSCA.           Then, it had been yours.
CORVINO. True. I do doubt this advocate
still.
MOSCA.                        I' faith,
You need not; I dare ease you of that
care.  75
CORVINO. I trust thee, Mosca.
MOSCA.           As your own soul, sir.
        [Exit CORVINO.]
CORBACCIO.                    Mosca!
MOSCA. Now for your business, sir.
CORBACCIO.        How! Ha' you business?
MOSCA. Yes, yours, sir.
CORBACCIO.    O, none else?
MOSCA.                None else, not I.
CORBACCIO. Be careful then.
MOSCA.                Rest you with
both your eyes, sir.
CORBACCIO. Dispatch it.
MOSCA.            Instantly.
CORBACCIO.            And look that all  80
Whatever be put in: jewels, plate, moneys,
Household stuff, bedding, curtains.
MOSCA.                Curtain-rings, sir;
Only the advocate's fee must be deducted.
CORBACCIO. I'll pay him now; you'll be
too prodigal.
MOSCA. Sir, I must tender it.
CORBACCIO.        Two chequins is well?  85
MOSCA. No, six, sir.
CORBACCIO. 'Tis too much.
MOSCA.            He talked a great while,
You must consider that, sir.
CORBACCIO.            Well, there's three—
MOSCA. I'll give it him.

45 face or color appearance or seeming.  49 fable
falsehood.  51 fleshed hardened, confirmed  52
constancy firm determination.  55 prodigies unnatural creatures, monsters  66 living income

71 other i.e., that he was pander for his wife  74
doubt suspect  78 none no one  79 Rest . . . eyes
"Don't worry about a thing"  80 Dispatch be
quick about  81 in i.e., in the inventory of Volpone's goods  85 tender give

CORBACCIO.  Do so, and there's for thee.
[*Gives* MOSCA *money and exits.*]
MOSCA. Bountiful bones! What horrid,
strange offense
Did he commit 'gainst nature in his youth, 90
Worthy this age? [*To* VOLTORE.] You see,
sir, how I work
Unto your ends; take you no notice.
VOLTORE.                              No,
I'll leave you.
MOSCA.    All is yours, [*exit* VOLTORE]—the
devil and all,
Good advocate!—[*to* LADY WOULDBE] Ma-
dam, I'll bring you home.
LADY WOULDBE. No, I'll go see your patron.
MOSCA.            That you shall not.   95
I'll tell you why: my purpose is to urge
My patron to reform his will, and for
The zeal you've shown today, whereas before
You were but third or fourth, you shall
be now
Put in the first; which would appear as
begged                                   100
If you were present. Therefore—
LADY WOULDBE.        You shall sway me.
[*Exeunt.*]


ACT V. *Scene 1*

[VOLPONE's *house. Enter* VOLPONE.]
VOLPONE. Well, I am here, and all this
brunt is past.
I ne'er was in dislike with my disguise
Till this fled moment. Here, 'twas good, in
private,
But in your public—*Cavè*, whilst I breathe.
'Fore God, my left leg 'gan to have the
cramp,                                    5
And I apprehended, straight, some power
had struck me
With a dead palsy. Well, I must be merry
And shake it off. A many of these fears
Would put me into some villainous disease

Should they come thick upon me. I'll prevent
'em.                                      10
Give me a bowl of lusty wine to fright
This humor from my heart. Hum, hum,
hum!                      (*He drinks.*)
'Tis almost gone already; I shall conquer.
Any device, now, of rare, ingenious knavery
That would possess me with a violent
laughter,                                 15
Would make me up again. So, so, so, so.
(*Drinks again.*)
This heat is life; 'tis blood by this time!
Mosca!

*Scene 2*

[*Enter* MOSCA.]
MOSCA. How now, sir? Does the day look
clear again?
Are we recovered? and wrought out of error
Into our way, to see our path before us?
Is our trade free once more?
VOLPONE.            Exquisite Mosca!
MOSCA. Was it not carried learnedly?
VOLPONE.            And stoutly.   5
Good wits are greatest in extremities.
MOSCA. It were a folly beyond thought
to trust
Any grand act unto a cowardly spirit.
You are not taken with it enough, methinks?
VOLPONE. O, more than if I had enjoyed
the wench.                                10
The pleasure of all womankind's not like it.
MOSCA. Why, now you speak, sir! We must
here be fixed;
Here we must rest. This is our masterpiece;
We cannot think to go beyond this.
VOLPONE.                 True,
Th'ast played thy prize, my precious Mosca.
MOSCA.                Nay, sir,   15
To gull the court—
VOLPONE.    And quite divert the torrent
Upon the innocent.

---

89 *Bountiful bones* This may be an exclamation of surprise at the physical and moral ugliness of Corbaccio, or it may refer ironically to his stinginess 91 *Worthy this age* "to have justified his horrible state in old age"  97 *reform* rewrite 101 *sway* persuade
V.1.1 *brunt* confusion, crisis  3 *fled* past  4 *Cavè* beware  6 *apprehended* felt; *straight* at once

16 *make me up* restore me  17 *heat ... time* According to the Renaissance physiology, food was turned by the liver into the four humors (see above, note II.2. 110–12) balanced in the blood. This blood then went to the heart where it created "vital heat" ...
V.2.6 *extremities* dangerous situations  7 *beyond thought* unthinkable  16 *gull* trick; *torrent* i.e., the law

MOSCA.　　　　　Yes, and to make
So rare a music out of discords—
　VOLPONE.　　　　　　　Right.
That yet to me 's the strangest; how th'ast
　borne it!
That these, being so divided 'mongst them-
　selves,　　　　　　　　　　　　20
Should not scent somewhat, or in me or thee,
Or doubt their own side.
　MOSCA.　　　　True, they will not see't.
Too much light blinds 'em, I think. Each
　of'em
Is so possessed and stuffed with his own hopes
That anything unto the contrary,　　　25
Never so true, or never so apparent,
Never so palpable, they will resist it—
　VOLPONE. Like a temptation of the devil.
　MOSCA.　　　　　　　Right, sir.
Merchants may talk of trade, and your great
　signiors
Of land that yields well; but if Italy　　30
Have any glebe more fruitful than these
　fellows,
I am deceived. Did not your advocate rare?
　VOLPONE. O—"My most honored fathers,
　my grave fathers,
Under correction of your fatherhoods,
What face of truth is here? If these strange
　deeds　　　　　　　　　　　　35
May pass, most honored fathers"—I had
　much ado
To forbear laughing.
　MOSCA.　　　'T seemed to me you sweat, sir.
　VOLPONE. In troth, I did a little.
　MOSCA.　　　　　　　But confess, sir;
Were you not daunted?
　VOLPONE.　　　　In good faith, I was
A little in a mist, but not dejected;　　40
Never but still myself.
　MOSCA.　　　　　I think it, sir.
Now, so truth help me, I must needs say
　this, sir,
And out of conscience for your advocate:
He's taken pains, in faith, sir, and deserved,

In my poor judgment, I speak it under
　favor,　　　　　　　　　　　　45
Not to contrary you, sir, very richly—
Well—to be cozened.
　VOLPONE.　　　Troth, and I think so too,
By that I heard him in the latter end.
　MOSCA. O, but before, sir, had you heard
　him first
Draw it to certain heads, then aggravate,　50
Then use his vehement figures—I looked still
When he would shift a shirt; and doing this
Out of pure love, no hope of gain—
　VOLPONE.　　　　　　　'Tis right.
I cannot answer him, Mosca, as I would,
Not yet; but for thy sake, at thy entreaty,　55
I will begin e'en now to vex 'em all,
This very instant.
　MOSCA.　　　　Good, sir.
　VOLPONE.　　　　　　Call the dwarf
And eunuch forth.
　MOSCA.　　　Castrone! Nano!
　　　[Enter CASTRONE and NANO.]
　NANO.　　　　　　　　　Here.
　VOLPONE. Shall we have a jig now?
　MOSCA.　　　　What you please, sir.
　VOLPONE.　　　　　　　　Go,
Straight give out about the streets, you
　two,　　　　　　　　　　　　60
That I am dead; do it with constancy,
Sadly, do you hear? Impute it to the grief
Of this late slander.
　　　[Exeunt CASTRONE and NANO.]
　MOSCA.　　　What do you mean, sir?
　VOLPONE.　　　　　　　　O,
I shall have instantly my vulture, crow,
Raven, come flying hither on the news　65

---

18 *discords* referring to the various fools each striving to be sole heir　19 *borne* managed　21 *or . . . or* either . . . or　23 *light* i.e., their greed and hopes　31 *glebe* land　32 *rare* rarely　40 *mist* dimness of eyesight caused by bodily disorders　41 *think* believe

45 *under favor* with permission　47 *cozened* bilked　48 *By . . . end* "to judge by the latter part of his speech." Volpone was brought in halfway through Voltore's performance　50 *Draw . . . heads* gather his material into topics; *aggravate* emphasize　51 *vehement figures* powerful rhetorical tropes　52 *shift a shirt* So violent were the actions Voltore used to accompany his speech that Mosca humorously compares him to a man trying to change a shirt; or perhaps he means that Voltore worked up such a sweat that he needed to change his shirt　54 *answer* repay　59 *jig* literally a dance, but a trick is meant. Jigs were the stock-in-trade of the low comedians in the Elizabethan theater, where performances usually ended with a jig　60 *Straight* at once　61 *with constancy* firmly, i.e., seriously　62 *Sadly* gravely

To peck for carrion, my she-wolf and all,
Greedy and full of expectation—
MOSCA. And then to have it ravished from
their mouths?
VOLPONE. 'Tis true. I will ha' thee put
on a gown,
And take upon thee as thou wert mine
heir;                                              70
Show 'em a will. Open that chest and reach
Forth one of those that has the blanks.
I'll straight
Put in thy name.
MOSCA.              It will be rare, sir.
VOLPONE.                          Ay,
When they e'en gape, and find themselves
deluded—
MOSCA. Yes.
VOLPONE. And thou use them scurvily!
Dispatch,                                          75
Get on thy gown.
MOSCA.            But what, sir, if they ask
After the body?
VOLPONE.       Say it was corrupted.
MOSCA. I'll say it stunk, sir; and was fain
t' have it
Coffined up instantly and sent away.
VOLPONE. Anything, what thou wilt.
Hold, here's my will.                              80
Get thee a cap, a count-book, pen and ink,
Papers afore thee; sit as thou wert taking
An inventory of parcels. I'll get up
Behind the curtain, on a stool, and hearken;
Sometime peep over, see how they do
look,                                              85
With what degrees their blood doth leave
their faces.
O, 'twill afford me a rare meal of laughter!
MOSCA. Your advocate will turn stark dull
upon it.

VOLPONE. It will take off his oratory's
edge.
MOSCA. But your *clarissimo*, old roundback,
he                                                 90
Will crump you like a hog-louse with the
touch.
VOLPONE. And what Corvino?
MOSCA.                    O sir, look for him
Tomorrow morning with a rope and dagger
To visit all the streets; he must run mad.
My lady too, that came into the court           95
To bear false witness for your worship—
VOLPONE.                              Yes,
And kissed me 'fore the fathers, when my
face
Flowed all with oils—
MOSCA.      And sweat, sir. Why, your gold
Is such another med'cine, it dries up
All those offensive savors! It transforms    100
The most deformed, and restores 'em lovely
As 'twere the strange poetical girdle. Jove
Could not invent t' himself a shroud more
subtle
To pass Acrisius' guards. It is the thing
Makes all the world her grace, her youth,
her beauty.                                        105
VOLPONE. I think she loves me.
MOSCA.                      Who? The lady, sir?
She's jealous of you.
VOLPONE.        Dost thou say so?
[*Knocking without.*]
MOSCA.                          Hark,
There's some already.
VOLPONE.          Look!
MOSCA [*peering out*].       It is the vulture;
He has the quickest scent.
VOLPONE.                  I'll to my place,
Thou to thy posture.

70 *take . . . thee* assume such manners and airs
75 *Dispatch* hurry    78 *was fain* it was necessary
81 *count-book* ledger  83 *parcels* parts (of his possessions)    84 *curtain* In Scene 3 Jonson has the
stage direction "Volpone peeps from behind a
traverse." Either he has retreated into an inner
stage across which a curtain is drawn, or a curtain is placed on a wire across the main part of
the stage. A "traverse" may be, however, a mov-
able screen of some variety. Whatever the arrangement, the "curtain" is probably the same
one used to cover the bed ordinarily, and the effect is once again to create a stage on a stage,
a theater within a theater

90 *clarissimo* Venetian of high rank; *round-back* i.e.,
Corbaccio, who obviously stoops    91 *crump you*
curl up  93 *rope and dagger* Carrying these props
was probably a standard symbol of extravagant
madness on the Elizabethan stage. . .  98 *sweat*
Mosca will not allow Volpone to forget that he
was nervous at the trial  102 *girdle* The reference
is to the girdle of Venus, mentioned by Homer in
*The Iliad*, into which was woven "love, desire,
sweetness, soft parley, gracefulness, persuasion,
and all the powers of Venus"  102–4 *Jove . . .
guards* Acrisius was the father of Danaë whom
Jove visited in the form of a shower of gold  110
*posture* pretense, act

MOSCA. I am set.
VOLPONE. But Mosca, 110
Play the artificer now, torture 'em rarely.

### Scene 3

[*Enter* VOLTORE.]
VOLTORE. How now, my Mosca?
MOSCA [*writing*]. Turkey carpets, nine—
VOLTORE. Taking an inventory? That is
well.
MOSCA. Two suits of bedding, tissue—
VOLTORE. Where's the will?
Let me read that the while.
[*Enter* BEARERS *carrying* CORBACCIO *in a chair*.]
CORBACCIO. So, set me down,
And get you home. [*Exeunt* BEARERS.]
VOLTORE. Is he come now, to trou-
ble us? 5
MOSCA. Of cloth of gold, two more—
CORBACCIO. Is it done, Mosca?
MOSCA. Of several vellets, eight—
VOLTORE. I like his care.
CORBACCIO. Dost thou not hear?
[*Enter* CORVINO.]
CORVINO. Ha! Is the hour come, Mosca?
VOLPONE [*aside*]. Ay, now they muster.
(*Peeps from behind a traverse*.)
CORVINO. What does the advocate here,
Or this Corbaccio?
CORBACCIO. What do these here?
[*Enter* LADY WOULDBE.]
LADY WOULDBE. Mosca! 10
Is his thread spun?
MOSCA. Eight chests of linen—
VOLPONE [*aside*]. O,
My fine Dame Wouldbe, too!
CORVINO. Mosca, the will,
That I may show it these and rid 'em hence.

111 *artificer* player (?), maker of schemes
V.3.1 *Turkey carpets* used during this period as
table covers 3 *suits* sets; *bedding* covers, hangings; *tissue* woven gold cloth 4 *the while* during
the time (the inventory continues) 7 *several
vellets* separate velvet hangings 9 Stage direction: *traverse* see note to V.2.84. 11 *thread spun*
Lady Wouldbe can never abandon her elaborate
and "learned" phrasing. The myth referred to
here is that of the Three Fates. The thread of
man's life was spun by Clotho, measured by
Lachesis, and then cut by Atropos

MOSCA. Six chests of diaper, four of
damask—There.
[*Gives them the will and continues to write.*]
CORBACCIO. Is that the will?
MOSCA. Down-beds, and bolsters—
VOLPONE [*aside*]. Rare! 15
Be busy still. Now they begin to flutter;
They never think of me. Look, see, see, see!
How their swift eyes run over the long deed
Unto the name, and to the legacies,
What is bequeathed them there.
MOSCA. Ten suits of hangings— 20
VOLPONE [*aside*]. Ay, i' their garters,
Mosca. Now their hopes
Are at the gasp.
VOLTORE. Mosca the heir!
CORBACCIO. What's that?
VOLPONE [*aside*]. My advocate is dumb;
look to my merchant.
He has heard of some strange storm, a ship
is lost,
He faints; my lady will swoon. Old glazen-
eyes 25
He hath not reached his despair, yet.
CORBACCIO. All these
Are out of hope; I'm sure the man.
CORVINO. But, Mosca—
MOSCA. Two cabinets—
CORVINO. Is this in earnest?
MOSCA. One
Of ebony—
CORVINO. Or do you but delude me?
MOSCA. The other, mother of pearl—I am
very busy. 30
Good faith, it is a fortune thrown upon me—
Item, one salt of agate—not my seeking.
LADY WOULDBE. Do you hear, sir?
MOSCA. A perfumed box—
Pray you forbear,
You see I'm troubled—made of an onyx—
LADY WOULDBE. How?
MOSCA. Tomorrow, or next day, I shall
be at leisure 35
To talk with you all.
CORVINO. Is this my large hope's issue?
LADY WOULDBE. Sir, I must have a fairer
answer.

14 *diaper* cloth woven with reiterated pattern
20–21 *hangings . . . garters* "hang themselves in
their own garters," a mocking formula for suicide
22 *gasp* last gasp 32 *salt* saltcellar

MOSCA. Madam!
Marry, and shall: pray you, fairly quit my
house.
Nay, raise no tempest with your looks; but
hark you,
Remember what your ladyship offered
me 40
To put you in an heir; go to, think on 't.
And what you said e'en your best madams did
For maintenance, and why not you? Enough.
Go home and use the poor Sir Pol, your
knight, well,
For fear I tell some riddles. Go, be melan-
cholic. [Exit LADY WOULDBE.] 45
VOLPONE [aside]. O my fine devil!
CORVINO. Mosca, pray you a word.
MOSCA. Lord! Will not you take your dis-
patch hence yet?
Methinks of all you should have been
th' example.
Why should you stay here? With what
thought? What promise?
Hear you: do not you know I know you an
ass, 50
And that you would most fain have been a
wittol
If fortune would have let you? That you are
A declared cuckold, on good terms? This
pearl, [holding up jewels]
You'll say, was yours? Right. This diamond?
I'll not deny't, but thank you. Much here
else? 55
It may be so. Why, think that these good
works
May help to hide your bad. I'll not betray
you,
Although you be but extraordinary,
And have it only in title, it sufficeth.
Go home, be melancholic too, or mad. 60
[Exit CORVINO.]
VOLPONE [aside]. Rare, Mosca! How his
villainy becomes him!

---

38 *fairly* this word has roughly the present-day
sense of "just" in "just leave the house" 40
*Remember . . . me* Lady Wouldbe has obviously
offered her favors to Mosca. This fact explains
the tone of line IV.6.101 47 *dispatch* dismissal
48 *example* i.e., by leaving first show the others
the way 51 *wittol* knowing cuckold 55 *else*
otherwise 58–59 *Although . . . sufficeth* "Although
you are an unusual cuckold, being one in title
but not in fact, this will do for you"

VOLTORE. Certain he doth delude all these
for me.
CORBACCIO. Mosca the heir?
[Still straining to read the will.]
VOLPONE [aside]. O, his
four eyes have found it!
CORBACCIO. I'm cozened, cheated, by a
parasite slave!
Harlot, th'ast gulled me.
MOSCA. Yes, sir. Stop your mouth, 65
Or I shall draw the only tooth is left.
Are not you he, that filthy, covetous wretch
With the three legs, that here, in hope of
prey,
Have, any time this three year, snuffed about
With your most grov'ling nose, and would
have hired 70
Me to the pois'ning of my patron, sir?
Are not you he that have, today, in court,
Professed the disinheriting of your son?
Perjured yourself? Go home, and die, and
stink.
If you but croak a syllable, all comes out. 75
Away, and call your porters! Go, go, stink.
[Exit CORBACCIO.]
VOLPONE [aside]. Excellent varlet!
VOLTORE. Now, my faithful Mosca,
I find thy constancy.
MOSCA. Sir?
VOLTORE. Sincere.
MOSCA. A table
Of porphyry—I mar'l you'll be thus trouble-
some.
VOLTORE. Nay, leave off now, they are
gone.
MOSCA. Why, who are you? 80
What! Who did send for you? O, cry you
mercy,
Reverend sir! Good faith, I am grieved for
you,
That any chance of mine should thus defeat
Your—I must needs say—most deserving
travails.
But I protest, sir, it was cast upon me, 85
And I could, almost, wish to be without it,
But that the will o' th' dead must be observed.
Marry, my joy is that you need it not;

---

65 *Harlot* malicious fellow—originally applied
to men 68 *three legs* Corbaccio uses a cane 69
*any time* at any time 79 *mar'l* marvel 81 *cry you
mercy* beg your pardon 83 *chance* luck

You have a gift, sir—thank your education—
Will never let you want while there are
men                                                    90
And malice to breed causes. Would I had
But half the like, for all my fortune, sir.
If I have any suits—as I do hope,
Things being so easy and direct, I shall not—
I will make bold with your obstreperous
aid;                                                    95
Conceive me, for your fee, sir. In meantime,
You that have so much law, I know ha' the
conscience
Not to be covetous of what is mine.
Good sir, I thank you for my plate; 'twill
help
To set up a young man. Good faith, you
look                                                   100
As you were costive; best go home and
purge, sir.              [*Exit* VOLTORE.]
    VOLPONE. Bid him eat lettuce well! My
    witty mischief,
              [*coming from behind curtain*]
Let me embrace thee. O that I could now
Transform thee to a Venus—Mosca, go,
Straight take my habit of *clarissimo*,        105
And walk the streets; be seen, torment 'em
more.
We must pursue as well as plot. Who would
Have lost this feast?
    MOSCA.             I doubt it will lose them.
    VOLPONE. O, my recovery shall recover all.
That I could now but think on some
disguise                                              110
To meet 'em in, and ask 'em questions.
How I would vex 'em still at every turn!
    MOSCA. Sir, I can fit you.
    VOLPONE.               Canst thou?
    MOSCA.                         Yes, I know
One o' th' *commendatori*, sir, so like you;
Him will I straight make drunk, and bring
you his habit.                                       115

VOLPONE. A rare disguise, and answering
thy brain!
O, I will be a sharp disease unto 'em.
    MOSCA. Sir, you must look for curses—
    VOLPONE.                    Till they burst;
The fox fares ever best when he is cursed.
                                      [*Exeunt.*]

*Scene 4*

[SIR POLITIC'*s house.*]
[*Enter* PEREGRINE *disguised, and three*
MERCHANTS.]
    PEREGRINE. Am I enough disguised?
    1ST MERCHANT.             I warrant you.
    PEREGRINE. All my ambition is to fright
    him only.
    2ND MERCHANT. If you could ship him
    away, 'twere excellent.
    3RD MERCHANT. To Zant, or to Aleppo?
    PEREGRINE.              Yes, and ha' his
Adventures put i' th' book of voyages,      5
And his gulled story registered for truth?
Well, gentlemen, when I am in a while,
And that you think us warm in our dis-
course,
Know your approaches.
    1ST MERCHANT.      Trust it to our care.
                        [*Exeunt* MERCHANTS.]
                        [*Enter* WOMAN.]
    PEREGRINE. Save you, fair lady. Is Sir Pol
    within?                                          10
    WOMAN. I do not know, sir.
    PEREGRINE.       Pray you say unto him,
Here is a merchant, upon earnest business,
Desires to speak with him.
    WOMAN.         I will see, sir.
    PEREGRINE.                Pray you.
                        [*Exit* WOMAN.]
I see the family is all female here.
                        [*Re-enter* WOMAN.]
    WOMAN. He says, sir, he has weighty affairs
    of state                                        15

91 *causes* lawsuits   94 *Things ... direct* i.e., the will being so clear and uncomplicated   95 *obstreperous* clamorous   96 *Conceive* understand; *for your fee* i.e., "I will not ask your services gratis but will pay the standard price"   97 *have* know   99 *plate* the one Voltore gave earlier as a present   101 *costive* constipated   102 *lettuce* a laxative   105 *habit* robe. Special dress was decreed for various social orders   108 *lose* get rid of   113 *fit you* "find just what you want"   114 *commendatori* sergeants, or minor officials, of the court

116 *answering* resembling (the rareness of Mosca's brain)   117 *sharp* painful   119 a proverbial saying
V.4.1 *warrant* assure   4 *Zant* one of the Ionian islands   5 *book of voyages* popular collections of foreign voyages such as Hakluyt's   9 *Know ... approaches* "come in at the right time"

That now require him whole; some other
time
You may possess him.

  PEREGRINE.    Pray you, say again,
If those require him whole, these will exact
him,
Whereof I bring him tidings. [*Exit* WOMAN.]
What might be
His grave affair of state now? How to
make           20
Bolognian sausages here in Venice, sparing
One o' th' ingredients?

     [*Re-enter* WOMAN.]

WOMAN.      Sir, he says he knows
By your word "tidings" that you are no
statesman,
And therefore wills you stay.

    PEREGRINE.    Sweet, pray you
return him:
I have not read so many proclamations  25
And studied them for words, as he has done,
But—Here he deigns to come.

    [*Enter* SIR POLITIC.]

  SIR POLITIC.    Sir, I must crave
Your courteous pardon. There hath chanced
today
Unkind disaster 'twixt my lady and me,
And I was penning my apology     30
To give her satisfaction, as you came now.

  PEREGRINE. Sir, I am grieved I bring you
worse disaster:
The gentleman you met at th' port today,
That told you he was newly arrived—

  SIR POLITIC.      Ay, was
A fugitive punk?

   PEREGRINE.  No, sir, a spy set on you,  35
And he has made relation to the Senate
That you professed to him to have a plot
To sell the state of Venice to the Turk.

  SIR POLITIC. O me!

  PEREGRINE.    For which warrants are
signed by this time
To apprehend you and to search your
study             40
For papers—

---

  SIR POLITIC. Alas, sir, I have none but notes
Drawn out of play-books—

  PEREGRINE.     All the better, sir.

  SIR POLITIC. And some essays. What shall
I do?

  PEREGRINE.       Sir, best
Convey yourself into a sugar-chest,
Or, if you could lie round, a frail were
rare,           45
And I could send you aboard.

  SIR POLITIC.    Sir, I but talked so
For discourse' sake merely. (*They knock
without.*)

  PEREGRINE.    Hark, they are there.

  SIR POLITIC. I am a wretch, a wretch!

  PEREGRINE.   What will you do, sir?
Ha' you ne'er a currant-butt to leap into?
They'll put you to the rack, you must be
sudden.          50

  SIR POLITIC. Sir, I have an engine—

  3RD MERCHANT [*calling from off-stage*]. Sir
Politic Wouldbe!

  2ND MERCHANT. Where is he?

  SIR POLITIC.    That I have thought
upon beforetime.

  PEREGRINE. What is it?

  SIR POLITIC.     I shall ne'er endure
the torture!
Marry, it is, sir, of a tortoise-shell,
Fitted for these extremities. Pray you, sir,
help me.         55

   [*He gets into a large tortoise shell.*]
Here I've a place, sir, to put back my legs;
Please you to lay it on, sir. With this cap
And my black gloves, I'll lie, sir, like a
tortoise,
Till they are gone.

  PEREGRINE.  And call you this an engine?

  SIR POLITIC. Mine own device—Good sir,
bid my wife's women     60
To burn my papers.

  (*They* [*the three* MERCHANTS] *rush in.*)

1ST MERCHANT.    Where's he hid?

3RD MERCHANT.      We must,
And will, sure, find him.

2ND MERCHANT.    Which is his study?

---

16 *require him whole* occupy his entire attention
17 *possess* Sir Pol's elaborate way of saying "see"
18 *exact* force  21 *sparing* leaving out  23 "*tidings*"
"intelligences" would be the statesman's word
24 *return him* "say to him in return"  35 *punk*
prostitute

42 *play-books* printed plays  45 *frail* rush basket
used for packing figs  47 *discourse'* conversation's
49 *currant-butt* cask for currants  51 *engine* device
55 *Fitted* The Quarto reads "apted," i.e., suited
57 *it* i.e., the shell

1ST MERCHANT. What
Are you, sir?

PEREGRINE. I'm a merchant that came here
To look upon this tortoise.

3RD MERCHANT. How!

1ST MERCHANT. St. Mark!
What beast is this?

PEREGRINE. It is a fish.

2ND MERCHANT [*striking the tortoise*]. Come
out here! 65

PEREGRINE. Nay, you may strike him, sir,
and tread upon him.
He'll bear a cart.

1ST MERCHANT. What, to run over him?

PEREGRINE. Yes.

3RD MERCHANT. Let's jump upon him.

2ND MERCHANT. Can he not go?

PEREGRINE. He creeps, sir.

1ST MERCHANT. Let's see him creep.
[*Prodding him*].

PEREGRINE. No, good sir, you
will hurt him.

2ND MERCHANT. Heart, I'll see him creep,
or prick his guts. 70

3RD MERCHANT. Come out here!

PEREGRINE [*aside to* SIR POLITIC]. Pray
you, sir, creep a little.

1ST MERCHANT. Forth!

2ND MERCHANT. Yet further.

PEREGRINE [*aside to* SIR POLITIC]. Good
sir, creep.

2ND MERCHANT. We'll see his legs.
(*They pull off the shell and discover him.*)

3RD MERCHANT. Godso, he has garters!

1ST MERCHANT. Ay, and gloves!

2ND MERCHANT. Is this
Your fearful tortoise?

PEREGRINE. Now, Sir Pol, we are even;
[*throwing off his disguise*]
For your next project I shall be prepared. 75
I am sorry for the funeral of your notes, sir.

1ST MERCHANT. 'Twere a rare motion to be
seen in Fleet Street.

2ND MERCHANT. Ay, i' the term.

1ST MERCHANT. Or Smithfield, in the fair.

3RD MERCHANT. Methinks 'tis but a melancholic sight.

PEREGRINE. Farewell, most politic tortoise!
[*Exeunt* PEREGRINE *and* MERCHANTS.]

SIR POLITIC. Where's my lady? 80
Knows she of this?

WOMAN. I know not, sir.

SIR POLITIC. Inquire.
[*Exit* WOMAN.]
O, I shall be the fable of all feasts,
The freight of the *gazetti*, ship-boys' tale,
And, which is worst, even talk for ordinaries.
[*Re-enter* WOMAN.]

WOMAN. My lady's come most melancholic
home, 85
And says, sir, she will straight to sea, for
physic.

SIR POLITIC. And I, to shun this place and
clime forever,
Creeping with house on back, and think it
well
To shrink my poor head in my politic shell.
[*Exeunt.*]

*Scene 5*

[VOLPONE'S *house.*]
[*Enter* VOLPONE *in the habit of a commendatore,* MOSCA *of a clarissimo.*]

VOLPONE. Am I then like him?

MOSCA. O sir, you are he;
No man can sever you.

VOLPONE. Good.

MOSCA. But what am I?

VOLPONE. 'Fore heav'n, a brave *clarissimo*,
thou becom'st it!
Pity thou wert not born one.

MOSCA. If I hold
My made one, 'twill be well.

VOLPONE. I'll go and see 5
What news, first, at the court [*Exit.*]

MOSCA. Do so. My fox
Is out on his hole, and ere he shall re-enter,

83 *freight* topic; *gazetti* newspapers  84 *ordinaries* taverns  86 *straight . . . sea* sail at once; *for physic* for health
V.5.1 *him* i.e., the commendatore  2 *sever* separate, distinguish  4 *hold* retain  5 *made one* assumed status (of clarissimo)  6-7 *fox . . . hole* Fox-in-the-hole was a game played by English boys. They hopped about on one leg and beat one another with gloves and pieces of leather tied on a string  7 *on* of

68 *go* walk  70 *Heart* a mild oath  72 Stage direction: *discover* disclose  76 *funeral* burning. The ironic comparison is to a funeral pyre  77 *motion* puppet show  78 *term* the period when the courts were in session and London filled with people; *Smithfield . . . fair* Bartholomew Fair, with many sideshows, was held in Smithfield

I'll make him languish in his borrowed case,
Except he come to composition with me.
Androgyno, Castrone, Nano!
[*Enter* ANDROGYNO, CASTRONE, *and* NANO.]
ALL. Here. 10
MOSCA. Go recreate yourselves abroad, go
sport. [*Exeunt the three.*]
So, now I have the keys and am possessed.
Since he will needs be dead afore his time,
I'll bury him, or gain by him. I'm his heir,
And so will keep me, till he share at least. 15
To cozen him of all were but a cheat
Well placed; no man would cònstrue it a sin.
Let his sport pay for 't. This is called the
fox-trap. [*Exit.*]

### Scene 6

[*A Venetian street.*]
[*Enter* CORBACCIO *and* CORVINO.]
CORBACCIO. They say the court is set.
CORVINO. We must maintain
Our first tale good, for both our reputations.
CORBACCIO. Why, mine's no tale! My son
would, there, have killed me.
CORVINO. That's true, I had forgot. Mine
is, I am sure.
But for your will, sir.
CORBACCIO. Ay, I'll come upon him 5
For that hereafter, now his patron's dead.
[*Enter* VOLPONE *in disguise.*]
VOLPONE. Signior Corvino! And Corbac-
cio! Sir,
Much joy unto you.
CORVINO. Of what?
VOLPONE. The sudden good
Dropped down upon you—
CORBACCIO. Where?
VOLPONE. And none knows how,
From old Volpone, sir.
CORBACCIO. Out, arrant knave! 10
VOLPONE. Let not your too much wealth,
sir, make you furious.

CORBACCIO. Away, thou varlet.
VOLPONE. Why, sir?
CORBACCIO. Dost thou mock me?
VOLPONE. You mock the world, sir; did
you not change wills?
CORBACCIO. Out, harlot!
VOLPONE. O! Belike you are the man,
Signior Corvino? Faith, you carry it well; 15
You grow not mad withal. I love your spirit.
You are not over-leavened with your fortune.
You should ha' some would swell now like
a wine-fat
With such an autumn—Did he gi' you all,
sir?
CORVINO. Avoid, you rascal.
VOLPONE. Troth, your wife has shown 20
Herself a very woman! But you are well,
You need not care, you have a good estate
To bear it out, sir, better by this chance.
Except Corbaccio have a share?
CORBACCIO. Hence, varlet.
VOLPONE. You will not be a'known, sir?
Why, 'tis wise. 25
Thus do all gamesters, at all games, dissemble.
No man will seem to win.
[*Exeunt* CORVINO *and* CORBACCIO.]
Here comes my vulture,
Heaving his beak up i' the air, and snuffing.

### Scene 7

[*Enter* VOLTORE *to* VOLPONE.]
VOLTORE. Outstripped thus, by a parasite!
A slave,
Would run on errands, and make legs for
crumbs?
Well, what I'll do—
VOLPONE. The court stays for your
worship.
I e'en rejoice, sir, at your worship's happiness,
And that it fell into so learned hands, 5
That understand the fingering—
VOLTORE. What do you mean?

---

8 *case* disguise 9 *Except* unless; *composition* agreement 11 *recreate* enjoy 12 *possessed* in possession 13 *will needs be* insists on being 15 *keep me*
remain 18 *Let . . . it* "Let the pleasure he is getting from all this pay him for what it is going to
cost"
V.6.1–2 *maintain . . . good* "continue to insist on
the truth of the tales told first in court" 5 *him*
i.e., Mosca

12 *varlet* low fellow; also the title for a sergeant
of the court 13 *change* exchange 17 *over-leavened*
puffed up 18 *fat* vat 19 *autumn* i.e., rich harvest 20 *Avoid* get out! 21 *very* true 23 *bear it
out* carry it off 24 *Except* unless 25 *a'known* acknowledged (the heir)
V.7.1 *Outstripped* outrun, beaten 2 *Would* "who
used to"; *legs* bows

VOLPONE. I mean to be a suitor to your worship
For the small tenement, out of reparations,
That at the end of your long row of houses,
By the *Pescheria*; it was, in Volpone's time, 10
Your predecessor, ere he grew diseased,
A handsome, pretty, customed bawdy-house
As any was in Venice—none dispraised—
But fell with him. His body and that house
Decayed together.
    VOLTORE. Come, sir, leave your prating. 15
    VOLPONE. Why, if your worship give me but your hand,
That I may ha' the refusal, I have done.
'Tis a mere toy to you, sir, candle-rents.
As your learned worship knows—
    VOLTORE.         What do I know?
    VOLPONE. Marry, no end of your wealth, sir, God decrease it.     20
    VOLTORE. Mistaking knave! What, mock'st thou my misfortune?
    VOLPONE. His blessing on your heart, sir; would 'twere more!   [*Exit* VOLTORE.]
Now, to my first again, at the next corner.

### Scene 8

[VOLPONE *remains on stage to one side.* COR-
    BACCIO *and* CORVINO *enter.*]
    [MOSCA *passes slowly across stage.*]
    CORBACCIO. See, in our habit! See the im-
    pudent varlet!
    CORVINO. That I could shoot mine eyes at him, like gunstones!   [*Exit* MOSCA.]
    VOLPONE. But is this true, sir, of the parasite?
    CORBACCIO. Again t' afflict us? Monster!
    VOLPONE.         In good faith, sir,
I'm heartily grieved a beard of your grave length     5
Should be so over-reached. I never brooked

That parasite's hair; methought his nose should cozen.
There still was somewhat in his look did promise
The bane of a *clarissimo*.
    CORBACCIO.         Knave—
    VOLPONE.         Methinks
Yet you, that are so traded i' the world,   10
A witty merchant, the fine bird Corvino,
That have such moral emblems on your name,
Should not have sung your shame, and dropped your cheese,
To let the fox laugh at your emptiness.
    CORVINO. Sirrah, you think the privilege of the place,     15
And your red, saucy cap, that seems to me
Nailed to your jolt-head with those two chequins,
Can warrant your abuses. Come you hither:
You shall perceive, sir, I dare beat you. Approach.
    VOLPONE. No haste, sir. I do know your valor well,     20
Since you durst publish what you are, sir.
    CORVINO.         Tarry,
I'd speak with you.
    VOLPONE.       Sir, sir, another time—
                    [*Backing away.*]
    CORVINO. Nay, now.
    VOLPONE.   O God, sir! I were a wise man
Would stand the fury of a distracted cuckold.
               (MOSCA *walks by 'em.*)
    CORBACCIO. What, come again!
    VOLPONE [*aside*].       Upon 'em,
    Mosca; save me.     25
    CORBACCIO. The air's infected where he breathes.
    CORVINO.         Let's fly him.

---

8 *reparations* repairs   10 *Pescheria* fish-market
12 *customed* well patronized   13 *none dispraised*
"not to say anything bad of the others"   17 *refusal* option; *have done* am finished (asking favors)
18 *toy* trifle; *candle-rents* rents from slums   20 *decrease* an intentional malapropism—he pretends
to mean "increase"
V.8.1 *our habit* i.e., the dress of a clarissimo   2
*gunstones* stone cannonballs   5 *beard ... length*
man as old and wise as you   6 *over-reached* out-
smarted; *brooked* could endure

8 *still* always; *somewhat* something   10 *traded* experienced   12–14 *moral emblems ... emptiness* In
the emblem books popular at this time, drawings
of various animals were used to symbolize human
vices, which were then explained in verses. Volpone has in mind here a picture of a crow dropping a piece of cheese while the fox below laughs
at him...   15 *privilege ... place* "the immunity
conferred by your rank"   16–17 *cap ... chequins*
a commendatore wore a red hat with two gilt
buttons on the front   17 *jolt-head* blockhead   18
*warrant* sanction   21 *what you are* i.e., a cuckold
24 *Would* "if I would"; *stand* oppose

[*Exeunt* CORVINO *and* CORBACCIO.]
VOLPONE. Excellent basilisk! Turn upon the vulture.

### Scene 9

[*Enter* VOLTORE.]
VOLTORE. Well, flesh-fly, it is summer with you now;
Your winter will come on.
MOSCA.                                Good advocate,
Pray thee not rail, nor threaten out of place thus;
Thou'lt make a solecism, as Madam says.
Get you a biggen more; your brain breaks
     loose.                         [*Exit.*]     5
VOLTORE. Well, sir.
VOLPONE.            Would you ha' me beat the insolent slave?
Throw dirt upon his first good clothes?
VOLTORE.                      This same
Is doubtless some familiar!
VOLPONE.            Sir, the court,
In troth, stays for you. I am mad; a mule
That never read Justinian, should get up    10
And ride an advocate! Had you no quirk
To avoid gullage, sir, by such a creature?
I hope you do but jest; he has not done 't;
This's but confederacy to blind the rest.
You are the heir?
VOLTORE.      A strange, officious,     15
Troublesome knave! Thou dost torment me.
VOLPONE [*aside*].            —I know—
It cannot be, sir, that you should be cozened;
'Tis not within the wit of man to do it.
You are so wise, so prudent, and 'tis fit
That wealth and wisdom still should go
     together.                        [*Exeunt.*]    20

---

27 *basilisk* a serpent believed to be able to kill with its glance
V.9.1 *flesh-fly* the meaning of "Mosca"   4 *Madam* i.e., Lady Wouldbe. See IV.2.43   5 *biggen* lawyer's cap; *more* i.e., to add to the one you have   7 *This same* i.e., Volpone   8 *familiar* evil spirit   9 *I am mad* "it is madness" (to believe that this has happened)   10 *Justinian* Roman legal code assembled at the order of the Emperor Justinian   11 *quirk* device   12 *gullage* being gulled, fooled   14 *confederacy* an agreement (between Voltore and Mosca)

### Scene 10

[*The Scrutineo.*]
[*Enter four* AVOCATORI, NOTARIO, COMMENDATORI, BONARIO, CELIA, CORBACCIO, CORVINO.]
1ST AVOCATORE. Are all the parties here?
NOTARIO.                All but the advocate.
2ND AVOCATORE. And here he comes.
[*Enter* VOLTORE, VOLPONE *following him.*]
AVOCATORI.                Then bring 'em forth to sentence.
VOLTORE. O my most honored fathers, let your mercy
Once win upon your justice, to forgive—
I am distracted—
VOLPONE [*aside*]. What will he do now?
VOLTORE.                      O,    5
I know not which t' address myself to first,
Whether your fatherhoods, or these innocents—
CORVINO [*aside*]. Will he betray himself?
VOLTORE.                Whom equally
I have abused, out of most covetous ends—
CORVINO. The man is mad!
CORBACCIO.      What's that?
CORVINO.                He is possessed.    10
VOLTORE. For which, now struck in conscience, here I prostrate
Myself at your offended feet, for pardon.
                              [*He kneels.*]
1ST, 2ND AVOCATORI. Arise.
CELIA.      O heav'n, how just thou art!
VOLPONE [*aside*].                I'm caught
I' mine own noose.
CORVINO [*aside to* CORBACCIO]. Be constant, sir, nought now
Can help but impudence.
1ST AVOCATORE.      Speak forward.
COMMENDATORE [*to the courtroom*]. Silence!    15

---

V.10.2 *Avocatori* The speech ascription here and in line 20 below reads in Quarto and Folio 1, "Avo." The usual practice of editors has been to assign this line to a particular *Avocatore*. Here and at line 20 it seems equally reasonable to have all the judges speak; *'em* i.e., Celia and Bonario   4 *win upon* overcome   9 *out . . . ends* because of covetous desires   10 *possessed* in the possession of the devil   14 *constant* "continue firm" (in your story)   15 *impudence* Latin *impudens*, shameless; *forward* on

VOLTORE. It is not passion in me, reverend
  fathers,
But only conscience, conscience, my good
  sires,
That makes me now tell truth. That parasite,
That knave, hath been the instrument of all.
  AVOCATORI. Where is that knave? Fetch
  him.
  VOLPONE. I go.             [*Exit.*]
  CORVINO.      Grave fathers,    20
This man's distracted, he confessed it now,
For, hoping to be old Volpone's heir,
Who now is dead—
  3RD AVOCATORE. How!
  2ND AVOCATORE.      Is Volpone dead?
  CORVINO. Dead since, grave fathers—
  BONARIO.      O sure vengeance!
  1ST AVOCATORE.          Stay.
Then he was no deceiver.
  VOLTORE.      O, no, none;    25
The parasite, grave fathers.
  CORVINO.        He does speak
Out of mere envy, 'cause the servant's made
The thing he gaped for. Please your father-
  hoods,
This is the truth; though I'll not justify
The other, but he may be some-deal
  faulty.                   30
  VOLTORE. Ay, to your hopes, as well as
  mine, Corvino.
But I'll use modesty. Pleaseth your wisdoms
To view these certain notes, and but confer
  them;          [*gives them notes*]
As I hope favor, they shall speak clear truth.
  CORVINO. The devil has entered him!
  BONARIO.      Or bides in you. 35
  4TH AVOCATORE. We have done ill, by a
  public officer
To send for him, if he be heir.
  2ND AVOCATORE.      For whom?
  4TH AVOCATORE. Him that they call the
  parasite.
  3RD AVOCATORE.    'Tis true,
He is a man of great estate now left.

  4TH AVOCATORE. Go you, and learn his
  name, and say the court    40
Entreats his presence here, but to the clearing
Of some few doubts.    [*Exit* NOTARIO.]
  2ND AVOCATORE. This same's a labyrinth!
  1ST AVOCATORE. Stand you unto your first
  report?
  CORVINO.             My state,
My life, my fame—
  BONARIO.    Where is't?
  CORVINO.          Are at the stake.
  1ST AVOCATORE. Is yours so too?
  CORBACCIO. The advocate's a knave,  45
And has a forkèd tongue—
  2ND AVOCATORE.    Speak to the point.
  CORBACCIO. So is the parasite too.
  1ST AVOCATORE.    This is confusion.
  VOLTORE. I do beseech your fatherhoods,
  read but those.
  CORVINO. And credit nothing the false spirit
  hath writ.
It cannot be but he is possessed, grave
  fathers.                   50

*Scene 11*

[*A street.* VOLPONE *alone.*]

VOLPONE. To make a snare for mine own
  neck! And run
My head into it wilfully, with laughter!
When I had newly 'scaped, was free and
  clear!
Out of mere wantonness! O, the dull devil
Was in this brain of mine when I devised it, 5
And Mosca gave it second; he must now
Help to sear up this vein, or we bleed dead.
  [*Enter* NANO, ANDROGYNO, *and* CASTRONE.]
How now! Who let you loose? Whither go
  you now?
What, to buy gingerbread, or to drown
  kitlings?
  NANO. Sir, Master Mosca called us out of
  doors,              10
And bid us all go play, and took the keys.
  ANDROGYNO.           Yes.

---

19 *instrument of all* arranger of everything   21
*distracted* out of his wits—see line 5 above   30
*some-deal* somewhat.   Quarto reads "somewhere"
32 *modesty* restraint   33 *certain* particular; *confer*
compare  35 *bides* abides, dwells  36–37 *We . . .
heir* Mosca's new dignity entitles him to a cere-
monious invitation, not a rude summons

41 *but to* only for  42 *doubts* questions  48 *those*
i.e., the notes he has given them  49 *credit* believe
V.11.4 *wantonness* playfulness  6 *gave it second*
seconded the idea  7 *sear* treat with a hot iron—
one method for closing cut veins  9 *kitlings* kit-
tens

VOLPONE. Did Master Mosca take the
keys? Why, so!
I am farther in. These are my fine conceits!
I must be merry, with a mischief to me!
What a vile wretch was I, that could not
bear                                             15
My fortune soberly; I must ha' my crotchets
And my conundrums! Well, go you and seek
him.
His meaning may be truer than my fear.
Bid him, he straight come to me to the court;
Thither will I, and if't be possible,            20
Unscrew my advocate, upon new hopes.
When I provoked him, then I lost myself.
                                   [Exeunt.]


                    *Scene 12*

              [*The Scrutineo.*]

[*Four* AVOCATORI, NOTARIO, VOLTORE,
BONARIO, CELIA, CORBACCIO, CORVINO.]
1ST AVOCATORE [*looking over* VOLTORE's
*notes*]. These things can ne'er be recon-
ciled. He here
Professeth that the gentleman was wronged,
And that the gentlewoman was brought
thither,
Forced by her husband, and there left.
    VOLTORE.                    Most true.
    CELIA. How ready is heav'n to those that
pray!
1ST AVOCATORE.              But that      5
Volpone would have ravished her, he holds
Utterly false, knowing his impotence.
    CORVINO. Grave fathers, he is possessed;
again, I say,
Possessed. Nay, if there be possession
And obsession, he has both.
    3RD AVOCATORE.          Here comes our
officer.                                       10
       [*Enter* VOLPONE, *still disguised.*]

VOLPONE. The parasite will straight be
here, grave fathers.
4TH AVOCATORE. You might invent some
other name, sir varlet.
3RD AVOCATORE. Did not the notary meet
him?
VOLPONE.                      Not that I know.
4TH AVOCATORE. His coming will clear all.
2ND AVOCATORE.              Yet, it is misty.
VOLTORE. May't please your fatherhoods—
VOLPONE.            Sir, the parasite    15
    (VOLPONE *whispers* [*to*] *the* ADVOCATE )
Willed me to tell you that his master lives;
That you are still the man; your hopes the
same;
And this was only a jest—
    VOLTORE.              How?
    VOLPONE.                 Sir, to try
If you were firm, and how you stood affected.
    VOLTORE. Art sure he lives?
    VOLPONE.          Do I live, sir?
    VOLTORE.                      O me!  20
I was too violent.
    VOLPONE.     Sir, you may redeem it:
They said you were possessed: fall down, and
seem so.
I'll help to make it good. God bless the man!
                        (VOLTORE *falls.*)
                   [*Aside to* VOLTORE.]
—Stop your wind hard, and swell—See, see,
see, see!
He vomits crooked pins! His eyes are set  25
Like a dead hare's hung in a poulter's shop!
His mouth's running away! Do you see,
signior?
Now, 'tis in his belly.
    CORVINO.          Ay, the devil!
    VOLPONE. Now, in his throat.

---

13 *farther in* deeper in (trouble); *conceits* ideas,
plans  16 *crotchets* fancies, whims  17 *conundrums*
puzzles—perhaps a reference to the puzzling of
the three disappointed heirs in scenes 6–9  18
"His intentions may be more honest than I fear
they are"  21 *Unscrew* i.e., "get him to change
his position again"—Voltore is pictured as being as crooked and as retentive as a screw, or
perhaps some variety of boring insect
V.12.5 *ready* available (to help)

12 *invent* find—because Mosca is now wealthy the
term parasite is no longer suitable  14 *clear* clear
up; *misty* confused  19 *stood affected* truly felt(?)
20 *Do . . . sir?* Considering the speed with which
Voltore changes at this point it seems likely that
Volpone manages to make Voltore pierce his
disguise  24 *Stop . . . wind* "hold your breath"
24–31 All of these details: swelling, vomiting
crooked pins, eyes strangely set, the appearance
of something running in the body from place to
place, and the expulsion of some strange animal
from the mouth were all taken as signs of possession by the devil. . . .  26 *poulter's* poultry seller's  27 *running away* awry and moving wildly

CORVINO.                Ay, I perceive it plain.

VOLPONE, 'Twill out, 'twill out! Stand
    clear. See where it flies!            30
In shape of a blue toad, with a bat's wings!
                              [*Pointing.*]
Do you not see it, sir?

CORBACCIO.         What? I think I do.

CORVINO. 'Tis too manifest.

VOLPONE.       Look! He comes t' himself.

VOLTORE. Where am I?

VOLPONE.               Take good heart,
    the worst is past, sir.
You are dispossessed.

1ST AVOCATORE.  What accident is this? 35

2ND AVOCATORE. Sudden, and full of won-
    der!

3RD AVOCATORE.             If he were
Possessed, as it appears, all this is nothing.
                          [*Waving notes.*]

CORVINO. He has been often subject to
    these fits.

1ST AVOCATORE. Show him that writing.
    —Do you know it, sir?

VOLPONE [*aside*]. Deny it sir, forswear it,
    know it not.                          40

VOLTORE. Yes, I do know it well, it is my
    hand;
But all that it contains is false.

BONARIO.              O practice!

2ND AVOCATORE. What maze is this!

1ST AVOCATORE.     Is he not guilty then,
Whom you, there, name the parasite?

VOLTORE.               Grave fathers,
No more than his good patron, old
    Volpone.                              45

4TH AVOCATORE. Why, he is dead.

VOLTORE.     O, no, my honored fathers.
He lives—

1ST AVOCATORE. How! Lives?

VOLTORE.                   Lives.

2ND AVOCATORE.       This is subtler yet!

3RD AVOCATORE. You said he was dead.

VOLTORE.     Never.

3RD AVOCATORE.     You said so!

CORVINO.               I heard so.

4TH AVOCATORE. Here comes the gentle-
    man, make him way.

[*Enter* MOSCA.]

3RD AVOCATORE.               A stool!

4TH AVOCATORE. A proper man and, were
    Volpone dead,                         50
A fit match for my daughter.

3RD AVOCATORE.        Give him way.

VOLPONE [*aside to* MOSCA]. Mosca, I was
    almost lost; the advocate
Had betrayed all; but now it is recovered.
All's o' the hinge again. Say I am living.

MOSCA. What busy knave is this? Most
    reverend fathers,                     55
I sooner had attended your grave pleasures,
But that my order for the funeral
Of my dear patron did require me—

VOLPONE [*aside*].               Mosca!

MOSCA. Whom I intend to bury like a
    gentleman.

VOLPONE [*aside*]. Ay, quick, and cozen me
    of all.

2ND AVOCATORE.       Still stranger! 60
More intricate!

1ST AVOCATORE.   And come about again!

4TH AVOCATORE [*aside*]. It is a match, my
    daughter is bestowed.

MOSCA [*aside to* VOLPONE]. Will you gi' me
    half?

VOLPONE [*half aloud*].       First I'll be
    hanged.

MOSCA [*aside*].               I know
Your voice is good, cry not so loud.

1ST AVOCATORE.             Demand
The advocate. Sir, did not you affirm    65
Volpone was alive?

VOLPONE.       Yes, and he is;
This gent'man told me so. [*Aside to* MOSCA.]
    Thou shalt have half.

MOSCA. Whose drunkard is this same?
    Speak, some that know him.
I never saw his face. [*Aside to* VOLPONE.]
    I cannot now

---

50 *proper* handsome    53 *recovered* Volpone uses
this word several times to mean "the problem
is solved"; but in a play where disguise and ob-
literating the truth with falsehood appear so con-
sistently, we must take the word in its literal
sense as well: covering reality over once more
with pretense    54 *o'* on    55 *busy* meddling    60
*quick* alive    61 *come . . . again* reversed once more
—i.e., having been declared dead, then living,
Volpone is once more dead    62 *bestowed* i.e., in
marriage    64 *Demand* question

---

33 *comes t' himself* revives    42 *practice* intrigue
47 *subtler* more intricate    49 *make him way*
"open a path for him"

Afford it you so cheap.

VOLPONE [*aside*].                    No?

1ST AVOCATORE [*to* VOLTORE]. What say
you?                                                                70

VOLTORE. The officer told me.

VOLPONE.                    I did, grave fathers,
And will maintain he lives with mine own life,
And that this creature told me. [*Aside.*] I was
born
With all good stars my enemies!

MOSCA.                    Most grave fathers,
If such an insolence as this must pass        75
Upon me, I am silent; 'twas not this
For which you sent, I hope.

2ND AVOCATORE.                    Take him away.

VOLPONE [*aside*]. Mosca!

3RD AVOCATORE.    Let him be whipped.

VOLPONE [*aside*].                    Wilt thou
betray me?
Cozen me?

3RD AVOCATORE. And taught to bear himself
Toward a person of his rank.

4TH AVOCATORE [*the* OFFICERS *seize*
VOLPONE].                    Away.    80

MOSCA. I humbly thank your fatherhoods.

VOLPONE [*aside*].    Soft, soft. Whipped?
And lose all that I have? If I confess,
It cannot be much more.

4TH AVOCATORE [*to* MOSCA]. Sir, are you
married?

VOLPONE [*aside*]. They'll be allied anon;
I must be resolute:
The fox shall here uncase. (*He puts off his
disguise.*)

MOSCA.                    Patron!

VOLPONE.                    Nay, now    85
My ruins shall not come alone; your match
I'll hinder sure. My substance shall not glue
you,
Nor screw you, into a family.

MOSCA.                    Why, patron!

VOLPONE. I am Volpone, and this is my
knave;
This, his own knave; this, avarice's fool;    90
This, a chimera of wittol, fool, and knave.

---

80 *his* i.e., Mosca's    81 *Soft, soft* "easy, easy"
84 *anon* soon    85 *uncase* take off disguise    87
*substance* fortune    89–91 *this . . . This* He points in
turn to Mosca, Voltore, Corbaccio, and Corvino
89 *knave* servant    91 *chimera* mythical beast, part
lion, goat and serpent

And, reverend fathers, since we all can hope
Nought but a sentence, let's not now despair
it.
You hear me brief.

CORVINO.                    May it please your fatherhoods—

COMMENDATORE.                    Silence.

1ST AVOCATORE. The knot is now undone
by miracle!                                                        95

2ND AVOCATORE. Nothing can be more
clear.

3RD AVOCATORE.                    Or can more prove
These innocent.

1ST AVOCATORE.    Give 'em their liberty.

BONARIO. Heaven could not long let such
gross crimes be hid.

2ND AVOCATORE. If this be held the highway to get riches,
May I be poor!

3RD AVOCATORE.    This's not the gain, but
torment.                                                            100

1ST AVOCATORE. These possess wealth as
sick men possess fevers,
Which trulier may be said to possess them.

2ND AVOCATORE. Disrobe that parasite.

CORVINO, MOSCA.    Most honored fathers—

1ST AVOCATORE. Can you plead aught to
stay the course of justice?
If you can, speak.

CORVINO, VOLTORE. We beg favor.

CELIA.                    And mercy.    105

1ST AVOCATORE. You hurt your innocence,
suing for the guilty.
Stand forth; and first the parasite. You
appear
T' have been the chiefest minister, if not
plotter,
In all these lewd impostures; and now,
lastly,
Have with your impudence abused the
court,                                                              110
And habit of a gentleman of Venice,
Being a fellow of no birth or blood.
For which our sentence is, first thou be
whipped;
Then live perpetual prisoner in our galleys.

VOLPONE. I thank you for him.

MOSCA.                    Bane to thy wolfish nature.    115

---

93 *let's . . . it* "don't disappoint us by delay"    94
*brief* (speak) briefly    108 *minister* agent    109 *lewd
impostures* base pretenses    115 *Bane to* a curse on

1ST AVOCATORE. Deliver him to the *Saffi*. [MOSCA *is taken out.*] Thou Volpone, By blood and rank a gentleman, canst not fall Under like censure; but our judgment on thee Is that thy substance all be straight confiscate To the hospital of the *Incurabili*. 120 And since the most was gotten by imposture, By feigning lame, gout, palsy, and such diseases, Thou art to lie in prison, cramped with irons, Till thou be'st sick and lame indeed. Remove him.

VOLPONE. This is called mortifying of a fox. 125

1ST AVOCATORE. Thou, Voltore, to take away the scandal Thou hast giv'n all worthy men of thy profession, Art banished from their fellowship, and our state. Corbaccio, bring him near! We here possess Thy son of all thy state, and confine thee 130 To the monastery of *San' Spirito;* Where, since thou knew'st not how to live well here, Thou shalt be learned to die well.

CORBACCIO [*cupping his ear*]. Ha! What said he?

COMMENDATORE. You shall know anon, sir.

1ST AVOCATORE. Thou, Corvino, shalt Be straight embarked from thine own house, and rowed 135 Round about Venice, through the Grand Canal, Wearing a cap with fair long ass's ears Instead of horns; and so to mount, a paper Pinned on thy breast, to the *Berlina*—

CORVINO. Yes, And have mine eyes beat out with stinking fish, 140 Bruised fruit, and rotten eggs—'Tis well, I'm glad I shall not see my shame yet.

1ST AVOCATORE. And to expiate Thy wrongs done to thy wife, thou art to send her Home to her father, with her dowry trebled. And these are all your judgments.

ALL. Honored fathers! 145

1ST AVOCATORE. Which may not be revoked. Now you begin, When crimes are done and past, and to be punished, To think what your crimes are. Away with them! Let all that see these vices thus rewarded, Take heart, and love to study 'em. Mischiefs feed 150 Like beasts, till they be fat, and then they bleed. [*Exeunt.*] [VOLPONE *comes forward.*]

VOLPONE. The seasoning of a play is the applause. Now, though the fox be punished by the laws, He yet doth hope there is no suff'ring due For any fact which he hath done 'gainst you. 155 If there be, censure him; here he doubtful stands. If not, fare jovially, and clap your hands.

THE END

---

116 *Saffi* bailiffs    119 *straight confiscate* instantly confiscated    120 *Incurabili* incurables    125 *mortifying* The literal meaning here is "humiliation," but two other senses apply. A cooking term; to mortify an animal was to allow it to hang after it had been killed until the meat became tender. But, as in our term "mortification of the flesh," the word also means subjecting the body and the passions to ascetic discipline and rigorous austerities    130 *state* property    131 *San' Spirito* the Monastery of the Holy Spirit, where Corbaccio, who has heretofore been completely without soul or spirit, will be painfully instructed to forget the things of this world and prepare his soul for the next    133 *learned* taught

135 *embarked* put on a boat    139 *Berlina* the stage on which malefactors were exposed, the pillory    140 *eyes beat out* the crowd threw refuse at those in pillory    155 *fact* crime

*Satirical Comedy*

The characters of *Volpone* are simplified almost as drastically as those of *Everyman* but in a different way. Instead of representing abstractions, such as Knowledge, or relationships, such as Kindred, they are people dominated by a single trait of character, such as jealousy or avarice. Jonson's method of characterization was much influenced by the popular theory of "humors," the four liquids in the body (blood, phlegm, choler, and melancholy) which were supposed to produce a normal temperament when they were in perfect balance. When there was an excess of one of them, however, the result was supposed to be a strong inclination to one emotional state such as anger or melancholy. By extension the term "humor" came to mean any dominant character trait or, sometimes, an affectation. It is Sir Pol's humor to claim omniscience about the countries where he has traveled, as it is Corvino's to be jealous of his wife.

To some extent, then, these are "humor" characters, but there are many characters in the play who share one dominant trait and yet are distinguished from each other in various ways. For example, a shocking majority of the characters are avaricious—a fact which several of the bird-and animal-names emphasize—but while one of the "birds of prey" is distinguished by his age (as indicated by farcical decrepitude) and another by his legal profession, the third is shown to be a jealous husband into the bargain. Each character is a type, but none of them is seen as exclusively the product of one humor.

In a variety of ways, which are worthy of analysis, Jonson manages to arrange these type-characters in groups. This technique emphasizes the themes of the play by producing a series of variations upon them such as the sequence of scenes in which Voltore, Corbaccio, and Corvino come to visit Volpone. The grouping of type-characters also creates a strong impression of coherence; each character, though a grotesque exaggeration, is so clearly related to others that very quickly an entire world is created to which they all belong. Again, the effect is somewhat comparable to one which we noticed in *Everyman.*

The world thus evoked is both familiar and fantastic. The human follies and vices emphasized in the play have been known at all times and in all places, and the original audience would readily have seen in Volpone's Venice a a mirror-image of their own London. Yet this element of realism is countered by the obvious distortion of character, the narrow range of types selected for presentation, and the arrangement of them in a formal pattern. If Jonson's comedy seems realistic by comparison with the romantic comedies of Shakespeare, it is far removed from the realism of more recent drama. No character in *Volpone* is nearly so credible a human being as Shaw's Barbara or Albee's Jerry.

Jonson's treatment of character supports a satirical view of human nature, which in turn gives a special coloration to the comedy. The vast majority of the characters are totally self-absorbed and unrelentingly materialistic. Any noble sentiments they may utter are immediately seen to be hypocrisy. Not only do we instinctively detach ourselves from these characters, as we do to some extent whenever we laugh at someone, but our laughter in this case is usually combined with contempt. If there is anything to admire it is only the cleverness of the trickery. Satirical comedy usually presents characters as ridiculous or repulsive, and thus evokes in the audience a more hostile response than do other sorts of comedy.

So long as the stage is filled with almost equally contemptible characters who are trying to impose upon each other, it is easy to remain quite uncommitted to one side or the other. In some scenes of *Volpone*, however, we see virtuous characters exposed to attack. When this happens, an important problem is raised about the nature of the comedy. Any interpretation of the play must deal with the effect of the scene in which Volpone attempts to rape Celia. It may seem that in the presence of such a heavenly nature as her name suggests, Volpone's schemes appear more sinister than laughable. It is a question, then, of whether Jonson oversteps the bounds he set himself when he said that comedy should "sport with human follies, not with crimes." We might also ask whether the didactic purpose served by Celia's rebuke betrays Jonson into a departure from the comic norm at least as serious as the one which worries him in the dedicatory epistle. Much will depend on how the actors playing the roles of Volpone and Celia read their lines, for the possibilities extend all the way from melodrama to farce. It is up to the reader to decide how the scene should be played in the ideal performance.

Whether or not this scene is too bitter to be funny, there is no doubt that in one respect it provides a superb example of poetic control. Volpone's courtship of Celia, including his famous song ("Come my Celia"), constitutes a subtle parody of the love poetry of Jonson's day. The undeniable beauty of the images is undercut by the stress on wealth and hedonism, and finally by the crude violence of Volpone's attack. Before this happens, however, the verbal surface makes Volpone's approaches attractive and repulsive in almost equal proportions. In the scene as a whole Volpone appears to be more dangerous but also more interesting—and possibly more real—than the usual butt of satire. The charlatan who can speak such poetry haunts the imagination.

## Selected Reading List for Jonson

Jonas A. Barish, ed., *Ben Jonson: A Collection of Critical Essays*. Englewood Cliffs, N.J.: Prentice-Hall, Inc., 1963.

John J. Enck, *Jonson and the Comic Truth*. Madison, Wis.: The University of Wisconsin Press, 1957.

Alvin Kernan, "The Satirist in the Theater," *The Cankered Muse*. New Haven: Yale University Press, 1959, pp. 141–91.

L. C. Knights, *Drama & Society in the Age of Jonson*. New York: Barnes & Noble, Inc., 1957.

L. C. Knights, "Ben Jonson, Dramatist," *The Age of Shakespeare*, *The Pelican Guide to English Literature*, II. Baltimore, Md: Penguin Books, 1963, 302–17.

Edward B. Partridge, *The Broken Compass*. New York: Columbia University Press, 1958.

# Molière and the French Classical Theater

In 1641, a year before the Puritans succeeded in having all the London theaters closed, a new theater was inaugurated in Paris. During the heyday of Elizabethan drama in England there had been very little dramatic activity in Paris. It had been discouraged by the monopoly of the theater held for many years by one company, and, possibly for this same reason, few talented authors had written for the stage. As England's greatest dramatic era was nearing its end, the situation in Paris began to change. Rival companies were allowed, theaters were improvised in various kinds of buildings, Pierre Corneille achieved recognition as a major playwright, and the court was taking an increasing interest in the drama. Cardinal Richelieu, one of the most powerful men in the country, was responsible for the theater which opened in 1641 in his own palace. At first it was a private theater, to which only the King and Queen and some of the greatest nobles were invited. After the cardinal's death, however, his palace became the Palais Royal, and in 1660 the King made the Théâtre du Palais Royal avaliable to Molière and his company. Here his most famous plays were performed.

This theater was different in every respect from the theater of Shakespeare and Jonson. It was a long room, decorated in classical style with columns and balustrades and lighted by chandeliers. The stage was at one end, framed by a flattened arch and two pilasters. In the center five steps led up to the stage from the floor. In a contemporary engraving (probably of the opening performance), we see the royal family seated in the middle of the hall at some distance from the stage, while most of the other spectators are crowded into the balconies which ran the length of the hall, two on each side. This engraving does not show that the floor of the auditorium rose in shallow steps, though we know that when the theater became public, there were benches at each level so that, as in a modern theater, those seated in back could see over the heads of the people in front.

Richelieu had seen to it that the stage was equipped after the Italian manner with painted scenery, usually consisting of side wings and a backdrop, and machines to change the scenery and create many spectacular effects. Although the fullest use of this kind of equipment was confined to the spectacular operas and ballets given for the court, no plays were performed without scenery, as in the Elizabethan theater. By the time that Molière came to the Palais Royal, the theater had several stock "sets"—a palace exterior, a room, a street—which sufficed for most plays, for classical taste was leading the dramatists to restrict the action of their plays to very few locations in order to preserve the "unity of place." Molière took advantage of the possibilities of spectacular staging in some of the entertainments he wrote for the court, and even in his important comedy, *Dom Juan*, several scene changes and a display of hell fire were required, but in *The Misanthrope* one set, a room in the house of Célimène, is all that is needed. To present it, a "box set" was probably used; that is, one consisting of three walls with practicable doors through which entrances could be made. In this case the scenery emphasizes the classical construction of the play, which is more strict than that of *Volpone*.

The theater for which Molière wrote was much more like the theater of today than were the theaters of Greece or of medieval and Elizabethan England. It was indoors and artificially lighted; architecturally the stage was separated

LE SOIR, LE ROI, ET LES PERSONNES DE LA COUR VONT A LA COMEDIE

*The engraving, executed by Van Lochom, is in the print collection of the Bibliothèque Nationale in Paris. The title may be translated: "In the evening the King and the people of the court go to the theater."*

from the auditorium and had a curtain which could be lowered to make the separation absolute. By means of scenery it could either make an appeal to the imagination or present a convincing imitation of the world the audience knew. This second kind of illusion was to be greatly developed in the nineteenth century.

Jean-Baptiste Poquelin, who later adopted the name of Molière, was born in Paris in 1622, the son of a well-to-do upholsterer. After going to a Jesuit school in Clermont, where he proved to be a good scholar, he began the study of law, but in 1643 he gave up not only the law but any idea of succeeding his father as upholsterer. He had become involved with a family of actors, the Béjarts, with whom he formed an acting company, called the Illustre Théâtre. Although this venture failed in Paris after a short time, many of the actors stayed together and toured the provinces. By 1658, when they returned to Paris and succeeded in establishing themselves there, Molière had become an accomplished actor, though never very successful in tragic roles. He had also begun writing plays, and it was a short farce of his own which insured the success of the company in Paris. From this time on they regularly performed Molière's plays, of which he wrote at least one and often two or three each year. Despite many battles with critics and censors who misunderstood the aim of his satire, Molière's comic genius was recognized by his contemporaries. Normally he took one of the principal parts in his comedies—he played Alceste in *The Misanthrope*—and he had acted in *Le Malade Imaginaire* on the night he died, February 17, 1673.

The glitter of the *salon* over which Célimène presides—including the physical glitter of crystal chandeliers, gilt furniture, and bright-colored silk and satin clothing—is part of the point of the play. We must imagine all of this and the formal gestures that accompany each gracefully-turned speech in order to appreciate the attractions and the absurdities of the world Alceste rejects. It is not easy to decide whether his condemnation is the product of clear vision or ill nature—whether his honesty is noble and heroic, as Éliante believes, or essentially spiteful, like that of Arsinoé.

# The Misanthrope

*A COMEDY*

## MOLIÈRE

### CHARACTERS

ALCESTE, *in love with* CÉLIMÈNE
PHILINTE, ALCESTE's *friend*
ORONTE, *in love with* CÉLIMÈNE
CÉLIMÈNE, ALCESTE's *beloved*
ÉLIANTE, CÉLIMÈNE's *cousin*
ARSINOÉ, *a friend of* CÉLIMÈNE's
ACASTE ⎫
CLITANDRE ⎬ *marquesses*
BASQUE, CÉLIMÈNE's *servant*

A GUARD *of the Marshalsea*[1]
DUBOIS, ALCESTE's *valet*

### ACT I. *Scene 1*

PHILINTE, ALCESTE.
PHILINTE. Now, what's got into you?
ALCESTE (*seated*).    Kindly leave me alone.
PHILINTE. Come, come, what is it? This
  lugubrious tone . . .

[1]*Marshalsea* a law-enforcement body roughly comparable to present-day police

ALCESTE. Leave me, I said; you spoil my solitude.

PHILINTE. Oh, listen to me, now, and don't be rude.

ALCESTE. I choose to be rude, Sir, and to be hard of hearing.

PHILINTE. These ugly moods of yours are not endearing;
Friends though we are, I really must insist . . .

ALCESTE (*abruptly rising*). Friends? Friends, you say? Well, cross me off your list.
I've been your friend till now, as you well know;
But after what I saw a moment ago
I tell you flatly that our ways must part.
I wish no place in a dishonest heart.

PHILINTE. Why, what have I done, Alceste? Is this quite just?

ALCESTE. My God, you ought to die of self-disgust.
I call your conduct inexcusable, Sir,
And every man of honor will concur.
I see you almost hug a man to death,
Exclaim for joy until you're out of breath,
And supplement these loving demonstrations
With endless offers, vows, and protestations;
Then when I ask you "Who was that?" I find
That you can barely bring his name to mind!
Once the man's back is turned, you cease to love him,
And speak with absolute indifference of him!
By God, I say it's base and scandalous
To falsify the heart's affections thus;
If I caught myself behaving in such a way,
I'd hang myself for shame, without delay.

PHILINTE. It hardly seems a hanging matter to me;
I hope that you will take it graciously
If I extend myself a slight reprieve,
And live a little longer, by your leave.

ALCESTE. How dare you joke about a crime so grave?

PHILINTE. What crime? How else are people to behave?

ALCESTE. I'd have them be sincere, and never part
With any word that isn't from the heart.

PHILINTE. When someone greets us with a show of pleasure,
It's but polite to give him equal measure,
Return his love the best that we know how,
And trade him offer for offer, vow for vow.

ALCESTE. No, no, this formula you'd have me follow,
However fashionable, is false and hollow,
And I despise the frenzied operations
Of all these barterers of protestations,
These lavishers of meaningless embraces,
These utterers of obliging commonplaces,
Who court and flatter everyone on earth
And praise the fool no less than the man of worth.
Should you rejoice that someone fondles you,
Offers his love and service, swears to be true,
And fills your ears with praises of your name,
When to the first damned fop he'll say the same?
No, no: no self-respecting heart would dream
Of prizing so promiscuous an esteem;
However high the praise, there's nothing worse
Than sharing honors with the universe.
Esteem is founded on comparison:
To honor all men is to honor none.
Since you embrace this indiscriminate vice,
Your friendship comes at far too cheap a price;
I spurn the easy tribute of a heart
Which will not set the worthy man apart:
I choose, Sir, to be chosen; and in fine,
The friend of mankind is no friend of mine.

PHILINTE. But in polite society, custom decrees
That we show certain outward courtesies. . . .

ALCESTE. Ah, no! we should condemn with all our force
Such false and artificial intercourse.
Let men behave like men; let them display
Their inmost hearts in everything they say;
Let the heart speak, and let our sentiments
Not mask themselves in silly compliments.

PHILINTE. In certain cases it would be uncouth
And most absurd to speak the naked truth;
With all respect for your exalted notions,
It's often best to veil one's true emotions.
Wouldn't the social fabric come undone
If we were wholly frank with everyone?

Suppose you met with someone you couldn't
  bear;
Would you inform him of it then and there?
  ALCESTE. Yes.
    PHILINTE.    Then you'd tell old Émilie
  it's pathetic
The way she daubs her features with cosmetic
And plays the gay coquette at sixty-four?
  ALCESTE. I would.
    PHILINTE.        And you'd call Dorilas
  a bore,
And tell him every ear at court is lame
From hearing him brag about his noble
  name?
  ALCESTE. Precisely.
    PHILINTE.        Ah, you're joking.
    ALCESTE.                *Au contraire:*
In this regard there's none I'd choose to spare.
All are corrupt; there's nothing to be seen
In court or town but aggravates my spleen.
I fall into deep gloom and melancholy
When I survey the scene of human folly,
Finding on every hand base flattery,
Injustice, fraud, self-interest, treachery. . . .
Ah, it's too much; mankind has grown
  so base,
I mean to break with the whole human race.
  PHILINTE. This philosophic rage is a
  bit extreme;
You've no idea how comical you seem;
Indeed, we're like those brothers in the play
Called *School for Husbands,*[2] one of whom was
  prey . . .
    ALCESTE. Enough, now! None of your
  stupid similes.
  PHILINTE. Then let's have no more tirades,
  if you please.
The world won't change, whatever you say
  or do;
And since plain speaking means so much to
  you,
I'll tell you plainly that by being frank
You've earned the reputation of a crank,
And that you're thought ridiculous when you
  rage
And rant against the manners of the age.
    ALCESTE. So much the better; just what I
  wish to hear.
No news could be more grateful to my ear.

---

[2]*School for Husbands* an earlier play by Molière

All men are so detestable in my eyes,
I should be sorry if they thought me wise.
  PHILINTE. Your hatred's very sweeping, is
  it not?
  ALCESTE. Quite right: I hate the whole de-
  graded lot.
  PHILINTE. Must all poor human creatures
  be embraced,
Without distinction, by your vast distaste?
Even in these bad times, there are surely a
  few . . .
  ALCESTE. No, I include all men in one dim
  view:
Some men I hate for being rogues; the others
I hate because they treat the rogues like
  brothers,
And, lacking a virtuous scorn for what is vile,
Receive the villain with a complaisant smile.
Notice how tolerant people choose to be
Toward that bold rascal who's at law with
  me.
His social polish can't conceal his nature;
One sees at once that he's a treacherous
  creature;
No one could possibly be taken in
By those soft speeches and that sugary grin.
The whole world knows the shady means by
  which
The low-brow's grown so powerful and rich,
And risen to a rank so bright and high
That virtue can but blush, and merit sigh.
Whenever his name comes up in conversa-
  tion,
None will defend his wretched reputation;
Call him knave, liar, scoundrel, and all the
  rest,
Each head will nod, and no one will protest.
And yet his smirk is seen in every house,
He's greeted everywhere with smiles and
  bows,
And when there's any honor that can be got
By pulling strings, he'll get it, like as not.
My God! It chills my heart to see the ways
Men come to terms with evil nowadays;
Sometimes, I swear, I'm moved to flee and
  find
Some desert land unfouled by humankind.
  PHILINTE. Come, let's forget the follies of
  the times
And pardon mankind for its petty crimes;
Let's have an end of rantings and of railings,

And show some leniency toward human fail-
ings.
This world requires a pliant rectitude;
Too stern a virtue makes one stiff and rude;
Good sense views all extremes with detesta-
tion,
And bids us to be noble in moderation.
The rigid virtues of the ancient days
Are not for us; they jar with all our ways
And ask of us too lofty a perfection.
Wise men accept their times without objec-
tion,
And there's no greater folly, if you ask me,
Than trying to reform society.
Like you, I see each day a hundred and one
Unhandsome deeds that might be better
done,
But still, for all the faults that meet my view,
I'm never known to storm and rave like you.
I take men as they are, or let them be,
And teach my soul to bear their frailty;
And whether in court or town, whatever the
scene,
My phlegm's as philosophic as your spleen.
    ALCESTE. This phlegm which you so elo-
quently commend,
Does nothing ever rile it up, my friend?
Suppose some man you trust should treach-
erously
Conspire to rob you of your property,
And do his best to wreck your reputation?
Wouldn't you feel a certain indignation?
    PHILINTE. Why, no. These faults of which
you so complain
Are part of human nature, I maintain,
And it's no more a matter for disgust
That men are knavish, selfish and unjust,
Than that the vulture dines upon the dead,
And wolves are furious, and apes ill-bred.
    ALCESTE. Shall I see myself betrayed,
robbed, torn to bits,
And not . . . Oh, let's be still and rest our wits.
Enough of reasoning, now. I've had my fill.
    PHILINTE. Indeed, you would do well, Sir,
to be still.
Rage less at your opponent, and give some
thought
To how you'll win this lawsuit that he's
brought.
    ALCESTE. I assure you I'll do nothing of the
sort.

    PHILINTE. Then who will plead your case
before the court?
    ALCESTE. Reason and right and justice will
plead for me.
    PHILINTE. Oh, Lord. What judges do you
plan to see?
    ALCESTE. Why, none. The justice of my
cause is clear.
    PHILINTE. Of course, man; but there's po-
litics to fear . . . .
    ALCESTE. No, I refuse to lift a hand.
That's flat.
I'm either right, or wrong.
    PHILINTE.              Don't count on that.
    ALCESTE. No, I'll do nothing.
    PHILINTE.           Your enemy's influence
Is great, you know . . .
    ALCESTE.        That makes no difference.
    PHILINTE. It will; you'll see.
    ALCESTE.        Must honor bow to guile?
If so, I shall be proud to lose the trial.
    PHILINTE. Oh, really . . .
    ALCESTE.          I'll discover by this case
Whether or not men are sufficiently base
And impudent and villainous and perverse
To do me wrong before the universe.
    PHILINTE. What a man!
    ALCESTE.          Oh, I could wish,
whatever the cost,
Just for the beauty of it, that my trial were
lost.
    PHILINTE. If people heard you talking so,
Alceste,
They'd split their sides. Your name would
be a jest.
    ALCESTE. So much the worse for jesters.
    PHILINTE.           May I enquire
Whether this rectitude you so admire,
And these hard virtues you're enamored of
Are qualities of the lady whom you love?
It much surprises me that you, who seem
To view mankind with furious disesteem,
Have yet found something to enchant your
eyes
Amidst a species which you so despise.
And what is more amazing, I'm afraid,
Is the most curious choice your heart has
made.
The honest Éliante is fond of you,
Arsinoé, the prude, admires you too;
And yet your spirit's been perversely led

To choose the flighty Célimène instead,
Whose brittle malice and coquettish ways
So typify the manners of our days.
How is it that the traits you most abhor
Are bearable in this lady you adore?
Are you so blind with love that you can't
   find them?
Or do you contrive, in her case, not to mind
   them?
   ALCESTE. My love for that young widow's
   not the kind
That can't perceive defects; no, I'm not blind.
I see her faults, despite my ardent love,
And all I see I fervently reprove.
And yet I'm weak; for all her falsity,
That woman knows the art of pleasing me,
And though I never cease complaining of her,
I swear I cannot manage not to love her.
Her charm outweighs her faults; I can but
   aim
To cleanse her spirit in my love's pure flame.
   PHILINTE. That's no small task; I wish you
   all success.
You think then that she loves you?
   ALCESTE.                    Heavens, yes!
I wouldn't love her did she not love me.
   PHILINTE. Well, if her taste for you is plain
   to see,
Why do these rivals cause you such despair?
   ALCESTE. True love, Sir, is possessive, and
   cannot bear
To share with all the world. I'm here today
To tell her she must send that mob away.
   PHILINTE. If I were you, and had your
   choice to make,
Éliante, her cousin, would be the one I'd take;
That honest heart, which cares for you
   alone,
Would harmonize far better with your own.
   ALCESTE. True, true: each day my reason
   tells me so;
But reason doesn't rule in love, you know.
   PHILINTE. I fear some bitter sorrow is in
   store;
This love . . .

### Scene 2

ORONTE, ALCESTE, PHILINTE.
ORONTE (to ALCESTE). The servants told me
   at the door

That Éliante and Célimène were out,
But when I heard, dear Sir, that you were
   about,
I came to say, without exaggeration,
That I hold you in the vastest admiration,
And that it's always been my dearest desire
To be the friend of one I so admire.
I hope to see my love of merit requited,
And you and I in friendship's bond united.
I'm sure you won't refuse—if I may be
   frank—
A friend of my devotedness—and rank.
   (During this speech of ORONTE's, ALCESTE
   is abstracted, and seems unaware that he is
   being spoken to. He only breaks off his
   reverie when ORONTE says:)
It was for you, if you please, that my words
   were intended.
   ALCESTE. For me, Sir?
   ORONTE.                    Yes, for you. You're
   not offended?
   ALCESTE. By no means. But this much sur-
   prises me . . . .
The honor comes most unexpectedly . . . .
   ORONTE. My high regard should not aston-
   ish you;
The whole world feels the same. It is your due.
   ALCESTE. Sir . . .
   ORONTE.                    Why, in all the State
   there isn't one
Can match your merits; they shine, Sir, like
   the sun
   ALCESTE. Sir . . .
   ORONTE.                    You are higher in my
   estimation
Than all that's most illustrious in the nation.
   ALCESTE. Sir . . .
   ORONTE.                    If I lie, may heaven strike
   me dead!
To show you that I mean what I have said,
Permit me, Sir, to embrace you most sincere-
   ly,
And swear that I will prize our friendship
   dearly.
Give me your hand. And now, Sir, if you
   choose,
We'll make our vows.
   ALCESTE.                    Sir . . .
   ORONTE.                    What! You refuse?
   ALCESTE. Sir, it's a very great honor you
   extend:

But friendship is a sacred thing, my friend;
It would be profanation to bestow
The name of friend on one you hardly know.
All parts are better played when well-re-
  hearsed;
Let's put off friendship, and get acquainted
  first.
We may discover it would be unwise
To try to make our natures harmonize.

ORONTE. By heaven! You're sagacious to
  the core;
This speech has made me admire you even
  more.
Let time, then, bring us closer day by day;
Meanwhile, I shall be yours in every way.
If, for example, there should be anything
You wish at court, I'll mention it to the
  King.
I have his ear, of course; it's quite well
  known
That I am much in favor with the throne.
In short, I am your servant. And now, dear
  friend,
Since you have such fine judgment, I intend
To please you, if I can, with a small sonnet
I wrote not long ago. Please comment on it,
And tell me whether I ought to publish it.

ALCESTE. You must excuse me, Sir; I'm
  hardly fit
To judge such matters.

ORONTE.                    Why not?

ALCESTE.                               I am, I fear,
Inclined to be unfashionably sincere.

ORONTE. Just what I ask; I'd take no satis-
  faction
In anything but your sincere reaction.
I beg you not to dream of being kind.

ALCESTE. Since you desire it, Sir, I'll speak
  my mind.

ORONTE. Sonnet. It's a sonnet ... Hope ...
  The poem's addressed
To a lady who wakened hopes within my
  breast.
Hope ... this is not the pompous sort of thing,
Just modest little verses, with a tender ring.

ALCESTE. Well, we shall see.

ORONTE.            Hope ... I'm anxious to hear
Whether the style seems properly smooth
  and clear,
And whether the choice of words is good or
  bad.

ALCESTE. We'll see, we'll see.

ORONTE.                  Perhaps I ought to add
That it took me only a quarter-hour to write
  it.

ALCESTE. The time's irrelevant, Sir: Kindly
  recite it.

ORONTE (reading).
  *Hope comforts us awhile, 'tis true,*
  *Lulling our cares with careless laughter,*
  *And yet such joy is full of rue,*
  *My Phyllis, if nothing follows after.*

PHILINTE. I'm charmed by this already:
  the style's delightful.

ALCESTE (sotto voce, to PHILINTE). How can
  you say that? Why the thing is frightful.

ORONTE.
  *Your fair face smiled on me awhile,*
  *But was it kindness so to enchant me?*
  *'Twould have been fairer not to smile,*
  *If hope was all you meant to grant me.*

PHILINTE. What a clever thought! How
  handsomely you phrase it!

ALCESTE (sotto voce, to PHILINTE). You know
  the thing is trash. How dare you
  praise it?

ORONTE.
  *If it's to be my passion's fate*
  *Thus everlastingly to wait,*
  *Then death will come to set me free:*
  *For death is fairer than the fair;*
  *Phyllis, to hope is to despair*
  *When one must hope eternally.*

PHILINTE. The close is exquisite—full of
  feeling and grace.

ALCESTE (sotto voce, aside). Oh, blast the
  close; you'd better close your face
Before you send your lying soul to hell.

PHILINTE. I can't remember a poem I've
  liked so well.

ALCESTE (sotto voce, aside). Good Lord!

ORONTE (to PHILINTE). I fear you're flattering me a bit.

PHILINTE. Oh, no!

ALCESTE (sotto voce, aside). What else d'you
  call it, you hypocrite?

ORONTE (to ALCESTE). But you, Sir, keep
  your promise now: don't shrink
From telling me sincerely what you think.

ALCESTE. Sir, these are delicate matters;
  we all desire
To be told that we've the true poetic fire.

But once, to one whose name I shall not
    mention,
I said, regarding some verse of his invention,
That gentlemen should rigorously control
That itch to write which often afflicts the
    soul;
That one should curb the heady inclination
To publicize one's little avocation;
And that in showing off one's works of art
One often plays a very clownish part.
    ORONTE. Are you suggesting in a devious
      way
That I ought not . . .
    ALCESTE.          Oh, that I do not say.
Further, I told him that no fault is worse
Than that of writing frigid, lifeless verse,
And that the merest whisper of such a
    shame
Suffices to destroy a man's good name.
    ORONTE. D'you mean to say my sonnet's
      dull and trite?
    ALCESTE. I don't say that. But I went on
      to cite
Numerous cases of once-respected men
Who came to grief by taking up the pen.
    ORONTE. And am I like them? Do I write
      so poorly?
    ALCESTE. I don't say that. But I told this
      person, "Surely
You're under no necessity to compose;
Why you should wish to publish, heaven
    knows.
There's no excuse for printing tedious rot
Unless one writes for bread, as you do not.
Resist temptation, then, I beg of you;
Conceal your pastimes from the public view;
And don't give up, on any provocation,
Your present high and courtly reputation,
To purchase at a greedy printer's shop
The name of silly author and scribbling
    fop."
These were the points I tried to make him
    see.
    ORONTE. I sense that they are also aimed
      at me;
But now—about my sonnet—I'd like to be
    told . . .
    ALCESTE. Frankly, that sonnet should be
      pigeonholed.
You've chosen the worst models to imitate.
The style's unnatural. Let me illustrate:

For example, *Your fair face smiled on*
    *me awhile,*
Followed by, *'Twould have been fairer*
    *not to smile!*
Or this: *such joy is full of rue;*
Or this: *For death is fairer than the*
    *fair;*
Or, *Phyllis, to hope is to despair*
    *When one must hope eternally!*
This artificial style, that's all the fashion,
Has neither taste, nor honesty, nor passion;
It's nothing but a sort of wordy play,
And nature never spoke in such a way.
What, in this shallow age, is not debased?
Our fathers, though less refined, had better
    taste;
I'd barter all that men admire today
For one old love song I shall try to say:
    *If the King had given me for my own*
    *Paris, his citadel,*
    *And I for that must leave alone*
    *Her whom I love so well,*
    *I'd say then to the Crown,*
    *Take back your glittering town;*
    *My darling is more fair, I swear,*
    *My darling is more fair.*
The rhyme's not rich, the style is rough and
    old,
But don't you see that it's the purest gold
Beside the tinsel nonsense now preferred,
And that there's passion in its every word?
    *If the King had given me for my own*
    *Paris, his citadel,*
    *And I for that must leave alone*
    *Her whom I love so well,*
    *I'd say then to the Crown,*
    *Take back your glittering town;*
    *My darling is more fair, I swear,*
    *My darling is more fair.*
There speaks a loving heart. (*To* PHILINTE.)
    You're laughing, eh?
Laugh on, my precious wit. Whatever you
    say,
I hold that song's worth all the bibelots
That people hail today with ah's and oh's.
    ORONTE. And I maintain my sonnet's very
      good.
    ALCESTE. It's not at all surprising that you
      should.
You have your reasons; permit me to have
    mine

For thinking that you cannot write a line.

ORONTE. Others have praised my sonnet to the skies.

ALCESTE. I lack their art of telling pleasant lies.

ORONTE. You seem to think you've got no end of wit.

ALCESTE. To praise your verse, I'd need still more of it.

ORONTE. I'm not in need of your approval, Sir.

ALCESTE. That's good; you couldn't have it if you were.

ORONTE. Come now, I'll lend you the subject of my sonnet;

I'd like to see you try to improve upon it.

ALCESTE. I might, by chance, write something just as shoddy;

But then I wouldn't show it to everybody.

ORONTE. You're most opinionated and conceited.

ALCESTE. Go find your flatterers, and be better treated.

ORONTE. Look here, my little fellow, pray watch your tone.

ALCESTE. My great big fellow, you'd better watch your own.

PHILINTE (*stepping between them*). Oh, please, please, gentlemen! This will never do.

ORONTE. The fault is mine, and I leave the field to you

I am your servant, Sir, in every way.

ALCESTE. And I, Sir, am your most abject valet.

#### Scene 3

PHILINTE, ALCESTE.

PHILINTE. Well, as you see, sincerity in excess

Can get you into a very pretty mess;

Oronte was hungry for appreciation . . .

ALCESTE. Don't speak to me.

PHILINTE. What?

ALCESTE. No more conversation.

PHILINTE. Really, now . . .

ALCESTE. Leave me alone.

PHILINTE. If I . . .

ALCESTE. Out of my sight!

PHILINTE. But what . . .

ALCESTE. I won't listen.

PHILINTE. But . . .

ALCESTE. Silence!

PHILINTE. Now, is it polite . . .

ALCESTE. By heaven, I've had enough. Don't follow me.

PHILINTE. Ah, you're just joking. I'll keep you company.

#### ACT II. *Scene 1*

ALCESTE, CÉLIMÈNE.

ALCESTE. Shall I speak plainly, Madam? I confess

Your conduct gives me infinite distress,

And my resentment's grown too hot to smother.

Soon, I foresee, we'll break with one another.

If I said otherwise, I should deceive you;

Sooner or later, I shall be forced to leave you,

And if I swore that we shall never part,

I should misread the omens of my heart.

CÉLIMÈNE. You kindly saw me home, it would appear,

So as to pour invectives in my ear.

ALCESTE. I've no desire to quarrel. But I deplore

Your inability to shut the door

On all these suitors who beset you so.

There's what annoys me, if you care to know.

CÉLIMÈNE. Is it my fault that all these men pursue me?

Am I to blame if they're attracted to me?

And when they gently beg an audience,

Ought I to take a stick and drive them hence?

ALCESTE. Madam, there's no necessity for a stick;

A less responsive heart would do the trick.

Of your attractiveness I don't complain;

But those your charms attract, you then detain

By a most melting and receptive manner,

And so enlist their hearts beneath your banner.

It's the agreeable hopes which you excite

That keep these lovers round you day and night;

Were they less liberally smiled upon,

That sighing troop would very soon be gone.

But tell me, Madam, why it is that lately

This man Clitandre interests you so greatly?
Because of what high merits do you deem
Him worthy of the honor of your esteem?
Is it that your admiring glances linger
On the splendidly long nail of his little finger?
Or do you share the general deep respect
For the blond wig he chooses to affect?
Are you in love with his embroidered hose?
Do you adore his ribbons and his bows?
Or is it that this paragon bewitches
Your tasteful eye with his vast German
    breeches?
Perhaps his giggle, or his falsetto voice,
Makes him the latest gallant of your choice?
    CÉLIMÈNE. You're much mistaken to resent
    him so.
Why I put up with him you surely know:
My lawsuit's very shortly to be tried,
And I must have his influence on my side.
    ALCESTE. Then lose your lawsuit, Madam,
    or let it drop;
Don't torture me by humoring such a fop.
    CÉLIMÈNE. You're jealous of the whole
    world, Sir.
    ALCESTE.                   That's true,
Since the whole world is well-received by
    you.
    CÉLIMÈNE. That my good nature is so un-
    confined
Should serve to pacify your jealous mind;
Were I to smile on one, and scorn the rest,
Then you might have some cause to be dis-
    tressed.
    ALCESTE. Well, if I mustn't be jealous, tell
    me, then,
Just how I'm better treated than other men.
    CÉLIMÈNE. You know you have my love.
    Will that not do?
    ALCESTE. What proof have I that what you
    say is true?
    CÉLIMÈNE. I would expect, Sir, that my
    having said it
Might give the statement a sufficient credit.
    ALCESTE. But how can I be sure that you
    don't tell
The selfsame thing to other men as well?
    CÉLIMÈNE. What a gallant speech! How
    flattering to me!
What a sweet creature you make me out to
    be!
Well then, to save you from the pangs of
    doubt,

All that I've said I hereby cancel out;
Now, none but yourself shall make a monkey
    of you:
Are you content?
    ALCESTE.         Why, why am I doomed to
    love you?
I swear that I shall bless the blissful hour
When this poor heart's no longer in your
    power!
I make no secret of it: I've done my best
To exorcise this passion from my breast;
But thus far all in vain; it will not go;
It's for my sins that I must love you so.
    CÉLIMÈNE. Your love for me is matchless,
    Sir; that's clear.
    ALCESTE. Indeed, in all the world it has
    no peer;
Words can't describe the nature of my pas-
    sion,
And no man ever loved in such a fashion.
    CÉLIMÈNE. Yes, it's a brand-new fashion,
    I agree:
You show your love by castigating me,
And all your speeches are enraged and rude.
I've never been so furiously wooed.
    ALCESTE. Yet you could calm that fury, if
    you chose.
Come, shall we bring our quarrels to a close?
Let's speak with open hearts, then, and
    begin . . .

### Scene 2

CÉLIMÈNE, ALCESTE, BASQUE.
    CÉLIMÈNE. What is it?
    BASQUE.             Acaste is here.
    CÉLIMÈNE.           Well, send him in.

### Scene 3

CÉLIMÈNE, ALCESTE.
    ALCESTE. What! Shall we never be alone
    at all?
You're always ready to receive a call,
And you can't bear, for ten ticks of the clock,
Not to keep open house for all who knock.
    CÉLIMÈNE. I couldn't refuse him: he'd be
    most put out.
    ALCESTE. Surely that's not worth worrying
    about.
    CÉLIMÈNE. Acaste would never forgive me
    if he guessed

That I consider him a dreadful pest.

ALCESTE. If he's a pest, why bother with him then?

CÉLIMÈNE. Heavens! One can't antagonize such men;

Why, they're the chartered gossips of the court,

And have a say in things of every sort.

One must receive them, and be full of charm;

They're no great help, but they can do you harm,

And though your influence be ever so great,

They're hardly the best people to alienate.

ALCESTE. I see, dear lady, that you could make a case

For putting up with the whole human race;

These friendships that you calculate so nicely . . .

### Scene 4

ALCESTE, CÉLIMÈNE, BASQUE.

BASQUE. Madam, Clitandre is here as well.

ALCESTE. Precisely.

CÉLIMÈNE. Where are you going?

ALCESTE. Elsewhere.

CÉLIMÈNE. Stay.

ALCESTE. No, no.

CÉLIMÈNE. Stay, Sir.

ALCESTE. I can't.

CÉLIMÈNE. I wish it.

ALCESTE. No, I must go.

I beg you, Madam, not to press the matter;

You know I have no taste for idle chatter.

CÉLIMÈNE. Stay: I command you.

ALCESTE. No, I cannot stay.

CÉLIMÈNE. Very well; you have my leave to go away.

### Scene 5

ÉLIANTE, PHILINTE, ACASTE,
CLITANDRE, ALCESTE, BASQUE.

ÉLIANTE (to CÉLIMÈNE). The Marquesses have kindly come to call.

Were they announced?

CÉLIMÈNE. Yes. Basque, bring chairs for all.

(BASQUE *provides the chairs, and exits.*)

(*To* ALCESTE.) You haven't gone?

ALCESTE. No; and I shan't depart

Till you decide who's foremost in your heart.

CÉLIMÈNE. Oh, hush.

ALCESTE. It's time to choose; take them, or me.

CÉLIMÈNE. You're mad.

ALCESTE. I'm not, as you shall shortly see.

CÉLIMÈNE. Oh?

ALCESTE. You'll decide.

CÉLIMÈNE. You're joking now, dear friend.

ALCESTE. No, no: you'll choose; my patience is at an end.

CLITANDRE. Madam, I come from court, where poor Cléonte

Behaved like a perfect fool, as is his wont.

Has he no friend to counsel him, I wonder,

And teach him less unerringly to blunder?

CÉLIMÈNE. It's true, the man's a most accomplished dunce;

His gauche behavior charms the eye at once;

And every time one sees him, on my word,

His manner's grown a trifle more absurd.

ACASTE. Speaking of dunces, I've just now conversed

With old Damon, who's one of the very worst;

I stood a lifetime in the broiling sun

Before his dreary monologue was done.

CÉLIMÈNE. Oh, he's a wondrous talker, and has the power

To tell you nothing hour after hour:

If, by mistake, he ever came to the point,

The shock would put his jawbone out of joint.

ÉLIANTE (*to* PHILINTE). The conversation takes its usual turn,

And all our dear friends' ears will shortly burn.

CLITANDRE. Timante's a character, Madam.

CÉLIMÈNE. Isn't he, though?

A man of mystery from top to toe,

Who moves about in a romantic mist

On secret missions which do not exist.

His talk is full of eyebrows and grimaces;

How tired one gets of his momentous faces;

He's always whispering something confidential

Which turns out to be quite inconsequential;

Nothing's too slight for him to mystify;

He even whispers when he says "good-by."
ACASTE. Tell us about Géralde.
   CÉLIMÈNE.           That tiresome ass.
He mixes only with the titled class,
And fawns on dukes and princes, and is bored
With anyone who's not at least a lord.
The man's obsessed with rank, and his dis-
   courses
Are all of hounds and carriages and horses;
He uses Christian names with all the great,
And the word Milord, with him, is out of date.
   CLITANDRE. He's very taken with Bélise,
      I hear.
   CÉLIMÈNE. She is the dreariest company,
      poor dear.
Whenever she comes to call, I grope about
To find some topic which will draw her out,
But, owing to her dry and faint replies,
The conversation wilts, and droops, and dies.
In vain one hopes to animate her face
By mentioning the ultimate commonplace;
But sun or shower, even hail or frost
Are matters she can instantly exhaust.
Meanwhile her visit, painful though it is,
Drags on and on through mute eternities,
And though you ask the time, and yawn,
   and yawn,
She sits there like a stone and won't be gone.
   ACASTE. Now for Adraste.
   CÉLIMÈNE.        Oh, that conceited elf
Has a gigantic passion for himself;
He rails against the court, and cannot bear it
That none will recognize his hidden merit;
All honors given to others give offense
To his imaginary excellence.
   CLITANDRE. What about young Cléon?
      His house, they say,
Is full of the best society, night and day.
   CÉLIMÈNE. His cook has made him pop-
      ular, not he:
It's Cléon's table that people come to see.
   ÉLIANTE. He gives a splendid dinner, you
      must admit.
   CÉLIMÈNE. But must he serve himself along
      with it?
For my taste, he's a most insipid dish
Whose presence sours the wine and spoils
   the fish.
   PHILINTE. Damis, his uncle, is admired no
      end.
What's your opinion, Madam?

   CÉLIMÈNE.          Why, he's my friend.
   PHILINTE. He seems a decent fellow, and
      rather clever.
   CÉLIMÈNE. He works too hard at clever-
      ness, however.
I hate to see him sweat and struggle so
To fill his conversation with bons mots.
Since he's decided to become a wit
His taste's so pure that nothing pleases it;
He scolds at all the latest books and plays,
Thinking that wit must never stoop to praise,
That finding fault's a sign of intellect,
That all appreciation is abject,
And that by damning everything in sight
One shows oneself in a distinguished light.
He's scornful even of our conversations:
Their trivial nature sorely tries his patience;
He folds his arms, and stands above the bat-
   tle,
And listens sadly to our childish prattle.
   ACASTE. Wonderful, Madam! You've hit
      him off precisely.
   CLITANDRE. No one can sketch a character
      so nicely.
   ALCESTE. How bravely, Sirs, you cut and
      thrust at all
These absent fools, till one by one they fall:
But let one come in sight, and you'll at once
Embrace the man you lately called a dunce,
Telling him in a tone sincere and fervent
How proud you are to be his humble servant.
   CLITANDRE. Why pick on us? *Madame's*
      been speaking, Sir,
And you should quarrel, if you must, with
   her.
   ALCESTE. No, no, by God, the fault is
      yours, because
You lead her on with laughter and applause,
And make her think that she's the more de-
   lightful
The more her talk is scandalous and spiteful.
Oh, she would stoop to malice far, far less
If no such claque approved her cleverness.
It's flatterers like you whose foolish praise
Nourishes all the vices of these days.
   PHILINTE. But why protest when someone
      ridicules
Those you'd condemn, yourself, as knaves or
      fools?
   CÉLIMÈNE. Why, Sir? Because he loves to
      make a fuss.

You don't expect him to agree with us,
When there's an opportunity to express
His heaven-sent spirit of contrariness?
What other people think, he can't abide;
Whatever they say, he's on the other side;
He lives in deadly terror of agreeing;
'Twould make him seem an ordinary being.
Indeed, he's so in love with contradiction,
He'll turn against his most profound convic-
tion
And with a furious eloquence deplore it,
If only someone else is speaking for it.

ALCESTE. Go on, dear lady, mock me as
you please;
You have your audience in ecstasies.

PHILINTE. But what she says is true: you
have a way
Of bridling at whatever people say;
Whether they praise or blame, your angry
spirit
Is equally unsatisfied to hear it.

ALCESTE. Men, Sir, are always wrong, and
that's the reason
That righteous anger's never out of season;
All that I hear in all their conversation
Is flattering praise or reckless condemna-
tion.

CÉLIMÈNE. But . . .

ALCESTE. No, no, Madam, I am
forced to state
That you have pleasures which I deprecate,
And that these others, here, are much to
blame
For nourishing the faults which are your
shame.

CLITANDRE. I shan't defend myself, Sir;
but I vow
I'd thought this lady faultless until now.

ACASTE. I see her charms and graces,
which are many;
But as for faults, I've never noticed any.

ALCESTE. I see them, Sir; and rather than
ignore them,
I strenuously criticize her for them.
The more one loves, the more one should
object
To every blemish, every least defect.
Were I this lady, I would soon get rid
Of lovers who approved of all I did,
And by their slack indulgence and applause
Endorsed my follies and excused my flaws.

CÉLIMÈNE. If all hearts beat according to
your measure,
The dawn of love would be the end of pleas-
ure;
And love would find its perfect consummation
In ecstasies of rage and reprobation.

ÉLIANTE. Love, as a rule, affects men oth-
erwise,
And lovers rarely love to criticize.
They see their lady as a charming blur,
And find all things commendable in her.
If she has any blemish, fault, or shame,
They will redeem it by a pleasing name.
The pale-faced lady's lily-white, perforce;
The swarthy one's a sweet brunette, of
course;
The spindly lady has a slender grace;
The fat one has a most majestic pace;
The plain one, with her dress in disarray,
They classify as *beauté négligée;*
The hulking one's a goddess in their eyes,
The dwarf, a concentrate of Paradise;
The haughty lady has a noble mind;
The mean one's witty, and the dull one's
kind;
The chatterbox has liveliness and verve,
The mute one has a virtuous reserve.
So lovers manage, in their passion's cause,
To love their ladies even for their flaws.

ALCESTE. But I still say . . .

CÉLIMÈNE. I think it would be nice
To stroll around the gallery once or twice.
What! You're not going, Sirs?

CLITANDRE AND ACASTE. No, Madam, no.

ALCESTE. You seem to be in terror lest
they go.
Do what you will, Sirs; leave, or linger on,
But I shan't go till after you are gone.

ACASTE. I'm free to linger, unless I should
perceive
*Madame* is tired, and wishes me to leave.

CLITANDRE. And as for me, I needn't go
today
Until the hour of the King's *coucher.*[3]

CÉLIMÈNE (*to* ALCESTE). You're joking,
surely?

ALCESTE. Not in the least; we'll see
Whether you'd rather part with them, or
me.

_____
[3] *coucher* ceremony attending the King's retire-
ment for the night

## Scene 6

ALCESTE, CÉLIMÈNE, ÉLIANTE,

ACASTE, PHILINTE, CLITANDRE, BASQUE.

BASQUE (*to* ALCESTE). Sir, there's a fellow
here who bids me state

That he must see you, and that it can't wait.

ALCESTE. Tell him that I have no such
pressing affairs.

BASQUE. It's a long tailcoat that this fellow
wears,

With gold all over.

CÉLIMÈNE (*to* ALCESTE). You'd best go down
and see.

Or—have him enter.

## Scene 7

ALCESTE, CÉLIMÈNE, ÉLIANTE, ACASTE,

PHILINTE, CLITANDRE, GUARD.

ALCESTE (*confronting the* GUARD). Well,
what do you want with me?

Come in, Sir.

GUARD. I've a word, Sir, for your ear.

ALCESTE. Speak it aloud, Sir; I shall strive
to hear.

GUARD. The Marshals have instructed me
to say

You must report to them without delay.

ALCESTE. Who? Me, Sir?

GUARD. Yes, Sir; you.

ALCESTE. But what do they want?

PHILINTE (*to* ALCESTE). To scotch your silly
quarrel with Oronte.

CÉLIMÈNE (*to* PHILINTE). What quarrel?

PHILINTE. Oronte and he have fallen out
Over some verse he spoke his mind about;
The Marshals wish to arbitrate the matter.

ALCESTE. Never shall I equivocate or
flatter!

PHILINTE. You'd best obey their summons;
come, let's go.

ALCESTE. How can they mend our quarrel,
I'd like to know?

Am I to make a cowardly retraction,

And praise those jingles to his satisfaction?

I'll not recant; I've judged that sonnet
rightly.

It's bad.

PHILINTE. But you might say so
more politely . . .

ALCESTE. I'll not back down; his verses
make me sick.

PHILINTE. If only you could be more politic!

But come, let's go.

ALCESTE. I'll go, but I won't unsay
A single word.

PHILINTE. Well, let's be on our way.

ALCESTE. Till I am ordered by my lord the
King

To praise that poem, I shall say the thing
Is scandalous, by God, and that the poet
Ought to be hanged for having the nerve to
show it.

(*To* CLITANDRE *and* ACASTE, *who are laughing.*)

By heaven, Sirs, I really didn't know
That I was being humorous.

CÉLIMÈNE. Go, Sir, go;
Settle your business.

ALCESTE. I shall, and when I'm through,
I shall return to settle things with you.

## ACT III. *Scene 1*

CLITANDRE, ACASTE.

CLITANDRE. Dear Marquess, how contented you appear;

All things delight you, nothing mars your
cheer.

Can you, in perfect honesty, declare

That you've a right to be so debonair?

ACASTE. By Jove, when I survey myself,
I find

No cause whatever for distress of mind.

I'm young and rich; I can in modesty

Lay claim to an exalted pedigree;

And owing to my name and my condition

I shall not want for honors and position.

Then as to courage, that most precious trait,

I seem to have it, as was proved of late

Upon the field of honor, where my bearing,

They say, was very cool and rather daring.

I've wit, of course; and taste in such perfection

That I can judge without the least reflection,

And at the theater, which is my delight,

Can make or break a play on opening night,

And lead the crowd in hisses or bravos,

And generally be known as one who knows.

I'm clever, handsome, gracefully polite;
My waist is small, my teeth are strong and
　　white;
As for my dress, the world's astonished eyes
Assure me that I bear away the prize.
I find myself in favor everywhere,
Honored by men, and worshiped by the fair;
And since these things are so, it seems to me
I'm justified in my complacency.
　　CLITANDRE. Well, if so many ladies hold
　　you dear,
Why do you press a hopeless courtship here?
　　ACASTE. Hopeless, you say? I'm not the
　　sort of fool
That likes his ladies difficult and cool.
Men who are awkward, shy, and peasantish
May pine for heartless beauties, if they wish,
Grovel before them, bear their cruelties,
Woo them with tears and sighs and bended
　　knees,
And hope by dogged faithfulness to gain
What their poor merits never could obtain.
For men like me, however, it makes no sense
To love on trust, and foot the whole ex-
　　pense.
Whatever any lady's merits be,
I think, thank God, that I'm as choice as she;
That if my heart is kind enough to burn
For her, she owes me something in return;
And that in any proper love affair
The partners must invest an equal share.
　　CLITANDRE. You think, then, that our host-
　　ess favors you?
　　ACASTE. I've reason to believe that that is
　　true.
　　CLITANDRE. How did you come to such a
　　mad conclusion?
You're blind, dear fellow. This is sheer delu-
　　sion.
　　ACASTE. All right, then: I'm deluded and
　　I'm blind.
　　CLITANDRE. Whatever put the notion in
　　your mind?
　　ACASTE. Delusion.
　　CLITANDRE.　　What persuades you that
　　you're right?
　　ACASTE. I'm blind.
　　CLITANDRE.　　But have you any proofs
　　to cite?
　　ACASTE. I tell you I'm deluded.
　　CLITANDRE.　　　　　Have you, then,

Received some secret pledge from Célimène?
　　ACASTE. Oh, no: she scorns me.
　　CLITANDRE.　　　Tell me the truth, I beg.
　　ACASTE. She just can't bear me.
　　CLITANDRE.　　　Ah, don't pull my leg.
Tell me what hope she's given you, I pray.
　　ACASTE. I'm hopeless, and it's you who win
　　the day.
She hates me thoroughly, and I'm so vexed
I mean to hang myself on Tuesday next.
　　CLITANDRE. Dear Marquess, let us have an
　　armistice
And make a treaty. What do you say to this?
If ever one of us can plainly prove
That Célimène encourages his love,
The other must abandon hope, and yield,
And leave him in possession of the field.
　　ACASTE. Now, there's a bargain that ap-
　　peals to me;
With all my heart, dear Marquess, I agree.
But hush.

### Scene 2

　　CÉLIMÈNE, ACASTE, CLITANDRE.
　　CÉLIMÈNE. Still here?
　　CLITANDRE.　　　'Twas love that stayed
　　our feet.
　　CÉLIMÈNE. I think I heard a carriage in
　　the street.
Whose is it? D'you know?

### Scene 3

　　CÉLIMÈNE, ACASTE, CLITANDRE, BASQUE.
　　BASQUE.　　　　　Arsinoé is here,
Madame.
　　CÉLIMÈNE.　　Arsinoé, you say? Oh, dear.
　　BASQUE. Éliante is entertaining her below.
　　CÉLIMÈNE. What brings the creature here,
　　I'd like to know?
　　ACASTE. They say she's dreadfully prudish,
　　but in fact
I think her piety . . .
　　CÉLIMÈNE.　　　It's all an act.
At heart she's worldly, and her poor success
In snaring men explains her prudishness.
It breaks her heart to see the beaux and
　　gallants
Engrossed by other women's charms and tal-
　　ents,
And so she's always in a jealous rage
Against the faulty standards of the age.

She lets the world believe that she's a prude
To justify her loveless solitude,
And strives to put a brand of moral shame
On all the graces that she cannot claim.
But still she'd love a lover; and Alceste
Appears to be the one she'd love the best.
His visits here are poison to her pride;
She seems to think I've lured him from her
    side;
And everywhere, at court or in the town,
The spiteful, envious woman runs me down.
In short, she's just as stupid as can be,
Vicious and arrogant in the last degree,
And . . .

## Scene 4

ARSINOÉ, CÉLIMÈNE, CLITANDRE, ACASTE.

CÉLIMÈNE. Ah! What happy chance has
    brought you here?
I've thought about you ever so much, my
    dear.
    ARSINOÉ. I've come to tell you something
    you should know.
CÉLIMÈNE. How good of you to think of
    doing so!
    (CLITANDRE and ACASTE go out, laughing.)

## Scene 5

ARSINOÉ, CÉLIMÈNE.

ARSINOÉ. It's just as well those gentlemen
    didn't tarry.
CÉLIMÈNE. Shall we sit down?
    ARSINOÉ.            That won't be necessary.
Madam, the flame of friendship ought to burn
Brightest in matters of the most concern,
And as there's nothing which concerns us
    more
Than honor, I have hastened to your door
To bring you, as your friend, some informa-
    tion
About the status of your reputation.
I visited, last night, some virtuous folk,
And, quite by chance, it was of you they
    spoke;
There was, I fear, no tendency to praise
Your light behavior and your dashing ways.
The quantity of gentlemen you see
And your by now notorious coquetry
Were both so vehemently criticized
By everyone, that I was much surprised.

Of course, I needn't tell you where I stood;
I came to your defense as best I could,
Assured them you were harmless, and de-
    clared
Your soul was absolutely unimpaired.
But there are some things, you must realize,
One can't excuse, however hard one tries,
And I was forced at last into conceding
That your behavior, Madam, is misleading,
That it makes a bad impression, giving rise
To ugly gossip and obscene surmise,
And that if you were more *overtly* good,
You wouldn't be so much misunderstood.
Not that I think you've been unchaste—
    no! no!
The saints preserve me from a thought so
    low!
But mere good conscience never did suffice:
One must avoid the outward show of vice.
Madam, you're too intelligent, I'm sure,
To think my motives anything but pure
In offering you this counsel—which I do
Out of a zealous interest in you.
    CÉLIMÈNE. Madam, I haven't taken you
    amiss;
I'm very much obliged to you for this;
And I'll at once discharge the obligation
By telling you about *your* reputation.
You've been so friendly as to let me know
What certain people say of me, and so
I mean to follow your benign example
By offering you a somewhat similar sample.
The other day, I went to an affair
And found some most distinguished people
    there
Discussing piety, both false and true.
The conversation soon came round to you.
Alas! Your prudery and bustling zeal
Appeared to have a very slight appeal.
Your affectation of a grave demeanor,
Your endless talk of virtue and of honor,
The aptitude of your suspicious mind
For finding sin where there is none to find,
Your towering self-esteem, that pitying face
With which you contemplate the human race,
Your sermonizings and your sharp aspersions
On people's pure and innocent diversions—
All these were mentioned, Madam, and, in
    fact,
Were roundly and concertedly attacked.
"What good," they said, "are all these out-
    ward shows,

When everything belies her pious pose?
She prays incessantly; but then, they say,
She beats her maids and cheats them of
their pay;
She shows her zeal in every holy place,
But still she's vain enough to paint her face;
She holds that naked statues are immoral,
But with a naked *man* she'd have no quarrel."
Of course, I said to everybody there
That they were being viciously unfair;
But still they were disposed to criticize you,
And all agreed that someone should advise
you
To leave the morals of the world alone,
And worry rather more about your own.
They felt that one's self-knowledge should be
great
Before one thinks of setting others straight;
That one should learn the art of living well
Before one threatens other men with hell,
And that the Church is best equipped, no
doubt,
To guide our souls and root our vices out.
Madam, you're too intelligent, I'm sure,
To think my motives anything but pure
In offering you this counsel—which I do
Out of a zealous interest in you.
    ARSINOÉ. I dared not hope for gratitude,
but I
Did not expect so acid a reply;
I judge, since you've been so extremely tart,
That my good counsel pierced you to the
heart.
    CÉLIMÈNE. Far from it, Madam. Indeed, it
seems to me
We ought to trade advice more frequently.
One's vision of oneself is so defective
That it would be an excellent corrective.
If you are willing, Madam, let's arrange
Shortly to have another frank exchange
In which we'll tell each other, *entre nous*,
What you've heard tell of me, and I of you.
    ARSINOÉ. Oh, people never censure you,
my dear;
It's me they criticize. Or so I hear.
    CÉLIMÉNE. Madam, I think we either
blame or praise
According to our taste and length of days.
There is a time of life for coquetry,
And there's a season, too, for prudery.
When all one's charms are gone, it is, I'm
sure,

Good strategy to be devout and pure:
It makes one seem a little less forsaken.
Some day, perhaps, I'll take the road you've
taken:
Time brings all things. But I have time
aplenty,
And see no cause to be a prude at twenty.
    ARSINOÉ. You give your age in such a gloat-
ing tone
That one would think I was an ancient
crone;
We're not so far apart, in sober truth,
That you can mock me with a boast of youth!
Madam, you baffle me. I wish I knew
What moves you to provoke me as you do.
    CÉLIMÈNE. For my part, Madam, I should
like to know
Why you abuse me everywhere you go.
Is it my fault, dear lady, that your hand
Is not, alas, in very great demand?
If men admire me, if they pay me court
And daily make me offers of the sort
You'd dearly love to have them make to
you,
How can I help it? What would you have
me do?
If what you want is lovers, please feel free
To take as many as you can from me.
    ARSINOÉ. Oh, come. D'you think the world
is losing sleep
Over that flock of lovers which you keep,
Or that we find it difficult to guess
What price you pay for their devotedness?
Surely you don't expect us to suppose
Mere merit could attract so many beaux?
It's not your virtue that they're dazzled by;
Nor is it virtuous love for which they sigh.
You're fooling no one, Madam; the world's
not blind;
There's many a lady heaven has designed
To call men's noblest, tenderest feelings out,
Who has no lovers dogging her about;
From which it's plain that lovers nowadays
Must be acquired in bold and shameless ways,
And only pay one court for such reward
As modesty and virtue can't afford.
Then don't be quite so puffed up, if you
please,
About your tawdry little victories;
Try, if you can, to be a shade less vain,
And treat the world with somewhat less dis-
dain.

If one were envious of your amours,
One soon could have a following like yours;
Lovers are no great trouble to collect
If one prefers them to one's self-respect.
    CÉLIMÈNE. Collect them then, my dear;
        I'd love to see
You demonstrate that charming theory;
Who knows, you might . . .
    ARSINOÉ.        Now, Madam, that will do;
It's time to end this trying interview.
My coach is late in coming to your door,
Or I'd have taken leave of you before.
    CÉLIMÈNE. Oh, please don't feel that you
        must rush away;
I'd be delighted, Madam, if you'd stay.
However, lest my conversation bore you,
Let me provide some better company for you;
This gentleman, who comes most apropos,
Will please you more than I could do, I
    know.


### Scene 6

ALCESTE, CÉLIMÈNE, ARSINOÉ.
    CÉLIMÈNE. Alceste, I have a little note to
        write
Which simply must go out before tonight;
Please entertain *Madame;* I'm sure that she
Will overlook my incivility.


### Scene 7

ALCESTE, ARSINOÉ.
    ARSINOÉ. Well, Sir, our hostess graciously
        contrives
For us to chat until my coach arrives;
And I shall be forever in her debt
For granting me this little tête-à-tête.
We women very rightly give our hearts
To men of noble character and parts,
And your especial merits, dear Alceste,
Have roused the deepest sympathy in my
    breast.
Oh, how I wish they had sufficient sense
At court, to recognize your excellence!
They wrong you greatly, Sir. How it must
    hurt you
Never to be rewarded for your virtue!
    ALCESTE. Why, Madam, what cause have
        I to feel aggrieved?

What great and brilliant thing have I
    achieved?
What service have I rendered to the King
That I should look to him for anything?
    ARSINOÉ. Not everyone who's honored by
        the State
Has done great services. A man must wait
Till time and fortune offer him the chance.
Your merit, Sir, is obvious at a glance,
And . . .
    ALCESTE.        Ah, forget my merit; I'm
        not neglected.
The court, I think, can hardly be expected
To mine men's souls for merit, and unearth
Our hidden virtues and our secret worth.
    ARSINOÉ. *Some* virtues, though, are far too
        bright to hide;
Yours are acknowledged, Sir, on every side.
Indeed, I've heard you warmly praised of late
By persons of considerable weight.
    ALCESTE. This fawning age has praise for
        everyone,
And all distinctions, Madam, are undone.
All things have equal honor nowadays,
And no one should be gratified by praise.
To be admired, one only need exist,
And every lackey's on the honors list.
    ARSINOÉ. I only wish, Sir, that you had
        your eye
On some position at court, however high;
You'd only have to hint at such a notion
For me to set the proper wheels in motion;
I've certain friendships I'd be glad to use
To get you any office you might choose.
    ALCESTE. Madam, I fear that any such
        ambition
Is wholly foreign to my disposition.
The soul God gave me isn't of the sort
That prospers in the weather of a court.
It's all too obvious that I don't possess
The virtues necessary for success.
My one great talent is for speaking plain;
I've never learned to flatter or to feign;
And anyone so stupidly sincere
Had best not seek a courtier's career.
Outside the court, I know, one must dispense
With honors, privilege, and influence;
But still one gains the right, foregoing these,
Not to be tortured by the wish to please.
One needn't live in dread of snubs and
    slights,

Nor praise the verse that every idiot writes,
Nor humor silly Marquesses, nor bestow
Politic sighs on Madam So-and-So.

ARSINOÉ. Forget the court, then; let the
matter rest.
But I've another cause to be distressed
About your present situation, Sir.
It's to your love affair that I refer.
She whom you love, and who pretends to
love you,
Is, I regret to say, unworthy of you.

ALCESTE. Why, Madam! Can you seriously
intend
To make so grave a charge against your
friend?

ARSINOÉ. Alas, I must. I've stood aside too
long
And let that lady do you grievous wrong;
But now my debt to conscience shall be paid:
I tell you that your love has been betrayed.

ALCESTE. I thank you, Madam; you're
extremely kind.
Such words are soothing to a lover's mind.

ARSINOÉ. Yes, though she *is* my friend,
I say again
You're very much too good for Célimène.
She's wantonly misled you from the start.

ALCESTE. You may be right; who knows
another's heart?
But ask yourself if it's the part of charity
To shake my soul with doubts of her sincerity.

ARSINOÉ. Well, if you'd rather be a dupe
than doubt her,
That's your affair. I'll say no more about
her.

ALCESTE. Madam, you know that doubt
and vague suspicion
Are painful to a man in my position;
It's most unkind to worry me this way
Unless you've some real proof of what you
say.

ARSINOÉ. Sir, say no more: all doubt shall
be removed,
And all that I've been saying shall be proved.
You've only to escort me home, and there
We'll look into the heart of this affair.
I've ocular evidence which will persuade you
Beyond a doubt, that Célimène's betrayed
you.
Then, if you're saddened by that revelation,
Perhaps I can provide some consolation.

## ACT IV. *Scene 1*

ÉLIANTE, PHILINTE.

PHILINTE. Madam, he acted like a stub-
born child;
I thought they never would be reconciled;
In vain we reasoned, threatened, and ap-
pealed;
He stood his ground and simply would not
yield.
The Marshals, I feel sure, have never heard
An argument so splendidly absurd.
"No, gentlemen," said he, "I'll not retract.
His verse is bad: extremely bad, in fact.
Surely it does the man no harm to know it.
Does it disgrace him, not to be a poet?
A gentleman may be respected still,
Whether he writes a sonnet well or ill.
That I dislike his verse should not offend
him;
In all that touches honor, I commend him;
He's noble, brave, and virtuous—but I fear
He can't in truth be called a sonneteer.
I'll gladly praise his wardrobe; I'll endorse
His dancing, or the way he sits a horse;
But, gentlemen, I cannot praise his rhyme.
In fact, it ought to be a capital crime
For anyone so sadly unendowed
To write a sonnet, and read the thing aloud."
At length he fell into a gentler mood
And, striking a concessive attitude,
He paid Oronte the following courtesies:
"Sir, I regret that I'm so hard to please,
And I'm profoundly sorry that your lyric
Failed to provoke me to a panegyric."
After these curious words, the two embraced,
And then the hearing was adjourned—in
haste.

ÉLIANTE. His conduct has been very
singular lately;
Still, I confess that I respect him greatly.
The honesty in which he takes such pride
Has—to my mind—its noble, heroic side.
In this false age, such candor seems out-
rageous;
But I could wish that it were more con-
tagious.

PHILINTE. What most intrigues me in our
friend Alceste

Is the grand passion that rages in his breast.
The sullen humors he's compounded of
Should not, I think, dispose his heart to
    love;
But since they do, it puzzles me still more
That he should choose your cousin to adore.
    ÉLIANTE. It does, indeed, belie the theory
That love is born of gentle sympathy,
And that the tender passion must be based
On sweet accords of temper and of taste.
    PHILINTE. Does she return his love, do you
      suppose?
    ÉLIANTE. Ah, that's a difficult question,
      Sir. Who knows?
How can we judge the truth of her devotion?
Her heart's a stranger to its own emotion.
Sometimes it thinks it loves, when no love's
    there;
At other times it loves quite unaware.
    PHILINTE. I rather think Alceste is in for
      more
Distress and sorrow than he's bargained for;
Were he of my mind, Madam, his affection
Would turn in quite a different direction,
And we would see him more responsive to
The kind regard which he receives from you.
    ÉLIANTE. Sir, I believe in frankness, and
      I'm inclined,
In matters of the heart, to speak my mind.
I don't oppose his love for her; indeed,
I hope with all my heart that he'll succeed,
And were it in my power, I'd rejoice
In giving him the lady of his choice.
But if, as happens frequently enough
In love affairs, he meets with a rebuff—
If Célimène should grant some rival's suit—
I'd gladly play the role of substitute;
Nor would his tender speeches please me less
Because they'd once been made without suc-
    cess.
    PHILINTE. Well, Madam, as for me, I
      don't oppose
Your hopes in this affair; and heaven knows
That in my conversations with the man
I plead your cause as often as I can.
But if those two should marry, and so re-
    move
All chance that he will offer you his love,
Then I'll declare my own, and hope to see
Your gracious favor pass from him to me.
In short, should you be cheated of Alceste,

I'd be most happy to be second best.
    ÉLIANTE. Philinte, you're teasing.
    PHILINTE.       Ah, Madam, never fear;
No words of mine were ever so sincere,
And I shall live in fretful expectation
Till I can make a fuller declaration.

### Scene 2

ALCESTE, ÉLIANTE, PHILINTE.

    ALCESTE. Avenge me, Madam! I must
      have satisfaction,
Or this great wrong will drive me to distrac-
    tion!
    ÉLIANTE. Why, what's the matter? What's
      upset you so?
    ALCESTE. Madam, I've had a mortal,
      mortal blow.
If Chaos repossessed the universe,
I swear I'd not be shaken any worse.
I'm ruined. . . . I can say no more. . . . . My
    soul . . .
    ÉLIANTE. Do try, Sir, to regain your self-
      control.
    ALCESTE. Just heaven! Why were so much
      beauty and grace
Bestowed on one so vicious and so base?
    ÉLIANTE. Once more, Sir, tell us . . . .
    ALCESTE.       My world has gone to wrack;
I'm—I'm betrayed; she's stabbed me in the
    back:
Yes, Célimène (who would have thought it
    of her?)
Is false to me, and has another lover.
    ÉLIANTE. Are you quite certain? Can you
      prove these things?
    PHILINTE. Lovers are prey to wild imagin-
      ings
And jealous fancies. No doubt there's some
    mistake . . . .
    ALCESTE. Mind your own business, Sir, for
      heaven's sake.
                (*To* ÉLIANTE.)
Madam, I have the proof that you demand
Here in my pocket, penned by her own hand.
Yes, all the shameful evidence one could want
Lies in this letter written to Oronte—
Oronte! whom I felt sure she couldn't love,
And hardly bothered to be jealous of.
    PHILINTE. Still, in a letter, appearances
      may deceive;

This may not be so bad as you believe.

ALCESTE. Once more I beg you, Sir, to let me be;

Tend to your own affairs; leave mine to me.

ÉLIANTE. Compose yourself; this anguish that you feel . . .

ALCESTE. Is something, Madam, you alone can heal.

My outraged heart, beside itself with grief,
Appeals to you for comfort and relief.
Avenge me on your cousin, whose unjust
And faithless nature has deceived my trust;
Avenge a crime your pure soul must detest.

ÉLIANTE. But how, Sir?

ALCESTE. Madam, this heart within my breast

Is yours; pray take it; redeem my heart from her,
And so avenge me on my torturer.
Let her be punished by the fond emotion,
The ardent love, the bottomless devotion,
The faithful worship which this heart of mine
Will offer up to yours as to a shrine.

ÉLIANTE. You have my sympathy, Sir, in all you suffer;

Nor do I scorn the noble heart you offer;
But I suspect you'll soon be mollified,
And this desire for vengeance will subside.
When some belovèd hand has done us wrong
We thirst for retribution—but not for long;
However dark the deed that she's committed,
A lovely culprit's very soon acquitted.
Nothing's so stormy as an injured lover,
And yet no storm so quickly passes over.

ALCESTE. No, Madam, no—this is no lovers' spat;

I'll not forgive her; it's gone too far for that;
My mind's made up; I'll kill myself before
I waste my hopes upon her any more.
Ah, here she is. My wrath intensifies.
I shall confront her with her tricks and lies,
And crush her utterly, and bring you then
A heart no longer slave to Célimène.

### Scene 3

CÉLIMÈNE, ALCESTE.

ALCESTE (aside). Sweet heaven, help me to control my passion.

CÉLIMÈNE (aside). Oh, Lord.

(To ALCESTE.)

Why stand there staring in that fashion?

And what d'you mean by those dramatic sighs,
And that malignant glitter in your eyes?

ALCESTE. I mean that sins which cause the blood to freeze

Look innocent beside your treacheries;
That nothing Hell's or Heaven's wrath could do
Ever produced so bad a thing as you.

CÉLIMÈNE. Your compliments were always sweet and pretty.

ALCESTE. Madam, it's not the moment to be witty.

No, blush and hang your head; you've ample reason,
Since I've the fullest evidence of your treason.
Ah, this is what my sad heart prophesied;
Now all my anxious fears are verified;
My dark suspicion and my gloomy doubt
Divined the truth, and now the truth is out.
For all your trickery, I was not deceived;
It was my bitter stars that I believed.
But don't imagine that you'll go scot-free;
You shan't misuse me with impunity.
I know that love's irrational and blind;
I know the heart's not subject to the mind,
And can't be reasoned into beating faster;
I know each soul is free to choose its master;
Therefore had you but spoken from the heart,
Rejecting my attentions from the start,
I'd have no grievance, or at any rate
I could complain of nothing but my fate.
Ah, but so falsely to encourage me—
That was a treason and a treachery
For which you cannot suffer too severely,
And you shall pay for that behavior dearly.
Yes, now I have no pity, not a shred;
My temper's out of hand; I've lost my head;
Shocked by the knowledge of your double-dealings,
My reason can't restrain my savage feelings;
A righteous wrath deprives me of my senses,
And I won't answer for the consequences.

CÉLIMÈNE. What does this outburst mean? Will you please explain?

Have you, by any chance, gone quite insane?

ALCESTE. Yes, yes, I went insane the day I fell

A victim to your black and fatal spell,

Thinking to meet with some sincerity
Among the treacherous charms that beck-
    oned me.
    CÉLIMÈNE. Pooh. Of what treachery can
    you complain?
    ALCESTE. How sly you are, how cleverly
    you feign!
But you'll not victimize me any more.
Look: here's a document you've seen before.
This evidence, which I acquired today,
Leaves you, I think, without a thing to say.
    CÉLIMÈNE. Is this what sent you into such
    a fit?
    ALCESTE. You should be blushing at the
    sight of it.
    CÉLIMÈNE. Ought I to blush? I truly don't
    see why.
    ALCESTE. Ah, now you're being bold as
    well as sly;
Since there's no signature, perhaps you'll
    claim . . .
    CÉLIMÈNE. I wrote it, whether or not it
    bears my name.
    ALCESTE. And you can view with equanim-
    ity
This proof of your disloyalty to me!
    CÉLIMÈNE. Oh, don't be so outrageous and
    extreme.
    ALCESTE. You take this matter lightly, it
    would seem.
Was it no wrong to me, no shame to you,
That you should send Oronte this billet-
    doux?
    CÉLIMÈNE. Oronte! Who said it was for
    him?
    ALCESTE.                     Why, those
Who brought me this example of your prose.
But what's the difference? If you wrote the
    letter
To someone else, it pleases me no better.
My grievance and your guilt remain the same.
    CÉLIMÈNE. But need you rage, and need
    I blush for shame,
If this was written to a *woman* friend?
    ALCESTE. Ah! Most ingenious. I'm im-
    pressed no end;
And after that incredible evasion
Your guilt is clear. I need no more persuasion.
How dare you try so clumsy a deception?
D'you think I'm wholly wanting in percep-
    tion?

Come, come, let's see how brazenly you'll try
To bolster up so palpable a lie:
Kindly construe this ardent closing section
As nothing more than sisterly affection!
Here, let me read it. Tell me, if you dare to,
That this is for a woman . . .
    CÉLIMÈNE.                     I don't care to.
What right have you to badger and berate
    me,
And so highhandedly interrogate me?
    ALCESTE. Now, don't be angry; all I ask of
    you
Is that you justify a phrase or two . . .
    CÉLIMÈNE. No, I shall not. I utterly refuse,
And you may take those phrases as you choose.
    ALCESTE. Just show me how this letter
    could be meant
For a woman's eyes, and I shall be content.
    CÉLIMÈNE. No, no, it's for Oronte; you're
    perfectly right.
I welcome his attentions with delight,
I prize his character and his intellect,
And everything is just as you suspect.
Come, do your worst now; give your rage
    free rein;
But kindly cease to bicker and complain.
    ALCESTE (*aside*). Good God! Could any-
    thing be more inhuman?
Was ever a heart so mangled by a woman?
When I complain of how she has betrayed me,
She bridles, and commences to upbraid me!
She tries my tortured patience to the limit;
She won't deny her guilt; she glories in it!
And yet my heart's too faint and cowardly
To break these chains of passion, and be free,
To scorn her as it should, and rise above
This unrewarded, mad, and bitter love.
                    (*To* CÉLIMÈNE.)
Ah, traitress, in how confident a fashion
You take advantage of my helpless passion,
And use my weakness for your faithless
    charms
To make me once again throw down my
    arms!
But do at least deny this black transgression;
Take back that mocking and perverse confes-
    sion;
Defend this letter and your innocence,
And I, poor fool, will aid in your defense.
Pretend, pretend, that you are just and true,
And I shall make myself believe in you.

CÉLIMÈNE. Oh, stop it. Don't be such a jealous dunce,
Or I shall leave off loving you at once.
Just why should I *pretend*? What could impel me
To stoop so low as that? And kindly tell me
Why, if I loved another, I shouldn't merely
Inform you of it, simply and sincerely!
I've told you where you stand, and that admission
Should altogether clear me of suspicion;
After so generous a guarantee,
What right have you to harbor doubts of me?
Since women are (from natural reticence)
Reluctant to declare their sentiments,
And since the honor of our sex requires
That we conceal our amorous desires,
Ought any man for whom such laws are broken
To question what the oracle has spoken?
Should he not rather feel an obligation
To trust that most obliging declaration?
Enough, now. Your suspicions quite disgust me;
Why should I love a man who doesn't trust me?
I cannot understand why I continue,
Fool that I am, to take an interest in you.
I ought to choose a man less prone to doubt,
And give you something to be vexed about.
  ALCESTE. Ah, what a poor enchanted fool I am;
These gentle words, no doubt, were all a sham;
But destiny requires me to entrust
My happiness to you, and so I must.
I'll love you to the bitter end, and see
How false and treacherous you dare to be.
  CÉLIMÈNE. No, you don't really love me as you ought.
  ALCESTE. I love you more than can be said or thought;
Indeed, I wish you were in such distress
That I might show my deep devotedness.
Yes, I could wish that you were wretchedly poor,
Unloved, uncherished, utterly obscure;
That fate had set you down upon the earth
Without possessions, rank, or gentle birth;
Then, by the offer of my heart, I might
Repair the great injustice of your plight;

I'd raise you from the dust, and proudly prove
The purity and vastness of my love.
  CÉLIMÈNE. This is a strange benevolence indeed!
God grant that I may never be in need. . . .
Ah, here's Monsieur Dubois, in quaint disguise.

*Scene 4*

CÉLIMÈNE, ALCESTE, DUBOIS.

  ALCESTE. Well, why this costume? Why those frightened eyes?
What ails you?
  DUBOIS. Well, Sir, things are most mysterious.
  ALCESTE. What do you mean?
  DUBOIS. I fear they're very serious.
  ALCESTE. What?
  DUBOIS. Shall I speak more loudly?
  ALCESTE. Yes; speak out.
  DUBOIS. Isn't there someone here, Sir?
  ALCESTE. Speak, you lout!
Stop wasting time.
  DUBOIS. Sir, we must slip away.
  ALCESTE. How's that?
  DUBOIS. We must decamp without delay.
  ALCESTE. Explain yourself.
  DUBOIS. I tell you we must fly.
  ALCESTE. What for?
  DUBOIS. We mustn't pause to say good-by.
  ALCESTE. Now what d'you mean by all of this, you clown?
  DUBOIS. I mean, Sir, that we've got to leave this town.
  ALCESTE. I'll tear you limb from limb and joint from joint
If you don't come more quickly to the point.
  DUBOIS. Well, Sir, today a man in a black suit,
Who wore a black and ugly scowl to boot,
Left us a document scrawled in such a hand
As even Satan couldn't understand.
It bears upon your lawsuit, I don't doubt;
But all hell's devils couldn't make it out.
  ALCESTE. Well, well, go on. What then? I fail to see
How this event obliges us to flee.
  DUBOIS. Well, Sir: an hour later, hardly more,

A gentleman who's often called before
Came looking for you in an anxious way.
Not finding you, he asked me to convey
(Knowing I could be trusted with the same)
The following message.... Now, what *was*
    his name?
    ALCESTE. Forget his name, you idiot.
    What did he say?
    DUBOIS. Well, it was one of your friends,
    Sir, anyway.
He warned you to begone, and he suggested
That if you stay, you may well be arrested.
    ALCESTE. What? Nothing more specific?
    Think, man, think!
    DUBOIS. No, Sir. He had me bring him pen
    and ink,
And dashed you off a letter which, I'm sure,
Will render things distinctly less obscure.
    ALCESTE. Well—let me have it!
    CÉLIMÈNE.        What *is* this all about?
    ALCESTE. God knows; but I have hopes of
    finding out.
How long am I to wait, you blitherer?
    DUBOIS (*after a protracted search for the letter*).
    I must have left it on your table, Sir.
    ALCESTE. I ought to ...
    CÉLIMÈNE.        No, no, keep your
    self-control;
Go find out what's behind his rigmarole.
    ALCESTE. It seems that fate, no matter
    what I do,
Has sworn that I may not converse with you;
But, Madam, pray permit your faithful lover
To try once more before the day is over.

## ACT V. *Scene 1*

ALCESTE, PHILINTE.

    ALCESTE. No, it's too much. My mind's
    made up, I tell you.
    PHILINTE. Why should this blow, however
    hard, compel you ...
    ALCESTE. No, no, don't waste your breath
    in argument;
Nothing you say will alter my intent;
This age is vile, and I've made up my mind
To have no further commerce with mankind.
Did not truth, honor, decency, and the laws
Oppose my enemy and approve my cause?
My claims were justified in all men's sight;
I put my trust in equity and right;

Yet, to my horror and the world's disgrace,
Justice is mocked, and I have lost my case!
A scoundrel whose dishonesty is notorious
Emerges from another lie victorious!
Honor and right condone his brazen fraud,
While rectitude and decency applaud!
Before his smirking face, the truth stands
    charmed,
And virtue conquered, and the law disarmed!
His crime is sanctioned by a court decree!
And not content with what he's done to me,
The dog now seeks to ruin me by stating
That I composed a book now circulating,
A book so wholly criminal and vicious
That even to speak its title is seditious!
Meanwhile Oronte, my rival, lends his credit
To the same libelous tale, and helps to
    spread it!
Oronte! a man of honor and of rank,
With whom I've been entirely fair and frank;
Who sought me out and forced me, willy-
    nilly,
To judge some verse I found extremely silly;
And who, because I properly refused
To flatter him, or see the truth abused,
Abets my enemy in a rotten slander!
There's the reward of honesty and candor!
The man will hate me to the end of time
For failing to commend his wretched rhyme!
And not this man alone, but all humanity
Do what they do from interest and vanity;
They prate of honor, truth, and right-
    eousness,
But lie, betray, and swindle nonetheless.
Come then: man's villainy is too much to
    bear;
Let's leave this jungle and this jackal's lair.
Yes! treacherous and savage race of men,
You shall not look upon my face again.
    PHILINTE. Oh, don't rush into exile prema-
    turely;
Things aren't as dreadful as you make them,
    surely.
It's rather obvious, since you're still at large,
That people don't believe your enemy's
    charge.
Indeed, his tale's so patently untrue
That it may do more harm to him than
    you.
    ALCESTE. Nothing could do that scoundrel
    any harm:

His frank corruption is his greatest charm,
And, far from hurting him, a further shame
Would only serve to magnify his name.

PHILINTE. In any case, his bald prevarica-
tion
Has done no injury to your reputation,
And you may feel secure in that regard.
As for your lawsuit, it should not be hard
To have the case reopened, and contest
This judgment . . .

ALCESTE.          No, no, let the verdict rest.
Whatever cruel penalty it may bring,
I wouldn't have it changed for anything.
It shows the times' injustice with such clarity
That I shall pass it down to our posterity
As a great proof and signal demonstration
Of the black wickedness of this generation.
It may cost twenty thousand francs; but I
Shall pay their twenty thousand, and gain
thereby
The right to storm and rage at human evil,
And send the race of mankind to the devil.

PHILINTE. Listen to me. . . .

ALCESTE.          Why? What can you
possibly say?
Don't argue, Sir; your labor's thrown away.
Do you propose to offer lame excuses
For men's behavior and the times' abuses?

PHILINTE. No, all you say I'll readily
concede:
This is a low, conniving age indeed;
Nothing but trickery prospers nowadays,
And people ought to mend their shabby ways.
Yes, man's a beastly creature; but must we
then
Abandon the society of men?
Here in the world, each human frailty
Provides occasion for philosophy,
And that is virtue's noblest exercise;
If honesty shone forth from all men's eyes,
If every heart were frank and kind and just,
What could our virtues do but gather dust
(Since their employment is to help us bear
The villainies of men without despair)?
A heart well-armed with virtue can en-
dure . . . .

ALCESTE. Sir, you're a matchless reasoner,
to be sure;
Your words are fine and full of cogency;
But don't waste time and eloquence on me.
*My* reason bids me go, for my own good.

My tongue won't lie and flatter as it should;
God knows what frankness it might next
commit,
And what I'd suffer on account of it.
Pray let me wait for Célimène's return
In peace and quiet. I shall shortly learn,
By her response to what I have in view,
Whether her love for me is feigned or true.

PHILINTE. Till then, let's visit Éliante upstairs.

ALCESTE. No, I am too weighed down with
somber cares.
Go to her, do; and leave me with my gloom
Here in the darkened corner of this room.

PHILINTE. Why, that's no sort of company,
my friend;
I'll see if Éliante will not descend.

*Scene 2*

CÉLIMÈNE, ORONTE, ALCESTE.

ORONTE. Yes, Madam, if you wish me to
remain
Your true and ardent lover, you must deign
To give me some more positive assurance.
All this suspense is quite beyond endurance.
If your heart shares the sweet desires of
mine,
Show me as much by some convincing sign;
And here's the sign I urgently suggest:
That you no longer tolerate Alceste,
But sacrifice him to my love, and sever
All your relations with the man forever.

CÉLIMÈNE. Why do you suddenly dislike
him so?
You praised him to the skies not long ago.

ORONTE. Madam, that's not the point.
I'm here to find
Which way your tender feelings are inclined.
Choose, if you please, between Alceste and
me,
And I shall stay or go accordingly.

ALCESTE (*emerging from the corner*). Yes,
Madam, choose; this gentleman's demand
Is wholly just, and I support his stand.
I too am true and ardent; I too am here.
To ask you that you make your feelings
clear.
No more delays, now; no equivocation;
The time has come to make your declaration.

ORONTE. Sir, I've no wish in any way to be
An obstacle to your felicity.

ALCESTE. Sir, I've no wish to share her heart with you;
That may sound jealous, but at least it's true.

ORONTE. If, weighing us, she leans in your direction . . .

ALCESTE. If she regards you with the least affection . . .

ORONTE. I swear I'll yield her to you there and then.

ALCESTE. I swear I'll never see her face again.

ORONTE. Now, Madam, tell us what we've come to hear.

ALCESTE. Madam, speak openly and have no fear.

ORONTE. Just say which one is to remain your lover.

ALCESTE. Just name one name, and it will all be over.

ORONTE. What! Is it possible that you're undecided?

ALCESTE. What! Can your feelings possibly be divided?

CÉLIMÈNE. Enough: this inquisition's gone too far:
How utterly unreasonable you are!
Not that I couldn't make the choice with ease;
My heart has no conflicting sympathies;
I know full well which one of you I favor,
And you'd not see me hesitate or waver.
But how can you expect me to reveal
So cruelly and bluntly what I feel?
I think it altogether too unpleasant
To choose between two men when both are present;
One's heart has means more subtle and more kind
Of letting its affections be divined,
Nor need one be uncharitably plain
To let a lover know he loves in vain.

ORONTE. No, no, speak plainly; I for one can stand it.
I beg you to be frank.

ALCESTE.                And I demand it.
The simple truth is what I wish to know,
And there's no need for softening the blow.
You've made an art of pleasing everyone,
But now your days of coquetry are done:
You have no choice now, Madam, but to choose,
For I'll know what to think if you refuse;

I'll take your silence for a clear admission
That I'm entitled to my worst suspicion.

ORONTE. I thank you for this ultimatum, Sir,
And I may say I heartily concur.

CÉLIMÈNE. Really, this foolishness is very wearing:
Must you be so unjust and overbearing?
Haven't I told you why I must demur?
Ah, here's Éliante; I'll put the case to her.

*Scene 3*

ÉLIANTE, PHILINTE, CÉLIMÈNE,
ORONTE, ALCESTE.

CÉLIMÈNE. Cousin, I'm being persecuted here
By these two persons, who, it would appear,
Will not be satisfied till I confess
Which one I love the more, and which the less,
And tell the latter to his face that he
Is henceforth banished from my company.
Tell me, has ever such a thing been done?

ÉLIANTE. You'd best not turn to me; I'm not the one
To back you in a matter of this kind:
I'm all for those who frankly speak their mind.

ORONTE. Madam, you'll search in vain for a defender.

ALCESTE. You're beaten, Madam, and may as well surrender.

ORONTE. Speak, speak, you must; and end this awful strain.

ALCESTE. Or don't, and your position will be plain.

ORONTE. A single word will close this painful scene.

ALCESTE. But if you're silent, I'll know what you mean.

*Scene 4*

ARSINOÉ, CÉLIMÈNE, ÉLIANTE,
ALCESTE, PHILINTE, ACASTE,
CLITANDRE, ORONTE.

ACASTE (*to* CÉLIMÈNE). Madam, with all due deference, we two
Have come to pick a little bone with you.

CLITANDRE (*to* ORONTE *and* ALCESTE). I'm glad you're present, Sirs; as you'll soon learn,

Our business here is also your concern.

ARSINOÉ (*to* CÉLIMÈNE). Madam, I visit
  you so soon again
Only because of these two gentlemen;
Who came to me indignant and aggrieved
About a crime too base to be believed.
Knowing your virtue, having such con-
  fidence in it,
I couldn't think you guilty for a minute,
In spite of all their telling evidence;
And, rising above our little difference,
I've hastened here in friendship's name to see
You clear yourself of this great calumny.

ACASTE. Yes, Madam, let us see with
  what composure
You'll manage to respond to this disclosure.
You lately sent Clitandre this tender note.

CLITANDRE. And this one, for Acaste, you
  also wrote.

ACASTE (*to* ORONTE *and* ALCESTE). You'll
  recognize this writing, Sirs, I think;
The lady is so free with pen and ink
That you must know it all too well, I fear.
But listen: this is something you should hear.

    *How absurd you are to condemn my
lightheartedness in society, and to accuse me
of being happiest in the company of others.
Nothing could be more unjust; and if you
do not come to me instantly and beg pardon
for saying such a thing, I shall never forgive
you as long as I live. Our big bumbling friend
the Viscount . . .*

What a shame that he's not here.

    *Our big bumbling friend the Viscount,
whose name stands first in your complaint,
is hardly a man to my taste; and ever since
the day I watched him spend three-quarters
of an hour spitting into a well, so as to make
circles in the water, I have been unable to
think highly of him. As for the little
Marquess . . .*

In all modesty, gentlemen, that is I.

    *As for the little Marquess, who sat squeez-
ing my hand for such a long while yesterday,
I find him in all respects the most trifling
creature alive; and the only things of value
about him are his cape and his sword.
As for the man with the green ribbons . . .*

    (*To* ALCESTE.)

It's your turn now, Sir.

    *As for the man with the green ribbons, he
amuses me now and then with his bluntness*
*and his bearish ill-humor; but there are
many times indeed when I think him the
greatest bore in the world. And as for the
sonneteer . . .*

    (*To* ORONTE.)

Here's your helping.

    *And as for the sonneteer, who has taken
it into his head to be witty, and insists
on being an author in the teeth of opinion,
I simply cannot be bothered to listen to him,
and his prose wearies me quite as much as
his poetry. Be assured that I am not
always so well-entertained as you suppose;
that I long for your company, more than
I dare to say, at all these entertainments to
which people drag me; and that the presence
of those one loves is the true and perfect
seasoning to all one's pleasures.*

CLITANDRE. And now for me.

    *Clitandre, whom you mention, and who
so pesters me with his saccharine speeches,
is the last man on earth for whom I could
feel any affection. He is quite mad to suppose
that I love him, and so are you, to doubt
that you are loved. Do come to your senses;
exchange your suppositions for his; and
visit me as often as possible, to help me
bear the annoyance of his unwelcome attentions.*

It's a sweet character that these letters show,
And what to call it, Madam, you well know.
Enough. We're off to make the world ac-
  quainted
With this sublime self-portrait that you've
  painted.

ACASTE. Madam, I'll make you no farewell
  oration;
No, you're not worthy of my indignation.
Far choicer hearts than yours, as you'll dis-
  cover,
Would like this little Marquess for a lover.

*Scene 5*

CÉLIMÈNE, ÉLIANTE, ARSINOÉ,
ALCESTE, ORONTE, PHILINTE.

ORONTE. So! After all those loving letters
  you wrote,
You turn on me like this, and cut my throat!
And your dissembling, faithless heart, I
  find,
Has pledged itself by turns to all mankind!

How blind I've been! But now I clearly see;
I thank you, Madam, for enlightening me.
My heart is mine once more, and I'm content;
The loss of it shall be your punishment.

(*To* ALCESTE.)

Sir, she is yours; I'll seek no more to stand
Between your wishes and this lady's hand.

### Scene 6

CÉLIMÈNE, ÉLIANTE, ARSINOÉ,
ALCESTE, PHILINTE.

ARSINOÉ (*to* CÉLIMÈNE). Madam, I'm
    forced to speak. I'm far too stirred
To keep my counsel, after what I've heard.
I'm shocked and staggered by your want of
    morals.
It's not my way to mix in others' quarrels;
But really, when this fine and noble spirit,
This man of honor and surpassing merit,
Laid down the offering of his heart before
    you,
How *could* you . . .

ALCESTE.          Madam, permit me, I
    implore you,
To represent myself in this debate.
Don't bother, please, to be my advocate.
My heart, in any case, could not afford
To give your services their due reward;
And if I chose, for consolation's sake,
Some other lady, 'twould not be you
    I'd take.

ARSINOÉ. What makes you think you could,
    Sir? And how dare you
Imply that I've been trying to ensnare you?
If you can for a moment entertain
Such flattering fancies, you're extremely vain.
I'm not so interested as you suppose
In Célimène's discarded gigolos.
Get rid of that absurd illusion, do.
Women like me are not for such as you.
Stay with this creature, to whom you're so
    attached;
I've never seen two people better matched.

### Scene 7

CÉLIMÈNE, ÉLIANTE, ALCESTE, PHILINTE.

ALCESTE (*to* CÉLIMÈNE). Well, I've been
    still throughout this exposé,
Till everyone but me has said his say.

Come, have I shown sufficient self-restraint?
And may I now . . .

CÉLIMÈNE.          Yes, make your just
    complaint.
Reproach me freely, call me what you will;
You've every right to say I've used you ill.
I've wronged you, I confess it; and in my
    shame
I'll make no effort to escape the blame.
The anger of those others I could despise;
My guilt toward you I sadly recognize.
Your wrath is wholly justified, I fear;
I know how culpable I must appear,
I know all things bespeak my treachery,
And that, in short, you've grounds for hating
    me.
Do so; I give you leave.

ALCESTE.          Ah, traitress—how,
How should I cease to love you, even now?
Though mind and will were passionately
    bent
On hating you, my heart would not consent.

(*To* ÉLIANTE *and* PHILINTE.)

Be witness to my madness, both of you;
See what infatuation drives one to;
But wait; my folly's only just begun,
And I shall prove to you before I'm done
How strange the human heart is, and how far
From rational we sorry creatures are.

(*To* CÉLIMÈNE.)

Woman, I'm willing to forget your shame,
And clothe your treacheries in a sweeter
    name;
I'll call them youthful errors, instead of
    crimes,
And lay the blame on these corrupting times.
My one condition is that you agree
To share my chosen fate, and fly with me
To that wild, trackless, solitary place
In which I shall forget the human race.
Only by such a course can you atone
For those atrocious letters; by that alone
Can you remove my present horror of you,
And make it possible for me to love you.

CÉLIMÈNE. What! I renounce the world at
    my young age,
And die of boredom in some hermitage?

ALCESTE. Ah, if you really loved me as you
    ought,
You wouldn't give the world a moment's
    thought;

Must you have me, and all the world beside?

CÉLIMÈNE. Alas, at twenty one is terrified
Of solitude. I fear I lack the force
And depth of soul to take so stern a course.
But if my hand in marriage will content
    you,
Why, there's a plan which I might well con-
    sent to,
And . . .

ALCESTE.    No, I detest you now. I
    could excuse
Everything else, but since you thus refuse
To love me wholly, as a wife should do,
And see the world in me, as I in you,
Go! I reject your hand, and disenthrall
My heart from your enchantments, once
    for all.

### Scene 8

ÉLIANTE, ALCESTE, PHILINTE.

ALCESTE (*to* ÉLIANTE). Madam, your vir-
    tuous beauty has no peer;
Of all this world, you only are sincere;
I've long esteemed you highly, as you know;
Permit me ever to esteem you so,

And if I do not now request your hand,
Forgive me, Madam, and try to understand.
I feel unworthy of it; I sense that fate
Does not intend me for the married state,
That I should do you wrong by offering you
My shattered heart's unhappy residue,
And that in short . . .

ÉLIANTE.    Your argument's well taken:
Nor need you fear that I shall feel forsaken.
Were I to offer him this hand of mine,
Your friend Philinte, I think, would not de-
    cline.

PHILINTE. Ah, Madam, that's my heart's
    most cherished goal,
For which I'd gladly give my life and soul.

ALCESTE (*to* ÉLIANTE *and* PHILINTE). May
    you be true to all you now profess,
And so deserve unending happiness.
Meanwhile, betrayed and wronged in every-
    thing,
I'll flee this bitter world where vice is king,
And seek some spot unpeopled and apart
Where I'll be free to have an honest heart.

PHILINTE. Come, Madam, let's do every-
    thing we can
To change the mind of this unhappy man.

## Comic Detachment

Molière's characters are less grotesque than Jonson's. Their very names proclaim the difference. Instead of animals or birds of prey we find elegant pseudo-
classical names such as characters were given in the fashionable romances of
Molière's day. And it is a fashionable world to which these characters belong.
The single set, representing a room in the house of Célimène, should remind us
constantly of the elevated social circle in which she and her friends move. We
are rapidly introduced to their literary interests, their love of gossip, and their
politeness, which Alceste considers inexcusable hypocrisy. Thus, although
several of the characters have eccentricities of temperament which might be
called humors, they are not walking embodiments of their humors as are
Corbaccio and Corvino. Their behavior is characteristic of a world which is
very special but nonetheless believable. Without being fully realistic, Alceste
and Célimène seem more human than Volpone and Celia.

Comedy which thus emphasizes the social milieu of its characters is often
called *comedy of manners*, and in the case of *The Misanthrope* manners become the
main theme of the play through Alceste's questioning of their value. In such a
comedy the satire is usually aimed at the customs of the society or at the failure
of certain people to master them completely. Thus one might make a super-
ficial distinction between *Volpone* and *The Misanthrope* by saying that whereas
Jonson satirizes greed, a major sin, Molière satirizes insincerity, a characteristic

encouraged by the society he depicts. However, this distinction, though right in part, misrepresents Molière's play by failing to indicate either the depth or the subtlety of the satire, and by leaving the impression that Alceste, the lover of sincerity, is the norm of behavior.

Another sort of distinction between Jonson and Molière has to do with their attitudes toward their characters. Although Molière's humor is often satirical, it is never bitter, and the Parisian society he ridicules seems attractive when compared to the brutal materialists of Jonson's Venice. At worst, the two marquesses are absurd, and Célimène is undeniably charming even when she is most malicious or hypocritical. Jonson, it will be recalled, wrote in the dedication to *Volpone* that it was "the office of a comic poet to imitate justice, and instruct to life," and on this basis defended the rather stern punishments of his offenders. In his comedy moral distinctions are more rigorous than in *The Misanthrope* and the laughter at the comic victims is more cruel. Because Molière is less overtly concerned with justice and instruction the tone of his comedy is considerably less harsh than that of Volpone. This difference is at least as important as the distinction between humors and manners.

Molière's exact attitude toward his characters is not easily defined, however. The case of Alceste is particularly troublesome, for he may be looked at in several ways. At the two extremes are the view of him as an obstinate egotist, absurdly rigid in his criticism of the way of the world, and the view of him as a hero, nobly choosing "that wild, trackless, solitary place" rather than compromise and Célimène. To interpret his last speeches in this heroic way is to evoke some of the mood of *King Lear* at the moment when the embittered king walks out onto the stormy heath rather than accept hospitality on the terms offered by Regan and Goneril. If this is Molière's view, his sympathies are with Alceste, and a serious injustice has been done. But Alceste's words strike a discordant note in the final scenes. His tone seems self-consciously heroic, and one is keenly aware that he is rejecting every effort to comfort or console him. In the face of Célimène's acceptance of his marriage proposal such stern adherence to principle appears slightly ludicrous if not masochistic. If Molière is sympathetic with Alceste, his sympathy is severely qualified.

The first of the two views described is essentially that of Philinte, the apologist for the way of the world. To understand Molière's attitude toward Alceste it is essential to decide whether Philinte is his spokesman. If he is, then the satire of the play is directed less at society than at the foolish idealist who believes in sincerity at all cost. In the opening dialogue we see Philinte and Alceste together. One of the best and most recent critics of Molière, Jacques Guicharnaud, has pointed out the importance of the listener in his plays.[1] Here Philinte listens to the diatribe of Alceste (strikingly similar to his last speeches in that he urges Philinte to go away and leave him in solitude), and Alceste listens to Philinte's justification of polite society. As each one speaks, the presence of the other reminds us of a contrary view. Each is undoubtedly a foil for the other, but is one of them finally right and the other wrong? Where Philinte is reasonable, Alceste is obsessed and hardly rational; where Alceste is concerned, Philinte is indifferent; where Alceste insists on individual integrity, Philinte defends the norm of social behavior. Since Molière has arranged so delicate a set of balances, it seems unlikely that Philinte, who is in one of the scales, is his spokesman.

Without disclosing his own attitude toward his characters, Molière delights

---

[1] *Molière: Une Aventure Théâtrale* (Paris: Gallimard, 1963), p. 11.

in situations in which they reveal their attitudes toward each other and toward their society. The scene in which Célimène entertains her listeners with her censorious portraits of absent friends is full of such revelations. Alceste, who wants Célimène to pay more attention to him, disapproves of the performance, though hardly on principle. Philinte asks:

> But why protest when someone ridicules
> Those you'd condemn, yourself, as knaves or fools?

And because Alceste, like everyone else, is charmed by Célimène, he directs his protest not at her but at the marquesses, who have done little but ask for Célimène's opinions and applaud her wit. Éliante and Philinte make feeble gestures to defend her victims, but in such a way that they almost encourage her to continue. If Alceste appears ill natured in comparison with her, because she manages to be so witty, Éliante and Philinte appear somewhat tame because they lack her enormous vivacity. The marquesses, having neither wit nor principles, are totally submerged in this little society and are unable to see beyond it. By juxtaposing all these attitudes, using each one to make us question another, Molière provides an unusually clear example of that special detachment which every writer must have when he depicts a person or an incident as comic.

Comic detachment is seen again to great advantage in the dramatic moment which ends the play. The characters of Alceste, Célimène, Philinte, and Éliante are nowhere more brilliantly delineated, and the differences between them are apparent above all in the contrasting tones of the voices we hear—Alceste's shrill declamation, Célimène's mocking frivolity, Éliante's cool reasonableness, and Philinte's compassion. If Philinte's attitude seems more praiseworthy than any of the others, we may still ask whether it has the author's unqualified endorsement. To hold every attitude up to question is the essence of Molière's comic technique.

## Selected Reading List for Molière

Jacques Guicharnaud, ed., *Molière: A Collection of Critical Essays*. Englewood Cliffs, N.J.: Prentice-Hall, Inc., 1964.
Jacques Guicharnaud, *Molière: Une Aventure Théâtrale*. Paris: Gallimard, 1963.
W. G. Moore, *Molière: A New Criticism*. Oxford: The Clarendon Press, 1962.

# Ibsen and the Realistic Theater

When the Italians first experimented with perspective scenery in the sixteenth century, the painted side wings and backdrop were placed entirely behind a rectangular acting area. Since the "buildings" upstage were drastically reduced in size to suggest distance, an actor standing next to them would have seemed out of scale and destroyed the effect. On such a stage the actors were between the audience and the scenery. In the seventeenth century perspective effects were sometimes so arranged that action could take place within the scenic framework, removing the actors from the audience into the world of stage illusion. The stage for *The Misanthrope* presented no distant views, but one room, of which the audience saw three walls. In all probability this was a "box set," and certainly the actors were not in front of the scenery but surrounded by it. The realistic conventions of the nineteenth century confirmed this separation of the theater into two distinct areas, that of the audience and that of the stage. The separation was marked physically by the proscenium arch and the curtain. An important psychological barrier was the lighting, for by this time it had become customary to darken the auditorium when the stage lights went up, whereas in the seventeenth century the auditorium had remained lighted. Realism erected one final barrier between audience and actors with the idea that the stage opening was to be considered an invisible fourth wall of the room depicted onstage. In the theaters devoted to the production of realistic plays in the late nineteenth century a new style of acting evolved with these developments in staging. At the first of them, the Théâtre Libre of Antoine, founded in 1887, actors were taught never to declaim their lines and never to address the audience directly, but to speak and act as if they were not being "overheard." It became necessary to pretend that the audience didn't exist in order to maintain the fictitious reality of the stage world.

To heighten the illusion, the walls of the box set were now made of more substantial material than painted canvas, and playwrights gave increasing attention to the furnishings of the rooms where their characters were to live. Ibsen gives minute details about the drawing room revealed by the rising curtain at the beginning of *Hedda Gabler*—the draperies, the oval table with an elegant table cover, the square piano, the whatnots, the hanging lamp with an iridescent shade. This scenery does more than tell us the social stratum to which the characters belong; it partially explains why they are what they are, and reveals something of what they want to be. We find that Hedda once said she liked this house, that Tesman has spent more than he can afford on it, and that his aunt has supervised the furnishing while they have been away. All these important facts about the characters are incorporated in the stage set, which becomes the visual symbol of their environment. By the time the action of the play is ending, this drawing room where it has all taken place has come to seem like a sort of trap in which the characters are caught. We may feel that to some extent it stands for the conventions of Ibsen's society, which operate like a modern equivalent of fate in determining the tragedy.

The aim of realism in nineteenth-century literature and drama was to banish the artificiality of the older conventions in the interest of a more truthful depiction of man. Some of the most significant developments occurred in France where the romantics, early in the century, proclaimed their independence of the classical "rules," and aimed at verisimilitude even in tragedy, where only elevated speech and decorous behavior had been allowed. A later generation found that romantic drama was still remote from the lives of ordinary people. Writers turned from the grand and the exotic to the familiar, and then finally to the mean and sordid.

This development was intimately related to the growth of scientific thought and its impact on nineteenth-century philosophy. By the end of the century Zola was advocating "naturalism" in fiction and in the theater, by which he meant a scientific depiction of men as the products of their heredity and environment. Even before this time, plays had begun to focus attention on social problems; now they took up clinical studies, and the cases were apt to be drawn from the lowest reaches of society. Though naturalism had a separate name and identity, it was in most respects a further development of tendencies inherent in realism.

One of the most influential French dramatists of the mid-nineteenth century was Eugène Scribe, who cared more about entertaining his spectators than making them think, but who was expert in constructing what came to be called the "well made play." He was a master of the scene which built up to an emotional climax, the act which ended just when some new development had taken place, the plot which was both surprising and completely logical. It was a highly successful formula, and though the naturalists protested against it as just one more theatrical artifice, it was successfully used by realists like Augier and Dumas *fils*, who had more to say than Scribe. By the time that Ibsen was writing his major plays, Scribe's structure was already associated with the drama of social problems.

Henrik Ibsen's theatrical career began at the age of twenty-three when he signed a contract as dramatic author and stage manager for the theater at Bergen. Born at Skien, Norway, in 1828, he had worked as a pharmacist after finishing school, since his family could not afford to send him to a university. However, he had written poetry and a couple of plays, the second of which had been performed and had attracted attention. During six years at Bergen he put on not only his own plays but those of many other playwrights, old and new, including several by Scribe, who became an important influence on his own work. His practical experience in the theater continued with five years as director of the Norwegian Theater in Christiania. He wrote the plays which brought him international fame during a long period of residence on the continent of Europe, and in 1865 the Norwegian government voted him a lifelong pension. Late in life he returned to Norway, where he died in 1906. His early plays, including such important ones as *Brand* and *Peer Gynt* were romantic, but with *The Pillars of Society* in 1877 he turned to realism and was one of the playwrights Antoine chose to perform in his Théâtre Libre. In his last plays he relied much more heavily upon symbolism. Some of his plays were banned in England, but they were read and admired by writers as different as Joyce and Shaw. *Hedda Gabler*, written in 1890, has been one of the most continuously successful of his plays on the stage. It is an excellent example of his realism in the form of a well-made play.

# Hedda Gabler

*A DRAMA IN FOUR ACTS*

## HENRIK IBSEN

### PERSONS IN THE PLAY

JÖRGEN TESMAN, *research fellow in the History of Civilization*

MRS. HEDDA TESMAN (née Gabler), *his wife*

MISS JULIANE TESMAN, *his aunt*

MRS. TÉA ELVSTED

JUDGE BRACK

EJLERT LÖVBORG

BERTE, *maid at* MR. *and* MRS. TESMAN'S

*The action takes place at the villa of* MR. *and* MRS. TESMAN *on the west side of Christiania (Oslo) in or about the year 1890.*

### ACT I

THE SETTING: *A spacious drawing room, decorated in somber colors, elegantly and tastefully furnished.*

*At the rear there is a wide doorway with portières that are drawn aside. This doorway leads into a smaller room which is decorated in the same style as the larger room. In the wall of the drawing room, left, is a folding door that leads to the entrance hall. In the opposite wall, right, is a glass door; this also has draperies which are drawn aside. Through the panes can be seen a part of an enclosed veranda and, outside, trees in autumn foliage. In the center of the room stands an oval-shaped table with an elegant table cover on it. About the table are grouped chairs.*

"Hedda Gabler" by Henrik Ibsen reprinted from *The Last Plays of Henrik Ibsen*, translated by Arvid Paulson, by permission of Bantam Books, Inc. © Copyright, 1960, by Arvid Paulson.

*Further downstage, at the wall on the left, is a wide, dark-colored porcelain stove, a high-backed armchair, a cushioned footstool, and two taborets.*

*In the rear corner, left, a sofa and a small, round table. Downstage, right, a sofa which protrudes from the wall at a slight angle. Beyond the glass door, a square piano. The doorway, rear, is flanked by whatnots with pieces of terra cotta and majolica.*

*Through the center doorway can be seen—against the wall in the inner room—a table and a couple of chairs. Above the sofa hangs a painting of a handsome, elderly man in the uniform of a general. Hanging over the table is a lamp with a glass shade of milky iridescence.*

*Throughout the larger room, an abundance of flowers in vases and glass bowls. Several bouquets lie on the tables. The floors in both rooms are covered with heavy carpets.*

*It is morning. The sunrays fall through the glass door into the room.*

MISS JULIANE TESMAN *comes in from the hall, followed by* BERTE. MISS TESMAN *is wearing a hat and carries a parasol;* BERTE *carries a bouquet of flowers wrapped in paper.*

MISS TESMAN *is a lady of about sixty-five, wholesome-looking and good-natured in appearance. She is dressed simply and wears a gray, tailored dress.*

BERTE *is somewhat advanced in years, of simple manner, and has the looks of one bred in the country.*

MISS TESMAN (*stops just inside the door, listens, and speaks in an undertone to* BERTE). Why, I believe they are not even up yet!

BERTE (*speaking in the same tone of voice*). Well, wasn't that what I said, Miss Tesman? And you know how late it was when the steamer came in last night—and think of all they had to do after that! My heavens—all the things the young mistress had to unpack before she could get herself to bed!

MISS TESMAN. Yes, yes—well, we'll let them have a good rest, then. But they must have fresh air when they get up—that they must! (*She goes over to the glass door and opens it wide.*)

BERTE (*by the table; she does not seem to know what to do with the bouquet which she holds in her hand*). So help me—I don't believe there's the least bit of room left anywhere . . . (*she looks around the room, uncertain as to where to put them*). I guess I'll have to put them down here, Miss Tesman. (*She places the bouquet on the piano.*)

MISS TESMAN. Well, now you have a new mistress, my dear Berte. God knows, having to part with you was harder than I can tell you.

BERTE (*on the verge of tears*). And for me, too, Miss Tesman! What more can I say . . . after the many years the Lord has let me be in the service of you and your sister . . .

MISS TESMAN. We must take it calmly, Berte. There is nothing else to do, you know. Jörgen simply has to have you in this house, you understand—he simply must. You know you have always looked after him ever since he was a little boy.

BERTE. Yes, but, Miss Tesman, I am always thinking about her who is lying there at home! The poor thing—lying there so helpless . . . And then—with that new maid! Never in the world will she learn to take decent care of your sick sister!

MISS TESMAN. Oh, don't worry, Berte, I'll manage to train her. And anyhow, I'll be doing most of the work myself, you understand. So you don't have to worry on account of my poor sister, my dear Berte.

BERTE. Yes, but there is still another matter, Miss Tesman. I am so terribly afraid I am not going to be able to please my new mistress.

MISS TESMAN. Oh, heavens—in the beginning there is always one thing or another that . . .

BERTE. For I have a feeling she is terribly particular.

MISS TESMAN (*with a smile*). Well, you can't expect anything else. She is General Gabler's daughter, you know. All the things she was used to—and could have while the General was alive! Do you remember how she used to ride down the road with her father—in that long black riding skirt of hers—and that feather in her hat?

BERTE. Oh yes, yes—I sure do! But to tell the truth, I never would have imagined that she would one day be married to your nephew . . .

MISS TESMAN. Nor would I. But, by the way, while I think of it, Berte, from now on you must not call my nephew *Mr.* Tesman—you must call him *Doctor* Tesman.

BERTE. Young Mrs. Tesman said something about that, too, last night—the moment they had come inside the door. Is that really true, Miss Tesman?

MISS TESMAN. It is, indeed! Think of it, Berte—they made him a doctor while he was abroad. Just recently, you understand. I hadn't heard a word about it—until he told me at the pier.

BERTE. Yes, yes—I'm sure he can be whatever he sets his mind on, a smart fellow like him. But I would never have thought he would take up curing people, too.

MISS TESMAN. Oh, no, Berte—he is not that kind of doctor. (*With a significant nod.*) Besides, you may soon be able to call him something even finer.

BERTE. You don't say! What in the world could that be, Miss Tesman?

MISS TESMAN (*smiles*). H'm—well, if you only knew! (*Moved.*) Oh, if my blessed brother Jochum could rise from his grave and see what his little son has made of himself! (*She looks around the room.*) But tell me, Berte —what made you do that—taking all the covers off the furniture?

BERTE. Mrs. Tesman told me to. She says she can't bear seeing the furniture covered.

MISS TESMAN. They plan to use this as a living room, do they?

BERTE. Yes—that's the way it sounded. At least when she—Mrs. Tesman—spoke. The doctor—he didn't say anything.

(JÖRGEN TESMAN *enters, humming, from the left in the inner room. He carries an open, empty traveling bag. He is a man of thirty-three, youthful in appearance, of medium height but a little plump, round-faced, and has an open, pleasant countenance. His hair and beard are light. He wears spectacles and is dressed in a comfortable though somewhat worn lounging suit.*)

MISS TESMAN (*warmly*). Good morning, good morning, Jörgen!

TESMAN (*in the doorway to the inner room*). Aunt Juliane! Dear Aunt Juliane! (*Goes over to her and shakes her hand.*) You've come all the way out here—so early in the morning, eh?

MISS TESMAN. Well—you can understand that I want to look after you a little . . .

TESMAN. And in spite of not having had a good rest last night!

MISS TESMAN. Oh, that does not matter in the least!

TESMAN. And you got home from the pier without difficulty, did you?

MISS TESMAN. Oh certainly. Thank heavens, Judge Brack was very nice to me—he saw me all the way to my home.

TESMAN. We were very sorry we couldn't take you along with us in the carriage. But you could see for yourself that Hedda had such a pile of boxes that she had to take with her.

MISS TESMAN. Yes, she did have a great many boxes . . .

BERTE (*to* TESMAN). Should I go in and ask Mrs. Tesman, perhaps, if there is anything I could help her with?

TESMAN. No, thank you, Berte. She said that she will ring, if she wants you.

BERTE (*walks toward the left*). Very well, then.

TESMAN. But here is something, Berte . . . You might take this bag with you.

BERTE (*takes the traveling bag*). I'll put it up in the attic. (*She goes out through the hall door.*)

TESMAN. Just think, Aunt Juliane, I had packed that bag to the brim with notes I had made. You have no idea how much material I have brought back with me from all the archives I have visited! Remarkable things from ancient times that no one even knew existed!

MISS TESMAN. Yes, yes—I don't think you have been wasting any time during your wedding trip . . .

TESMAN. No, I dare say I haven't. But do take off your hat, Aunt Juliane . . . Here—let me help you untie the bow. Eh?

MISS TESMAN (*while he is doing this*). Oh, Lord! This is exactly as if you still were at home with us!

TESMAN (*turns and twists the hat in his hand*). Oh, but what a nice, elegant hat you have got yourself!

MISS TESMAN. I bought this hat on Hedda's account.

TESMAN. On Hedda's account? Eh?

MISS TESMAN. Yes—so that Hedda wouldn't have to be ashamed of me if we should be going out for a walk together.

TESMAN (*patting her on the cheek*). You certainly think of everything, you certainly do, Aunt Juliane! (*He puts down the hat on one of the chairs by the table.*) And now—come over here—and let us sit down on the sofa. And then we can have a few words together before Hedda comes. (*They seat themselves. She puts her parasol in the corner of the sofa.*)

MISS TESMAN (*clasping both his hands and gazing intently at him*). What a blessing it is to have a chance to look at you again and see that you are alive, Jörgen! Ah, Jörgen—my blessed brother Jochum's own son!

TESMAN. And what a joy to see you again, Aunt Juliane! You have been both father and mother to me . . .

MISS TESMAN. Yes, I know you will always have affection for your old aunts . . .

TESMAN. But Aunt Rina—she still isn't any better, eh?

MISS TESMAN. No, Jörgen dear—I'm afraid we can't hope for any improvement in her condition, poor dear! She is still lying there, the way she has all these years. I only pray that the Lord will let me have her with me a little longer . . . If He shouldn't, then,—for me—life wouldn't be worth living, Jörgen—especially now that I don't have you to look after any more.

TESMAN (*patting her on the back*). Now, now, now . . .

MISS TESMAN (*suddenly changing the subject*). And to think that you are now a married man, Jörgen! And who would have thought that *you* would be the one to carry off Hedda Gabler—the beautiful Hedda Gabler, who always had so many beaux after her!

TESMAN (*smiles a self-satisfied smile and hums a little*). Yes—I can't help feeling I have several good friends about town who now go around envying me . . . Eh?

MISS TESMAN. And then this extensive wedding trip that you took! Over five months—almost six months!

TESMAN. Yes—but it was a sort of educational trip for me also. All the many archives I did research in, Aunt Juliane—and the enormous lot of books I had to wade through!

MISS TESMAN. Yes, of course, of course. (*In a confidential and somewhat lower tone of voice.*) But tell me, Jörgen—haven't you—haven't you anything—anything special to tell me?

TESMAN. About our stay abroad?

MISS TESMAN. Y—e—s.

TESMAN. No—nothing except what I wrote to you in my letters. That I took my doctor's degree while abroad—that I remember telling you yesterday.

MISS TESMAN. Oh, yes, that you told me—but I mean—what I mean is—if you have . . . Have you no—no special—expectations?

TESMAN. Expectations?

MISS TESMAN. For heaven's sake, Jörgen—after all, I am your old aunt, am I not?

TESMAN. Why, of course, I have expectations, naturally!

MISS TESMAN (*with anticipation*). Well?

TESMAN. My prospects for becoming a professor one of these days are the most excellent . . .

MISS TESMAN. Oh, professor—well . . .

TESMAN. As a matter of fact—I think I can say with certainty that I will be made a professor. But, dear Aunt Juliane, you already know that!

MISS TESMAN (*with a smile*). Of course I do. You are right. (*Changing the subject.*) But we were talking about your trip abroad, Jörgen. It must have cost a good deal of money, Jörgen, didn't it?

TESMAN. Good Lord, yes . . . however, the generous fellowship award helped considerably.

MISS TESMAN. But how you ever made it last for you both is more than I can understand.

TESMAN. Yes, yes—I can well understand you might find it a little hard to believe, eh?

MISS TESMAN. And especially when traveling with a lady—it makes it infinitely more expensive, I am told.

TESMAN. Yes, that goes without saying—it makes it a little more expensive. No doubt about that. But Hedda simply *had* to take this trip, Aunt Juliane. She just *had* to! It would not have looked well otherwise!

MISS TESMAN. No, no—I suppose it wouldn't . . . A wedding trip seems almost to be a part of the marriage ceremony nowadays. But tell me—have you had a chance to look over the house completely?

TESMAN. Yes, to be sure, I have. I have been busy since early this morning.

MISS TESMAN. And what do you think of it?

TESMAN. Splendid! Just splendid! There is only one thing I am a little puzzled about. I don't know what we are going to use the two empty rooms for—the ones between Hedda's bedroom and the inner room there. (*He points to the room in the rear.*)

MISS TESMAN (*with a smile*). Ah, Jörgen dear, you will find use for them, no doubt—when the time comes.

TESMAN. Yes, you are quite right, Aunt Juliane; as my collection of books keeps growing, why . . . Eh?

MISS TESMAN. Yes, yes! It was your books I was thinking of.

TESMAN. But, Aunt Juliane, I am most happy now for Hedda's sake. Before we were engaged, she would always say she didn't want to live anywhere but in the villa that belonged to the widow of Mr. Falk, the former cabinet minister.

MISS TESMAN. Yes, and just imagine—it so happened that it was for sale—just after you had left.

TESMAN. Yes, Aunt Juliane, we certainly were in luck, eh?

MISS TESMAN. But it will be expensive, Jörgen dear! It will be expensive for you—all this!

TESMAN (*looks at her a little timidly*). Yes, it may be . . . perhaps it will, aunt dear . . .

MISS TESMAN. Oh, good heavens!

TESMAN. Have you any idea how much it will amount to? I mean approximately. Eh?

MISS TESMAN. No, I have absolutely no idea until I get all the bills.

TESMAN. Well, luckily Judge Brack was able to obtain terms that are very advantageous. He himself wrote and told Hedda.

MISS TESMAN. But you must not worry about it, my boy. And as far as the furniture and the carpets and rugs are concerned, I have given security for them.

TESMAN. Security? You? Dear Aunt Juliane—what sort of security could you possibly give?

MISS TESMAN. I have ordered the money to be paid out of our income.

TESMAN (jumps up). What! Out of yours and Aunt Rina's income?

MISS TESMAN. Yes. I didn't know how else to manage it, don't you see?

TESMAN (face to face with her). But, Aunt Juliane, have you completely lost your reason? That income is all you and Aunt Rina have to live on!

MISS TESMAN. Well, now—you must not get so excited about it. The whole thing is merely a formality, you see. Judge Brack made that plain to me; and it was he who was nice enough to arrange the matter for me. Merely a formality, that's what he said.

TESMAN. Oh well, it may be nothing but that—but nevertheless . . .

MISS TESMAN. And from now on you will have your own salary to fall back on. And—good Lord!—what of it? Even if we should have to contribute a little in the beginning—even if we should have to economize a little more—Rina and I would consider that a joy, a blessing!

TESMAN. Oh, Aunt Juliane—you never tire of making sacrifices for me!

MISS TESMAN (gets up and places her hands on his shoulders). What other happiness in this world have I but to try to make your path a little easier, dear boy? You have had neither father nor mother to watch over you. And now, Jörgen dear—now we are coming close to our goal . . . There have been times when things looked black, but now—God be praised, Jörgen—now you are at the top of the tree.

TESMAN. Yes, it is really amazing the way everything has turned out.

MISS TESMAN. Yes—and those who stood in your way and tried to close the door on you—they will now be left behind. They have all fallen by the wayside, Jörgen! And he who was your most formidable rival—he was the one who fell hardest. And now the poor misguided creature lies in the ditch he dug for himself.

TESMAN. Have you had any news of Ejlert? I mean—since he went away?

MISS TESMAN. Nothing except that he has had a new book published—so they say.

TESMAN. What's that you say? Ejlert Lövborg? Now—lately? Eh?

MISS TESMAN. Yes—that's what they say. God knows whether it is anything to brag about, though . . . Oh, but—when your new book comes out—that will be something! What will be the subject of your new book, Jörgen?

TESMAN. It will be about the native industry of Brabant during the Middle Ages.

MISS TESMAN. Just think of that! That you can write about such things, too!

TESMAN. But it may take quite a while yet before I have it finished. You see—I have all this enormous collection of notes that I must put in order first.

MISS TESMAN. Yes, to collect and put in order—you certainly are good at that! You are not my blessed brother Jochum's son for nothing!

TESMAN. It will be a great joy to get started on it! Especially now that I have a comfortable home of my own to work in.

MISS TESMAN. But the most important thing of all is that you now have a wife, the woman your heart desired, Jörgen dear.

TESMAN (embracing her). Ah, yes, yes, Aunt Juliane . . . Hedda—she is the most precious of all! (He glances in the direction of the doorway.) I think it is she coming now, eh?

(HEDDA enters through the center doorway from the right in the inner room. She is a woman of twenty-nine. Both her figure and features indicate dignity and distinction. Her complexion has an opaque pallor; her eyes are steel-gray and betoken a cool, imperturbable composure. She has beautiful hair of a medium brown color but it is not particularly thick. She is dressed in an attractive, rather loose-fitting morning gown.)

MISS TESMAN (gets up to greet HEDDA). Good

morning, dear Hedda! From the bottom of my heart—good morning!

HEDDA (*extends her hand to* MISS TESMAN). Good morning, dear Miss Tesman! Coming to visit us so early? That was considerate of you.

MISS TESMAN (*a little embarrassed*). Well . . . and did my little niece sleep well in her new home?

HEDDA. Oh yes, thank you! Tolerably.

TESMAN (*with a chuckle*). Tolerably! Well, I like that, Hedda! You were fast asleep like a rock when I got up.

HEDDA. As luck would have it, yes. But then we have to accustom ourselves to anything new, Miss Tesman, little by little. (*She gazes toward the right.*) Huh—the maid has left the veranda door wide open and the sun is just *pouring* in!

MISS TESMAN (*starts for the door*). Well, then we'll close it.

HEDDA. No, no—don't shut it! Tesman, dear, draw the curtains—it will give a softer light.

TESMAN (*by the door*). So it will, so it will! (*He closes the curtains.*) There, Hedda—now you will have both shade and fresh air!

HEDDA. Yes, we certainly need some fresh air—with all these blessed flowers . . . But, heavens, won't you sit down, Miss Tesman?

MISS TESMAN. No—thank you ever so much. Now, thank God, I am satisfied that everything is in order here—and I think it's time for me to start for home. My poor sister will be lying there waiting for me—anxiously waiting for me.

TESMAN. Don't forget to give her my love—and tell her I'll be over to see her later in the day.

MISS TESMAN. Oh no, I won't forget. But, Jörgen . . . Oh, wait a minute . . . (*She searches for something in her skirt pocket.*) It almost slipped my mind . . . I brought something with me for you.

TESMAN. What did you bring, Aunt Juliane, eh?

MISS TESMAN (*pulls out a flat parcel wrapped in newspaper and hands it to* TESMAN.) Here you are, my dear boy.

TESMAN (*opens the parcel*). Oh heavens! You saved my slippers for me, Aunt Juliane—

you did! Hedda, this is really touching—isn't it, Hedda? Eh?

HEDDA (*by the whatnot on the left*). Yes, dear, what is it?

TESMAN. My old slippers—my bedroom slippers!

HEDDA. Is that so? I remember you often conversed about them on our honeymoon.

TESMAN. Yes—I missed them frightfully! (*He goes over to her with the slippers.*) Here they are, Hedda! Look at them!

HEDDA (*moves over to the stove*). No, thank you, I am not interested.

TESMAN (*following her*). Think of it—Aunt Rina embroidered them for me, ill as she is, and bedridden—lying in her bed . . . Oh, you have no idea how many memories are bound up with them . . .

HEDDA (*by the table*). Hardly for me.

MISS TESMAN. I would say Hedda is right, Jörgen.

TESMAN. Yes, but it seems to me now—that she is one of the family . . .

HEDDA (*abruptly*). But that servant—we shall never be able to do with her, Tesman.

MISS TESMAN. Never be able to do with Berte?

TESMAN. Dearest—what makes you say that, eh?

HEDDA (*pointing to* MISS TESMAN'*s hat on one of the chairs*). Look at that! She has left her old hat on the chair!

TESMAN (*shocked, he drops the slippers on the floor*). But, Hedda—Hedda . . .

HEDDA. Imagine, if anyone should come in and see it lying there!

TESMAN. But Hedda, Hedda—it's Aunt Juliane's hat!

HEDDA. Oh!

MISS TESMAN (*takes her hat*). It is, indeed! And for that matter, it is not old, my dear Mrs. Tesman!

HEDDA. I am sorry—I didn't look at it closely.

MISS TESMAN (*puts on her hat and ties the ribbons into a bow*). To tell the truth, I am wearing this hat for the first time. And the good Lord knows I am telling the truth.

TESMAN. And it certainly is elegant—it's really gorgeous!

MISS TESMAN. Oh, now, you mustn't exaggerate, Jörgen dear . . . (*She looks around.*) My parasol? Ah, there it is. (*She takes it.*) For the parasol is mine, too . . . (*Muttering to herself.*) Not Berte's.

TESMAN. New hat and new parasol! Think of that, Hedda!

HEDDA. And quite nice and pretty.

TESMAN. Yes, aren't they, eh? But before you go, take a good look at Hedda, Aunt Juliane. Isn't she lovely and beautiful to look at? Isn't she? Eh?

MISS TESMAN. Oh, dear me, that's not news to me. Hasn't Hedda always been beautiful! (*She nods and walks over to the left.*)

TESMAN (*following her*). Yes—but don't you notice how she has filled out—how plump and rounded she has grown—how she has blossomed out during the journey?

HEDDA (*walks over to the other side of the room*). Oh, stop it!

MISS TESMAN (*stops and turns around*). Filled out? Rounded?

TESMAN. Well, you may not notice it so much now while she is dressed in that morning dress—but I, who have plenty of opportunity to . . .

HEDDA (*standing over by the glass door; impatiently*). Oh, you have no opportunity for anything!

TESMAN. It must have been the mountain air down there in the Tyrolean Alps . . .

HEDDA (*interrupting him; curtly*). I am exactly as I was when I left.

TESMAN. Well—yes, that's what you say . . . But I say differently. I say you are not. Don't you agree with me, Aunt Juliane?

MISS TESMAN (*she gazes at* HEDDA *intently, her hands clasped*). Yes—Hedda is beautiful—beautiful—beautiful . . . (*She goes up to her and, bending her head down, she presses a kiss on her hair.*) May God bless and keep Hedda Tesman—for Jörgen's sake!

HEDDA (*gently releasing herself*). Please don't.

MISS TESMAN (*quietly; moved*). I shall be over to see you both every single day from now on . . .

TESMAN. Yes, you must, you must, Aunt Juliane! Eh!

MISS TESMAN. Good-by—good-by!

(*She goes out through the hall door.* TESMAN *accompanies her, leaving the door partly open.* TESMAN *can be heard repeating his greetings and message to* AUNT RINA *and his thanks for the slippers. While* MISS TESMAN *and* TESMAN *are conversing in the hall,* HEDDA *is pacing up and down in the room. She raises her arms, clenching her hands as if in a rage, and goes over to the glass door. Then she impetuously flings back the curtains and remains standing there, gazing out. Soon after,* TESMAN *comes into the room again, closing the door to the hall after him.*)

TESMAN (*picking up the slippers from the floor*). What are you looking at?

HEDDA (*now calm and controlled*). I am just looking at the leaves on the trees. They have all turned yellow—yellow and withered.

TESMAN (*wraps up the slippers and puts them on the table*). Well, we are now in September, you know.

HEDDA (*again showing signs of restlessness*). Yes, imagine—we are already—already in September!

TESMAN. Didn't you think Aunt Juliane seemed a little strange today? Almost solemn? What do you think could have been the trouble? Eh?

HEDDA. Why, I scarcely know her. Isn't she always like that?

TESMAN. No—not the way she behaved today.

HEDDA (*going away from the glass door*). Do you think she was offended because of this incident with the hat?

TESMAN. No, I shouldn't think so . . . Perhaps a little—for the moment . . .

HEDDA. But what a way to behave—to throw one's hat on a chair in the drawing room. It just is not done.

TESMAN. Well, you may be sure Aunt Juliane won't do it again.

HEDDA. Anyhow, I'll try to make up for it to her.

TESMAN. Dear, darling Hedda—yes, I wish you would!

HEDDA. When you go to see your aunts later in the day, you might ask her to come by this evening.

TESMAN. Oh, I most certainly will. And

there is one thing more you could do that would please her no end.

HEDDA. What is that?

TESMAN. If you could only persuade yourself to call her by her first name . . . For my sake, Hedda? Eh?

HEDDA. No—no, Tesman . . . please don't ask me to do that. I have told you that before. I will try to call her aunt—and that will have to be sufficient.

TESMAN. Well—very well . . . But it seems to me that now that you are in the family, you . . .

HEDDA (*in an undertone, to herself*). H'm. I don't know about that . . . (*She goes across the room to the center doorway, leading to the inner room.*)

TESMAN (*after a silence*). Is there anything the matter with you, Hedda, eh?

HEDDA. I am just looking at my old piano. It doesn't seem to fit in with the rest of the furniture.

TESMAN. As soon as I draw my salary, we'll see about getting it exchanged.

HEDDA. No, no—I don't mean that. I won't part with my piano. We might try to put it in here . . . (*she points to the inner room*) . . . and then get another one for the drawing room—I mean when we can afford it.

TESMAN (*somewhat timidly*). Why—yes, we *could* do that . . .

HEDDA (*picks up the bouquet of flowers on the piano*). These flowers weren't here last night when we came home.

TESMAN. I believe Aunt Juliane brought them for you.

HEDDA (*looking at the bouquet*). Here is somebody's visiting card. (*She holds it up and reads:*) "Shall come back later today." Can you guess from whom it is?

TESMAN. No—from whom? Eh?

HEDDA. The card says "From Mrs. Elvsted."

TESMAN. You don't say? Mrs. Elvsted! She was Miss Rysing before she married.

HEDDA. Precisely. She had a mop of hair that was most irritating to me and she used it to attract attention. She was an old flame of yours, I have heard.

TESMAN (*with a smile*). Ah well, that didn't last long! And that was before I met you,

Hedda. Just imagine—her being in town.

HEDDA. Curious that she should pay us a visit. I scarcely know her—it was practically only at school we met.

TESMAN. And, as a matter of fact, I haven't seen her either for God knows how long! I can't understand how she endures it up there in that out-of-the-way place. Eh?

HEDDA (*reflecting, she suddenly says*). Tell me, Tesman—isn't it somewhere up there that *he* lives—Ejlert Lövborg?

TESMAN. Yes, so it is—somewhere up there.

(BERTE *appears in the doorway to the hall.*)

BERTE. She is here again, Mrs. Tesman—the lady who was here before and left those flowers. (*She points to the flowers.*) Those you have there in your hand . . .

HEDDA. Oh, is she? Well, ask her to come in.

(BERTE *opens the door for* MRS. ELVSTED, *then leaves.* MRS. ELVSTED *is a young woman of a slight, slender figure and with delicate, attractive features. She has large, round, rather protuberant eyes of a light blue color which have a frightened, searching expression. Her hair is strikingly golden, almost platinum white, and unusually thick and wavy. She is a couple of years younger than* HEDDA. *She is dressed in a dark afternoon dress; while in good taste, it is not in the latest fashion.* HEDDA *goes to meet her; cordially.*)

HEDDA. How do you do, dear Mrs. Elvsted. How nice to see you again!

MRS. ELVSTED (*trying not to show her nervousness*). Yes, it is quite a long time since we saw each other.

TESMAN (*greets her with a handshake*). And since *I* saw you, too. Eh?

HEDDA. Thank you for those pretty flowers.

MRS. ELVSTED. Oh, don't mention it. I had intended to come to see you yesterday; but then I heard you had been abroad and had not returned yet.

TESMAN. Did you just come to town, eh?

MRS. ELVSTED. I came late yesterday afternoon. Oh, and I was so upset when I heard you were not at home.

HEDDA. Upset? For what reason?

TESMAN. But my dear, dear Mrs. Rysing—I meant to say Mrs. Elvsted . . .

HEDDA. There isn't anything wrong, is there?

MRS. ELVSTED. Yes, there is. And I know of no living soul that I can turn to but you . . .

HEDDA (*puts the bouquet on the table*). Come—and let us sit down here on the sofa . . .

MRS. ELVSTED. Oh, I can't . . . I am much too upset . . .

HEDDA. Oh, yes, you can—come and sit down . . . (*She pulls* MRS. ELVSTED *down on the sofa and seats herself beside her.*)

TESMAN. Well? And now, ladies . . .

HEDDA. Is it anything particular that has happened up there where you live?

MRS. ELVSTED. Yes—it is and it isn't . . . Oh—if I could only be absolutely certain that you would not misunderstand me . . .

HEDDA. That's why you had best tell me exactly what your trouble is, Mrs. Elvsted.

TESMAN. And I suppose that's why you have come to us. Eh?

MRS. ELVSTED. Yes. Yes, that's right. And now I can tell you—if you don't know already—that Ejlert Lövborg also is in town.

HEDDA. Is Lövborg . . . ?

TESMAN. You don't say? Has Ejlert Lövborg come back to town? Think of that, Hedda!

HEDDA. My God! Don't you think I can hear!

MRS. ELVSTED. He has been here a whole week. Think of it—a whole week! Alone—in a city so full of temptations—among all the vicious people here!

HEDDA. But, dear Mrs. Elvsted—how, exactly, does this concern you?

MRS. ELVSTED (*gazes frightened at her and quickly responds*). He has been the children's tutor.

HEDDA. Your children's?

MRS. ELVSTED. My husband's. I have no children.

HEDDA. Your stepchildren's tutor, in other words.

MRS. ELVSTED. Yes.

TESMAN (*with a slight hesitation*). Was he sufficiently—I don't just know how to express myself—was he—was he sufficiently regular in his habits to be trusted to perform such duties? Eh?

MRS. ELVSTED. During the past two years there has been no reason for complaint.

TESMAN. You don't say? Think of that, Hedda!

HEDDA. I heard.

MRS. ELVSTED. Not in the least, I assure you. Not in any way whatsoever. But just the same —now that I know he is here—in the big city—and having quite a lot of money with him . . . I can't help being terribly disturbed about him.

TESMAN. But why didn't he stay where he was—up there—with you and your husband? Eh?

MRS. ELVSTED. After his book had been published, he seemed to find no peace up there with us any longer—he became restless.

TESMAN. Oh yes—my Aunt Juliane mentioned he had had a new book published.

MRS. ELVSTED. Yes—a new, big book. It's about the development of civilization; it gives a complete outline. It came out a couple of weeks ago. And because it sold so well and was bought by so many, and attracted such a lot of attention . . .

TESMAN. It did, did it? Then I suppose it must have been something he had written and put aside—something from his better days.

MRS. ELVSTED. You mean—something he had written previously?

TESMAN. Yes.

MRS. ELVSTED. No! He wrote the book while he was with us. Every line of it—during the past year.

TESMAN. Well, I am glad to hear that. Why, think of that, Hedda!

MRS. ELVSTED. Yes—but I only hope he will keep on writing!

HEDDA. Have you seen him since you have come to town?

MRS. ELVSTED. No, I haven't. I have had such a difficult time finding out where he is staying. But I found out this morning, at last.

HEDDA (*gazes at her searchingly*). To tell the truth, doesn't it seem a little strange that your husband . . . h'm . . .

MRS. ELVSTED (*she gives a nervous start*). My husband? What about my husband?

HEDDA. . . . that he should send you to the city on an errand like this—that he doesn't come himself to look after his friend?

MRS. ELVSTED. Oh no, no—my husband has no time for that. And, anyhow, I—I had some shopping to do here . . .

HEDDA (*with a faint smile*). Oh well, that's a different matter.

MRS. ELVSTED (*rising quickly, and ill at ease*). And now I beg of you, Mr. Tesman—I implore you—if Ejlert Lövborg should come to see you—receive him with kindliness! And I am sure he will come to see you. Why, you used to be such good friends at one time—and besides, you are both interested in the same studies, and the same subjects, as far as I can see.

TESMAN. Well, at any rate, we used to be.

MRS. ELVSTED. Yes—and that is why I ask you also to try to keep an eye on him. You will do that, Mr. Tesman, promise me you will!

TESMAN. Yes, I'll be more than glad to, Mrs. Rysing.

HEDDA (*corrects him*). Elvsted.

TESMAN. I shall, indeed, do everything I possibly can for Ejlert. You can depend on that.

MRS. ELVSTED. Oh, how wonderfully kind of you! (*She presses his hands.*) Thank you, thank you, thank you! (*With a frightened expression.*) You see, my husband is so terribly fond of him!

HEDDA (*gets up*). You ought to write to him, Tesman. He is not likely to come here otherwise.

TESMAN. Yes, Hedda, I presume that would be the proper thing to do. Eh?

HEDDA. And don't put it off. Why not do it immediately?

MRS. ELVSTED (*imploringly*). Oh yes, do—please!

TESMAN. I shall write to him without delay. Have you his address, Mrs. . . . Mrs. Elvsted?

MRS. ELVSTED (*she takes a piece of note paper from her pocket and hands it to him*). Yes. Here it is.

TESMAN. Splendid! Splendid! I'll go inside then . . . (*He looks around.*) Oh, I forgot. My slippers? Ah, there they are! (*He takes the parcel and starts to go.*)

HEDDA. Be sure to write a friendly, cordial note to him—and make it a nice, long letter!

TESMAN. Yes, I'll do my very best.

MRS. ELVSTED. But don't mention that I asked you to—don't say a word about that!

TESMAN. Why, of course not, that's understood. Eh?

(*He goes out through the center doorway to the left.*)

HEDDA (*goes to* MRS. ELVSTED, *smiles and says in an undertone*). Now then! We've killed two birds with one stone.

MRS. ELVSTED. What do you mean?

HEDDA. Couldn't you see that I wanted to get rid of him?

MRS. ELVSTED. Oh—so he could write the letter . . .

HEDDA. And so that I could have a chance to talk to you, alone.

MRS. ELVSTED (*perplexed*). About what? About—all this?

HEDDA. Precisely—yes.

MRS. ELVSTED (*apprehensively*). But I have told you everything, Mrs. Tesman. There is nothing more to tell! Really!

HEDDA. Oh yes, there is! There is a good deal more to it! Of that I am certain. Come over here—and then let us have a nice, cozy little chat together. (*She forces* MRS. ELVSTED *down into the armchair by the stove and seats herself on one of the taborets.*)

MRS. ELVSTED (*looks at her watch anxiously*). But my dear, dear Mrs. Tesman—I really must be going . . .

HEDDA. Oh, you can't really be in such a hurry. Well, tell me now a little about yourself—tell me about your home . . .

MRS. ELVSTED. Oh, that is what I least of all want to talk about!

HEDDA. But to me, my dear . . . We were at school together, weren't we!

MRS. ELVSTED. Yes, but you were in the class ahead of me . . . Oh, I used to be dreadfully afraid of you at that time.

HEDDA. Afraid—of me?

MRS. ELVSTED. Yes, terribly so! Whenever we met on the stairs, you would always pull my hair.

HEDDA. Did I do that?

MRS. ELVSTED. Yes, you did, and once you even said you would set fire to it and burn it all off.

HEDDA. Oh, I only said that in jest; it was nothing but a silly threat!

MRS. ELVSTED. Well, I was very naïve and gullible in those days ... And after our school days, we went our different ways. We moved in such different circles, you know.

HEDDA. But now we must see that we come closer to each other again. Listen to me now! You remember, at school we always used to call each other by our first names ...

MRS. ELVSTED. Oh no, you must be mistaken.

HEDDA. Not at all! Not at all! I remember distinctly—and so we must not keep any secrets from each other—just as during our school days. (*Moves the taboret, on which she is sitting, closer to* MRS. ELVSTED.) And now ... (*She kisses* MRS. ELVSTED *on the cheek.*) Now you must call me Hedda again.

MRS. ELVSTED (*pressing* HEDDA'*s hands and patting them*). Oh, you are so good. I am not used to such kindness.

HEDDA. There, there, there! (*Patting* MRS. ELVSTED'*s hand.*) And just as I used to, I shall call you by your first name—I shall call you my dear Tora.

MRS. ELVSTED (*slightly hurt; timidly*). My name is Téa.

HEDDA. Why, of course, of course! I meant Téa, of course! (*Looking at her with sympathy.*) So you say you are not being treated with kindness, my dear Téa? Not even in your own home?

MRS. ELVSTED. Oh—if I only *had* a home ... But I haven't. I have never had a home ...

HEDDA (*regards her for a moment*). I had a faint suspicion something was wrong.

MRS. ELVSTED (*staring helplessly into space*). Yes—yes—yes.

HEDDA. I can't exactly remember now—but weren't you first employed up there at the Sheriff's as housekeeper? Weren't you?

MRS. ELVSTED. I really went there as governess. But his wife—I mean his wife at the time—she was an invalid and most of the time confined to her bed, so that I had to take charge of the household as well.

HEDDA. But then—it ended by your becoming mistress in the house.

MRS. ELVSTED (*in a dull voice*). Yes.

HEDDA. Let me see—how long ago was that?

MRS. ELVSTED. Since I married him?

HEDDA. Yes.

MRS. ELVSTED. It is now about five years.

HEDDA. Yes, you are right—it must be that long.

MRS. ELVSTED. Oh, these five years—and especially the last two or three! Oh, Mrs. Tesman, if you could only imagine what a ...

HEDDA (*taps her lightly on the hand*). Mrs. Tesman! Now, now, have you forgot, Téa?

MRS. ELVSTED. Yes, yes—I'll try to remember. Yes, if you—if you, Hedda, could only imagine—if you could only realize ...

HEDDA (*in a purposely casual tone of voice*). Hasn't Ejlert Lövborg also been up there for about three years?

MRS. ELVSTED (*looks at her hesitantly*). Ejlert Lövborg? Yes—yes, he has.

HEDDA. Did you know him before—here in the city?

MRS. ELVSTED. Only very casually. Well, that is to say—I knew him by name, of course.

HEDDA. But up there in the country—there he was in your house, of course.

MRS. ELVSTED. Well, he came to our house every day. He was the children's tutor, you understand. For after a while I found it impossible to manage all the duties by myself.

HEDDA. I can quite understand. And your husband—I expect he is frequently called away from home, isn't he?

MRS. ELVSTED. Yes, Mrs. Tesman—I mean Hedda—you understand he has to travel about in his district because of his official duties.

HEDDA (*leaning against the arm of* MRS. ELVSTED'*s chair*). Téa—poor dear little Téa! You must tell me everything—exactly as things are—from beginning to end.

MRS. ELVSTED. Well—if you—if you will tell me what you want to know.

HEDDA. First of all, what kind of man is your husband, Téa? I mean—how is he in his relations with you? Is he good to you?

MRS. ELVSTED (*evasively*). I imagine he thinks he treats me as well as he should.

HEDDA. But isn't he rather too old for you? I've heard he is more than twenty years older.

MRS. ELVSTED (*caustically; with bitterness*). That, too! That is only one of the things! Everything about him is distasteful to me! There is nothing we have in common! Not a thing in the world—nothing!

HEDDA. But isn't he fond of you just the same? In his own particular way?

MRS. ELVSTED (*petulantly*). Oh, I don't know what he is! I think he simply uses me. And I am no expense to him—I don't cost him much!

HEDDA. That's stupid of you.

MRS. ELVSTED. I couldn't be anything but stupid—being around him. I don't believe he really cares for anyone but himself. And perhaps he likes the children a little.

HEDDA. And then there is Ejlert Lövborg, Téa!

MRS. ELVSTED (*looking at her*). Ejlert Lövborg! What makes you think that?

HEDDA. But Téa dear—it seems to me that if he sends you all the way to the city to find him . . . (*With an almost imperceptible smile.*) Wasn't that what you told Tesman?

MRS. ELVSTED (*with a nervous twitch*). Did I? Yes, I'm afraid I did. (*Vehemently, in a subdued tone of voice.*) Oh—I may as well tell you the whole truth! For it's bound to come out sooner or later . . .

HEDDA. But my dear Téa . . .

MRS. ELVSTED. Yes, I may as well tell you! My husband doesn't know I am here in the city.

HEDDA. What's that you say? Your husband doesn't know!

MRS. ELVSTED. No, certainly not! For that matter, he was not at home. He, too, had gone traveling. Oh, Hedda, I couldn't stand it any longer! I just couldn't! I couldn't stand being alone up there after what has happened!

HEDDA. Well—and so . . .

MRS. ELVSTED. And so I packed a few of my belongings—the things I needed most—and without telling anyone, I left!

HEDDA. As simple as that!

MRS. ELVSTED. Yes. And then I took the next train in here, to the city.

HEDDA. But my sweet, dear Téa—how did you get the courage to do it?

MRS. ELVSTED (*rises and walks about the room*). What else was there for me to do?

HEDDA. But what do you think your husband will say when you return home?

MRS. ELVSTED (*stops at the table and looks at her*). When I return home?

HEDDA. Why, yes—yes.

MRS. ELVSTED. I shall never go back to him again.

HEDDA (*rises and gazes at her*). Then you have definitely, unalterably, made up your mind to leave your home and your husband?

MRS. ELVSTED. Yes. There doesn't seem to be anything else for me to do.

HEDDA. But to leave—and so openly . . .

MRS. ELVSTED. Well, no matter how I were to do it, it wouldn't remain a secret very long.

HEDDA. But what do you think people will say about you, Téa?

MRS. ELVSTED. They may say what in God's name they like! (*She seats herself, tired and depressed, on the sofa.*) For what I have done, I *had* to do.

HEDDA (*after a brief silence*). What do you plan to do now? What are you going to do?

MRS. ELVSTED. I don't know yet. All I know is that I must live here where Ejlert Lövborg is, if I am to live at all.

HEDDA (*moves one of the chairs by the table and places it close by* TÉA; *then sits down on it and strokes* TÉA's *hands*). Tell me, Téa—how did this—this friendship between you and Ejlert Lövborg—start?

MRS. ELVSTED. Oh, it grew—little by little. I found myself getting a sort of power over him.

HEDDA. So-o?

MRS. ELVSTED. He gave up his old habits. Not because I asked him to—for that I could never have done—but he undoubtedly noticed that I did not approve of them. And so he gave them up.

HEDDA (*with an involuntary, scornful smile, which she is trying to hide*). In short, you have rehabilitated him, reformed him, as they say, Téa dear.

MRS. ELVSTED. Yes, that's what he says himself, at least. And he, in turn, has almost made me into a real human being—has taught me to think—and to understand a great many things.

HEDDA. And did he give *you* a few lessons, too?

MRS. ELVSTED. No, he didn't exactly give me lessons but he talked to me—talked to me about such a lot of different things. And then came that happy, wonderful time when I was allowed to take part in his work—when he allowed me to help him!

HEDDA. He let you do that?

MRS. ELVSTED. Yes, whenever he was writing, he wanted me to be with him and help him.

HEDDA. Like two good comrades, in short.

MRS. ELVSTED (*with animation*). Comrades—yes! Why, that's exactly the word *he* used, too! Oh, I ought to be very, very happy, of course—but I just can't. For I don't know how long it will last.

HEDDA. Have you no more confidence in him than that?

MRS. ELVSTED (*gloomily*). Something stands between Ejlert Lövborg and myself—a dark shadow—a woman!

HEDDA (*looking at her tensely*). Who can that be?

MRS. ELVSTED. I don't know. Somebody that he—that he knew before. Probably someone he has never forgotten completely.

HEDDA. Has he ever said anything to you—about this woman?

MRS. ELVSTED. Only once—and then very casually—have I heard him allude to her.

HEDDA. Oh! And what did he say?

MRS. ELVSTED. He made the remark that when they parted, she threatened to shoot him with a pistol.

HEDDA (*with complete control*). Oh, heavens! People don't do such things here!

MRS. ELVSTED. No, and that is why I think it must be that redheaded singer whom he once . . .

HEDDA. Yes, it could very well be.

MRS. ELVSTED. And I remember having heard she used to go about with loaded pistols.

HEDDA. Well, then of course *she* must be the one.

MRS. ELVSTED (*wringing her hands*). Oh but—think of it, Hedda, now I hear that this woman—that she is in the city again! Oh—I don't know what to do . . .

HEDDA (*with a glance toward the inner room*). Sh! Here comes Tesman . . . (*She rises and whispers to* MRS. ELVSTED.) Everything we have said, Téa, is in confidence—between you and me . . .

MRS. ELVSTED (*jumps up*). Oh yes—yes—for God's sake!

(JÖRGEN TESMAN *enters from the left in the rear room, holding a letter in his hand.*)

TESMAN. There now—now I have written the letter!

HEDDA. That's splendid! But I think Mrs. Elvsted is anxious to leave . . . Will you wait here while I see her to the garden gate . . .

TESMAN (*waving the letter*). Oh, Hedda—perhaps Berte could go to the post box with this?

HEDDA (*taking the letter from him*). I'll tell her.

(BERTE *enters from the hall.*)

BERTE. Judge Brack is here and says he would like to see Mr. and Mrs. Tesman.

HEDDA. Yes, ask the Judge to be good enough to come in. And then—put this letter in the post box.

BERTE (*taking the letter*). I will, Mrs. Tesman.

(BERTE *holds the door open for* JUDGE BRACK *and then leaves.* JUDGE BRACK *is a man of forty-five. He is a stocky, well-built man and moves with limberness. He has a rounded face; his profile has distinction. His hair is cut short and has scarcely any gray in it; it is carefully groomed. His eyes sparkle and indicate dash and vivacity; his eyebrows are thick, as is his well-trimmed mustache. He is impeccably dressed in a walking suit which, however, seems more in style for a man some years younger. He wears a monocle which he occasionally lets drop out of his eye.*)

JUDGE BRACK (*with hat in hand, he greets them*). May one have the temerity to call so early in the day?

HEDDA. One may, indeed!

TESMAN (*pressing his hand*). You are always welcome to us. (*Presenting him to* MRS. ELVSTED.) Judge Brack—Miss Rysing . . .

HEDDA. Oh . . .

JUDGE BRACK (*with a bow*). Ah—it is a great pleasure . . .

HEDDA (*looks at him and smiles*). It is rather a pleasure to have a chance to look at you in daylight, Judge Brack!

JUDGE BRACK. You think I look—different, do you?

HEDDA. Yes—a little younger, it seems to me.

JUDGE BRACK. Thank you for the compliment!

TESMAN. But what do you think about Hedda? Eh? Don't you think she looks ravishing? She positively . . .

HEDDA. I wish you would leave me out of the conversation. Why don't you instead thank Judge Brack for all the trouble he has gone to . . .

JUDGE BRACK. Why, I was very glad to be of service.

HEDDA. Yes, you are indeed a loyal soul. But my friend here is anxious to get away. Forgive me, Judge—I'll be back in just a moment.

(Good-bys are exchanged. MRS. ELVSTED and HEDDA go out through the hall door.)

JUDGE BRACK. Well—is your wife pleased . . . ?

TESMAN. Yes—and we can't thank you enough. Of course, I think she will want to rearrange things here and there—and there are a few items we shall have to get. We'll probably have to buy one or two other little things . . .

JUDGE BRACK. Oh, really?

TESMAN. But that is something you won't have to trouble yourself about. Hedda said she would take care of that herself. Wouldn't you like to sit down? Eh?

JUDGE BRACK. Thank you, but just for a moment. (They seat themselves at the table.) There is something I would like to talk to you about, my dear Tesman.

TESMAN. Oh yes, I understand . . . (They sit down.) I assume it's the—the thorns—the thorns in our bed of roses—we are coming to now, eh?

JUDGE BRACK. Oh, there is no special hurry about settling our accounts. However, I wonder whether it would not have been wiser if we had been a little more careful, a little more economical in our selections.

TESMAN. But that would never have done. My dear Judge Brack, think about Hedda! You know her so well. Why, I couldn't possibly have asked her to live in ordinary bourgeois surroundings, could I?

JUDGE BRACK. Why, no—that's where the difficulty lies.

TESMAN. But fortunately—it can't be long before I receive my appointment.

JUDGE BRACK. Well—you know, such matters can often drag on interminably.

TESMAN. You haven't heard anything more about it, have you? Eh?

JUDGE BRACK. Nothing very definite . . . (He suddenly breaks off.) But come to think of it, I have one piece of news I can tell you.

TESMAN. Oh?

JUDGE BRACK. Your old friend Ejlert Lövborg has come to town.

TESMAN. Yes, I know he has.

JUDGE BRACK. Oh? Who told you?

TESMAN. Mrs. . . . the lady who just left with Hedda.

JUDGE BRACK. Oh . . . so? What was her name again? I didn't quite catch it.

TESMAN. Mrs. Elvsted.

JUDGE BRACK. Aha—then she is the Sheriff's wife. Why, yes—I believe he has been staying up there in the country with them.

TESMAN. And think of it—I hear he has become a completely respectable person again, and I am delighted!

JUDGE BRACK. Yes, that's what I hear.

TESMAN. And I also hear he has had a new book published. Eh?

JUDGE BRACK. Yes, indeed!

TESMAN. And what's more, it has caused a sensation . . .

JUDGE BRACK. It has created an extraordinary sensation!

TESMAN. Think of that! It makes me very glad to hear it! He is an exceptionally gifted man! I was so terribly sorry to think that his future was done for completely.

JUDGE BRACK. I imagine that was what people generally thought.

TESMAN. But I can't imagine what he will be turning to now . . . What in the world will he do for a living? Eh?

(As HEDDA comes back from the hall, she overhears TESMAN's last remark.)

HEDDA (to BRACK with a rather sarcastic smile). Tesman is always going about worrying how to make both ends meet.

TESMAN. Good God—we are sitting here talking about that poor Ejlert Lövborg, you know.

HEDDA (with a quick glance at him). Ah! (She seats herself in the armchair by the stove and asks indifferently.) What is the matter with him?

TESMAN. Well—I think he spent his inheritance long ago. And he can't write a new book every year, can he? Eh? And that's why I ask: What's going to become of him?

JUDGE BRACK. Perhaps I can enlighten you on that score a little.

TESMAN. So-o?

JUDGE BRACK. You must remember that he has relatives who have considerable influence.

TESMAN. Oh, but unfortunately they—his relatives—refuse to have anything to do with him.

JUDGE BRACK. There was a time when he was looked upon as the pride of the family.

TESMAN. In the past, yes! But all that he has ruined!

HEDDA. Who knows? (*With a faint smile.*) Up there at Sheriff Elvsted's they have made a new man of him . . .

JUDGE BRACK. And then this book he has just published . . .

TESMAN. Yes, yes, I only wish and hope his relatives might help him in one way or another. I have just written to him. Oh, Hedda—I asked him to come out to see us this evening.

JUDGE BRACK. But, my dear Tesman, you are coming to my house this evening! (*To* HEDDA.) I am having some men friends in. (*Again to* TESMAN.) Have you forgot you promised me last night at the pier?

HEDDA. Did you forget, Tesman?

TESMAN. Yes, it slipped my mind completely.

JUDGE BRACK. Anyhow, you can be assured he won't come.

TESMAN. What makes you think that? Eh?

JUDGE BRACK (*after hestitating for a moment, he rises and leans against the back of his chair*). My dear Tesman—and you, too, Mrs. Tesman—I feel it my duty to let you know about something that—that . . .

TESMAN. Is it something that has to do with Ejlert Lövborg? Eh?

JUDGE BRACK. Not only Ejlert Lövborg but yourself as well.

TESMAN. But, my dear Judge, let us hear what it is!

JUDGE BRACK. I must caution you not to rely on your appointment to come quite as soon as you had hoped for and expected.

TESMAN (*jumps up; anxiously*). Has anything happened to upset it? Eh?

JUDGE BRACK. There is a possibility that the appointment may have to be decided by a competition . . .

TESMAN. A competition? Think of that, Hedda!

HEDDA (*leaning farther and farther back in her chair*). Ah! Think of that!

TESMAN. A competition with whom? Certainly not with Ejlert Lövborg?

JUDGE BRACK. Yes—just that—with Ejlert Lövborg.

TESMAN (*striking his hands together*). Oh—no! No! This is completely unthinkable! It just can't be! Eh?

JUDGE BRACK. H'm. Nevertheless we may find it to be so.

TESMAN. Oh but, Judge Brack—that would prove to be the grossest kind of outrage —and disrespect for me! (*Gesticulating with his arms.*) Yes, it would! Remember—I am a married man, you know! Hedda and I married on the strength of my prospects. We've gone into debt—have borrowed a great deal! We have borrowed from Aunt Juliane, too! And, good Lord!—all because the position was as good as promised to me! Eh?

JUDGE BRACK. Well, well, well—you will undoubtedly get the position. But it will have to be by competition.

HEDDA (*sitting motionless in the armchair*). Just think, Tesman—it will be almost like a game of sport . . .

TESMAN. But, Hedda dearest, how can you treat a matter like this with such indifference?

HEDDA (*as before*). But I am not in the least indifferent. It will be quite exciting to see who will come out ahead.

JUDGE BRACK. In any case, Mrs. Tesman, it is in your interest to know just how matters stand. I mean—before you start making those little purchases I understand you were contemplating.

HEDDA. They wouldn't make much difference.

JUDGE BRACK. Oh? Then I have nothing more to say. Good-by! (*To* TESMAN.) When I go for my usual walk this afternoon, I'll drop by and call for you.

TESMAN. Oh yes—yes . . . I—I don't know what to do.

HEDDA (*reclining, she holds out her hand to* BRACK *without changing her position*). Good-by, Judge. We are always glad to see you.

JUDGE BRACK. I thank you. Good-by—good-by.

TESMAN (*seeing him to the door*). Good-by, my dear Judge! I hope you will excuse me . . .

(BRACK *leaves through the hall door*.)

TESMAN (*pacing the floor*). Oh, Hedda—one should never venture into the land of adventures. Eh?

HEDDA (*looks at him and smiles*). Is that what you have done?

TESMAN. Yes, Hedda—there is no use denying it—to go and get married and start housekeeping on nothing but expectations—that is an adventure.

HEDDA. You may be right.

TESMAN. Well, Hedda, at any rate we still have our comfortable home! Think of it, the home we both dreamed of—yes, and longed for! Eh?

HEDDA (*she rises slowly and wearily*). It was understood that we were to be active socially, to entertain, and to . . .

TESMAN. Yes, good God, I looked forward to that, too! To see you as a hostess to a select circle . . . Eh? Think of it! Well, well, well! Now we will have to be satisfied with each other—keep to ourselves—try to entertain each other . . . From time to time we can have Aunt Juliane come to see us. Oh, Hedda, I wanted you to have it so very differently, so very differently!

HEDDA. That means, first of all, of course, I shan't get the liveried servant!

TESMAN. No, I am afraid not! We couldn't possibly think of having a manservant now, you understand, Hedda.

HEDDA. And the riding horse I was to have . . .

TESMAN (*horrified*). The riding horse!

HEDDA. I suppose I have to do without that, too.

TESMAN. Yes, for God's sake—that's entirely out of the question!

HEDDA (*pacing the floor*). Well—there is one thing at least I can amuse myself with for the time being.

TESMAN (*with a happy smile*). Oh, thank God for that! What is that, Hedda. Eh?

HEDDA (*stopping in the doorway, she looks at him with hidden scorn*). My pistols, Jörgen.

TESMAN (*frightened*). Your pistols!

HEDDA (*with a cold stare*). General Gabler's pistols.

(*She goes out through the near room and to the right.*)

TESMAN (*runs up to the doorway, calling after her*). Oh, Hedda, my dearest, please don't touch those dangerous things! For my sake, Hedda! Eh?

## ACT II

THE SETTING.—*The same as in Act I, except that the piano has been replaced by a small, elegant writing table with a rack for books. A smaller table is placed by the sofa, at the right. Most of the flowers have been removed.* MRS. ELVSTED'S *bouquet now stands on the large table in the center of the room. It is afternoon of the same day.*

HEDDA, *dressed in an afternoon dress, is alone on the stage. She is standing by the open glass door, right, and is loading an automatic magazine pistol. An identical pistol lies in an open pistol case on the writing table.*

HEDDA (*looks down into the garden below and calls to* JUDGE BRACK). Glad to see you again, Judge Brack!

JUDGE BRACK (*is heard answering from below, a distance away*). The same to you, Mrs. Tesman!

HEDDA (*raises the pistol, aiming it in his direction*). Now I am going to shoot you, Judge Brack!

JUDGE BRACK (*with a shout from below*). No-no-no! You mustn't aim your pistol at me like that!

HEDDA. That's what happens when people enter by the back way! (*She fires the pistol.*)

JUDGE BRACK (*now not so far away*). Have you gone absolutely mad!

HEDDA. Oh, good God, did I hit you? Did I?

JUDGE BRACK (*still from outside*). Stop playing these foolish tricks of yours!

HEDDA. Then come on in, Judge.

(JUDGE BRACK, *now dressed less formally, enters through the veranda glass door. On his arm he carries a light fall coat.*)

JUDGE BRACK. What the devil! You still keep playing with those pistols? What is it you are shooting at?

HEDDA. Oh, I am merely aiming at the blue sky.

JUDGE BRACK (*he gently takes the pistol from her*). Please, Mrs, Tesman. (*He looks at the pistol.*) Ah, this pistol—how well I know it! (*Looks around.*) Where is the case for it? Ah, here it is. (*He puts the pistol in its case and closes it.*) And we are not going to have any more of this nonsense today.

HEDDA. Well—what in Heaven's name do you expect me to do with myself?

JUDGE BRACK. Don't you have people come to see you?

HEDDA (*closing the glass door*). Not a soul. I suppose all our friends are still away in the country.

JUDGE BRACK. What about Tesman? Isn't he at home either?

HEDDA (*at the writing table, puts away the pistol case in the table drawer and closes it*). No. As soon as he had had his lunch, he rushed off to his aunts. He didn't expect you quite so early.

JUDGE BRACK. H'm. Why didn't I think of that? How stupid of me!

HEDDA (*turning her head, she looks at him*). Why stupid?

JUDGE BRACK. Because in that case I would have come even a little earlier.

HEDDA (*walks across the room*). And then you wouldn't have seen anyone, for I've been busy ever since lunch—changing my dress.

JUDGE BRACK. And is there not so much as a tiny crack in the door through which a fellow could carry on a negotiation?

HEDDA. *That* is one thing you forgot to arrange!

JUDGE BRACK. That, too, was stupid of me!

HEDDA. Well, at any rate, let us sit down and wait .For I don't think Tesman will be back for a while yet.

JUDGE BRACK. Well, good Lord—I won't be impatient!

(HEDDA *seats herself in the corner of the sofa.* BRACK *hangs his overcoat across the back of a nearby chair and sits down also, holding his hat in his hand. There is a brief pause, during which they regard each other silently.*)

HEDDA. Well?

JUDGE BRACK (*in the same tone of voice*). Well?

HEDDA. I was the one to ask first.

JUDGE BRACK (*leaning forward a trifle*). Well, let us have a cozy little chat now, Mrs. Hedda.

HEDDA (*leaning farther back in her corner*). Doesn't it seem like an eternity since you and I last had a talk? I am not speaking of the few words we had together last night and this morning . . .

JUDGE BRACK. But a more—a more intimate conversation, you mean? Between the two of us—alone?

HEDDA. Well—yes. Something like that.

JUDGE BRACK. I have been praying for your return every single day you have been away.

HEDDA. And I have wished for the same—every single day.

JUDGE BRACK. You? Is it really true, Mrs. Hedda? And all the time I thought you were enjoying yourself wonderfully on your trip.

HEDDA. I only wish I had!

JUDGE BRACK. That's what Tesman kept saying in his letters—that you were having a wonderful trip.

HEDDA (*derisively*). He would! For him, the height of ecstasy in this world is to go snooping about in libraries and to sit fixed there, copying pages of old parchment manuscripts, or whatever it might be.

JUDGE BRACK (*with a touch of maliciousness*). Well, that is his mission in this world—or something of the sort.

HEDDA. Well, I suppose it is. And I dare say that one may . . . But as for me, my dear Judge—no, no! I have been horribly bored!

JUDGE BRACK (*sympathetically*). You really mean it? Are you serious?

HEDDA. Yes, I am. You ought to understand that yourself! To have to spend six whole months without meeting a single person who would be acceptable to our circle of friends and to whom one could talk about the sort of things that interest us!

JUDGE BRACK. Yes, yes! I agree with you. I would feel as you do.

HEDDA. But most intolerable of all was to . . .

JUDGE BRACK. What?

HEDDA. . . . to have to be everlastingly together with one and the same person . . .

JUDGE BRACK( *with an encouraging nod*). Day in and day out—yes ... Think of it, from early morning till late at night!

HEDDA. I said *everlastingly*, didn't I?

JUDGE BRACK. Yet, as far as Tesman is concerned, it seems to me that one certainly should be able to ...

HEDDA. Tesman is a professional pedant, my dear Judge.

JUDGE BRACK. No denying that!

HEDDA. And to travel with a pedantic scholar is not much of a pleasure. Not for very long, at least.

JUDGE BRACK. Not even if you are in love with such a person?

HEDDA. Ugh! Don't use that disgusting word *love*!

JUDGE BRACK (*taken aback*). Why, Mrs. Hedda!

HEDDA (*with a smile, yet showing annoyance*). Well—I only wish you yourself could have a taste of it! From morning till night—all I hear is the history of civilization!

JUDGE BRACK. Over and over ...

HEDDA. Yes, yes, yes! And then all about the native industry during the Middle Ages! *That* is worse than anything else I have to listen to!

JUDGE BRACK (*looking at her searchingly*). But tell me—how am I to understand your ... ? H'm ...

HEDDA. You mean—Jörgen Tesman and I marrying?

JUDGE BRACK. Well, yes—let us call it that.

HEDDA. Good God! Does that seem so very strange to you?

JUDGE BRACK. I could answer both *yes* and *no* to that—Mrs. Hedda!

HEDDA. I have danced practically all my life—and I was getting tired, my dear Judge. My summer was up ... (*She catches herself.*) Oh no—I mustn't talk that way—and I mustn't think that way, either!

JUDGE BRACK. There is no reason whatever why you should.

HEDDA. Reason—oh! (*She looks at him with a somewhat inquiring expression.*) And Jörgen Tesman—well, after all, you must admit he is in every respect a proper, correct person.

JUDGE BRACK. By all means, he is that—and respectable.

HEDDA. And I can find nothing ludicrous about him ... Can you?

JUDGE BRACK. Ludicrous? No-o. I wouldn't exactly call it that ...

HEDDA. Well—and no matter what you may think, you can't deny he is an exceedingly painstaking collector. In time, he might very well go far.

JUDGE BRACK (*looks at her rather quizzically*). I thought that you, like everybody else, were convinced he would some day be a very distinguished man?

HEDDA (*with an expression of fatigue*). Yes, so I did. And I saw no reason why I shouldn't accept his proposal when he persistently pleaded to provide for me.

JUDGE BRACK. No, no—as far as that is concerned ...

HEDDA. After all, it was more than my other beaux offered to do, my dear Judge.

JUDGE BRACK (*with a smile*). Well, of course, I cannot answer for your other admirers, but as for myself, you must know that I have always had a—a certain respect for the marriage bond generally speaking, Mrs. Hedda.

HEDDA (*in jest*). Oh, I have never really had any expectations as far as *you* are concerned.

JUDGE BRACK. All I ask for is to have a circle of good, loyal friends to whom I can be of service by deed and with advice and to whom I can come and go—as a trusted friend ...

HEDDA. A trusted friend—of the head of the house, you mean?

JUDGE BRACK (*with a bow*). Frankly speaking —preferably of the mistress of the house. But, of course, also of the husband. Do you know, such a relationship—I might call it a triangular relationship—is in reality a great convenience to all concerned.

HEDDA. Yes—I often missed not having a third person with us on the journey. To be alone with the same man in a railway compartment ... Ugh!

JUDGE BRACK. But now, fortunately, your wedding trip is over ...

HEDDA (*shaking her head*). The journey has only begun! It is far from being over! We have merely come to a road stop ...

JUDGE BRACK. Well, then you can jump off

and exercise a bit, and give yourself an airing.

HEDDA. I never jump off.

JUDGE BRACK. You don't say?

HEDDA. No. There is always someone waiting at the road stop who . . .

JUDGE BRACK (*with a smile*). . . . whose interest is focused on your ankles, you mean?

HEDDA. Just that, yes.

JUDGE BRACK. Well, but . . . Good God . . .

HEDDA (*with a deprecating gesture*). No—that sort of thing has no appeal for me. Then I'd rather stay where I am and not stir from my position—and keep looking at the same face.

JUDGE BRACK. Ah, but suppose a third person were to enter and join the couple?

HEDDA. Well—that would be quite a different matter!

JUDGE BRACK. A friend of understanding, one who had proved himself . . .

HEDDA. . . . and who was entertaining and high-spirited and could converse interestingly on a variety of topics . . .

JUDGE BRACK. . . . and who had not the slightest trace of the professional academician —or of the bookworm!

HEDDA (*with an audible deep sigh*). That would, indeed, be a relief!

JUDGE BRACK (*hearing the entrance door opening, he looks in that direction*). The triangle is complete.

HEDDA (*in a subdued tone of voice*). And now the train is on its way again.

(JÖRGEN TESMAN, *in a gray walking suit and wearing a soft felt hat, comes in from the hall. He carries a bundle of unbound books under his arm, and there are also books in his pockets.*)

TESMAN (*crosses to the table by the sofa in the corner*). Whew! Carrying all these books certainly makes you warm. I am literally perspiring, Hedda. (*He puts down the books on the table.*) Ah, but see . . . You are already here, my dear Judge! Eh? Berte didn't say anything to me . . .

JUDGE BRACK (*gets up*). I came in through the garden.

HEDDA. What are these books you just brought home with you?

TESMAN (*turning over some of the leaves*). They are new works by experts in my field

—professional books I simply must have.

HEDDA. Professional books?

JUDGE BRACK. Aha, they are professional books, Mrs. Tesman! (BRACK *and* HEDDA *exchange glances. They smile knowingly to each other.*)

TESMAN. Yes, Hedda dear, one can't have enough. One has to keep abreast of what is being written and published.

HEDDA. Yes, I suppose one must.

TESMAN (*poking among the books*). And look here! Here is Ejlert Lövborg's new book, too! (*He holds it up.*) Would you like to look at it, Hedda? Eh?

HEDDA. No, thank you . . . Yes—perhaps later.

TESMAN. I glanced through it on my way home.

JUDGE BRACK. Well—what do you think of it, as an expert?

TESMAN. I think it is remarkable how soberly and objectively he has treated his subject. He never wrote with such clarity before. (*He picks up the books.*) And now I'll take them all inside. I can't wait to cut the leaves! And then I must put on another suit. (*To* BRACK.) We don't have to leave immediately, do we? Eh?

JUDGE BRACK. Oh, heavens, no—take all the time you like.

TESMAN. Very well, then I won't hurry. (*He starts off with the books, but turns in the doorway and stops.*) Oh, I forgot, Hedda—Aunt Juliane will not be over to see you this evening.

HEDDA. No? Does she still feel hurt about the hat?

TESMAN. Oh, not at all. How can you think anything like that about Aunt Juliane? No —but, you see, Aunt Rina is so very sick.

HEDDA. Isn't she always that?

TESMAN. Yes, but today she is really quite sick—she is very, very ill, poor soul.

HEDDA. Well, then her sister naturally ought to be with her. That's understandable, and I'll have to try to bear it.

TESMAN. But you can't imagine how terribly happy Aunt Juliane was to see you looking so healthy and vigorous and filled out after our journey!

HEDDA (*in an undertone as she rises*). Oh! These everlasting aunts!

TESMAN. Eh?

HEDDA (*going over to the glass door*). Nothing.

TESMAN. Well . . . Very well, then.

(*He goes through the center doorway to the left in the inner room.*)

JUDGE BRACK. What was that I heard you mention about a hat?

HEDDA. Oh, it was something that happened this morning when Miss Tesman was here. She had put her hat on that chair there. (*She points and looks at him and smiles.*) And I made her believe I thought it was the maid's.

JUDGE BRACK (*shaking his head*). But my dear Mrs. Hedda, how could you do such a thing? And to such a nice old lady?

HEDDA (*nervously moving about the room.*) Well, you see—when I get a sudden notion like that, I just can't resist it. (*Throws herself into the armchair by the stove.*) Oh, I just don't know how to explain it . . .

JUDGE BRACK (*behind the armchair*). You are not really happy—that's the whole trouble with you.

HEDDA (*gazing straight ahead*). There is no real reason why I should be. Can you tell me why I should be happy?

JUDGE BRACK. Yes. If for no other reason, because you now have the very home you always wanted.

HEDDA (*looks at him and smiles*). Do you really believe in such fairy tales, do you?

JUDGE BRACK. Didn't yours come true?

HEDDA. Oh, I suppose there is some truth in it.

JUDGE BRACK. Well, then?

HEDDA. It is true that I used Tesman last summer to escort me home from parties . . .

JUDGE BRACK. Unfortunately for me, I lived in an entirely different direction.

HEDDA. Yes, I know. Last summer your path led elsewhere.

JUDGE BRACK (*smiles*). Shame on you, Mrs. Hedda! Well—but to return to you and Tesman . . . ?

HEDDA. Well—one evening we happened to pass by this house. And Tesman—the poor fellow—he turned and twisted and didn't know what to talk about. And I felt sorry for the learned creature . . .

JUDGE BRACK (*with a smile of doubt*). Did you? H'm . . .

HEDDA. Yes, I actually did. And then, trying to help him out of his misery, I foolishly made the remark that this was the house I should like to live in—here, in this villa.

JUDGE BRACK. And that was all you said?

HEDDA. That was all—that evening.

JUDGE BRACK. And how about afterward?

HEDDA. Well—afterward my foolish remark had consequences, my dear Judge.

JUDGE BRACK. That, unfortunately, is what foolishness only too often leads to, Mrs. Hedda.

HEDDA. Ha! So, you see, it was through this capricious appetite, this passionate love for the villa of the widow of the late Cabinet Minister Falk that Jörgen Tesman's soul and mine met in mutual understanding! In the wake of it followed engagement, marriage, honeymoon and all the rest. Yes, yes, Judge Brack, as one makes one's bed, so one has to lie, as the saying goes.

JUDGE BRACK. This is really amusing! And actually, perhaps you didn't have the slightest desire to live in this house.

HEDDA. You are quite right—I didn't.

JUDGE BRACK. Yes, but now—now that we have managed to have it arranged so comfortably for you . . .

HEDDA. Whew! In every room there seems to be a scent of lavender and dried rose petals. But it may be the scent is lingering from Aunt Juliane's visits.

JUDGE BRACK (*with a smile*). No, I would rather think it might be handed down from the widow of the Cabinet Minister—Mrs. Falk.

HEDDA. There is something stale about it— something musty. It reminds me of dead flowers. (*She folds her hands behind her head, leans back in her chair and gazes at him.*) Oh, my dear Judge—you will never know how bored I am going to be out here!

JUDGE BRACK. But isn't there something or other you could occupy yourself with?

HEDDA. To occupy myself with? Something that would be interesting to me—something intriguing, exciting . . .

JUDGE BRACK. Preferably—of course!

HEDDA. God knows what that could be. I have often thought that . . . (*Interrupts herself.*) But I'm afraid that wouldn't work out, either.

JUDGE BRACK. Who knows? Let me hear what it is.

HEDDA. I have been thinking—if I could persuade Tesman to go into politics. That's what I've been thinking.

JUDGE BRACK (*with a laugh*). Tesman! Oh no, that's too amusing! Politics is the last thing he would be fitted for—the very last!

HEDDA. I'm quite sure you are right. But suppose I could persuade him nevertheless?

JUDGE BRACK. Yes, but—what satisfaction could you possibly get from that, since he has no qualifications? Why would you want him to enter politics?

HEDDA. Because I am bored, you understand! Bored! (*After a moment's silence.*) Do you really think it would be completely unthinkable that Tesman could become prime minister, do you?

JUDGE BRACK. H'm. You see, my dear Mrs. Hedda—in order to become prime minister, he must first of all be a reasonably rich man.

HEDDA (*rising impatiently*). Yes—there's the rub! It is this lack of money that is at the root of our problems . . . (*Pacing the floor.*) . . . and which makes life so miserable—so fantastically ridiculous! Yes, there's where the trouble lies!

JUDGE BRACK. I am inclined to think the fault lies elsewhere.

HEDDA. Then where?

JUDGE BRACK. You have never experienced anything that could stimulate you—to make you come *really* alive.

HEDDA. You mean—something of a downright serious nature?

JUDGE BRACK. Yes, you might call it that. But I dare say you will now.

HEDDA (*tossing her head back*). Oh, you are thinking of the difficulites in connection with this silly professorship! But that is Tesman's own affair. I don't intend to waste any of my time on that, you may be sure.

JUDGE BRACK. No, no, forget about that. But what about now, when you find yourself faced with what we in starched, pompous language call profoundly grave and serious responsibilities? (*With a smile.*) New responsibilities, dear Mrs. Hedda?

HEDDA (*angered*). Be quiet! That's something you will not live to see!

JUDGE BRACK (*cautiously*). We might talk about that a year from now—at the very latest.

HEDDA (*curtly*). I have no inclination in that direction, Judge Brack. I want no responsibilities of any kind!

JUDGE BRACK. Haven't you, like most women, a capacity for a duty such as . . .

HEDDA (*at the glass door*). Oh, keep quiet, I tell you! I often feel as though I had a capacity for only one thing in this world.

JUDGE BRACK (*coming closer to her*). And what is that, if I may ask?

HEDDA (*gazing outside*). To bore myself to death! Now you know. (*She turns, looks in the direction of the inner room, and smiles.*) Yes, just what I expected! Here we have the professor.

JUDGE BRACK (*in an admonishing undertone to her*). Now, now, now, Mrs. Hedda!

(JÖRGEN TESMAN, *in dinner jacket and carrying his hat and gloves, enters from the left through the inner room.*)

TESMAN. Hedda—has Ejlert Lövborg sent a message that he can't come this evening? Eh?

HEDDA. No.

TESMAN. Well, I'm sure he will be here before long.

JUDGE BRACK. You really think he will come, do you?

TESMAN. Yes—I am almost certain he will. I can't believe that what you told us this morning is anything but idle rumors.

JUDGE BRACK. Oh?

TESMAN. Yes—at least Aunt Juliane said she could never believe he would stand in my way again. Think of that!

JUDGE BRACK. Well, then you have nothing to worry about, do you?

TESMAN (*places his hat and gloves on a chair at the left*). However, I really ought to see him . . . I'll wait as long as I can.

JUDGE BRACK. We still have plenty of time. I don't expect anyone to arrive before seven —seven-thirty.

TESMAN. Well, then we can keep Hedda company for a while and see if he comes. Eh?

HEDDA (*takes* BRACK'S *hat and overcoat and is about to put them on the sofa in the corner*). And if the worst should happen, Mr. Lövborg can spend the evening here with me.

JUDGE BRACK (*offering to take the things from her*). Oh, please—let me, Mrs. Hedda! What do you mean when you say "If the worst should happen"?

HEDDA. If he doesn't wish to go with you and Tesman.

TESMAN (*looking suspiciously at her*). But, Hedda dear—do you think it would be proper to have him remain here with you? Eh? Remember that Aunt Juliane won't be here . . .

HEDDA. No, but Mrs. Elvsted will be coming. And the three of us can have a cup of tea together.

TESMAN. Oh, well, in that case it will be quite proper.

JUDGE BRACK (*with a smile*). And it would no doubt be the best thing for his health.

HEDDA. Why so?

JUDGE BRACK. Good Lord, Mrs. Hedda, how often haven't you taunted me about my little bachelor parties! You always insisted they were suited only for those who had the very highest of principles and an indomitable strength of character.

HEDDA. But I should think Mr. Lövborg would now have sufficient strength of character and principle. A sinner who has reformed . . .

(BERTE *appears in the door to the hall.*)

BERTE. There is a gentleman who would like to see you, Mrs. Tesman.

HEDDA. Yes—show him in.

TESMAN (*in an undertone*). It must be he! I feel sure it is! Think of it!

(EJLERT LÖVBORG *enters from the hall. He is slender and emaciated. Although of the same age as* TESMAN, *he looks older and rather worn. His hair and beard are dark brown; his face is pale and narrow, but on the cheekbones there is a patch of red. He is dressed in a new, black, smartly tailored suit. In his hand he carries a pair of dark gloves and a top hat. He remains standing near the door and makes a nervous bow. Evidently he is a little embarrassed.*)

TESMAN (*goes up to him and shakes him by the hand*). Well, my dear Ejlert! To think that we would meet once more!

LÖVBORG (*speaking in a low tone of voice*). Thank you, Jörgen, for the letter! (*He goes up to* HEDDA.) May I offer my hand to you also, Mrs. Tesman?

HEDDA (*takes his hand*). Welcome, Mr. Lövborg. (*With a gesture.*) I don't know whether you two gentlemen . . . ?

LÖVBORG (*with a slight bow*). Judge Brack, I believe.

JUDGE BRACK (*with a similar bow*). We have met before—some years ago.

TESMAN (*to* LÖVBORG, *placing his hands on his shoulders*). And now you must behave exactly as if this were your own home, Ejlert! Isn't that right, Hedda? For I understand you intend to live here in the city again. Eh?

LÖVBORG. I would like to.

TESMAN. Well, that's quite natural. Oh, I have bought your new book. But to tell the truth, I haven't had time to read it yet.

LÖVBORG. You ought to save yourself the trouble, I think.

TESMAN. What do you mean by that?

LÖVBORG. There is nothing very extraordinary about it.

TESMAN. Just think—that you yourself should say a thing like that!

JUDGE BRACK. But I've heard it's being highly praised.

LÖVBORG. That's exactly what I was aiming for. And so I wrote the book in such a way that everybody would accept it.

JUDGE BRACK. A very wise thing to do!

TESMAN. But my dear Ejlert . . .

LÖVBORG. For what I have in mind now is to try to build up a new reputation for myself, starting from scratch.

TESMAN (*slightly embarrassed*). Yes, I imagine you probably would want to do that. Eh?

LÖVBORG (*smiles, puts down his hat and takes out a large envelope, wrapped in paper, from his coat pocket*). But when *this* book is published, Jörgen Tesman—then you must read it! For this is a book—an honest book. I have put my soul into this one!

TESMAN. Have you really? And what is this book about?

LÖVBORG. This is the continuation.

TESMAN. The continuation? Of what?

LÖVBORG. Of the first one.

TESMAN. Of the new book?

LÖVBORG. Yes—just that!

TESMAN. Yes but, my dear Ejlert—that book covers the whole of civilization up to the present time!

LÖVBORG. So it does. And my new book—this one—(*waving the manuscript before him*)—deals with the future.

TESMAN. The future! But—my God! What do we know about that? We don't know a thing about that!

LÖVBORG. No—but there are a few things that can be said about it all the same. (*He unwraps the packet and takes out the manuscript from the envelope.*) Here you will see . . .

TESMAN. But this is not in your handwriting.

LÖVBORG. I have dictated it . . . (*He turns over the pages.*) I have divided the book into two parts. The first part is about the civilizing forces of the future—and the second part . . . (*he turns to the pages of Part II*) . . . the second part deals with the progress and development of civilization in the ages to come.

TESMAN. This is astonishing! It would never have occurred to me to write about anything like that!

HEDDA (*by the glass door; she is drumming on the pane*). H'm. Oh no!

LÖVBORG (*puts the manuscript back into the envelope and lays it in the wrapper on the table*). I brought it with me and thought I might read a part of it to you this evening.

TESMAN. Well, that was thoughtful of you, Ejlert—but this evening . . . (*With a glance at BRACK.*) I don't know just how we can arrange it . . .

LÖVBORG. Well—some other time then. There is no hurry.

JUDGE BRACK. I must explain to you, Mr. Lövborg, that I am having a few friends in this evening. I am really giving this party for Tesman, you see . . .

LÖVBORG (*looking around for his hat*). Ah—then I won't . . .

JUDGE BRACK. Well—but what about coming with us? It would be a pleasure to have you come along with us.

LÖVBORG (*his answer is short and definite*). No, I can't do that. Thanks just the same.

JUDGE BRACK. Oh, why don't you come with us? Do come! It's just a few close friends. And you can be sure we shall have a "lively time"—as Mrs. Hed . . . as Mrs. Tesman calls it.

LÖVBORG. I don't doubt that. Nevertheless . . .

JUDGE BRACK. And you could take your manuscript with you and read to Tesman from it at the same time. If you want privacy, I have enough rooms.

TESMAN. Yes, think of that, Ejlert. Couldn't you do that, eh?

HEDDA (*interrupting*). But, dear, don't you understand that Mr. Lövborg doesn't care to go! I think Mr. Lövborg would much prefer to stay here and have dinner with me.

LÖVBORG (*glancing at her*). With you, Mrs. Tesman?

HEDDA. And with Mrs. Elvsted.

LÖVBORG. Ah! (*In a purposely careless tone.*) I met her quite casually at noontime today.

HEDDA. Oh, did you? Well, she is coming here also. And so you see you almost *have* to stay, Mr. Lövborg—else she will have no one to take her home.

LÖVBORG. That's true. Well, then—thank you, Mrs. Tesman, then I'll stay.

HEDDA. Now I just want to tell the maid so that she knows. (*She goes over to the hall door and rings.* BERTE *comes in.* HEDDA *speaks to her in subdued tones, pointing toward the inner room.* BERTE *nods and goes out.*)

TESMAN (*to* LÖVBORG). Tell me, Ejlert—this new subject of yours—about what is to happen in the future . . . Is it about this you are planning to lecture?

LÖVBORG. Yes.

TESMAN. Yes, I heard about it in the bookshop . . . You are going to deliver a series of lectures this fall?

LÖVBORG. That's what I intend. You don't disapprove, I hope?

TESMAN. Oh, heavens—no! But . . .

LÖVBORG. Of course, I can well understand that it might be a little embarrassing to you.

TESMAN (*depressed; timidly*). Oh, I can't expect that you—for my sake—should . . .

LÖVBORG. However, I am not going to give these lectures until after you have received your appointment.

TESMAN. What? You will wait . . . Well, then . . . Well, but aren't you going to compete with me for it? Eh?

LÖVBORG. No. All I want is that I come out the victor—in the public's opinion.

TESMAN. Good Lord! Then—then Aunt Juliane was right, after all! Oh, I knew it!

I knew it! Hedda! Think of it! Ejlert Lövborg has not the least intention of standing in our way!

HEDDA (*crisply*). In our way? Keep me out of it, please!

(*She goes toward the inner room where* BERTE *is in the midst of placing a tray with decanters and glasses on the table.* HEDDA *gives an approving nod and goes back to her seat.* BERTE *goes out.*)

TESMAN (*simultaneously with the above pantomime*). But what do *you* say, Judge Brack—what do you say about all this? Eh?

JUDGE BRACK. Well, I say that honor and victory—h'm—are well and good in themselves . . .

TESMAN. Yes, that's true enough—but nevertheless . . .

HEDDA (*looking at* TESMAN *with a frigid smile*). You stand there as if you had been struck by lightning.

TESMAN. Well—not far from it. I almost think . . .

JUDGE BRACK. But then you *might* say a thunderstorm did pass over us just now, Mrs. Tesman.

HEDDA (*pointing to the rear room*). Won't you gentlemen step inside and have a glass of cold punch . . .

JUDGE BRACK (*looking at his watch*). As a parting cup? Yes, that's not a bad idea.

TESMAN. A splendid idea, Hedda! Quite perfect for the happy mood I am in now . . .

HEDDA. Won't you have a glass, too, Mr. Lövborg? (*She pours and offers him a glass.*)

LÖVBORG (*refusing it with a gesture*). No, thank you very much. None for me.

JUDGE BRACK. But good Lord—a glass of cold punch won't poison anyone.

LÖVBORG. Perhaps not—not everyone!

HEDDA. Well, then—I'll try to keep Mr. Lövborg company in here.

TESMAN. Yes, yes, Hedda dear, you do that.

(TESMAN *and* BRACK *go into the inner room and seat themselves, drinking punch, smoking cigarettes, and carrying on an animated conversation during the following scene.*)

HEDDA (*her voice somewhat louder than usual*). If you care to look at them, I would like to show you some photographs. Tesman and I made a tour through the Tyrol on our way home . . . (*She takes an album from the writing table to the table by the sofa, then sits down in the upper corner of the latter.* EJLERT LÖVBORG *takes a few steps toward her, stops and gazes at her; then draws up a chair and seats himself on her right, his back toward the inner room.*)

HEDDA (*opening the album*). You see this mountain ridge here, Mr. Lövborg? This is the Ortler group. Tesman has written the name underneath. See—the Ortler group near Meran.

LÖVBORG (*who has been gazing intently at her throughout, says slowly and softly*). Hedda—Gabler!

HEDDA (*gives him a swift glance*). Sh!

LÖVBORG (*again softly*). Hedda Gabler!

HEDDA (*her eyes on the album*). Yes—that was my name when—when we two knew each other.

LÖVBORG. And from now on—and for the rest of my life—I must efface from my memory the name of Hedda Gabler . . .

HEDDA (*keeps turning the leaves in the album*). Yes, so you must. And I think you ought to begin practicing in time—the sooner the better.

LÖVBORG (*his voice full of indignation*). Hedda Gabler married! And to—to Jörgen Tesman!

HEDDA. Yes—that's the way it goes.

LÖVBORG. Oh, Hedda, Hedda! How could you throw yourself away like that?

HEDDA (*looking at him sharply*). None of that, if you please!

LÖVBORG. Of what, do you mean? (TESMAN *comes from the inner room and walks over toward the sofa.*)

HEDDA (*hearing him approach, says in a casual tone of voice*). And this photograph—this is the Ampezzo Valley. Just look at those mountain tops! (*With a tender look at* TESMAN.) What is it these remarkable looking pinnacles are called, Tesman?

TESMAN. Let me look. Oh, those are the Dolomites, that's what they are!

HEDDA. Oh, of course—they are the Dolomites, Mr. Lövborg.

TESMAN. Oh, Hedda, don't you think we ought to bring in some punch to you just the same? At least, for yourself, eh?

HEDDA. Thank you—yes. And perhaps some little cakes.

TESMAN. No cigarettes?

HEDDA. No.

TESMAN. Very well. (*He goes into the room inside, and toward the right.* BRACK *still sits at the table; now and then he casts a glance toward* HEDDA *and* LÖVBORG.)

LÖVBORG (*still speaking in a subdued tone of voice*). But answer me, Hedda—how could you have done this?

HEDDA (*outwardly absorbed in the album*). If you persist in using my first name, I shan't speak to you!

LÖVBORG. Won't you let me call you Hedda even when we are alone?

HEDDA. No. You may think of me as Hedda —but you must not say it.

LÖVBORG. Ah, I begin to understand. It dampens your love for Jörgen Tesman.

HEDDA (*glancing at him and smiling*). Love? Don't be ridiculous!

LÖVBORG. Then it is not love?

HEDDA. And that does not mean that I am unfaithful. I want to stay clear of anything like that.

LÖVBORG. Hedda—let me ask you one thing—just one thing . . .

HEDDA. Sh!

(TESMAN *enters from the inner room, carrying a serving tray.*)

TESMAN. Here you are! Here are the delectables. (*He puts the tray on the table.*)

HEDDA. Why do you bring it yourself?

TESMAN (*filling the glasses*). Because it is such a joy to wait on you, Hedda.

HEDDA. But you have filled both glasses. And you know Mr. Lövborg doesn't drink.

TESMAN. No, but Mrs. Elvsted will soon be here, I expect.

HEDDA. Oh yes, Mrs. Elvsted—that's true.

TESMAN. Had you forgot she was coming? Eh?

HEDDA. We have been sitting here completely engrossed in these photographs . . . . (*She holds up the album and points to a photograph in it.*) You remember this little country village? Do you?

TESMAN. Oh, that's the village at the foot of the Brenner Pass! It was there we stayed overnight . . .

HEDDA. . . . and where we met all those gay tourists.

TESMAN. Yes, so it was. Think of it—if we could only have had you along with us, Ejlert! Well . . . (*He returns to the inner room and seats himself again with* BRACK.)

LÖVBORG. I'd like you to answer one question, Hedda.

HEDDA. Well?

LÖVBORG. Was there no love in your relationship with me, either? Not in the least —not even a semblance of love there either?

HEDDA. I wonder whether there was— really? I have the feeling we were just good comrades—two truly devoted friends. (*She smiles.*) You—you in particular—were uncommonly frank and openhearted—extremely so.

LÖVBORG. It was you who prompted me to be frank.

HEDDA. As I look back on those days, there was something beautiful, something enticing —yes, it seems to me there was something courageous about this clandestine intimacy of ours . . . this comradeship which no one had even the merest suspicion of.

LÖVBORG. Yes, there really was, Hedda, wasn't there? The way I would come to your home in the afternoons—the general sitting over by the window reading his newspaper, with his back turned to us . . .

HEDDA. And you and I sitting on the corner sofa . . .

LÖVBORG. Always with the same illustrated periodical in front of us . . .

HEDDA. For lack of an album, yes!

LÖVBORG. Yes, Hedda! And all the things I used to confess to you—telling you things about myself I had told no one else—revealing how I had been out carousing for days and nights—day in and day out. Oh, Hedda— what was there about you that made me open my heart so completely to you—holding nothing back?

HEDDA. Do you believe that I possessed some special power?

LÖVBORG. Yes—how else could I explain it? —And all those questions—those roundabout, subtle questions you put to me . . .

HEDDA. And which you—which you understood and relished . . .

LÖVBORG. How could you ask such questions—with such cool, deliberate presumption?

HEDDA. Don't forget—I asked them in a roundabout way!

LÖVBORG. Yes—but with presumption nevertheless . . . Asked me questions about—about things like that . . .

HEDDA. And why did you answer them, Mr. Lövborg?

LÖVBORG. Well, looking back—that is just what I can't understand. But tell me now, Hedda—wasn't it love that was at the bottom of our relationship? Could it be that you wanted to wash me clean, so to speak, when I came to you with my confession?

HEDDA. No—not entirely.

LÖVBORG. What was your reason then?

HEDDA. Does it seem so strange to you that a young girl—if she can do it in secret—might like to . . .

LÖVBORG. Well?

HEDDA. . . . might like to take a peep into a world—that . . .

LÖVBORG. That . . . ?

HEDDA. That is out of bounds—that is forbidden to us?

LÖVBORG. So that was what made you do it . . .

HEDDA. That too! It was probably one reason—I think.

LÖVBORG. A comradeship based on our common urge for a taste of life. But why did our comradeship not last?

HEDDA. You are the one to be blamed for that.

LÖVBORG. It was you who broke it off.

HEDDA. Yes—when I realized our relationship was on the verge of becoming too intimate. Shame on you, Ejlert Lövborg! How could you possibly have wanted to commit such an outrage against—against your trusting comrade!

LÖVBORG (wringing his hands). Oh, why didn't you carry out your threat! Why didn't you shoot me?

HEDDA. Because—I have a horror of scandal.

LÖVBORG. Yes, Hedda—you are at heart a coward.

HEDDA. A frightful coward! (In a different tone.) But it was a fortunate thing for you, don't you think? Now that you have been so beautifully consoled up there at the Elvsteds'.

LÖVBORG. Téa has told me what she confided to you.

HEDDA. And perhaps you have confided to her something about our relationship?

LÖVBORG. Not a word! She is too stupidly innocent to understand things like that.

HEDDA. Stupid? Innocent?

LÖVBORG. When it comes to things of that sort—yes.

HEDDA. And I am a coward . . . . (Leans close to him and, without looking him in the eye, she says softly.) But now I'll confide something to you.

LÖVBORG (tensely). Well?

HEDDA. That I did not have the courage to shoot you that evening . . .

LÖVBORG. Well?

HEDDA. . . . that was not my most cowardly act!

LÖVBORG (gazes at her for a moment, then he understands and whispers passionately to her). Oh, Hedda! Hedda Gabler! At last I am about to solve the mystery: I see what lay at the core of our relationship—the relations between you and me! No matter what you say, it was nature making itself felt in you . . .

HEDDA (softly, with a trenchant look at him). Take care! Don't believe anything of the kind! (It is beginning to get dark. The hall door is opened by BERTE from the outside. HEDDA closes the album and calls out with a smile.) Well, at last! Téa, my dearest—do come in!

(MRS. ELVSTED enters from the hall. She is wearing an evening dress. The door is closed by BERTE.)

HEDDA (on the sofa, holds out her arms to MRS. ELVSTED). Dear little Téa, you can't imagine how I have been waiting for you to come.

(MRS. ELVSTED, in passing, exchanges a casual greeting with TESMAN and JUDGE BRACK in the rear room; then goes up to the table and shakes hands with HEDDA. EJLERT LÖVBORG gets up. He and MRS. ELVSTED greet each other silently with a nod.)

MRS. ELVSTED. Perhaps I ought to go in and say a few words to your husband?

HEDDA. Oh no, that isn't necessary. Let them sit there. They'll soon be leaving.

MRS. ELVSTED. Leaving?

HEDDA. Yes, they are going to a drinking party.

MRS. ELVSTED (*quickly, worried, to* LÖVBORG). But you are not, are you?

LÖVBORG. No.

HEDDA. Mr. Lövborg, he—he stays here—with us.

MRS. ELVSTED (*takes a chair and is about to place it next to* LÖVBORG). Oh, how glad I am to be here!

HEDDA. No, no, my dear little Téa—not there! You come over here and sit down nicely beside me. I want to sit between you and Mr. Lövborg.

MRS. ELVSTED. Well, just as you say. (*She walks around the table and seats herself on the left side of* HEDDA *on the sofa.* LÖVBORG *sits down again.*)

LÖVBORG (*after a brief silence, to* HEDDA). Isn't she lovely to look at?

HEDDA (*lightly stroking* MRS. ELVSTED'S *hair*). To look at? Only to look at?

LÖVBORG. Oh, we two—she and I—we are real comrades. We have such absolute faith in each other; and we have such cheerful talks together . . .

HEDDA. Without going roundabout, Mr. Lövborg?

LÖVBORG. Oh well . . .

MRS. ELVSTED (*softly, moving closer to* HEDDA). Oh, Hedda—I am so very happy! And just think—he even says I have been his inspiration!

HEDDA (*looking at her, with a smile*). Why—does he say that—really?

LÖVBORG. And Téa has courage—the courage to act! Yes, that she certainly has, Mrs. Tesman.

MRS. ELVSTED. Oh God! I—courage!

LÖVBORG. No end of it—when she wants to do something for her comrade . . .

HEDDA. Courage! Yes—yes! If one only had courage!

LÖVBORG. What then? What do you mean?

HEDDA. Then, perhaps, one could really live. (*Suddenly changing the subject.*) But now, dearest little Téa—now you must have a glass of this refreshing, cold punch.

MRS. ELVSTED. Thank you—no, I never touch anything like that.

HEDDA. Well, then—you will have a glass, Mr. Lövborg, won't you?

LÖVBORG. No, thank you. None for me, either.

MRS. ELVSTED. No, none for him either!

HEDDA (*with a challenging look at him*). But if I should—if I should coax you?

LÖVBORG. It would be of no use.

HEDDA (*with a smile*). Am I so completely powerless over you then, poor woman that I am?

LÖVBORG. Yes. When it comes to that!

HEDDA. Seriously speaking, I think you ought to have a drink. It would do you good.

MRS. ELVSTED. Why, Hedda!

LÖVBORG. How so?

HEDDA. Or, perhaps, I should say, people would talk if you didn't.

LÖVBORG. So-o?

HEDDA. Yes, one might easily get the idea that you weren't quite so strong-minded and self-reliant as you should be—that you didn't have complete confidence in yourself.

MRS. ELVSTED (*softly, to* HEDDA). Oh but, Hedda . . .

LÖVBORG. People may think whatever they like—for the time being.

MRS. ELVSTED (*cheerfully*). Yes, I say the same.

HEDDA. I noticed it so plainly by the way Judge Brack acted just now . . .

LÖVBORG. How?

HEDDA. He smiled so contemptuously when you didn't have the nerve to join them inside.

LÖVBORG. Didn't have the nerve! Why, I just preferred to stay here and talk with you, of course.

MRS. ELVSTED. That was quite natural, Hedda, wasn't it?

HEDDA. But I imagine the Judge didn't think so. And I noticed him smile faintly and that he gave Tesman a furtive glance when you so timidly declined the invitation to his silly party.

LÖVBORG. Timidly? Do you imply I am afraid to go?

HEDDA. Why no—not I! I say that's the way Judge Brack interpreted it.

LÖVBORG. Then let him!

HEDDA. And so you are not going with them?

LÖVBORG. I am staying here with you and Téa.

MRS. ELVSTED. Why, of course, Hedda—you know he would want to.

HEDDA (*smiles, nodding approvingly to* LÖVBORG). Not to be swerved in his principles! Firm as bedrock! Unto eternity! That is what I call a man! (*She turns to* MRS. ELVSTED *and gives her a pat.*) Well—wasn't that what I told you this morning when you came here so frightfully wrought up?

LÖVBORG (*aghast*). Wrought up?

MRS. ELVSTED (*horrified*). Hedda—Hedda —why . . .

HEDDA (*to* MRS. ELVSTED). There you see— you can see for yourself now! You have absolutely no cause for being so dreadfully upset and worried . . . And now—now let us be happy—all of us—all three of us!

LÖVBORG (*taken aback*). Oh but—just what is the meaning of all this, Mrs. Tesman?

MRS. ELVSTED. Oh God, Hedda! Oh God! What have you done, Hedda? What have you been saying?

HEDDA. Sh! Don't get so excited! That disgusting Judge Brack is sitting there watching you.

LÖVBORG (*to* MRS. ELVSTED). So-o? Dreadfully upset and worried—on my account!

MRS. ELVSTED (*with a suppressed moan*). Oh, Hedda—you have made life miserable for me!

LÖVBORG (*gazes at her steadily for a moment or two, his face distorted*). So this is what you call keeping faith—the faith of a trusting comrade . . .

MRS. ELVSTED (*pleading with him*). Oh, but— Ejlert dear! First you must listen to me . . .

LÖVBORG (*takes one of the filled glasses, raises it and says in a low, husky voice*). To your health, Téa! (*He empties the glass, puts it down and picks up the other glass.*)

MRS. ELVSTED (*to* HEDDA, *with suppressed emotion*). Oh, Hedda, Hedda! That you could want to do such a thing!

HEDDA. Want to? I want to? Are you mad?

LÖVBORG. And a toast to you, Mrs. Tesman, too! Thank you for letting me know the truth! (*He drains his glass and is about to pour himself another drink.*)

HEDDA (*laying her hand on his arm*). Now, Mr. Lövborg—you shouldn't take too much, should you? Remember you are going to the party.

MRS. ELVSTED. No, no, no!

HEDDA (*to* MRS. ELVSTED). Not so loud! They are sitting in there watching you!

LÖVBORG (*puts down his glass*). Now, Téa! I want you to tell me the truth!

MRS. ELVSTED. Yes . . .

LÖVBORG. Did Sheriff Elvsted know that you went to the city after me?

MRS. ELVSTED (*wringing her hands*). Oh, Hedda—do you hear what he asks me?

LÖVBORG. Was it agreed between you and your husband, the Sheriff, that you should go to the city and keep an eye on me? Was it? Could it be it was he himself who had you come after me? Oh yes—yes—he had need of me at the office again, I suppose! Or perhaps he missed me at the card table?

MRS. ELVSTED (*gently, quietly, in utter distress*). Oh, Lövborg, Lövborg!

LÖVBORG (*snatches a glass and starts to fill it*). Let's drink a toast to the old Sheriff, also!

HEDDA (*gently taking the decanter from him*). No—no more, don't forget you are going to read from your new manuscript to Tesman.

LÖVBORG (*quiets down and puts away the glass*). I've been a fool, Téa, acting like this! There is no reason for me to behave this way. I hope you will forgive me, Téa—my dear, dear comrade! You shall see—and not only you but all the others—that even though I once was a defeated man that I—that I now have raised myself up again. And it is you, Téa, who have helped me!

MRS. ELVSTED (*radiantly*). Oh, God be praised! (*At this moment* BRACK *looks at his watch. He and* TESMAN *rise from their seats and come into the drawing room.*)

JUDGE BRACK (*takes his hat and overcoat*). Well, Mrs. Tesman, our time is up.

HEDDA. I imagine it is.

LÖVBORG (*gets up*). Mine, too, Judge Brack.

MRS. ELVSTED (*in a subdued, pleading voice to* LÖVBORG). Oh, Lövborg—please don't!

HEDDA (*pinching* MRS. ELVSTED's *arm*). Quiet! (*Under her breath.*) They'll hear you!

MRS. ELVSTED (*with a low cry of pain*). Ouch!

LÖVBORG (*to* BRACK). You were kind enough to ask me to come along . . .

JUDGE BRACK. Oh, so you have decided to come with us, after all?

LÖVBORG. Yes—thank you.

JUDGE BRACK. I am delighted to have you come.

LÖVBORG (*puts the packet with his manuscript in his pocket and says to* TESMAN). I am very anxious to show you one or two things in it before I send it off to the publishers.

TESMAN. Why, think of that! I would enjoy that! But, Hedda dear, how is Mrs. Elvsted going to get home? Eh?

HEDDA. Oh, she'll get home somehow.

LÖVBORG (*looking in the direction of the ladies*). Mrs. Elvsted? Why, I'll take her home, of course. I'll come back for her. (*Going toward them.*) About ten, would you say? Would that be agreeable?

HEDDA. Yes, of course. That's perfect.

TESMAN. Well, now everything is arranged then. But you musn't expect *me* home quite that early, Hedda.

HEDDA. Oh, you stay, dear—stay as long as you like.

MRS. ELVSTED (*trying to conceal her anxiety*). Then I'll wait here until you come and call for me, Mr. Lövborg.

LÖVBORG (*with his hat in his hand*). Yes, that's right, Mrs. Elvsted.

JUDGE BRACK. And now, gentlemen—now, the reception committee has to be on its way. I hope the party will be as lively as a certain fair lady expects it to be.

HEDDA. Alas, I only wish the fair lady could be with you—without being seen!

JUDGE BRACK. Why unseen?

HEDDA. So that she might take a peep at some of your untamed conviviality.

JUDGE BRACK (*smiling*). That's something I wouldn't prescribe for the fair lady.

TESMAN (*also with a smile*). Oh, Hedda, now you are being clever! Think of that!

JUDGE BRACK. Well, good-by then! Good-by, ladies!

LÖVBORG (*bowing to* HEDDA *and* MRS. ELVSTED). About ten o'clock, then.

(JUDGE BRACK, TESMAN, *and* LÖVBORG *go out through the hall door. At the same time* BERTE *enters from the inner room with a lighted lamp which she places on the drawing-room table, center. She then leaves by the way she entered.*)

MRS. ELVSTED (*has risen and is pacing the floor restlessly*). Oh, Hedda, Hedda! What will happen now?

HEDDA. At ten o'clock—at ten o'clock he will be here—with vine leaves in his hair! Burning with passion and full of courage!

MRS. ELVSTED. Yes—if it were only so.

HEDDA. And *then*, you see—*then* he will have regained the power over himself. *Then* he will be a *free* man for the rest of his days . . .

MRS. ELVSTED. Oh, if he only would! Please, God, send him back like that!

HEDDA. That is the way he will come—and no other way! (*She rises and goes up close to* MRS. ELVSTED.) Doubt him if you like—as much as you like . . . I believe in him. And now we shall see . . .

MRS. ELVSTED. There is something mysterious about you, Hedda, and about all this . . .

HEDDA. So there is. For once in my life, I wish to hold the fate of a human being in my hands.

MRS. ELVSTED. Don't you already?

HEDDA. No—nor have I ever.

MRS. ELVSTED. But you have your husband!

HEDDA. Why should I care about him! Oh! If you only knew how starved, how destitute I am! And you—you are allowed to be so—so satisfied—to have so much! (*She throws her arms hysterically round* MRS. ELVSTED *and draws her tightly to her.*) I think I shall set fire to your hair, after all!

MRS. ELVSTED (*frightened out of her wits*). Let me go! Let me go! You frighten me, Hedda!

BERTE (*appears in the center doorway*). Tea is served in the dining room, Mrs. Tesman.

HEDDA. Very well. We are coming . . .

MRS. ELVSTED. No-no-no! I want to go home—I'll go home alone—now—immediately . . .

HEDDA. Nonsense! First you'll sip your tea, you stupid little goose! And then—at ten o'clock—then Ejlert Lövborg will be back . . . He will be here, with vine leaves in his hair . . .

(*She almost drags* MRS. ELVSTED *toward the center opening and into the inner room.*)

## ACT III

THE SETTING.—*The same as in the preceding acts. The portières in the doorway to the inner room and the draperies before the glass door are opened. The lamp with the shade on the large table gives a faint light. The door to the porcelain stove is open, showing the fading embers.*

MRS. ELVSTED, *with a large shawl covering her, sits close by the stove. She is reclining in the armchair, her feet on a footstool.* HEDDA *is asleep on the sofa; she is fully dressed. A steamer rug covers her.*

MRS. ELVSTED (*after a pause, she suddenly sits up and listens anxiously. She then leans back in her chair again, murmuring in a low, weary voice*). Not yet back. Oh God! Oh God—he hasn't come yet.

(BERTE *steals quietly, cautiously, into the room through the hall door. She holds a letter her in hand.*)

MRS. ELVSTED (*turns to* BERTE *and whispers tensely*). Did anyone—did anyone come?

BERTE (*in a low voice*). Yes, a girl was here just now with this letter.

MRS. ELVSTED (*nervously, eagerly, reaching for the letter*). A letter! Give it to me!

BERTE. No, it's for Doctor Tesman, Mrs. Elvsted.

MRS. ELVSTED. Oh, for the doctor . . .

BERTE. It was Miss Tesman's maid who came here with it. I'll put it here on the table.

MRS. ELVSTED. Do that—yes.

BERTE (*puts the letter on the table*). I'd better put out the lamp, I think. It's beginning to smoke. I can smell it.

MRS. ELVSTED. Yes, put it out. It won't be long before the sun is up.

BERTE (*blows out the flame*). It's already daylight.

MRS. ELVSTED. Already! And still not back!

BERTE. Yes, God knows—I knew that would happen!

MRS. ELVSTED. You did?

BERTE. Yes—the moment I saw that a certain somebody was back in the city again —and saw him march off with Doctor Tesman and the Judge . . . For everyone has heard enough tales about *that* gentleman in years gone by.

MRS. ELVSTED. Don't talk so loud. You'll wake Mrs. Tesman.

BERTE (*looks over toward the sofa and sighs*). Yes, yes—let her get her sleep, poor soul. Shall I put some more wood on the fire?

MRS. ELVSTED. No, thank you—not for my sake.

BERTE. Oh, very well, then . . .

(*She goes out noiselessly through the hall door.*)

HEDDA (*awakens as* BERTE *closes the door, and looks up*). What was that?

MRS. ELVSTED. It was only the maid . . .

HEDDA (*looking around*). Oh, I—I am in here! Oh yes—now I remember . . . (*She sits up, stretches herself and seats herself on the sofa. She rubs her eyes.*) What time is it, Téa?

MRS. ELVSTED (*looks at her watch*). It's past seven now.

HEDDA. What time was it when Tesman came back?

MRS. ELVSTED. He hasn't come yet.

HEDDA. Not home yet?

MRS. ELVSTED (*rising*). Nobody has come. Not a soul.

HEDDA. And here we sat up, waiting and waiting, until four in the morning!

MRS. ELVSTED (*wringing her hands*). And I —waiting—waiting for him to come!

HEDDA (*covering a yawn with her hands*). Well, yes—we might have saved ourselves all that trouble . . .

MRS. ELVSTED. Did you get any sleep at all?

HEDDA. Oh yes, I think I got a little—I slept quite well. And you?

MRS. ELVSTED. I didn't get a wink of sleep. I just couldn't sleep, Hedda.

HEDDA (*gets up and goes toward her*). Now, now, now! There is nothing to be worried about. I understand perfectly what has happened.

MRS. ELVSTED. What do you think has happened? Tell me!

HEDDA. Why, of course, they just kept drinking at Judge Brack's until the wee hours.

MRS. ELVSTED. Oh, God in heaven, yes—I knew it. But all the same . . .

HEDDA. And then Tesman, you see, didn't want to come home and disturb us by ringing the bell in the middle of the night. (*She smiles meaningfully.*) Perhaps he didn't care to show himself—having just come from such a lusty party.

MRS. ELVSTED. But, Hedda dear—where could he be then?

HEDDA. He has gone to his aunts, of course. They still keep his old room for him, where he can sleep. He has gone to bed there, naturally.

MRS. ELVSTED. Oh no, he couldn't have gone to them, for a letter came for him from Miss Tesman just a moment ago. It's lying over there. (*She points to it.*)

HEDDA. Oh! (*She looks at the envelope.*) Yes, so it is—it's Aunt Juliane's handwriting. Well, then I suppose he has remained with Judge Brack. And Ejlert Lövborg is sitting there, with vine leaves in his hair, reading to Tesman from his manuscript.

MRS. ELVSTED. Oh, Hedda, you are just talking! You don't believe a word you are saying!

HEDDA. You are an imbecile, Téa. An imbecile!

MRS. ELVSTED. Yes, so I am, sad to say!

HEDDA. And how tired you look! You look frightfully tired!

MRS. ELVSTED. Yes—and I *am*—horribly tired!

HEDDA. Well, then, you do as I tell you now. Go into my room and lie down on my bed for a while!

MRS. ELVSTED. Oh no, no! It'll do me no good—I couldn't sleep anyhow.

HEDDA. Oh yes, you can.

MRS. ELVSTED. Oh, but your husband is bound to come home any minute now. And then I'll find out . . .

HEDDA. You don't have to worry—I'll let you know as soon as he comes.

MRS. ELVSTED. Well, will you promise me that, Hedda?

HEDDA. Yes, you can depend on me. You just go into my room now and get your sleep.

MRS. ELVSTED. Thank you! I'll try to get some rest, then.

(*She goes out through the back room.* HEDDA *goes over to the glass door and pulls the curtains aside. Outside is broad daylight, and the light fills the room. Then she picks up a small hand mirror from the writing table; she looks at herself and arranges her hair. Having done this, she walks over to the hall door and presses the bell button. Soon after,* BERTE *appears at the door to the hall.*)

BERTE. Anything I can do for you, Mrs. Tesman?

HEDDA. Yes, put some more wood on the fire. I'm freezing.

BERTE. Merciful heavens! I'll see to it this minute. (*She rakes the fire and puts a fresh log on it. Suddenly she stops and listens.*) I heard the bell at the front door, Mrs. Tesman.

HEDDA. Then go and open it. I'll take care of the fire.

BERTE. The fire will soon be coming up now. (*She goes out through the hall door.*)

(HEDDA, *kneeling on the footstool, puts a few more logs on the fire. After a brief pause,* JÖRGEN TESMAN *enters from the hall. He looks tired and seems to be in a rather serious mood. He steals in on tiptoe. When he is in the center doorway and tries to disappear through the* portières, HEDDA *sees him.*)

HEDDA (*at the stove, without looking up*). Good morning.

TESMAN (*turning*). Hedda! (*He takes a few steps toward her.*) What in the world! Are you up so early? Eh?

HEDDA. Yes, I am up early today, unusually early.

TESMAN. And I was so certain you were still in bed and fast asleep. Think of that, Hedda!

HEDDA. Don't talk so loud—Mrs. Elvsted is asleep in my room.

TESMAN. Has Mrs. Elvsted spent the night here?

HEDDA. Yes. No one came to take her home.

TESMAN. No, nobody did, I suppose.

HEDDA (*closing the door to the stove, she gets up*). Well, did you have a good time at Judge Brack's?

TESMAN. You didn't worry about me, did you? Eh?

HEDDA. No, why should I? But I asked you whether you had a good time.

TESMAN. Yes, in a way. For once, it . . . But it was the early part of the evening I enjoyed most, as I think of it. Because then Ejlert read to me from his manuscript. Think of that! We arrived more than an hour too soon! And Brack had a great many things to attend to, and so Ejlert read to me.

HEDDA (*seating herself to the left of the large table*). Well? Tell me all about it . . .

TESMAN (*seating himself on a taboret by the stove*). Well, Hedda, you can't imagine what sort of book it's going to be! I think it is one of the most remarkable books ever written! Think of that!

HEDDA. Yes, yes—I'm not interested in that . . .

TESMAN. And I am going to confess something to you, Hedda . . . When he had finished reading, an ugly feeling took hold of me . . .

HEDDA. An ugly feeling, you say?

TESMAN. Yes—I sat there with envy in my heart—envying Ejlert for having been able to write a book such as this! Think of that, Hedda!

HEDDA. Yes, yes, I'm thinking, I'm thinking!

TESMAN. And then to know that he—with all his gifts and his ability—nevertheless is hopelessly done for.

HEDDA. You mean, I suppose, that he possesses greater courage to cope with life than the rest of you?

TESMAN. No, good Lord—but you see he has absolutely no restraint when it comes to pleasures.

HEDDA. And what happened? How did it end?

TESMAN. Well, the only way to describe it, Hedda, would be to call it an orgy, a bacchanalian orgy.

HEDDA. Did he have vine leaves in his hair?

TESMAN. Vine leaves? No—I saw nothing like that; but he made a long, rambling speech about the woman who had been his inspiration during the time he wrote his book. Yes—that's the way he expressed it.

HEDDA. Did he mention who she was?

TESMAN. No, he did not. But I can't imagine it could have been anyone but Mrs. Elvsted. So there you are!

HEDDA. Well—where did you leave him?

TESMAN. On the way home. We all left at the same time—that is, those of us who stayed throughout the party. And Brack came along with us—he wanted to get a little fresh air. And it was then we thought we had best see to it that Ejlert got home—for he was really quite drunk. Yes, he was quite drunk!

HEDDA. I presume he was.

TESMAN. But now I am coming to something that happened—something quite amazing, Hedda—yes, I should call it tragic. Oh, I am almost ashamed—for Ejlert's sake—to tell you about it . . .

HEDDA. Well, what happened?

TESMAN. Well, you see, as we were walking along, I momentarily lagged behind the others. But only for a couple of minutes! Think of that!

HEDDA. Yes, yes, good God! And then . . .

TESMAN. And then—as I hurried to catch up with the others—can you imagine what I found at the side of the road? Eh?

HEDDA. No, how could I!

TESMAN. Don't say a word about it to anyone, Hedda! Do you hear? You must promise me that—for Ejlert's sake! (*He takes a packet wrapped in paper from his coat pocket.*) This is what I found! Think of it!

HEDDA. Isn't that the manuscript he brought with him here yesterday?

TESMAN. Yes, Hedda! It is his priceless manuscript—every page of it—and it could never be replaced! And he goes and loses it —without even noticing it! Just think of it, Hedda! It's sad!

HEDDA. But why didn't you give it back to him the moment you found it?

TESMAN. In the condition he was in—I thought it best not to.

HEDDA. Didn't you tell any of the others you had found it?

TESMAN. Oh no, I would never have done that! For Ejlert's sake, you understand!

HEDDA. Then no one—no one knows you have Ejlert Lövborg's manuscript?

TESMAN. No—and no one must know, either.

HEDDA. What did you talk to him about— afterward?

TESMAN. I had no chance to say a word to him after that, Hedda. We lost him and two or three of the others in one of the streets on the way, lost them completely. Think of that!

HEDDA. Oh? Well, I suppose they helped him to get home, then?

TESMAN. Yes, I presume so—that was their intention. And Brack disappeared also.

HEDDA. And where have you been keeping yourself after that?

TESMAN. Why, I and some of the others

went to the home of one of the men at the party and had an early breakfast there. Or perhaps I should say, more properly, a predawn snack. Eh? But now, after I have had a little rest, and as soon as I think poor Ejlert has had sufficient sleep, I must bring the manuscript to him.

HEDDA (*reaching for the packet*). No—don't give it back! I mean—not immediately! Let me read it first.

TESMAN. No, Hedda, my darling, I can't let you do that! My conscience wouldn't allow that!

HEDDA. Your conscience . . . ?

TESMAN. Yes! Can't you imagine how despondent, how desperately frantic Ejlert will be when he wakes up and finds his manuscript missing? For, you know, he has no copy of it. He told me so himself!

HEDDA (*giving him a scrutinizing look*). Couldn't a work like this be written again? He could write it again, couldn't he?

TESMAN. No, I don't think he could. It takes inspiration, you know . . .

HEDDA. Yes, yes, precisely—I suppose it does . . . (*Indicating the letter on the table.*) But I forgot—a letter came for you. (*She goes to fetch it.*)

TESMAN. Why, think of that!

HEDDA (*handing him the letter*). It arrived early this morning.

TESMAN. From Aunt Juliane, Hedda! I wonder what it can be? (*He puts the manuscript packet on the other taboret, opens the letter, reads it and jumps to his feet.*) Oh, Hedda! She writes that poor Aunt Rina is lying on her deathbed!

HEDDA. You didn't expect anything else?

TESMAN. And she says that if I wish to see her, I must waste no time . . . I have to hurry over at once—I have to run . . .

HEDDA (*suppressing a smile*). Will you really run?

TESMAN. Oh, Hedda, my dearest—I wish you could bring yourself to come with me! Think of it!

HEDDA (*rising, she dismisses his suggestion in a weary voice*). No, no! Don't ask me to do anything of the sort. I don't want to look at sickness and death! I want to stay away from anything that is ugly and repulsive.

TESMAN. Good Lord . . . Yes, well—in that case . . . (*He excitedly rushes about in the room.*) My hat? My overcoat? Oh yes—in the hall . . . Oh, I do hope I won't be too late, Hedda! Eh?

HEDDA. Oh, if you keep running, you will . . .

(BERTE *enters from the hall.*)

BERTE. Judge Brack is outside and he asks if he can come in.

TESMAN. At this hour! No—I can't possibly see him now.

HEDDA. But I can. (*To* BERTE.) Ask the Judge to come in.

(BERTE *goes out.*)

HEDDA (*blurts out in a whisper to* TESMAN). The manuscript, Tesman! (*She snatches it from the taboret.*)

TESMAN. Yes—give it to me!

HEDDA. No, no—I'll keep it safe till you return. (*She goes over to the writing table and hides it among the books on the bookrack.* TESMAN *keeps fussing about and cannot get his gloves on.* JUDGE BRACK *enters from the hall.* HEDDA *greets him with a nod.*) Well, you are indeed an early bird.

JUDGE BRACK. Yes, that I am, don't you think? (*To* TESMAN.) So you are on the move, too, this morning?

TESMAN. Yes, I have to go to my aunts. Think of it! Aunt Rina, who has always been so sick, poor soul, is not expected to live.

JUDGE BRACK. Oh, good heavens, you don't say! Then don't let me keep you. When anything so serious as that . . .

TESMAN. Yes, I must be going—I must be going . . . Good-by—good-by!

(*He hurries out through the hall door.*)

HEDDA (*walking up toward* JUDGE BRACK). I think your party last night must have been more exhilarating than usual, Judge Brack.

JUDGE BRACK. You can see I haven't been out of my clothes even.

HEDDA. Not you, either?

JUDGE BRACK. No, as you see. But what did Tesman tell you about last night's happenings?

HEDDA. Oh, what he told me sounded awfully dull and uninteresting—something about having gone somewhere for an early breakfast with some of your guests.

JUDGE BRACK. Yes, I know about that. But I don't think Ejlert Lövborg was among them.

HEDDA. No, they had helped him home first.

JUDGE BRACK. Tesman, too?

HEDDA. No, some of the others from your party.

JUDGE BRACK. (with a smile). Jörgen Tesman is indeed a child at heart, Mrs. Hedda.

HEDDA. Yes, God knows he is that. But did anything mysterious happen last night?

JUDGE BRACK. That depends upon how you look at it.

HEDDA. Well, then, my dear Judge, tell me about it. And let us sit down—you'll be more at ease. (She seats herself to the right of the table, while BRACK sits close to her at the long side of the table.) Now, then?

JUDGE BRACK. I had particular reasons for keeping track of where my guests were going —or rather, I should say, certain of my guests—after my party was over.

HEDDA. And perhaps Ejlert Lövborg was one of these?

JUDGE BRACK. I have to confess that he was.

HEDDA. Now you are really whetting my appetite.

JUDGE BRACK. Do you know where he and a couple of the others spent the rest of the night, Mrs. Hedda?

HEDDA. If you feel you can tell me, do so.

JUDGE BRACK. Oh heavens, there is no reason why I shouldn't. Well, they turned up at a rather bawdy nocturnal party.

HEDDA. Of the more lively kind?

JUDGE BRACK. Of the most lively kind!

HEDDA. Tell me some more about it, Judge Brack . . .

JUDGE BRACK. Lövborg had been invited beforehand—just as some of the others. I knew all about it. But he had declined the invitation; for, as you know, he has now been rehabilitated.

HEDDA. Up at Sheriff Elvsted's, yes. Yet he went, nevertheless?

JUDGE BRACK. Yes, you see, Mrs. Hedda— unfortunately, the spirits took possession of him when he was at my home last night . . .

HEDDA. Yes, I understand he became inspired.

JUDGE BRACK. Quite violently inspired!

Well, I suppose he had a change of heart. Sad to say, we males are not always so firm in our principles as we should be.

HEDDA. Oh, I am sure you are an exception to the rule, Judge Brack. And so, Lövborg . . .

JUDGE BRACK. Well, to make a long story short, it ended by his landing at that Miss Diana's.

HEDDA. Miss Diana?

JUDGE BRACK. Yes, she was entertaining a select circle of female friends and admirers.

HEDDA. Is she a redheaded woman?

JUDGE BRACK. Exactly.

HEDDA. Some sort of—singer?

JUDGE BRACK. Oh yes, she is that, too. And in addition, an experienced huntress—after men, Mrs. Hedda. You must have heard of her. Ejlert Lövborg was one of her most ardent patrons in his days of affluence.

HEDDA. And how did it all end?

JUDGE BRACK. In a less than friendly manner, I hear. After having been received most tenderly by Miss Diana, I am told it ended by her attacking him.

HEDDA. Attacking Lövborg?

JUDGE BRACK. Yes, he accused Miss Diana or her female friends of having robbed him. He said his wallet had disappeared—and also some other belongings. In short, he caused a frightful rumpus, I am told.

HEDDA. And what was the outcome of it all?

JUDGE BRACK. It led to a scuffle between everybody. Not only the men but the women took part in it. Luckily the police came and put an end to it.

HEDDA. The police came?

JUDGE BRACK. Yes. And I'm afraid it will be a costly night of pleasures for that mad fellow Lövborg.

HEDDA. Oh!

JUDGE BRACK. They say he made violent resistance to the police, and I am told he struck one of the policemen on the ear and ripped his uniform coat to pieces. It was then they took him to the police station.

HEDDA. Where did you learn all this?

JUDGE BRACK. From the police themselves.

HEDDA (looking straight ahead). And that is how it happened . . . And so he had no vine leaves in his hair.

JUDGE BRACK. Vine leaves, did you say?

HEDDA (*in a changed tone of voice*). But tell me, Judge Brack, just what is your reason for going about tracking down and spying on Lövborg?

JUDGE BRACK. First of all, I can't remain indifferent to the fact that he came directly from a party at my home—in case this should be brought out during the hearings in court.

HEDDA. You mean there will be a court hearing?

JUDGE BRACK. Oh, of course. However, these things will take care of themselves. I only felt that I—as a friend of yours and your husband's—ought to give you and Tesman a full account of Lövborg's nocturnal escapades.

HEDDA. Why so, Judge Brack?

JUDGE BRACK. Because I have a strong suspicion that he will use you as a sort of alibi.

HEDDA. Why, how could you possibly think that?

JUDGE BRACK. Oh, good Lord—we are not blind, Mrs. Hedda. You must be careful! This Mrs. Elvsted—I am sure she won't be leaving town so very soon.

HEDDA. Well, if there were anything between her and Lövborg, there must be a great many other places where they could meet.

JUDGE BRACK. Not in anyone's home. Every respectable home in town will from now on be closed to Ejlert Lövborg.

HEDDA. And so mine ought to be closed to him also, you mean!

JUDGE BRACK. Yes, I must confess it would be more than painful to me if this individual should be able to come and go here as he pleased. If he, worthless and irresponsible as he is, should try to force himself into . . .

HEDDA. Into the triangle!

JUDGE BRACK. Just so. That—for me—would be the same as to be a man without a home.

HEDDA (*with a smile, looking at him*). So—to be the cock of the walk—that is what you are after?

JUDGE BRACK (*with a slow nod and in a lowered voice*). Yes—that is my goal. And for that I will fight—with all the means in my possession.

HEDDA (*her smile fading*). When your own interests are at stake, I think you are really quite a dangerous person.

JUDGE BRACK. Is that what you think?

HEDDA. Yes, I am now beginning to think so. And I rejoice that you have no hold of any kind over me.

JUDGE BRACK (*with an ambiguous smile*). Well, well, Mrs. Hedda—you may be right. But if that had been the case, who knows what I might have done.

HEDDA. Oh, but really, Judge Brack! One might think you were threatening me.

JUDGE BRACK. (*rising*). Far from it! The triangle, you see—the triangle should preferably be a tower of strength, and should be defended voluntarily.

HEDDA. That is the way I look at it, too.

JUDGE BRACK. Well, now that I have said what I came to say, I think I'd best be on my way home. Good-by, Mrs. Hedda! (*He walks toward the glass door.*)

HEDDA (*getting up*). Are you leaving by the garden?

JUDGE BRACK. Yes, it saves a few steps.

HEDDA. Yes—and it's also the back way.

JUDGE BRACK. Ah, quite so. I don't object to that. The back way can sometimes be tantalizing.

HEDDA. You mean, when bullets are flying?

JUDGE BRACK (*standing in the doorway, with a smile*). Oh, people don't shoot their tame prize cocks, do they?

HEDDA (*also with a smile*). Oh no! Not when there is only one, for then . . .

(*They laughingly say good-by to each other with a nod, and* BRACK *leaves.* HEDDA *closes the door after him. She looks serious and stands for a moment looking out through the glass door. Then she goes up and peeps through the portières at the center doorway. She crosses to the writing table, takes* LÖVBORG's *manuscript packet from the bookrack and starts to glance through the pages. Just then* BERTE, *in a loud voice, can be heard talking to someone in the hall.* HEDDA *turns, listening. She quickly puts the manuscript in the table drawer and locks it, laying the key on the inkstand.* EJLERT LÖVBORG, *wearing an overcoat and holding his hat in his hand, bursts into the room. He looks confused and excited.*)

LÖVBORG (*facing the hall*). I tell you I have to—I intend to see them! That's all! (*He shuts the door, turns and sees* HEDDA. *Immediately he controls himself and greets* HEDDA.)

HEDDA (*at the writing table*). Well, Mr. Lövborg, you are rather late in calling for Téa.

LÖVBORG. And a little early in calling on you. I hope you will forgive me.

HEDDA. How do you know that Téa is still here?

LÖVBORG. I found out at her lodgings she had not yet returned.

HEDDA (*goes over to the large center table*). Did you notice anything in the expression on their faces when they told you this?

LÖVBORG (*looking at her inquiringly*). The expression on their faces?

HEDDA. I mean—did it seem as if her staying out all night had given them some kind of wrong impression?

LÖVBORG (*suddenly understanding*). Why, of course—that never occurred to me! I'll ruin her reputation also! However, there was nothing in their manner that ... I don't suppose Tesman is up yet?

HEDDA. No—I don't think he is ...

LÖVBORG. What time was it when he came home?

HEDDA. It was terribly late.

LÖVBORG. Did he tell you anything?

HEDDA. Well, I heard you had a really gay time at Judge Brack's.

LÖVBORG. Was that all?

HEDDA. Yes, I think that was all he said. But I was so terribly sleepy ...

(MRS. ELVSTED *enters from the rear room. She goes to* LÖVBORG.)

MRS. ELVSTED. Oh, Lövborg! At last!

LÖVBORG. Yes, at last—and too late!

MRS. ELVSTED (*anxiously regarding him*). Too late? What is too late?

LÖVBORG. Everything—everything is too late now! I am done for!

MRS. ELVSTED. Oh, no, no! Don't say that!

LÖVBORG. You'll say the same when you hear what ...

MRS. ELVSTED. I don't want to hear ...

HEDDA. Perhaps you would rather speak with her alone—so I'll leave you to yourselves.

LÖVBORG. No, I would like you to stay—I beg you to stay.

MRS. ELVSTED. Oh, but I tell you I don't want to hear!

LÖVBORG. It is not about last night's escapades I want to talk ...

MRS. ELVSTED. No? What then?

LÖVBORG. Only about this: we must part.

MRS. ELVSTED. Part?

HEDDA (*involuntarily*). I knew it!

LÖVBORG. I no longer have any need for you, Téa.

MRS. ELVSTED. And you can stand there and say that to me! No more need for me! You mean you no longer want me to help you? You mean we are not going to work together as we have been ... ?

LÖVBORG. I shall never write again.

MRS. ELVSTED (*desperately*). Then what will I live for?

LÖVBORG. You must try to live your life as if you had never known me.

MRS. ELVSTED. How can I?

LÖVBORG. You have to, Téa. You must return to your home ...

MRS. ELVSTED (*rebelliously; in agitation*). Never in this world! I want to be with you wherever you are ... I won't let you drive me away like this ... I want to be here—with you—when the book comes out.

HEDDA (*anxiously, in a scarcely audible voice*). Yes—the book!

LÖVBORG (*gazing at her*). Mine and Téa's—for that's what it is.

MRS. ELVSTED. Yes—it is—I feel it is. And that's why I feel I have the right to be with you when it's published! I want to see you showered with respect and honors once more ... And the joy—I will share your joy with you!

LÖVBORG. Our book, Téa—our book will never see the light of day!

HEDDA. Ah!

MRS. ELVSTED. Never see the light of day?

LÖVBORG. It never will—it never can!

MRS. ELVSTED (*fearing the worst, in anguish*). Lövborg—what have you done with the manuscript?

HEDDA (*looking at him in suspense*). Yes, the manuscript?

MRS. ELVSTED. Where is it?

LÖVBORG. Oh, Téa—don't ask me!

MRS. ELVSTED. Yes, yes—I want to know—I have a right to know.

LÖVBORG. I may as well tell you . . . I tore it up—tore it to bits . . .

MRS. ELVSTED (*with a scream*). Oh no, no!

HEDDA (*temporarily losing control of herself*). But that's not the . . .

LÖVBORG (*glancing at her*). Not true, you think?

HEDDA (*again in control of herself*). Since you say so yourself, I suppose it must be. But it sounded so incredible.

LÖVBORG. It is true, nevertheless.

MRS. ELVSTED (*wringing her hands*). Oh God! Oh God! Tearing his own work to pieces, Hedda!

LÖVBORG. I've torn my life to pieces. Then why shouldn't I destroy my life's work also?

MRS. ELVSTED. And that's what you've been doing tonight!

LÖVBORG. Yes, that's what I did! I tore it up—tore it page by page and scattered the pieces on the fjord—far, far out, where the water is clean and the sea is salty. There I let them drift—with the current and the wind—until at last they sink—deeper and deeper—just as I am sinking, Téa . . .

MRS. ELVSTED. You must know, Lövborg, that what you have done with your book is . . . is as if you had done away with a little child . . . For the rest of my days I shall grieve for it . . .

LÖVBORG. You are right . . . it is much like murdering a child!

MRS. ELVSTED. But how could you then! I helped to give it life, didn't I?

HEDDA (*almost inaudibly*). The child . . .

MRS. ELVSTED (*breathing heavily*). Then this is the end . . . yes—yes . . . I'm going, Hedda.

HEDDA. But you are not leaving town, are you?

MRS. ELVSTED. Oh, I have no idea what I'll do. Everything seems so dark just now . . .

(*She goes out through the hall door.*)

HEDDA (*stands silent for a moment*). You don't intend to see her home, Mr. Lövborg?

LÖVBORG. I—Ejlert Lövborg? You wouldn't want people to see her walking in the street with me, would you?

HEDDA. I have no idea what else may have happened last night. But whatever it was—would it be so completely impossible to put it right?

LÖVBORG. The trouble is it won't be the last time. I know it won't. But just the same —it is not the sort of life I care to live. Not any more . . . The courage, the defiance that life had endowed me with . . . She has broken that—it's gone . . .

HEDDA (*gazing straight ahead*). That insipid little fool, playing with a man's destiny! (*Looking at* LÖVBORG.) But, just the same, how could you be so heartless to her?

LÖVBORG. Oh, don't say I was heartless!

HEDDA. To destroy what was dearest to her—all that she had cherished for so long—don't you call that being heartless?

LÖVBORG. Hedda! To you, Hedda, I can tell the truth.

HEDDA. The truth?

LÖVBORG. You must first promise me—you must give me your word that you will never let Téa know what I now confide to you.

HEDDA. I give you my word.

LÖVBORG. Very well. And so I shall tell you that what I said a moment ago was not true.

HEDDA. About the manuscript, you mean?

LÖVBORG. Yes—I did not tear it up and I did not throw it in the fjord . . .

HEDDA. But—but where is it then?

LÖVBORG. . . . but I have done away with it nevertheless—done away with it forever.

HEDDA. I don't understand . . .

LÖVBORG. Téa made the remark just now that what I had done, was like taking the life of a little child.

HEDDA. Yes, that's what she said.

LÖVBORG. But to deprive a child of its life—that is not the worst crime a father can commit.

HEDDA. That is not the worst?

LÖVBORG. No. It was from knowing this worst of crimes that I wanted to spare Téa.

HEDDA. What then is this worst of crimes?

LÖVBORG. Let's suppose, Hedda, that a man—after a night of drinking and carousing —came home to his child's mother in the early morning hours and said: I have been here and I have been there—at such and such a place. And I have had my child with me—both here and there. Then I lost our child—yes, lost it. God knows into whose hands it has fallen. And who is at the bottom of it all.

HEDDA. Be that as it may—but this was merely a book . . .

LÖVBORG. Téa's pure soul was in it.

HEDDA. Yes, I understand that.

LÖVBORG. Then you will also understand that there can be no future for Téa and me together.

HEDDA. What do you plan to do then?

LÖVBORG. Nothing. I simply want to end it all. The sooner the better.

HEDDA (coming a step closer to him). Ejlert Lövborg—listen to me! Will you promise me one thing: that you do it beautifully?

LÖVBORG. Beautifully? (He smiles.) With vine leaves in my hair, as you always used to say . . .

HEDDA. No, no—I put no faith in vine leaves any more. But nonetheless—for once—do it beautifully! And now—you must go . . . Good-by! And do not come here again.

LÖVBORG. Good-by, Mrs. Tesman. And give my regards to Jörgen Tesman. (He starts to leave.)

HEDDA. No, wait! I must give you something to remember me by. (She goes to the writing table, opens the drawer and takes out the pistol case. From the latter she removes a pistol which she gives to LÖVBORG.)

LÖVBORG (regarding her). A pistol? Is that your remembrance?

HEDDA (slowly nodding). Do you recall it? It once was aimed at you.

LÖVBORG. You should have used it that time.

HEDDA. It's yours! You use it now! (He puts the pistol in his breast pocket.)

LÖVBORG. I thank you.

HEDDA. And remember! Do it beautifully, Ejlert Lövborg. You must promise me to do it beautifully!

LÖVBORG. Good-by, Hedda Gabler!

(He goes out through the hall door. For a moment HEDDA stands at the door, listening to his steps; then she goes over to the writing table and takes out the packet with the manuscript, peeps into the envelope, pulls several sheets of paper halfway out and glances at them. She takes the packet and goes over to the armchair

by the stove. She sits down in the armchair, holding the packet in her lap. After a brief silence, she opens the door to the stove, and a moment or two later, the manuscript packet. She then throws one of the sheets into the fire, whispering to herself.)

HEDDA. Now I am burning your child, Téa! You with your frizzy hair! (She throws a few more sheets into the fire.) Your child—yours and Ejlert Lövborg's . . . (She throws the rest of the manuscript into the stove.) Now I am burning it—burning the child!

## ACT IV

THE SETTING.—The same as in the previous acts. It is evening. There is no light in the drawing room, but the room in the back is illuminated by the light from the lamp hanging over the table. The draperies before the glass door are closed.

HEDDA, dressed in mourning, is idly walking to and fro in the dark drawing room. She enters the rear room and walks over to the right, out of sight. A moment later, one hears a few chords played on the piano. Then she reappears and returns to the drawing room.

BERTE enters from the left in the inner room, carrying a lighted lamp which she places on the table in front of the sofa in the corner of the drawing room. Her eyes are red from weeping; and her maid's cap is trimmed with black crêpe. She leaves silently and unobtrusively by the door, left. HEDDA walks over to the glass door, moves the draperies a little to one side and peers out into the darkness. Soon after, MISS TESMAN comes in from the hall. She is dressed in mourning, with a black hat and black crêpe veil. HEDDA goes to meet her and extends her hand in greeting.

MISS TESMAN. Well, Hedda, I come to you in my darkest hour, dressed in mourning. For my poor sister has now at last found her rest.

HEDDA (alluding to her dress). As you can see, I already know. Tesman sent word to me.

MISS TESMAN. Yes, he promised he would. Just the same, I felt I owed it to you, Hedda, to bring you the sad news of her death myself —you, Hedda, who live here in this house of life.

HEDDA. That was very thoughtful of you.

MISS TESMAN. I only wish that Rina hadn't passed away just at this time. Hedda's house should not be a house of mourning at a time like this.

HEDDA (*trying to divert her thoughts*). She died very peacefully, Miss Tesman, didn't she?

MISS TESMAN. Oh, she died so beautifully! She said good-by to this world so peacefully. And then she had the unspeakable joy of seeing Jörgen once more, and bidding a final good-by to him! Perhaps he hasn't come home yet? Has he?

HEDDA. No. He wrote that I shouldn't expect him immediately. But do sit down.

MISS TESMAN. No, thank you, dear, blessed Hedda! I would like to, but I can't. She has to be laid out and I have to make her as pretty as I can. I want her to look her best when she is lowered into her grave.

HEDDA. Isn't there anything I can help you with?

MISS TESMAN. Oh, you mustn't bother yourself about that! This is not a chore for the hands of Hedda Tesman! And it isn't anything her thoughts should have to dwell on either. No, not at a time like this!

HEDDA. Oh, my thoughts . . . It isn't easy to master one's thoughts . . .

MISS TESMAN (*still continuing in the same vein*). Lord—yes, that's the way it goes in this world. At my house we'll be sewing a shroud for Rina—and here you'll soon be sewing, too—only something else, if I am not wrong —yes, praise be to God!

(JÖRGEN TESMAN *enters from the hall.*)

HEDDA. Well, I'm glad you finally got here.

TESMAN. Are you here, Aunt Juliane? With Hedda? Think of that!

MISS TESMAN. I was just about to leave, my dear boy. Well, did you do the errands as you promised?

TESMAN. No, I'm afraid I forgot half of them. I have to drop over and see you again tomorrow. Today I am completely in a state of confusion. I just can't think!

MISS TESMAN. But, Jörgen dear, you mustn't let it affect you that way.

TESMAN. Why—what do you mean?

MISS TESMAN. You must accept sorrow with joy. You must rejoice in what has come to be, as I do.

TESMAN. Oh yes, yes—you are thinking of Aunt Rina.

HEDDA. It will be lonely for you now, Miss Tesman.

MISS TESMAN. In the beginning yes; but that feeling will soon pass, I hope. I shan't let my poor blessed Rina's room stand vacant for long.

TESMAN. Oh? Whom are you going to put in it? Eh?

MISS TESMAN. Oh, you can always find some poor soul who is sick who needs to be helped and cared for.

HEDDA. Would you really want to take a burden like that upon yourself again?

MISS TESMAN. Burden? May God forgive you, child—it was never a burden to me.

HEDDA. But now—if you should take in a stranger—why . . .

MISS TESMAN. Oh, it doesn't take long to become friends with people who are sick. And I simply have to have someone to live for, I simply must. Well, God be praised, in time there will also be something in this house an old aunt could lend a hand to . . .

HEDDA. Oh, don't be thinking about us, please.

TESMAN. Just think what a wonderful time we three could have together if . . .

HEDDA. If . . . ?

TESMAN (*uneasily*). Oh, it wasn't anything. But I am sure everything will turn out well. At least I hope so. Eh?

MISS TESMAN. Yes, yes. I can see you two have something you want to talk about. (*She smiles meaningfully.*) And I shouldn't be surprised if Hedda had something to tell you, Jörgen. Good-by! Now I must go home to Rina. (*At the door, she turns.*) Oh Lord! How strange it seems when I think of it! Now Rina is together with our blessed brother Jochum in heaven—and still she is here with me.

TESMAN. Yes, think of that, Aunt Juliane! Eh?

(MISS TESMAN *goes out through the hall door.*)

HEDDA (*following* TESMAN *with cold, withering glances*). I almost think you take her death more to heart than her sister does.

TESMAN. Oh, it isn't only her death that upsets me. I am so terribly worried about Ejlert.

HEDDA (*quickly*). Have you heard anything new about him?

TESMAN. I had intended to tell him the manuscript was in safe hands, and went to see him this afternoon.

HEDDA. Well, did you find him in?

TESMAN. No, he wasn't at home. But soon after, I met Mrs. Elvsted, and she told me he had been here at our house early this morning.

HEDDA. Yes, shortly after you left.

TESMAN. And I understand he had torn his manuscript into bits. Eh?

HEDDA. Yes, that's what he said.

TESMAN. But, good God, then he must have been clear out of his mind! And in that case I suppose you hesitated to give it back to him, Hedda?

HEDDA. Yes—I didn't give it to him.

TESMAN. But I presume you told him we had it.

HEDDA. No. (*Nervously.*) You didn't tell Mrs. Elvsted, did you?

TESMAN. No, I had no reason to do that. But you should have told Lövborg. Just think, if he in desperation should go and do himself some harm! Let me have the manuscript, Hedda. I'll run over and give it to him at once. Where is it?

HEDDA (*cold and immovable, she stands leaning against the armchair*). I haven't got it.

TESMAN. You haven't the manuscript! What in the world do you mean by that?

HEDDA. I have burned it—burned every page of it.

TESMAN (*in terror, with a shriek*). Burned! You have burned Ejlert's manuscript!

HEDDA. Don't scream! The maid might hear you.

TESMAN. Burned it! Merciful God! No, no, no—I can't believe it!

HEDDA. Nevertheless I have.

TESMAN. And do you realize what you have done, Hedda! You have committed an illegal act, you have appropriated another's property. Think of that! Just ask Judge Brack—he will tell you.

HEDDA. I would advise you not to mention anything about it either to Judge Brack or to anyone else.

TESMAN. But how could you—how could you do anything so—so monstrous? How could you even think of such a thing? Whatever possessed you to do it? Answer me! Eh?

HEDDA (*with an almost imperceptible smile which she tries to suppress*). I did it for you, Jörgen—for your sake.

TESMAN. For my sake?

HEDDA. When you came home this morning and told me Lövborg had read to you . . .

TESMAN. Yes—yes? Well?

HEDDA. You told me you envied him for having written such a book.

TESMAN. Oh, God in heaven, I didn't mean that so literally.

HEDDA. No matter what, I couldn't bear seeing you put in the shade by someone else.

TESMAN (*in an outburst of mingled joy and doubt*). Hedda! Oh, can it be true what you say? Yes, but . . . yes, but—you have never showed any such love for me before. Think of that!

HEDDA. And now perhaps I'd best tell you that—that I am . . . (*She vehemently breaks off.*) No, no—ask your Aunt Juliane—she'll tell you.

TESMAN. Oh, Hedda, I believe I understand! (*He claps his hands.*) Good Lord! Can it be possible, Hedda? Eh?

HEDDA. Don't shout like that! The maid will hear you!

TESMAN (*with a smile, unable to repress his joy*). The maid! Now that's really priceless, Hedda! The maid—why, that's Berte—that's Berte, I know! I am going to tell her myself!

HEDDA (*clenching her hands in desperation*). Oh, I can't bear all this! I shall die!

TESMAN. What's the matter, Hedda? Eh?

HEDDA (*with cold self-control*). All this—this ludicrous business—Jörgen!

TESMAN. Ludicrous? That I should show how overjoyed it makes me! But perhaps, after all, I'd better say nothing to Berte.

HEDDA. Oh yes—why not tell her everything?

TESMAN. No, no, not yet. But I think I ought to tell Aunt Juliane . . . And to think that you have started to call me by my first name, too! Think of that! Oh, Aunt Juliane will be so happy—so happy!

HEDDA. Also when she hears that I have burned Ejlert Lövborg's manuscript—for your sake?

TESMAN. Oh, I forgot about the manuscript! No—nobody must know a thing about the manuscript, of course. But that you should have such a burning love for me—*that* I shall certainly have to tell Aunt Juliane! I wonder —can such a thing be a common occurrence among newly married women, do you think? Eh?

HEDDA. Ask your Aunt Juliane about that, too, why don't you?

TESMAN. I'll do that, yes—as soon as I have a chance. (*Again he seems apprehensive and ill at ease.*) Oh but—oh but the manuscript! God in heaven, when I think of poor Ejlert, it makes me feel horrible, horrible!

(MRS. ELVSTED, *dressed as on her first visit, wearing a hat and coat, enters from the hall.*)

MRS. ELVSTED (*with a hurried greeting, in agitation*). Oh, Hedda dear, I hope you will forgive me for coming here once more today.

HEDDA. What has happened, Téa? Has anything happened to you?

TESMAN. Has it to do with Ejlert Lövborg? Eh?

MRS. ELVSTED. Yes, it has. I am so terribly afraid he has met with an accident.

HEDDA (*seizing her by the arm*). You say—an accident!

TESMAN. Oh but—in Heaven's name— what makes you think so, Mrs. Elvsted?

MRS. ELVSTED. I heard people at my lodgings talking about him—just as I returned home. Oh, there are all kinds of unbelievable rumors circulating about him in town today.

TESMAN. Yes, I heard that, too! Think of that! And I can testify that he went straight home and went to bed.

HEDDA. Well, what did they say at your lodgings?

MRS. ELVSTED, Oh, I didn't find out anything, really. I don't know whether they actually knew anything or not—or whether ... At any rate, as soon as they saw me, they stopped discussing him and I didn't dare ask them.

TESMAN (*moving about uneasily*). Let us hope for the best—let us hope you have heard wrong, Mrs. Elvsted.

MRS. ELVSTED. No, no, I am certain it was he they were discussing. And, besides, I heard them say something about the hospital, or ...

TESMAN. The hospital?

HEDDA. No—that couldn't possibly be!

MRS. ELVSTED. Oh—I was so frightfully concerned about him that I went to his lodgings and asked for him ...

HEDDA. Did you really do that, Téa?

MRS. ELVSTED. Yes, what else could I do? I couldn't bear the uncertainty any longer!

TESMAN. And I suppose you didn't find him there, did you? Eh?

MRS. ELVSTED. No. And nobody could tell me anything about him. He hadn't been at home since yesterday afternoon, they said.

TESMAN. Yesterday afternoon? That they could say a thing like that! Think of that!

MRS. ELVSTED. Oh, something must have happened to him—something terrible—I am sure of that!

TESMAN. Hedda dear—don't you think I ought to go and make a few inquiries here and there ...

HEDDA. No, no—don't you get involved in this!

(JUDGE BRACK, *with hat in hand, comes in through the hall door which* BERTE *holds open and closes after him. His mien is grave and he greets them silently.*)

TESMAN. Oh, it's you, my dear Judge? Eh?

JUDGE BRACK. Yes, it is absolutely necessary that I see you without delay.

TESMAN. I can see that you have received Aunt Juliane's message with the sad news.

JUDGE BRACK. That too, I received—yes.

TESMAN. Isn't it sad, don't you think? Eh?

JUDGE BRACK. Well, my dear Tesman, that depends on how you look at it.

TESMAN (*looking at him with a vague expression*). Has anything else happened?

JUDGE BRACK. Yes, it has.

HEDDA (*tensely*). Anything of a painful nature?

JUDGE BRACK. Again, that depends on how you look at it.

MRS. ELVSTED (*in an uncontrollable outburst*). Oh! It has something to do with Ejlert Lövborg!

JUDGE BRACK (*with a momentary glance at her*). What makes you think so? Perhaps you already know something about it?

MRS. ELVSTED (*in confusion*). No, no, I don't know a thing—but ...

TESMAN (*to* BRACK). But for God's sake, tell us what it is!

JUDGE BRACK (*with a shrug of the shoulders*). Well, I am sorry to say—Ejlert Lövborg has been taken to the hospital. He may not have long to live.

MRS. ELVSTED (*with a scream*). Oh God! Oh God!

TESMAN. To the hospital! And he is dying!

HEDDA (*involuntarily*). So quickly!

MRS. ELVSTED (*wailing*). And we parted in anger, Hedda!

HEDDA (*in a whisper to her*). But Téa—Téa!

MRS. ELVSTED (*ignoring her*). I must go to him! I must see him while he is still alive!

JUDGE BRACK. It's no use, Mrs. Elvsted. He is not permitted to have visitors.

MRS. ELVSTED. Oh, but please tell me what's happened to him! What's happened to him?

TESMAN. Yes, tell us! You don't mean that he has—that he has . . . ? Eh?

HEDDA. Yes, I'm sure that's what he has done!

TESMAN. Hedda—how can you . . . !

JUDGE BRACK (*looking fixedly at her*). I am sorry to say—you have guessed correctly, Mrs. Tesman.

MRS. ELVSTED. Oh, how frightful!

TESMAN. Suicide! Think of that!

HEDDA. Shot himself!

JUDGE BRACK. Again you guessed right, Mrs. Tesman.

MRS. ELVSTED (*in an attempt to be calm*). When did it happen, Judge Brack?

JUDGE BRACK. This afternoon. Between three and four.

TESMAN. But, good God—where—where did he do it? Eh?

JUDGE BRACK (*hesitatingly*). Where? Why, I imagine—I imagine he did it at his lodgings.

MRS. ELVSTED. No, he couldn't have done it there, for I stopped in there myself between six and seven.

JUDGE BRACK. Well, it may have been some other place, then. I don't know exactly. All I know is that they found him . . . He had shot himself—in the heart.

MRS. ELVSTED. Oh, how frightful! That he should come to an end like that!

HEDDA (*to* BRACK). He shot himself in the heart?

JUDGE BRACK. Yes, as I said.

HEDDA. And not in the temple?

JUDGE BRACK. In the heart, Mrs. Tesman.

HEDDA. Yes—yes—the heart is a good place, too.

JUDGE BRACK. What did you say, Mrs. Tesman?

HEDDA (*evasively*). Oh—it was nothing.

TESMAN. And you say the injury will prove fatal? Eh?

JUDGE BRACK. There is no chance for him to survive. He may already have died.

MRS. ELVSTED. Yes, yes, I have a feeling he is already gone! He is gone! Gone! Oh, Hedda!

TESMAN. But tell me—where did you hear all this?

JUDGE BRACK (*curtly*). From a police official I consulted.

HEDDA (*aloud*). At last—at last he has done something sublime!

TESMAN (*terrified*). God have mercy! What are you saying, Hedda?

HEDDA. I say there is beauty in this . . .

JUDGE BRACK. H'm, Mrs. Tesman . . .

TESMAN. Beauty! Why—think of that!

MRS. ELVSTED. Oh, Hedda, how can you say such things after what's happened!

HEDDA. Ejlert Lövborg has settled his account with life. He has had the courage to do—what had to be done.

MRS. ELVSTED. No, don't ever believe it happened that way! He was not in his right mind when he did it!

TESMAN. He did it in a moment of despair.

HEDDA. No, no! I am certain it was not that!

MRS. ELVSTED. Yes—he did it in despair! Just as when he tore the manuscript to pieces!

JUDGE BRACK (*startled*). The manuscript? Did you say the manuscript? He destroyed it!

MRS. ELVSTED. Yes—he did—last night.

TESMAN (*in a low whisper to* HEDDA). Oh, Hedda, we'll never get out of this.

JUDGE BRACK. H'm. This is really strange.

TESMAN (*walking to and fro*). Who would have thought that Ejlert Lövborg would leave this world in that way! And without leaving behind him this work of his that would have brought him enduring fame!

MRS. ELVSTED. Oh, if it could only be put together again!

TESMAN. Yes, think of it, if it could be put together! I would give anything to . . .

MRS. ELVSTED. Perhaps you could do it, Mr. Tesman?

TESMAN. What do you mean?

MRS. ELVSTED (searching in her pockets). Look—here! I have saved the notes he used when he dictated.

HEDDA (coming a step closer to them). Ah!

TESMAN. Oh, you have kept all the notes, Mrs. Elvsted? Have you really? Eh?

MRS. ELVSTED. Yes, I have them here. I brought them with me when I left home, and I have been keeping them in my pocket . . .

TESMAN. Oh—let me see them!

MRS. ELVSTED (hands him a batch of small paper notes). But they are all in disorder—all mixed up.

TESMAN. Think of it, if we could put them in order and make something out of this despite the difficulties! Perhaps—if we two could help each other, we . . .

MRS. ELVSTED. Oh yes—at any rate, let us try . . .

TESMAN. We must do it! We must! I shall dedicate my life to this task!

HEDDA. You, Jörgen? Your life?

TESMAN. Yes, or perhaps I should say, I'll give all my spare time to it. My own work will have to wait. Hedda—you understand my feelings, don't you? Eh? This is something I owe to Ejlert Lövborg's memory.

HEDDA. Perhaps you do.

TESMAN. And now, my dear Mrs. Elvsted, let us pull ourselves together. Good heavens, it's no use brooding over what has happened. Eh? We must try to calm ourselves sufficiently so that we . . .

MRS. ELVSTED. Yes, yes, Mr. Tesman. I'll do my best.

TESMAN. Well, then let us start. We must waste no time. We must go over his notes without delay. Where should we sit? Here? No, let's go into the other room. Pardon me, Judge Brack . . . You come with me, Mrs. Elvsted . . .

MRS. ELVSTED. Oh God! How I wish it could be done!

(TESMAN and MRS. ELVSTED go into the room in the back. She removes her hat and coat. They seat themselves at the table beneath the hanging lamp and immediately become engrossed in examining the notes. HEDDA goes over toward the stove and seats herself in the armchair. A moment later, JUDGE BRACK comes over to her.)

HEDDA (in a low tone of voice). Oh, Judge Brack—what a relief, what a consolation it gives me to know what Ejlert Lövborg has done!

JUDGE BRACK. Relief—consolation, Mrs. Hedda. Yes—for him, undoubtedly, it means freedom from . . .

HEDDA. I mean, it gives me a feeling of relief to know that in spite of everything there are people in this world who voluntarily, without compulsion, will do something courageous—something that is illumined by a gleam of sublime, perfect beauty!

JUDGE BRACK (with a smile). H'm, my dear Mrs. Hedda . . .

HEDDA. Oh, I know what you are going to say. For, after all, you are also one of those professional men—who, just as . . . Oh, well!

JUDGE BRACK (looking intently at her). Ejlert Lövborg has been more to you than you are willing to admit to yourself. Or could I be mistaken?

HEDDA. That's something I don't care to answer. All I know is that Ejlert Lövborg had the courage to live life as he wanted to. And now—this ending—this heroic act of his, with its aura of beauty, gives proof to me that he had the strength and the will to break away from the pleasures of life—at so young an age.

JUDGE BRACK. It pains me to do it, Mrs. Hedda—but I shall have to disillusion you of the beautiful picture you have created . . .

HEDDA. Disillusion?

JUDGE BRACK. . . . and which you would soon have seen destroyed, anyway.

HEDDA. What makes you say that?

JUDGE BRACK. He did not shoot himself—of his own free will.

HEDDA. Not of his own free will!

JUDGE BRACK. No. The death of Ejlert Lövborg did not occur exactly the way I told you.

HEDDA (tensely; emotionally). You have been

concealing something? What have you concealed?

JUDGE BRACK. For the sake of Mrs. Elvsted, I had to change some of the facts.

HEDDA. What is the truth, then?

JUDGE BRACK. First of all—he is already dead.

HEDDA. He died at the hospital?

JUDGE BRACK. Yes, and without regaining consciousness.

HEDDA. What else have you kept from us?

JUDGE BRACK. The incident did not take place at his lodgings.

HEDDA. Well, that really is of no great importance.

JUDGE BRACK. I wouldn't say that. For I must tell you that—that Ejlert Lövborg was found shot—in Miss Diana's boudoir.

HEDDA (is about to jump up but sinks back in her chair). Why, it can't be, Judge Brack! He couldn't have been there today again!

JUDGE BRACK. He was there this afternoon. He went there to call for something he insisted had been taken from him. He spoke confusedly about having lost his child.

HEDDA. Ah—that's the reason he . . .

JUDGE BRACK. I thought at first he must have meant his manuscript—but now that I hear he destroyed it, I can only suppose he was speaking of his wallet.

HEDDA. Yes, perhaps so. And you say—it was there they found him.

JUDGE BRACK. Yes, there's where they found him—with a discharged pistol in his breast pocket—and mortally wounded.

HEDDA. He shot himself in the heart—yes.

JUDGE BRACK. No—in the abdomen.

HEDDA (looking at him with an expression of disgust). That, too! Oh—everything I touch seems to be cursed—it turns into nothing but what is ludicrous and vulgar.

JUDGE BRACK. And to that you may add another thing, Mrs. Hedda. Something that fits into that same beastly category.

HEDDA. And what is that?

JUDGE BRACK. The pistol that was found in his breast pocket.

HEDDA (breathlessly). Well? What about it?

JUDGE BRACK. He must have stolen it.

HEDDA (jumps up). Stolen it? That's not true! He did not steal it!

JUDGE BRACK. There is no other explanation. He must have stolen it! Sh!

(TESMAN and MRS. ELVSTED have got up from the table in the rear room and come into the drawing room.)

TESMAN (with sheets of notebook paper in both hands). Hedda dear—it's almost impossible to see by that lamp in there. Think of that!

HEDDA. I'm thinking.

TESMAN. Perhaps you wouldn't mind if we sat at your writing table? Eh?

HEDDA. By all means! (Quickly.) No, wait! Let me tidy it up first.

TESMAN. Oh, don't bother to do that, Hedda. We'll have room enough.

HEDDA. No, no—let me clear it off first, I tell you. Let me put these things in the other room—on the piano. There!

(She pulls out a portfolio with scores of music from under the bookrack, puts a few other scores on top of the portfolio and takes them into the rear room, going toward the right. TESMAN spreads the notebook sheets on the writing table and moves the lamp from the corner table over to it. He and MRS. ELVSTED sit down and again set to work. HEDDA enters again.)

HEDDA (standing behind TÉA, gently runs her fingers through MRS. ELVSTED's hair and rumples it). Well, my sweet little Téa—how are you progressing with your memorial to Ejlert Lövborg?

MRS. ELVSTED (looks up at her with an expression of discouragement). Oh God! I'm afraid it's going to be a very difficult task.

TESMAN. It must be done—no matter how hard. And to put in order and classify and systematize methodically other people's writings—that is just the task for me.

(HEDDA moves over to the stove and sits down on one of the taborets. BRACK leans over her, bracing himself against the armchair.)

HEDDA (in a whisper). What was that you said about the pistol?

JUDGE BRACK (in a low voice). That he must have stolen it.

HEDDA. Why must he have stolen it?

JUDGE BRACK. Because any other explanation simply is out of the question.

HEDDA. Really?

JUDGE BRACK (with a glance at her). Ejlert

Lövborg was here this morning. Wasn't he?

HEDDA. Yes.

JUDGE BRACK. Were the two of you alone?

HEDDA. Yes—for a short time.

JUDGE BRACK. Did you leave the room while he was here? Did you?

HEDDA. No.

JUDGE BRACK. Think carefully. Weren't you out of the room for even a moment?

HEDDA. Well—I may have left for a moment —just to go out into the hall.

JUDGE BRACK. Where was your pistol case during that time?

HEDDA. It was inside the . . .

JUDGE BRACK. Where—Mrs. Hedda?

HEDDA. The case was standing over there —on the writing table.

JUDGE BRACK. Have you opened it since, to see whether both pistols were in it?

HEDDA. No.

JUDGE BRACK. And there is no need to. I have seen the pistol that was found on Lövborg. It was the same pistol you had yesterday. I had seen it on other occasions as well and I recognized it immediately.

HEDDA. Have you the pistol?

JUDGE BRACK. No, the police have it.

HEDDA. What will the police do with it?

JUDGE BRACK. They will make every effort to find the owner.

HEDDA. Do you think they will?

JUDGE BRACK (in a whisper, bending low over her). No, Hedda Gabler—not so long as I say nothing.

HEDDA (shrinking, she looks at him quizzically). And if you should not keep silent—what then?

JUDGE BRACK (with a shrug of the shoulders). There is always a way out—by saying the pistol was stolen.

HEDDA (firmly). I would rather die!

JUDGE BRACK (smiling). People say such things . . . But they don't do them.

HEDDA (does not reply). And consequently, since the pistol is not stolen—and if the owner should be found—what will happen then?

JUDGE BRACK. Well, Hedda—then there will be a scandal . . .

HEDDA. Scandal?

JUDGE BRACK. A scandal, yes—of which you have such a deadly fear. Naturally, you would have to appear in court—both you

and Miss Diana. She will have to testify how it all happened—whether it was an accident or a murder. Did Lövborg try to pull the pistol out of his pocket to intimidate or threaten her—and did the pistol go off? Or did she take it away from him and then shoot him, afterward putting the pistol back in his breast pocket? It would not be surprising if she had done just that. For she is a solidly built female, this Miss Diana!

HEDDA. This is all so revolting to me, and it does not concern me.

JUDGE BRACK. No—but you will have to answer when the question is put to you: Why did you give Ejlert Lövborg the pistol? And what conclusions will people draw from the fact that you gave him the pistol?

HEDDA (lowering her head). That is true. I hadn't thought of that.

JUDGE BRACK. Well, fortunately, you are in no danger so long as I say nothing.

HEDDA (looking up at him). So now I am in your clutches, Judge . . . From now on, you own me—body and soul . . .

JUDGE BRACK (whispering softly to her). Hedda, my dearest—believe me, I shall never misuse my privilege . . .

HEDDA. Nevertheless, I am in your power— subject to your demands, and your will. No longer free! Your slave! Your creature! (She rises violently.) No! That's something I could never endure! Never!

JUDGE BRACK (with a look, tinged with sarcasm) People usually learn to endure what is inevitable—somehow.

HEDDA (looking at him in the same way). Yes— perhaps they do. (She goes over to the writing table. Suppressing an involuntary smile and parroting TESMAN's intonations.) Well, Jörgen? Are you having any luck? Eh?

TESMAN. God knows, Hedda. In any case, it will mean many months of work.

HEDDA (as before). Well, think of that! (She softly runs her hands through MRS. ELVSTED's hair.) Doesn't this seem strange to you, Téa— sitting here with Tesman as you used to sit with Ejlert Lövborg?

MRS. ELVSTED. Oh God, I only wish I could inspire your husband in the same way.

HEDDA. I have no doubt that will come— with time.

TESMAN. Yes, to tell the truth, Hedda—I am actually beginning to feel as if I were. But go back and sit down with Judge Brack again . . .

HEDDA. Is there nothing I can do for you two—nothing I can help with?

TESMAN. No, not a thing. (*He turns his head.*) From now on, you will have to keep Hedda company, my dear Judge.

JUDGE BRACK (*with a glance at* HEDDA). That I will do with the utmost pleasure!

HEDDA. Thanks. But I am tired tonight. I am going inside and lie down on the sofa for a while.

TESMAN. Yes, do that, my dear. Eh?

(HEDDA *goes into the room in the back. She closes the portières after her. There is a brief pause. Suddenly wild dance music is heard being played within on the piano.*)

MRS. ELVSTED (*jumps up from her chair*). My God! What's that?

TESMAN (*rushes over to the center doorway*). But Hedda, my dearest—how can you be playing music like that at this time! Think of Aunt Rina! And of Ejlert, too!

HEDDA (*her head protruding from between the portières*). And don't forget Aunt Juliane! And the whole lot of them! But from now on I shan't disturb you any more . . . (*She pulls the portières together and withdraws from view.*)

TESMAN (*at the writing table*). I don't think she likes the idea of our doing this painful work . . . You know what we'll do, Mrs.

Elvsted! You go and live with Aunt Juliane. Then I'll come there in the evenings, and then we can work there. Eh?

MRS. ELVSTED. Yes, perhaps that is what we ought to do.

HEDDA (*from the inner room*). I hear what you say, Tesman. But what shall I be doing then to pass the time out here?

TESMAN (*searching among his notes and papers*). Oh, I am sure, Judge Brack will not neglect you.

JUDGE BRACK (*in the armchair, calls out jovially*). No, I'll be over every blessed evening, Mrs. Tesman! I am sure we two will have a very good time together!

HEDDA (*pointedly*). Yes—isn't that what you hope, Judge? You—the prize cock o' the walk . . .

(*A shot is heard from within.* TESMAN, MRS. ELVSTED, *and* BRACK *jump up from their seats, startled.*)

TESMAN. Oh, now Hedda is playing with those pistols again!

(*He draws the portières and runs inside, followed by* MRS. ELVSTED. HEDDA *is lying lifeless on the sofa. There is confusion, and sounds of consternation and shock are heard.* BERTE *enters, terror-stricken, from the left.*)

TESMAN (*shrieks to* BRACK). Shot herself! Shot herself in the temple! Think of that!

JUDGE BRACK (*sinking into the armchair, overcome with shock*). But—merciful God! People just don't do things like that!

## Tragedy in a Social Context

Most of Ibsen's realistic plays dealt with social problems and hence gave rise to the term "problem plays." The frankness of his presentation of divorce in *A Doll's House* and venereal disease in *Ghosts* so shocked his contemporaries that it obscured almost every other feature of the plays. However, he did not consider *Hedda Gabler* a problem play in spite of the importance he had given to the social situation. Writing to Moritz Prozor in 1890 he said: "It was not really my desire to deal in this play with so-called problems. What I principally wanted to do was to depict human beings, human emotions, and human destinies, upon a groundwork of certain of the social conditions and principles of the present day." *Hedda Gabler* is unquestionably a tragedy, but the playwright who studies character in the context of contemporary "social conditions and principles" is doing something very different from what was expected of the tragic poet by classical critics—to depict a great man of history or myth coming to misfortune through "error or frailty." Much as this Aristotelian formulation was discussed (and sometimes disagreed with), it was a common assumption that universal moral or religious principles, rather than social ones, were the "groundwork" of tragedy. It was comedy that usually dealt with manners and with departures from a social norm. It was also comedy that usually presented such a milieu as the middle-class academic world of Jörgen Tesman. A few "domestic" tragedies in the seventeenth and eighteenth centuries had dealt with such unheroic characters, but usually with the aim of pointing a plain moral in simpler terms than those of standard tragedy. Ibsen's play presents an experience totally unlike that of preceding comedy or tragedy.

For Shaw the novelty of Ibsen's plays was the introduction of discussion—that is, the dramatization of the issues underlying the situation. In some of Ibsen's plays there is overt discussion, as in the last scene of *A Doll's House*, but in *Hedda Gabler* most of the discussion is implicit in the presentation of the opposed ideals of Tesman, Hedda, Téa, and the others. Shaw wrote that in Ibsen "the drama arises through a conflict of unsettled ideals," but he pointed out that the "conflict is not between clear right and wrong." He thought the value of this technique lay in its challenge to the unconsidered moral assumptions of the audience. *Hedda Gabler* was one of a group of plays in which he believed that Ibsen had shown the dangers of idealism. It is open to question whether these statements of Shaw's lead to a completely satisfactory interpretation of the play, but they call attention to one of its salient features, the portrayal of Hedda's paradoxical relationship to the society in which she lives, fearing its disapproval while hating its restrictions—dreaming of something greater, and yet making a hideous and absurd mess of her attempt to inspire a great rebel.

Like Alceste, Hedda is totally disgusted with society, and like him she seems to have a somewhat greater stature than the defenders of things as they are, such as her pathetically unimaginative husband or her hypocritical would-be lover, Judge Brack, whose comment on her suicide ends the play with a crashing irony: "But—merciful God! People just don't do things like that!" Hedda frees herself from these people only by self-destruction. It is this pistol shot which differentiates her most sharply from Molière's misanthropist. Though she has lacked the courage of her convictions in the past, as when she refused Lövborg's advances, her pseudo-Byronic ideals finally push her to a desperation more genuine than we feel in Alceste's threat to retreat from the world.

The pistol shot is a highly theatrical stroke, testifying to what Ibsen learned from Scribe and other adroit play-makers. But it is far from mere sensationalism. Not only do all the lines of the plot meet in this final act, but the moment is charged with the cumulative significance of all the relationships with which the play has been concerned. It is Hedda's admission of defeat in her attempt to transform Ejlert Lövborg into a Greek god with vine leaves in his hair, and at the same time it is her own enactment of the scene she wanted him to play at the end—"Do it beautifully." It is also her answer to the blackmail of Judge Brack and a refutation of what he has offered her. The presence of Tesman and Téa on the stage adds many ironic overtones to the scene. The nobility of their project of reconstructing Lövborg's manuscript is somewhat undercut by Tesman's bad conscience over his indirect responsibility for the burning. His act is not so selfless as it is made to sound in his promise to dedicate his life to it. Téa is the real expert in self-sacrifice, however. Though there is no reason to doubt the genuineness of her idealism, there is grim comedy in Hedda's observation that

Téa has now transferred her field of operations from Lövborg to Tesman, and in Téa's starry-eyed reply: "Oh God, I only wish I could inspire your husband in the same way." The pistol shot is a terrible reminder of the difference between these two and Hedda. For it is above all her way of asserting the heroic and aristocratic values of General Gabler, whose pistol she uses and whose picture stares at us from the drawing room wall. There are few plays in which the author has managed to concentrate so much of his meaning into one dramatic moment.

### Selected Reading List for Ibsen

Robert Brustein, "Henrik Ibsen," *The Theatre of Revolt*. Boston: Little, Brown & Co., 1964, pp. 37–83.

John Gassner, "The Realistic Phase," *Form and Idea in Modern Theatre*. New York: The Dryden Press, 1956, pp. 3–76.

Janko Lavrin, *Ibsen, An Approach*. London: Methuen and Co., Ltd., 1950.

Bernard Shaw, *The Quintessence of Ibsenism*. New York: Hill and Wang, 1957.

Maurice Valency, *The Flower and the Castle*. New York: The Macmillan Company, 1963, pp. 58–237.

Hermann Weigand, *The Modern Ibsen*. New York: E. P. Dutton & Co. Inc., 1960.

# Chekhov and Stanislavski

In 1898 the most famous of all the theaters devoted to realistic drama, the Moscow Art Theater, was founded by Konstantin Stanislavski and Vladimir Nemirovich-Danchenko, eleven years after the opening of Antoine's Théâtre Libre in Paris. Stanislavski was concerned with every aspect of theatrical production, but especially with acting style. Like Antoine, he had been impressed with the innovations of a private company of actors belonging to the Duke of Saxe-Meinigen, who had toured Europe in the seventies and eighties, making themselves famous for the historical accuracy of their costumes and sets, for their ensemble acting, and for their crowd scenes, in which each actor was an individual and yet a carefully calculated part of the total effect. Stanislavski went on to develop still further acting techniques which give the impression of the utmost verisimilitude—techniques which continue to be influential in the theaters of Europe and America today. "The Method," as it is often called, has helped to form the acting style of a very large proportion of Broadway, Hollywood, and television actors. (In the Appendix, pp. 488–92, are selections from his book, *An Actor Prepares*, in which he discusses the principles of his approach to acting in the fictional form of an actor's reminiscences of his training with a director named Tortsov, the representative of Stanislavski himself.)

Stanislavski insisted that the actor live his part, familiarizing himself wherever possible with the most minute details of the milieu to which the character belongs, and seeking in his own experience equivalents for the character's emotions, in order to express them on the stage with complete conviction. Because of his emphasis on psychological truth, Stanislavski has been accused of being opposed to the more conventional kinds of training in diction, voice-projection, and bodily movement, but in fact, he was fully aware of the importance of this aspect of technique. What he opposed was the mechanical acting which could result from exclusive concentration on externals. However, even more important than any of the devices he used to develop realistic acting was his basic concern with the unity of effect to which every detail of acting and production must contribute. His notes describe the hours of planning for a single set, in order to provide the perfect background for certain lines and pieces of stage business; the additional hours devoted to the lighting and sound effects necessary to project the mood of the scene. No one has ever been a more effective advocate of the total theatrical experience.

One of the first great successes of the Moscow Art Theater in 1898 was *The Seagull*, which had failed two years before when it was put on by another company. The success of this performance established the new acting group and made the reputation of a playwright who up to that time had won little recognition. Anton Chekhov was born in a small provincial town in Russia in 1860. Twenty-four years later he took his medical degree from the University of Moscow, but writing, especially writing for the theater, interested him more than medicine. He had written twelve plays before *The Seagull*, but was so discouraged by its initial failure that he decided to give up playwriting. Nemirovich-Danchenko's interest in the play persuaded him to allow the Moscow Art Theater to revive it, and their success encouraged him to write three other plays before his death in 1904: *Uncle Vanya*, *Three Sisters*, and *The Cherry Orchard*. All were performed at the Moscow Art Theater.

Like the French realists and like Stanislavski, Chekhov was disgusted by the artificiality of the theater of his day. He believed that art should show "life as it is," and thought that even Ibsen was guilty of falsifying for the sake of dramatic effect. He did not wish to be associated with the naturalists, however, who seemed to him (as they did to Ibsen) to cultivate the sordid for its own sake. Chekhov sought for a faithfulness to life which was not mere reportage, and a dramatic form which was effective without being meretricious.

The little episode of Treplev's play in the first act of *The Seagull* provides an insight into Chekhov's concept of the theater. Treplev objects to the artifice, the banality, and the moral shallowness of the contemporary theater, and it is important to notice that the plays he despises are not romantic extravaganzas but realistic plays of an earlier generation, such as *La Dame aux Camélias* by Dumas *fils*: "When the curtain goes up, and by artificial light, in a room with three walls, these great geniuses, the devotees of holy art, represent how people eat, drink, love, move about, and wear their jackets; when from these commonplace sentences and pictures they try to draw a moral . . ." and so forth. He is offended by the egotism of the actors (including his mother) and by the falseness and vulgarity of the stage picture of life. On the other hand, his own play is pretentiously arty in its situation, dialogue, and even the attempt to use nature itself—the lake—as the backdrop. Nina, sympathetic as she is, points out that "there are no living characters" in the play, and Madame Arkadin's laughter, though cruel, is deserved. We may infer that Chekhov had no more sympathy with this sort of symbolist experiment (especially such an amateurish one) than with obvious contrivance or uninspired imitation of everyday life. His own realism incorporated symbols such as the seagull without destroying the impression of verisimilitude, but it did much more than reproduce surfaces; it penetrated to the inner life of his characters, which it was Stanislavski's aim to bring out by his method of acting.

From the very first speech to the last we must try to hear the intonations of the speakers and listen for the overtones which reveal unspoken truths about the characters or hint at such themes as the difference between true art and mere contrivance. Ideally, then, we must be simultaneously attuned to a subtle variety of realism in character portrayal and to a more abstract discussion of the problems of the artist. What seems to be the most casual flow of conversation may contribute to the understanding of both topics.

# The Seagull

### A COMEDY IN FOUR ACTS

## ANTON CHEKHOV

## CHARACTERS*

IRINA NIKOLAYEVNA ARKADIN (I-rí-na Ni-ko-lá-yev-na Ar-ká-din) (MA-DAME TREPLEV) (Trep-lyóf) *an actress*

KONSTANTIN GAVRILOVITCH TREPLEV (Kon-stan-tín Ga-vrí-lo-vitch Trep-lyóf) *her son, a young man*

PYOTR NIKOLAYEVITCH SORIN (Pyó-tr Ni-ko-lá-ye-vitch Só-rin) *her brother*

NINA MIHAILOVNA ZARETCHNY (Ní-na Mi-háï-lov-na Za-rétch-ny) *a young girl, the daughter of a wealthy Landowner*

ILYA AFANASYEVITCH SHAMRAEV (Il-yá A-fa-ná-sye-vitch Sham-rá-yef) *a retired Lieutenant,* SORIN'S *Steward*

POLINA ANDREYEVNA (Pó-li-na An-dré-yev-na) *his wife*

MASHA (Má-sha) *his daughter*

BORIS ALEXEYEVITCH TRIGORIN (Bo-rís Al-ex-é-ye-vitch Tri-gó-rin) *a literary man*

YEVGENY SERGEYEVITCH DORN (Yev-ghé-ny Ser-ghé-ye-vitch Dorn) *a doctor*

SEMYON SEMYONOVITCH MEDVEDENKO

---

*The Seagull* by Anton Chekhov, translated by Constance Garnett. Reprinted by permission of Chatto & Windus Ltd. and of the estate of Constance Garnett.
* (The pronunciation in parentheses following each name has been added by the editor. Vowel sounds are pronounced approximately as in French or German.)

(Sem-yón Sem-yó-no-vitch Med-ve-dén-ko) *a schoolmaster*

YAKOV (Yá-kof) *a labourer*

A MAN COOK

A HOUSEMAID

*The action takes place in* SORIN'S *house and garden. Between the third and fourth acts there is an interval of two years.*

## ACT I

*Part of the park on* SORIN'S *estate. Wide avenue leading away from the spectators into the depths of the park towards the lake is blocked up by a platform roughly put together for private theatricals, so that the lake is not visible. To right and left of the platform, bushes. A few chairs, a little table.*

*The sun has just set.* YAKOV *and other labourers are at work on the platform behind the curtain; there is the sound of coughing and hammering.* MASHA *and* MEDVEDENKO *enter on the left, returning from a walk.*

MEDVEDENKO. Why do you always wear black?

MASHA. I am in mourning for my life. I am unhappy.

MEDVEDENKO. Why? (*Pondering.*) I don't understand . . . You are in good health; though your father is not very well off, he has got enough. My life is much harder than yours. I only get twenty-three roubles a month, and from that they deduct something for the pension fund, and yet I don't wear mourning. (*They sit down.*)

MASHA. It isn't money that matters. A poor man may be happy.

MEDVEDENKO. Theoretically, yes; but in practice it's like this: there are my two

358

sisters and my mother and my little brother and I, and my salary is only twenty-three roubles. We must eat and drink, mustn't we? One must have tea and sugar. One must have tobacco. It's a tight fit.

MASHA (*looking round at the platform*). The play will soon begin.

MEDVEDENKO. Yes. Miss Zaretchny will act: it is Konstantin Gavrilitch's play. They are in love with each other and to-day their souls will be united in the effort to realise the same artistic effect. But your soul and mine have not a common point of contact. I love you. I am so wretched I can't stay at home. Every day I walk four miles here and four miles back and I meet with nothing but indifference from you. I can quite understand it. I am without means and have a big family to keep.... Who would care to marry a man who hasn't a penny to bless himself with?

MASHA. Oh, nonsense! (*Takes a pinch of snuff.*) Your love touches me, but I can't reciprocate it—that's all. (*Holding out the snuff-box to him.*) Help yourself.

MEDVEDENKO. I don't feel like it (*a pause*).

MASHA. How stifling it is! There must be a storm coming.... You're always discussing theories or talking about money. You think there is no greater misfortune than poverty, but to my mind it is a thousand times better to go in rags and be a beggar than ... But you wouldn't understand that. though....

(SORIN *and* TREPLEV *enter on the right.*)

SORIN (*leaning on his walking-stick*). I am never quite myself in the country, my boy, and, naturally enough, I shall never get used to it. Last night I went to bed at ten and woke up this morning at nine feeling as though my brain were glued to my skull, through sleeping so long (*laughs*). And after dinner I accidentally dropped off again, and now I am utterly shattered and feel as though I were in a nightmare, in fact....

TREPLEV. Yes, you really ought to live in town.(*Catches sight of* MASHA *and* MEDVEDENKO.) When the show begins, my friends, you will be summoned, but you mustn't be here now. You must please go away.

SORIN (*to* MASHA). Marya Ilyinishna, will you be so good as to ask your papa to tell them to take the dog off the chain?—it howls. My sister could not sleep again last night.

MASHA. Speak to my father yourself; I am not going to. Please don't ask me. (*To* MEDVEDENKO.) Come along!

MEDVEDENKO (*to* TREPLEV). So you will send and let us know before it begins. (*Both go out.*)

SORIN. So I suppose the dog will be howling all night. What a business it is! I have never done as I liked in the country. In old days I used to get leave for twenty-eight days and come here for a rest and so on, but they worried me so with all sorts of trifles that before I had been here two days I was longing to be off again (*laughs*). I've always been glad to get away from here.... But now I am on the retired list, and I have nowhere else to go, as a matter of fact. I've got to live here whether I like it or not....

YAKOV (*to* TREPLEV). We are going to have a bathe, Konstantin Gavrilitch.

TREPLEV. Very well; but don't be more than ten minutes (*looks at his watch*). It will soon begin.

YAKOV. Yes, sir (*goes out*).

TREPLEV (*looking round the stage*). Here is our theatre. The curtain, then the first wing, then the second, and beyond that—open space. No scenery of any sort. There is an open view of the lake and the horizon. We shall raise the curtain at exactly half-past eight, when the moon rises.

SORIN. Magnificent.

TREPLEV. If Nina is late it will spoil the whole effect. It is time she was here. Her father and her stepmother keep a sharp eye on her, and it is as hard for her to get out of the house as to escape from prison (*puts his uncle's cravat straight*). Your hair and your beard are very untidy. They want clipping or something....

SORIN (*combing out his beard*). It's the tragedy of my life. Even as a young man I looked as though I had been drinking for days or something of the sort. I was never a favorite with the ladies (*sitting down*). Why is your mother out of humour?

TREPLEV. Why? Because she is bored (*sitting down beside him*). She is jealous. She is set against me, and against the performance, and against my play because Nina is acting in it, and she is not. She does not know my play, but she hates it.

SORIN (*laughs*). What an idea!

TREPLEV. She is annoyed to think that even on this little stage Nina will have a triumph and not she (*looks at his watch*). My mother is a psychological freak. Unmistakably talented, intelligent, capable of sobbing over a book, she will reel off all Nekrassov[1] by heart; as a sick nurse she is an angel; but just try praising Duse[2] in her presence! O-ho! You must praise no one but herself, you must write about her, make a fuss over her, be in raptures over her extraordinary acting in "La Dame aux Camélias"[3] or the "Ferment of Life"; but she has none of this narcotic in the country, she is bored and cross, and we are all her enemies—we are all in fault. Then she is superstitious—she is afraid of three candles, of the number thirteen. She is stingy. She has got seventy thousand roubles in a bank at Odessa—I know that for a fact—but ask her to lend you some money, and she will burst into tears.

SORIN. You imagine your mother does not like your play, and you are already upset and all that. Don't worry; your mother adores you.

TREPLEV (*pulling the petals off a flower*). Loves me, loves me not; loves me, loves me not; loves me, loves me not (*laughs*). You see, my mother does not love me. I should think not! She wants to live, to love, to wear light blouses; and I am twenty-five, and I am a continual reminder that she is no longer young. When I am not there she is only thirty-two, but when I am there she is forty-three, and for that she hates me. She knows, too, that I have no belief in the theatre. She loves the stage, she fancies she is working for

humanity, for the holy cause of art, while to my mind the modern theatre is nothing but tradition and conventionality. When the curtain goes up, and by artificial light in a room with three walls, these great geniuses, the devotees of holy art, represent how people eat, drink, love, move about, and wear their jackets; when from these commonplace sentences and pictures they try to draw a moral—a petty moral, easy of comprehension and convenient for domestic use; when in a thousand variations I am offered the same thing over and over again—I run away as Maupassant ran away from the Eiffel Tower which weighed upon his brain with its vulgarity.

SORIN. You can't do without the stage.

TREPLEV. We need new forms of expression. We need new forms, and if we can't have them we had better have nothing (*looks at his watch*). I love my mother—I love her very much—but she leads a senseless sort of life, always taken up with this literary gentleman, her name is always trotted out in the papers—and that wearies me. And sometimes the simple egoism of an ordinary mortal makes me feel sorry that my mother is a celebrated actress, and I fancy that if she were an ordinary woman I should be happier. Uncle, what could be more hopeless and stupid than my position? She used to have visitors, all celebrities—artists and authors—and among them all I was the only one who was nothing, and they only put up with me because I was her son. Who am I? What am I? I left the University in my third year—owing to circumstances "for which we accept no responsibility," as the editors say; I have no talents, I haven't a penny of my own, and on my passport I am described as an artisan of Kiev. You know my father was an artisan of Kiev, though he too was a well-known actor. So, when in her drawing-room all these artists and authors graciously noticed me, I always fancied from their faces that they were taking the measure of my insignificance—I guessed their thoughts and suffered from the humiliation. . . .

SORIN. And, by the way, can you tell me, please, what sort of man this literary gentle-

---

[1] *Nekrassov* (Nikolai Alexeyevitch, 1821–1877), Russian poet; a peoples' poet, idol of the reformers [2]*Duse* (Eleonora, 1859–1924), in 1897 gave a famous performance of *La Dame aux Camélias;* associated with Sarah Bernhardt as one of the two greatest actresses of her time [3]*La Dame aux Camélias* the best play of Dumas *fils* (1824–1895), written in 1848

man is? There's no making him out. He never says anything.

TREPLEV. He is an intelligent man, good-natured and rather melancholy, you know. A very decent fellow. He is still a good distance off forty, but he is already celebrated and has enough and to spare of everything. As for his writings . . . what shall I say? They are charming, full of talent, but . . . after Tolstoy or Zola you do not care to read Trigorin.

SORIN. Well, I am fond of authors, my boy. At one time I had a passionate desire for two things: I wanted to get married, and I wanted to become an author; but I did not succeed in doing either. Yes, it is pleasant to be even a small author, as a matter of fact.

TREPLEV (*listens*). I hear steps . . . (*embraces his uncle*). I cannot live without her. . . . The very sound of her footsteps is lovely. . . . I am wildly happy (*goes quickly to meet* NINA ZARETCHNY *as she enters*). My enchantress— my dream. . . .

NINA (*in agitation*). I am not late. . . . Of course I am not late. . . .

TREPLEV (*kissing her hands*). No, no, no!

NINA. I have been uneasy all day. I was so frightened. I was afraid father would not let me come. . . . But he has just gone out with my stepmother. The sky is red, the moon is just rising, and I kept urging on the horse (*laughs*). But I am glad (*shakes* SORIN'S *hand warmly*).

SORIN (*laughs*). Your eyes look as though you have been crying. . . . Fie, fie! That's not right!

NINA. Oh, it was nothing. . . . You see how out of breath I am. I have to go in half an hour. We must make haste. I can't stay, I can't! For God's sake don't keep me! My father doesn't know I am here.

TREPLEV. It really is time to begin. We must go and call the others.

SORIN. I'll go this minute (*goes to the right, singing* "To France two grenadiers." *Looks round*). Once I sang like that, and a deputy prosecutor said to me, "You have a powerful voice, your Excellency"; then he thought a little and added, "but not a pleasant one" (*laughs and goes off*).

NINA. My father and his wife won't let me come here. They say it is so Bohemian here . . . they are afraid I shall go on the stage. . . . But I feel drawn to the lake here like a seagull. . . . My heart is full of you (*looks round*).

TREPLEV. We are alone.

NINA. I fancy there is someone there.

TREPLEV. There's nobody. (*They kiss.*)

NINA. What tree is this?

TREPLEV. An elm.

NINA. Why is it so dark?

TREPLEV. It's evening; everything is getting dark. Don't go away early, I entreat you!

NINA. I must.

TREPLEV. And if I come to you, Nina, I'll stand in the garden all night, watching your window.

NINA. You can't; the watchman would notice you. Trésor is not used to you, and he would bark.

TREPLEV. I love you!

NINA. Sh-h. . . .

TREPLEV (*hearing footsteps*). Who is there? You, Yakov?

YAKOV (*behind the stage*). Yes, sir.

TREPLEV. Take your places. It's time to begin. Is the moon rising?

YAKOV. Yes, sir.

TREPLEV. Have you got the methylated spirit? Have you got the sulphur? When the red eyes appear there must be a smell of sulphur. (*To* NINA.) Go, it's all ready. Are you nervous?

NINA. Yes, awfully! Your mother is all right—I am not afraid of her—but there's Trigorin . . . I feel frightened and ashamed of acting before him . . . a celebrated author. . . . Is he young?

TREPLEV. Yes.

NINA. How wonderful his stories are.

TREPLEV (*coldly*). I don't know. I haven't read them.

NINA. It is difficult to act in your play. There are no living characters in it.

TREPLEV. Living characters! One must depict life not as it is, and not as it ought to be, but as we see it in our dreams.

NINA. There is very little action in your play—nothing but speeches. And to my mind there ought to be love in a play. (*Both go behind the stage.*)

(*Enter* POLINA ANDREYEVNA *and* DORN.)

POLINA. It is getting damp. Go back and put on your goloshes.

DORN. I am hot.

POLINA. You don't take care of yourself. It's obstinacy. You are a doctor, and you know perfectly well that damp air is bad for you, but you want to make me miserable; you sat out on the verandah all yesterday evening on purpose. . . .

DORN (*hums*). "Do not say that youth is ruined."

POLINA. You were so absorbed in conversation with Irina Nikolayevna. . . you did not notice the cold. Own up . . . you are attracted by her.

DORN. I am fifty-five.

POLINA. Nonsense! That's not old for a man. You look very young for your age, and are still attractive to women.

DORN. Well, what would you have?

POLINA. All you men are ready to fall down and worship an actress, all of you!

DORN (*hums*). "Before thee once again I stand." If artists are liked in society and treated differently from merchants, for example, that's only in the nature of things. It's idealism.

POLINA. Women have always fallen in love with you and thrown themselves on your neck. Is that idealism too?

DORN (*shrugs his shoulders*). Well, in the attitude of women to me there has been a great deal that was good. What they principally loved in me was a first-rate doctor. You remember that ten or fifteen years ago I was the only decent accoucheur in the district. Then, too, I have always been an honest man.

POLINA (*seizes him by the hand*). Dearest!

DORN. Sh-h! They are coming.

(*Enter* MADAME ARKADIN *arm in arm with* SORIN, TRIGORIN, SHAMRAEV, MEDVEDENKO *and* MASHA.)

SHAMRAEV. In the year 1873 she acted marvellously at the fair at Poltava. It was a delight! She acted exquisitely! Do you happen to know, madam, where Pavel Semyonitch Tchadin, a comic actor, is now? His Rasplyuev was inimitable, even finer than Sadovsky's, I assure you, honoured lady. Where is he now?

MADAME ARKADIN. You keep asking me about antediluvians. How should I know? (*Sits down.*)

SHAMRAEV (*with a sigh*). Pashka Tchadin! There are no such actors now. The stage has gone down, Irina Nikolayevna! In old days there were mighty oaks, but now we see nothing but stumps.

DORN. There are few actors of brilliant talents nowadays, that's true; but the average level of acting is far higher than it was.

SHAMRAEV. I can't agree with you. But, of course, it's a matter of taste. *De gustibus aut bene aut nihil.*[4]

(TREPLEV *comes out from behind the stage.*)

MADAME ARKADIN (*to her son*). My dear son, when is it going to begin?

TREPLEV. In a minute. I beg you to be patient.

MADAME ARKADIN (*recites from* "Hamlet").
"Oh, Hamlet, speak no more!
Thou turn'st mine eyes into my
    very soul;
And there I see such black and
    grained spots
As will not leave their tinct."

TREPLEV (*from* "Hamlet").
"And let me wring your heart, for
    so I shall,
If it be made of penetrable stuff."[5]

(*A horn is sounded behind the stage.*)

TREPLEV. Ladies and gentlemen, we begin! I beg you to attend (*a pause*). I begin (*taps with a stick and recites aloud*). Oh, you venerable old shadows that float at nighttime over this lake, lull us to sleep and let us dream of what will be in two hundred thousand years!

SORIN. There will be nothing in two hundred thousand years.

---

[4] *De gustibus aut bene aut nihil* Shamraev is apparently confusing two Latin proverbs, "*De gustibus non est disputandum*" ("There is no disputing about tastes") and "*De mortuis nil nisi bonum*" ("Of the dead speak kindly or not at all"), and the motto, "*Aut Caesar aut nihil*" ("Either Caesar or nothing") [5] Quotations from *Hamlet*: III.4.89–92; III.4.36–7

TREPLEV. Then let them present that nothing to us.

MADAME ARKADIN. Let them. We are asleep. (*The curtain rises; the view of the lake is revealed; the moon is above the horizon, its reflection in the water;* NINA ZARETCHNY, *all in white, is sitting on a big stone.*)

NINA. Men, lions, eagles and partridges, horned deer, geese, spiders, silent fish that dwell in the water, starfishes and creatures which cannot be seen by the eye—all living things, all living things, all living things, having completed their cycle of sorrow, are extinct.... For thousands of years the earth has borne no living creature on its surface, and this poor moon lights its lamp in vain. On the meadow the cranes no longer waken with a cry, and there is no sound of the May beetles in the lime trees. It is cold, cold, cold! Empty, empty, empty! Dreadful, dreadful, dreadful! (*a pause.*) The bodies of living creatures have vanished into dust, and eternal matter has transformed them into rocks, into water, into clouds, while the souls of all have melted into one. That world-soul I am—I.... In me is the soul of Alexander the Great, of Cæsar, of Shakespeare and of Napoleon, and of the lowest leech. In me the consciousness of men is blended with the instincts of the animals, and I remember all, all, all! And I live through every life over again in myself! (*Will-of-the-wisps appear.*)

MADAME ARKADIN (*softly*). It's something decadent.

TREPLEV (*in an imploring and reproachful voice*). Mother!

NINA. I am alone. Once in a hundred years I open my lips to speak, and my voice echoes mournfully in the void, and no one hears.... You too, pale lights, hear me not. ... The stagnant marsh begets you before daybreak and you wander until dawn, but without thought, without will, without the tremor of life. For fear that life should spring up in you the father of eternal matter, the devil, keeps the atoms in you, as in the stones and in the water, in continual flux, and you are changing perpetually. For in all the universe nothing remains permanent and unchanged but the spirit (*a pause*).

Like a prisoner cast into a deep, empty well I know not where I am and what awaits me. All is hidden from me but that in the cruel, persistent struggle with the devil—the principle of the forces of matter—I am destined to conquer, and, after that, matter and spirit will be blended in glorious harmony and the Kingdom of the Cosmic Will will come. But that will come only little by little, through long, long thousands of years when the moon and the bright Sirius and the earth are changed to dust.... Till then—terror, terror... (*a pause; two red spots appear upon the background of the lake*). Here my powerful foe, the devil, is approaching. I see his dreadful crimson eyes....

MADAME ARKADIN. There's a smell of sulphur. Is that as it should be?

TREPLEV. Yes.

MADAME ARKADIN (*laughs*). Oh, it's a stage effect!

TREPLEV. Mother!

NINA. He is dreary without man—

POLINA (*to* DORN). You have taken your hat off. Put it on or you will catch cold.

MADAME ARKADIN. The doctor has taken his hat off to the devil, the father of eternal matter.

TREPLEV (*firing up, aloud*). The play is over! Enough! Curtain!

MADAME ARKADIN. What are you cross about?

TREPLEV. Enough! The curtain! Let down the curtain! (*Stamping.*) Curtain! (*The curtain falls.*) I am sorry! I lost sight of the fact that only a few of the elect may write plays and act in them. I have infringed the monopoly. I...I... (*Tries to say something more, but with a wave of his hand goes out on left.*)

MADAME ARKADIN. What's the matter with him?

SORIN. Irina, you really must have more consideration for youthful vanity, my dear.

MADAME ARKADIN. What did I say to him?

SORIN. You hurt his feelings.

MADAME ARKADIN. He told us beforehand that it was a joke, and I regarded his play as a joke.

SORIN. All the same...

MADAME ARKADIN. Now it appears that he has written a great work. What next! So he has got up this performance and smothered us with sulphur not as a joke but as a protest. . . He wanted to show us how to write and what to act. This is getting tiresome! These continual sallies at my expense—these continual pinpricks would put anyone out of patience, say what you like. He is a vain, whimsical boy!

SORIN. He meant to give you pleasure.

MADAME ARKADIN. Really? He did not choose an ordinary play, however, but made us listen to this decadent delirium. For the sake of a joke I am ready to listen to delirium, but here we have pretensions to new forms and a new view of art. To my thinking it's no question of new forms at all, but simply bad temper.

TRIGORIN. Everyone writes as he likes and as he can.

MADAME ARKADIN. Let him write as he likes and as he can, only let him leave me in peace.

DORN. Jupiter! you are angry. . . .

MADAME ARKADIN. I am not Jupiter—I am a woman (*lights a cigarette*). I am not angry—I am only vexed that a young man should spend his time so drearily. I did not mean to hurt his feelings.

MEDVEDENKO. No one has any grounds to separate spirit from matter, seeing that spirit itself may be a combination of material atoms. (*With animation, to* TRIGORIN.) But you know someone ought to write a play on how we poor teachers live, and get it acted. We have a hard, hard life.

MADAME ARKADIN. That's true, but don't let us talk either of plays or of atoms. It is such a glorious evening! Do you hear? There is singing! (*Listens.*) How nice it is!

POLINA. It's on the other side of the lake (*a pause*).

MADAME ARKADIN (*to* TRIGORIN). Sit down beside me. Ten or fifteen years ago there were sounds of music and singing on that lake continually almost every night. There are six country houses on the shores of the lake. I remember laughter, noise, shooting, and love affairs without end. . . . The *jeune premier* and the idol of all those six households was in those days our friend here, the doctor (*motions with her head towards* DORN), Yevgeny Sergeitch. He is fascinating still, but in those days he was irresistible. But my conscience is beginning to

trouble me. Why did I hurt my poor boy's feelings? I feel worried. (*Aloud.*) Kostya! Son! Kostya!

MASHA. I'll go and look for him.

MADAME ARKADIN. Please do, my dear.

MASHA (*going to the left*). Aa-oo! Konstantin Gavrilitch! Aa-oo! (*goes off*).

NINA (*coming out from behind the stage*). Apparently there will be no going on, and I may come out. Good evening! (*Kisses* MADAME ARKADIN *and* POLINA ANDREYEVNA.)

SORIN. Bravo! Bravo!

MADAME ARKADIN. Bravo! Bravo! We admired you. With such an appearance, with such a lovely voice, you really cannot stay in the country; it is a sin. You must have talent. Do you hear? It's your duty to go on the stage.

NINA. Oh, that's my dream! (*Sighing.*) But it will never be realised.

MADAME ARKADIN. Who knows? Here, let me introduce Boris Alexeyevitch Trigorin.

NINA. Oh, I am so glad . . . (*overcome with embarrassment*). I am always reading your . . .

MADAME ARKADIN (*making her sit down beside them*). Don't be shy, my dear. He is a celebrity, but he has a simple heart. You see, he is shy himself.

DORN. I suppose we may raise the curtain; it's rather uncanny.

SHAMRAEV (*aloud*). Yakov, pull up the curtain, my lad. (*The curtain goes up.*)

NINA (*to* TRIGORIN). It is a queer play, isn't it?

TRIGORIN. I did not understand it at all. But I enjoyed it. You acted so genuinely. And the scenery was delightful (*a pause*). There must be a lot of fish in that lake.

NINA. Yes.

TRIGORIN. I love angling. There is nothing I enjoy so much as sitting on the bank of a river in the evening and watching the float.

NINA. But I should have thought that for anyone who has known the enjoyment of creation, no other enjoyment can exist.

MADAME ARKADIN (*laughing*). Don't talk like that. When people say nice things to him he is utterly floored.

SHAMRAEV. I remember one evening in the opera theatre in Moscow the celebrated Silva took the lower *C!* As it happened, there was sitting in the gallery the bass of our church choir, and all at once—imagine our intense astonishment—we heard from the gallery "Bravo, Silva!" a whole octave lower—like this: (*in a deep bass*) "Bravo, Silva!" The audience sat spellbound (*a pause*).

DORN. The angel of silence has flown over us.

NINA. It's time for me to go. Good-bye.

MADAME ARKADIN. Where are you off to? Why so early? We won't let you go.

NINA. My father expects me.

MADAME ARKADIN. What a man, really ... (*kisses her*). Well, there is no help for it. I am sorry—I am sorry to let you go.

NINA. If you knew how grieved I am to go.

MADAME ARKADIN. Someone ought to see you home, my little dear.

NINA (*frightened*). Oh, no, no!

SORIN (*to her, in an imploring voice*). Do stay!

NINA. I can't, Pyotr Nikolayevitch.

SORIN. Stay for an hour. What is there in that?

NINA (*thinking a minute, tearfully*). I can't! (*Shakes hands and hurriedly goes off.*)

MADAME ARKADIN. Unfortunate girl she is, really. They say her mother left her father all her immense property—every farthing of it—and now the girl has got nothing, as her father has already made a will leaving everything to his second wife. It's monstrous!

DORN. Yes, her father is a pretty thorough scoundrel, one must do him the justice to say so.

SORIN (*rubbing his cold hands*). Let us go too, it's getting damp. My legs ache.

MADAME ARKADIN. They seem like wooden legs, you can hardly walk. Let us go, unlucky old man! (*Takes his arm.*)

SHAMRAEV (*offering his arm to his wife*). Madame?

SORIN. I hear that dog howling again. (*To* SHAMRAEV.) Be so kind, Ilya Afanasyitch, as to tell them to let it off the chain.

SHAMRAEV. It's impossible, Pyotr Nikolayevitch, I am afraid of thieves getting into the barn. Our millet is there. (*To* MEDVEDENKO *who is walking beside him.*) Yes, a whole octave lower: "Bravo, Silva!" And he not a singer—simply a church chorister!

MEDVEDENKO. And what salary does a chorister get? (*All go out except* DORN.)

DORN (*alone*). I don't know, perhaps I know

nothing about it, or have gone off my head, but I like the play. There is something in it. When that girl talked about loneliness and afterwards when the devil's eyes appeared, I was so excited that my hands trembled. It is fresh, naïve.... Here he comes, I believe. I want to say all the nice things I can to him.

TREPLEV (*enters*). They have all gone.

DORN. I am here.

TREPLEV. Mashenka is looking for me all over the park. Insufferable creature she is!

DORN. Konstantin Gavrilitch, I liked your play extremely. It's a strange thing, and I haven't heard the end, and yet it made a strong impression! You are a gifted man—you must persevere.

(TREPLEV *presses his hand warmly and embraces him impulsively.*)

DORN. Fie, what an hysterical fellow! There are tears in his eyes! What I mean is this. You have taken a subject from the realm of abstract ideas. So it should be, for a work of art ought to express a great idea. A thing is only fine when it is serious. How pale you are!

TREPLEV. So you tell me to persevere?

DORN. Yes.... But write only of what is important and eternal. You know, I have had varied experiences of life, and have enjoyed it; I am satisfied, but if it had been my lot to know the spiritual heights which artists reach at the moment of creation, I should, I believe, have despised my bodily self and all that appertains to it and left all things earthly as far behind as possible.

TREPLEV. Excuse me, where is Nina?

DORN. And another thing. In a work of art there ought to be a clear definite idea. You ought to know what is your aim in writing, for if you go along that picturesque route without a definite goal you will be lost and your talent will be your ruin.

TREPLEV (*impatiently*). Where is Nina?

DORN. She has gone home.

TREPLEV (*in despair*). What am I to do? I want to see her ... I must see her.... I must go....

(*Enter* MASHA.)

DORN (*to* TREPLEV). Calm yourself, my boy.

TREPLEV. But I am going all the same. I must go.

MASHA. Come indoors, Konstantin Gavrilitch. Your mother wants you. She is worried.

TREPLEV. Tell her that I have gone away. And I beg you—all of you—leave me in peace! Let me alone! Don't follow me about!

DORN. Come, come, come, dear boy. . . . You can't go on like that. . . . That's not the thing.

TREPLEV (*in tears*). Good-bye, doctor. Thank you . . . (*goes off*).

DORN (*with a sigh*). Youth! youth!

MASHA. When people have nothing better to say, they say, "Youth! youth!" . . . (*Takes a pinch of snuff.*)

DORN (*takes her snuff-box from her and flings it into the bushes*). That's disgusting! (*a pause*). I believe they are playing the piano indoors. We must go in.

MASHA. Wait a little.

DORN. What is it?

MASHA. I want to tell you once more. I have a longing to talk . . . (*growing agitated*). I don't care for my father . . . but I feel drawn to you. For some reason I feel with all my heart that you are very near me. . . . Help me. Help me, or I shall do something silly, I shall make a mock of my life and ruin it. . . . I can't go on. . . .

DORN. What is it? Help you in what?

MASHA. I am miserable. No one, no one knows how miserable I am! (*Laying her head on his breast, softly.*) I love Konstantin!

DORN. How hysterical they all are! How hysterical! And what a lot of love. . . . Oh, the sorcery of the lake! (*Tenderly.*) But what can I do, my child? What? What?

CURTAIN


## ACT II

*A croquet lawn. The house with a big verandah in the background on the right, on the left is seen the lake with the blazing sun reflected in it.*

*Flower beds. Midday. Hot.* MADAME ARKADIN, DORN *and* MASHA *are sitting on a garden seat in the shade of an old lime tree on one side of the croquet lawn.* DORN *has an open book on his knee.*

MADAME ARKADIN (*to* MASHA). Come, let us stand up. (*They both get up.*) Let us stand side by side. You are twenty-two and I am nearly twice as old. Yevgeny Sergeitch, which of us looks the younger?

DORN. You, of course.

MADAME ARKADIN. There! And why is it? Because I work, I feel I am always on the go, while you stay always in the same place and have no life at all. . . . And it is my rule never to look into the future. I never think about old age or death. What is to be, will be.

MASHA. And I feel as though I had been born long, long ago; I trail my life along like an endless train. . . . And often I have not the slightest desire to go on living (*sits down*). Of course, that's all nonsense. I must shake myself and throw it all off.

DORN (*hums quietly*). "Tell her, my flowers."

MADAME ARKADIN. Then I am as particular as an Englishman. I keep myself in hand, as they say, my dear, and am always dressed and have my hair done *comme il faut*. Do I allow myself to go out of the house even into the garden in a dressing-gown, or without my hair being done? Never! What has preserved me is that I have never been a dowdy, I have never let myself go, as some women do . . . (*walks about the lawn with her arms akimbo*). Here I am, as brisk as a bird. I could take the part of a girl of fifteen.

DORN. Nevertheless, I shall go on (*takes up the book*). We stopped at the corn merchant and the rats. . . .

MADAME ARKADIN. And the rats. Read (*sits down*). But give it to me, I'll read. It is my turn (*takes the book and looks in it*). And rats. . . . Here it is. . . . (*Reads*) "And of course for society people to spoil novelists and to attract them to themselves is as dangerous as for a corn merchant to rear rats in his granaries. And yet they love them. And so, when a woman has picked out an author whom she desires to captivate, she lays siege to him by means of compliments, flattery and favours . . ." Well, that may be so with the French, but there is nothing like that with us, we have no set rules. Among us, before a woman sets to work to captivate an author, she is generally head over ears in love herself, if you please. To go no further, take Trigorin and me. . . .

(*Enter* SORIN, *leaning on his stick and with*

*him* NINA; MEDVEDENKO *wheels an empty bath-chair in after them.*)

SORIN (*in a caressing tone, as to a child*). Yes? We are delighted, aren't we? We are happy to-day at last? (*To his sister.*) We are delighted! Our father and stepmother have gone off to Tver, and we are free now for three whole days.

NINA (*sits down beside* MADAME ARKADIN *and embraces her*). I am happy! Now I belong to you.

SORIN (*sits down in his bath-chair*). She looks quite a beauty to-day.

MADAME ARKADIN. Nicely dressed and interesting. ... That's a good girl (*kisses* NINA). But we mustn't praise you too much for fear of ill-luck. Where is Boris Alexeyevitch?

NINA. He is in the bathing-house, fishing.

MADAME ARKADIN. I wonder he doesn't get sick of it! (*is about to go on reading*).

NINA. What is that?

MADAME ARKADIN. Maupassant's "Sur l'eau," my dear (*reads a few lines to herself*). Well, the rest isn't interesting or true (*shuts the book*). I feel uneasy. Tell me, what's wrong with my son? Why is he so depressed and ill-humoured? He spends whole days on the lake and I hardly ever see him.

MASHA. His heart is troubled. (*To* NINA, *timidly.*) Please, do read us something out of his play!

NINA (*shrugging her shoulders*). Would you like it? It's so uninteresting.

MASHA (*restraining her enthusiasm*). When he reads anything himself his eyes glow and his face turns pale. He has a fine mournful voice, and the gestures of a poet.

(*There is a sound of* SORIN *snoring.*)

DORN. Good night!

MADAME ARKADIN. Petrusha!

SORIN. Ah?

MADAME ARKADIN. Are you asleep?

SORIN. Not a bit of it (*a pause*).

MADAME ARKADIN. You do nothing for your health, brother, and that's not right.

SORIN. I should like to take something, but the doctor won't give me anything.

DORN. Take medicine at sixty!

SORIN. Even at sixty one wants to live!

DORN (*with vexation*). Oh, very well, take valerian drops!

MADAME ARKADIN. It seems to me it would do him good to go to some mineral springs.

DORN. Well, he might go. And he might not.

MADAME ARKADIN. What is one to make of that?

DORN. There's nothing to make of it. It's quite clear (*a pause*).

MEDVEDENKO. Pyotr Nikolayevitch ought to give up smoking.

SORIN. Nonsense!

DORN. No, it's not nonsense. Wine and tobacco destroy the personality. After a cigar or a glass of vodka, you are not Pyotr Nikolayevitch any more but Pyotr Nikolayevitch plus somebody else; your ego is diffused and you feel towards yourself as to a third person.

SORIN (*laughs*). It's all very well for you to argue! You've lived your life, but what about me? I have served in the Department of Justice for twenty-eight years, but I haven't lived yet, I've seen and done nothing as a matter of fact, and very naturally I want to live very much. You've had enough and you don't care, and so you are inclined to be philosophical, but I want to live, and so I drink sherry at dinner and smoke cigars and so on. That's all it comes to.

DORN. One must look at life seriously, but to go in for cures at sixty and to regret that one hasn't enjoyed oneself enough in one's youth is frivolous, if you will forgive my saying so.

MASHA (*gets up*). It must be lunch-time (*walks with a lazy, lagging step*). My leg is gone to sleep (*goes off*).

DORN. She will go and have a couple of glasses before lunch.

SORIN. She has no personal happiness, poor thing.

DORN. Nonsense, your Excellency.

SORIN. You argue like a man who has had all he wants.

MADAME ARKADIN. Oh, what can be more boring than this sweet country boredom! Hot, still, no one ever doing anything, everyone airing their theories. ... It's nice being with you, my friends, charming to listen to you, but ... to sit in a hotel room somewhere and learn one's part is ever so much better.

NINA (*enthusiastically*). Delightful! I understand you.

SORIN. Of course, it's better in town. You sit in your study, the footman lets no one in unannounced, there's a telephone ... in the streets there are cabs and everything. . . .

DORN (*hums*). "Tell her, my flowers."

(ENTER SHAMRAEV, *and after him* POLINA ANDREYEVNA.)

SHAMRAEV. Here they are! Good morning! (*Kisses* MADAME ARKADIN'S *hand and then* NINA'S.) Delighted to see you in good health. (*To* MADAME ARKADIN.) My wife tells me that you are proposing to drive into town with her to-day. Is that so?

MADAME ARKADIN. Yes, we are thinking of it.

SHAMRAEV. Hm! that's splendid, but how are you going, honoured lady? They are carting the rye to-day; all the men are at work. What horses are you to have, allow me to ask?

MADAME ARKADIN. What horses? How can I tell which?

SORIN. We've got carriage horses.

SHAMRAEV (*growing excited*). Carriage horses! But where am I to get collars for them? Where am I to get collars? It's a strange thing! It passes my understanding! Honoured lady! forgive me, I am full of reverence for your talent. I would give ten years of my life for you, but I cannot let you have the horses!

MADAME ARKADIN. But if I have to go! It's a queer thing!

SHAMRAEV. Honoured lady! you don't know what farming means.

MADAME ARKADIN (*flaring up*). That's the old story! If that's so, I go back to Moscow to-day. Give orders for horses to be hired for me at the village, or I'll walk to the station.

SHAMRAEV (*flaring up*). In that case I resign my position! You must look for another steward (*goes off*).

MADAME ARKADIN. It's like this every summer; every summer I am insulted here! I won't set my foot in the place again (*goes off at left where the bathing shed is supposed to be; a minute later she can be seen entering the house.* TRIGORIN *follows her, carrying fishing rods and tackle, and a pail*).

SORIN (*flaring up*). This is insolence! It's beyond everything. I am thoroughly sick of it. Send all the horses here this minute!

NINA (*to* POLINA ANDREYEVNA). To refuse Irina Nikolayevna, the famous actress! Any wish of hers, any whim even, is of more consequence than all your farming. It's positively incredible!

POLINA (*in despair*). What can I do? Put yourself in my position: what can I do?

SORIN (*to* NINA). Let us go to my sister. We will all entreat her not to go away. Won't we? (*Looking in the direction in which* SHAMRAEV *has gone*.) Insufferable man! Despot!

NINA (*preventing him from getting up*). Sit still, sit still. We will wheel you in. (*She and* MEDVEDENKO *push the bath-chair*.) Oh, how awful it is!

SORIN. Yes, yes, it's awful. But he won't leave, I'll speak to him directly. (*They go out;* DORN *and* POLINA ANDREYEVNA *are left alone on the stage*.)

DORN. People are tiresome. Your husband ought to be simply kicked out, but it will end in that old woman Pyotr Nikolayevitch and his sister begging the man's pardon. You will see!

POLINA. He has sent the carriage horses into the fields too! And there are misunderstandings like this every day. If you only knew how it upsets me! It makes me ill; see how I am trembling. . . . I can't endure his rudeness. (*In an imploring voice*.) Yevgeny, dearest, light of my eyes, my darling, let me come to you. . . . Our time is passing, we are no longer young, and if only we could lay aside concealment and lying for the end of our lives, anyway . . . (*a pause*).

DORN. I am fifty-five; it's too late to change my life.

POLINA. I know you refuse me because there are other women too who are as near to you. You can't take them all to live with you. I understand. Forgive me, you are tired of me.

(NINA *appears near the house; she is picking flowers*.)

DORN. No, it's all right.

POLINA. I am wretched from jealousy. Of course you are a doctor, you can't avoid women. I understand.

DORN (to NINA, who comes up to them). How are things going?

NINA. Irina Nikolayevna is crying and Pyotr Nikolayevitch has an attack of asthma.

DORN (gets up). I'd better go and give them both valerian drops.

NINA (gives him the flowers). Please take these.

DORN. Merci bien (goes towards the house).

POLINA (going with him). What charming flowers! (Near the house, in a smothered voice.) Give me those flowers! Give me those flowers! (On receiving them tears the flowers to pieces and throws them away; both go into the house.)

NINA (alone). How strange it is to see a famous actress cry, and about such a trivial thing! And isn't it strange? A famous author, adored by the public, written about in all the papers, his photographs for sale, his works translated into foreign languages— and he spends the whole day fishing and is delighted that he has caught two gudgeon. I thought famous people were proud, unapproachable, that they despised the crowd, and by their fame and the glory of their name, as it were, revenged themselves on the vulgar herd for putting rank and wealth above everything. But here they cry and fish, play cards, laugh and get cross like everyone else!

TREPLEV (comes in without a hat on, with a gun and a dead seagull). Are you alone here?

NINA. Yes.

(TREPLEV lays the seagull at her feet.)

NINA. What does that mean?

TREPLEV. I was so mean as to kill this bird to-day. I lay it at your feet.

NINA. What is the matter with you? (Picks up the bird and looks at it.)

TREPLEV (after a pause). Soon I shall kill myself in the same way.

NINA. You have so changed, I hardly know you.

TREPLEV. Yes, ever since the day when I hardly knew you. You have changed to me, your eyes are cold, you feel me in the way.

NINA. You have become irritable of late, you express yourself so incomprehensibly, as it were in symbols. This bird is a symbol too, I suppose, but forgive me, I don't understand it (lays the seagull on the seat). I am too simple to understand you.

TREPLEV. This began from that evening when my play came to grief so stupidly. Women never forgive failure. I have burnt it all; every scrap of it. If only you knew how miserable I am! Your growing cold to me is awful, incredible, as though I had woken up and found this lake had suddenly dried up or sunk into the earth. You have just said that you are too simple to understand me. Oh, what is there to understand? My play was not liked, you despise my inspiration, you already consider me commonplace, insignificant, like so many others ... (stamping). How well I understand it all, how I understand it! I feel as though I had a nail in my brain, damnation take it together with my vanity which is sucking away my life, sucking it like a snake ... (sees TRIGORIN, who comes in reading a book). Here comes the real genius, walking like Hamlet and with a book too. (Mimics.) "Words, words, words." ... The sun has scarcely reached you and you are smiling already, your eyes are melting in its rays. I won't be in your way (goes off quickly).

TRIGORIN (making notes in his book). Takes snuff and drinks vodka. Always in black. The schoolmaster is in love with her. ...

NINA. Good morning, Boris Alexeyevitch!

TRIGORIN. Good morning. Circumstances have turned out so unexpectedly that it seems we are setting off to-day. We are hardly likely to meet again. I am sorry. I don't often have the chance of meeting young girls, youthful and charming; I have forgotten how one feels at eighteen or nineteen and can't picture it to myself, and so the young girls in my stories and novels are usually false. I should like to be in your shoes just for one hour to find out how you think, and altogether what sort of person you are.

NINA. And I should like to be in your shoes.

TRIGORIN. What for?

NINA. To know what it feels like to be a famous, gifted author. What does it feel like to be famous? How does it affect you, being famous?

TRIGORIN. How? Nohow, I believe. I have

never thought about it. (*After a moment's thought*.) It's one of two things: either you exaggerate my fame, or it never is felt at all.

NINA. But if you read about yourself in the newspapers?

TRIGORIN. When they praise me I am pleased, and when they abuse me I feel out of humour for a day or two.

NINA. What a wonderful world! If only you knew how I envy you! How different people's lots in life are! Some can scarcely get through their dull, obscure existence, they are all just like one another, they are all unhappy; while others—you, for instance—you are one out of a million, have an interesting life full of brightness and significance. You are happy.

TRIGORIN. I? (*Shrugging his shoulders*.) Hm. . . . You talk of fame and happiness, of bright interesting life, but to me all those fine words, if you will forgive my saying so, are just like a sweetmeat which I never taste. You are very young and very good-natured.

NINA. Your life is splendid!

TRIGORIN. What is there particularly nice in it? (*Looks at his watch*.) I must go and write directly. Excuse me, I mustn't stay . . . (*laughs*). You have stepped on my favourite corn, as the saying is, and here I am beginning to get excited and a little cross. Let us talk though. We will talk about my splendid bright life. . . . Well, where shall we begin? (*After thinking a little*.) There are such things as fixed ideas, when a man thinks days and night, for instance, of nothing but the moon. And I have just such a moon. I am haunted day and night by one persistent thought: I ought to be writing, I ought to be writing, I ought . . . I have scarcely finished one novel when, for some reason, I must begin writing another, then a third, after the third a fourth. I write incessantly, post haste, and I can't write in any other way. What is there splendid and bright in that, I ask you? Oh, it's an absurd life! Here I am with you; I am excited, yet every moment I remember that my unfinished novel is waiting for me. Here I see a cloud that looks like a grand piano. I think that I must put into a story somewhere that a cloud sailed by that looked like a grand piano. There is a scent of heliotrope. I hurriedly make a note: a sickly smell, a widow's flower, to be mentioned in the description of a summer evening. I catch up myself and you at every sentence, every word, and make haste to put those sentences and words away into my literary treasure-house—it may come in useful! When I finish work I race off to the theatre or to fishing; if only I could rest in that and forget myself. But no, there's a new subject rolling about in my head like a heavy iron cannon ball, and I am drawn to my writing table and must make haste again to go on writing and writing. And it's always like that, always. And I have no rest from myself, and I feel that I am eating up my own life, and that for the sake of the honey I give to someone in space I am stripping the pollen from my best flowers, tearing up the flowers themselves and trampling on their roots. Don't you think I am mad? Do my friends and acquaintances treat me as though I were sane? "What are you writing? What are you giving us?" It's the same thing again and again, and it seems to me as though my friends' notice, their praises, their enthusiasm—that it's all a sham, that they are deceiving me as an invalid and I am somehow afraid that they will steal up to me from behind, snatch me and carry me off and put me in a mad-house. And in those years, the best years of my youth, when I was beginning, my writing was unmixed torture. A small writer, particularly when he is not successful, seems to himself clumsy, awkward, unnecessary; his nerves are strained and overwrought. He can't resist hanging about people connected with literature and art, unrecognised and unnoticed by anyone, afraid to look anyone boldly in the face, like a passionate gambler without any money. I hadn't seen my reader, but for some reason I always imagined him hostile, and mistrustful. I was afraid of the public, it alarmed me, and when I had to produce my first play it always seemed to me that all the dark people felt hostile and all the fair ones were coldly indifferent. Oh, how awful it was! What agony it was!

NINA. But surely inspiration and the very

process of creation give you moments of exalted happiness?

TRIGORIN. Yes. While I am writing I enjoy it. And I like reading my proofs, but . . . as soon as it is published I can't endure it, and I see that it is all wrong, a mistake, that it ought not to have been written at all, and I feel vexed and sick about it . . . (laughing). And the public reads it and says: "Yes, charming, clever. Charming, but very inferior to Tolstoy," or, "It's a fine thing, but Turgenev's 'Fathers and Children' is finer." And it will be the same to my dying day, only charming and clever, charming and clever—and nothing more. And when I die my friends, passing by my tomb, will say, "Here lies Trigorin. He was a good writer, but inferior to Turgenev."

NINA. Forgive me, but I refuse to understand you. You are simply spoiled by success.

TRIGORIN. What success? I have never liked myself; I dislike my own work. The worst of it is that I am in a sort of delirium, and often don't understand what I am writing. I love this water here, the trees, the sky. I feel nature, it arouses in me a passionate, irresistible desire to write. But I am not simply a landscape painter; I am also a citizen. I love my native country, my people; I feel that if I am a writer I am in duty bound to write of the people, of their sufferings, of their future, to talk about science and the rights of man and so on, and so on, and I write about everything. I am hurried and flustered, and on all sides they whip me up and are angry with me; I dash about from side to side like a fox beset by hounds. I see life and culture continually getting farther and farther away while I fall farther and farther behind like a peasant too late for the train; and what it comes to is that I feel I can only describe scenes and in everything else I am false to the marrow of my bones.

NINA. You are overworked and have not the leisure nor the desire to appreciate your own significance. You may be dissatisfied with yourself, but for others you are great and splendid! If I were a writer like you, I should give up my whole life to the common herd, but I should know that there could be no greater happiness for them than to rise

to my level, and they would harness themselves to my chariot.

TRIGORIN. My chariot, what next! Am I an Agamemnon, or what?[6] (Both smile.)

NINA. For such happiness as being a writer or an artist I would be ready to endure poverty, disappointment, the dislike of those around me; I would live in a garret and eat nothing but rye bread, I would suffer from being dissatisfied with myself, from recognising my own imperfections, but I should ask in return for fame . . . real, resounding fame . . . (covers her face with her hands). It makes me dizzy. . . . Ough!

(The voice of MADAME ARKADIN from the house.)

MADAME ARKADIN. Boris Alexeyevitch!

TRIGORIN. They are calling for me. I suppose it's to pack. But I don't want to leave here. (Looks round at the lake.) Just look how glorious it is! It's splendid!

NINA. Do you see the house and garden on the other side of the lake?

TRIGORIN. Yes.

NINA. That house was my dear mother's. I was born there. I have spent all my life beside this lake and I know every little islet on it.

TRIGORIN. It's very delightful here! (Seeing the seagull) And what's this?

NINA. A seagull. Konstantin Gavrilitch shot it.

TRIGORIN. A beautiful bird. Really, I don't want to go away. Try and persuade Irina Nikolayevna to stay (makes a note in his book).

NINA. What are you writing?

TRIGORIN. Oh, I am only making a note. A subject struck me (putting away the notebook). A subject for a short story: a young girl, such as you, has lived all her life beside a lake; she loves the lake like a seagull, and is as free and happy as a seagull. But a man comes by chance, sees her, and having nothing better to do, destroys her like that seagull here (a pause).

(MADAME ARKADIN appears at the window.)

---

6 "Am I an Agamemnon, or what?" cf. also p. 376; like Agamemnon with Clytemnestra, Trigorin shows his susceptibility to women's flattery

MADAME ARKADIN. Boris Alexeyevitch, where are you?

TRIGORIN. I am coming. (*Goes and looks back at* NINA. *To* MADAME ARKADIN *at the window.*) What is it?

MADAME ARKADIN. We are staying.

(TRIGORIN *goes into the house.*)

NINA (*advances to the footlights; after a few moment's meditation*). It's a dream!

CURTAIN

## ACT III

*The dining-room in* SORIN'S *house. Doors on right and on left. A sideboard. A medicine cupboard. A table in the middle of the room. A portmanteau and hat-boxes; signs of preparation for departure.* TRIGORIN *is having lunch;* MASHA *stands by the table.*

MASHA. I tell all this to you as a writer. You may make use of it. I am telling you the truth: if he had hurt himself seriously I would not have gone on living another minute. But I have pluck enough all the same. I just made up my mind that I would tear this love out of my heart, tear it out by the roots.

TRIGORIN. How are you going to do that?

MASHA. I am going to be married. To Medvedenko.

TRIGORIN. That's the schoolmaster?

MASHA. Yes.

TRIGORIN. I don't understand what's the object of it.

MASHA. To love without hope, to spend whole years waiting for something. . . . But when I marry, there will be no time left for love, new cares will smother all the old feelings. And, anyway, it will be a change, you know. Shall we have another?

TRIGORIN. Won't that be too much?

MASHA. Oh, come! (*fills two glasses*). Don't look at me like that! Women drink much oftener than you imagine. Only a small proportion drink openly as I do, the majority drink in secret. Yes. And it's always vodka or brandy. (*Clinks glasses.*) My best wishes! You are a good-hearted man; I am sorry to be parting from you. (*They drink.*)

TRIGORIN. I don't want to go myself.

MASHA. You should beg her to stay.

TRIGORIN. No, she won't stay now. Her son is behaving very tactlessly. First, he shoots himself, and now they say he is going to challenge me to a duel. And whatever for? He sulks, and snorts, and preaches new forms of art. . . . But there is room for all—new and old—why quarrel about it?

MASHA. Well, there's jealousy too. But it is nothing to do with me.

(*A pause.* YAKOV *crosses from right to left with a portmanteau.* NINA *enters and stands by the window.*)

MASHA. My schoolmaster is not very brilliant, but he is a good-natured man, and poor, and he is very much in love with me. I am sorry for him. And I am sorry for his old mother. Well, let me wish you all happiness. Don't remember evil against me (*shakes hands with him warmly*). I am very grateful for your friendly interest. Send me your books and be sure to put in an inscription. Only don't write, "To my honoured friend," but write simply, "To Marya who belongs nowhere and has no object in life." Good-bye! (*Goes out.*)

NINA (*stretching out her arm towards* TRIGORIN, *with her fist clenched*). Odd or even?

TRIGORIN. Even.

NINA (*with a sigh*). Wrong. I had only one pea in my hand. I was trying my fortune whether to go on the stage or not. I wish someone would advise me.

TRIGORIN. It's impossible to advise in such a matter (*a pause*).

NINA. We are parting and . . . perhaps we shall never meet again. Won't you please take this little medallion as a parting gift? I had your initials engraved on one side of it . . . and on the other the title of your book, "Days and Nights."

TRIGORIN. How exquisite! (*Kisses the medallion.*) A charming present!

NINA. Think of me sometimes.

TRIGORIN. I shall think of you. I shall think of you as you were on that sunny day—do you remember?—a week ago, when you were wearing a light dress . . . we were talking . . . there was a white seagull lying on the seat.

NINA (*pensively*). Yes, a seagull . . . (*a pause*).

We can't talk any more, there's someone coming. . . . Let me have two minutes before you go, I entreat you . . . (*goes out on the left*).

(*At the same instant* MADAME ARKADIN, SORIN *in a dress coat with a star of some order on it, then* YAKOV, *occupied with the luggage, enter on the right.*)

MADAME ARKADIN. Stay at home, old man. With your rheumatism you ought not to go gadding about. (*To* TRIGORIN.) Who was that went out? Nina?

TRIGORIN. Yes.

MADAME ARKADIN. *Pardon*, we interrupted you (*sits down*). I believe I have packed everything. I am worn out.

TRIGORIN (*reads on the medallion*). " 'Days and Nights', page 121, lines 11 and 12."

YAKOV (*clearing the table*). Am I to pack your fishing things too, sir?

TRIGORIN. Yes, I shall want them again. You can give away the hooks.

YAKOV. Yes, sir.

TRIGORIN (*to himself*). Page 121, lines 11 and 12. What is there in those lines? (*To* MADAME ARKADIN.) Are there copies of my books in the house?

MADAME ARKADIN. Yes, in my brother's study, in the corner bookcase.

TRIGORIN. Page 121 . . . (*goes out*).

MADAME ARKADIN. Really, Petrusha, you had better stay at home.

SORIN. You are going away; it will be dreary for me at home without you.

MADAME ARKADIN. And what is there in the town?

SORIN. Nothing particular, but still . . . (*laughs*). There will be the laying of the foundation-stone of the Zemstvo-hall, and all that sort of thing. One longs to shake oneself free from this stagnant existence, if only for an hour or two. I've been too long on the shelf like some old cigarette-holder. I have ordered the horses for one o'clock; we'll set off at the same time.

MADAME ARKADIN (*after a pause*). Come, stay here, don't be bored and don't catch cold. Look after my son. Take care of him. Give him good advice (*a pause*). Here I am going away and I shall never know why Konstantin tried to shoot himself. I fancy jealousy was the chief cause, and the sooner I get Trigorin away from here, the better.

SORIN. What can I say? There were other reasons too. It's easy to understand; he is young, intelligent, living in the country, in the wilds, with no money, no position and no future. He has nothing to do. He is ashamed of his idleness and afraid of it. I am very fond of him indeed, and he is attached to me, yet in spite of it all he feels he is superfluous in the house, that he is a dependent, a poor relation. It's easy to understand, it's *amour propre*. . . .

MADAME ARKADIN. He is a great anxiety to me! (*Pondering*.) He might go into the service, perhaps.

SORIN (*begins to whistle, then irresolutely*). I think that quite the best thing would be if you were to . . . let him have a little money. In the first place he ought to be able to be dressed like other people and all that. Just look at him, he's been going about in the same wretched jacket for the last three years and he has no overcoat . . . (*laughs*). It would do him no harm to have a little fun . . . to go abroad or something. . . . It wouldn't cost much.

MADAME ARKADIN. But all the same . . . I might manage the suit, perhaps, but as for going abroad . . . No, just at the moment I can't even manage the suit. (*Resolutely*.) I have no money!

(SORIN *laughs*.)

MADAME ARKADIN. No!

SORIN (*begins to whistle*). Quite so. Forgive me, my dear, don't be cross. I believe you. . . . You are a generous, noble-hearted woman.

MADAME ARKADIN (*weeping*). I have no money.

SORIN. If I had money, of course I would give him some myself, but I have nothing, not a half-penny (*laughs*). My steward takes all my pension and spends it all on the land and the cattle and the bees, and my money is all wasted. The bees die, and the cows die, they never let me have horses. . . .

MADAME ARKADIN. Yes, I have money, but you see I am an actress; my dresses alone are enough to ruin me.

SORIN. You are a kind, good creature . . . I respect you. . . . Yes . . . but there, I got a touch of it again . . . (*staggers*). I feel dizzy (*clutches at the table*). I feel ill and all that.

MADAME ARKADIN (*alarmed*). Petrusha! (*trying to support him*). Petrusha, my dear! (*Calling.*) Help! help!

(*Enter* TREPLEV *with a bandage round his head and* MEDVEDENKO.)

MADAME ARKADIN. He feels faint!

SORIN. It's all right, it's all right! (*smiles and drinks some water*). It's passed off . . . and all that.

TREPLEV (*to his mother*). Don't be frightened, mother, it's not serious. Uncle often has these attacks now. (*To his uncle.*) You must lie down, uncle.

SORIN. For a little while, yes. . . . But I am going to the town all the same. . . . I'll lie down a little and then set off. . . . It's quite natural (*goes out leaning on his stick*).

MEDVEDENKO (*gives him his arm*). There's a riddle: in the morning on four legs, at noon on two, in the evening on three. . . .

SORIN (*laughs*). Just so. And at night on the back. Thank you, I can manage alone. . . .

MEDVEDENKO. Oh come, why stand on ceremony! (*Goes out with* SORIN.)

MADAME ARKADIN. How he frightened me!

TREPLEV. It is not good for him to live in the country. He gets depressed. If you would be generous for once, mother, and lend him fifteen hundred or two thousand roubles, he could spend a whole year in town.

MADAME ARKADIN. I have no money. I am an actress, not a banker (*a pause*).

TREPLEV. Mother, change my bandage. You do it so well.

MADAME ARKADIN (*takes out of the medicine cupboard some iodoform and a box with bandaging material*). The doctor is late.

TREPLEV. He promised to be here at ten, and it is midday already.

MADAME ARKADIN. Sit down (*takes the bandage off his head*). It's like a turban. Yesterday a stranger asked in the kitchen what nationality you were. But you have almost completely healed. There is the merest trifle left (*kisses him on the head*). You won't do anything naughty again while I am away, will you?

TREPLEV. No, mother. It was a moment of mad despair when I could not control myself. It won't happen again. (*Kisses her hand.*) You have such clever hands. I remember, long

ago, when you were still acting at the Imperial Theatre—I was little then—there was a fight in our yard and a washerwoman, one of the tenants, was badly beaten. Do you remember? She was picked up senseless . . . you looked after her, took her remedies and washed her children in a tub. Don't you remember?

MADAME ARKADIN. No (*puts on a fresh bandage*).

TREPLEV. Two ballet dancers lived in the same house as we did at the time. . . . They used to come to you and have coffee. . . .

MADAME ARKADIN. I remember that.

TREPLEV. They were very pious (*a pause*). Just lately, these last days, I have loved you as tenderly and completely as when I was a child. I have no one left now but you. Only why, why do you give yourself up to the influence of that man?

MADAME ARKADIN. You don't understand him, Konstantin. He is a very noble character. . . .

TREPLEV. And yet when he was told I was going to challenge him, the nobility of his character did not prevent him from funking it. He is going away. Ignominious flight!

MADAME ARKADIN. What nonsense! It is I who am asking him to go.

TREPLEV. A very noble character! Here you and I are almost quarrelling over him, and at this very moment he is somewhere in the drawing-room or the garden laughing at us . . . developing Nina, trying to convince her finally that he is a genius.

MADAME ARKADIN. You take a pleasure in saying unpleasant things to me. I respect that man and beg you not to speak ill of him before me.

TREPLEV. And I don't respect him. You want me to think him a genius too, but forgive me, I can't tell lies, his books make me sick.

MADAME ARKADIN. That's envy. There's nothing left for people who have pretension without talent but to attack real talent. Much comfort in that, I must say!

TREPLEV (*ironically*). Real talent! (*Wrathfully.*) I have more talent than all of you put together if it comes to that! (*tears the bandage off his head*). You, with your hackneyed conventions, have usurped the supremacy in art and consider nothing real and legitimate but what you do yourselves; everything else you stifle and suppress. I don't believe in you! I don't believe in you or in him!

MADAME ARKADIN. Decadent!

TREPLEV. Get away to your charming theatre and act there in your paltry, stupid plays!

MADAME ARKADIN. I have never acted in such plays. Let me alone! You are not capable of writing even a wretched burlesque! You are nothing but a Kiev shopman! living on other people!

TREPLEV. You miser!

MADAME ARKADIN. You ragged beggar!

(TREPLEV *sits down and weeps quietly.*)

MADAME ARKADIN. Nonentity! (*walking up and down in agitation*). Don't cry.... You mustn't cry (*weeps*). Don't ... (*kisses him on the forehead, on the cheeks and on the head*). My dear child, forgive me.... Forgive your sinful mother. Forgive me, you know I am wretched.

TREPLEV (*puts his arms round her*). If only you knew! I have lost everything! She does not love me, and now I cannot write ... all my hopes are gone....

MADAME ARKADIN. Don't despair ... Everything will come right. He is going away directly, she will love you again (*wipes away his tears*). Give over. We have made it up now.

TREPLEV (*kisses her hands*). Yes, mother.

MADAME ARKADIN (*tenderly*). Make it up with him too. You don't want a duel, do you?

TREPLEV. Very well. Only, mother, do allow me not to meet him. It's painful to me —it's more than I can bear. (*Enter* TRIGORIN.) Here he is ... I am going ... (*rapidly puts away the dressings in the cupboard*). The doctor will do the bandaging now.

TRIGORIN (*looking in a book*). Page 121 ... lines 11 and 12. Here it is. (*Reads.*) "If ever my life can be of use to you, come and take it."

(TREPLEV *picks up the bandage from the floor and goes out.*)

MADAME ARKADIN (*looking at her watch*). The horses will soon be here.

TRIGORIN (*to himself*). "If ever my life can be of use to you, come and take it."

MADAME ARKADIN. I hope all your things are packed?

TRIGORIN (*impatiently*). Yes, yes. (*Musing.*) Why is it that I feel so much sorrow in that appeal from a pure soul and that it wrings my heart so painfully? "If ever my life can be of use to you, come and take it." (*To* MADAME ARKADIN.) Let us stay one day longer.

(MADAME ARKADIN *shakes her head.*)

TRIGORIN. Let us stay!

MADAME ARKADIN. Darling, I know what keeps you here. But have control over yourself. You are a little intoxicated, try to be sober.

TRIGORIN. You be sober too, be sensible and reasonable, I implore you; look at it all as a true friend should. (*Presses her hand.*) You are capable of sacrifice. Be a friend to me, let me be free!

MADAME ARKADIN (*in violent agitation*). Are you so enthralled?

TRIGORIN. I am drawn to her! Perhaps it is just what I need.

MADAME ARKADIN. The love of a provincial girl? Oh, how little you know yourself!

TRIGORIN. Sometimes people sleep as they talk—that's how it is with me, I am talking to you and yet I am asleep and dreaming of her.... I am possessed by sweet, marvellous dreams.... Let me be free....

MADAME ARKADIN (*trembling*). No, no! I am an ordinary woman, you can't talk like that to me. Don't torture me, Boris. It terrifies me.

TRIGORIN. If you cared to, you could be not ordinary. Love—youthful, charming, poetical, lifting one into a world of dreams— that's the only thing in life that can give happiness! I have never yet known a love like that.... In my youth I never had time, I was always hanging about the editors' offices struggling with want. Now it is here, that love, it has come, it beckons to me. What sense is there in running away from it?

MADAME ARKADIN (*wrathfully*). You have gone mad!

TRIGORIN. Well, let me?

MADAME ARKADIN. You are all in a conspiracy together to torment me to-day! (*weeps*).

TRIGORIN (*clutching at his heart*). She does not understand! She won't understand!

MADAME ARKADIN. Am I so old and ugly that you don't mind talking of other women to me? (*Puts her arms round him and kisses him.*) Oh, you are mad! My wonderful, splendid darling. . . . You are the last page of my life! (*falls on her knees*). My joy, my pride, my bliss! . . . (*embraces his knees*). If you forsake me even for one hour I shall not survive it, I shall go mad, my marvellous, magnificent one, my master. . . .

TRIGORIN. Someone may come in (*helps her to get up*).

MADAME ARKADIN. Let them, I am not ashamed of my love for you (*kisses his hands*). My treasure, you desperate boy, you want to be mad, but I won't have it, I won't let you . . . (*laughs*). You are mine . . . mine. . . . This forehead is mine, and these eyes, and this lovely silky hair is mine too . . . you are mine all over. You are so gifted, so clever, the best of all modern writers, you are the one hope of Russia. . . . You have so much truthfulness, simplicity, freshness, healthy humour. . . . In one touch you can give all the essential characteristics of a person or a landscape, your characters are living. One can't read you without delight! You think this is exaggerated? That I am flattering you? But look into my eyes . . . look. . . . Do I look like a liar? You see, I am the only one who can appreciate you; I am the only one who tells you the truth, my precious, wonderful darling . . . Are you coming? Yes? You won't abandon me? . . .

TRIGORIN. I have no will of my own . . . I have never had a will of my own. . . . Flabby, feeble, always submissive—how can a woman care for such a man? Take me, carry me off, but don't let me move a step away from you. . . .

MADAME ARKADIN (*to herself*). Now he is mine! (*In an easy tone as though nothing had happened.*) But, of course, if you like, you can stay. I'll go by myself and you can come afterwards, a week later. After all, why should you be in a hurry?

TRIGORIN. No, we may as well go together.

MADAME ARKADIN. As you please. Let us go together then (*a pause*).

(TRIGORIN *makes a note.*)

MADAME ARKADIN. What are you writing?

TRIGORIN. I heard a good name this morning, "The Maiden's Forest." It may be of use (*stretches*). So we are to go then? Again there will be railway carriages, stations, refreshment bars, mutton chops, conversations. . . .

SHAMRAEV (*enters*). I have the honour to announce, with regret, that the horses are ready. It's time, honoured lady, to set off for the station; the train comes in at five minutes past two. So please do me a favour, Irina Nikolayevna, do not forget to inquire what has become of the actor Suzdaltsev. Is he alive and well? We used to drink together at one time. . . . In "The Plundered Mail" he used to play incomparably . . . I remember the tragedian Izmaïlov, also a remarkable personality, acted with him in Elisavetograd. . . . Don't be in a hurry, honoured lady, you need not start for five minutes. Once they were acting conspirators in a melodrama and when they were suddenly discovered Izmaïlov had to say, "We are caught in a trap," but he said, "We are caught in a tap!" (*Laughs.*) A tap!

(*While he is speaking* YAKOV *is busy looking after the luggage. The maid brings* MADAME ARKADIN *her hat, her coat, her umbrella and her gloves; they all help* MADAME ARKADIN *to put on her things. The man-cook looks in at the door on left and after some hesitation comes in. Enter* POLINA ANDREYEVNA, *then* SORIN *and* MEDVEDENKO.)

POLINA (*with a basket*). Here are some plums for the journey. . . . Very sweet ones. You may be glad to have something nice. . . .

MADAME ARKADIN. You are very kind, Polina Andreyevna.

POLINA. Good-bye, my dear! If anything has not been to your liking, forgive it (*weeps*).

MADAME ARKADIN (*embraces her*). Everything has been nice, everything! But you mustn't cry.

POLINA. The time flies so fast!

MADAME ARKADIN. There's no help for it.

SORIN (*in a great-coat with a cape to it, with his hat on and a stick in his hand, enters from door on left, crossing the stage*). Sister, it's time to start, or you may be too late after all. I am going to get into the carriage (*goes out*).

MEDVEDENKO. And I shall walk to the station . . . to see you off. I'll be there in no time . . . (*goes out*).

MADAME ARKADIN. Good-bye, dear friends.
. . . If we are all alive and well, we shall meet
again next summer. (*The maid, the cook and*
YAKOV *kiss her hand.*) Don't forget me. (*Gives
the cook a rouble.*) Here's a rouble for the three
of you.

THE COOK. We humbly thank you, madame!
Good journey to you! We are very grateful
for your kindness!

YAKOV. May God give you good luck!

SHAMRAEV. You might rejoice our hearts
with a letter! Good-bye, Boris Alexeyevitch!

MADAME ARKADIN. Where is Konstantin?
Tell him that I am starting; I must say good-
bye. Well, don't remember evil against me.
(*To* YAKOV.) I gave the cook a rouble. It's
for the three of you.

(*All go out on right. The stage is empty.
Behind the scenes the noise that is usual when
people are being seen off. The maid comes back
to fetch the basket of plums from the table and
goes out again.*)

TRIGORIN (*coming back*). I have forgotten
my stick. I believe it is out there, on the
verandah (*goes and, at door on left meets* NINA
*who is coming in*). Is that you? We are going.

NINA. I felt that we should see each other
once more. (*Excitedly.*) Boris Alexeyevitch,
I have come to a decision, the die is cast,
I am going on the stage. I shall be gone from
here to-morrow; I am leaving my father, I am
abandoning everything, I am beginning a
new life. Like you, I am going . . . to Moscow. We shall meet there.

TRIGORIN (*looking round*). Stay at the "Slav-
yansky Bazaar" . . . Let me know at once . . .
Molchanovka, Groholsky House. . . . I am
in a hurry . . . (*a pause*).

NINA. One minute more. . . .

TRIGORIN (*in an undertone*). You are so
lovely. . . . Oh, what happiness to think that
we shall see each other soon! (*She sinks on his
breast.*) I shall see again those wonderful eyes,
that inexpressibly beautiful tender smile . . .
those soft features, the expression of angelic
purity. . . . My darling . . . (*a prolonged kiss*).

CURTAIN

(*Betweeen the third and fourth acts there is an
interval of two years.*)

ACT IV

*One of the drawing-rooms in* SORIN'S *house,
which has been turned into a study for* KONSTANTIN
TREPLEV. *On the right and left, doors leading to
inner apartments. In the middle, glass door leading
on to the verandah. Besides the usual drawing-room
furniture there is, in corner on right, a writing table,
near door on left, a sofa, a bookcase and books in
windows and on the chairs. Evening. There is a
single lamp alight with a shade on it. It is half dark.
There is the sound of the trees rustling, and the wind
howling in the chimney. A watchman is tapping.
Enter* MEDVEDENKO *and* MASHA.

MASHA (*calling*). Konstantin Gavrilitch!
Konstantin Gavrilitch! (*Looking round.*) No,
there is no one here. The old man keeps
asking every minute, where is Kostya, where
is Kostya? He cannot live without him. . . .

MEDVEDENKO. He is afraid of being alone.
(*Listening.*) What awful weather! This is the
second day of it.

MASHA (*turns up the lamp*). There are waves
on the lake. Great big ones.

MEDVEDENKO. How dark it is in the garden!
We ought to have told them to break up that
stage in the garden. It stands as bare and
ugly as a skeleton, and the curtain flaps in the
wind. When I passed it yesterday evening, it
seemed as though someone were crying in it.

MASHA. What next . . . (*a pause*).

MEDVEDENKO. Let us go home, Masha.

MASHA (*shakes her head*). I shall stay here for
the night.

MEDVEDENKO (*in an imploring voice*). Masha,
do come! Our baby must be hungry.

MASHA. Nonsense. Matryona will feed him
(*a pause*).

MEDVEDENKO. I am sorry for him. He has
been three nights now without his mother.

MASHA. You are a bore. In old days you
used at least to discuss general subjects, but
now it is only home, baby, home, baby—
that's all one can get out of you.

MEDVEDENKO. Come along, Masha!

MASHA. Go by yourself.

MEDVEDENKO. Your father won't let me
have a horse.

MASHA. Yes, he will. You ask, and he will.

MEDVEDENKO. Very well, I'll ask. Then
you will come to-morrow?

MASHA (*talking a pinch of snuff*). Very well, to-morrow. How you pester me.

(*Enter* TREPLEV *and* POLINA ANDREYEVNA; TREPLEV *brings in pillows and a quilt, and* POLINA ANDREYEVNA *sheets and pillow-cases; they lay them on the sofa, then* TREPLEV *goes to his table and sits down.*)

MASHA. What's this for, mother?

POLINA. Pyotr Nikolayevitch asked us to make a bed for him in Kostya's room.

MASHA. Let me do it (*makes the bed*).

POLINA (*sighing*). Old people are like children (*goes up to the writing table, and leaning on her elbow, looks at the manuscript; a pause*).

MEDVEDENKO. Well, I am going then. Good-bye, Masha (*kisses his wife's hand*). Good-bye, mother (*tries to kiss his mother-in-law's hand*).

POLINA (*with vexation*). Come, if you are going, go.

MEDVEDENKO. Good-bye, Konstantin Gavrilitch.

(TREPLEV *gives him his hand without speaking;* MEDVEDENKO *goes out.*)

POLINA (*looking at the MS.*). No one would have guessed or thought that you would have become a real author, Kostya. And now, thank God, they send you money from the magazines. (*Passes her hand over his hair.*) And you have grown good-looking too. . . . Dear, good Kostya, do be a little kinder to my Mashenka!

MASHA (*as she makes the bed*). Leave him alone mother.

POLINA (*to* TREPLEV). She is a nice little thing (*a pause*). A woman wants nothing, you know, Kostya, so long as you give her a kind look. I know from myself.

(TREPLEV *gets up from the table and walks away without speaking.*)

MASHA. Now you have made him angry. What induced you to pester him?

POLINA. I feel so sorry for you, Mashenka.

MASHA. Much use that is!

POLINA. My heart aches for you. I see it all, you know, I understand it all.

MASHA. It's all foolishness. There is no such thing as hopeless love except in novels. It's of no consequence. The only thing is one mustn't let oneself go and keep expecting something, waiting for the tide to turn. . . . When love

gets into the heart there is nothing to be done but to clear it out. Here they promised to transfer my husband to another district. As soon as I am there, I shall forget it all. . . . I shall tear it out of my heart.

(*Two rooms away a melancholy waltz is played.*)

POLINA. That's Kostya playing. He must be depressed.

MASHA (*noiselessly dances a few waltz steps*). The great thing, mother, is not to have him before one's eyes. If they only give my Semyon his transfer, trust me, I shall get over it in a month. It's all nonsense.

(*Door on left opens.* DORN *and* MEDVEDENKO *wheel in* SORIN *in his chair.*)

MEDVEDENKO. I have six of them at home now. And flour is two kopeks per pound.

DORN. You've got to look sharp to make both ends meet.

MEDVEDENKO. It's all very well for you to laugh. You've got more money than you know what to do with.

DORN. Money? After thirty years of practice, my boy, troublesome work during which I could not call my soul my own by day or by night, I only succeeded in saving two thousand roubles, and that I spent not long ago abroad. I have nothing.

MASHA (*to her husband*). You have not gone?

MEDVEDENKO (*guiltily*). Well, how can I when they won't let me have a horse?

MASHA (*with bitter vexation in an undertone*). I can't bear the sight of you.

(*The wheel-chair remains in the left half of the room;* POLINA ANDREYEVNA, MASHA *and* DORN *sit down beside it,* MEDVEDENKO *moves mournfully to one side.*)

DORN. What changes there have been here! The drawing-room has been turned into a study.

MASHA. It is more convenient for Konstantin Gavrilitch to work here. Whenever he likes, he can walk out into the garden and think there.

(*A watchman taps.*)

SORIN. Where is my sister?

DORN. She has gone to the station to meet Trigorin. She will be back directly.

SORIN. Since you thought it necessary to send for my sister, I must be dangerously ill.

(*After a silence.*) It's a queer thing, I am dangerously ill and here they don't give me any medicines.

DORN. Well, what would you like to have? Valerian drops? Soda? Quinine?

SORIN. Ah, he is at his moralising again! What an infliction it is! (*With a motion of his head towards the sofa.*) Is that bed for me?

POLINA. Yes, it's for you, Pyotr Nikolaye-vitch.

SORIN. Thank you.

DORN (*hums*). "The moon is floating in the midnight sky."

SORIN. I want to give Kostya a subject for a story. It ought to be called "The Man who Wished"—*L'homme qui a voulu.* In my youth I wanted to become a literary man—and didn't; I wanted to speak well—and I spoke horribly badly, (*mimicking himself*) "and all the rest of it, and all that, and so on, and so forth" ... and I would go plodding on and on, trying to sum up till I was in a regular perspiration; I wanted to get married—and I didn't; I always wanted to live in town and here I am ending my life in the country—and so on.

DORN. I wanted to become an actual civil councillor—and I have.

SORIN (*laughs*). That I had no hankerings after. That happened of itself.

DORN. To be expresssing dissatisfaction with life at sixty-two is really ungracious, you know.

SORIN. What a persistent fellow he is! You might understand that one wants to live!

DORN. That's just frivolity. It's the law of nature that every life must have an end.

SORIN. You argue like a man who has had enough. You are satisfied and so you are indifferent to life, nothing matters to you. But even you will be afraid to die.

DORN. The dread of death is an animal fear. One must overcome it. A rational fear of death is only possible for those who believe in eternal life and are conscious of their sins. And you, in the first place, don't believe, and, in the second, what sins have you to worry about? You have served in the courts of justice for twenty-five years—that's all.

SORIN (*laughs*). Twenty-eight. ...

(TREPLEV *comes in and sits down on a stool at* SORIN's *feet.* MASHA *never takes her eyes off him.*)

DORN. We are hindering Konstantin Gavrilitch from working.

TREPLEV. Oh no, it doesn't matter (*a pause*).

MEDVEDENKO. Allow me to ask you, doctor, what town did you like best abroad?

DORN. Genoa.

TREPLEV. Why Genoa?

DORN. The life in the streets is so wonderful there. When you go out of the hotel in the evening, the whole street is packed with people. You wander aimlessly zigzagging about the crowd, backwards and forwards; you live with it, are psychologically at one with it and begin almost to believe that a world-soul is really possible, such as was acted by Nina Zaretchny in your play. And, by the way, where is she now? How is she getting on?

TREPLEV. I expect she is quite well.

DORN. I was told that she was leading a rather peculiar life. How was that?

TREPLEV. That's a long story, doctor.

DORN. Well, tell it us shortly (*a pause*).

TREPLEV. She ran away from home and had an affair with Trigorin. You know that?

DORN. I know.

TREPLEV. She had a child. The child died. Trigorin got tired of her and went back to his old ties, as might have been expected. Though, indeed, he had never abandoned them, but in his weak-willed way contrived to keep both going. As far as I can make out from what I have heard, Nina's private life was a complete failure.

DORN. And the stage?

TREPLEV. I fancy that was worse still. She made her début at some holiday place near Moscow, then went to the provinces. All that time I did not lose sight of her, and wherever she went I followed her. She always took big parts, but she acted crudely, without taste, screamingly, with violent gestures. There were moments when she uttered a cry successfully or died successfully, but they were only moments.

DORN. Then she really has some talent?

TREPLEV. It was difficult to make it out. I suppose she has. I saw her but she would not see me, and the servants would not admit me at the hotel. I understood her state of mind and did not insist on seeing her (*a pause*). What more can I tell you? Afterwards, when I was back at home, I had some letters from her—warm, intelligent, interesting letters. She did not complain, but I felt that she was profoundly unhappy; every line betrayed sick overstrained nerves. And her imagination is a little unhinged. She signed herself the Seagull. In Pushkin's "Mermaid" the miller says that he is a raven, and in the same way in her letters she kept repeating that she was a seagull. Now she is here.

DORN. Here? How do you mean?

TREPLEV. In the town, staying at an inn. She has been there for five days. I did go to see her, and Marya Ilyinishna here went too, but she won't see anyone. Semyon Semyonitch declares he saw her yesterday afternoon in the fields a mile and a half from here.

MEDVEDENKO. Yes, I saw her. She went in that direction, towards the town. I bowed to her and asked her why she did not come to see us. She said she would come.

TREPLEV. She won't come (*a pause*). Her father and stepmother refuse to recognise her. They have put watchmen about so that she may not even go near the house (*walks away with the doctor towards the writing table*). How easy it is to be a philosopher on paper, doctor, and how difficult it is in life!

SORIN. She was a charming girl.

DORN. What?

SORIN. She was a charming girl, I say. Actual Civil Councillor Sorin was positively in love with her for a time.

DORN. The old Lovelace.

(SHAMRAEV's *laugh is heard*.)

POLINA. I fancy our people have come back from the station. . . .

TREPLEV. Yes, I hear mother.

(*Enter* MADAME ARKADIN, TRIGORIN *and with them* SHAMRAEV.)

SHAMRAEV (*as he enters*). We all grow old and dilapidated under the influence of the elements, while you, honoured lady, are still young . . . a light blouse, sprightliness, grace.

MADAME ARKADIN. You want to bring me ill-luck again, you tiresome man!

TRIGORIN. How do you do, Pyotr Nikolayevitch! So you are still poorly? That's bad!

(*Seeing* MASHA, *joyfully*.) Marya Ilyinishna!

MASHA. You know me, do you? (*shakes hands*).

TRIGORIN. Married?

MASHA. Long ago.

TRIGORIN. Are you happy? (*Bows to* DORN *and* MEDVEDENKO, *then hesitatingly approaches* TREPLEV.) Irina Nikolayevna has told me that you have forgotten the past and are no longer angry.

(TREPLEV *holds out his hand*.)

MADAME ARKADIN (*to her son*). Boris Alexeyevitch has brought the magazine with your new story in it.

TREPLEV (*taking the magazine, to* TRIGORIN). Thank you, you are very kind (*They sit down*.)

TRIGORIN. Your admirers send their greetings to you. . . . In Petersburg and Moscow there is great interest in your work and I am continually being asked questions about you. People ask what you are like, how old you are, whether you are dark or fair. Everyone imagines, for some reason, that you are no longer young. And no one knows your real name, as you always publish under a pseudonym. You are as mysterious as the Iron Mask.

TREPLEV. Will you be able to make a long stay?

TRIGORIN. No, I think I must go back to Moscow to-morrow. I am obliged to. I am in a hurry to finish my novel, and besides, I have promised something for a collection of tales that is being published. It's the old story, in fact.

(*While they are talking* MADAME ARKADIN *and* POLINA ANDREYEVNA *put a card-table in the middle of the room and open it out.* SHAMRAEV *lights candles and sets chairs. A game of lotto is brought out of the cupboard.*)

TRIGORIN. The weather has not given me a friendly welcome. There is a cruel wind. If it has dropped by to-morrow morning I shall go to the lake to fish. And I must have a look at the garden and that place where— you remember?—your play was acted. I've got a subject for a story, I only want to revive my recollections of the scene in which it is laid.

MASHA (*to her father*). Father, let my husband have a horse! He must get home.

SHAMRAEV (*mimicking*). Must get home—a horse! (*Sternly.*) You can see for yourself: they have just been to the station. I can't send them out again.

MASHA. But there are other horses. (*Seeing that her father says nothing, waves her hand.*) There's no doing anything with you.

MEDVEDENKO. I can walk, Masha. Really.

POLINA (*with a sigh*). Walk in such weather ... (*sits down to the card-table*). Come, friends.

MEDVEDENKO. It is only four miles. Good-bye (*kisses his wife's hand*). Good-bye, mother. (*His mother-in-law reluctantly holds out her hand for him to kiss.*) I wouldn't trouble anyone, but the baby ... (*bows to the company*). Good-bye ... (*goes out with a guilty step*).

SHAMRAEV. He can walk right enough. He's not a general.

POLINA (*tapping on the table*). Come, friends. Don't let us waste time, we shall soon be called to supper.

(SHAMRAEV, MASHA *and* DORN *sit down at the table.*)

MADAME ARKADIN (*to* TRIGORIN). When the long autumn evenings come on, they play lotto here. Look, it's the same old lotto that we had when our mother used to play with us, when we were children. Won't you have a game before supper? (*sits down to the table with* TRIGORIN). It's a dull game, but it is not so bad when you are used to it (*deals three cards to everyone*).

TREPLEV (*turning the pages of the magazine*). He has read his own story, but he has not even cut mine (*puts the magazine down on the writing table, then goes towards door on left; as he passes his mother he kisses her on the head*).

MADAME ARKADIN. And you, Kostya?

TREPLEV. Excuse me, I would rather not ... I am going out (*goes out*).

MADAME ARKADIN. The stake is ten kopeks. Put it down for me, doctor, will you?

DORN. Right.

MASHA. Has everyone put down their stakes? I begin ... Twenty-two.

MADAME ARKADIN. Yes.

MASHA. Three!

DORN. Right!

MASHA. Did you play three? Eight! Eighty-one! Ten!

SHAMRAEV. Don't be in a hurry!

MADAME ARKADIN. What a reception I had in Harkov! My goodness! I feel dizzy with it still.

MASHA. Thirty-four!

(*A melancholy waltz is played behind the scenes.*)

MADAME ARKADIN. The students gave me an ovation. ... Three baskets of flowers ... two wreaths and this, see (*unfastens a brooch on her throat and lays it on the table*).

SHAMRAEV. Yes, that is a thing. ...

MASHA. Fifty!

DORN. Exactly fifty?

MADAME ARKADIN. I had a wonderful dress. ... Whatever I don't know, I do know how to dress.

POLINA. Kostya is playing the piano; he is depressed, poor fellow.

SHAMRAEV. He is awfully abused in the newspapers.

MASHA. Seventy-seven!

MADAME ARKADIN. As though that mattered!

TRIGORIN. He never quite comes off. He has not yet hit upon his own medium. There is always something queer and vague, at times almost like delirium. Not a single living character.

MASHA. Eleven!

MADAME ARKADIN (*looking round at* SORIN). Petrusha, are you bored? (*A pause.*) He is asleep.

DORN. The actual civil councillor is asleep.

MASHA. Seven! Ninety!

TRIGORIN. If I lived in such a place, beside a lake, do you suppose I should write? I should overcome this passion and should do nothing but fish.

MASHA. Twenty-eight!

TRIGORIN. Catching perch is so delightful!

DORN. Well, I believe in Konstantin Gavrilitch. There is something in him! There is something in him! He thinks in images; his stories are vivid, full of colour and they affect me strongly. The only pity is that he has not got definite aims. He produces an impression and that's all, but you can't get far with nothing but an impression. Irina Nikolayevna, are you glad that your son is a writer?

MADAME ARKADIN. Only fancy, I have not

read anything of his yet. I never have time.

MASHA. Twenty-six!

(TREPLEV *comes in quietly and sits down at his table.*)

SHAMRAEV (*to* TRIGORIN). We have still got something here belonging to you, Boris Alexeyevitch.

TRIGORIN. What's that?

SHAMRAEV. Konstantin Gavrilitch shot a seagull and you asked me to get it stuffed for you.

TRIGORIN. I don't remember! (*Pondering.*) I don't remember!

MASHA. Sixty-six! One!

TREPLEV (*flinging open the window, listens*). How dark it is! I don't know why I feel so uneasy.

MADAME ARKADIN. Kostya, shut the window, there's a draught.

(TREPLEV *shuts the window.*)

MASHA. Eighty-eight!

TRIGORIN. The game is mine!

MADAME ARKADIN (*gaily*). Bravo, bravo!

SHAMRAEV. Bravo!

MADAME ARKADIN. That man always has luck in everything (*gets up*). And now let us go and have something to eat. Our great man has not dined to-day. We will go on again after supper. (*To her son.*) Kostya, leave your manuscripts and come to supper.

TREPLEV. I don't want any, mother, I am not hungry.

MADAME ARKADIN. As you like. (*Wakes* SORIN.) Petrusha, supper! (*Takes* SHAMRAEV's *arm.*) I'll tell you about my reception in Harkov.

(POLINA ANDREYEVNA *puts out the candles on the table. Then she and* DORN *wheel the chair. All go out by door on left; only* TREPLEV, *sitting at the writing table, is left on the stage.*)

TREPLEV (*setting himself to write; runs through what he has written already*). I have talked so much about new forms and now I feel that little by little I am falling into a convention myself. (*Reads.*) "The placard on the wall proclaimed. . . . The pale face in its setting of dark hair." Proclaimed, setting. That's stupid (*scratches out*). I will begin where the hero is awakened by the patter of the rain, and throw out all the rest. The description of the moonlight evening is long and overelaborate.

Trigorin has worked out methods for himself, it's easy for him now. . . . With him the broken bottle neck glitters on the dam and the mill-wheel casts a black shadow—and there you have the moonlight night, while I have the tremulous light, and the soft twinkling of the stars, and the far-away strains of the piano dying away in the still fragrant air. . . . It's agonising (*a pause*). I come more and more to the conviction that it is not a question of new and old forms, but that what matters is that a man should write without thinking about forms at all, write because it springs freely from his soul. (*There is a tap at the window nearest to the table.*) What is that? (*Looks out of window.*) There is nothing to be seen . . . (*opens the glass door and looks out into the garden*). Someone ran down the steps. (*Calls.*) Who is there? (*Goes out and can be heard walking rapidly along the verandah; returns half a minute later with* NINA ZARETCHNY.) Nina, Nina!

(NINA *lays her head on his breast and weeps with subdued sobs.*)

TREPLEV (*moved*). Nina! Nina! It's you . . . you. . . . It's as though I had foreseen it, all day long my heart has been aching and restless (*takes off her hat and cape*). Oh, my sweet, my precious, she has come at last. Don't let us cry, don't let us!

NINA. There is someone here.

TREPLEV. No one.

NINA. Lock the doors, someone may come in.

TREPLEV. No one will come in.

NINA. I know Irina Nikolayevna is here. Lock the doors.

TREPLEV (*locks the door on right, goes to door on left*). There is no lock on this one. I'll put a chair against it (*puts an armchair against the door*). Don't be afraid, no one will come.

NINA (*looking intently into his face*). Let me look at you. (*Looking round.*) It's warm, it's nice. . . . In old days this was the drawing-room. Am I very much changed?

TREPLEV. Yes . . . You are thinner and your eyes are bigger. Nina, how strange it is that I should be seeing you. Why would not you let me see you? Why haven't you come all this time? I know you have been here almost a week. . . . I have been to you several times every day; I stood under your window like a beggar.

NINA. I was afraid that you might hate me. I dream every night that you look at me and don't know me. If only you knew! Ever since I came I have been walking here . . . by the lake. I have been near your house many times and could not bring myself to enter it. Let us sit down. (*They sit down.*) Let us sit down and talk and talk. It's nice here, it's warm and snug. Do you hear the wind? There's a passage in Turgenev, "Well for the man on such a night who sits under the shelter of home, who has a warm corner in safety." I am a seagull. . . . No, that's not it (*rubs her forehead*). What was I saying? Yes . . . Turgenev . . . "And the Lord help all homeless wanderers!" . . . It doesn't matter (*sobs*).

TREPLEV. Nina, you are crying again. . . . Nina!

NINA. Never mind, it does me good . . . I haven't cried for two years. Yesterday, late in the evening, I came into the garden to see whether our stage was still there. It is still standing. I cried for the first time after two years and it eased the weight on my heart and made it lighter. You see, I am not crying now (*takes him by the hand*). And so now you are an author. . . . You are an author, I am an actress. . . . We too have been drawn into the whirlpool. I lived joyously like a child—I woke up singing in the morning; I loved you and dreamed of fame, and now? Early tomorrow morning I must go to Yelets third-class . . . with peasants, and at Yelets the cultured tradesmen will pester me with attentions. Life is a coarse business!

TREPLEV. Why to Yelets?

NINA. I have taken an engagement for the whole winter. It is time to go.

TREPLEV. Nina, I cursed you, I hated you, I tore up your letters and photographs, but I was conscious every minute that my soul is bound to yours for ever. It's not in my power to leave off loving you, Nina. Ever since I lost you and began to get my work published my life has been unbearable—I am wretched. . . . My youth was, as it were, torn away all at once and it seems to me as though I have lived for ninety years already. I call upon you, I kiss the earth on which you have walked; wherever I look I see your face, that tender smile that lighted up the best days of my life.

NINA (*distractedly*). Why does he talk like this, why does he talk like this?

TREPLEV. I am alone in the world, warmed by no affection. I am as cold as though I were in a cellar, and everything I write is dry, hard and gloomy. Stay here, Nina, I entreat you, or let me go with you!

(NINA *rapidly puts on her hat and cape.*)

TREPLEV. Nina, why is this? For God's sake, Nina! (*Looks at her as she puts her things on; a pause.*)

NINA. My horses are waiting at the gate. Don't see me off, I'll go alone. . . . (*Through her tears.*) Give me some water. . . .

TREPLEV (*gives her some water*). Where are you going now?

NINA. To the town (*a pause*). Is Irina Nikolayevna here?

TREPLEV. Yes. . . . Uncle was taken worse on Thursday and we telegraphed for her.

NINA. Why do you say that you kissed the earth on which I walked? I ought to be killed. (*Bends over table.*) I am so tired! If I could rest . . . if I could rest! (*Raising her head.*) I am a seagull. . . . No, that's not it. I am an actress. Oh, well! (*Hearing* MADAME ARKADIN *and* TRIGORIN *laughing, she listens, then runs to door on left and looks through the keyhole.*) He is here too. . . . (*Turning back to* TREPLEV.) Oh, well . . . it doesn't matter . . . no. . . . He did not believe in the stage, he always laughed at dreams and little by little I left off believing in it too, and lost heart. . . . And then I was fretted by love and jealousy, and continually anxious over my little one. . . . I grew petty and trivial, I acted stupidly. . . . I did not know what to do with my arms, I did not know how to stand on the stage, could not control my voice. You can't understand what it feels like when one knows one is acting disgracefully. I am a seagull. No, that's not it. . . . Do you remember you shot a seagull? A man came by chance, saw it and, just to pass the time, destroyed it. . . . A subject for a short story. . . . That's not it, though (*rubs her forehead*). What was I saying? . . . I am talking of the stage. Now I am not like that. I am a real actress, I act with enjoyment, with enthusiasm, I am intoxicated when I am on the stage and feel that I am splendid. And since I have been here, I keep walking about and thinking, thinking and feeling that my soul is getting stronger every day. Now I know, I understand, Kostya, that in our work—in acting or writing—what matters is not fame, not glory, not what I dreamed of, but knowing how to be patient. To bear one's cross and have faith. I have faith and it all doesn't hurt so much, and when I think of my vocation I am not afraid of life.

TREPLEV (*mournfully*). You have found your path, you know which way you are going, but I am still floating in a chaos of dreams and images, not knowing what use it is to anyone. I have no faith and don't know what my vocation is.

NINA (*listening*). 'Sh-sh . . . I am going. Good-bye. When I become a great actress, come and look at me. Will you promise? But now . . . (*presses his hand*) it's late. I can hardly stand on my feet. . . . I am worn out and hungry. . . .

TREPLEV. Stay, I'll give you some supper.

NINA. No, no. . . . Don't see me off, I will go by myself. My horses are close by. . . . So she brought him with her? Well, it doesn't matter. When you see Trigorin, don't say anything to him. . . . I love him! I love him even more than before. . . . A subject for a short story . . . I love him, I love him, passionately, I love him to despair. It was nice in old days, Kostya! Do you remember? How clear, warm, joyous and pure life was, what feelings we had—feelings like tender, exquisite flowers. . . . Do you remember? (*Recites.*) "Men, lions, eagles, and partridges, horned deer, geese, spiders, silent fish that dwell in the water, starfishes, and creatures which cannot be seen by the eye—all living things, all living things, all living things, have completed their cycle of sorrow, are extinct. . . . For thousands of years the earth has borne no living creature on its surface, and this poor moon lights its lamp in vain. On the meadow the cranes no longer waken with a cry and there is no sound of the May beetles in the lime trees . . ." (*impulsively embraces* TREPLEV *and runs out of the glass door*).

TREPLEV (*after a pause*). It will be a pity if someone meets her in the garden and tells mother. It may upset mother. . . .

(*He spends two minutes in tearing up all his manuscripts and throwing them under the table; unlocks the door on right and goes out.*)

DORN (*trying to open the door on left*). Strange. The door seems to be locked . . . (*comes in and puts the armchair in its place*). An obstacle race.

(*Enter* MADAME ARKADIN *and* POLINA ANDREYEVNA, *behind them* YAKOV *carrying a tray with bottles;* MASHA; *then* SHAMRAEV *and* TRIGORIN.)

MADAME ARKADIN. Put the claret and the beer for Boris Alexeyevitch here on the table. We will play as we drink it. Let us sit down, friends.

POLINA (*to* YAKOV). Bring tea too at the same time (*lights the candles and sits down to the card-table*).

SHAMRAEV (*leads* TRIGORIN *to the cupboard*). Here's the thing I was speaking about just now (*takes the stuffed seagull from the cupboard*). This is what you ordered.

TRIGORIN (*looking at the seagull*). I don't remember it. (*Musing.*) I don't remember.

(*The sound of a shot coming from right of stage; everyone starts.*)

MADAME ARKADIN (*frightened*). What's that?

DORN. That's nothing. It must be something in my medicine-chest that has gone off. Don't be anxious (*goes out at door on right, comes back in half a minute*). That's what it is. A bottle of ether has exploded. (*Hums.*) "I stand before thee enchanted again. . . ."

MADAME ARKADIN (*sitting down to the table*). Ough, how frightened I was. It reminded me of how . . . (*hides her face in her hands*). It made me quite dizzy. . . .

DORN (*turning over the leaves of the magazine, to* TRIGORIN). There was an article in this two months ago—a letter from America—and I wanted to ask you, among other things (*puts his arm round* TRIGORIN's *waist and leads him to the footlights*) as I am very much interested in the question. . . . (*In a lower tone, dropping his voice.*) Get Irina Nikolayevna away somehow. The fact is, Konstantin Gavrilitch has shot himself. . . .

CURTAIN

## Between Comedy and Tragedy

There is an offstage pistol shot at the end of *The Seagull* as there is at the end of *Hedda Gabler*, but the meaning of the two shots is as different as Treplev is from Hedda. He is not the victim of some grand but false ideal; he is a writer of unfortunately limited talents and uncertain objectives. Chekhov wrote of him: "Treplev has no definite aims and that has led to his destruction." He himself says something very similar to Nina in the fourth act. Here and in the scene of his quarrel with his mother we are aware of an immaturity which, at twenty-five, is at times ludicrous, at times pathetic. The question is whether the suicide of such a character constitutes tragedy, and the question is basic to the interpretation of the play.

Shortly before Treplev's suicide, Nina's situation appears more tragic than his. She is the seagull whom a man has seen by chance, and "having nothing better to do," has destroyed, and yet Nina, despite her unhappy love affair, or because of it, has grown more certain of herself, and in her last scene with Treplev, rejects the symbolism of the seagull: "Now I am not like that. I am a real actress, I act with enjoyment, with enthusiasm . . . ." Her confidence in the future makes Treplev's weakness the more conspicuous. Chekhov has avoided the most obvious potentiality for tragedy in the play.

Furthermore, the effect of the pistol shot onstage undercuts its tragic implications. *Hedda Gabler* ends with the horrified response of the principal characters. Here only Dorn knows what has happened, and to spare Madame Arkadin's feelings (perhaps also thinking of the scene she would make), explains the sound as a bottle exploding in his medicine chest. There is no terrible realization, nothing to magnify the significance of the episode. Its dimensions are cut down to the smallest possible. For the audience it is a shocking and sad conclusion, but not one which is as comprehensive or as final as the conclusion of *Hedda Gabler*. Nina has escaped; Madame Arkadin and Trigorin will go on—for better or for worse—much as before, once the initial shock has worn off.

Chekhov called the play a comedy. If that is what it is, the usual notion of comedy needs to be considerably extended, but it may be useful to recall that Jonson believed comedy should show people as they are, and that both he and Molière maintained an attitude of detachment from their characters. In these respects Chekhov adheres to a very old concept of comedy. We have seen that he believed in showing "life as it is," but he also spoke of putting his characters on trial before the jury of readers or spectators. Such objectivity combined with an interest in exposing weakness would have been quite comprehensible to Jonson and Molière.

What makes the nature of a Chekhov play so difficult to define is the combination of comic exposure with a sympathetic understanding of the human being exposed. The opening of *The Seagull* is an excellent example. Masha, hopelessly in love with Treplev, is swathed in black. When Medvedenko asks her why, she says: "I am mourning for my life." The extravagance of her words can only provoke a smile, and yet, snuffbox and all, Masha is not merely a grotesque. Her anguish is moving as well as funny, and provides the ideal introduction to the mood of the play. Treplev's scene with his mother in the third act is a similar combination. It is a "big scene" of quarrel and reconciliation, emotionally persuasive and ludicrous at the same time. In both cases the doubleness of effect is due in part to our awareness of acting. Masha dramatizes herself, and Madame Arkadin is always the actress, whether on or off the stage. To the extent that we see them as playing roles we can watch their performances without giving them full sympathy. But judgment is complicated by another factor which becomes more apparent as the play progresses—the strength which Madame Arkadin and later Nina derive from their histrionic ability. There is a genuineness in their artifice, so to speak, which makes them finally less vulnerable than Treplev, who succeeds neither in art nor in life. The complexity of judgment which Chekhov invites makes it difficult to define the nature of one's response to his plays. It is not the characteristic response to tragedy, but neither, in spite of the resemblances noted, is it exactly the usual response to comedy.

Congenial as Chekhov and Stanislavski were, they disagreed sharply about the tone of the plays Chekhov wrote for the Moscow Art Theater. Although the author insisted that *The Seagull* and *The Cherry Orchard* were comedies, Stanislavski directed them as tragedies, and it is in this way that they are usually performed today. Thus Chekhov's play raises a problem we have encountered before: the response of the audience will be conditioned by the emphasis of the performance. Stanislavski was one of the first of a long line of autocratic directors who have felt justified in imposing their interpretations upon an author's work (though they would not express it in those terms). It is possible, of course, that Chekhov's interpretations of his plays were less valid than those of his talented director. In such a case the reader must be his own director and decide how he would have the scenes played.

## Selected Reading List for Chekhov and Stanislavski

Robert Brustein, "Anton Chekhov," *The Theatre of Revolt*. Boston: Little, Brown & Co., 1964, pp. 137–79.

David Magarshack, *Chekhov the Dramatist*. New York: Hill and Wang, 1960.

David Magarshack, *Stanislavsky: A Life*. New York: Chanticleer Press, 1951.

Constantin Stanislavski, *An Actor Prepares*, trans. Elizabeth Reynolds Hapgood. New York: Theatre Arts Books, 1963.

Constantin Stanislavski, *My Life in Art*, trans. J. J. Robbins. New York: Theatre Arts Books, n.d.

*experiments
which
shaped today's
theater*

SECTION III

# Strindberg and Expressionism

The theatrical career of August Strindberg is superficially similar to that of Ibsen. Born in Stockholm in 1849 (and hence a little more than twenty years Ibsen's junior), he began writing for the theater just as Ibsen was becoming known. His first important plays, *The Father* and *Miss Julie*, basically realistic in style, were written in the eighties, when Ibsen was at the height of his reputation as a realistic playwright. In their later plays both Ibsen and Strindberg broke away from realism. Strindberg was no admirer of Ibsen, however; for, on the basis of *A Doll's House* and other plays, he considered Ibsen to be a champion of the "emancipated woman." (Strindberg's profound distrust and even fear of women is evident in the two plays already mentioned.) Furthermore, he believed that Ibsen had caricatured him in some of his plays. Both of these convictions were based on misunderstanding.

Such fears and hostilities were characteristic of Strindberg's emotional instability. His mother, who died when he was thirteen, was an object of adoration and bitter resentment. His three marriages ended in divorce. An unbeliever in his youth, he went through a spiritual crisis in the nineties, leading to a religious conversion. These upheavals of his inner life are clearly reflected in his drama as well as in novels, letters, and diaries. His crisis was followed by a period of intensive composition, 1898–1909, during which he wrote over thirty plays. He died of cancer in 1912.

Even in the realistic plays of his early period Strindberg paid far less attention than did Ibsen to the social background of his characters, and concentrated on psychological problems. After his crisis he moved further from a concern with external reality. In 1907 he founded with August Falck the Intimate Theater in Stockholm and wrote for production there the brief so-called "chamber plays," of which *The Ghost Sonata* is one. The designation "chamber plays" was intended as an analogy to chamber music. The plays were written for a small theater and aimed at an effect of unity and intensity; there were to be no intermissions. The development of a theme was to take precedence over the portrayal of character or telling a story, and the theme was to be developed without regard to the demands of verisimilitude. In his preface to *A Dream Play*, written five years earlier, he had said: "Anything may happen; everything is possible and probable." As Walter H. Sokel has pointed out,[1] some dehumanization is inevitable when writers take music as the primary art, and hence as their model; for music is the most absolute of the arts. Idea and form are one. In *The Ghost Sonata* the importance of the musical analogy is proclaimed in the title and can readily be seen in the structure. Although only the most tenuous strands of plot relate the

---

NOTE: The introductions to the plays in the third section combine the sorts of background material contained in previous introductions and in the discussions following the plays. In the place of additional discussions by the editor to follow these last three plays, three essays by men of major importance in the modern theater are reprinted in the Appendix. Though only the last of these bears directly upon one of the plays in the third section, all of them illustrate, as do the plays themselves, what has been happening in the drama in this century. But since these essays deal with basic problems—the technique of acting and the nature of theatrical illusion—they are relevant to the earliest drama as well as to the latest.

[1] *The Writer in Extremis* (New York: McGraw-Hill Book Co., 1964), p. 35.

last scene to the two preceding scenes, the principal themes of the play are recapitulated as they are in the last section of a sonata.

In this experimental drama, therefore, we do not encounter characters who are convincing human beings. Most of them are given impersonal names such as The Milkmaid, The Young Lady, The Lady in Black. They are not exaggerations of a particular temperament, though old Hummel, in his hypocrisy and greed, is slightly reminiscent of a Jonsonian humor character. Neither are they such allegorical characters as we find in *Everyman*, though the predominance of theme in the two plays is similar. The characters in *The Ghost Sonata* have the fantastic quality of figures in a dream. The Milkmaid, we discover, is a ghost, sometimes seen by one person, sometimes by another. Some characters are grotesques who collapse, shrivel up, and die when certain words are spoken. Two of them are described as vampires, and several others are in some sense living off other people. The Young Lady seems at first to be an ideal woman, but this impression is changed by the developments in the last scene. Only The Student approaches a kind of human wholeness, and even he is not so much a real person as a spokesman for an idea. His rhapsodic speeches at the end, informed by the religious beliefs of Strindberg's last years, leave the familiar style of everyday conversation far behind, and use a more formal rhetoric to present their theme.

In a number of his later plays Strindberg used the stage set, not to give the illusion of actual places in which his characters lived, but to support the themes of the play by providing visual symbols and a certain mood or atmosphere. In *A Dream Play* a castle grows, puts forth a chrysanthemum flower, and bursts into flames. The house in *The Ghost Sonata* is clearly symbolic. As viewed from the outside in the first scene, it represents the ultimate in beauty and luxury to The Student. The round room, into which we can see when the curtains are drawn, becomes the location of the second scene, in which everyone is stripped of his pretenses. The shift from outside to inside reinforces the contrast between appearance and reality. The third scene takes place still farther within the house, in the hyacinth room, where The Young Lady lives. The symbolism of the hyacinths is more complex. To Strindberg they represented a beauty which is overpoweringly sweet and hence enervating—almost poisonous. At the same time they are bulbs like the shallot seen onstage in the lap of the Buddha, and The Student explains how both the hyacinth and the shallot are images of the relationship between earth and heaven. The reality of the hyacinth room is not merely the paring away of false appearances but the penetration into an ultimate mystery. After the last words of the play have been spoken there is a final shift of scenery: the hyacinth room disappears, to be replaced by a reproduction of Boecklin's painting, "The Island of the Dead." The stage itself makes the last comment.

Strindberg was the first to make extensive use of the combination of dramatic techniques, exemplified by *The Ghost Sonata*, which has come to be known as "expressionism," a term first applied to the French painters who revolted against the impressionists and their concern with surfaces. Later it was used as the name of a movement which began about the time of the First World War and flourished largely in Germany. An expressionist was an artist who sought to *express* his feeling, his vision, his ideas, rather than to create an exact replica of anything. The implied contrast with the realist is partly false, since very few realists were solely concerned with imitation. Nevertheless, the techniques of expressionism were distinctive. In the plastic arts the most conspicuous were gross distortion and unnatural color. Expressionistic playwrights, taking their lead from Strindberg, began to depersonalize their characters, disregard probability in devising the action, return to a kind of poetic dialogue similar in some ways to that of the Elizabethan theater, and give a free rein to fantasy in the design of the stage set.

Expressionism as an organized movement did not last long, but expressionistic techniques appear in plays as different as Eugene O'Neill's *The Hairy Ape*, Thornton Wilder's *Our Town*, Arthur Miller's *Death of a Salesman*, Friedrich Dürrenmatt's *The Visit*, and Jean Genêt's *The Blacks*. Thus, directly or indirectly, Strindberg continues to influence the theater of today.

# The Ghost Sonata

*OPUS THREE OF THE CHAMBER PLAYS*

## AUGUST STRINDBERG

### CHARACTERS

THE OLD MAN, *Mr. Hummel*[1]

THE STUDENT, *Arkenholz*[2]

THE MILKMAID, *an apparition*

THE SUPERINTENDENT'S WIFE

THE SUPERINTENDENT

THE DEAD MAN, *formerly a Consul*

THE WOMAN IN BLACK, *daughter of* THE DEAD MAN *and* THE SUPERINTENDENT'S WIFE

THE COLONEL

THE MUMMY, THE COLONEL'S *wife*

THE YOUNG LADY, THE COLONEL'S *daughter, actually* THE OLD MAN'S *daughter*

BARON SKANSKORG, *engaged to* THE WOMAN IN BLACK

JOHANSSON, *Hummel's servant*

BENGTSSON, THE COLONEL'S *manservant*

THE FIANCÉE, *Hummel's former fiancée, now a white-haired old woman*

THE COOK

BEGGARS

A HOUSEMAID

(SCENE: *Stockholm*)

"The Ghost Sonata," translated by Evert Sprinchorn, from the book *The Chamber Plays* by August Strindberg, translated by Evert Sprinchorn and Seabury Quinn, Jr. Copyright, ©, 1962 by Evert Sprinchorn and Seabury Quinn, Jr. Reprinted by permission of E. P. Dutton & Co., Inc. The notes, unless otherwise indicated, are those of the translator, sometimes abbreviated because of space restrictions. A few others have been added by the editor.

[1] *Hummel* He was modeled in part on a Stockholm merchant, Isaac Hirsh, whose ostentatious philanthropy irritated Strindberg. The name Hummel may possibly have been suggested by a famous case of 1905, involving an American criminal lawyer, Abraham Henry Hummel, who was convicted on charges of conspiracy. There is also a Hummel who figures prominently in Beethoven's life   [2] *Arkenholz* The name of The Student reinforces the impression we have of him as a religious figure in the action of the play. He tries to save people from catastrophes

## SCENE 1

*The first two floors of a façade of a new house on a city square. Only the corner of the house is visible, the ground floor terminating in a round room, the second floor in a balcony with a flagpole.*

*When the curtains are drawn and the windows opened in the round room, one can see a white marble statue of a young woman surrounded by palms and bathed in sunlight. On the windowsill farthest to the left are pots of hyacinths—blue, white, pink.*

*Hanging on the railing of the balcony on the second story are a blue silk bedspread and two white pillowcases. The windows to the left are covered with sheets, signifying a death in the house. It is a bright Sunday morning.*

*A green park bench is downstage toward the left. Downstage right is a drinking fountain, with a long-handled drinking cup hanging at its side. To the left a kiosk, plastered with advertisements. A telephone booth is also onstage.*

*The main entrance to the house is at the right. The stairs leading up from the sidewalk to the door are of marble and the railings are of mahogany and brass. On the sidewalk on both sides of the entryway are tubs with small laurels.*

*The corner of the house with the round room also faces a side street which runs upstage.*

*On the first floor to the left of the entryway is a window with a special mirror, quite common in Sweden around the turn of the century, which enables those inside to view the passing scene without sticking their heads out the window.*

### At Rise

*The bells of several churches can be heard ringing in the distance.*

*The double doors in the entryway are wide open.*

THE WOMAN IN BLACK *stands motionless in the doorway.*

THE SUPERINTENDENT's WIFE *is sweeping the stairs and the sidewalk in front of the house. Having finished that, she polishes the brass in the entryway and then waters the laurels.*

*Sitting in a wheelchair near the kiosk is* THE OLD MAN, *reading a newspaper. He has white hair and beard and is wearing glasses.*

THE MILKMAID *comes in from around the corner, carrying a wire basket filled with bottles. She is wearing a summer dress, with brown shoes, black stockings and white cap. She takes off her cap and hangs it on the drinking fountain; wipes the sweat from her brow; takes a drink from the cup; washes her hands; arranges her hair, using the water in the fountain as a mirror.*

*The ringing of a steamship bell is heard, and now and then the silence is broken by the deep notes of the organs in the nearby churches.*

*After a few moments of silence, and after* THE MILKMAID *has finished arranging her hair,* THE STUDENT *enters from the left. He is unshaven and looks as if he had not had any sleep. He goes directly to the drinking fountain.*

*Pause.*

THE STUDENT. Could I borrow the cup, please?

(THE MILKMAID *hugs the cup to herself.*) Aren't you through using it?

(THE MILKMAID *stares at him in terror.*)

THE OLD MAN (*to himself*). Who on earth is he talking to?—I don't see anyone!—Is he crazy? (*He continues to stare at them in amazement.*)

THE STUDENT. What are you looking at? Do I look so awful?—Well, I haven't slept a wink all night, I suppose you think that I've been out doing the town. . . .

(THE MILKMAID *still stares at him in terror.*) Think I've been drinking, don't you?—Do I smell like it?

(THE MILKMAID *as before.*) I haven't had a chance to shave, I know that. . . . Come on, let me have a drink of water. After last night, I think I've earned it. (*Pause.*) I guess I have to tell you the whole story. I've spent the whole night bandaging wounds and taking care of the injured people. You see, I was there when the house collapsed last night. . . . Well, that's it.

(THE MILKMAID *rinses the cup and offers him a drink of water.*)

Thanks!

(THE MILKMAID *does not move.*)

(THE STUDENT *continues, slowly.*) I wonder if you would do me a big favor? (*Pause.*) The thing is, my eyes are inflamed, as you can see—but I've had my hands on wounds and on corpses —so I don't want to risk using my hands to wash my eyes. . . . I was wondering if you would take this clean handkerchief, dip it in that fresh water, and bathe my poor eyes with it?—Would you do that?—Will you play the Good Samaritan for me?

(THE MILKMAID *hesitates for a moment before doing as asked.*)

That's very kind of you. And here's something for your trouble—(*He has taken his wallet out and is about to offer her some money.* THE MILKMAID *makes a gesture of refusal.*) I'm sorry. Forgive me. I'm still in a daze. . . .

THE OLD MAN (*to* THE STUDENT). Forgive my speaking to you, but I could not help hearing you say you were in on that terrible accident yesterday evening. I was just sitting here reading about it in the paper.

THE STUDENT. Is it already in the paper?

THE OLD MAN. The whole story! And they've got a picture of you too. But they regret they were unable to obtain the name of the courageous young student. . . .

THE STUDENT (*looking at the paper*). So that's me! What do you know!

THE OLD MAN. Who . . . who was that you were talking to just now?

THE STUDENT. Didn't you see?

(*Pause.*)

THE OLD MAN. I suppose I'm being nosey, but would you do me the honor of giving me your name?

THE STUDENT. Why do you want to know that? I don't care for publicity. First they praise you, then they blame you. Running people down has been built up into one of the fine arts. Besides, I'm not looking for any reward.

THE OLD MAN. Rich, I suppose?

THE STUDENT. Not at all! I haven't got a dime to my name.

THE OLD MAN. It's strange . . . but I can't help thinking that I've heard your voice before. . . . When I was a young man I had a friend who couldn't pronounce window,[3] he always said winder. I've only met one person who said that, and that was him. The other is you, of course. Is it possible that you are related to Arkenholz, the wholesale dealer?

THE STUDENT. He was my father.

---

[3] *window* Although The Student has not said "window" previously, this is not a mere oversight; the window becomes a significant motif [Ed]

THE OLD MAN. Isn't fate strange? Then I have seen you when you were a child—under very difficult circumstances.

THE STUDENT. I suppose so. I understand I came into the world right in the middle of bankruptcy proceedings.

THE OLD MAN. Exactly!

THE STUDENT. May I ask what your name is?

THE OLD MAN. My name is Hummel.

THE STUDENT. Hummel? Then you're— Yes, I remember. . . .

THE OLD MAN. You've heard my name mentioned in your family?

THE STUDENT. Yes.

THE OLD MAN. And mentioned, perhaps, with a certain antipathy?

(THE STUDENT *remains silent.*)

I can well imagine! . . . No doubt you heard that I was the man who ruined your father? . . . Everyone who is ruined by stupid speculations comes to realize sooner or later that he was actually ruined by someone he couldn't fool. (*Pause.*) The truth of the matter is that your father fleeced me of seventeen thousand crowns, every cent I had saved up at the time.

THE STUDENT. It's remarkable how the same story can be told in two exactly opposite ways.

THE OLD MAN. Surely you don't think I'm being untruthful?

THE STUDENT. What do you think? My father didn't lie.

THE OLD MAN. That's true, a father never lies. . . . But I too am a father, and consequently . . .

THE STUDENT. What're you getting at?

THE OLD MAN. I saved your father from the worst possible misery, and he repaid me with all the terrible hatred of a man who feels obliged to be grateful. He taught his family to speak ill of me.

THE STUDENT. Maybe you made him ungrateful. The help you gave him was probably poisoned with unnecessary humiliations.

THE OLD MAN. My dear young man, all help is humiliating.

THE STUDENT. What do you want of me?

THE OLD MAN. Don't worry, I'm not asking for the money back. But if you would render me a few small services, I would consider myself well repaid. You see that I'm a cripple —some say it's my own fault—others blame my parents—personally I blame it all on life itself, with all its traps—in avoiding one you fall right into the next one. Anyway, I can't run up and down stairs—can't even pull bell cords. And so I ask you: help me!

THE STUDENT. What can I do?

THE OLD MAN. Well, first of all you might give my chair a push so that I can read the posters. I want to see what's playing to-night.

THE STUDENT (*pushing the wheelchair*). Don't you have a man who takes care of you?

THE OLD MAN. Yes, but he's off on an errand ... Be right back. ... You a medical student?

THE STUDENT. No, I'm studying languages. But I really don't know what I want to be.

THE OLD MAN. Aha!—How are you at mathematics?

THE STUDENT. Fairly good.

THE OLD MAN. Good! Good!—Would you possibly be interested in a job?

THE STUDENT. Sure, why not?

THE OLD MAN. Splendid! (*Reading the posters.*) They're giving *Die Walküre*[4] at the matinée. ... That means that the Colonel will be there with his daughter. And since he always sits on the aisle in the sixth row, I'll put you next to him. ... You go into that telephone booth over there and order a ticket for seat number eighty-two in the sixth row.

THE STUDENT. You expect me to go to the opera in the middle of the day?

THE OLD MAN. That's right! Just you do as I tell you and you won't regret it. I want to see you happy—rich and respected. Your début last night as the courageous rescuer is the beginning of your fame. From now on your very name will be a great asset.

THE STUDENT (*going toward the telephone booth*). I don't know what I'm getting into. It's crazy!

THE OLD MAN. Aren't you a gambler?

THE STUDENT. Yes, unfortunately. I always lose.

---

[4] *Die Walküre* the second opera in Wagner's cycle, *The Ring of the Nibelung*, is named for the Valkyries, the legendary horsewomen of the air, who bear to Valhalla the bodies of dead heroes [Ed]

THE OLD MAN. This will change your luck! —Go and telephone!

(*He picks up his newspaper and starts to read. In the meantime* THE LADY IN BLACK *has come out on the sidewalk and is talking with* THE SUPERINTENDENT'S WIFE. THE OLD MAN *listens furtively, but the audience hears nothing.* THE STUDENT *returns.*)

All set?

THE STUDENT. It's all taken care of.

THE OLD MAN. Take a look at that house.

THE STUDENT. I already have looked at it—very carefully. ... I went by here yesterday, when the sun was glittering on the panes—and dreaming of all the beauty and luxury there must be in that house, I said to my friend, "Imagine having an apartment there, four flights up, and a beautiful wife, and two pretty kids, and twenty thousand crowns in dividends every year."

THE OLD MAN. Did you now? Did you say that? Well, well! I too am very fond of that house. ...

THE STUDENT. Do you speculate in houses?

THE OLD MAN. Mmm—yes! But not in the way you think. ...

THE STUDENT. Do you know the people who live there?

THE OLD MAN. Every single one. At my age you know everyone, including their fathers and their grandfathers—and you always find you're related to them somehow. I've just turned eighty. ... But no one knows me, not really. ... I take a great interest in human destinies. ...

(*The curtains in the round room are drawn up.* THE COLONEL *is seen inside, dressed in civilian clothes. After having looked at the thermometer he moves away from the window and stands in front of the marble statue.*)

Look, there's the Colonel! You'll sit next to him this afternoon.

THE STUDENT. Is that him—the Colonel? I don't understand anything that's going on. It's like a fairy tale.

THE OLD MAN. My whole life, my dear young man, is like a book of fairy tales. But although the stories are different, one thread ties them all together and the same leitmotif recurs constantly.

THE STUDENT. Who is that marble statue in there?

THE OLD MAN. That's his wife, naturally. . . .

THE STUDENT. Was she so wonderful? Did he love her so much?

THE OLD MAN. Hmm yes . . . yes, of course.

THE STUDENT. Well, tell me!

THE OLD MAN. Come now, you know we can't judge other people. . . . Suppose I were to tell you that she left him, that he beat her, that she came back again and married him again, and that she is sitting in there right now like a mummy, worshiping her own statue, you would think I was crazy.

THE STUDENT. I can't understand it!

THE OLD MAN. That doesn't surprise me!— And over there we have the hyacinth window. That's where his daughter lives. She's out horseback riding, but she'll be home soon. . . .

THE STUDENT. Who's the lady in black that's talking to the caretaker?

THE OLD MAN. Well, that's a little complicated. But it's connected with the dead man upstairs, there where you see the white sheets.

THE STUDENT. And who was he?

THE OLD MAN. A human being, like the rest of us. The most conspicuous thing about him was his vanity. . . . Now if you were a Sunday child, you would soon see him come out of that very door just to look at the consulate flag at half-mast for himself. Yes, you see, he was a consul. Liked nothing better than coronets and lions, plumed hats and colored ribbons.

THE STUDENT. Sunday child, did you say? I was actually born on a Sunday, so I'm told.

THE OLD MAN. Really! Are you—! I should have guessed it. I could tell by the color of your eyes. . . . But—then you can see . . . what others can't see, haven't you noticed that?

THE STUDENT. I don't know what others see. But sometimes—Well, there are some things you don't talk about!

THE OLD MAN. I knew it, I knew it! But you can talk to me about it. I understand— things like that. . . .

THE STUDENT. Yesterday, for example. . . . I was drawn to that little side street where the house collapsed afterwards. . . . I walked down the street and stopped in front of a house that I had never seen before. . . . Then I noticed a crack in the wall. I could hear the floor beams snapping in two. I leaped forward and grabbed up a child that was walking under the wall. . . . The next moment the house collapsed. . . . I escaped—but in my arms—where I thought I had the child— there wasn't anything. . . .

THE OLD MAN. Remarkable. Remarkable. . . . I always knew that. . . . But tell me something: why were you making all those gestures just now at the fountain? And why were you talking to yourself?

THE STUDENT. Didn't you see the milkmaid I was talking to?

THE OLD MAN (in horror). Milkmaid!?

THE STUDENT. Yes, of course. She handed me the cup.

THE OLD MAN. Indeed? . . . so that's the way it is? . . . Very well, I may not have second sight, but I have other powers. . . .

(A white-haired woman sits down at the window with the mirror.)

Look at the old lady in the window! Do you see her? . . . Good, good! That was my fiancée—once upon a time—sixty years ago. . . . I was twenty. Don't be afraid, she doesn't recognize me. We see each other every day, but it doesn't mean a thing to me —although we once vowed to love each other forever. Forever!

THE STUDENT. How foolish you were in those days! Nowadays we don't tell girls things like that.

THE OLD MAN. Forgive us, young man. We didn't know any better! . . . But can you see that that old woman was once young and beautiful?

THE STUDENT. No, I can't . . . Well, maybe. I like the way she turns her head to look at things . . . I can't see her eyes.

(THE SUPERINTENDENT'S WIFE comes out carrying a basket of spruce greens, which she strews on the sidewalk, in accordance with Swedish custom at funerals.)

THE OLD MAN. Aha, the wife of the superintendent! The lady in black is her daughter by the dead man upstairs. That's why her husband got the job as superintendent. . . . But the lady in black has a lover—very aristocratic and waiting to inherit a fortune. Right now he's in the process of getting a divorce—from his present wife, who is giving him a town house just to get rid of him. The aristocratic lover is the son-in-law of the dead man, and you see his bedclothes being aired on the balcony up there.—Complicated, don't you think?

THE STUDENT. It's damned complicated!

THE OLD MAN. Yes, indeed it is, inside and outside, although it all looks so simple.

THE STUDENT. But then who is the dead man?

THE OLD MAN. You just asked me and I told you. If you could look around the corner where the service entrance is, you'd see a pack of poor people whom he used to help—when he felt like it.

THE STUDENT. Then I suppose he was a kind and charitable man?

THE OLD MAN. Oh, yes—sometimes.

THE STUDENT. Not always?

THE OLD MAN. No, that's how people are!—Listen, will you give me a little push over there in the sun? I'm so terribly cold. When you never get to move around, the blood congeals. I'm going to die soon, I know that. But before I do there are a few things I want to take care of.—Feel my hand, just feel how cold I am.

THE STUDENT. My god! It's unbelievable! (*He tries to free his hand but* THE OLD MAN *holds on to it.*)

THE OLD MAN. Don't leave me, I beg you— I'm tired, I'm lonely—but it hasn't always been this way, I tell you.—I have an infinitely long life behind me—infinitely long—I've made people unhappy and people have made me unhappy, the one cancels out the other. But before I die I want to make you happy. . . . Our destinies are tangled together through your father—and other things.

THE STUDENT. Let go, let go of my hand—you are drawing all my strength from me—you're freezing me to death—what do you want of me?

THE OLD MAN. Patience. You'll soon see and understand. . . . There she comes.—

THE STUDENT. The Colonel's daughter?

THE OLD MAN. Yes! *His* daughter! Just look

at her!—have you ever seen such a master-piece?

THE STUDENT. She looks like the marble statue in there.

THE OLD MAN. She should. That's her mother!

THE STUDENT. Incredibly beautiful! "Can woman be so fair?" . . . "*Und selig, wer das gute Schicksal hat, als Bräutigam sie heimzuführen!*"[5]

THE OLD MAN. Yes, indeed. "Happy the man whose luck it is to bear her home to wedded bliss."—I see you appreciate her beauty. Not everyone recognizes it. . . . Well, then, it is ordained!

(THE YOUNG LADY *enters from the left dressed in a riding habit, in the manner of a modern English amazon, and, without taking notice of anyone, crosses slowly over to the door of the house. Before entering, she stops and says a few words to* THE SUPERINTENDENT'S WIFE.

THE STUDENT *covers his eyes with his hands.*)
Are you crying?

THE STUDENT. When I see how far beyond my reach my happiness is, what can I feel but despair?

THE OLD MAN. But I can open doors—and hearts—if only I can find an arm to do my will. Serve me, and you shall be a lord of creation!

THE STUDENT. A devil's bargain? You want me to sell my soul?

THE OLD MAN. Sell nothing!—Don't you understand, all my life I have *taken, taken!* Now I crave to give, to give! But nobody will take what I have to offer. I'm a rich man, very rich—and without any heirs.—Oh, yes, I have a good-for-nothing son who torments the life out of me. . . . You could become my son, become my heir while I'm still alive, enjoy life while I'm here to see it—at least from a distance.

THE STUDENT. What do you want me to do?

THE OLD MAN. First, go and hear *Die Walküre!*

_____
[5] "*Can woman . . . heimzuführen!*" in the Witch's Kitchen scene of Goethe's *Faust*, Part I, Faust, on seeing the vision of the beautiful woman, exclaims, "Can woman be so fair?" The reply (which is not in German in Strindberg's original) is given by Mephistopheles [Ed]

THE STUDENT. That's already been taken care of. What else?

THE OLD MAN. This evening you shall be sitting in there—in the round room!

THE STUDENT. How do you expect me to get in?

THE OLD MAN. By way of *Die Walküre!*

THE STUDENT. Why did you pick me for your—your medium? Did you know me before?

THE OLD MAN. Of course, of course! I've had my eyes on you for a long time. . . . Ah! Look up there, on the balcony, where the maid is raising the flag to half-mast for the Consul—and now she's turning over the bedclothes. . . . Do you see that blue quilt? It was made for two to sleep under, and now it covers only one. . . .

(THE YOUNG LADY, *in a change of clothes, appears at the window to water the hyacinths.*)

There's my dear little girl. Look at her, just look at her! . . . She's talking to the flowers now. Isn't she just like a blue hyacinth herself? She gives them water to drink, the purest water, and they transform the water into color and perfume.—Here comes the Colonel with a newspaper. . . . Now he's pointing to your picture! She's reading about your heroic deed.—It's starting to cloud over. Suppose it starts to rain? I'll be in a pretty mess if Johansson doesn't come back soon.

(*It grows cloudy and dark.* THE OLD WOMAN *at the window mirror closes her window.*)

I see my fiancée is closing up shop. . . . Seventy-nine years. . . . That window mirror is the only mirror she ever uses. That's because she can't see herself in it, only the outside world and from two directions at once. But the world can see her. She doesn't realize that. . . . All the same, not bad-looking for an old woman.

(*Now,* THE DEAD MAN, *wrapped in a winding sheet, is seen coming out of the main door.*)

THE STUDENT. Oh my god, what—?

THE OLD MAN. What do you see?

THE STUDENT. Don't *you* see? Don't you see, in the doorway, the dead man?

THE OLD MAN. No, I don't see anything. But I'm not surprised. Tell me exactly what—

THE STUDENT. He's stepping out into the street. . . . (*Pause.*) Now he's turning his head and looking up at the flag.

THE OLD MAN. What did I tell you? Watch, he will count every wreath and read every calling card. I pity whoever is missing!

THE STUDENT. Now he's turning the corner. . . .

THE OLD MAN. He's gone to count the poor people at the service entrance. The poor add such a nice touch to an obituary: "Received the blessings of the populace!" Yes, but he won't receive my blessing!—Just between us, he was a big scoundrel.

THE STUDENT. But benevolent.

THE OLD MAN. A benevolent scoundrel. Always thinking of his own magnificent funeral. . . . When he could feel his end was near, he embezzled fifty thousand crowns from the state. . . . Now his daughter is running around with another woman's husband and wondering about the will. . . . The scoundrel can hear every word we're saying. I hope he gets an earful!—Here's Johansson.

(JOHANSSON *enters from the left.*)

Report!

(JOHANSSON *speaks to* THE OLD MAN, *but the audience cannot hear what he says.*)

What do you mean, not at home? You're an ass!—What about the telegram?—Not a word! . . . go on, go on! . . . six o'clock this evening? That's good!—An extra edition? —With all the details about him? . . . Arkenholz, student . . . born . . . his parents. . . . Splendid! . . . It's beginning to rain, I think. . . . And what did he say? . . . Really, really!—He didn't *want* to? Well, he's going to have to!—Here comes the Baron, or whatever he is!—Push me around the corner, Johansson. I want to hear what the poor people are saying.—And Arkenholz! Don't go away. Do you understand?—Well, come on, come on, what are you waiting for!

(JOHANSSON *pushes the wheelchair around the corner.* THE STUDENT *has turned to look at* THE YOUNG LADY *who is loosening the earth in the hyacinth pots. Dressed in mourning,* BARON SKANSKORG *enters and speaks to* THE LADY IN BLACK, *who has been walking up and down the sidewalk.*)

BARON SKANSKORG. What can we do about it? We simply have to wait.

LADY IN BLACK (*intensely*). But I can't wait, don't you understand?

BARON SKANSKORG. Well, if that's the way it is, you'll have to go to the country.

LADY IN BLACK. I don't want to do that!

BARON SKANSKORG. Come over here. Otherwise they'll hear what we're saying.

(*They move over toward the advertisement column and continue their conversation unheard by the audience.* JOHANSSON *enters from the right.*)

JOHANSSON (*to* THE STUDENT). My master asks you to forget that other matter. . . .

THE STUDENT (*warily*). Just a minute—I want to know something first. Tell me, exactly what is your employer's business?

JOHANSSON. What can I say? He's so many things, and he's been everything.

THE STUDENT. He's not crazy, is he?

JOHANSSON. What does it mean to be crazy? All his life he's been looking for a Sunday child. That's what he says—but he might be making it up. . . .

THE STUDENT. What's he after? Money?

JOHANSSON. Power.—All day long he rides around in his chariot like the great god Thor.[6] . . . He keeps his eye on houses, tears them down, opens up streets, builds up city squares. But he also breaks into houses,[7] sneaks in through the windows, ravages human lives, kills his enemies, and forgives nothing and nobody. . . . Can you imagine that that little cripple was once a Don Juan. But no woman would ever stick with him.

THE STUDENT. Sounds inconsistent.

JOHANSSON. Oh, no. You see, he was so sly that he knew how to get the women to leave when he got bored with them. But that was a long time ago. Now he's more like a horse thief at a slave market. He steals people—in more ways than one. . . . He literally stole me out of the hands of the law. I made a little

mistake—that's all—and he was the only one who knew about it. But instead of putting me in jail, he made me his slave. I slave for him just for my food—which isn't the best in the world.

THE STUDENT. What's he got up his sleeve? What's he want to do in this house?

JOHANSSON. I wouldn't want to say! I wouldn't even know where to begin!

THE STUDENT. I think I'd better get out while the getting is good.

JOHANSSON. Look at the young lady! She's dropped her bracelet out of the window.

(*Her bracelet has fallen off* THE YOUNG LADY's *arm and through the open window.* THE STUDENT *crosses over slowly, picks up the bracelet and hands it to* THE YOUNG LADY, *who thanks him stiffly.* THE STUDENT *goes back to* JOHANSSON.)

I thought you said you were leaving. It isn't as easy as you think once *he* has slipped his net over your head. . . . And he's afraid of nothing between heaven and earth—yes, one thing—or rather one person.

THE STUDENT. I bet I know.

JOHANSSON. How can you know?

THE STUDENT. Just guessing! Could it be . . . he's afraid of a little Milkmaid?

JOHANSSON. He turns his head away whenever he sees a milk wagon. . . . Sometimes he talks in his sleep. He must have been in Hamburg once. . . .

THE STUDENT. Can I depend on him?

JOHANSSON. You can depend on him—to do anything and everything!

THE STUDENT. What's he up to around the corner?

JOHANSSON. Eavesdropping on the poor. . . . Planting a word here and there, chipping away at one stone at a time—until the whole house falls—metaphorically speaking. Oh yes, I've had an education. And I used to be a bookseller. . . . Are you leaving or staying?

THE STUDENT. I don't like to be ungrateful. This man once saved my father, and all he's asking for now is a little favor in return.

JOHANSSON. What is that?

THE STUDENT. He wants me to go and see *Die Walküre.*

JOHANSSON. That's beyond me. . . . He's always got something up his sleeve. . . . Look

---

[6] *Thor* in Norse mythology, the god of thunder, war, and strength, the son of Odin [Ed]   [7] *breaks into houses* The description of old Hummel as a housebreaker may be an allusion to Joel 2: 9: "They shall climb up into the houses; they shall enter in at the windows like a thief." Glossing this passage, Swedenborg says "to steal means to deprive others of the truths of their faith"

at him, he's talking to the policeman. He's always in with the police. He makes use of them, gets them involved in his business, ties them hand and foot with false promises of future possibilities. And all the while he's pumping them, pumping them.—Mark my words, before the night is over he'll be received in the round room.

THE STUDENT. What does he want in there? What's he got to do with the Colonel?

JOHANSSON. I'm not sure, but I've got my ideas. You'll be able to see for yourself when you go there!

THE STUDENT. I'll never get in there. . . .

JOHANSSON. That depends on you! Go to *Die Walküre.*

THE STUDENT. Is that the way?

JOHANSSON. If he said so, it is!—Look at him, just look at him! Riding his war chariot, drawn in triumph by the beggars, who don't get a cent for it, just a hint that something might come their way at his funeral!

(THE OLD MAN *enters standing in his wheelchair, drawn by one of* THE BEGGARS, *and followed by the others.*)

THE OLD MAN. Let us hail the noble youth, who risked his own life to save so many in yesterday's accident! Hail Arkenholz!

(THE BEGGARS *bare their heads but do not cheer.* THE YOUNG LADY, *standing in the window, waves her handkerchief.* THE COLONEL *looks at the scene from his window.* THE FIANCÉE *stands up at her window.* THE HOUSEMAID *on the balcony raises the flag to the top.*)

Hail the hero, my fellow citizens! I know indeed it is Sunday, but the ass in the pit and the ear in the field absolve us. And though I may not be a Sunday child, I can see into the future and I can heal the sick. I have even brought a drowned soul back to life. . . . That happened in Hamburg, yes, on a Sunday morning, just like this—

(THE MILKMAID *enters, seen only by* THE STUDENT *and* THE OLD MAN. *She stretches her arms above her head like a drowning person and stares fixedly at* THE OLD MAN. THE OLD MAN *sits down, and shrivels up in fear and terror.*)

Get me out of here, Johansson! Quick—Arkenholz, don't you forget *Die Walküre!*

THE STUDENT. What is all this?

JOHANSSON. We shall see! We shall see!

## SCENE 2

*In the round room. At the back of the stage a stove of white glazed porcelain, its mantel decorated with a mirror, a pendulum clock, and candelabra. At the right side of the stage a hallway can be seen and through it a view of a green room with mahogany furniture. At the left of the stage stands the statue in the shadow of the palm trees, and with a curtain which can be drawn to conceal it. In the rear wall to the left of the stove is the door to the hyacinth room, where* THE YOUNG LADY *is seen reading.* THE COLONEL'*s back can be seen in the green room, where he is writing at his desk.*

THE COLONEL'*s valet,* BENGTSSON, *wearing livery, enters from the hall, accompanied by* JOHANSSON, *who is dressed very formally as a waiter.*

BENGTSSON. Now, Johansson, you'll have to wait on the table while I take care of the coats. Have you done this before?

JOHANSSON. During the day I push that war chariot, as you know, but in the evenings I work as a waiter at receptions. It's always been my dream to get into this house. . . . They're peculiar people, aren't they?

BENGTSSON. Well, yes, I think one might say that they're a little strange.

JOHANSSON. Are we going to have a musicale this evening? Or what is the occasion?

BENGTSSON. Just the ordinary ghost supper, as we call it. They drink tea, without saying a word, or else the Colonel talks all by himself. And they champ their biscuits and crackers all at once and all in unison. They sound like a pack of rats in an attic.

JOHANSSON. Why do you call it the ghost supper?

BENGTSSON. They all look like ghosts. . . . This has been going on for twenty years—always the same people, always saying the same things. Or else keeping silent to avoid being embarrassed.

JOHANSSON. Where's the lady of the house? Isn't she around?

BENGTSSON. Oh, yes. But she's crazy. She keeps herself shut up in a closet because her eyes can't stand the light. She's sitting in there right now. (*He points to a wall-papered door.*[8])

JOHANSSON. In there?

BENGTSSON. I told you they were a little peculiar.

JOHANSSON. What on earth does she look like?

BENGTSSON. Like a mummy. Do you want to see her? (*He opens the papered door.*) There she sits!

JOHANSSON. Je-sus!

THE MUMMY (*babbling*). Why do you open the door? Didn't I tell you to keep it closed?

BENGTSSON (*as if talking to a baby*). Ta, ta, ta, ta, ta!—Is little chickadee going to be nice to me? Then little chickadee will get something good!—Pretty polly!

THE MUMMY (*like a parrot*). Pretty polly! Are you there, Jacob? Jacob? Cluck, cluck!

BENGTSSON. She thinks she's a parrot—and maybe she is. (*To* THE MUMMY.) Come on, polly, whistle for us!

(THE MUMMY *whistles.*)

JOHANSSON. I thought I had seen everything, but this tops it all.

BENGTSSON. Well, when a house grows old, it turns moldy and rotten, and when people are together too much and torment each other too long, they go crazy. Take the lady in this house—shut up, polly!—this mummy has been sitting here for forty years—the same husband, same furniture, same relatives, same friends.... (*Closing the door on* THE MUMMY.) And imagine what's gone on in this house! Even I don't know the whole story.... Look at this statue. That's the lady of the house as a young girl!

JOHANSSON. Oh my god!—Is that the mummy?

BENGTSSON. Yes. It's enough to make one cry! But this lady—carried away by her imagination or something—has acquired certain of the peculiarities of the prating parrot. She can't stand cripples, for instance —or sick people. She can't even stand the sight of her own daughter because she's sick.

JOHANSSON. Is that young girl sick?

BENGTSSON. Yes. Didn't you know?

JOHANSSON. No. . . . What about the Colonel? Who is he?

BENGTSSON. Wait a while and you'll see!

JOHANSSON (*looking at the statue*). It's terrifying to realize that—How old is the lady now?

BENGTSSON. Who knows? But I've heard it said that when she was thirty-five she looked like she was nineteen.—And she convinced the Colonel that she was ... here in this house.... Do you know what that black Japanese screen[9] by the couch is for? It's called a death screen, and when somebody's going to die, it's placed around them, same as in a hospital.

JOHANSSON. What a horrible house.... That poor student thought that when he entered this house he would be entering paradise.

BENGTSSON. Which student? Oh, yes, of course! The one that's coming here tonight. The Colonel and his daughter met him at the opera and were captivated by him.... Hm. ... But let me ask you a couple of questions. Who's your master? The financier in the wheelchair?

JOHANSSON (*nodding*). Yes, that's right.—Is he coming here too?

BENGTSSON. He's not invited.

JOHANSSON. Then he'll come uninvited—if necessary!

(THE OLD MAN *appears in the hallway, dressed in frock coat and high hat. He moves silently forward on his crutches, like a black spider, and eavesdrops on the servants.*)

BENGTSSON. I'll bet he's a real old mean one.

JOHANSSON. A perfect specimen!

BENGTSSON. He looks like the devil incarnate!

JOHANSSON. And he's a black magician, I

---

[8] *wall-papered door* Doors concealed by wallpaper were common in Sweden in the nineteenth century. See Strindberg's *The Father*, for another example. The wall-papered door is *not* one of the bizarre elements in the *Sonata*

[9] *black Japanese screen* A Japanese screen caught Strindberg's eye when he visited his sister's apartment and was linked up in his mind with a description given by one of his nieces, who was a nurse, of what was done in the hospital when someone died. (See Gunnar Ollén, *Strindberg's dramatik*, 2d ed., Stockholm, 1961, p. 469)

tell you. He can go through locked doors—

THE OLD MAN (*coming forward and grabbing* JOHANSSON *by the ear*). Fool! Hold your tongue! (*To* BENGTSSON.) Announce me to the Colonel!

BENGTSSON. But we're expecting company here.

THE OLD MAN. I know you are! My visit is not unexpected—although undesired.

BENGTSSON. I see. What was the name? Mr. Hummel?

THE OLD MAN. That's right! Precisely!

(BENGTSSON *goes down the hall into the green room and closes the door.*) (*To* JOHANSSON.) Disappear!

(JOHANSSON *hesitates.*)

Vanish!

(JOHANSSON *vanishes down the hall.* THE OLD MAN *inspects the room. Stops in front of the statue. Much amazed.*)

Amelia! . . . It is she! . . . Amelia! (*He roams about the room fingering objects. Stops in front of the mirror to adjust his wig. Returns to the statue.*)

THE MUMMY (*from within the closet*). Pretty polly!

THE OLD MAN (*startled*). What on earth! Sounded like a parrot in the room. But I don't see any.

THE MUMMY. You there, Jacob?

THE OLD MAN. Place is haunted.

THE MUMMY. Jacob!

THE OLD MAN. It's enough to frighten one! . . . So that's the kind of secrets they've been keeping in this house! (*With his back to the closet he studies a portrait on the wall.*) There he is!—The old Colonel himself!

THE MUMMY (*coming out of the closet, goes up to* THE OLD MAN *from behind and gives his wig a pull*). Cluck, cluck. Cluck, cluck. Are you dumb cluck—cluck?

THE OLD MAN (*frightened out of his skin*). Oh my god in heaven!—Who are you?

THE MUMMY (*speaking in her normal voice*). Is that you, Jacob?

THE OLD MAN. Yes. My name is Jacob.

THE MUMMY (*movingly*). And my name is Amelia!

THE OLD MAN. Oh no. . . . No, no. . . . Oh my god! . . .

THE MUMMY. Yes, this is how I look!—And that's how I did look once upon a time. Life gives one a great education. Most of my life

I've spent in the closet, so that I won't have to see—or be seen. . . . But you, Jacob, what are you looking for here?

THE OLD MAN. My child! Our child!

THE MUMMY. She's sitting in there.

THE OLD MAN. Where?

THE MUMMY. In there, in the hyacinth room.

THE OLD MAN (*looking at* THE YOUNG LADY). Yes, there she is! (*Pause.*) And what does her father think of her—I mean, the Colonel—your husband?

THE MUMMY. I had a quarrel with him once, and told him everything. . . .

THE OLD MAN. And? . . .

THE MUMMY. He didn't believe me. He said, "That's what all women say when they want to murder their husbands." . . . All the same it was a terrible crime. His whole life has been falsified, including his family tree. When I look at his family record in the peerage, I say to myself she's no better than a runaway servant girl with a false birth certificate, and girls like that are sent to the reformatory.

THE OLD MAN. A lot of people forge their birth certificates. I seem to remember that even you falsified the date of your birth.

THE MUMMY. It was my mother who put me up to it. I'm not to blame for that! . . . And furthermore, you played the biggest part in our crime.

THE OLD MAN. Not true! Your husband started it all when he stole my fiancée from me! I was born unable to forgive until I have punished. I've always looked upon it as an imperative duty. And I still do!

THE MUMMY. What do you expect to find in this house? What do you want here? And how did you get in?—Does your business concern my daughter? Keep your hands off her, I warn you, or you'll die!

THE OLD MAN. I wish her nothing but the best!

THE MUMMY. And you must have consideration for her father, too!

THE OLD MAN. Never!

THE MUMMY. Then you must die. In this room. Behind that screen.

THE OLD MAN. Be that as it may. But I'm a bulldog. I never let go.

THE MUMMY. You want to marry her to that student. Why? He has nothing; he is nothing.

THE OLD MAN. He'll be a rich man, thanks to me.

THE MUMMY. Are you one of the invited guests tonight?

THE OLD MAN. No, but I've decided to invite myself to this ghost supper!

THE MUMMY. Do you know who'll be here?

THE OLD MAN. Not entirely.

THE MUMMY. The Baron—who lives upstairs, and whose father-in-law was buried this afternoon—

THE OLD MAN. Yes, the Baron—who is getting a divorce in order to marry the daughter of the superintendent's wife. The Baron—who was once—your lover!

THE MUMMY. And then there'll be your former fiancée—whom my husband seduced.

THE OLD MAN. A very select gathering. . . .

THE MUMMY. Oh god, why can't we die? If only we could die!

THE OLD MAN. Then why do you keep seeing each other?

THE MUMMY. Our crimes and our secrets and our guilt bind us together! We have split up and gone our separate ways an infinite number of times. But we're always drawn back together again. . . .

THE OLD MAN. I believe the Colonel is coming.

THE MUMMY. Then I'll go in to Adele. . . . (*Pause.*) Jacob, don't do anything foolish! Be considerate toward him. . . .

(*A pause. She leaves.*)

THE COLONEL (*enters, cold and reserved*). Please sit down.

(THE OLD MAN *takes his time seating himself. A pause.* THE COLONEL *stares at him.*)
Did you write this letter?

THE OLD MAN. I did.

THE COLONEL. And your name is Hummel?

THE OLD MAN. It is.

(*Pause.*)

THE COLONEL. Since it's clear that you have bought up all my outstanding promissory notes, it follows that I'm completely at your mercy. Now what do you want?

THE OLD MAN. I want to be paid—in one way or another.

THE COLONEL. In what way?

THE OLD MAN. A very simple way. Don't let's talk about money. Allow me to come and go in your house—as a guest.

THE COLONEL. If that's all it takes to satisfy you—

THE OLD MAN. Thank you!

THE COLONEL. And what else?

THE OLD MAN. Dismiss Bengtsson!

THE COLONEL. Why? Bengtsson is my devoted servant. He's been with me during my whole career. The army awarded him a medal for faithful service. Why should I dismiss him?

THE OLD MAN. I have no doubt he's a very fine man in your eyes. But he's not the man he seems to be!

THE COLONEL. Who is?

THE OLD MAN (*taken aback*). True!—But Bengtsson must go!

THE COLONEL. Are you going to give orders in my house?

THE OLD MAN. Yes! Since I own everything that you can lay your eyes on—furniture, curtains, service, linen . . . and other things.

THE COLONEL. What other things?

THE OLD MAN. Everything. I own it all. Everything that you see here is mine!

THE COLONEL. I can't argue that. But my family honor, my coat of arms and my good name are things you cannot take from me!

THE OLD MAN. Yes, I can. They don't belong to you. (*Pause.*) You are not a nobleman.

THE COLONEL. I shall give you the opportunity of withdrawing those words!

THE OLD MAN (*producing a piece of paper*). If you will take the trouble to read this extract from the standard book of genealogy, you will see that the family whose name you have assumed has been extinct for over a century.

THE COLONEL (*reading*). Of course I've heard rumors like this before. But it was my father's name before it was mine. . . . (*Reading on.*) I can't deny it. You are quite right. . . . I am not a nobleman! Not even that. . . . Therefore I shall take this signet ring from off my hand—Oh, but of course, excuse me: it belongs to you. There you are.

THE OLD MAN (*putting the ring in his pocket*).

Let us continue.—You are not a colonel either!

THE COLONEL. Am I not?

THE OLD MAN. No! You held a temporary commission as a colonel in the American Volunteers; but at the end of the Spanish-American War and the reorganization of the Army, all such titles were abolished.

THE COLONEL. Is that true?

THE OLD MAN (*reaching into his pocket*). Do you want to see for yourself?

THE COLONEL. No, it won't be necessary. . . . Who are you? What gives you the right to sit there and strip me naked in this way?

THE OLD MAN. Patience, my good man! And as far as stripping is concerned—do you really want to know who you are?

THE COLONEL. Have you no decency?

THE OLD MAN. Take off that wig of yours and have a look at yourself in the mirror. And while you're at it, take out those false teeth and shave off that moustache and let Bengtsson unlace your metal corset, and then we shall see if a certain valet, Mr. *X*, won't recognize himself—a valet in a certain house who flirted with the maids in order to scrounge in the kitchen.

(THE COLONEL *reaches for the bell on the table.* THE OLD MAN *stops him, saying:*)

I wouldn't touch that if I were you. If you call Bengtsson I'll order him arrested. . . . I believe your guests are arriving. Now let us be calm, and go on playing our old roles for a while longer.

THE COLONEL. Who are you? I've seen your eyes and heard your voice before.

THE OLD MAN. Never mind that. Be silent and do as you're told!

THE STUDENT (*enters and bows to* THE COLONEL). How do you do, sir!

THE COLONEL. Welcome to my house, young man! Your heroism at that terrible accident has brought your name to everybody's lips. I deem it an honor to receive you in my house.

THE STUDENT. You're very kind, sir. It's a great honor for me, sir. I've never expected—well, my humble birth—and your illustrious name and your noble birth. . . .

THE COLONEL. Mr. Hummel, may I introduce Mr. Arkenholz, who is a student at the university. The ladies are in there, Mr. Arkenholz—if you care to join them. I have a few more things I wanted to say to Mr. Hummel.

(THE COLONEL *shows* THE STUDENT *in to the hyacinth room where he remains visible to the audience, engaged in shy conversation with* THE YOUNG LADY.)

An excellent young man—musical, sings, writes poetry. . . . If it weren't for his birth and social position I certainly wouldn't have anything against—my. . . .

THE OLD MAN. Against what?

THE COLONEL. Having my daughter—

THE OLD MAN. *Your* daughter! . . . Apropos of her, why does she always sit in that room?

THE COLONEL. She feels she has to sit in the hyacinth room whenever she's in the house. A peculiarity of hers. . . . Here comes Miss Beatrice von Holsteinkrona. Charming woman. Very active in the church and with an income that perfectly suits her position and circumstances. . . .

THE OLD MAN (*to himself*). My fiancée!

(THE FIANCÉE *enters, white-haired and giving every appearance of being crazy.*)

THE COLONEL. Miss Holsteinkrona—Mr. Hummel.

(THE FIANCÉE *curtsies and takes a seat.* BARON SKANSKORG *enters next—dressed in mourning and with a strange look on his face—and sits down.*)

Baron Skanskorg—

THE OLD MAN (*in an aside, without rising*). A jewel thief, if ever I saw one. (*To* THE COLONEL.) Now let the mummy in, and the party can begin.

THE COLONEL (*in the doorway to the hyacinth room*). Polly!

THE MUMMY (*enters*). Cluck, cluck! Dumbcluck!

THE COLONEL. Shall we invite the young people, too?

THE OLD MAN. No! Not the young people! They shall be spared.

(*They seat themselves in a circle. Silence.*)

THE COLONEL. Shall I ring for the tea?

THE OLD MAN. Why bother? No one cares for tea. Why play games?

(*Pause.*)

THE COLONEL. Then perhaps we should start a conversation?

THE OLD MAN (*slowly, deliberately and with frequent pauses*). About the weather? Which we know. Ask each other how we're feeling? Which we also know. I prefer silence . . : in which one can hear thoughts and see the past. Silence cannot hide anything—which is more than you can say for words. I read the other day that the differences in languages originated among the primitive savages who sought to keep their secrets from the other tribes. Languages are therefore codes, and he who finds the key can understand all the languages of the world. But that doesn't mean that secrets cannot be discovered without a key. Especially in those cases where paternity must be proved. Legal proof is of course a different matter. Two false witnesses[10] provide complete proof of whatever they agree to say. But in the kind of escapades I have in mind one doesn't take witnesses along. Nature herself has planted in man a blushing sense of shame, which seeks to hide what should be hidden. But we slip into certain situations without intending to, and chance confronts us with moments of revelation, when the deepest secrets are revealed, the mask is ripped from the impostor and the villain stands exposed. . . .

(*Pause. All look at each other in silence.*) Extraordinary, how silent you all are! (*Long silence.*) Take this house, for example. In this estimable house, in this elegant home, where beauty, wealth, and culture are united . . . (*Long silence.*) All of us sitting here, we know who we are, don't we? . . . I don't have to tell you. . . . And you know me although you pretend ignorance. . . . Sitting in that room is my daughter, yes mine, you know that too. . . . She had lost all desire to live, without knowing why. . . . She was withering away because of the air in this house, which reeks of crime, deception, and deceits of every kind. . . . That is why I had to find a friend for her, a friend from whose very presence she would apprehend the warmth and light radiated by a noble deed. . . . (*Long silence.*)

That was my mission in this house. To pull up the weeds, to expose the crimes, to settle the accounts, so that these young people might make a new beginning in this home, which is my gift to them! (*Long silence.*) Listen to the ticking of the clock, like a deathwatch beetle in the wall! Listen to what it's saying: "time's-up, time's-up! . . ." When it strikes—in just a few moments— your time is up. Then you may go—not before. But the clock raises its arm before it strikes.

(*The clock can be heard preparing to strike the hour.*)

—Listen! It's warning you: "Clocks can strike!"—And I can strike too! (*He strikes the table with his crutch.*) Do you understand?

(*Silence.*)

THE MUMMY (*goes over to the clock and stops its pendulum. In her normal voice, speaking seriously*). But I can stop time in its course. I can wipe out the past, and undo what is done. Not with bribes, not with threats—but through suffering and repentance. (*Approaching* THE OLD MAN.) We are poor miserable creatures, we know that. We have erred, we have transgressed, we, like all the rest. We are not what we seem to be. At bottom we are better than ourselves, since we abhor and detest our misdeeds. But when you, Jacob Hummel, with your false name, come here to sit in judgment over us, that proves that you are more contemptible than we! And you are not the one you seem to be! You are a slave trader, a stealer of souls! You once stole me with false promises. You murdered the Consul who was buried today, you strangled him with debts. You have stolen the student and shackled him with an imaginary debt of his father's, who never owed you a penny. . . .

(THE OLD MAN *has tried to rise and speak but has collapsed in his chair and shriveled up, and, like a dying insect, he shrivels up more and more during the following dialogue.*)

But there is one dark spot in your life, which I'm not sure about—although I have my suspicions. . . . I think that Bengtsson might help us. (*She rings the bell on the table.*)

THE OLD MAN. No! Not Bengtsson! Not him!

THE MUMMY. Then it is true? He does know! (*She rings again*).

[10] *Two false witnesses* not an uncommon saying, but it may be another glance at Goethe's *Faust* (the scene in Martha's house)

(THE LITTLE MILKMAID *appears in the door to the hall, unseen by all except* THE OLD MAN, *who shies in terror.* THE MILKMAID *disappears when* BENGTSSON *enters.*)

Bengtsson, do you know this man?

BENGTSSON. Yes, I know him and he knows me. Life has its ups and downs, as we all know, and I have been in his service, and once he was in mine. To be exact, he was a sponger in my kitchen for two whole years. Since he had to be out of the house by three o'clock, dinner had to be ready at two, and those in the house had to eat the warmed-up food left by that ox. Even worse, he drank up the pure soup stock and the gravy, which then had to be diluted with water. He sat there like a vampire, sucking all the marrow out of the house, and turned us all into skeletons. And he nearly succeeded in putting us into prison, when we accused the cook of being a thief.... Later I met this man in Hamburg under another name. He had become a usurer or bloodsucker. And it was there that he was accused of having lured a young girl out onto the ice in order to drown her, for she was the only witness to a crime which he was afraid would come to light. ...

THE MUMMY (*passes her hand over* THE OLD MAN's *face*). That is the real you! Now empty your pockets of the notes and the will!

(JOHANSSON *appears in the door to the hall and watches* THE OLD MAN *intently, knowing that his slavery is coming to an end.* THE OLD MAN *produces a bundle of papers which he throws on the table.*)

(THE MUMMY, *stroking* THE OLD MAN's *back.*) Pretty bird! Where's Jacob![11]

THE OLD MAN (*like a parrot*). Jacob's here! (*Crows like a rooster.*)

THE MUMMY. Can clocks strike?

THE OLD MAN (*making clucking sounds*). Clocks can strike! (*He imitates a cuckoo clock.*) Coo-coo! Coo-coo! Coo-coo! ...

THE MUMMY (*opening the papered door to the closet*). Now the clock has struck! Stand up, and enter the closet where I have sat for twenty years,[12] crying over our misdeeds. You'll find a rope in there, which can represent the one you strangled the Consul with, and with which you intended to strangle your benefactor. ... Go in!

(THE OLD MAN *goes into the closet.* THE MUMMY *closes the door.*)

Bengtsson! Put up the screen! The death screen!

(BENGTSSON *places the screen in front of the door.*)

It is over!—May god have mercy on his soul!

ALL. Amen!

(*Long silence.*)

(*In the hyacinth room* THE YOUNG LADY *can be seen sitting at a harp on which she accompanies* THE STUDENT. *After a prelude played by* THE YOUNG LADY, THE STUDENT *recites.*)

THE STUDENT. I saw the sun
    And from its blaze
    There burst on me
    The deepest truth:

    Man reaps as he sows;
    Blessed is he
    Who sows the good.

    For deeds done in anger
    Kindness alone
    Can make amends.

    Bring cheer to those
    Whom you have hurt,
    And kindness reaps
    Its own rewards.

    The pure in heart
    Have none to fear.
    The harmless are happy.
    The guileless are good.[13]

---

[11] *Jacob* In view of Hummel's transformation into a parrot, his first name is not without its relevance. Gray parrots with scarlet tails were usually called Jacob because their cry sounded like "Jacob" ...

[12] *twenty years* Like Hamlet's age, the length of time The Mummy has sat in the closet varies from point to point. On page 399, the time was forty years. I don't see any inconsistency, however. The Mummy knows better than Bengtsson how long she has been there. Furthermore, Bengtsson may be referring to the length of time The Mummy has been a member of the family, not to her time in the closet  [13] *I saw ... are good* This song consists mostly of lines taken from "The Song of the Sun" in the *Elder Edda* ...

## SCENE 3

*A room decorated in a bizarre style, predominantly oriental. A profusion of hyacinths in all colors fills the room. On the porcelain tiled stove sits a large Buddha with a bulb of a shallot* (allium ascalonicum) *in its lap. The stem of the shallot rises from this bulb and bursts into a spherical cluster of white, starlike flowers. In the rear to the right a door leads to the round room.* THE COLONEL *and* THE MUMMY *can be seen in there sitting motionless and silent. A part of the death screen is also visible. To the left in the rear a door to the pantry and the kitchen.* THE STUDENT *and* THE YOUNG LADY (ADELE) *are near a table, she seated at her harp, he standing beside her.*

THE YOUNG LADY. Now you must sing a song to my flowers!

THE STUDENT. Is this the flower of your soul?

THE YOUNG LADY. The one and only! Don't you love the hyacinth?

THE STUDENT. I love it above all other flowers—its stem rising straight and slender, like a young maiden, from the round bulb, which floats on water and reaches its white rare roots down into clear, colorless nothingness. I love it for its colors: the snow-white, innocent and pure—the golden yellow, sweet as honey—the sky pink, the ripe red—but above all the blue ones—blue as morning mist, deep-eyed blue, ever-faithful blue. I love them all—more than gold and pearls. Have loved them ever since I was a child, have worshiped them because they possess all the virtues I lack . . . But still—

THE YOUNG LADY. What?

THE STUDENT. My love is not returned. These beautiful blossoms hate and detest me.

THE YOUNG LADY. How?

THE STUDENT. Their fragrance—as strong and clear as the first winds of spring, sweeping down from the fields of melting snow—confuse my senses—they deafen me, blind me, drive me out of my mind—impale me with their poisonous arrows that stab my heart and set my head afire! . . .

Don't you know the legend of that flower?[14]

THE YOUNG LADY. No. Tell me.

THE STUDENT. First I must tell you what it means as a symbol. The bulb is the earth, whether floating on water or buried deep in black humus. Here the stalk shoots up, straight as the axis of the world, and here at its upper end are gathered together the six-pointed star flowers.

THE YOUNG LADY. Above the earth, the stars! How sublime! How did you know that? Where did you discover that?

THE STUDENT. I don't know. Let me think. —In your eyes! . . . So you see, it's an image of the whole cosmos. That's why Buddha sits there with the bulb of the earth in his lap, watching it constantly in order to see it shoot up and burst forth and be transformed into a heaven. This poor earth shall become a heaven! That is what Buddha is waiting for!

THE YOUNG LADY. Of course! I see that now!—And don't the snowflakes have six points like the hyacinth?

THE STUDENT. Exactly! Then snowflakes are falling stars—

THE YOUNG LADY. And the snowdrop is a snow-star—growing out of the snow.

THE STUDENT. And Sirius, the largest and most beautiful of all the stars in the firmament, golden-red Sirius is the narcissus with its golden-red chalice and its six white rays—

THE YOUNG LADY. Have you seen the shallot burst into bloom?

THE STUDENT. Yes, of course I have! It hides its blossoms in a ball—a globe just like the celestial globe, strewn with white stars.

THE YOUNG LADY. How heavenly! Wonderful! Whose idea was it?

THE STUDENT. Yours!

THE YOUNG LADY. Yours!

THE STUDENT. Ours. We have given birth to something together. We are wedded. . . .

THE YOUNG LADY. No, not yet. . . .

THE STUDENT. Why not? What else?

---

14 *that flower* The Student's allusion to the legend of the hyacinth portends the death of The Young Lady. In the myth, the beautiful young Hyacinthus was killed accidentally by his lover Apollo. In the *Sonata* the girl will be killed more or less accidentally by her lover, The Student, and homosexuality will play a part in her death

THE YOUNG LADY. Time—testing—patience.

THE STUDENT. Very well! Put me to the test! (*Pause.*) So silent? ... Why do your parents sit in there, silent, without saying a single word?

THE YOUNG LADY. Because they have nothing to say to each other, because they don't believe what the other says. My father explains it this way: He says, "What good does talking do, we can't fool each other anyway."

THE STUDENT. It makes me sick to hear things like that. . . .

THE YOUNG LADY. The cook is coming this way. . . . Look at her, how big and fat she is. . . .

THE STUDENT. What does she want?

THE YOUNG LADY. She wants to ask me about dinner. I've been managing the house during my mother's illness.

THE STUDENT. What have we got to do with the kitchen?

THE YOUNG LADY. We have to eat, don't we? . . . Look at her, look at her. I can't bear to. . . .

THE STUDENT. Who is that bloated monster?

THE YOUNG LADY. She belongs to the Hummel family of vampires. She's eating us up. . . .

THE STUDENT. Why don't you fire her?

THE YOUNG LADY. She won't leave! We can't control her. We got her because of our sins. . . . Don't you see that we're wasting away, withering?

THE STUDENT. Don't you get enough food to eat?

THE YOUNG LADY. We get course after course, but all the strength is gone from the food. She boils the beef until there's nothing left of it and serves us the sinews swimming in water while she herself drinks the stock. And when we have a roast, she cooks all the juice out of it and drinks it and eats the gravy. Everything she touches loses its flavor. It's as if she sucked it up with her very eyes. We get the grounds when she has finished her coffee. She drinks the wine and fills up the bottles with water.[15]

---

[15] *We get . . . with water* When writing the chamber plays, Strindberg had trouble getting anyone to cook properly for him . . .

THE STUDENT. Get rid of her!

THE YOUNG LADY. We can't!

THE STUDENT. Why not?

THE YOUNG LADY. We don't know! She won't leave! No one can control her. . . . She has taken all our strength from us.

THE STUDENT. Let me get rid of her for you.

THE YOUNG LADY. Oh, no! I guess this is how it's supposed to be. . . . Here she is! She'll ask me what we're having for dinner— I'll tell her this and that—she'll make objections—and finally we'll have what she says.

THE STUDENT. Then let her decide in the first place!

THE YOUNG LADY. She won't do that.

THE STUDENT. What a strange house! It's haunted, isn't it?

THE YOUNG LADY. Yes.—She's turning back now. She saw you!

THE COOK (*in the doorway*). Hah, that ain't why! (*Grinning so that all her teeth show.*)

THE STUDENT. Get out!

THE COOK. When I feel like it I will! (*Pause.*) Now I feel like it!

(*She vanishes.*)

THE YOUNG LADY. Don't lose your temper. Learn to be patient. She's part of the trials and tribulations we have to go through in this home. And we've got a housemaid, too! Whom we have to clean up after!

THE STUDENT. I can feel myself sinking into the earth!—*Cor in aethere!*—Let's have music!

THE YOUNG LADY. Wait!

THE STUDENT. No! Music now!

THE YOUNG LADY. Patience!—This room is called the testing room. It's beautiful to look at, but it's full of imperfections.

THE STUDENT. I don't believe it. But if it's true we'll just have to ignore them. It's beautiful, but a little cold. Why don't you start the fire?

THE YOUNG LADY. Because it smokes up the room.

THE STUDENT. Can't you have the chimney cleaned?

THE YOUNG LADY. It doesn't help! . . . Do you see that writing table?

THE STUDENT. What an extraordinarily handsome piece!

THE YOUNG LADY. But it wobbles. Every day I lay a piece of cork under that foot, but the housemaid takes it away when she sweeps, and I have to cut a new piece. The penholder is covered with ink every morning, and so is the inkstand, and I have to clean them up after her, as regularly as the sun goes up. (*Pause.*) What do you hate most to do?

THE STUDENT. To sort the week's wash! (*Grimaces in disgust.*)

THE YOUNG LADY. That's what I have to do! (*Grimacing in disgust.*)

THE STUDENT. What else?

THE YOUNG LADY. To be awakened in the middle of the night, to have to get up and close the banging window—which the housemaid forgot to close.

THE STUDENT. Go on.

THE YOUNG LADY. To climb up on a ladder and fix the damper on the stovepipe after the maid broke off the cord.

THE STUDENT. Go on.

THE YOUNG LADY. To sweep up after her, to dust after her, and to start the fire in the stove after her—all she does is throw on some wood! To adjust the damper, to dry the glasses, to set the table *over* again, to pull the corks out of the bottles, to open the windows and air the rooms, to make and remake my bed, to rinse the water bottle when it's green with sediment, to buy matches and soap, which we're always out of, to wipe the chimneys and trim the wicks to keep the lamps from smoking—and to keep the lamps from going out I have to fill them myself when we have company. . . .

THE STUDENT. Let's have music!

THE YOUNG LADY. You have to wait!— First comes the drudgery, the drudgery of keeping oneself above the dirt of life.

THE STUDENT. But you're well off. You've got two servants!

THE YOUNG LADY. Doesn't make any difference! Even if we had three! Living is such a nuisance, and I get so tired at times. . . . Imagine, if on top of it all one had a nursery and a baby crib.

THE STUDENT. The dearest of joys!

THE YOUNG LADY. The dearest in more ways than one. . . . Is life really worth so much trouble?

THE STUDENT. I suppose that depends on the reward you expect for all your troubles. . . . There's nothing I wouldn't do to win your hand.

THE YOUNG LADY. Don't say that! You can never have me!

THE STUDENT. Why not?

THE YOUNG LADY. You mustn't ask.

(*Pause.*)

THE STUDENT. You dropped your bracelet out of the window. . . .

THE YOUNG LADY. Because my hand has grown so thin.

(*Pause.* THE COOK *appears with a Japanese bottle in her hand.*)

She's the one who's eating me—and all the rest of us.

THE STUDENT. What is she holding in her hand?

THE YOUNG LADY. It's a bottle of coloring matter. It's got letters on it that look like scorpions. It's filled with soya sauce—which takes the place of gravy, which is transformed into soup, which serves as stock for cooking cabbage in, which is used to make mock turtle soup. . . .

THE STUDENT. Get out!

THE COOK. You suck the sap from us, and we from you. We take the blood and give you back water—with coloring added. This is the coloring!—I'm leaving now, but that doesn't mean I haven't stayed as long as I wanted to.

(*She leaves.*)

THE STUDENT. Why was Bengtsson given a medal?

THE YOUNG LADY. Because of his great merits.

THE STUDENT. Has he no faults?

THE YOUNG LADY. Yes, many great ones. But you don't get medals for them.

(*They smile at each other.*)

THE STUDENT. You have a great many secrets in this house.

THE YOUNG LADY. As in all houses. Permit us to keep ours.

(*Pause.*)

THE STUDENT. Do you admire frankness?

THE YOUNG LADY. Yes, within moderation.

THE STUDENT. Sometimes there comes over me a crazy desire to say everything I'm thinking. But I know the world would collapse completely if one were completely honest. (*Pause.*) I went to a funeral the other day.... In church.... Very solemn, very beautiful.

THE YOUNG LADY. Mr. Hummel's funeral?

THE STUDENT. Yes, my false benefactor's. At the head of the coffin stood an old friend of the deceased. He carried the mace. The priest impressed me especially, his dignified manner and his moving words. I cried. We all cried. And afterwards we went to a restaurant.... And there I learned that the macebearer had been the lover of the dead man's son.

(THE YOUNG LADY *stares at him, trying to understand him.*)

And that the dead man had borrowed money from his son's admirer.... (*Pause.*) The day after that, they arrested the priest for embezzling church funds! It's a pretty story, isn't it?

(THE YOUNG LADY *turns her head away in disgust. Pause.*)

Do you know what I think of you now?

THE YOUNG LADY. You must not tell me or I'll die!

THE STUDENT. But I must or I'll die!

THE YOUNG LADY. In an asylum they say whatever they feel like.

THE STUDENT. Exactly right! That's where my father ended up—in a madhouse.

THE YOUNG LADY. Was he ill?

THE STUDENT. No, he was quite healthy. But he was crazy! It just came over him. Let me tell you how it happened.... Like all of us, he had his circle of acquaintances, whom for convenience' sake he called his friends. Of course they were a pretty sorry bunch of good-for-nothings—like most people. But he had to have some acquaintances, he couldn't just sit alone. Now one doesn't tell a person what one really thinks of him, not in ordinary conversation anyway—and my father didn't either. He knew how false they were. He saw through their deceitfulness right to the bottom of their souls. But he was an intelligent man, brought up to behave properly, and so he was always polite. But one day he held a big party. It was in the evening, he was tired after a day's work, and under the strain of forcing himself to hold his tongue half the time and of talking nonsense with his guests the other half....

(THE YOUNG LADY *shudders in fear.*)

Well, whatever the reason, at the dinner table he rapped for silence, raised his glass, and began to make a speech. ... Then something loosed the trigger, and in a long oration he stripped naked every single person there, one after another. Told them of all their deceits. And at the end, exhausted, he sat right down in the middle of the table and told them all to go to hell!

(THE YOUNG LADY *moans.*)

I was there and heard it all, and I shall never forget what happened afterwards.... Father and Mother began to fight, the guests rushed for the door—and my father was taken off to the madhouse where he died! (*Pause.*) If you keep silent too long, stagnant water begins to accumulate and things begin to rot. That's what's happening in this house. Something's rotting here. And I thought it was paradise when I saw you come in here for the first time.... It was a Sunday morning, and I stood looking into these rooms. I saw a colonel who wasn't a colonel. I had a magnanimous benefactor who turned out to be a bandit and had to hang himself. I saw a mummy who wasn't one, and a maiden who—speaking of which, where can one find virginity? Where is beauty to be found? In nature, and my mind when it's all dressed up in its Sunday clothes. Where do honor and faith exist? In fairy tales and children's games! Where can you find anything that fulfills its promise? Only in one's imagination! ...Now your flowers have poisoned me, and I have passed the poison back. I begged you to become my wife in my home. We played and we sang. We created poetry together. And then came the cook.... *Sursum corda!*[16] Try just once again to pluck fire and brightness from the golden harp! Please try! I beg you, I implore you on my knees! ... Very well. Then I shall do it myself (*He takes the harp but no sound comes from the strings.*) It is silent and deaf. Tell me, why are beautiful

---

[16] *Sursum corda* "Lift up your hearts" (from the Roman Catholic Mass) [Ed]

flowers so poisonous, and the most beautiful the most deadly? Why? The whole of creation, all of life, is cursed and damned. . . . Why would you not become my bride? Because you are sick, infected at the very core of life. . . . Now I can feel that vampire in the kitchen beginning to suck the blood from me. She must be one of those lamias that suck the blood of suckling babes. It's always in the kitchen that the children are nipped in the bud. And if not there, then in the bedroom. . . . There are poisons that seal the eyes and poisons that open them. I must have been born with the latter kind in my veins, because I cannot see what is ugly as beautiful and I cannot call what is evil good. I cannot. They say that Christ harrowed hell. What they really meant was that he descended to earth, to this penal colony, to this madhouse and morgue of a world. And the inmates crucified Him when He tried to free them. But the robber they let free. Robbers always win sympathy. . . . Woe! Woe to all of us! Saviour of the World, save us! We are perishing!

(THE YOUNG LADY *has collapsed more and more during this speech. She is obviously dying. She rings the bell.* BENGTSSON *enters.*)

THE YOUNG LADY. Bring the screen. Quickly! I'm dying.

(BENGTSSON *returns with the screen, opens it, and places it in front of* THE YOUNG LADY.)

THE STUDENT. Your liberator is coming! Welcome, pale and gentle one. . . . And you, you beautiful, innocent, lost soul, who suffer for no fault of your own, sleep, sleep a dreamless sleep. And when you wake again . . . may you be greeted by a sun that doesn't scorch, in a home without dust, by friends without faults, and by a love without flaw. . . . Buddha, wise and gentle Buddha, sitting there waiting for a heaven to grow out of the earth, grant us the purity of will and the patience to endure our trials, that your hopes will not come to nought.

(*The harp strings begin to move and hum. Pure white light pours into the room.*)

I saw the sun
And from its blaze
There burst on me
The deepest truth:

Man reaps as he sows;
Blessed is he
Who sows the good.

For deeds done in anger
Kindness alone
Can make amends.

Bring cheer to those
Whom you have hurt,
And kindness reaps
Its own rewards.

The pure in heart
Have none to fear
The harmless are happy.
The guileless are good.

(*A moaning is heard from behind the screen.*) You poor little child! Child of this world of illusion and guilt and suffering and death— this world of eternal change and disappointment and never-ending pain! May the Lord of Heaven have mercy on you as you journey forth. . . .

(*The room vanishes. In the distance Boecklin's* The Island of the Dead *appears. Music— soft, pleasant, and melancholy—is heard coming from the island.*)

CURTAIN

## Selected Reading List for Strindberg

Eric Bentley, "August Strindberg," *The Playwright as Thinker.* New York: Meridian Books, 1955, pp. 158–80.

Robert Brustein, "August Strindberg," *The Theatre of Revolt.* Boston: Little, Brown & Co., 1964, pp. 87–134.

John Gassner, "From Realism to Expressionism," *Form and Idea in Modern Theatre.* New York: The Dryden Press, 1956, pp. 79–130.

Cyrus Hoy, *The Hyacinth Room.* New York: Alfred A. Knopf, 1964, pp. 281–318.

Walter H. Sokel, *The Writer in Extremis.* New York: McGraw-Hill Book Company, 1959.

Maurice Valency, *The Flower and the Castle.* New York: The Macmillan Company, 1963, pp. 238–403.

# Brecht and Epic Theater

Bertolt Brecht grew up in the Germany of the First World War. He was sixteen when the war began, and got into serious trouble in his school for writing a pacifist essay. After studying medicine in Munich he was made a medical orderly, an experience which confirmed his hatred of war. During the terrible aftermath of the war he became a social rebel and a Marxist. Leading a bohemian sort of life, he gradually gave up his medical studies and began writing plays, poems, and songs. He sometimes sang his ballads in cafés, accompanying himself on the guitar. His first success on the stage was a play called *Drums in the Night*, performed in Munich in 1922. Five years later he began the collaboration with the composer, Kurt Weill, which resulted in 1928 in *The Threepenny Opera*, Brecht's adaptation of John Gay's *The Beggar's Opera*. The performance of this musical, the most popular of all Brecht's works, was also the beginning of his association with the important German director, Erwin Piscator and a theater in what is now East Berlin. Like the plays, Brecht's musical entertainments were conspicuous for their satirical view of capitalistic, bourgeois society. Hence, when the Nazis came to power in 1933, Brecht was forced to flee to other European countries and finally, in 1941, to the United States. After the war he returned to East Berlin, where he died in 1956.

*Mother Courage* (1939) is one of several important plays which Brecht wrote during his exile. It is an example of what he and Piscator called "epic theater." The most obvious meaning of the term is illustrated by the structure of the play—a series of episodes stretching out over a period of twelve years and thus achieving dimensions comparable with those of the great epics of the past, the *Odyssey* or the *Aeneid*. But the epic theater was also a revolt against the theatrical styles current in Germany around 1920. Brecht's characters were not the individuals of the realistic theater, whose speech and actions were intended to give the illusion of living people. He often used types such as the great majority of the characters in *Mother Courage*, and his dialogue was a mixture of colloquial and poetic speech, frequently interspersed with songs. In *Mother Courage* a revolving stage and colored projections thrown on the cyclorama were used to give the effect of traveling, and the summaries of setting and action which precede each scene were flashed on a screen like the subtitles of cinema. In one production of the play, signs giving the locality of each scene were suspended overhead. These techniques were similar to those of the expressionists, but Brecht was not interested in fantasies or dream-plays, whose intense subjectivism seemed to him a perversion of the proper purpose of the theater. He believed that a play should confront the spectator with some aspect of the actual world and force him to think about it. Epic theater was therefore deeply concerned with social conditions and made use of realistic detail in costume and stage setting even though it did not attempt to construct an illusionistic picture. What Brecht objected to in both the realistic and the expressionistic theater of his day was the creation of an illusory world into which the audience was lured as if by a magic spell. The spectator was tricked into identifying himself with a character in this world of illusion, and once he had done that, he was no longer in a state to think clearly or make rational judgments about what was happening on the stage. By rejecting the techniques of both realists and expressionists Brecht hoped to create a theater which would be more truly realistic—which would present facts and require judgment of them.

By various means, then, Brecht tried to destroy illusion and, so to speak, keep the audience at a distance. His songs often served this purpose. Those in *Mother Courage*, for instance, were to be understood as deliberate insertions, not growing out of the situations organically, and not intensifying the emotions of a moment, as in opera, but interrupting, destroying the mood with music-hall entertainment. The lighting for the play was as brilliant as possible, so as "to get rid of any remnants of 'atmosphere,' "as Brecht said. But most important of all was the style of acting described in his essay, "Alienation Effects in Chinese Acting," reprinted in the Appendix (pp. 492–97). The actor was not to "be" the character, as Stanislavski would have him, but rather to remind the audience that he was still an actor. "Alienation" only conveys in part what is meant by Brecht's word, *Verfremdung*, which more literally means "estranging" or "making strange." "The artist's object is to appear strange and even surprising," as Brecht put it. The audience might be moved by the performance but never in such a way as to forget that the stage was a stage. In short, Brecht's aim was, paradoxically, to restore the theatricality of the theater in order to arrive at "realistic images of human social life."[1]

In some respects this attack on illusion is a return to the theater of Shakespeare's and Jonson's time. Brecht's actors, like theirs, address the audience directly, and the "alienation effect" is not so different as it is sometimes thought to be from the awareness of stage artifice encouraged by the conventions of the Elizabethan theater.

The Author's Notes to *Mother Courage* and the excerpts from an earlier version testify to the troubles Brecht had in keeping his audiences from identifying with his protagonist. Even in the revised version, where her "villainy" is made more obvious, it is difficult to restrain a certain admiration for the sheer doggedness with which she pursues her materialistic ends. We are faced again, as in *Everyman*, with the curious fact that a didactic play may be extraordinarily effective even when the response of the audience is not at all the one desired by the author. In the case of *Mother Courage*, there is no danger of missing Brecht's savage indictment of war, but this "lesson" may finally seem to be only one component of the experience of the play. Its distinctive quality may be explicable, as Martin Esslin has suggested, in "the tug-of-war between the intended and the actual reaction of the audience."[2] It inheres certainly in situations like the death of Kattrin, to which we respond with pity, horror, and an ironic awareness of the futility of her heroism.

---

[1] "From the Mother Courage Model," *Brecht on Theatre*, trans. John Willett (New York: Hill and Wang, 1964), p. 219.
[2] *Brecht* (New York: Doubleday & Company, Inc., 1961), p. 141.

# Mother Courage and Her Children

*A CHRONICLE OF THE THIRTY YEARS' WAR*

### BERTOLT BRECHT

## CHARACTERS

MOTHER COURAGE
KATTRIN, *her dumb daughter*
EILIF, *her elder son*
SWISS CHEESE, *her younger son*
RECRUITING OFFICER
SERGEANT
COOK
SWEDISH COMMANDER
CHAPLAIN
ORDNANCE OFFICER
YVETTE POTTIER
MAN WITH THE BANDAGE
ANOTHER SERGEANT
OLD COLONEL
CLERK
YOUNG SOLDIER
OLDER SOLDIER
PEASANT
PEASANT WOMAN
YOUNG MAN
OLD WOMAN
ANOTHER PEASANT
ANOTHER PEASANT WOMAN
YOUNG PEASANT
LIEUTENANT
VOICE

## SCENE 1

*SPRING, 1624. IN DALARNA, THE SWEDISH COMMANDER OXENSTIERNA IS RECRUITING FOR THE CAMPAIGN IN POLAND. THE CANTEEN WOMAN ANNA FIERLING, COMMONLY KNOWN AS MOTHER COURAGE, LOSES A SON.*

(*Highway outside a town. A* SERGEANT *and a* RECRUITING OFFICER *stand shivering.*)

THE RECRUITING OFFICER. How the hell can you line up a squadron in a place like this? You know what I keep thinking about, Sergeant? Suicide. I'm supposed to knock four platoons together by the twelfth—four platoons the Chief's asking for! And they're so friendly around here, I'm scared to go to sleep at night. Suppose I do get my hands on some character and squint at him so I don't notice he's pigeon-chested and has varicose veins. I get him drunk and relaxed, he signs on the dotted line. I pay for the drinks, he steps outside for a minute. I have a hunch I should follow him to the door, and am I right? Off he's shot like a louse from a scratch. You can't take a man's word any more, Sergeant. There's no loyalty left in the world, no trust, no faith, no sense of honor. I'm losing my confidence in mankind, Sergeant.

THE SERGEANT. What they could use around here is a good war. What else can you expect with peace running wild all over the place? You know what the trouble with

413

peace is? No organization. And when do you get organization? In a war. Peace is one big waste of equipment. Anything goes, no one gives a damn. See the way they eat? Cheese on pumpernickel, bacon on the cheese? Disgusting! How many horses have they got in this town? How many young men? Nobody knows! They haven't bothered to count 'em! That's peace for you! I've been in places where they haven't had a war for seventy years and you know what? The people haven't even been given names! They don't know who they are! It takes a war to fix that. In a war, everyone registers, everyone's name's on a list. Their shoes are stacked, their corn's in the bag, you count it all up—cattle, men, *et cetera*—and you take it away! That's the story: no organization, no war!

THE RECRUITING OFFICER. It's the God's truth.

THE SERGEANT. Of course, a war's like any good deal: hard to get going. But when it does get moving, it's a pisser, and they're all scared of peace, like a dice player who can't stop—'cause when peace comes they have to pay up. Of course, *until* it gets going, they're just as scared of war, it's such a novelty!

THE RECRUITING OFFICER. Hey, look, here's a canteen wagon. Two women and a couple of fellows. Stop the old lady, Sergeant. And if there's nothing doing this time, you won't catch me freezing my ass in the April wind any longer.

(*A harmonica is heard. A canteen wagon rolls on, drawn by two young fellows.* MOTHER COURAGE *is sitting on it with her dumb daughter,* KATTRIN.)

MOTHER COURAGE. A good day to you, Sergeant!

THE SERGEANT (*barring the way*). Good day to *you*! Who d'you think *you* are?

MOTHER COURAGE. Tradespeople.

(*She sings.*)

Stop all the troops: here's Mother Courage!
Hey, Captain, let them come and buy!
For they can get from Mother Courage
Boots they will march in till they die!
Your marching men do not adore you
(Packs on their backs, lice in their hair)
But it's to death they're marching for you

And so they need good boots to wear!
Christians, awake! Winter is gone!
The snows depart! Dead men sleep on!
Let all of you who still survive
Get out of bed and look alive!

Your men will walk till they are dead,
But cannot fight, sir, unless they eat.
The blood they spill for you is red,
What fires that blood, sir, is my red meat.
Cannon is rough on empty bellies:
First with my meat they should be crammed
Then let them go and find where hell is
And give my greetings to the damned!
Christians, awake! Winter is gone!
The snows depart! Dead men sleep on!
Let all of you who still survive
Get out of bed and look alive!

THE SERGEANT. Halt! Where are you from, riffraff?

EILIF. Second Finnish Regiment!

THE SERGEANT. Where are your papers?

MOTHER COURAGE. Papers?

SWISS CHEESE. But this is Mother Courage!

THE SERGEANT. Never heard of her. Where'd she get a name like that?

MOTHER COURAGE. They call me Mother Courage 'cause I was afraid I'd be ruined, so I drove through the bombardment of Riga like a madwoman, with fifty loaves of bread in my cart. They were going moldy, what else could I do?

THE SERGEANT. No funny business! Where are your papers?

MOTHER COURAGE (*rummaging among papers in a tin box and clambering down from her wagon*). Here, Sergeant! Here's a missal—I got it in Altötting to wrap my cucumbers in. Here's a map of Moravia—God knows if I'll ever get there—the birds can have it if I don't. And here's a document saying my horse hasn't got hoof and mouth disease—pity he died on us, he cost fifteen guilders, thank God I didn't pay it. Is that enough paper?

THE SERGEANT. Are you pulling my leg? Well, you've got another guess coming. You need a license and you know it.

MOTHER COURAGE. Show a little respect for a lady and don't go telling these grown children of mine I'm pulling anything of yours. What would I want with you? My license in the Second Protestant Regiment is an honest face. If *you* wouldn't know how to read it, that's not my fault, I want no rubber stamp on it anyhow.

THE RECRUITING OFFICER. Sergeant, we have a case of insubordination on our hands. Do you know what we need in the army? Discipline!

MOTHER COURAGE. I was going to say sausages.

THE SERGEANT. Name?

MOTHER COURAGE. Anna Fierling.

THE SERGEANT. So you're all Fierlings.

MOTHER COURAGE. I was talking about me.

THE SERGEANT. And I was talking about your children.

MOTHER COURAGE. Must they all have the same name? (*Pointing to the elder son.*) This fellow, for instance, I call him Eilif Noyocki. Why? He got the name from his father who told me he was called Koyocki. Or was it Moyocki? Anyhow, the lad remembers him to this day. Only the man he remembers is someone else, a Frenchman with a pointed beard. But he certainly has his father's brains—that man could whip the breeches off a farmer's backside before he could turn around. So we all have our own names.

THE SERGEANT. You're all called something different?

MOTHER COURAGE. Are you pretending you don't understand?

THE SERGEANT (*pointing at the younger son*). He's Chinese, I suppose.

MOTHER COURAGE. Wrong again. Swiss.

THE SERGEANT. After the Frenchman?

MOTHER COURAGE. Frenchman? What Frenchman? Don't confuse the issue, Sergeant, or we'll be here all day. He's Swiss, but he happens to be called Feyos, a name that has nothing to do with his father, who was called something else—a military engineer, if you please, and a drunkard.

(SWISS CHEESE *nods, beaming; even* KATTRIN *smiles.*)

THE SERGEANT. Then how come his name's Feyos?

MOTHER COURAGE. Oh, Sergeant, you have no imagination. *Of course* he's called Feyos:

when he came, I was with a Hungarian. He didn't mind. He had a floating kidney, though he never touched a drop. He was a very *honest* man. The boy takes after him.

THE SERGEANT. But that wasn't his father!

MOTHER COURAGE. I said: he took after him. I call him Swiss Cheese. Why? Because he's good at pulling wagons. (*Pointing to her daughter.*) And that is Kattrin Haupt, she's half German.

THE SERGEANT. A nice family, I must say!

MOTHER COURAGE. And we've seen the whole wide world together—this wagonload and me.

THE SERGEANT. We'll need all that in writing. (*He writes.*) You're from Bamberg in Bavaria. What are you doing *here?*

MOTHER COURAGE. I can't wait till the war is good enough to come to Bamberg.

THE RECRUITING OFFICER. And you two oxen pull the cart. Jacob Ox and Esau Ox! D'you ever get out of harness?

EILIF. Mother! May I smack him in the puss? I'd like to.

MOTHER COURAGE. I'd like *you* to stay where you are. And now, gentlemen, what about a brace of pistols? Or a belt? Sergeant? Yours is worn clean through.

THE SERGEANT. It's something else *I'm* looking for. These lads of yours are straight as birch trees, strong limbs, massive chests. ... What are such fine specimens doing out of the army?

MOTHER COURAGE (*quickly*). A soldier's life is not for sons of mine!

THE RECRUITING OFFICER. Why not? It means money. It means fame. Peddling shoes is woman's work. (*To* EILIF.) Step this way and let's see if that's muscle or chicken fat.

MOTHER COURAGE. It's chicken fat. Give him a good hard look, and he'll fall right over.

THE RECRUITING OFFICER. Yes, and kill a calf in the falling! (*He tries to hustle* EILIF *away.*)

MOTHER COURAGE. Let him alone! He's not for you!

THE RECRUITING OFFICER. He called my face a puss. That is an insult. The two of us will now go and settle the affair on the field of honor.

EILIF. Don't worry, Mother, I can handle him.

MOTHER COURAGE. Stay here. You're never happy till you're in a fight. He has a knife in his boot and he knows how to use it.

THE RECRUITING OFFICER. I'll draw it out of him like a milk tooth. Come on, young fellow!

MOTHER COURAGE. Officer, I'll report you to the Colonel, and he'll throw you in jail. His lieutenant is courting my daughter.

THE SERGEANT. Go easy. (*To* MOTHER COURAGE.) What have you got against the service, wasn't his own father a soldier? Didn't you say he died a soldier's death?

MOTHER COURAGE. This one's just a baby. You'll lead him like a lamb to the slaughter. I know you, you'll get five guilders for him.

THE RECRUITING OFFICER (*to* EILIF). First thing you know, you'll have a lovely cap and high boots, how about it?

EILIF. Not from you.

MOTHER COURAGE. "Let's you and me go fishing," said the angler to the worm. (*To* SWISS CHEESE.) Run and tell everybody they're trying to steal your brother! (*She draws a knife.*) Yes, just you try, and I'll cut you down like dogs! We sell cloth, we sell ham, we are peaceful people!

THE SERGEANT. You're peaceful all right: your knife proves that. Why, you should be ashamed of yourself. Give me that knife, you hag! You admit you live off the war, what else *could* you live off? Now tell me, how can we have a war without soldiers?

MOTHER COURAGE. Do they have to be mine?

THE SERGEANT. So that's the trouble. The war should swallow the peach stone and spit out the peach, hm? Your brood should get fat off the war, but the poor war must ask nothing in return, it can look after itself, can it? Call yourself Mother Courage and then get scared of the war, your breadwinner? Your sons aren't scared, I know that much.

EILIF. Takes more than a war to scare me.

THE SERGEANT. Correct! Take me. The soldier's life hasn't done *me* any harm, has it? I enlisted at seventeen.

MOTHER COURAGE. You haven't reached seventy.

THE SERGEANT. I will, though.

MOTHER COURAGE. Above ground?

THE SERGEANT. Are you trying to rile me, telling me I'll die?

MOTHER COURAGE. Suppose it's the truth? Suppose I see it's your fate? Suppose I *know* you're just a corpse on furlough?

SWISS CHEESE. She can look into the future. Everyone says so.

THE RECRUITING OFFICER. Then by all means look into the sergeant's future. It might amuse him.

THE SERGEANT. I don't believe in that stuff.

MOTHER COURAGE. Helmet!

(*The* SERGEANT *gives her his helmet.*)

THE SERGEANT. It means less than a crap in the grass. Anything for a laugh.

MOTHER COURAGE (*taking a sheet of parchment and tearing it in two*). Eilif, Swiss Cheese, Kattrin! So shall we all be torn in two if we let ourselves get too deep into this war! (*To the* SERGEANT.) I'll give you the bargain rate, and do it free. Watch! Death is black, so I draw a black cross.

SWISS CHEESE. And the other she leaves blank, see?

MOTHER COURAGE. I fold them, put them in the helmet, and mix 'em up together, the way we're all mixed up together from our mother's womb on. Now draw!

(*The* SERGEANT *hesitates.*)

THE RECRUITING OFFICER (*to* EILIF). I don't take just anybody. I'm choosy. And you've got guts, I like that.

THE SERGEANT (*fishing around in the helmet*). It's silly. Means as much as blowing your nose.

SWISS CHEESE. The black cross! Oh, his number's up!

THE RECRUITING OFFICER. Don't let them get under your skin. There aren't enough bullets to go around.

THE SERGEANT (*hoarsely*). You cheated me!

MOTHER COURAGE. You cheated yourself the day you enlisted. And now we must drive on. There isn't a war every day in the week, we must get to work.

THE SERGEANT. Hell, you're not getting away with this! We're taking that bastard of yours with *us*!

EILIF. I'd like that, Mother.

MOTHER COURAGE. Quiet—you Finnish devil, you!

EILIF. And Swiss Cheese wants to be a soldier, too.

MOTHER COURAGE. That's news to me. I see I'll have to draw lots for all three of you. (*She goes to the back to draw the crosses on bits of paper.*)

THE RECRUITING OFFICER (*to* EILIF). People've been saying the Swedish soldier is religious. That kind of loose talk has hurt us a lot. One verse of a hymn every Sunday—and then only if you have a voice . . .

MOTHER COURAGE (*returning with the slips and putting them in the* SERGEANT's *helmet*). So they'd desert their old mother, would they, the scoundrels? They take to war like a cat to cream. But I'll consult these slips, and they'll see the world's no promised land, with a "Join up, son, you're officer material!" Sergeant, I'm afraid for them, very afraid they won't get through this war. They have terrible qualities, all three. (*She holds the helmet out to* EILIF.) There. Draw your lot. (EILIF *fishes in the helmet, unfolds a slip. She snatches it from him.*) There you have it: a cross. Unhappy mother that I am, rich only in a mother's sorrows! He dies. In the springtime of his life, he must go. If he's a soldier, he must bite the dust, that's clear. He's too brave, like his father. And if he doesn't use his head, he'll go the way of all flesh, the slip proves it. (*Hectoring him.*) Will you use your head?

EILIF. Why not?

MOTHER COURAGE. It's using your head to stay with your mother. And when they make fun of you and call you a chicken, just laugh.

THE RECRUITING OFFICER. If you're going to wet your pants, I'll try your brother.

MOTHER COURAGE. I told you to laugh. Laugh! Now it's your turn, Swiss Cheese. You should be a better bet, you're honest. (*He fishes in the helmet.*) Why are you giving that slip such a funny look? You've drawn a blank for sure. It can't be there's a cross on it. It can't be I'm going to lose *you*. (*She takes the slip.*) A cross? Him too! Could it be 'cause he's so simple? Oh, Swiss Cheese, you'll be a goner too, if you aren't honest, honest, honest the whole time, the way I

always brought you up to be, the way you always bring me all the change when you buy me a loaf. It's the only way you can save yourself. Look, Sergeant, if it isn't a black cross!

THE SERGEANT. It's a cross! I don't understand how *I* got one. I always stay well in the rear. (*To the* OFFICER.) But it can't be a trick: it gets *her* children too.

SWISS CHEESE. It gets me too. But I don't accept it!

MOTHER COURAGE (*to* KATTRIN). And now all I have left for certain is you, you're a cross in yourself, you have a good heart. (*She holds the helmet up high toward the wagon but takes the slip out herself.*) Oh, I could give up in despair! There must be some mistake, I didn't mix them right. Don't be too kind, Kattrin, just don't, there's a cross in your path too. Always be very quiet, it can't be hard, you can't speak. Well, so now you know, all of you: be careful, you'll need to be. Now let's climb on the wagon and move on. (*She returns the helmet to the* SERGEANT *and climbs on the wagon.*)

THE RECRUITING OFFICER (*to the* SERGEANT). Do something!

THE SERGEANT. I don't feel very well.

THE RECRUITING OFFICER. Maybe you caught a chill when you handed over your helmet in this wind. Get her involved in a business transaction! (*Aloud.*) That belt, Sergeant, you could at least take a look at it. These good people live by trade, don't they? Hey, all of you, the sergeant wants to buy the belt!

MOTHER COURAGE. Half a guilder. A belt like that is worth two guilders. (*She clambers down again from the wagon.*)

THE SERGEANT. It isn't new. But there's too much wind here. I'll go and look at it behind the wagon. (*He does so.*)

MOTHER COURAGE. I don't find it windy.

THE SERGEANT. Maybe it's worth half a guilder at that. There's silver on it.

MOTHER COURAGE (*following him behind the wagon*). A solid six ounces worth!

THE RECRUITING OFFICER (*to* EILIF). And we can have a drink, just us men. I'll advance you some money to cover it. Let's go.

(EILIF *stands undecided.*)

MOTHER COURAGE. Half a guilder, then.

THE SERGEANT. I don't understand it. I always stay in the rear. There's no safer spot for a sergeant to be. You can send the others on ahead in quest of fame. My appetite is ruined. I can tell you right now: I won't be able to get anything down.

MOTHER COURAGE. You shouldn't take on so, just because you can't eat. Just stay in the rear. Here, take a slug of brandy, man. (*She gives him brandy.*)

THE RECRUITING OFFICER (*taking* EILIF *by the arm and making off toward the back*). Ten guilders in advance and you're a soldier of the king and a stout fellow and the women will be mad about you. And you can give me a smack in the puss for insulting you.

(*Both leave. Dumb* KATTRIN *jumps down from the wagon and lets out harsh cries.*)

MOTHER COURAGE. Coming, Kattrin, coming! The sergeant's just paying up. (*She bites the half guilder.*) I'm suspicious of all money, I've been badly burned, Sergeant. But this money's good. And now we'll be going. Where's Eilif?

SWISS CHEESE. Gone with the recruiting officer.

MOTHER COURAGE (*standing quite still, then*). Oh, you simpleton! (*To* KATTRIN.) You *can't* speak, I know. You are innocent.

THE SERGEANT. That's life. Take a slug yourself, Mother. Being a soldier isn't the worst that could happen. You want to live off war and keep you and yours out of it, do you?

MOTHER COURAGE. You must help your brother now, Kattrin.

(*Brother and sister get into harness together and pull the wagon.* MOTHER COURAGE *walks at their side. The wagon gets under way.*)

THE SERGEANT (*looking after them*).
When a war gives you all you earn
One day it may claim something in return!

## SCENE 2

IN THE YEARS 1625 AND 1626 MOTHER COURAGE JOURNEYS THROUGH POLAND IN THE BAGGAGE TRAIN OF THE SWEDISH ARMY. SHE MEETS HER SON AGAIN BEFORE THE FORTIFIED TOWN OF WALL-HOF—OF THE SUCCESSFUL SALE OF A CAPON AND GREAT DAYS FOR THE BRAVE SON.

(*Tent of the* SWEDISH COMMANDER. *Kitchen next to it. Thunder of cannon. The* COOK *is quarreling with* MOTHER COURAGE, *who is trying to sell him a capon.*)

THE COOK. Sixty hellers for that miserable bird?

MOTHER COURAGE. Miserable bird? This fat fowl? Your Commander is a glutton. Woe betide you if you've nothing for him to eat. This capon is worth sixty hellers to you.

THE COOK. They're ten hellers a dozen on every corner.

MOTHER COURAGE. A capon like this on every corner! With a siege going on and people all skin and bones? Maybe you can get a field rat! I said maybe. Because we're all out of *them* too. Don't you see the soldiers running five deep after one hungry little field rat? All right then, in a siege, my price for a giant capon is fifty hellers.

THE COOK. But we're not "in a siege," we're doing the besieging, it's the other side that's "in a siege," when will you get this into your head?

MOTHER COURAGE. A fat lot of difference that makes, *we* haven't got a thing to eat either. They took everything into the town with them before all this started, and now they've nothing to do but eat and drink, I hear. It's us I'm worried about. Look at the farmers around here, they haven't a thing.

THE COOK. Certainly they have. They hide it.

MOTHER COURAGE (*triumphant*). They have not! They're ruined, that's what. They're so hungry I've seen 'em digging up roots to eat. I could boil your leather belt and make their mouths water with it. That's how things are around here. And I'm expected to let a capon go for forty hellers!

THE COOK. Thirty. Not forty. I said thirty hellers.

MOTHER COURAGE. I say this is no ordinary capon. It was a talented animal, so I hear. It would only feed to music—one march in particular was its favorite. It was so intelligent it could count. Forty hellers is too much for all this? I know *your* problem: if you don't find something to eat and quick, the Chief will—cut—your—fat—head—off!

THE COOK. All right, just watch. (*He takes a piece of beef and lays his knife on it.*) Here's a piece of beef, I'm going to roast it. I give you one more chance.

MOTHER COURAGE. Roast it, go ahead, it's only one year old.

THE COOK. One *day* old! Yesterday it was a cow. I saw it running around.

MOTHER COURAGE. In that case it must have started stinking before it died.

THE COOK. I don't care if I have to cook it for five hours. We'll see if it's still hard after that. (*He cuts into it.*)

MOTHER COURAGE. Put plenty of pepper in, so the Commander won't smell the smell.

(*The* SWEDISH COMMANDER, *a* CHAPLAIN, *and* EILIF *enter the tent.*)

THE COMMANDER (*clapping* EILIF *on the shoulder*). In the Commander's tent with you, my son! Sit at my right hand, you happy warrior! You've played a hero's part, you've served the Lord in his own Holy War, *that's* the thing! And you'll get a gold bracelet out of it when we take the town if *I* have any say in the matter! We come to save their souls and what do they do, the filthy, shameless peasant pigs? Drive their cattle away from *us*, while they stuff their priests with beef at both ends! But you showed 'em. So here's a can of red wine for you, we'll drink together! (*They do so.*) The chaplain gets the dregs, he's pious. Now what would you like for dinner, my hearty?

EILIF. How about slice of meat?

THE COMMANDER. Cook, meat!

THE COOK. Nothing to eat, so he brings company to eat it!

(MOTHER COURAGE *makes him stop talking; she wants to listen.*)

EILIF. Tires you out, skinning peasants. Gives you an appetite.

MOTHER COURAGE. Dear God, it's my Eilif!

THE COOK. Who?

MOTHER COURAGE. My eldest. It's two years since I saw him, he was stolen from me in the street. He must be in high favor if the Commander's invited him to dinner. And what do you have to eat? Nothing. You hear

what the Commander's guest wants? Meat! Better take my advice, buy the capon. The price is one guilder.

(*The* COMMANDER *has sat down with* EILIF *and the* CHAPLAIN.)

THE COMMANDER (*roaring*). Cook! Dinner, you pig, or I'll have your head!

THE COOK. This is blackmail. Give me the damn thing!

MOTHER COURAGE. A miserable bird like this?

THE COOK. You were right. Give it here. It's highway robbery, fifty hellers.

MOTHER COURAGE. I said one guilder. Nothing's too high for my eldest, the Commander's guest of honor.

THE COOK (*giving her the money*). Well, you might at least pluck it till I have a fire going.

MOTHER COURAGE (*sitting down to pluck the capon*). I can't wait to see his face when he sees me. This is my brave and clever son. I have a stupid one as well but he's honest. The daughter is nothing. At least, she doesn't talk: we must be thankful for small mercies.

THE COMMANDER. Have another can, my son, it's my favorite Falernian. There's only one cask left—two at the most—but it's worth it to meet a soldier that still believes in God! The shepherd of our flock here just looks on, he only preaches, he hasn't a clue how anything gets done. So now, Eilif, my son, give us the details: tell us how you fixed the peasants and grabbed the twenty bullocks. And let's hope they'll soon be here.

EILIF. In one day's time. Two at the most.

MOTHER COURAGE. Now that's considerate of Eilif—to bring the oxen tomorrow—otherwise my capon wouldn't have been so welcome today.

EILIF. Well, it was like this. I found out that the peasants had hidden their oxen and —on the sly and chiefly at night—had driven them into a certain wood. The people from the town were to pick them up there. I let them get their oxen in peace—they ought to know better than me where they are, I said to myself. Meanwhile I made my men crazy for meat. Their rations were short and I made sure they got shorter. Their mouths'd water at the sound of any word beginning with MEA . . . , like measles.

THE COMMANDER. Smart fella.

EILIF. Not bad. The rest was a snap. Only the peasants had clubs and outnumbered us three to one and made a murderous attack on us. Four of them drove me into a clump of trees, knocked my good sword from my hand, and yelled, "Surrender!" What now, I said to myself, they'll make mincemeat of me.

THE COMMANDER. What did you do?

EILIF. I laughed.

THE COMMANDER. You what?

EILIF. I laughed. And so we got to talking. I came right down to business and said: "Twenty guilders an ox is too much, I bid fifteen." Like I wanted to buy. That foxed 'em. So while they were scratching their heads, I reached for my good sword and cut 'em to pieces. Necessity knows no law, huh?

THE COMMANDER. What do *you* say, shepherd of the flock?

THE CHAPLAIN. Strictly speaking, that saying is not in the Bible. Our Lord made five hundred loaves out of five so that no such necessity would arise. When he told men to love their neighbors, their bellies were full. Things have changed since his day.

THE COMMANDER (*laughing*). Things have changed! A swallow of wine for those wise words, you pharisee! (*To* EILIF.) You cut 'em to pieces in a good cause, our fellows were hungry and you gave 'em to eat. Doesn't it say in the Bible "Whatsoever thou doest for the least of these my children, thou doest for me?" And what *did* you do for 'em? You got 'em the best steak dinner they ever tasted. Moldy bread is not what they're used to. They always ate white bread, and drank wine in their helmets, before going out to fight for God.

EILIF. I reached for my good sword and cut 'em to pieces.

THE COMMANDER. You have the makings of a Julius Caesar, why, you should be presented to the King!

EILIF. I've seen him—from a distance of course. He seemed to shed a light all around. I must try to be like him!

THE COMMANDER. I think you're succeeding, my boy! Oh, Eilif, you don't know how I value a brave soldier like you! I treat such a chap as my very own son. (*He takes him to the map.*) Take a look at our position, Eilif, it isn't all it might be, is it?

(MOTHER COURAGE *has been listening and is now plucking angrily at her capon.*)

MOTHER COURAGE. He must be a very bad Commander.

THE COOK. Just a gluttonous one. Why bad?

MOTHER COURAGE. Because he needs *brave* soldiers, that's why. If his plan of campaign was any good, why would he need *brave* soldiers, wouldn't plain, ordinary soldiers do? Whenever there are great virtues, it's a sure sign something's wrong.

THE COOK. You mean, it's a sure sign something's right.

MOTHER COURAGE. I mean what I say. Why? When a general or a king is stupid and leads his soldiers into a trap, they need this virtue of courage. When he's tightfisted and hasn't enough soldiers, the few he does have need the heroism of Hercules—another virtue. And if he's slovenly and doesn't give a damn about anything, they have to be as wise as serpents or they're finished. Loyalty's another virtue and you need plenty of it if the king's always asking too much of you. All virtues which a well-regulated country with a good king or a good general wouldn't need. In a good country virtues wouldn't be necessary. Everybody could be quite ordinary, middling, and, for all I care, cowards.

THE COMMANDER. I bet your father was a soldier.

EILIF. I've heard he was a great soldier. My mother warned me. I know a song about that.

THE COMMANDER. Sing it to us. (*Roaring.*) Bring that meat!

EILIF. It's called The Song of the Wise Woman and the Soldier.

(*He sings and at the same time does a war dance with his saber.*)

A shotgun will shoot and a jackknife will
  knife,
If you wade in the water, it will drown you,
Keep away from the ice, if you want my
  advice,
Said the wise woman to the soldier.

But that young soldier, he loaded his gun,
And he reached for his knife, and he started
    to run:
For marching never could hurt him!
From the north to the south he will march
    through the land
With his knife at his side and his gun in
    his hand:
That's what the soldiers told the wise
    woman.

Woe to him who defies the advice of
    the wise!
If you wade in the water, it will drown you!
Don't ignore what I say or you'll rue it
    one day,
Said the wise woman to the soldier.

But that young soldier, his knife at his side
And his gun in his hand, he steps into the
    tide:
For water never could hurt him!
When the new moon is shining on yonder
    church tower
We are all coming back: go and pray for
    that hour:
That's what the soldiers told the wise
    woman.

(MOTHER COURAGE *continues the song from
her kitchen, beating on a pan with a spoon.*)

Then the wise woman spoke: you will
    vanish like smoke
Leaving nothing but cold air behind you!
Just watch the smoke fly! Oh God, don't
    let him die!
Said the wise woman to the soldier.

EILIF. What's that?

MOTHER COURAGE (*singing on.*)

And the lad who defied the wise woman's
    advice,
When the new moon shone, floated down
    with the ice:
He waded in the water and it drowned him.

The wise woman spoke, and they vanished
    like smoke,
And their glorious deeds did not warm us.
Your glorious deeds do not warm us!

THE COMMANDER. What a kitchen I've got!
There's no end to the liberties they take!

(EILIF *has entered the kitchen and embraced
his mother.*)

EILIF. To see you again! Where are the
others?

MOTHER COURAGE (*in his arms*). Happy as
ducks in a pond. Swiss Cheese is paymaster
with the Second Regiment, so at least he
isn't in the fighting. I couldn't keep him out
altogether.

EILIF. Are your feet holding up?

MOTHER COURAGE. I've a bit of trouble
getting my shoes on in the morning.

(*The* COMMANDER *has come over.*)

THE COMMANDER. So you're his mother!
I hope you have more sons for me like this
fellow.

EILIF. If I'm not the lucky one: to be
feasted by the Commander while you sit
listening in the kitchen!

MOTHER COURAGE. Yes. I heard all right.
(*She gives him a box on the ear.*)

EILIF (*his hand to his cheek*). Because I took
the oxen?

MOTHER COURAGE. No. Because you didn't
surrender when the four peasants let fly at
you and tried to make mincemeat of you!
Didn't I teach you to take care of yourself?
You Finnish devil, you!

(*The* COMMANDER *and the* CHAPLAIN *stand
laughing in the doorway.*)

## SCENE 3

*THREE YEARS PASS AND MOTHER COUR-
AGE, WITH PARTS OF A FINNISH REGI-
MENT, IS TAKEN PRISONER. HER DAUGH-
TER IS SAVED. HER WAGON LIKEWISE,
BUT HER HONEST SON DIES.*

(*A camp. The regimental flag is flying from a
pole. Afternoon. All sorts of wares hanging on
the wagon.* MOTHER COURAGE'S *clothesline is
tied to the wagon at one end, to a cannon at
the other. She and* KATTRIN *are folding the
washing on the cannon. At the same time she
is bargaining with an* ORDNANCE OFFICER
*over a bag of bullets.* SWISS CHEESE, *in paymaster's uniform now, looks on.* YVETTE POT-
TIER, *a very good-looking young person, is
sewing at a colored hat, a glass of brandy before her. She is in stocking feet. Her red boots
are near by.*)

THE OFFICER. I'm letting you have the bullets for two guilders. Dirt cheap. 'Cause I need the money. The Colonel's been drinking with the officers for three days and we're out of liquor.

MOTHER COURAGE. They're army property. If they find 'em on me, I'll be court-martialed. You sell your bullets, you bastards, and send your men out to fight with nothing to shoot with.

THE OFFICER. Oh, come on, you scratch my back, and I'll scratch yours.

MOTHER COURAGE. I won't take army stuff. Not at *that* price.

THE OFFICER. You can resell 'em for five guilders, maybe eight, to the Ordnance Officer of the Fourth Regiment. All you have to do is to give him a receipt for twelve. He hasn't a bullet left.

MOTHER COURAGE. Why don't you do it yourself?

THE OFFICER. I don't trust him. We're friends.

MOTHER COURAGE (*taking the bag*). Give it here. (*To* KATTRIN.) Take it around to the back and pay him a guilder and a half. (*As the* OFFICER *protests.*) I said a guilder and a half! (KATTRIN *drags the bag away. The* OFFICER *follows.* MOTHER COURAGE *speaks to* SWISS CHEESE.) Here's your underwear back, take care of it; it's October now, autumn may come at any time; I purposely don't say it must come, I've learned from experience there's nothing that must come, not even the seasons. But your books *must* balance now you're the regimental paymaster. *Do* they balance?

SWISS CHEESE. Yes, Mother.

MOTHER COURAGE. Don't forget they made you paymaster because you're honest and so simple you'd never think of running off with the cash. Don't lose that underwear.

SWISS CHEESE. No, mother. I'll put in under the mattress. (*He starts to go.*)

THE OFFICER. I'll go with you, paymaster.

MOTHER COURAGE. Don't teach him any monkey business.

(*Without a good-by the* OFFICER *leaves with* SWISS CHEESE.)

YVETTE (*waving to him*). You might at least say good-by!

MOTHER COURAGE (*to* YVETTE). I don't like that. *He's* no sort of company for my Swiss Cheese. But the war's not making a bad start. Before all the different countries get into it, four or five years'll have gone by like nothing. If I look ahead and make no mistakes, business will be good. Don't you know you shouldn't drink in the morning with your illness?

YVETTE. Who says I'm ill? That's libel!

MOTHER COURAGE. They all say so.

YVETTE. They're all liars. I'm desperate, Mother Courage. They all avoid me like a stinking fish. Because of those lies. So what am I arranging my hat for? (*She throws it down.*) That's why I drink in the morning. I never used to, it gives you crow's feet. But what's the difference? Every man in the regiment knows me. I should have stayed at home when my first was unfaithful. But pride isn't for the likes of us, you eat dirt or down you go.

MOTHER COURAGE. Now don't you start again with your friend Peter and how it all happened—in front of my innocent daughter.

YVETTE. She's the one that should hear it. So she'll get hardened against love.

MOTHER COURAGE. That's something no one ever gets hardened against.

YVETTE. I'll tell you about it, and get it off my chest. I grew up in Flanders' fields, that's where it starts, or I'd never even have caught sight of him and I wouldn't be here in Poland today. He was an army cook, blond, a Dutchman, but thin. Kattrin, beware of thin men! I didn't. I didn't even know he'd had another girl before me and she called him Peter Piper because he never took his pipe out of his mouth the whole time, it meant so little to him.

(*She sings "The Fraternization Song".*)

When I was almost seventeen
The foe came to our land
And laying aside his saber
He took me gently by the hand.

First came the May Day Rite
Then came the May Day night.
The pipes played and the drums did beat.
The foe paraded down the street.
And then with us they took their ease
And fraternized behind the trees.

Our foes they came in plenty.
A cook was my own foe.
I hated him by daylight
But in the dark I loved him so.

    First comes the May Day Rite
    Then comes the May Day night.
    The pipes play and the drums do beat.
    The foe parades down every street.
    And then with us they take their ease
    And fraternize behind the trees.

The heavens seemed to open
Such passion did I feel.
But my people never understood
The love I felt was real.

    One day the sun rose slow
    On all my pain and woe.
    My loved one, with the other men,
    Presented arms and stood at ease
    Then marched away past all those trees
    And never did come back again.

I made the mistake of running after him, I never found him. It's five years ago now. (*With swaying gait she goes behind the wagon.*)

MOTHER COURAGE. You've left your hat.

YVETTE. For the birds.

MOTHER COURAGE. Let this be a lesson to you, Kattrin, never start anything with a soldier. The heavens do seem to open, so watch out! Even with men who're not in the army life's no honeypot. He tells you he'd like to kiss the ground under your feet—did you wash 'em yesterday, while we're on the subject?—and then if you don't look out, your number's up, you're his slave for life. Be glad you're dumb, Kattrin: you'll never contradict yourself, you'll never want to bite your tongue off because you spoke out of turn. Dumbness is a gift from God. Here comes the Commander's cook, what's bothering *him*?

    (*Enter the* COOK *and the* CHAPLAIN.)

THE CHAPLAIN. I bring a message from your son Eilif. The cook came with me. You've made, ahem, an impression on him.

THE COOK. I thought I'd get a little whiff of the balmy breeze.

MOTHER COURAGE. You're welcome to that if you behave yourself, and even if you don't

I think I can handle you. But what does Eilif want? I don't have any money.

THE CHAPLAIN. Actually, I have something to tell his brother, the paymaster.

MOTHER COURAGE. He isn't here. And he isn't anywhere else either. He's not his brother's paymaster, and I won't have him led into temptation. Let Eilif try it on with someone else! (*She takes money from the purse at her belt.*) Give him this. It's a sin. He's speculating in mother love, he ought to be ashamed of himself.

THE COOK. Not for long. He has to go with his regiment now—to his death maybe. Send some more money, or you'll be sorry. You women are hard—and sorry afterward. A glass of brandy wouldn't cost very much, but you refuse to provide it, and six feet under goes your man and you can't dig him up again.

THE CHAPLAIN. All very touching, my dear cook, but to fall in this war is not a misfortune, it's a blessing. This is a war of religion. Not just any old war but a special one, a religious one, and therefore pleasing unto God.

THE COOK. Correct. In one sense it's a war because there's fleecing, bribing, plundering, not to mention a little raping, but it's different from all other wars because it's a war of religion. That's clear. All the same, it makes you thirsty.

THE CHAPLAIN (*to* MOTHER COURAGE, *pointing at the* COOK). I tried to hold him off but he said you'd bewitched him. He dreams about you.

THE COOK (*lighting a clay pipe*). Brandy from the fair hand of a lady, that's for me. And don't embarrass me any more: the stories the chaplain was telling me on the way over still have me blushing.

MOTHER COURAGE. A man of his cloth! I must get you both something to drink or you'll be making improper advances out of sheer boredom.

THE CHAPLAIN. That is indeed a temptation, said the court chaplain, and gave way to it. (*Turning toward* KATTRIN *as he walks.*) And who is this captivating young person?

MOTHER COURAGE. She's not a captivating young person, she's a respectable young person.

(*The* CHAPLAIN *and the* COOK *go with* MOTHER COURAGE *behind the cart, and one hears them talk politics.*)

MOTHER COURAGE. The trouble here in Poland is that the Poles *would* keep meddling. It's true our King moved in on them with man, beast, and wagon, but instead of keeping the peace the Poles attacked the Swedish King when he was in the act of peacefully withdrawing. So they were guilty of a breach of the peace and their blood is on their own heads.

THE CHAPLAIN. Anyway, our King was thinking of nothing but freedom. The Kaiser enslaved them all, Poles and Germans alike, so our King *had* to liberate them.

THE COOK. Just what *I* think. Your health! Your brandy is first-rate, I'm never mistaken in a face.

(KATTRIN *looks after them, leaves the washing, goes to the hat, picks it up, sits down, and takes up the red boots.*)

And the war is a war of religion. (*Singing while* KATTRIN *puts the boots on.*) "A mighty fortress is our God . . ." (*He sings a verse or so of Luther's hymn.*) And talking of King Gustavus, this freedom he tried to bring to Germany cost him a pretty penny. Back in Sweden he had to levy a salt tax, the poorer folks didn't like it a bit. Then, too, he had to lock up the Germans and even cut their heads off, they clung so to slavery and their Kaiser. Of course, if no one had *wanted* to be free, the King would have got quite mad. First it was just Poland he tried to protect from bad men, especially the Kaiser, then his appetite grew with eating, and he ended up protecting Germany too. Now Germany put up a pretty decent fight. So the good King had nothing but worries in return for his outlay and his goodness, and of course he had to get his money back with taxes, which made bad blood, but he didn't shrink even from that. For he had one thing in his favor anyway, God's Holy Word, which was all to the good, because otherwise they could have said he did it for profit. That's how he kept his conscience clear. He always put conscience first.

MOTHER COURAGE. It's plain you're no Swede, or you'd speak differently of the Hero King.

THE CHAPLAIN. What's more, you eat his bread.

THE COOK. I don't eat his bread. I bake his bread.

MOTHER COURAGE. He's unbeatable. Why? His men believe in him. (*Earnestly.*) To hear the big fellows talk, they wage war from fear of God and for all things bright and beautiful, but just look into it, and you'll see they're not so silly: they want a good profit out of it, or else the little fellows like you and me wouldn't back 'em up.

THE COOK. That's right.

THE CHAPLAIN. And as a Dutchman you'd do well to see which flag's flying here before you express an opinion!

MOTHER COURAGE. All good Protestants forever!

THE COOK. A health!

(KATTRIN *has begun to strut about with* YVETTE's *hat on, copying* YVETTE's *sexy walk. Suddenly cannon and shots. Drums.* MOTHER COURAGE, *the* COOK, *and the* CHAPLAIN *rush around to the front of the cart, the last two with glasses in their hands. The* ORDNANCE OFFICER *and a* SOLDIER *come running to the cannon and try to push it along.*)

MOTHER COURAGE. What's the matter? Let me get my washing off that gun, you slobs! (*She tries to do so.*)

THE OFFICER. The Catholics! Surprise attack! We don't know if we can get away! (*To the* SOLDIER.) Get that gun! (*He runs off.*)

THE COOK. For heaven's sake! I must go to the Commander. Mother Courage, I'll be back in a day or two—for a short conversation. (*He rushes off.*)

MOTHER COURAGE. Hey, you've left your pipe!

THE COOK (*off*). Keep it for me, I'll need it!

MOTHER COURAGE. This *would* happen just when we were making money.

THE CHAPLAIN. Well, I must be going too. Yes, if the enemy's so close, it can be dangerous. "Blessed are the peacemakers," a good slogan in war time! If only I had a cloak.

MOTHER COURAGE. I'm lending no cloaks. Not even to save a life, I'm not. I've had experience in that line.

THE CHAPLAIN. But I'm in special danger. Because of my religion.

MOTHER COURAGE (*bringing him a cloak*). It's against my better judgment. Now run!

THE CHAPLAIN. I thank you, you're very generous, but maybe I'd better stay and sit here. If I run, I might attract the enemy's attention, I might arouse suspicion.

MOTHER COURAGE (*to the* SOLDIER). Let it alone, you dolt, who's going to pay you for this? It'll cost you your life, let me hold it for you.

THE SOLDIER (*running away*). You're my witness: I tried!

MOTHER COURAGE. I'll swear to it! (*Seeing* KATTRIN *with the hat.*) What on earth are you up to—with a whore's hat! Take it off this minute! Are you mad? With the enemy coming? (*She tears the hat off her head.*) Do you want them to find you and make a whore of you? And she has the boots on too, straight from Babylon. I'll soon fix that. (*She tries to get them off.*) Oh God, Chaplain, help me with these boots, I'll be right back. (*She runs to the wagon.*)

YVETTE (*entering and powdering her face*). What's that you say: the Catholics are coming? Where's my hat? Who's been trampling on it? I can't run around in that, what will they think of me? And I don't even have a mirror. (*To the* CHAPLAIN.) How do I look—too much powder?

THE CHAPLAIN. Just, er, right.

YVETTE. And where are my red boots? (*She can't find them because* KATTRIN *is hiding her feet under her skirt.*) I left them here! Now I've got to go barefoot to my tent, it's a scandal! (*Exit.*)

(SWISS CHEESE *comes running in carrying a cash box.* MOTHER COURAGE *enters with her hands covered with ashes.*)

MOTHER COURAGE (*to* KATTRIN). Ashes! (*To* SWISS CHEESE.) What have you got there?

SWISS CHEESE. The regimental cash box.

MOTHER COURAGE. Throw it away! Your paymastering days are over!

SWISS CHEESE. It's a trust! (*He goes to the back.*)

MOTHER COURAGE (*to the* CHAPLAIN). Off with your pastor's coat, Chaplain, or they'll recognize you, cloak or no cloak. (*She is rubbing ashes into* KATTRIN'S *face.*) Keep still. A little dirt, and you're safe. A calamity! The

sentries were drunk. Well, one must hide one's light under a bushel, as they say. When a soldier sees a clean face, there's one more whore in the world. Especially a Catholic soldier. For weeks on end, no grub. Then, when the plundering starts and they steal some, they jump on top of the womenfolk. That should do. Let me look at you. Not bad. Looks like you've been rolling in muck. Don't tremble. Nothing can happen to you now. (*To* SWISS CHEESE.) Where've you left the cash box?

SWISS CHEESE. I thought I'd just put it in the wagon.

MOTHER COURAGE (*horrified*). What! In my wagon? God punish you for a prize idiot! If I just look away for a moment! They'll hang all three of us!

SWISS CHEESE. Then I'll put it somewhere else. Or escape with it.

MOTHER COURAGE. You'll stay where you are. It's too late.

THE CHAPLAIN (*still changing his clothes*). For heaven's sake: the flag!

MOTHER COURAGE (*taking down the flag*). God in heaven! I don't notice it any more. I've had it twenty-five years.

(*The thunder of cannon grows.*)

(*Three days later. Morning. The cannon is gone.* MOTHER COURAGE, KATTRIN, *the* CHAPLAIN, *and* SWISS CHEESE *sit anxiously eating.*)

SWISS CHEESE. This is the third day I've been sitting here doing nothing, and the Sergeant, who's always been patient with me, may be slowly beginning to ask, "Where on earth is Swiss Cheese with that cash box?"

MOTHER COURAGE. Be glad they're not on the trail.

THE CHAPLAIN. What about me? I can't hold a service here or I'll be in hot water. It is written, "Out of the abundance of the heart, the tongue speaketh." But woe is me if *my* tongue speaketh!

MOTHER COURAGE. That's how it is. Here you sit—one with his religion, the other with his cash box, I don't know which is more dangerous.

THE CHAPLAIN. We're in God's hands now!

MOTHER COURAGE. I hope we're not *that* desperate, but it *is* hard to sleep nights.

'Course it'd be easier if *you* weren't here, Swiss Cheese, all the same I've not done badly. I told them I was against the Antichrist, who's a Swede with horns on his head. I told them I noticed his left horn's a bit threadbare. When they cross-examined me, I always asked where I could buy holy candles a bit cheaper. I know these things because Swiss Cheese's father was a Catholic and made jokes about it. They didn't quite believe me but they needed a canteen, so they turned a blind eye. Maybe it's all for the best. We're prisoners. But so are lice in fur.

THE CHAPLAIN. The milk is good. As far as quantity goes, we may have to reduce our Swedish appetites somewhat. We are defeated.

MOTHER COURAGE. Who's defeated? The defeats and victories of the fellows at the top aren't always defeats and victories for the fellows at the bottom. Not at all. There've been cases where a defeat is a victory for the fellows at the bottom, it's only their honor that's lost, nothing serious. In Livonia once, our Chief took such a knock from the enemy, in the confusion I got a fine gray mare out of the baggage train, it pulled my wagon seven months—till we won and there was an inventory. But in general both defeat and victory are a costly business for us that haven't got much. The best thing is for politics to get stuck in the mud. (*To* SWISS CHEESE.) Eat!

SWISS CHEESE. I don't like it. How will the sergeant pay his men?

MOTHER COURAGE. Soldiers in flight don't get paid.

SWISS CHEESE. Well, they could claim to be. No pay, no flight. They can refuse to budge.

MOTHER COURAGE. Swiss Cheese, your sense of duty worries me. I've brought you up to be honest because you're not very bright. But don't overdo it. And now I'm going with the chaplain to buy a Catholic flag and some meat. There's no one can hunt out meat like him, sure as a sleepwalker. He can tell a good piece of meat from the way his mouth waters. A good thing they let me stay in the business. In business you ask what price, not what religion. And Protestant trousers keep you just as warm.

THE CHAPLAIN. As the mendicant monk said when there was talk of the Lutherans turning the whole world upside down: Beggars will *always* be needed. (MOTHER COURAGE *disappears into the wagon.*) She's worried about the cash box. Up to now they've ignored us—as if we were part of the wagon—but can it last?

SWISS CHEESE. I can get rid of it.

THE CHAPLAIN. That's almost *more* dangerous. Suppose you're seen. They have spies. Yesterday morning one jumped out of the very hole I was relieving myself in. I was so scared I almost broke out in prayer—*that* would have given me away all right! I believe their favorite way of finding a Protestant is smelling his excrement. The spy was a little brute with a bandage over one eye.

MOTHER COURAGE (*clambering out of the wagon with a basket*). I've found you out, you shameless hussy! (*She holds up* YVETTE'S *red boots in triumph.*) Yvette's red boots! She just swiped them—because you went and told her she was a captivating person. (*She lays them in the basket.*) Stealing Yvette's boots! But *she* disgraces herself for money, *you* do it for nothing—for pleasure! I told you, you must wait for the peace. No soldiers! Save your proud peacock ways for peacetime!

THE CHAPLAIN. I don't find her proud.

MOTHER COURAGE. Prouder than she can afford to be. I like her when people say "I never noticed the poor thing." I like her when she's a stone in Dalarna, where there's nothing but stones. (*To* SWISS CHEESE.) Leave the cash box where it is, do you hear? And pay attention to your sister, she needs it. Between the two of you, you'll be the death of me yet. I'd rather take care of a bag of fleas.

(*She leaves with the* CHAPLAIN. KATTRIN *clears the dishes away.*)

SWISS CHEESE. Not many days more when you can sit in the sun in your shirtsleeves. (KATTRIN *points to a tree.*) Yes, the leaves are yellow already. (*With gestures,* KATTRIN *asks if he wants a drink.*) I'm not drinking, I'm thinking. (*Pause.*) She says she can't sleep. So I *should* take the cash box away. I've found a place for it. I'll keep it in the mole hole by the river till the time comes. I might get it tonight before sunrise and take it to the regiment. How far can they have fled in three days? The Sergeant's eyes'll pop out of his head. "I give you the cashbox to take care of, and what do you do," he'll say, "but hand it right back to me: you've disappointed me most pleasantly, Swiss Cheese." Yes, Kattrin, I *will* have a glass now!

(*When* KATTRIN *reappears behind the wagon two men confront her. One of them is a* SERGEANT. *The other doffs his hat and flourishes it in a showy greeting. He has a bandage over one eye.*)

THE MAN WITH THE BANDAGE. Good morning, young lady. Have you seen a man from the Second Protestant Regiment?

(*Terrified,* KATTRIN *runs away, spilling her brandy. The two men look at each other and then withdraw after seeing* SWISS CHEESE.)

SWISS CHEESE (*starting up from his reflection*). You're spilling it! What's the matter with you, have you hurt your eye? I don't understand. Yes, and I must be going, too. I've decided it's the thing to do. (*He stands up. She does all she can to make him aware of the danger he is in. He only pushes her away.*) I'd like to know what you mean. I know you mean well, poor thing, you just can't get it out. And don't trouble yourself about the brandy, I'll live to drink so much of it, what's one glass? (*He takes the cash box out of the wagon and puts it under his coat.*) I'll be back right away. But don't hold me up or I'll have to scold you. Yes, I know you mean well. If you could only speak!

(*When she tries to hold him back he kisses her and pulls himself free. Exit. She is desperate and runs up and down, emitting little sounds.* MOTHER COURAGE *and the* CHAPLAIN *return.* KATTRIN *rushes at her mother.*)

MOTHER COURAGE. What *is* it, what *is* it, Kattrin? Control yourself! Has someone done something to you? Where is Swiss Cheese? (*To the* CHAPLAIN.) Don't stand around, get that Catholic flag up! (*She takes a Catholic flag out of her basket and the* CHAPLAIN *runs it up the pole.*)

THE CHAPLAIN (*bitterly*). All good Catholics forever!

MOTHER COURAGE. Now, Kattrin, calm down and tell all about it, your mother understands you. What, that little bastard of mine's taken the cash box away? I'll box his ears for him, the rascal! Now take your time and don't try to talk, use your hands. I don't like it when you howl like a dog, what'll the chaplain think of you? You're giving him the creeps. A man with one eye was here?

THE CHAPLAIN. That fellow with one eye is an informer! Have they caught Swiss Cheese? (KATTRIN *shakes her head, shrugs her shoulders.*) This is the end.

(*Voices off. The two men bring in* SWISS CHEESE.)

SWISS CHEESE. Let me go. I've nothing on me. You're breaking my shoulder! I am innocent.

THE SERGEANT. This is where he comes from. These are his friends.

MOTHER COURAGE. Us? Since when?

SWISS CHEESE. I don't even know 'em. I was just getting my lunch here. Ten hellers it cost me. Maybe you saw me sitting on that bench. It was too salty.

THE SERGEANT. Who *are* you people, anyway?

MOTHER COURAGE. Law-abiding citizens! It's true what he says. He bought his lunch here. And it was too salty.

THE SERGEANT. Are you pretending you don't know him?

MOTHER COURAGE. I can't know all of them, can I? *I* don't ask, "What's your name and are you a heathen?" If they pay up, they're not heathens to me. Are you a heathen?

SWISS CHEESE. Oh, no!

THE CHAPLAIN. He sat there like a law-abiding fellow and never once opened his mouth. Except to eat. Which is necessary.

THE SERGEANT. Who do you think *you* are?

MOTHER COURAGE. Oh, he's my barman. And you're thirsty, I'll bring you a glass of brandy. You must be footsore and weary!

THE SERGEANT. No brandy on duty. (*To* SWISS CHEESE:) You were carrying something. You must have hidden it by the river. We saw the bulge in your shirt.

MOTHER COURAGE. Sure it was him?

SWISS CHEESE. I think you mean another fellow. There *was* a fellow with something under his shirt, I saw him. I'm the wrong man.

MOTHER COURAGE. I think so too. It's a misunderstanding. Could happen to anyone. Oh, I know what people are like, I'm Mother Courage, you've heard of me, everyone knows about me, and I can tell you this: he looks honest.

THE SERGEANT. We're after the regimental cash box. And we know what the man looks like who's been keeping it. We've been looking for him two days. It's you.

SWISS CHEESE. No, it's not!

THE SERGEANT. And if you don't shell out, you're dead, see? Where is it?

MOTHER COURAGE (urgently). 'Course he'd give it to you to save his life. He'd up and say, *I've* got it, here it is, you're stronger than me. He's not *that* stupid. Speak, little stupid, the sergeant's giving you a chance!

SWISS CHEESE. What if I haven't got it?

THE SERGEANT. Come with us. We'll get it out of you. (*They take him off.*)

MOTHER COURAGE (shouting after them). He'd tell you! He's not *that* stupid! And don't you break his shoulder! (*She runs after them.*)

(*The same evening. The* CHAPLAIN *and* KATTRIN *are rinsing glasses and polishing knives.*)

THE CHAPLAIN. Cases of people getting caught like this are by no means unknown in the history of religion. I am reminded of the Passion of Our Lord and Savior. There's an old song about it.

(*He sings "The Song of the Hours".*)
In the first hour of the day
Simple Jesus Christ was
Presented as a murderer
To the heathen Pilate.

Pilate found no fault in him
No cause to condemn him
So he sent the Lord away.
Let King Herod see him!

Hour the third: the Son of God
Was with scourges beaten
And they set a crown of thorns
On the head of Jesus.

And they dressed him as a king
Joked and jested at him

And the cross to die upon
He himself must carry

Six: they stripped Lord Jesus bare.
To the cross they nailed him.
When the blood came gushing, he
Prayed and loud lamented.

Each upon his cross, two thieves
Mocked him like the others.
And the bright sun crept away
Not to see such doings.

Nine: Lord Jesus cried aloud
That he was forsaken!
In a sponge upon a pole
Vinegar was fed him.

Then the Lord gave up the ghost
And the earth did tremble.
Temple curtain split in twain.
Cliffs fell in the ocean.

Evening: they broke the bones
Of the malefactors.
Then they took a spear and pierced
The side of gentle Jesus.

And the blood and water ran
And they laughed at Jesus.
Of this simple son of man
Such and more they tell us.

MOTHER COURAGE (entering, excited). It's life and death. But the Sergeant will still listen to us. The only thing is, he mustn't know it's our Swiss Cheese, or they'll say we helped him. It's only a matter of money, but where can *we* get money? Isn't Yvette here yet? I talked to her on the way over. She's picked up a Colonel who may be willing to buy her a canteen business.

THE CHAPLAIN. You'd sell the wagon, everything?

MOTHER COURAGE. Where else would I get the money for the Sergeant?

THE CHAPLAIN. What are you to live off?

MOTHER COURAGE. That's just it.

(*Enter* YVETTE *with a hoary old* COLONEL.)

YVETTE (embracing MOTHER COURAGE). *Dear* Mistress Courage, we meet again. (*Whispering.*) He didn't say no. (*Aloud.*) This is my friend, my, um, business adviser. I happened to hear you might sell your wagon. Due to special circumstances, I'd like to think about it.

MOTHER COURAGE. I want to pawn it, not sell it. And nothing hasty. In war time you don't find another wagon like that so easy.

YVETTE (*disappointed*). Only pawn it? I thought you wanted to sell. I don't know if I'm interested. (*To the* COLONEL.) What do *you* think, my dear?

THE COLONEL. I quite agree with you, bunny.

MOTHER COURAGE. It's only for pawn.

YVETTE. I thought you *had* to have the money.

MOTHER COURAGE (*firmly*). I do have to have it. But I'd rather wear my feet off looking for an offer than just sell. Why? We live off the wagon. It's an opportunity for you, Yvette. Who knows when you'll have another such? Who knows when you'll find another business adviser?

THE COLONEL. Take it, take it!

YVETTE. My friend thinks I should go ahead, but I'm not sure, if it's only for pawn. You think we should buy it outright, don't you?

THE COLONEL. I do, bunny, I do!

MOTHER COURAGE. Then you must go and find something that's for sale. Maybe you'll find it—if you have the time, and your friend goes with you, let's say in about a week, or two weeks, you may find the right thing.

YVETTE. Yes, we can certainly look around for something. I love going around looking, I love going around with you, Poldy . . .

THE COLONEL. Really? Do you?

YVETTE. Oh, it's lovely! I could take two weeks of it!

THE COLONEL. Really, could you?

YVETTE. If you get the money, when are you thinking of paying it back?

MOTHER COURAGE. In two weeks. Maybe one.

YVETTE. I can't make up my mind. Poldy, advise me, *chéri*! (*She takes the* COLONEL *to one side.*) She'll *have* to sell, don't worry. That Lieutenant—the blond one, you know the one I mean—he'll lend me the money. He's

mad about me, he says I remind him of someone. What do you advise?

THE COLONEL. Oh, I have to warn you against *him*. He's no good. He'll exploit the situation. I told you, bunny, I told you *I'd* buy you something, didn't I tell you that?

YVETTE. I simply can't let you!

THE COLONEL. Oh, please, please!

YVETTE. Well, if you think the Lieutenant might exploit the situation I *will* let you!

THE COLONEL. I do think so.

YVETTE. So you advise me to?

THE COLONEL. I do, bunny, I do!

YVETTE (*returning to* MOTHER COURAGE). My friend says all right. Write me out a receipt saying the wagon's mine when the two weeks are up—with everything in it. I'll just run through it all now, the two hundred guilders can wait. (*To the* COLONEL.) You go ahead to the camp, I'll follow, I must go over all this so nothing'll be missing later from *my* wagon!

THE COLONEL. Wait, I'll help you up! (*He does so.*) Come soon, honey bun! (*Exit.*)

MOTHER COURAGE. Yvette, Yvette!

YVETTE. There aren't many boots left!

MOTHER COURAGE. Yvette, this is no time to go through the wagon, yours or not yours. You promised you'd talk to the Sergeant about Swiss Cheese. There isn't a minute to lose. He's up before the court-martial one hour from now.

YVETTE. I just want to count these shirts again.

MOTHER COURAGE (*dragging her down the steps by the skirt*). You hyena, Swiss Cheese's life's at stake! And don't say who the money comes from. Pretend he's your sweetheart, for heaven's sake, or we'll all get it for helping him.

YVETTE. I've arranged to meet One Eye in the bushes. He must be there by now.

THE CHAPLAIN. And don't hand over all two hundred, a hundred and fifty's sure to be enough.

MOTHER COURAGE. Is it your money? I'll thank you to keep your nose out of this, I'm not doing *you* out of your porridge. Now run, and no haggling, remember his life's at stake. (*She pushes* YVETTE *off.*)

THE CHAPLAIN. I didn't want to talk you

into anything, but what are we going to live on? You have an unemployable daughter around your neck.

MOTHER COURAGE. I'm counting on that cash box, smart aleck. They'll pay his expenses out of it.

THE CHAPLAIN. You think she can work it?

MOTHER COURAGE. It's in her own interest: I pay the two hundred and she gets the wagon. She knows what she's doing, she won't have her Colonel on the string forever. Kattrin, go and clean the knives, use pumice stone. And don't *you* stand around like Jesus in Gethsemane. Get a move on, wash those glasses. There'll be over fifty cavalrymen here tonight, and you'll be saying you're not used to being on your feet. "Oh my poor feet, in church I never had to run around like this!" I think they'll let us have him. Thanks be to God they're corruptible. They're not wolves, they're human and after money. God is merciful, and men are bribable, that's how His will is done on earth as it is in Heaven. Corruption is our only hope. As long as there's corruption, there'll be merciful judges and even the innocent may get off.

(YVETTE *comes in panting.*)

YVETTE. They'll do it for two hundred if you make it snappy—these things change from one minute to the next. I'd better take One Eye to my Colonel at once. He confessed he had the cash box, they put the thumb-screws on him. But he threw it in the river when he noticed them coming up behind him. So it's gone. Shall I run and get the money from my Colonel?

MOTHER COURAGE. The cash box gone? How'll I ever get my two hundred back?

YVETTE. So you thought you could get it from the cash box? I *would* have been sunk. Not a hope, Mother Courage. If you want your Swiss Cheese, you'll have to pay. Or should I let the whole thing drop, so you can keep your wagon?

MOTHER COURAGE. I wasn't figuring on this. But you needn't hound me, you'll get the wagon, it's yours already, and it's been mine seventeen years. I need a minute to think it over, it's all so sudden. What can I do? I *can't* pay two hundred. You *should* have haggled with them. I must hold on to some-

thing, or any passer-by can kick me in the ditch. Go and say I'll pay a hundred and twenty or the deal's off. Even then I lose the wagon.

YVETTE. They won't do it. And anyway, One Eye's in a hurry. He keeps looking over his shoulder all the time, he's so worked up. Hadn't I better give them the whole two hundred?

MOTHER COURAGE (*desperate*). I can't pay it! I've been working thirty years. She's twenty-five and still no husband. I have her to think of. So leave me alone. I know what I'm doing. A hundred and twenty or no deal.

YVETTE. You know best. (*She runs off.*)

(MOTHER COURAGE *turns away and slowly walks a few paces to the rear. Then she turns around, looks neither at the* CHAPLAIN *nor her daughter, and sits down to help* KATTRIN *polish the knives.*)

MOTHER COURAGE. Don't break the glasses, they're not ours. Watch what you're doing, you're cutting yourself. Swiss Cheese will be back, I'll give two hundred, if I have to. You'll get your brother back. With eighty guilders we could pack a hamper with goods and begin again. It wouldn't be the end of the world.

THE CHAPLAIN. The Bible says: the Lord will provide.

MOTHER COURAGE. Rub them dry, I said.

(*They clean the knives in silence.*)

They say the war will stop soon. How would it? I ask. And no one can answer me. (*Slowly.*) The King and the Pope are mortal enemies, their Faith is different. They must go for each other till one of them drops dead, neither of them can relax till then. Even so they can't get on with it. Why not? The Emperor is in the way, and they both have something against him. They're not going to fight each other to the death with the Emperor lurking about till they're half dead so he can fall on both of 'em! No, they're banding together against the Emperor so he'll drop dead first and they can go for each other.

(*Suddenly* KATTRIN *runs sobbing behind the wagon.*)

Someone once offered me five hundred guilders for the wagon. I didn't take it. My

Eilif, wherever he may be, thought I'd taken it and cried all night.

(YVETTE *comes running in.*)

YVETTE. They won't do it. I warned you. One Eye was going to drop it then and there. There's no point, he said. He said the drums would roll any second now and that's the sign a verdict has been reached. I offered a hundred and fifty, he didn't even shrug. I could hardly get him to stay there while I came here.

MOTHER COURAGE. Tell him I'll pay two hundred. Run!

(YVETTE *runs.* MOTHER COURAGE *sits, silent. The* CHAPLAIN *has stopped doing the glasses.*)

I believe—I've haggled too long.

(*In the distance, a roll of drums. The* CHAPLAIN *stands up and walks toward the rear.* MOTHER COURAGE *remains seated. It grows dark. It gets light again.* MOTHER COURAGE *has not moved.* YVETTE *appears, pale.*)

YVETTE. Now you've done it—with your haggling. You can keep the wagon now. He got eleven bullets in him. I don't know why I still bother about you, you don't deserve it, but I just happened to learn they don't think the cash box is really in the river. They suspect it's here, they think you're connected with him. I think they're going to bring him here to see if you'll give yourself away when you see him. You'd better not know him or we're in for it. And I'd better tell you straight, they're just behind me. Shall I keep Kattrin away? (MOTHER COURAGE *shakes her head.*) Does she know? Maybe she never heard the drums or didn't understand.

MOTHER COURAGE. She knows. Bring her.

(YVETTE *brings* KATTRIN, *who walks over to her mother and stands by her.* MOTHER COURAGE *takes her hand. Two men come on with a stretcher; there is a sheet on it and something underneath. Beside them, the* SERGEANT. *They put the stretcher down.*)

THE SERGEANT. Here's a man we can't identify. But he has to be registered to keep the records straight. He bought a meal from you. Look at him, see if you know him. (*He pulls back the sheet.*) Do you know him? (MOTHER COURAGE *shakes her head.*) What?

You never saw him before he took that meal? (MOTHER COURAGE *shakes her head.*) Lift him up. Throw him in the carrion pit. He has no one that knows him.

(*They carry him off.*)

## SCENE 4

*MOTHER COURAGE SINGS THE SONG OF THE GREAT CAPITULATION*

(*Outside an officer's tent.* MOTHER COURAGE *waits. A* CLERK *looks out of the tent.*)

THE CLERK. I know you. You had a Protestant paymaster with you, he was hiding out with you. Better make no complaint.

MOTHER COURAGE. But I'm innocent and if I give up it'll look as if I have a bad conscience. They cut everything in my wagon to ribbons with their sabers and then claimed a fine of five thalers for nothing and less than nothing.

THE CLERK. For your own good, keep your trap shut. We haven't many canteens, so we let you stay in business, especially if you've a bad conscience and have to pay a fine now and then.

MOTHER COURAGE. I'm going to file a complaint.

THE CLERK. As you wish. Wait here till the Captain has time.

(*He withdraws into tent.*)

(*A YOUNG SOLDIER comes storming in.*)

THE YOUNG SOLDIER. Screw the Captain! Where *is* the son of a bitch? Swiping my reward, spending it on brandy for his whores, I'll rip his belly open!

AN OLDER SOLDIER (*coming after him*). Shut your hole, you'll wind up in the stocks.

THE YOUNG SOLDIER. Come out, you thief, I'll make lamb chops out of you! I was the only one in the squad who swam the river and *he* grabs my money, I can't even buy myself a beer. Come on out! And let me slice you up!

THE OLDER SOLDIER. Holy Christ, he'll destroy himself!

THE YOUNG SOLDIER. Let me go or I'll run *you* down too. This has got to be settled!

THE OLDER SOLDIER. Saved the Colonel's horse and didn't get the reward. He's young, he hasn't been at it long.

MOTHER COURAGE. Let him go. He doesn't have to be chained, he's not a dog. Very reasonable to want a reward. Why else should he want to shine?

THE YOUNG SOLDIER. He's in there pouring it down! You're all nice. I've done something special, I want the reward!

MOTHER COURAGE. Young man, don't scream at *me*, I have my own troubles. And go easy with your voice, you may need it when the Captain comes. The Captain'll come and you'll be hoarse and can't make a sound, so he'll have to deny himself the pleasure of sticking you in the stocks till you pass out. The screamers don't scream long, only half an hour, after which they have to be sung to sleep, they're all in.

THE YOUNG SOLDIER. I'm not all in, and sleep's out of the question. I'm hungry. They're making their bread out of acorns and hempseed, and not even much of that. He's whoring on my money, and I'm hungry. I'll murder him!

MOTHER COURAGE. I understand: you're hungry. Last year your Commander ordered you people out of the streets and into the fields. So the crops got trampled down. I could have got ten guilders for boots, if anyone'd had ten guilders, and if I'd had any boots. He didn't expect to be around this year, but he is, and there's famine. I understand: you're angry.

THE YOUNG SOLDIER. It's no use your talking. I won't stand for injustice!

MOTHER COURAGE. You're quite right. But how long? How long won't you stand for injustice? One hour? Or two? you haven't asked yourself that, have you? And yet it's the main thing. It's pure misery to sit in the stocks. Especially if you leave it till then to decide you do stand for injustice.

THE YOUNG SOLDIER. I don't know why I listen to you. Screw that Captain! Where is he?

MOTHER COURAGE. You listen because you know I'm right. Your rage has calmed down already. It was a short one and you'd need a long one. But where would you find it?

THE YOUNG SOLDIER. Are you trying to say it's not right to ask for the money?

MOTHER COURAGE. Just the opposite. I only say, your rage won't last. You'll get nowhere with it, it's a pity. If your rage was a long one, I'd urge you on. Slice him up, I'd advise you. But what's the use if you *don't* slice him up because you can feel your tail between your legs? You stand there and the Captain lets you have it.

THE OLDER SOLDIER. You're quite right, he's crazy.

THE YOUNG SOLDIER. All right, we'll see whether I slice him up or not. (*He draws his sword.*) When he comes out, I slice him up!

THE CLERK (*looking out*). The Captain will be out in a minute. (*In the tone of military command.*) Be seated!

(*The* YOUNG SOLDIER *sits.*)

MOTHER COURAGE. And he *is* seated. What did I tell you? You are seated. They know us through and through. They know how they must work it. Be seated! And we sit. And in sitting there's no revolt. Better not stand up again—not the way you did before—don't stand up again. And don't be embarrassed in front of me, I'm no better, not a scrap. They've drawn our teeth, haven't they? If we say boo, it's bad for business. Let me tell you about the great capitulation.

(*She sings "The Song of the Great Capitulation".*)

Long ago when I was a green beginner
I believed I was a special case.

(None of your ordinary run of the mill girls, with my looks and my talent, and my love of the higher things in life!)

And if I picked a hair out of my
    dinner
I would put the cook right in his
    place.

(All or nothing. Anyhow, never the second best. I am the master of my Fate. I'll take no orders from no one.)

Then a little bird whispered in my ear:
"That's all very well, but wait a year
And you will join the big brass band
And with your trumpet in your hand
You'll march in lockstep with the rest.

Then one day, look! The battalions
    wheel!
The whole thing swings from east to
    west!
And falling on your knees, you'll
    squeal:
The Lord God, He knows best!
(But don't give *me* that!)"

And a month or two before that year
    was over
I had learned to drink their cup of tea.

(Two children round your neck, and the
price of bread and what all!)

And the day soon came when I was
    to discover
They had me just where they wanted
    me.

(You must get in good with people. If you
scratch my back, I'll scratch yours. Don't
stick your neck out.)

And that little bird whispered in my
    ear:
"You didn't even take a year!
And you have joined the big brass
    band
And with your trumpet in your hand
You marched in lockstep with the rest.
But one day, look! The battalions
    wheeled!
The whole thing swung from east to
    west!
And falling on your knees, you
    squealed:
The Lord God, He knows best!
(But don't give *me* that!)"

Yes, our hopes are high, our plans
    colossal!
And we hitch our wagon to a star!

(Where there's a will there's a way. One
can't hold a good man down.)

We can move mountains, says St.
    Paul the great Apostle
And yet: how heavy one cigar!

(We must cut our coat according to our
cloth.)

For that little bird whispers in your
    ear:
"That's all very well but wait a year
And we will join the big brass band
And with our trumpet in our hand
We march in lockstep with the rest.
But one day, look! The battalions
    wheel!
The whole thing swings from east to
    west!
And falling on our knees, we squeal:
The Lord God, He knows best!
(But don't give *me* that!)"

And so I think you should stay here with
your sword drawn if you're set on it and
your anger is big enough. You have good
cause, I admit. But if your anger is a short
one, you'd better go.

THE YOUNG SOLDIER. Kiss my ass. (*He
stumbles off, the other* SOLDIER *following him.*)

THE CLERK (*sticking his head out*). The
Captain is ready now. You can file your
complaint.

MOTHER COURAGE. I've thought better of
it. I'm not complaining. (*Exit.*)

(*The* CLERK *looks after her, shaking his head.*)

## SCENE 5

*TWO YEARS HAVE PASSED. THE WAR
COVERS WIDER AND WIDER TERRITORY.
FOREVER ON THE MOVE, THE LITTLE
WAGON CROSSES POLAND, MORAVIA,
BAVARIA, ITALY, AND AGAIN BAVARIA.
1631. TILLY'S VICTORY AT MAGDEBURG
COSTS MOTHER COURAGE FOUR OFFI-
CERS' SHIRTS.*

(*The wagon stands in a war-ravaged village.
Faint military music from the distance. Two
SOLDIERS are being served at a counter by
KATTRIN and MOTHER COURAGE. One of
them has a woman's fur coat about his
shoulders.*)

MOTHER COURAGE. What, you can't pay?
No money, no brandy! They can play victory
marches, they should pay their men.

THE FIRST SOLDIER. I want my brandy!
I arrived too late for plunder. The Chief

allowed one hour to plunder the town, it's a swindle. He's not inhuman, he says. So I suppose they bought him off.

THE CHAPLAIN (*staggering in*). There are more in the farmhouse. A family of peasants. Help me someone. I need linen!

> *The second* SOLDIER *goes with him.* KATTRIN *is getting very excited. She tries to get her mother to bring linen out.*

MOTHER COURAGE. I have none. I sold all my bandages to the regiment. I'm not tearing up my officer's shirts for these people.

THE CHAPLAIN (*calling over his shoulder*). I said I need linen!

MOTHER COURAGE (*stopping* KATTRIN *from entering the wagon*). Not a thing! They can't pay, and why? They have nothing and they pay nothing!

THE CHAPLAIN (*to a* WOMAN *he is carrying in*). Why did you stay out there in the line of fire?

THE WOMAN. Our farm—

MOTHER COURAGE. Think they'd ever let go of *anything*? And now I'm supposed to pay. Well, I won't!

THE FIRST SOLDIER. They're Protestants, why should they be Protestants?

MOTHER COURAGE. Protestant, Catholic, what do *they* care? Their farm's gone, that's what.

THE SECOND SOLDIER. They're not Protestants anyway, they're Catholics.

THE FIRST SOLDIER. In a bombardment we can't pick and choose.

A PEASANT (*brought on by the* CHAPLAIN). My arm's gone.

THE CHAPLAIN. Where's that linen?

> (*All look at* MOTHER COURAGE, *who does not budge.*)

MOTHER COURAGE. I can't give you any. With all I have to pay out—taxes, duties, bribes. . . . (KATTRIN *takes up a board and threatens her mother with it, emitting gurgling sounds.*) Are you out of your mind? Put that board down or I'll let you have one, you lunatic! I'm giving nothing, I don't dare, I have myself to think of. (*The* CHAPLAIN *lifts her bodily off the steps of the wagon and sets her down on the ground. He takes out shirts from the wagon and tears them in strips.*) My shirts, my officer's shirts!

> (*From the house comes the cry of a child in pain.*)

THE PEASANT. The child's still in there.

> (KATTRIN *runs in.*)

THE CHAPLAIN (*to the* WOMAN). Stay where you are. She's getting it for you.

MOTHER COURAGE. Hold her back, the roof may fall in!

THE CHAPLAIN. I'm not going back in there!

MOTHER COURAGE (*pulled in both directions*). Go easy on my expensive linen.

> (*The* SECOND SOLDIER *holds her back.* KATTRIN *brings a baby out of the ruins.*)

MOTHER COURAGE. Another baby to drag around, you must be pleased with yourself. Give it to its mother this minute! Or do I have to fight you again for hours till I get it from you? Are you deaf? (*To the* SECOND SOLDIER.) Don't stand about gawking, go back there and tell 'em to stop that music, I can see their victory without it. I have nothing but losses from your victory!

THE CHAPLAIN (*bandaging*). The blood's coming through.

> (KATTRIN *is rocking the child and half humming a lullaby.*)

MOTHER COURAGE. There she sits, happy as a lark in all this misery. Give the baby back, the mother is coming to! (*She sees the* FIRST SOLDIER. *He had been handling the drinks, and is now trying to make off with the bottle.*) God's truth! You beast! You want another victory, do you? Then pay for it!

THE FIRST SOLDIER. I have nothing.

MOTHER COURAGE (*snatching the fur coat back*). Then leave this coat, it's stolen goods anyhow.

THE CHAPLAIN. There's still someone in there.

## SCENE 6

*BEFORE THE CITY OF INGOLSTADT IN BAVARIA MOTHER COURAGE IS PRESENT AT THE FUNERAL OF THE FALLEN COMMANDER, TILLY. CONVERSATIONS TAKE PLACE ABOUT WAR HEROES AND THE DURATION OF THE WAR. THE CHAPLAIN COMPLAINS THAT HIS TALENTS ARE LYING FALLOW AND KATTRIN GETS THE RED BOOTS. THE YEAR IS 1632.*

> (*The inside of a canteen tent. The inner*

*side of a counter at the rear. Rain. In the distance, drums and funeral music. The* CHAPLAIN *and the regimental* CLERK *are playing draughts.* MOTHER COURAGE *and her daughter are taking an inventory.*)

THE CHAPLAIN. The funeral procession is just starting out.

MOTHER COURAGE. Pity about the Chief—twenty-two pairs of socks—getting killed that way. They say it was an accident. There was a fog over the fields that morning, and the fog was to blame. The Chief called up another regiment, told 'em to fight to the death, rode back again, missed his way in the fog, went forward instead of back, and ran smack into a bullet in the thick of the battle—only four lanterns left. (*A whistle from the rear. She goes to the counter. To a* SOLDIER.) It's a disgrace the way you're all skipping your Commander's funeral! (*She pours a drink.*)

THE CLERK. They shouldn't have handed the money out before the funeral. Now the men are all getting drunk instead of going to it.

THE CHAPLAIN (*to the* CLERK). Don't you have to be there?

THE CLERK. I stayed away because of the rain.

MOTHER COURAGE. It's different for you, the rain might spoil your uniform. I hear they wanted to ring the bells for his funeral, which is natural, but it came out that the churches had been shot up by his orders, so the poor Commander won't be hearing any bells when they lower him in his grave. Instead, they'll fire off three shots so the occasion won't be *too* sober—sixteen leather belts.

A VOICE FROM THE COUNTER. Service! One brandy!

MOTHER COURAGE. Your money first. No, you *can't* come inside the tent, not with those boots on. You can drink outside, rain or no rain. I only let officers in here. (*To the* CLERK.) The Chief had his troubles lately, I hear. There was unrest in the Second Regiment because he didn't pay 'em. He said it was a war of religion and they must fight it free of charge.

(*Funeral march. All look toward the rear.*)

THE CHAPLAIN. Now they're filing past the body.

MOTHER COURAGE. I feel sorry for a Commander or an Emperor like that—when he might have had something special in mind, something they'd talk about in times to come, something they'd raise a statue to him for. The conquest of the world now, *that's* a goal for a Commander, he wouldn't know any better. . . . Lord, worms have got into the biscuits. . . . In short, he works his hands to the bone and then it's all spoiled by the common riffraff that only wants a jug of beer or a bit of company, not the higher things in life. The finest plans have always been spoiled by the littleness of them that should carry them out. Even Emperors can't do it all by themselves. They count on support from their soldiers and the people round about. Am I right?

THE CHAPLAIN (*laughing*). You're right, Mother Courage, till you come to the soldiers. They do what they can. Those fellows outside, for example, drinking their brandy in the rain, I'd trust 'em to fight a hundred years, one war after another, two at a time if necessary. And I wasn't trained as a commander.

MOTHER COURAGE. . . . Seventeen leather belts. . . . Then you don't think the war might end?

THE CHAPLAIN. Because a commander's dead? Don't be childish, they grow on trees. There are always heroes.

MOTHER COURAGE. Well, I wasn't asking for the sake of argument. I was wondering if I should buy up a lot of supplies. They happen to be cheap just now. But if the war ended, I might just as well throw them away.

THE CHAPLAIN. I realize you are serious, Mother Courage. Well, there've always been people going around saying some day the war will end. I say, you can't be sure the war will *ever* end. Of course it may have to pause occasionally—for breath, as it were—it can even meet with an accident—nothing on this earth is perfect—a war of which we could say it left nothing to be desired will probably never exist. A war can come to a sudden halt—from unforeseen causes—you can't think of everything—a little oversight, and the war's in the hole, and someone's got to pull it out again! The someone is the Emperor or the King or the Pope. They're such friends in need, the war has really nothing to worry about, it can look forward to a prosperous future.

A SOLDIER (*singing at the counter*).
One schnapps, mine host, make haste!
We have no time to waste:
We must be shooting, shooting, shooting
Our Emperor's foes uprooting!

Make it a double. This is a holiday.

MOTHER COURAGE. If I was sure you're right . . .

THE CHAPLAIN. Think it out for yourself: how *could* the war end?

THE SOLDIER (*off-stage*).
Two breasts, mine host, make haste!
For we have no time to waste:
We must be hating, hating, hating
We cannot keep our Emperor waiting!

THE CLERK (*suddenly*). What about peace? Yes, peace. I'm from Bohemia. I'd like to get home once in a while.

THE CHAPLAIN. Oh, you would, would you? Dear old peace! What happens to the hole when the cheese is gone?

THE SOLDIER (*off-stage*).
Your blessing, priest, make haste!
For we have no time to waste:
We must be dying, dying, dying
Our Emperor's greatness glorifying!

THE CLERK. In the long run you can't live without peace!

THE CHAPLAIN. Well, I'd say there's peace even in war, war has its islands of peace. For war satisfies *all* needs, even those of peace, yes, they're provided for, or the war couldn't keep going. In war—as in the very thick of peace—you can take a crap, and between one battle and the next there's always a beer, and even on the march you can snatch a nap—on your elbow maybe, in a gutter— something can always be managed. Of course you can't play cards during an attack, but neither can you while ploughing the fields in peace time: it's when the victory's won that there are possibilities. You have your leg shot off, and at first you raise quite an outcry as if it *was* something, but soon you calm down or take a swig of brandy, and you end up hopping about, and the war is none

the worse for your little misadventure. And can't you be fruitful and multiply in the thick of slaughter—behind a barn or some-where? Nothing can keep you from it very long in any event. And so the war has your offspring and can carry on. War is like love, it always finds a way. Why *should* it end?

(KATTRIN *has stopped working. She stares at the* CHAPLAIN.)

MOTHER COURAGE. Then I *will* buy those supplies, I'll rely on you. (KATTRIN *suddenly bangs a basket of glasses down on the ground and runs out.* MOTHER COURAGE *laughs.*) Kattrin! Lord, Kattrin's still going to wait for peace. I promised her she'll get a husband—when it's peace. (*She runs after her.*)

THE CLERK (*standing up*). I win. You were talking. You pay.

MOTHER COURAGE (*returning with* KATTRIN). Be sensible, the war'll go on a bit longer, and we'll make a bit more money, then peace'll be all the nicer. Now you go into the town, it's not ten minutes walk, and bring the things from the Golden Lion, just the more expen-sive ones, we can get the rest later in the wagon. It's all arranged, the clerk will go with you, most of the soldiers are at the Commander's funeral, nothing can happen to you. Do a good job, don't lose anything, Kattrin, think of your trousseau!

(KATTRIN *ties a cloth around her head and leaves with the* CLERK.)

THE CHAPLAIN. You don't mind her going with the clerk?

MOTHER COURAGE. She's not so pretty anyone would want to ruin her.

THE CHAPLAIN. The way you run your business and always come through is highly commendable, Mother Courage—I see how you got your name.

MOTHER COURAGE. The poor need courage. Why? They're lost. That they even get up in the morning is something—in *their* plight. Or that they plough a field—in war time. Even their bringing children into the world shows they have courage, for they have no prospects. They have to hang each other one by one and slaughter each other in the lump, so if they want to look each other in the face once in a while, well, it takes courage. That they put up with an Emperor and a Pope, that takes an unnatural amount of courage, for *they* cost you your life. (*She sits, takes a small pipe from her pocket and smokes it.*) You might chop me a bit of firewood.

THE CHAPLAIN (*reluctantly taking his coat off and preparing to chop wood*). Properly speaking, I'm a pastor of souls, not a woodcutter.

MOTHER COURAGE. But I don't have a soul. And I do need wood.

THE CHAPLAIN. What's that little pipe you've got there?

MOTHER COURAGE. Just a pipe.

THE CHAPLAIN. I think it's a very particular pipe.

MOTHER COURAGE. Oh?

THE CHAPLAIN. The cook's pipe in fact. The cook from the Oxenstierna Regiment.

MOTHER COURAGE. If you know, why beat about the bush?

THE CHAPLAIN. Because I don't know if you've been *aware* that's what you've been smoking. It was possible you just rummaged among your belongings and your fingers just lit on a pipe and you just took it. In pure absent-mindedness.

MOTHER COURAGE. How do you know that's not it?

THE CHAPLAIN. It isn't. You *are* aware of it. (*He brings the ax down on the block with a crash.*)

MOTHER COURAGE. What if I was?

THE CHAPLAIN. I must give you a warning, Mother Courage, it's my duty. You are unlikely to see the gentleman again but that's no pity, you're in luck. Mother Courage, he did not impress me as trustworthy. On the contrary.

MOTHER COURAGE. Really? He was such a nice man.

THE CHAPLAIN. Well! So that's what you call a nice man. I do not. (*The ax falls again.*) Far be it from me to wish him ill, but I cannot—cannot—describe him as nice. No, no, he's a Don Juan, a cunning Don Juan. Just look at that pipe if you don't believe me. You must admit it tells all.

MOTHER COURAGE. I see nothing special in it. It's been used, of course.

THE CHAPLAIN. It's bitten halfway through! He's a man of great violence! It is the pipe of a man of great violence, you can see *that* if

you've any judgment left! (*He deals the block a tremendous blow.*)

MOTHER COURAGE. Don't bite my chopping block halfway through!

THE CHAPLAIN. I told you I had no training as a woodcutter. The care of souls was my field. Around here my gifts and capabilities are grossly misused. In physical labor my God-given talents find no—um—adequate expression—which is a sin. You haven't heard me preach. Why, I can put such spirit into a regiment with a single sermon that the enemy's a mere flock of sheep to them and their own lives no more than smelly old shoes to be thrown away at the thought of final victory! God has given me the gift of tongues. I can preach you out of your senses!

MOTHER COURAGE. I need my senses. What would I do without them?

THE CHAPLAIN. Mother Courage, I have often thought that—under a veil of plain speech—you conceal a heart. You are human, you need warmth.

MOTHER COURAGE. The best way of warming this tent is to chop plenty of firewood.

THE CHAPLAIN. You're changing the subject. Seriously, my dear Courage, I sometimes ask myself how it would be if our relationship should be somewhat more firmly cemented. I mean, now the wild wind of war has whirled us so strangely together.

MOTHER COURAGE. The cement's pretty firm already. I cook your meals. And you lend a hand—at chopping firewood, for instance.

THE CHAPLAIN (*going over to her, gesturing with the ax*): You know what I mean by a close relationship. It has nothing to do with eating and woodcutting and such base necessities. Let your heart speak!

MOTHER COURAGE. Don't come at me like that with your ax, that'd be *too* close a relationship!

THE CHAPLAIN. This is no laughing matter, I am in earnest. I've thought it all over.

MOTHER COURAGE. Dear Chaplain, be a sensible fellow. I like you, and I don't want to heap coals of fire on your head. All I want is to bring me and my children through in that wagon. It isn't just mine, the wagon, and anyway I've no mind to start any adventures. At the moment I'm taking quite a risk buying these things when the Commander's fallen and there's all this talk of peace. Where would you go, if I was ruined? See? You don't even know. Now chop some firewood and it'll be warm of an evening, which is quite a lot in times like these. What was that? (*She stands up.* KATTRIN *enters, breathless, with a wound across the eye and forehead. She is dragging all sorts of articles, parcels, leather goods, a drum, etc.*) What is it, were you attacked? On the way back? She was attacked on the way back! I'll bet it was that soldier who got drunk on my liquor. I should never have let you go. Dump all that stuff! It's not bad, the wound is only a flesh wound. I'll bandage it for you, it'll all be healed up in a week. They're worse than aminals.

(*She bandages the wound.*)

THE CHAPLAIN. I reproach them with nothing. At home they never did these shameful things. The men who start the wars are responsible, they bring out the worst in people.

MOTHER COURAGE. Didn't the clerk walk you back home? That's because you're a respectable girl, he thought they'd leave you alone. The wound's not at all deep, it will never show. There: all bandaged up. Now, I've got something for you, rest easy. I've been keeping them secret. (*She digs* YVETTE's *red boots out of a bag.*) Well, what do you see? You always wanted them. Now you have them. (*She helps her to put the boots on.*) Put them on quick, before I change my mind. It will never show, though it wouldn't bother *me* if it did. The ones they like fare worst. They drag them around till they're finished. Those they don't care for they leave alone. I've seen so many girls, pretty as they come in the beginning, then all of a sudden they're so ugly they'd scare a wolf. They can't even go behind a tree on the street without having something to fear from it. They lead a frightful life. Like with trees: the tall, straight ones are cut down for roof timber, and the crooked ones can enjoy life. So this wound here is really a piece of luck. The boots have kept well. I gave them a good cleaning before I put them away.

(KATTRIN *leaves the boots and creeps into the wagon.*)

THE CHAPLAIN (*when she's gone*). I hope she won't be disfigured?

MOTHER COURAGE. There'll be a scar. She needn't wait for peace now.

THE CHAPLAIN. She didn't let them get any of the stuff.

MOTHER COURAGE. Maybe I shouldn't have made such a point of it. If only I ever knew what went on inside her head. Once she stayed out all night, once in all the years. Afterward she seemed much the same, except that she worked harder. I could never get out of her what happened. I worried about it for quite a while. (*She picks up the things* KATTRIN *spilled and sorts them angrily.*) This is war. A nice source of income, I must say!

(*Cannon shots.*)

THE CHAPLAIN. Now they're lowering the Commander into his grave! A historic moment.

MOTHER COURAGE. It's a historic moment to me when they hit my daughter over the eye. She's all but finished now, she'll never get a husband, and she's so mad about children! Even her dumbness comes from the war. A soldier stuck something in her mouth when she was little. I'll never see Swiss Cheese again, and where my Eilif is the Good Lord knows. Curse the war!

## SCENE 7

*MOTHER COURAGE AT THE HEIGHT OF HER BUSINESS CAREER*

(*A highway. The* CHAPLAIN, MOTHER COURAGE, *and her daughter* KATTRIN *pull the wagon, and new wares are hanging from it.* MOTHER COURAGE *wears a necklace of silver coins.*)

MOTHER COURAGE. I won't let you spoil my war for me. Destroys the weak, does it? Well, what does peace do for 'em, huh? War feeds its people better.

(*She sings.*)

If war don't suit your disposition
When victory comes, you will be dead.
War is a business proposition:
But not with cheese, with steel instead!

Christians, awake! Winter is gone!
The snows depart! Dead men sleep on!
Let all of you who still survive
Get out of bed and look alive!

And staying in one place won't help either.
Those who stay at home are the first to go.
(*She sings.*)
Too many seek a bed to sleep in:
Each ditch is taken, and each cave
And he who digs a hole to creep in
Finds he has dug an early grave.
And many a man spends many a minute
In hurrying toward some resting place.
You wonder, when at last he's in it
Just why the fellow forced the pace.
(*The wagon proceeds.*)

## SCENE 8

1632. *IN THIS SAME YEAR GUSTAVUS ADOLPHUS FELL IN THE BATTLE OF LÜTZEN. THE PEACE THREATENS MOTHER COURAGE WITH RUIN. HER BRAVE SON PERFORMS ONE HEROIC DEED TOO MANY AND COMES TO A SHAMEFUL END.*
(*A camp. A summer morning. In front of the wagon, an* OLD WOMAN *and her son. The son is dragging a large bag of bedding.*)
MOTHER COURAGE (*from inside the wagon*). Must you come at the crack of dawn?
THE YOUNG MAN. We've been walking all night, twenty miles it was, we have to be back today.
MOTHER COURAGE (*still inside*). What do I want with bed feathers? People don't even have houses.
THE YOUNG MAN. At least wait till you see 'em.
THE OLD WOMAN. Nothing doing here either, let's go.
THE YOUNG MAN. And let 'em sign away the roof over our heads for taxes? Maybe she'll pay three guilders if you throw in that bracelet. (*Bells start ringing.*) You hear, mother?
VOICES (*from the rear*). It's peace! The King of Sweden's been killed!
(MOTHER COURAGE *sticks her head out of the wagon. She hasn't done her hair yet.*)
MOTHER COURAGE. Bells! What are the bells for, middle of the week?

THE CHAPLAIN (*crawling out from under the wagon*). What's that they're shouting?
THE YOUNG MAN. It's peace.
THE CHAPLAIN. Peace!
MOTHER COURAGE. Don't tell me peace has broken out—when I've just gone and bought all these supplies!
THE CHAPLAIN (*calling, toward the rear*). Is it peace?
VOICE (*from a distance*). They say the war stopped three weeks ago. I've only just heard.
THE CHAPLAIN (*to* MOTHER COURAGE). Or why would they ring the bells?
VOICE. A great crowd of Lutherans have just arrived with wagons—they brought the news.
THE YOUNG MAN. It's peace, mother. (*The* OLD WOMAN *collapses.*) What's the matter?
MOTHER COURAGE (*back in the wagon*). Kattrin, it's peace! Put on your black dress, we're going to church, we owe it to Swiss Cheese! Can it be true?
THE YOUNG MAN. The people here say so too, the war's over. Can you stand up? (*The* OLD WOMAN *stands up, dazed.*) I'll get the harness shop going again now, I promise you. Everything'll be all right, father will get his bed back.... Can you walk? (*To the* CHAPLAIN.) She felt ill, it was the news. She didn't believe there'd ever be peace again. Father always said there would. We're going home.
(*They leave.*)
MOTHER COURAGE (*off*). Give her some brandy.
THE CHAPLAIN. They've left already.
MOTHER COURAGE (*still off*). What's going on in the camp over there?
THE CHAPLAIN. They're all getting together. I think I'll go over. Shall I put my pastor's coat on again?
MOTHER COURAGE. Better get the exact news first, and not risk being taken for the Antichrist. I'm glad about the peace even though I'm ruined. At least I've got two of my children through the war. Now I'll see my Eilif again.
THE CHAPLAIN. And who may this be coming down from the camp? Well, if it isn't our Swedish Commander's cook!

THE COOK (*somewhat bedraggled, carrying a bundle*). Who's here? The chaplain!

THE CHAPLAIN. Mother Courage, a visitor!

(MOTHER COURAGE *clambers out.*)

THE COOK. Well, I promised I'd come over for a brief conversation as soon as I had time. I didn't forget your brandy, Mrs. Fierling.

MOTHER COURAGE. Jesus, the Commander's cook! After all these years! Where is Eilif, my eldest?

THE COOK. Isn't he here yet? He went on ahead yesterday, he was on his way over.

THE CHAPLAIN. I *will* put my pastor's coat on. I'll be back.

(*He goes behind the wagon.*)

MOTHER COURAGE. He may be here any minute then. (*She calls toward the wagon:*) Kattrin, Eilif's coming! Bring a glass of brandy for the cook, Kattrin! (KATTRIN *doesn't come.*) Just pull your hair over it. Mr. Lamb is no stranger. (*She gets the brandy herself.*) She won't come out. Peace is nothing to her, it was too long coming. They hit her right over the eye. You can hardly see it now. But she thinks people stare at her.

THE COOK. Ah yes, war! (*He and* MOTHER COURAGE *sit.*)

MOTHER COURAGE. Cook, you come at a bad time. I'm ruined .

THE COOK. What? That's terrible!

MOTHER COURAGE. The peace has broken my neck. On the chaplain's advice I've gone and bought a lot of supplies. Now everybody's leaving and I'm holding the baby.

THE COOK. How could you listen to the chaplain? If I'd had time—but the Catholics were too quick for me—I'd have warned you against him. He's a windbag. Well, so now he's the big man round here!

MOTHER COURAGE. He's been doing the dishes for me and helping with the wagon.

THE COOK. With the wagon—him! And I'll bet he's told you a few of his jokes. He has a most unhealthy attitude to women. I tried to influence him but it was no good. He isn't sound.

MOTHER COURAGE. Are you sound?

THE COOK. If I'm nothing else, I'm sound. Your health!

MOTHER COURAGE. Sound! Only one person around here was ever sound, and I never had to slave as I did then. He sold the blankets off the children's beds in the spring, and he called my harmonica unchristian. You aren't recommending yourself if you *admit* you're sound.

THE COOK. You fight tooth and nail, don't you? I like that.

MOTHER COURAGE. Don't tell me you've been dreaming of my teeth and nails.

THE COOK. Well, here we sit, while the bells of peace do ring, and you pouring your famous brandy as only you know how!

MOTHER COURAGE. I don't think much of the bells of peace at the moment. I don't see how they can hand out all this pay that's in arrears. And then where shall I be with my famous brandy? Have you all been paid?

THE COOK (*hesitating*). Not exactly. That's why we disbanded. In the circumstances, I thought, why stay? For the time being, I'll look up a couple of friends. So here I sit—with you.

MOTHER COURAGE. In other words, you're broke.

THE COOK (*annoyed by the bells*). It's about time they stopped that racket! I'd like to set myself up in some business. I'm fed up with being their cook. I'm supposed to make do with tree roots and shoe leather, and then they throw my hot soup in my face! Being a cook nowadays is a dog's life. I'd sooner be a soldier, but of course, it's peace now. (*As the* CHAPLAIN *turns up, wearing his old coat.*) We'll talk it over later.

THE CHAPLAIN. The coat's pretty good. Just a few moth holes.

THE COOK. I don't know why you take the trouble. You won't find another pulpit. Who could you incite now to earn an honest living or risk his life for a cause? Besides, I have a bone to pick with you.

THE CHAPLAIN. Have you?

THE COOK. I have. You advised a lady to buy superfluous goods on the pretext that the war would never end.

THE CHAPLAIN (*hotly*). I'd like to know what business it is of yours?

THE COOK. It's unprincipled behavior! How can you give unwanted advice? And interfere with the conduct of other people's business?

THE CHAPLAIN. Who's interfering now, I'd like to know? (*To* MOTHER COURAGE.) I had no idea you were such a close friend of this gentleman and had to account to *him* for everything.

MOTHER COURAGE. Now don't get excited. The cook's giving his personal opinion. You can't deny your war was a flop.

THE CHAPLAIN. You have no respect for peace, Courage. You're a hyena of the battlefield!

MOTHER COURAGE. A what?

THE COOK. Who insults my girl friend insults me!

THE CHAPLAIN. I am *not* speaking to you, your intentions are only too transparent! (*To* MOTHER COURAGE.) But when I see *you* take peace between finger and thumb like a snotty old hanky, my humanity rebels! It shows that you want war, not peace, for what you get out of it. But don't forget the proverb: he who sups with the devil must use a long spoon!

MOTHER COURAGE. Remember what one fox said to another that was caught in a trap? "If you stay there, you're just asking for trouble!" There isn't much love lost between me and the war. And when it comes to calling me a hyena, you and I part company.

THE CHAPLAIN. Then why all this grumbling about the peace just as everyone's heaving a sigh of relief? Is it for the junk in your wagon?

MOTHER COURAGE. My goods are not junk. I live off them. *You've* been living off them.

THE CHAPLAIN. You live off war. Exactly.

THE COOK (*to the* CHAPLAIN). As a grown man, you should know better than to go around advising people. (*To* MOTHER COURAGE.) Now, in your situation you'd be smart to get rid of certain goods at once— before the prices sink to nothing. Get ready and get going, there isn't a moment to lose!

MOTHER COURAGE. That's sensible advice, I think I'll take it.

THE CHAPLAIN. Because the cook says so.

MOTHER COURAGE. Why didn't *you* say so? He's right, I must get to the market. (*She climbs into the wagon.*)

THE COOK. One up for me, Chaplain. You have no presence of mind. You should have said, "*I* gave you advice? Why, I was just

talking politics!" And you shouldn't take me on as a rival. Cockfights are not becoming to your cloth.

THE CHAPLAIN. If you don't shut your trap, I'll murder you, cloth or no cloth!

THE COOK (*taking his boots off and unwinding the wrappings on his feet*). If you hadn't degenerated into a godless tramp, you could easily get yourself a parsonage, now it's peace. Cooks won't be needed, there's nothing to cook, but there's still plenty to believe, and people will go right on believing it.

THE CHAPLAIN. Mr. Lamb, please don't drive me out! Since I became a tramp, I'm a somewhat better man. I couldn't preach to 'em any more.

(YVETTE POTTIER *enters, decked out in black, with a stick. She is much older, fatter, and heavily powdered. Behind her, a* SERVANT.)

YVETTE. Hullo, everybody! Is this Mother Courage's establishment?

THE CHAPLAIN. Quite right. And with whom have we the pleasure?

YVETTE. I am Madame Colonel Starhemberg, good people. Where's Mother Courage?

THE CHAPLAIN (*calling to the wagon*). Madame Colonel Starhemberg wants to speak to you!

MOTHER COURAGE (*from inside*). Coming!

YVETTE (*calling*). It's Yvette!

MOTHER COURAGE (*inside*). Yvette!

YVETTE. Just to see how you're getting on! (*As the* COOK *turns around in horror.*) Peter!

THE COOK. Yvette!

YVETTE. Of all things! How did *you* get here?

THE COOK. On a cart.

THE CHAPLAIN. Well! You know each other? Intimately?

YVETTE. I'll say. (*Scrutinizing the* COOK.) You're fat.

THE COOK. For that matter, *you're* no beanpole.

YVETTE. Anyway, it's lucky we've met, tramp. Now I can tell you what I think of you.

THE CHAPLAIN. Do so, tell him all, but wait till Mother Courage comes out.

THE COOK. Now don't make a scene . . .

MOTHER COURAGE (*coming out, laden with goods*). Yvette! (*They embrace.*) But why are you in mourning?

YVETTE. Doesn't it suit me? My husband, the colonel, died several years ago.

MOTHER COURAGE. The old fellow that nearly bought my wagon?

YVETTE. His elder brother.

MOTHER COURAGE. So you're not doing badly. Good to see one person who got somewhere in the war.

YVETTE. I've had my ups and downs.

MOTHER COURAGE. Don't let's speak ill of colonels. They make money like hay.

THE CHAPLAIN (*to the* COOK). If I were you, I'd put my shoes on again. (*To* YVETTE.) You promised to give us your opinion of this gentleman.

THE COOK. Now, Yvette, don't make a stink!

MOTHER COURAGE. He's a friend of mine, Yvette.

YVETTE. He's—Peter Piper, that's who.

MOTHER COURAGE. What!

THE COOK. Cut the nicknames. My name's Lamb.

MOTHER COURAGE (*laughing*). Peter Piper? Who turned the women's heads? And I've been keeping your pipe for you.

THE CHAPLAIN. And smoking it.

YVETTE. Lucky I can warn you against him. He's a bad lot. You won't find worse on the whole coast of Flanders. He got more girls in trouble than . . .

THE COOK. That's a long time ago, it isn't true any more.

YVETTE. Stand up when you talk to a lady! Oh, how I loved that man; and all the time he was having a little bowlegged brunette. He got *her* into trouble too, of course.

THE COOK. I seem to have brought *you* luck!

YVETTE. Shut your trap, you hoary ruin! And you take care, Mother Courage, this type is still dangerous even in decay!

MOTHER COURAGE (*to* YVETTE). Come with me, I must get rid of this stuff before the prices fall.

YVETTE (*concentrating on the* COOK). Miserable cur!

MOTHER COURAGE. Maybe you can help me at army headquarters, you have contacts.

YVETTE. Seducer!

MOTHER COURAGE (*shouting into the wagon*). Kattrin, church is all off, I'm going to market!

YVETTE. Whore hunter!

MOTHER COURAGE (*still to* KATTRIN). When Eilif comes, give him something to drink!

YVETTE. That a man like him should have been able to turn me from the straight and narrow! I have my own star to thank that I rose none the less to the heights! But I've put an end to your tricks, Peter Piper, and one day—in a better life than this—the Lord God will reward me! Come, Mother Courage! (*She leaves with* MOTHER COURAGE.)

THE CHAPLAIN. As our text this morning let us take the saying: the mills of God grind slowly. And you complain of my jokes!

THE COOK. I never have any luck. I'll be frank, I was hoping for a good hot dinner, I'm starving. And now they'll be talking about me, and she'll get a completely wrong picture. I think I should go before she comes back.

THE CHAPLAIN. I think so too.

THE COOK. Chaplain, peace makes me sick. Mankind must perish by fire and sword, we're born and bred in sin! Oh, how I wish I was roasting a great fat capon for the Commander—God knows where *he's* got to—with mustard sauce and those little yellow carrots . . .

THE CHAPLAIN. Red cabbage—with capon, red cabbage.

THE COOK. You're right. But he always wanted yellow carrots.

THE CHAPLAIN. He never understood a thing.

THE COOK. You always put plenty away.

THE CHAPLAIN. Under protest.

THE COOK. Anyway, you must admit, those were the days.

THE CHAPLAIN. Yes, that I might admit.

THE COOK. Now you've called her a hyena, there's not much future for you here either. What are you staring at?

THE CHAPLAIN. It's Eilif!

(*Followed by two soldiers with halberds,* EILIF *enters. His hands are fettered. He is white as chalk.*)

THE CHAPLAIN. What's happened to you?

EILIF. Where's mother?

THE CHAPLAIN. Gone to town.

EILIF. They said she was here. I was allowed a last visit.

THE COOK (to the SOLDIERS). Where are you taking him?

A SOLDIER. For a ride.

(The other SOLDIER makes the gesture of throat cutting.)

THE CHAPLAIN. What has he done?

THE SOLDIER. He broke in on a peasant. The wife is dead.

THE CHAPLAIN. Eilif, how could you?

EILIF. It's no different. It's what I did before.

THE COOK. That was in war time.

EILIF. Shut your hole. Can I sit down till she comes?

THE SOLDIER. No.

THE CHAPLAIN. It's true. In war time they honored him for it. He sat at the Commander's right hand. It was bravery. Couldn't we speak with the military police?

THE SOLDIER. What's the use? Stealing cattle from a peasant, what's brave about that?

THE COOK. It was just stupid.

EILIF. If I'd been stupid, I'd have starved, smarty.

THE COOK. So you were bright and paid for it.

THE CHAPLAIN. At least we must bring Kattrin out.

EILIF. Let her alone. Just give me some brandy.

THE SOLDIER. No.

THE CHAPLAIN. What shall we tell your mother?

EILIF. Tell her it was no different. Tell her it was the same. Oh, tell her nothing.

(The SOLDIERS take him away.)

THE CHAPLAIN. I'll come with you, I'll . . .

EILIF. I don't need a priest!

THE CHAPLAIN. You don't know—yet. (He follows him.)

THE COOK (calling after him). I'll have to tell her, she'll want to see him!

THE CHAPLAIN. Better tell her nothing. Or maybe just that he was here, and he'll return, maybe tomorrow. Meantime I'll be back and can break the news. (He leaves quickly.)

(The COOK looks after him, shakes his head, then walks about uneasily. Finally, he approaches the wagon.)

THE COOK. Hello! Won't you come out? You want to sneak away from the peace, don't you? Well, so do I! I'm the Swedish Commander's cook, remember me? I was wondering if you've got anything to eat in there—while we're waiting for your mother. I wouldn't mind a bit of bacon—or even bread—just to pass the time. (He looks in.) She's got a blanket over her head.

(The thunder of cannon. MOTHER COURAGE runs in, out of breath, still carrying the goods.)

MOTHER COURAGE. Cook, the peace is over, the war's on again, has been for three days! I didn't get rid of this stuff after all, thank God! There's a shooting match in the town already—with the Lutherans. We must get away with the wagon. Pack, Kattrin! What's on your mind? Something the matter?

THE COOK. Nothing.

MOTHER COURAGE. But there is. I see it in your face.

THE COOK. Because the war's on again, most likely. May it last till tomorrow evening, so I can get something in my belly!

MOTHER COURAGE. You're not telling me.

THE COOK. Eilif was here. Only he had to go away again.

MOTHER COURAGE. He was here? Then we'll see him on the march. I'll be with our side this time. How'd he look?

THE COOK. The same.

MOTHER COURAGE. He'll never change. And the war couldn't get him, he's bright. Help me with the packing. (She starts it.) Did he tell you anything? Is he well in with the Provost? Did he tell you about his heroic deeds?

THE COOK (darkly). He's done one of them again.

MOTHER COURAGE. Tell me about it later. (KATTRIN appears.) Kattrin, the peace is over, we're on the move again. (To the COOK.) What is the matter with you?

THE COOK. I'll enlist.

MOTHER COURAGE. A good idea. Where's the Chaplain?

THE COOK. In the town. With Eilif.

MOTHER COURAGE. Stay with us a while, Lamb, I need a bit of help.

THE COOK. This matter of Yvette . . .

MOTHER COURAGE. Hasn't done you any harm at all in my eyes. Just the opposite. Where there's smoke, there's fire, they say. You'll come?

THE COOK. I may as well.

MOTHER COURAGE. The Twelfth Regiment's under way. Into harness with you! Maybe I'll see Eilif before the day is out, just think! That's what I like best. Well, it wasn't such a long peace, we can't grumble. Let's go!

(*The* COOK *and* KATTRIN *are in harness.*)

MOTHER COURAGE (*sings*).

From Ulm to Metz, past dome and steeple
My wagon always moves ahead.
The war can care for all its people
So long as there is steel and lead.
Though steel and lead are stout supporters
A war needs human beings too.
Report today to your headquarters!
If it's to last, this war needs you!


## SCENE 9


*THE GREAT WAR OF RELIGION HAS LASTED SIXTEEN YEARS AND GERMANY HAS LOST HALF ITS INHABITANTS. THOSE WHO ARE SPARED IN BATTLE DIE BY PLAGUE. OVER ONCE BLOOMING COUNTRYSIDE HUNGER RAGES. TOWNS ARE BURNED DOWN. WOLVES PROWL THE EMPTY STREETS. IN THE AUTUMN OF 1634 WE FIND MOTHER COURAGE IN THE FICHTELGEBIRGE NOT FAR FROM THE ROAD THE SWEDISH ARMY IS TAKING. WINTER HAS COME EARLY AND IS HARD. BUSINESS IS BAD. ONLY BEGGING REMAINS. THE COOK RECEIVES A LETTER FROM UTRECHT AND IS SENT PACKING.*

(*In front of a half-ruined parsonage. Early winter. A gray morning. Gusts of wind.* MOTHER COURAGE *and the* COOK *at the wagon in shabby clothes.*)

THE COOK. There are no lights on. No one's up.

MOTHER COURAGE. But it's a parsonage. The parson'll have to leave his feather bed and ring the bells. Then he'll have some hot soup.

THE COOK. Where'll he get it from? The whole village is starving.

MOTHER COURAGE. The house is lived in. There was a dog barking.

THE COOK. If the parson has anything, he'll hang on to it.

MOTHER COURAGE. Maybe if we sang him something . . .

THE COOK. I've had enough. (*Suddenly.*) I didn't tell you, a letter came from Utrecht. My mother's died of cholera, the inn is mine. There's the letter, if you don't believe me. I'll show it to you, though my aunt's railing about me and my ups and downs is none of your business.

MOTHER COURAGE (*reading*). Lamb, I'm tired of wandering, too. I feel like a butcher's dog taking meat to my customers and getting none myself. I've nothing more to sell and people have nothing to pay with. In Saxony someone tried to force a chestful of books on me in return for two eggs. And in Württemberg they would have let me have their plough for a bag of salt. Nothing grows any more, only thorn bushes. In Pomerania I hear the villagers have been eating their younger children. Nuns have been caught committing robbery.

THE COOK. The world's dying out.

MOTHER COURAGE. Sometimes I see myself driving through hell with this wagon and selling brimstone. And sometimes I'm driving through heaven handing our provisions to wandering souls! If only we could find a place where there's no shooting, me and my children—what's left of 'em—we might rest a while.

THE COOK. We could open this inn together. Think about it, Courage. *My* mind's made up. With or without you, I'm leaving for Utrecht. And today too.

MOTHER COURAGE. I must talk to Kattrin, it's a bit sudden, and I don't like to make my decisions in the cold on an empty stomach. (KATTRIN *emerges from the wagon.*) Kattrin, I've something to tell you. The cook and I want to go to Utrecht, he's been left an inn. You'd be able to stay put and get to know some people. Many a man'd be prepared to take on a girl with a position. Looks aren't everything. I like the idea. I get on well with the cook. I'll say this for him: he has a head for business. We'd be sure of our dinner, that would be all right, wouldn't it? You'd have your own bed, what do you think of *that*? In the long run, this is no life, on the road. You might be killed any time. You're eaten up with lice as it is. And we must decide now, because otherwise we go north with the Swedes. They must be over there somewhere. (*She points left.*) I think we'll decide to go, Kattrin.

THE COOK. Anna, I must have a word with you alone.

MOTHER COURAGE. Go back inside, Kattrin.

(KATTRIN *does so.*)

THE COOK. I'm interrupting because there's a misunderstanding, Anna. I thought I wouldn't have to say it right out, but I see I must. If you're bringing *her*, it's all off. Do we understand each other?

(KATTRIN *has her head out of the back of the wagon and is listening.*)

MOTHER COURAGE. You mean I leave Kattrin behind?

THE COOK. What do you think? There's no room in the inn, it isn't one of those places with three counters. If the two of us look lively we can earn a living, but three's too many. Let Kattrin keep your wagon.

MOTHER COURAGE. I was thinking we might find her a husband in Utrecht.

THE COOK. Don't make me laugh. With that scar? And old as she is? And dumb?

MOTHER COURAGE. Not so loud!

THE COOK. Loud or soft, what is, is. That's another reason I can't have her in the inn. Customers don't like having something like that always before their eyes. You can't blame them.

MOTHER COURAGE. Shut up. I told you not to talk so loud.

THE COOK. There's a light in the parsonage, we can sing now!

MOTHER COURAGE. Cook, how could she pull the wagon by herself? The war frightens her. She can't bear it. She has terrible dreams. I hear her groan at night, especially after battles. What she sees in her dreams I don't know. She suffers from sheer pity. The other day I found her with a hedgehog that we'd run over.

THE COOK. The inn's too small. (*Calling.*) Worthy Sir, menials, and all within! We now present the song of Solomon, Julius Caesar, and other great souls who came to no good, so you can see we're law-abiding folk too, and have a hard time getting by, especially in winter.

(*He sings "The Song of the Great Souls of this Earth"*:)

King Solomon was very wise,
So what's his history?
He came to view this life with scorn,
Yes, he came to regret he ever had
    been born
Declaring: all is vanity.
King Solomon was very wise,
But long before the day was out
The consequence was clear, alas:
His wisdom 'twas that brought him to
    this pass.
A man is better off without.

For the virtues are dangerous in this world, as our fine song tells. You're better off without, you have a nice life, breakfast included—some good hot soup maybe . . . I'm an example of a man who's not had any, and I'd like some, I'm a soldier, but what good did my bravery do me in all those battles? None at all. I might just as well have wet my pants like a poltroon and stayed at home. For why?

Old Julius Caesar, he was brave.
His fame shall never cease.
He sat like a god on an altar piece.
Yet they tore brave old Julius limb
    from valiant limb
And Brutus helped to slaughter him.
Old Julius was very brave
But long before the day was out
The consequence was clear, alas:
His bravery 'twas that brought him
    to this pass.
A man is better off without.

(*Under his breath.*) They don't even look out. (*Aloud.*) Worthy Sir, menials, and all within! You could say, no, courage isn't the thing to fill a man's belly, try honesty, that should be worth a dinner, at any rate it must have *some* effect. Let's see.

You all know honest Socrates
Who always spoke the truth.
They owed him thanks for that, you'd
  think,
But what happened? Why, they put
  hemlock in his drink
And swore that he misled the youth.
How honest was this Socrates!
Yet long before the day was out
The consequence was clear, alas:
His honesty had brought him to this
  pass.
A man is better off without.

Yes, we're told to be unselfish and share what we have, but what if we have nothing? And those who do share it don't have an easy time either, for what's left when you're through sharing? Unselfishness is a very rare virtue—it doesn't pay.

Unselfish Martin could not bear
His fellow creatures' woes.
He met a poor man in the snows
And he gave this poor fellow half his
  cloak to wear:
So both of them fell down and froze.
His brothers' woes he could not bear,
So long before the day was out
The consequence was clear, alas:
Unselfishness had brought him to this
  pass.
A man is better off without.

That's how it is with us. We're law-abiding folk, we keep to ourselves, don't steal, don't kill, don't burn the place down. And in this way we sink lower and lower and the song proves true and there's no soup going. And if we were different, if we were thieves and killers, maybe we could eat our fill! For virtues bring no reward, only vices. Such is the world, need it be so?

God's ten commandments we have
  kept
And acted as we should.
It has not done us any good.
All you people who sit beside a
  roaring fire
O help us in our need so dire!

The ten commandments we have kept
And long before the day was out
The consequence was clear, alas:
Our godliness has brought us to this
  pass.
A man is better off without.

VOICE (*from above*). You there! Come up! There's some soup here for you!

MOTHER COURAGE. Lamb, I couldn't swallow a thing. I don't say what you said is unreasonable, but was it your last word? We've always understood each other.

THE COOK. Yes, Anna. Think it over.

MOTHER COURAGE. There's nothing to think over. I'm not leaving her here.

THE COOK. You're going to be silly, but what can I do? I'm not inhuman, it's just that the inn's a small one. And now we must go up, or there'll be nothing doing here too, and we've been singing in the cold for nothing.

MOTHER COURAGE. I'll fetch Kattrin.

THE COOK. Better stick something in your pocket for her. If there are three of us, they'll get a shock.

(*Exeunt.* KATTRIN *clambers out of the wagon with a bundle. She makes sure they are both gone. Then, on a wagon wheel, she lays out a skirt of her mother's and a pair of the cook's trousers side by side and easy to see. She has just finished, and has picked up her bundle, when* MOTHER COURAGE *returns.*)

MOTHER COURAGE (*with a plate of soup*). Kattrin! Stay where you are, Kattrin! Where do you think you're going with that bundle? (*She examines the bundle.*) She's packed her things. Were you listening? I told him there was nothing doing, he can *have* Utrecht and his lousy inn, what would we want with a lousy inn? (*She sees the skirt and trousers.*) Oh, you're a stupid girl, Kattrin, what if I'd seen that and you gone? (*She takes hold of* KATTRIN *who is trying to leave.*) And don't think I've sent him packing on your account. It was the wagon. You can't part us, I'm too used to it, it wasn't you, it was the wagon. Now we're leaving, and we'll put the cook's things here where he'll find 'em, the stupid man. (*She clambers up and throws a couple of things down to go with the trousers.*) There! He's fired. The last man I'll take into *this* business! Now let's be going, you and me. This winter'll pass, like all the others. Get into harness, it looks like snow.

(*They harness themselves to the wagon, turn it around, and start out. A gust of wind. Enter the* COOK, *still chewing. He sees his things.*)

## SCENE 10

*DURING THE WHOLE OF* 1635 *MOTHER COURAGE AND KATTRIN PULL THE WAGON ALONG THE ROADS OF CENTRAL GERMANY IN THE WAKE OF THE EVER MORE TATTERED ARMIES.*

(*On the highway.* MOTHER COURAGE *and* KATTRIN *are pulling the wagon. They come to a prosperous farmhouse. Someone inside is singing.*)

THE VOICE.

In March a bush we planted
To make the garden gay.
In June we were enchanted:
A lovely rose was blooming
The balmy air perfuming!
Blest are they
Who have gardens gay!
In June we were enchanted.

When snow falls helter-skelter
And loudly blows the storm
Our farmhouse gives us shelter.
The winter's in a hurry
But we've no cause to worry.
We are warm
In the midst of the storm!
Our farmhouse gives us shelter.

(MOTHER COURAGE *and* KATTRIN *have stopped to listen. Then they start out again.*)

## SCENE 11

*JANUARY,* 1636. *CATHOLIC TROOPS THREATEN THE PROTESTANT TOWN OF HALLE. THE STONE BEGINS TO SPEAK. MOTHER COURAGE LOSES HER DAUGHTER AND JOURNEYS ONWARD ALONE. THE WAR IS NOT YET NEAR ITS END.*

(*The wagon, very far gone now, stands near a farmhouse with a straw roof. It is night. Out of the woods come a* LIEUTENANT *and three* SOLDIERS *in full armor.*)

THE LIEUTENANT. And there mustn't be a sound. If anyone yells, cut him down.

THE FIRST SOLDIER. But we'll have to knock—if we want a guide.

THE LIEUTENANT. Knocking's a natural noise, it's all right, could be a cow hitting the wall of the cowshed.

(*The* SOLDIERS *knock at the farmhouse door. An* OLD PEASANT WOMAN *opens. A hand is clapped over her mouth. Two* SOLDIERS *enter.*)

A MAN'S VOICE. What is it?

(*The* SOLDIERS *bring out an* OLD PEASANT *and his son.*)

THE LIEUTENANT (*pointing to the wagon on which* KATTRIN *has appeared*). There's one. (*A* SOLDIER *pulls her out.*) Is this everybody that lives here?

THE PEASANTS (*alternating*). That's our son. And that's a girl that can't talk. Her mother's in town buying up stocks because the shopkeepers are running away and selling cheap. They're canteen people.

THE LIEUTENANT. I'm warning you. Keep quiet. One sound and we'll crack you over the head with a pike. And I need someone to show us the path to the town. (*He points to the* YOUNG PEASANT.) You! Come here!

THE YOUNG PEASANT. I don't know any path!

THE SECOND SOLDIER (*grinning*). He don't know any path!

THE YOUNG PEASANT. I don't help Catholics.

THE LIEUTENANT (*to the* SECOND SOLDIER). Let him feel your pike in his side.

THE YOUNG PEASANT (*forced to his knees, the pike at his throat*). I'd rather die!

THE SECOND SOLDIER (*again mimicking*). He'd rather die!

THE FIRST SOLDIER. I know how to change his mind. (*He walks over to the cowshed.*) Two cows and a bull. Listen, you. If you aren't going to be reasonable, I'll saber your cattle.

THE YOUNG PEASANT. Not the cattle!

THE PEASANT WOMAN (*weeping*). Spare the cattle, Captain, or we'll starve!

THE LIEUTENANT. If he must be pigheaded!

THE FIRST SOLDIER. I think I'll start with the bull.

THE YOUNG PEASANT (*to the old one*). Do I have to? (*The older one nods.*) I'll do it.

THE PEASANT WOMAN. Thank you, thank you, Captain, for sparing us, for ever and ever, Amen.

(*The* OLD MAN *stops her going on thanking him.*)

THE FIRST SOLDIER. I knew the bull came first all right!

(*Led by the* YOUNG PEASANT, *the* LIEUTENANT *and the* SOLDIERS *go on their way.*)

THE OLD PEASANT. I wish we knew what it was. Nothing good, I suppose.

THE PEASANT WOMAN. Maybe they're just scouts. What are you doing?

THE OLD PEASANT (*setting a ladder against the roof and climbing up*). I'm seeing if they're alone. (*On the roof.*) Things are moving—all over. I can see armor. And a cannon. There must be more than a regiment. God have mercy on the town and all within!

THE PEASANT WOMAN. Are there lights in the town?

THE OLD PEASANT. No, they're all asleep. (*He climbs down.*) There'll be an attack, and they'll all be slaughtered in their beds.

THE PEASANT WOMAN. The watchman'll give warning.

THE OLD PEASANT. They must have killed the watchman in the tower on the hill or he'd have sounded his horn before this.

THE PEASANT WOMAN. If there were more of us . . .

THE OLD PEASANT. But being that we're alone with that cripple . . .

THE PEASANT WOMAN. There's nothing we can do, is there?

THE OLD PEASANT. Nothing.

THE PEASANT WOMAN. We can't get down there. In the dark.

THE OLD PEASANT. The whole hillside's swarming with 'em.

THE PEASANT WOMAN. We could give a sign?

THE OLD PEASANT. And be cut down for it?

THE PEASANT WOMAN. No, there's nothing we can do. (*To* KATTRIN.) Pray, poor thing, pray! There's nothing we can do to stop this bloodshed, so even if you can't talk, at least pray! He hears, if no one else does. I'll help you. (*All kneel,* KATTRIN *behind.*) Our Father, which art in Heaven, hear our prayer, let not the town perish with all that lie therein asleep

and fearing nothing. Wake them, that they rise and go to the walls and see the foe that comes with fire and sword in the night down the hill and across the fields. (*Back to* KATTRIN.) God protect our mother and make the watchman not sleep but wake ere it's too late. And save our son-in-law too, O God, he's there with his four children, let them not perish, they're innocent, they know nothing —(*to* KATTRIN, *who groans*)—one of them's not two years old, the eldest is seven. (KATTRIN *rises, troubled.*) Heavenly Father, hear us, only Thou canst help us or we die, for we are weak and have no sword nor nothing; we cannot trust our own strength but only Thine, O Lord; we are in Thy hands, our cattle, our farm, and the town too, we're all in Thy hands, and the foe is nigh unto the walls with all his power.

(KATTRIN, *unperceived, has crept off to the wagon, has taken something out of it, put it under her apron, and has climbed up the ladder to the roof.*)

Be mindful of the children in danger, especially the little ones, be mindful of the old folk who cannot move, and of all Christian souls, O Lord.

THE OLD PEASANT. And forgive us our trespasses as we forgive them that trespass against us. Amen.

(*Sitting on the roof,* KATTRIN *takes a drum from under her apron and starts to beat it.*)

THE PEASANT WOMAN. Heavens, what's she doing?

THE OLD PEASANT. She's out of her mind!

THE PEASANT WOMAN. Get her down, quick.

(*The* OLD PEASANT *runs to the ladder but* KATTRIN *pulls it up on the roof.*)

She'll get us in trouble.

THE OLD PEASANT. Stop it this minute, you silly cripple!

THE PEASANT WOMAN. The soldiers'll come!

THE OLD PEASANT (*looking for stones*). I'll stone you!

THE PEASANT WOMAN. Have you no pity, have you no heart? We have relations there too, four grandchildren, but there's nothing we can do. If they find us now, it's the end, they'll stab us to death!

(KATTRIN *is staring into the far distance, toward the town. She goes on drumming.*)

THE PEASANT WOMAN (*to the* PEASANT). I told you not to let that riffraff in your farm. What do *they* care if we lose our cattle?

THE LIEUTENANT (*running back with* SOLDIERS *and the* YOUNG PEASANT). I'll cut you all to bits!

THE PEASANT WOMAN. We're innocent, sir, there's nothing we can do. She did it, a stranger!

THE LIEUTENANT. Where's the ladder?

THE OLD PEASANT. On the roof.

THE LIEUTENANT (*calling*). Throw down the drum. I order you! (KATTRIN *goes on drumming.*) You're all in this, but you won't live to tell the tale.

THE OLD PEASANT. They've been cutting down fir trees around here. If we bring a tall enough trunk we can knock her off the roof.

THE FIRST SOLDIER (*to the* LIEUTENANT). I beg leave to make a suggestion. (*He whispers something to the* LIEUTENANT, *who nods.*) Listen, you! We have an idea—for your own good. Come down and go with us to the town. Show us your mother and we'll spare her.

(KATTRIN *goes on drumming.*)

THE LIEUTENANT (*pushing him away*). She doesn't trust you, no wonder with your face. (*He calls up to* KATTRIN.) Hey, you! Suppose I give you my word? I'm an officer, my word's my bond!

(KATTRIN *drums harder.*)

Nothing is sacred to her.

THE YOUNG PEASANT. Sir, it's not just because of her mother!

THE FIRST SOLDIER. This can't go on, they'll hear it in the town as sure as hell.

THE LIEUTENANT. We must make another noise with something. Louder than that drum. What can we make a noise with?

THE FIRST SOLDIER. But we mustn't make a noise!

THE LIEUTENANT. A harmless noise, fool, a peacetime noise!

THE OLD PEASANT. I could start chopping wood.

THE LIEUTENANT. That's it! (*The* PEASANT *brings his ax and chops away.*) Chop! Chop harder! Chop for your life!

(KATTRIN *has been listening, beating the drum less hard. Very upset, and peering around, she now goes on drumming.*)

It's not enough. (*To the* FIRST SOLDIER.) You chop too!

THE OLD PEASANT. I've only one ax. (*He stops chopping.*)

THE LIEUTENANT. We must set fire to the farm. Smoke her out.

THE OLD PEASANT. That's no good, Captain. When they see fire from the town, they'll know everything.

(*During the drumming* KATTRIN *has been listening again. Now she laughs.*)

THE LIEUTENANT. She's laughing at us, that's too much, I'll have her guts if it's the last thing I do. Bring a musket!

(*Two* SOLDIERS *off.* KATTRIN *goes on drumming.*)

THE PEASANT WOMAN. I have it, Captain. That's their wagon over there, Captain. If we smash that, she'll stop. It's all they have, Captain.

THE LIEUTENANT (*to the* YOUNG PEASANT). Smash it! (*Calling.*) If you don't stop that noise, we'll smash your wagon!

(*The* YOUNG PEASANT *deals the wagon a couple of feeble blows with a board.*)

THE PEASANT WOMAN (*to* KATTRIN). Stop, you little beast!

(KATTRIN *stares at the wagon and pauses. Noises of distress come out of her. But she goes on drumming.*)

THE LIEUTENANT. Where are those sons of bitches with that gun?

THE FIRST SOLDIER. They can't have heard anything in the town or we'd hear their cannon.

THE LIEUTENANT (*calling*). They don't hear you. And now we're going to shoot you. I'll give you one more chance: throw down that drum!

THE YOUNG PEASANT (*dropping the board, screaming to* KATTRIN). Don't stop now! Or they're all done for. Go on, go on, go on . . .

(*The* SOLDIER *knocks him down and beats him with his pike.* KATTRIN *starts crying but goes on drumming.*)

THE PEASANT WOMAN. Not in the back, you're killing him!

(*The* SOLDIERS *arrive with the musket.*)

THE SECOND SOLDIER. The Colonel's foaming at the mouth. We'll be court-martialed.

THE LIEUTENANT. Set it up! Set it up!

(*Calling while the musket is set up on forks.*)
Once and for all: stop that drumming!

> (*Still crying,* KATTRIN *is drumming as hard as she can.*)

Fire!

> (*The* SOLDIERS *fire.* KATTRIN *is hit. She gives the drum another feeble beat or two, then slowly collapses.*)

THE LIEUTENANT. That's an end to the noise.

> (*But the last beats of the drum are lost in the din of cannon from the town. Mingled with the thunder of cannon, alarm bells are heard in the distance.*)

THE FIRST SOLDIER. She made it.

### SCENE 12

*Toward morning. The drums and pipes of troops on the march, receding. In front of the wagon* MOTHER COURAGE *sits by* KATTRIN's *body. The* PEASANTS *of the last scene are standing near.*

THE PEASANT. You must leave, woman. There's only one regiment to go. You can never get away by yourself.

MOTHER COURAGE. Maybe she's fallen asleep.

> (*She sings.*)
> Lullaby, baby, what's that in the hay?
> The neighbor's kids cry but mine are
>     gay.
> The neighbor's kids are dressed in
>     dirt:
> Your silks are cut from an angel's
>     skirt.
> They are all starving: you have a pie.
> If it's too stale, you need only cry.
> Lullaby, baby, what's rustling there?
> One lad fell in Poland. The other
>     is—where?

You shouldn't have told her about the children.

THE PEASANTS. If you hadn't gone off to the town to get your cut, maybe it wouldn't have happened.

MOTHER COURAGE. She's asleep now.

THE PEASANTS. She's not asleep, it's time you realized. She's gone. You must get away. There are wolves in these parts. And the bandits are worse.

MOTHER COURAGE. That's right.

> (*She goes and fetches a cloth from the wagon to cover up the body.*)

THE PEASANT WOMAN. Have you no one now? Someone you can go to?

MOTHER COURAGE. There's one. My Eilif.

THE PEASANT (*while* MOTHER COURAGE *covers the body*). Find him then. Leave *her* to us. We'll give her a proper burial. You needn't worry.

MOTHER COURAGE. Here's money for the expenses.

> (*She pays the* PEASANT. *The* PEASANT *and his son shake her hand and carry* KATTRIN *away.*)

THE PEASANT WOMAN (*also taking her hand, and bowing, as she goes away*). Hurry!

MOTHER COURAGE (*harnessing herself to the wagon*). I hope I can pull the wagon by myself. Yes, I'll manage, there's not much in it now. I must get back into business.

> (*Another regiment passes at the rear with pipe and drum.* MOTHER COURAGE *starts pulling the wagon.*)

MOTHER COURAGE. Hey! Take me with you!

> (*Soldiers are heard singing.*)
> Dangers, surprises, devastations!
> The war moves on, but will not quit.
> And though it last three generations,
> We shall get nothing out of it.
> Starvation, filth, and cold enslave us.
> The army robs us of our pay.
> But God may yet come down and save
>     us:
> His holy war won't end today.
>     Christians, awake! Winter is gone!
>     The snows depart! Dead men sleep
>       on!
>     Let all of you who still survive
>     Get out of bed and look alive!

## Editorial Notes

*Mother Courage and Her Children* was copyrighted in the U.S. in 1940, and first published here, not in German, but in English, in 1941: the translation was by H. R. Hays, and the play appeared in an anthology of new writing entitled *New Directions, 1941*, published by New Directions. An Eric Bentley version of the play, with the cuts made by Brecht for the German production, appeared in *The Modern Theatre*, volume two (Doubleday, Anchor, 1955). A second Bentley version, even more heavily cut for a projected American production, appeared in *Seven Plays by Bertolt Brecht* (Grove Press, 1961).

The world première of the play (and this was in German) took place in 1941 at the Zürich Schauspielhaus; the director was Leopold Lindtberg.

The now famous production of the Berlin Ensemble dates back to 1949 (though the Ensemble did not yet exist) when Erich Engel and Bertolt Brecht put the play on at the Deutsches Theater in Berlin with Helene Weigel (Mrs. Bertolt Brecht) in the title role. When the play was last given (1960), Frau Weigel was one of the few performers from the original cast who were still in the show.

The first Broadway production of *Mother Courage and Her Children*, in a version by Eric Bentley, opened at the Martin Beck Theatre, New York City, on March 28, 1963. Produced by Cheryl Crawford and Jerome Robbins, directed by Jerome Robbins, and with the music of Paul Dessau, it starred Anne Bancroft, Zohra Lampert, and Barbara Harris. Other professional productions of the play, adapted by Eric Bentley, have been staged in London, Bristol, Dublin, Cleveland, and San Francisco. It has also been presented by BBC-TV.

The music to the world première in Zürich was by Paul Burkhard, and there is an as yet unused score by Darius Milhaud, composed expressly for English lyrics of Eric Bentley, but the music generally associated with the play is that of Paul Dessau, for which the lyrics in the present text were written. Part of Dessau's score can be heard, with the words in French, on a Vanguard Record (VRS-9022); part with the words sung in German by the Berlin cast, on East German records usually available from Deutsche Schallplatten, Deutscher Buch Export, Lenin-strasse 16, Leipzig C.I. Two lyrics from the play, one set by Dessau, the other by Hanns Eisler, are to be found on *Bentley on Brecht* (Riverside Records, RM 7017).

## Author's Notes

The world première of *Mother Courage and Her Children* in Zürich during the Hitler War, with the outstanding Therese Giehse in the title role, made it possible, despite the antifascist and pacifist stand of the Zürich Schauspielhaus (mainly staffed with German emigrants), for the bourgeois press to speak of a Niobe tragedy and of the overwhelming vital strength of the mother animal. Duly warned, the playwright made some changes for the Berlin production. The original text follows.

*From Scene 1, pages 413–418*

MOTHER COURAGE. . . . all of you: be careful, you'll need to be. Now let's climb on the wagon and move on.

SERGEANT. I don't feel very well.

RECRUITING OFFICER. Maybe you caught a chill when you handed over your helmet in all this wind.

(*The* SERGEANT *grabs his helmet.*)

MOTHER COURAGE. And you give me my papers. Someone else might ask for them and I'll be without. (*She collects them in her tin.*)

RECRUITING OFFICER (*to* EILIF). You can at least take a look at the boots. And we can have a drink, just us men. I can advance you money: come behind the wagon, and I'll prove it.

(*They go behind the wagon.*)

SERGEANT. I don't understand. I always stay in the rear. There's no safer spot for a sergeant to be. You can send the others on ahead in quest of fame. My appetite is ruined. I can tell you right now, I won't be able to get anything done.

MOTHER COURAGE (*going over to him*). You shouldn't take on so, just because you can't eat. Just stay in the rear. Here, take a slug of brandy, man, and no offence. (*She gives him something to drink from the wagon.*)

RECRUITING OFFICER (*who has taken* EILIF'S *arm and is making off toward the back*). You die anyway. You drew a cross, so what? Ten guilders in advance and you're a soldier of the king and a stout fellow and the women will be mad about you. And you can give me a smack in the puss for insulting you.

(*Both leave. Dumb* KATTRIN *lets out harsh cries, for she has seen the abduction.*)

MOTHER COURAGE. Coming, Kattrin, coming. The Sergeant isn't well, he's superstitious, I didn't know that. And now we'll be going. Where's Eilif?

SWISS CHEESE. He must have gone with the recruiting officer. He was talking with him the whole time.

*From Scene 5, pages 433–434*

MOTHER COURAGE. What, you can't pay? No money, no brandy! They can play victory marches, they should pay their men!

SOLDIER (*threateningly*). I want my brandy!

I arrived too late for plunder. The Chief allowed one hour for plunder. He's not inhuman, he says. So I suppose they bought him off.

(*The* CHAPLAIN *staggers in.*)

CHAPLAIN. There are more in the farmhouse. A family of peasants. Help me, someone, I need linen!

(*The* SECOND SOLDIER *goes off with him.*)

MOTHER COURAGE. I have none. I sold all my bandages to the regiment. I'm not tearing up my officers' shirts for these people.

CHAPLAIN (*calling back*). I said I need linen!

MOTHER COURAGE (*rummaging around in her wagon*). Not a thing! They have nothing, and they pay nothing!

(*The* CHAPLAIN *stoops over a* WOMAN *whom he has brought on.*)

CHAPLAIN. Why did you stay out there in the line of fire?

WOMAN (*weakly*). Our farm . . .

MOTHER COURAGE. Expect *them* to leave? My beautiful shirts. My officers will be coming tomorrow, and I won't have a thing for them. (*She throws some stuff down.* KATTRIN *takes it to the* PEASANT WOMAN.) What am I doing, giving stuff away? I didn't start the war.

FIRST SOLDIER. They're Protestants. Why should they be Protestants?

MOTHER COURAGE. Protestant, Catholic, what do *they* care? Their farm's gone, that's what.

SECOND SOLDIER. They're not Protestants anyway: they're Catholics.

FIRST SOLDIER. In a bombardment we can't pick and choose.

(*A* PEASANT *is brought in by the* CHAPLAIN.)

PEASANT. My arm's gone.

(*From the house comes the cry of a child in pain.*)

CHAPLAIN (*to the* PEASANT WOMAN). Don't get up.

MOTHER COURAGE. Get the child out of there.

(KATTRIN *runs off.*)

MOTHER COURAGE (*tearing up shirts*). Half a guilder a shirt. I'm ruined. Don't move her when you're bandaging, it may be her back. (*To* KATTRIN *who has brought a young baby out of the ruins and is rocking it as she walks around.*)

Another baby to drag around—you must be pleased with yourself! Give it to its mother this minute. Or do I have to fight you again for hours till I get it from you? Are you deaf? (KATTRIN *ignores all this*.) I have nothing but losses from your victories. Now, make do with this, Chaplain, don't waste any of my linen, do you hear?

CHAPLAIN. I need more. The blood's coming through.

MOTHER COURAGE (*referring to* KATTRIN). There she sits, happy as a lark in all this misery. Give the baby back, the mother is coming to! (*As* KATTRIN *finally and reluctantly gives the child back to the* PEASANT WOMAN, MOTHER COURAGE *rips up a new shirt*.) I'm giving nothing, I *can* give nothing, I have myself to think of. (*To the* SECOND SOLDIER.) Don't stand around gawking, go back there and tell them to stop that music, I can see their victory without it. Have yourself a glass of brandy, Chaplain, don't say no, I have enough to cope with. (*She has to get down from the wagon to snatch her daughter from the* FIRST SOLDIER, *who is drunk*.) You beast! You want another victory, do you? Well, you don't get away from me without paying up! (*To the* PEASANT.) Your child is all right. (*Pointing to the* WOMAN.) Get something down her. (*To the* FIRST SOLDIER.) Then leave this coat. It's stolen goods anyhow.

(FIRST SOLDIER *staggers away*. MOTHER COURAGE *goes on ripping shirts*.)

CHAPLAIN. There's still someone in there.

MOTHER COURAGE. Don't worry, I'll tear up all I have.

*From Scene 7, pages 438–439*
(*A highway. The* CHAPLAIN, MOTHER COURAGE, *and* KATTRIN *pull the wagon. It is dirty and neglected, but new wares are hanging from it.*)

MOTHER COURAGE (*sings*).
So many seek a bed to sleep in:
Each ditch is taken, and each cave,
And he who seeks a hole to creep in
Finds he has dug an early grave.
And many a man spends many a minute
In hurrying toward some resting place.
You wonder, when at last he's in it,
Just why the fellow forced the pace.
(*She plays the refrain,* "Christians, awake!" *on the harmonica.*)

*From Scene 12, page 450*
PEASANTS. You must leave, woman. There's only one regiment to go. You can never get away by yourself.

MOTHER COURAGE. She's still breathing. Maybe she's fallen asleep.

Of the Peasants' War,[1] which was the greatest misfortune of German history, one may say that, socially considered, it pulled the teeth of the Reformation. Its legacy was cynicism and business as usual. Mother Courage (let it be said to help performances in the theatre) recognizes, as do her friends and guests and nearly everyone, the purely commercial character of the war: this is precisely what attracts her. She believes in the war to the end. It never occurs to her that one must have a big pair of scissors to take one's cut of a war. Those who look on at catastrophes wrongly expect those involved to learn something. So long as the masses are the *object* of politics they cannot regard what happens to them as an experiment but only as a fate. They learn as little from catastrophe as a scientist's rabbit learns of biology. It is not incumbent on the playwright to give Mother Courage insight at the end—she sees something, around the middle of the play, at the close of the sixth scene, then loses again what she has seen—his concern is that the spectator should see.

B. B.

---

[1] Brecht is referring to the Thirty Years' War.

## Selected Reading List for Brecht

Eric Bentley, "From Strindberg to Bertolt Brecht," *The Playwright as Thinker.* New York: Meridian Books, 1955, pp. 209–31.

*Brecht on Theatre*, trans. John Willett. New York: Hill and Wang, 1964.

Robert Brustein, "Bertolt Brecht," *The Theatre of Revolt.* Boston: Little, Brown and Company, 1964, pp. 231–78.

Martin Esslin, *Brecht: The Man and his Work.* New York: Doubleday & Company, Inc., 1961.

John Willett, *The Theatre of Bertolt Brecht.* New York: New Directions, 1964.

# Pirandello: Illusion and Reality

*Six Characters in Search of an Author*, written in 1921, is as much a play of ideas as *Major Barbara*, but its ideas concern a different topic. Shaw is concerned with flaws in the economic structure of society and with conflicting theories of how to deal with them. Evangelism and materialism are brought to a head-on confrontation. Pirandello is concerned with a more metaphysical problem—the nature of reality. As he explains in the preface to the play (reprinted in the Appendix, pp. 498–505), the problem presented itself to him in the form of characters whose story he had never been able to complete, but whom he had nevertheless imagined with such clarity that they seemed to have a life of their own. The play is a dramatization of their desire to escape from the limbo of incomplete artistic existence to which they have been condemned by their author's rejection of them. When these characters confront the living actors and, in a sense, the audience as well, the conflict is between different kinds of reality.

With such a theme as this it is not surprising that Pirandello, like Strindberg and Brecht, but for different reasons, broke with the conventions of the realistic stage, which were designed to mirror the reality of everyday rather than to challenge it. In his early work he had been a naturalist, greatly influenced by his fellow Sicilians, Giovanni Verga and Luigi Capuana, two of the chief exponents of the Italian naturalistic movement called *verismo*. Luigi Pirandello was born at Girgenti in 1867. After studying in Rome he went to the University of Bonn and then returned to Rome, where he met some of the important Italian writers of the turn of the century. At this period he wrote novels and short stories based on Sicilian life. He did not become widely known until the time of the first World War when he was taking an increasing interest in the theater and was developing an individual style in which realism was blended with unrealistic elements. In the plays for which he is best known, such as *Six Characters in Search of an Author*, *Right You Are if You Think You Are*, and *Henry IV*, all written in the twenties, he used this distinctive combination of techniques to present the ambiguous borderland of truth and delusion, sanity and madness. In 1934, two years before his death, he was awarded the Nobel Prize for literature.

*Six Characters in Search of an Author* raises not only the question, "what is reality?" but also "what is stage realism?" When the spectators enter the theater they find, as the stage direction informs us, "the curtain raised and the stage as it usually is during the day time." Soon the actors and the manager arrive as if for a rehearsal. In one sense this is thoroughly realistic, for it presents an exact image of a familiar situation. Yet in being realistic about the means of producing plays it lays bare the artifice which underlies realism in the theater, reminding us that this seeming reality is an illusion.

The main themes of the play grow logically out of the initial paradox. The six characters introduce a plane of reality which corresponds neither to the stage nor to the life which the stage represents, for these characters are embodiments of the author's imagination. Their entrance is an impressive moment. "A tenuous light surrounds them," as the stage direction informs us, "almost as if irradiated by them—the faint breath of their fantastic reality." In search of the author, they pause with the actors in the hope of at least living in the performance of their story, which they begin to tell. In the attempt of the actors to present these characters Pirandello dramatizes the puzzling relationship between the playwright's conception and its realization in a performance which may falsify it. Here the characters, incomplete and unrealized as they are, seem more real than the actors' imitation of them.

When the characters themselves perform two scenes from their story, another aspect of the problem of reality is presented. Such life as they have can only be realized in the enactment and re-enactment of their drama, in which each one seeks to justify his understanding of its meaning. While they are condemned to endless repetition of their big scenes, it is their tragedy that the meaning is forever incomplete, since the author himself gave up the attempt to find it. Thus, even when the danger of misinterpretation by the actors is removed, there remains the question of what meaning and even what reality a series of events has outside of the interpretative mind of some individual.

The dilemma of the characters is in part the consequence of their belonging to the world of art, and they complain of the way they have been caught in the fixed form of the story devised for them; yet their feeling is analogous to the protests of actual people against the roles they are forced to play in life. In a similar way the disagreement among the characters about the meaning of their drama is an analogue to the bewilderment of people who look for some intelligible design in the events of their lives. Pirandello contrives to make every implicit statement about art a challenge to one's assumptions about life.

The six characters fasten their hopes to the enactment of the crucial episodes of their lives—the scene at Madame Pace's, the scene in the garden. These are in every sense of the term their dramatic moments. Pirandello makes it clear that whatever meaning there may be in the lives of his characters is concentrated in these moments. In fact only in these moments do they live at all. The example is extreme and hence startling, but it is nonetheless characteristic of all drama. It is in such dramatic moments that we truly feel the existence of Oedipus or Lear and glimpse the meaning of their tragedies. Pirandello succeeds not only in posing his questions about the nature of reality but in giving a demonstration of how the drama achieves its effects.

# Six Characters in Search of an Author

*A COMEDY IN THE MAKING*

## LUIGI PIRANDELLO

### CHARACTERS OF THE COMEDY IN THE MAKING

THE FATHER
THE MOTHER
THE STEP-DAUGHTER
THE SON
THE BOY
THE CHILD
(*The last two do not speak*)
MADAME PACE

### ACTORS OF THE COMPANY

THE MANAGER
LEADING LADY
LEADING MAN
SECOND LADY LEAD
L'INGÉNUE
JUVENILE LEAD
OTHER ACTORS AND ACTRESSES
PROPERTY MAN
PROMPTER
MACHINIST
MANAGER'S SECRETARY
DOOR-KEEPER
SCENE-SHIFTERS

*Daytime. The Stage of a Theatre*
*N. B.   The Comedy is without acts or scenes. The performance is interrupted once, without the curtain being lowered, when the manager and the chief characters withdraw to arrange the scenario. A second interruption of the action takes place when, by mistake, the stage hands let the curtain down.*

### ACT I

*The spectators will find the curtain raised and the stage as it usually is during the day time. It will be half dark, and empty, so that from the beginning the public may have the impression of an impromptu performance.*

*Prompter's box and a small table and chair for the manager.*

*Two other small tables and several chairs scattered about as during rehearsals.*

*The* ACTORS *and* ACTRESSES *of the company enter from the back of the stage: first one, then another, then two together; nine or ten in all. They are about to rehearse a Pirandello play: Mixing It Up.[1] Some of the company move off towards their dressing rooms. The* PROMPTER *who has the "book" under his arm, is waiting for the manager in order to begin the rehearsal.*

*The* ACTORS *and* ACTRESSES, *some standing, some sitting, chat and smoke. One perhaps reads a paper; another cons his part.*

[1] I.e., *Il giuoco delle parti.*

*Finally,* THE MANAGER *enters and goes to the table prepared for him. His* SECRETARY *brings him his mail, through which he glances. The* PROMPTER *takes his seat, turns on a light, and opens the "book."*

THE MANAGER (*throwing a letter down on the table*). I can't see (*To* PROPERTY MAN.) Let's have a little light, please!

PROPERTY MAN. Yes sir, yes, at once. (*A light comes down on to the stage.*)

THE MANAGER (*clapping his hands*). Come along! Come along! Second act of "Mixing It Up." (*Sits down.*)

(*The* ACTORS *and* ACTRESSES *go from the front of the stage to the wings, all except the three who are to begin the rehearsal.*)

THE PROMPTER (*reading the "book"*). "Leo Gala's house. A curious room serving as dining-room and study."

THE MANAGER (*to* PROPERTY MAN). Fix up the old red room.

PROPERTY MAN (*noting it down*). Red set. All right!

THE PROMPTER (*continuing to read from the "book"*). "Table already laid and writing desk with books and papers. Book-shelves. Exit rear to Leo's bedroom. Exit left to kitchen. Principal exit to right."

THE MANAGER (*energetically*). Well, you understand: The principal exit over there; here, the kitchen. (*Turning to actor who is to play the part of Socrates.*) You make your entrances and exits here. (*To* PROPERTY MAN.) The baize doors at the rear, and curtains.

PROPERTY MAN (*noting it down*). Right!

PROMPTER (*reading as before*). "When the curtain rises, Leo Gala, dressed in cook's cap and apron is busy beating an egg in a cup. Philip, also dressed as a cook, is beating another egg. Guido Venanzi is seated and listening."

LEADING MAN (*to* MANAGER). Excuse me, but must I absolutely wear a cook's cap?

THE MANAGER (*annoyed*). I imagine so. It says so there anyway. (*Pointing to the "book."*)

LEADING MAN. But it's ridiculous!

THE MANAGER (*jumping up in a rage*). Ridiculous? Ridiculous? Is it my fault if France won't send us any more good comedies, and we are reduced to putting on Pirandello's works, where nobody understands anything, and where the author plays the fool with us all? (*The* ACTORS *grin.* THE MANAGER *goes to* LEADING MAN *and shouts.*) Yes sir, you put on the cook's cap and beat eggs. Do you suppose that with all this egg-beating business you are on an ordinary stage? Get that out of your head. You represent the shell of the eggs you are beating! (*Laughter and comments among the* ACTORS.) Silence! and listen to my explanations, please! (*To* LEADING MAN.) "The empty form of reason without the fullness of instinct, which is blind."—You stand for reason, your wife is instinct. It's a mixing up of the parts, according to which you who act your own part become the puppet of yourself. Do you understand?

LEADING MAN. I'm hanged if I do.

THE MANAGER. Neither do I. But let's get on with it. It's sure to be a glorious failure anyway. (*Confidentially.*) But I say, please face three-quarters. Otherwise, what with the abstruseness of the dialogue, and the public that won't be able to hear you, the whole thing will go to hell. Come on! come on!

PROMPTER. Pardon sir, may I get into my box? There's a bit of a draught.

THE MANAGER. Yes, yes, of course!

(*At this point, the* DOOR-KEEPER *has entered from the stage door and advances towards the manager's table, taking off his braided cap. During this manoeuvre, the six* CHARACTERS *enter and stop by the door at back of stage, so that when the* DOOR-KEEPER *is about to announce their coming to* THE MANAGER, *they are already on the stage. A tenuous light surrounds them, almost as if irradiated by them—the faint breath of their fantastic reality.*

*This light will disappear when they come forward towards the actors. They preserve, however, something of the dream lightness in which they seem almost suspended; but this does not detract from the essential reality of their forms and expressions.*

*He who is known as* THE FATHER *is a man of about 50: hair, reddish in colour, thin at the temples; he is not bald, however; thick moustaches, falling over his still fresh mouth, which often opens in an empty and uncertain smile. He is fattish, pale; with an especially wide forehead. He has blue, oval-shaped eyes, very clear and piercing. Wears light trousers and a dark jacket. He is alternatively mellifluous and violent in his manner.*

THE MOTHER *seems crushed and terrified as if by an intolerable weight of shame and abasement. She is dressed in modest black and wears a thick widow's veil of crêpe. When she lifts this, she reveals a wax-like face. She always keeps her eyes downcast.*

THE STEP-DAUGHTER, *is dashing, almost impudent, beautiful. She wears mourning too, but with great elegance. She shows contempt for the timid half-frightened manner of the wretched* BOY *[14 years old, and also dressed in black]; on the other hand, she displays a lively tenderness for her little sister, THE CHILD [about four], who is dressed in white, with a black silk sash at the waist.*

THE SON *[22] tall, severe in his attitude of contempt for* THE FATHER, *supercilious and indifferent to* THE MOTHER. *He looks as if he had come on the stage against his will.)*

DOOR-KEEPER *(cap in hand).* Excuse me, sir . . .

THE MANAGER *(rudely).* Eh? What is it?

DOOR-KEEPER *(timidly).* These people are asking for you, sir.

THE MANAGER *(furious).* I am rehearsing, and you know perfectly well no one's allowed to come in during rehearsals! *(Turning to the* CHARACTERS.) Who are you, please? What do you want?

THE FATHER *(coming forward a little, followed by the others who seem embarrassed).* As a matter of fact . . . we have come here in search of an author . . .

THE MANAGER *(half angry, half amazed).* An author? What author?

THE FATHER. Any author, sir.

THE MANAGER. But there's no author here. We are not rehearsing a new piece.

THE STEP-DAUGHTER *(vivaciously).* So much the better, so much the better! We can be your new piece.

AN ACTOR *(coming forward from the others).* Oh, do you hear that?

THE FATHER *(to STEP-DAUGHTER).* Yes, but if the author isn't here . . . *(to MANAGER)* unless you would be willing . . .

THE MANAGER. You are trying to be funny.

THE FATHER. No, for Heaven's sake, what are you saying? We bring you a drama, sir.

THE STEP-DAUGHTER. We may be your fortune.

THE MANAGER. Will you oblige me by going away? We haven't time to waste with mad people.

THE FATHER *(mellifluously).* Oh sir, you know well that life is full of infinite absurdities, which, strangely enough, do not even need to appear plausible, since they are true.

THE MANAGER. What the devil is he talking about?

THE FATHER. I say that to reverse the ordinary process may well be considered a madness: that is, to create credible situations, in order that they may appear true. But permit me to observe that if this be madness, it is the sole *raison d'être* of your profession, gentlemen. *(The* ACTORS *look hurt and perplexed.)*

THE MANAGER *(getting up and looking at him).* So our profession seems to you one worthy of madmen then?

THE FATHER. Well, to make seem true that which isn't true . . . without any need . . . for a joke as it were. . . . Isn't that your mission, gentlemen: to give life to fantastic characters on the stage?

THE MANAGER *(interpreting the rising anger of the* COMPANY). But I would beg you to believe, my dear sir, that the profession of the comedian is a noble one. If today, as things go, the playwrights give us stupid comedies to play and puppets to represent instead of men, remember we are proud to have given life to immortal works here on these very boards! *(The* ACTORS, *satisfied, applaud their* MANAGER.)

THE FATHER *(interrupting furiously).* Exactly, perfectly, to living beings more alive than those who breathe and wear clothes: beings less real perhaps, but truer! I agree with you entirely. *(The* ACTORS *look at one another in amazement.)*

THE MANAGER. But what do you mean? Before, you said . . .

THE FATHER. No, excuse me, I meant it for you, sir, who were crying out that you had no time to lose with madmen, while no one better than yourself knows that nature uses the instrument of human fantasy in order to pursue her high creative purpose.

THE MANAGER. Very well,—but where does all this take us?

THE FATHER. Nowhere! It is merely to show you that one is born to life in many forms, in many shapes, as tree, or as stone, as water, as butterfly, or as woman. So one may also be born a character in a play.

THE MANAGER (*with feigned comic dismay*). So you and these other friends of yours have been born characters?

THE FATHER. Exactly, and alive as you see! (MANAGER *and* ACTORS *burst out laughing.*)

THE FATHER (*hurt*). I am sorry you laugh, because we carry in us a drama, as you can guess from this woman here veiled in black.

THE MANAGER (*losing patience at last and almost indignant*). Oh, chuck it! Get away please! Clear out of here! (*To* PROPERTY MAN.) For Heaven's sake, turn them out!

THE FATHER (*resisting*). No, no, look here, we . . .

THE MANAGER (*roaring*). We come here to work, you know.

LEADING ACTOR. One cannot let oneself be made such a fool of.

THE FATHER (*determined, coming forward*). I marvel at your incredulity, gentlemen. Are you not accustomed to see the characters created by an author spring to life in yourselves and face each other? Just because there is no "book" (*pointing to the* PROMPTER's *box*) which contains us, you refuse to believe . . .

THE STEP-DAUGHTER (*advances towards* MANAGER, *smiling and coquettish*). Believe me, we are really six most interesting characters, sir; side-tracked however.

THE FATHER. Yes, that is the word! (*To* MANAGER *all at once.*) In the sense, that is, that the author who created us alive no longer wished, or was no longer able, materially to put us into a work of art. And this was a real crime, sir; because he who has had the luck to be born a character can laugh even at death. He cannot die. The man, the writer, the instrument of the creation will die, but his creation does not die. And to live for ever, it does not need to have extraordinary gifts or to be able to work wonders. Who was Sancho Panza? Who

was Don Abbondio?[2] Yet they live eternally because—live germs as they were—they had the fortune to find a fecundating matrix, a fantasy which could raise and nourish them: make them live for ever!

THE MANAGER. That is quite all right. But what do you want here, all of you?

THE FATHER. We want to live.

THE MANAGER (*ironically*). For Eternity?

THE FATHER. No, sir, only for a moment . . . in you.

AN ACTOR. Just listen to him!

LEADING LADY. They want to live, in us . . . !

JUVENILE LEAD (*pointing to* THE STEP-DAUGHTER). I've no objection, as far as that one is concerned!

THE FATHER. Look here! look here! The comedy has to be made. (*To* THE MANAGER.) But if you and your actors are willing, we can soon concert it among ourselves.

THE MANAGER (*annoyed*). But what do you want to concert? We don't go in for concerts here. Here we play dramas and comedies!

THE FATHER. Exactly! That is just why we have come to you.

THE MANAGER. And where is the "book"?

THE FATHER. It is in us! (*The* ACTORS *laugh.*) The drama is in us, and we are the drama. We are impatient to play it. Our inner passion drives us on to this.

THE STEP-DAUGHTER (*disdainful, alluring, treacherous, full of impudence*). My passion, sir! Ah, if you only knew! My passion for him! (*Points to* THE FATHER *and makes a pretence of embracing him. Then she breaks out into a loud laugh.*)

THE FATHER (*angrily*). Behave yourself! And please don't laugh in that fashion.

THE STEP-DAUGHTER. With your permission, gentlemen, I, who am a two months' orphan, will show you how I can dance and sing. (*Sings and then dances* Prenez garde à Tchou-Tchin-Tchou.)

   Les chinois sont un peuple malin,
   De Shangaï à Pékin,

---

[2] *Don Abbondio* a character in *The Betrothed* (*I Promessi Sposi*), a novel by Alessandro Manzoni (1785–1873)

Ils ont mis des écriteaux partout:
Prenez garde à Tchou-Tchin-Tchou.[3]

ACTORS AND ACTRESSES. Bravo! Well done! Tip-top!

THE MANAGER. Silence! This isn't a café concert, you know! (*Turning to* THE FATHER *in consternation.*) Is she mad?

THE FATHER. Mad? No, she's worse than mad.

THE STEP-DAUGHTER (*to* MANAGER). Worse? Worse? Listen! Stage this drama for us at once! Then you will see that at a certain moment I . . . when this little darling here . . . (*takes* THE CHILD *by the hand and leads her to* THE MANAGER). Isn't she a dear? (*Takes her up and kisses her.*) Darling! Darling! (*Puts her down again and adds feelingly.*) Well, when God suddenly takes this dear little child away from that poor mother there; and this imbecile here (*seizing hold of* THE BOY *roughly and pushing him forward*) does the stupidest things, like the fool he is, you will see me run away. Yes, gentlemen, I shall be off. But the moment hasn't arrived yet. After what has taken place between him and me (*indicates* THE FATHER *with a horrible wink*) I can't remain any longer in this society, to have to witness the anguish of this mother here for that fool. . . . (*Indicates* THE SON.) Look at him! Look at him! See how indifferent, how frigid he is, because he is the legitimate son. He despises me, despises him (*pointing to* THE BOY), despises this baby here; because . . . we are bastards. (*Goes to* THE MOTHER *and embraces her.*) And he doesn't want to recognize her as his mother—she who is the common mother of us all. He looks down upon her as if she were only the mother of us three bastards. Wretch! (*She says all this very rapidly, excitedly. At the word "bastards" she raises her voice, and almost spits out the final "Wretch!"*)

THE MOTHER (*to* THE MANAGER, *in anguish*). In the name of these two little children, I beg you . . . (*she grows faint and is about to fall*). Oh God!

THE FATHER (*coming forward to support her*

as do some of the ACTORS). Quick, a chair, a chair for this poor widow!

THE ACTORS. Is it true? Has she really fainted?

THE MANAGER. Quick, a chair! Here!

(*One of the* ACTORS *brings a chair, the others proffer assistance.* THE MOTHER *tries to prevent* THE FATHER *from lifting the veil which covers her face.*)

THE FATHER. Look at her! Look at her!

THE MOTHER. No, no; stop it please!

THE FATHER (*raising her veil*). Let them see you!

THE MOTHER (*rising and covering her face with her hands, in desperation*). I beg you, sir, to prevent this man from carrying out his plan which is loathsome to me.

THE MANAGER (*dumbfounded*). I don't understand at all. What is the situation? Is this lady your wife? (*To* THE FATHER.)

THE FATHER. Yes, gentlemen: my wife!

THE MANAGER. But how can she be a widow if you are alive? (*The* ACTORS *find relief for their astonishment in a loud laugh.*)

THE FATHER. Don't laugh! Don't laugh like that, for Heaven's sake. Her drama lies just here in this: she has had a lover, a man who ought to be here.

THE MOTHER (*with a cry*). No! No!

THE STEP-DAUGHTER. Fortunately for her, he is dead. Two months ago as I said. We are in mourning, as you see.

THE FATHER. He isn't here you see, not because he is dead. He isn't here—look at her a moment and you will understand—because her drama isn't a drama of the love of two men for whom she was incapable of feeling anything except possibly a little gratitude—gratitude not for me but for the other. She isn't a woman, she is a mother, and her drama—powerful sir, I assure you—lies, as a matter of fact, all in these four children she has had by two men.

THE MOTHER. I had them? Have you got the courage to say that I wanted them? (*To the company.*) It was his doing. It was he who gave me that other man, who forced me to go away with him.

THE STEP-DAUGHTER. It isn't true.

THE MOTHER (*startled*). Not true, isn't it?

---

[3] *Les Chinois . . . Tchou-Tchin-Tchou* The Chinese are a mischievous people, / From Shanghai to Peking; / Everywhere they have put notices: / Beware of Tchou-Tchin-Tchou

THE STEP-DAUGHTER. No, it isn't true, it just isn't true.

THE MOTHER. And what can you know about it?

THE STEP-DAUGHTER. It isn't true. Don't believe it. (*To* MANAGER.) Do you know why she says so? For that fellow there. (*Indicates* THE SON.) She tortures herself, destroys herself on account of the neglect of that son there; and she wants him to believe that if she abandoned him when ·he was only two years old, it was because he (*indicates* THE FATHER) made her do so.

THE MOTHER (*vigorously*). He forced me to it, and I call God to witness it. (*To the* MANAGER.) Ask him (*indicates* HUSBAND) if it isn't true. Let him speak. You (*to* DAUGH-TER) are not in a position to know anything about it.

THE STEP-DAUGHTER. I know you lived in peace and happiness with my father while he lived. Can you deny it?

THE MOTHER. No, I don't deny it . . .

THE STEP-DAUGHTER. He was always full of affection and kindness for you. (*To* THE BOY, *angrily*.) It's true, isn't it? Tell them! Why don't you speak, you little fool?

THE MOTHER. Leave the poor boy alone. Why do you want to make me appear un-grateful, daughter? I don't want to offend your father. I have answered him that I didn't abandon my house and my son through any fault of mine, nor from any wilful passion.

THE FATHER. It is true. It was my doing.

LEADING MAN (*to the company*). What a spectacle!

LEADING LADY. We are the audience this time.

JUVENILE LEAD. For once, in a way.

THE MANAGER (*beginning to get really inter-ested*). Let's hear them out. Listen!

THE SON. Oh yes, you're going to hear a fine bit now. He will talk to you of the Demon of Experiment.

THE FATHER. You are a cynical imbecile. I've told you so already a hundred times. (*To* THE MANAGER.) He tries to make fun of me on account of this expression which I have found to excuse myself with.

THE SON (*with disgust*). Yes, phrases! phrases!

THE FATHER. Phrases! Isn't everyone consoled when faced with a trouble or fact he doesn't understand, by a word, some simple word, which tells us nothing and yet calms us?

THE STEP-DAUGHTER. Even in the case of remorse. In fact, especially then.

THE FATHER. Remorse? No, that isn't true. I've done more than use words to quieten the remorse in me.

THE STEP-DAUGHTER. Yes, there was a bit of money too. Yes, yes, a bit of money. There were the hundred lire he was about to offer me in payment, gentlemen. . . . (*Sensation of horror among the* ACTORS.)

THE SON (*to* THE STEP-DAUGHTER). This is vile.

THE STEP-DAUGHTER. Vile? There they were in a pale blue envelope on a little mahogany table in the back of Madame Pace's shop. You know Madame Pace—one of those ladies who attract poor girls of good family into their ateliers, under the pretext of their selling *robes et manteaux*.[4]

THE SON. And he thinks he has bought the right to tyrannize over us all with those hundred lire he was going to pay; but which, fortunately—note this, gentlemen—he had no chance of paying.

THE STEP-DAUGHTER. It was a near thing, though, you know! (*Laughs ironically*.)

THE MOTHER (*protesting*). Shame, my daughter, shame!

THE STEP-DAUGHTER. Shame indeed! This is my revenge! I am dying to live that scene. . . . The room . . . I see it. . . . Here is the window with the mantles exposed, there the divan, the looking-glass, a screen, there in front of the window the little mahogany table with the blue envelope containing one hundred lire. I see it. I see it. I could take hold of it. . . . But you, gentlemen, you ought to turn your backs now: I am almost nude, you know. But I don't blush: I leave that to him. (*Indicating* FATHER.)

THE MANAGER. I don't understand this at all.

THE FATHER. Naturally enough. I would ask you, sir, to exercise your authority a little

————

[4] *robes et manteaux* dresses and coats

here, and let me speak before you believe all she is trying to blame me with. Let me explain.

THE STEP-DAUGHTER. Ah yes, explain it in your own way.

THE FATHER. But don't you see that the whole trouble lies here. In words, words. Each one of us has within him a whole world of things, each man of us his own special world. And how can we ever come to an understanding if I put in the words I utter the sense and value of things as I see them; while you who listen to me must inevitably translate them according to the conception of things each one of you has within himself. We think we understand each other, but we never really do. Look here! This woman (*indicating* THE MOTHER) takes all my pity for her as a specially ferocious form of cruelty.

THE MOTHER. But you drove me away.

THE FATHER. Do you hear her? I drove her away! She believes I really sent her away.

THE MOTHER. You know how to talk, and I don't; but, believe me, sir (*to* MANAGER), after he had married me . . . who knows why? . . . I was a poor insignificant woman.

THE FATHER. But, good Heavens! it was just for your humility that I married you. I loved this simplicity in you. (*He stops when he sees she makes signs to contradict him, opens his arms wide in sign of desperation, seeing how hopeless it is to make himself understood.*) You see she denies it. Her mental deafness, believe me, is phenomenal, the limit: (*touches his forehead*) deaf, deaf, mentally deaf! She has plenty of feeling. Oh yes, a good heart for the children; but the brain—deaf, to the point of desperation——!

THE STEP-DAUGHTER. Yes, but ask him how his intelligence has helped us.

THE FATHER. If we could see all the evil that may spring from good, what should we do? (*At this point the* LEADING LADY *who is biting her lips with rage at seeing the* LEADING MAN *flirting with* THE STEP-DAUGHTER, *comes forward and says to* THE MANAGER.)

LEADING LADY. Excuse me, but are we going to rehearse today?

MANAGER. Of course, of course; but let's hear them out.

JUVENILE LEAD. This is something quite new.

L'INGÉNUE. Most interesting!

LEADING LADY. Yes, for the people who like that kind of thing. (*Casts a glance at* LEADING MAN.)

THE MANAGER (*to* FATHER). You must please explain yourself quite clearly. (*Sits down.*)

THE FATHER. Very well then: listen! I had in my service a poor man, a clerk, a secretary of mine, full of devotion, who became friends with her. (*Indicating* THE MOTHER.) They understood one another, were kindred souls in fact, without, however, the least suspicion of any evil existing. They were incapable even of thinking of it.

THE STEP-DAUGHTER. So he thought of it—for them!

THE FATHER. That's not true. I meant to do good to them—and to myself, I confess, at the same time. Things had come to the point that I could not say a word to either of them without their making a mute appeal, one to the other, with their eyes. I could see them silently asking each other how I was to be kept in countenance, how I was to be kept quiet. And this, believe me, was just about enough of itself to keep me in a constant rage, to exasperate me beyond measure.

THE MANAGER. And why didn't you send him away then—this secretary of yours?

THE FATHER. Precisely what I did, sir. And then I had to watch this poor woman drifting forlornly about the house like an animal without a master, like an animal one has taken in out of pity.

THE MOTHER. Ah yes . . . !

THE FATHER (*suddenly turning to* THE MOTHER). It's true about the son anyway, isn't it?

THE MOTHER. He took my son away from me first of all.

THE FATHER. But not from cruelty. I did it so that he should grow up healthy and strong by living in the country.

THE STEP-DAUGHTER (*pointing to him ironically*). As one can see.

THE FATHER (*quickly*). Is it my fault if he has grown up like this? I sent him to a wet nurse in the country, a peasant, as *she* did not seem to me strong enough, though she is of humble origin. That was, anyway, the reason I married her. Unpleasant all this may be, but how can it be helped? My mistake possibly, but there we are! All my life I have had these confounded aspirations towards a certain moral sanity. (*At this point* THE STEP-DAUGHTER *bursts into a noisy laugh.*) Oh, stop it! Stop it! I can't stand it.

THE MANAGER. Yes, please stop it, for Heaven's sake.

THE STEP-DAUGHTER. But imagine moral sanity from him, if you please—the client of certain ateliers like that of Madame Pace!

THE FATHER. Fool! That is the proof that I am a man! This seeming contradiction, gentlemen, is the strongest proof that I stand here a live man before you. Why, it is just for this very incongruity in my nature that I have had to suffer what I have. I could not live by the side of that woman (*indicating* THE MOTHER) any longer; but not so much for the boredom she inspired me with as for the pity I felt for her.

THE MOTHER. And so he turned me out—.

THE FATHER. —well provided for! Yes, I sent her to that man, gentlemen . . . to let her go free of me.

THE MOTHER. And to free himself.

THE FATHER. Yes, I admit it. It was also a liberation for me. But great evil has come of it. I meant well when I did it; and I did it more for her sake than mine. I swear it. (*Crosses his arms on his chest; then turns suddenly to* THE MOTHER.) Did I ever lose sight of you until that other man carried you off to another town, like the angry fool he was? And on account of my pure interest in you . . . my pure interest, I repeat, that had no base motive in it . . . I watched with the tenderest concern the new family that grew up around her. She can bear witness to this. (*Points to* THE STEP-DAUGHTER.)

THE STEP-DAUGHTER. Oh yes, that's true enough. When I was a kiddie, so so high, you know, with plaits over my shoulders and knickers longer than my skirts, I used to see him waiting outside the school for me to come out. He came to see how I was growing up.

THE FATHER. This is infamous, shameful!

THE STEP-DAUGHTER. No. Why?

THE FATHER. Infamous! infamous! (*Then excitedly to* MANAGER *explaining.*) After she (*indicating* MOTHER) went away, my house seemed suddenly empty. She was my incubus, but she filled my house. I was like a dazed fly alone in the empty rooms. This boy here (*indicating* THE SON) was educated away from home, and when he came back, he seemed to me to be no more mine. With no mother to stand between him and me, he grew up entirely for himself, on his own, apart, with no tie of intellect or affection binding him to me. And then—strange but true—I was driven, by curiosity at first and then by some tender sentiment, towards her family, which had come into being through my will. The thought of her began gradually to fill up the emptiness I felt all around me. I wanted to know if she were happy in living out the simple daily duties of life. I wanted to think of her as fortunate and happy because far away from the complicated torments of my spirit. And so, to have proof of this, I used to watch that child coming out of school.

THE STEP-DAUGHTER. Yes, yes. True. He used to follow me in the street and smiled at me, waved his hand, like this. I would look at him with interest, wondering who he might be. I told my mother, who guessed at once. (THE MOTHER *agrees with a nod.*) Then she didn't want to send me to school for some days; and when I finally went back, there he was again—looking so ridiculous—with a paper parcel in his hands. He came close to me, caressed me, and drew out a fine straw hat from the parcel, with a bouquet of flowers—all for me!

THE MANAGER. A bit discursive this, you know!

THE SON (*contemptuously*). Literature! Literature!

THE FATHER. Literature indeed! This is life, this is passion!

THE MANAGER. It may be, but it won't act.

THE FATHER. I agree. This is only the part leading up. I don't suggest this should be staged. She (*pointing to* THE STEP-DAUGHTER), as you see, is no longer the flapper with plaits down her back—.

THE STEP-DAUGHTER. —and the knickers showing below the skirt!

THE FATHER. The drama is coming now,

sir; something new, complex, most interesting.

THE STEP-DAUGHTER. As soon as my father died . . .

THE FATHER. —there was absolute misery for them. They came back here, unknown to me. Through her stupidity! (*Pointing to* THE MOTHER.) It is true she can barely write her own name; but she could anyhow have got her daughter to write to me that they were in need . . .

THE MOTHER. And how was I to divine all this sentiment in him?

THE FATHER. That is exactly your mistake, never to have guessed any of my sentiments.

THE MOTHER. After so many years apart, and all that had happened . . .

THE FATHER. Was it my fault if that fellow carried you away? It happened quite suddenly; for after he had obtained some job or other, I could find no trace of them; and so, not unnaturally, my interest in them dwindled. But the drama culminated unforeseen and violent on their return, when I was impelled by my miserable flesh that still lives.... Ah! what misery, what wretchedness is that of the man who is alone and disdains debasing *liaisons!* Not old enough to do without women, and not young enough to go and look for one without shame. Misery? It's worse than misery; it's a horror; for no woman can any longer give him love; and when a man feels this.... One ought to do without, you say? Yes, yes, I know. Each of us when he appears before his fellows is clothed in a certain dignity. But every man knows what unconfessable things pass within the secrecy of his own heart. One gives way to the temptation, only to rise from it again, afterwards, with a great eagerness to re-establish one's dignity, as if it were a tombstone to place on the grave of one's shame, and a monument to hide and sign the memory of our weaknesses. Everybody's in the same case. Some folks haven't the courage to say certain things, that's all!

THE STEP-DAUGHTER. All appear to have the courage to do them though.

THE FATHER. Yes, but in secret. Therefore, you want more courage to say these things. Let a man but speak these things out, and folks at once label him a cynic. But it isn't true. He is like all the others, better indeed, because he isn't afraid to reveal with the light of the intelligence the red shame of human bestiality on which most men close their eyes so as not to see it.

Woman—for example, look at her case! She turns tantalizing inviting glances on you. You seize her. No sooner does she feel herself in your grasp than she closes her eyes. It is the sign of her mission, the sign by which she says to man: "Blind yourself, for I am blind."

THE STEP-DAUGHTER. Sometimes she can close them no more: when she no longer feels the need of hiding her shame to herself, but dry-eyed and dispassionately, sees only that of the man who has blinded himself without love. Oh, all these intellectual complications make me sick, disgust me—all this philosophy that uncovers the beast in man, and then seeks to save him, excuse him . . . I can't stand it, sir. When a man seeks to "simplify" life bestially, throwing aside every relic of humanity, every chaste aspiration, every pure feeling, all sense of ideality, duty, modesty, shame . . . then nothing is more revolting and nauseous than a certain kind of remorse—crocodiles' tears, that's what it is.

THE MANAGER. Let's come to the point. This is only discussion.

THE FATHER. Very good, sir! But a fact is like a sack which won't stand up when it is empty. In order that it may stand up, one has to put into it the reason and sentiment which have caused it to exist. I couldn't possibly know that after the death of that man, they had decided to return here, that they were in misery, and that she (*pointing to* THE MOTHER) had gone to work as a modiste, and at a shop of the type of that of Madame Pace.

THE STEP-DAUGHTER. A real high-class modiste, you must know, gentlemen. In appearance, she works for the leaders of the best society; but she arranges matters so that these elegant ladies serve her purpose . . . without prejudice to other ladies who are . . . well . . . only so so.

THE MOTHER. You will believe me, gentlemen, that it never entered my mind that the old hag offered me work because she had her eye on my daughter.

THE STEP-DAUGHTER. Poor mamma! Do you know, sir, what that woman did when I brought her back the work my mother had finished? She would point out to me that I had torn one of my frocks, and she would give it back to my mother to mend. It was I who paid for it, always I; while this poor creature here believed she was sacrificing herself for me and these two children here, sitting up at night sewing Madame Pace's robes.

THE MANAGER. And one day you met there . . .

THE STEP-DAUGHTER. Him, him. Yes sir, an old client. There's a scene for you to play! Superb!

THE FATHER. She, the Mother arrived just then . . .

THE STEP-DAUGHTER (treacherously). Almost in time!

THE FATHER (crying out). No, in time! in time! Fortunately I recognized her . . . in time. And I took them back home with me to my house. You can imagine now her position and mine; she, as you see her; and I who cannot look her in the face.

THE STEP-DAUGHTER. Absurd! How can I possibly be expected—after that—to be a modest young miss, a fit person to go with his confounded aspirations for "a solid moral sanity"?

THE FATHER. For the drama lies all in this—in the conscience that I have, that each one of us has. We believe this conscience to be a single thing, but it is many-sided. There is one for this person, and another for that. Diverse consciences. So we have this illusion of being one person for all, of having a personality that is unique in all our acts. But it isn't true. We perceive this when, tragically perhaps, in something we do, we are as it were, suspended, caught up in the air on a kind of hook. Then we perceive that all of us was not in that act, and that it would be an atrocious injustice to judge us by that action alone, as if all our existence were summed up in that one deed. Now do you understand the perfidy of this girl? She surprised me in a place, where she ought not to have known me, just as I could not exist for her; and she now seeks to attach to me a reality such as I could never suppose I should have to assume for her in a shameful and fleeting moment of my life. I feel this above all else. And the drama, you will see, acquires a tremendous value from this point. Then there is the position of the others . . . his . . . (indicating THE SON).

THE SON (shrugging his shoulders scornfully). Leave me alone! I don't come into this.

THE FATHER. What? You don't come into this?

THE SON. I've got nothing to do with it, and don't want to have; because you know well enough I wasn't made to be mixed up in all this with the rest of you.

THE STEP-DAUGHTER. We are only vulgar folk! He is the fine gentleman. You may have noticed, Mr. Manager, that I fix him now and again with a look of scorn while he lowers his eyes—for he knows the evil he has done me.

THE SON (scarcely looking at her). I?

THE STEP-DAUGHTER. You! I owe my life on the streets to you. Did you or did you not deny us, with your behaviour, I won't say the intimacy of home, but even that mere hospitality which makes guests feel at their ease? We were intruders who had come to disturb the kingdom of your legitimacy. I should like to have you witness, Mr. Manager, certain scenes between him and me. He says I have tyrannized over everyone. But it was just his behaviour which made me insist on the reason for which I had come into the house,—this reason he calls "vile"—into his house, with my mother who is his mother too. And I came as mistress of the house.

THE SON. It's easy for them to put me always in the wrong. But imagine, gentlemen, the position of a son, whose fate it is to see arrive one day at his home a young woman of impudent bearing, a young woman who inquires for his father, with whom who knows what business she has. This young man has then to witness her return bolder than ever, accompanied by that child there. He is obliged to watch her treat his father in an equivocal and confidential manner. She asks money of him in a way that lets one suppose he must give it her, *must*, do you understand, because he has every obligation to do so.

THE FATHER. But I have, as a matter of fact, this obligation. I owe it to your mother.

THE SON. How should I know? When had I ever seen or heard of her? One day there arrive with her (*indicating* STEP-DAUGHTER) that lad and this baby here. I am told: "This is *your* mother too, you know." I divine from her manner (*indicating* STEP-DAUGHTER *again*) why it is they have come home. I had rather not say what I feel and think about it. I shouldn't even care to confess to myself. No action can therefore be hoped for from me in this affair. Believe me, Mr. Manager, I am an "unrealized" character, dramatically speaking; and I find myself not at all at ease in their company. Leave me out of it, I beg you.

THE FATHER. What? It is just because you are so that . . .

THE SON. How do you know what I am like? When did you ever bother your head about me?

THE FATHER. I admit it. I admit it. But isn't that a situation in itself? This aloofness of yours which is so cruel to me and to your mother, who returns home and sees you almost for the first time grown up, who doesn't recognize you but knows you are her son . . . (*pointing out* THE MOTHER *to* THE MANAGER). See, she's crying!

THE STEP-DAUGHTER (*angrily, stamping her foot*). Like a fool!

THE FATHER (*indicating* STEP-DAUGHTER). She can't stand him you know. (*Then referring again to* THE SON.) He says he doesn't come into the affair, whereas he is really the hinge of the whole action. Look at that lad who is always clinging to his mother, frightened and humiliated. It is on account of this fellow here. Possibly his situation is the most painful of all. He feels himself a stranger more than the others. The poor little chap feels mortified, humiliated at being brought into a home out of charity as it were. (*In confidence.*) He is the image of his father. Hardly talks at all. Humble and quiet.

THE MANAGER. Oh, we'll cut him out. You've no notion what a nuisance boys are on the stage . . .

THE FATHER. He disappears soon, you know. And the baby too. She is the first to vanish from the scene. The drama consists finally in this: when that mother re-enters my house, her family born outside of it, and shall we say superimposed on the original, ends with the death of the little girl, the tragedy of the boy and the flight of the elder daughter. It cannot go on, because it is foreign to its surroundings. So after much torment, we three remain: I, the mother, that son. Then, owing to the disappearance of that extraneous family, we too find ourselves strange to one another. We find we are living in an atmosphere of mortal desolation which is the revenge, as he (*indicating* SON) scornfully said of the Demon of Experiment, that unfortunately hides in me. Thus, sir, you see when faith is lacking, it becomes impossible to create certain states of happiness, for we lack the necessary humility. Vaingloriously, we try to substitute ourselves for this faith, creating thus for the rest of the world a reality which we believe after their fashion, while, actually, it doesn't exist. For each one of us has his own reality to be respected before God, even when it is harmful to one's very self.

THE MANAGER. There is something in what you say. I assure you all this interests me very much. I begin to think there's the stuff for a drama in all this, and not a bad drama either.

THE STEP-DAUGHTER (*coming forward*). When you've got a character like me.

THE FATHER (*shutting her up, all excited to learn the decision of* THE MANAGER). You be quiet!

THE MANAGER (*reflecting, heedless of interruption*). It's new . . . hem . . . yes . . .

THE FATHER. Absolutely new!

THE MANAGER. You've got a nerve though, I must say, to come here and fling it at me like this . . .

THE FATHER. You will understand, sir, born as we are for the stage . . .

THE MANAGER. Are you amateur actors then?

THE FATHER. No. I say born for the stage, because . . .

THE MANAGER. Oh, nonsense. You're an old hand, you know.

THE FATHER. No sir, no. We act that rôle for which we have been cast, that rôle which we are given in life. And in my own case, passion itself, as usually happens, becomes a trifle theatrical when it is exalted.

THE MANAGER. Well, well, that will do. But you see, without an author ... I could give you the address of an author if you like ...

THE FATHER. No, no. Look here! You must be the author.

THE MANAGER. I? What are you talking about?

THE FATHER. Yes, you, you! Why not?

THE MANAGER. Because I have never been an author: that's why.

THE FATHER. Then why not turn author now? Everybody does it. You don't want any special qualities. Your task is made much easier by the fact that we are all here alive before you ...

THE MANAGER. It won't do.

THE FATHER. What? When you see us live our drama ...

THE MANAGER. Yes, that's all right. But you want someone to write it.

THE FATHER. No, no. Someone to take it down, possibly, while we play it, scene by scene! It will be enough to sketch it out at first, and then try it over.

THE MANAGER. Well ... I am almost tempted. It's a bit of an idea. One might have a shot at it.

THE FATHER. Of course. You'll see what scenes will come out of it. I can give you one, at once ...

THE MANAGER. By Jove, it tempts me. I'd like to have a go at it. Let's try it out. Come with me to my office. (Turning to the ACTORS.) You are at liberty for a bit, but don't step out of the theatre for long. In a quarter of an hour, twenty minutes, all back here again! (To THE FATHER.) We'll see what can be done. Who knows if we don't get something really extraordinary out of it?

THE FATHER. There's no doubt about it. They (indicating the CHARACTERS) had better come with us too, hadn't they?

THE MANAGER. Yes, yes. Come on! come on! (Moves away and then turning to the ACTORS.) Be punctual, please! (MANAGER and the six CHARACTERS cross the stage and go off. The other ACTORS remain, looking at one another in astonishment.)

LEADING MAN. Is he serious? What the devil does he want to do?

JUVENILE LEAD. This is rank madness.

THIRD ACTOR. Does he expect to knock up a drama in five minutes?

JUVENILE LEAD. Like the improvisers!

LEADING LADY. If he thinks I'm going to take part in a joke like this ...

JUVENILE LEAD. I'm out of it anyway.

FOURTH ACTOR. I should like to know who they are. (Alludes to CHARACTERS.)

THIRD ACTOR. What do you suppose? Madmen or rascals!

JUVENILE LEAD. And he takes them seriously!

L'INGÉNUE. Vanity! He fancies himself as an author now.

LEADING MAN. It's absolutely unheard of. If the stage has come to this ... well I'm ...

FIFTH ACTOR. It's rather a joke.

THIRD ACTOR. Well, we'll see what's going to happen next.

(Thus talking, the ACTORS leave the stage; some going out by the little door at the back; others retiring to their dressing-rooms.

The curtain remains up.

The action of the play is suspended for twenty minutes.)

## ACT II

The stage call-bells ring to warn the company that the play is about to begin again.

(THE STEP-DAUGHTER comes out of THE MANAGER's office along with THE CHILD and THE BOY. As she comes out of the office, she cries:—)

Nonsense! nonsense! Do it yourselves! I'm not going to mix myself up in this mess. (Turning to THE CHILD and coming quickly with her on to the stage.) Come on, Rosetta, let's run!

(THE BOY follows them slowly, remaining a little behind and seeming perplexed.)

THE STEP-DAUGHTER (stops, bends over THE CHILD and takes the latter's face between her hands). My little darling! You're frightened, aren't you? You don't know where we are, do you? (Pretending to reply to a question of THE CHILD.)

What is the stage? It's a place, baby, you know, where people play at being serious, a place where they act comedies. We've got to act a comedy now, dead serious, you know; and you're in it also, little one. (*Embraces her, pressing the little head to her breast, and rocking* THE CHILD *for a moment.*) Oh darling, darling, what a horrid comedy you've got to play! What a wretched part they've found for you! A garden . . . a fountain . . . look . . . just suppose, kiddie, it's here. Where, you say? Why, right here in the middle. It's all pretence you know. That's the trouble, my pet: it's all make-believe here. It's better to imagine it though, because if they fix it up for you, it'll only be painted cardboard, painted cardboard for the rockery, the water, the plants. . . . Ah, but I think a baby like this one would sooner have a make-believe fountain than a real one, so she could play with it. What a joke it'll be for the others! But for you, alas! not quite such a joke: you who are real, baby dear, and really play by a real fountain that is big and green and beautiful, with ever so many bamboos around it that are reflected in the water, and a whole lot of little ducks swimming about. . . . No, Rosetta, no, your mother doesn't bother about you on account of that wretch of a son there. I'm in the devil of a temper, and as for that lad . . . (*seizes* BOY *by the arm to force him to take one of his hands out of his pockets*). What have you got there? What are you hiding? (*Pulls his hand out of his pocket, looks into it and catches the glint of a revolver.*) Ah! where did you get this? (THE BOY, *very pale in the face, looks at her, but does not answer.*) Idiot! If I'd been in your place, instead of killing myself, I'd have shot one of those two, or both of them: father and son. (THE FATHER *enters from the office, all excited from his work.* THE MANAGER *follows him.*)

THE FATHER. Come on, come on dear! Come here for a minute! We've arranged everything. It's all fixed up.

THE MANAGER (*also excited*). If you please, young lady, there are one or two points to settle still. Will you come along?

THE STEP-DAUGHTER (*following him towards the office*). Ouff! what's the good, if you've arranged everything.

(THE FATHER, MANAGER *and* STEP-DAUGHTER *go back into the office again* [*off*] *for a moment. At the same time,* THE SON, *followed by* THE MOTHER, *comes out.*)

THE SON (*looking at the three entering office*). Oh this is fine, fine! And to think I can't even get away!

(THE MOTHER *attempts to look at him, but lowers her eyes immediately when he turns away from her. She then sits down.* THE BOY *and* THE CHILD *approach her. She casts a glance again at* THE SON, *and speaks with humble tones, trying to draw him into conversation.*)

THE MOTHER. And isn't my punishment the worst of all? (*Then seeing from* THE SON'S *manner that he will not bother himself about her.*) My God! Why are you so cruel? Isn't it enough for one person to support all this torment? Must you then insist on others seeing it also?

THE SON (*half to himself, meaning* THE MOTHER *to hear, however*). And they want to put it on the stage! If there was at least a reason for it! He thinks he has got at the meaning of it all. Just as if each one of us in every circumstance of life couldn't find his own explanation of it! (*Pauses.*) He complains he was discovered in a place where he ought not to have been seen, in a moment of his life which ought to have remained hidden and kept out of the reach of that convention which he has to maintain for other people. And what about my case? Haven't I had to reveal what no son ought ever to reveal: how father and mother live and are man and wife for themselves quite apart from that idea of father and mother which we give them? When this idea is revealed, our life is then linked at one point only to that man and that woman; and as such it should shame them, shouldn't it?

(THE MOTHER *hides her face in her hands. From the dressing-rooms and the little door at the back of the stage the* ACTORS *and* STAGE MANAGER *return, followed by the* PROPERTY MAN *and the* PROMPTER. *At the same moment,* THE MANAGER *comes out of his office, accompanied by* THE FATHER *and* THE STEP-DAUGHTER.)

THE MANAGER. Come on, come on, ladies and gentlemen! Heh! you there, machinist!

MACHINIST. Yes sir?

THE MANAGER. Fix up the white parlor with the floral decorations. Two wings and a drop with a door will do. Hurry up!

(*The* MACHINIST *runs off at once to prepare the scene, and arranges it while* THE MANAGER *talks with the* STAGE MANAGER, *the* PROPERTY MAN, *and the* PROMPTER *on matters of detail.*)

THE MANAGER (*to* PROPERTY MAN). Just have a look, and see if there isn't a sofa or divan in the wardrobe . . .

PROPERTY MAN. There's the green one.

THE STEP-DAUGHTER. No no! Green won't do. It was yellow, ornamented with flowers—very large! and most comfortable!

PROPERTY MAN. There isn't one like that.

THE MANAGER. It doesn't matter. Use the one we've got.

THE STEP-DAUGHTER. Doesn't matter? It's most important!

THE MANAGER. We're only trying it now. Please don't interfere. (*To* PROPERTY MAN.) See if we've got a shop window—long and narrowish.

THE STEP-DAUGHTER. And the little table! The little mahogany table for the pale blue envelope!

PROPERTY MAN (*to* MANAGER). There's that little gilt one.

THE MANAGER. That'll do fine.

THE FATHER. A mirror.

THE STEP-DAUGHTER. And the screen! We must have a screen. Otherwise how can I manage?

PROPERTY MAN. That's all right, Miss. We've got any amount of them.

THE MANAGER (*to* THE STEP-DAUGHTER). We want some clothes pegs too, don't we?

THE STEP-DAUGHTER. Yes, several, several!

THE MANAGER. See how many we've got and bring them all.

PROPERTY MAN. All right!

(*The* PROPERTY MAN *hurries off to obey his orders. While he is putting the things in their places,* THE MANAGER *talks to the* PROMPTER *and then with the* CHARACTERS *and the* ACTORS.)

THE MANAGER (*to* PROMPTER). Take your seat. Look here: this is the outline of the scenes, act by act. (*Hands him some sheets of paper.*) And now I'm going to ask you to do something out of the ordinary.

PROMPTER. Take it down in shorthand?

THE MANAGER (*pleasantly surprised*). Exactly! Can you do shorthand?

PROMPTER. Yes, a little.

THE MANAGER. Good! (*Turning to a* STAGE HAND.) Go and get some paper from my office, plenty, as much as you can find.

(*The* STAGE HAND *goes off, and soon returns with a handful of paper which he gives to the* PROMPTER.)

THE MANAGER (*to* PROMPTER). You follow the scenes as we play them, and try and get the points down, at any rate the most important ones. (*Then addressing the* ACTORS.) Clear the stage, ladies and gentlemen! Come over here (*pointing to the left*) and listen attentively.

LEADING LADY. But, excuse me, we . . .

THE MANAGER (*guessing her thought*). Don't worry! You won't have to improvise.

LEADING MAN. What have we to do then?

THE MANAGER. Nothing. For the moment you just watch and listen. Everybody will get his part written out afterwards. At present we're going to try the thing as best we can. They're going to act now.

THE FATHER (*as if fallen from the clouds into the confusion of the stage*). We? What do you mean, if you please, by a rehearsal?

THE MANAGER. A rehearsal for them. (*Points to the* ACTORS.)

THE FATHER. But since we are the characters . . .

THE MANAGER. All right: "characters" then, if you insist on calling yourselves such. But here, my dear sir, the characters don't act. Here the actors do the acting. The characters are there, in the "book" (*pointing towards* PROMPTER's *box*)—when there is a "book"!

THE FATHER. I won't contradict you; but excuse me, the actors aren't the characters. They want to be, they pretend to be, don't they? Now if these gentlemen here are fortunate enough to have us alive before them . . .

THE MANAGER. Oh this is grand! You want to come before the public yourselves then?

THE FATHER. As we are . . .

THE MANAGER. I can assure you it would be a magnificent spectacle!

LEADING MAN. What's the use of us here anyway then?

THE MANAGER. You're not going to pretend that you can act? It makes me laugh! (*The* ACTORS *laugh*.) There, you see, they are laughing at the notion. But, by the way, I must cast the parts. That won't be difficult. They cast themselves. (*To the* SECOND LADY LEAD.) You play the Mother. (*To* THE FATHER.) We must find her a name.

THE FATHER. Amalia, sir.

THE MANAGER. But that is the real name of your wife. We don't want to call her by her real name.

THE FATHER. Why ever not, if it is her name? . . . Still, perhaps, if that lady must . . . (*makes a slight motion of the hand to indicate the* SECOND LADY LEAD). I see this woman here (*means* THE MOTHER) as Amalia. But do as you like. (*Gets more and more confused.*) I don't know what to say to you. Already, I begin to hear my own words ring false, as if they had another sound . . .

THE MANAGER. Don't you worry about it. It'll be our job to find the right tones. And as for her name, if you want her Amalia, Amalia it shall be; and if you don't like it, we'll find another! For the moment though, we'll call the characters in this way: (*to* JUVENILE LEAD) You are the Son. (*To the* LEADING LADY.) You naturally are the Step-Daughter . . .

THE STEP-DAUGHTER (*excitedly*). What? what? I, that woman there? (*Bursts out laughing.*)

THE MANAGER (*angry*). What is there to laugh at?

LEADING LADY (*indignant*). Nobody has ever dared to laugh at me. I insist on being treated with respect; otherwise I go away.

THE STEP-DAUGHTER. No, no, excuse me . . . I am not laughing at you . . .

THE MANAGER (*to* STEP-DAUGHTER). You ought to feel honored to be played by . . .

LEADING LADY (*at once, contemptuously*). "That woman there" . . .

THE STEP-DAUGHTER. But I wasn't speaking of you you know. I was speaking of myself— whom I can't see at all in you! That is all.

I don't know . . . but . . . you . . . aren't in the least like me . . .

THE FATHER. True. Here's the point. Look here, sir, our temperaments, our souls . . .

THE MANAGER. Temperament, soul, be hanged! Do you suppose the spirit of the piece is in you? Nothing of the kind!

THE FATHER. What, haven't we our own temperaments, our own souls?

THE MANAGER. Not at all. Your soul or whatever you like to call it takes shape here. The actors give body and form to it, voice and gesture. And my actors—I may tell you—have given expression to much more lofty material than this little drama of yours, which may or may not hold up on the stage. But if it does, the merit of it, believe me, will be due to my actors.

THE FATHER. I don't dare contradict you, sir; but, believe me, it is a terrible suffering for us who are as we are, with these bodies of ours, these features to see . . .

THE MANAGER (*cutting him short and out of patience*). Good heavens! The make-up will remedy all that, man, the make-up . . .

THE FATHER. Maybe. But the voice, the gestures . . .

THE MANAGER. Now, look here! On the stage, you as yourself, cannot exist. The actor here acts you, and that's an end to it!

THE FATHER. I understand. And now I think I see why our author who conceived us as we are, all alive, didn't want to put us on the stage after all. I haven't the least desire to offend your actors. Far from it! But when I think that I am to be acted by . . . I don't know by whom . . .

LEADING MAN (*on his dignity*). By me, if you've no objection!

THE FATHER (*humbly, mellifluously*). Honored, I assure you, sir. (*Bows.*) Still, I must say that try as this gentleman may, with all his good will and wonderful art, to absorb me into himself . . .

LEADING MAN. Oh chuck it! "Wonderful art!" Withdraw that, please!

THE FATHER. The performance he will give, even doing his best with make-up to look like me . . .

LEADING MAN. It will certainly be a bit difficult! (*The* ACTORS *laugh.*)

THE FATHER. Exactly! It will be difficult to act me as I really am. The effect will be rather—apart from the make-up—according as to how he supposes I am, as he senses me—if he does sense me—and not as I inside of myself feel myself to be. It seems to me then that account should be taken of this by everyone whose duty it may become to criticize us ...

THE MANAGER. Heavens! The man's starting to think about the critics now! Let them say what they like. It's up to us to put on the play if we can. (*Looking around.*) Come on! come on! Is the stage set? (*To the* ACTORS *and* CHARACTERS.) Stand back—stand back! Let me see, and don't let's lose any more time! (*To* THE STEP-DAUGHTER.) Is it all right as it is now?

THE STEP-DAUGHTER. Well, to tell the truth, I don't recognize the scene.

THE MANAGER. My dear lady, you can't possibly suppose that we can construct that shop of Madame Pace piece by piece here? (*To* THE FATHER.) You said a white room with flowered wall-paper, didn't you?

THE FATHER. Yes.

THE MANAGER. Well then. We've got the furniture right more or less. Bring that little table a bit further forward. (*The* STAGE HANDS *obey the order. To* PROPERTY MAN.) You go and find an envelope, if possible, a pale blue one; and give it to that gentleman. (*Indicates* FATHER.)

PROPERTY MAN. An ordinary envelope?

MANAGER AND FATHER. Yes, yes, an ordinary envelope.

PROPERTY MAN. At once, sir. (*Exit.*)

THE MANAGER. Ready, everyone! First scene—the Young Lady. (*The* LEADING LADY *comes forward.*) No, no, you must wait. I meant her (*indicating* THE STEP-DAUGHTER). You just watch—

THE STEP-DAUGHTER (*adding at once*). How I shall play it, how I shall live it! ...

LEADING LADY (*offended*). I shall live it also, you may be sure, as soon as I begin!

THE MANAGER (*with his hands to his head*). Ladies and gentlemen, if you please! No more useless discussions! Scene I: the young lady with Madame Pace: Oh! (*Looks around as if lost.*) And this Madame Pace, where is she?

THE FATHER. She isn't with us, sir.

THE MANAGER. Then what the devil's to be done?

THE FATHER. But she is alive too.

THE MANAGER. Yes, but where is she?

THE FATHER. One minute. Let me speak! (*Turning to the* ACTRESSES.) If these ladies would be so good as to give me their hats for a moment ...

THE ACTRESSES (*half surprised, half laughing, in chorus*).
What?
Why?
Our hats?
What does he say?

THE MANAGER. What are you going to do with the ladies' hats? (*The* ACTORS *laugh.*)

THE FATHER. Oh nothing. I just want to put them on these pegs for a moment. And one of the ladies will be so kind as to take off her mantle ...

THE ACTORS. Oh, what d'you think of that? Only the mantle?
He must be mad.

SOME ACTRESSES. But why?
Mantles as well?

THE FATHER. To hang them up here for a moment. Please be so kind, will you?

THE ACTRESSES (*taking off their hats, one or two also their cloaks, and going to hang them on the racks*). After all, why not?
There you are!
This is really funny.
We've got to put them on show.

THE FATHER. Exactly; just like that, on show.

THE MANAGER. May we know why?

THE FATHER. I'll tell you. Who knows if, by arranging the stage for her, she does not come here herself, attracted by the very articles of her trade? (*Inviting the* ACTORS *to look towards the exit at back of stage.*) Look! Look!

(*The door at the back of stage opens and* MADAME PACE *enters and takes a few steps forward. She is a fat, oldish woman with puffy oxygenated hair. She is rouged and powdered, dressed with a comical elegance* in black silk. Round her waist is a long silver chain from which hangs a pair of scissors. THE STEP-DAUGHTER runs over to her at once amid the stupor of the actors.)

THE STEP-DAUGHTER (turning towards her). There she is! There she is!

THE FATHER (radiant). It's she! I said so, didn't I? There she is!

THE MANAGER (conquering his surprise, and then becoming indignant). What sort of a trick is this?

LEADING MAN (almost at the same time). What's going to happen next?

JUVENILE LEAD. Where does she come from?

L'INGÉNUE. They've been holding her in reserve, I guess.

LEADING LADY. A vulgar trick!

THE FATHER (dominating the protests). Excuse me, all of you! Why are you so anxious to destroy in the name of a vulgar, commonplace sense of truth, this reality which comes to birth attracted and formed by the magic of the stage itself, which has indeed more right to live here than you, since it is much truer than you—if you don't mind my saying so? Which is the actress among you who is to play Madame Pace? Well, here is Madame Pace herself. And you will allow, I fancy, that the actress who acts her will be less true than this woman here, who is herself in person. You see my daughter recognized her and went over to her at once. Now you're going to witness the scene!

(But the scene between THE STEP-DAUGHTER and MADAME PACE has already begun despite the protest of the actors and the reply of THE FATHER. It has begun quietly, naturally, in a manner impossible for the stage. So when the ACTORS, called to attention by THE FATHER, turn round and see MADAME PACE, who has placed one hand under THE STEP-DAUGHTER's chin to raise her head, they observe her at first with great attention, but hearing her speak in an unintelligible manner their interest begins to wane.)

THE MANAGER. Well? well?

LEADING MAN. What does she say?

LEADING LADY. One can't hear a word.

JUVENILE LEAD. Louder! Louder please!

THE STEP-DAUGHTER (leaving MADAME PACE, who smiles a Sphinx-like smile, and advancing towards the ACTORS). Louder? Louder? What are you talking about? These aren't matters which can be shouted at the top of one's voice. If I have spoken them out loud, it was to shame him and have my revenge. (Indicates FATHER.) But for Madame it's quite a different matter.

THE MANAGER. Indeed? indeed? But here, you know, people have got to make themselves heard, my dear. Even we who are on the stage can't hear you. What will it be when the public's in the theatre? And anyway, you can very well speak up now among yourselves, since we shan't be present to listen to you as we are now. You've got to pretend to be alone in a room at the back of a shop where no one can hear you.

(THE STEP-DAUGHTER coquettishly and with a touch of malice makes a sign of disagreement two or three times with her finger.)

THE MANAGER. What do you mean by no?

THE STEP-DAUGHTER (sotto voce, mysteriously). There's someone who will hear us if she (indicating MADAME PACE) speaks out loud.

THE MANAGER (in consternation). What? Have you got someone else to spring on us now? (The ACTORS burst out laughing.)

THE FATHER. No, no sir. She is alluding to me. I've got to be here—there behind that door, in waiting; and Madame Pace knows it. In fact, if you will allow me, I'll go there at once, so I can be quite ready. (Moves away.)

THE MANAGER (stopping him). No! Wait! wait! We must observe the conventions of the theatre. Before you are ready . . .

THE STEP-DAUGHTER (interrupting him). No, get on with it at once! I'm just dying, I tell you, to act this scene. If he's ready, I'm more than ready.

THE MANAGER (shouting). But, my dear young lady, first of all, we must have the scene between you and this lady . . . (indicates MADAME PACE). Do you understand? . . .

THE STEP-DAUGHTER. Good Heavens! She's been telling me what you know already: that mamma's work is badly done again, that the material's ruined; and that if I want her to continue to help us in our misery I must be patient . . .

MADAME PACE (*coming forward with an air of great importance*). Yes indeed, sir, I no wanta take advantage of her, I no wanta be hard . . .

> (*Note.* MADAME PACE *is supposed to talk in a jargon half Italian, half English.*)

THE MANAGER (*alarmed*). What? What? She talks like that? (*The* ACTORS *burst out laughing again.*)

THE STEP-DAUGHTER (*also laughing*). Yes yes, that's the way she talks, half English, half Italian! Most comical it is!

MADAME PACE. Itta seem not verra polite gentlemen laugha atta me eef I trya best speaka English.

THE MANAGER. *Diamine!*[5] Of course! Of course! Let her talk like that! Just what we want. Talk just like that, Madame, if you please! The effect will be certain. Exactly what was wanted to put a little comic relief into the crudity of the situation. Of course she talks like that! Magnificent!

THE STEP-DAUGHTER. Magnificent? Certainly! When certain suggestions are made to one in language of that kind, the effect is certain, since it seems almost a joke. One feels inclined to laugh when one hears her talk about an "old signore" "who wanta talka nicely with you." Nice old signore, eh, Madame?

MADAME PACE. Not so old my dear, not so old! And even if you no lika him, he won't make any scandal!

THE MOTHER (*jumping up amid the amazement and consternation of the* ACTORS *who had not been noticing her. They move to restrain her*). You old devil! You murderess!

THE STEP-DAUGHTER (*running over to calm her* MOTHER). Calm yourself, Mother, calm yourself! Please don't . . .

THE FATHER (*going to her also at the same time*). Calm yourself! Don't get excited! Sit down now!

THE MOTHER. Well then, take that woman away out of my sight!

THE STEP-DAUGHTER (*to* MANAGER). It is impossible for my mother to remain here.

---

[5] *Diamine* the deuce! What the dickens !

THE FATHER (*to* MANAGER). They can't be here together. And for this reason, you see: that woman there was not with us when we came. . . . If they are on together, the whole thing is given away inevitably, as you see.

THE MANAGER. It doesn't matter. This is only a first rough sketch—just to get an idea of the various points of the scene, even confusedly . . . (*turning to* THE MOTHER *and leading her to her chair*). Come along, my dear lady, sit down now, and let's get on with the scene . . .

> (*Meanwhile,* THE STEP-DAUGHTER, *coming forward again, turns to* MADAME PACE.)

THE STEP-DAUGHTER. Come on, Madame, come on!

MADAME PACE (*offended*). No, no, *grazie*! I not do anything witha your mother present.

THE STEP-DAUGHTER. Nonsense! Introduce this "old signore" who wants to talk nicely to me. (*Addressing the company imperiously.*) We've got to do this scene one way or another, haven't we? Come on! (*To* MADAME PACE.) You can go!

MADAME PACE. Ah yes! I go'way! I go'way! Certainly! (*Exits furious.*)

THE STEP-DAUGHTER (*to* THE FATHER). Now you make your entry. No, you needn't go over here. Come here. Let's suppose you've already come in. Like that, yes! I'm here with bowed head, modest like. Come on! Out with your voice! Say "Good morning, Miss" in that peculiar tone, that special tone . . .

THE MANAGER. Excuse me, but are you the Manager, or am I? (*To* THE FATHER, *who looks undecided and perplexed.*) Get on with it, man! Go down there to the back of the stage. You needn't go off. Then come right forward here.

> (THE FATHER *does as he is told, looking troubled and perplexed at first. But as soon as he begins to move, the reality of the action affects him, and he begins to smile and to be more natural. The* ACTORS *watch intently.*)

THE MANAGER (*sotto voce, quickly to the* PROMPTER *in his box*). Ready! ready? Get ready to write now.

THE FATHER (*coming forward and speaking in a different tone*). Good afternoon, Miss!

THE STEP-DAUGHTER (*head bowed down*

*slightly with restrained disgust*). Good afternoon!

THE FATHER (*looks under her hat which partly covers her face. Perceiving she is very young, he makes an exclamation, partly of surprise, partly of fear lest he compromise himself in a risky adventure*). Ah . . . but . . . ah . . . I say . . . this is not the first time that you have come here, is it?

THE STEP-DAUGHTER (*modestly*). No sir.

THE FATHER. You've been here before, eh? (*Then seeing her nod agreement.*) More than once? (*Waits for her to answer, looks under her hat, smiles, and then says.*) Well then, there's no need to be so shy, is there? May I take off your hat?

THE STEP-DAUGHTER (*anticipating him and with veiled disgust*). No sir . . . I'll do it myself. (*Takes it off quickly.*)

(THE MOTHER, *who watches the progress of the scene with* THE SON *and the other two children who cling to her, is on thorns; and follows with varying expressions of sorrow, indignation, anxiety, and horror the words and actions of the other two. From time to time she hides her face in her hands and sobs.*)

THE MOTHER. Oh, my God, my God!

THE FATHER (*playing his part with a touch of gallantry*). Give it to me! I'll put it down. (*Takes hat from her hands.*) But a dear little head like yours ought to have a smarter hat. Come and help me choose one from the stock, won't you?

L'INGÉNUE (*interrupting*). I say . . . those are our hats you know.

THE MANAGER (*furious*). Silence! silence! Don't try and be funny, if you please. . . . We're playing the scene now I'd have you notice. (*To* THE STEP-DAUGHTER.) Begin again, please!

THE STEP-DAUGHTER (*continuing*). No thank you, sir.

THE FATHER. Oh, come now. Don't talk like that. You must take it. I shall be upset if you don't. There are some lovely little hats here; and then—Madame will be pleased. She expects it, anyway, you know.

THE STEP-DAUGHTER. No, no! I couldn't wear it!

THE FATHER. Oh, you're thinking about what they'd say at home if they saw you come in with a new hat? My dear girl, there's always a way round these little matters you know.

THE STEP-DAUGHTER (*all keyed up*). No, it's not that I couldn't wear it because I am . . . as you see . . . you might have noticed . . . (*Showing her black dress.*)

THE FATHER. . . . in mourning! Of course: I beg your pardon: I'm frightfully sorry . . .

THE STEP-DAUGHTER (*forcing herself to conquer her indignation and nausea*). Stop! Stop! It's I who must thank you. There's no need for you to feel mortified or specially sorry. Don't think any more of what I've said. (*Tries to smile.*) I must forget that I am dressed so . . .

THE MANAGER (*interrupting and turning to the* PROMPTER). Stop a minute! Stop! Don't write that down. Cut out that last bit. (*Then to* THE FATHER *and* STEP-DAUGHTER.) Fine! it's going fine! (*To* THE FATHER *only.*) And now you can go on as we arranged. (*To the* ACTORS.) Pretty good that scene, where he offers her the hat, eh?

THE STEP-DAUGHTER. The best's coming now. Why can't we go on?

THE MANAGER. Have a little patience! (*To the* ACTORS.) Of course, it must be treated rather lightly.

LEADING MAN. Still, with a bit of go in it!

LEADING LADY. Of course! It's easy enough! (*To* LEADING MAN.) Shall you and I try it now?

LEADING MAN. Why, yes! I'll prepare my entrance. (*Exit in order to make his entrance.*)

THE MANAGER (*to* LEADING LADY). See here! The scene between you and Madame Pace is finished. I'll have it written out properly after. You remain here . . . oh, where are you going?

LEADING LADY. One minute. I want to put my hat on again. (*Goes over to hat-rack and puts her hat on her head.*)

THE MANAGER. Good! You stay here with your head bowed down a bit.

THE STEP-DAUGHTER. But she isn't dressed in black.

LEADING LADY. But I shall be, and much more effectively than you.

THE MANAGER (*to* STEP-DAUGHTER). Be quiet please, and watch! You'll be able to learn something. (*Clapping his hands.*) Come on! come on! Entrance, please!

> (*The door at rear of stage opens, and the* LEADING MAN *enters with the lively manner of an old gallant. The rendering of the scene by the* ACTORS *from the very first words is seen to be quite a different thing, though it has not in any way the air of a parody. Naturally,* THE STEP-DAUGHTER *and* THE FATHER, *not being able to recognize themselves in the* LEADING LADY *and the* LEADING MAN, *who deliver their words in different tones and with a different psychology, express, sometimes with smiles, sometimes with gestures, the impression they receive.*)

LEADING MAN. Good afternoon, Miss . . .

THE FATHER (*at once unable to contain himself*). No! no!

> (THE STEP-DAUGHTER *noticing the way the* LEADING MAN *enters, bursts out laughing.*)

THE MANAGER (*furious*). Silence! And you please just stop that laughing. If we go on like this, we shall never finish.

THE STEP-DAUGHTER. Forgive me, sir, but it's natural enough. This lady (*indicating* LEADING LADY) stands there still; but if she is supposed to be me, I can assure you that if I heard anyone say "Good afternoon" in that manner and in that tone, I should burst out laughing as I did.

THE FATHER. Yes, yes, the manner, the tone . . .

THE MANAGER. Nonsense! Rubbish! Stand aside and let me see the action.

LEADING MAN. If I've got to represent an old fellow who's coming into a house of an equivocal character . . .

THE MANAGER. Don't listen to them, for Heaven's sake! Do it again! It goes fine. (*Waiting for the* ACTORS *to begin again.*) Well?

LEADING MAN. Good afternoon, Miss.

LEADING LADY. Good afternoon.

LEADING MAN (*imitating the gesture of* THE FATHER *when he looked under the hat, and then expressing quite clearly first satisfaction and then fear*). Ah, but . . . I say . . . this is not the first time that you have come here, is it?

THE MANAGER. Good, but not quite so heavily. Like this. (*Acts himself.*) "This isn't the first time that you have come here." . . .

(*To* LEADING LADY.) And you say: "No, sir."

LEADING LADY. No, sir.

LEADING MAN. You've been here before, more than once.

THE MANAGER. No, no, stop! Let her nod "yes" first. "You've been here before, eh?" (*The* LEADING LADY *lifts up her head slightly and closes her eyes as though in disgust. Then she inclines her head twice.*)

THE STEP-DAUGHTER (*unable to contain herself*). Oh my God! (*Puts a hand to her mouth to prevent herself from laughing.*)

THE MANAGER (*turning round*). What's the matter?

THE STEP-DAUGHTER. Nothing, nothing!

THE MANAGER (*to* LEADING MAN). Go on!

LEADING MAN. You've been here before, eh? Well then, there's no need to be so shy, is there? May I take off your hat?

> (*The* LEADING MAN *says this last speech in such a tone and with such gestures that* THE STEP-DAUGHTER, *though she has her hand to her mouth, cannot keep from laughing.*)

LEADING LADY (*indignant*). I'm not going to stop here to be made a fool of by that woman there.

LEADING MAN. Neither am I! I'm through with it!

THE MANAGER (*shouting to* STEP-DAUGHTER). Silence! for once and all, I tell you!

THE STEP-DAUGHTER. Forgive me! forgive me!

THE MANAGER. You haven't any manners: that's what it is! You go too far.

THE FATHER (*endeavouring to intervene*). Yes, it's true, but excuse her . . .

THE MANAGER. Excuse what? It's absolutely disgusting.

THE FATHER. Yes, sir, but believe me, it has such a strange effect when . . .

THE MANAGER. Strange? Why strange? Where is it strange?

THE FATHER. No, sir; I admire your actors —this gentleman here, this lady; but they are certainly not us!

THE MANAGER. I should hope not. Evidently they can not be you, if they are actors.

THE FATHER. Just so: actors! Both of them act our parts exceedingly well. But, believe me, it produces quite a different effect on us.

They want to be us, but they aren't, all the same.

THE MANAGER. What is it then anyway?

THE FATHER. Something that is . . . that is theirs—and no longer ours . . .

THE MANAGER. But naturally, inevitably. I've told you so already.

THE FATHER. Yes, I understand . . . I understand . . .

THE MANAGER. Well then, let's have no more of it! (*Turning to the* ACTORS.) We'll have the rehearsals by ourselves, afterwards, in the ordinary way. I never could stand rehearsing with the author present. He's never satisfied! (*Turning to* FATHER *and* STEP-DAUGHTER.) Come on! Let's get on with it again; and try and see if you can't keep from laughing.

THE STEP-DAUGHTER. Oh, I shan't laugh any more. There's a nice little bit coming for me now: you'll see.

THE MANAGER. Well then: when she says "Don't think any more of what I've said. I must forget, etc.," you (*addressing* THE FATHER) come in sharp with "I understand, I understand"; and then you ask her . . .

THE STEP-DAUGHTER (*interrupting*). What?

THE MANAGER. Why she is in mourning.

THE STEP-DAUGHTER. Not at all! See here: when I told him that it was useless for me to be thinking about my wearing mourning, do you know how he answered me? "Ah well," he said, "then let's take off this little frock."

THE MANAGER. Great! Just what we want, to make a riot in the theatre!

THE STEP-DAUGHTER. But it's the truth!

THE MANAGER. What does that matter? Acting is our business here. Truth up to a certain point, but no further.

THE STEP-DAUGHTER. What do you want to do then?

THE MANAGER. You'll see, you'll see! Leave it to me.

THE STEP-DAUGHTER. No sir! What you want to do is to piece together a little romantic sentimental scene out of my disgust, out of all the reasons, each more cruel and viler than the other, why I am what I am. He is to ask me why I'm in mourning; and I'm to answer with tears in my eyes, that it is just two months, since papa died. No sir, no! He's got to say to me; as he did say: "Well, let's take off this little dress at once." And I; with my two months' mourning in my heart, went there behind that screen, and with these fingers tingling with shame . . .

THE MANAGER (*running his hands through his hair*). For Heaven's sake! What are you saying?

THE STEP-DAUGHTER (*crying out excitedly*). The truth! The truth!

THE MANAGER. It may be. I don't deny it, and I can understand all your horror; but you must surely see that you can't have this kind of thing on the stage. It won't go.

THE STEP-DAUGHTER. Not possible, eh? Very well! I'm much obliged to you—but I'm off!

THE MANAGER. Now be reasonable! Don't lose your temper!

THE STEP-DAUGHTER. I won't stop here! I won't! I can see you've fixed it all up with him in your office. All this talk about what is possible for the stage . . . I understand! He wants to get at his complicated "cerebral drama," to have his famous remorses and torments acted; but I want to act my part, *my part!*

THE MANAGER (*annoyed, shaking his shoulders*). Ah! Just *your* part! But, if you will pardon me, there are other parts than yours: His (*indicating* THE FATHER) and hers! (*Indicating* THE MOTHER.) On the stage you can't have a character becoming too prominent and overshadowing all the others. The thing is to pack them all into a neat little framework and then act what is actable. I am aware of the fact that everyone has his own interior life which he wants very much to put forward. But the difficulty lies in this fact: to set out just so much as is necessary for the stage, taking the other characters into consideration, and at the same time hint at the unrevealed interior life of each. I am willing to admit, my dear young lady, that from your point of view it would be a fine idea if each character could tell the public all his troubles in a nice monologue or a regular one hour lecture. (*Good humoredly.*) You must restrain yourself, my dear, and in your own interest, too; because this fury of yours, this exaggerated disgust you show, may make a bad impression, you know. After you have confessed to me that there were others before him at Madame Pace's and more than once.

THE STEP-DAUGHTER (*bowing her head, impressed*). It's true. But remember those others mean him for me all the same.

THE MANAGER (*not understanding*). What? The others? What do you mean?

THE STEP-DAUGHTER. For one who has gone wrong, sir, he who was responsible for the first fault is responsible for all that follow. He is responsible for my faults, was, even before I was born. Look at him, and see if it isn't true!

THE MANAGER. Well, well! And does the weight of so much responsiblity seem nothing to you? Give him a chance to act it, to get it over!

THE STEP-DAUGHTER. How? How can he act all his "noble remorses," all his "moral torments," if you want to spare him the horror of being discovered one day—after he had asked her what he did ask her—in the arms of her, that already fallen woman, that child, sir, that child he used to watch come out of school? (*She is moved.*)

(THE MOTHER *at this point is overcome with emotion, and breaks out into a fit of crying. All are touched. A long pause.*)

THE STEP-DAUGHTER (*as soon as* THE MOTHER *becomes a little quieter, adds resolutely and gravely*). At present, we are unknown to the public. Tomorrow, you will act us as you wish, treating us in your own manner. But do you really want to see drama, do you want to see it flash out as it really did?

THE MANAGER. Of course! That's just what I do want, so I can use as much of it as is possible.

THE STEP-DAUGHTER. Well then, ask that Mother there to leave us.

THE MOTHER (*changing her low plaint into a sharp cry*). No! No! Don't permit it, sir, don't permit it!

THE MANAGER. But it's only to try it.

THE MOTHER. I can't bear it. I can't.

THE MANAGER. But since it has happened already . . . I don't understand!

THE MOTHER. It's taking place now. It happens all the time. My torment isn't a pretended one. I live and feel every minute of my torture. Those two children there—have you heard them speak? They can't speak any more. They cling to me to keep up my torment actual and vivid for me. But for themselves, they do not exist, they aren't any more. And she (*indicating* THE STEP-DAUGHTER) has run away, she has left me, and is lost. If I now see her here before me, it is only to renew for me the tortures I have suffered for her too.

THE FATHER. The eternal moment! She (*indicating* THE STEP-DAUGHTER) is here to catch me, fix me, and hold me eternally in the stocks for that one fleeting and shameful moment of my life. She can't give it up! And you sir, cannot either fairly spare me it.

THE MANAGER. I never said I didn't want to act it. It will form, as a matter of fact, the nucleus of the whole first act right up to her surprise. (*Indicates* THE MOTHER.)

THE FATHER. Just so! This is my punishment: the passion in all of us that must culminate in her final cry.

THE STEP-DAUGHTER. I can hear it still in my ears. It's driven me mad, that cry!— You can put me on as you like; it doesn't matter. Fully dressed, if you like—provided I have at least the arm bare; because, standing like this (*she goes close to* THE FATHER *and leans her head on his breast*) with my head so, and my arms round his neck, I saw a vein pulsing in my arm here; and then, as if that live vein had awakened disgust in me, I closed my eyes like this, and let my head sink on his breast. (*Turning to* THE MOTHER.) Cry out mother! Cry out! (*Buries head in* FATHER'S *breast, and with her shoulders raised as if to prevent her hearing the cry, adds in tones of intense emotion.*) Cry out as you did then!

THE MOTHER (*coming forward to separate them*). No! My daughter, my daughter! (*And after having pulled her away from him.*) You brute! you brute! She is my daughter! Don't you see she's my daughter?

THE MANAGER (*walking backwards towards footlights*). Fine! fine! Damned good! And then, of course—curtain!

THE FATHER (*going towards him excitedly*).

Yes, of course, because that's the way it really happened.

THE MANAGER (*convinced and pleased*). Oh, yes, no doubt about it. Curtain here, curtain! (*At the reiterated cry of* THE MANAGER, *the* MACHINIST *lets the curtain down, leaving the* MANAGER *and* THE FATHER *in front of it before the footlights.*)

THE MANAGER. The darned idiot! I said "curtain" to show the act should end there, and he goes and lets it down in earnest. (*To* THE FATHER, *while he pulls the curtain back to go on to the stage again.*) Yes, yes, it's all right. Effect certain! That's the right ending. I'll guarantee the first act at any rate.

## ACT III

*When the curtain goes up again, it is seen that the stage hands have shifted the bit of scenery used in the last part, and have rigged up instead at the back of the stage a drop, with some trees, and one or two wings. A portion of a fountain basin is visible.* THE MOTHER *is sitting on the right with the two children by her side.* THE SON *is on the same side, but away from the others. He seems bored, angry, and full of shame.* THE FATHER *and* THE STEP-DAUGHTER *are also seated towards the right front. On the other side* (*left*) *are the* ACTORS, *much in the positions they occupied before the curtain was lowered. Only* THE MANAGER *is standing up in the middle of the stage, with his hand closed over his mouth in the act of meditating.*

THE MANAGER (*shaking his shoulders after a brief pause*). Ah yes: the second act! Leave it to me, leave it all to me as we arranged, and you'll see! It'll go fine!

THE STEP-DAUGHTER. Our entry into his house (*indicates* FATHER) in spite of him . . . (*indicates* THE SON).

THE MANAGER (*out of patience*). Leave it to me, I tell you!

THE STEP-DAUGHTER. Do let it be clear, at any rate, that it is in spite of my wishes.

THE MOTHER (*from her corner, shaking her head*). For all the good that's come of it . . .

THE STEP-DAUGHTER (*turning towards her quickly*). It doesn't matter. The more harm done us, the more remorse for him.

THE MANAGER (*impatiently*). I understand!

Good Heavens! I understand! I'm taking it into account.

THE MOTHER (*supplicatingly*). I beg you, sir, to let it appear quite plain that for conscience' sake I did try in every way . . .

THE STEP-DAUGHTER (*interrupting indignantly and continuing for* THE MOTHER). . . . to pacify me, to dissuade me from spiting him. (*To* MANAGER.) Do as she wants: satisfy her, because it is true! I enjoy it immensely. Anyhow, as you can see, the meeker she is, the more she tries to get at his heart, the more distant and aloof does he become.

THE MANAGER. Are we going to begin this second act or not?

THE STEP-DAUGHTER. I'm not going to talk any more now. But I must tell you this: you can't have the whole action take place in the garden, as you suggest. It isn't possible!

THE MANAGER. Why not?

THE STEP-DAUGHTER. Because he (*indicates* THE SON *again*) is always shut up alone in his room. And then there's all the part of that poor dazed-looking boy there which takes place indoors.

THE MANAGER. Maybe! On the other hand, you will understand—we can't change scenes three or four times in one act.

THE LEADING MAN. They used to once.

THE MANAGER. Yes, when the public was up to the level of that child there.

THE LEADING LADY. It makes the illusion easier.

THE FATHER (*irritated*). The illusion! For Heaven's sake, don't say illusion. Please don't use that word, which is particularly painful for us.

THE MANAGER (*astounded*). And why, if you please?

THE FATHER. It's painful, cruel, really cruel; and you ought to understand that.

THE MANAGER. But why? What ought we to say then? The illusion, I tell you, sir, which we've got to create for the audience . . .

THE LEADING MAN. With our acting.

THE MANAGER. The illusion of a reality.

THE FATHER. I understand; but you, perhaps, do not understand us. Forgive me! You see . . . here for you and your actors, the thing is only—and rightly so . . . a kind of game . . .

THE LEADING LADY (*interrupting indignantly*). A game! We're not children here, if you please! We are serious actors.

THE FATHER. I don't deny it. What I mean is the game, or play, of your art, which has to give, as the gentleman says, a perfect illusion of reality.

THE MANAGER. Precisely—!

THE FATHER. Now, if you consider the fact that we (*indicates himself and the other five* CHARACTERS), as we are, have no other reality outside of this illusion . . .

THE MANAGER (*astonished, looking at his* ACTORS, *who are also amazed*). And what does that mean?

THE FATHER (*after watching them for a moment with a wan smile*). As I say, sir, that which is a game of art for you is our sole reality. (*Brief pause. He goes a step or two nearer* THE MANAGER *and adds.*) But not only for us, you know, by the way. Just you think it over well. (*Looks him in the eyes.*) Can you tell me who you are?

THE MANAGER (*perplexed, half smiling*). What? Who am I? I am myself.

THE FATHER. And if I were to tell you that that isn't true, because you and I . . . ?

THE MANAGER. I should say you were mad—! (*The* ACTORS *laugh.*)

THE FATHER. You're quite right to laugh: because we are all making believe here. (*To* MANAGER.) And you can therefore object that it's only for a joke that that gentleman there (*indicates the* LEADING MAN), who naturally is himself, has to be me, who am on the contrary myself—this thing you see here. You see I've caught you in a trap! (*The* ACTORS *laugh.*)

THE MANAGER (*annoyed*). But we've had all this over once before. Do you want to begin again?

THE FATHER. No, no! That wasn't my meaning! In fact, I should like to request you to abandon this game of art (*looking at the* LEADING LADY *as if anticipating her*) which you are accustomed to play here with your actors, and to ask you seriously once again: who are you?

THE MANAGER (*astonished and irritated, turning to his* ACTORS). If this fellow here hasn't got a nerve! A man who calls himself a character comes and asks me who I am!

THE FATHER (*with dignity, but not offended*). A character, sir, may always ask a man who he is. Because a character has really a life of his own, marked with his especial characteristics; for which reason he is always "somebody." But a man—I'm not speaking of you now—may very well be "nobody."

THE MANAGER. Yes, but you are asking these questions of me, the boss, the manager! Do you understand?

THE FATHER. But only in order to know if you, as you really are now, see yourself as you once were with all the illusions that were yours then, with all the things both inside and outside of you as they seemed to you—as they were then indeed for you. Well, sir, if you think of all those illusions that mean nothing to you now, of all those things which don't even *seem* to you to exist any more, while once they *were* for you, don't you feel that—I won't say these boards —but the very earth under your feet is sinking away from you when you reflect that in the same way this *you* as you feel it today—all this present reality of yours—is fated to seem a mere illusion to you tomorrow?

THE MANAGER (*without having understood much, but astonished by the specious argument*). Well, well! And where does all this take us anyway?

THE FATHER. Oh, nowhere! It's only to show you that if we (*indicating the* CHARACTERS) have no other reality beyond the illusion, you too must not count overmuch on your reality as you feel it today, since, like that of yesterday, it may prove an illusion for you tomorrow.

THE MANAGER (*determining to make fun of him*). Ah, excellent! Then you'll be saying next that you, with this comedy of yours that you brought here to act, are truer and more real than I am.

THE FATHER (*with the greatest seriousness*). But of course; without doubt!

THE MANAGER. Ah, really?

THE FATHER. Why, I thought you'd understand that from the beginning.

THE MANAGER. More real than I?

THE FATHER. If your reality can change from one day to another . . .

THE MANAGER. But everyone knows it

can change. It is always changing, the same as anyone else's.

THE FATHER (*with a cry*). No, sir, not ours! Look here! That is the very difference! Our reality doesn't change: it can't change! It can't be other than what it is, because it is already fixed for ever. It's terrible. Ours is an immutable reality which should make you shudder when you approach us if you are really conscious of the fact that your reality is a mere transitory and fleeting illusion, taking this form today and that tomorrow, according to the conditions, according to your will, your sentiments, which in turn are controlled by an intellect that shows them to you today in one manner and tomorrow . . . who knows how? . . . Illusions of reality represented in this fatuous comedy of life that never ends, nor can ever end! Because if tomorrow it were to end . . . then why, all would be finished.

THE MANAGER. Oh for God's sake, will you *at least* finish with this philosophizing and let us try and shape this comedy which you yourself have brought me here? You argue and philosophize a bit too much, my dear sir. You know you seem to me almost, almost . . . (*stops and looks him over from head to foot*). Ah, by the way, I think you introduced yourself to me as a—what shall . . . we say—a "character," created by an author who did not afterward care to make a drama of his own creations.

THE FATHER. It is the simple truth, sir.

THE MANAGER. Nonsense! Cut that out, please! None of us believes it, because it isn't a thing, as you must recognize yourself, which one can believe seriously. If you want to know, it seems to me you are trying to imitate the manner of a certain author whom I heartily detest—I warn you—although I have unfortunately bound myself to put on one of his works. As a matter of fact, I was just starting to rehearse it, when you arrived. (*Turning to the* ACTORS.) And this is what we've gained—out of the frying-pan into the fire!

THE FATHER. I don't know to what author you may be alluding, but believe me I feel what I think; and I seem to be philosophizing only for those who do not think what they feel, because they blind themselves with their own sentiment. I know that for many people this self-blinding seems much more "human"; but the contrary is really true. For man never reasons so much and becomes so introspective as when he suffers; since he is anxious to get at the cause of his sufferings, to learn who has produced them, and whether it is just or unjust that he should have to bear them. On the other hand, when he is happy, he takes his happiness as it comes and doesn't analyze it, just as if happiness were his right. The animals suffer without reasoning about their sufferings. But take the case of a man who suffers and begins to reason about it. Oh no! it can't be allowed! Let him suffer like an animal, and then—ah yes, he is "human"!

THE MANAGER. Look here! Look here! You're off again, philosophizing worse than ever.

THE FATHER. Because I suffer, sir! I'm not philosophizing: I'm crying aloud the reason of my sufferings.

THE MANAGER (*makes brusque movement as he is taken with a new idea*). I should like to know if anyone has ever heard of a character who gets right out of his part and perorates and speechifies as you do. Have you ever heard of a case? I haven't.

THE FATHER. You have never met such a case, sir, because authors, as a rule, hide the labour of their creations. When the characters are really alive before their author, the latter does nothing but follow them in their action, in their words, in the situations which they suggest to him; and he has to will them the way they will themselves—for there's trouble if he doesn't. When a character is born, he acquires at once such an independence, even of his own author, that he can be imagined by everybody even in many other situations where the author never dreamed of placing him; and so he acquires for himself a meaning which the author never thought of giving him.

THE MANAGER. Yes, yes, I know this.

THE FATHER. What is there then to marvel at in us? Imagine such a misfortune for characters as I have described to you: to be born of an author's fantasy, and be denied life by him; and then answer me if these characters left alive, and yet without life, weren't right in doing what they did do and are doing now, after they have attempted everything in their power to persuade him to give them their stage life. We've all tried him in turn, I, she (*indicating* THE STEP-DAUGHTER) and she (*indicating* THE MOTHER).

THE STEP-DAUGHTER. It's true. I too have sought to tempt him, many, many times, when he has been sitting at his writing table, feeling a bit melancholy, at the twilight hour. He would sit in his armchair too lazy to switch on the light, and all the shadows that crept into his room were full of our presence coming to tempt him. (*As if she saw herself still there by the writing table, and was annoyed by the presence of the* ACTORS.) Oh, if you would only go away, go away and leave us alone—mother here with that son of hers—I with that Child—that Boy there always alone—and then I with him (*just hints at* THE FATHER)—and then I alone, alone . . . in those shadows! (*Makes a sudden movement as if in the vision she has of herself illuminating those shadows she wanted to seize hold of herself.*) Ah! my life! my life! Oh, what scenes we proposed to him—and I tempted him more than any of the others!

THE FATHER. Maybe. But perhaps it was your fault that he refused to give us life: because you were too insistent, too troublesome.

THE STEP-DAUGHTER. Nonsense! Didn't he make me so himself? (*Goes close to* THE MANAGER *to tell him as if in confidence.*) In my opinion he abandoned us in a fit of depression, of disgust for the ordinary theatre as the public knows it and likes it.

THE SON. Exactly what it was, sir; exactly that!

THE FATHER. Not at all! Don't believe it for a minute. Listen to me! You'll be doing quite right to modify, as you suggest, the excesses both of this girl here, who wants to do too much, and of this young man, who won't do anything at all.

THE SON. No, nothing!

THE MANAGER. You too get over the mark occasionally, my dear sir, if I may say so.

THE FATHER. I? When? Where?

THE MANAGER. Always! Continuously! Then there's this insistence of yours in trying to make us believe you are a character. And then too, you must really argue and philosophize less, you know, much less.

THE FATHER. Well, if you want to take away from me the possibility of representing the torment of my spirit which never gives me peace, you will be suppressing me: that's all. Every true man, sir, who is a little above the level of the beasts and plants does not live for the sake of living, without knowing how to live; but he lives so as to give a meaning and a value of his own to life. For me this is *everything*. I cannot give up this, just to represent a mere fact as she (*indicating* THE STEP-DAUGHTER) wants. It's all very well for her, since her "vendetta" lies in the "fact." I'm not going to do it. It destroys my *raison d'être*.

THE MANAGER. Your *raison d'être*! Oh, we're going ahead fine! First she starts off, and then you jump in. At this rate, we'll never finish.

THE FATHER. Now, don't be offended! Have it your own way—provided, however, that within the limits of the parts you assign us each one's sacrifice isn't too great.

THE MANAGER. You've got to understand that you can't go on arguing at your own pleasure. Drama is action, sir, action and not confounded philosophy.

THE FATHER. All right. I'll do just as much arguing and philosophizing as everybody does when he is considering his own torments.

THE MANAGER. If the drama permits! But for Heaven's sake, man, let's get along and come to the scene.

THE STEP-DAUGHTER. It seems to me we've got too much action with our coming into his house. (*Indicating* FATHER.) You said, before, you couldn't change the scene every five minutes.

THE MANAGER. Of course not. What we've got to do is to combine and group up all the facts in one simultaneous, close-knit, action. We can't have it as you want, with your little brother wandering like a ghost from room to room, hiding behind doors and meditating a project which—what did you say it did to him?

THE STEP-DAUGHTER. Consumes him, sir, wastes him away!

THE MANAGER. Well, it may be. And then at the same time, you want the little girl there to be playing in the garden . . . one in the house, and the other in the garden: isn't that it?

THE STEP-DAUGHTER. Yes, in the sun; in the sun! That is my only pleasure: to see her happy and careless in the garden after the misery and squalor of the horrible room where we all four slept together. And I had to sleep with her—I, do you understand?—with my vile contaminated body next to hers; with her folding me fast in her loving little arms. In the garden, whenever she spied me, she would run to take me by the hand. She didn't care for the big flowers, only the little ones; and she loved to show me them and pet me.

THE MANAGER. Well then, we'll have it in the garden. Everything shall happen in the garden; and we'll group the other scenes there. (*Calls a* STAGE HAND.) Here, a backcloth with trees and something to do as a fountain basin. (*Turning round to look at the back of the stage.*) Ah, you've fixed it up. Good! (*To* STEP-DAUGHTER.) This is just to give an idea, of course. The Boy, instead of hiding behind the doors, will wander about here in the garden, hiding behind the trees. But it's going to be rather difficult to find a child to do that scene with you where she shows you the flowers. (*Turning to* THE BOY.) Come forward a little, will you please? Let's try it now! Come along! come along! (*Then seeing him come shyly forward, full of fear and looking lost.*) It's a nice business, this lad here. What's the matter with him? We'll have to give him a word or two to say. (*Goes close to him, puts a hand on his shoulders, and leads him behind one of the trees.*) Come on! come on! Let me see you a little! Hide here . . . yes, like that. Try and show your head just a little as if you were looking for someone. . . . (*Goes back to observe the effect, when* THE BOY *at once goes through the action.*) Excellent! fine! (*Turning to* STEP-DAUGHTER.) Suppose the little girl there were to surprise him as he looks round, and run over to him, so we could give him a word or two to say?

THE STEP-DAUGHTER. It's useless to hope he will speak, as long as that fellow there is here . . . (*indicates* THE SON). You must send him away first.

THE SON (*jumping up*). Delighted! Delighted! I don't ask for anything better. (*Begins to move away.*)

THE MANAGER (*at once stopping him*). No! No! Where are you going? Wait a bit!

(THE MOTHER *gets up alarmed and terrified at the thought that he is really about to go away. Instinctively she lifts her arms to prevent him, without, however, leaving her seat.*)

THE SON (*to* MANAGER *who stops him*). I've got nothing to do with this affair. Let me go please! Let me go!

THE MANAGER. What do you mean by saying you've got nothing to do with this?

THE STEP-DAUGHTER (*calmly, with irony*). Don't bother to stop him: he won't go away.

THE FATHER. He has to act the terrible scene in the garden with his mother.

THE SON (*suddenly resolute and with dignity*). I shall act nothing at all. I've said so from the very beginning. (*To* THE MANAGER.) Let me go!

THE STEP-DAUGHTER (*going over to* THE MANAGER). Allow me? (*Puts down* THE MANAGER'S *arm which is restraining* THE SON.) Well, go away then, if you want to! (THE SON *looks at her with contempt and hatred. She laughs and says.*) You see, he can't, he can't go away! He is obliged to stay here, indissolubly bound to the chain. If I, who fly off when that happens which has to happen, because I can't bear him—if I am still here and support that face and expression of his, you can well imagine that he is unable to move. He has to remain here, has to stop with that nice father of his, and that mother whose only son he is. (*Turning to* THE MOTHER.) Come on, mother, come along! (*Turning to* MANAGER *to indicate her.*) You see, she was getting up to keep him back. (*To* THE MOTHER, *beckoning her with her hand.*) Come on! come on! (*Then to* MANAGER.) You can imagine how little she wants to show these actors of yours what she really feels; but so eager is she to get near him that. . . . There, you see? She is willing to act her part. (*And in fact,* THE MOTHER *approaches him; and as soon as* THE STEP-DAUGHTER *has finished speaking, opens her arms to signify that she consents.*)

THE SON (*suddenly*). No! no! If I can't go away, then I'll stop here; but I repeat: I act nothing!

THE FATHER (*to* MANAGER *excitedly*). You can force him, sir.

THE SON. Nobody can force me.

THE FATHER. I can.

THE STEP-DAUGHTER. Wait a minute, wait. . . . First of all, the baby has to go to the fountain . . . (*runs to take* THE CHILD *and leads her to the fountain*).

THE MANAGER. Yes, yes of course; that's it. Both at the same time.

(*The* SECOND LADY LEAD *and the* JUVENILE LEAD *at this point separate themselves from the group of* ACTORS. *One watches* THE MOTHER *attentively; the other moves about studying the movements and manner of* THE SON *whom he will have to act.*)

THE SON (*to* MANAGER). What do you mean by both at the same time? It isn't right. There was no scene between me and her. (*Indicates* THE MOTHER.) Ask her how it was!

THE MOTHER. Yes, it's true. I had come into his room . . .

THE SON. Into my room, do you understand? Nothing to do with the garden.

THE MANAGER. It doesn't matter. Haven't I told you we've got to group the action?

THE SON (*observing the* JUVENILE LEAD *studying him*). What do you want?

THE JUVENILE LEAD. Nothing! I was just looking at you.

THE SON (*turning towards the* SECOND LADY LEAD). Ah! she's at it too: re-act her part! (*Indicating* THE MOTHER.)

THE MANAGER. Exactly! And it seems to me that you ought to be grateful to them for their interest.

THE SON. Yes, but haven't you yet perceived that it isn't possible to live in front of a mirror which not only freezes us with the image of ourselves, but throws our likeness back at us with a horrible grimace?

THE FATHER. That is true, absolutely true. You must see that.

THE MANAGER (*to* SECOND LADY LEAD *and* JUVENILE LEAD). He's right! Move away from them!

THE SON. Do as you like. I'm out of this!

THE MANAGER. Be quiet, you, will you? And let me hear your mother! (*To* MOTHER.) You were saying you had entered . . .

THE MOTHER. Yes, into his room, because I couldn't stand it any longer. I went to empty my heart to him of all the anguish that tortures me . . . . But as soon as he saw me come in . . .

THE SON. Nothing happened! There was no scene. I went away, that's all! I don't care for scenes!

THE MOTHER. It's true, true. That's how it was.

THE MANAGER. Well now, we've got to do this bit between you and him. It's indispensable.

THE MOTHER. I'm ready . . . when you are ready. If you could only find a chance for me to tell him what I feel here in my heart.

THE FATHER (*going to* SON *in a great rage*). You'll do this for your mother, for your mother, do you understand?

THE SON (*quite determined*). I do nothing!

THE FATHER (*taking hold of him and shaking him*). For God's sake, do as I tell you! Don't you hear your mother asking you for a favor? Haven't you even got the guts to be a son?

THE SON (*taking hold of* THE FATHER). No! No! And for God's sake stop it, or else . . . (*general agitation.* THE MOTHER, *frightened, tries to separate them*).

THE MOTHER (*pleading*). Please! please!

THE FATHER (*not leaving hold of* THE SON). You've got to obey, do you hear?

THE SON (*almost crying from rage*). What does it mean, this madness you've got? (*They separate.*) Have you no decency, that you insist on showing everyone our shame? I won't do it! I won't! And I stand for the will of our author in this. He didn't want to put us on the stage, after all!

THE MANAGER. Man alive! You came here . . .

THE SON (*indicating* FATHER). He did! I didn't!

THE MANAGER. Aren't you here now?

THE SON. It was his wish, and he dragged us along with him. He's told you not only the things that did happen, but also things that have never happened at all.

THE MANAGER. Well, tell me then what did happen. You went out of your room without saying a word?

THE SON. Without a word, so as to avoid a scene!

THE MANAGER. And then what did you do?

THE SON. Nothing ... walking in the garden ... (*Hesitates for a moment with expression of gloom.*)

THE MANAGER (*coming closer to him, interested by his extraordinary reserve*). Well, well ... walking in the garden ...

THE SON (*exasperated*). Why on earth do you insist? It's horrible! (THE MOTHER *trembles, sobs, and looks towards the fountain.*)

THE MANAGER (*slowly observing the glance and turning towards* THE SON *with increasing apprehension*). The baby?

THE SON. There in the fountain ...

THE FATHER (*pointing with tender pity to* THE MOTHER). She was following him at the moment ...

THE MANAGER (*to* THE SON *anxiously*). And then you ...

THE SON. I ran over to her; I was jumping in to drag her out when I saw something that froze my blood ... the boy standing stock still, with eyes like a madman's, watching his little drowned sister, in the fountain! (THE STEP-DAUGHTER *bends over the fountain to hide* THE CHILD. *She sobs.*) Then ... (*a revolver shot rings out behind the trees where* THE BOY *is hidden*).

THE MOTHER (*with a cry of terror runs over in that direction together with several of the* ACTORS *amid general confusion*). My son! My son! (*Then amid the cries and exclamations one hears her voice.*) Help! Help!

THE MANAGER (*pushing the* ACTORS *aside while they lift up* THE BOY *and carry him off.*) Is he really wounded?

SOME ACTORS. He's dead! dead!

OTHER ACTORS. No, no, it's only make believe, it's only pretence!

THE FATHER (*with a terrible cry*). Pretence? Reality, sir, reality!

THE MANAGER. Pretence? Reality? To hell with it all! Never in my life has such a thing happened to me. I've lost a whole day over these people, a whole day!

CURTAIN.

## Selected Reading List for Pirandello

Eric Bentley, "Pirandello's Joy and Torment," *In Search of Theater*. New York: Vintage Books, 1954, pp. 279–95.

Francis Fergusson, "Action as Theatrical," *The Idea of a Theater*. New York: Doubleday Company, Inc., 1949, pp. 198–206.

Walter Starkie, *Luigi Pirandello*. Berkeley: University of California Press, 1965.

Domenico Vittorini, *The Drama of Luigi Pirandello*. New York: Dover Publications, Inc., 1957.

*appendix*

# When Acting Is an Art

## CONSTANTIN STANISLAVSKI

Today we were called together to hear the Director's criticism of our performance. He said:

"Above all look for what is fine in art and try to understand it. Therefore, we shall begin by discussing the constructive elements of the test. There are only two moments worth noting; the first when, Maria threw herself down the staircase with the despairing cry of 'Oh, help me!' and the second, more extended in time, when Kostya Nazvanov said 'Blood, Iago, blood!' In both instances, you who were playing, and we who were watching, gave ourselves up completely to what was happening on the stage. Such successful moments, by themselves, we can recognize as belonging to the art of living a part."

"And what is this art?" I asked.

"You experienced it yourself. Suppose you state what you felt."

"I neither know nor remember," said I, embarrassed by Tortsov's praise.

"What! You do not remember your own inner excitement? You do not remember that your hands, your eyes and your whole body tried to throw themselves forward to grasp something; you do not remember how you bit your lips and barely restrained your tears?"

"Now that you tell me about what happened, I seem to remember my actions," I confessed.

"But without me you could not have

understood the ways in which your feelings found expression?"

"No, I admit I couldn't."

"You were acting with your subconscious, intuitively?" he concluded.

"Perhaps. I do not know. But is that good or bad?"

"Very good, if your intuition carries you along the right path, and very bad if it makes a mistake," explained Tortsov. "During the exhibition performance it did not mislead you, and what you gave us in those few successful moments was excellent."

"Is that really true?" I asked.

"Yes, because the very best that can happen is to have the actor completely carried away by the play. Then regardless of his own will he lives the part, not noticing *how* he feels, not thinking about *what* he does, and it all moves of its own accord, subconsciously and intuitively. Salvini said: 'The great actor should be full of feeling, and especially he should feel the thing he is portraying. He must feel an emotion not only once or twice while he is studying his part, but to a greater or lesser degree every time he plays it, no matter whether it is the first or the thousandth time.' Unfortunately this is not within our control. Our subconscious is inaccessible to our consciousness. We cannot enter into that realm. If for any reason we do penetrate into it, then the subconscious becomes conscious and dies.

"The result is a predicament; we are supposed to create under inspiration; only our subconscious gives us inspiration; yet we apparently can use this subconscious only through our consciousness, which kills it.

"Fortunately there is a way out. We find

Excerpts from "When Acting is an Art," from *An Actor Prepares* by Constantin Stanislavski, translated by Elizabeth Reynolds Hapgood. © 1936 by Theatre Arts, Inc. © 1948 by Elizabeth Reynolds Hapgood. Reprinted by permission of Theatre Arts Books, New York, N.Y.

the solution in an oblique instead of a direct approach. In the soul of a human being there are certain elements which are subject to consciousness and will. These accessible parts are capable in turn of acting on psychic processes that are involuntary.

"To be sure, this calls for extremely complicated creative work. It is carried on in part under the control of our consciousness, but a much more significant proportion is subconscious and involuntary.

"To rouse your subconscious to creative work there is a special technique. We must leave all that is in the fullest sense subconscious to nature, and address ourselves to what is within our reach. When the subconscious, when intuition, enters into our work we must know how not to interfere.

"One cannot always create subconsciously and with inspiration. No such genius exists in the world. Therefore our art teaches us first of all to create consciously and rightly, because that will best prepare the way for the blossoming of the subconscious, which is inspiration. The more you have of conscious creative moments in your role the more chance you will have of a flow of inspiration.

" 'You may play well or you may play badly; the important thing is that you should play truly,' wrote Shchepkin to his pupil Shumski.

"To play truly means to be right, logical, coherent, to think, strive, feel and act in unison with your role.

"If you take all these internal processes, and adapt them to the spiritual and physical life of the person you are representing, we call that living the part. This is of supreme significance in creative work. Aside from the fact that it opens up avenues for inspiration, living the part helps the artist to carry out one of his main objectives. His job is not to present merely the external life of his character. He must fit his own human qualities to the life of this other person, and pour into it all of his own soul. The fundamental aim of our art is the creation of this inner life of a human spirit, and its expression in an artistic form.

"That is why we begin by thinking about the inner side of a role, and how to create its spiritual life through the help of the internal process of living the part. You must live it by actually experiencing feelings that are analogous to it, each and every time you repeat the process of creating it."

"Why is the subconscious so dependent on the conscious?" said I.

"It seems entirely normal to me," was the reply. "The use of steam, electricity, wind, water and other involuntary forces in nature is dependent on the intelligence of an engineer. Our subconscious power cannot function without its own engineer—our conscious technique. It is only when an actor feels that his inner and outer life on the stage is flowing naturally and normally, in the circumstances that surround him, that the deeper sources of his subconscious gently open, and from them come feelings we cannot always analyse. For a shorter or longer space of time they take possession of us whenever some inner instinct bids them. Since we do not understand this governing power, and cannot study it, we actors call it simply nature.

"But if you break the laws of normal organic life, and cease to function rightly, then this highly sensitive subconscious becomes alarmed, and withdraws. To avoid this, plan your role consciously at first, then play it truthfully. At this point realism and even naturalism in the inner preparation of a part is essential, because it causes your subconscious to work and induces outbursts of inspiration."

"From what you have said I gather that to study our art we must assimilate a psychological technique of living a part and that this will help us to accomplish our main object, which is to create the life of a human spirit," Paul Shustov said.

"That is correct but not complete," said Tortsov. "Our aim is not only to create the life of a human spirit, but also to 'express it in a beautiful, artistic form.' An actor is under the obligation to live his part inwardly, and then to give to his experience an external embodiment. I ask you to note especially that the dependence of the body on the soul is particularly important in our school of art. *In order to express a most delicate and largely subconscious life it is necessary to have control of an unusually responsive, excellently prepared vocal and physical apparatus.* This apparatus must be ready instantly and exactly to reproduce most delicate and all but intangible feelings with great sensitiveness and directness. *That is why an actor of our type is obliged to work so much more than others,* both on his inner equipment, which creates the life of the part, and also on his outer physical apparatus, which should reproduce the results of the creative work of his emotions with precision.

"Even the externalizing of a role is greatly influenced by the subconscious. In fact no artificial, theatrical technique can even compare with the marvels that nature brings forth.

"I have pointed out to you today, in general outlines, what we consider essential. Our experience has led to a firm belief that only our kind of art, soaked as it is in the living experiences of human beings, can artistically reproduce the impalpable shadings and depths of life. Only such art can completely absorb the spectator and make him both understand and also inwardly experience the happenings on the stage, enriching his inner life, and leaving impressions which will not fade with time.

"Moreover, and this is of primary importance, *the organic bases of the laws of nature on which our art is founded will protect you in the future from going down the wrong path.* Who knows under what directors, or in what theatres, you will work? Not everywhere, not with everyone, will you find creative work based on nature. In the vast majority of theatres the actors and producers are constantly violating nature in the most shameless manner. But if you are sure of the limits of true art, and of the organic laws of nature, you will not go astray, you will be able to understand your mistakes and correct them. That is why a study of the foundations of our art is the beginning of the work of every student actor."

"Yes, yes," I exclaimed, "I am so happy that I was able to take a step, if only a small one, in that direction."

"Not so fast," said Tortsov, "otherwise you will suffer the bitterest disillusion. Do not mix up living your part with what you showed us on the stage."

"Why, what did I show?"

"I have told you that in all that big scene from *Othello* there were only a few minutes in which you succeeded in living the part. I used them to illustrate to you, and to the other students, the foundations of our type of art. However, if we speak of the whole scene between Othello and Iago, we certainly cannot call it our type of art."

"What is it, then?"

"That is what we call forced acting," defined the Director.

"And what, really, is that?" said I, puzzled.

"When one acts as you did," he explained, "there are individual moments when you suddenly and unexpectedly rise to great artistic heights and thrill your audience. In such moments you are creating according to your inspiration, improvising, as it were; but would you feel yourself capable enough, or strong enough spiritually or physically, to play the five great acts of *Othello* with the same lift with which you accidentally played part of that one short scene?"

"I do not know," I said, conscientiously.

"I know, unquestionably, that such an undertaking would be far beyond the strength not only of a genius with an extraordinary temperament, but even of a very Hercules," answered Tortsov. "For our purposes you must have, in addition to the help of nature, a well worked-out psychological technique, an enormous talent, and great physical and nervous reserves. You have not all these things, any more than do the personality actors who do not admit technique. They, as you did, rely entirely on inspiration. If this inspiration does not turn up then neither you nor they have anything with which to fill in the blank spaces. You have long stretches of nervous let-down in playing your part, complete artistic impotence, and a naïve amateurish sort of acting. At such times your playing is lifeless, stilted. Consequently high moments alternate with over-acting."

Today we heard some more from Tortsov about our acting. When he came to the classroom he turned to Paul and said to him:

"You too gave us some interesting moments, but they were rather typical of the 'art of representation.'

"Now since you successfully demonstrated this other way of acting, Paul, why not recall for us how you created the role of Iago?" suggested the Director.

"I went right at the role for its inner content, and studied that for a long time," said Paul. "At home it seemed to me that I really did live the part, and at some of the rehearsals there were certain places in the role that I seemed to feel. Therefore I do not know what the art of 'representation' has to do with it."

"In it the actor also lives his part," said Tortsov. "This partial identity with our method is what makes it possible to consider this other type also true art.

"Yet his objective is different. He lives his part as a preparation for perfecting an external form. Once that is determined to his satisfaction he reproduces that form through the aid of mechanically trained muscles. Therefore, in this other school, living your role is not the chief moment of creation as it is with us, but one of the preparatory stages for further artistic work. . . .

"You should first of all assimilate the model. This is complicated. You study it from the point of view of the epoch, the time, the country, condition of life, background, literature, psychology, the soul, way of living, social position, and external appearance; moreover, you study character, such as custom, manner, movements, voice, speech, intonations. All this work on your material will help you to permeate it with your own feelings. Without all this you will have no art.

"When, from this material, a living image of the role emerges, the artist of the school of representation transfers it to himself. This work is concretely described by one of the best representatives of this school, the famous French actor, Coquelin the elder: . . . 'The actor creates his model in his imagination, and then, just as does the painter, he takes every feature of it and transfers it, not onto canvas, but onto himself.' . . . He sees Tartuffe's costume and puts it on himself; he notices his gait and imitates it; he sees his physiognomy and adapts it to himself; he adapts his own face to it. He speaks with the same voice that he has heard Tartuffe use; he must make this person he has put together

move, walk, gesticulate, listen and think like Tartuffe, in other words, hand over his soul to him. The portrait ready, it needs only to be framed; that is, put on the stage, and then the public will say either, 'That is Tartuffe,' or, 'The actor has not done a good job.' . . ."

"But all that is frightfully difficult and complicated," said I with feeling.

"Yes, Coquelin himself admits it. He says: 'The actor does not live, he plays. He remains cold toward the object of his acting but his art must be perfection.' . . . And to be sure," added Tortsov, "the art of representation demands perfection if it is to remain an art.

"The confident answer by the school of representation is that 'art is not real life, nor is it even its reflection. Art is in itself a creator, it creates its own life, beautiful in its abstraction, beyond the limits of time, and space.' Of course we cannot agree to such a presumptuous defiance of that unique, perfect, and unattainable artist, our creative nature.

"Artists of the Coquelin school reason this way: The theatre is a convention, and the stage is too poor in resources to create the illusion of real life; therefore the theatre should not avoid conventions. . . . This type of art is less profound than beautiful, it is more immediately effective than truly powerful; in it the form is more interesting than its content. It acts more on your sense of sound and sight than on your soul. Consequently it is more likely to delight than to move you.

"You can receive great impressions through this art. But they will neither warm your soul nor penetrate deeply into it. Their effect is sharp but not lasting. Your astonishment rather than your faith is aroused. Only what can be accomplished through surprising theatrical beauty, or picturesque pathos, lies within the bounds of this art. But delicate and deep human feelings are not subject to such technique. They call for natural emotions *at the very moment* in which they appear before you in the flesh. *They call for the direct cooperation of nature itself.* . . .

"*. . . never allow yourself externally to portray anything that you have not inwardly experienced and which is not even interesting to you.*

"An artistic truth is hard to draw out, but it never palls. It becomes more pleasing, penetrates more deeply, all the time, until it embraces the whole being of an artist, and of his spectators as well. A role which is built of truth will grow, whereas one built on stereotype will shrivel."

# Alienation Effects in Chinese Acting

## BERTOLT BRECHT

The following is intended to refer briefly to the use of the alienation effect in traditional Chinese acting. This method was most recently used in Germany for plays of a non-Aristotelian (not dependent on empathy) type as part of the attempts[1] being made to evolve an epic theatre. The efforts in question were directed to playing in such a way that the audience was hindered from simply identifying itself with the characters in the play. Acceptance or rejection of their actions and utterances was meant to take place on a conscious plane, instead of, as hitherto, in the audience's subconscious.

This effort to make the incidents represented appear strange to the public can be seen in a primitive form in the theatrical and pictorial displays at the old popular fairs. The way the clowns speak and the way the panoramas are painted both embody an act of alienation. The method of painting used to reproduce the picture of "Charles the Bold's flight after the Battle of Murten," as shown at many German fairs, is certainly mediocre; yet the act of alienation which is achieved here (not by the original) is in no wise due to the mediocrity of the copyist. The fleeing commander, his horse, his retinue and the landscape are all quite consciously painted in such a way as to create the impression of an abnormal event, an astonishing disaster. In spite of his inadequacy the painter succeeds brilliantly in bringing out the unexpected. Amazement guides his brush.

Traditional Chinese acting also knows the alienation effect, and applies it most subtly. It is well known that the Chinese theatre uses a lot of symbols. Thus a general will carry little pennants on his shoulder, corresponding to the number of regiments under his command. Poverty is shown by patching the silken costumes with irregular shapes of different colours, likewise silken, to indicate that they have been mended. Characters are distinguished by particular masks, i.e. simply by painting. Certain gestures of the two hands signify the forcible opening of a door, etc. The stage itself remains the same, but articles of furniture are carried in during the action. All this has long been known, and cannot very well be exported.

It is not all that simple to break with the habit of assimilating a work of art as a whole. But this has to be done if just one of a large number of effects is to be singled out and studied. The alienation effect is achieved in the Chinese theatre in the following way.

Above all, the Chinese artist never acts as

[1]Brecht uses the word "Versuche."

if there were a fourth wall besides the three surrounding him. He expresses his awareness of being watched. This immediately removes one of the European stage's characteristic illusions. The audience can no longer have the illusion of being the unseen spectator at an event which is really taking place. A whole elaborate European stage technique, which helps to conceal the fact that the scenes are so arranged that the audience can view them in the easiest way, is thereby made unnecessary. The actors openly choose those positions which will best show them off to the audience, just as if they were *acrobats*. A further means is that the artist observes himself. Thus if he is representing a cloud, perhaps, showing its unexpected appearance, its soft and strong growth, its rapid yet gradual transformation, he will occasionally look at the audience as if to say: isn't it just like that? At the same time he also observes his own arms and legs, adducing them, testing them and perhaps finally approving them. An obvious glance at the floor, so as to judge the space available to him for his act, does not strike him as liable to break the illusion. In this way the artist separates mime (showing observation) from gesture (showing a cloud), but without detracting from the latter, since the body's attitude is reflected in the face and is wholly responsible for its expression. At one moment the expression is of well-managed restraint; at another, of utter triumph. The artist has been using his countenance as a blank sheet, to be inscribed by the gest of the body.

The artist's object is to appear strange and even surprising to the audience. He achieves this by looking strangely at himself and his work. As a result everything put forward by him has a touch of the amazing. Everyday things are thereby raised above the level of the obvious and automatic. A young woman, a fisherman's wife, is shown paddling a boat. She stands steering a nonexistent boat with a paddle that barely reaches to her knees. Now the current is swifter, and she is finding it harder to keep her balance; now she is in a pool and paddling more easily. Right: that is how one manages a boat. But this journey in the boat is apparently historic, celebrated in many songs, an exceptional journey about which everybody knows. Each of this famous girl's movements has probably been recorded in pictures; each bend in the river was a well-known adventure story, it is even known which particular bend it was. This feeling on the audience's part is induced by the artist's attitude; it is this that makes the journey famous. The scene reminded us of the march to Budejovice in Piscator's production of *The Good Soldier Schweik*. Schweik's three-day-and-night march to a front which he oddly enough never gets to was seen from a completely historic point of view, as no less noteworthy a phenomenon than, for instance, Napoleon's Russian expedition of 1812. The performer's self-observation, an artful and artistic act of self-alienation, stopped the spectator from losing himself in the character completely, i.e. to the point of giving up his own identity, and lent a splendid remoteness to the events. Yet the spectator's empathy was not entirely rejected. The audience identifies itself with the actor as being an observer, and accordingly develops his attitude of observing or looking on.

The Chinese artist's performance often strikes the Western actor as cold. That does not mean that the Chinese theatre rejects all representation of feelings. The performer portrays incidents of utmost passion, but without his delivery becoming heated. At those points where the character portrayed is deeply excited the performer takes a lock of hair between his lips and chews it. But this is like a ritual, there is nothing eruptive about it. It is quite clearly somebody else's repetition of the incident: a representation, even though an artistic one. The performer shows that this man is not in control of himself, and he point to the outward signs. And so lack of control is decorously expressed, or if not decorously at any rate decorously for the stage. Among all the possible signs certain particular ones are picked out, with careful and visible consideration. Anger is naturally different from sulkiness, hatred from distaste, love from liking; but the corresponding fluctuations of feeling are portrayed economically. The coldness comes from the actor's holding himself remote from the character portrayed, along the lines described. He is careful not to make its sensations into those of the spectator. Nobody gets raped by the individual he portrays; this individual is not the spectator himself but his neighbour.

The Western actor does all he can to bring his spectator into the closest proximity to the events and the character he has to portray. To this end he persuades him to identify himself with him (the actor) and uses every energy to convert himself as completely as possible into a different type, that of the character in question. If this complete conversion succeeds then his art has been more or less expended. Once he has become the bank-clerk, doctor, or general concerned he will need no more art than any of these people need "in real life."

This complete conversion operation is extremely exhausting. Stanislavski puts forward a series of means—a complete system —by which what he calls "creative mood" can repeatedly be manufactured afresh at every performance. For the actor cannot usually manage to feel for very long on end that he really is the other person; he soon gets exhausted and begins just to copy various superficialities of the other person's speech and hearing, whereupon the effect on the public drops off alarmingly. This is certainly due to the fact that the other person has been created by an "intuitive" and accordingly murky process which takes place in the subconscious. The subconscious is not at all responsive to guidance; it has as it were a bad memory.

These problems are unknown to the Chinese performer, for he rejects complete conversion. He limits himself from the start to simply quoting the character played. But with what art he does this! He only needs a minimum of illusion. What he has to show is worth seeing even for a man in his right mind. What Western actor of the old sort (apart from one or two comedians) could demonstrate the elements of his art like the Chinese actor Mei Lan-fang, without special lighting and wearing a dinner jacket in an ordinary room full of specialists? It would be like the magician at a fair giving away his tricks, so that nobody ever wanted to see the act again. He would just be showing how to disguise oneself; the hypnotism would vanish and all that

would be left would be a few pounds of ill-blended imitation, a quickly-mixed product for selling in the dark to hurried customers. Of course no Western actor would stage such a demonstration. What about the sanctity of Art? The mysteries of metamorphosis? To the Westerner what matters is that his actions should be unconscious; otherwise they would be degraded. By comparison with Asiatic acting our own art still seems hopelessly parsonical. Nonetheless it is becoming increasingly difficult for our actors to bring off the mystery of complete conversion; their subconscious's memory is getting weaker and weaker, and it is almost impossible to extract the truth from the uncensored intuitions of any member of our class society even when the man is a genius.

For the actor it is difficult and taxing to conjure up particular inner moods or emotions night after night; it is simpler to exhibit the outer signs which accompany these emotions and identify them. In this case, however, there is not the same automatic transfer of emotions to the spectator, the same emotional infection. The alienation effect intervenes, not in the form of absence of emotion, but in the form of emotions which need not correspond to those of the character portrayed. On seeing worry the spectator may feel a sensation of joy; on seeing anger, one of disgust. When we speak of exhibiting the outer signs of emotion we do not mean such an exhibition and such a choice of signs that the emotional transference does in fact take place because the actor has managed to infect himself with the emotions portrayed, by exhibiting the outer signs; thus, by letting his voice rise, holding his breath and tightening his neck muscles so that the blood shoots to his head, the actor can easily conjure up a rage. In such a case of course the effect does not occur. But it does occur if the actor at a particular point unexpectedly shows a completely white face, which he has produced mechanically by holding his face in his hands with some white make-up on them. If the actor at the same time displays an apparently composed character, then his terror at this point (as a result of this message, or that discovery) will give rise to an alienation effect.

Acting like this is healthier and in our view less unworthy of a thinking being; it demands a considerable knowledge of humanity and worldly wisdom, and a keen eye for what is socially important. In this case too there is of course a creative process at work; but it is a higher one, because it is raised to the conscious level.

The alienation effect does not in any way demand an unnatural way of acting. It has nothing whatever to do with ordinary stylization. On the contrary, the achievement of of an A-effect absolutely depends on lightness and naturalness of performance. But when the actor checks the truth of his performance (a necessary operation, which Stanislavski is much concerned with in his system) he is not just thrown back on his "natural sensibilities," but can always be corrected by a comparison with reality (is that how an angry man really speaks? is that how an offended man sits down?) and so from outside, by other people. He acts in such a way that nearly every sentence could be followed by a verdict of the audience and practically every gesture is submitted for the public's approval.

The Chinese performer is in no trance. He can be interrupted at any moment. He won't have to "come round." After an interruption he will go on with his exposition from that point. We are not disturbing him at the "mystic moment of creation"; when he steps on to the stage before us the process of creation is already over. He does not mind if the setting is changed around him as he plays. Busy hands quite openly pass him what he needs for his performance. When Mei Lan-fang was playing a death scene a spectator sitting next me exclaimed with astonishment at one of his gestures. One or two people sitting in front of us turned round indignantly and sshhh'd. They behaved as if they were present at the real death of a real girl. Possibly their attitude would have been all right for a European production, but for a Chinese it was unspeakably ridiculous. In their case the A-effect had misfired.

It is not entirely easy to realize that the Chinese actor's A-effect is a transportable piece of technique: a conception that can be prised loose from the Chinese theatre. We see

this theatre as uncommonly precious, its portrayal of human passions as schematized, its idea of society as rigid and wrong-headed; at first sight this superb art seems to offer nothing applicable to a realistic and revolutionary theatre. Against that, the motives and objects of the A-effect strike us as odd and suspicious.

When one sees the Chinese acting it is at first very hard to discount the feeling of estrangement which they produce in us as Europeans. One has to be able to imagine them achieving an A-effect among their Chinese spectators too. What is still harder is that one must accept the fact that when the Chinese performer conjures up an impression of mystery he seems uninterested in disclosing a mystery to us. He makes his own mystery from the mysteries of nature (especially human nature): he allows nobody to examine how he produces the natural phenomenon, nor does nature allow him to understand as he produces it. We have here the artistic counterpart of a primitive technology, a rudimentary science. The Chinese performer gets his A-effect by association with magic. "How it's done" remains hidden; knowledge is a matter of knowing the tricks and is in the hands of a few men who guard it jealously and profit from their secrets. And yet there is already an attempt here to interfere with the course of nature; the capacity to do so leads to questioning; and the future explorer, with his anxiety to make nature's course intelligible, controllable and down-to-earth, will always start by adopting a standpoint from which it seems mysterious, incomprehensible and beyond control. He will take up the attitude of somebody wondering, will apply the A-effect. Nobody can be a mathematician who takes it for granted that "two and two makes four"; nor is anybody one who fails to understand it. The man who first looked with astonishment at a swinging lantern and instead of taking it for granted found it highly remarkable that it should swing, and swing in that particular way rather than any other, was brought close to understanding the phenomenon by this observation, and so to mastering it. Nor must it simply be exclaimed that the attitude here proposed is all right for science but not for art. Why shouldn't art try, by its *own* means of course, to further the great social task of mastering life?

In point of fact the only people who can profitably study a piece of technique like Chinese acting's A-effect are those who need such a technique for quite definite social purposes.

The experiments conducted by the modern German theatre led to a wholly independent development of the A-effect. So far Asiatic acting has exerted no influence.

The A-effect was achieved in the German epic theatre not only by the actor, but also by the music (choruses, songs) and the setting (placards, film etc.). It was principally designed to historicize the incidents portrayed. By this is meant the following:

The bourgeois theatre emphasized the timelessness of its objects. Its representation of people is bound by the alleged "eternally human." Its story is arranged in such a way as to create "universal" situations that allow Man with a capital M to express himself: man of every period and every colour. All its incidents are just one enormous cue, and this cue is followed by the "eternal" response: the inevitable, usual, natural, purely human response. An example: a black man falls in love in the same way as a white man; the story forces him to react with the same expression as the white man (in theory this formula works as well the other way round); and with that the sphere of art is attained. The cue can take account of what is special, different; the response is shared, there is no element of difference in it. This notion may allow that such a thing as history exists, but it is none the less unhistorical. A few circumstances vary, the environments are altered, but Man remains unchanged. History applies to the environment, not to Man. The environment is remarkably unimportant, is treated simply as a pretext; it is a variable quantity and something remarkably inhuman; it exists in fact apart from Man, confronting him as a coherent whole, whereas he is a fixed quantity, eternally unchanged. The idea of man as a function of the environment and the environment as a function of man, i.e. the breaking up of the environment into relationships between men, corresponds to a new way of

thinking, the historical way. Rather than be sidetracked into the philosophy of history, let us give an example. Suppose the following is to be shown on the stage: a girl leaves home in order to take a job in a fair-sized city (Piscator's *American Tragedy*). For the bourgeois theatre this is an insignificant affair, clearly the beginning of a story; it is what one has to have been told in order to understand what comes after, or to be keyed up for it. The actor's imagination will hardly be greatly fired by it. In a sense the incident is universal: girls take jobs (in the case in question one can be keyed up to see what in particular is going to happen to her). Only in one way is it particular: this girl goes away (if she had remained what comes after would not have happened). The fact that her family lets her go is not the object of the inquiry; it is understandable (the motives are understandable). But for the historicizing theatre everything is different. The theatre concentrates entirely on whatever in this perfectly everyday event is remarkable, particular and demanding inquiry. What! A family letting one of its members leave the nest to earn her future living independently and without help? Is she up to it? Will what she has learnt here as a member of the family help her to earn her living? Can't families keep a grip on their children any longer? Have they become (or remained) a burden? Is it like that with every family? Was it always like that? Is this the way of the world, something that can't be affected? The fruit falls off the tree when ripe: does this sentence apply here? Do children always make themselves independent? Did they do so in every age? If so, and if it's something biological, does it always happen in the same way, for the same reasons and with the same results? These are the questions (or a few of them) that the actors must answer if they want to show the incident as a unique, historical one: if they want to demonstrate a custom which leads to conclusions about the entire structure of a society at a particular (transient) time. But how is such an incident to be represented if its historic character is to be brought out? How can the confusion of our unfortunate epoch be striking? When the mother, in between warnings and moral injunctions, packs her daughter's case—a very small one—how is the following to be shown: So many injunctions and few clothes? Moral injunctions for a lifetime and bread for five hours? How is the actress to speak the mother's sentence as she hands over such a very small case—"There, I guess that ought to do you"—in such way that it is understood as a historic dictum? This can only be achieved if the A-effect is brought out. The actress must not make the sentence her own affair, she must hand it over for criticism, she must help us to understand its causes and protest. The effect can only be got by long training. In the New York Yiddish Theater, a highly progressive theatre, I saw a play by S. Ornitz showing the rise of an East Side boy to be a big crooked attorney. The theatre could not perform the play. And yet there were scenes like this in it: the young attorney sits in the street outside his house giving cheap legal advice. A young woman arrives and complains that her leg has been hurt in a traffic accident. But the case has been bungled and her compensation has not yet been paid. In desperation she points to her leg and says: "It's started to heal up." Working without the A-effect, the theatre was unable to make use of this exceptional scene to show the horror of a bloody epoch. Few people in the audience noticed it; hardly anyone who reads this will remember that cry. The actress spoke the cry as if it were something perfectly natural. But it is exactly this—the fact that this poor creature finds such a complaint natural—that she should have reported to the public like a horrified messenger returning from the lowest of all hells. To that end she would of course have needed a special technique which would have allowed her to underline the historical aspect of a specific social condition. Only the A-effect makes this possible. Without it all she can do is to observe how she is not forced to go over entirely into the character on the stage.

In setting up new artistic principles and working out new methods of representation we must start with the compelling demands of a changing epoch; the necessity and the possiblity of remodelling society loom ahead. All incidents between men must be noted, and everything must be seen from a social point of view. Among other effects that a new theatre will need for its social criticism and its historical reporting of completed transformations is the A-effect.

NOTE: This essay, though unpublished in German till 1949, appeared (in Mr. Eric White's translation) in *Life and Letters*, London, in the winter of 1936. A pencilled note on the typescript (Brecht-Archive 332/81) says: "This essay arose out of a performance by Mei Lan-fang's company in Moscow in spring 1935." Brecht had seen the performance that May, during his Moscow visit, though the essay itself cannot have been completed till after his return from New York.

Almost certainly this, rather than the following item (as I wrongly suggested in my book on Brecht), is the first mention in his writings of the term "Verfremdungseffekt." ... The formula itself is a translation of the Russian critic Viktor Shklovskij's phrase "Priem Ostrannenija," or "device for making strange," and it can hardly be a coincidence that it should have entered Brecht's vocabulary after his Moscow visit. So far as Mrs. Hauptmann can remember he had not spoken of "Verfremdung" earlier, even in conversation. It was indeed virtually a neologism, for Grimm's dictionary gives only two obscure early examples for the use of "verfremden" as a transitive verb.

According to Professor Eric Bentley the play by Samuel Ornitz was called *Haunch, Paunch and Fowl* and was performed in 1935 by the Artef Players' collective. The incident with the leg seems to anticipate the water-carrier's injury in *Der gute Mensch von Sezuan*.

Piscator's adaptation of Dreiser's *An American Tragedy* was produced by the Group Theater in New York in 1936 under the title *The Case of Clyde Griffiths*, with Lee Strasberg directing. Harold Clurman wrote of it in *The Fervent Years* (London, 1946, p. 174) that "It was schematic in a cold way that to my mind definitely went across the American grain. ... It was nevertheless technically intriguing and capable of being fashioned into a novel type of stage production."

# Preface to *Six Characters in Search of an Author*

## LUIGI PIRANDELLO

It seems like yesterday but is actually many years ago that a nimble little maidservant entered the service of my art. However, she always comes fresh to the job.

She is called Fantasy.

A little puckish and malicious, if she likes to dress in black no one will wish to deny that she is often positively bizarre and no one will wish to believe that she always does everything in the same way and in earnest. She sticks her hand in her pocket, pulls out a cap and bells, sets it on her head, red as a cock's comb, and dashes away. Here today, there tomorrow. And she amuses herself by bringing to my house—since I derive stories and novels and plays from them—the most disgruntled tribe in the world, men, women, children, involved in strange adventures which they can find no way out of; thwarted in their plans; cheated in their hopes; with whom, in short, it is often torture to deal.

Well, this little maidservant of mine, Fantasy, several years ago, had the bad inspiration or ill-omened caprice to bring a family into my house. I wouldn't know where she fished them up or how, but, according to her, I could find in them the subject for a magnificent novel.

I found before me a man about fifty years old, in a dark jacket and light trousers, with a frowning air and ill-natured, mortified eyes; a poor woman in widow's weeds leading by one hand a little girl of four and by the other a boy of rather more than ten; a cheeky and "sexy" girl, also clad in black but with an equivocal and brazen pomp, all atremble with a lively, biting contempt for the mortified old man and for a young fellow of twenty who stood on one side closed in on himself as if he despised them all. In short, the six characters who are seen coming on stage at the beginning of the play. Now one of them and now another—often beating down one another—embarked on the sad story of their adventures, each shouting his own reasons, and projecting in my face his disordered passions, more or less as they do in the play to the unhappy Manager.

What author will be able to say how and why a character was born in his fantasy? The mystery of artistic creation is the same as that of birth. A woman who loves may desire to become a mother; but the desire by itself, however intense, cannot suffice. One fine day she will find herself a mother without having any precise intimation when it began. In the same way an artist imbibes very many germs of life and can never say how and why, at a certain moment, one of these vital germs inserts itself into his fantasy, there to become a living creature on a plane of life superior to the changeable existence of every day.

I can only say that, without having made

any effort to seek them out, I found before me, alive—you could touch them and even hear them breathe—the six characters now seen on the stage. And they stayed there in my presence, each with his secret torment and all bound together by the one common origin and mutual entanglement of their affairs, while I had them enter the world of art, constructing from their persons, their passions, and their adventures a novel, a drama, or at least a story.

Born alive, they wished to live.

To me it was never enough to present a man or a woman and what is special and characteristic about them simply for the pleasure of presenting them; to narrate a particular affair, lively or sad, simply for the pleasure of narrating it; to describe a landscape simply for the pleasure of describing it.

There are some writers (and not a few) who do feel this pleasure and, satisfied, ask no more. They are, to speak more precisely, historical writers.

But there are others who, beyond such pleasure, feel a more profound spiritual need on whose account they admit only figures, affairs, landscapes which have been soaked, so to speak, in a particular sense of life and acquire from it a universal value. These are, more precisely, philosophical writers.

I have the misfortune to belong to these last.

I hate symbolic art in which the presentation loses all spontaneous movement in order to become a machine, an allegory—a vain and misconceived effort because the very fact of giving an allegorical sense to a presentation clearly shows that we have to do with a fable which by itself has no truth either fantastic or direct; it was made for the demonstration of some moral truth. The spiritual need I speak of cannot be satisfied—or seldom, and that to the end of a superior irony, as for example in Ariosto[1]—by such allegorical symbolism. This latter starts from a concept, and from a concept which creates or tries to create for itself an image. The former on the other hand seeks in the image—which must remain alive and free throughout—a meaning to give it value.

[1] *Ariosto* (Lodovico, 1474–1533) Italian poet, author of *Orlando Furioso*

Now, however much I sought, I did not succeed in uncovering this meaning in the six characters. And I concluded therefore that it was no use making them live.

I thought to myself: "I have already afflicted my readers with hundreds and hundreds of stories. Why should I afflict them now by narrating the sad entanglements of these six unfortunates?"

And, thinking thus, I put them away from me. Or rather I did all I could to put them away.

But one doesn't give life to a character for nothing.

Creatures of my spirit, these six were already living a life which was their own and not mine any more, a life which it was not in my power any more to deny them.

Thus it is that while I persisted in desiring to drive them out of my spirit, they, as if completely detached from every narrative support, characters from a novel miraculously emerging from the pages of the book that contained them, went on living on their own, choosing certain moments of the day to reappear before me in the solitude of my study and coming—now one, now the other, now two together—to tempt me, to propose that I present or describe this scene or that, to explain the effects that could be secured with them, the new interest which a certain unusual situation could provide, and so forth.

For a moment I let myself be won over. And this condescension of mine, thus letting myself go for a while, was enough, because they drew from it a new increment of life, a greater degree of clarity and addition, consequently a greater degree of persuasive power over me. And thus as it became gradually harder and harder for me to go back and free myself from them, it became easier and easier for them to come back and tempt me. At a certain point I actually became obsessed with them. Until, all of a sudden, a way out of the difficulty flashed upon me.

"Why not," I said to myself, "present this highly strange fact of an author who refuses to let some of his characters live though they have been born in his fantasy, and the fact that these characters, having by now life in their veins, do not resign themselves to remaining excluded from the world of art? They are detached from me; live on their own; have acquired voice and movement; have by themselves—in this struggle for existence that they have had to wage with me—become dramatic characters, characters that can move and talk on their own initiative; already see themselves as such; have learned to defend themselves against me; will even know how to defend themselves against others. And so let them go where dramatic characters do go to have life: on a stage. And let us see what will happen."

That's what I did. And, naturally, the result was what it had to be: a mixture of tragic and comic, fantastic and realistic, in a humorous situation that was quite new and infinitely complex, a drama which is conveyed by means of the characters, who carry it within them and suffer it, a drama, breathing, speaking, self-propelled, which seeks at all costs to find the means of its own presentation; and the comedy of the vain attempt at an improvised realization of the drama on stage. First, the surprise of the poor actors in a theatrical company rehearsing a play by day on a bare stage (no scenery, no flats). Surprise and incredulity at the sight of the six characters announcing themselves as such in search of an author. Then immediately, afterwards, through that sudden fainting fit of the Mother veiled in black, their instinctive interest in the drama of which they catch a glimpse in her and in the other members of the strange family, an obscure, ambiguous drama, coming about so unexpectedly on a stage that is empty and unprepared to receive it. And gradually the growth of this interest to the bursting forth of the contrasting passions of Father, of Step-Daughter, of Son, of that poor Mother, passions seeking, as I said, to overwhelm each other with a tragic, lacerating fury.

And here is the universal meaning at first vainly sought in the six characters, now that, going on stage of their own accord, they succeed in finding it within themselves in the excitement of the desperate struggle which each wages against the other and all wage against the Manager and the actors, who do not understand them.

Without wanting to, without knowing it, in the strife of their bedevilled souls, each of them, defending himself against the accusations of the others, expresses as his own living passion and torment the passion and torment which for so many years have been the pangs of my spirit: the deceit of mutual understanding irremediably founded on the empty abstraction of the words, the multiple personality of everyone corresponding to the possibilities of being to be found in each of us, and finally the inherent tragic conflict between life (which is always moving and changing) and form (which fixes it, immutable).

Two above all among the six characters, the Father and the Step-Daughter, speak of that outrageous unalterable fixity of their form in which he and she see their essential nature expressed permanently and immutably, a nature that for one means punishment and for the other revenge; and they defend it against the factitious affectations and unaware volatility of the actors, and they try to impose it on the vulgar Manager who would like to change it and adapt it to the so-called exigencies of the theatre.

If the six characters don't all seem to exist on the same plane, it is not because some are figures of first rank and others of the second, that is, some are main characters and others minor ones—the elementary perspective necessary to all scenic or narrative art—nor is it that any are not completely created—for their purpose. They are all six at the same point of artistic realization and on the same level of reality, which is the fantastic level of the whole play. Except that the Father, the Step-Daughter, and also the Son are realized as mind; the Mother as nature; the Boy as a presence watching and performing a gesture and the Baby unaware of it all. This fact creates among them a perspective of a new sort. Unconsciously I had had the impression that some of them needed to be fully realized (artistically speaking), others less so, and others merely sketched in as elements in a narrative or presentational sequence: the most alive, the most completely created, are the Father and the Step-Daughter who naturally stand out more and lead the way, dragging themselves along beside the almost dead weight of the others—first, the Son, holding back; second, the Mother, like a victim resigned to her fate, between the two children who have hardly any substance beyond their appearance and who need to be led by the hand.

And actually! actually they had each to appear in that stage of creation which they had attained in the author's fantasy at the moment when he wished to drive them away.

If I now think about these things, about having intuited that necessity, having unconsciously found the way to resolve it by means of a new perspective, and about the way in which I actually obtained it, they seem like miracles. The fact is that the play was really conceived in one of those spontaneous illuminations of the fantasy when by a miracle all the elements of the mind answer to each other's call and work in divine accord. No human brain, working "in the cold," however stirred up it might be, could ever have succeeded in penetrating far enough, could ever have been in a position to satisfy all the exigencies of the play's form. Therefore the reasons which I will give to clarify the values of the play must not be thought of as intentions that I conceived beforehand when I prepared myself for the job and which I now undertake to defend, but only as discoveries which I have been able to make afterwards in tranquillity.

I wanted to present six characters seeking an author. Their play does not manage to get presented—precisely because the author whom they seek is missing. Instead is presented the comedy of their vain attempt with all that it contains of tragedy by virtue of the fact that the six characters have been rejected.

But can one present a character while rejecting him? Obviously, to present him one needs, on the contrary, to receive him into one's fantasy before one can express him. And I have actually accepted and realized the six characters: I have, however, accepted and realized them as rejected: in search of *another* author.

What have I rejected of them? Not themselves, obviously, but their drama, which doubtless is what interests them above all but which did not interest me—for the reasons already indicated.

And what is it, for a character—his drama?

Every creature of fantasy and art, in order to exist, must have his drama, that is, a drama in which he may be a character and for which he *is* a character. This drama is the character's *raison d'être*, his vital function, necessary for his existence.

In these six, then, I have accepted the "being" without the reason for being. I have taken the organism and entrusted to it, not its own proper function, but another more complex function into which its own function entered, if at all, only as a datum. A terrible and desperate situation especially for the two—Father and Step-Daughter—who more than the others crave life and more than the others feel themselves to be characters, that is, absolutely need a drama and therefore their own drama—the only one which they can envisage for themselves yet which meantime they see rejected: an "impossible" situation from which they feel they must escape at whatever cost; it is a matter of life and death. True, I have given them another *raison d'être*, another function: precisely that "impossible" situation, the drama of being in search of an author and rejected. But that this should be a *raison d'être*, that it should have become their real function, that it should be necessary, that it should suffice, they can hardly suppose; for they have a life of their own. If someone were to tell them, they wouldn't believe him. It is not possible to believe that the sole reason for our living should lie in a torment that seems to us unjust and inexplicable.

I cannot imagine, therefore, why the charge was brought against me that the character of the Father was not what it should have been because it stepped out of its quality and position as a character and invaded at times the author's province and took it over. I who understand those who don't quite understand me see that the charge derives from the fact that the character expresses and makes his own a torment of spirit which is recognized as mine. Which is entirely natural and of absolutely no significance. Aside from the fact that this torment of spirit in the character of the Father derives from causes, and is suffered and lived for reasons, that have nothing to do with the drama of my personal experience, a fact which alone removes all substance from the criticism, I want to make it clear that the inherent torment of my spirit is one thing, a torment which I can legitimately—provided that it be organic—reflect in a character, and that the activity of my spirit as revealed in the realized work, the activity that succeeds in forming a drama out of the six characters in search of an author is another thing. If the Father participated in this latter activity, if he competed in forming the drama of the six characters without an author, then and only then would it by all means be justified to say that he was at times the author himself and therefore not the man he should be. But the Father suffers and does not create his existence as a character in search of an author. He suffers it as an inexplicable fatality and as a situation which he tries with all his powers to rebel against, which he tries to remedy: hence it is that he is a character in search of an author and nothing more, even if he expresses as his own the torment of my spirit. If he, so to speak, assumed some of the author's responsibilities, the fatality would be completely explained. He would, that is to say, see himself accepted, if only as a rejected character, accepted in the poet's heart of hearts, and he would no longer have any reason to suffer the despair of not finding someone to construct and affirm his life as a character. I mean that he would quite willingly accept the *raison d'être* which the author gives him and without regrets would forego his own, throwing over the Manager and the actors to whom in fact he runs as his only recourse.

There is one character, that of the Mother, who on the other hand does not care about being alive (considering being alive as an end in itself). She hasn't the least suspicion that she is *not* alive. It has never occurred to her to ask how and why and in what manner she lives. In short, she is not aware of being a character, inasmuch as she is never, even for a moment, detached from her role. She doesn't know she has a role.

This makes her perfectly organic. Indeed,

her role of Mother does not of itself, in its natural essence, embrace mental activity. And she does not exist as a mind. She lives in an endless continuum of feeling, and therefore she cannot acquire awareness of her life—that is, of her existence as a character. But with all this, even she, in her own way and for her own ends, seeks an author, and at a certain stage seems happy to have been brought before the Manager. Because she hopes to take life from him, perhaps? No: because she hopes the Manager will have her present a scene with the Son in which she would put so much of her own life. But it is a scene which does not exist, which never has and never could take place. So unaware is she of being a character, that is, of the life that is possible to her, all fixed and determined, moment by moment, in every action, every phrase.

She appears on stage with the other characters but without understanding what the others make her do. Obviously, she imagines that the itch for life with which the husband and the daughter are afflicted and for which she herself is to be found on stage is no more than one of the usual incomprehensible extravagances of this man who is both tortured and torturer and—horrible, most horrible—a new equivocal rebellion on the part of that poor erring girl. The Mother is completely passive. The events of her own life and the values they assume in her eyes, her very character, are all things which are "said" by the others and which she only once contradicts, and that because the maternal instinct rises up and rebels within her to make it clear that she didn't at all wish to abandon either the son or the husband: the Son was taken from her and the husband forced her to abandon him. She is only correcting data; she explains and knows nothing.

In short, she is nature. Nature fixed in the figure of a mother.

This character gave me a satisfaction of a new sort, not to be ignored. Nearly all my critics, instead of defining her, after their habit, as "unhuman"—which seems to be the peculiar and incorrigible characteristic of all my creatures without exception—had the goodness to note "with real pleasure" that at last a *very human* figure had emerged from my fantasy. I explain this praise to myself in the following way: since my poor Mother is entirely limited to the natural attitude of a Mother with no possibility of free mental activity, being, that is, little more than a lump of flesh completely alive in all its functions—procreation, lactation, caring for and loving its young—without any need therefore of exercising her brain, she realizes in her person the true and complete "human type." That must be how it is, since in a human organism nothing seems more superfluous than the mind.

But the critics have tried to get rid of the Mother with this praise without bothering to penetrate the nucleus of poetic values which the character in the play represents. A very human figure, certainly, because mindless, that is, unaware of being what she is or not caring to explain it to herself. But not knowing that she is a character doesn't prevent her from being one. That is her drama in my play. And the most living expression of it comes spurting out in her cry to the Manager who wants her to think all these things have happened already and therefore cannot now be a reason for renewed lamentations: "No, it's happening now, it's happening always! My torture is not a pretence, signore! I am alive and present, always, in every moment of my torture: it is renewed, alive and present, always!" This she *feels*, without being conscious of it, and feels it therefore as something inexplicable: but she feels it so terribly that she doesn't think it *can* be something to explain either to herself or to others. She feels it and that is that. She feels it as pain, and this pain is immediate; she cries it out. Thus she reflects the growing fixity of life in a form—the same thing, which in another way, tortures the Father and the Step-Daughter. In them, mind. In her, nature. The mind rebels and, as best it may, seeks an advantage; nature, if not aroused by sensory stimuli, weeps.

Conflict between life-in-movement and form is the inexorable condition not only of the mental but also of the physical order. The life which in order to exist has become fixed in our corporeal form little by little kills that

form. The tears of a nature thus fixed lament the irreparable, continuous aging of our bodies. Hence the tears of the Mother are passive and perpetual. Revealed in three faces, made significant in three distinct and simultaneous dramas, this inherent conflict finds in the play its most complete expression. More: the Mother declares also the particular value of artistic form—a form which does not delimit or destroy its own life and which life does not consume—in her cry to the Manager. If the Father and Step-Daughter began their scene a hundred thousand times in succession, always, at the appointed moment, at the instant when the life of the work of art must be expressed with that cry, it would always be heard, unaltered and unalterable in its form, not as a mechanical repetition, not as a return determined by external necessities, but on the contrary, alive every time and as new, suddenly born *thus forever!* embalmed alive in its incorruptible form. Hence, always, as we open the book, we shall find Francesca alive and confessing to Dante her sweet sin, and if we turn to the passage a hundred thousand times in succession, a hundred thousand times in succession Francesca will speak her words, never repeating them mechanically, but saying them as though each time were the first time with such living and sudden passion that Dante every time will turn faint. All that lives, by the fact of living, has a form, and by the same token must die—except the work of art which lives forever insofar as it *is* form.

The birth of a creature of human fantasy, a birth which is a step across the threshold between nothing and eternity, can also happen suddenly, occasioned by some necessity. An imagined drama needs a character who does or says a certain necessary thing; accordingly this character is born and is precisely what he had to be. In this way Madame Pace is born among the six characters and seems a miracle, even a trick, realistically portrayed on the stage. It is no trick. The birth is real. The new character is alive not because she was alive already but because she is now happily born as is required by the fact of her being a character—she is obliged to be as she is. There is a break here, a sudden change in the level of reality of the scene, because a character can be born in this way only in the poet's fancy and not on the boards of a stage. Without anyone's noticing it, I have all of a sudden changed the scene: I have gathered it up again into my own fantasy without removing it from the spectator's eyes. That is, I have shown them, instead of the stage, my own fantasy in the act of creating—my own fantasy in the form of this same stage. The sudden and uncontrollable changing of a visual phenomenon from one level of reality to another is a miracle comparable to those of the saint who sets his own statue in motion: it is neither wood nor stone at such a moment. But the miracle is not arbitrary. The stage—a stage which accepts the fantastic reality of the six characters—is no fixed, immutable datum. Nothing in this play exists as given and preconceived. Everything is in the making, is in motion, is a sudden experiment: even the place in which this unformed life, reaching after its own form, changes and changes again contrives to shift position organically. The level of reality changes. When I had the idea of bringing Madame Pace to birth right there on the stage, I felt I could do it and I did it. Had I noticed that this birth was unhinging and silently, unnoticed, in a second, giving another shape, another reality to my scene, I certainly wouldn't have brought it about. I would have been afraid of the apparent lack of logic. And I would have committed an ill-omened assault on the beauty of my work. The fervor of my mind saved me from doing so. For despite appearances, with their specious logic, this fantastic birth is sustained by a real necessity in mysterious, organic relation with the whole life of the work.

That someone now tells me it hasn't all the value it could have because its expression is not constructed but chaotic, because it smacks of romanticism, makes me smile.

I understand why this observation was made to me: because in this work of mine the presentation of the drama in which the six characters are involved appears tumultuous and never proceeds in an orderly manner. There is no logical development, no concatenation of the events. Very true. Had I hunted it with a lamp I couldn't have found a more disordered, crazy, arbitrary, complicated, in short, romantic way of presenting "the drama in which the six characters are involved." Very true. But I have not presented that drama. I have presented another—and I won't undertake to say again what!—in which, among the many fine things that everyone, according to his tastes, can find, there is a discreet satire on romantic procedures: in the six characters thus excited to the point where they stifle themselves in the roles which each of them plays in a certain drama while I present them as characters in another play which they don't know and don't suspect the existence of, so that this inflammation of their passions—which belongs to the realm of romantic procedures—is humorously "placed," located in the void. And the drama of the six characters presented not as it would have been organized by my fantasy had it been accepted but in this way, as a rejected drama, could not exist in the work except as a "situation," with some little development, and could not come out except in indications, stormily, disorderedly, in violent foreshortenings, in a chaotic manner: continually interrupted, sidetracked, contradicted (by one of its characters), denied, and (by two others) not even seen.

There is a character indeed—he who denies the drama which makes him a character, the Son—who draws all his importance and value from being a character not of the comedy in the making—which as such hardly appears—but from the presentation that I made of it. In short, he is the only one who lives solely as "a character in search of an author"—inasmuch as the author he seeks is not a dramatic author. Even this could not be otherwise. The character's attitude is an organic product of my conception, and it is logical that in the situation it should produce greater confusion and disorder and another element of romantic contrast.

But I had precisely to *present* this organic and natural chaos. And to present a chaos is not at all to present chaotically, that is, romantically. That my presentation is the reverse of confused, that it is quite simple, clear, and orderly, is proved by the clarity which the intrigue, the characters, the fantastic and realistic, dramatic and comic levels of the work have had for every public in the world and by the way in which, for those with more searching vision, the unusual values enclosed within it come out.

Great is the confusion of tongues among men if criticisms thus made find words for their expression. No less great than this confusion is the intimate law of order which, obeyed in all points, makes this work of mine classical and typical and at its catastrophic close forbids the use of words. Though the audience eventually understands that one does not create life by artifice and that the drama of the six characters cannot be presented without an author to give them value with his spirit, the Manager remains vulgarly anxious to know how the thing turned out, and the "ending" is remembered by the Son in its sequence of actual moments, but without any sense and therefore not needing a human voice for its expression. It happens stupidly, uselessly, with the going-off of a mechanical weapon on stage. It breaks up and disperses the sterile experiment of the characters and the actors, which has apparently been made without the assistance of the poet.

The poet, unknown to them, as if looking on at a distance during the whole period of the experiment, was at the same time busy creating—with it and of it—his own play.